PUBLIC CONTROL OF ECONOMIC ENTERPRISE

PUBLIC CONTROL OF ECONOMIC ENTERPRISE

HAROLD KOONTZ
School of Business Administration
University of California, Los Angeles

RICHARD W. GABLE
School of Public Administration
University of Southern California

McGRAW-HILL BOOK COMPANY, INC.
New York Toronto London
1956

PUBLIC CONTROL OF ECONOMIC ENTERPRISE

Library of Congress Catalog Card Number 55-11173

To

MARY AND MYRA

PREFACE

The questions of policy and action involved in public control of economic enterprise are among the most vital facing the American citizen. Being an aspect of freedom, even though limited primarily to the economic sphere of human conduct, government controls over economic affairs naturally strike at the heart of the American social philosophy of government in its relationships with individuals. While American traditions have clearly favored private ownership and control of economic activities, there has always been an acknowledgment that individual business freedom of the few may properly be curtailed if by so doing freedom for the many is enhanced. In addition to this goal of increasing *total* economic freedom, other objectives have arisen, primarily in the past several decades, from the belief that government controls are justified as means for safeguarding the successful functioning of the economic system in the interests of full employment, stable prosperity, and national defense. While there is little doubt as to the validity of these goals for public policy, there is ever the question as to whether particular measures designed to accomplish these objectives do so effectively and with a minimum of unsought consequences.

Public control of economic enterprise is, therefore, an area of inquiry and analysis which is not only of significance to persons in business, but also to the general public whose material wants the economic system is designed to satisfy and whose economic freedom is often closely related to political and social freedom. Consequently, the intelligent citizen, whether or not immediately concerned with the making of business policies, who would follow his own self-interest and who would play a discerning role in molding political action will find it necessary to understand the essence and implications of this phase of public control.

This book is designed to describe and analyze the field of public control of economic enterprise in the United States. The word "control" has been interpreted to apply, in addition to specific regulation of business, to the intervention of government into economic affairs through aids and ownership and through broader fiscal monetary controls designed to influence the entire economy. The authors have attempted to obtain unity and perspective in this tremendously complex field by first introducing the subject through presenting briefly the evolution of the problem and the constitutional and administrative framework in which it has operated, and then by analyzing the major areas of control. Special emphasis has been given to transportation and public utilities not only because of the importance and thoroughness of control in these industries, but also because they have furnished much which has become a pattern for positive control when it has been extended to other businesses. Likewise, considerable emphasis has been placed on the programs of control to maintain competition, since the essential importance of this kind of regulation has been enhanced by the practice of utilizing in other fields many of the patterns of control in this area. In addition to these major areas, special attention is given to controls as they affect the investor and the worker, to the significantly expanded controls involved in public promotion and ownership, and to the important public control of the entire economy in peace as well as in war.

This book is to some extent a revision of *Government Control of Business*, published by the senior author in 1941, a revision which has long been generously urged by many users of the original book. But it is far more than a revision. While owing much in concept and organization to its predecessor, the present book has been completely rewritten and widely reorganized, to bring material up to date and to cast into proper perspective the major developments of the intervening years. Not the least of these developments are the maturation of public control of economic activities and the increased emphasis on programs applying to the total economy.

In a field which encompasses so much experience and so many issues as public control of private enterprise, it is clearly impossible to do everything within the limits of a single volume. The authors recognize that there are several valid approaches. One which has been widely used is to paint the principal public issues with a broad brush and to deal extensively with their philosophical implications. Another is to deal mainly with issues of competition and its control, leaving the analysis of controls in other areas to specialized books on such subjects as transportation, public utilities, labor, and banking. Still another approach is to concentrate on administrative aspects of government action. The authors have chosen to deal broadly with the areas of control and to place primary emphasis on an orderly presentation of the rationale, legal bases, techniques, and effects of control, with as much attention as possible to the broader implications of control, particularly in view of their bearing on the efficiency and effectiveness of the economic system. It is believed that a reasonably thorough understanding of the development and nature of controls must precede an intelligent formulation and understanding of broader issues and that, with this basic understanding, the reader or instructor will be in a better position to formulate and evaluate the social issues involved.

The preparation of this book has naturally caused the authors to be indebted to so many persons that it is impossible, without appearing encyclopedic, to acknowledge this debt to all by name. The research of many scholars has been utilized and footnotes call attention to their specific contributions. Numerous officials of government agencies and business associations have generously responded to requests for information. Associates at Colgate University, Stanford, the University of California, and the University of Southern California, as well as colleagues in other universities, have contributed to this book through their intelligent analysis of public issues and their willingness to discuss them with the authors. Likewise, many teachers who used the earlier book have offered suggestions from time to time, and students in the authors' classes have contributed much by their searching questions and frank criticisms.

Considerable assistance has been given the authors by certain authorities in the field who have patiently and intelligently read and criticized portions of the manuscript. It is a pleasure to record the debt owed these men. Dean Henry Reining, Jr., of the School of Public Administration of the University of Southern California read Parts I, III, and IV, and the authors have benefited greatly by his help in these areas as well as his counsel throughout the preparation of the book. Dr. Michael F. Conant of the University of California at Berkeley was of great assistance in reading and criticizing in detail certain chapters on public utilities and the entire section on maintaining competition. Dr. Frank P. Sherwood of the University of Southern California kindly criticized the chapter on wartime economic controls, and Dr. Ernest A. Englebert of the University of California at Los Angeles made many helpful suggestions on the chapter on government aids in agriculture. Dr. C. Fred Weston of the University of California at Los Angeles read the chapter on control for economic stability and growth and his incisive observations, as well as those of his colleague Dr. Frank W. Norton, greatly improved the material there presented. Among the business and government executives who contributed their help, special mention should be made of Mr. Charles Chase of the Bank of America who read the chapter on regulation of financial organizations and Mr. Charles M. Rehmus of the United States Mediation and Conciliation Service who generously read and made many suggestions on the chapters on labor.

The authors are grateful to Mrs. Eleanor M. Rohrbeck who so intelligently and patiently supervised the preparation of the entire manuscript and for the assistance of Mrs. Nadine H. Daniels and Miss Elizabeth Barker. The authors also appreciate the assistance of Mrs. Beatrice Markey and Mr. Evangelos Rizos who painstakingly checked the many references used.

HAROLD KOONTZ
RICHARD W. GABLE

CONTENTS

PART SEVEN. PUBLIC PROMOTION AND OWNERSHIP OF ECONOMIC ENTERPRISE

PART EIGHT. PUBLIC CONTROL OF THE TOTAL ECONOMY

PART ONE

THE SETTING OF ECONOMIC CONTROL

1

THE PROBLEM AND ITS DEVELOPMENT

The paradox of American experience with economic controls is that, while government has been traditionally distrusted, increased reliance has been placed on it to solve economic and social problems. With the apparent willingness of individuals to give government increased authority over their economic life, understanding the nature and implications of public control over economic enterprise becomes a prerequisite of intelligent citizenship as well as of effective business leadership.

The Problem of Economic Control

On the domestic scene in the United States today, one of the most pressing and complex problems of public policy is to find an answer to the question: "What is the proper role of government in relation to the economy?"

Government is only one among several institutions of social control. Government is the agent, the mechanism by which the ends of the people associated in the state are pursued. And the state is only one of many human associations in society. Among others are the family, the church, the club, the business firm—all groups of people organized for a common end.

The state has three characteristics that distinguish it from other forms of human association.[1] First, a person is always a member of some state. He can withdraw from other associations, but he cannot avoid being a member of a state. Then, the state always exists. Governments may change, private associations may disappear, but people living in a definite territory, with some kind of government, make up a continuing association. Finally, unlike other associations, the state is sovereign, legally supreme.

To say that the state is sovereign does not mean that it is all-powerful. It is superior to other associations in society only in the area of public affairs. Moreover, it does not follow that government must regulate *every* activity of public concern. That decision must take into account the prob-

[1] For an analysis of the distinction between the state and other associations, see John Dewey, *The Public and Its Problems* (Chicago: Gateway Books, 1946), chap. 1.

lem to be solved, the degree to which the need for action is felt, the responsiveness of the policy-making process, the alternative instruments of social control that might be used, and the desires and values of the people which influence the choice of instruments and the way they might be employed.

The economic system of a people—the economy in its broadest sense—consists of all associations and institutions involved in the conversion of resources into goods and services, their distribution, and the consumption of these products. Decisions regarding the relation of government to the economy may be called "public economic policy," or simply "economic policy."

In the area of economic policy, perhaps more than any other area of public policy, confusion, misunderstanding, and conflict often arise. People have different conceptions about the nature of the state and the competence of government. To many persons government is an evil, although a necessary one, and therefore an improper agent to regulate the economy. To others it is the salvation of all earthly cares. In reality, there is nothing inherently evil—or, on the other hand, inherently good—about government. Likewise, no function is peculiarly appropriate or inappropriate to government. Nor is the fact that government engages in planning inherently wrong or bad, for planning is essential for rational policy. The problem of the desirability of a particular economic policy cannot be solved simply by reference to any inherent quality of government.

Moreover, democracy does not imply what the economic policies of government should be. As Charles Merriam has said, "There is no necessary relationship between democracy as a form of political association and any special form of economic association or organization." [2] A democratic government is committed to no economic system or doctrine of state function. Decisions regarding the relation of government to the economy are worked out through the democratic process. This is not to say that one economic system may not be more wise or reasonable than another in terms of what the community accepts. The wisdom or reasonableness of the democratic process does not lie in any specific program of economic regulation but in the method by which majority decisions are reached.

By distinguishing between democracy, as a political arrangement which locates political power in the hands of the people, and the extent of economic control that may be exerted by a democratic government, the relation of government to the economy can be properly regarded as a problem of public policy to be worked out through the democratic process.

The decision, on one hand, to have no economic regulation, or, on the other hand, the decision to have extensive and detailed regulation of a

[2] *The New Democracy and The New Despotism* (New York: McGraw-Hill Book Company, Inc., 1939), p. 69.

particular economic enterprise or transaction are conceivable policy decisions that could be made through the democratic process. The substance of democratic economic policy is limited by the restraints inherent in the process by which democratic decisions are made and by the predominant values of the people. If other restraints existed, the ability of the people to work out the problems of their economy through public means would be impaired.

Government control of economic enterprise is not new. Despite a tendency on the part of many to regard it as a New Deal phenomenon, sparked by a series of emergencies in the past quarter century, the exercise of government restrictions on business is virtually as old as business itself. The perspective of history illuminates many of the problems of economic control, and the next section will trace its development. The following section will discuss the various political doctrines which prescribe what the relationship of government to the economy ought to be and how those doctrines have been applied in practice.

The Development of Control

In sketching the development of economic control, the influence exerted by moral force in the economic activity of primitive peoples need only be noted.[3] Many economic functions were regulated by government in ancient Greece, as Aristotle pointed out in his *Athenian Constitution*. A code of law governing economic relations was developed under the Roman Empire, and many principles were deduced and applied to business by early governments and the early Catholic Church. From the point of view of modern government control of business in the United States, the significant developments date largely from the rise of towns and trade in the eleventh century.

The instances of government control of business are so numerous in the years since the eleventh century that a brief review can do no more than bring into focus the regulatory characteristics of four important periods.

MEDIEVAL BUSINESS REGULATIONS

Although central control of political life virtually disappeared with the breakup of the Roman Empire, economic controls continued to exist during the Middle Ages. Under the feudal system political and economic life were closely interwoven under the direction of the overlord. Regard for custom also dominated economic activity. Workers were expected to follow in the path of their fathers. Prices were supposed to be based upon previous prices, and the producer was entitled only to a wage which

[3] See Melville Herskovits, *The Economic Life of Primitive Peoples* (New York: Alfred A. Knopf, Inc., 1940).

would allow him to maintain himself in the customary standard of living for his class.

With the organization of guilds and the rise of municipal governments further sources of economic controls appeared. The guilds were of two sorts, merchant and craft guilds. Although merchant guilds were known in continental Europe in the ninth century, their real rise dates from the eleventh century, and by 1300 they could be found in practically every town in England and Western Europe. Originally they were formed for the purpose of protecting a group of traders from the hazards of a journey and disbanded at the end of the trip. In time they became permanent and closely regulated the economic conduct of their members. Eventually the merchant guilds became part of the town governments as the towns saw the advantage they could obtain from encouraging and protecting trade.

Independent artisans in the towns banded together to form craft guilds. These associations rose to prominence somewhat after merchant guilds. Craft guilds were combinations of trade union, manufacturers' association, mutual benefit society, and professional society. They regulated the work of the craft, governed the amount and type of production, fixed the price and method of production, enforced contracts of members, and restricted advertising and aggressive selling methods. A craft guild enjoyed the exclusive right to practice a trade in a given area. Political authorities protected the attainment of monopolistic power and enforced guild regulations because of the advantages to them of complete organization of craft workers for purposes of regulation and taxation. Often these guilds became a regular part of town governments.

The forerunner of modern economic control by the state is regulation by the towns. Between roughly 1400 and 1550, besides protecting guild monopolies, towns undertook the licensing of traders and the regulation of the time, place, buildings, and commodities of markets. Fairs, or large wholesale markets, were usually held only by permission of the king or some high noble. They were limited to a number of days, and trading in nearby towns was ordinarily suspended during that time. In addition, certain towns were selected in the thirteenth and fourteenth centuries for the carrying on of foreign trade in such commodities as wool, leather, hides, and tin. These towns were called "staple towns."

In both the fairs and the staple towns trade was closely supervised. A body of rules, called the "law merchant" and based largely upon custom, was administered in the fairs by a court of piepoudre and in the staple towns by a staple court. These rules were for the most part business regulations covering weights, measures, just price, fraudulent sales, business contracts, and such trade practices as forestalling, regrating, and engrossing. Because merchants were transient, these courts had complete jurisdiction, dealing with both criminal and civil cases. The law merchant, a sort of business common law, developed over the years until it covered not only the law of contracts, notes, and bills of exchange, but widespread regulation of prices, service obligations, and liabilities of those in "common," or public, and "private" callings. In the laws against regrating (buying commodities in bulk to sell again in the same market), forestalling (purchasing commodities in advance outside the market), and engrossing (buying in quantities in order to corner the market) are found the origins of Anglo-Saxon hostility toward combination and monopoly.

Another source of economic regulation during the Middle Ages was the Catholic Church. Besides directing man's spiritual life, it also exercised control over certain economic activities, but this control was basically ethical rather than economic. The Church forbade charging interest, since it was regarded as usury and hence "sinful." It also insisted upon the doctrine of the "just price," a price that would reflect what the producer or seller needed by way of income to maintain him in the economic status in which he was born.

The character of medieval business regulations in each case varied somewhat with the authority concerned. The feudal lord was dominated by the need for revenue or by the desire to exalt his position or the standing of the territory over which he ruled. The force of custom was partly an outgrowth of the dogmas of the Church and partly an evidence of the conservative characteristics of the Middle Ages. A practice was generally regarded as good, and hence to be observed, if it had been adhered to in the past. The town was guided by the desire to protect consumers, the guilds by the interests of their members, and the Church by the precepts of Christianity.

THE NATION-STATE AND MERCANTILISM

Like other social changes, the transition from feudalism to the nation-state system was gradual. The growing importance of cities, many of which bought themselves out of feudalism; the changed methods of warfare, which necessitated the employment of a permanent professional army; the growing sense of national consciousness; the assumption of authority by a central ruling group—all these contributed to the transformation.

The king needed revenue to support the standing army under his control and to maintain his position in the state, so national taxation replaced feudal dues and services. A service-and-subsistence economy gave place to a money economy as wages and rents succeeded feudal payments. When it became apparent that sufficient revenue was not available in Europe, colonies were sought to provide a continuing source of money. Hence, royal power was intimately involved in economic activity.

The desired goal was a large supply of money. Since precious metals were the most acceptable medium of exchange, they were looked upon as being the most desirable form of wealth for a nation to have. The assumption was that only by exporting goods of more value than could be imported could a large supply of money come into the country. In order to encourage manufacture for export and secure a favorable balance of trade, extensive regulations were formulated. In England this policy was known as "mercantilism"; in France, as "Colbertism" (after the man who, although he did not originate the policy, systematized it); and in the Germanic states, as "cameralism."

The state supported shipbuilding and encouraged navigation. Duties on goods arriving in foreign bottoms helped domestic carriers. Manufacturing was assisted by protective duties as well as given stimulation by bounties, special privileges, and patent and monopoly grants. Wages were regulated to keep down labor costs. Furthermore, the state aided the discovery and exploitation of new sources of raw materials and promoted colonization by chartering trading companies with exclusive privileges. The colonies, which supplied the crude products, were then expected to purchase the finished goods so that the desired balance of trade could be maintained.

In studying the problem of government control of business in the United States, an understanding of the historic role of mercantilism gives better perspective. The laissez-faire theory of government was originally nothing more than a revulsion against the errors and excesses of mercantilism. The mercantilist policies of England were among the causes that led to the American Revolution. The American colonists were aroused by the requirement to trade with the mother country on English ships, by attempts to keep the colonies as sources of raw material through forbidding the importing of machinery, and by tax policies designed to enrich English treasuries. Because the drives for economic freedom and for political independence were reactions against mercantilism and because both occurred at the same time, a prejudice against control over business by any government influenced the framers of the American Constitution and colored the character of early American business morality.

THE PERIOD OF LIMITED CONTROL

Gradually many people came to the conclusion that full advantage could not be taken of the economic and technological developments that were revolutionizing industry in the eighteenth and nineteenth centuries if the excessive controls of the mercantilist state were continued. The period of limited control was characterized at first by the glorification of individual freedom in business and by the repeal of governmental restraints upon economic activity. But as the industrial revolution gained momentum and economic life became more complex, this period witnessed the introduction of business controls on a limited basis for the purpose of curtailing what were regarded as the abuses of individual business freedom. As business became still more complicated and social welfare more dependent upon large privately owned industries, the shortcomings of the economic system led to public insistence for government regulation, aid, and sometimes ownership of business.

Laissez faire. The development of *laissez faire* in the latter part of the eighteenth century had both a practical and an ideological basis. The rise of industry and trade and a class of enterprisers looking for means of increasing their profits led to a revolt against the restrictions of the mercantilist states and the local controls which had survived nationalism. The search for laws of nature in the physical and biological fields led to the belief that "natural" laws might be found in human relationships. To those who found the restrictions of mercantilism burdensome, it was not difficult to conceive that such restraints interfered with the natural and beneficent action of economic forces. It remained, however, for Adam Smith, a Scottish professor, to popularize this point of view and show that the traditional mercantilist approach really hampered the very development of wealth it was supposed to encourage.

In his *Wealth of Nations*, published in 1776, Adam Smith called attention to certain economic principles based upon natural law [4] and indicated the proper duties and functions of government toward business. These principles, in so far as they relate to governmental economic policy, constitute what has been called *laissez faire*, because the conclusion drawn from them was that, on the whole, wealth will be increased by letting the individual alone in his selfish quest for profit. Adam Smith, like the mercantalists, desired a strong and healthy nation. But, in contrast to them, he claimed that the wealth of nations would be greater under a system in which government did as little as possible, particularly in the area of business.

Adam Smith's works, and those of other economists who made refinements in his compilation of economic principles, were widely read and did much to influence government policy. Smith himself was at one time engaged as an adviser to the government. The time was ripe for a revolt against mercantilism. The growth of capitalism, the rise of a class of busi-

[4] The idea of natural law permeates Smith's work. He felt that men had been endowed with a self-interest by which public good would be promoted. Self-interest, if allowed freely to influence actions, would act as a sort of "invisible hand" to promote greater wealth. Thus, the natural propensity to trade and barter leads to a division of labor, and this to greater efficiency in production. The natural desire for profit leads businessmen to invest capital in enterprises for production of goods which society wants. For a discussion of this philosophy in Smith's works, see James Bonar, *Philosophy and Political Economy* (New York: The Macmillan Company, 1893), book II, chaps. 8 and 9.

nessmen who chafed under mercantilist regulation, and the existence of a period of intellectual revolt all contributed to the popular success of Adam Smith's teachings.

According to Adam Smith, the duties and functions of government are few. It should protect the nation against foreign violence or invasion. It should protect the individual through the administration of justice. It might establish and maintain certain public works, such as streets, canals, and harbors. It might contribute to schools and churches. If absolutely necessary for national defense, import duties might be levied to ensure self-sufficiency in such things as war supplies and shipping. The liberty of those engaged in banking might be restrained in the interests of liberty of the whole society. Interest rates might be fixed by law to prevent usury. The government might provide free schools for those who could not afford private education. Certain regulations in favor of labor might be fair and equitable.

It is difficult to say how much further Smith would have gone in increasing the scope of governmental activity. One can say that he did favor governmental assistance to encourage the production in his home country of such goods as might be needed to repel an invasion and would not be produced domestically without assistance. Moreover, he favored government operation of such enterprises as might be needed by the people but would not be undertaken privately because of lack of prospective profits.

However, Adam Smith and the laissez-faire economists of the eighteenth and nineteenth centuries placed their main reliance on the individual. An individual, left to his own desires, would buy what he wanted as cheaply as possible, sell for as much as he could get, engage in work most profitable to himself, produce goods in which the greatest profit lay, and conserve those goods the scarcity of which made their prices high. Thus he would gain the greatest material income with the least cost. From this position, it was deduced that a nation of such individuals would be a nation in which there would be the maximum of satisfaction with a minimum of pain.

To safeguard the community against adverse effects of individual selfishness, competition among sellers, buyers, and producers, including workers, would furnish the necessary control. In other words, if competition could be made free and governmental restraints reduced or eliminated, individuals could intelligently exert force to keep human greed in check.

Industrial revolution and *laissez faire*. The exponents of economic freedom, although standing at the very threshold of the industrial revolution, did not visualize the evils of the factory system, the development of the business corporation, or the effects of huge enterprises, such as the railroads and other public utilities, or great industrial combinations, upon public welfare. *Laissez faire* had no chance for trial, even though the restrictions of the mercantilist period were swept away in favor of a high degree of free trade, free competition, and free private enterprise. For as soon as a measure of freedom was introduced, the advance of productive technique, the increased scale of business operations, and the lack of an understanding of the science of management raised problems which called for regulation. Before Great Britain had razed the last barrier to free foreign trade, government regulation of factory labor conditions had started. In 1846, the protective import duties on grain were repealed, bringing to success the efforts of the free traders. But as early as 1802 the national government had begun to regulate the hours of work of factory apprentices. By 1853 England had passed a whole series of factory acts designed to limit the working hours of women and children and to improve the conditions of their work.

In America, also, *laissez faire* has never been fully tried. Protection to American industry was granted in the very first tariff measure passed in 1789, and by 1824 the protective tariff as a governmental aid to industry was strongly embedded in American politics and legislation. As early as 1791 the national government chartered the United States Bank as a semi-publicly owned bank. Various states also engaged in banking in the early nineteenth century. Congress prohibited foreign-owned ships from engaging in the coastal trade. State governments, with state funds, built turnpikes, canals, and railroads or contributed heavily to those enterprises.[5] In order to protect its investment in the Erie Canal, New York prohibited certain railroads from carrying freight until 1851. Charters granted to canal and railroad companies also usually included direct regulation of rates.

The United States of the nineteenth century has been thought of as genuinely individualistic. But at no time had a laissez-faire policy been tried fully. The very development of business, beginning with the demand of industry for the protective tariff, has been accompanied by the growth of governmental control through ownership, subsidy, or regulation. To be sure, labor regulation and regulation of railroads, beyond that found in the early charters, came in the last half of the nineteenth century. But the industrial revolution was hardly in effect before that time in this country. Even banking regulation, tried in various forms since the founding of the republic, did not become very effective until after 1850.

The granger movement. As early as 1836, Rhode Island created a commission with power to inquire into railroad "transactions and proceedings" so that the people of that state might "secure . . . the full and equal privileges of the transportation of passengers and property . . . granted

[5] For a discussion of these excursions into business, see W. M. Persons, *Government Experimentation in Business* (New York: John Wiley & Sons, Inc., 1934), chap. 3.

. . . to the citizens of another state or states." Commissions with like powers were established before 1860 in New Hampshire, Connecticut, Vermont, New York, and Maine. The Massachusetts commission, created in 1869, was little more than a group to advise the state whether the railroads were living up to their charters, to suggest policies of public interest to them, to require uniform accounts and reports, and to recommend needed legislation.

The real stimulus for more positive regulation came with the granger movement of the late 1860s and the 1870s. Farmers in the West and South, disgruntled at high transportation rates which reduced their profits, inflamed at paying higher rates than industrialists did at competitive railroad points, and aroused by the arrogant attitude of railroad executives whose roads the money of small communities had helped to build, took political action to curb the railroads. In 1871 Illinois passed laws that set maximum rates and prohibited discriminating fares or charges by railroads and grain elevators. Similar laws were passed in Minnesota, Wisconsin, and Iowa in the same decade.

Using the interstate-commerce power for the first time for positive regulation, the federal government, stimulated by the granger movement and the failure of granger laws to regulate railroads extending their lines over state borders, entered the field of railroad regulation in 1887. This recognition of the failure of *laissez faire* is important, not only because it marked the placing of one of the nation's largest industries under federal control, but also because the experience with railroad regulation has made the country realize how powerful the interstate-commerce power can be in regulating businesses which affect interstate commerce.

Monopoly and "trust busting." The granger movement brought about regulation of rates and practices in those businesses which have come to be regarded as "affected with the public interest" and in which monopoly is not only likely but often desirable. A few years later, with passage of the antitrust laws about 1890, the cloak of regulation was thrown over businesses other than quasi-public ones. However, the policy used was fundamentally different. While railroads were ordinarily regulated by limiting rates and prohibiting certain practices, the antitrust laws were aimed at breaking up combinations of business so that freer competition might be restored to safeguard public interest.

The growth of business combinations after the War between the States was a natural result of business development and of the apparently unlimited opportunities for the exploitation of natural resources. Paced by the privateering tactics of the Standard Oil combination, the combinations in tobacco, steel, whisky, sugar, and other fields gained virtual control of the production and marketing of many commodities of general use. To meet this threat to the competitive system, individualistic America, although claiming that it was promoting business freedom, threw overboard practical belief in *laissez faire*. With state and federal laws passed in 1887 to 1914, the dislike of freeborn Americans for the power of "trusts" was crystallized into a vigorous legislative policy to break these combinations into competitive parts. When industrial leadership found new ways to conspire against the consumer and to monopolize business, new regulations were devised, often belatedly, to further the policy of "trust busting."

Contend as one might that the antitrust laws were designed to restore economic individualism and free competition, in reality they represented an excursion into the field of government control which has not been retracted and which has led to further government control through regulation of unfair competition. The attempt to control big business and to keep it from conspiring to restrain trade brought about the regulation of trade practices of small businesses as well.

THE MODERN PERIOD OF CONTROL

It was only a step from the correction of the abuses of public utilities and monopolies to the modern period of control when an emergency created by the Depression, followed by the emergencies caused by World War II and the postwar period, brought the feeling that a free system of business enterprise could not be trusted to meet the problems of want and security. This period has been characterized throughout the world by rapid expansion of government power over business and by the concentration of this power in strong central governments. In some respects the present era of control is reminiscent of the period of the nation-states in the fifteenth to eighteenth centuries, when strong governments controlled the details of economic life to bring about wealth and national strength. In other respects, the present period may be regarded as a logical expansion of the limited controls of the nineteenth and early twentieth century.

The increased tempo of government control in the United States since 1933 has led some people to believe that nothing less than a revolution has taken place. To the extent that a revolution is really the accentuation of forces set in motion at an earlier date, this is a fair characterization. In reality, the roots of this new day of government control over business may be found in earlier developments.

Regulation of public-utility holding companies in this modern period is an outgrowth of public-utility regulation, which in turn may be traced to the unwillingness of nineteenth-century American shippers to see railroad businesses operating according to free competition. Use of subsidies in such industries as agriculture and airlines are little more than a large-scale application of principles incorporated in tariff policies and in earlier subsidies to road, canal, and railroad building. Strict banking regulation, credit-control measures, stock-exchange regulation, and security-issue restrictions are not unusual developments of the century-old struggle for sound money, banking, and investment. Motor-carrier, airline, and water-carrier regulations are understandable as expansions of transportation control. Laws to enforce competition begin with breaking up large monopolies and proceed to regulations to keep all business from interfering with what comes to be regarded as "fair" competition. Labor laws, first designed to keep women and children from working unconscionably long hours, grow into regulations to keep the employer from working men too long, setting wages too low, or interfering with labor's rights to organize. Price control, once regarded as applicable only to those few businesses "affected with a public interest," and the one kind of control which so long distinguished quasi-public and private businesses, has now become one of the kinds of control which government can apply to any business. "Emergency" controls of price and output, used at first to meet the crisis of World War II, have now become an almost standard means of control as emergency conditions continue.

One could go over the entire field of present controls and find in practically every case some precedent in the last century embodying similar principles. Once people have come to the conclusion that the code of *lasisez faire* or the rules of modified free enterprise do not protect them from political and social problems, their natural impulse is to turn to governmental measures to gain protection. In addition, since progress brings new business techniques, new economic problems, and greater complications in the operation of a system of competitive private enterprise, it is only natural that government controls should increase. The continual emergencies of the past twenty years have furnished a setting in which the freedom of business decision making has been increasingly circumscribed by government action.

Economic Controls: Doctrine and Practice

TYPES OF POLITICAL DOCTRINES

Inevitably, in a discussion of economic control, the question arises of what the relation of government to the economy *ought* to be. When we turn from a factual presentation of what the relationship of government to the economy *is* to what it *ought* to be, we enter the realm of political doctrine. Political doctrine is concerned with the justification of existing or proposed political arrangements.[6]

The subject matter of political doctrine varies with time and circum-

[6] Here followed is the terminology used by Harold D. Lasswell and Abraham Kaplan in *Power and Society, A Framework for Political Inquiry* (New Haven, Conn.: Yale University Press, 1950), p. xi. Political doctrine and political philosophy, which includes doctrine as well as the logical analysis of doctrine and science, make up the subject matter of political theory.

stance as people's interests change. During the Middle Ages man speculated about spiritual problems and the relation of the church to the state. In the age of the Enlightenment the concern was with freeing man from political despotism. Today, the relation between government and the economy is a central problem. Some men maintain that government ought not be an instrument to control economic life. Others insist that the economy ought to be completely controlled by government. Conflicting judgments of what "ought to be" are products of differing assumptions concerning the nature of men, the state, and government and consequently different views about the ways the ends of the state can be achieved.

In some cases, a political doctrine has developed out of a controversy over the merit of rival economic policies and serves as justification for a particular policy. In other cases, the doctrine may outline a desirable program of action. To put it another way, sometimes ideas are a product of socioeconomic conditions, and sometimes ideas govern the development of social institutions. In both cases, there is often little consistency between doctrine and practice. Most persons are not consistent believers in any one political doctrine. Consequently, political doctrines seldom exist in pure form. But they should be examined in the study of economic policy, for they make up the myths and values which guide the selection of programs to achieve the ends of government. A political doctrine serves as a goal to be achieved and as a convenient set of symbols to be employed in political action.

While it is impossible here to differentiate in detail between doctrines of state economic functions, some insight may be obtained by a brief examination of the leading types.

Anarchism. The simplest doctrine of state functions is anarchism, which would abolish the state entirely. The thread of anarchist writing runs from the Stoics of ancient Greece through the various sects of the Middle Ages down to the anarchists of modern times, such as Michael Bakunin, Prince Kropotkin, and Count Leo Tolstoi. Hostility to the state is the point of agreement among all anarchists. Some would also destroy private property and the church. Most anarchists agree in the assumption that human nature is essentially good, except that it is corrupted by such evil influences as government, private property, or the church. There is less agreement as to the methods by which the state should be overthrown and the nature of the regime which should replace it.

The anarchists do succeed in pointing to certain evils in our society. The utopian character of some of their writings is optimistic and inspirational. But their basic doctrines are built on fallacious assumptions, and the solutions proposed are impossible to accomplish.

Individualism. The individualist agrees with the anarchist that the state is evil, but he regards it as necessary to perform certain functions. The individualist is primarily concerned with imposing limits on the authority of government even though that authority may be derived from the people through democratic processes.

The various doctrines of individualism differ according to the time and conditions under which they are advocated and the particular rights that are being asserted. In general there is agreement that the individual is the focus for all social and political action and that his well-being can be enhanced by restricting state activity. It is assumed that each person is a rational, mature individual who is the best judge of his own interests. He knows what he wants out of life and, if left free from outside interference, can accomplish his ends. Since individual interests are held to yield results for the highest welfare of society, the state must be prohibited from disturbing the natural equilibrium. Government control is necessary only to prevent one individual from encroaching upon the rights of others, to protect life and property from natural hazards, and to defend the state from external dangers.

There is an economic and a political aspect of individualism. Individualism came into prominence during the eighteenth century as a reaction to the excessive government controls in all aspects of daily life. On the economic side the protest against mercantilism resulted in the doctrine of the physiocrats in France and the classical school of economists in England, which traces its origins back to Adam Smith. On the political side individualism provided the philosophic support for revolutionary and evolutionary movements that culminated in democratic government.

Like economic individualism, political individualism is based on the natural-law assumption that man knows his own interests and should be left free to exercise his inherent freedom. Autocratic government and the doctrine of divine right of kings imposed political restraints on man's independence. To protect his freedom man placed limitations on government. Thus, out of political individualism developed constitutionalism—an arrangement by which government is regularly and legally limited. Simultaneously, the movement for popular government was in the making, and constitutionalism became a necessary part of democracy. But not every limited government is a democracy. Democracy refers to the arrangement by which the control of government is kept in the hands of the people. Limitations on government are one way to perpetuate this control.

However, the individualist is not necessarily a supporter of democratic government. The fear that popular government would alter existing social and economic arrangements led some individualists to seek to limit government actions that reflect majority will. Moreover, efforts are made by individualists to identify liberty in the political sense, which is essential to the functioning of democratic government, with economc freedom.

Socialism. Whereas the individualist regards each man as his own keeper and expects every man to satisfy his needs, the socialist looks to society organized in the state for assistance in promoting individual welfare and bringing about a more equitable distribution of goods and services.

In simplest terms socialism is a system under which the means of production and distribution of goods and services are owned and operated by instruments of the state. The specific character of the doctrine depends upon the assumptions and values that underlie it. A form of socialism known as Fabianism gained wide support in England. The Fabian's basic assumption is that value is the creation of society rather than of workers. The classical economists as well as the Marxists hold that the value of any product or service depends upon the amount of labor that goes into it. The object of Fabian socialism is to obtain for all members of society, through gradual and democratic means, the values which society creates.

Guild socialism also gained popularity in England and, as a corrective to increasing centralization, proposed the organization of the state into guilds of workers and consumers for the ownership and control of productive property. Syndicalism holds that the workers alone must control the conditions under which they work and live and that social change can be accomplished by their own efforts—principally through the general strike. Syndicalism is largely identified with elements of the trade-union movement in France, although its influence was felt in the Industrial Workers of the World in the United States, in certain labor developments in Britain, and in aspects of the government of Fascist Italy.

Communism. Communism is a complex doctrine that is rooted in a philosophy of dialectic materialism. It contains a critique of capitalism and a program of revolutionary action and violence to replace it with the Communist state. As applied in Russia, it resulted in the establishment of a totalitarian state. The state, which according to Lenin would eventually wither away, has shown no signs of disappearing. To run the state the Communist party became a highly centralized bureaucracy. Drama, music, literature, religion—every aspect of community life is subject to some state direction. The Five Year Plans imposed tight economic controls. Collective and cooperative farming were introduced to stimulate output.

In a state with a limited government, government is only one of many regulatory institutions in the community. Constitutional sanction is given to the distinction between the community and the state. Under a totalitarian state like the Soviet Union this distinction is denied. The state is made equivalent to the community, so that no aspect of life is above or beyond the reach of the state.[7]

[7] See Robert MacIver, *The Web of Government* (New York: The Macmillan Company, 1947), pp. 192–208.

POLITICAL DOCTRINE IN PRACTICE

Now that National Socialist Germany and Fascist Italy have been destroyed by World War II, the prime example of the operation of totalitarian principles is the Soviet Union, although such countries as Spain, Argentina, and China have traveled far down the totalitarian road. The U.S.S.R. has, of course, gone furthest in its application of collectivistic principles, with its universal public ownership of business in mining, agriculture, trade, transportation, and other fields of economic activity. But even the Soviet Union has retained some of the features of individualism through private ownership in income, unequal compensation, piecework wages, and bonuses. In other totalitarian countries, one usually finds private ownership of property and income predominating, although the state controls the economic system through fixing prices, regulating wages, limiting profits, directing the allocation of capital resources into industries, and determining to some extent the quantities of goods which should be produced.

Most of the democratic nations, including the United States, but especially the Scandinavian countries and Great Britain, have adopted socialist principles. But much individual freedom in business and political matters may still be found in these countries. To be sure, the government of the United Kingdom has rapidly increased the tempo toward a socialist society, through nationalization of some basic industries, its national health program, international bartering of some basic commodities, and other programs which replace the forces of competition and industrial business decision with the planning and action of a central government. In the United States, one can see strong tendencies toward socialism in municipal utilities, public power projects, and the like. These tendencies have not yet embraced the nationalization of any basic industries and are not likely to do so, but a series of emergencies over the past quarter century have led to detailed regulation of wages, prices, and production and the domination of many sectors of the economy by the state. Many of these regulations which are now accepted as a matter of course were unthinkable to most people a few years ago. While many regulations are accepted because of the existence of emergencies, one wonders to what extent the way toward socialism is a one-way street and whether continual emergencies will occur to replace those which pass.

Even so, the application of socialist principles in the United States has not gone nearly to the extent which has been prevalent in the totalitarian countries. Businessmen still enjoy much freedom. Most goods are sold at prices and in quantities fairly free from control of government. Even much of the emergency price-control legislation and its administration had little real controlling influence on prices. Wages tend to be pretty largely determined by the forces of competition and collective bargaining, and emergency stabilization controls often do no more than act as a brake. The way in which things are produced, the places they are produced, and the persons who produce them are among some of the fundamental aspects of economic activity which are still subject to much individual freedom, despite the pattern of material allocations of World War II and the defense programs of recent years.

Americans do not adhere unalterably to one political doctrine for the solution of all their public problems. Through the democratic process they have chosen the solution which they think will best solve a particular problem. The approach has been largely pragmatic, rather than being guided by a fixed dogma. As John Dewey put it, "There is no antecedent universal proposition which can be laid down because of which the functions of the state should be limited or should be expanded. Their scope is something to be critically and experimentally determined." [8] As a result, the American economy is best characterized as a "mixed" economy. Certain sectors of the economic system are private, others are subject to extensive government regulation while ultimate control rests in private hands, and still other sectors are publicly owned and operated. Yet, this mixed economy continues to be molded by the force of an enlightened public opinion operating in a system of free expression and free use of the ballot.

Conclusions

The history of economic controls points up the fact that economic life has always been subject to some form of social control. Political and social life was never a separate sphere of activity from the economic. Private enterprise played a role in ancient Greece and Rome, but always in the presence of more powerful political control. During the Middle Ages and under mercantilism the tendency was decidedly away from private enterprise. Only the period of *laissez faire* was unique in the history of political economy. What was unusual about that period was the contradiction between the theoretical insistence upon minimization of economic controls by government and the reality of their existence.

Since the beginning of recorded history it has been far too late to ask *whether* government should control the economy. The questions that must be faced by an intelligent citizenry today are: "In what areas, to what extent, and in what ways should government control the economic system?"

[8] *Op. cit.*, p. 74.

Selected References

Beard, Charles A., "The Myth of Rugged American Individualism," 164 *Harper's Magazine* 13–22 (December, 1931).

Becker, Carl L., *Modern Democracy*. New Haven, Conn.: Yale University Press, 1941.

Clark, John M., *Social Control of Business*, 2d ed., chaps. 1–4. New York: McGraw-Hill Book Company, Inc., 1939.

Cole, G. D. H., "Laissez-faire," in *Encyclopedia of the Social Sciences*, vol. IX, pp. 15–20.

Commager, Henry Steele, *Majority Rule and Minority Rights*. New York: Oxford University Press, 1943.

Dahl, Robert A., and Charles E. Lindblom, *Politics, Economics, and Welfare*. New York: Harper & Brothers, 1953.

Dewey, John, *The Public and Its Problems*. Chicago: Gateway Books, 1946.

Finer, Herman, *The Road to Reaction*. Boston: Little, Brown & Company, 1946.

Hayek, Friedrich A., *The Road to Serfdom*. Chicago: University of Chicago Press, 1944.

Knight, Frank H., *Freedom and Reform*. New York: Harper & Brothers, 1947.

Lauterbach, Albert, *Economic Security and Individual Freedom*. Ithaca, N.Y.: Cornell University Press, 1948.

Lindsay, A. D., "Individualism," in *Encyclopedia of the Social Sciences*, vol. VIII, pp. 674–680.

MacIver, Robert M., *Democracy and the Economic Challenge*. New York: Alfred A. Knopf, Inc., 1952.

———, *The Web of Government*. New York: The Macmillan Company, 1947.

Mason, Alpheus T., "American Individualism: Fact and Fiction," 46 *American Political Science Review* 1–18 (March, 1952).

Schumpeter, Joseph A., *Capitalism, Socialism, and Democracy*. New York: Harper & Brothers, 1947.

Steiner, George A., *Government's Role in Economic Life*. New York: McGraw-Hill Book Company, Inc., 1953.

Whittaker, Edmund, *A History of Economic Ideas*. New York: Longmans, Green & Co., Inc., 1940.

2

THE CONSTITUTIONAL FRAMEWORK FOR ECONOMIC CONTROL

An analysis of government control of economic enterprise in the United States cannot be made without some understanding of the constitutional framework within which these controls operate. Because of its paramount importance, the present discussion will be confined to the federal Constitution. It has influenced the wording of the state constitutions, and its grants of power to the federal government and its restrictions on authority are binding on state and national governments alike.

One should not forget that the whole of constitutional law includes much more than the written Constitution itself. Interpretations of it by the courts, the elaborate statutory enactments filling in the details of the written document, and the element of custom in giving meaning to terminology, form a part of the constitutional law in its entirety. This chapter will point out only the legal foundations of government control over business.

The Constitution of the United States consists of three elements: (1) it provides a structure of government by establishing a federal system of government and outlining the establishment of a Congress, the presidency, and the judiciary at the federal level; (2) it prescribes and describes the powers of the three branches of the federal government and defines the division of power between the states and the federal government; and (3) it imposes certain legal limitations on both the federal and state governments to protect the people against arbitrary government. Each of these elements will be discussed in so far as it pertains to economic control.

The Structure of Government

THE FEDERAL SYSTEM

One of the most striking features of the American Constitution is the federal system it establishes. The Founding Fathers preserved the states, each with its own government, while at the same time creating a new federal level of government. Each level has certain powers and is subject to certain restraints. The powers of the national government are expressly granted to it, and all powers not so granted are reserved to the states, unless otherwise prohibited by the federal Constitution. Certain powers, such as the power to tax and the power to enact bankruptcy laws, are shared concurrently by both the states and the federal government. In case of a conflict between state and federal authority the Constitution provides that the Constitution, and all laws and treaties made under the Constitution, shall be "the supreme law of the land."

The constitutionality of federal economic regulation has frequently been attacked on the grounds that it encroaches upon the powers reserved to the states. However, the states'-rights argument has sometimes been used when the real issue is whether control should be exercised at all. The defenders of states' rights in turn become their opponents if the states undertake economic control. Moreover, while the power reserved to the states was broad, it was not intended to stand in the way of the full exercise of the authority granted to the federal government.

SEPARATION OF BRANCHES AND THE POWERS OF EACH

The Constitution set up a federal government of separate but coordinate branches. This pattern has been followed in the state governments. All legislative power is vested in the Congress, the President is vested with executive power, and judicial power is vested in the Supreme Court and such inferior courts as Congress chooses to establish. The purpose of dividing the powers of government among three branches, rather than vesting all powers in one branch, as is the case in the British Cabinet form of government, was to prevent government from becoming too strong.[1] To preserve the equilibrium between the branches of government and prevent one from becoming too strong, each branch has a share in the powers of the other. This arrangement is known as "checks and balances." The President shares in lawmaking through his power to propose legislation and to sign or veto bills. The Senate shares in the ratification of treaties and consents to presidential appointments. Congress controls the organization and jurisdiction of the federal courts, and the President appoints federal judges. The President and federal judges may be removed by congressional impeachment proceedings. To prevent any one branch from becoming too weak, the independence of each was guaranteed by measures which limited the arrest of members of Congress, provided that the President have a fixed salary during his term of office, and assured judges of life tenure during good behavior.

[1] Madison wrote in *The Federalist*, No. 47: "The accumulation of all powers, legislative, executive, and judiciary, in the same hands, whether of one, a few, or many, and whether hereditary, self-appointed, or elective, may justly be pronounced the very definition of tyranny."

The limitations imposed by separation of powers tend to be offset by certain developments, although the general restrictive influence of the doctrine persists. The rise of political parties and the assertion of political leadership by the President has brought Congress and the executive branch into a closer working relationship. The rise of independent regulatory commissions has bridged certain of the gaps created by the establishment of separate branches. And the increasing willingness of the Supreme Court to accept certain kinds of congressional delegation of authority to the executive branch has further closed the gaps. For example, contingent legislation authorizing the executive to act on the determination of certain facts, has been uniformly supheld. Skeleton legislation, the details of which are filled in by the executive branch in accordance with certain limitations, has also been generally upheld.

Legislative power. The Constitution (Art. I, sec. 8) delegates to Congress certain enumerated powers, sometimes referred to as "express" powers. If Congress were confined to enacting laws only in pursuance of these specifically delegated powers, its authority would be greatly limited. However, Congress also has the power (Art. I, sec. 8, par. 18) "to make all laws which shall be necessary and proper for carrying into execution the foregoing powers." The Supreme Court long ago ruled, in a case testing the authority of Congress to incorporate a bank, which power was not expressly granted to Congress: "Let the end be legitimate, let it be within the scope of the Constitution, and all means which are appropriate, which are plainly adapted to that end, which are not prohibited, but consist with the letter and spirit of the Constitution, are constitutional." [2] The implied powers of Congress have been the principal basis for the expansion of the authority of the national government.

Executive power. The President is not only the Chief Executive of the United States, but he is also the Commander in Chief of the armed forces, chief of foreign relations, and legislative leader.[3] As Chief Executive the President is directed to "take care that the laws be faithfully executed" (Art. II, sec. 3). The only powers specifically vested in the President to aid him in executing all laws is the power to appoint, by and with the advice and consent of the Senate, "ambassadors, other public ministers and consuls, judges of the Supreme Court and all other officers of the United States" (Art. II, sec. 2, par. 2). In addition, the President alone may appoint "inferior officers" subordinate to the heads of departments or the courts of law. The power to remove has been implied from the power to appoint.[4] However, the authority of the President to remove appointees to the

[2] *McCulloch v. Maryland*, 4 Wheat. 316 (1819).

[3] See Edward S. Corwin, *The President, Office and Powers* (New York: New York University Press, 1941).

[4] *Myers v. United States*, 272 U.S. 52 (1926).

regulatory commissions, who exercise quasi-legislative and quasi-judicial powers, may be limited by statutory restrictions.[5]

In time of war the powers of the President as Commander in Chief are extensive. Lincoln argued that his war powers gave him expanded civil authority. On this basis he issued the Emancipation Proclamation depriving slave owners of their property. Wilson exercised vast powers, largely conferred on him by Congress. Franklin Roosevelt asserted that he possessed civil powers in time of war that in peacetime would require congressional authorization. Thus, industrial relations were governed during World War II on the basis of an agreement he entered into with employers and employees.

The question has arisen as to whether the President has any inherent executive power beyond that expressly granted in the Constitution. In one case the Supreme Court ruled that the President may exercise a power without any specific constitutional authorization.[6] However, when President Truman seized the steel mills in 1952 without prior congressional authorization, the Supreme Court, without going so far as to deny the existence of inherent power, held that the President had exceeded his constitutional authority.[7]

Judicial power. In addition to settling legal disputes the judiciary has the power to declare laws unconstitutional. This authority was not expressly embodied in the Constitution and, in so far as the power of the central courts to invalidate acts of the central legislature is concerned, is unique among modern governments.

Chief Justice Marshall first enunciated the theory of judicial review in 1803 when he declared that an act of Congress repugnant to the Constitution is void.[8] Prior to the War between the States, only one other act of Congress was declared unconstitutional.[9] Since that time there have been seventy-six cases in which all or part of an act of Congress has been invalidated.

Although there has been much dispute over the authority of the courts to declare acts of the federal government unconstitutional, there is no question that if federal supremacy is to be maintained, state laws can be invalidated when they conflict with the Constitution. Since the Supreme Court first asserted its right to pass on state actions in 1793,[10] hundreds of state laws have been invalidated. They have been invalidated either because they were in conflict with express constitutional limitations upon the states,

[5] *Humphrey's Executor (Rathbun) v. United States*, 295 U.S. 602 (1935).
[6] *In re Neagle*, 135 U.S. 1 (1890).
[7] *Youngstown Sheet & Tube Co. v. Sawyer*, 343 U.S. 579 (1952).
[8] *Marbury v. Madison*, 1 Cranch 137 (1803).
[9] *Dred Scott v. Standford*, 19 How. 393 (1857).
[10] *Chisholm v. Georgia*, 2 Dall. 419 (1793).

such as the taking of life, liberty, and property without due process of law, or because they encroached upon the sphere of federal authority as determined by the Constitution.

The courts' power of judicial review has sometimes been described as a principal way by which the Constitution has been expanded. Actually, this assertion is not completely accurate. It must be remembered that, before a court ever reviews a statute, a need for legislation has usually been felt by the public. If the Court upholds an act which expands the authority of government, it appears that the Court was responsible for the expansion. But the initial expansion resulted from legislative action. Only in rare instances has the Supreme Court enunciated a principle expanding governmental power without some prior legislative determination.[11]

Since 1937 [12] the scope of judicial review has been greatly narrowed by the policy of the Supreme Court to refrain from invalidating the acts of the elected representatives of the people unless overriding evidence of the unconstitutionality is presented. This policy of judicial self-restraint operates in the entire sphere of economic regulation. Only in the area of civil liberties does the presumption of unconstitutionality still orient the Court's review of a statute.

The Power of Congress

THE COMMERCE POWER

In the regulation of business by the national government, perhaps no power of Congress is more important and has more possibilities for expansion than the control of interstate and foreign commerce. Of the many regulations of business in recent years, few can be found which do not rest in part upon this grant of power.

The clause. The clause of the Constitution (Art. I, sec. 8, par. 3) in which power is delegated to Congress states that Congress may "regulate commerce with foreign nations, and among the several states, and with the Indian tribes." Of particular significance is the phrase referring to interstate commerce. Passed by the framers of the Constitution without debate, this section was probably designed by them to give the national government authority to prevent the states from placing burdens on the free flow of commerce between states and with foreign countries. Except for some control over navigable waters, largely negative in that it merely forbade certain interferences with free commerce, the commerce power was little used for nearly a century after the ratification of the Constitution. The beginning of its use for positive regulation of business in reality dates from

[11] For example, *Thornhill v. Alabama*, 310 U.S. 88 (1940); *The Genessee Chief*, 12 How. 443 (1851).

[12] Actually since 1934 in the case of state laws.

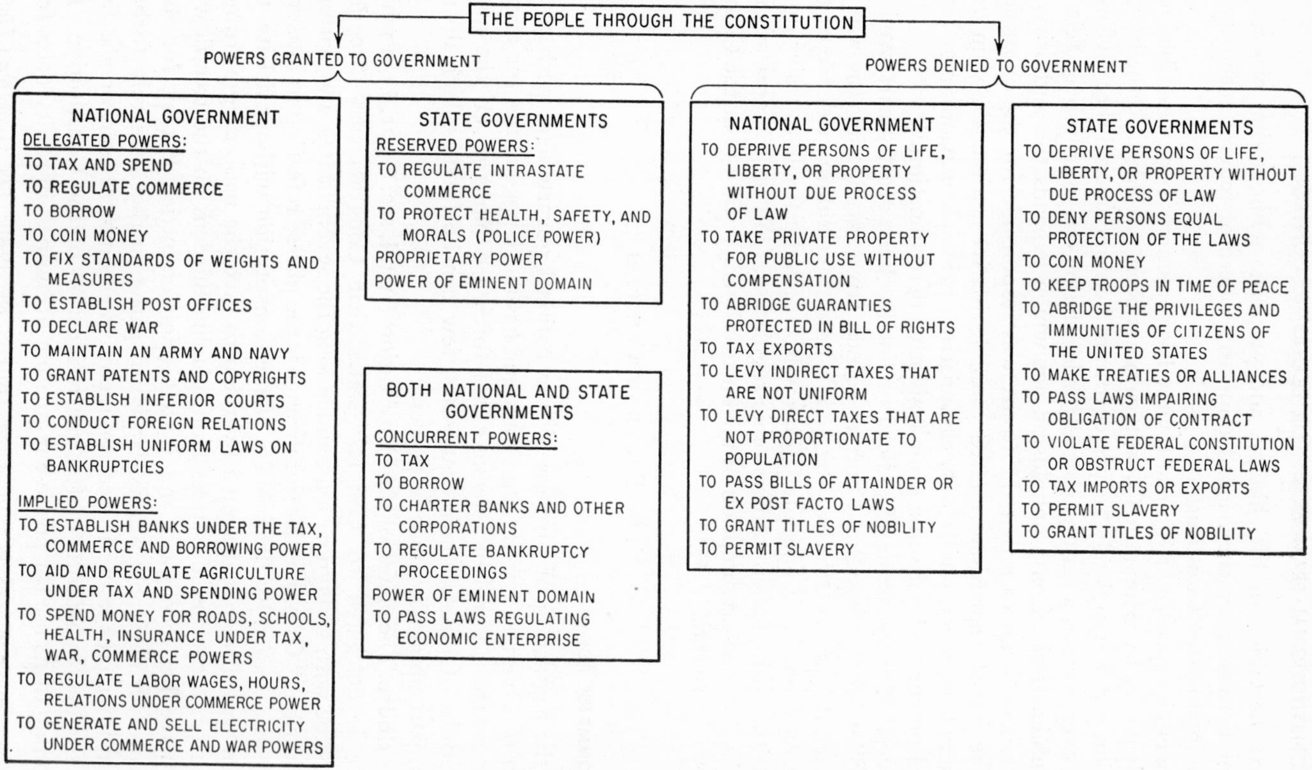

THE PEOPLE THROUGH THE CONSTITUTION

POWERS GRANTED TO GOVERNMENT

NATIONAL GOVERNMENT

DELEGATED POWERS:

TO TAX AND SPEND
TO REGULATE COMMERCE
TO BORROW
TO COIN MONEY
TO FIX STANDARDS OF WEIGHTS AND MEASURES
TO ESTABLISH POST OFFICES
TO DECLARE WAR
TO MAINTAIN AN ARMY AND NAVY
TO GRANT PATENTS AND COPYRIGHTS
TO ESTABLISH INFERIOR COURTS
TO CONDUCT FOREIGN RELATIONS
TO ESTABLISH UNIFORM LAWS ON BANKRUPTCIES

IMPLIED POWERS:

TO ESTABLISH BANKS UNDER THE TAX, COMMERCE AND BORROWING POWER
TO AID AND REGULATE AGRICULTURE UNDER TAX AND SPENDING POWER
TO SPEND MONEY FOR ROADS, SCHOOLS, HEALTH, INSURANCE UNDER TAX, WAR, COMMERCE POWERS
TO REGULATE LABOR WAGES, HOURS, RELATIONS UNDER COMMERCE POWER
TO GENERATE AND SELL ELECTRICITY UNDER COMMERCE AND WAR POWERS

STATE GOVERNMENTS

RESERVED POWERS:

TO REGULATE INTRASTATE COMMERCE
TO PROTECT HEALTH, SAFETY, AND MORALS (POLICE POWER)
PROPRIETARY POWER
POWER OF EMINENT DOMAIN

BOTH NATIONAL AND STATE GOVERNMENTS

CONCURRENT POWERS:

TO TAX
TO BORROW
TO CHARTER BANKS AND OTHER CORPORATIONS
TO REGULATE BANKRUPTCY PROCEEDINGS
POWER OF EMINENT DOMAIN
TO PASS LAWS REGULATING ECONOMIC ENTERPRISE

POWERS DENIED TO GOVERNMENT

NATIONAL GOVERNMENT

TO DEPRIVE PERSONS OF LIFE, LIBERTY, OR PROPERTY WITHOUT DUE PROCESS OF LAW
TO TAKE PRIVATE PROPERTY FOR PUBLIC USE WITHOUT COMPENSATION
TO ABRIDGE GUARANTIES PROTECTED IN BILL OF RIGHTS
TO TAX EXPORTS
TO LEVY INDIRECT TAXES THAT ARE NOT UNIFORM
TO LEVY DIRECT TAXES THAT ARE NOT PROPORTIONATE TO POPULATION
TO PASS BILLS OF ATTAINDER OR EX POST FACTO LAWS
TO GRANT TITLES OF NOBILITY
TO PERMIT SLAVERY

STATE GOVERNMENTS

TO DEPRIVE PERSONS OF LIFE, LIBERTY, OR PROPERTY WITHOUT DUE PROCESS OF LAW
TO DENY PERSONS EQUAL PROTECTION OF THE LAWS
TO COIN MONEY
TO KEEP TROOPS IN TIME OF PEACE
TO ABRIDGE THE PRIVILEGES AND IMMUNITIES OF CITIZENS OF THE UNITED STATES
TO MAKE TREATIES OR ALLIANCES
TO PASS LAWS IMPAIRING OBLIGATION OF CONTRACT
TO VIOLATE FEDERAL CONSTITUTION OR OBSTRUCT FEDERAL LAWS
TO TAX IMPORTS OR EXPORTS
TO PERMIT SLAVERY
TO GRANT TITLES OF NOBILITY

Figure 2—1. Division of Powers in the Federal System

the Interstate Commerce Act of 1887, under which railroads were subjected to national control.

As one writer has pointed out: [13]

> Following the Interstate Commerce Act came a veritable deluge of legislation under the commerce power. In the exercise of that power Congress has not only regulated the railroads, but has prohibited contracts and combinations in restraint of trade and certain "unfair" business practices, and extended federal jurisdiction over stockyards, boards of trade, aviation, communication, warehouses, and securities exchanges. It has regulated the quality of foods and drugs and the standards for articles shipped in interstate commerce, such as meats, cotton, grain, etc. It has regulated the shipment of liquor into "dry" states and prohibited the movement in interstate commerce of prison-made goods, kidnapped persons, white slaves, and stolen automobiles. It has chartered railroads and determined who shall construct dams and power plants on navigable waters. Indeed, the commerce power has come to be the principal means which the national government has at its disposal for the regulation of private business, the chief fount of federal power, perhaps the most benign gift of the Constitution.

What is interstate commerce? The interstate-commerce clause, while concise, is a direct and complete grant of power to the federal government. But the questions of what is "commerce" and what is "interstate" have been exceedingly difficult to answer and have occupied much of the attention of the federal courts for more than a century. Because of the possible varieties of meaning attaching to these two words, particularly in specific cases, the real import of the interstate-commerce clause has depended singularly upon interpretation by the courts. While this interpretation has at times appeared restrictive, it has generally been expansive. In the past two decades, the interpretation has been expansive; the courts have found in the interstate-commerce clause an authority so inclusive as virtually to allow the federal government a broad power to legislate in the interests of the public health, morals, safety, and welfare. This "benign gift of the Constitution" has, indeed, been interpreted so extensively that the dividing line between intrastate and interstate matters has all but disappeared.

1. *Interstate exchange.* In the first case in which the Supreme Court attempted interpretation of the interstate-commerce power, Chief Justice Marshall held that "commerce, undoubtedly, is traffic, but it is something more; it is intercourse. It describes the commercial intercourse between nations and parts of nations, *in all its branches*, and is regulated by prescribing rules for carrying on that intercourse." [14] What the Chief Justice

[13] M. G. Lee, *The Government's Hand in Business* (New York: Baker, Voorhis and Company, 1937), pp. 6–8.

[14] *Gibbons v. Ogden*, 9 Wheat. 1, 68 (1824). (Italics added.)

was endeavoring to emphasize was that the concept of commerce included more than mere buying and selling over state boundaries; it includes the whole process by which the exchange is carried on. In this case, the Supreme Court found that interstate navigation was an essential part of this broader view of exchange. In other cases, the Supreme Court emphasized that all interstate communication or trade by any means is included in the legal concept of commerce.[15]

2. *Interstate commerce extends to agencies or instrumentalities.* Although a particular agency or instrumentality may be inside the boundaries of a state, the Supreme Court early held that it still may be engaged in interstate commerce and thus be subject to the power of Congress. In a famous case in 1871 the Supreme Court held that a steamship which carried goods within the boundaries of a state was an instrumentality of interstate commerce because it handled goods traveling in interstate commerce.[16] This recognition of participation in the flow of commerce by agencies operating entirely within a state can well be regarded as one of the philosophical bases for the present wide expansion of the interstate-commerce power. Even before the wide expansion following 1937, one finds a gradual expansion. In 1922, the Supreme Court held that local grain elevators which purchased grain and reshipped to an out-of-state market were in the "flow" of interstate commerce.[17] The "same practical conception of interstate commerce" was given to federal regulation of stockyards.[18] Here the Supreme Court found that the stockyards of the country, being an agency through which interstate commerce flowed, were but an "incident" in the current of commerce from state to state and were subject to the power of Congress to regulate interstate commerce.

3. *Removing obstructions to interstate commerce.* Having established the concept that commerce between the states is a "flow" or "current" of business over state boundaries, the Supreme Court has found a useful legal precedent for giving Congress authority to preserve the freedom of this commerce. Although the concept that the interstate-commerce power encompassed the protection of a free flow of commerce cannot be said to be new with the stockyards case, the idea of preserving the current

[15] *Pensacola Tel. Co. v. Western Un. Tel. Co.*, 96 U.S. 1 (1877); *Federal Radio Commission v. Nelson Bros.*, 289 U.S. 266 (1933); *Electric Bond and Share Co. v. SEC*, 303 U.S. 419 (1938); *United States v. South Eastern Underwriters Assoc.*, 322 U.S. 533 (1944).

[16] *The Daniel Ball*, 10 Wall. 557. Here the Court held that the steamship "was employed as an instrument of that [interstate] commerce; for whenever an article has begun to issue as an article of trade from one state to another, commerce in that commodity between the states has commenced"; and that "to the extent in which each agency acts in that transportation, it is subject to the regulation of Congress."

[17] *Lemke v. Farmers' Grain Company*, 258 U.S. 50 (1922).

[18] *Stafford v. Wallace*, 258 U.S. 495 (1922).

of interstate commerce was materially clarified and enlarged in that case.[19]

Certainly the most far-reaching Supreme Court decision affecting the interstate-commerce power was the case decided in 1937 which found the National Labor Relations Act constitutional.[20] Despite a solid background of precedent that mining and manufacture were not commerce, the Supreme Court found grounds to hold that the manufacturing activities of the Jones and Laughlin Steel Corporation were "organized on a national scale," that their "relation to interstate commerce" was the dominant factor" in its business activities, and that interstate commerce could constitutionally be protected "from the paralyzing consequences of industrial war." Consequently, held the Court, not only could Congress remove obstructions in the form of labor strife from the flow of interstate commerce, but the labor practices of this steel manufacturer, in view of its "far-flung activities," had an effect on interstate commerce which was not "indirect or remote."

Following the Jones and Laughlin case, a number of businesses have been found to fall within the purview of the interstate-commerce power. The Supreme Court had little trouble in finding that the labor practices of a clothing manufacturer,[21] a trailer manufacturer,[22] and a fruit-packing company with only 37 per cent of its output in interstate commerce[23] affect interstate commerce enough to admit of control by Congress. It is interesting how, as time went on, the special circumstances which made the Jones and Laughlin Steel Corporation, with its integrated and far-flung activities, a good case for discovering obstructions to commerce, began to disappear. The source of raw materials lying in the channels of interstate commerce and the sales of finished goods in interstate commerce were forgotten in the application of the removal-of-obstruction doctrine to smaller and more local businesses.[24]

Even the distinction between "direct" and "indirect" effects on commerce, outlined by Chief Justice Hughes in the Jones and Laughlin Steel

[19] For example, in 1904, the Court held that attempts to monopolize trade interfered with the freedom of interstate commerce. See *Northern Securities Co. v. United States*, 193 U.S. 197 (1904); also *Swift and Co. v. United States*, 196 U.S. 375 (1905). In certain railroad cases, the Supreme Court had upheld the power of Congress to regulate intrastate rates to the extent necessary to remove burdens on the movement of commodities in interstate commerce. See especially *Railroad Commission v. Chicago B. & Q. Rwy. Co.*, 257 U.S. 563 (1922), and *Shreveport Rate Cases*, 234 U.S. 342 (1914).

[20] *NLRB v. Jones and Laughlin Steel Corp.*, 301 U.S. 1 (1935).

[21] *NLRB v. Friedman-Harry Marks Clothing Co.*, 301 U.S. 58 (1937).

[22] *NLRB v. Fruehauf Trailer Co.*, 301 U.S. 49 (1937).

[23] *Santa Cruz Fruit Packing Co. v. NLRB*, 303 U.S. 453 (1938).

[24] See e.g., *NLRB v. Fainblatt*, 306 U.S. 601 (1939); *NLRB v. Bradford Dyeing Ass'n.*, 310 U.S. 318 (1940); *Polish National Alliance v. NLRB*, 332 U.S. 643 (1944).

case, seems to have been forgotten. In this connection Chief Justice Hughes made the following point: [25]

> Undoubtedly the scope of this power must be considered in the light of our dual system of government and may not be extended so as to embrace effects upon interstate commerce so indirect and remote that to embrace them, in view of our complex society, would effectually obliterate the distinction between what is national and what is local and create a completely centralized government.

However, federal price control over local milk producers was later upheld as an appropriate device for giving needed protection to federally regulated prices in interstate trade.[26]

The tendency to obliterate the difference between indirect and direct effects is exemplified in cases under the acreage-allotment program of the Agricultural Adjustment Act. This law provides, among other things, for a system of acreage allotments to farmers to limit the production of agricultural products and thereby increase market prices and the return to the farmer. The national character of the agriculture problem and the use of marketing quotas controlling the flow of products into markets to solve this problem were held by the Supreme Court to be an appropriate use of the commerce power in 1939.[27] At that time, the Court held that the law merely aimed to control sales of agricultural products so as to prevent the flow of commerce from harming the public welfare. But three years later, the Supreme Court held that the production of wheat not for sale but for use on the farm fell within the interstate-commerce power if, in the judgment of Congress, such control was necessary to accomplish effective federal control of the marketing process.[28] No more remote effect upon interstate commerce can be imagined.

Such a line of decision seems to place little or no limit upon the reach of the federal interstate-commerce power, if relationship between the regulation of a local business and a national policy can be found. Virtually any program of federal business regulation can be supported as affecting, at least to some extent, the free flow of commerce. The integrated character of economic life would appear to form a basis for placing any business in the flow of commerce if a farmer growing wheat for use on his own farm can be regulated under the extension of this doctrine.

4. *Policing interstate commerce.* The flow-of-commerce interpretation of the interstate-commerce clause tends to merge into the power of Con-

[25] *NLRB v. Jones and Laughlin Steel Corp.*, 301 U.S. 1 (1937).

[26] *United States v. Wrightwood Dairy Co.*, 315 U.S. 110 (1942). On other local sales see *United States v. Rock Royal Cooperative, Inc.*, 307 U.S. 533 (1939); *Sunshine Anthracite Coal Co.*, 310 U.S. 381 (1940).

[27] *Mulford v. Smith*, 307 U.S. 38 (1939).

[28] *Wickard v. Filburn*, 317 U.S. 11 (1942).

gress to keep the channels of interstate commerce free of traffic which is injurious to public health, morals, and safety. Thus, Congress has constitutionally excluded from interstate commerce lottery tickets,[29] impure food and drugs,[30] stolen automobiles,[31] below-standard grain,[32] and the transport of women for immoral purposes.[33] But, until 1941, the Supreme Court had held that the article to be excluded must be such as to "promote immorality, dishonesty or the spread of any evil or harm to the people of other States from the State of origin." [34] For example, in a case involving the prohibition of goods produced by child labor from interstate commerce, the Supreme Court decided in 1918 that, since these goods were harmless in and of themselves and since the prohibition really involved regulation of local business, the goods could not be excluded from interstate commerce.[35]

However, in a line of cases beginning in 1941, the Court has held that the power of Congress to prohibit use of the channels of interstate commerce extends beyond the nature of the goods themselves to the evils under which they are produced. Instead of the emphasis being on the articles of commerce, the Court has agreed that Congress might deny the channels of commerce to any activity regarded as an evil. The first case to open wide the power of Congress to exclude businesses from the channels of interstate commerce overruled the 1918 child-labor case and upheld the right of Congress to exclude from interstate commerce articles produced under substandard working conditions (i.e., not in accordance with legislatively established minimum wages and maximum hours).[36] The Court has likewise supported Congress in excluding certain public-utility holding-company activities from interstate commerce on the grounds that Congress may take necessary steps to make sure that the channels of interstate commerce are not used by companies that violate a desired standard of business operations.[37]

Recent developments of the interstate-commerce power have been far-reaching. With the current interpretations that the interstate-commerce power includes the authority to remove obstructions and the authority to

[29] *Champion v. Ames*, 188 U.S. 321 (1902).

[30] *Hipolite Egg Co. v. United States*, 220 U.S. 45 (1910).

[31] *Brooks v. United States*, 267 U.S. 432 (1924).

[32] *Lemke v. Farmers' Grain Co.*, 258 U.S. 50 (1922).

[33] *Hoke v. United States*, 227 U.S. 308 (1912).

[34] *Brooks v. United States*, 267 U.S. 432.

[35] *Hammer v. Dagenhart*, 247 U.S. 251 (1918).

[36] *United States v. Darby Lumber Co.*, 312 U.S. 100 (1941).

[37] See *North American Co. v. SEC*, 327 U.S. 686 (1946) and *American Power & Light Co. v. SEC*, 329 U.S. 90 (1946). For an excellent analysis of the implications of these cases see Henry Rottschaefer, *The Constitution and Socio-economic Change* (Ann Arbor, Mich.: University of Michigan Law School, 1948), pp. 68–79.

deny channels to meet any kind of danger to public health, safety, or welfare, it seems safe to say that Congress virtually has a general police power. While the courts still often give lip service to the concept that effects on interstate commerce must be substantial, the cases indicate that some fairly negligible effects are found to be substantial. The cases also have indicated that, if Congress has reason to believe that public policy demands exclusion of articles from commerce or that regulation is necessary to prevent evils of national importance, the Court will not normally question the motives of Congress, for these are matters of legislative judgment over which the courts have recently claimed no control.

State control over interstate commerce. Although the power of the federal government over interstate commerce is superior to that of the states, the courts have held that states, under their police and taxing powers, may enact laws which incidentally affect that commerce. This power is subject to several limitations: the laws can be made only in the absence of federal legislation on the subject unless they are completely consistent with expressed federal policy; they must be concerned with matters which are primarily intrastate in nature; and the states may not substantially burden interstate commerce by passing such laws.

THE TAX AND SPENDING POWER

The Constitution (Art. I, sec. 8, par. 1) delegates to Congress the power "to lay and collect taxes, duties, imposts and excises." This power is actually broader than the commerce power, because there is no constitutional requirement to work out a sharing arrangement with the states.

Certain limits on the tax power are included in the Constitution. No tax may be levied on exports (Art. I, sec. 9, par. 5). All duties, imposts, and excises must be levied uniformly throughout the country (that is, must take no account of geography), and direct taxes (Art. I, sec. 9, par. 4), except for income taxes (Sixteenth Amendment), must be levied on the basis of population.

The purpose of taxation is to raise revenue, but the courts have been willing to allow the tax power to be used for regulatory purposes as well. High taxes have been upheld to drive out of existence the sale of colored oleomargarine, white-phosphorus matches, and sawed-off shotguns and to control the traffic in narcotics.[38] In these cases, the Supreme Court took the position that so long as the tax was on its face a revenue measure, the Court would not look into the motives of the legislature in levying it.

During the 1920s and early 1930s, the regulatory use of taxation was sharply restricted. The attempt to regulate child labor by levying a tax

[38] *McCray v. United States*, 195 U.S. 27 (1904); *United States v. Doremus*, 249 U.S. 87 (1919); *Nigro v. United States*, 276 U.S. 332 (1928); *Sonzinsky v. United States*, 300 U.S. 506 (1937).

on businesses which employed children contrary to established standards was struck down as being an improper use of the tax power. The Court viewed the tax as an instrument of coercion rather than for revenue.[39] Several New Deal measures met the same fate. The Guffey Coal Act, under which producers who agreed to certain price and labor provisions of the coal code were entitled to a credit of 90 per cent of a tax levied, was found unconstitutional in 1936.[40] The Supreme Court held that the taxes and exemption were not intended for revenue purposes but for regulation in a field in which the national government was not empowered to act. In the same year, the Court upset the processing taxes by which agricultural control was to be effected under the first Agricultural Adjustment Act.[41] The Court held that these taxes were not really taxes because they were levied for the benefit of a particular group (the cooperating farmers) rather than for the general welfare and because they were used for regulating "a purely local activity." The decision in the Butler case was a close one, and this was the last case in which the use of the federal taxing power has been invalidated because its ultimate purpose has been to regulate rather than raise revenue.

From this line of decisions it is clear that the federal taxing power is extremely broad. While there still exists in the law the principle that Congress may not use the tax power to invade the powers reserved to the states, it is difficult to conceive what would constitute such an invasion.

The spending power constitutes another limitation on the tax power. The full grant of power to Congress reads: ". . . to lay and collect taxes, duties, imposts and excises, to pay the debts and provide for the common defense and general welfare of the United States." The tax power is linked to the spending power and can be used only for the purposes designated in the spending power. But what is the scope of the spending power?

There are few restrictions in the Constitution on spending. An appropriation for armies is not to be made for a period of longer than two years, salaries of federal judges may not be reduced during their continuance in office, and no money may be spent except by appropriation of Congress. Beyond those restraints, the interpretation given to the term "general welfare" constitutes the limitation. Can Congress tax and spend only to the extent necessary to carry into execution the other specifically delegated powers, or can Congress tax and spend for other purposes if those purposes promote the general welfare? The Supreme Court never faced this question until 1936, when it affirmed the broader view. At that time the Court held that the government spending power was not restricted to the subjects of the other delegated powers but was subject only to the

[39] *Bailey v. Drexel Furniture Co.*, 259 U.S. 20 (1922).

[40] *Carter v. Carter Coal Co.*, 298 U.S. 238 (1936).

[41] *United States v. Butler*, 297 U.S. 1 (1936).

limitations that funds be appropriated properly and that they be for the general welfare.[42]

This broad interpretation opens wide the area of economic life which can be subject to congressional control under its power to tax and spend. Thus, the federal government can tax and spend money in support of unemployment insurance, to provide old-age pensions, or to loan money to municipalities to enable them to erect their own electric plants.[43] Moreover, like the taxing power, the spending power may apparently be used to permit the federal government to regulate intrastate and local problems if these are related to some situation of national importance.[44]

FISCAL-MONETARY POWERS

If the tax revenues are not adequate to meet current obligations, Congress has the authority to borrow money (Art. I, sec. 8, par. 2). Although it might be expected that borrowing authority would be limited to providing money for the common defense and the general welfare, the only constitutional restraint is that borrowing be "on the credit of the United States."

Congress has also the authority to "coin money, regulate the value thereof" (Art. I, sec. 8, par. 5), and "provide for the punishment of counterfeiting the securities and current coin of the United States" (Art. I, sec. 8, par. 6). These provisions make up the fiscal-monetary powers of the federal government. These powers have become of strategic importance to the country in the managed-money economy of the past two decades.

By virtue of these powers the national government has been able to enter the banking field, put the functions of national banks beyond the reach of the taxing power of the states, control the private banking business to the most minute detail, issue paper money and confer upon it the quality of legal tender for debts, tax the notes of issue of state banks out of existence, and establish a Federal Reserve System, a Farm Loan Bank, and the like.[45]

Like other delegated powers, this power is plenary. When Congress de-

[42] *Ibid.* While asserting this broader position, the Court found the first Agricultural Adjustment Act unconstitutional.

[43] *Steward Machine Co. v. Davis*, 301 U.S. 548 (1937); *Helvering v. Davis*, 301 U.S. 619 (1937); *Alabama Power Co. v. Ickes*, 302 U.S. 364 (1938).

[44] Note that in *Oklahoma v. United States Civil Serv. Com.*, 330 U.S. 127 (1947), the Supreme Court upheld a provision of the Hatch (political-activity) Act which required a reduction in a federal grant-in-aid if a state did not suspend a state official found to be in violation of the Act.

[45] *McCulloch v. Maryland*, 4 Wheat. 316 (1819); *Knox v. Lee*, 12 Wall. 457 (1871); *Veazie Bank v. Fenno*, 8 Wall. 533 (1869); *Smith v. Kansas City T. and T. Co.*, 255 U.S. 180 (1921); *Smyth v. United States*, 302 U.S. 329 (1937).

valued the currency by reducing the gold content of the dollar, the Supreme Court not only upheld this action as a valid use of the money power but unhesitatingly agreed that contracts payable in gold of a certain weight and fineness were rendered invalid in this respect as an interference with the money power of Congress.[46]

When the fiscal-monetary powers are considered in conjunction with the tax and spending power, it is readily seen that the federal government has ample authority to control the ebb and flow of credit and thereby control the course of basic economic conditions. These powers furnish the constitutional basis for the managed-currency economics expounded by John Maynard Keynes, whose doctrines of credit and money management have so deeply influenced the course of national policy in the United States and Great Britain as well as in many other countries.

THE WAR POWER

One of the most important constitutional bases for economic regulation in recent years has been the war power of Congress. The constitutional grant of authority to Congress (Art. I, sec. 8, pars. 11–16) and the powers that have been implied therefrom provide the federal government with ample basis for prosecuting war. In reality, the national government possesses the power to prosecute war as an inherent attribute of national sovereignty, and the constitutional provisions merely regulate the use of these powers.[47] This power is unaffected by the rights and prerogatives of the state.

The plenary nature of the war power was clearly stated by the Supreme Court in two cases handed down in 1944. In one, upholding rent controls, the Court pointed out that "a nation which can demand the lives of its men and women in the waging of that war is under no constitutional necessity of providing a system of price control on the domestic front which will assure each landlord a 'fair return' on his property." [48] In another case, upholding the Emergency Price Control Act of 1942, the Supreme Court went so far as to deny an accused violator the right to contest the constitutionality of the statute in the same trial in which his guilt or innocence was being determined.[49]

The nature of the war power can be illustrated from several cases. In 1948, the Supreme Court held, in approving the rent-control provisions of the Housing and Rent Act of 1947, that the war power includes the power to handle problems resulting from war and may be employed as long as

[46] *Norman v. Baltimore & Ohio R.R.*, 294 U.S. 240 (1935); *Holyoke Power Co. v. American Paper Co.*, 300 U.S. 324 (1937).

[47] *United States v. Curtiss-Wright Export Corp.*, 299 U.S. 304 (1936).

[48] *Bowles v. Willingham*, 321 U.S. 503, 519 (1944).

[49] *Yakus v. United States*, 321 U.S. 414 (1944).

war-induced emergencies last.[50] In upholding the Renegotiation Act of 1942, the Court held that, if the federal government can conscript men, it can certainly conscript property and profits.[51] And in another case, the seizure of the property of enemy aliens was upheld on the grounds that, with the total nature of modern warfare, "every resource within the ambit of sovereign power is subject to use for the national defense." [52]

Thus, it appears that in time of war, or in the case of serious problems resulting from war, or in the interest of national defense, the authority of the federal government becomes broad enough to encompass virtually any regulation of economic activity. That this power is important, particularly with the apparent willingness of the courts to extend the war power to long periods after the end of hostilities, is beyond doubt. With world affairs disturbed and the continuing existence of defense emergencies, the possibilities for centralization of business controls in the federal government seem to be restricted primarily by legislative desires rather than constitutional limitations.

WEIGHTS AND MEASURES

Further control over business has been exercised through the constitutional provision (Art. I, sec. 8, par. 5) giving Congress power to "fix the standard of weights and measures." This power has been used largely as a means of aiding business by securing scientific exactness of standards, by making various tests in connection with standards, and by facilitating the adoption of standardized materials, parts, and sizes. In a few cases, such as basket sizes and the use of the term "sterling," definite standards are enforced by law.

BANKRUPTCIES

The Constitution (Art. I, sec. 8, par. 4) gives Congress the power to establish "uniform laws on the subject of bankruptcies throughout the United States." Since 1898, and particularly by acts in 1933, 1934, and 1935, the federal bankruptcy law has been growing in importance. To what extent Congress can go in granting relief to bankrupts under this power is uncertain. In a Supreme Court case in 1935 the Court found invalid a bankruptcy law which seemed so unfair to creditors as to take property without due process of law.[53]

[50] *Woods v. Miller*, 333 U.S. 138 (1948).

[51] *Lichter v. United States*, 334 U.S. 742 (1948).

[52] *Silesian-American Corp. v. Clark*, 332 U.S. 469 (1947).

[53] The first Frazier-Lemke Act, by which farmers were granted mortgage extensions under excessively liberal terms, was held unconstitutional in *Louisville Land Bank v. Radford*, 295 U.S. 555 (1935). A later act safeguarding creditors more amply was upheld in 1937.

In spite of the fact that the bankruptcy power carries no limitation of any sort, the Supreme Court in a close decision in 1936 declared unconstitutional a municipal bankruptcy law on the ground that Congress could not extend its bankruptcy power to the political subdivisions of the states.[54] However, this power has shown itself to be a real source of governmental control, particularly in the reorganization of railroads and in justifying laws aimed at regulating credit dealings.

The states are allowed to make bankruptcy laws of their own so long as they do not conflict with federal laws. This is a particularly valuable construction of the federal power in that the states may make many additional bankruptcy provisions with which the federal laws does not deal.

POST OFFICES AND POST ROADS

The only provision of the Constitution which can be construed as an outright grant to the national government to enter business is that (Art. I, sec. 8, par. 7) "to establish post offices and post roads." This power has been widely used to exert control over business, and there are those who see in it possibilities for further expansion of governmental intervention.

To what extent the postal power can be adopted to regulate matters not clearly within the other powers of the federal government is not clear. Congress may disallow the use of the mails for securities which are fraudulent or "unfair to investors." [55] But it is doubtful if it can exclude businesses from using the mails if they cannot be regulated under any other power. In one case in 1913 the Supreme Court specifically held that the postal power must be "construed in the light of definite prohibitions in the Constitution." [56] The power is apparently limited to control over the matter mailed, including prevention of injury to the recipient. However, Congress has been able to exert control over companies doing business with the post office. Contracts with air, water, and railway carriers ordinarily contain provisions involving far-reaching control over these agencies. Through contracts with builders and companies furnishing supplies, the government has also been able to impose extensive restrictions which have loomed large in the area of government controls as federal expenditures have become so extensive and heavy.

PATENTS AND COPYRIGHTS

The Constitution (Art I, sec. 8, par. 8) entrusts to Congress the promotion of "progress of science and useful arts" by authorizing grants of patents and copyrights "for limited times." Notice that the Constitution

[54] *Ashton v. Cameron County Water Imp. Dist.*, 298 U.S. 513 (1936).

[55] That is, under the Securities Act of 1933. This is clear from the decision in *Electric Bond & Share Co. v. SEC*, 303 U.S. 419 (1938).

[56] *Lewis Pub. Co. v. Morgan*, 229 U.S. 288, 313 (1913).

gives Congress no power to register trade-marks, this being undertaken as a regulation of interstate and foreign commerce. The courts here have held that these rights are exclusive only as are any property rights and that without permission of Congress they cannot be used for purposes which would be unlawful.[57] However, as a property holder the patentee may refuse to allow the use of his patent.

TREATIES

Power to make treaties with foreign governments is given (Art. II, sec. 2, par. 2) to the President "by and with the advice and consent of the Senate—provided two thirds of the senators present concur." The treaties made and ratified are a part of the "supreme law of the land" (Art. VI, sec. 2) and as such are enforceable by the courts. Some students of government have claimed that the treaty power would make possible the passing of regulations in fields outside the specifically delegated powers of Congress. Many lawyers claim that the federal government can be given no power through treaties to do anything which the Constitution as a whole seems to forbid. Indeed, in 1855 the Supreme Court suggested that a treaty which would encroach upon powers reserved to the states would be unconstitutional.[58] Actually, the Court has upheld treaties which involved intrastate regulations. Regulation of migratory birds within a state was upheld as a valid control under a treaty between the United States and Canada.[59]

Powers of States under the Constitution

Those powers which are not delegated to the federal government by the Constitution are reserved to the states, unless some constitutional provision specifically prohibits the states from exercising that power (Tenth Amendment). These so-called reserved powers include the police power, proprietary powers, and the power of eminent domain.

THE POLICE POWER

One of the most important and comprehensive of all governmental powers is the police power. The police power embraces two main areas: the promotion of the fundamental objects of social welfare, including public health, safety, and morals; and the promotion of economic welfare. The former area is the traditional scope of the police power and is much

[57] For example, a patent right does not entitle holders of several patents to join together to restrain trade in opposition to the antitrust laws. See *National Harrow Co. v. Hench*, 83 Fed. 36 (1897).

[58] *Prevost v. Greneaux*, 19 How. 1 (1855).

[59] *Missouri v. Holland*, 252 U.S. 416 (1920).

more fundamental than the latter. While the federal government has what amounts to a national police power incidental to the exercise of the powers delegated to Congress, the police power of the states is much broader and more general.

Unlike other reserved powers of the state, such as the power of eminent domain, which requires that a just compensation be given, the police power can be used to take property when the private use of such property is deemed detrimental to the public, and no compensation need be given. However, the police power must meet the requirements of due process of law, which will be discussed in a later section. The states may even exercise a police power which indirectly affects interstate commerce, as long as that regulation is local in character and does not conflict with federal regulation.

By virtue of the police power, states have prohibited the sale of unwholesome or adulterated foods, required the inspection of milk, meat, and other foods, established quarantines, required vaccinations, regulated the entrance into occupations, curbed gambling, intoxication, and obscenity, provided for safety features in buildings, stores, and the like, and enacted laws introducing racial distinctions. All state business and labor regulations are based on the police power.

PROPRIETARY POWER

Every sovereign government has the power to engage in undertakings which it regards as necessary to the functioning of government. This may be limited to the construction and operation of public buildings or the granting of contracts for public supplies, or it may extend to the building and operation of a barge canal or the construction of a system of state-operated elevators.[60] The state may also incorporate private businesses, or it may grant to its subdivisions such as counties and municipalities the authority to enter into practically any kind of business. The extent to which a given state may lawfully become a proprietor of businesses seems to be limited mainly by its constitution and the sanction of its people and legislature. To the extent that due process requires that taxation be for a public purpose, and because states may hardly enter business without resorting to taxation, the idea that the business must be for the general welfare would seem to follow as a further limitation.

EMINENT DOMAIN

The power of a state to take private property for public purpose, upon payment of just compensation, is "an attribute of sovereignty," "inheres

[60] That this is perfectly consistent with the federal Constitution was shown in *Green v. Frazier*, 253 U.S. 233 (1920), by which state ownership of grain elevators and mills was upheld.

in every sovereign state," and "so often necessary for the proper performance of governmental functions that the power is deemed to be essential to the life of the states." [61] The only real limitations on this power are that property taken must be for a public use and that a fair compensation must be paid for it. The power is different from the regulatory or taxing power of a state in that the exercise of the latter does not require such compensation.

The state may take property by eminent domain, or it may allow any of its subdivisions or any privately owned business to do so; no matter which of these methods is adopted, the main limitation is that the taking be for a public use. The states have granted this power not only to public utilities but also to such private concerns as mining and timber companies needing a right of way from their property. In doing so they have been upheld by the United States Supreme Court.[62] Apparently, so far as the federal Constitution is concerned, the determination of what is public use is left largely to the states under their constitutions and the interpretation of their courts.

Constitutional Limitations

Any constitution worthy of the name is more than a source of power and a framework of government. A constitution is a restrictive instrument, imposing legal limitations on the exercise of power. This is especially true in the United States because the framers of the Constitution had a healthy distrust of men in positions of power.

LIMITATIONS ON THE FEDERAL GOVERNMENT

Delegated powers. The act of delegating certain powers to the federal government constitutes a limitation on its powers in that it is restricted to exercising only those specifically delegated powers. Those powers not delegated to Congress and not prohibited to the states are reserved to the states (Tenth Amendment).

In addition, certain enumerated powers were hedged in by other requirements. Direct taxes must be apportioned among the several states according to population, and indirect taxes must be uniform (Art. I, sec. 9, par. 4). No taxes may be levied on exports (Art. I, sec. 9, par. 5). Money may not be spent except through the appropriation process of Congress (Art. I, sec. 9, par. 7).

Due process of law. The most important restriction on the economic powers of the federal government is the requirement in the Fifth Amend-

[61] *State of Georgia v. Chattanooga*, 264 U.S. 472 (1924).

[62] See, e.g., as to gold mining, *Strickley v. Highland Boy Gold Mining Co.*, 200 U.S. 527 (1906).

ment that "no person shall . . . be deprived of life, liberty or property, without due process of law; nor shall private property be taken for public use without compensation." The last part of this restriction presents little difficulty, meaning only that the government under its inherent power of eminent domain shall pay a reasonable price for any property it takes for public use. Thus, when private property was needed for the building of the Tennessee Valley dams, the property could be taken, but a reasonable compensation, as determined by agreement of the government and the owner, or by a jury of appraisers, had to be paid.

The amendment prohibiting the taking of life, liberty, or property without due process of law has been of tremendous significance in American legal history. The same restriction was applied to state actions by the Fourteenth Amendment to the Constitution, and so far as due process is concerned most of what is discussed here applies to the powers of states.

The Fifth Amendment declares not that private property and liberty cannot be taken but that the federal government cannot take them without due process of law. This restriction has been construed to be applicable to all enumerated powers, regardless of how complete they seem to be.

The phrase "due process of law" was borrowed by the framers of the Constitution from the English common law. Under the latter it meant that a person's property or liberty could not be taken by government unless it was done according to "the law of the land." [63] This was merely another way of stating that a person had the right to a fair hearing by a fair and impartial court of competent jurisdiction. Thus, "due process" under the common law was *procedural* due process in that all it implied was that an accused should have "his day in court." Procedural due process applies to acts of judges, legislators, regulatory commissions, and executive officers and is designed to safeguard against tyrannical or arbitrary practices which are substituted for legal customs of fairness and impartiality.

Following the War between the States and until 1937, the courts broadened their construction of due process to include not only restrictions as to the *form* of procedure but also the principle that laws and their administration should not violate the *substance* of individual rights, liberty, and property.[64] Indications that the Supreme Court took this position are found in dicta in cases in 1870 and 1878,[65] and in 1884 the Court decided a case on the principle that the due-process clause of the Fourteenth

[63] For discussion see J. R. Commons, *Legal Foundations of Capitalism* (New York: The Macmillan Company, 1924), pp. 331 ff.

[64] See *ibid.*, pp. 333 ff. The first case in which a law was found unconstitutional on the basis that due process meant more than due procedure was *Wynehamer v. New York*, 13 N.Y. 378 (1856).

[65] See *Hepburn v. Griswold*, 8 Wall. 603 (1870) and *Davidson v. New Orleans*, 96 U.S. 97 (1878).

Amendment was not restricted to procedural matters but included also the substance of individual rights, liberty, and property.[66]

The interpretation that due process involved substantive fairness forced the courts to become arbiters of what line could be drawn between reasonable use of enumerated powers of Congress and the police powers of the states and cases where the exercise of these powers took property or other rights unreasonably. This interpretation of due process led the courts to invalidate many state and federal laws regulating economic life.

But in 1937, when criticism of the Supreme Court as an agency of reaction standing in the way of needed social legislation reached its height, the Court, in a revolutionary line of cases, decided that the element of substantive due process should not override the legislative will to protect the health, safety, morals, and welfare of the people. In a case upholding the minimum wage law of the state of Washington, the court said: [67]

> The Constitution does not speak of freedom of contract. It speaks of liberty and prohibits the deprivation of liberty without due process of law. In prohibiting that deprivation the Constitution does not recognize an absolute and uncontrollable liberty. Liberty in each of its phases has its history and connotations. But the liberty safeguarded is liberty in a social organization which requires the protection of law against the evils which menace the health, safety, morals and welfare of the people. Liberty under the Constitution is thus necessarily subject to the restraints of due process, and regulation which is reasonable in relation to its subject and is adopted in the interests of the community is due process.

Since that time, the Supreme Court has not declared invalid any state or federal business regulations on the grounds that substantive due process has been impaired. While the Court has not hesitated to examine closely requirements of procedural due process, has spent much time and effort in interpreting federal regulatory statutes, and has declared state laws which interfere with such federal powers as interstate commerce to be invalid,

[66] *Hurtado v. California*, 110 U.S. 516.

[67] *West Coast Hotel Co. v. Parrish*, 300 U.S. 379, at p. 391. In a sense, the departure from substantive due process can be said to date from 1934, when the Supreme Court held valid price fixing of milk and said, in *Nebbia v. New York*, 291 U.S. 502, at p. 537, "But there can be no doubt that upon proper occasion and by appropriate measures the state may regulate a business in any of its aspects, including the prices to be charged for the products or commodities it sells. So far as the requirement of due process is concerned, and in the absence of other constitutional restrictions, a state is free to adopt whatever economic policy may reasonably be deemed to promote the public welfare, and to enforce that policy by legislation adapted to its purpose. The courts are without authority either to declare such policy, or, when it is declared by the legislature, to override it." Regardless of the importance of the decision in this case, the use of substantive due process to invalidate legislative policy between 1934 and 1937, and the fact that substantive due process has not been used since 1937 to override legislative policy, make the West Coast Hotel case one of pivotal importance.

the Court has taken the position, as Justice Frankfurter recently said, that it "is not a tribunal for the relief from the crudities and inequities of complicated economic legislation." [68]

LIMITATIONS ON THE STATES

Limitations on state taxes. The federal Constitution places some restrictions on the taxing powers of states. Except where absolutely necessary for inspection purposes, the Constitution (Art. I, sec. 10, par. 2) forbids states "without the consent of Congress" to "lay any imposts or duties on imports or exports." The purpose of this limitation is to restrain the states from interfering with the free flow of commerce, and in deciding whether a state tax falls under this clause the courts have generally looked for undue interference with interstate commerce. As a matter of fact, particularly with the growth of state sales and use taxes, and other taxes designed to force interstate businesses to contribute to state treasuries, the interstate-commerce power has become one of the principal deterring forces to state taxing policy.

Additional restriction on state taxation has resulted from the doctrine that all taxes, state and federal, must be for a public purpose. With regard to state taxation, this doctrine is not found in the Constitution but has been firmly established by a line of judicial decisions.[69] While this restriction clearly exists in principle, the current reluctance of the courts to look behind the motives of the legislature would seem to give the limitation little substance if a legislature declared the taxation to be for a public purpose.

Limitations on state money powers. Besides granting money powers to the national government, the Constitution (Art. I, sec. 10, par. 1) forbids the states to coin money, issue bills of credit, or make anything but gold and silver coin tender for payment of debts. This in itself does not prohibit the states from chartering banks with the privilege of issuing notes, but the federal government has practically prohibited it through levying a high tax on such notes. Nor does the Constitution restrict state-chartered banks from such activities as using demand deposits as a medium of exchange. However, if the national government wished to impose this and other restrictions, it is clear that its plenary power over money could be used to do so.

Obligation of contracts. One of the most important restrictions on the states imposed by the federal Constitution is that (Art. I, sec. 10, par. 1) forbidding the states to pass a law impairing the obligation of contracts. The term "contract" has been interpreted broadly. It includes contracts between a state and private parties. Thus a franchise, charter, or other

[68] *Secretary of Agriculture v. Central Roig Refining Co.*, 338 U.S. 604 (1950).
[69] See particularly *Loan Association v. Topeka*, 20 Wall. 655 (1874).

privilege obtained by private corporations from the legislature is construed to be a contract within the meaning of this clause. This interpretation has economic and social significance, because many such privileges have been held to be inviolable rights which the state may not later impair. For example, a street railway in New York City was granted a perpetual franchise for use of the city streets. By its terms there was no practicable way, except by condemnation proceedings under eminent domain, that the state legislature could divest the company of its rights without impairing the obligation of contracts.[70] On the other hand, charters granted by the state to its subdivisions are not held to be contracts, nor is the appointment of an individual to public office at a fixed salary for a certain term held to be one.[71]

The obligation of a contract is impaired when its value has been diminished as the result of legislation.[72] But a legislature may change the procedure of enforcing a contractual claim, so long as the value of the contract is not changed, without impairing the obligation of contracts.[73]

As a general proposition the states may not contract away their police power. All contracts are held to be made in accordance with both present and future regulations which may be found necessary for the protection of public health, morals, safety, and welfare. A brewing company's right to manufacture and sell beer under its charter was held to be subject to the morals or health of the people as protected by a prohibition law passed subsequent to the company's incorporation.[74] A lottery charter granted to a company has been held to be subject to later laws prohibiting lotteries.[75]

While the restrictions in impairment of contract obligations apply specifically to the states alone, the federal government has been limited in practically the same way. Contract rights are regarded as property. Consequently, under the substantive interpretation given to the due-process clause of the Fifth Amendment, the courts have held that the property represented by contracts cannot be taken by the federal government without due process of law.[76]

Interstate privileges and immunities of citizens. The Constitution grants (Art. IV, sec. 2, par. 1) to citizens of each state "all privileges and immunities of citizens in the several states." These privileges and immunities

[70] Although the state was allowed to dissolve the corporation, the franchise was held to be irrevocable. *People v. O'Brien*, 111 N.Y. 1 (1888).

[71] See *Trenton v. New Jersey*, 262 U.S. 182 (1923), and *Butler v. Pennsylvania*, 10 How. 402 (1850).

[72] *Planters' Bank v. Sharp*, 6 How. 327 (1848).

[73] *Oshkosh Water Works v. Oshkosh*, 187 U.S. 437 (1903).

[74] *Beer Co. v. Massachusetts*, 97 U.S. 25 (1877).

[75] *Stone v. Mississippi*, 101 U.S. 814 (1879).

[76] See *Sinking Fund Cases*, 99 U.S. 700, 718, 719 (1879).

include, among other things, "the right of a citizen of one state to pass through or to reside in any other state, for purposes of trade, agriculture, professional pursuits, or otherwise; . . . to institute and maintain actions of any kind in the courts of a state; to take, hold and dispose of property, either real or personal; and an exemption from higher taxes or impositions than are paid by other citizens of the state." [77]

The restriction upon state discrimination against citizens of other states is important to business. But the courts have allowed some prejudicial laws which they found to be a reasonable exercise of the state police power. Thus, a state law refusing a liquor dealer's license to citizens of another state was upheld,[78] and one requiring an individual or at least one firm member conducting a bank to be a state resident has also been upheld.[79] These exceptions were allowed because effective regulation in certain fields depended in part on having citizens of the state concerned in the business.

Furthermore, a corporation of one state, being "a mere creature of local law," is not regarded as a citizen within the scope of this clause, and a state may refuse to allow corporations from other states to do business within it, or it may regulate foreign corporations differently from domestic ones.[80] But where the foreign corporation is engaging in interstate or foreign commerce from outside a state, that state may not exclude its commerce, for to do so would be an interference with interstate commerce. A mail-order business incorporated in Illinois, for instance, could not be excluded from Indiana if its business were done entirely by mail.

Due process of law. The Fourteenth Amendment to the Constitution, ratified by the states shortly after the War between the States, provides, among other things, that no state shall "deprive any person of life, liberty or property without due process of law." This restriction placed upon the states is practically identical with that placed on the federal government by the Fifth Amendment.

While this provision was formerly of major importance in defining the scope of state police power, so far as the subject matter and character of regulation is concerned, it is now primarily a check upon the use of arbitrary methods of hearing, trial, and enforcement.[81] As such, it is an important restriction upon the states, but it has become far less significant

[77] *Corfield v. Caryell*, 4 Wash. C.C. 371 (1825).

[78] *DeGrazier v. Stephens*, 101 Tex. 194 (1907). Also in *Mette v. McGuckin*, 18 Nebr. 323 (1885), affirmed by a divided United States Supreme Court in 149 U.S. 781 (1892).

[79] *State v. Richcreek*, 167 Ind. 217 (1906).

[80] *Paul v. Virginia*, 8 Wall. 168 (1868).

[81] Of course state courts have often invalidated laws on the grounds of substantive due process, and they still do. See F. H. Sherwood, "State Constitutional Law in 1948–49," 43 *American Political Science Review* 735, 761 (August, 1949).

than restrictions imposed by the growth of federal powers and the constitutional provision requiring equal protection of the laws.

Equal protection of the laws. The Fourteenth Amendment (section 1) forbids any state to "deny to any person within its jurisdiction the equal protection of the laws." Here also the word "person" includes both natural and corporate persons. The equal protection of the laws so guaranteed means that any person within a state "is entitled to stand before the law upon equal terms, to enjoy the same rights as belong to, and to bear the same burdens as are imposed upon, other persons in a like situation." [82] This clause was inserted in the Constitution primarily to protect Negroes from discriminatory legislation. But it has been resorted to increasingly, particularly with the devitalization of substantive due process, for the protection of businesses from laws which discriminate against one business in favor of another.

Equal protection of the law does not mean that legislation may not classify subjects for regulation. A state law which permitted railroads operating less than 50 miles of road to employ smaller crews than longer railroads was held not to involve an unreasonable classification.[83] State laws imposing higher taxes on chain stores than on other stores have been upheld on the ground that enough difference exists between chain stores and other stores to satisfy the requirements of equal protection of the laws.[84]

But where the classification appears to the courts to be clearly arbitrary or to remove any semblance of equal protection, the regulation has been found unconstitutional, even in recent years. In 1920, a tax applying more heavily to corporations doing business both within and outside a state than those doing business entirely inside it was held to make for unequal protection of the laws.[85] A similar tax applying to foreign corporations but exempting domestic corporations was invalidated in 1949.[86]

Selected References

Carr, Robert K., *The Supreme Court and Judicial Review.* New York: Rinehart & Company, Inc., 1942.

Commons, John R., *Legal Foundations of Capitalism.* New York: The Macmillan Company, 1924.

Corwin, Edward S., *The Constitution and What It Means Today.* Princeton, N. J.: Princeton University Press, 1947.

[82] *Southern R.R. Co. v. Greene*, 216 U.S. 400, 412 (1910).

[83] *Chicago, Rock Island and Pac. Rwy. Co. v. Arkansas*, 219 U.S. 453 (1911).

[84] *Indiana v. Jackson*, 283 U.S. 527 (1931).

[85] *Royster Guano Co. v. Virginia*, 253 U.S. 412.

[86] *Wheeling Steel Corp. v. Glander*, 337 U.S. 562.

——, *The Twilight of the Supreme Court.* New Haven, Conn.: Yale University Press, 1934.

Gavit, Bernard C., *The Commerce Clause of the United States Constitution.* Bloomington, Ind.: The Principia Press, Inc., 1932.

Hale, Robert L., *Freedom through Law.* New York: Columbia University Press, 1952.

Jackson, Robert H., *The Struggle for Judicial Supremacy.* New York: Alfred A. Knopf, Inc., 1941.

Kellenbach, J. E., *Federal Cooperation with the States under the Commerce Clause.* Ann Arbor, Mich.: University of Michigan Press, 1942.

Kelly, Alfred H., and Winfred A. Harbison, *The American Constitution: Its Origins and Development.* New York: W. W. Norton & Company, Inc., 1948.

Mathews, John M., *The American Constitutional System.* New York: McGraw-Hill Book Company, Inc., 1940.

Pound, Roscoe, *Social Control through Law.* New Haven, Conn.: Yale University Press, 1942.

Pritchett, C. Herman, *The Roosevelt Court—A Study in Judicial Politics and Values, 1937–1947.* New York: The Macmillan Company, 1948.

Schwartz, Louis B., *Free Enterprise and Economic Organization: Legal and Related Materials.* Brooklyn, N. Y.: The Foundation Press, Inc., 1952.

Stauss, James H., "The Supreme Court and the Architects of Economic Legislation," *Journal of Political Economy,* vol. 56 (April, 1948).

Swisher, Carl B., *American Constitutional Development.* Boston: Houghton Mifflin Company, 1954.

Warren, C., *The Supreme Court in United States History,* 2 vols. Boston: Little, Brown & Company, 1937.

Wood, Virginia, *Due Process of Law, 1932–1949.* Baton Rouge, La.: Louisiana State University Press, 1951.

Wright, Benjamin F., *The Contract Clause of the Constitution.* Cambridge, Mass.: Harvard University Press, 1938.

——, *The Growth of American Constitutional Law.* New York: Reynal & Hitchcock, Inc., 1942.

3

THE TECHNIQUES AND TYPES OF PUBLIC CONTROL

Public control in its broadest sense includes every governmental decision or action which seeks to aid, promote, guide, limit, restrict, or prohibit individuals or groups engaged in private enterprise so as to influence or determine the direction of private economic endeavor. A wide variety of techniques and types of public control is possible. Techniques and types vary with the purposes to be achieved, the extent of control intended, the problems encountered in exercising control, and the business being controlled. Of course, several techniques and types may be used at one time in regulating a single area of business.

The reader should bear in mind that a more complete analysis of the techniques, types, and problems of control must wait for the discussion of each of the substantive fields of regulation. It is hoped, however, that this chapter will aid the reader in recognizing when and where the techniques and types are being used and to comprehend better the administrative problems involved.

In the sections that follow, the discussion of techniques is concerned with those instrumentalities through which control is exercised; under Types of Control are analyzed the more common objects or purposes of control. For example, administrative regulation is treated as a *technique* of controlling public utilities, and control over rates and service is considered a *type* of economic control.

Techniques of Control

INFORMAL CONTROLS

Formal controls are primarily those exercised through the official machinery of government, backed by the force of law. But behind formal controls lie innumerable forces which exert some influence on the economy, such as custom, tradition, religion, public opinion, prestige, status, and the like.[1] Although mention of informal controls may appear out of

[1] For an excellent discussion of informal controls, see John M. Clark, *Social Control of Business* (New York: McGraw-Hill Book Company, Inc., 2d ed., 1939), chaps. 12, 13.

place in a book on government control, they are a consideration in the formulation of economic policy. Some people believe that we would get on better if the only controls ever used were the informal ones. Therefore, the decision to continue to rely upon them, or not to do so, is basic to the development of economic policy. Furthermore, in the event of their failure, the need for government action may be felt and intensified pressure for public control exerted.

Control by such informal methods as custom or public opinion has the advantage of being inexpensive and prompt. But it may be highly irrational and often needs formal institutions to give it consistency, persistence, and the advantage of expert knowledge. There is always the danger that informal controls may not be in the public interest.

CODES

Codes are a bridge between informal self-regulation and formal control by government. Under this method of control, business is given the opportunity to regulate itself, subject to supervision by the government. The code of fair competition, a set of ethical practices approved by a trade, is an outgrowth of the attempt by trade associations to stabilize practices in a particular field of business. Even before 1933, many of these codes were accepted by the Federal Trade Commission as embodying a standard of fair competition in a field. With the passage of the National Industrial Recovery Act in 1933, the code became a dominant form of business self-regulation under governmental supervision. Although the Recovery Act was short-lived, the code as a method of control has not succumbed.

Codes are an advantageous method of control in that they represent, to some degree, self-regulation by the businesses concerned. Such regulation should consequently include provisions of importance and interest to the group. Because the regulation comes from the trade, compliance should be made easier. On the other hand, for a code to be effective the government must have an agency empowered to enforce it. Also, because the members of the group which formulate the code are likely to consider their own interests to the exclusion of other businessmen and consumers, protection of the latter groups may greatly complicate the machinery of arriving at a code truly cognizant of the public interest. Furthermore, the multiplicity of codes and code provisions is likely to result in an all too burdensome mass of regulations, the interpretation, administration, and harmonizing of which might be extremely difficult.

INVESTIGATION AND PUBLICITY

Investigation and publicity constitute methods of government control fully as much as other formal controls, but they do not rely on legal coercion. Investigations of business by federal and state legislatures are commonplace, and it is not unusual for administrative commissions and administrative officers to make public investigations of business practices and conditions. To be sure, most investigations are undertaken to gain expert data on conditions so that regulatory laws can be passed to meet the needs so exposed. But often the most important effect of investigations is to force business, under the spur of public opinion, to make changes in practices and policies in advance of, or without recourse to, statutory measures.

While many of the investigations of the Federal Trade Commission have been used as the basis of new legislation, one of their most significant results has been to cause discontinuance of certain practices. For example, investigation of public-utility holding companies disclosed practices inimical to effective regulation of local public-utility operating companies.[2] Even before the national government passed a law regulating these holding companies in 1935, publicity had forced many of the companies to discontinue the practices involved.

The Federal Power Commission's investigation of electric rates also did much to cause reduction of rates which appeared to be relatively high.[3] The investigation of civil liberties undertaken by a Senate subcommittee, in which employers' methods of spying upon and interfering with labor unions were exposed, has definitely affected labor policies of most of the companies concerned.[4]

Effective as this method of control may be in certain cases, the inquisitorial nature of some investigations, plus the fact that practices of all the businesses in a field can seldom be publicized, make it one to be used sparingly. Too often large businesses are forced by public opinion to give up certain practices, while smaller businesses escaping investigation can continue without restraint. Moreover, in some matters where regulation may be needed, the force of public opinion may not be an adequate goad.

FRANCHISES AND LICENSES

The franchise, as the term is used here, denotes the grant by a sovereign government of a special privilege to an individual or corporation, which could not otherwise be exercised legally and which ordinarily rests exclusively with the state. As such, power to establish corporations is a franchise given to incorporators. If a corporation or an individual wishes to lay gas, water, electricity, or telephone lines under or over public streets, the privilege of so doing is likewise a franchise. Closely akin to the franchise is the license or permit, by which permission is given to individuals by some

[2] FPC, *Utility Corporations*, S. Doc. 92, 70th Cong., 1st Sess. (1928–1937).

[3] FPC, *Electrical Rate Survey* (1937).

[4] U.S. Senate, Subcommittee of Committee on Education and Labor, *Violation of Free Speech and the Rights of Labor*, 75th, 76th Cong. (1937–1939).

competent authority, conferring the right to perform some act which would otherwise be illegal.

By requiring franchises, licenses, or permits for engaging in business, any government can exercise regulatory powers through laying down conditions for granting or revocation of these permissions.[5] As a method of control, the franchise has been particularly important in the public-utility field, but the conditions upon which franchises to corporations have been granted make the corporate-charter type of franchise also of significance. In recent years, too, the tendency to require licensing of various types of businesses, and to revoke those licenses when certain conditions are not met, has made this method of control of increasing moment.

As a way of control, however, the franchise, the license, and the permit are inflexible, in that they do not and cannot make complete provision for the varying conditions which government control is certain to encounter. While still widely used, they are now generally accompanied by an administrator or an administrative commission to interpret and apply phraseology purposely made elastic.

The public-utility franchise has been largely superseded as an instrument of regulatory control by the development of commissions. The experience with such franchises amply indicates their weaknesses. To be at all effective in a field where fairly complete control is necessary, the franchise must include so many provisions and must be so carefully drawn to take care of future exigencies that, unless it is accompanied by commission regulation, it is likely to be a hindrance to protection of the public interest. It must be remembered that a franchise is a contract between a governmental authority and an individual or a corporation. Unless enough safeguards are placed in it to make future change in the public interest legal, its provisions may be held enforceable in spite of their defects or outmoded nature. If a franchise is made elastic enough to allow for future conditions not envisaged at the time, administrative treatment of its provisions by some body, such as a commission, is necessitated. If a franchise is drawn up in detail to care for needed regulation, but its term made short to safeguard the public, the prospect of losing franchise privileges is not conducive to the economic embarkation of capital in such enterprises as railroads and gas and electric companies.

Furthermore, legislators who grant franchise rights are not usually trained to care well for the legal or business details necessarily included in a well-drawn contract. Too often companies, with their superior knowledge of the business and ability to hire good lawyers, have outwitted unsuspecting state legislators or city councilmen into making concessions which do not safeguard the public. In addition, the granting of franchises

[5] A license can be differentiated from a franchise: the former is an imposed device of regulation; the latter is a grant of privilege.

in the past has often been accompanied by bribery to legislators for favorable votes. A franchise granted in 1884 to operate street railways on New York's Broadway was admittedly obtained by means of large-scale bribery, but its perpetual and irrevocable character was upheld by New York's highest court.[6]

INSPECTION

Inspection is one of the most common methods of regulation at all levels of government. It is an old technique dating back to the inspection of quality, price, and weight in medieval markets by town authorities and, in the United States, to the inspection of town markets in the early nineteenth century.[7] Inspection is essentially a method of examining and evaluating some matter in terms of established standards. It may precede the issuance of a license, or it may be conducted later to see if the licensee has lived up to his requirements. The inspection of foods, ventilation, and sanitary facilities in the interests of health is one example of the use to which inspection is put, and the inspection of elevators, factories, and transportation equipment in the interests of safety is another example.

While inspection is buttressed by legal forms of coercion, including revocation of license, fine, and even imprisonment, it usually seeks compliance through noncoercive means. These noncoercive techniques include education, persuasion, exhortation, mediation, and conferences.

JUDICIAL DECISIONS

The English common law is a body of legal doctrine developed from the accepted decisions of the courts. Since judges are likely to decide in line with prevailing customs, especially in the absence of a written constitution, the English common law has been as much as anything a body of principles of fairness in accordance with these customs. Under this system of law there were many legal principles which in effect regulated business. Contracts intended to monopolize were generally regarded as unenforceable. The laws of partnerships and negotiable instruments were brought into the common law from the early law merchant. The concept of a common carrier and his obligation to serve adequately, safely, and at a reasonable charge was also embodied in the common law. Common-law principles were developed for liability and the prosecution of damage suits; these were in reality laws regulating business. For example, while the common law recognized that the employer should use reasonable care in protecting his employees and was liable for injuries in the absence of such care, an employee could not receive damages where the injury was

[6] *People v. O'Brien*, 111 New York 1 (1888).

[7] See Leonard D. White, *Introduction to the Study of Public Administration* (New York: The Macmillan Company, 1955), pp. 471–474.

due to inherent occupational hazards or where he had contributed to it by his own negligence.

Regulation of business according to common-law principles means that the method of control is through judicial decision; an aggrieved party must sue the aggressor. Some regulation of business could be effected in this way. As a matter of fact, such regulation was common prior to the middle of the nineteenth century and is not at all uncommon today. Even though a constitution or the legislature should lay down general principles to be applied in regulating business, interpretation of these principles would be ultimately, if not immediately, a matter of judicial decision.

For really effective regulation of business, judicial decision is grossly inadequate. Legal proceedings are expensive, slow, and likely to be inexpert. The ordinary user of a railroad, for example, could hardly afford to institute a lawsuit if he felt that the rates were too high or the service poor. Moreover, months and sometimes years elapse before a final decision can be reached in legal proceedings. Courts lack administrative machinery for handling the variety of problems arising in business regulation; they do not ordinarily have a staff of trained engineers, accountants, and financial experts at their disposal. When one considers the intricacies of the law itself, one can hardly expect a judge to be trained in law and also in public-utility problems, competitive practices of business, holding-company matters, or many other difficult aspects of business control.

Limited as they are by judicial precedents, judges are seldom free to make decisions which look to the future and to the growth of a constructive regulatory program. The principles which they apply usually limit them to passing upon the question in a general way. Thus, under laws of common carriage they may find a carrier to have discriminated unreasonably against a particular customer, but they cannot lay down a detailed procedure of reasonable discrimination. In finding a rate unreasonable, the courts are customarily limited to this finding alone and may not declare what a reasonable rate would be.

Obviously, as an exclusive method for government control of business, judicial decision is unsatisfactory. Regulation is something which should be continuous, not sporadic. For if regulatory control is to follow any line of public policy, it must involve constant supervision. This is a legislative and administrative function, not one for the courts.

LEGISLATION

Businesses may be regulated by direct legislative action. It is not beyond possibility for federal and state legislatures and municipal councils to enact a governmental-regulation program by passing detailed statutes and ordinances involving the myriad of details necessary. State legislatures have made such attempts in many cases. Before general incorporation laws were enacted, new corporations were chartered by direct legislative action. In the latter part of the nineteenth century it was also common for such matters as railway rates to be regulated by statutes. Muncipal ordinances even today often include many detailed regulations of local businesses.

Like control by judicial decision, control through detailed legislation is likely to be unsatisfactory. Legislators have enough to do to pass wise general laws and the numerous private bills which call for direct action. Furthermore, control by statutes is likely to be sporadic and subject to delay. State legislatures seldom meet in continuous session throughout the year, and continuing supervision can hardly be provided. Again, the control of business, especially as its scope has broadened in recent years, calls for specialized and expert attention. Legislators do not usually have adequate staffs of experts available, and there is certainly little chance that any one legislator could be adequately trained in the variety of fields over which the government exerts control.

Regulation of business calls for an administrative type of organization, with a personnel able to apply general principles to particular cases. This is indeed a different function from that of legislatures, whose job it is to lay down fair laws of general application in an even wider field than government control of business.

ADMINISTRATIVE REGULATION

While investigation, licensing, inspection, and law enforcement are all forms of administrative action, rule making and adjudication are a form of administrative regulation, associated with the rise of regulatory agencies, which has assumed special importance today.[8] Although the regulatory agency is often headed by a commission or board of several members, it is not uncommon for the functions of rule making and adjudication to be exercised by one commissioner.

The outstanding characteristic of rule-making and adjudicatory agencies is the blending of executive, legislative, and judicial powers in one agency. The purpose of a regulatory agency is to enforce the law as set down by the legislature, and in such capacity it is acting as an executive body. Often the agency is given rather detailed guides as to how the law is to be executed. But usually a large range of discretion is entrusted to it as to how the will of the legislature is to be enforced. When an agency formulates an administrative rule or regulation within the standards established by the legislature, it is exercising quasi-legislative powers. The power of the Interstate Commerce Commission to regulate railroad accounts, for instance, grows out of a statutory provision which is exceedingly general.

[8] For an extensive treatment of the administration of economic control, see Emmette S. Redford, *Administration of National Economic Control* (New York: The Macmillan Company, 1952).

The Commission has laid down numerous rules for the keeping of these accounts; in doing so, it is acting as a lawmaking body.

Regulatory agencies also have judicial characteristics. Hearings are held, much like judicial hearings, in which evidence is introduced, although the agencies are not usually limited by rules of evidence as strictly as are the courts. The entire commission, a section of it, or a representative in the form of an examiner presides who acts like a judge in ruling on the admissibility of evidence, keeping order, and formulating a preliminary determination. If a person is found to have violated a law or administrative rule, an order of individual application is issued. This quasi-judicial process is referred to as "administrative adjudication."

The mixed character of regulatory agencies has been opposed as being inconsistent with the doctrine of separation of powers. Various authorities have from time to time taken the position that the fundamental structure of the administrative system is unconstitutional.[9] The Supreme Court, however, has never held that combination in a single agency of legislative, judicial, and executive powers is unconstitutional, and the day is long past when the Court would even give serious consideration to an argument to that effect. The validity of administrative rule making has been sustained against the charge that it involved an unconstitutional delegation of legislative power. The Court declared in this instance that "the authority to make administrative rules is not a delegation of legislative power, nor are such rules raised from an administrative to a legislative character because the violation thereof is punished as a public offense." [10] As for the judicial powers of regulatory agencies, they have been held to be no more than incidental to legislative or administrative power, and not to destroy the fundamental separation of powers.

Development in the United States. The development of administrative regulation has been interesting. Commissioners (or "superintendents") of banking and insurance have long been granted administrative powers over banks and insurance companies by many states. Railroad commissions were set up before 1850 to guard the public interest (at first as an organ of publicity or "advice") as these new transport agencies grew in importance.

The earliest federal regulatory commission was the Interstate Commerce Commission, which was originally established in 1887 to administer railroad regulation. Its scope, in terms both of forms of transport and of objects of regulation, has been increased, until today there is hardly any commission with more experience or greater importance in the field of

[9] The unconstitutionality of all federal administrative agencies is the basic thesis of James M. Beck's *Our Wonderland of Bureaucracy* (New York: The Macmillan Company, 1913).

[10] *United States v. Grimaud*, 220 U.S. 506, 521 (1911).

control. The commission movement was given impetus by the adoption of commissions for state public-utility regulation in the decade prior to World War I. In the same period many federal commissions were created. The Federal Reserve Board, with powers over central-banking policy and national-bank practices, was established in 1914, the same year in which the Federal Trade Commission, with powers over competitive practices of business in or affecting interstate commerce, was set up. Since that time, and particularly in the past two decades, commission-type regulation has been greatly extended. Prior to World War II, such important commissions were established as the Federal Power Commission in 1930, the Securities and Exchange Commission and the Federal Communications Commission in 1934, and the National Labor Relations Board in 1935. During World War II, wide use was made of the techniques of administrative regulation. The War Production Board, the Office of Price Administration, the War Labor Board, the Office of Defense Transportation, and many other similar agencies, some headed by a plural executive and others by a single administrator, all had as their principal purpose the administration of regulatory statutes.

While most of the World War II regulatory agencies were abolished or their functions transferred after the end of the war, they reappeared in the postwar defense program with the establishment of such agencies as the National Production Authority, the Office of Price Stabilization, and the Wage Stabilization Board. Likewise, with the maintenance and expansion of peacetime controls on both the national and the state levels, there has come such a multiplicity of regulatory bodies, both inside and independent of established departments, as to be a source of confusion to the student and to the business manager subject to their control.

An important administrative development is the increasing use of the single commissioner or administrator in place of the multiheaded board or commission. The practice itself is not new, as is indicated from the long existence of commissioners of banking and insurance, the Comptroller of Currency, the Patent Commissioner, the single-headed Food and Drug Administration, and the regulatory activities of the administrative departments of the federal executive branch. The defense agencies of World War II and of recent years have often been headed by a single commissioner, although he has sometimes been aided by an advisory board. This development may well be an indication that the objectives and methods of control have become well understood and accepted, or that the job of administration has become less judicial and more managerial in character, or that legislators have become less concerned with the dangers of abuse of commission power. In other words, the tendency toward the single administrator of a regulatory program seems to indicate that the emphasis is being placed more on effective management, an area in which the plural executive is notoriously inefficient, and less on the element of distrust in placing power in the hands of one individual.

Table 3–1. Federal Regulatory Commissions

Agency	*Date established*	*Number of members*	*Terms, years*	*Jurisdiction*
Interstate Commerce Commission	1887	11	7	Railroads; motor carriers; shipping by coastwise, intercoastal and inland waters; pipelines (except natural gas and water); express companies; carriers using rail-and-water routes; sleeping-car companies
Board of Governors of the Federal Reserve System	1913	7	14	Determines general monetary, credit, and operating policies for System; influences credit conditions and supervises Federal Reserve banks and member banks
Federal Trade Commission	1914	5	7	Regulates competition to keep it free and fair
Federal Power Commission	1920, 1930	5	5	Water-power sites, electric power, natural-gas pipelines
Securities and Exchange Commission	1934	5	5	Securities and financial markets
Federal Communications Commission	1934	7	7	Radio, telephone, telegraph, cables
National Labor Relations Board	1935	5	5	Labor-management relations
Civil Aeronautics Authority	1938	Board, 5; Administration, 1	6	Airlines, airways, and airports
Federal Maritime Board	1950	3	4	Shipping in foreign commerce

Advantages of administrative regulation. The regulatory agency is particularly suited to most fields of economic control. As contrasted to reliance on judicial decision, it makes possible prescription of action to safeguard the public interest *before* injury to that interest. It is better to set public-utility rates on a reasonable level than to rely on customers' suing for a return of money expended on extortionate rates. It is better to ensure physicians' competence in advance by licensing them than to wait for patients harmed by a quack doctor to sue for damages.

In the second place, administrative regulation makes possible continuing supervision. Usually, where government control is found necessary, continual contact with the industry is important. With the furnishing of public-utility service, or with the application of labor regulations, problems are seldom *finally* solved, and changing conditions call for an almost ceaseless regulatory treatment. The administrative agency may keep in close contact with these problems. The informal nature of administrative regulation, whereby commissioners or commission representatives can work out in advance solutions to these problems, without recourse to courtroom technicalities or legislative politics, helps to explain how this kind of supervision can remain so uninterrupted.

A third advantage of administrative regulation is that administration of general regulatory principles *can* be handled by a group of experts. If those entrusted with railroad regulation in a state are experts in this field, the advantage for efficient public regulation is obvious. Because the regulatory agency is usually limited to a narrow field, its membership can include men who are experts in this line.[11] Moreover, the commission may, for the same reason, as well as because of the constant nature of its activities, make efficient use of a staff of expert assistants. It would obviously be excessively costly for the courts or legislatures to hire experts to advise them in all the fields with which they might deal. But a public-utility commission or a securities commission has its jurisdiction limited to a certain type of regulation, and its staff of experts will likewise be limited to this narrower field.

Dangers in administrative regulation. One of the dangers in administrative regulation is that it can become the basis for a complicated bureaucracy. Not only can the field of government regulation be extended, but the jurisdictions of commissions may be so broken down and the number of commissions so increased, for the purpose of obtaining expert control, that the businessman or customer has to deal with altogether too many of them. This may become so confusing to persons subject to regulatory agencies, and so much red tape may result, that much of the efficiency of the administrative regulation may be lost.

The regulatory agency has often been criticized as being legislator, prosecutor, judge, and jury. In a sense this may be true. On certain matters the agency must make rules to aid in the administration of a law. Most agencies are empowered to make investigations into the activities of persons under their jurisdictions. On the basis of these investigations, regu-

[11] Or who become expert as the result of long familiarity with certain problems. Practically, this experience in the agency may be the most important source of expertness.

latory agencies often decide what they believe to be the law and whether they find a violation of it. Having made this decision, an order is usually issued. If it is not obeyed, the agency may then bring suit against the violator in a court. There do seem to be possibilities for abuse in an administrative device of this sort.

Actually, however, most regulatory agencies took care to divide these functions, and the Administrative Procedures Act of 1946 now requires this separation. A member of the agency staff, ordinarily an examiner, gathers the facts for the investigation. The agency itself sits as a sort of jury and judge to decide whether these facts justify a finding of violation of the law. If, on issuance of an order, compliance is not forthcoming, the legal staff of the agency brings proper suit. Hence, to the extent that these different functions are divided within the organization of the commission and its staff, it is not correct to say that the membership of the commission itself combines them all.

If the regulatory agency does not separate these functions within its organization, or if in making its finding it places undue emphasis upon evidence presented by examiners, unfairness can easily result. While abuse of administrative power may be curtailed by resorting to the courts or to the legislature which created the agency, this is likely to be little solace to the small businessman or customer who feels that he has been treated arbitrarily and unfairly. He may not be able to afford an appeal to the courts, or he may find it difficult to convince a court, in the absence of a clear legal mistake by the agency, that the latter's conclusions from the facts were unjustly reached. After all, the administrative body must have some discretion in applying the law to the facts. This discretion, however, may be open to abuse. The danger of such abuse seems particularly great with the tendency in recent years for the courts to withdraw from examination of administrative decisions. The recently developed reluctance of the Supreme Court to go beyond matters of procedure in weighing due process may leave the aggrieved businessman or consumer little recourse to abuse of administrative power other than the ballot; and this recourse means rather little in cases of individual mistreatment.

One of the best methods of ensuring fairness and effectiveness of administrative regulation is to be sure that its members are competent in the field and not subject to undue political control. In many states public-utility commissioners are still elected by popular vote. In cases where commissioners are appointed, in both the state and federal governments, the appointment is too often looked upon as a way to repay political debts. When political factors cause incompetent or prejudiced men to be placed on commissions, effective regulation is threatened. The unfair baiter of business is as dangerous as the influenced conniver with business. Moreover, since regulatory agencies are generally regarded as protectors of the "public," particularly the organized pressure groups of the "public," there is likely to be a bias in its favor at the expense of the less effectively organized business manager.

Judicial review of administrative regulation. In the United States, any decision of an administrative agency on a point of law is open to review by the courts.[12] In some cases the legislature defines the procedure of appeal, but no legislature, state or federal, could refuse to grant the right of appeal. To do so would be to take liberty or property without due process of law.

It has always been a well-established judicial principle that the courts do not sit as boards of revision to substitute their judgment of the facts for that of the administrative body. However, under the interpretation of due process as a substantive matter, which was prevalent until 1937, the federal courts had taken the position that due process requires the decisions of regulatory agencies to be supported by evidence upon which reasonable men might have reached a judgment and to result in a finding which meets the test of due process in substance, as well as in procedure. As a consequence of this position, the federal courts found themselves reviewing the findings of fact of administrative agencies, including not only the evidence used but also the methods employed in dealing with the evidence.

Although this legal position often resulted in court reexamination of the evidence placed before regulatory agencies, some avoidance of duplication of the quasi-judicial work of the administrative bodies was accomplished by the procedure of remanding cases where the facts were regarded as questionable. The legal skirmishes which followed or accompanied administrative regulation have been exceedingly costly in terms of effective regulation. When a telephone-rate case was kept in the judicial air for more than a decade before any decision was reached, as was true in a case finally decided in 1934,[13] the crippling effect of slow court action becomes readily apparent.

While there is no assurance that even the United States Supreme Court will not look beyond administrative procedure to the result of the action in deciding whether to grant judicial review, and many of the lower federal courts and the state courts have not adopted so extensive a view, the present attitude of the Supreme Court toward due process and its avowed reluctance to interfere in legislative matters have brought a new freedom to regulatory agencies. This attitude of the Supreme Court has especially been apparent in the field of price regulation. After many decades of imposition of judicial standards of reasonableness on public-utility rate-setting methods of regulatory agencies, the Supreme Court

[12] For an excellent treatment, see J. Roland Pennock, *Administration and the Rule of Law* (New York: Rinehart & Company, Inc., 1941).

[13] See *Lindheimer v. Bell Telephone Co.*, 292 U.S. 151 (1934).

apparently abandoned such interference in 1944.[14] Even though the Court indicated that it might still look at the *result* of administrative action to determine whether property had been taken without due process of law, the fact that the Court has not interfered with the substantive determinations of regulatory agencies since, plus the Court's attitude on due process in other matters, indicates that Supreme Court interference with administrative action will occur only if (1) the requirements of procedural due process are infringed; (2) the agency acts without statutory power; or (3) the agency action violates some specific constitutional prohibition.[15]

PUBLIC AID

Grants of public aid, whether in terms of cash, special privilege, government services, or advantageous enabling laws, very often carry with them certain conditions upon which the gift will be made. With the government extending aid on a wider front to business of all sorts, it is only natural that control through such aid should increase.

A perhaps insidious feature of control by this method is that the recipient of government aid may be so happy to receive the help that the strings attached to it may not seem to be important. Furthermore, a question exists as to whether the emergency character of much government aid will ever pass over. There are those who believe that such emergency grants, especially in the field of credit facilities, will become permanent, and that this method of control will take an important place along with those methods which are admittedly more direct.

TAXATION

While taxation in order to be valid must be for revenue purposes or be one of many devices to carry into effect some power possessed by a government, its method of application, especially in regard to exemptions, is one of the most important means of exerting regulation. Customs duties on selected imports are certainly used to regulate the flow of foreign trade and aid the development of domestic industry. Taxes on certain commodities, such as colored oleomargarine, opium, and white-phosphorus

[14] *Federal Power Com. v. Hope Natural Gas Co.*, 320 U.S. 591 (1944).

[15] It is interesting that at least four of the nine justices sitting on the Supreme Court in 1944 had advocated a return to the doctrine of *Munn v. Illinois*, 94 U.S. 113 (1877), by which judicial review of legislative or commission action is limited to securing compliance with the procedural requirements of due process. See opinions of Justices Black, Murphy, Douglas, and Frankfurter in *Federal Power Com. v. Hope Natural Gas Co.*, and in *McCart v. Indianapolis Water Co.*, 302 U.S. 419 (1938) and *Driscoll v. Edison Lt. & Pwr. Co.* 307 U.S. 104 (1939). There is hardly any doubt but that this is the position of the Court now. However, there are cases where state and federal courts have refused to go along with this concept of noninterference. See, e.g., *Utah Pwr. & Lt. Co. v. Public Serv. Com.*, 152 P. 2d 542 (1945).

matches, are probably more valuable as regulatory devices than for revenue. Taxes on chain stores are also imposed in the interests of restricting the effectiveness of this method of merchandising as compared to that of the independent retailer.

Taxes must also conform to certain standards in order to be valid. They must apply uniformly. Within reason, as stated above, they must be for revenue purposes. But reasonable exemptions from the operation of the tax can be laid down, so that its regulatory force can be applied on certain subjects, as desired.

GOVERNMENT OWNERSHIP

Some may object to the inclusion of government-ownership methods as a means of government control of business. But the fact that the government directly or indirectly goes into business is sure to have a controlling effect upon certain aspects of business. The government in business is no ordinary competitor or monopolist. The way it does business, the conditions it makes for others to do business with it, the political power behind it, and its practically unlimited financial backing make it a formidable agent of control.

Government ownership is often frankly used for yardstick purposes. Either private business brought into line by the danger of government competition, or the supposed inefficiency or imprudence of private management is "exposed" by the government plant. Yardstick regulation has been recommended particularly in the public-utility field.

Types of Control

The techniques of control of economic enterprise are closely related to the types of control, and the two may be regarded as comprising the machinery through which public control is exercised. Even though both are necessarily dependent upon the economic enterprise regulated and the public purposes envisaged, one does find a pattern of administrative approach in all kinds of controls. While this pattern is discernible, and experience and principles are carried from one field to another, the substantive application of regulation, which is the subject of succeeding chapters of this book, necessarily depends upon the nature of the economic activity controlled.

Most government controls are partial in nature, in the sense that they aim to bring under public regulation a particular phase of economic activity. In some industries, such as the railroad industry, these partial controls have become so comprehensive that they amount virtually to industry management, and the private managers may have to reckon with the government in virtually every major policy area. In other cases, the combination of types of control which the government undertakes may be grouped along functional lines, with application to virtually all industries in accordance with a certain function. Thus, during World War II the price policy of all businesses was controlled along a given set of principles by the Office of Price Administration and matériel-procurement and -utilization policy by the War Production Board.

But what distinguishes these types of partial control is that they are aimed at bringing under control some major decision area of economic enterprise. The completely unregulated private business manager would freely reach policy decisions in such major areas as the determination of the nature of the product to be offered, the market in which to sell it, the volume to be offered for sale, the price at which to sell it, the methods and practices of production and sale, the methods of financing capital investment, and the utilization of material and human resources in production and sale. The regulated business manager would have one or more of these major areas of policy determination circumscribed to a greater or lesser degree by the government.

In addition to partial controls, public policy has aimed at over-all control of the economy. While partial controls are sometimes utilized in accomplishing over-all control by the government just as production control may contribute to over-all control of a business operation by a manager, there are additionally certain over-all controls, such as control of the fiscal-monetary system, undertaken by government to accomplish objectives related to the economy as a whole. These are aimed at the health of the economy as a whole in terms of full employment or effective national defense much in the same way as profit-and-loss controls or the standard of controlling a business through the yardstick of return on investment are often utilized by business managers to control the over-all economic health of a business enterprise.

ENTRY INTO SERVICE

Perhaps no type of business control is more common than that exercised by the government over entry into service. Physicians, dentists, beauty experts, and barbers must usually obtain permits before setting up in business. Taxicab operators, bus companies, telephone companies, railroads, electric light and power companies, and others also receive some kind of permit before they can begin business. Persons who would open a bank, an insurance company, or a brokerage agency usually must get permission to do so. A moment's reflection may bring to mind even more examples where entry into business is not a right to be freely exercised without getting some permission from the state.

Sometimes the purpose of requiring permits or licenses before entry into business is largely for the revenue that can be obtained. More often, however, regulation of entry is designed to protect the public interest in some way and is a use of a state's police power or of the federal government's power to police those matters within its jurisdiction. Thus, obtaining competent physicians, dentists, or even barbers is a matter of public concern. Because telephone, bus, and other public-utility companies use public streets and highways, the public has an interest in keeping these facilities from being crowded with competing companies. Moreover, in the public-utility field it has been found that the most efficient service to the public can ordinarily be obtained by encouraging monopoly. For this purpose, permission to enter the business has been required. In this and other fields, the necessity of protecting public property, or of obtaining efficient production of important public services, or of ensuring that the business will be responsibly operated, has been held to justify the regulation and restriction of entry into service.

Controlling entry into service can also be used as an administrative device to enforce a program of regulation. If a government agency may require a license to enter a field, it may normally cancel that license or refuse to issue it as a penalty for an infraction. Many proposals have been made for general federal licensing of businesses. In 1951, for example, the Office of Price Stabilization proposed such licensing as a means of enforcing the vast program of defense price controls. To date, such attempts at general licensing have been refused by Congress on the grounds that this gives an administrative or regulatory agency, especially one handling a program applying to the majority of American businesses, far too much power over the life and death of American industry.

NATURE OF PRODUCT

In many cases, regulation of the nature of product has been found necessary in the public interest. Pure-food and -drug laws have been passed with the hope of safeguarding the innocent consumer, who may be duped into accepting not only adulterated substitutes but goods positively injurious to his health. Wherever a monopoly is granted to a private company, as to an electric light and power company, the quality of the product is ordinarily subject to regulation; this may be in terms of minimum and maximum voltages, interruptions of service, or accuracy of meters. Specified standards of quality of service are also customarily required of other public utilities. Blue-sky laws, whereby the honesty of security issuance is regulated, are also an example of an attempt to regulate quality of product.

The wide expansion of this type of control came in World War II. In order to channel scarce materials into the war program and into the most essential civilian production, the War Production Board set up a system of elaborate controls over the use of materials. Although not completely relaxed after the end of the war, most of these controls were eliminated. But with the emergency presented as the result of defense rearming, a large number of the quantity of materials controls were reinstated under the National Production Authority, created in the Department of Commerce in 1950. Thus, the wide application of this type of control seems to be well established whenever an "emergency" appears to demand them.

ABANDONMENT OF SERVICE

A type of control applicable to public-service companies and to common carriers is the restriction on free abandonment of service. In these fields a company may not withdraw from service whenever or to whatever extent it wishes. Because these companies have embarked upon a business which the public regards as necessary, and because they are often given monopoly privileges, their right to abandon service is limited. In order to quit such service, they must receive permission from the administrative agency in charge of their regulation. This type of control is not found in other business fields, although liquidation of such businesses as banking or insurance is accompanied by many legal technicalities.

REASONABLE PRICE

One of the most important types of control is regulation to obtain a reasonable price. Because price has been regarded as the heart of a contract, and freedom of contract indispensable for a system of free private enterprise, extension of regulation of price to new fields has been strongly resisted. At first applied in this country only to common carriers and public utilities, enforcement of reasonable price has been introduced to new subjects of regulation. Regulation of wages and bargaining conditions of laborers have incorporated the idea of reasonable price. Production control in agriculture and other industries has been dominated in part by the desire to obtain a reasonable price. Regulation of bank interest charges and insurance-company rates are further examples of the application of this type of control.

Even before World War II, price control had been fairly widely expanded, but always on the basis of a special case being made for each commodity or service brought under control. During the war, however, the government embarked upon a wide program of general control of prices as a device to prevent the spiraling and dangerous effects of inflation. The Office of Price Administration was charged with setting up this program in the field of prices, as was the War Production Board in the field of materials. As in the case of materials, the prolongation of certain "emergency" conditions after the war, especially in rental housing, was used to justify the continuance of some general price control until the emergency conditions of 1950 again brought under the federal government the control of virtually all prices, a control not terminated until 1953. Thus, this kind of control appears to be well grounded in the pattern of government regulation, at least if an "emergency" can be found to exist. With the probability that emergencies will periodically recur, one may wonder whether future "emergencies" must be as serious as those in the past to justify reappearance of a program of general price control.

It might be noted here that, of all types of control, perhaps none has caused more difficulty than the attempt to set reasonable prices. Because of its close connection with the very essence of property and contract, and because reasonableness of price is not a matter of formula, lawmakers, administrative officers, commissions, and judges have found the concept of price not easily subject to definition. Moreover, because prices are myriad, the task of administering any very broad controls, especially under a system strongly motivated by private enterprise, is immeasurably great.

DISCRIMINATION IN PRICE AND SERVICE

Strict business privacy would imply that the businessman may deal with whomever he pleases and upon what terms he pleases. In other words, the right to discriminate between customers as to either price or service is one of the traditional elements of privacy. In certain fields, however, government control has taken the form of forbidding unreasonable discrimination in price or service between customers. Note that discrimination is modified to include only that which is unreasonable. For example, it is unreasonable for a telephone company to take toll calls from one resident user but refuse to take them from another, or to charge two users in exactly the same position different rates. But it is not unreasonable to charge a different rate to resident and business users, since the type of service required, or other factors, makes this discrimination reasonable in the opinion of the public.

Limitations on unreasonable discrimination in price or service has ordinarily been confined to common carriers and public-service companies. Because their service has been regarded as so necessary to the public, and because they often operate under certain public grants of privilege, such requirement is deemed to be in the public interest. This type of control has been extended to general business through various fair-trade laws, so that the manufacturer or wholesaler who would charge or serve two customers differently may find himself faced with this type of control.

HONEST AND PRUDENT FINANCING

Because of increased public interest in the ways in which certain businesses are operated, control for purposes of securing honesty or prudence in financing has been growing in importance. Where price has been regulated, such control has been found necessary for its more accurate determination. In some cases, notably the public-utility holding company, the public has found that financing methods have thwarted the purpose of administration of government regulation. In other cases, even where the businesses were dominantly private, some control over financial practices has been necessary for protection from fraudulent security issuance.

RESTRAINT OF TRADE

Because relative freedom of trade has been regarded as desirable in most fields, many aspects of government control have been devoted to removing restraints from the freedom of doing business. These restraints are usually those of monopoly or monopolistic practices which interfere with the effectiveness of competition. This type of control does not envisage the removal of all restraints upon the freedom of trade. The advantage to the public of patents and copyrights is an exception. Monopoly has also been allowed in business where the growth has appeared to courts and commissions as being natural rather than artificially stimulated.

Moreover, in some fields restraint of trade has actually been encouraged. Extension of the monopoly principle in the public-service industry (electric, gas, water, telephone, etc.) has been encouraged because it has seemed that the public interest in adequate service and reasonable rates lies in this direction. It is important to remember, however, that, where restraint of trade is actually promoted, increased regulation to prevent injury to the public from monopolistic practices is a necessary concomitant.

UNFAIR PRACTICES

Introduced in this country as a type of control to aid in gaining ethical freedom of trade, prohibition of unfair practices has become an increasingly important regulatory device. Not only is it used to limit businessmen in taking such advantage of rivals as "unfairly" to reduce the freedom of doing business, but the concept has been extended to other fields. Most important is the unfair labor practice, where an employer is forbidden to interfere with the privilege of self-organization and collective bargaining by employees through freely selected unions.

What is an unfair practice is a matter of the prevailing mores, as these come to be recognized by legislatures and administrative commissions and as they are supported by the courts. It is interesting to note how this type of control in the field of competition was at first limited to practices which were unfair in that they artificially stimulated monopolies. But under the National Industrial Recovery Act, an unfair practice became an act of nonconformity with a monopolistic business code. And under recent "fair-trade laws," an unfair practice has become refusal to sell a trade-marked good at a fixed price set by a manufacturer, a procedure which smacks of monopoly.

GOVERNMENT SERVICES

In addition to the many services government renders to the community generally, such as protection of health and safety and provision of educational facilities, government supplies certain services which are essential to economic enterprises. These include the construction of roads and waterways, promotion of shipping and foreign trade, protection of property, establishment of standards of weights and measure, and the collection and distribution of statistical data. Indirect financial aid is provided by means of tariffs, and direct financial assistance is made available through the provision of credit facilities and direct subsidies.

MAINTENANCE OF A FRAMEWORK FOR BUSINESS OPERATION

Another type of government economic activity is the establishment and maintenance of a framework for business operation. This includes protection of property and contract, maintenance of a monetary system, provision for incorporation, provision of debt relief through bankruptcy procedures, and the extension of patent, copyright, and trade-mark privileges. Without these general aids business would be virtually unable to operate.

FISCAL-MONETARY CONTROL

Perhaps the most used type of over-all control is that having to do with tax, credit, and spending activities of the government. These may be aimed at the encouragement or discouragement of a given industry but are more ordinarily aimed at the maintenance of the economy as a whole on a level desired by public policy. These controls are based on the facts that the flow of credit or the level of expenditures for businesses generally may be controlled by the government and that, in so doing, the level of business activity may be expanded, retracted, or stabilized. In so controlling the flow of funds between the government and private industry and, as is often the case, establishing criteria by which government credit may be obtained or taxes affected, the economy as a whole is influenced. Thus, more funds can be made available for construction, or less, or more or less funds may be available for consumer expenditures. In some cases, too, individual industries may be influenced, as happened when high taxes were placed on passenger transportation and on night clubs during World War II or when the government in 1954 liberalized the terms applicable for credit for new home construction.

The Administrative Problem of Control

It is not unreasonable to say that the United States appears to have embarked upon the road to becoming an administrative state.[16] Whether this may be the same as the "welfare state" or the more nebulous idea of "big government" is rather unimportant. The significant fact is that the present system is hardly one of free enterprise, in view of the extent to which economic activities have been brought under government control, nor can it be regarded as authoritarian, since considerable freedom in economic life exists and, more importantly, the ballot remains almost completely free from autocratic political control.

But the tendency toward the administrative state is great indeed. Virtually every business transaction is touched by the hand of government. Practically every business decision must be made in the environment of government controls. Taxes of all kinds take approximately 26 per cent of the national income; the actual nondefense activities of federal, state, and local governments accounted for approximately 10 per cent of the national income in 1953; and nonmilitary government service occupied the time of 6.4 million nonmilitary employees, or 11 per cent of the employed civilian working force.[17]

It would be very surprising if such a tremendous program of government did not bring administrative complexities and problems. The largest private corporation in the world, the General Motors Corporation, with its 551,000 employees, $10 billion sales, and forty major operating divisions, is dwarfed by the size of government. Since the job of management is primarily that of coordinating the efforts of people, it is perfectly clear that the managerial job alone involved in government may well be beyond human ability. In any event, the sheer size of the managerial task and the necessity of dividing the job to be done make necessary the existence of numerous governmental units. Complexity becomes unavoidable. Duplication and wastes of administration, while seldom justifiable, become understandable. It is not surprising that, even after several decades of administrative improvement in the federal service,[18] the Hoover Commission recommended further improvements in administration and management of the federal government that promised to effect savings of approximately $3 billion per year.

[16] For a definition of administrative state, see Joseph Rosenfarb, *Freedom and the Administrative State* (New York: Harper & Brothers, 1948), p. 74: "It constitutes the ultimate conscious integration of our differentiated economy by the state."

[17] U.S. Department of Commerce, *National Income, 1954 Edition* (1954), pp. 163, 171, 203.

[18] A fact which is often overlooked is that, in many of the federal government agencies, much time and effort have been intelligently applied to problems of management engineering.

In fact, the job of managing an administrative state has become so great as to add another factor to the considerations which the intelligent voter should face in supporting a program of control. For in addition to such questions as to whether the social and economic benefits of control will outweigh the costs in loss of economic efficiency and individual freedom, the citizen must face the problem of whether the government can, as an organization, do the job effectively and at reasonable cost.

Selected References

Blachly, Frederick F., and Miriam E. Oatman, *Administrative Legislation and Adjudication.* Washington, D.C.: Brookings Institution, 1934.

——— and ———, *Federal Regulatory Action and Control.* Washington, D.C.: Brookings Institution, 1940.

Commission on Organization of the Executive Branch of Government, *Task Force Report on Regulatory Commissions* (Appendix N), Government Printing Office, 1949.

Committee on Administrative Procedure, appointed by the Attorney General, *Administrative Procedure in Government Agencies,* Doc. 8, 77th Cong., 1st Sess. (1941).

Cooper, Robert M., "Techniques of Public Control—An Appraisal of Methods," 201 *The Annals of the American Academy of Political and Social Science* 1–16 (January, 1939).

Cushman, Robert E., *The Independent Regulatory Commissions.* New York: Oxford University Press, 1941.

Davis, Kenneth C., *Administrative Law.* St. Paul, Minn.: West Publishing Co., 1951.

Dimock, Marshall E., "Government Corporations: A Focus of Policy and Administration," 43 *American Political Science Review* 899–921, 1145–1164 (October, December, 1949).

Gellhorn, Walter, *Federal Administrative Proceedings.* Baltimore: Johns Hopkins Press, 1941.

Landis, James M., *The Administrative Process.* New Haven, Conn.: Yale University Press, 1938.

Leiserson, Avery, *Administrative Regulation: A Study in Representation of Interests.* Chicago: University of Chicago Press, 1942.

McDiarmid, John, *Government Corporations and Federal Funds.* Chicago: University of Chicago Press, 1938.

Pegrum, Dudley F., "The Public Corporation as a Regulatory Device," 16 *Journal of Land and Public Utility Economics* 335 (August, 1940).

Pennock, J. Roland, *Administration and the Rule of Law.* New York: Farrar & Rinehart, Inc., 1941.

Pritchett, C. Herman, "The Regulatory Commissions Revisited," 43 *American Political Science Review* 978 (October, 1949).

Redford, Emmette S., *Administration of National Economic Control.* New York: The Macmillan Company, 1952.

Seidman, Harold, "The Theory of the Autonomous Government Corporation: A Critical Appraisal," 12 *Public Administration Review* 89–96 (Spring, 1952).

Thurston, John, *Government Proprietary Corporations in the English Speaking Countries*. Cambridge, Mass.: Harvard University Press, 1937.

Warren, George (ed.), *The Federal Administrative Procedure Act and the Administrative Agencies*. New York: New York University School of Law, 1947.

PART TWO

TRANSPORTATION

4

TRANSPORT REGULATION: EVOLUTION OF A PATTERN

In no field of government control of business is the development of a pattern of regulation more clear or complete than in the field of transportation. With the possible exception of money and banking regulation, the earliest control over business of a continuing and supervisory nature was exercised in the transportation field. Space forbids tracing the growth of all types of regulation treated in this book. The history of transport regulation is traced, however, since it is especially illustrative of the expanding nature of government controls and discloses how gaps in regulation tend to be continually filled as new problems arise and regulatory weaknesses appear. Moreover, the real beginnings of continuing regulation in the United States and the development of many regulatory principles, later applied to other fields of control, have been found in the control of transportation businesses.

The primary pattern of transport regulation began with controls placed on the railroads. While canal and turnpike regulation antedated control of railroads, it was sporadic and limited largely to enforcement of charter provisions. But from the establishment of state railroad commissions in the middle of the nineteenth century and the passage of national legislation with the Interstate Commerce Act of 1887, a pattern for government control of an industry was developed. From regulation of the railroad industry, control expanded to cover all forms of transportation, so that today the regulatory pattern may be said to be complete.

In this field of regulation, both the states and the federal government have exerted control. But with the expansion of transport facilities into interstate commerce, and with the enlargement of the legal concept of interstate commerce, the control exercised by the federal government has been far more than that exercised by the states. Thus, most of the attention given to the development of transport regulation will be directed at federal government control. In later chapters, where the regulation of the public-service companies will be discussed, more attention will be given to the principles and problems of state regulation, since these companies have operated so largely in intrastate commerce.

Development of a Pattern: Early Regulation

Early regulation is characterized by legislative attempts to establish the objectives of regulation, by trial of legal issues in the courts, by the development of administrative devices to accomplish effective regulation, and by the repair of existing legislation found to be inadequate for its purposes. Regulations of this period, extending from the first establishment of "advisory" state railroad commissions before the middle of the nineteenth century until the adoption of the Transportation Act of 1920, were primarily punitive in nature, aimed at bringing under control the excessive power of the railroads over the economic growth of the nation.

REGULATION PRIOR TO 1887

Effective regulation, even by the states, did not come before the 1870s, although some regulation was found in charter limitations and early "advisory" railroad commissions. Many railroad charters included limitations on maximum charges and rate of profits, but these maxima were usually so high as to be of no significance as regulatory measures. Moreover, such regulation as resulted did not touch the problem of rate discrimination, or adequacy or equality of service. The charters were also a weak form of regulation in that, even in the same state, charters differed in their provisions and no uniformity in policy was possible.

Railroad commissions were first created in Rhode Island in 1839, New Hampshire in 1844, Connecticut in 1853, Vermont in 1855, and Maine in 1858. These commissions have been called "advisory" in that their main purpose was not to regulate but to advise legislators, administrators, and railway officials on certain matters. They usually had the duty of seeing that railroads lived up to charter provisions; they appraised land taken by railroads through eminent domain; they reported accidents, adopted measures to reduce accidents, and gathered what financial and operating statistics they could. Some also attempted to help the railroads in apportioning receipts and expenditures in interstate traffic.

Positive control over railroads did not come until the so-called granger legislation of the 1870s. This was brought on by an agrarian revolt against certain railroad practices, a revolt which has come to be known as the "granger movement." While the "Grange," an organization of farmers especially popular in the Middle West, did not sponsor railroad legislation, discussion of railroad problems by its members had much to do with solidifying opinion in favor of regulation of the railroads.

Actually, the granger movement was brought about by the agricultural depression of the late 1860s and 1870s, which was caused by a decline in agricultural prices. While the railroads were not to blame for this depression, the farmers, angered by railroad practices, felt that relief lay in the direction of railroad regulation. They believed that unreasonably high rail rates contributed to low farm prices, that the railroads discriminated against them by charging lower rates to competitive points and to certain favored shippers, and that control of the railroads by Eastern capitalists had robbed them of the beneficial effects of railroads, many of which they had helped to build through taxes and direct investment.

As a result, strong regulatory measures were passed by legislatures in most Middle Western states. These included strict regulation of maximum charges, usually by direct legislative action, prorata clauses by which rates lower for a long haul than for a short haul were prohibited, provisions prohibiting granting of free passes to public officials, and clauses forbidding combination of competing railroads.

Although upheld in 1877 by the United States Supreme Court as a constitutional regulation of business "affected with a public interest,"[1] the granger laws were repealed in the late 1870s by most of the states. The depression of 1873, together with effective propaganda efforts by the railroads, as well as the difficulty of effectively administering the crudely drawn laws, caused the public to wonder whether it had actually been helped or hindered by this legislation. State regulation was revived in the 1880s. However, by that time the federal government had entered the field, and it has since overshadowed, though not entirely displaced, the states in regulation of the railroads.

THE INTERSTATE COMMERCE ACT OF 1887

For some years before 1887, Congress had investigated the feasibility of providing for federal regulation of railroads. In 1874 a congressional committee had reported that the abuses in the railroad system could best be met by government competition and recommended the improvement of natural waterways, the construction of canals, and the building of a railroad from the Mississippi River to the Atlantic seaboard.[2] Since no action was taken following this report and the demand for regulation became imperative, a second committee was selected to study the question; its findings were reported in 1886.[3]

The report of this committee, as well as the decision of the Supreme Court in the Wabash case,[4] led to the adoption of the act of 1887. The committee described widespread abuses and emphasized that the extension of railway facilities made the problem of regulation an interstate rather than an intrastate one. Overbuilding of railroads, industrialization

[1] *Munn v. Illinois*, 94 U.S. 113 (1877).

[2] This interesting report may be found in *Transportation Routes to the Seaboard*, S. Rept. 307, 43d Cong., 1st Sess.

[3] *Report of the Senate Select Committee on Interstate Commerce*, S. Rept. 46, 49th Cong., 1st Sess.

[4] *Wabash Rwy. Co. v. Illinois*, 118 U.S. 557 (1886).

of the Middle West, and the depression of 1873 had led to cutthroat competition between railroads. This competitive struggle had given rise to rate discrimination and to the organization of pooling arrangements which impressed the popular mind as placing the small shipper and the consumer in danger of monopolistic exploitation. Competitive construction had been accompanied by fraudulent financial practices and excessive promotion profits, with a resultant threat to the solvency of railroad investment.

The decision in the Wabash case also hastened the enactment of federal legislation. In this case the Supreme Court held that a state could not regulate rates on interstate traffic. Since much of the traffic was interstate, a large part of the railroad business was left unregulated. This situation, in the face of popular demand for regulation of the railroads, made federal legislation necessary.

The act of 1887 created a commission of five members to administer the new law. The legislation was made applicable to all common carriage by railroads operating in interstate and foreign commerce, as well as to interstate and foreign common carriage by water and rail where through traffic was involved. Since few railroads engaged exclusively in intrastate commerce, most of them carrying some interstate traffic, the act really applied to all railroads.

On the subject of rates, the act prohibited "unjust and unreasonable" charges; forbade discrimination between persons; prohibited unjust discrimination between places or kinds of traffic; and outlawed higher charges made "under substantially similar circumstances and conditions, for a shorter than for a longer distance over the same line, in the same direction, the shorter being included within the longer distance." [5] In addition, the act required publication of rates and fares and ten days' public notice of rate increases. Pooling of traffic or of revenue of competing carriers was forbidden.

The Interstate Commerce Commission was also to function as a board of investigation and was authorized to inquire into railroad management. For this purpose it might require the presence and testimony of witnesses, and the production of books and documents relating to the subject under investigation. The Commission was in addition empowered to require annual reports and to prescribe a uniform system of accounting. Enforcement of any Commission order necessitated application to a federal circuit court.

WEAKENING AND REPAIR OF THE ACT OF 1887

While the act of 1887 showed promise of being an effective regulatory law, a series of court decisions soon brought out its feeble character. In

[5] The Commission was empowered to grant relief from the operation of this section when in its discretion such exemption seemed in the public interest.

the first place, the Supreme Court in 1892 upheld refusals of witnesses to testify on the grounds that their testimony might incriminate them and that the law gave them no immunity from criminal prosecution upon this testimony.[6] This deficiency was removed by legislation passed in 1893, but the amendment was not upheld by the Supreme Court until 1896.[7] A second handicap for the Commission, in addition to the necessity of carrying its orders through the courts before they could be enforced, was the refusal by the latter to accept its findings of fact as final. Until a Supreme Court decision in 1896,[8] the lower federal courts treated every case as being original, and allowed the railroads to introduce new evidence which they had advantageously withheld in earlier hearings before the Commission. This hindrance to effective regulation was also partly removed by the passage of the Expediting Act of 1903, under which appeals to the Supreme Court were hastened.

A serious blow was dealt to the Commission's authority under the act of 1887 when the Supreme Court held in 1897 that it had no power to fix rates, whether maximum or minimum, and that it could only find certain rates unreasonable or unjust.[9] This meant that effective rate regulation was impossible, for once the Commission had obtained court sanction to its order that a rate was unreasonable, nothing could stop a carrier from setting the rate slightly lower. If the rate were still unreasonable, the same process would have to be repeated. This disability was not removed until 1906, when power to set maximum rates was specifically given to the Commission.

The act of 1887 was further emasculated by a Supreme Court decision in 1897 concerned with the long- and short-haul clause.[10] In this case the Interstate Commerce Commission had attempted to forbid a carrier to charge a lower rate for a long haul than for a shorter haul over the same line. The carrier claimed that competition with another railroad forced the discrimination. Obviously, most of these low long-haul rates were due to competitive influences, and no effective prohibition of them could permit such influences. But the Supreme Court held that the phrase "under substantially similar circumstances and conditions" signified that dissimilarity could result from competition between railroads. This decision meant that the Commission could do little about long- and short-haul discriminations, a lack of power which was not remedied until 1910.

The two decades after passage of the act of 1887 brought little in the way of regulation of any permanent importance. Some of the weaknesses

[6] *Counselman v. Hitchcock*, 142 U.S. 547 (1892).
[7] *Brown v. Walker*, 161 U.S. 591 (1896).
[8] *Cincinnati, New Orleans and Texas Pac. Rwy. Co. v. ICC*, 162 U.S. 184 (1896).
[9] *ICC v. Cincinnati, New Orleans and Texas Pac. Rwy. Co.*, 167 U.S. 479 (1897).
[10] *ICC v. Alabama Midland Rwy. Co.*, 168 U.S. 144 (1897).

of the act were removed, but the major obstacles to effective control remained. Even the Elkins Act of 1903 did little to increase this effectiveness; under it, fines were provided for the granting of rebates and the nonpublishing of tariffs, published tariffs were made binding, and the recipient of a rebate was made equally liable for punishment with the giver.

THE HEPBURN ACT OF 1906

Regulatory revision was provided by the Hepburn Act of 1906. The jurisdiction of the Interstate Commerce Commission was extended to express companies, sleeping-car companies, pipelines other than water and gas, and accessorial services such as private-car companies. The Commission was enlarged from five to seven members, and the salary of commissioners was increased. Power to establish maximum rates, to regulate through routes and joint rates, and to require annual reports and uniform accounts was granted in unequivocal terms. In order to give the Commission more time for investigation and to ensure publicity of rates, thirty days' notice of all rate changes was required. Subject to specified exceptions, issuance of free passes was prohibited. Stricter penalties in the form of imprisonment and higher fines were included. Moreover, in order to remove one of the main causes for personal discrimination the law contained the so-called "commodities clause," designed to keep railroads from carrying products of businesses in which they had an ownership interest.

The changes in procedure included in the Hepburn Act are also important. Orders of the Interstate Commerce Commission, except those involving the payment of money, were to become effective in thirty days, unless the carrier obtained a court order staying execution. Disobedience of the Commission's order brought a high fine. Such procedure meant that the burden was placed upon the carrier to obey the order or to institute court proceedings.

THE MANN-ELKINS ACT OF 1910

Intended to stop some of the gaps left by the Hepburn Act, the Mann-Elkins Act of 1910 was in effect a part of the movement for strong regulation represented by the Hepburn Act. The long- and short-haul clause, made meaningless by court decisions, was revitalized by the elimination of the phrase "under substantially similar circumstances and conditions," thus making the prohibition practically absolute unless special permission were given by the Interstate Commerce Commission. To keep the railroads from killing water-borne competition, the law provided that if low long-haul rates were put into effect to meet such competition, the carriers could not later ask to increase these rates unless for some other reason than the elimination of water competition. To aid the Interstate Commerce Commission in making a rate investigation and to protect the shipper who might be overcharged in the event a rate was later found unreasonable, the law included provisions for suspension of proposed changes in rates for an initial period not exceeding 120 days, and for a second period of like length if the first period was insufficient.

LEGISLATION, 1910 TO 1920

The decade 1910–1920 witnessed the passage of a few isolated pieces of transportation regulation. The Panama Canal Act of 1912 is notable because it forbade any railroad or other common carrier under the jurisdiction of the Commission to control by ownership or otherwise any passenger or freight vessel operating through the Panama Canal or elsewhere when in competition with such carrier. This measure was obviously designed to protect water carriers from extinction or limitation by competing railroads.

Until 1916, the federal government exerted no positive economic regulation of water carriers. Regulation for safe service had been imposed on the water carriers for many years by both the state and federal governments. Navigation controls have dated from the ratification of the Constitution. Federal steamboat inspection had been provided for fairly early in the nineteenth century. Regulation of water-carrier rates, finance, and service has been provided in many states for local commerce for many years. However, even the better state laws touched only upon intrastate rates and rate practices, with only occasional regulations of finance. These regulations also applied ordinarily only to common carriers, and the requirement of a certificate or permit to operate had been relatively rare. Consequently, with the exception of safety regulation, there existed no effective program of regulation of water carriers on either the state or the federal government level.

In 1916, however, the national government, by the Shipping Act of 1916, established the United States Shipping Board and charged it with supervision over rate discrimination and other discriminatory practices of water common carriers; for interstate common carriers, the Board was given the power to fix maximum rates. The scope of the act was limited to carriage on the high seas, on the Great Lakes, and in interstate coastwise traffic. Thus, intercoastal and inland waterways other than on the Great Lakes, as well as contract and private carriers, were excluded. Not only was this partial economic regulatory program of the water-carrier industry, while representing an attempt to supplement railroad regulation with control of its principal competitor, inadequate to accomplish control, but the Shipping Board (and its successors the Maritime Commission in 1936 and the Federal Maritime Board in 1950) was so preoccupied with the administration of shipping subsidies that little regulation resulted.

Emergence of a National Transportation Policy

As has been noted, until 1920 the approach of the federal government to the problem of railroad regulation had been primarily punitive. However, the experience with government operation of the railroads during World War I had disclosed serious economic weaknesses in this essential industry. The railroads' financial difficulties, the unsolved labor and rate problems remaining from the war, and the public recognition that an adequate and financially sound railroad system was a need of national importance, led to a demand for a constructive and positive approach to the problem of regulation. Furthermore, there had been a long-felt need for new regulatory measures over issuance of railroad securities, minimum rates, new construction and abandonment, and fair return on the private property used for the railroad service. The result was that Congress passed the Transportation Act of 1920 which, although aimed almost exclusively at the regulation of railroads, for the first time established the framework for a positive national transportation policy. As Chief Justice Taft said in 1924: [11]

> . . . The new act seeks affirmatively to build up a system of railways prepared to handle promptly all the interstate traffic of the country. It aims to give the owners of the railways an opportunity to earn enough to maintain their properties and equipment in such a state of efficiency that they can carry well this burden. To achieve this great purpose, it puts the railroad systems of the country more completely under the fostering guardianship and control of the Commission. . . .

One of the most important provisions of the act was that respecting rate making. For the first time, Congress set up a guiding rule for the Interstate Commerce Commission to follow in setting rates so that adequate revenues might be obtained for the carriers. In order to meet the problem of strong and weak railroads, partial recapture of excess earnings of the more prosperous railroads was authorized, these recaptured earnings to be used for loans to needy railroads. The rate-making power of the Commission was extended to the fixing of minimum rates, so that with the previously granted authority over maximum rates it could set the absolute charge.

A new legislative policy regarding combinations was included in the act. Pooling agreements found by the Interstate Commerce Commission to be in the public interest and not unduly restricting competition were to be allowed. Elaborate provisions were made for the encouragement of consolidation under Commission control and according to a plan which would preserve competition "as fully as possible." Authority over acqui-

[11] *Dayton-Goose Creek Rwy. Co. v. United States*, 263 U.S. 456, 478 (1924).

sitions of control by methods other than consolidation was given to the Commission. Further power over financial practices was granted by bringing the issuance of securities under its supervision.

In the field of railroad service, control over abandonments and new construction was placed in the Interstate Commerce Commission's jurisdiction, including power to require, under certain conditions, extension of railroad facilities. The Commission was also empowered to require joint use by several railroads of terminal facilities. Other service regulations included increased authority over railroad car-service rules and practices, and authority to order railroad carriers to install certain safety devices.

Except for emergency legislation passed in the Great Depression after 1932 and the development of special statutory measures affecting transport labor, the principal provisions of the Transportation Act furnish the pattern for regulation found in the transportation field today. Under the Emergency Transportation Act of 1933 some rather significant changes were made. Controls over combinations were enlarged so that railroad holding companies could not gain control of railroads without consent of the Interstate Commerce Commission. Noncarrier companies controlling railroads were placed under the accounting and securities regulations imposed on the railroads. The rule of rate making was changed by dropping all reference to definite standards such as "fair return" and "fair value," and the Commission was given wide discretion to set rates which it should find to be in the interest of both the carriers and the public. Because of the impracticable and disputed nature of the clause covering recapture of excess earnings, it was repealed.

Special Labor Legislation

The essential character of the railroad industry, the strong unions found in the industry even before World War I, and the disruptive effects of labor disputes on the national economy led to the establishment of special regulations affecting railroad labor. These regulations have tended to become the pattern for the extensive entrance into the field of labor relations undertaken by the federal government in the 1930s. Most of this legislation has been undertaken in the interest of settling railway labor disputes either by providing machinery for their settlement or by legislating special concessions to labor.

EARLY RAILROAD LABOR LEGISLATION

As early as 1888, Congress passed legislation providing for the settlement of railway labor disputes through voluntary arbitration and impartial investigation. With the failure of this legislation in the great Pullman strike of 1894, Congress enacted the Erdman Act in 1898. This law maintained provisions for voluntary arbitration and provided for mediation by the Chairman of the Interstate Commerce Commission and the United States Commissioner of Labor. Under the pressure of a labor dispute in 1913, Congress rushed through the Newlands Act designed to give some stability and permanence to the mediation and arbitration procedures of the earlier laws. But when, in 1916, a general strike was called, Congress, again under pressure, passed the Adamson Act, which ostensibly gave train-service workers the eight-hour day but was actually a wage law, since it allowed for more than a basic eight-hour day with the payment of an overtime premium for work beyond this basic day.

The Transportation Act of 1920 provided for the establishment of a tripartite nine-member United States Railroad Labor Board with power to hear and issue decisions on labor disputes but with no power to enforce any of its decisions. After the Board's decisions had been repudiated by carrier and labor groups alike, representatives of management and labor agreed upon the draft of new legislation which was enacted by Congress in 1926 as the Railway Labor Act. This law not only has furnished the legal basis for government's role in labor relations in the railroad industry and in the transportation industry generally but has pretty largely become the pattern for federal government intervention in labor disputes in other industries.[12]

THE RAILWAY LABOR ACT OF 1926

To some extent the legislation passed in 1926 returned to the principles of the earliest labor legislation. Without describing the machinery in detail, the Railroad Labor Act of 1926 provided for the following: (1) principal reliance was placed upon settlement of disputes by joint conference of the disputants with the government providing mediators, either on request of interested parties or upon its own motion; (2) upon failure of mediation, the Mediation Board established by the law is to encourage arbitration of the dispute; (3) should arbitration fail, the act requires the continuance of the *status quo* in the dispute for an additional thirty days; (4) should the Mediation Board feel that the dispute threatens substantially to interrupt interstate commerce, it may notify the President, who may appoint an emergency board to report to him its findings in the dispute; and (5) while the parties are not bound by the findings of the emergency board appointed by the President, no change may be made by either party in the conditions giving rise to the dispute for thirty days allotted to the emergency board's investigation and for thirty days thereafter. Thus the Railway Labor Act placed its reliance for the settlement of labor disputes upon voluntary settlement by the contending parties, but-

[12] See below, Chapter 22.

tressed by government intervention in the interests of conciliation and by the force of public opinion.

Among the most significant provisions of the Railway Labor Act of 1926 are those protecting the right of railroad employees to collective bargaining. The law requires that representatives of each of the respective parties be chosen without interference, influence, or coercion of the other party. Employees are specifically given the right to organize, company unions are outlawed, and contracts making employment contingent upon nonunion affiliation ("yellow-dog contracts") are prohibited. Thus, in the field of collective bargaining as in others, regulation of the railroad industry set a pattern for national legislation applicable to industry generally. The collective-bargaining provisions of the act of 1926 became the pattern for the Wagner Act of 1935, which applied to all private businesses in interstate commerce.

THE RAILROAD LABOR ACT OF 1934

Certain defects in the 1926 labor law were supposedly remedied by amendments made in 1934. Most of the new amendments introduced no new principles and affected procedure only. The main provisions of this amendment to the act of 1926 were (1) to outlaw "company unions" and to ensure, so far as possible, that the national labor organizations would handle all collective bargaining; and (2) to establish the National Adjustment Board. This board was charged with the interpretation of working rules and agreements and was given a compulsory jurisdiction over this class of dispute, and while its awards were made enforceable in the courts, no provision was made for judicial review of any awards. The National Adjustment Board [13] was established at the insistence of railroad labor, has applied to railroad employees only, has handled a huge volume of grievances and controversies, and has been the source for hundreds of awards of additional pay to labor under its interpretation of the complicated rules and procedures of railroad labor agreements.

RAILROAD RETIREMENT AND UNEMPLOYMENT-INSURANCE ACTS

Special acts for retirement and unemployment-insurance benefits have been passed by Congress for workers in organizations subject to the Interstate Commerce Act. Railroad retirement acts were passed in 1934, 1935, and 1937. The 1934 law was found to be unconstitutional, and the 1935 law was quickly replaced by the 1937 act which incorporated a plan agreed upon by management and labor. Interesting features of this law are that the retirement system for railroad employees is separate from the general Social Security Act applying to other businesses and that the railroad retirement taxes and allowances are higher than those applicable

[13] See below, pp. 151–152.

to workers in other industries. Likewise, railroad labor has obtained its own special unemployment-compensation law, passed in 1938 and administered by the Railroad Retirement Board, rather than by the separate states as is provided for other industries. In general, also, this law is somewhat more favorable to labor than are the state laws.

Emergency Legislation in the Great Depression

The spirit of the Transportation Act of 1920 affirmatively to build up a strong transportation system through federal government intervention was followed in several pieces of emergency legislation passed during the Great Depression.

THE RECONSTRUCTION FINANCE CORPORATION ACT OF 1932

One of the general relief measures of the Hoover administration was the establishment of the Reconstruction Finance Corporation in 1932. This corporation was created to lend funds to various business and government borrowers, among which were the railroads and other transportation companies. In the early days of the Depression, and to some extent much later, it was instrumental in keeping many railroads, water carriers, and truck lines out of bankruptcy.

THE BANKRUPTCY ACTS OF 1933 AND 1935

To aid the reorganization of bankrupt railroads a special bankruptcy act was passed in 1933, and some amendments were added in 1935. A special bankruptcy procedure was provided to expedite sound railroad reorganization. It enabled all interested parties to be heard in order to arrive at a plan fair to all classes of creditors and stockholders; it made it less possible for minority groups to block desirable reorganization; and it gave to the Interstate Commerce Commission authority to participate in the formulation of the plan in the hope of gaining a sounder financial structure than had theretofore existed. What is especially interesting about these reorganization laws is not only that they were specially designed for the railroads but that the Interstate Commerce Commission was placed in an important role whereby it was expected to use the bankruptcy procedure as an effective regulatory device for remaking railroad financial structures.

Completion of the Regulatory Pattern

Although the pattern of economic regulation of the railroads was fairly complete with the passage of the Transportation Act of 1920 and was supplemented by the Railroad Labor Act of 1926, there was little effective regulation of transportation by water, highway, and air until the 1930s. While oil pipelines were placed under the jurisdiction of the Interstate Commerce Commission in 1906, water-rail operations had been under some control since the act of 1887, and certain common-carrier water transport had been subject to regulation since the Shipping Act of 1916, the actual regulation of these carriers was perfunctory and generally ineffective.

MOTOR-TRANSPORT REGULATION BEFORE 1935

In the field of motor transportation, reliance was placed on state regulation until 1935. In view of the local origins of this industry, this early reliance upon the power of the states is understandable. Even after the federal government entered the field in 1935, state regulations have continued to be of primary importance in the field. Because of the intrastate nature of so large a portion of the industry, and because of the natural reluctance of the federal government to employ the stream-of-interstate-commerce theory of constitutional law to an industry with so many thousands of operators, state control will continue to be of great importance. Although the economic regulatory programs of the states varied considerably before 1935 and still do today, safety, service, and rate regulation, especially of common carriers, have been fairly complete.

However, state regulation has been difficult to enforce, even where adequate authority is found on the statute books. The tremendous number of motor-carrier operators and motor vehicles makes the job exceedingly difficult. This fact, the lack of funds of state commissions for enforcement, and apathetic cooperation of local officials have long served to make many state laws ineffective. When these factors are considered along with the wide variety of state laws, one is surprised that state motor-vehicle regulation has been as effective as it has.

But, until 1935, state control of motor-carrier operations was subject, in addition, to the same kind of disability that state control of railroads had experienced before 1887. In cases decided in 1925 the Supreme Court held that states could not place a direct burden on interstate commerce by regulating the business of interstate motor carriage.[14] In each session of Congress from 1925 to 1935 bills proposing federal motor-carrier regulation were proposed. During this decade, the difficulty of framing an acceptable law for this complex industry and the opposition of certain interested groups kept Congress from passing any law, despite the increasingly pressing need for control. This opposition came from farmers who feared that federal control would interfere with their trucking operations to markets; from some parts of the motor-carrier industry where it was feared that control would interfere with the freedom to do business; and

[14] *Buck v. Kuykendall*, 267 U.S. 307 (1925), and *Buck v. Maloy*, 267 U.S. 317 (1925).

from motor-vehicle manufacturers who feared that this fast-growing industry would be restricted by being placed in a straitjacket of regulation.

AIR-TRANSPORT REGULATION BEFORE 1938

In the field of air transportation, the federal government had no definite program for regulation before 1926. Even when the Air Commerce Act of 1926 was passed, regulation by the federal government was limited to safety measures, including registration and licensing of aircraft and pilots, and establishment of air-traffic rules. No economic regulations were provided. To be sure, under the various air-mail acts, some regulation was applied to air carriers. As early as 1925, when the Postmaster General was given power to grant air-mail contracts to private companies, the giving or withholding of these contracts had regulatory force. It was the Watres Act of 1930, however, that gave the Postmaster General a wide range of authority over mail carriers: he could make extensions or consolidations of routes, and select routes for mail transport; he could stipulate the character of passenger services to be performed by mail planes; he was empowered to prescribe accounts and make requirements respecting airline personnel and equipment. While this authority was limited to air-mail carriers, these were the only commercial carriers of any significance in the period. Yet this program was hardly a program of regulation, but more a summary of the authority of a government officer who had the right to make subsidy contracts with private businesses.

WATER-TRANSPORT REGULATION BEFORE 1940

The limited nature of water-carrier regulation before the 1930s has already been noted.[15] Until 1940, when water-carrier regulation was effectively fitted into the over-all pattern of federal transportation control, the condition of water-carrier regulation was chaotic. The Shipping Act of 1916 left free of regulation all economic matters except maximum rates of common interstate carriers and rate and other discriminatory practices. Moreover, it was limited to carriage only on the high seas, on the Great Lakes, and in interstate coastwise traffic. Even the Intercoastal Shipping Act of 1933 extended this regulation only to the intercoastal service. The Merchant Marine Act of 1936 set up the Maritime Commission to succeed the Shipping Board to take over all water regulation except that under the Interstate Commerce Commission.

The confused condition of water-carrier regulation before the Transportation Act of 1940 was passed may be made somewhat clearer by pointing out the jurisdictions of the Interstate Commerce Commission and the Maritime Commission at that time. The former had jurisdiction only over interstate and foreign common carriers of persons or property,

[15] See above, p. 81.

partly by railroad and partly by water, when both were used under a common control, management, or arrangement for a continuous carriage or shipment. The Interstate Commerce Commission also had complete jurisdiction over any water carrier owned or controlled by a railroad to the same extent as it had over railroads. The Maritime Commission had jurisdiction, except where the Interstate Commerce Commission already possessed it, over (1) interstate and foreign commerce in oceanic ("by the high seas"), coastwise, intercoastal, and Great Lakes traffic; and (2) contract carriers in the intercoastal trade. This left unregulated by the federal government intrastate water carriers, interstate inland water carriers except on the Great Lakes, all private carriers, and all contract carriers except in the intercoastal trade.

The regulations applicable to types of carriers in each kind of service also varied to a great degree. The jurisdictions of the Interstate Commerce Commission and the Maritime Commission were confused and overlapping. Regulation under the Shipping Board and its successor, the Maritime Commission, was mixed in with the administration of subsidy policies toward the merchant marine. Indeed, these two bodies were so busy with the problem of subsidy allocation that regulation was not very effective. In fact, according to a statement of a Shipping Board official, the Board, at least before 1933, did little in the way of regulation.[16]

THE MOTOR CARRIER ACT OF 1935

The motor-carrier industry was fitted into the ever more enveloping pattern of federal transportation regulation by the Motor Carrier Act of 1935. By this law, regulation of interstate motor carriers was placed under the Interstate Commerce Commission. The policy of Congress in enacting the law was shown in section 202, which provided as follows:

> . . . It is hereby declared to be the policy of Congress to regulate transportation by motor carriers in such manner as to recognize and preserve the inherent advantages of, and foster sound economic conditions in, such transportation and among such carriers in the public interest; promote adequate, economical, and efficient service by motor carriers, and reasonable charges therefor, without discrimination, undue preferences or advantages, and unfair or destructive competitive practices; improve the relations between, and coordinate transportation by and regulation of, motor carriers and other carriers; develop and preserve a highway transportation system properly adapted to the needs of the commerce of the United States and of the national defense; and cooperate with the several states and the duly authorized officials thereof and with any organization of motor carriers in the administration and enforcement of this part.

[16] P. M. Zeis, *American Shipping Policy* (Princeton, N.J.: Princeton University Press, 1938), p. 168.

This statement of policy is interesting because it represents a modern approach to regulation. It indicates a seeing of the problem as a whole. Railroad regulation has been evolved by trial and error over a period of years. When motor-carrier regulation was authorized in 1935, the forty-eight years of experience with railroad regulation made it possible for Congress to draw up a comprehensive law, based on long-developed principles. Not only is this apparent from the statement of policy, but it can also be seen in the provisions of the law. This does not mean that the Motor Carrier Act is a model piece of transportation legislation. As early as 1938, amendments were made which were mainly procedural and for the purpose of expediting and facilitating administrative action. By the Transportation Act of 1940, further amendments were enacted for the purpose of clarifying the meaning of the law, especially in regard to classes of carriers, exemptions, rates, and accounts.

The Transportation Act of 1940 also repealed the statement of policy which headed the Motor Carrier Act. But a statement of policy, drawn along similar lines, was placed at the head of the entire Interstate Commerce Act to serve as the broad policy for the Interstate Commerce Commission to follow in regulating all rail, water, and motor carriers under its jurisdiction. Although this admirable policy has become the congressional mandate to the Commission for treatment of all carriers under its control, the statutes applicable to the various carriers are still almost as individual as they were before 1940.

In contrast to the results of development of railroad regulation, Congress intimated in the original statement of motor-carrier policy, and directs in the Motor Carrier Act's provisions, that the federal government is not to crowd state regulation from the field. Cooperation with state officials is required, and later in the act the Interstate Commerce Commission is plainly told that it has no power to regulate intrastate rates as a part of the control over interstate rates.

While certain carriers operating in the general field of interstate commerce are exempt from a part of the law, no such carrier is exempted from the provisions which authorize the Interstate Commerce Commission to fix safety standards of employees, operation, or equipment. Exempted from provisions other than safety regulation are (1) motor vehicles operated by farmers for transportation of farm produce and supplies; (2) motor vehicles used exclusively for carrying livestock, fish, or agricultural products, but not including articles manufactured from these products; (3) motor vehicles owned or controlled by agricultural cooperatives; (4) trucks handling newspapers exclusively; (5) vehicles used exclusively in connection with aircraft operations; (6) local carriers, such as school busses, taxicabs, trolley busses, hotel busses; and (7) vehicles used by the Department of the Interior in the national parks. Except for safety regulation, the Commission is further empowered, to the extent it deems wise, to exempt (1) interstate operations within a municipal area; and (2) casual, occasional, or reciprocal transportation for compensation by any person not engaged in motor transportation as a regular occupation or business.

Private carriers are not subject to the law except for regulations regarding qualifications and hours of service of employees, standards of equipment, and safety of operation. In this respect the economic regulations of the act are limited to for-hire carriers, with primary emphasis on the common carrier. Even in regulations affecting contract carriers, the law is based on the principle that they be regulated only to the extent necessary to prevent undue interference with common carriage.

In general, at least for common carriers, the regulatory program of the Motor Carrier Act followed the provisions already applicable to the railroad industry. The right freely to enter service was restricted, although carriers in operation at the effective date of the act were given "grandfather" rights to continue in operation upon application. Power to promulgate safety regulations affecting employees, equipment, and operations was placed in the hands of the Interstate Commerce Commission, as was control over rates, rate and service discrimination, financial matters, and combinations.

But in certain respects the act is considerably different from the law applicable to the railroads. This difference is due largely to the fact that in the railroad industry virtually all carriers are common carriers, that is, they hold themselves out for hire to serve all who can use their services. In the motor carrier industry, the common carrier is important, but the major portion of the industry's business is done by the contract and private carriers. The contract carrier limits its service to particular shippers and makes contracts for definite carriage over a definite period of time, restricting itself to handling goods specifically contracted for. The private carrier makes no contract or offering to serve others, limiting its business to the commodities of an owner.

While safety legislation applies to all types of carriers, the economic phases of regulation apply to the contract carriers to a much lesser degree than to the common carriers and are not applicable to the private carrier. Even for the contract carrier, the theory of regulation is to control it only to the extent necessary to protect the common carrier, who is looked upon as especially important to the public interest since he serves the public generally. Thus, the law provides only for minimum rate regulation of the contract carrier to ensure against destructive and unreasonable competition with the common carriers. At the same time the law is clear in its intent that protection to common carriers should not be followed to the extent of denying shippers the economic advantages of contract carriage.

THE CIVIL AERONAUTICS ACT OF 1938

As the result of a lack of a federal regulatory program in the air-transport field, the growth of the industry to important size in the 1930s, and the obvious fact that the states could not control an industry so clearly interstate in nature, Congress passed the first comprehensive control of air transportation when the Civil Aeronautics Act became law in 1938. Unlike the regulation of interstate motor carriers and the revamping of water-carrier regulation in 1940, the federal control program was not placed under the Interstate Commerce Commission. This young industry was believed to be so unique in its techniques and problems as to require a specialized administrative commission, and it was feared that a commission dominated by surface-carrier thinking would not do justice to this new transport industry.

As modified by administrative reorganizations made under the Reorganization Act of 1939, air-carrier regulation has been set up under two administrative agencies. The Civil Aeronautics Board of five members operates as an independent commission. It has the quasi-judicial and quasi-legislative functions of promulgating and administering economic regulations as well as the making of air-transport safety rules. The Civil Aeronautics Administration, under a single administrator, subject to the direction and supervision of the Secretary of Commerce, is made responsible for administering the promotional programs of the federal government with respect to airports and air navigational facilities. It also is responsible for issuance and amendment of airman, aircraft, and air-carrier certificates, the registration of aircraft, and the enforcement of air safety rules. Thus, the Board handles all economic regulations and makes the air safety rules; the Administration handles promotional activities and administers safety regulation.

The field of safety regulation is more completely occupied by the federal government and is more detailed than in the case of any other transport agency. Economic regulations are not quite so broad as those applicable to the railroad field. Except for the lack of specific regulation over contract carriers,[17] however, the economic regulations are somewhat

[17] The Civil Aeronautics Act made no reference to contract-carrier operations, although by inference from definitions of "air carrier" and "air transportation" the economic regulations of the act are made to apply only to common carrier operations or to any carrier operations involving the carriage of mail. Through the determination of what constitutes common carriage and the exclusion of others from the economic controls of the law, the Civil Aeronautics Board has exerted control over the large

similar to those over motor-carrier operations. The economic regulations which apply to common-carrier operations include the usual provisions such as control over entry of service through requirement of a certificate of convenience and necessity, control over abandonments, regulation of rates and service, and control over accounting, finance, and combinations.

As in the case of the Motor Carrier Act, the Civil Aeronautics Act set up a positive statement of policy to guide the regulating commission. The law requires that the following things, among others, should be considered:

(a) The encouragement and development of an air-transportation system properly adapted to the present and future needs of the foreign and domestic commerce of the United States, of the Postal Service, and of the national defense;

(b) The regulation of air transportation in such manner as to recognize and preserve the inherent advantages of, assure the highest degree of safety in, and foster sound economic conditions in, such transportation, and to improve the relations between, and coordinate transportation by, air carriers;

(c) The promotion of adequate, economical, and efficient service by air carriers at reasonable charges, without unjust discriminations, undue preferences or advantages, or unfair or destructive competitive practices;

(d) Competition to the extent necessary to assure the sound development of an air-transportation system properly adapted to the needs of the foreign and domestic commerce of the United States, of the Postal Service, and of the national defense;

(e) The regulation of air commerce in such manner as to best promote its development and safety; and

(f) The encouragement and development of civil aeronautics.

The rule of rate making found in the act of 1938 is similar to the rules provided by law to guide the Interstate Commerce Commission in regulating the level of railroad and motor-carrier rates. Noteworthy, however, is the recognition given to the need for mail subsidies. Unlike other rules of rate making, the act of 1938 requires the commission, in setting mail rates, to consider the need of the carrier for compensation sufficient to ensure the performance of the standard of air service required and, together with other revenues, to enable the carrier, under honest, economical, and efficient management, to maintain and continue the development of air transportation of the extent and quality required by commercial, postal, and national-defense needs of the nation.

---

number of irregular, or nonscheduled, carriers who have held themselves out for hire. These carriers, operating without the benefit of a certificate of convenience and necessity, are thus at the mercy of the Board which may at any time hold that they are not really contract operators and must meet the requirements of the act. However, if any of these carriers can prove themselves to be in fact contract carriers, rather than common carriers, the economic regulations of the law would not apply to them.

In addition, rather special controls over combination are provided. The law requires not only the normal kind of approvals by the Civil Aeronautics Board but also positive showing of promotion of public interest in the case of combination of an air carrier and a surface carrier.

A rather unusual provision of the law is the provision that the Civil Aeronautics Board may exempt any air carrier from its economic regulations, with certain minor exceptions, if the Board finds that application of such provisions would place an undue burden on the carrier. This exemption provision is not found in the Interstate Commerce Act, applicable to other interstate carriers, and is an interesting regulatory practice, probably justifiable for an industry which in 1938 (and even today) had a large number of relatively unimportant for-hire interstate operators for whom economic regulation would be meaningless and unduly burdensome.

WATER-CARRIER REGULATION UNDER THE TRANSPORTATION ACT OF 1940

The Transportation Act of 1940 made progress in the attempt to unify under one commission the regulation of interstate transportation in the United States. The jurisdiction of the Interstate Commerce Commission was extended quite generally over water-carrier regulation, and the chaotic condition of regulation over certain segments of water transportation was replaced by controls similar to those long in existence in the railroad industry and placed over motor carriers in 1935. It should be noted, however, that promotional aspects of government policy were kept under the jurisdiction of the Maritime Commission. Water safety regulation was kept in the Department of Commerce, and the limited existing economic control over common carriers in foreign commerce remained with the Maritime Commission. However, in 1950, regulatory functions were transferred to a newly created Federal Maritime Board and promotional activities were allocated to the Maritime Administration, an agency within the Department of Commerce.

However, the efficacy of the water regulation program was reduced by the numerous exemptions made in the 1940 law. Local and small operations in interstate commerce were excepted. Contract carriers which did not compete "actually and substantially" with other types of transport agencies were placed outside the law. Private carriers were exempted. The act went so far as to exempt common carriers which transport goods in bulk in cargo space used for not more than three commodities, and common carriers of liquid cargoes in bulk in tank vessels. Although the act ostensibly applies to operations in interstate and foreign commerce, transportation to or from points outside the United States is not included, at least to the extent of the portion of the movement outside the United States. Furthermore, the act explicitly forbids the Interstate Commerce Commission to regulate the rates and services of any intrastate carrier, even where advisable to remove discriminations against interstate commerce. In fact, the exemptions from the act are so considerable that the Commission has estimated that only approximately 10 per cent of the total water tonnage is subject to the law.[18]

But where the water-carrier regulation is applicable, the pattern of control is similar to controls over railroads and motor carriers. Rates, routes, and service of common carriers are regulated almost to the degree found in railroad control. Rates of contract carriers are regulated in much the same way as those of contract motor carriers. Common carriers must obtain certificates of convenience and necessity before entering into service, and contract carriers must obtain permits. Strict accounting regulation is also imposed. The long- and short-haul clause, long applicable to railroads, is extended to common carriers by water under the law. Combination of water carriers by pooling, mergers, acquisitions of control, or other means is placed under the same general kind of control as is applied to railroads.

The Transportation Regulatory Pattern

The transportation regulatory pattern has developed since 1887 until all forms of interstate transport have been placed under federal government control, although the extent and nature of controls vary somewhat and several government agencies participate in the administration of these regulations. With the exception of air-carrier regulation, most interstate aspects of common-carrier railroads and motor carriers and of certain water-transport companies are subject to the jurisdiction of the Interstate Commerce Commission. Through the Transportation Act of 1940, a single policy of "fair and impartial regulation of all modes of transportation" has been expressed with the avowed purpose of "developing, coordinating, and preserving a national transportation system by water, highway, rail, as well as other means, adequate to meet the needs of the commerce of the United States, of the Postal Service, and of the national defense."

Thus, while the pattern and objectives are uniform, the actual control has necessarily been far from uniform. For one thing, regulation of carriers other than railroads has been long in developing. Another factor, amply evident from the sketches of regulation above, is the exemptions from regulation in the case of water, highway, and air carriers. Some of these exclusions merely reflect the economic characteristics of these industries which, unlike the railroads, have many enterprises engaging in private- and contract-carrier operations. Other exclusions are due to the political pressures brought to bear by the exempt and to the administrative complexities of bringing under regulation a large number of relatively small

[18] ICC, *60th Annual Report, 1946,* p. 36.

enterprises. In addition to these exclusions, there are of necessity variations in control in the actual administration of regulations established by statute. Experience with control engenders adeptness, not only on the part of the commissions involved but on the part of the businesses controlled. One could hardly expect the thoroughness and quality of control in other transport industries which has characterized the railroad industry with its nearly seven decades of federal regulation.

But what the pattern of transport regulation evolution does show is the tendency for regulation to spread. To be sure, much of this tendency is due to the rise of new industries and to their position of national prominence. But some of the control comes from the self-generating tendency of controls to expand. The water-transport industry, for example, is hardly a new one; yet, after bringing the railroad industry under such complete federal regulation, it seemed clearly fair and in the interests of the development of a sound national transportation policy to bring much of the water-transport industry under restrictions similar to those applied to the railroads. Nevertheless, even though lawmakers have sought to extend controls broadly over the interstate transport industry, one can easily ascertain wide areas, such as those of the private and common carriers, where the uncontrolled compete strongly with the regulated.

Selected References

Bigham, T. C., and M. J. Roberts, *Transportation*, chaps. 7–10. New York: McGraw-Hill Book Company, Inc., 1952.

Daggett, Stuart, *Principles of Inland Transportation*, 3d ed., chaps. 29, 30. New York: Harper & Brothers, 1941.

Fair, M. L., and E. W. Williams, Jr., *Economics of Transportation*, chaps. 24–28. New York: Harper & Brothers, 1950.

Interstate Commerce Commission, *Interstate Commerce Commission Activities, 1887–1937*. Government Printing Office, 1937.

Landon, C. E., *Transportation*, chaps. 22–24. New York: William Sloane Associates, 1951.

Locklin, D. P., *Economics of Transportation*, 4th ed., chaps. 10–14, 31, 34, 36. Homewood, Ill.: Richard D. Irwin, Inc., 1952.

Sharfman, I. L., *The Interstate Commerce Commission*, vol. I. New York: The Commonwealth Fund, 1931.

Troxel, Emery, *Economics of Transport*, chaps. 15–16. New York: Rinehart & Company, Inc., 1955.

Van Metre, T. W., *Transportation in the United States*, 2d ed., chaps. 19–22. Brooklyn, N. Y.: The Foundation Press, Inc., 1950.

5

REGULATION OF TRANSPORT RATES

One of the most important portions of the work of any regulatory commission is the regulation of price. This has been especially true of the work of the Interstate Commerce Commission in its regulation of railroad rates, and it is becoming increasingly true in the regulation of motor-carrier and water-carrier rates. Likewise, as the airlines serve more and more of the nation's passenger and freight businesses, the problem of rate regulation shows signs of far overshadowing such time-consuming tasks of the Civil Aeronautics Board as the establishment and modification of routes in this young and growing industry. Even some of the other work of the transport regulatory commissions, such as accounting control, regulation of security issuance, and control of combinations, has been undertaken largely as an aid to rate regulation.

The economic and legal nature of the transport industry has tended to make much of rate regulation necessary. These businesses in general and the railroad and water-transport businesses in particular are ones in which the elements of overhead and joint costs play an important role. Operation under such conditions tends to lead to price and service discrimination in order to increase volume of traffic at any rate in excess of out-of-pocket costs. This characteristic of the transport business is of special meaning to the public served by the transportation industry, because the economic welfare of individuals and groups may be dependent upon the terms by which they can reach their markets. The abuses of railroads in rate matters before the era of regulation and the continuing cases before the regulatory commissions involving alleged rate discriminations are ample evidence of public interest in the economic effects of transportation. Even with the rise in competition between the various forms of transport and the increasing strength of competition between companies, competition has not been complete enough to safeguard against rate and service discriminations, although there is reason to believe that in the past two decades the general level of transportation rates has been controlled more by competition than by regulation.

Regulation of transportation rates is also grounded upon legal factors. Most transportation rests upon the use of power of eminent domain to get facilities which might not have been obtainable otherwise except at exorbitant prices. Public aid, in terms of land grants, credit extensions, investment of public funds in operating facilities, and outright subsidies, has been given to transport companies. These and other aids give the public a more than ordinary interest in the rates charged.

Even without these many public favors, most transport agencies subject to regulation would still be recognized at law as common carriers. This term implies a class of transport business which serves all who may come. For centuries the English common law has recognized that these carriers, by professing to serve, are subject to obligations to serve adequately, continuously, at reasonable rates, and without discrimination. The common carrier is traditionally, and not without good reason, the most public of all the privately owned businesses. With this interest in the common carrier, it is no wonder that economic regulation has been extended to more limited carriers, such as the contract carrier, with a view to protecting the public interest in the common carrier.

The Rate Level and the Rate Structure

Transport rate regulation, like all regulation of price in the public-service field, falls into two main divisions, the rate level and the rate structure. The former of these has to do with the financial adequacy of rates in general. The problem of reasonableness here is whether the rates taken as a whole are high enough to support on a sound financial basis the cost of an adequate transport system. Yet the rate level should not be excessive in the sense of exacting more than this from rate payers.

Regulation of the rate structure, on the other hand, is concerned with particular rates. Because these apply as between places, commodities, persons, or kinds of traffic, they may discriminate in some way so as to give an unearned or unreasonable economic advantage. The central problem here is to adjust individual rates or groups of rates so that discrimination does not result or, if inevitable, will be reasonable. This is a complex task. While passenger rates are fairly simple, freight rates are based upon thousands of different types of freight to which distance rates, as modified by many competitive influences, are applied for every possible haul. In addition to the problem of discriminatory rates within the rate structure, individual rates must also be reasonable per se. But as will be shown, the standard of reasonableness applied to individual rates differs from that applied to the level of rates.

Rate regulation is not separated completely into that of levels and that of structures. As a matter of fact, these two aspects are closely related. Very seldom can a shift in the rate level be undertaken without upsetting many of the individual rate adjustments. For example, when the Interstate Commerce Commission allowed a general increase in the level of railroad rates in 1938, it recognized that competition with other forms of transport, as well as possible discrimination against localities, made a blanket increase of a certain percentage applied to all rates impracticable.[1]

THE RATE LEVEL

ECONOMIC BASIS OF A REASONABLE RATE LEVEL

If the rates of any privately owned business are to be regulated and private ownership is to be preserved, the rate level must be adequate to support the transportation service desired by the public and to cover all expenses necessary to ensure efficient operation. Imprudent expenses should not be added to the rate payer's bill. But all prudent operating expenses, including an adequate allowance for depreciation and taxes and for experimental work, should be allowed. In addition, the rates should be sufficient to make possible a return on capital invested, whether by bondholder or stockholder, adequate to keep capital flowing into the industry. If private capital is to be relied on in the railroad field, any level of rates which does not induce private capital to be invested there is not a reasonable one. On the other hand, a higher rate level would require the public to pay in excess of reasonable total cost, and the object of regulation is to avoid higher charges.

The economic basis is simply that a reasonable rate is one which covers the *cost* of furnishing a service demanded by the public. If the public demands expensive service, then a rate level in order to be reasonable must cover the cost of that service. Not only will the adequacy and stability of that return determine to a great extent the cost of the capital, but the public must pay enough to keep capital flowing into the industry if improvements involving new investment are wanted by it. As a matter of interest, there have been cases in recent years where economic realities and political expediency have required the regulatory commission to allow rates which will furnish some funds for capital additions. For example, in 1951, the Interstate Commerce Commission, in approving a rise in freight rates, took note of the fact that both the government and the shipping public, with national defense primarily in mind, were encouraging huge capital outlays, some of which must be expected from rates.[2]

LEGAL BASIS OF A REASONABLE RATE LEVEL

Interpretation of the due-process clauses of the Constitution by the Supreme Court has given the legal basis for a reasonable rate level in a publicly regulated, though privately owned, business. While some property right is clearly taken away from a transportation-company stock-

[1] *Fifteen Per Cent Case*, 226 I.C.C. 41 (1938).

[2] *Increased Freight Rates, 1951,* 280 I.C.C. 179 and 281 I.C.C. 557 (1951).

holder if the company may not charge what it pleases for service, the courts early discerned regulation which destroyed property without due process of law.[3] There has never been a question that due process of law permitted the taking of property in so far as it was necessary to protect the public against unreasonable charges. And the courts have traditionally held that property was taken without due process if the rate level did not cover the reasonable cost of the service to the public. As the Supreme Court said in 1898, "the corporation may not be required to use its property for the benefit of the public without receiving just compensation for the services rendered by it." [4] But recent decisions cast some doubt upon *when* a rate level may be so low as to result in confiscation. Consistent with the tendency of the Supreme Court to limit the meaning of due process to procedural matters, decisions of recent years lead to the belief that regulation may seldom, if ever, be so restrictive as to be confiscatory. These decisions appear to grant to commissions the power to determine reasonableness unhampered by legal doctrine so long as their findings are based upon evidence.[5] In any case it is clear that the Court will not find confiscation so long as the end result of regulation is a company able to operate successfully and maintain its financial integrity.

COMMISSION AUTHORITY OVER THE RATE LEVEL

Until the Transportation Act of 1920, the Interstate Commerce Commission had no very definite guide to follow in setting the level of railroad rates. The Act of 1887 had required only that rates be just and reasonable. Later laws gave the Commission power to fix maximum rates and to suspend rates pending investigation. But this gave the Commission no criteria as to how reasonableness was to be measured. Having no positive duty to see that a reasonable level of rates was fixed and with the burden of proof for any increase on the railroads, the Commission needed no guide other than to hold rates just above the level which would result in confiscation as defined by the courts.

With the adoption of a positive program of regulation in 1920, definite criteria were established. These were furnished by a rule of rate making incorporated in the Transportation Act of 1920. With some changes, this rule is essentially the same as those for rail, water, and highway transport written by Congress in the Transportation Act of 1940 and employed since by the Interstate Commerce Commission in its regulatory activities

[3] See *Stone v. Farmers' Loan and Trust Co.*, 116 U.S. 307 (1886). At p. 331 the Court said: ". . . it is not to be inferred that this power of limitation or regulation is itself without limit. This power to regulate is not a power to destroy, and limitation is not the equivalent of confiscation."

[4] *Smyth v. Ames*, 169 U.S. 466, at 546.

[5] This seems to be the import of *Federal Power Commission v. Hope Natural Gas Co.*, 320 U.S. 591 (1944).

over the various forms of transport enterprises. While separate rules of rate making are found in the Interstate Commerce Act for rail, water, and highway transport, all provide that the Commission, in the exercise of its power to prescribe just and reasonable rates, must give due consideration to the following factors, among others:

1. The effect of rates on the movement of traffic by the carrier or carriers for which the rates are prescribed.
2. The need, in the public interest, for adequate and efficient transportation service at the lowest cost consistent with the furnishing of such service.
3. The need for revenues sufficient to enable the carriers, under honest, economical, and efficient management, to provide such service.

In addition, the rule of rate making applicable to motor carriers provides that the Commission must pay attention to the inherent advantages of transportation by common motor carriers. This additional provision is designed to admonish the Commission that in setting rates the special economic and service features of the motor-carrier industry must not be forgotten.

A similar rule of rate making is provided for the guidance of the Civil Aeronautics Board in its regulation of air carriers. The only differences are the requirement that the Board must take into account the inherent advantages of air transport, as in the case of motor carriers, and that the Board must take into account the special standards and quality of service which may be required by law. This latter provision is, of course, aimed at the special safety standards required of air transport.

While the statutory rules of rate making for the various modes of transportation are essentially the same, the rather special place of mail-rate determination in the case of the airlines should be noted. Under the Interstate Commerce Commission, mail rates of carriers are subject to the same rules as any other rates, except that any railroad may enter into a contract to carry the mail for less than the rate set by the Commission. But for the airline industry, the Civil Aeronautics Act provides in the determination of mail rates that the Board must consider carrier need (under honest, economical, and effective operation) for mail revenues to furnish the kind of service required for national commerce, postal service, and defense.

Analysis of these rules of rate making will show how broad they are. Essentially, they set no formula or standard for commission action. Except for the special case of air-mail rates, these rules require of a commission the same kind of approach which a responsible business manager would use. They, in effect, request the commissions concerned not to price a carrier out of its market and yet to keep in mind the requirements for revenues adequate to preserve a strong and adequate transportation system for the needs of the shipping and traveling public. Yet this positive approach, apparently solicitous of the need for adequate rates, when administered in the light of the regulatory provisions requiring the establishment of reasonable rates, gives the commissions ample grounds for holding rates to reasonably low levels in the interests of the users of transportation.

FACTORS CONSIDERED IN FIXING RATE LEVELS

Under the different rules of rate making, and indeed before any rule was promulgated by Congress, the Interstate Commerce Commission has based its decisions with respect to the rate level on certain factors. Except for mail-rate determination, a subsidy problem to be discussed later, the Civil Aeronautics Board has had before it few cases in which to analyze and make decisions upon the airline rate-level problem. In such cases as it has had, consideration has been given to the same kind of factors that the Interstate Commerce Commission has utilized in its long experience in regulating the rates of the much more complicated rail, water, and highway industries. These factors will be discussed briefly at this point.

Other means of increasing revenues. In considering a fair level of rates, commissions have studied how the level of rates can be made reasonable by increasing revenues through other means than the raising of rates. While these other means might be just as important to consider in the event that the problem is one of lowering the rate level, as a matter of fact cases have usually arisen from requests for an increase in rates.

In several cases involving railroads, the Interstate Commerce Commission has suggested ways by which the railroads could increase revenues.[6] Some of the methods which have been suggested are the readjustment of unremunerative individual rates, curtailment of free transportation, reduction of allowances to shippers for special services performed by them, increases of charges for lighterage and other special ancillary services, and increases of rates made too low by competition between railroads.

In many of the rate-level cases, the Interstate Commerce Commission has indicated that its refusal to grant higher increases has been tempered by the belief that the carriers had not done all they could to increase revenues. But definite orders to do so have been rare. In making a special investigation in 1933 of certain practices of the carriers which affected revenues, the Commission did order that excessive payments for rental of private cars of shippers and the furnishing of storage services at less than prevailing rates should cease.[7]

Operating expenses. One factor always considered in arriving at a decision respecting the rate level is the size and validity of operating expenses.

[6] See, e.g., *Five Per Cent Case,* 31 I.C.C. 351, 407; 32 I.C.C. 325, 334 (1914).

[7] *Use of Privately Owned Refrigerator Cars,* 201 I.C.C. 323 (1934), and *Practices of Carriers Affecting Operating Revenues or Expenses* (part VI), 198 I.C.C. 134 (1933).

While some control over them has come about indirectly through accounting regulation (such as the requirement that depreciation allowances shall be made), the Interstate Commerce Commission has actually done little to interfere with charges made for these expenses. On the whole, its examination of operating expenses has disclosed that those incurred have been reasonable.

The Commission has called attention of the railroads to differences in operating costs between different carriers for the same service and has questioned whether this may not indicate that greater efficiency or economy could be practiced.[8] During the Great Depression, the Commission also encouraged pooling of traffic and reduction of wasteful competitive practices.[9] Likewise, in recent rate cases the Commission called for more effective reduction of operating expenses. In allowing increases in 1949, for example, the Commission asked the railroads to look into the cost reductions possible through investigating terminal operations and abandonment of unprofitable passenger services or substitution of motor services.[10]

Perhaps the most effective recent controls over operating expenses have come indirectly, through the studies of the Commission's Bureau of Accounts and Cost Finding and its Bureau of Transport Economics and Statistics. Through study and publicity of results on such matters as comparative costs between carriers, analysis of depreciation reserves, and the economics of motive power, these bureaus have had an undoubted indirect effect on industry practices, and they have also affected the decisions of the Commission in rate-level cases.[11]

The Civil Aeronautics Board has been more active than the Interstate Commerce Commission in considering operating expenses of air carriers in rate-regulation actions. To be sure, the Board has been in a role somewhat different from that of the Commission in that all the cases involved were those having to do with mail rates, which required the expenditure of government funds for subsidy purposes. But in many cases, particularly those which dealt with claims for back mail pay, the Board has

[8] See e.g., *Advances in Rates—Eastern Case*, 20 I.C.C. 243, 279 (1911).

[9] See *Fifteen Per Cent Case, 1931*, 178 I.C.C. 639, 585 (1931).

[10] *Increases of Rates*, 276 I.C.C. 9 (1949).

[11] Perhaps the most important direct program of the government to influence the cost practices of the railroads was the establishment of the office of the Federal Coordinator of Transportation by the Emergency Transportation Act of 1933. During the three-year existence of his office, the Federal Coordinator made many recommendations, including the consolidation of less-than-carload freight and express services, pooling of rail and highway transportation, unification of stations and terminals, pooling of freight cars, and many other programs of cost saving. Although some results came from informal pressure, none of the moves recommended was ever ordered to be put into effect.

scrutinized air-carrier operating expenses closely and has disallowed, for mail-rate purposes, expenses regarded as imprudent.

The validity of operating expenses in setting a reasonable level of rates is exceedingly important. In the railroad industry, the average percentage of operating revenues going for operating expenses have ranged from 62 per cent in prosperous 1942 to approximately 80 per cent in postwar years. This ratio ran much higher for motor carriers, averaging above 95 per cent in recent years for those motor carriers reporting to the Interstate Commerce Commission, and nearly the same high average percentage for water and air carriers. But operating expenses are largely determined by economic and political conditions (notably changes in the price level), by the pressure of labor for higher wages, by the quality and effectiveness of management, and by formal or informal industrial price fixing. The size of tax expenses is largely beyond the control of the carriers and the commissions regulating them.

Even though commissions have power to control more completely than they do the expenditure of proceeds from rates, it is questionable whether such regulation would be desirable. The existence of private ownership implies that some discretion in operating expenses must be left to carrier managers. Even the specification by law of the maintenance of honest, economical, and efficient management, now found in the rules of rate making, can hardly be interpreted as meaning that control over operating expenses should be taken away from management. On the other hand, continued study and scrutiny of operating expenses and the practices which give rise to them do seem to be an appropriate commission function. If an industry is to be regulated, it would seem that the government is entitled to some means of ensuring, in general, that operating expenses are valid.

Fair return on fair value. In 1898 the United States Supreme Court injected into the field of rate-level regulation a concept which was to be of absorbing interest in regulation of quasi-public businesses for almost a half century until, as will be noted, the same court removed it from the scene. In attempting to find a formula for determining when rate regulation took property without due process of law, the Court held in 1898 that ". . . the basis of all calculations as to the reasonableness of rates to be charged by a corporation maintaining a highway under legislative sanction must be fair value of the property being used by it for the convenience of the public." [12] Largely on the basis of this legal doctrine, the Transportation Act of 1920 required that the Interstate Commerce Commission provide rates for the railroads which would, among other things, allow for the companies to receive a fair return on the fair value of their properties used in the public service. Although this requirement was

[12] *Smyth v. Ames*, 169 U.S. 466, 546.

excluded from the rule of rate making in 1933, the Commission has continued to consider the fair-value requirement in establishing rate levels.

After a long, complex, and controversial history, the United States Supreme Court in 1944 removed the fair-return-on-fair-value formula from the legal requirement for commission determination of a reasonable rate level.[13] At this time, and on occasions later, the Court has made clear that it is not the formula which is important but rather whether the impact of the orders regulating rates is such as to be unreasonable and arbitrary. Moreover, there is some doubt that the Court will interfere at all with commission rate-level regulation, so long as the commission is acting in accordance with a statute properly constituted, and so long as the commission's actions follow all the requirements of procedural due process. Even though the requirement of fair-value determination no longer exists either in the rules of rate making controlling transport regulation or in the doctrine of the Supreme Court, the Interstate Commerce Commission continues to take the position that value is "indispensable to the proper performance of a number" of its most important regulatory functions, including "the more comprehensive proceedings relating to general rate levels." [14]

As a practical matter among the transport agencies the rate and fair-value questions have assumed real regulatory importance only in the case of the railroads. The Commission has done relatively little rate regulation of the pipelines, and the level of rates of interstate motor and water carriers has generally been geared to that of the railroads. The rate-level problem of air carriers has likewise been largely subordinated to the same competitive factors which have held down motor and water rates. While rate-level problems arise with motor, water, and air carriers, the rate of return in these industries has normally been so low that it does not act to place a regulatory ceiling on the requests for increases.

The Interstate Commerce Commission has considered problems of fair return, particularly in the rate-level cases since 1920. Some evidence exists that the Commission, aided by congressional opinion,[15] allowed too low a rate of return in the 1920s, since the railroads as a whole made less than 6 per cent on their fair value during all these years. In the 1930s, the rate of return was notably low, ranging from a little over 1 to approximately 3 per cent during these years. But during these years the elasticity of demand for railroad service was such that the Commission could probably not have allowed or encouraged a higher rate level if it had wished. In the 1940s,

[13] *Federal Power Com. v. Hope Natural Gas Co.*, 320 U.S. 591.

[14] ICC, *63rd Annual Report* (1949), p. 69.

[15] Note that the Hoch-Smith resolution, passed in 1925, directed the Commission to make such rate changes as would promote the movement of products of agriculture affected by the depression in that industry.

however, with the pressure of wartime traffic, higher returns were earned. But even in this decade, the return on what is probably a conservative fair value (return on investment less depreciation) ranged from 3 per cent in 1940 and 1949 to a high of almost 7 per cent in 1942, with the decade and the years through 1954 averaging close to 4 per cent.

Thus, if one were to judge the results of Commission regulation by the return enjoyed by the railroad industry as a whole, it cannot be said that the Commission has allowed very generous returns even when a higher rate level could have been collected as was doubtless the case in the 1920s and the 1940s. However, there is evidence that the Commission has been impressed with the rate of return of the industry and in recent years particularly has allowed a number of rate-level increases. It has done so despite the protestations of other government agencies, such as the Department of Agriculture, the World War II Office of Price Administration, and the postwar Office of Price Stabilization. Nevertheless, the complexities of rate structures, the existence of certain strong carriers among weak carriers, the inflexibilities in so large an industry, and the elasticities of demand are among the factors which explain why rates cannot automatically be raised upon a mere determination that the rate of return is too low.

Earnings adequacy as measured by operating ratio. An interesting factor has been considered in rate-level cases involving motor carriers. When the Interstate Commerce Commission found it impracticable to apply the usual fair-return factors to the motor-carrier industry, it used the operating ratio as a guide to determining the adequacy of rates. In one case, the Commission held that if operating expenses were only 93 per cent of operating revenues, it could be presumed that the remaining margin would allow enough to keep the industry financially healthy.[16] As a matter of fact, this method of setting a reasonable-earnings standard makes much sense. The primary obligation of a regulatory commission is to do what it can to allow rate levels which will ensure a financially healthy industry. If study can be undertaken to show what operating ratio is necessary for this purpose, a simple and sensible measure can be developed.

Effect of rates on traffic. As rate regulation of an industry becomes thoroughly developed, there is evidence that the effect of rates on traffic becomes an increasingly important factor. This has been especially true in the regulation of railroad rate levels by the Interstate Commerce Commission. With the rate-level increases allowed the railroads during World War II and after, the Commission has become increasingly concerned with the problem of compounding rate increases. In 1949, after a series of post-

[16] *Increased Common Carrier Truck Rates in the East*, 42 M.C.C. 633 (1943). The same method was used in other cases. See e.g., *Increased Common Carrier Rates in New England*, 43 M.C.C. 13 (1943).

war increases, the effect of cumulative rate increases on traffic led the Commission to question whether or not the processes of production and distribution may not be so disturbed as to cause "permanent changes in the economic map of the country." [17]

This is intelligent concern for the results which might be expected from general rate-level increases. None of the rate-level increases of the past decade could be applied percentagewise to every rate, because competitive and other factors make it impossible to do so. Consequently, the dangers of economic dislocation from an unavoidable unequal increase in rates can have a disrupting effect upon the nation's industry. But this problem places the Commission in an interesting dilemma. With rises in costs, it cannot refuse rate-level increases. Yet, since increases must be somewhat unequal, the complexity of the railroad rate structure plus the complexities of the rate structures of other modes of transport make it impracticable to study the effects of every increase of every rate on the movement of traffic.

The question has been raised as to how far any commission *should* go in giving effect to traffic in setting rates. It is often declared that a commission is invading managerial discretion by insisting upon deciding when a lower rate, or a moderate increase, in the face of uncontested need, will bring an increased return. It is said that the central function of management is to determine how an increased return can be obtained, so long as the existing return is too low, and so far as a rate structure does not result which would be discriminatory.

Two students who have analyzed this problem have come to the conclusion that the Interstate Commerce Commission, at least, "has, in effect, served as a board of directors for the nation's railroads with respect to general pricing policies." [18] They point out that the Commission has substituted its own judgment for that of railroad management on such important factors as the effect of rates upon the general economy of the country, the competitive position of the carriers, and the public-relations standing of the companies desiring to raise rates.

There are two schools of thought on this question. One position is presented by those who claim that, if private property is to endure, some faith must be placed in private management to set rates which will be most profitable for it. Unless the rates requested by private management are excessive (in terms of allowing more earnings than necessary to maintain financial health), or unduly discriminatory, a commission, while perhaps warning the carriers that it believes the change to be unwise, should grant the rate pleas. In other words, more responsibility should be placed

[17] ICC, *op. cit.*, pp. 2–3.

[18] C. L. Dearing and W. Owen, *National Transportation Policy* (Washington, D.C.: Brookings Institution, 1949), p. 273.

on carrier management to work out compensatory rates than has been the case.

The other school of thought maintains that a commission has a responsibility to fix rates so that carriers will be able to furnish adequate transportation service, without at the same time putting shippers under a burden of transportation charges which would impede economic readjustment. In other words, the job of a regulatory agency is to harmonize what it conceives to be the long-run interests of carriers and shippers. If it seems to a commission that lower rates than those asked for by carriers would stimulate business and aid shippers, it should use the rule of rate making as a "flexible instrument of public policy" to attain this end.[19]

The latter policy, which more nearly conforms to the actual policy of the Interstate Commerce Commission in its regulation of railroad rates, places a regulatory agency in the position of judging when rates will make for adequate revenues. The basic difference between the two schools of thought lies in this point. Is this exercise of judgment proper regulatory policy, or is this a responsibility which should rest with private management?

Rate Structures

Regulation of carrier rate structures is an extremely complicated phase of government control. The prescription of rates for particular commodities and between particular points would be difficult enough if a commission had only to decide whether the rates per se were just and reasonable. But when it must decide in addition that particular rates do not cause "undue" discrimination between persons, localities, ports, markets, areas, or gateways, the problem becomes almost impossible to comprehend.

THE ECONOMICS OF RATE DISCRIMINATION

If the transportation business were one in which all costs were variable, there would be no problem of rate discrimination, because it would be uneconomical to carry any traffic which did not pay its full cost. The importance of overhead costs in relation to total costs varies among the modes of transportation. But they are exceedingly important in all the larger carrier businesses subject to regulation. As a matter of fact, it is surprising how important overhead costs are in all the transport industries.[20] Logically, one would expect variable costs to be proportionately

[19] For an elaboration of this position, see I. L. Sharfman, *The Interstate Commerce Commission* (New York: The Commonwealth Fund, 1936), vol. IIIB, pp. 290–308.

[20] Analysis of expenses of carriers reporting to the Interstate Commerce Commission and the Civil Aeronautics Board indicates that expenses not variable with the volume

more important in the airline, motor-vehicle, and water-carrier industries because these companies usually do not furnish their rights of way. However, in the airline business, for example, where air is the way and federal navigational facilities are used without cost, the domestic trunk-line carriers still expended in 1954, a typical year, approximately 11 per cent of their operating expenses on depreciation, 3 per cent on advertising and publicity, 9 per cent on sales activity, 6 per cent on general and administrative, and approximately 10 per cent on other ground activities not directly related to the volume of flying.

In addition to the importance of costs not varying directly with the volume of operations, the transportation companies generally have an important element of joint and common costs in their operations. Empty car-miles are necessary by-products of full car-miles in railroad operations. Empty or partially filled backhauls are usual phenomena in motor-carrier and water-carrier operations. And there is no product so perishable as an empty railroad coach or airplane seat or an unsold available ton-mile. Unfilled capacity of operating equipment is necessarily produced jointly with the production of revenue service, although careful scheduling and good management can reduce this lost service. Other costs are common to several services. For example, certain railroad way expenses are common to both passenger and freight services, and the cost of operating a locomotive is largely common to the various cars in the train.

In any case, when the importance of overhead, common, or joint costs is considered, one can easily find economic motives for selling certain additional transportation service at special prices in order to maximize profits. To be sure, a carrier should realize its out-of-pocket costs in pricing such special services, but if it can obtain more than this, without endangering the price structure of other services, the carrier will improve its profit position by establishing a price below average costs if necessary to obtain the traffic. This situation explains the cost motives for rate discrimination.

If the business of transportation were perfectly competitive, rate discrimination would hardly be possible. The fact that more than out-of-pocket costs can be obtained from some kinds of traffic is evidence not only that transport services are different and not freely substitutable but that restraint exists in competition. For if competition worked perfectly, in the short run at least, there would be a tendency for all rates to fall to

of operations are the following approximate percentages of total operating expenses: railroads, 25 per cent; motor carriers, 27 per cent; water carriers, 20 per cent; air carriers, 40 per cent. However, when interest and rentals are added to expenses, the proportion of fixed expenses of the railroads rises markedly, to approximately 40 per cent of total costs. Moreover, it should be emphasized that the above percentages are approximate and necessarily depend upon the range of time and operations considered.

out-of-pocket costs. Hence, the very existence of discrimination indicates some imperfectly competitive, or monopolistic, elements in the transport business, plus the existence of unused productive capacity.

PUBLIC INTEREST IN RATE DISCRIMINATION

Public interest in rate discrimination arises from several causes. Where a carrier occupies a monopolistic position, it might be in the interests of maximum profits to charge a rate which would seem to the public to be unduly burdensome to shippers or passengers. Where competitive factors enter in, the course of cutthroat competition might lead to preferences being given to certain geographical locations and to certain persons, a practice which might seem unreasonable and burdensome to others and might cause impairment in carrier service, with ultimate extinction of weaker lines.

Differential pricing, however, may well be in the public interest if it means that traffic could not move unless something less than fully allocated costs were charged. A rate slightly more than out-of-pocket costs for traffic, which could not move without such a rate, does not burden other traffic, but it instead reduces the share of overhead costs that the latter might have to bear. Moreover, the public interest is served by a financially healthy transportation industry, and it is clearly in the direction of profit maximization to charge discriminatory rates. But where this differential pricing becomes arbitrary, capricious, or "unfair," discrimination becomes an evil that regulation properly aims to eradicate. In other words, laws against discrimination should not and do not forbid all differential pricing, but merely pricing inconsistent with what is conceived by legislature, commission, or court as incompatible with the public interest.

COMMISSION AUTHORITY OVER RATE STRUCTURES

The legislative basis for regulation of individual rates of railroad, highway, water, and pipeline operations is found in several parts of the Interstate Commerce Act. The Interstate Commerce Commission has power to set just and reasonable rates for all common carriers and reasonable minimum rates of contract water and highway carriers. With respect to all common carriers, the law forbids undue or unjust discrimination against persons, places, or commodities. The comprehensiveness of this prohibition against discrimination may be seen by quoting the statute which provides that it shall be unlawful for a common carrier

> . . . to make, give, or cause any undue or unreasonable preference or advantage to any particular person, company, firm, corporation, association, locality, port, port district, gateway, transit point, region, district, territory, or description of traffic in any respect whatsoever; or to subject any particular person, port, port district, gateway, transit point, company, firm, corporation, associa-

tion, locality, region, district, territory, or description of traffic to any unjust discrimination or any undue or unreasonable prejudice or disadvantage in any respect whatsoever: *Provided, however,* That this paragraph shall not be construed to apply to the discriminations, prejudice, or disadvantage to the traffic of any other carrier of whatever description.

Note that, except for possible discrimination against the traffic of a competitive carrier, the prohibition covers every phase of rate discrimination. Almost identical language is used in the Civil Aeronautics Act of 1938 in its control over common carriers by air.

UNDERLYING PRINCIPLES IN SETTING PARTICULAR RATES

Since the law does not prohibit all discrimination but only that which is "undue" or "unreasonable," the burden of determining the extent of lawful rate discrimination necessarily lies with the commissions charged with the regulation of transportation rates. In the setting of particular rates and in determining the reasonableness of discrimination involved, unlike cases involving the level of rates, a commission is not immediately concerned with the over-all profitability of a carrier's operations. As the Supreme Court has pointed out: [21]

> . . . Where the rates as a whole are under consideration, there is a possibility of deciding with more or less certainty, whether the total earnings afford a reasonable return. But whether the carrier earned dividends or not sheds little light on the question as to whether the rate on a particular article is reasonable. For, if the carrier's total income enables it to declare a dividend, that would not justify an order requiring it to haul one class of goods for nothing, or for less than a reasonable rate. On the other hand, if the carrier earned no dividend, it would not have warranted an order fixing an unreasonably high rate on such article.

Although certain underlying principles which have guided commissions in fixing particular carrier rates can be selected, it is not to be inferred that they represent the basis for an accurate formula applicable to the rate structure. The procedure of commission regulation is not subject to rigid formulas. Various principles are given varying weight as the circumstances of each case demand. The "zone of reasonableness," either of rates per se or of relationships of rates with each other, is broad. It must be remembered that regulation of transportation rates is a highly practical matter. Economic development of entire industries has been materially influenced by transportation rates, and any commission hardly dares upset these fine balances by rigorously applying a single theory or an inflexible set of principles of rate-structure regulation.

Cost. As has already been indicated, the reason for a problem of rate structures and rate discrimination is that, as a general rule in transporta-

[21] *ICC v. Union Pacific R.R. Co.*, 222 U.S. 541, 549 (1912).

tion and particularly in the railroad field, individual rates cannot be fixed upon an over-all cost basis. Because an individual rate makes good economic and management sense if it brings an increase in traffic at a return above the cost incurred in obtaining it, the commissions, as well as carrier management, must pay attention to the promotional effects of rates.

The Interstate Commerce Commission has recognized this problem by admitting that there is a "zone of reasonableness" within which rates should fall. It has held that railroads may voluntarily, in certain situations, fix rates which will little more than cover variable costs.[22] This is the practical minimum at which rates can be fixed. The practical maximum is that rates may not be set so high as to bring unrestricted monopoly profits. As a matter of fact, this maximum is more usually a question of relationship between rates, that is, a problem of discrimination, than a problem of reasonableness per se.

The Civil Aeronautics Board has likewise recognized the practical aspects of rate making. The Board has permitted considerable experimentation not only in air freight rates but also in air passenger fares, with its sympathetic hearing to coach fares and service and to such promotional schemes as family fares on the middle three days of the week. At the same time, the Board has required the carriers to prove that out-of-pocket costs would be covered, that some contribution would be made to overhead, and that the differential rates would not harm the earnings of the airlines as a whole.

Value of service. Another factor which underlies the setting of a particular rate is the value of the service to shippers. To say that value of service is a variable factor is simply another way of saying that the demand for transportation services is, in some degree, elastic. Except for rare cases, transportation by a particular method or carrier is not indispensable for shippers. The value of service measures the degree of dispensability. If carriage of a particular kind of traffic is not much affected by the freight rate, its value of service is high and its elasticity of demand is low. If, however, traffic (by a given kind of carrier) is sensitive to rates in that changes in them would greatly affect the volume carried, this is evidence that the value of its service is low and its elasticity of demand high.

One factor influencing the value of transportation service is the difference in cost of producing the same article at the two points between which shipment is considered.[23] The measure of value of such service

[22] *American National Live Stock Assoc. v. Atchison T. & S. F. Rwy. Co.*, 122 I.C.C. 609, 617 (1927).

[23] But those who know business practices are aware that articles made in town A are often shipped to town B, where an article physically the same is made, and the articles from B may be shipped to A. This shipment of goods cannot be explained in terms of cost alone. The answer to this apparent economic dilemma is found in the develop-

must also take into account competition of other carriers. With some products this competition may not be important, but the development of other agencies of transport has immeasurably increased the elasticity of demand for railroad service.

It is quite true that the value of service for a high-priced commodity may be higher than that for a low-priced one. This is so because the part of the former commodity's costs which is represented by freight is not enough to make much relative difference in price. This difference in value of a commodity is important in determining value of service but is not a factor separate from the effect of elasticity of demand in fixing rates.

The elasticity of demand for goods themselves will affect the value of transportation service. If a good has an inelastic demand, the demand for transportation service may be inelastic unless the good can be produced at almost any point. If the demand for a good is elastic, the demand for transportation service will also tend to be elastic. However, the demand for railroad service may not be the same as the transportation demand for the good, since the use of alternative transport agencies almost inevitably increases the elasticity of demand for railroad services.

Social need. Some individuals claim that, since a carrier controls economic development and affects prices so much through the rates charged, these should be fixed with a view to social need. Indeed, there is evidence that the Interstate Commerce Commission has given some effect to social need in fixing rates, although this is estimated to have exerted only a minor influence.[24] In passing the Hoch-Smith resolution in 1925, Congress showed that it desired the Commission to pay attention to the need for favorable rail rates by the depressed agricultural industry. In some of the cases growing out of this resolution, the Commission demonstrated that it was not unmindful of this charge. In more recent cases, particularly in the 1931 freight-rate case, it gave some effect to the need of industry for freedom from burdensome freight rates.

Some effect to what might be termed social need is given in connection with certain competitive rates. The Commission has fairly consistently refused to allow rates which would take away a natural economic advantage of a particular locality. Moreover, rates have been fixed at times to encourage development of an industry. But the element of social need has perhaps actually played its greatest part in curtailment by the Commission of wasteful transportation hauls induced by competitive rates, which increase the volume of ton-mileage without increasing the utility of goods to the consumer.

---

ment of product differentiation. Although physically identical and having like manufacturing costs, it is not unusual for X brand of shoes, manufactured in A, to be sold in B, where Y brand of shoes is made, and for Y brand to be sold in A.

[24] Sharfman, *op. cit.*, pp. 519–521.

Transportation Rate Regulation: An Evaluation

Of all problems in the transportation business, rate determination is perhaps the most difficult. As was pointed out in the discussion of the economics of individual rates, transportation is an unusual business, since its product is a service which varies in nature as between persons and things and as between the countless possibilities of pairs of points between which persons and property are transported. Because of the economic nature of the business, rate uniformity is impossible. While it is conceivable that all manner of passengers and freight might be carried for a uniform rate per pound per mile, the nature of costs and value of service make a pure weight-distance standard an economic impossibility. Moreover, the transportation business is normally much more competitive than is usually realized, with a large number of different companies engaged in transportation by various means. In the case of highway, water, and air transportation, the problem of competition is complicated by the existence of a substantial volume of private and contract operations in addition to the traditional common-carrier operations.

It is consequently almost impossible to evaluate the role of government in transport rate policy. In so competitive and complex a business, the authority over rates cannot be placed in a government agency. Carrier managements necessarily have a real part in rate making. Users of the service exert an extraordinarily important influence, and competitive and business conditions have also been responsible.

Furthermore, the effect of government has been variable as between carriers. The oldest adequate statutory basis for rate regulation exists in the case of railroad rates, and the influence of government policy can most easily be seen in this field. Although statutory authority was early placed over oil pipelines,[25] the actual regulation has been very small, partly because of Interstate Commerce Commission preoccupation with railroad regulation and partly because most of the pipelines have been subsidiaries of large oil-refining companies and have been treated, despite legal edict to the contrary, as private carriers. Likewise, effective control over interstate motor-carrier rate making has had a short history, dating from 1935. Air-carrier rate regulation by the federal government did not come until 1938, and only a shadow of rate authority existed over interstate water carriers until 1940.

With such variation in experience, it might be well to look at the experience with regulation by types of carriers.

[25] Natural-gas pipelines were placed under the control of the Federal Power Commission in 1938, thirty-two years after oil pipelines were placed under the Interstate Commerce Commission.

RAILROAD RATE REGULATION

In the field of individual rate regulation, including problems of rate discrimination, there is no doubt but that the Interstate Commerce Commission has exerted an enormous influence. It has been well said that the Commission's role and the basic purpose of the law is "to make the transportation system, as a whole, function as an impartial service agency for the national economy." [26] This influence has been felt by direct action on rates and even broad investigations of rate structures.[27] It has also been felt by the legal requirements that all tariffs must be filed and that rates can be suspended upon complaint or upon the Commission's own motion. Such action naturally leads to considerable publicity in rate making, with an important regulatory effect on the carriers and shippers involved.[28]

While the regulatory effect on individual rates has been great, the Interstate Commerce Commission has had to be realistic in administering rate regulation. It has been forced by realities to allow differential pricing which would more than cover out-of-pocket costs and yet give effect to competitive and other value-of-service factors. In removing discriminations as being unreasonable or unjust, the Commission has generally insisted that the discrimination or disadvantage be something that is created by the rate rather than by the commercial or geographical disadvantage of the shipper. Moreover, the Commission has shown admirable restraint in not adjusting rates to meet the commercial needs of shippers and localities. But in the case of joint water-rail rates, the Commission has, under prodding from Congress, been guilty of establishing rates clearly designed to discriminate in favor of water transportation and localities dependent upon such transport.[29]

As for the regulation of the railroad rate level, the results of commission regulation are not so clear. In evaluating the regulation of railroad rates, one should look to the results of this task in terms of the adequacy of

[26] Dearing and Owen, *op. cit.*, p. 233.

[27] See, e.g., *Class Rate Investigation and Consolidated Freight Classification*, 262 I.C.C. 447 (1945).

[28] In 1954, for example, the Interstate Commerce Commission received for filing 142,050 publications concerning rate changes, of which it is estimated that much more than half had to do with the railroad rates. Although suspension proceedings were initiated on only 1,851 of these filings, the publicity of rates plus the chance of suspension has a policing effect on the making of individual rates. See ICC, *68th Annual Report* (1954), pp. 105–106.

[29] *Rail and Barge Joint Rates*, 270 I.C.C. 591 (1948). In this case the Commission approved lower rail-water rates than all-rail rates, even though many transportation authorities believed this to be economically unsound as a forced diversion from more economical rail routes. Among other reasons for the decision, the Commission mentioned (at p. 612) the benefits of pioneering and the fact that Congress had been supporting the development of the inland waterways involved.

these rates to support an efficient service needed by the public. There can be no doubt that the railroad industry meets this test, and experience with this industry in World War II and in the defense effort thereafter amply supports this fact.

On the other hand, railroad rates have not been particularly adequate, even in recent heavy traffic years, as measured by return on investment. While the average rate of return for all railroads does not show the individual cases of higher or lower returns, it does serve to show that serious question exists as to the adequacy of rates, except during the years of World War II. In only two years since 1920 (1942 and 1943) have the railroads earned an average return of 6 per cent on their investment less depreciation. During most of the period, and particularly in the 1930s when the rate dropped to 1.4 per cent in 1932, the return has been lamentably low, ranging ordinarily from 2 to 4½ per cent.

The Interstate Commerce Commission has been criticized by some persons for not allowing the railroads to charge higher rates during the 1920s and 1940s when, it is contended, higher rates could have been collected. The low rate of return earned by the railroads has often been compared with the much more prosperous rates earned by local public utilities and industrial companies. On the other hand, other persons feel this criticism to be unreasonable in the light of the demonstrated ability of the railroads to raise capital for necessary extensions and betterments.[30]

It is true that the railroads were able to obtain new capital during the 1920s and the 1940s; some were even able to do so by the sale of stock. But in both these decades, most of the new capital has been obtained by borrowing, although the railroads were able to obtain much capital from reinvestment of earnings during the extraordinarily profitable years of World War II, as well as the funds made available from swelling depreciation charges.[31]

But is this an adequate criterion? The railroads are subject to the business cycle and to competitive influences. Even in prosperous 1954 operating expenses, taxes, and fixed charges took 92 per cent of total revenues. It probably would not take too sharp a drop in traffic again to plunge many of the railroads in the red and perhaps bring on another era of bankruptcies reminiscent of the 1930s, when approximately one-third of the nation's railroad mileage was operated by companies in receivership or

[30] Sharfman, *op. cit.*, p. 305, finds this criticism "largely wanting in substance when tested by reference to the basic objective of maintaining such railroad credit as is necessary for adequate and efficient service."

[31] For example, in 1950 the railroads spent $1,065 million on additions and betterments of which $430 million came from depreciation reserves, $285 million from earnings, $75 million from bonds, and $275 million from equipment trust obligations. See *Railroads, 1951* (New York: Merrill Lynch, Pierce, Fenner & Beane, 1951), p. 10.

trusteeship. While the nation's railroads are much better off from the standpoint of debt load and fixed charges than they were before 1930, and the depression brought great advances in railroad cost control, the present level of railroad profits is not such as to ensure financial health in depression as well as prosperity.

However, it must be said that in recent years the Interstate Commerce Commission has shown more understanding of the problem of rate levels. Even though applications for rate increases tend to be protracted, the Commission has approved a number of rate-level increases in the post-World War II years of rapid inflation. From 1946 to 1948, the Commission allowed freight-rate increases totaling approximately 57 per cent, and additional increases were allowed in 1950 and 1951, so that the permitted increases in the five years from 1946 to 1951 amounted to approximately 67 per cent.[32] Yet this rise and slight rises since 1951 have not kept pace with the general rise in prices, especially when it is considered that the level of railroad freight rates in 1946 was approximately the same as in 1939. Even in 1954, the average revenue per ton-mile of freight was barely 50 per cent above that in 1939, the lesser rise in average revenues reflecting primarily the carriers' inability or unwillingness to put allowed increases into effect.

MOTOR CARRIERS

When the Interstate Commerce Commission was given regulatory control over motor-carrier rates in 1935, it found an industry of many small companies, highly competitive, generally unprofitable, and with no tradition of commodity classifications and tariffs such as had so long been a part of the railroad business. Moreover, unlike the railroad business, the Commission found an industry complicated by the existence of contract and private carriers which competed vigorously for the business handled by the common carriers. It is no wonder, therefore, that the progress of rate regulation has appeared to be slow and relatively ineffective, as judged by railroad standards.

One of the first acts of the Commission, in 1936, was to require the filing and publication of tariffs, an action which led to the preparation of a national motor freight classification and the development of tariff bureaus. With the rates finally filed, the Commission set to work to bring them into conformity with its regulations respecting individual rates. This progress has been slow, and the Commission has proceeded cautiously.

In order to meet the most pressing problem of the industry, that of destructive rate cutting, the Commission undertook early the prescription of minimum rates. In order to bring some rate stability into the industry, the Commission between 1937 and 1941 set minimum rates for motor

[32] ICC, *63rd Annual Report* (1949), p. 2, and 30 *Railroad Data* 33 (Aug. 17, 1951).

carriers throughout a large part of the United States.[33] These rates were admittedly of an emergency character, were imposed without complete study of costs or rates, and were based either upon railroad rates or upon the rate minima recommended by associations of motor carriers. With the advent of World War II and the feeling on the part of the Commission that rate cutting had practically ceased, these orders were vacated in 1943, and since that time the Commission has dealt with the problem of minimum rates more on an individual basis.

While the regulation of motor-carrier rates has not been as complete as that in the railroad field, it can hardly be said to be inadequate. Regulation has assisted in bringing some order out of chaos in the motor-carrier industry. Through requirements for filing rates, and through constant examination to remove cases of destructively low rates, discrimination, and unreasonably high rates, the Commission has had more influence than the open record might indicate. Moreover, it must be recognized that rail rates tend to set the standard and that motor-carrier rates are, to a great extent, established to compete with rail rates. This tendency cannot be avoided, although the Commission has been insisting increasingly upon adequate cost data to support the reasonableness of rates of the highway carriers.

The rate-level problem has not had the place in motor-carrier regulation that it has had in the railroad industry. Where level increases have been requested, the Commission has been fairly liberal in granting them. But the principal problem is one again of competition, primarily competition with the railroads. Through continual control to see that the motor carriers do not impoverish themselves by too low rates to meet competition, the Commission is doing what can be expected to protect the level of rates. How successful this policy has been is difficult to tell. It is certain that the interstate operators reporting to the Commission are in far better financial health than they were before the era of regulation started in 1935. Much of this financial improvement is due to the prosperity of the war years and the postwar defense years, but certainly some part of it may fairly be ascribed to the stability induced by regulation.

PIPELINES

Commission regulation of any of the aspects of pipeline companies has not been great, despite the fact that since 1906 the Interstate Commerce Commission has had virtually the same authority over oil pipelines that it has had over railroads. As a matter of fact, the economic and organizational characteristics of the pipeline industry are such that few of these lines conform to the pattern of common carriers, even though at law they

[33] See cases at 4 M.C.C. 68 (1937); 8 M.C.C. 287 (1938); 24 M.C.C. 501 (1940); and 27 M.C.C. 297 (1941).

are held to be such. Most of the pipelines are subsidiaries of large producing or refining oil companies and have naturally been built where they would most conveniently serve the parent companies. As a result of this status most of the pipeline carriers handle little oil and gasoline except that of the producing companies which own them.

In order to buttress this position, the pipeline companies have charged relatively high rates and have required high minimum tenders of oil. The Commission has, on two occasions, held that the minimum tender should be reduced from 100,000 barrels to 10,000 barrels. Such a finding was made in 1922, but the order of the Commission was so restricted that it had little effect on industry practices.[34] A similar decision was made in 1940 after an industry-wide investigation, and a show-cause order was issued,[35] but with the advent of the war, the Commission postponed its final decision. Because the war made many of the facts obsolete, and for other reasons not readily apparent, the Commission had by 1955 never issued its proposed order to reduce these tender requirements.

Likewise, in the field of direct rate control the Commission has not been active. The pipelines have been extraordinarily profitable, earning returns on investment after depreciation of approximately 24 per cent throughout the 1930s and approximately 15 per cent during the 1940s. Despite these ample returns, which would seem to support the thesis that the pipelines are really not open to the independent companies on a reasonably economical basis, since high rates have little meaning to the parent companies, the Commission has not acted really to control rates. In 1940 it did find that the rates of most of the companies were excessive and that a reasonable rate would be one allowing an 8 per cent return on the value of the lines.[36] But this finding, like that regarding minimum tender, has not been translated into an effective order.

The reluctance of the Interstate Commerce Commission to do something effective about pipeline rates and practices decades ago is not easily explained. To be sure, few complaints have been filed, the other phases of the Commission's regulatory jurisdiction have kept it busy, and World War II intervened to halt the rate work the Commission did undertake. Watkins has suggested that the paucity of complaints is due to the fear by small producing customers of discriminatory reprisals by large oil companies owning pipelines.[37] Also, it is true that pipeline rates have been much lower than those of railroads and trucks; but even though uniform and low by comparison, they appear to be somewhat high as judged by

[34] *Brundred Bros. v. Prairie Pipe Line Co.*, 68 I.C.C. 458.

[35] *Reduced Pipe Line Rates and Charges*, 243 I.C.C. 115.

[36] *Ibid.*

[37] M. W. Watkins, *Oil: Stabilization or Conservation?* (New York: Harper & Brothers, 1937).

cost. If they are, the independent producer or refiner is being subjected to discrimination, for these rates have only paper significance to the owner of a pipeline who transports the oil he produces.

WATER CARRIERS

Before the passage of the Transportation Act of 1940, there was little effective rate regulation of water carriers, except for those under the control of the railroads and under the jurisdiction of the Interstate Commerce Commission. Most of the regulation was industry self-regulation through agreements or conferences. Long practiced by American and foreign shipping lines, these conferences were legalized by the Shipping Act of 1916 and were placed outside the national antitrust laws, if filed with and approved by the Shipping Board (after 1936 the Maritime Commission and since 1950 the Federal Maritime Board).

Even with the passage of the Transportation Act of 1940, actual Commission regulation of water-carrier rates has not been extensive. The situation with respect to the water carriers is analogous to that with respect to the motor carriers. Water-carrier earnings have long been low, so that there can hardly be a charge of excessive rates. Water-carrier service is sharply competitive with that of the railroads. As a result, individual rates and the rate level tend to follow railroad practice, with enough differential to allow for the slowness and circuity of water transport. Since all common carriers by water must file their rates and rate classifications, the mere act of filing, with its attendant publicity, has had an important regulatory effect.

Most of the rate regulation has been in the direction of controlling the minimum rates of contract carriers by water in order to make sure that the common carriers will not be placed at an unsupportable disadvantage. Except for the general order applicable to intercoastal common carriers by the Maritime Commission in 1940 [38] and establishing minimum rates in this field of shipping, no general orders have been issued setting minimum rates for common or contract carriers. However, in dealing with individual rate cases and in meeting objections to rates filed by common and contract carriers, the Commission has attempted to eliminate chaotic rate-cutting practices which have so long threatened the economic existence of the water carriers.

AIR CARRIERS

As has been indicated, the principal rate-regulation activities of the Civil Aeronautics Board have had to do with mail rates.

In a sense, the Board has really exercised most of its influence on airline rates through its expansion of airline routes and the resulting competition

[38] *Intercoastal Rate Structure*, 2 U.S. M.C. 285.

which has followed. Before the airline business became as competitive as it has in the post–World War II years, there was a wide variety of rate levels among the carriers and significant differences in the way passenger fares were calculated. Not only has the new competition between airlines forced upon the industry a rather uniform fare structure, but the newness of the industry, the fact that it has been predominantly a passenger-carrying industry, and the action of the Civil Aeronautics Board to stabilize freight rates have led to a rate structure for passengers and freight which is extraordinarily simple. One finds, for example, few of the complicated freight classifications which so characterize the railroad industry.

As a general rule, the Civil Aeronautics Board has permitted the airlines to develop their own level of passenger fares. To be sure, in 1943, when the lines were making extraordinarily high profits, the Board did serve a show-cause order asking why passenger fares should not be reduced by 10 per cent.[39] When several of the airlines made reductions in fares of 6 to 10 per cent and competition forced most other carriers to follow, the Board dropped the proposed investigation. Moreover, in 1947 and 1948, when mounting losses of the trunk-line carriers became serious, the Board informally took some leadership in assisting the airlines to raise their rates.[40] When passenger-load factors of the airlines remained low, several of the airlines undertook a number of promotional services and fares.

The Board wisely permitted the airlines to undertake these experiments but felt it necessary to exert some restraint on the imposition of low "coach" fares. Pointing out that "there is little indication that the airline industry is in a position to enter the air coach business on a broad and indiscriminate basis,"[41] the Board placed restrictions on coach service, and the coach service of each of the certificated carriers was specifically approved by the Board for limited periods of time. In so doing, the Board was able to limit the amount of coach service, to control the time of offering the service, and to see in general that the first-class fare structure of the airlines was not destroyed by unwise and uneconomical extensions of the service. In the past few years, however, the Board has continually renewed coach-service authorizations and has greatly liberalized restrictions on the quality of the service as the airlines have been able to prove the profitability of their coach services.

In the field of air freight, the Board has also influenced rates. Regular air-freight operations of the certificated airlines date from 1944 and were put into effect after the noncertificated cargo carriers had developed a considerable volume of business. With increased freight operations by the certificated passenger carriers, the newly (1947) certificated cargo

[39] CAB Docket No. 850 (1943).

[40] CAB, *Annual Report, 1948*, pp. 2–3.

[41] CAB, *Policy Statement on Coach and Promotional Tariffs* (1949).

carriers, and the noncertificated carriers, a highly competitive situation developed. Two of the passenger carriers proposed in 1947 freight rates of 12 cents per ton-mile, a rate much lower than ever offered before, although competitive with the rates being charged by the cargo carriers. Fearing a destructively competitive situation, the Board intervened in 1948 to establish minimum rates ranging from 13 to 16 cents per ton-mile.[42] The Board followed this minimum rate order, however, with a series of orders which provided for lower minimum rates where found to be necessary to promote utilization of space on low-load-factor back-hauls.

As can be seen, the influence of the Board has not been considerable in the case of passenger and freight rates of the air carriers. One would not expect otherwise. With many airlines charging rates generally inadequate to make profits in normal years without subsidy mail pay, the level could hardly be accused of being unreasonably high. Yet, in view of competitive factors, and the profit position of the larger airlines, the Board has not wished to impose its judgment on the airline managements and insist upon higher fare levels than these managements believed to be wise.

In the area of individual rates and rate discriminations, the relative simplicity of airline rates and the small part which air freight has played in the national freight picture have left rather little for a regulatory commission to do. What the Board has done is to place a restraining hand upon competitive excesses. While even doing this is dangerous government policy in a new and growing industry, since it may hamper experimentation, the record indicates that the Board's action has not been harmful but has rather been helpful to the industry as a whole.

Selected References

Bigham, T. C., and M. J. Roberts, *Transportation*, chaps. 6, 11–17. New York: McGraw-Hill Book Company, Inc., 1952.

Daggett, Stuart, *Principles of Inland Transportation*, 3d ed., chaps. 15–17. New York: Harper & Brothers, 1941.

Dearing, C. L., and W. Owen, *National Transportation Policy*, chaps. 11–13. Washington, D.C.: Brookings Institution, 1949.

Fair, M. L., and E. W. Williams, Jr., *Economics of Transportation*, chaps. 18–23. New York: Harper & Brothers, 1950.

Frederick, J. H., *Commercial Air Transportation*, 4th ed., chaps. 8–9. Homewood, Ill.: Richard D. Irwin, Inc., 1955.

[42] *Air Freight Rate Investigation*, 9 C.A.B. 340 (1948). This order set a minimum rate of 16 cents per ton-mile for the first 1,000 freight ton-miles of any shipment and 13 cents for those ton-miles in excess of 1,000.

Healy, K. T., *Economics of Transportation*, chaps. 10–13, 20–22. New York: The Ronald Press Company, 1940.

Landon, C. E., *Transportation*, chaps. 13–21. New York: William Sloane Associates, 1951.

Locklin, D. P., *Economics of Transportation*, 4th ed., chaps. 16–22. Homewood, Ill.: Richard D. Irwin, Inc., 1954.

McDowell, C. E., and H. M. Gibbs, *Ocean Transportation*, chap. 19. New York: McGraw-Hill Book Company, Inc., 1954.

Nicholson, J. L., *Air Transportation Management*, chap. 9. New York: John Wiley & Sons, Inc., 1951.

Taff, C. A., *Commercial Motor Transportation*, chap. 9. Homewood, Ill.: Richard D. Irwin, Inc., 1951.

Troxel, Emery, *Economics of Transport*, chaps. 18–19. New York: Rinehart & Company, Inc., 1955.

6

REGULATION OF TRANSPORT SERVICE

The problem of rates cannot be separated from the problem of service, for rates have little significance unless related to the character, quality, adequacy, and safety of service. By the same token the pattern of service required and permitted by the public interest has a strong influence on rates and upon the financial profitability of the carriers involved. This is nowhere more clear than in the case of the airline industry, whose pattern of service has been more influenced by public authority than that of any other mode of transport since effective federal regulation was instituted in 1938 when the industry was in its infancy.

At the same time, service regulation has not been as complicated as rate regulation, except perhaps in the case of the air carriers. This is partly due to the fact that adequate jurisdiction over railroad service did not come until 1920, over highway-carrier service until 1935, and over water-carrier service until 1940, well after these industries were well developed. In the case of the pipelines, even though considerable statutory authority existed as early as 1906 and certainly by 1940, the Interstate Commerce Commission has exercised very little control over the industry. In addition to these factors as explaining the relative lack of control over service of most of the carrying agencies, it must be remembered that the transport industry has long been fairly competitive and that competition has served to promote high service standards.

Entry into Service: Railroads

Although several state governments, beginning with New York in 1892, passed laws forbidding the building of new railways or extensions of existing ones, this legislation was inadequate to meet the problem of entry into service by interstate railways. Even this regulation came too late to prevent much uneconomical extension of intrastate railroad building. It is rather surprising that the federal government should not have entered this field before 1920, because notorious cases of competitive and unsound building of railroads were clearly evident years before. The building of the West Shore Railroad across the Hudson River from the New York Central, and the construction of the New York, Chicago, and St. Louis parallel to the Lake Shore and Michigan Southern are examples of speculative building to force the older roads to buy the newer at a profit to the promoters, in order to avoid disastrous competition.

LEGISLATION ON NEW CONSTRUCTION

The Interstate Commerce Commission was granted jurisdiction over new construction and extensions in 1920; this is limited to interstate carriers. Nevertheless, where proposed construction is entirely within a state but is to be done by an interstate carrier or is closely related to interstate commerce, it falls under the jurisdiction of the Commission. The law requires a carrier to obtain a certificate of convenience and necessity before it may embark on new construction. In granting this certificate the Commission may attach such terms and conditions as future public convenience and necessity seem to require. Ordinary construction of such facilities as spur, industrial, team, switch, or side tracks is excepted from the law.

The law respecting entry into service also gives the Interstate Commerce Commission the authority to require a railroad to extend its lines. To order such extension the Commission must find that "it is reasonably required in the interest of public convenience and necessity" and that the "expense involved therein will not impair the ability of the carrier to perform its duty to the public." This provision of the law represents an apparent expansion of the common-law obligation of common carriers to serve adequately their respective territories. However, there is nothing in the statute itself which would limit the Commission to ordering extension of lines in the territory a railroad professes to serve.

VOLUNTARY CONSTRUCTION

In administering the law in respect to voluntary extension the Commission has laid down several principles. It will not allow new construction in territory where service is already adequate and may be had on reasonable terms. But it will do so in territories previously served exclusively by one carrier if the new line will improve service, serve new communities, or shorten routes.

The Commission has even approved of competitive building where there is evidence that competition will stimulate an existing carrier to improve its services.[1] A number of the members of the Commission, however, have dissented from this position. In general their opinion is based upon the argument that competition implies some duplication of facilities, a result which the Transportation Act of 1920 was designed to avoid, through placing emphasis on an adequate and efficient national system of transportation. To this might be added the argument that regulation of

[1] *Construction by Wenatchee Southern Rwy. Co.*, 90 I.C.C. 237 (1924).

the railroads along monopolistic principles implies encouragement to monopoly. The recognition of competition as a goad to adequate service or reasonable rates appears to be an admission that regulation cannot be successfully accomplished by direct administrative action.

Another principle followed by the Commission in allowing new construction is that the new line must show promise of being self-sustaining. The application of this test is usually made in conjunction with the need for service. For example, the Commission refused to allow construction of a new line between Pittsburgh and New York because it believed not only that there was no need for an additional trunk line between these points but that the return on the capital invested would be inadequate.[2]

INVOLUNTARY CONSTRUCTION

There are, in fact, relatively few cases where the Interstate Commerce Commission has ordered a railroad to extend its lines. In most instances when shippers have complained that existing facilities were inadequate and have asked for extensions, the Commission has refused to require them, largely because of the uncertain financial results of the projects.

In one case, the Commission ordered a rather extensive construction. In 1927 the Public Service Commission of Oregon asked it to require construction of a 185-mile connecting line to serve the central part of the state. The federal commission ordered a subsidiary of the Union Pacific Railroad to undertake the construction after finding that the line was needed and that the expense would not impair the Union Pacific in its duty to the public; the Commission even maintained that the extension would be profitable to that railroad.[3] However, the order was set aside by the Supreme Court, largely on grounds of statutory construction.[4] The majority of the Court held that the power of the Interstate Commerce Commission to require new construction "is confined to extensions within the undertaking of the carrier to serve, and cannot be extended to embrace the building of what is essentially a new line to reach new territory."[5] The Court based its conclusion in the first place on the fact that the law placed extension of car service and of lines in the same clause, not thereby making clear that extension of lines into new territory was intended. In the second place, the Court pointed to the legal doctrine that public-utility extensions cannot be required into areas which the public utility has not held itself out to serve and held that the Transportation Act of 1920 must have been enacted with this constitutional principle in mind.

[2] *Construction of New York, Pittsburgh and Chicago R.R. Co.*, 187 I.C.C. 598 (1932).

[3] *Public Serv. Comm. of Oregon v. Central Pac. Rwy. Co.*, 159 I.C.C. 630 (1929).

[4] *ICC v. Oregon-Wash. R.R. and Nav. Co.*, 288 U.S. 14 (1933).

[5] *Ibid.*, p. 40.

Entry into Service: Highway and Water Carriers

Because of the similarity of the problems and legislative jurisdiction over highway and water carriers, the control over entry into service of these two industries can well be discussed together. The regulatory pattern of these two industries reflects certain economic and organization characteristics. Highway and water carriers fall into three general classifications: common carriers, contract carriers, and private carriers. Both common and contract carriers operate a for-hire business, that is, they carry goods or persons for pay. The private carrier handles traffic of the owning company only.

With the exception of a few lines, such as lumbering railroads, all railroads are common carriers. This situation is practically reversed in the highway- and water-transport field. A rather small portion of their business is done by common carriers, the larger part being done by contract and private carriers.

ECONOMIC CHARACTERISTICS AND THE PUBLIC INTEREST

As contrasted to the railroad business, the motor- and water-transport businesses (like the air-carrier business) are interesting hybrids. Nature plus considerable public expenditures furnish the way, and the operator need only invest in moving equipment and sometimes terminal and station structures. This fact has marked economic effects. In the first place, regulation of carriers is not actually complete regulation of supply. Granting a certificate of convenience and necessity is merely the giving of permission to operate over a line already there. Permission to build a public highway, a waterway, or an airway has not been required yet by any transport regulatory authority. Once the way is built and is being maintained, a transportation facility exists. To refuse to allow its use would hardly be economical. Whether certificates allowing entry into this field are granted or not affects mainly the number of operators using the highways, waterways, or airways and has a limited influence on the actual supply of transportation.

The hybrid nature of these businesses has its effect on the size of the operating units. While an ocean-going ship represents a large investment, as does a large lake ship, these investments are small relative to railroad investments, and many of the ships operated (especially when bought from government surpluses) represent little more investment that a large truck-and-trailer combination. And an investment in a small fleet of trucks is small compared to the large investment required in the railroad business. This means, of course, that these industries tend to have a large number of relatively small operators and that the economies of large size are not pronounced.

The smallness of the efficient operating unit, especially in the highway-transport field, and the lesser significance of investment and other fixed costs have interesting implications for regulation. Compared to railroads, there is less tendency for rate discrimination, although the existence of unutilized capacity leads to some desire for differential pricing. Moreover, these industries are likely to be highly competitive. In fact, the motive of regulation is not often to protect against unreasonably high rates and limited service, but rather to limit competitive excesses which can lead to financially irresponsible and undependable service. In any industry as essential to other businesses and to the public welfare as the transportation industry, such factors explain public need for detailed regulation.

STATUTORY BASIS OF CONTROL

The Motor Carrier Act of 1935 provides that common carriers must receive "certificates of convenience and necessity," and contract carriers must receive "permits" to operate. To meet the problem presented by the fact that thousands of carriers were already in the field, the law gave "grandfather" rights to these carriers. For carriers operating on and since June 1, 1935, as bona fide common carriers, the law directed the Commission to grant certificates of convenience and necessity without question if application was made within 120 days after October 1, 1935. For contract carriers, a permit would also be forthcoming automatically on the same basis, except that they must have operated on and since July 1, 1935.

For carriers which could not qualify under the grandfather clauses, certain requirements were set up by the law upon which a permit or certificate should be granted. The act provided that certificates may be issued to common carriers if (1) "the applicant is fit, willing, and able properly to perform the service proposed and to conform to" the provisions of the law and rules of the Commission; (2) the Commission finds the "proposed service . . . is or will be required by future convenience and necessity." Permits are to be given to contract carriers if the Commission finds (1) the applicant to be "fit, willing, and able"; and (2) the proposed operation to be "consistent with the public interest and the policy" of Congress in formulating the law. Thus, the only difference between the requirement for a certificate and that for a permit lies in the service of a common carrier being *required* for public convenience and necessity and the service of a contract carrier being *consistent* with the general policy of the law. The contract carrier apparently need not make as strict a showing of the necessity of service as the common carrier, though it should be remembered that the law contemplates a healthy growth of motor transport and coordination of motor and other forms of carriage.

Almost identical statutory control was provided for the interstate water carriers by the Transportation Act of 1940, except that, of course, the effective date for grandfather clauses was made January 1, 1940.

COMMISSION ADMINISTRATION OF CONTROL

The bestowal of grandfather rights robbed the Commission of much of its power to control the character and the supply of motor- and water-transportation service. If uneconomical duplication existed when the respective acts went into effect, or if a number of economically inefficient or undependable operators were in business at that time, the Commission was fairly powerless to do anything about it. Even so, by setting up high standards of performance, in rate, finance, and service regulation, some of the uneconomical carriage has been eliminated and and other inefficient operators have dropped from the industry with the passage of time.

In administering the certificate programs for the motor and water carriers, the Commission has taken the position that competition is desirable, whether motor or water carriers are considered alone or with other transport agencies.[6] At the same time it has recognized that excessive competition may result in poorer and unstable transport businesses. Where the Commission has evidence that the existing carrier, whether rail, highway, or water, is adequately and efficiently serving the territory in question, and that the traffic would not support another carrier, applications for operation have been denied. Even under the guise of emergency conditions, the Commission has been loath to approve applications for emergency authority to operate where adequate service is already available.[7]

On the other hand, the Commission is inclined to grant a certificate for operation if the carrier can prove that it is qualified financially, if it appears that the traffic diverted will not seriously harm existing carriers, and if the proposed operation shows promise of operating at a profit. Much emphasis is placed upon the ability to operate profitably. This has been criticized as placing too much emphasis on profit and not enough on the public need for the service. While there are grounds for this position, the Commission is persuasive when it points out that the promise of profitability is an indication of need for the service. Furthermore, with legislative policy favoring competition, placing strong reliance on profitability and allowing additional carriers to operate under such circumstances would seem to represent intelligent support of this policy.

[6] See *Pan-American Bus Lines Operation*, 1 M.C.C. 190, 208 (1936).

[7] See, e.g., discussion of this point with respect to water carriers in ICC, *63rd Annual Report, 1949*, p. 129.

Entry into Service: Air Carriers

There has probably been no more important aspect of air-carrier regulation than the government controls over the right of an air carrier to engage in business over certain routes. As compared to the railroads, which must construct their way at great expense, the investment required to enter the airline business is relatively small, although costs of modern equipment and the cost of ground facilities for maintenance, passenger and freight handling, and sales may be very large.[8] However, at the end of World War II, the cost of practically new surplus transport aircraft, particularly for veterans, was so low that it took little capital to enter the business.

Moreover, the ability of an airplane to go between any pair of suitable airports tends to make the business very competitive, and in the absence of control over entry into the service, a destructively competitive situation might develop. Because of the extraordinary hazards of air transportation and the public interest in high standards of service and safety, as well as the importance of an economically healthy aviation industry for purposes of defense and commerce, there is admittedly strong grounds for public control of entry into this field of business.

The government's control over the right to enter business and over the prescription of routes is also of exceptional importance to the airline companies. The kind of market which an airline has is determined by its route structure. An individual company may engage in all the tools of sales promotion, including such features as a high-quality service, attractive pricing programs, and heavy advertising, but if it is not allowed to serve an adequate traffic-generating market, managerial ability cannot make operations successful. This is especially important in the airline business, since much of the traffic moves between relatively few points. For example, in a sample traffic analysis, made by the Civil Aeronautics Board, it was found that 84 per cent of the passenger traffic of trunk-line air carriers came from 50 cities out of a total of 430 then served in the United States.[9] Of the more than 15,000 pairs of cities served, 100 pairs of cities, or less than 1 per cent, had 47 per cent of the nation's total air traffic.

While it has been pointed out that effective control over airline routes

[8] Thus a modern large airplane, like the Constellation, may cost approximately $2 million and a smaller modern airplane like the Convairliner approximately $750,000. Moreover, new transport jet airplanes are being priced at more than $4,500,000 each. However, the surplus of certain transport aircraft after World War II caused prices to be low on these aircraft, with C-47 types selling from $20,000 to $50,000 and large C-54s selling often for around $100,000. Of course, with the advent of the Korean conflict, these bargains disappeared and prices for such aircraft rose manyfold.

[9] CAB, *Airline Traffic Survey for March, 1949* (1950), vol. I.

dates from the Civil Aeronautics Act of 1938, the federal government did exert considerable influence on commercial airline route structures before that date. Until recent years it has been virtually impossible for anyone to engage in commercial air transportation without a mail contract. As early as 1926 the federal government entered into contracts for the transportation of mail by private companies and several of the trunk airlines of today trace their history to that year. As the result of these contracts, in 1938 there were 16 domestic trunk-line air carriers operating 33,400 route miles; the 13 domestic carriers which comprised the trunk-line industry in 1955 were either these same companies or combinations of them. However, it is true that in 1955 there were 13 local-service airlines and 2 all-cargo carriers which had been newly certificated for domestic service since World War II.

Despite the fact the earlier air-mail contracts had done much to set the route pattern of air carriers, the expansion of the industry since 1938 through route additions and changes and new routes has given the Civil Aeronautics Board ample opportunity to mold much of the air-route pattern of the present time.

STATUTORY BASIS OF CONTROL

The statutory basis of control over entry into service, provided by the Civil Aeronautics Act of 1938, was similar in most respects to that established for railroads. Unlike motor-carrier and water-carrier regulation, the Act provides only for certificates of convenience and necessity for common carriers (or carriers of mail) plus permits for carriers owned by foreign nationals and operating in foreign commerce.

For interstate and foreign air carriers owned and operated by nationals of the United States, the certificate of convenience and necessity may be granted if the Board finds that (1) the applicant is fit, willing, and able to perform the applied-for service properly; and (2) such service is required by the public convenience and necessity. Carriers in operation in 1938 under air-mail contracts were given certificates under traditional "grandfather" rights. Transfers of certificates are subject to the approval of the Board.

Foreign carriers (i.e., those air carriers operated by foreign nationals in foreign commerce) are required to have a permit to operate into ports of the United States. Permits issued under the Air Commerce Act of 1926 and in effect in 1938 were protected under the usual "grandfather" rights. New permits require a finding that the applicant is "fit, willing, and able" and that the service would be in the public interest. Unlike applications of domestic operators it should be noted that the latter provision does not require that the service *be required* by the public convenience and necessity.

Of unusual nature and importance is the provision of the Act (section 801) that the President of the United States must approve the "issuance, denial, transfer, amendment, . . . of . . . any certificate authorizing an air carrier to engage in overseas or foreign air transportation, or air transportation between places in the same Territory or possession. . . ." Thus, this provision gives to the President of the United States authority to determine the foreign and overseas, as well as territorial, routes of United States carriers. While the extent of this power might at first sight seem strange, it is understandable in the light of the international-relations aspects of foreign air transportation.

BOARD POLICY: DOMESTIC TRUNK AIRLINES

Administration of the legislative provisions regarding airline routes and entry of carriers into service may be analyzed along the lines of the main classes of service: (1) route expansion and modification of the domestic trunk lines; (2) certification of domestic cargo carriers; (3) routes for American Flag operators in foreign commerce; (4) provision of feeder or local service routes, including helicopter routes in metropolitan areas; and (5) the problem of permitting irregular air-carrier operations. While all these operations are common carrier in nature, the problems of route expansion and the principles involved in each field have been somewhat different.

Even though new route applications were acted on, for the most part, on a piecemeal basis and not in conformity with a national route pattern, there have been a number of principles which have guided the Board's actions. In its first case involving new routes, the Board emphasized the principle of restricting competition in the airline industry, while permitting an orderly development of the route pattern. In this connection, the Board said:[10]

> . . . it was not the Congressional intent that the air transportation system of the country should be "frozen" to its present pattern. On the other hand, it is equally apparent that Congress intended the Authority to exercise a firm control over the expansion of air transportation routes in order to prevent the scramble for routes which might occur under a "laissez-faire" policy. Congress, in defining the problem, clearly intended to avoid the duplication of transportation facilities and services, the wasteful competitive practices, such as the opening of non-productive routes, and other uneconomic results which characterized the development of other modes of transportation prior to the time of their governmental regulation.

This policy of balanced and limited competition has continually been given lip service by the Board, but other factors which played so large a

[10] *Duluth–Twin Cities Operation*, 1 C.A.A. 573 (1940).

part in its deliberations after 1944 have made the Board appear to favor a far less limited competition. It is true that the Board has been extremely careful, except for the certification of local-service lines after 1946, not to allow new carriers into the air-transport field.[11] As a matter of fact, no new carrier has been permitted entry into domestic trunk-line operations (combined passenger and cargo carriers) since the act of 1938 was passed. Only one new carrier was permitted in the foreign field, although numerous local-service operators were certificated between 1946 and 1949 and four new operators were certificated for all-cargo transport in 1949.

But the real expansion of the trunk airline system has come through new routes and privileges of existing carriers by the Board's interpretation of the statutory declaration (section 2[d]) in favor of competition "to the extent necessary to assure the sound development of an air-transportation system." In following out this mandate, the Board has allowed route extensions of existing carriers when it appeared to the Board that the traffic potential warranted additional carrier service, that competitive carriers would not be unduly harmed, and the benefits to be derived from improved service, equipment, and methods promised to offset any of the inevitable costs of traffic diversion.

In following out its policy of route expansion, the Board has also been influenced by the problem of strong and weak carriers. As a result, the smaller carriers have, as a percentage to their size in 1938, received more mileage of the new routes and route extensions than the larger carriers. American and Eastern, for example, have received small percentage increases in routes, although Trans World received much more, presumably to place it on a more nearly equal footing with its larger carrier competitors. But even though the smaller airlines were expanded percentagewise much more than the larger—and this has been the conscious policy of the Board [12]—none of the smaller domestic carriers has grown to the point of even approaching the Big Four (American, United, Eastern, and Trans World) in size. Moreover, much of the expansion undertaken to strengthen the smaller airlines was in weak traffic markets or in markets dominated by

[11] Note that, in 1941, the Board said that "the number of air carriers now operating appears to be sufficient to insure against monopoly in respect to the average new route case, and we believe that the present air transportation system can by proper supervision be integrated and expanded in a manner that will in general afford the competition necessary for the development of that system in the manner contemplated by the Act. In the absence of peculiar circumstances presenting an affirmative reason for a new carrier there appears to be no inherent desirability of enlarging the present number of carriers merely for the purpose of numerically enlarging the industry." *Delta Air Corporation et al.*, 2 C.A.B. 447, 480 (1941).

[12] See, e.g., *Atlantic Seaboard Operations*, 4 C.A.B. 552 (1944), and *Mid-Continent Airlines, Kansas City–New Orleans*, 6 C.A.B. 253 (1945).

the heavily scheduled service of the Big Four. Consequently, while geographic size of operations was expanded, often the economic strength of the carrier was undermined.

The Board has also given much weight in certificate cases to the need for service, including such strongly advanced factors as the need for service to a city not being served and the need for one-carrier service between two points being served by two or more interconnecting carriers. Likewise, the Board has, as is naturally the case in certificate cases, given weight to such factors as the promised traffic potential, the cost of the proposed service, and the likelihood of profitable operations.

While the principles which the Board has followed in allowing expansion of the domestic route structure are sound, the result of their application leaves much to be desired. Board members, like most other persons familiar with aviation, were entirely too optimistic as to airline traffic potentials, especially from some of the smaller cities which were placed on routes. The Board, particularly from 1945 to 1947, was also placed under great pressure by local civic organizations and politicians to extend the benefit of air service to communities which could not support such service, to allow one-carrier service between points not justifying it, and to bring the benefits of competition to route segments which could barely support the one or two carriers already serving them. Thus, from 1938 to 1944, the mileage of domestic air-mail routes expanded from approximately 39,000 miles to 63,000 miles; but from 1945 to 1950 the route mileage of the sixteen trunk carriers expanded to 131,000 miles.[13] In addition, the Board had certificated some 31,000 miles of interstate local-service airline routes and 210,000 miles of international and overseas air routes. Although airline route mileage remained fairly constant from 1950 to 1955, the increase in air traffic and the improved economic condition of most trunk airlines led the Board to expand route mileage materially in 1955.

There is a fair degree of unanimity that much of the airline difficulties of the latter 1940s was due to the excessive competition permitted by the Board.[14] There is no doubt that the Board has duplicated and triplicated certain routes. Study of the effect of increased competition on the fifty

[13] *Facts and Figures* (Washington, D.C.: Air Transport Association, 1951), p. 6. It should be noted that, in some respects, these data exaggerate the route mileage. Actually, in 1950, the trunk airlines operated over 55,946 daily route miles. See CAB, *Annual Report, 1950*, p. 44. The difference is in the way routes are counted. Thus, an airline may operate over two routes between the same points, one stopping at intermediate points and the other nonstop between the two points. While the ability to operate both with stops and nonstop is more advantageous than to operate in one manner only, it is hardly accurate to count the route miles separately.

[14] F. W. Gill and G. L. Bates, *Airline Competition* (Boston: Harvard University Graduate School of Business Administration, 1949), pp. 618–623.

most important traffic-generating pairs of cities in 1940 and in 1948 showed that 54 per cent of the traffic was noncompetitive in 1940; that 20 per cent was subject to two-carrier competition; and 26 per cent, to three-carrier competition. In 1948, only 9 per cent of the traffic was noncompetitive, 29 per cent had two carriers, 50 per cent was subject to three carriers, and 12 per cent was open to four carriers.[15]

Other study of the problem of economic factors which account for the subsidy needs of the air carriers indicates that the problem is not so much a matter of excessive competition as it is a matter of the overexpansion of airline routes to points which cannot support air service.[16] Analysis indicates that the four largest airlines (American, United, Eastern, and Trans World) have domestic route structures which will support an unsubsidized air service. Yet, as measured by the 100 most important traffic-generating pairs of cities, these airlines are, on the average, subject to more competition than the smaller airlines of the industry. The difference between an economically sound route and one which would apparently indefinitely require subsidy appears not to be competition, at least to the extent to which it has gone, but rather the fact that some airlines serve important traffic-generating pairs of cities and other airlines do not. In other words, the extension of routes to weak traffic-generating points without the ability to include enough of the strong traffic-generating route segments appears to lie at the bottom of the airline route problem.

BOARD POLICY: CERTIFICATED CARGO CARRIERS

In 1949, the Civil Aeronautics Board certificated for a temporary period of five years four all-cargo common carriers for service to all principal freight points in the United States.[17] For three of the four carriers (Slick, Flying Tiger, and U.S. Airlines), the Board provided for certification between certain points but provided principally for service from a given area to another given area. Thus, points in California were grouped, as were other points in the New England area. A carrier certificated to serve these two areas might serve any point in one area and any other point, whether specifically named in the order or not, in another area. This novel approach was designed to permit the cargo carriers flexibility of picking

[15] Testimony of C. R. Smith, President of American Airlines in *Air Line Industry Investigation* (U.S. Senate, Committee on Interstate and Foreign Commerce, 1949).

[16] See Harold Koontz, "Economic and Managerial Factors Underlying Subsidy Needs of Domestic Trunk Line Air Carriers," 18 *Journal of Air Law and Commerce* 127–156 (Spring, 1951). In their analysis of the shortcomings of the Board's route policy, Dearing and Owen emphasize the overexpansion of routes as being the critical factor and not excessive competition. See C. L. Dearing, and W. Owen, *National Transportation Policy* (Washington, D.C.: Brookings Institution, 1949), pp. 200–218.

[17] *Air Freight Case*, 10 C.A.B. 572 (1949).

up and delivering freight in a given area. The certification of the cargo carriers is also noteworthy in that the new routes were granted with the understanding that the carriers would not carry mail and would not be eligible for mail subsidies.

This important decision of the Board, from which two of the five members dissented, was based largely upon the Board's belief that (1) the potential of air freight justified having all-cargo carriers as well as the freight operations of the certificated passenger-cargo carriers; (2) the traffic diversion from existing carriers would not be great, as was indicated by the fact the freight business of the passenger-cargo carriers had grown fast while the cargo carriers, then uncertificated, had developed a large volume of traffic; (3) the competition of unsubsidized freight carriers should stimulate the quality and volume of air-freight business; (4) such new service would serve as an interesting "yardstick" for the Board; and (5) the evidence indicated that the needs of national defense for a rapidly growing fleet of commercial cargo airplanes would be served.

BOARD POLICY: FOREIGN CARRIERS

As has already been noted, the authority of the Board over foreign routes of American Flag carriers is circumscribed by the power of the President to approve or deny any route authorization or modification. As a result, it is difficult to discern Board policy as against presidential policy in this field. However, the Board has passed upon several important cases involving foreign operations of American-owned air carriers, and some observations may be made in connection with these. It should be noted that these principles apply to American Flag carriers. Air carriers operating from foreign countries are required to have permits. The issuance of these is largely a formality for the Board, since the selection of the routes is a matter handled by bilateral agreement between the countries concerned.

In one of the earliest cases decided by the Board, it was held that the policy of competition of the act of 1938 extended to international operations and that the competitive spur of foreign-owned carriers could not replace that of two or more American carriers in the same field.[18] Thus, as early as 1940, the Board repudiated a "chosen instrument" policy in international air transportation. Despite the strong opposition of Pan American Airways and a bitter fight which reached into the halls of Congress, the Board held to this policy in 1945. In the North Atlantic Route Case of that year, the Board granted certificates to Trans World Airlines and American Export Airlines, as well as to Pan American, for services to Europe, North Africa, and Asia.[19] This policy has been fol-

[18] *American Export Air Trans-Atlantic Service*, 2 C.A.B. 16 (1940).
[19] 6 C.A.B. 319 (1945).

lowed with additional route authorizations to other parts of the world, so that Pan American, which had pioneered a wide network of foreign routes, now has competition of other American operators over most of its routes.

The significance of the policy of competition in international service may be seen from the rapid growth of route mileage. In 1941, there were 61,000 route miles in operation, and by 1950, American Flag carriers operated over 210,000 miles of certificated routes.[20] While it has been the policy of the Board to support competition between carriers, many of the new routes certificated are not directly competitive with other routes. Thus, Pan American serves the Orient through Honolulu and through Europe and Asia, United operates only to Honolulu, and Northwest serves the Orient through Alaska and Japan. Braniff serves South America over somewhat different routes from those of Pan American or Panagra, although all serve some common points. The same situation exists to some extent in Europe and Asia in the competition of Pan American and Trans World. The Board has increased materially the common points served; in 1950 both carriers were given rights to serve such important points as London, Paris, Frankfurt, and Rome.[21]

In respects other than the policy of competition, which has been especially significant in the certification of carriers in foreign transportation, the Board's considerations have been similar to those involved in all new-route and route-extension cases. The Board bases its recommendations to the President on such other matters as traffic potential, costs of the service, the dangers of traffic diversion, and the ability of the applying carrier to fulfill the obligations to serve. Of course, in taking into account the public interest in the route, the Board and the President are likely to be more concerned with the national policy considerations than with the economic. For example, the route of Pan American to South Africa is barely justifiable on economic grounds but is believed to be justified amply by the national policy aspects involved.

BOARD POLICY: LOCAL-SERVICE CARRIERS

One of the most interesting experiments in the development of a new service has been the case of the certification of the local-service, or feeder, lines. During World War II and immediately after, there developed in this country a strong and optimistic feeling that the air age had dawned and that the benefits of air-carrier service should be extended to the smaller communities. The support of local business interests for such a service was vigorously pressed on Congress and the Board, and those who opposed such extension were often accused of protecting the "monopoly"

[20] CAB, *Annual Report, 1950*, p. 23.

[21] *North Atlantic Route Transfer Case*, CAB Docket No. 3589, Serial No. E-4410 (July 11, 1950).

of the trunk-line carriers. Proponents often placed the need for such service on the same grounds as the costly, although widely accepted, rural free delivery of mail. Others felt that air service to small communities would pay in the course of time.

Analysis of the economics of feeder-line routes did not promise well for such a service. Investigation made by the staff of the Civil Aeronautics Board and incorporated into an examiners' report (which still recommended certification of feeder lines) disclosed that (1) passenger traffic prospects are "not reassuring"; (2) the Post Office Department found the trunk-line network "sufficient to meet the . . . requirements of the Postal Service"; and (3) little financial help could be expected from cargo.[22]

It is true that, in addition to most of the certificated trunk lines, there were by the end of 1943 more than 200 applicants for feeder-line routes.[23] There can be no doubt that most of the applications of the trunk lines for feeder stops were dominated by the fear that, if new local-service carriers were certificated, these carriers might later develop into trunk-line competition. Other applicants believed that the service could be made profitable without subsidy, and others felt that the business would be made profitable by ample mail pay.

Despite the rather dismal outlook for economic success, the Board approved a large volume of feeder-line service between 1946 and 1949. By 1950, the local-service airlines had a route mileage exceeding 31,000 miles, and a large number of smaller cities had been added to the routes of the trunk-line carriers.[24] The Board's reasons for embarking upon such a program in the face of discouraging economic facts, while questionable, are understandable. Yielding to the pressure for spreading the advantages of air transportation to smaller communities and to the optimistic forecasts of traffic volume, the Board also saw in the local-service extensions a chance to experiment with air transportation.

In order to keep this program on an experimental basis, the Board limited the certificates to short periods, usually three years, and placed the bulk of the feeder-line operations in the hands of new carriers. On the latter action, the Board was impressed that this was a new kind of service gauged to the needs of small communities and that it would be helped by the managerial ingenuity of the independent local operator.[25]

After considerable experience with the feeder-line experiment, some tentative conclusions can be drawn, and most of them are not favorable

[22] *Investigation of Local Feeder and Pick-up Air Service*, Report of Examiners in CAB Docket No. 857 (1944).

[23] *Ibid.*

[24] *Air Transport Facts and Figures*, 1950, p. 6.

[25] *Rocky Mountain States Air Service*, 6 C.A.B. 695 (1946).

to this type of service. It is true that many communities without air service have received this service and that some of the service has been of a high order. It is also true that some of the local-service airlines have brought into the industry innovations such as efficient ground handling of passengers and cargo. But the industry is still dependent upon large mail payments, and even the most successful of the carriers could not exist without subsidies. Moreover, the feeder lines themselves, finding the serving of many small light-traffic stations to be economically burdensome have increasingly applied for abandonment of service to these stations; in doing so, they tend to approach the trunk airline route structure, against which it was not the intention of the Board to have them compete. Furthermore, the Board, again inconsistently with the original concept of the lines as carriers in a local area, has permitted mergers tending in some cases toward the development of systems which take on the appearance of trunk airlines.

In spite of the questionable success of a large part of the local-service routes, the Board has shown little disposition to abandon the experiment. Most of the certificates have recently been up for renewal, and with a few exceptions renewals for varying periods of time have been made. Where a carrier has actually instituted service and has made an effort to develop an efficient operation, the Board has been disposed to continue the certificate, although in most instances some modification of the routes has been made.

Abandonment of Service

In the early common law, there was apparently no obligation of a common carrier to continue service. So long as he professed to serve, he was under obligation to serve adequately, but he might withdraw from the service completely. With the granting of corporate charters and powers of eminent domain to railroads, however, the right of any business affected with the public interest to abandon service became restricted. For example, in a Connecticut case in 1885, the court held that the sovereign powers conferred on a railroad corporation by the state were granted upon the theory that they were to be used to promote the public welfare, and that when a corporation had exercised these powers it had no right to abandon the enterprise against the will of the state.[26]

The free right of railroads to abandon their property was admittedly restricted before the Transportation Act of 1920, although the Supreme Court has held that where the company was compelled to continue operating at a loss, it was deprived of its property without due process of law.[27] Abandonment of railroad property was largely a matter of state-

[26] *Gates v. Boston and N. Y. Air Line*, 53 Conn. 333 (1885).

[27] *Brooks Scanlon Co. v. Railroad Com. of Louisiana*, 251 U.S. 396 (1920).

commission jurisdiction and railroad-charter provision before 1920, at which time the Interstate Commerce Commission was given authority over abandonments in interstate commerce.

The problem of abandonment has been predominantly one applicable to the railroad industry. In the first place, this is a large industry with extensive fixed investment of interest to local taxing authorities. Secondly, the long organization of its employees into a few national unions has given the employees a more effective voice in abandonment policy and practice. A third factor, of course, is the tremendous economic importance of the railroad industries to the economy of localities. As a matter of fact, one finds no legislative provision on abandonment of water carriers or motor carriers, these carriers apparently having authority completely to abandon an operation at will. The Civil Aeronautics Board has authority, however, over abandonment of airline service, although the problem has had little significance in the regulation of the airlines.

LEGISLATION CONCERNING ABANDONMENT

The Transportation Act of 1920 forbids the abandonment of "all or any portion of a line of railroad, or the operation thereof, unless and until there shall first have been obtained from the commission a certificate that the present or future public convenience and necessity permit of such abandonment." The law specifically excepts industrial, spur, team, or switching tracks located within one state, as well as street, suburban, and interurban electric railways not operated as a part of the general system of any carrier subject to the act. As in the case of new construction, the Commission may attach such conditions as it desires, and the railroad may abandon without securing the approval of any other agency.

The provisions regarding railroads, it should be noted, apply to partial, as well as complete, abandonment. While the Interstate Commerce Commission has no authority over the abandonment of motor-carrier or water-carrier operations, it could doubtless proceed against a carrier which abandoned its routes partially on the grounds of inadequate service.

The Civil Aeronautics Act gives the Civil Aeronautics Board complete authority over the abandonment of any route, or portion of a route, for which a certificate has been issued. The act of 1938 provides that the Board may grant a petition for abandonment if it is found to be in the public interest.

RELATION OF STATE AND FEDERAL AUTHORITY

Some difficulty has arisen over the question as to when federal authority is controlling in railroad abandonments. Most such abandonments remove lucrative taxable property from the rolls of state subdivisions, and in many cases they cause relative hardship to small-business groups. As a consequence, political pressure has been brought to bear on state authorities to block the abandonment.

After some litigation, the Supreme Court has laid down some general principles on the controversy respecting federal and state powers in an abandonment proceeding. Even though intrastate trackage is involved, the Interstate Commerce Commission may authorize abandonment if continued operation would burden interstate commerce. In a leading case,[28] the Supreme Court upheld an order of the Commission allowing abandonment of intrastate operation of a branch line where, in the Commission's judgment, continued operation would affect the ability of the carrier to carry on its interstate business. The Supreme Court pointed out that it was unnecessary for the Commission to prove that the operation of the branch line would impair the ability of the carrier to earn a just compensation. The sole test made in the statute was public convenience and necessity, and so long as the Commission found adequate evidence to support its order, its judgment respecting the applicability of this test was controlling.

ADMINISTRATION OF ABANDONMENT POLICY

Virtually all the commission administration of transportation abandonments is limited to abandonment of railroad line under the Interstate Commerce Commission. Some proceedings for abandonment of airline stops have been handled by the Civil Aeronautics Board, but these are normally made a part of a route-modification case or are handled in a rather routine fashion as temporary or permanent suspensions of service. However, with the overcertification of airline routes and with traffic demands for smaller points not materializing, it is expected that airline abandonment proceedings will assume increasing importance in the future.

From 1920 to the end of 1954, the Interstate Commerce Commission approved the abandonment of 39,344 miles of railroad.[29] In practically every case abandonment came as the result of operating losses on the lines, these usually being due to exhaustion of natural resources in the area which the line was built to serve, highway competition, excessive railroad competition, and other factors causing a decline of traffic. Most abandonments have been branch lines, tap lines, or other short lines which were a part of a single interstate carrier's system.

In allowing abandonments, the Commission attempts to balance carrier and community interests. Where abandonment will not seriously inconvenience the public, the request of the railroad will be approved almost invariably. On the whole, the Commission allows abandonment where

[28] *Colorado v. United States*, 271 U.S. 153 (1926).

[29] ICC, *67th Annual Report, 1953*, p. 183, and ICC, *68th Annual Report, 1954*, p. 168.

operation of a branch line will seriously affect the earnings of the carrier system. But losses on a part of a carrier's line are not adequate basis for allowing abandonment if the railroad serves a definite public need. Even in these cases, the Commission has indicated that there is a point beyond which unprofitable operation cannot go, regardless of the prosperity of the carrier system. Where reasonably adequate substitute services are available, or where the losses incurred are clear evidence of the lack of great public need for the line, the Commission usually allows abandonment. But where there seems to be a possibility that the continuance of service will bring improvement, either from special attempts to increase traffic or from the institution of economies, the Commission ordinarily rejects the application, at least for a trial period.

Adequacy of Service

Under the common law a common carrier was required to furnish reasonably adequate service in the sense of convenient accommodations, safe facilities, and continuous and nondiscriminatory service. The duty to serve adequately was thus not an absolute one but rather one to serve "reasonably." Thus, the Supreme Court has held that the right of a shipper to obtain adequate service "is not an absolute right and the carrier is not liable if its failure to furnish cars was the result of sudden and great demands and which it could not reasonably have been expected to meet in full." [30]

LEGISLATIVE BASIS FOR ADEQUACY OF SERVICE

In the case of most of the carriers, statutes are somewhat general in their definition of power to require adequate service. Motor carriers and water carriers have imposed on them little more than the common-law obligations for adequate service, and the main legislative provision applicable to the airlines is the requirement that they furnish service adequate for the carriage of mail.

In the case of the railroads, however, the service regulations covered by the statutes are more complete and definite than with the other forms. Not only does the Interstate Commerce Commission have the power to require extension of new line and track, but it also has been given specific power to establish reasonable rules with respect to car service. Because car service is interpreted to mean "use, control, supply, movement, distribution, exchange, interchange, and return of locomotive cars, and other vehicles used in the transportation of property" [31] it is clear that

[30] *Pennsylvania R.R. Co. v. Puritan Coal Co.*, 237 U.S. 121, 123 (1915).
[31] Interstate Commerce Act, part I, sec. 1 (10).

this provision gives the Commission power to deal with most of the problems concerning the adequacy of railroad service, at least so far as it applies to the freight service.

In case of emergency in which the Interstate Commerce Commission believes immediate action to be necessary, the law grants it authority to suspend existing car-service rules and to issue new ones without regard to ownership rights of carriers, so long as the rules are designed to "promote the service in the interest of the public and the convenience of the people." These emergency powers are extensive. They, in effect, give the Commission the authority to manage the railroads and to subordinate carrier rights to public interest.

ADMINISTRATIVE CONTROL FOR ADEQUATE SERVICE

Despite a lack of definiteness over the quantity and quality of service in the Civil Aeronautics Act of 1938, the Civil Aeronautics Board has, perhaps with one exception to be noted presently, exerted more peacetime control over air service than the Interstate Commerce Commission has over the service of the carriers under its jurisdiction. The exceptional case is the close supervision of the Commission over railroad car service in periods of emergencies, especially since World War II.

The Civil Aeronautics Board has, however, exerted almost managerial control over airline service. There have been cases in which the Board has said that the minimum service to a point on a route is two stops in each direction.[32] Through its control over mail pay, the Board has practically controlled the scheduling policies of many carriers by expressing, sometimes prior to a mail-pay case, the opinion that costs of certain schedules cannot be included in mail pay.[33]

Normally, in exercising its control over the adequacy of service, the Interstate Commerce Commission has cooperated with the railroads. The latter have generally been allowed to take the initiative in instituting changes in car-service rules and in asking for joint use of facilities. Competition has been an effective stimulus for giving adequate service.

[32] For example, in the *Texas-Oklahoma Case*, 7 C.A.B. 481 (1946), at 529, the Board said: ". . . experience has demonstrated in ordinary circumstances that less than a minimum of two daily round trips serving all points on a route does not constitute service adequate to meet the needs of commerce and the postal service, and we deem it desirable that the routes herein authorized be provided with at least that quantum of service."

[33] This has been a usual consideration in mail-rate cases. Note that in *Capital Airlines, Inc., Mail Rates*, 10 C.A.B. 705 (1949), at 711, the Board said: "These facts support the conclusion that Capital operated schedules in excess of those reasonably required for the commerce, the postal service, and the national defense." Of course, in a subsidized situation, where the government is underwriting a service, the Board would be derelict if it did not disallow practices believed to be uneconomical.

DIRECT CONTROL OF SERVICE IN EMERGENCIES

Until World War II, the power of the Commission to assume direct control over railroad car service was rather sparingly used. When the effective movement of freight was impaired by strikes in 1920 and 1922, the Commission exercised its emergency powers on a country-wide basis. Orders were issued for roads to expedite movement of traffic over the fastest routes, regardless of instructions of shippers or carriers, or ownership of cars. Preferential shipment of certain commodities to consignees most in need was directed. In effect the Commission assumed managerial control over service. These powers have also been assumed in restricted areas where strikes, floods, or other conditions have threatened to impair the efficient movement of traffic.

The lack of use of this emergency power is partly due to action taken by the industry itself. The railroads operating as an industry have established rules designed to bring about an effective utilization of cars. During periods of emergency, the Car Service Division of the Association of American Railroads, which administers these rules for the railroads, has authority to permit or require departure from the rules. While the rules and their administration are established under a voluntary agreement, so successful has this program been that the Interstate Commerce Commission has normally supported the Car Service Division with service orders when necessary. Also during the emergency of World War II, both the Commission and the Office of Defense Transportation entrusted much of the control of car service to the Division.

In addition to the important role of the Association of American Railroads in administering controls over railroad service, both the Commission and the Office of Defense Transportation, an emergency agency established to coordinate all aspects of transportation, exercised emergency controls over the railroad business. Most emergency measures taken both during the war and in the postwar defense period have aimed at accomplishing objectives through cooperation. But extensive orders were issued, particularly during World War II, requiring prompt loading and unloading of cars, the pooling of freight and passenger equipment, higher minimum carloads, elimination of crosshauling, discontinuance of poorly utilized trains, and other measures looking toward the more effective utilization of transport facilities.

Safety of Service

The federal government has armed the Interstate Commerce Commission, the Department of Commerce, the Civil Aeronautics Board, and the Civil Aeronautics Administration with wide control over safety requirements, but where Congress has not acted, the states under their police power have authority to pass laws reasonably designed to promote safety. The states are still an important factor in safety regulations applicable to railroads and motor carriers. As for the former, they have passed laws regulating the minimum number of crew members on a railroad train, a few have attempted to limit the length of trains, and the protection of grade crossings is still largely a matter of state control. In the motor-carrier industry states exercise safety controls affecting speed, weights of vehicles, length and width, lights, and many other matters. But as the safety regulations of the federal government have expanded, the state governments, as in many other controls, have had to give way.

EXTENSIVENESS OF AUTHORITY TO REQUIRE SAFETY

There is probably more thoroughness and equality of regulation in the case of controls for safety than in any other phase of transport regulation. All the modes of interstate transport are subject to extensive regulation in behalf of the safety of passengers and freight. Unlike regulation in many economic areas, safety controls in aviation apply to all types of carriers—common, contract, and private.

As might be expected, most safety regulations have applied to equipment, operational techniques, and the hours of service of operating employees. In addition, through its inspection activities and its thorough investigation of accidents, the government has had a control in behalf of safety which extends beyond the regulations found in the statutes. Indeed, in some cases, the administration of safety regulation has been more important than the statutory bases of control. In administering certain safety regulations, such as the requirements for safe aircraft performance, the government has often substituted its judgment for that of an informed industry and has often materially affected the economics of the transportation business, sometimes without making any real contribution to safety.

During the first years of operation of the Motor Carrier Act, the Interstate Commerce Commission was forced to prescribe regulations without complete study. But through investigation of accidents and research, as well as the cooperation of motor-vehicle associations and state officials, the regulations have been continually improved. After fifteen years of operation of the Act, the Commission has been able to bring a surprisingly uniform set of reasonable safety regulations to the motor carriers of the country. In this complex industry with its thousands of operators, such a contribution is considerable. One of the most encouraging aspects of this program has been the tendency of the states to remold their laws to fit federal requirements. If similar action could be taken in the field of weight limits, truck-and-trailer lengths, and similar safety-related items of tremendous economic importance, many of the barriers to efficient interstate movement of motor traffic might be removed.

SPECIAL SAFETY REGULATIONS FOR AIR CARRIERS

As might be expected in this young and somewhat hazardous [34] industry, the role of government in safety regulation has been more extensive in the case of the airlines than in any other industry. Government safety regulations prescribe many of the operating procedures, the qualifications of operating employees, the design of equipment, the use of many ground facilities, and many other features of the air-transportation business. Indeed, the attention paid by management to problems of safety and the detailed regulation for safety undertaken by the government probably determine the economics of the air-transportation business more than any single factor other than the routes a carrier is allowed to serve.

The administration of the regulation of airline safety is somewhat confused and unusual. The Civil Aeronautics Board has the functions of establishing regulations on safety matters and of investigating accidents. The Civil Aeronautics Administration is responsible for administering the safety regulations and for undertaking research in the field of safety. This interesting case of dual responsibility necessarily causes serious problems of coordination. In the first place, the Board must rely upon the Administration for the information necessary to make and change safety regulations. In the second place, the Administration must interpret and administer rules for which it has had little responsibility in making. As a matter of fact, there is more coordination between the two agencies than might be expected, and in addition the rules made by the Board are often general, or it delegates certain authority, so that many detailed rules of safety regulation are actually made by the agency which administers them.[35] At the same time, this dual responsibility makes fundamental changes of rules difficult, and the safety regulations of the airlines are replete with obsolete safety requirements which place a heavy burden on the airlines.

There is hardly a detail of aircraft design, operation of commercial aircraft in airline service, or their maintenance which is not subject to some rule or regulation of the federal government. Much of this detailed control may be necessary. But as the airline business matures and as aircraft design becomes more perfected, it seems entirely appropriate for the

[34] Although, according to safety statistics, not nearly as hazardous as the nation's most popular form of transportation, the passenger automobile. For example, in 1953, the domestic airlines had a fatality rate of 0 6 per 100 million passenger miles, while the rate on passenger automobiles and taxicabs was 2.9. The rate on the railroads was, however 0.16 that year. See *Air Transport Facts and Figures*, 1955, p. 18.

[35] For a good discussion of these relationships, see E. C. Sweeney, "Safety Regulations and Accident Investigation: Jurisdictional Conflicts of CAB and CAA," 17 *Journal of Air Law and Commerce* 141–150, 269–282 (Spring, Summer, 1950).

government to relax some of its controls. There is some reason to believe that even a well-manned government agency is less qualified to meet the many problems encountered by airline operation than the management and personnel of the airlines. Perhaps the trend of recent years from general rules to detailed and specific rules should be reversed. But in this field of control, as in so many others in which the government has imposed regulations, the one-way trend of regulation to dig more deeply into the field of private management is a most difficult one to change. Rules tend to beget additional rules in order to patch deficiencies and interpret uncertainties; seldom does the reverse occur.

Selected References

Bigham, T. C., and M. J. Roberts, *Transportation*, chap. 18. New York: McGraw-Hill Book Company, Inc., 1952.

Daggett, Stuart, *Principles of Inland Transportation*, 3d ed., chaps. 12–13. New York: Harper & Brothers, 1941.

Dearing, C. L., and W. Owen, *National Transportation Policy*, chap. 10. Washington, D.C.: Brookings Institution, 1949.

Frederick, J. H., *Commercial Air Transportation*, 4th ed., chaps. 6, 7, 10, 11. Homewood, Ill.: Richard D. Irwin, Inc., 1955.

Locklin, D. P., *Economics of Transportation*, 4th ed., chaps. 26, 32, 34, 36. Homewood, Ill.: Richard D. Irwin, Inc., 1952.

McDowell, C. E., and H. M. Gibbs, *Ocean Transportation*, chaps. 17, 20–22. New York: McGraw-Hill Book Company, Inc., 1954.

Troxel, Emery, *Economics of Transport*, chap. 17. New York: Rinehart & Company, Inc., 1955.

Westmeyer, R. E., *Economics of Transportation*, chaps. 16, 19–20, 24, 28. New York: Prentice-Hall, Inc., 1952.

Wilson, G. L., and L. A. Bryan, *Air Transportation*, chaps. 9, 10–11, 21, 23. New York: Prentice-Hall, Inc., 1949.

7

REGULATION OF TRANSPORT LABOR, FINANCE, AND COMBINATION

As might be expected, the principal emphasis of transport regulation has been in the areas of rates and service. However, partly to make the regulation of these areas effective and partly to effectuate policy desired by organized groups, such as transport labor, extensive regulations have been applied in the fields of labor, finance, and combinations. In some respects, these controls are similar to those now applied to business generally, and the main discussion of these points is reserved for later chapters. However, certain of the governmental restrictions applicable to transportation are more stringent than those imposed on businesses generally, and most of them were applied to transportation, the railroad industry particularly, in advance of their being placed on other businesses.

To some extent, then, the transportation industry and the railroads in particular have been used as a kind of proving ground for federal government business regulation. This is especially apparent in the field of railroad labor, where a special set of regulations has been established, usually in advance of controls extending to industry generally, covering the settlement of disputes, the limitation of hours, unemployment benefits, accident and sickness benefits, retirement pay, and protection from loss of jobs due to business merger or abandonment. Moreover, the thorough control over security issuance and the administrative supervision over combinations to justify their removal from the antitrust laws appear to be programs which may well influence the course of future federal legislative policy.

Government Policy and Transport Labor

As was pointed out in Chapter 4, in which the evolution of transport regulation was sketched, the series of laws dealing with railroad and airline labor provided for machinery for (1) the *making* of labor agreements, and (2) the *interpretation* of these agreements. In the making of agreements it will be recalled that the law provides for mediation, for voluntary arbitration, and for the establishment of fact-finding boards if all other methods of intervention fail and if a work stoppage threatens to impair the flow of interstate commerce. In the case of the interpretation of agreements, the law provides for the establishment of a National Railroad Adjustment Board with power to interpret these agreements and to make awards to employees who have been harmed by any misinterpretation by the carriers. While the National Mediation Board has the power to establish a National Air Transport Adjustment Board, it has not done so. Consequently a governmentally constituted board to interpret union-management agreements exists only in the case of the railroad industry. The provisions respecting the making of agreements apply, however, to the airlines as well as the railroads.

In addition to these basic provisions of the law in the handling of labor disputes, during the years of World War II and in recent years the government used another technique. Falling back on the powers granted by the Army Appropriations Act of 1916, the President, from time to time, has taken temporary possession of the railroads subject to strike and, through his authority to enjoin strikes against the government, has exerted a strong power to halt strikes and force the settlement of disputes. The railroads and airlines are not subject to the Labor-Management Relations Act of 1947 (the Taft-Hartley Act), although much that is in this law has been patterned after the experience with the railroads.[1] Moreover, railroad employees are not subject to the national social-security program, but have had special unemployment-insurance and old-age-benefit programs provided for them by the law. Nor do the differences between treatment of railroad labor and other labor stop here. As will be noted presently, railroad labor has been given special protection against loss of jobs or pay through combination of railroads or abandonment of services.

THE EFFECTIVENESS OF FACT-FINDING BOARDS

The creation of emergency boards to investigate disputes failing of mediation or arbitration and to make recommendations was authorized by the Railway Labor Act of 1926 and is an important feature of railroad and airline labor control today. Between 1926 and 1940, six major disputes went to a fact-finding board, and in all these cases no strike resulted. With this exceptional record, the railway labor laws came to be regarded as "model" legislation. But the interesting fact is that in these cases all the findings were favorable to railroad labor, and carrier management, unwilling to assume responsibility for a major strike, accepted them.

Beginning in 1941, however, the fact-finding procedure has proved to be largely ineffective. Since that time almost every report of a fact-finding board established for a major dispute has been found to be unacceptable to carrier labor, and the union organizations concerned have continued

[1] See below, Chapter 22.

with their strike plans. While many of these findings granted a portion of the increases requested by unions, one can draw no other conclusion from recent years than that this procedure failed to meet the test as a formula for settling labor disputes.

Most of this failure can be traced to the permissive nature of the law and the inadequate force of public opinion, although most failures have occurred during periods of national emergency when the force of public opinion should be at its strongest. Some of the failure can likewise be attributed to the fact that the President has not fully supported the findings of the boards. In the first major dispute in which employees rejected the opinion of a fact-finding board, that involving the nonoperating railroad organizations in 1941, the President, instead of supporting the board, asked that it be reconvened and virtually dictated a higher award which the unions accepted. Having found that appeal to the President against findings believed to be inadequate proved to be successful, the unions have naturally continued in this course.

However, in recent years, the White House has been less willing to override the boards and, in important cases, has stopped the strike by taking over the companies in the name of the government. In other cases, the President has shown a disposition to let the strike take its course and thereby force the parties to reach an agreement themselves.

The failure of the dispute-settling machinery of the railroad and airline businesses is also highlighted by the tendency in the past few years for disputes arising out of grievances and the interpretation of agreements to go to fact-finding boards rather than through the established adjustment channels. This tendency of the carriers and the unions to allow grievances to go to the strike stage when adequate machinery is provided for their settlement is especially disruptive. As one of the fact-finding boards has said: [2]

> It seems inconceivable to us that a coercive strike should occur on one of the nation's major transportation systems, with all of the losses and hardships that would follow, in view of the fact that the Railway Labor Act provides an orderly, efficient and complete remedy for the fair and just settlement of the matters in dispute. Grievances of the character here under discussion are so numerous and of such frequent occurrence on all railroads that the general adoption of the policy pursued by the organizations in this case would soon result in the complete nullification of the Railway Labor Act.

The failure of the Railway Labor Act to settle major disputes and the essential relation of the transportation business to the nation's economy have led to many proposals for overhaul of the law. Despite the exten-

[2] *Report to the President by the Emergency Board* (in the case of the operating organizations against the Missouri Pacific Railroad Company), August, 1949, quoted in NMB, *16th Annual Report, 1950*, p. 25.

sion of compulsion involved and the loss of freedom implied, the only proposal which offers a solution for the problem of interruption of a vital industry appears to be some kind of compulsory arbitration. This could be done by providing that the findings of the presidential fact-finding boards shall be binding on both parties. To do so would be to limit the compulsory features to those cases which cannot be settled by any other means and which have a material bearing on the economy of the nation. Since interruptions of such consequence cannot be permitted anyway and the government must resort to such subterfuges as taking over control of the carriers involved, this proposal makes reasonable sense despite the long tradition of freedom in labor-relations matters.

NATIONAL RAILROAD ADJUSTMENT BOARD

Although the decisions of the National Railroad Adjustment Board have not been spectacular, they have been extremely important when taken as a whole. Most of the decisions arise as the result of minor disputes, since they have to do with the interpretation and application of agreements and working rules. The cases often result in outright awards of cash to aggrieved employees who feel that they have not been receiving adequate wage allowance for particular work done.

Occasionally cases settled by the Adjustment Board involve large sums of money and result in decisions materially affecting railroad costs. One of the most sensational cases which resulted from interpretation of an operating rule was that of the Lehigh Valley awards made in 1937. Because an operating rule was interpreted to mean that a day's run ended when a train reached the terminal, over $241,000 was awarded to fifty Lehigh Valley trainmen and engineers to give a full day's pay for the short trip from the Pennsylvania Station in New York to the yards in Long Island, a distance of about four miles.

It is difficult to appraise the work of the National Adjustment Board. Thousands of cases of minor character have been handled, and perhaps much has been done to make smoother the course of railroad labor relations. But most of the cases are brought at the instigation of labor unions who want to "get something" for their members. Only those cases where labor may gain by favorable interpretation of the rules seem to be brought to the Board. As a result, the decisions have perhaps been on the whole favorable to labor. Moreover, the curious administrative provision, amply supported by the courts,[3] that only labor can appeal to the courts to force carrier performance of awards of the Board, has tended to favor labor. This denial of appeal by the carriers, plus the fact that unions tend to overcome the disadvantages of unfavorable decisions by threatening

[3] *Slocum v. Delaware L. & W. R.R. Co.*, 339 U.S. 239 (1950), and *Order of Rwy. Conductors v. Southern Rwy. Co.*, 339 U.S. 250 (1950).

strikes, have naturally been the source of violent criticism from the railroad industry.

UNEMPLOYMENT FROM RAILROAD COMBINATION

Strictly speaking, until the passage of the Transportation Act of 1940, the federal government had no law requiring compensation to railroad workers displaced by combination. But in the Transportation Act of 1933 creating the temporary office of Federal Coordinator of Transportation, that official was directed not to order coordinations which would cause displacement of railroad workers. When the office of Coordinator was allowed to lapse in 1936, the railway executives did draw up a "voluntary" dismissal-compensation agreement, rather than risk the almost certain passage of a more rigorous law by Congress.

Under this agreement, employees affected by coordination or consolidation were to be given ninety days' notice of their dismissal. Depending upon his previous service, a displaced employee was to be given 60 per cent of his usual rate of pay for periods of six to sixty months, or to accept a lump-sum settlement of three to twelve months' full salary.

At the same time, and before any specific statutory authority was made available, the Interstate Commerce Commission inserted similar requirements in certain of its orders. Under its power to approve combinations found to be "in the public interest," the Commission insisted that railroad labor displaced by a combination be cared for if the public interest was to be satisfied.

These policies were written into the Interstate Commerce Act by the Transportation Act of 1940. By this legislation the Commission was directed not only to take into account the interests of railroad employees affected by combination, but also to require a fair and equitable arrangement to protect these interests. Moreover, the law required that the Commission make sure that, during four years from the effective date of an order, a combination will not result in the employees of a railroad concerned being in a worse position than before with respect to employment. The only exception allowed was for employees whose service with the railroad has been less than four years, in which case the protection of the law extends only for a period in the future equal to the employees' length of service.

Although this labor provision causes an important impediment to combination of railroads and seems unnecessary in view of the voluntary dismissal-compensation agreement and the power of the Commission to condition approval of combinations on the public interest (as it sees this), the special statutory provision is perhaps even more interesting as an example of congressional intent to protect workers of one industry from unemployment. It also indicates the strength of the railroad-labor lobbies in

Washington as early as the 1930s, and gives an idea as to what can be done with respect to other industries in case unemployment becomes a serious threat again.

As yet, however, no statutory limitation to unemployment is found in any other business. Even the state and federal governments reserve the right to cause unemployment when, in the pursuance of administrative reorganization of governmental agencies, efficiency may be obtained.

One may question such a restriction upon employment from several points of view. Regardless of the social justice in such an arrangement, it can hardly be upheld as sound regulatory policy. Care of workers displaced by progress would seem to be a cost that society as a whole ought to bear. Not only do the special limitations on railroad combination saddle one privately owned industry with a social cost not similarly borne by other industries, but they tend to retard combinations that might otherwise economically be made.

Moreover, question might be raised from the point of view of the employees themselves. By impeding efficiency which could be obtained from combination, workers may actually be increasing costs and diminishing the possibility of the railroad industry's maintaining or enlarging employment. The law does not prohibit the laying off of employees owing to a decline in business or inability to meet payrolls, nor does it protect against them other than through unemployment insurance. Such layoffs may be the indirect result of wastes which could be removed by combination.

UNEMPLOYMENT FROM ABANDONMENT

Although the special statutory provision regarding displaced railroad personnel applies only in the case of combinations, the Interstate Commerce Commission has in some cases extended this protection where abandonment was involved. As with combinations, the Commission is empowered to give its approval only when it finds the abandonment to be in the public interest. Until 1942, the Commission had held that it had no power to impose conditions for the protection of employees adversely affected by abandonment. But in a case which involved the abandonment of some lines and the substitution of motor service, the courts held that the Commission did have authority to consider employee interests in abandonment proceedings.[4]

[4] In *Railway Labor Executives' Assn. v. United States*, 38 F. Supp. 818 (1941), a federal district court held (at p. 824) that, if "abandonment like consolidation tends to increase the earnings of the corporate applicant, . . . it is difficult to recognize any distinction between such a case and one of consolidation. . . ." The Supreme Court upheld the district court in *ICC v. Railway Labor Executives' Assn.*, 315 U.S. 373 (1942), stating that the Commission had authority to impose conditions for the protection of persons displaced by railroad abandonments, to the extent and in those cases which the Commission felt the public interest demanded.

Following the determination by the courts that the Commission had such authority, it has adopted a policy of imposing conditions to protect displaced personnel as the result of partial abandonment. As the Commission has explained, it does not impose any such conditions in the case of abandonment of an entire line or system. But in the case particularly of branch lines, in which it has appeared that employees would be adversely affected, the Commission has followed the practice of prescribing conditions similar to those utilized in combination cases.[5]

SPECIAL RAILROAD UNEMPLOYMENT-INSURANCE AND RETIREMENT BENEFITS

Although the analysis of government programs of social security applicable to industry generally will be discussed later,[6] it is worth noting at this point that special unemployment-insurance and retirement-benefit programs have been established for railroad employees. While there are some valid reasons for these programs, particularly since regular unemployment insurance has been handled by the states and many railroad workers operate in more than one state, the principal reason for these special programs was the strong political position of railroad unions in Washington during the 1930s. Additionally, so far as retirement benefits are concerned, many railroads had pension plans in existence at the time social-insurance legislation was passed for industry generally, and railroad employees naturally feared that federal government entry into the field might weaken their established position.

The railroad retirement plan originally provided for pensions and taxes considerably above those established for other industry by the Social Security Act. While increases made in recent years in the general social-security program have tended to close this gap, the benefits payable to railroad employees have been considerably above those paid to workers in other industries. It should be recognized, however, that the railroad retirement program is more costly both to employers and employees. With total payroll taxes, split between employee and employer, in 1954 at 12½ per cent of annual earnings up to $3,600, the tax levied for railroad pensions was much higher than the 4 per cent being then levied for general social security.

PUBLIC POLICY AND TRANSPORT LABOR

In surveying the main points of impact of public policy on transport labor, one notes that this labor, particularly railroad labor, has obtained laws more favorable than those applying to other industries. In no other industry has the force of government been brought to play on programs

[5] For an explanation of the Commission's policy, see ICC, *60th Annual Report, 1946,* p. 63, and *Chicago B. & Q. R.R. Co. Abandonment,* 257 I.C.C. 700 (1945).

[6] See Chapter 21.

to increase efficiency through combinations and abandonments. In no other industry has pressure been brought to bear—at least, not as effectively—to place the burden for displacement of labor through progress directly upon the industry rather than upon society in general.

Railroad employees have also been provided with more benefits than other workers in the matter of retirement pay, although the cost to them and their employers has apparently been high enough to cover these benefits. But the serious problem is the inequity between industries in matters of taxes. It cannot be argued that the benefits are too high, especially with the rise in prices in the past decade. But to levy such high taxes on a single industry is hardly equitable government fiscal policy or sound competitive economics.

Favorable labor laws become particularly questionable when they involve make-work legislation, such as unreasonable full-crew laws, and when they encourage a system of adjudicating operating rules, such as that under the National Railroad Adjustment Board, which operates to burden an industry with inefficient practices. It is encouraging that these programs of the government have not extended much beyond the railroad industry. But there are signs of their development in other industry, where both labor and management hope to find a solution for their differences in government intervention.

What cannot be forgotten by labor, management, or the government is that the demand for labor by a single industry is not perfectly inelastic. Reducing efficiency is not a means of increasing employment or total wages. Through increasing sales of transport service, reducing costs per unit of output is the surest method of increasing employment and wages. To be sure, if a small group of transport workers protected from loss of jobs through seniority rules can keep wage rates inflexible and labor inefficient, this group may be able to gain for its members a larger portion of the national income than would otherwise be possible. Even for them, however, the highly elastic character of demand for the service of a particular transport agency may make their real interests lie in undertaking methods for the increase of efficiency of transport service.

In the area of labor disputes and work stoppages, what seems to be needed in a field so essential to the nation's economy is a labor law which recognizes that labor is as much dedicated to the public service as capital. Strikes which cripple transportation should be outlawed as being opposed to the public interest in uninterrupted interstate commerce. Major disputes should be settled by compulsory arbitration and handled by a completely nonpartisan board. While such a disputes board might be independent of the regulatory commissions responsible for economic controls, consistency would seem to require that this aspect of regulation, as well as the other features of labor regulation, should be placed under the same commission which handles other regulatory matters.

Control of Transport Finance

In discussing regulation of transport securities and finance, a distinction should be drawn between this particular field of government interference and the regulation of security issuance as undertaken by the state "blue-sky" commissions and the Federal Securities and Exchange Commission. In the public-service businesses, in which the transport industry may be classified, emphasis is primarily on soundly financed companies capable of efficient and continuous service. In the regulation of financial practices of other types of industries, the fundamental purpose is to safeguard the security-buying public. To be sure, transport and other public-utility investors are given some protection by financial regulation, for issuance of securities and other financial transactions are subject to the same safeguards as those applicable to business generally. But regulation in the quasi-public industries is also based upon public interest in rates and service.

PURPOSE OF FINANCIAL CONTROLS

One clear purpose of instituting controls over finance of publicly regulated companies, such as transportation enterprises, is to prevent overcapitalization and weak financial standing, which could interfere with the ability of a company to serve the public efficiently. Another is to make sure that costs and revenues are properly reflected in the books of the carriers as an aid to accurate rate regulation, the administration of subsidy policies, and the avoidance of financial instability in so essential an industry.

EXTENT OF SECURITY REGULATIONS

Because the principal purpose of security regulation in the public service industries is to prevent the saddling of properties with an unnecessary burden of fixed charges or dividend commitments, control over security issuance in these businesses encompasses Commission approval of private-company security issuance and often approval of the methods of sale, the price received, the amount of securities issued, the kind of securities, and the utilization of the proceeds of sale.

The desirability of federal regulation was recognized shortly after the Interstate Commerce Act was passed. The problems of financial abuses received the attention and condemnation of a congressional investigating committee as early as 1874, but belief that such control was within the proper province of the federal government did not become current until

1907.[7] Congress appointed a commission to study this question in 1910, but its report, rendered in 1911, opposed federal control and suggested instead more stringent state control.[8] State regulation not meeting this problem any better than in the past, general opinion continued to grow in favor of federal controls. The Interstate Commerce Commission repeated its recommendation in favor of security-issuance control each year from 1907 to 1919, and Congress finally imposed the control on railroads in 1920.

The control over transport security issues instituted by the Transportation Act of 1920 applies primarily to the railroads. Certain limited control exists over motor carriers, but no special control of security issuance applies to water carriers, pipelines, or air carriers.

With respect to railroads, the Interstate Commerce Act makes it unlawful for any such carrier to issue securities or assume obligations with respect to securities of other corporations unless by authorization of the Interstate Commerce Commission. The law covers the issuance of securities by a company itself, whether stocks, bonds, notes, or other evidence of ownership or indebtedness, as well as the assumption of guarantee under lease or contract of the securities of other companies. The only exception allowed is the issuance of short-term notes with maturities of not more than two years and totaling not more than 5 per cent of the par value of outstanding securities. The obvious purpose of allowing this exception is to permit railroads freedom from delay and formality in doing current and temporary business financing. With respect to the issuance of securities by common and contract motor carriers operating in interstate commerce, similar controls are provided, except that issues not exceeding $500,000 are exempt from regulation; this exception is clearly designed to exclude the many small companies in the field.

In approving the issuance of securities, the Commission is given wide discretion to attach conditions which are believed to be in the public interest. Even the statement of principles which the Commission is directed to follow in authorizing a proposed transaction is exceedingly broad. It must find the security issue or assumption of obligation to be for some lawful object, consistent with the proper performance of common-carrier service and compatible with the public interest, and reasonably necessary and appropriate for these purposes. By this grant of power the Commission not only may use wide discretion as to whether the securities may be

[7] In an investigation in 1907, the Interstate Commerce Commission declared that "the time has come when some reasonable regulation should be imposed upon the issuance of securities by railways engaged in interstate commerce." *Consolidations and Combinations of Carriers*, 12 I.C.C. 277, 306 (1907).

[8] *Report of Railroad Securities Commission*, H. Doc. 256, 62d Cong., 2d Sess. (1911).

issued or obligations assumed at all, but may also decide whether the particular proposal will reasonably meet the object for which it is designed. Furthermore, the law gives it authority to deny the petition in part, make modifications as a condition of approval, and make supplemental orders whenever new developments make such a move wise. Thus, with such discretionary powers, the Interstate Commerce Commission has ample grounds for fixing the amount, kind, and character of securities, the conditions of sale, and the application of proceeds from it.

PROBLEMS IN SECURITY CONTROL

With a power so broad, the Interstate Commerce Commission has naturally had to deal with a wide variety of financial problems. Although only a few of the leading problems can be mentioned here, it must be recognized that the positive control provided by the act of 1920 makes it possible for nearly every practice of railroad and large motor carrier finance to be brought under the regulation of the Commission.

As a general rule, the Interstate Commerce Commission has strictly limited the issuance of securities to investments made for transportation service. New expenditure for road and equipment, including betterments made on leased property which is virtually owned, working capital reasonably needed, and investments in affiliated carrier property, such as joint ownership of terminals, are all allowed as proper items for capitalization. But attempts to capitalize outlays properly belonging to operating expenses, stock or bond discount, and the cost of issuing and selling securities have been rejected.

The Commission has held to the principle that investments in noncarrier property or securities are not capitalizable, on the ground that they are not held for transportation service and do not necessarily represent a permanent part of railroad capital, since they may be liquidated and the cash be used for other purposes. Along the same line of reasoning, the Commission has disapproved capitalization of government bonds, special cash deposits, sinking funds, or other reserve funds. As it has declared, capitalizable assets are those "which have been provided and which are intended for continuing productive use in service of transportation." [9]

In granting authorizations for sale of stock, the Interstate Commerce Commission has generally disapproved of the practice of limiting voting power of classes of security holders. The policy of giving no voting power to holders of preferred stock and of some classes of common stock was not unusual in the 1920s, and was used as a method of extending

[9] *Securities of L. and N. R.R. Co.*, 76 I.C.C. 718, 720 (1923). In this case the Commission discussed the principles to which it has generally adhered in determining capitalizable assets.

control by groups with a minor portion of investment. The Commission has taken the position that disenfranchisement of stockholders leads to a concentration of control which is contrary to the public interest.

The Commission has approved of the issuance of stock dividends in most cases. But the contention of some railroads that this is an absolute legal right so long as a surplus exists has been denied. The Commission's policy has been to determine whether and to what extent a surplus exists and to allow only a portion of the surplus to be capitalized. As it has pointed out, "a substantial surplus should remain uncapitalized as a support for the applicant's credit, providing for emergency needs, offsetting obsolescence and necessary investments in non-revenue-producing property, and serving as a general financial balance-wheel." [10]

The reliance of the railroads on debt financing has been a long-standing policy. In 1910, 54.9 per cent of capitalization was represented by funded debt, and in 1930 it was 56.1 per cent. Even after the debt-paring effects of railroad reorganizations following the Great Depression and the high-earning period of the 1940s, the railroad funded debt stood at 49.6 per cent in 1953.[11] The reasons for this policy are many. They include the desire to protect common-stockholder control, the profitability in getting capital at low interest rates from a vast reservoir of banking, trust, and insurance-company funds, and the lack of market for stocks at many times during the development of the railroads. However, this policy has borne hard on the railroads, particularly during the years of low earnings before World War II. By forcing many carriers into bankruptcy, by harming railroad credit, and by endangering the very existence of railroad service in many localities, this financial policy is shown to be of real public concern.

The extent to which the Interstate Commerce Commission can be held responsible for the continuance of this debt-financing policy is difficult to say. The Commission has no apparent power to force the remaking of railroad capital structure, except in cases of bankruptcy, as will be noted presently. However, in its control over security issues it can exert a material influence on capitalization. Although the Commission has clearly favored the issuance of stock instead of bonds, there is little evidence that this position has had much effect. In the 1920s and in the latter 1940s and 1950s, when many industrial companies were able to keep their capital structures relatively free of long-term debt, the railroads have still continued to carry a high proportion of their capital structure in such debt. The Commission has been more successful, however, in forcing new rail

[10] *Stock of D., L. and W. R.R.*, 67 I.C.C. 426, 433 (1921).

[11] ICC, *43d Annual Report, 1929*, p. 120; ICC, *54th Annual Report, 1940*, p. 148; and ICC, *68th Annual Report, 1954*, p. 153.

bond issues to carry sinking-fund provisions so that, where practicable, these bonds may be gradually retired rather than be left to the uncertainties of refunding upon maturity. Moreover, in fairness to the Commission and to the railroads, the extraordinary favorable bond market, especially immediately after World War II, has made for low capital costs, and the Commission has been reluctant to force the railroads away from this type of financing.

REGULATION OF ACCOUNTING AND REPORTS

Both the Interstate Commerce Commission and the Civil Aeronautics Board have ample authority over accounting and reports. The original Interstate Commerce Act of 1887 had authorized the Commission to require annual and other reports and prescribe uniform accounts, since the framers of the law recognized that these controls are essential to effective regulation. Obviously, unless a Commission can obtain reliable revenue, cost, and investment data, uniform and comparable among carriers, regulation can hardly be accurate or effectual.

Because the enforcement provisions of the act of 1887 were weak, real accounting regulation did not come until after Congress, in 1906, gave the Interstate Commerce Commission complete power over railway accounts and reports. By this law it was empowered to prescribe, require compliance under penalty, and police a uniform system of accounts and to prescribe under penalty the nature of reports to be filed. Similar provisions of the act were applied to pipelines and water carriers. The Motor Carrier Act of 1935 and the Civil Aeronautics Act of 1938 made such controls applicable to motor carriers and air carriers.

Control over accounts and reports is sometimes regarded as of minor importance because of the obvious necessity of such regulation. While no one would dispute the essential nature of these controls, it is sometimes forgotten how important they are to the regulated carriers. Much of the traditional freedom of accounting procedure and method is lost, and there is a tendency for accounts and reports to reflect the need of regulatory commissions rather than the need of management. In the railroad business, for example, the student of management is struck with the fact that the elaborate system of accounts and reports leaves much to be desired from the standpoint of managerial control. Many of the accounts and reports are not suitable for tracing organizational responsibility for costs or for developing financial planning or budgeting which would best enable managers to control costs and the expenditure of funds. Too often accountants in the regulated industries and in the administrative commissions forget that the accounting system should be designed for effective management as well as effective government control.

The Economics of Transport Combination [12]

There are certain economic characteristics of transport agencies, particularly the railroads, which account for a natural tendency toward vigorous, if not indeed ruinous, competition. Owing to the relatively large fixed investment required and the large proportion of fixed costs (fixed charges on bonds and under leases, as well as constant operating expenses), railroads usually operate under conditions of decreasing cost. Much the same condition exists in the pipelines, whose proportion of constant costs is probably even greater than the railroads. Even though the airlines have little investment for way, their huge investment in flight equipment and in maintenance and ground facilities, plus the important element of constant operating expenses, tend to place them in a situation of decreasing costs. Even the highway and water carriers, especially the larger common carriers, have to make large investments in equipment and terminal facilities, so that there is some tendency toward decreasing cost in their operations, although this tendency is far less than that of the other carriers.

In addition to the influence on costs of fixed charges and constant operating expenses, all forms of transport are affected by the economic results of common costs for several kinds of service. Both constant and variable costs may become relatively fixed for a given quantum of available ton-miles or seat-miles produced.[13] Consequently, the available capacity of transportation service produced and unsold furnishes a strong impetus for increasing profits or reducing losses through lowering rates and expanding sales.

The tendencies toward decreasing cost by more complete utilization of transport plant have never been more apparent than in the profit realization of the transport industry during World War II and the high profits experienced by many carriers with the defense program accompanying the Korean conflict. Between 1939 and 1942, for example, the operating

[12] The term "combination" is used in a broad sense to include any device whereby a management group, acting in concert, controls all or a part of the policies of two or more carriers. In some cases the combination is complete and its management controls every detail of policy. In other cases, it is partial, in that the constituent carriers combine for certain purposes, but beyond these each carrier retains its independence. The most common methods of complete combination are outright consolidation by merger or amalgamation, acquisition of control through lease or stock ownership, and control through the use of the nonoperating holding company. Partial combination usually results through informal agreements, pooling agreements, equipment interchange, and interlocking directorates or officers, although the last device might be employed for complete combination.

[13] See discussion of this point in connection with rates, pp. 108–110.

revenues of the Class I railways rose from $4 billion to $7.5 billion, while operating expenses plus fixed taxes and charges rose from $3.9 billion to $6.6 billion, thus increasing net income from $93 million in 1939 to $902 million in 1942. And during the Korean conflict the revenues of the domestic trunk-line air carriers rose within a year from a level of approximately $476 million annually to a level of $599 million, while expenses rose only from $449 million to $502 million. While the full effects of this leverage were dulled by rising prices, the existence of decreasing cost is a dramatic and real fact.

There are also some tendencies toward cost reduction through economies of scale. As a general rule, a double-track railroad can handle more than twice the traffic of a single-track line, and a four-track line more than four times as much. Also, an airline able to operate large modern airplanes can carry traffic at a lower cost than an airline with smaller airplanes. Yet, despite the unmistakable advantages of large-scale production in most transportation enterprises, the economies of scale are not so great as is often supposed. Problems of effective management of large enterprises create diseconomies of scale, so that the most efficient transportation unit is probably smaller than many operators realize.

In addition, there is some real doubt that the existence of decreasing cost, whether due to more complete plant utilization or to scale of operations, in the transportation industry is much different from that in other industry. The same influences can be found in the automobile-manufacturing and steel industries, as well as in many other industries where large capital investment is involved. Economic tendencies toward decreasing costs, noted in the airline or other transportation industries, are not peculiar to transportation.

As for the entire transport system within a particular area, there is reason for believing that the most efficient operation and best service could be obtained by combination. If this is true, it is evidence of a somewhat natural tendency toward monopoly. From the point of view of service, a single carrier could probably give better coordinated and more efficient service than could several in a particular area. With some modes of transport, such as the railroads, the limited number of most desirable sites for terminals and line would tend to make it possible for a single carrier to give better and more efficient service than several carriers. Because most transport agencies must have equipment and other facilities for peak demands, because regular schedules must be adhered to, and because for some kinds of transport terminal facilities are usually scarce, there are reasons for decreasing cost through combination. While this tendency may not be so pronounced with highway and water carriers and even though it is not a tendency unique to the transportation industry, the evidence leads one to believe that a coordinated rail-water-highway-air service, under central management, should have advantages in lower cost and improved service.

Considering the cost of wasteful competitive operations, particularly in normal times, it is not at all certain that the user of transportation service is benefited by competition between agencies for the traffic of each other. Substantial benefits to the user would seem to follow from the development of *total* transportation business.

Nevertheless, one may well question such a course of action for public policy. In the first place, there is real question whether regional transportation monopolies could be well managed because of the sheer size and complexity of the managerial job. In the second place, the spur of competition in the transportation business has certainly been considerable enough to bring about improvements in facilities, operations, and service which might not have occurred without this competition.

In the third place, the monopolistic tendencies in transportation can be overrated. While individual localities may be subject to a single railroad or a single airline, the developments of competitive services have lessened the hold of any monopolistically inclined transportation company. The *fact* is that the transportation business generally in the United States is highly competitive. This competition has been due to the freedom which has often characterized entry into the transportation business, the jealousies of transport managers who have been loath to merge themselves out of a position, the development of new means of transportation, and the policy of government control in this field.

The policy of the government of encouraging competition by permitting new carriers to enter the field has already been discussed.[14] At this point, interest is directed primarily to the control of combination. As might be expected, a great portion of this control has been aimed at the railroads and most of the control has been undertaken by the federal government.

Control of Intra-agency Combination

The control of transport combinations has tended to develop rather differently depending on whether the combination envisaged is between carriers of the same type or between carriers of different types. In other words, public policy regarding the combination of one railroad with another has differed from that regarding the combination of a railroad with a motor carrier or an air carrier. The former type of combination may be referred to as intra-agency combination and is discussed in this section. The latter type may be regarded as interagency combination and is discussed separately in the next section.

[14] See above, pp. 125–126, 129, 132–135, 138–139.

COMBINATIONS UNDER THE ANTITRUST LAWS

While in recent years regulation of combinations among transport agencies has been in the hands of the Interstate Commerce Commission or Civil Aeronautics Board, some four decades ago the most important control came from the enforcement of the federal antitrust laws by the U.S. Department of Justice. Even today, the Justice Department exercises some control, although it has gradually been forced to defer to the regulatory commission concerned. Since the antitrust laws [15] apply to all businesses the combination of which affects interstate commerce, the more detailed study of antitrust policy is reserved for a later chapter.[16]

As might be expected, the regulation of carrier combinations has been largely removed from the antitrust laws, as the regulatory commissions have been given increased control over combination activities. While the antitrust laws still apply to combinations in restraint of trade, unless specifically exempted by law, and are a factor to be considered by the management of any transport business, the rather complete control of combination now incorporated in the Interstate Commerce Act and the Civil Aeronautics Act tends to place the transportation industry outside the antitrust laws.

Under the Transportation Act of 1920 the railroads were relieved from the operation of the antitrust laws so far as necessary to allow consolidation and cooperative agreements between them. This exemption was extended by the Reed-Bulwinkle Act of 1948, providing that agreements among carriers relating to rates, fares, classifications, divisions, allowances, or charges would be outside the antitrust act if approved by the Interstate Commerce Commission. Similar provisions exist for the motor carriers, water carriers, and airlines.

While such broad exemption of the interstate carriers from the federal antitrust laws has been criticized as being inimical to the operation of competition,[17] it is difficult to conceive a system of regulation in which such exemption would not be made. If carrier combination is to be closely regulated by regulatory commissions, and if rates, both minimum and maximum, are to be regulated in the interests of protecting against the ravages of ruinous competition or dangerous monopoly, a policy of plac-

[15] The first antitrust law was the Sherman Act, passed in 1890. This law declared "every contract, combination in the form of trust or otherwise, or conspiracy in restraint of trade or commerce among the several states or with the foreign nations" to be illegal.

[16] See below, Chapter 14.

[17] See, e.g., V. A. Mund, *Government and Business* (New York: Harper & Brothers, 1950), pp. 255–261. Mund sees in such exemptions a "long step" toward "a universal system of legalized private monopoly."

ing the power to force strict competition among carriers in another agency of government is strange government regulation indeed.

INTERCHANGE AGREEMENTS

The practice of providing for through service over the lines of two or more carriers through interchange of equipment or route facilities has been fairly widely used in the transportation industry. A variation of pooling, these interchanges are usually handled by voluntary agreements among carriers, although there have been occasions when they have been forced on carriers by commissions.

The reasons for the wide use of interchange agreements are clear. In the first place, the transportation business is one in which provision of through service improves the quality of product and the limited facilities of one carrier can easily be supplemented by the facilities of another carrier. In the second place, such agreements, unlike outright consolidation, retain the identities of the contracting parties and are therefore much easier to consummate.

Interchange agreements take many forms. In the railroad business, among the most common are arrangements for the pooled use of freight cars and passenger cars, for trackage rights, for switch connections, and for the establishment of through routes and rates. Interchange has likewise become important in the airline business. Because of the advantage of through service between any pair of cities able to justify it, and the disadvantage of excessive competition which would result if one-carrier service were certificated to all such points, airlines have found it profitable to interchange equipment. Thus, through service is offered between Florida and California in the same plane, although two or three separate airlines participate in the service. This kind of interchange is really a limited pooling of equipment with some pooling of sales and servicing facilities.

Both the Interstate Commerce Act and the Civil Aeronautics Act give commissions power to order the establishment of reasonable through routes and rates between common carriers by each mode of transport. The law also requires such cooperation between railroads and water carriers, and the commissions are given power to approve voluntarily made joint arrangements between other forms of transport. The law does not require motor carriers of property to set up joint routes and rates with other motor carriers.

The Interstate Commerce Commission has power to require railroads to enter into interchange agreements and provide facilities for the interchange of traffic where necessary in the public interest and where not unduly burdensome to them. The Commission also has power to require physical connection between rail lines and water lines. Both the Interstate Commerce Act and the Civil Aeronautics Act have the power to approve almost any other cooperative agreements voluntarily made between carriers.

Both the Interstate Commerce Commission and the Civil Aeronautics Board have rather freely approved agreements between carriers where the effect has been to improve service or reduce costs. The power of the commissions to require, rather than merely to approve, certain cooperative arrangements, such as joint routes and rates and joint use of terminals, has not been extensively used. Cooperation through establishment of joint routes and rates has been forced on the railroads in a number of cases, as have requirements for the interchange of freight. But by far the largest volume of commission action has come in the approving of the countless voluntary agreements made by carriers for mutual improvement of service and costs. Commission approval has been an especially important means of preserving reasonable competition between carriers, of avoiding plans for the unjustified harm of a competitor, and of protecting users from monopolistic practices. On the whole, however, a high degree of coordination between carriers has resulted from these agreements, service has improved to the public, and costs have been reduced. It is doubtful, however, that the carriers themselves have explored the service and cost improvements possible through cooperative agreements to the extent that efficiency in operating the national transportation system would seem to warrant.

INTERLOCKING DIRECTORATES

The possibility of obtaining unified control of several "independent" corporations through interlocking directors and officers has long been recognized. Corporate entities may be kept separate, but a community of interest and unity of policy can easily be obtained by having the same person act in a directorial capacity for two or more companies. Even where only one or two officers or directors are the same, there is always the possibility that these individuals can act as a liaison between the companies.

In many cases the existence of interlocking directorates is beneficial. A director with experience on the boards of other carriers may be very valuable to a company. Where two carriers have somewhat identical interests or may be competitive, a certain cooperation in policy may be advantageous for efficiency and economy. Where representatives of investment bankers sit on the boards of several companies, the financial advice these individuals are able to give may be beneficial to successful financing of the various companies.

Since the carriers have been subjected to the federal antitrust law, and since interlocking directorates are combinations within the meaning of that law, the use of this device has been unlawful where the effect was unduly to restrain competition. The Transportation Act of 1920 made it unlawful for any individual to hold the position of officer or director in more than one carrier unless the Interstate Commerce Commission permitted it as being compatible with the public and private interest.

The law against interlocking directorates was strengthened in 1940 by giving the Commission wider powers over the acquisition of control through the ownership of stock. Under the Transportation Act of 1940, it is made unlawful for any person to accomplish control or management of two or more carriers by any means whatever without obtaining permission of the Commission.

Similar limitations on interlocking relationships are incorporated in the Civil Aeronautics Act of 1938. As a matter of fact, the prohibitions in regard to airlines are, if anything, more thorough than those in regard to the surface carriers. The act of 1938 excludes the interlocking not only between airline companies but between them and a company in "any phase of aeronautics." The inclusiveness of this phrase is understandable when it is realized that one of the compelling reasons for the passage of the law was the removal of interlocking relationships between the airline business and the aircraft-manufacturing industry.

In the three decades since the Interstate Commerce Commission was given authority to allow or disallow interlocking directors or officers, and in the lesser time which the Civil Aeronautics Board has been in existence, relatively few of the applications to sit on the boards or act as officers of other companies have been denied. In the case of the Interstate Commerce Commission, some 95 per cent have been approved, and most of the others were withdrawn rather than denied. This record for approval is not necessarily an indication of liberality on the part of the Commission, for relatively few applications have been made where the grounds seemed in conflict with the purpose of the law.

As might be expected, the Civil Aeronautics Board has had a higher proportion of cases where the interlocking relationships have not been approved. In attempting to develop commission policy under the law, many applications for interlocking relationships have been made which would not have been made had the Board's policy been clear.

In the case of both the Interstate Commerce Commission and the Civil Aeronautics Board, similar principles have been followed in passing on applications for interlocking relationships. Where carriers are in direct competition with each other, an authorization is almost surely denied. Where they are not in competition an application may be denied if there is a likehood that the interlocking arrangement will lead to discrimination in interchange of traffic between carriers concerned and other carriers. Possible financial mismanagement has also been a ground for denial.

As a general rule, commissions look at the application from the standpoint of its effect upon competition. For example, the Civil Aeronautics Board has observed that the typical case coming before it was one seeking approval of an interlocking relationship between an air carrier and a steamship company wherein the steamship company operated over some of the routes of the air carrier but restricted itself to the carriage of freight, while the air carrier was predominantly a carrier of passengers. The Board pointed out that in such cases the arrangement could at most involve only a situation of "negligible competition" to the air carrier; as a result the Board has approved such interlocking relationships as not being adverse to the public interest.[18]

DIRECT ACQUISITIONS OF CONTROL

Whether by use of a long-term lease, by the acquisition of control by stock ownership, or by outright consolidation of the carrier properties, direct acquisition of control of one company by another is the means most often employed in bringing about combination of carriers. The use of these devices is nowhere better illustrated than in the railroad industry, where large "systems" have been put together. In some cases, the operating railroad has bought up controlling interest in the voting stock of another railroad and has proceeded to operate it as a part of the system. In other cases, an operating railroad contracts with another railroad for the long-time use of its facilities, at a stated annual rental or at a guaranteed dividend on stocks and interest on bonds. Often these two methods are used together. In some cases stock control has been obtained, and then, by virtue of it, a long-term lease contract has been entered into. In other cases, of course, consolidation has been effected through merger or amalgamation, although even in these cases the consolidation has usually been preceded by stock control.

Even though no consolidation takes place, direct acquisitions through lease or stock ownership have been very important, especially in the railroad field. This may be seen from examination of the Pennsylvania Railroad Company.[19] Investment in stocks of affiliated companies operated as a part of the Pennsylvania system is over $400 million, or approximately one-fourth of the amount invested in road and equipment of the company. Moreover, the return applied to leases or guaranties of securities of companies operating as a part of the company's system constitutes an amount one and one-half times as much as the interest on the company's own funded debt.

As might be expected, the powers of the Interstate Commerce Commission and the Civil Aeronautics Board over stock ownership, leases, and

[18] CAB, *Annual Report, 1949*, pp. 27–28.
[19] The Pennsylvania Railroad Co., *108th Annual Report, 1954.*

outright consolidation are complete. While the former commission had no power to approve acquisitions of control until 1920 and did not gain plenary powers until 1940, complete power was written into the Civil Aeronautics Act of 1938. These powers apply to all kinds of common carriers, with the exception that combinations of certain small companies in the motor-carrier field are exempt from the law. The Motor Carrier Act of 1935 excluded from the combination regulations cases where the total number of vehicles involved in a combination was less than twenty, this exclusion being given to lessen the administrative load of the Commission in cases of little public interest.

For those surface carriers falling under the Interstate Commerce Commission, the law directs the Commission, in approving a unification, to consider the public interest, the effect upon competition, the effect upon the public interest of including (or failing to include) other carriers in the territory involved, the total fixed charges resulting, and the interests of the employees concerned. The Civil Aeronautics Board is enjoined by the law, before approving combinations of air carriers, to find that the combination will be in the public interest and will not result in "creating a monopoly or monopolies and thereby restrain competition or jeopardize another air carrier not a party" to the combination. As will be noted presently, the law on combinations places special requirements for combination of carriers in different modes of transport.

Under its broad grant of discretion, the Interstate Commerce Commission has forged some fairly definite principles as to when acquisition of control or consolidation is in the public interest. One distinct requirement is that there must be a clear showing of public gain. This has been taken to mean not only that competition must not be unduly repressed and channels of trade not unreasonably disturbed but that the unification should show possibilities of improving service and reducing costs. The Interstate Commerce Commission has also required that the general financial plan for a unification be just and reasonable in terms both of sound finance and of protection of minority interests.

As the Civil Aeronautics Act of 1938 was written, the provisions for approval of unifications are somewhat more complex than are those in the Interstate Commerce Act. Although there is some doubt that Congress meant the language to be so interpreted, the Board has properly, in view of the language, held that it may approve combinations, even though they restrain competition and threaten to jeopardize another carrier, so long as these effects do not ensue from a condition of monopoly.[20] Rejecting the concept of monopoly as used in the antitrust laws as equivalent to restraint of competition, the Board has defined monopoly as control

[20] *United Air Lines–Western Air Express Interchange of Equipment*, 1 C.A.A. 723 (1940).

of the market. In actual practice, this concept has taken on two meanings. In one case, the Board turned down a merger proposal on the grounds that, while the size of the combination proposed would not be excessive, it would result in too much single-carrier control of certain markets.[21] In another case, the Board refused to approve a merger proposal where the two airlines did not serve the same markets, but where the merger would make the nation's largest airline still larger and where the Board saw no possibilities of service or cost improvements through integration of the two systems.[22]

Control of Interagency Combinations

Examination of the holdings of any large railroad will disclose ownership interests in highway motor carriers and water lines, and at times in the past in airlines. A study made in 1934 showed that 209 steam and electric railways were engaged to some extent in motor-vehicle operations; most coastwise water lines were owned by the railroads, as were many ferry and lighterage companies; and several railroads held large investments in airlines.[23]

As competitors to railroads have developed and grown strong, the rail carriers have naturally sought to bring them under control, not only for protection from competition, but in order to utilize facilities for which the public had expressed a demand. Most water carriers were early brought under the control of the railroads. Until restrictive legislation was passed in 1912, practically every coastwise, intercoastal, and inland water carrier was owned or otherwise controlled by the railroads. When the motor truck and bus gained importance after 1920, most railroads were slow to use this form of transport, since railroad managements regarded the motor vehicle as an unimportant competitor and an unnecessary adjunct to rail service. As late as 1927 only 745 buses were operated directly, through subsidiaries, or by contract, by Class I railways, but this number had increased to 3,100 in 1933.[24] Even in the development of the trunk airlines of the country, railroads played a part, although most had relinquished their ownership interests by the late 1930s and very few railroads attempted to develop air service as a transportation adjunct.

Because of the fear that the more powerful railroads would destroy the water lines, and because of the belief that water competition would

[21] *Acquisition of Western Air Express by United Air Lines*, 1 C.A.A. 739 (1940).

[22] *American Airlines, Inc., Acquisition of Control of Mid-Continent Airlines*, 7 C.A.B. 365 (1946).

[23] *Regulation of Transportation Agencies*, S. Doc. 152, 73d Cong., 2d Sess. (1934), Appendixes A and E.

[24] *Ibid.*, p. 284.

have a salutary effect on rail rates, Congress early provided for the maintenance of competition between these two agencies of transport. In 1912, as the Panama Canal was nearing completion, Congress made it unlawful for any railroad or other common carrier subject to the Interstate Commerce Act to control in any way water carriers with which such common carrier did or might compete for traffic. Except for water-line operation through the Panama Canal, where the restriction was absolute, the Interstate Commerce Commission was empowered to allow the continuance of control where the service was in the public interest and did not prevent, exclude, or reduce competition on the water lines.

Under the Motor Carrier Act of 1935, special restrictions were placed upon combinations of any other form of transport with motor carriers. In the case of combinations between motor carriers, it will be recalled that the law requires only that the Commission find the combination to be consistent with the public interest. But if the carrier attempting to acquire a motor carrier is "other than a motor carrier," [25] the law provided that the Commission, to approve the combination, must find not only that the unification is consistent with the public interest but also that it "will enable such carrier to use service by motor vehicle to public advantage in its operations and will not unduly restrain competition." Thus, the mere economy or consistency with the public interest is not enough in acquisitions of motor-carrier lines by railroads; the combination must be approved only with the additional proof that the service of the railroad to the public will be *improved* by its utilization of motor vehicles.

Similar special restrictions against the free acquisition of air-carrier companies is incorporated in the Civil Aeronautics Act of 1938. In this law, Congress provided that if an applicant for acquisition of control over an airline was a carrier other than an airline, the Board must find that the combination will *promote* the public interest by enabling such carrier to use aircraft to public advantage in its operation, and that such combination will not restrain competition. Unifications between airlines, on the other hand, need only show that they will be consistent with the public interest in order to obtain approval.

COMMISSION POLICY IN INTERCARRIER COMBINATIONS

The policy of Congress severely to limit intercarrier combinations, and in the case of railroad ownership of water carriers operating through the Panama Canal to forbid it, has received strong support from the Interstate Commerce Commission and the Civil Aeronautics Board. Both

[25] The Transportation Act of 1940 changed this slightly by having the restriction apply to "a carrier by railroad . . . , or any person which is controlled by such a carrier, or affiliated therewith. . . ." (Interstate Commerce Act, as amended, part I, sec. 5.)

commissions have taken the point of view that Congress has intended to protect each mode of transport from suppression by another agency and that the healthy growth of each form of transport depended upon development free from domination of one form by another.

The Interstate Commerce Commission has been called on many times to approve railroad operation and control of water carriers. A finding of actual or potential competition between the rail and the water carrier is above all necessary for the combination to be ruled unlawful, for if such competition does not exist, there can be no infraction of the law by railroad control.

In finding competition to be actual or potential, the Commission has used as a practical test the determination of whether divorcement of control would result in competition which had not previously existed. When the rail line is using the water line to stifle competition or is not operating it in the best interests of the public, a finding of unlawful competitive relationship is likely to be made.[26] Thus, the Southern Pacific was allowed to maintain its ownership in water lines operating from the Atlantic Coast to Gulf ports and the New Haven Railroad was permitted to own the New England Steamship Company, operating from Boston to New York. In both these cases the Commission found that water competition would not be increased by the divorcement of ownership. On the other hand, railroads controlling water lines on the Great Lakes were forced to give up their control because of evidence that they were strengthening their own traffic at the expense of the water carriers.

In authorizing railroad ownership of motor-carrier lines since 1935, the Interstate Commerce Commission has followed a policy similar to that applied to railroad ownership of water carriers. Principles for deciding such authorizations were enunciated in the so-called "Barker" case. In this case the Commission said: [27] "Approved operations are those which are auxiliary or supplementary to train service. Except as hereinafter indicated, non-approved operations are those which otherwise compete with the railroad itself, those which compete with an established motor carrier, or which invade to a substantial degree a territory already adequately served by another rail carrier." This principle has been followed in a number of cases, and authorization has been denied where competition between rail and motor carriers would be affected. Some authorizations have been granted with the condition that the railroad-controlled motor carrier limit its activities to auxiliary or supplemental services.

The Civil Aeronautics Board has been even more strict in its application of the separation principle. While the Board has had few cases of inter-carrier combination before it, the principles involved have often been

[26] *Southern Pac. Co. Ownership of Oil Steamers*, 37 I.C.C. 528 (1916).

[27] *Pennsylvania Truck Lines, Inc.–Control–Barker*, 5 M.C.C. 9, 11–12 (1937).

expressed in cases in which railroads or steamship lines have sought route certificates. In one major case, the Board required a steamship line to divest itself of its control of an airline primarily on the grounds that Congress intended the two modes of transport to be separate and that surface carriers could acquire an air carrier only if air operations were "incidental to the surface operations." [28]

RELATION OF INTERCARRIER-COMBINATION POLICY TO APPLICATIONS FOR NEW CERTIFICATES

Interestingly enough, the statutes controlling requirements for entry into service do not place any special restrictions on one type of carrier asking for rights to establish and operate another form of transportation. The laws providing for the granting of certificates of convenience and necessity place no barriers in the way of a railroad asking for rights to operate a motor carrier or an airline subsidiary.

However, both the Interstate Commerce Commission and the Civil Aeronautics Board have tended to interpret the requirements for certificates of necessity and convenience in the light of the restrictions placed on intercarrier combination. Of course, many major motor-carrier operations are still under railroad control, having been obtained under the "grandfather" rights incorporated in the Motor Carrier Act of 1935. In the cases of new operations, the Commission is likely to allow the service if the railroads can show that the ownership of a motor-carrier operation will improve service, lower costs, be auxiliary and supplementary to the railroad service, and not be harmful to established motor carriers operating in the territory.[29] While cases have been decided which vary widely from this principle, it is interesting that the approach of the Commission is to make the policies followed in unification and in entry into service similar.

At first, the Civil Aeronautics Board took the view that the law imposed no special limitation on applications for certificates for new service from surface carriers.[30] However, after the federal Circuit Court of Appeals made the observation that the Board should consider the restriction in the unification sections of the law,[31] the Board adopted a strict interpretation of the requirements of public convenience and necessity. As a

[28] *American Export Lines, Control of American Export Airlines*, 4 C.A.B. 104 (1943).

[29] Note especially *Kansas City Southern Transport Co. Inc., Common Carrier Application*, 10 M.C.C. 221 (1938), 28 M.C.C. 5 (1941).

[30] In *American Export Airlines, Inc., Certificate*, 2 C.A.B. 16 (1940), the Board approved the application of a steamship-line subsidiary for an international operating certificate, taking the position that, since the law imposed no special restrictions on a surface carrier, the Board was not justified in excluding it.

[31] *Pan American World Airways v. CAB*, 121 F.2d 810 (1941).

result of this change in policy and also of change in the personnel and thinking of the Board, it has since been the consistent practice of the Board to exclude surface carriers from serious consideration in granting new routes for air-carrier service. Thus, the separation requirements of the unification provisions have become, by interpretation of apparent congressional intent, a part of the provisions controlling entry into the airline business.

TRANSPORT COORDINATION AND INTERCARRIER COMBINATION

Since the depression of the 1930s, much attention has been given to the desirability and economy of transport coordination. Differences exist as to just what is meant by "transport coordination." Some regard it as meaning merely a kind of cooperation between carriers of the same kind to reduce wasteful duplication of service. But perhaps the more acceptable use of the term is "the assignment, by whatever means, of each facility to those transport tasks which it can perform better than other facilities, under conditions which will insure its fullest development in the place so found." [32]

If transport coordination, as broadly perceived, is sound and should tend to promote efficiency and excellence of service, it is a little strange that government policy should try to insulate the various modes of transportation from each other. There can hardly be doubt that, if the same management were permitted to use rail, water, highway, and air carrying facilities, the drive to use the most economical and best service for each traffic demand would bring about coordination of transportation as no government policy could. Likewise, some of the wasteful competitive practices of intercarrier rivalry would tend to be eliminated, and the emphasis of competition would be placed on the development of total traffic and the fitting of facilities to the particular traffic demand. On the other hand, the point is often made, with some conviction, that elimination of barriers to interagency combination would lead to railroad dominance of the newer forms of transportation. It is felt by some that this dominance would tend to hold progress in check and that the desire of managers of older forms to protect the validity of their capital investment would result in strangulation of the newer forms.

While the government policy of curtailing intercarrier combination was originally reasonably based upon the fear of railroad dominance, there is justice in the position of the railroads that they should not be hamstrung in offering a complete service to the public. The fear of railroad dominance is of questionable soundness, especially in the light of the extensive transport competition existing, the commission controls over

[32] G. S. Peterson, "Transport Coordination: Meaning and Purpose," 38 *Journal of Political Economy* 660 (1930).

transportation in effect, and the fact that permitting intercarrier combination need not materially reduce competition. Indeed, in continuing a government policy based upon a fear of monopoly engendered in the nineteenth century, the public may be paying a high, and unnecessary, price in terms of transportation costs and service.

Selected References

Bigham, T. C., and M. J. Roberts, *Transportation*, chaps. 19–21. New York: McGraw-Hill Book Company, Inc., 1952.

Daggett, Stuart, *Principles of Inland Transportation*, 3d ed., chaps. 24–28. New York: Harper & Brothers, 1941.

Dearing, C. L., and W. Owen, *National Transportation Policy*, chaps. 14–15. Washington, D.C.: Brookings Institution, 1949.

Fair, M. L., and E. W. Williams, Jr., *Economics of Transportation*, chaps. 31–34. New York: Harper & Brothers, 1950.

Frederick, J. H., *Commercial Air Teansportation*, 4th ed., chaps. 7, 12. Homewood, Ill.: Richard D. Irwin, Inc., 1955.

Landon, C. E., *Transportation*, chaps. 25, 27, 28. New York: William Sloane Associates, 1951.

Locklin, D. P., *Economics of Transportation*, 4th ed., chaps. 24, 25, 37, 38. Homewood, Ill.: Richard D. Irwin, Inc., 1952.

Westmeyer, R. E., *Economics of Transportation*, chaps. 14, 15, 17. New York: Prentice-Hall, Inc., 1952.

Troxel, Emery, *Economics of Transport*, chaps. 23–24. New York: Rinehart & Company, Inc., 1955.

8

NATIONAL TRANSPORTATION POLICY

The Transportation Industry

The character and extent of the transportation industry have been commented upon in previous chapters, and certain economic features have been pointed out. If total costs are considered, transportation is a business in which fixed and common costs are exceedingly important. Consequently, the cost characteristics of the industry are such as to lead to vigorous price competition—in fact, a kind of competition so aggressive that, in the absence of government restraints, monopolistic combinations might result. However, the presence of government regulation and the fact that government owns the ways for all carriers except railroads and pipelines have tended to limit combinations, and the industry has remained extremely competitive.

The nature of the transport field is also confused by the existence of carriers which are not common carriers. Practically all railroads are common carriers. Most of the volume of commercial air transport is done by common carriers. Pipelines, while generally held to be common carriers, have in fact operated more nearly as private carriers. Water and motor carriage are spread among all classes of operation, with the common carrier much less important than the contract or private carrier.

Regulation, as has been noted, has proceeded unevenly, at different times for different agencies, in different degrees for different kinds of carriers, and with variance between federal and state provisions. Whether this regulation has been effective depends upon what it should do. One can be sure only that it has not been faultless, that reform measures can be offered with ease, and that a wholly satisfactory policy and program will probably never exist. Prior to World War II, the very solvency of the transportation industry was a matter of great public concern. The pipelines have always operated at profitable levels, but other forms of transportation operated either at very moderate profits or at losses which forced many companies, particularly railroads, into bankruptcy. The unprecedented traffic demands of World War II and the postwar defense programs and the high level of industrial prosperity which has prevailed in recent years have so improved profits in the transportation industry as to remove or camouflage the marginal character of the economic operations of this industry.

It should not be inferred that the marginally profitable status of the transportation industry is due entirely to regulation or lack of it; the causative factors are many and complex. It is clear, however, that the whole policy of the government toward transport is open to suspicion. If any features of regulation or promotion have contributed to the unhealthful state of the industry, they should be sought out and corrected.

What Should Government Do?

The aim of government regulatory or promotional policy does not seem to be difficult to formulate. Transportation is primarily an economic machine. The ideal transportation is that by which adequate service is furnished at the lowest cost to society. Both adequacy of service and reasonableness of cost are highly dynamic matters; they are interdependent, for the quality and adequacy of service demanded depend in large part on its cost. Given certain standards of service, the interest of society lies in getting it at the lowest cost as measured by expenditure of human effort and natural resources. Upon this basis, cost covers expenditures by private enterprise and outlays by the public as well. The aim of the government, whether in regulatory or promotional policy, should be, then, to obtain the highest standard of service at the lowest cost.

Control over transportation facilities, whether in public or private hands, involves such great power over general economic welfare that government must curtail abuses of it. Shippers may be placed at disadvantages not consistent with economic welfare. Investors may be caused to suffer loss from unwise or dishonest use of this power. Laborers may be exploited or be subjected to undue dangers. Different carriers may be discriminated against in ways not for the social good. The consuming public may be made poorer by abuse of the power over transportation facilities.

So long as the principal reliance is placed on private enterprise to operate transport facilities, an equality of opportunity to conduct business efficiently should be afforded by government policy. Subsidizing the inefficient or placing unequal restrictions on classes and types of carriers not only is poor economic policy but is unsound treatment of private enterprise.

To be sure, even an ideal policy toward transportation would take into account social needs which are not economic; the military and cultural features of transportation also cannot be overlooked. Yet its main task is an economic one.

Fundamental Weaknesses in Transportation Regulation

As each agency of transportation has been studied, criticism of regulatory and promotional policies has been made. In some cases the weaknesses emphasized are peculiar to the field of transport regulation concerned. Often they lie in the statutory basis of control. Sometimes they may be attributed to its administration.

INADEQUATE CONTROL OVER SUPPLY

In viewing the whole sphere of government and transportation, certain weaknesses appear which seem fundamental. In the first place, control of the supply of transportation facilities is inadequate. Were competition allowed to rule, maladjustment in supply would be solved by the hard principle of survival of the fittest; some such adjustment is going on irrespective of government control. As a general matter, however, the public by regulating transportation has necessarily taken on the task of control of supply. To some extent supply is regulated by government. Railroads have had to obtain certificates from the federal government to enter or abandon service since 1920. Highway carriers have had to obtain certificates to enter new service since 1935. Certain air carriers have had to get such permission since 1938 and certain water carriers since 1940.

Experience with government control of supply leaves much to be desired. In every field where certificates or permits have been required, except perhaps with air carriers, the control has come after extensive development of the industry. Even now in the railroad field, control extends only to the mileage of track to be operated and only partially to the amount of service using it. In the highway and airway industries, regulatory jurisdiction does not apply to the supply of road facilities or vehicles, but only, at best, to the *number* of contract carriers and the *number* and *routes* of common carriers. Noteworthy regulation of the supply of water carriers has just commenced. The supply of private carriage in any field is not limited by regulation.

One very important gap in control of supply has arisen from the determination of promotional policy. The economic need for new highways, waterways, or airways for a national transportation system has played too minor a part in the decision as to their being built. This situation is made even more serious by the fact that once these facilities are built they might as well be used, irrespective of the effect on the total supply of transportation. With the lack of regulatory control over supply and the fact that promotional policy has not been made consistent with economic need for transportation service, there is little wonder that an oversupply of transport facilities exists in many places and that the industry is, at times, demoralized.

REGULATION AS MONOPOLIES WHILE INSISTING ON COMPETITION

Regulatory policy in transportation has been characterized by an inconsistency which, perhaps more than any other feature of regulation, has contributed to economic weaknesses. On one hand, competition is encouraged and enforced. Ever since the passage of the Interstate Commerce Act of 1887 and the Sherman Anti-trust Act of 1890, the federal government as well as the states has maintained a fundamental policy of enforcing competition. On the other hand, many carriers are kept from competing effectively by application of the same rate and service regulations found in the regulated monopoly field. Clearly, if competition is to be the policy, then restraints not found in competitive "private" business should be removed; if carriers are to be regulated as monopolies, then encouragement should be given to monopoly.

A policy in either direction could logically be supported. One leading to monopoly would seem to have some advantages. Wastes of competition would be eliminated. With monopoly of all transport in a particular area—and area monopolies would be all that is required to gain such benefits—coordination of facilities according to their basic economic advantages would be a normal business action. Certain other economies might be effected through large-scale operation and fuller utilization of facilities. Regulation would be somewhat simplified, since practices arising from competition would no longer need regulatory attention. The government commission charged with control would have very few companies to supervise, and this simplification of the task would surely more than make up for the increased vigilance required. The economics of government promotion of transport might be brought into a clearer light. The rivalry between modes of transport and users of the various forms for government subsidy of waterways, airlines, and other facilities would tend to disappear.

Likewise, a policy recognizing the existence of competition would have advantages through removing the shackles which now bind the carrier manager. The policy of maintaining competition in transportation has in fact led to the existence of a highly competitive industry. If the advantages of competition are to be gained in transportation as they have in many other industries, managements must be permitted to meet competition with price, service, plant expansion, labor, and marketing policies suitable to profit maximization. If the spur of competition has been so successful in yielding maximum satisfactions at minimum costs in manufacturing, retailing, and many other industries, it might well be in the public interest to consider a more thorough competition in transportation.

Traditional public policy has in any case been inconsistent. Perhaps a certain degree of such inconsistency is wise. Perhaps it is in the public interest to promote competition, while at the same time placing obstacles to the free play of competitive forces in an industry, such as transportation, where competitive excesses might impair the entire economy. But the inconsistency should be recognized and its manifestations in controls carefully weighed. It is certainly dangerous public policy to encourage competition with one set of controls and to take away from carrier managers the power to compete effectively with another.

INTERFERENCE WITH EFFECTIVE MANAGEMENT

Many of the economic difficulties of the transportation industry are laid at the feet of company managements. Normally, those who are responsible for the course of a business should be held accountable for its success or failure. But in the transportation industry, some of the inadequacies of management can be attributed to public policy. The problems of meeting competition with the shackles of monopoly-type regulation were pointed out above. In addition, there are many other areas where regulation weakens management.

One of these is the preoccupation with controls which regulation forces on a carrier manager. Most business policies of transport companies have regulatory implications. The attention paid by railroad companies to auditing and reauditing freight bills, even items of negligible financial import, the cumbersome machinery for changing rates, the interferences with accounting and financial procedures, the complicated legalistic approach to working conditions involved in government adjudication of railroad operating rules, and many other features of regulation require so much of the energy of carrier managers that many have little time or inclination to undertake effectively the more important job of running their companies. Observation of many regulated companies, particularly those in the railroad industry, sometimes leads one to the cynical conclusion that these companies are run for the purpose of meeting regulations and not to produce the best kind of service demanded at the lowest cost, and with the highest profits.

The interference of regulation extends far beyond the preoccupation of management and the matter of managerial objectives. It affects even the tools of management. The detailed prescription of accounts and reports by regulatory authorities may require so much expense and effort on the part of the managers of a company that they neglect the statistical and accounting tools by which they may sharpen the quality of their planning and control. The lack of cost accounting in much of the transportation industry is a case at point.

Furthermore, the power of regulatory commissions to establish rates, to set service standards, to limit the right of entry into a market, and to stop a company from eliminating an unprofitable service, along with the many other substantive applications of control, interferes with the traditional area of decision making of the normal business. With so little control over their own destinies, many transport managers understandably feel thwarted in planning and executing courses of action designed to improve their companies' operations. Moreover, in some long-regulated companies, this kind of frustration has led to a lack of aggressiveness and intelligence in handling the problems wrought by social, physical, and biological change, problems with which every enterprise must cope if it is to maintain its successful existence.

Moreover, these decisions must be made quickly if the enterprise is to meet the pace of change of its environment. Delays in reaching decisions are inherent in the regulatory process where requirements of due process make it necessary that all concerned with a matter be heard and where a group of men and their staff must take time to assimilate evidence and reach conclusions. In addition, for the job they are required to do, most regulatory commissions are understaffed and many members of the commission untrained in the field. These factors likewise cause delay. But, while the delays in reaching decisions are understandable, the fact that commission procedure is not conducive to arriving at business decisions expeditiously is not always appreciated.

It should not be implied that all transportation companies are so circumscribed by regulation that there is no room for good management. Even within the maze of regulations which permeate commercial transportation, one sees the effect of various qualities of management in the differences between individual companies. Excellently managed companies exist alongside poorly managed companies in the same regulated industries. But, just as differences in the quality of management should not be attributed entirely to regulation, it should not be forgotten how serious is the interference of regulation with effective management.

INCONSISTENCIES BETWEEN REGULATION AND PROMOTION

Promotional activities of the federal and state governments have been spread over numerous agencies. While these agencies are not now as numerous as they were several years ago and most of them have been brought under the jurisdiction of the Department of Commerce, it is still true that administration of promotion policy is far from centralized. Moreover, even with the tendency to concentrate the administration of promotional activities, it is still customary to deal with promotional projects and policies piecemeal. Government appropriations are made for specific projects, and most of these have in no wise been related to the picture of transportation as a whole. The federal promotional program has not been evaluated in terms of the relative merits of spending for one type of facility over another, and there is no evidence that the effect of new facilities upon present operations is considered seriously.[1]

At the same time regulation has been developing along more paternalistic lines, with the government assuming more positive responsibility for the development and maintenance of economical transport service. The statements of policy in the Motor Carrier Act of 1935 and the Civil Aeronautics Act of 1938 instruct commissions to regulate so as to "foster" sound economic conditions in the field of transport. Such a policy was, of course, a part of the Transportation Act of 1920, applying to railroads and oil pipelines, and it was rewritten to apply uniformly to all carriers by the Transportation Act of 1940.

If regulation is to foster economic transportation development, the independent, uncoordinated, and uneconomic program of promotional expenditures must be changed. The present policy leads to the government's furnishing facilities without regard to their effect on a plan of regulation. Promotional activities have been designed to develop individual forms of transport rather than a unified system. If regulatory policy is to become one by which transport agencies may be coordinated along economical lines, the policy of promotion should be made consistent with it.

ADMINISTRATIVE DIVISIONS IN THE FIELD OF REGULATION

Effective and sound regulation is definitely thwarted by the way in which this field is split. The federal system of government in the United States means that there are fifty governments to deal with the problem of transportation: the federal government, the forty-eight states, and the District of Columbia. The federal government has gained the dominant position. Nevertheless, the vexing problem of distinguishing between federal and state jurisdiction remains. Some carriers are in interstate commerce and some in intrastate commerce. In the railroad field, the federal government has been permitted to extend its jurisdiction over intrastate carriers where they have much effect upon, or are in the flow of, interstate commerce. In the motor-carrier and water-carrier industries, the federal law expresses the desire to keep the scope of federal control limited. What does this mean? It means that a unified program of regulation is not possible except by cooperation between governments—a device of questionable effectiveness.

Within the several state governments, and especially within the federal government, regulation of carriers is divided between different commissions. Under these, regulation is further applied with varying force. Some carrying agencies are subject to more regulation than are others, and of a

[1] See, e.g., C. L. Dearing and W. Owen, *National Transportation Policy* (Washington, D.C.: Brookings Institution, 1949), pp. 353–361.

different kind. Statutory provisions and their administration have differed markedly as between railroads, water carriers, and air carriers in particular. Some kinds of carriers within each of these fields are regulated in different ways from others. Common carriers are ordinarily under much more rigorous regulation than contract carriers; private carriers are subject to no economic regulation at all.

With such variance in the scope and nature of regulation, one can hardly wonder at the condition of the transportation industry and the problem of government policy. A unified and consistent national policy should embrace all commercial carriage, especially intercity as contrasted to intraterminal, whether across state lines or within the states.

LEGISLATION BY GROUP INTEREST

A fundamental weakness in transportation regulation, as perhaps in all regulation, is that legislation is the result of pressure by interested groups. This is equally true of promotional legislation. If the farmers wish relief, they get a resolution passed asking the Interstate Commerce Commission to reduce railroad rates on agricultural products, or press for free waterways at government expense. Labor finds it profitable to get a basic eight-hour day made law, a full-crew bill enacted, or a provision passed to limit layoffs in coordination and consolidation projects. Chambers of commerce and local politicians in cities situated on waterways find that they "get something" by pressing for harbor improvements, canals, and dredging at government expense. Shippers believe it to be to their interest to keep laws enforcing competition on the statute books, for lower rates are believed to result. This may mean that shippers will have to put up with higher rates or poorer service in the future, but the future is far beyond the horizon. Management groups often fight regulation, good or bad, unless such legislation seems to give them a competitive advantage over certain other carriers.

Study of the genesis of transportation legislation would disclose many more examples of lawmaking by interested groups. In a sense, if groups are equally powerful and if they represent wide enough interests, the laws thus made may really be to the public interest. But this is not the case. At various times certain groups have been so powerful as to get pretty much what they want. Moreover, the consuming public, as a highly interested group, is seldom represented in the councils of lawmakers.

Transportation regulation has almost never been viewed as a whole. The relationship of one policy to another has seldom been recognized; long-run effects are usually sacrificed to short-run needs. The result has been a fairly uncoordinated patchwork.

Investigations Proposing Reforms

In view of the importance of transportation to the national economy, the financial difficulties which the various companies in the field have faced from time to time, and the fact that in no other business, with the possible exception of banking, has public policy played a greater and longer role, it is not surprising to find the history of transport regulation a series of investigations and proposals for reform. Before the depression following 1929, these were usually aimed at the solution of the "railroad" problem. Since that time, proposals have tended to be concerned with the whole sphere of transportation.

TRANSPORTATION INVESTIGATIONS, 1933–1954

So many investigations, studies, and proposals have been made that it would be impossible to summarize them all here. There has seldom been a time, particularly since 1929, that the transportation problem has not been under investigation by government or other public agencies. A number of reports outlining proposals for reform have been made. Among the more important of these are the National Transportation Committee report in 1933; [2] the report of the Federal Coordinator of Transportation in 1934; [3] the report of a special Interstate Commerce Commission Committee (the Splawn committee) in 1938; [4] the report of the Committee of Six, a committee of three railroad management and three railroad union members, in 1938; [5] the reports of the Board of Investigation and Research, established by the Transportation Act of 1940; [6] the study of the National Resources

[2] The report and conclusions of the committee are found in H. G. Moulton and others, *American Transportation Problem* (Washington, D.C.: Brookings Institution, 1933). This committee was comprised of five eminent businessmen and statesmen (Calvin Coolidge, Alfred E. Smith, Bernard M. Baruch, Clark Howell, and Alexander Legge) who undertook the assignment at the invitation of sixty-five insurance companies, banking and business associations, and other large institutional investors.

[3] This report was published in two parts: *Regulation of Railroads*, S. Doc. 119, 73d Cong., 2d Sess. (1934); and *Regulation of Transportation Agencies*, S. Doc. 152, 73d Cong., 2d Sess. (1934).

[4] The report is printed as *Immediate Relief for Railroads*, H. Doc. 583, 75th Cong., 3d Sess. (1938).

[5] *Report of Committee Appointed September 20, 1938, by the President of the United States to Submit Recommendations upon the General Transportation Situation (1938)*.

[6] Although most of its reports dealt with aspects of transport economics rather than broad transport policy, and many of its reports were not published, some of the more significant published reports include *Public Aids to Domestic Transportation*, H. Doc. 159, 79th Cong., 1st Sess. (1945); *Comparison of Rail, Motor, and Water Carrier Costs*, S. Doc. 84, 79th Cong., 1st Sess. (1944); *The National Traffic Pattern*, S. Doc. 83, 79th Cong., 1st Sess. (1945); *Report on Interterritorial Freight Rates*, H. Doc. 303, 78th Cong., 1st Sess. (1943).

Planning Board, published in 1942;[7] the President's Air Policy Commission[8] and the Congressional Aviation Policy Boards[9] of 1948; the reports of the President's Air Coordinating Committee in 1947 and 1954;[10] the report of the President's Advisory Committee on the Merchant Marine in 1947;[11] the National Transportation Inquiry of the House of Representatives in 1946;[12] the special report of the Secretary of Commerce in 1949;[13] and the special investigation and study of the Cabinet Committee on Transport Policy in 1955.[14]

PRIVATE-AGENCY CONTRIBUTIONS TO REFORM

In addition to these agencies, major contributions to the proposals for reform of public policy in the transportation field have been made by such private agencies as the Brookings Institution and the Transportation Association of America. The former agency, a nonprofit research and educational organization, has been called in by several of the governmental or other committees investigating transport policy to undertake the necessary staff work for them. Consequently, the Brookings reports have usually been available to the committees and have certainly influenced their findings. But in addition to this assistance, the Brookings Institution has from time to time published recommendations on transportation reform, the most noteworthy recent report being a study published in 1949.[15]

The Transportation Association of America, a private nonprofit organization, is composed of all kinds of parties having an interest in a sound and efficient national transportation system, including not only carrier managers, but also users of transportation, investors, educators, and others. Thus, this organization represents an unusual cross section of interests in the area of transportation and through its various studies, panel discussions, legislative analyses, and other activities has contributed importantly to a program of public policy based upon broad public interests and the successful maintenance of the principle of competitive private ownership. With so many divergent interests represented, one is not surprised to find that many of the proposals made by the Associa-

[7] *Transportation and National Policy* (National Resources Planning Board, 1942).

[8] *Survival in the Air Age* (President's Air Policy Commission, 1948).

[9] *National Aviation Policy*, Joint Committee Print, 80th Cong., 2d Sess. (1948).

[10] *Civil Air Policy* (President's Air Coordinating Committee, 1954).

[11] *Report of the President's Advisory Committee on the Merchant Marine* (1947).

[12] *National Transportation Inquiry*, H. Rept. 2735, 79th Cong., 2d Sess. (1946).

[13] Secretary of Commerce, *Issues Involved in a Unified and Coordinated Federal Program of Transportation* (1949).

[14] *Revision of Federal Transport Policy*, a report prepared by the Presidential Advisory Committee on Transport Policy and Organization (released Apr. 18, 1955).

[15] Dearing and Owen, *op. cit.*

tion represent compromises and often neglect clearly desirable courses of action which might be to the disadvantage of a particular interest. Yet, despite this rather natural infirmity, the organization has done much to develop an informed public policy based on broad interests rather than the narrow considerations of affected groups.

The objectives of the Association are perhaps no better expressed than in the purposes stated for the National Cooperative Project, a program designed to study and debate the issues of transport policy through panels of interested parties in all parts of the country. This project was established by the Association to assist the House of Representatives in its study of policy and has had such an influence in Congress as almost to constitute a quasi-governmental organization. The purposes of the project have been summarized as follows: [16]

1. Make regulation work more effectively in the public interest—freeing burdened forms of transportation rather than adding restrictions to others.
2. Straighten out the conflicts and delays now involved in government procedures to help assure a solvent industry.
3. Assure more even conditions of competition between forms of transportation.
4. Make it possible for management, under private ownership, to provide the best possible service at the lowest possible cost.
5. Develop the cooperative mechanism for the future adjudication of basic issues and the closest possible partnership between private enterprise and government to that end.

One of the encouraging aspects of the program of the Transportation Association of America is that its program attacks transportation regulation, keeping its objectives in mind, on a specific basis. Specific changes in regulation are studied, recommendations to the Association's Board of Directors made by the panels of the National Cooperative Project are acted on by the Board, even in the face of strong dissenting votes. While a position on a piece of legislative reform may be unpopular in some quarters and this dissent may be so well pressed in Congress as to negate the recommendations of the Association, its influence on legislation has been considerable and should continue to be even greater in the future.

PATTERN OF RECOMMENDATIONS FOR REFORM

While it is clearly impossible to summarize the large number of changes in transport policy recommended by the various public and quasi-public committees, boards, and other agencies, some rather interesting patterns of reform have developed. In the period between the depression following 1929 and World War II, these proposals took the direction of recom-

[16] *Sound Transportation for the National Welfare* (Chicago: Transportation Association of America, 1953), p. iii.

mending a curbing of competition, and many of the committees came out strongly for regional monopolies of transportation as a means for bringing about efficiency in operation and coordinated use of the various modes of transport. They also recommended the strengthening of regulation and its equal application to all the forms of transport, an aim which was partially fulfilled by the passage of the Transportation Act of 1940. Furthermore, these reports were fairly consistent in recommending a reexamination of the promotional policies of the government toward transportation with a view to bringing consistency between the supply of transport facilities, the payment for them by users, and the coordination of transportation on the basis of true economies. In order to accomplish this last objective, many of the recommendations favored the establishment of a central government transportation agency to handle all promotional activities and a centralized, though separate, agency to handle all regulatory duties.

In the recommendations made since World War II, one notes a slight change of direction. While there is a desire to equalize regulation, to improve the efficiency of transportation, and to bring about a coordinated service in the interest of the shipping public, the direction taken by most investigatory agencies is toward freer competition and equality of regulation through removing shackles on the more regulated rather than adding them to the less regulated. Also, there is much less concern with the problem of oversupply of transportation facilities than was the case before World War II, the expansion of the economy having eliminated much of the oversupply which characterized the 1930s. Moreover, the stabilization and continued growth of the motor-carrier industry and the rapid rise of the airline industry in the postwar period, along with the virtual doubling of traffic demands in the past two decades, have so established a tradition of workable competition that the idea of regional monopoly in transportation is seldom advanced as a cure for the transportation problem. In fact, competitive private enterprise has become so well established in the transportation industry that many of the proposals for reform are aimed at making this competition more effective.

RECOMMENDATIONS OF THE EISENHOWER CABINET COMMITTEE, 1955

The tone of recommendations for reform of transportation policy in recent years is reflected in the study and recommendations made by the Special Committee on Transportation Policy and Organization in 1955. This committee, appointed by President Eisenhower in 1954 with the task of recommending reforms in transportation policy, included on its membership the secretaries of Commerce, Treasury, Defense, and Agriculture, and the Postmaster General, the Budget Director, and the Director of Defense Mobilization. Although this report was to have been made public late in 1954, its departure from previous government policy naturally gave rise to a number of controversial questions, and the President withheld publication of the report until April, 1955. In general, the report recommended a departure from the paternalistic attitude of government toward transportation and the freeing of transportation companies from many of the regulatory restrictions against their ability to compete.

The Cabinet Committee report is based on the theory that, since there is no monopoly in the transportation field, the public no longer needs the strict regulations which have so long been applied to the transportation industry, particularly the railroads. It is the philosophy of the report that present regulatory policy interferes with the efficient operation of the nation's transportation system and that greater reliance on private management under competitive conditions will improve the efficiency of carrier operation, reduce the cost of service to the public, and improve the quality of service. It was the Committee's recommendation that the regulatory commission be "expected to act as an adjudicator, not a business manager."

The Committee philosophy is well illustrated in its suggested revision of the national transportation policy, which it would have read as follows:

It is hereby declared to be the national transportation policy of the Congress:

(1) To provide for and develop, under the free enterprise system of dynamic competition, a strong, efficient and financially sound national transportation industry by water, highway and rail, as well as other means, which is and will at all times remain fully adequate for national defense, the Postal Service and commerce;

(2) To encourage and promote full competition between modes of transportation at charges not less than reasonable minimum charges, or more than reasonable maximum charges, so as to encourage technical innovations, the development of new rate and service techniques, and the increase of operating and managerial efficiency, full use of facilities and equipment, and the highest standards of service, economy, efficiency and benefit to the transportation user and the ultimate consumer, but without unjust discrimination, undue preference or advantage, or undue prejudice, and without excessive or unreasonable charges on non-competitive traffic;

(3) To cooperate with the several States and the duly authorized officials thereof, and to encourage fair wages and equitable working conditions;

(4) To reduce economic regulation of the transportation industry to the minimum consistent with the public interest to the end that the inherent economic advantages, including cost and service advantages, of each mode of transportation, may be realized in such a manner so as to reflect its full competitive capabilities; and

(5) To require that such minimum economic regulation be fair and impartial, without special restrictions, conditions or limitations on individual modes of transport.

All the provisions of this Act shall be construed, administered and enforced with a view of carrying out the above declaration of policy.

In more specific terms, the program of deregulation recommended by the Committee would strip from the regulatory commissions their power to fix exact rates, although keeping power to set minimum rates at direct cost and limit maximum rates to an amount ascertained to be just and reasonable, although not below a carrier's full cost. The Committee would retain in government hands the power to investigate rates and to prevent rates which discriminate unfairly against certain shippers and carriers. In addition to this philosophy of relatively free pricing, the Committee implied that present arbitrary restraints placed upon one form of transportation in its use of another form be relaxed. The Committee recommendations included many other specific items aimed at freeing transportation companies of unequal regulatory burdens. Among these were recommendations in favor of permitting establishment of volume rates based on cost differences, clarifying and limiting agricultural exemptions in trucking, sharpening the definitions of contract and private carriage so as to assure the bona fide nature of these operations, and empowering the Interstate Commerce Commission to override state service requirements, such as railroad abandonment denials by states, where they unduly burden interstate commerce.

The Committee recommendations were criticized in some quarters as being unduly favorable to the railroad industry. While this might seem to be the case on the first reading of the report, one cannot but be impressed that the report consistently argues in favor of equal transportation opportunity free of regulation not needed to protect the public interest. It is only natural that, since the railroad industry has perhaps been fettered to a greater extent than other portions of the transportation industry, the Cabinet Committee recommendations would seem to favor the railroads.

Toward a Sound National Policy

There is certainly adequate evidence that the present status of public policy and its operations in the transportation field are unsatisfactory. While the transportation industry is generally in a sounder financial position that it has been since 1929, many of the companies in it operate at narrow profit margins, or depend on government subsidies, or operate at such low returns as to limit the availability of capital for needed expansion. Looked upon as a socioeconomic instrument, there is real doubt that the transportation industry is giving a maximum of service at a minimum of cost. Since government has for so many years regulated and promoted this industry, some of the shortcomings must be laid at its doorstep. While the solution for this problem is too complex to be mapped in any detail here, a few major measures within the power of government which can be undertaken to develop a sounder and more economical transportation system may be outlined. These might be summarized as a three freedoms for transportation: freedom to be efficient, freedom to compete, and freedom from uneconomical or unnecessary government subsidy.

FREEDOM TO BE EFFICIENT

Unless important public policy indicates otherwise—and it must be recognized that efficiency is not the only measure of success in the public interest—government controls should be so designed as to permit a business to operate efficiently. As a general rule, the public interest will be served best if the product desired is made available at the lowest cost consistent with the demands for that service. There may be exceptions to this rule, although even in times of emergency there is some question whether the tendency to toss aside considerations of cost may always be wise, particularly when the requirement of adequate service is taken into account.

In the transportation industry, there is seldom any justification for public policy which interferes with efficiency. And where the requirements of the public, as in local airline or rural mail service, loom so large as to force private enterprise to furnish a service at a cost not justified by the revenues, this should be regarded as a service to be paid for by the public through tax revenues. Granted that common carriers have been traditionally required to give adequate service in the area for which they have held themselves out to serve, this requirement does not imply that the service be furnished below cost.

There are a number of places where the operation of public policy has thwarted transport managements in their quest for efficiency. Among these are the blocks which have been placed in the way of abandonment of unprofitable service or line. In the railroad business, for example, many costly passenger services are forced to continue, and many unprofitable branch lines are kept in operation, because a government agency will not allow the abandonment or places such impediments that a management cannot permit abandonment. In the motor-carrier and air-carrier businesses in particular, and even in the railroad business, government controls force many companies to stick to obsolete route patterns and deny other companies the right to follow the most efficient routes or enter markets which would lower their costs and improve their service. While much of the restriction on route changes and new routes may be justified on the grounds that unlimited competition would so weaken some carriers as to harm the industry and its service as a whole, the fact still remains that these limitations fetter efficiency. Furthermore, many of the limitations and the excessive procedural requirements for changes restrict efficiency with rather little justification.

In the same category are limitations placed by public policy on efficient combinations of carriers and on the freedom of individual companies to utilize the best available tools for the job to be done. The artificial separation of railroads, water carriers, motor carriers, and airlines, and the extreme difficulty with which a company engaged in one type of business may utilize the methods of another instrument of transportation are curious interferences with efficiency. It is as though a forge shop were debarred from utilizing centrifugal casting in making machine parts.

But the present interferences with efficiency take other forms than those arising from public interest in maintaining service or competition or encouraging a form of transportation. The cumbersome procedures of rate changes typical in transport regulation, the difficulties in making changes in accounting systems to reflect management needs, and the kind of detailed and inflexible safety regulations found in air transportation are examples of the restrictions placed on private management, to a great extent unnecessarily, which impede efficiency.

Regulations—the manifestations of public policy—and the policies which underlie them need a careful review to determine whether their costs in terms of inefficient operations are justified by clearly demonstrable public needs. Private enterprise depends for its successful existence upon the relentless pursuit of the best product at the lowest cost. Even the ablest transportation managers cannot accomplish this objective if fettered by needless public interference.

FREEDOM TO COMPETE

Regulatory policy of the government in the transportation field has clearly been inconsistent. On the one hand, controls require the maintenance of competition; yet, on the other hand, they regulate companies in detail as though they were monopolies and do not let them compete. Prices are carefully controlled, service standards are subject to regulation, and availability of markets is carefully restricted through route limitations. It is certainly reasonable to argue that government policy should either consistently aim at making competition effective or at promoting monopoly and gaining its fruits. It should hardly try to do both.

Admittedly, a public policy encouraging monopoly in transportation has much to commend it. Monopoly, whether regional or national, has great possibilities for lower costs in an industry like transportation where fixed costs tend to be high. Also, the tasks of regulation would probably be simplified because of the fewness of companies involved and the lack of so many competitively inspired deviations from regulatory standards of reasonableness.

But the fact is that the transportation industry in the United States has developed as competitive enterprise. Nor is this believed to be an undesirable development. Competition has proved to furnish the spur for an efficient and progressive business in transportation, as it has in other areas of industrial enterprise. One need only compare the tremendously effective system of transportation in the United States today with that in most foreign nations, particularly where government-owned transport companies have been customary, to find how dependent American prosperity and industrial efficiency are upon ample and relatively efficient transportation facilities.

There is, therefore, neither the justification nor the inclination to depart from the tradition of competition in American transportation industry. Under these circumstances, restrictions on free competition in transportation should be reexamined in the light of clearly defined public needs to ascertain whether it would not truly be in the public interest to give companies more freedom to compete. It is doubtful whether detailed rate regulation is longer necessary, and it is probable that mere outlawing of unfair price discrimination of the kind applicable to businesses generally would protect the public in a freer transport economy. Perhaps the protections of antitrust regulations would be adequate to maintain effective competition in transportation as it does in many other industries. Almost certainly, freer entry into markets might be in the public interest, so long as safeguards are placed to protect the public against poor or dishonest service by irresponsible operators.

One must recognize that the peculiar nature of transportation, by which it affects so many other industries and the economy as a whole, may ever require that this industry be regulated to a greater extent than most others. It is entirely possible that limitations of location, heavy capital requirements, and the pervasive effects of price and service discrimination may make it unwise to allow the industry to be as free to serve the public as is the case with the drug, soap, or even the automobile-manufacturing industries. But if the transportation business is to continue as a competitive one, and if the public is to gain the economies and service advantages of competition, regulation should be patterned to suit. It is certainly not reasonable to continue controls perfected at the turn of the twentieth century when the railroads, as an agency of transport, and many companies in this industry, were often monopolistic.

FREEDOM FROM UNECONOMICAL AND UNNECESSARY GOVERNMENT SUBSIDY

It is obviously not enough to free the transportation industry from shackles to inefficient management and blocks against competitive behavior if the federal and state governments do not also set up an environment conducive to fair and open competition. A major impediment to this environment within the power of government lies in public financing of transportation improvements and government subsidy of carriers. Clearly, if any company or method of transportation is given a subsidy or is not levied its fair share of cost for transportation improvements, while other companies or modes of transportation are paying their full share, the government is establishing an environment where free and effective competition under private management cannot exist. Unequal government support of transportation exists not only in such obvious cases as airmail subsidies but in the far less obvious instances of financing public road or waterway improvements out of public funds without regard to levying costs fairly upon the beneficiaries.

While the principle for obtaining freedom from uneconomical subsidy is clear, it is recognized that there may be cases where the broader public interest in such subsidies far outweighs a narrower public interest in transportation policy. One would hardly deny, for example, that the subsidy element existing in rural free postal delivery service and in the provision of airways, with their clear use for defense purposes, are in the public interest. In the zeal, then, to equalize opportunity in the transportation field, the citizen and legislator must distinguish between subsidies for the benefit of individuals and those aids based upon a strong public need the benefits of which can only, or should, be levied on the public at large. The criterion of necessity, then, should be to weigh public aids in the light of the ability and desirability of transportation users to pay for them versus the desirability of payment by the public generally through tax funds. It is just as fair to have transportation facilities and services paid for by the public at large when the benefits so accrue as it is to require that the cost of transportation be borne by the immediate user when the benefits accrue to him. But clearly, in applying this guide, those persons responsible for public policy must consider the costs carefully against the benefits obtained.

Selected References

Bigham, T. C., and M. J. Roberts, *Transportation*, 2d ed., chap. 24. New York: McGraw-Hill Book Company, Inc., 1952.

Dearing, C. L., and Wilfred Owen, *National Transportation Policy*. Washington, D.C.: Brookings Institution, 1949.

Fair, M. L., and E. W. Williams, Jr., *Economics of Transportation*, chaps. 34–36. New York: Harper & Brothers, 1950.

Federal Coordinator of Transportation, *Regulation of Transportation Agencies*, S. Doc. 152, 73d Cong., 2d Sess. (1934).

Koontz, Harold, "Returning Railroad Management to Railroad Managers," 39 *Proceedings, Pacific Railway Club* 9–28 (May, 1955).

Middleton, P. H., *Sound Policies in Transportation.* Chicago: Railway Business Association, 1953.

National Resources Planning Board, *Transportation and National Policy.* Government Printing Office, 1942.

Pegrum, Dudley F., "The Economic Basis of Public Policy for Motor Transport," 28 *Land Economics* 244–263 (August, 1952).

Presidential Advisory Committee on Transport Policy and Organization, *Revision of Federal Transportation Policy.* 1955.

President's Air Coordinating Committee, *Civil Air Policy.* 1954.

Secretary of Commerce, *Issues Involved in a Unified and Coordinated Federal Program for Transportation.* 1950.

Transportation Association of America, *Sound Transportation for the National Welfare.* Chicago: Transportation Association of America, 1953.

U. S. Senate, Committee on Interstate and Foreign Commerce, *Domestic Land and Water Transportation*, S. Rept. 1039, 82d Cong., 1st Sess. (1951).

Westmeyer, R. E., *Economics of Transportation*, chaps. 32–33. New York: Prentice-Hall, Inc., 1952.

Wilcox, Clair, *Public Policies toward Business*, chap. 22. Homewood, Ill.: Homewood, Ill. Richard D. Irwin, Inc., 1955.

PART THREE

PUBLIC UTILITIES

9

THE PUBLIC-UTILITY CONCEPT

Certain businesses, including transportation agencies, have come to be designated in law as "public utilities." This term applies to all those businesses that legislative, administrative, and judicial bodies regard as being so impressed with peculiar public interest as to justify intensive government regulation of practically every detail of their activities.

Every business is affected with some measure of public interest. But as a general rule, entry into business is unrestricted by government, except where certain qualifications demand licensing to protect the public interest.[1] Usually, too, businessmen are free, so far as government is concerned, to charge what prices they please and to extend service as they wish. When regulation occurs, it is ordinarily to promote the safety, health, or welfare of the public. In the public-utility field, however, a business is expected to serve all comers, at a reasonable rate and without discrimination. Therefore, its rates, services, finances, accounting, and other activities usually regarded as private are carefully regulated.

Since the public-utility concept is essentially a legal concept, the process by which a particular business acquires public-utility status is the political process by which a felt need is satisfied through government action. The path leading to legal controls is marked by the growth of public opinion in favor of the regulation, followed by legislative enactment of the control. A regulatory commission may be vested with the authority to define the business practices affected by the policy and to administer the details of regulation. In time the question whether this regulation is within the limits of the due-process clauses of the Fifth and Fourteenth Amendments may reach the courts.

Until the early 1930s the courts held generally that detailed rate and service regulation was valid only if the business so regulated was one "affected with a public interest." This phrase was the practical equivalent of saying that a business was a public utility. Thus, regulation was dependent upon defining a "public utility." The courts took the position that only a small group of businesses were public utilities, as distinguished

[1] See *Occupational Licensing Legislation in the States* (Chicago: Council of State Governments, 1952).

from the vast number of private businesses. Only on public utilities could legislatures impose certain economic regulations without violating due process.

Since the 1930s the public-utility concept, as a constitutional limitation on the power of government to control prices and service, has been passing, although it continues to exist as a politicoeconomic classification of business regulation. The present tendency of the courts is to hold that there is no special group of businesses that is unusually affected with a public interest. Any business apparently may be subjected to special obligations and regulations without violating the due-process clause if, in the judgment of the legislature, the consequences of unrestricted business activity are undesirable.

There have been two distinct problems involved in the decision to impose detailed rate and service regulations on a particular business or industry. The first has been the public-policy question of whether a legislature should impose public-utility controls in a given business area. The second has been the constitutional question of whether the regulation conforms to the requirements of the Constitution that a person may not be deprived of his property without due process of law. The first section of this chapter will trace the legal development of the public-utility concept as the courts grappled with the question of the constitutionality of certain economic controls. The following section will examine the various criteria legislatures have used, and the courts have accepted, in deciding to enact rate and service regulations. The public-policy criteria assume greater importance now that the courts are showing a willingness to accept the judgment of the legislature as to the need for regulation.

Legal Development of the Public-utility Concept

The meaning of the public-utility concept is best understood by reviewing some of the outstanding cases in the history of its legal development.[2] Nourished by the Supreme Court's ruling in *Munn v. Illinois*, the concept came into full flower in the decade preceding *Nebbia v. New York*. Since 1934 the traditional concept has been withering away.

FLOWERING OF THE CONCEPT

***Munn v. Illinois* (1877).**[3] In the Munn case the Supreme Court was faced for the first time with the problem of state control of the rates in a privately owned business. In 1870, the Illinois legislature, as a result of the granger movement, passed a law prescribing maximum rates for grain stor-

[2] For an extended treatment, see Ford P. Hall, *The Concept of a Business Affected with a Public Interest* (Bloomington, Ind.: The Principia Press, Inc., 1940), pp. 4–6.

[3] 94 U.S. 113.

age and requiring warehouse operators to obtain a license and post a bond to ensure performance of their lawful duties as public warehousemen. Munn and Scott, owners of a grain warehouse in Chicago, maintained they operated a private business and contested the law on the grounds that it was a deprivation of property without due process of law.

The attorney for Munn and Scott supported his case by relying on a two-century-old treatise by Lord Hale, then Lord Chief Justice of England, in which he distinguished between "public" and "private" wharves. The Lord Chief Justice had held that a person might charge what he wanted for use of a wharf set up for his "private advantage," but that, if the wharf were one to which all persons must come for loading and unloading, the wharf had become "affected with a public interest" and the rate charged should be just and reasonable.[4] The lawyer for Munn and Scott argued that the doctrine of Lord Hale proved that his clients' business was not one which was subject to such obligations under the common law, because no precedent could be found for the regulation of grain elevators. Therefore, the Illinois statute must be an unconstitutional deprivation of property without due process of law.

The majority of the Supreme Court made use of the reference to Lord Hale's essay.[5] But they found in it a legal basis for holding the regulation of Munn and Scott's warehouse to be constitutional. The Court decided that, as Lord Hale had indicated, when private property becomes "clothed with a public interest" and affects "the community at large," the owner of the property has in effect granted the public an interest in that use and "must submit to be controlled by the public for the common good."

The Court found grounds for believing these Chicago warehousemen to be in a business "clothed with a public interest." The facts had shown that warehouses on the Chicago waterfront were virtual "gateways of commerce" which took "toll from all who pass." The Court was clearly impressed by the fact that these operators were in a monopolistic position and were furnishing a service practically indispensable to the public.

The significance of the majority decision does not lie in the legal logic by which the police power of the state was broadened. Rather it is important because the Court recognized the practical necessity for regulation in the particular circumstance and accepted the legislature's judgment. Unfortunately, Lord Hale's principle, although employed by the

[4] See W. H. Hamilton, "Affectation with Public Interest," 39 *Yale Law Journal* 1089–1112 (June, 1930); and B. P. McAllister, "Lord Hale and Businesses Affected with a Public Interest," 43 *Harvard Law Review* 759–791 (March, 1930).

[5] As Professor Hamilton aptly remarked: "So Mr. Chief Justice Waite, with a rare impartiality, accepted the rule of law from the plaintiffs-in-error, affected grain elevators with a public interest, and handed the decision to the state of Illinois." *Op cit.*, p. 1096.

Court, did not contribute a precise standard by which the legitimate exercise of state police power could be determined.

The doctrine of affectation with the public interest came to be the basis upon which state power over a host of businesses was upheld. Immediately after the decision in *Munn v. Illinois*, railroads were held to be businesses affected with a public interest.[6] From the precedent in the Munn case, regulation of a water company was found to come under the public-interest formula.[7] Grist mills were likewise found to be clothed with such public interest as to permit regulation.[8]

The principles of *Munn v. Illinois* were also employed by state and lower courts in finding various businesses affected with a public interest. The public-utility concept was broadened to include, among others, stockyards,[9] gas companies,[10] telephone companies,[11] and electric companies.[12]

***Brass v. North Dakota* (1894).**[13] The public-utility concept was further extended in another case involving the regulation of grain elevators. In *Brass v. North Dakota* the Supreme Court upheld a state law fixing maximum rates for grain storage, but its reasoning differed from that in *Munn v. Illinois.* Rather than examine the monopolistic character of the warehouse business, which might make regulation necessary, the Court simply held that the judgment of the North Dakota legislature to regulate warehouse rates was the deciding factor. Mr. Justice Shiras wrote, ". . . we have no right to revise the wisdom or expediency of the law . . ." and ". . . we would not be justified in imputing an improper exercise of discretion to the legislature of North Dakota." [14]

***German Alliance Insurance Co. v. Kansas* (1914).**[15] One of the broadest definitions was given to the public-utility concept when the Supreme Court upheld a comprehensive regulation of fire-insurance rates by a 1909 Kansas law. The Court repeated the doctrine of *Munn v. Illinois* and ruled that the insurance business had come to hold "such a peculiar relation to

[6] *Chicago B. and Q. R.R. Co. v. Iowa*, 94 U.S. 155 (1877), and *Peik v. Chicago and N.W. Rwy. Co.*, 94 U.S. 164 (1877).

[7] *Spring Valley Water Works v. Schottler*, 110 U.S. 347 (1884).

[8] *Burlington v. Beasley*, 94 U.S. 314 (1877).

[9] *Ratcliff v. Wichita Union Stock Yards Co.*, 74 Kan. 1, 86 Pac. 150 (1906).

[10] *Zanesville v. Zanesville Gas Light Co.*, 47 Ohio St. 1 (1889); *In re Pryor*, 55 Kan. 724, 41 Pac. 960 (1895).

[11] *Western Union Tel. Co. v. Pendleton*, 95 Ind. 12 (1883); *Chesapeake Tel. Co. v. Baltimore Tel. Co.*, 66 Md. 399, 7 Atl. 809 (1886); *Missouri v. Bell Tel. Co.* 23 Fed. 539 (1885).

[12] *Cincinnati R.R. Co. v. Bowling Green*, 57 Ohio St. 336, 49 N.E. 123 (1896); *State v. Spokane Rwy. Co.*, 89 Wash. 605, 154 Pac. 1110 (1916).

[13] 153 U.S. 391.

[14] 153 U.S. 403.

[15] 233 U.S. 389.

the public interests that there is superinduced upon it the right of public regulation." A realistic consideration of the nature of the insurance business was the basis for this decision. The Court contended that the insurance business is necessary to business and personal life, that its effect is widespread, since most of the country's wealth is protected by it; that the purchaser has little influence over rates as he negotiates for a necessity; and that the solvency and efficiency of insurance companies is of the widest public interest.

The three dissenting justices pointed to the obvious fact that the insurance business was not like the transportation, communications, and other public-utility businesses that previously had been found to be affected with a public interest (nor did the majority find any similarity). The minority found no monopolistic conditions (nor did the majority say anything about a "virtual monopoly" existing, which had been the reason for declaring the warehouse business of Munn and Scott a public utility). If the price of fire insurance could be regulated, they suggested, " . . . then the price of everything within the circle of business transactions can be regulated." Therefore, they concluded that the law should be declared void.

***Wolff Packing Co. v. Kansas* (1923).**[16] Until 1923, it seemed that the concept of a public utility had no practical limits. In the decade following 1923, however, the inclusiveness of the concept was severely limited. Before this time there seemed to be little except the attitude of state legislatures that kept a business from being regarded as affected with a public interest and hence subject to economic regulation.

In 1920, Kansas enacted a law declaring all businesses concerned with the manufacture, preparation or transport of food, clothing, and fuel to be affected with a public interest. The statute provided that in those businesses there should be compulsory arbitration of disputes involving wages and other conditions of employment. The Wolff Packing Company refused to comply with an order increasing wages issued under the law, claiming that, since it was a private business, this order constituted deprivation of property without due process. The Supreme Court unanimously upheld the packing company. Since the Court found no monopoly, no emergency, and no assumption of obligation to the public in this business, the Court held that it could not be regarded as one affected with a public interest. The Court emphasized that a business becomes clothed with a public interest by its very nature and its relations to the public, not by the declaration of a legislature. This reasoning stands in marked contrast to that in the Brass decision.

The Wolff case is significant for the attempt by Chief Justice Taft to define affectation with a public interest. He divided into three classes

[16] 262 U.S. 522.

business said to be clothed with a public interest and thereby justifying some public regulation: (1) railroads and other common carriers which operate under "the authority of a public grant of privileges" which imposes "either expressedly or impliedly" the duty of rendering a public service; (2) certain occupations, such as keepers of inns, cabs, and grist mills, which have been recognized from earliest times as public callings subject to special obligations; (3) "businesses which, though not public at their inception, may be fairly said to have risen to be such, and have become subject in consequence to some government regulation."[17]

Subsequent cases. After the Wolff case the Supreme Court could find few businesses sufficiently affected with a public interest to justify government regulation. In *Tyson v. Banton*[18] the Supreme Court accepted the argument of theater-ticket brokers that their business was a private one so that price fixing would deprive them of their property and liberty without due process of law. Justice Holmes, in dissenting, followed the Brass precedent. He maintained that the New York legislature should be allowed to do "whatever it sees fit to do unless it is restrained by some express prohibition in the constitution." It seemed to him that "government does not go beyond its sphere in attempting to make life livable. . . . I am far from saying that I think this particular law a wise and rational provision. That is not my affair. But if the people of the State of New York speaking by their authorized voice say that they want it, I see nothing in the Constitution of the United States to prevent their having their will."[19]

The Tyson decision was used by the Court the next year in declaring unconstitutional a 1918 New Jersey law which regulated the fees charged by private employment agencies.[20] They were considered to be simply brokerage businesses, little different from theater-ticket brokers. The Court did admit that the evils of extortion, fraud, and discrimination existed in the business of employment agencies. However, it held that "these are grounds for regulation but not for price fixing."

Mr. Justice Stone, writing for the minority, found that the business of the employment agency differed markedly from that of the ticket broker. He pointed to the great number and widespread effect of evils of private employment agencies. He called attention to general enactment of regulation of these agencies and to the fact that controls, other than price, had been upheld. He challenged the reasoning of the majority by which

[17] 262 U.S. 535. Chief Justice Taft's definition is not an exposition of the criteria by which affection with a public interest can be determined. Instead, it is a categorical summary of the businesses which had been accepted as public utilities at that time.

[18] 273 U.S. 418 (1927).

[19] 273 U.S. 447.

[20] *Ribnik v. McBride*, 227 U.S. 350 (1928).

they distinguished between price controls and other regulations, and declared that there was no valid difference "between reasonable regulation of price, if appropriate to the evil to be remedied, and other forms of appropriate regulation which curtail liberty of contract or the use and enjoyment of property." Mr. Justice Stone felt that price regulation was an appropriate means for removing some of the evils of the employment agency.[21]

A Tennessee statute which fixed the prices of gasoline was held invalid in 1929 on the grounds that the selling of gasoline was not a business affected with a public interest.[22] The Court found that "gasoline is one of the ordinary commodities of trade, differing so far as the question here is affected, in no essential respect from a great variety of other articles commonly bought and sold by merchants and private dealers in the country."

A final example of this development is the New State Ice Company case.[23] The Supreme Court refused to include the ice business in the category of public business so that an Oklahoma requirement of a license as a condition of entry could be upheld as constitutional. The Court pointed out that the ice business was an ordinary one, no grant of special privileges was involved, no monopoly or emergency existed, and protection of natural resources was not an issue. Therefore, the ice business was private, and a person could not be kept from beginning an ice business because he did not obtain a license.

Mr. Justice Brandeis, with Mr. Justice Stone concurring, dissented in an opinion that is a classic statement of the "liberal" interpretation of the police power. He declared that public welfare may often demand creation of monopolies to curb wastes and dangers of "unbridled competition." The requirement of a certificate of public convenience and necessity in the ice business has as its purpose avoidance of duplication of facilities, waste, and poor service. Whether local conditions justify such control is primarily a concern of the legislature, and should not be overruled unless the latter has acted in a clearly unreasonable or arbitrary fashion.

As for the manufacture of ice in Oklahoma, Mr. Justice Brandeis found ice to be "an article of primary necessity . . . partaking of the fundamental character of electricity, gas, water, transportation, and communication." He questioned whether "means of manufacturing ice for private use are within the reach of all persons who are dependent on it." He saw in this legislation a case where extension of public control might be desirable and where a state could "try novel social and economic experi-

[21] When the same issue was presented to the Supreme Court thirteen years later in *Olsen v. Nebraska*, 313 U.S. 236 (1941), the Ribnik decision was specifically reversed.

[22] *Williams v. Standard Oil Co.*, 278 U.S. 235 (1929).

[23] *New State Ice Co. v. Liebman*, 285 U.S. 262 (1932).

ments without risk to the rest of the country." He chided the majority for using its power to prevent experimentation on the ground that a statute is "arbitrary, capricious, or unreasonable." In the exercise of this power, Mr. Justice Brandeis said, "we must be ever on our guard, lest we erect our prejudices into legal principles."

THE WITHERING OF THE CONCEPT

***Nebbia v. New York* (1934).**[24] In 1933, the New York legislature enacted a statute which declared the milk business to be one affected with a public interest. It also created a Milk Control Board charged with the duty of fixing minimum wholesale and retail prices of milk. The board fixed 9 cents as the lawful price in Rochester. Leo Nebbia, a Rochester grocer, sold two quarts of milk and a loaf of bread for 18 cents. He was convicted of violation of the law, and the case was carried to the Supreme Court on the ground that fixing the sale price of milk took property and liberty without due process of law.

In a 5-to-4 decision, the United States Supreme Court upheld the New York law. The decision is quite different from that in the ice-company case two years prior, and it probably represents the effect of the economic depression upon the judicial mind. The majority of the Supreme Court found adequate basis for more than ordinary public interest in the New York milk industry. They agreed that milk was an essential item of diet, that the failure of producers to receive a reasonable return over a period of time threatened relaxation of vigilance against contamination, and that the production and distribution of milk largely affects the health and prosperity of people of New York State.

At the same time, the Court held that the dairy business is not, "in the accepted phrase, a public utility." Nevertheless, if the industry is subject to regulation generally, the Court believed that no "constitutional principle bars the state from correcting existing maladjustments by legislation touching prices." Holding that the due-process clause makes no mention of prices any more than other incidents of property, the majority intimated that there is nothing particularly "sacrosanct" about price as an object of regulation. As for the phrase "affected with a public interest," it was interpreted to mean "no more than that an industry, for adequate reason, is subject to control for the public good."

Reading for the majority, Mr. Justice Roberts summed up the reasoning of the Court as follows:

> If the law-making body within its sphere of government concludes that the conditions or practices in an industry make unrestricted competition an inadequate safeguard of the consumer's interests, produce waste harmful to the

[24] 291 U.S. 538.

public, threaten ultimately to cut off the supply of a commodity needed by the public, or portend the destruction of the industry itself, appropriate statutes passed in an honest effort to correct the threatened consequences may not be set aside because the regulation adopted fixes prices reasonably deemed by the legislature to be fair to those engaged in the industry and to the consuming public.

Thus, by the Nebbia decision the affected-with-a-public-interest test of economic regulation appears to have been discarded. It is important to note that prior to this case the public-interest status was assigned a business to protect the consumer by regulating rates and services. In this case, however, producers asked for the price fixing as a protection against the effects of competition. As Emery Troxel points out, the milk-control boards were dominated by milk-producer associations determined to get higher incomes for dairy farmers. After the Nebbia decision they did not show any particular interest in consumer welfare. When "the Supreme Court approved milk price control, it gave its support to a kind of monopolistic pricing. The pricing practices of milk producer associations were monopolistic before the case was decided and the dominant milk distributors in most American cities preferred price agreements to competitive pricing. Managerial administration of milk prices was strengthened by the Nebbia decision." [25]

Nevertheless, *Nebbia v. New York* is an epochal case, not only because regulation under the state police power was once again upheld, but also because it makes a departure from the Court's use of the "public-interest" category of business to justify regulation.

Subsequent cases. The distinction between private and public business, as a criterion for testing the validity of price and service regulation in the latter group, has tended to be broken down by Supreme Court decisions since the Nebbia case. In an impressive number of cases [26] culminating in the Hope Natural Gas decision,[27] the Supreme Court has taken the position that the Fifth and Fourteenth Amendments are not bars to price and service regulation that is reasonably appropriate to the evil to be remedied. In the Hope case the Court held that the typical rate case does not contain issues that fall legitimately within the purview of the Court.

A few cases may be noted for illustrative purposes. In them the Court followed the Nebbia doctrine and held that the due-process clause does not hinder the federal government from fixing minimum milk prices or

[25] Emery Troxel, *Economics of Public Utilities* (New York: Rinehart & Company, Inc., 1947), p. 23.

[26] For an extensive list see the minority opinion in *FPC v. Natural Gas Pipeline Co.*, 315 U.S. 575 (1942).

[27] *FPC v. Hope Natural Gas Co.*, 320 U.S. 591. See below pp. 251–253.

coal prices. While these later cases involved the federal government rather than the state governments, they do indicate that a business is not deprived of its property without due process of law if the public interest in safety, health, or welfare demands price regulation.

In a case decided in 1939, the United States Supreme Court upheld the fixing of minimum milk prices according to a plan set up by the Secretary of Agriculture under authority of the federal Agricultural Marketing Agreement Act.[28] In this case the Court pointed out that the series of price-regulation cases beginning with *Munn v. Illinois* had been reexamined and that the decision in *Nebbia v. New York* meant that, when the public interest demanded, price regulation could be undertaken without trespassing upon the due-process provisions.

Measures to fix prices of bituminous coal in interstate commerce were also supported by the United States Supreme Court in 1940.[29] This case involved a federal law designed to stabilize coal prices and production through strong regulatory devices applied to the bituminous coal industry. The Court pointed out that price control is one of the means available to the states and to Congress for the protection and promotion of the welfare of the economic system.

The Court completed its reversal when, in *Olsen v. Nebraska*,[30] it upheld state regulation of private employment agencies and expressly reversed the Ribnik decision. Justice Douglas called attention to the trend away from previous holdings in this field and cited many cases in which an increasing number of industries were being subjected to economic regulation. Rather than concern himself with unreal and difficult-to-identify categories of private and public business, he emphasized that considerations of the wisdom, need, or appropriateness of legislation should be left to the legislature.

The concept today. Although the traditional distinctions between public and private businesses is withering, this process is not, in the words of Horace Gray, "likely to proceed rapidly. It [the public utility concept] is deeply rooted in our law and social traditions; powerful economic organizations have a vested interest in its preservation as a protective device; and, as a people, our capacity for 'institutional inventiveness' is poorly developed." [31] The courts must still occasionally concern themselves with

[28] *United States v. Rock Royal Cooperative, Inc.*, 307 U.S. 533 (1939). See discussion of this law and the case, in Chapter 24.

[29] *Sunshine Anthracite Coal Co. v. Adkins*, 310 U.S. 381 (1940). The control of oil production through proration schemes has also been upheld as valid exercise of the state police power. See *Champlin Ref. Co. v. Corporation Com.*, 286 U.S. 210 (1932), and *Railroad Com. v. Rowan & Nichols Oil Co.*, 310 U.S. 573 (1940).

[30] 313 U.S. 236 (1941).

[31] "The Passing of the Public Utilities Concept," 16 *Journal of Land and Public*

the question of what constitutes public service or public use, especially in regard to common carriers.[32] For example, a Court of Appeals found that an aviation company engaged in the business of spraying farm lands is not a common carrier, since the carrying of insecticide to fields is incidental to the performance of a special service.[33] A New York court ruled that the publishing of a classified directory by an operating telephone company is not affected with a public interest sufficient to subject the publisher to regulation as to rates or nondiscriminatory service.[34] A nonprofit community club which supplied water to the residents of a tract of land for a flat rate was held not to be a public utility where it did not hold itself out to serve the public generally.[35]

But none of these cases was of major importance, and they were seldom appealed. Frequently, the state utility commission is successful in settling the issue so that a judicial determination is not necessary. For example, the Massachusetts commission found garbage collecting a public utility where the fee was paid by the producers of the waste rather than by the city.[36] The towing of floating cranes, dredges, pile drivers, and the like was found to be within the commission's jurisdiction in California. However, the turning of ships by towboats, which is usually the pulling of vessels away from docks so that they can proceed under their own power, was not.[37] As a final illustration, the Wisconsin commission ruled that a street-directory information service by a telephone company was not a public-utility service and therefore could be discontinued without commission approval.[38]

Economic Criteria for Policy Decisions

This historical survey of the legal development of the public-utility concept reveals that before the Nebbia case the Supreme Court was unable to agree upon any reliable criteria that could be used for determining whether a business was affected with a public interest. After the Nebbia decision the Court allowed legislative and administrative bodies much

Utility Economics 8–20 (February, 1940). See also Howard R. Smith, "The Rise and Fall of the Public Utility Concept," 23 *Journal of Land and Public Utility Economics* 117–131 (May, 1947).

[32] See, for examples, *Annual Digest of Public Utilities Reports, New Series* (Washington, D.C.: Public Utilities Reports, 1953), pp. 226–230.

[33] *Marsh Aviation Co. v. State Corporation Commission*, 228 P.2d 959 (1951).

[34] *Abco Moving & Storage Corp. v. New York Telephone Co.*, 106 N.Y.S.2d 90 (1951).

[35] *Schall v. Glenburn Community Club*, 94 P.U.R. (n.s.) 393 (1951).

[36] *Re Callahan*, D.P.U. 9167, May 15, 1951.

[37] *Re Coggeshall Launch Co.*, 92 P.U.R. (n.s.) 237 (1951).

[38] *Re Wisconsin Telephone Co.*, 93 P.U.R. (n.s.) 490 (1952).

greater discretion to decide that the rates of a business may be regulated without violating the due-process clauses.

In formulating an economic policy of price and service control, legislative bodies have employed various criteria. The tests that have been used take into account the growth and development of the economy and its impact on society.

THE TEST OF NECESSITY

The necessity of a particular business has frequently been the standard used to assign public-utility status. Modern life finds the services of many businesses practically indispensable. A moment's reflection will bring to mind the various ways in which modern social and industrial living depends upon electric, water, gas, communication, and local-transport services. In addition, it is conceivable that a legislature, under certain circumstances, might find food, clothing, shelter—or almost any other good or service—a necessity.

Legislatures and the courts have recognized the essential character of a number of enterprises. The service of warehousemen was regarded as necessary to farmers in *Munn v. Illinois*. The same essential character was found to inhere in the fire-insurance business in the German Alliance case. At one time the majority of the Supreme Court found nothing necessary to the public in the theater-ticket-agency (Tyson case), ice (New State Ice case), or employment-agency (Ribnik case) businesses, but the opinion in the last case was later reversed.

THE TEST OF STRUCTURAL MONOPOLY

The existence of a monopoly or a "virtual monopoly" has been a guide for determining when the public interest in a business is sufficient to justify regulation. Where competition is absent or conspicuously ineffective, three alternatives face government. The attempt may be made to restore competition through antitrust proceedings; the business may be taken over and operated by government; or the monopoly may be retained and controlled because it is more efficient than competition in the particular instance. In the latter case, government must do what competition is otherwise expected to do, that is, protect the consumer from exploitation by those in a monopolistic position. Hence, government regulates rates and services.

There are several reasons why some utility monopolies may be regarded as more efficient than competition. Public utilities tend to be industries requiring a relatively large capital outlay. Production facilities and distribution lines are extremely costly. The importance of this capital investment is apparent when one compares the rates of capital turnover.[39]

[39] Capital turnover $= \dfrac{\text{annual gross revenues}}{\text{total capital invested in the enterprise}}$

Capital may turn over eight times annually in a chain-store business, once a year in an automobile-manufacturing business, and once in three years in a steel plant, but a public utility will have a capital turnover of once in four or five years. With such large capital outlay, fixed investment and maintenance costs are very important. Moreover, in the operations themselves a large proportion of costs are relatively fixed.

The importance of fixed costs means that costs per unit of output tend to be markedly lower as the plant capacity is approached. Decreasing costs are also encountered as the plants become larger, as well as with full utilization of existing plants. For example, a 1,000,000-kilowatt generating station does not carry twice the investment or operating cost of a 500,000-kilowatt station. Although distribution costs may tend to increase as the size of a public-utility plant increases, the cost per unit of service apparently does not, and in some cases (as where high-tension lines may be used by an electric company) it may actually decrease.

A further cause for decreasing per-unit costs with the larger public-utility plants comes from the character of demands made on them by customers. Obviously, a public utility must have investment in facilities adequate to meet peak demands. The more customers a plant has, the less likely it is that all or most of them will want their maximum service at the same time. This means that the capital investment per customer will tend to be less and the cost of serving will also be lower through the more efficient utilization of the plant.[40]

The fact that costs per unit of service are generally lower with the larger plant means that monopoly, rather than competition, tends to be more efficient for the public. Monopoly is more efficient also in its use of the city streets and other facilities. If competitive telephone, gas, water, electricity, or street-railway lines were allowed to build multiple lines down the city streets or across property, the result would be a confusing and inefficient mass of duplicating facilities. These might not only hamper use of the streets but impair the quality of service.

Competition is also not conducive to the lowest costs of investment capital. A single monopolistic company can become better known and occupy a better position in the investment market than rival companies. Because of the inevitable cutthroat character of competition which would grow out of the high fixed costs of rival companies, earnings would be

[40] The telephone industry is one which is sometimes pointed out as being operated under conditions of increasing costs as the size of plant increases. It is said that the cost per subscriber in a system of 10,000 subscribers is greater than in one of 1,000. The reason given is that the number of possible connections increases in a geometric ratio. However, if the service actually given is taken into account, the telephone industry still seems to be one in which costs decrease with increasing size. While the cost per *subscriber* may increase, the cost per possible call or per call-mile-minute would seem to decrease.

impaired and financial stability threatened. Such a situation would cause investors to want a higher return for their capital before embarking it in an enterprise.

Competition would be ineffective as well as inefficient. With high fixed costs per unit, costs would be lower with more complete utilization. Per-unit costs would also tend to be lower as the result of production on a larger scale. Both these types of decreasing costs would cause a strong competition for business. Unless restricted by an effective agreement among operators—a move tantamount to monopoly—the struggle for business would probably give rise to cutthroat competition. The economic minimum of price being out-of-pocket, or direct, costs, this competition could be carried on only at a loss. The ultimate result of such rivalry would probably be monopoly, with the strongest company surviving.

Thus competition cannot be relied on to protect the public, even if it were not an expensive way of conducting the public-utility business. Moreover, the quality of service given to patrons would probably be impaired. This is particularly well dramatized by experience in the telephone field. When two or more telephone companies are in a locality, adequate service means that each customer must have telephones of each company.

Being aware of the value of monopoly in certain enterprises, the Supreme Court has accepted the appropriateness of legislative action to safeguard the public against the dangers inherent in monopoly. In *Munn v. Illinois* the Court recognized the monopolistic position of warehousemen in Chicago and therefore upheld the exercise of state police power to fix grain-elevator rates. On the other hand, the Court maintained that monopoly was lacking in the businesses of meat packing (Wolff case), ice (New State Ice case), and gasoline (Williams case).

The test of structural monopoly, however, is too narrow a guide in all the instances in which utility regulation is appropriate. Railroads, motor carriers, taxicabs, hotels, grain elevators, and insurance companies have been held to be public businesses sufficient to justify rate regulation, even though they were competitive. Obviously, this criterion is not a complete one.

THE TEST OF EXCESSIVE COMPETITION

The discussion of certain advantages of monopoly has called attention to the evils of excessive or cutthroat competition. Congress has been cognizant of such dangers. In the Sunshine Anthracite case the Supreme Court approved the extension of public-utility status to the coal industry, because "overproduction and savage, competitive warfare wasted the industry." [41] It should be noted that this test is not always designed to protect the consuming public, who may benefit from the low prices that result

[41] *Sunshine Anthracite Coal Co. v. Adkins*, 310 U.S. 395 (1940).

from excessive competition. Instead, this test sometimes protects competitors who may be injured by competition.

THE TEST OF CONSUMER'S DISADVANTAGE

A generalized test for the public-interest character of business was suggested by R. G. Tugwell. He referred to it as "a theory of consumer's disadvantage." [42] It could be argued that all the previously discussed tests are subsumed under this general criterion. The basic question is: "Will the consumer suffer from this particular business if it continues to operate and serve the public under present conditions?" If the service is so essential to his life that the consumer should not be subjected to the rates and service set at the whims of private operators, or if the monopolistic position of the enterprise causes him to suffer discriminatory practices and exorbitant prices, or if excessive competition results in injury to the consumer, then the test of consumer's disadvantage would indicate that the business is clothed with a public interest. But, in addition, the test can be used to sanction regulation even when these economic conditions are not present, on the grounds that the normal competitive controls operate to the disadvantage of the consumer.

The theory of consumer's disadvantage has never received explicit recognition from the courts, but it has been implicit in the reasoning of many decisions. Justice Stone, dissenting in the Tyson case, declared that the element common to all lawful price regulation has been "the existence of a situation or a combination of circumstances materially restricting the regulative force of competition, so that buyers or sellers are placed at such a disadvantage in the bargaining struggle that serious economic consequences result to a very large number of members of the community." [43] For one reason or another, the consumer was found to be at a disadvantage in a number of businesses in which utility regulation was held to be appropriate. In the case of grain warehouses it was because of the strategic position of the business; in the case of fire insurance, because of the predetermination of prices; and in the case of the milk business, because of the threatened shortage of an essential product. The majority in the Nebbia case implicitly recognized the validity of this test when it said the "phrase 'affected with a public interest' can, in the nature of things, mean no more than that an industry, for adequate reason, is subject to control for the public good." [44]

THE GENERAL-WELFARE TEST

Sometimes the concern expressed for the welfare of the consumer in the above test is broadened to encompass the welfare of the entire com-

[42] R. G. Tugwell, *The Economic Basis of Public Interest* (Menasha, Wis.: George Banta Publishing Company, 1922).

[43] 273 U.S. 451–452 (1927).

[44] 291 U.S. 536.

munity. In time of war or emergency the national public interest extends to many businesses normally considered private. Regulation of rents in Washington, D.C., during World War I was upheld on this basis in *Block v. Hirsh*;[45] so was rent regulation in New York.[46] One of the bases for permitting the regulation of milk prices in the Nebbia case was the existence of an emergency.

Even in normal times concern for the welfare of the nation has been sufficient reason to justify the regulation of certain businesses. The Supreme Court emphasized the strategic importance of the coal industry in the national economy in the Sunshine Anthracite Coal case. And, in upholding the Agricultural Marketing Agreement Act in the Rock Royal decision, the Court said: ". . . the disruption of the orderly exchange of commodities in interstate commerce impairs the purchasing power of farmers, thus destroying the value of agricultural assets to the detriment of the national public interest."[47]

The general-welfare test was given its fullest and most explicit expression by Justice Brandeis in his New State Ice Company case dissent:[48]

> . . . The business of supplying to others, for compensation any article or service whatsoever may become a matter of public concern. Whether it is or is not depends upon the conditions existing in the community affected. If it is a matter of public concern it may be regulated, whatever the business. The public's concern may be limited to a single feature of the business, so that the needed protection can be secured by a relatively slight degree of regulation. . . . On the other hand, the public concern about a particular business may be so pervasive and varied as to require constant and detailed supervision and a very high degree of regulation.

The Public-utility Concept: Conclusions

Prior to the Nebbia case the central problem in public-utility regulation was a constitutional one. The Supreme Court took the position that detailed rate and service regulation was valid only if the Court found that the enterprise being regulated was in the category of businesses "affected with a public interest." Unfortunately, from a legal point of view, this category of business lacked clear and precise standards.

Since the Nebbia case the distinction between businesses clothed with a public interest and private business has been virtually abandoned, and the decision as to which businesses should be regulated has been largely conceded to the legislature. Subsequent decisions of both state and federal courts give the distinct impression that they feel that the power to

[45] 256 U.S. 135 (1921).

[46] *People v. La Fetra*, 130 N.E. 601, 230 N.Y. 429 (1921).

[47] 307 U.S. 543 (1939).

[48] 285 U.S. 262 (1932).

regulate should be commensurate with the need for regulation. Where the legislature has determined that there is a direct dependence of the community on a particular enterprise, that abuses exist or threaten because of the monopolistic character of the business, that the consumer is placed at a disadvantage, or that the welfare of the whole community is endangered, the Court has ruled that economic regulation does not violate the Constitution.

Whether the present position of the Supreme Court represents a complete denial of the time-honored public-utility concept is difficult to say. It cannot yet be concluded that the Court will never again invalidate actions of legislature or regulatory commissions on due-process grounds. The fiction of public-utility status has an enduring quality. The present-day significance of the concept is that a recognizable body of obligations and regulations applicable to businesses designated as "public utilities" exists. This set of controls is the concern of the three chapters that follow. Since the transportation agencies have already been treated separately in Part II, the discussion will be devoted largely to communications, gas, and electric utilities. Most of the regulatory experience in the public-utility field has pertained to control over these utilities. At the same time, the extent, principles, and problems of control are applicable to other businesses in the public-utility field.

Selected References

Arteaburn, Norman F., "The Origin and First Test of Public Callings," 75 *University of Pennsylvania Law Review* 411 (March, 1927).

Barnes, Irston, *The Economics of Public Utility Regulation*, chaps. 1, 3. New York: Appleton-Century-Crofts, Inc., 1942.

Clemens, Eli Winston, *Economics and Public Utilities*, chap. 2. New York: Appleton-Century-Crofts, Inc., 1950.

Glaeser, M. G., "The Meaning of Public Utility—A Sociological Interpretation," 1 *Journal of Land and Public Utility Economics* 176 (April, 1925).

Gray, H. M., "The Passing of the Public Utilities Concept," 16 *Journal of Land and Public Utility Economics* 8–20 (February, 1940).

Hall, Ford P., *The Concept of a Business Affected with a Public Interest.* Bloomington, Ind.: The Principia Press, Inc., 1940.

Hamilton, W. H., "Affectation with Public Interest," 39 *Yale Law Journal* 1089–1112 (June, 1930).

Harbeson, R. W., "The Public Interest Concept in Law and in Economics," 37 *Michigan Law Review* 181–208 (December, 1938).

Lyon, L. S., V. Abramson, and others, *Government and Economic Life*, vol. II, chap. 21. Washington, D.C.: Brookings Institution, 1940.

McAllister, Breck P, "Lord Hale and Businesses Affected with a Public Interest," 43 *Harvard Law Review* 759–791 (March, 1930).

Mosher, William E., and Finla G. Crawford, *Public Utility Regulation*, chap. 1. New York: Harper & Brothers, 1933.

Smith, Howard R., "The Rise and Fall of the Public Utility Concept," 23 *Journal of Land and Public Utility Economics* 117–131 (May, 1947).

Troxel, Emery, *Economics of Public Utilities*, chaps. 1, 2. New York: Rinehart & Company, Inc., 1947.

10

REGULATION OF PUBLIC-UTILITY SERVICE

The purpose of public-utility regulation is to promote and protect the interest of consumers, investors, and the general public. This purpose is accomplished by regulating the quality and quantity of service, rates charged, and the finance and combinations of public-utility companies. The methods of control have included direct regulation by the courts and legislatures, charters and franchises, and state and federal commissions.[1] Today public-utility regulation is largely in the hands of appointed or elected regulatory commissions.

State and Federal Jurisdiction over Utility Regulation

The responsibility for regulating public utilities is shared by the states and the federal government. The legal basis for state action is found in the police power, which is reserved to the states, and for federal regulation in the powers delegated to Congress and the powers that have been implied therefrom.[2] The principal restrictions on the exercise of these powers are the due-process clauses of the Fourteenth Amendment (which applies to the states) and the Fifth Amendment (which applies to the federal government) and the limitations implied in the concept of federalism. The discussion of the public-utility concept indicated the extent to which the courts believed economic regulation could go without contravening due process. A detailed consideration of the limitations inherent in the division of powers between the federal and state levels of government is beyond the scope of this book.

For the purposes of this discussion it is sufficient to point out briefly the difficulties involved in deciding which level of government has jurisdiction over public utilities. Except for transportation agencies, regulation of public utilities has been generally regarded as a matter for the states. Even the communication agencies, especially the telephone, have been subject to more state than federal control. Although some interstate

[1] See Chapter 3.
[2] See Chapter 2.

communication by telephone or telegraph was placed under a measure of federal regulation as early as were the railroads, a positive program of such control did not emerge until the 1930s. Not until the 1930s were certain aspects of the electric and gas businesses brought under federal regulation; however, there was earlier federal regulation of power producers using water sites on or affecting navigable streams.

Even though large quantities of natural gas and electricity enter interstate commerce, practically all is sold at wholesale and distributed by an intrastate public-utility company. The local and long-distance telephone and telegraph services are closely interwoven, with relatively few companies handling the major portion of them. Radio is, of course, not limited to local market areas, especially within states; yet a fairly large proportion of commercial broadcasting is aimed at a narrow market near the station.

Therefore, because of the nature of the utilities being regulated, federal and state powers overlap and jurisdictional conflicts have occurred. On one hand, the divided responsibility has permitted greater flexibility and an opportunity for experimentation in areas where government has never before entered. On the other hand, the division of authority has been an obstacle to the accomplishment of regulation that has been desired by a majority of the people and necessary to the economic progress of the nation. To an increasing extent the economic problems of this country transcend state boundaries and require federal action. The jurisdictional conflict that arises is not so much a conflict between federal and state levels of government as it is an excuse used by those who oppose regulation per se. In the defense of states' rights is found a stronghold against federal regulation.

Recognizing that interstate and intrastate public-utility activities cannot be marked off into independent spheres, Congress has attempted to divide the jurisdiction of some federal and state commissions. In the Communications Act of 1934, the Public Utility Act of 1935, and the Natural Gas Act of 1938 Congress provided machinery, such as joint committees, for cooperative action.[3] This approach does much to reduce the conflict over spheres of authority, but the role which the federal government is likely to play in future public-utility regulation seems to be enlarging.[4] However, if the present tendency continues, federal action will supplement, rather than supplant, state control. The federal commis-

[3] For a detailed consideration of this cooperation, see Karl Bosworth, "Federal-State Administrative Relations in the Regulation of Public-Service Enterprises," 36 *American Political Science Review* 215–240 (1942).

[4] In *FPC v. East Ohio Gas Co.*, 338 U.S. 464 (1950), the Supreme Court extended the Federal Power Commission's jurisdiction to include some intrastate natural-gas transactions. However, Congress revised this ruling by a measure enacted in 1954.

sions will be in a better position to develop financial and statistical data which are needed by the state commissions to perform their functions properly but which have been beyond their reach. And regulation on the national level will bring greater uniformity to the procedures and principles of state utility control.

Whether a public-utility business is controlled by the federal government or by the states, many of the economic and legal problems—the concepts of adequate service, fair price, and sound finance, for example—are pretty much the same.

State Regulation of Service

The primary interest of public-utility consumers is in securing good service. This fact has sometimes been overlooked in controversies over rates, financial practices, and public ownership; yet these matters are really secondary to the quality of service. To be sure, under private enterprise public-utility service in this country has reached a high standard, and consumers have found relatively little basis for complaint. This has perhaps been due to the stimulus of profit, to a degree of competition between public utilities in instances where a customer has an alternative choice, to the fear of public ownership, and to regulatory supervision. Nevertheless, particularly in some localities, service standards leave something to be desired, and effective control by commissions is ever necessary to ensure high quality. Customers are far more likely to complain of the price of service than of its quality. Regulatory commissions are also more prone to give price and its attendant problems more scrutiny than they give to service.

Service and rates are closely related. A high standard of service involves high costs, and rates must reflect this expense. Low rates may induce a utility to lower its quality of service unless the latter is safeguarded. Should a commission be initially successful in forcing a higher-grade service than rates can support, the resultant effect upon earnings almost inevitably leads to impaired service. It is often poor economy to insist upon reduced rates without taking into account the character of service demanded by the public and the cost of furnishing it.

The common-law service obligations of the common carrier [5] were transferred to other businesses affected with a public interest. They have become the basis of service regulation in the public-utility field. If no statutory service regulation were provided, or if the existing statutes were incomplete, an aggrieved customer could sue for damages under common law if a public utility did not serve adequately, continuously, expeditiously, and without unreasonable discrimination. Although breaches of

[5] See Chapter 6.

these obligations are thus causes for action and would therefore have some regulatory effect in the absence of statutory controls, effective regulation depends upon continuous supervision by a fully authorized commission. The individual customer who feels that he has a grievance cannot always afford a lawsuit, nor will he always go to the trouble of suing for redress.

Commission regulation of public-utility service has been similar to that placed on transportation agencies. Its main aspects are controls over entry into service, abandonment of service, extension of facilities, discrimination in service, and service standards. Relatively less attention has been given to regulation for safety than with carriers, because the public safety is not so much involved. On the other hand, more supervision of the standards of service has been undertaken, probably because of the more monopolistic position of the local utilities and their closer relations with the public. A further difference is found in the practice of safeguarding public utilities against competition of like service to a greater degree than is characteristic of transportation.

SCOPE OF STATE REGULATION OF SERVICE

There is naturally much difference in the scope of regulatory jurisdiction over service among the forty-eight states and the District of Columbia. All these governments now have commissions which exert some control over privately owned utilities. The commissions of Delaware, Minnesota, Iowa, South Dakota, Florida, Mississippi, and Texas have limited jurisdiction. As of 1954, including the District of Columbia, six states gave commissions no jurisdiction over electric utility service; eight placed no control over natural gas, and eight no control over manufactured gas utilities; thirteen excluded street railways; seven did not regulate water companies; two excepted telephone and telegraph companies; and only four states had no jurisdiction over motor common carriers.[6]

As might be expected, service regulation even where found is not uniform. The character of commission jurisdiction varies, and the extent of actual regulation through similar powers differs between commissions. Most states have power to authorize establishment and abandonment of service, to prevent discrimination, and to define adequacy of service. Power to require extensions within municipal limits is customary, and many states empower commissions to require private utilities to make extensions into rural areas. While most states establish service standards for public utilities, relatively few commissions maintain systematic inspection, grading, and policing of these standards.

[6] FPC, *State Commission Jurisdiction and Regulation of Electric and Gas Utilities*, (1948); Council of State Governments, *The Book of the States, 1954–1955* (Chicago, 1954), p. 218.

ENTRY INTO SERVICE

Private enterprise is not free to embark upon the business of furnishing public-utility service. Under the common law, such entry was restricted; today, practically all states require that permission from the public-utility commission be obtained. In some states, the public also has no right to enter the field by construction or purchase of a municipally owned plant, unless approval is obtained from the state agency. As in the carrier field, this approval takes the form of the grant of a certificate of convenience and necessity; the purpose of this, of course, is the certification that the public interest requires the service and that the applicant is in a position to serve consistently with that interest.

In most jurisdictions, a public-utility company needs more than a certificate of convenience and necessity from the state commission. In order to use the public streets and other facilities, municipal corporations or other state subdivisions require the obtaining of a franchise. This instrument customarily grants special rights to supply service and to use streets for lines to distribute it. In addition, it often contains provisions respecting rates, kinds of service, and other matters. Although the franchise is a contractual right to use public facilities for utility service, modern regulatory statutes make actual commencement of service contingent, in the last analysis, upon the receipt of a certificate of convenience and necessity from the state commission.

As has been noted in a previous chapter,[7] franchises vary from short-term contract grants to perpetual grants. When franchises were the principal form by which the local authority regulated public utilities, control of their length of term and detailed provisions was of the utmost importance. With development of commission regulation the franchise has become far less important, and its regulatory features have been largely superseded.

The primary purpose of requiring a certificate of convenience and necessity is found in the economics of monopoly. Attention has already been called to the injurious and uneconomical nature of competition in the public-utility field.[8] The ultimate losers if restrained competition were allowed appear to be the customers themselves. So great has been the public interest in avoiding wastes and evils of competition that modern statutes do not leave this control to municipalities and state subdivisions but place it in the hands of a state commission.

Restriction of entry into service also has other purposes. Commissions consider the financial standing and responsibility of applicants and do much to stimulate good service by refusing to grant certificates to those

[7] See Chapter 3.

[8] See pp. 208–211.

who do not have the required qualifications. Favorable action on an application has often been contingent upon approval of the financial plan of the new company. By refusing to approve where the investors seem to be subject to too great dangers, commissions have used the certificate as a means of protecting them. Because a certificate does not grant an exclusive right to do business, and a commission can allow others to enter the same field, it has sometimes found the threat of approving the application of a competing company to be an effective means of control.

EXTENSION OF SERVICE

Most commissions require that a public utility obtain a certificate of convenience and necessity for voluntary extension of service. In most cases where the extension is into territory already served or into adjacent territory not served by another company, certificates are not required. Where they are, they are handled much like permits to enter service and present no particularly difficult problems.

Far more difficulty is encountered where a commission orders a public utility to extend its service involuntarily. The great majority of commissions have statutory power to require such extension, even into rural areas. This follows from the common-law obligation to serve adequately. This power, however, is not without limitation. Under well-established legal doctrine, the United States Supreme Court has held that a public utility cannot be required to extend service into areas which it has not held itself out to serve.[9] The bounds of a territory which a utility has professed to serve are determined by the facts in each case; actual doing of business, franchise limits, and the definition of territory in the corporate charter are elements of such evidence.

Where extensions are ordered into sparsely settled areas, whether in municipal or rural territory, commissions have been rather careful to safeguard orders by setting up rules whereby customers will compensate the utility for the service. In rural electric extensions, commissions often require a minimum number of subscribers per mile of line, a high minimum bill, or part payment of the cost of construction by the customers. If the extension appears to be compensatory at a higher rate than that currently charged, and if it appears that the higher rate can be collected, the courts have sustained commissions in ordering extension of service.[10]

ABANDONMENT OF SERVICE

Complete abandonment. The legal rule is well established that states may require public-service companies to obtain a certificate allowing

[9] See *ICC v. Oregon-Wash. R.R. and Nav. Co.*, 288 U.S. 14 (1932), and cases there cited.

[10] *Woodhaven Gas and Light Co. v. Public Serv. Com.*, 269 U.S. 244, 249 (1925).

abandonment, whether total or partial.[11] Protection of public welfare under the police power gives a ground for this rule. Since the service is likely to be comparatively indispensable, this safeguard would seem to be entirely lawful. Nevertheless, where the abandonment contemplated is complete and follows a period of losses, a commission cannot ordinarily refuse to grant the certificate within a reasonable time.

One exception to the right for complete withdrawal may be noted. Where a public utility has agreed to a franchise by which it has assumed the contractual obligation to serve for a period of time under specified circumstances, it may be compelled to operate in spite of loss.[12] The courts tend to interpret such contracts strictly, however, and the obligation of the public utility must be clearly shown. One might note that in case of bankruptcy of the utility, abandonment could legally follow irrespective of such contracts.

Partial abandonment. Most of the difficulty regarding abandonment is encountered when a utility desires to discontinue a part of the service found to be unprofitable. A public utility has no legal right to abandon a part of the service, even though this portion be carried on at a loss.[13] However, so long as it continues to operate, it is obligated to perform reasonably adequate service. Where a portion of the service causes loss large enough to affect the return on the property as a whole, the question of right to abandonment is a little confused. In one case, the Supreme Court said that "a carrier cannot be compelled to carry on even a branch of business at a loss, much less the whole business of carriage." [14] In another case, however, the Court took the position that a utility might not discontinue a portion of its service even though this is operated at a loss and "the system as a whole fails to earn a fair return upon the value of the property." [15] In the light of the often stated opinion that a public utility cannot continue to exercise privileges granted by its charter and refuse to serve adequately, even at some pecuniary loss on a part of the business, the latter position would seem to represent the prevailing legal view.[16]

[11] See O. P. Field, "The Withdrawal from Service of Public Utility Companies," 35 *Yale Law Journal* 169–190 (December, 1925). See also *Western and Atlantic R.R. v. Georgia P.S. Com.*, 267 U.S. 493 (1925).

[12] *Georgia Power Co. v. Decatur*, 281 U.S. 505 (1930).

[13] *Fort Smith Lt. and Tr. Co. v. Bourland*, 267 U.S. 330 (1925).

[14] *Brooks-Scanlon Co. v. Railroad Com.*, 251 U.S. 399 (1920).

[15] *Fort Smith Lt. and Tr. Co. v. Bourland*, 267 U.S. 333 (1925).

[16] See *United Fuel Gas Co. v. Railroad Com. of Kentucky*, 278 U.S. 300 (1929); *Texas R.R. Com. v. Eastern Texas R.R. Co.*, 264 U.S. 79 (1924); *Atlantic Coast Line R.R. Co. v. North Carolina Corp. Com.*, 206 U.S. 1 (1907); *Missouri Pac. R.R. Co. v. Kansas*, 216 U.S. 262 (1910). Although some of these are railroad cases, the principles would seem equally applicable to all public utilities.

In spite of the power of a commission to compel continuance of service at a loss, this authority should be administered sparingly. The company and the commission have the public obligation to search for means of making a losing portion of service pay its way. A public-utility company cannot long serve other customers well if it cannot be operated at a profit. If it cannot be made to pay, if it places a burden on the financial soundness of all operations, and if its discontinuance would not cause too great public harm, the commission should issue the needed permit for abandonment.

SERVICE DISCRIMINATION

Considering the problem broadly, the law against service discrimination involves the obligation of a public utility to serve all customers within its professed territory and to serve them equally.

The duty to serve all. The general rule is that public utilities must serve all who apply for service and who are in the territory which a utility professes to serve. In some cases, a public utility may properly refuse to do so. A public utility is, of course, not bound to serve those who do not pay for their service or who delay longer than a certain period in meeting their bills. Where a gas or water company has a diminishing supply and an adequate one cannot be obtained at a reasonable capital outlay, courts and commissions have allowed it to refuse to serve new customers. Courts have also upheld public utilities in refusing to serve a competitor, whether the competing company is a private manufacturer selling surplus electricity or water, or a public-service company.[17] Refusal to serve has also been upheld where a customer used abusive and obscene language over the telephone or telegraph, and where a message was in aid of an illegal purpose. It is well settled that public utilities may make reasonable rules for the conduct of their business, including requirement of a cash deposit, and refuse to serve where these rules are not obeyed.

Public utilities have been ordered to serve in many cases where at first they refused to do so. Courts and commissions have quite generally held that a public utility cannot continue to refuse to serve after a customer has paid his back bills or complied with rules which he had previously not obeyed. Financial embarrassment is ordinarily not held to be an excuse for failure to serve, and it is generally agreed that the proper remedy lies in application for increased rates.

The duty to serve equally. Most cases of refusal to serve are those in which customers are not served equally; in addition to these, there are some cases where a utility serves classes of customers, or certain customers within a class, differently. Here the company has not refused to serve but

[17] See *Rogers Iron Works v. Public Service Com.*, 323 Mo. 122 (1929), and cases there cited.

is serving discriminately. As with the duty to serve all, the obligation to serve equally is subject to a rule of reasonableness. This type of discrimination is closely related to rate discrimination. Most differences in service present differences in costs and rates. The claim is often made, then, that the rates are discriminatory rather than that unreasonable differences exist in service.

STANDARDS OF SERVICE

The common-law obligation to serve adequately has been translated by modern public-utility laws into the establishment of certain minimum standards of service. Nearly all the state commissions have power to establish such service standards, although the scope of this authority differs. Rather few commissions who set up standards have appropriations large enough to exercise continuous supervision by inspection and grading. The engineering staffs of the more modern commissions have done much work in this field. They have been assisted to a great degree by research of the companies themselves, the U.S. Bureau of Standards, trade associations such as the American Gas Association and the Edison Electric Institute, and the National Association of Railroad and Utilities Commissioners.

STATE REGULATION OF SERVICE: CONCLUSIONS

Service is obviously as important to a public-utility customer as are rates. Yet beyond matters of entry and abandonment of service, the efforts at regulation have not been nearly so great in this sphere. This difference may be due to several factors. Measurement of adequate service is not subject to the objective calculation possible with rates and finance. Regulation of service on a broad and effective scale calls for much work and expense; most public-utility commissions have not been granted appropriations to provide for adequate and expert staffs to undertake research, inspection, and grading of service. Furthermore, private enterprise in the United States has had a good and improving record for a high grade of public-utility service, and the demand for regulation has not been great. Whether the service has been as good as modern technical progress makes possible is another question. The significant point is that the utilities have adopted enough of this technical advance to cause service to improve consistently.

The record in control of entry into service has been good, as measured by the economic advantages of monopolistic production in public-utility service. A few of the more modern commissions have made excellent progress in regulating for adequate service. In other cases, a need appears for more effective enforcement machinery. The tendency to except municipally owned utilities from service regulation is also open to question. As service requirements come to be better understood and as technical improvements become more standardized, a more adequate system of regulation will probably be developed. It should be remembered that a high grade of service is the primary goal of public-utility regulation.

Federal Regulation of Service: Communications [18]

Whereas the public-utility businesses that are regulated in each of the several states are usually controlled by one commission, at the federal level regulation of public utilities is in the hands of several commissions, each of which specializes in only one business area. Therefore, in discussing federal regulation of service it will also be necessary to describe briefly the origin and jurisdiction of each of the various commissions. For this reason, the approach will be in terms of areas of regulation rather than types of service regulations.

The economic characteristics of businesses in the communications field, except for radio and television broadcasting, are similar to those of common carriers in the transportation businesses. As a matter of fact, communication companies serving the public have been referred to as transporters of ideas and as carriers analogous to railways and steamships. Whether by telegraph, telephone, or wireless, most operators of communication facilities hold themselves out to serve the public in much the same way that a railroad does; their relation to the public is close, their capital investment is relatively large, and they have similar tendencies toward monopoly.

In contrast to other carriers, these monopolistic tendencies have shown more concrete results. The American Telephone and Telegraph Company, an operating and holding company, occupies a preeminent position in this field. Though control of more than 200 corporations, the company supervises in the United States between 80 and 90 per cent of local telephone service, 98 per cent of long-distance telephone wires, practically all the wire facilities used by radio broadcasting, and all the transoceanic radiotelephone service.[19]

REGULATION OF WIRE COMMUNICATIONS

As early as 1866, Congress provided in the Post Roads Act for the granting of federal franchise for the operation of telegraph lines over public domain, post roads, and navigable streams. Further regulation was

[18] For a comprehensive treatment of the subject, see J. G. Mosher and Richard Lavine, *Radio and the Law* (Los Angeles: Parke & Co., 1947).

[19] FCC, *Investigation of the Telephone Industry in the U.S.*, H. Doc. 340, 76th Cong., 1st Sess. (1939), p. xxiii.

provided in 1888. At this time the Interstate Commerce Commission was authorized to require telegraph companies that received a government subsidy for construction to operate as common carriers, and to make interconnections with other companies that had submitted to the Post Roads Act of 1866.

The Mann-Elkins Act of 1910 placed the interstate, but not foreign, transmission of messages by wire (and wireless) within many of the parts of the law applicable to railroads. The control of telephone, telegraph, and cable utilities by the Interstate Commerce Commission was not particularly aggressive. It found few complaints raised in interstate wire-communications matters, and it was so engaged in railroad regulatory problems that it had little time to investigate communication affairs. In the twenty-four years during which communication companies were under the Commission, it dealt with only fourteen rate cases.[20]

The relatively ineffective regulation of telephone, telegraph, and cable companies by the Commission should not be blamed entirely upon that body. The laws under which it was operating had so many omissions that effective administration was practically impossible. The Interstate Commerce Commission continued to regulate telegraph, telephone, and cable companies until the passage of the Communications Act of 1934. This law is far from being a counterpart of the federal railroad statutes, since the breadth and depth of control provisions found in the latter are lacking.

Under the Act, all common carriers of messages by wire (or wireless) are required to furnish reasonably adequate service upon a request for it. To supervise the adequacy of service, the then Federal Communications Commission was empowered to take action for the establishment of physical connection between carriers and for through routes. Construction of new lines or extension of existing ones, with certain exceptions, was subjected to the obtaining of a certificate of convenience and necessity from the Commission. The Commission was also authorized to require the extension of common-carrier communication lines when found to be in the public interest but not to involve so great an expense as to impair the ability of a carrier to perform its duty of service to the public. The act applied to wireless- as well as wire-communications companies.

REGULATION OF WIRELESS COMMUNICATIONS

Between 1910 and 1934, the control of radio communications developed along somewhat different lines from wire-communications regulation. When regulation came, it was at the request of the radio businesses to be regulated for their own protection, although there was no agreement on the form and method of regulation. Also, radio communication is the

[20] J. M. Herring and G. C. Gross, *Telecommunications* (New York: McGraw-Hill Book Company, Inc., 1936), p. 220.

only public utility controlled exclusively by the federal government, so jurisdictional questions have never arisen. Division of responsibility between the federal and state governments is impossible. Only the national government is in a position to assign the limited number of wave lengths that are available and to police their use.

Early legislation in the field of radio was not regulatory. In the interests of safety Congress passed a law in 1910 requiring that every vessel carrying fifty or more passengers from any port in the United States be equipped with wireless apparatus. The Act was administered by the Bureau of Navigation in the Department of Commerce and Labor. A law of 1912 required all radio operators and stations to be licensed, and measures were included to avoid interference, maintain secrecy in messages, and give government stations certain preferences.

With the rapid development of commercial broadcasting in the early 1920s this early legislation proved inadequate. No special provision for assigning wave lengths had been included. Two adverse court decisions, coupled with a ruling of the Attorney General, brought an end to attempts by Secretary of Commerce Hoover to bring some kind of order into broadcasting. In 1923, the Circuit Court of Appeals of the District of Columbia held that the Secretary had no authority to refuse a license to a wireless station.[21] Three years later the Attorney General ruled that radio stations could use different hours and frequencies from those assigned to them by the Secretary of Commerce.[22] Also in 1926, a district court held that the Secretary had no power under existing law to make any regulations affecting radio licenses.[23] Broadcasters proceeded to "jump" their licenses and use whatever frequencies, hours, and powers they chose regardless of what other stations were doing. Inevitably, anarchy reigned in the ether.

Congress was forced to act.[24] In 1927 a Federal Radio Commission was created and given certain control over all kinds of interstate and foreign radio communication for one year's time. Two years later it was put on indefinite tenure, and the policy of year-by-year probation was abandoned.

Administrative responsibility was divided between the Federal Radio Commission and the Secretary of Commerce. The Commission was given authority to assign frequencies, power output, and time divisions, to establish regulations to prevent interference, to regulate the construction of new stations, and to equalize broadcasting facilities by preventing their

[21] *Hoover, Sec. of Commerce v. Intercity Radio Co., Inc.*, 286 Fed. 1003 (1923).

[22] 35 *Op. Atty. Gen.* 126 (1926).

[23] *United States v. Zenith Radio Corp.*, 12 F.2d 617 (1926).

[24] See Carl J. Friedrich and Evelyn Sternberg, "Congress and the Control of Radio Broadcasting," 37 *American Political Science Review* 797–818, 1014–1026 (October and December, 1943).

monopolization by a particular section of the United States. The purely administrative powers were left in the hands of the Secretary. He was to license and regulate operators, designate call letters, prohibit willful or malicious interference with radio communication, and inspect radio transmitting equipment.[25]

The administration of this act by the Federal Radio Commission tended to bring order out of chaos in the radio industry. But a comprehensive program of regulation of radio as a public utility, similar to that developed with railroads and electric companies, was not possible. The Interstate Commerce Commission still held its nominal power over radio-message rates, and the Department of Commerce had a share in radio regulation.

The Communications Act of 1934 abolished the Federal Radio Commission and transferred its powers to the Federal Communications Commission [26] created under the Act. A comprehensive program of public-utility regulation for radio-broadcasting, and now television-broadcasting, companies did not result from this statute. However, it did serve to consolidate previous laws under one commission and to make some improvement on existing statutes.

SPECIAL RADIO- AND TELEVISION-BROADCASTING REGULATION

In certain important respects radio and television broadcasting is different from wire and wireless message communications and therefore is not subjected to requirements that apply to common carriers in the businesses of transmitting messages. As a consequence, the Federal Communications Commission has no power to regulate rates, discrimination, or consolidation of broadcasting companies. Control is limited to entry into service. The reasons for control, however, are somewhat different from those basic to the regulation of other public utilities.

Special control has been felt necessary because radio waves know no bounds and can be used to reach practically any person possessing a receiving set. The available frequencies are fairly limited. Radio is susceptible to many uses in addition to transmission of private messages, especially government, shipping, police, and entertainment communication. The very fact that radio and television broadcasting is a source of public education and entertainment distinguishes this field of communication from the others. The democratic process itself is dependent upon its informational functions, and when one considers that broadcasting for public consumption has been undertaken on a commercial basis with

[25] For a further discussion of this act and its administration, see Herring and Gross, *op. cit.*, pp. 295–320.

[26] For a recent description, see Herbert Brattar, "Meet the FCC," 41 *Public Utilities Fortnightly* 399–410 (Mar. 29, 1951).

advertising paying the way, the complexity and importance of the regulatory problem loom even larger.

These factors have their economic consequences. As opposed to most transportation and communication services, commercial broadcasting gains its greatest economic importance from its suitability as an advertising medium. The persons who use radio and television facilities and the way in which they are used are of far more public significance than in other public utilities. While broadcasting has been likened to a newspaper and as such, it is claimed, should be given the greatest possible freedom from state action, the broadcasting station is really using channels belonging to the public and should be required to employ these for public benefit.

On the other hand, the nature of commercial broadcasting may not make necessary the same type of regulation as that found in the public-utility field. Since one class of receivers of the service—the listening public—pays nothing for the entertainment, no price regulation is necessary. Because the price of time for commercial users is more or less competitively determined, rate regulation is not necessary to protect them. As matters stand now, the way radio and television is used and the practices employed in the industry are of more public interest than the charges made.

Licensing power. The greatest single instrument of power which the Federal Communications Commission holds over broadcasting companies is the authority to grant, revoke, or withhold licenses to operate radio and television stations. No person is permitted by the present law to operate a station unless he has a license to do so. The law specifically states that these licenses are to be granted for a limited time—three years is the maximum for broadcasting licenses, and five years for other licenses—and that no licensee is to have any property right in a radio channel beyond the terms, conditions, and periods of the license.

In granting new licenses or renewing old ones the Commission must make a finding that the public interest, convenience, or necessity will be served thereby. Therefore, the Commission must inquire into the moral, technical, and financial responsibility of applicants. The Commission is empowered to revoke licenses if a licensee does not operate according to the conditions of his permit, or if he violates any regulation of the Commission authorized by law. Licenses may be suspended for willful damage to broadcasting apparatus, for superfluous or profane communications, or for willful or malicious interference with other radio communication. Broadcasters are prohibited from using radio or television facilities for advertisement of or information concerning any lottery. Where broadcast matter is paid for, or furnished, the station is required to announce the fact and the name of the person so doing. In cases where a licensee is convicted for violation of any of the antitrust laws, because of attempts to monopolize or restrain trade, the Commission is directed to cancel the license.

In granting a license the Federal Communications Commission assigns a frequency and operation time to the broadcaster. In addition, the Commission may prescribe the nature of service to be rendered by the various classes of stations, the minimum and maximum power, and the location of stations. The quality of apparatus employed may be regulated with a view to obtaining pure and sharp transmission and reducing interference. The Commission may prescribe qualifications for station operators and require their licensing. Station facilities can be constructed only after permits are obtained from the Commission, and inspection of facilities and personnel is provided for.

In general, the Commission operates in the area of licensing on the assumption that the interests of the *listening* public are superior to those of broadcasters.[27]

Censorship versus standards of performance. The broad power of the Commission over entry into broadcasting service naturally gives rise to several problems. If a license is to be granted on the basis of public interest, convenience, and necessity, the Commission is placed in the position of selecting the stations which it believes to be most capable of meeting these requirements. But in doing so it has often been accused of acting as a censor of what the station broadcasts. This question was raised in an early case before the Federal Radio Commission. On appeal to the courts, the Commission's refusal to renew a license on the ground that a part of the station's programs was not in the public interest was upheld as a reasonable exercise of the Commission's power. This action did not constitute censorship, since inspection of programs was not made in advance.[28]

In a more recent case the National Broadcasting Company argued that the licensing power of the Federal Communications Commission violated the First Amendment. The Supreme Court ruled:[29]

> The right of free speech does not include, however, the right to use the facilities of radio without a license. The licensing system established by Congress in the Communications Act of 1934 was a proper exercise of its power over commerce. The standard it provided for the licensing of stations was the "public interest, convenience, or necessity." Denial of a station license on that ground, if valid under the Act, is not a denial of free speech.

The Commission itself has taken the position that it does not have the

[27] See Jacob M. Edelman, *The Licensing of Radio Services in the United States, 1927 to 1947; A Study in Administrative Formulation of Policy* (Urbana, Ill.: University of Illinois Press, 1948).

[28] *KFKB Broadcasting Assoc. v. Federal Radio Com.*, 47 F.2d 670 (1931).

[29] *National Broadcasting Co. v. United States*, 319 U.S. 227 (1943).

authority to make regulations governing the content of programs because of the prohibition in the Communications Act against censorship. On the other hand, it has emphasized that it would taken into consideration the past conduct of licensees, including the content and character of programs they have broadcast, in considering applications for renewal of licenses. Actually, relatively few cases exist where the Commission has not renewed licenses.[30] The principal basis for these actions have been false, fraudulent, or misleading advertising or indecent and defamatory utterances.

A more significant and useful power than the refusal to renew licenses is the threat not to renew. By setting standards of performance and threatening not to renew licenses of stations that do not conform to these standards the Federal Communications Commission could exert considerable influence over program content. The stations, of course, contest any effort to control program content and contend that self-regulation is fully adequate. Furthermore, the Commission is in danger of imposing previous restraints that border on censorship rather than examining past conduct.

Nevertheless, the Commission does have an obligation to promote the public interest. Radio programs, and now television shows, have often been criticized for being scaled to the lowest common denominator. The desire to avoid all controversy results in utter banality. The commercials are often claimed to be too loud, too long, too obnoxious, and too illiterate. Furthermore, the station is largely dependent upon the advertiser or the advertising agency for the preparation of programs. The advertiser and its agent think in terms of high sales rather than high intellectual content. Therefore, it is argued that, in fulfillment of its obligation, the Commission should be more aggressive in bringing about improvement of broadcasting standards.

Steps along this line were taken in 1945 when the Commission announced a policy of a more detailed review of broadcast station performance when passing upon applications for license renewal. The following year the Federal Communications Commission issued its widely publicized "blue book," in which it recognized the value of self-regulation: "It is to the stations and networks rather than to Federal regulation that listeners must primarily turn for improved standards of program service." However, ". . . The Commission has a statutory responsibility for the public interest, of which it cannot divest itself." [31] Therefore, in issuing and renewing licenses of broadcast stations the Commission proposed to give particular consideration to four program factors:

[30] But see, for example, *Re McGlashan (KGFJ) et al.*, 2 F.C.C. 145 (1935), and *Re Morris et al.*, 2 F.C.C. 269 (1936).

[31] FCC, *Public Service Responsibility of Broadcast Licensees* (1946); see also FCC, *12th Annual Report, 1946,* p. 2.

1. The carrying of sustaining programs.
2. The carrying of local live programs.
3. The carrying of programs devoted to the discussion of public issues.
4. The elimination of advertising excesses.

Despite repeated declarations regarding the importance of a balanced program schedule, the Commission has not used its power to enforce its policy. Not a single station has been denied a license renewal on this ground, although many stations have been serious offenders judging from the Commission's own statements.

Another aspect of the Commission's control over program content has been the endeavor to prevent censorship on the part of radio and television stations. The problem is simply that the fortunate few who are successful in obtaining a license are in a position to advocate their own convictions and exclude those of their opponents. A rule promulgated in 1938 provided that, while no station is obligated to allow its facilities to be used by a candidate for a public office, if it does so, equal opportunities must be afforded to all other candidates for that office. In 1940 the Commission announced in its famous Mayflower decision that radio stations were to maintain a neutral attitude in their own broadcasts.

The decision stated:[32]

> . . . With the limitations of frequencies inherent in the nature of radio, the public interest can never be served by a dedication of any broadcast facility to the support of his [the broadcaster's] own partisan ends. Radio can serve as an instrument of democracy only when devoted to the communication and the exchange of ideas fairly and objectively presented. A truly free radio cannot be used to support the candidacies of his friends. It cannot be devoted to the support of principles he happens to regard most favorably.
>
> In brief, the broadcaster cannot be an advocate.

This decision is a carefully reasoned, sound ruling which is based on an awareness of the special public-interest character of radio broadcasting. However, considerable opposition to the Mayflower decision was generated, and in 1949 the Commission modified its position. It affirmed the right of broadcast licensees to editorialize as part of their presentation of public issues, but reiterated that such views may not be used to achieve a partisan or one-sided objective.[33] In practice, this proves to be a difficult standard to enforce.

Concentration of control in broadcasting. In granting licenses, operating channels, and frequencies, the Federal Communications Commission has

[32] *In re Mayflower Broadcasting Corporation, Yankee Networks Inc.*, 8 F.C.C. 340 (1940).

[33] *In re Editorializing by Broadcast Licenses,* 1 Pike and Fischer Radio Reg. 91:204 (1949).

found it necessary as a practical matter to give some stations a better channel and power than others. Stations with strong power, being better advertising media, have tended to prosper to a much greater extent than others. The larger and more prosperous stations become the leaders, with an advantage over other stations, in getting the more expensive national advertising programs. The smaller stations find that their best chance to get advertising and good programs is to lease their time to a national chain. Often the networks purchased an ownership interest in the affiliated station. The consequence of placing some stations in a more advantageous economic position has been to promote a concentration of control in radio broadcasting.

The first effort to attack concentration of control occurred in 1938 when the Commission announced that applicants who do not own newspapers should be favored over those who do, in order to promote diversification in the media of public information. In a number of cases the fact of newspaper ownership weighed rather heavily against an applicant, but the policy has not been applied zealously where counteracting considerations were present.[34]

Another attempt to combat monopoly in the broadcasting industry appeared in a series of rules adopted by the Commission in 1941. By 1938, the National Broadcasting Company and the Columbia Broadcasting System dominated the broadcasting industry. Of the 660 commercial stations, 160 were affiliated with NBC and 107 with CBS. This was 40 per cent of the total. Stations representing 86 per cent of the total nighttime power were affiliated with one of the two major networks.[35] The cry of monopoly was raised. In 1938, the Commission ordered an investigation of chain broadcasting and monopoly in radio broadcasting. A final report was issued after three years of study, which served as basis for new regulation.[36] Exclusive affiliation contracts were prohibited, and affiliation contracts were limited to two years, instead of five years for the stations and one year for the networks as had been the case. The Commission prohibited contracts by which networks bound themselves not to offer a program to another station in a given area if the affiliated station had rejected it. The networks were prevented from owning more than one station in a locality or owning any station in a locality where existing stations were of such unequal desirability that competition would be precluded. The National Broadcasting Company was ordered to dispose of one of the two networks it owned, and stations were to be allowed to set their own advertising rates without regard for network restrictions.

[34] Edelman, *op. cit.*, p. 11.

[35] T. P. Robinson, *Radio Networks and the Federal Government* (New York: Columbia University Press, 1943), pp. 208–209.

[36] FCC, *Report on Chain Broadcasting*, Com. Order No. 37 (1941).

These regulations were challenged in the courts by NBC and CBS. In *National Broadcasting Company v. United States*, Justice Frankfurter upheld the rules, stating that the Communications Act gave the Commission "not niggardly but expansive powers" over financial and contractual practices of radio stations and over the conditions under which network programs were distributed.[37]

Broadcasting regulation: conclusions. The power of the Federal Communications Commission to grant or refuse licenses is exceedingly great. Its discretion is limited only by the standard of "public interest, convenience, and necessity." The Commission is denied the power of censorship—the prior examination of broadcast matter—but the effect is much the same if it can refuse renewal of a license because of the nature of the programs in the past. Indeed, radio operators maintain that this is worse than censorship, for they do not know what the Commission dislikes.

This power of the Commission is one of the greatest in the hands of any regulatory agency. To date, there is no probative evidence that it has been abused. As Fainsod and Gordon put it: "On the whole, a good case can be made out for the proposition that the Commission has been more zealous in guarding the freedom of the air, particularly in the case of political broadcasting, than have individual broadcasters." [38] This raises the question of how much responsibility the Commission should assume for the content of programs. Immediately a conflict results over the question of what the public *wants* and what the public *should have*. So long as radio is left to private enterprise, one cannot overlook the fact that the successful station is one which gets the most advertising revenue, and advertising revenue depends to a great extent upon formulating programs that the people want—or will not strenuously object to. Even if the government should take over the operation of radio stations, as is occasionally suggested, it would still have to pay some attention to what the public desires. But between the two extremes of government operation on one hand and, on the other, self-regulation, with minimal control of program content by the Commission as is now the case, there is a considerable gap and much room for improvement without having to resort to government operation.

Federal Regulation of Service: Electricity

The federal government entered the field of public control of electric utilities in 1920 by the passage of the Federal Water Power Act. The Act applied only to the use of hydroelectric sites on navigable waters of the

[37] 319 U.S. 219 (1943).

[38] Merle Fainsod and Lincoln Gordon, *Government and the American Economy* (New York: W. W. Norton & Company, Inc., 1941), pp. 394–395.

United States. Its primary purpose was the conservation of these natural resources and the assurance that they be used for the benefit of the public. Several alternatives were suggested for the development of hydroelectric sites. Some groups held that the government should erect dams and power stations and sell the current directly to consumers or to private companies for resale to consumers. Others believed that the development of water resources should be left to private enterprise, with no regulation except that coming from state public-utility commissions. Still other groups felt that the federal government should retain title to the sites but lease them to private companies for development.

When the issue was decided in 1920, the last alternative was adopted. The Federal Power Act provided that the federal government should lease the sites to private companies, retaining the right to buy them back upon payment of just compensation, and that the principal regulatory job should be left to the state commissions.

THE FEDERAL WATER POWER ACT OF 1920

The law created the Federal Power Commission.[39] It was composed of the Secretaries of War, Agriculture, and Interior—each of the Cabinet officers who exercised some control over the use of navigable waters. Administration of the Act was not particularly effective, because Cabinet officers could give little time to the many complex problems arising and could not develop any very well defined principles upon which to proceed. Moreover, since political considerations may play a large part in the granting of power sites and apparently did so, the administration of such an act by political officers, rather than by an independent commission, was not conducive to the best attainment of its purposes. The Commission was subsequently reorganized in 1930, and an independent body of five full-time commissioners was created.

Under the act of 1920 the Commission was empowered to grant licenses to private persons or government bodies for the development of water-power resources under federal jurisdiction and to collect information on the nature and possible utilization of water-power resources.

Permits and licenses. Before anyone can use any of the navigable waters or waters on public lands of the United States for the development of water power, permission must be obtained from the Federal Power Commission. The applicant is given a preliminary permit which ensures for him, for a period of three years, priority over other persons who may wish to use the same resources. After receiving this permit he must hand in detailed information as to the nature, constructional specifications, legal and financial arrangements, and estimated disposition of power from

[39] For a recent description, see Salley Alley, "What Makes the FPC Tick," 45 *Public Utilities Fortnightly* 142–149 (Feb. 2, 1950).

the project. If these data lead the Commission to believe that the project is in the public interest, a license may be issued.

In issuing the license, which may run for a period as long as fifty years, the Federal Power Commission must give preference to government agencies, and can issue other licenses only to citizens of the United States or corporations organized under state or federal law. The licensee must pay a sum, fixed by the Commission, to the United States government each year, for defraying the costs of administering the law, paying the government for the use of lands and property, and recapturing excess profits where the state does not do so.

By June 30, 1954, the Federal Power Commission had issued licenses covering 657 projects involving 9,252,000 horsepower of installed generating capacity, and representing a total claimed cost of approximately $2,123 million. Of the 657 licenses, 219 were for major projects (involving more than 100 horsepower), 139 for minor projects, 36 for minor parts of complete projects, and 263 for transmission lines across federal lands. During 1954 the Commission collected $1,322,000 in license fees for the use of water resources.[40]

The law provides that the federal government may take over the property of any licensee at the end of the license term. It also expressly reserves to the federal and state governments the right to acquire the property of any licensee by condemnation on the payment of just compensation. Moreover, the government may take over the property by mutual consent between it and the licensee. If a licensee does not live up to the terms of his agreement, the government may assume the license and purchase the property or issue the license to some other person.

Except for its important power to allocate natural resources, through the issuance of licenses, and to force licensees to keep an accurate investment record, the Commission's jurisdiction over licensees is rather limited. Most of the regulation is left to the states, so the Commission can do little to check on the character of licensees' operations and satisfy itself that they are in the public interest.

Investigations. Some of the most meritorious work of the Federal Power Commission in its control of water-power sites, as well as its regulation of interstate transmission of electricity and gas, has been its fact-finding activities. From time to time since 1920, the Commission has made investigations of developed and undeveloped water resources, of costs of development, of possible markets for electric power, and of power needs for national defense. It has made studies of the way in which licensees have made use of their privilege and has made an extensive study of rates for electric light and power under both private and public ownership throughout the United States. In response to the Flood Control Act of

[40] FPC, *34th Annual Report, 1954,* pp. 45–46, 210.

1938, the Commission has also been making an investigation of possible flood-control dams and reservoirs.

The investigatory activities of the Commission have furnished the basis for much legislative and commission policy. In addition, they have had some direct effect on regulation. The studies of electric rates, for example, by showing up differences in rates between localities, did much to cause certain companies to lower rates voluntarily.

THE FEDERAL WATER POWER ACT OF 1935

The Federal Water Power Act was amended in 1935 to give the Power Commission control over interconnection, consolidation, security issues, accounts, rates, service, and interlocking directorates of electric companies transmitting and selling power at wholesale in interstate commerce.

Scope of federal control. In placing regulation of electric utilities engaged in interstate commerce under the Federal Power Commission, Congress, by declaration of policy in Title II of the Public Utility Act of 1935, stated that such regulation was "to extend only to those matters which are not subject to regulation by the states." It was to apply to "the transmission of electric energy in interstate commerce and to the sale of electric energy at *wholesale* in interstate commerce, but shall not apply to any other sale of electric energy or deprive a state or state commission of its lawful authority now exercised over the exportation of hydro-electric energy which is transmitted across a state line." [41] The federal law also exempts government-owned public utilities, whether owned by the United States, a state, its subdivision, or a government corporation.[42]

Since the framers of federal legislation in 1935 believed that state regulation of interstate *retail* sales of electric power could be adequate, they did not grant the federal government jurisdiction in this area. This provision is interesting as an evidence of the intent of Congress not to disturb but to supplement state control.

Interconnection and coordination of facilities. The law of 1935 directs the Federal Power Commission to divide the country into regional districts for interconnection and coordination of electric production and transmission facilities; these districts are to be made up of such areas as the Commission feels can be served economically. The interconnections and coordinations within these districts are to be effected voluntarily if possible. However, upon application of a state commission, or any person

[41] Italics added.

[42] In certain matters such as accounting and special credit contracts, the Federal Power Commission has jurisdiction over the Tennessee Valley Authority. The Commission also has the authority to approve the rate schedules of the Bonneville Administration and the Fort Peck Dam project under the Bureau of Reclamation of the Department of the Interior.

engaged in the transmission of electric energy, and after notice and hearing of interested parties, the Federal Power Commission may order a public utility to make physical connection of its transmission lines with the facilities of other public utilities engaged in the transmission or sale of electricity. Before doing so the Commission must find that no undue burden will thereby be placed upon such public utility, and it cannot make an interconnection order which would compel a public utility to enlarge its generating facilities or would impair its ability to render adequate service to its customers. Ironically, the act has had the effect in some instances of decreasing interconnections by utilities seeking to escape commission jurisdiction. Some emergency interconnections were ordered by the Commission during World War II.

Adequate service. The Federal Power Commission has a somewhat limited authority over the quality of service of electric companies operating in interstate commerce. In case it is requested to do so by a state commission, the Commission, after notice and hearing, and after a finding that service is inadequate or insufficient, may determine and order such service as it finds to be proper, adequate, or sufficient. This order may embrace extension or increase of service. However, in exercising this power it is given no authority to compel the enlargement of generating facilities or to do anything which would impair the ability of a public utility to render adequate service to its customers.

Cooperation with states. Care has been taken in the law to leave state regulation much as it was and to impose federal control to stop the gaps in state regulation. To encourage cooperation with state commissions, the law of 1935 allows the Federal Power Commission to set up joint boards of state and federal commissioners. Each of these is given full commission powers on matters delegated to it by the Federal Power Commission. In addition, the Commission is authorized to confer with state commissions regarding rates, costs, accounts, and other regulations of utilities in which both state and federal governments have an interest. Furthermore, it may hold joint hearings with state commissions on matters with which the federal board is authorized to deal and in which state authorities have an interest.[43]

The Federal Power Commission is also directed to make available to state commissions such information and reports, or staff experts, as may be of assistance in the state regulation of public utilities.

FEDERAL REGULATION OF INTERSTATE POWER: CONCLUSIONS

The federal government's control over hydroelectric developments rests upon two bases—the ownership of land having hydroelectric resources, and control under the commerce clause over navigable waters, including

[43] See Bosworth, *op. cit.*

waters that can be made navigable with reasonable improvements. The foundation for the regulation of the transmission of electric energy in interstate commerce or the sale of electric energy at wholesale in interstate commerce is clearly the commerce clause.

Primarily because of its limited jurisdiction, the service regulations of the Federal Power Commission in regard to the electric industry have not been as far-reaching as those of state regulatory commissions. The major part of its activity and accomplishment has been in the field of investigation. The numerous investigations of the electric-power industry and the detailed reports published have been of inestimable value to state regulatory commissions and to other federal agencies interested in the electric-utility industry.

Federal Regulation of Service: Natural Gas

Not until 1938 did the federal government enter upon a program of regulation of gas-operating public utilities, although the Holding Company Act of 1935 dealt with companies controlling gas as well as electric companies.

The demand for regulation of the natural-gas industry by the federal government arises from several factors.[44] In the first place, interstate commerce in this commodity has been increasing, particularly since 1926. By 1938, natural gas moved from five principal areas over a network of 50,000 miles of line to thirty-seven of the forty-eight states. The interstate nature of such operations caused many state public-utility commissions difficulty in regulating local gas companies obtaining their supply from interstate companies. Many commissions were rebuffed by the courts in their attempts to regulate the interstate companies and found it almost impossible to obtain information from these companies for use in local rate regulation.[45]

Another reason for federal regulation was the refusal of certain interstate companies to supply cities with an adequate supply of natural gas. Finally, because the supply is limited, and because of the prevalence of wasteful practices from time to time in the industry, regulation was demanded by some in the interests of conservation.

THE SCOPE OF FEDERAL REGULATION

The Natural Gas Act of 1938 deals only with natural-gas operations, although these include cases where any mixture of natural and artificial

[44] M. M. Rice, "Gas and Government," 22 *Public Utilities Fortnightly* 483–490 (Oct. 13, 1938).

[45] *West v. Kansas Nat. G. Corp.* 221 U.S. 229 (1911); *Haskell v. Kansas Nat. G. Co.* 224 U.S. 217 (1912); *Public U. Com. v. Landon*, 249 U.S. 236 (1919); *Pennsylvania v. West Virginia*, 262 U.S. 553 (1923).

gas is involved. The law applies to transportation of gas in interstate commerce and to sale for resale for "ultimate public consumption." The law specifically excludes production or gathering of natural gas and the local distribution of gas. This means that the Federal Power Commission, to which the administration of the law is entrusted, has no regulatory control over two general phases of natural-gas operations—production and local distribution—and that its authority is limited to the third phase, transmission. Even with this phase, the business must be interstate.

Throughout the Natural Gas Act, as was the case in the electric-power law, there is clear evidence of the intent of Congress that the federal government is not to supersede the states in regulation but to complement them.

PROVISIONS SIMILAR TO ELECTRIC-POWER REGULATION

Certain parts of the Natural Gas Act are very similar to provisions in the Federal Power Act of 1935. The rate-regulation provisions are practically identical with those of the electric-power law and are fairly standard in their coverage of reasonable rates, rate discriminations, changes, filing, publication, suspension, and determination of costs. The law respecting accounting and reports is similar, too.

The service-regulation authority is also much the same, with exceptions to be mentioned below, and the power of the Federal Power Commission to order extensions is subject also to the restriction that these orders may not impair the ability of a company to render adequate service to its customers. The Natural Gas Act similarly provides for the establishment of joint boards and for other means of cooperating with state commissions.

DIFFERENCES BETWEEN ELECTRIC AND GAS LAWS

The regulation of gas companies is not so extensive as that of interstate electric utilities. The Federal Power Commission has no authority over consolidations, mergers, sale of gas property, security issuance, or interlocking directorates. The Natural Gas Act does not envisage a planned national system of interconnected lines over certain regions. Interconnection of gas lines cannot be ordered even under emergency conditions.

The law dealing with entry, extension, and abandonment of gas service is somewhat different from and more specific than that covering electric companies. Under the electric-utility law, the Federal Power Commission is authorized only to approve acquisitions and disposals of property and to order extensions. When an electric company wishes to construct a line, extend its facilities, or abandon them, apparently it must obtain a certificate of convenience and necessity from the state commission. But gas utilities under the jurisdiction of the Commission must obtain its approval for extensions and abandonment. Abandonments may be approved after finding that there is depletion in the gas supply or that the present or future public convenience and necessity permit such stoppage. Under the 1938 law, gas companies were required to obtain certificates of convenience and necessity only when they built lines into areas that already were served by other firms. If the service was not competitive, no certificate was needed. Congress plugged this loophole by an amendment in 1942 which requires gas companies to obtain certificates for all interstate construction, extensions, or acquisitions of natural-gas lines.

ISSUANCE OF CERTIFICATES

In passing upon application for certificates of convenience and necessity, the Commission seeks to protect the interests of the natural-gas consumer. The tests developed by the Commission to determine the "public convenience and necessity" are commonplace standards, framed in the public-utility tradition, to fit the economic and physical characteristics of the natural-gas industry. The applicant must have adequate sources of natural gas available; it must have a potential market in the area to be served; it must have adequate financial resources to ensure the construction and satisfactory maintenance of the proposed transmission line and other facilities; and the rates proposed must be both reasonable for the consumer and adequate for the company.[46]

The real importance of the certificate power, Ralph Huitt suggests,[47] lies in the fact that issues raised in Commission proceedings have transcended the scope of these standards and involve an attempt to redefine the public interest in respect to natural gas. The Commission allowed interested parties in certificate cases to intervene extensively until they became the battleground upon which coal, labor, and railroad interests sought to withstand the invasion by natural gas of coal-burning market areas. Their case for restricting the growth of the natural-gas industry was based on the fact that the supply of gas reserves is limited as compared to the almost inexhaustible coal reserves. Hence, it was suggested that natural gas should be kept out of markets adequately supplied by coal and the certificate power should be used for the selective control of end uses of gas. These contentions raised issues that went beyond the intention of Congress in the Natural Gas Act. Therefore, the Federal Power Commission conducted an extensive investigation in 1945 and 1946 at which all interested persons and groups were given an opportunity to be heard.

Commissioners Leland Olds and Claude L. Draper recommended that

[46] *Kansas Pipe Line and Gas Co. et al.*, 2 F.P.C. 29 (1939).

[47] "Federal Regulation of the Uses of Natural Gas," 46 *American Political Science Review* 455–469 (June, 1952).

the Commission give "increased consideration to the conservation aspects in the delivery of natural gas" from gas-producing states to coal-producing regions. Commissioners Nelson Lee Smith and Harrington Wimberly confined themselves to counseling the producing states and the industry to cooperate in increased efforts to conserve natural gas, and the industry to develop alternative supplies of gas fuel to replace natural gas, as and when natural-gas reserves decline.[48]

Federal Regulation of Service: Conclusions

Recent years have seen the emergence of a definite and enlarged pattern of federal control of public utilities. This statement applies not only to the regulation of services, under consideration in this chapter, but also to regulation of rates, finances, and combinations by the federal government. The regulatory laws are scattered and somewhat piecemeal. Communication utilities are placed under one commission; interstate electric and gas operations are placed under another, along with the licensing of use of natural water-power resources. But transactions of holding companies in the electric and gas industries are placed under the jurisdiction of the Securities and Exchange Commission, together with the general regulation of security sales of private industry.[49] In addition, of course, there are the many state commissions with powers over local communication, gas, electricity, and water companies. Perhaps this scattering of administration between state and national commissions is inevitable under the federal system of government. Nevertheless, a question can be raised about the present allocation of authority to the federal commissions. It may not be wise to have electric and gas holding companies under one commission and interstate electric and gas operations under another. Furthermore, placing the regulation of interstate electric-power companies and radio companies in commissions also empowered to promote these industries may not be the best administrative policy. Yet the Federal Power Commission is charged with the allocation, and promotion of use, of natural resources, and the Federal Communications Commission is required to study new uses for radio and to encourage its wider and more effective employment.

There are those who believe that the cause of regulation has been weakened by the tendency of the federal laws to defer to state control. They see the rapid increase in interstate aspects of public-utility business. Attention is also called at times to the fact that state regulatory bodies have neither sufficient tenure of office nor adequate staffs to administer a law as effectively as can a federal commission. Moreover, the legal basis

[48] *Ibid.*, p. 466.
[49] See Chapter 12.

of some state regulation is not complete enough for effective control. While the commissions in Massachusetts, Wisconsin, and Illinois may be doing an effective job, there are many more states where various limitations do not permit it.

On the other hand, state commissions fear that the federal commissions will eventually encroach upon their jurisdictions, until they find themselves in the inferior position they now occupy with respect to railroads. Since consumer contact with these companies is generally local, with local distributing companies, the states may be in a better position to deal with regulation than is the federal government.

Whatever the relative merits of federal and state regulation are, the future of public-utility control seems to point to increase of federal activity and relative decline in state control. One fact leading in this direction is the enlargement of interstate commerce in the utility field; economic development is no respecter of political boundaries. Another is that regulation seldom goes backward. Now that the federal government has entered the field, it finds that certain loopholes exist for the thwarting of effective control. As these are filled, the position of the federal government must necessarily become more powerful. Possibly, too, the public-utility industry itself may ask for the federal government to assume the leading role in regulation in order to escape dealing with too many commissions and laws. Regulation at the request of the regulated is not new in the development of government control.

Selected References

Barnes, Irston, *The Economics of Public Utility Regulation*, chaps. 5, 21, 22. New York: Appleton-Century-Crofts, Inc., 1942.

Bauer, John, *Transforming Public Utility Regulation.* New York: Harper & Brothers, 1950.

Baum, Robert D., *The Federal Power Commission and State Utility Regulation.* Washington, D.C.: Public Affairs Press, 1942.

Clemens, Eli, *Economics and Public Utilities*, chaps. 16, 17, 18. New York: Appleton-Century-Crofts, Inc., 1950.

Edelman, Jacob M., *The Licensing of Radio Services in the United States, 1927 to 1947; A Study in Administrative Formulation of Policy.* Urbana, Ill.: University of Illinois Press, 1950.

Fesler, James W., *The Independence of State Regulatory Agencies.* Chicago: Public Administration Service, 1942.

Friedrich, Carl J., and Jeanette Sayre, *The Development of the Control of Advertising on the Air.* Cambridge, Mass.: Harvard University Press, 1940.

——— and Evelyn Sternberg, "Congress and the Control of Radio-broadcasting," 37 *American Political Science Review* 797–818, 1014–1026 (October and December, 1943).

Herring, J. M., and G. C. Gross, *Telecommunications*, chaps. 9–15. New York: McGraw-Hill Book Company, Inc., 1936.

Mosher, J. G., and Richard A. Lavine, *Radio and the Law*. Los Angeles: Parke & Co., 1947.

Mosher, William E., "Public Utility Regulation," in George A. Graham and Henry Reining, Jr. (eds.), *Regulatory Administration*. New York: John Wiley & Sons, Inc., 1943.

Robinson, T. P., *Radio Networks and the Federal Government*. New York: Columbia University Press, 1943.

Rose, C. B., Jr., *National Policy for Radio Broadcasting*. New York: Harper & Brothers, 1940.

Ruggles, C. O., *Aspects of the Organization, Functioning, and Financing of State Public Utility Commissions*. Cambridge, Mass.: Harvard University Press, 1937.

Siepmann, C. A., *Radio's Second Chance*. Boston: Little, Brown & Company, 1946.

Troxel, Emery, *Economics of Public Utilities*, chaps. 5, 28. New York: Rinehart & Company, Inc., 1947.

Twentieth Century Fund, *The Power Industry and the Public Interest*. New York: The Twentieth Century Fund, Inc., 1944.

White, Llewellyn, *The American Radio*. Chicago: University of Chicago Press, 1947.

11

REGULATION OF PUBLIC-UTILITY RATES

Like common carriers, public utilities are obligated under common law to serve at reasonable rates. This obligation has been carried over into state and federal statutes, along with provisions authorizing regulatory commissions to determine what constitutes just and reasonable rates. Most of the controversies over public-utility control have focused on this problem of rate regulation.

The purpose of public-utility rate regulation is threefold: (1) to protect the rate payer from unreasonable and discriminatory charges; (2) to compensate fairly the investing public to assure an adequate flow of capital into the industry; and (3) to ensure that the public utility will be able to serve the public adequately. The first objective is essential, because public utilities are usually guaranteed by government a highly monopolistic position, which, in the absence of strict regulation, would permit these companies to charge exorbitant rates.[1]

Important as the first objective has been in motivating government to undertake rate regulation, the other two goals have usually set the standards for determining what constitutes a just and reasonable rate. In other words, the controversies have commonly been over whether the investor is fairly compensated or whether the companies receive a return that is adequate to serve the public rather than over whether the rates are reasonable to the customer.

From 1898 to 1944, regulation of the level of public-utility rates was guided by the rule set forth in *Smyth v. Ames*:[2] a rate order must assure an efficiently and honestly operated company of a fair rate of return on the fair value of its property, over and above reasonable operating expenses, or the company is being deprived of its property without due process of law. Under the Smyth rule, utility rate making involved the

[1] This is a situation decidedly dissimilar to that existing in the carrier business, where rate levels of many companies would not be excessive if regulation were much more lax. At the same time, many public utilities have a more elastic demand facing them than is often supposed; some managements have found, after contesting a lowering of rate levels, that their profits after rates have been reduced were greater than before.

[2] 169 U.S. 466 (1898).

determination of three things: (1) fair value of property used and useful for the public service; (2) fair rate of return; and (3) reasonable operating expenses, including taxes and depreciation allowances. Each of these factors will be discussed separately in succeeding sections of this chapter.

Since the principles of rate fixing are the same whether a state or federal commission is exercising the authority, it will be unnecessary to discuss the procedure for each level of government. A brief section will be devoted to the scope of state rate regulation, and in the final section some special problems of federal rate making will be considered.

Valuation

The most difficult element to determine in rate regulation, and the center of greatest dispute at least until recent years, is *fair property value*. The fair value of a given public-utility property depends on two sets of information: (1) the method used to measure the value; and (2) the property items included in a computation of what is used and useful for public service.

METHODS OF MEASURING FAIR VALUE

There are various methods of determining property value. The student of economics might conceive value to be an exchange value, or the power of a good to command another in free and voluntary exchange. But public-utility properties are seldom bought and sold in a free and competitive market. Even if they were, their sale price would reflect the earnings that the company had been making; the earnings in turn would be affected by the rates fixed. Clearly, exchange value cannot be used, even if it were known, as a basis for public-utility rate control. As a result, a variety of other methods have been used.

Cost of reproduction. The determination of fair value by reference to reproduction costs is by far the most difficult method to employ, even after agreement is reached on its exact meaning. Perhaps the reason for the utility companies' preference for this formula is its complexity and the confusion that results from interpreting it in different ways. The valuation engineers of public utilities have always been able to come up with different and substantially higher valuations than the state commissions by using cost of reproduction.

Measurement of value by a cost-of-reproduction standard involves the determination of the cost of reproducing the property at present prices. It is essentially an appraisal method, as opposed to the determination of original costs, which may be referred to as an accounting method. To arrive at cost of reproduction, valuation engineers usually take an inventory of the physical property, apply present prices thereto, and add estimated amounts for the cost of intangible property items. The latter necessitates an inquiry into numerous elements of intangible value, such as franchise value, water rights, leaseholds, patents, going value, and good will.

Determination of reproduction cost is an expensive, slow, and complicated matter. Besides the problem of making an accurate inventory, questions arise over what prices to use (competitive bidding cannot be simulated), when the plant is to be reproduced, and what intangible items to include. Strict compliance with the principles of reproduction cost would seem to make necessary using prices as of the date of valuation. These current equipment prices and construction costs are called "spot" prices. Yet prices may change during the period while a difficult valuation is being made, or the spot prices may not be normal in terms of past prices. A variation is to take an average of a three-year, five-year, or even of a ten-year period of past prices.

The reliance on past or present prices is actually a fairly unrealistic measure of reproduction costs, because the replacement of utility plants is a continuous process. Deteriorated and obsolete equipment is replaced as the occasion requires. Seldom does a utility company replace a whole plant at one time. Most of the real reproduction costs are incurred at some future time. Therefore, a realistic interpretation of reproduction costs would be in terms of a hypothetical plant constructed at probable future prices. But it is impossible to predict accurately future prices, especially if the kinds of equipment, methods of construction, and other technological developments that will become available are not known.

Other problems arise. For example, should the cost of tearing up pavement to lay mains be included, even though the mains were actually laid before the street was paved? Should the cost of replacing machinery of an old type be calculated when actual reproduction would call for using modern machines?

Still another problem is whether the cost should be that of reproducing the existing plant or that of reproducing the existing service capacity. Using modern equipment and techniques, it may be possible to build a plant which is entirely different from the existing one but which furnishes the same service. This method would necessitate engineering estimates of the cost of building a new plant, despite the fact that construction of new facilities is not contemplated. Questions would arise as to just what design is most efficient in view of costs. Much work and expense would be incurred in making purely hypothetical estimates.

Original cost. The method of original cost is also subject to varying interpretations, but it has the advantage of being easier to employ and relatively inexpensive. Original cost refers to the actual cost to the company of the present property allocable to the capital account. The method is essentially an accounting technique. If the books are accurately kept according to accepted accounting principles, the actual cost should be the same as the book cost.

Three variations can be noted: (1) "first" original cost, or the cost of property when it was first devoted to public-utility service; (2) "investment" cost, or the actual cost to the existing company; and (3) "prudent investment" cost, or the investment cost which is adjusted for unwise or fraudulent investments. When the "first" cost, or "initial-use," definition is followed, the property exchanges between utility companies as well as arbitrary write-ups in property values are ignored. The "investment" cost formula measures the total investment in the existing plant including new construction work, arm's-length transactions between unaffiliated companies, and reasonable transactions between affiliated companies. In other words, "investment" cost takes into account the investment additions to the "first" original cost values.

Prudent investment. The "prudent investment" formula combines both the accounting and appraisal methods. The doctrine starts from an original cost, determined by reference to the accounts, and eliminates costs which are appraised as those which would not have been made by a competent and prudent businessman.

In evaluating all three variations on the method of original costs, it can be said that, in contrast with other methods, determinations are not based on the judgments of appraisal engineers, commissioners, or judges. Disagreement may arise over imprudent investments or reasonable additions to the "first" original cost. But most valuation data are gathered from accounting records. This information can be kept up to date easily, since original cost valuation of separate items does not change and valuations studies are inexpensive to run. Since companies and commissions seldom dispute these valuations, many fewer commission decisions are appealed to the courts.

Index numbers. To give effect to present-day cost without going to the trouble and expense of reproduction-cost calculations, the use of index numbers of prices has been suggested. At least one commission, the Maryland Public Service Commission, adopted this method.[3] By it, costs are taken at actual amounts and are translated into present-cost estimates by applying price index numbers. Where original costs are not obtainable over the full history of a public utility, an agreed-upon valuation as of a certain date is taken and trended by price indexes, and all additions and betterments are taken at actual cost and the price indexes applied. The greatest problem in using this method, aside from the question of

[3] With lack of legal success, as will be shown below in the discussion of *West v. Chesapeake and Potomac Tel. Co.*, 295 U.S. 662 (1935); see below, p. 250.

its acceptance as lawful evidence, is that agreement upon accurate and suitable price indexes for public-utility property is difficult.

VALUATION AND THE LAW

Prior to the Hope decision of 1944,[4] the regulatory commissions' job of rate fixing was continuously and carefully scrutinized by the courts. Whenever a public-utility commission set a rate using one method of determining the rate base, and the company, employing another measure, complained that the rate was too low, the company had little difficulty in getting a hearing before the courts. The federal courts furnished the principal stage for these suits, for the usual complaint was that the rate level was so low that private property was being taken without due process of law in violation of the Fifth or Fourteenth Amendment. Seldom did a rate case reach the courts in which the crux of the disagreement was not the rate base. In order to appreciate the complexity of the valuation problem and its legal aspects, one must look at the decisions in a few of the leading cases.

***Smyth v. Ames* (1898).** *Smyth v. Ames* furnished the basis for the measure of fair value in the whole field of rate regulation. In a decision from which no justices dissented, the Supreme Court held that a privately owned business was entitled to rates which would cover reasonable operating expenses plus a fair return upon the fair value of the property being used for the convenience of the public. Ominously pointing out that the question of fair value "will always be an embarrassing question," the Court undertook to indicate some of the "necessary elements" in determining fair value. The Court said:[5]

> And in order to ascertain that value, the original cost of construction, the amount expended in permanent improvements, the amount and market value of its bonds and stocks, the present as compared with the original cost of construction, the probable earning capacity of the property under particular rates prescribed by statute, and the sum required to meet operating expenses, are all matters for consideration, and are to be given such weight as may be just and right in each case. We do not say that there may not be other matters to be regarded in estimating the value of the property.

Thus, the Court suggested both the original-cost and reproduction-cost methods of measuring property value, but no indication was given as to when one or the other was to be employed or how they could be synthesized. Earning power and market value of securities obviously depend to a large extent on the rate allowed by the regulatory authorities. They consequently have little bearing on the determination of value for rate-

[4] *FPC v. Hope Natural Gas Co.*, 320 U.S. 591 (1944).

[5] 169 U.S. 466, 546–547.

making purposes and have seldom been used. The Court also left the way clear for the introduction of other measures of value.

Judicial supervision of valuation. The Smyth doctrine was adhered to in many decisions between 1898 and 1923.[6] However, the Court did not show exclusive preference for the original-cost or reproduction-cost formulas during this period.

With the rise in prices during World War I, and with a level afterward materially above that of 1914, public-utility companies found good reason to ask for valuations based upon these higher prices—i.e., present cost, or cost of reproduction. In 1923, the Supreme Court decided three cases in each of which the cost-of-reproduction formula was considered but not used as the determining factor by the state commissions.[7] The Southwestern Bell Telephone Company case is one in which it was employed and is typical of the struggle between companies and commissions in this postwar period. The Supreme Court found that the state commission's valuation was far too low in that it did not accord "any weight to the greatly enhanced costs of material, labor, supplies, etc." Declaring that "an honest and intelligent forecast of probable future values made up in view of all the relevant circumstances is essential," it held that "such a forecast becomes impossible" if the "element of present costs is wholly disregarded." The majority insisted that "estimates for tomorrow cannot ignore prices of today." [8]

The Southwestern Bell case is also important for the minority opinion. Justices Brandeis and Holmes, in a dissent written by Brandeis, agreed that the rates were confiscatory, not because the regulatory commission overlooked present costs, but because the rates would not return a fair profit upon the amount *prudently invested* in the business. Brandeis found the "rule of Smyth v. Ames legally and economically unsound," as well as impracticable to use.

Insistence upon commission consideration of reproduction costs in arriving at fair value reached a new high in the case of *McCardle v. Indianapolis Water Company*,[9] decided in 1926. The Court declared that "in determining present value, consideration must be given to prices and wages prevailing at the time of the investigation," and that "there must be an honest and intelligent forecast as to probable price and wage levels during a reasonable period in the immediate future." [10] Thus, both present

[6] Among others, *Willcox v. Consolidated Gas Co.*, 212 U.S. 19 (1909); *Minnesota Rate Cases*, 230 U.S. 352 (1913); *Denver v. Denver Union Water Co.*, 246 U.S. 178 (1918).

[7] *Southwestern Bell Tel. Co. v. Public Serv. Com. of Missouri*, 262 U.S. 276; *Bluefield W. Works & Improvement Co. v. Public Serv. Com. of W. Vir.*, 262 U.S. 679; *Georgia Ry. & P. Co. v. Railroad Com. of Georgia*, 262 U.S. 625.

[8] 262 U.S. 288.

[9] 272 U.S. 400.

[10] 272 U.S. 408.

or "spot" prices *and* future prices were to be considered, especially when original costs no longer reflected present costs. Justices Brandeis and Holmes again dissented, pointing out that the rule of *Smyth v. Ames* did not make value tantamount to reproduction cost.

The Los Angeles Gas and Electric case [11] of 1933 marks an important turning point in the Supreme Court's view of the valuation controversy. It is especially significant for the clear statement the Court made about its role in the regulation of utility rates. The majority of the Court pointed out that it did "not sit as a board of revision, but to enforce constitutional rights," and that it was not concerned with either the method used by a commission to calculate rates or the determination itself, "so long as constitutional limitations are not transgressed." While the Court did not disavow the doctrine of *Smyth v. Ames,* it emphasized that the question of confiscation should be decided in view of the *results* of a rate order, rather than the *method* employed.

Following this line of reasoning, the Supreme Court was convinced that the California Commission rate order was not confiscatory. The Commission had given predominant weight to historical cost, but it had considered reproduction cost. Since most of the construction of plant had taken place in years before the fall of prices in 1929 to 1933, the Court held that historical cost probably gave liberal effect to present prices.

A unique deviation from the original- and reproduction-cost formulas was the attempt to rely upon index numbers. The Maryland Public Service Commission was administered a rebuff in the Supreme Court in 1935 [12] in a case which again beclouded the legal aspects of fair value after the comparatively clarifying language of the Los Angeles case. For several years, the Maryland Commission had used a price index number to give effect to present costs without going to the expense of estimating reproduction cost. It had ascertained historical cost from the books of the company or upon investigation, as of a certain date, and had prescribed accounting so that thereafter books would accurately show historical cost. When rate making required finding fair value, the Commission merely translated these cost figures, according to the year of capital investments, into a present value by applying index numbers.

The Supreme Court found that the use of index numbers was improper for the ascertainment of value, since they were not designed for appraisal purposes.

The decline of judicial supervision. In the Driscoll case of 1939,[13] two members of the Supreme Court termed the Smyth formula "useless" and

[11] *Los Angeles G. and E. Corp. v. Railroad Com. of Calif.*, 289 U.S. 287.
[12] *West v. Chesapeake and Potomac Tel. Co.*, 295 U.S. 662.
[13] *Driscoll v. Edison Lt. and Power Co.*, 307 U.S. 104, 122 (1939).

"mischievous" and urged the Court to withdraw from the valuation tangle, but the majority was not so inclined at the time. An important step was taken three years later in the Natural Gas Pipeline case.[14] Since the Court was not confronted with a property valuation controversy, a clean break with the Smyth rule was not possible. The significance of the case lies in the judgment that property valuation was perhaps a useful, but not an indispensable, means of measuring earnings. Chief Justice Stone spoke for the majority:[15]

> The Constitution does not bind rate-making bodies to the service of any single formula or combination of formulas. Agencies to whom this legislative power has been delegated are free, within the ambit of their statutory authority, to make the pragmatic adjustments which may be called for by particular circumstances. Once a fair hearing has been given, proper findings made and other statutory requirements satisfied, the courts cannot intervene in the absence of a clear showing that the limits of due process have been overstepped.

The majority of the court did not directly overrule the Smyth doctrine and therefore left the status of property valuation in a nebulous position. The minority judges concurred in the decision but wanted to go all the way and break with the Smyth rule. Moreover, these judges felt that an "expert" commission rather than the courts should "prescribe what formula should be used." In effect, they desired to revert to the position of the Court in the Munn case[16] and curtail judicial review of rate regulation in preference to legislative and administrative control. The courts ". . . should be reduced to the barest minimum which is consistent with the statutory mandate for judicial review. . . ." The minority recognized that this case ". . . starts a new chapter in the regulation of utility rates. . . ."

The rise of administrative supervision. Two years later the Supreme Court faced a valuation question and settled it without equivocation. In the Hope Natural Gas case[17] the Court renounced the title conferred upon it by Professor John R. Commons—"The Authoritative Faculty of Political Economy for the United States." Without mentioning *Smyth v. Ames*, the fair-value rule was repudiated and the determination of the reasonableness of earnings was renounced—at least, partially—as not a subject for judicial review.

The use of the prudent-investment formula was upheld, but the Court declined to espouse it. The majority agreed on reiterating the principle

[14] *FPC v. Natural Gas Pipeline Co.*, 315 U.S. 575 (1942).

[15] 315 U.S. 586.

[16] *Munn v. Illinois*, 94 U.S. 113 (1877).

[17] *FPC v. Hope Natural Gas Co.*, 320 U.S. 591 (1944). The Court was highly divided in this case. Two members of the majority (Black and Murphy) wrote a separate concurring opinion. Each member of the minority (Reed, Frankfurter, and Jackson) wrote a separate dissent, for a total of five separate opinions.

of the Natural Gas case that "the Constitution does not bind rate-making bodies to the service of any single formula or combination of formulas." Any formula—or no formula at all—was satisfactory as long as the earnings were reasonable. Justice Douglas wrote:[18]

> Under the statutory standard of "just and reasonable" it is the result reached not the method employed which is controlling. It is not theory but the impact of the rate order which counts. If the total effect of the rate order cannot be said to be unjust and unreasonable, judicial inquiry under the Act is at an end. The fact that the method employed to reach that result may contain infirmities is not then important.

This is the doctrine of "end result" or "total effect of the rate order." Thus, the regulatory commissions are left with greater freedom to fix rates. They may still use the rate-base procedure, but if they do not choose to do so, the authority of the Fourteenth Amendment cannot be invoked to nullify a reasonable rate. As Robert L. Hale pointed out,[19] the Hope case laid at rest the myth that the power to regulate rates is not a power to destroy any part of the value of properties. It is! The purpose of regulation is to reduce excessive rates, and such reduction lessens earnings. Prior to the Hope decision, the Court maintained that such reduction could not diminish the value of property which yielded those earnings, for that action would be "taking of the use" of property. But effective rate regulation must deprive companies of some part of the value of its property. Hale writes: ". . . to permit reductions when, and only when, the previously anticipated earnings amount to more than a fair return on value is the same thing as to permit no reductions whatever in anticipated earnings."[20] Any lesser rate would certainly amount to less than a fair return on previous value. Since the true value of property depends on anticipated earnings, the lower rate would necessarily diminish value.

The Hope decision held rate making to be an exercise of the police power rather than of the power of eminent domain. Therefore, the utility rate-fixing process no longer consists of the determination of just compensation for taking of property, but rather of determining what is a just and reasonable price for the service or product which the utility will furnish to its customers.[21] Justice Douglas suggested as a guide: "Rates

[18] 320 U.S. 602.

[19] "Utility Regulation in the Light of the Hope Natural Gas Case," 44 *Columbia Law Review* 488–489 (July, 1944).

[20] *Ibid.*, p. 489.

[21] The weakness of the Smyth formula was that it made little distinction between unreasonable rates and confiscatory rates. It was based on the assumption that the regulation of utility rates was the legal equivalent to the exercise of the power of eminent domain. Therefore, the rates prescribed must assure just compensation for the taking of property or they would be confiscatory. See Herbert T. Ferguson, "Why Is a Rate Base?" 39 *Public Utilities Fortnightly* 811–812 (June 19, 1947).

which enable the company to operate successfully, to maintain its financial integrity, to attract capital, and to compensate its investors for the risks assumed. . . ." [22]

Such a standard of reasonable earnings focuses attention on the financial background of a company—its market position, financial obligations, credit standing, and past dividends—and "involves a balancing of the investor and the consumer interests." [23] In this particular case Douglas deemed the return adequate for capital-raising purposes by relating it to the amount and type of outstanding securities.

Obviously, new controveries will develop over what is and what is not "just and reasonable" under the end-result doctrine. The majority of the Court attempted to free itself from these controversies by shifting the responsibility for deciding on the reasonableness of earnings to the commissions. The Court said of the rate order in this case: "It is the product of expert judgment which carries a presumption of validity." [24]

But the Supreme Court did not renounce entirely its power to declare rates unconstitutional. If the Court chooses to review a commission's concept of reasonableness, as it may do, some method must be employed to study the end result of rates. If, on the other hand, the Court intends to follow the Munn precedent which asserted that ". . . the law itself . . . may be changed at the will, or even at the whim, of the legislature, unless prevented by constitutional limitations. . . ," then the Court will probably refrain from intruding on rate matters. It will be recalled that the Court said in the Munn decision: "For protection against abuses by legislatures the people must resort to the polls, not to the courts." [25]

Valuation since the Hope decision. The Supreme Court's decision to withdraw from valuation problems and not bind the regulatory commissions to any specific valuation formula would seem to enlarge greatly the discretion of state commissions. However, statutory limitations on the powers of many of the state regulatory bodies with reference to valuation of utility property preclude them from freely using their own methods in obtaining a rate base.

The state statutes pertaining to valuation fall into three categories: (1) nine state commissions are required by law to consider reproduction cost, but in no state is it required to be the exclusive or controlling consideration;[26] (2) the commissions in nine other states must find some sort of "fair" or "reasonable" value;[27] (3) in the rest of the states, except for the

[22] 320 U.S. 605.

[23] 320 U.S. 603.

[24] 320 U.S. 602.

[25] 94 U.S. 134 (1877).

[26] Alabama, Indiana, Kentucky, New Mexico, North Carolina, Oklahoma (constitutional), Nebraska (telephone), Ohio, and North Dakota.

[27] Connecticut, Kansas, Maine, Maryland (telephone), Michigan, New York, Pennsylvania, Washington, and Texas (gas only).

eight that do not regulate gas or electric utilities,[28] the commissions seem to be allowed to use their own methods in obtaining a rate order.[29]

Obviously, the commissions in group 1 are not affected by the Hope decision, since the laws are specific and definite. Two months after the Hope decision the Supreme Court of North Dakota said: "There can be no doubt today, but that, in so far as the Federal courts are concerned, the 'ghost of Smyth v. Ames had been laid.' That circumstance, however, has no bearing upon the question before us now. We are concerned with the law of this state as enacted in 1919." [30]

The regulatory bodies in groups 2 and 3 might, or might not, be affected—depending on court interpretation of state statutes. The Hope decision would have effect in the states where the statutes require the commissions to find some sort of "fair" or "reasonable" value, only if the courts would retroactively interpret the intent of the respective legislatures as anticipating the eventual no-formula rule laid down in the Hope case. Since the courts have traditionally adhered to the Smyth rule under these statutes, this interpretation is unlikely to be made. For example, two months before the Hope decision, the Pennsylvania Superior Court anticipated the Supreme Court's holding in the Hope case and said: ". . . even though the Supreme Court of the United States, as presently constituted, may, in the near future, overrule some of its former decisions and uphold as constitutional something other than fair value as a rate base, such change of position would not effect a change in the law of this commonwealth." [31] In 1952, the Maryland Court of Appeals upheld the use of reproduction cost [32] and, in 1953, the Maine Supreme Court overruled the regulatory commission when it failed to consider current values.[33]

The twenty-five states in group 3 are required to fix rates that are just and reasonable, but no definition for "just and reasonable" is given. It must be remembered that all these laws were passed before the Hope case. The framers of these statutes probably did not have in mind the kind of theory set forth in the Hope decision when they drafted them. For years the state courts have generally been following *Smyth v. Ames*. It could be argued that the courts in these states would deny the intent of the framers of these laws if they adhered to the Hope rule too closely.

Recently the Wisconsin Public Service Commission dispensed with any formula in arriving at reasonable earnings in a case involving the Com-

[28] Delaware, Florida, Iowa, Minnesota, Mississippi, Nebraska, South Dakota, and Texas (electric).

[29] For a summary of these laws, see Charles A. Fsser, "State Laws in Relation to the Hope Natural Gas Decision," 34 *Public Utilities Fortnightly* 70 (July 20, 1944).

[30] *Northern States Power Co. v. Public Service Com.*, 13 N.W.2d 779 (1944).

[31] *Peoples Nat. Gas Co. v. Public U.C.*, 51 P.U.R. (n.s.) 129, 138 (1943).

[32] *Chesapeake & Potomac Tel. Co. v. Public S.C.*, 95 P.U.R. (n.s.) 129.

[33] *New England Tel. & Tel. Co. v. Public U.C.*, CCH 1953 Utilities, Par. 16,389.

monwealth Telephone Company. Prudent investment was expressly renounced, as was a given rate of return on any kind of rate base. The court reversed the commission for relying on the "trance method" of rate fixing.[34] The Supreme Court of Illinois reversed the state commission for not considering current values.[35] But other state courts, like the Supreme Court of Utah,[36] permit value to be found in any way which the United States Supreme Court may view as permissible under the due-process clause.

Between 1946 and 1953, about seventy-five court decisions were handed down on appeals of rate cases. In more than half the cases the commission order was affirmed. Under the latitude permitted by the Hope decision there has been a tendency, where state law permits, to allow the use of original cost in determining rate base.[37]

Fair Rate of Return

The formula most commonly used for arriving at reasonable earnings is to multiply a fair valuation of the property used and useful for public service by a fair rate of return. Therefore, once a rate base has been determined, a regulatory commission must decide upon a rate of return that is "fair." Prior to the Hope decision, the greatest emphasis was on the rate base. Since 1944 there has been a shift of emphasis to the rate of return component in the formula, a shift which was especially noticeable during 1952.[38] Postwar inflation has been another reason for the emphasis on the rate of return. Utility corporations have felt the impact of inflation particularly hard, because it has cost more to add new customer facilities than it did before the war. The regulatory commissions of such states as Utah, Colorado, and California [39] have made allowances for this cost in the rate of return.

Certainly the rate of return is as significant as the rate base. A small change in the rate of return may be equivalent to a large change in the valuation total. For example, a rate of 6 per cent on a fair value of $10 million returns the same amount as a rate of 5 per cent on a fair value of $12 million.

[34] *City of Two Rivers v. Commonwealth Tel. Co.*, 70 P.U.R. (n.s.) 5 (1947); *Commonwealth Tel. Co. v. Wisconsin P.S.C.*, 71 P.U.R. (n.s.) 65 (1947).

[35] *Illinois Bell Tel. Co. v. Commerce Com.*, CCH 1953 Utilities, Par. 16,347.

[36] See *Utah Power & Light Co. v. Public S.C.*, 56 P.U.R. (n.s.) 136 (1945).

[37] See *Chicopee Mfg. Co. v. Public S.C.*, CCH 1953 Utilities, Par. 16,364; and for a general discussion, John P. Randolph, "The Status of Public Utility Regulation," 51 *Public Utilities Fortnightly* 740–746 (June 4, 1953).

[38] See, for example, *Re Washington Gas Light Co.*, P.U.S. No. 3517, Formal Case No. 414, Order No. 3876, Mar. 27, 1952.

[39] See *P.G. & E. Co.*, 51 Cal. P.U.C. 130 (1951).

Actual rates fixed by commissions have varied from 5 to 9 per cent, according to several studies which have been made.[40] The majority of rates of return have fallen between 5 and 8 per cent, with the average being around 6 per cent or slightly below. As of 1948, the Arizona commission allowed rates between 6 and 8 per cent, and the Oklahoma commission fixed them as low as 5¼ per cent. The rest of the state commissions set them at 5½ to 6 or 6½ per cent. In 1952, the Federal Power Commission limited one gas company to a 5½ per cent rate of return and another to 6 per cent.[41] Up until that time the Commission fixed rates of return by categories. That is, in the early 1940s it was allowing 6½ per cent for all natural-gas companies and 6 per cent for all electric companies. Now it is individualizing rates by companies. Furthermore, there is a trend to adopt a test period for fixing rates for the future, which is the latest twelve months' recorded experience adjusted for known changes.

The function of the courts in reviewing rates fixed by commissions is not to fix fair rates but to determine whether the rates are reasonable.[42] However, the courts have on many occasions found that a reasonable rate of return would be no less than a certain per cent.[43]

Although lower rates of return have been allowed in recent years,[44] courts generally have shown a tendency to look with disfavor upon those

[40] For a summary of some of these studies, see F. X. Welch and others, *Cases on Utility Regulation* (Washington, D.C.: Public Utilities Reports, Inc., 1936), pp. 434–438, and supplement (1940). Also see Nelson Lee Smith, *The Fair Rate of Return in Public Utility Regulation* (Boston: Houghton Mifflin Company, 1932); FCC, *The Problem of the "Rate of Return" in Public Utility Regulation* (1938); FPC, *State Commission Jurisdiction and Regulation of Electric and Gas Utilities* (1948), p. 11.

[41] *Northern Natural Gas Co.*, F.P.C. Opinion No. 228, June 11, 1952, 95 P.U.R. (n.s.) 289; *Mississippi River Fuel Corporation*, F.P.C. Opinion No. 234, July 29, 1952, 95 P.U.R. (n.s.) 435.

[42] The test of reasonableness was best stated by the Supreme Court in 1923: "A public utility is entitled to such rates as will permit it to earn a return on the value of the property which it employs for the convenience of the public equal to that generally being made at the same time and in the same general part of the country on investments in other business undertakings which are attended by corresponding risks and uncertainties. . . . The return should be reasonably sufficient to assure confidence in the financial soundness of the utility and should be adequate, under efficient and economical management, to maintain and support its credit and enable it to raise money necessary for the proper discharge of its public duties." *Bluefield W.W. and Imp. Co. v. West Virginia*, 262 U.S. 692–693.

[43] For example, in the United Railways and Electric Company case (280 U.S. 234, at 252), the Supreme Court found that a rate of return of less than 7.44 per cent (the amount suggested by the company) would be confiscatory.

[44] In *Peoples Gas Light and Coke Co. v. Slattery*, 373 Ill. 31 (1939), the Illinois Supreme Court refused to deny the validity of a 5 per cent rate of return. The United States Supreme Court denied a petition for appeal. *Peoples Gas Light and Coke Co. v. Hart*, 309 U.S. 634 (1940).

of less than 6 per cent. However, in a dissenting opinion, Mr. Justice Stone suggested in 1935 that, in view of capital-market conditions, a company might have difficulty in proving that a return of 4½ per cent was so low as to be confiscatory.[45]

In 1942, when it handed down the Natural Gas Pipeline decision, the Court approved the Illinois Commission's choice of a 6½ per cent return. Moreover, for the first time, the Court tied the rate of property depreciation and rate of return together, implying that amortization of plant investments through depreciation charges should influence the choice of a reasonable rate.[46] The Supreme Court was not primarily concerned with rate-of-return problems in the Hope case and contented itself with repeating the language of previous decisions on this issue. The Court did not sanction any one method of determining fair rates but preferred to leave the matter to the discretion of regulatory commissions.

Reasonable Operating Expenses

Traditionally, operating expenses have been regarded as peculiarly within the discretion of private management. It has been felt that management would have as much incentive as the public to keep these costs at a low level so that relatively little attention has been paid to the regulation of operating expenses. However, as was noted in beginning the discussion of rate regulation, the general rule in rate cases has been that due process requires a fair return over and above reasonable operating expenses. Operating expenses commonly are one-half to three-quarters of the total costs. If depreciation allowances, service contracts, and other operating expenses are excessive, the company would receive more than its just earnings. Rate regulation would be meaningless without examination of operating expenses. Thus, the Supreme Court recognized as early as 1892 that the power to set fair rates included the right to review operating expenses.[47] Only recently, however, has the regulation of operating expenses been effective.

In general, regulatory commissions' powers are limited to disallowing certain expenses as not being proper for furnishing public service. Disallowance means that these expenditures will be excluded in the computation of a reasonable rate level. It does not mean, however, that the public utility may not continue making these expenses. Very rarely can a commission prevent a utility from incurring improper operating expenses. Only if a company is legally required to submit a budget for commission approval does a regulatory agency have prior knowledge of them.

[45] *West v. Chesapeake and Potomac Tel. Co.*, 295 U.S. 662, 683.

[46] *FPC v. Natural Gas Pipeline Co. of America*, 315 U.S. 597.

[47] *Chicago and Grand Trunk Ry. v. Wellman*, 143 U.S. 339 (1892).

THE DEPRECIATION ALLOWANCE

Because depreciation allowances loom large among the operating expenses of public utilities, the importance of commission review of them is apparent.[48] And because the proper amount to be charged against operations for loss in value during a year is not capable of objective and accurate calculation, it is a subject of much disagreement between companies and commissions. Since accountants, who traditionally deal with original cost, calculate it by multiplying the percentage of annual loss against original cost, commissions have insisted that computation of depreciation expense be done in this way. But the Supreme Court, in one of the few cases on this subject, upheld the contention of a public-utility company that present value, rather than original cost, should be used for the depreciation base.[49] This decision had to do with the question of confiscation in a rate case. Hence, it was for *rate-making* purposes that the calculation of depreciation allowance could not be limited to original costs. Where control of accounts is concerned and depreciation allowances are prescribed in accounts, the calculation may lawfully be made on original cost.[50]

OTHER OPERATING EXPENSES

With very few exceptions, little has been done by state public-utility commissions with regard to other operating expenses. There are scattered cases where various expenses have been disallowed in rate cases. These include excessive amounts for salaries, pensions, advertising expenses, bad debts, public donations, and political contributions.

An interesting question is whether public utilities can pass on to the consumer as an operating expense the costs of combating commission regulation. These expenses might include not only the cost of gathering evidence, conducting property valuation studies, hiring lawyers, and so forth, but also the expense, if necessary, of carrying a case into the courts. If these costs are allowed, a company's temptation to fight every disadvantageous rate change would be heightened, for the firm would have nothing to lose.

In 1935 the Supreme Court ruled that a company should be reimbursed for the expense of presenting its case to a regulatory commission, although it did suggest that the case might be different if the company's case had

[48] In 1948, forty states—that is, all states having commissions with the power to regulate charges for electric and gas service, except North Dakota—had the power to prescribe depreciation methods. Of these, twenty-five established a method for computing depreciation. Seventeen states prescribed the straight-line method for general use. Only four states established depreciation rates. FPC, *State Commission Jurisdiction and Regulation of Electric and Gas Utilities*, pp. 12, 13.

[49] *United Rwy. & Elec. Co. v. West*, 280 U.S. 234 (1930).

[50] *American Tel. & Tel. Co. v. United States*, 299 U.S. 232 (1936).

been unfounded.[51] Four years later the Court said, "Even where the rates in effect are excessive, . . . we are of the view that the utility should be allowed its fair and proper expenses for presenting its side to the commission." [52] The Court approved amortization of the rate expenses over a ten-year period.

Economic and Administative Aspects of Rate Regulation

From an economic point of view, the return allowed by a regulatory commission should be adequate to keep capital flowing into the industry. Therefore, its economic soundness must be judged primarily in the light of long-time considerations and competition for investment capital. A return which may seem adequate to attract capital at one time may not be high enough to protect credit standing over a period of years.

To attract investment capital in a competitive capital market, the public-utility return should not be frozen at a fixed dollar income for a certain dollar investment. It is true that some commentators have argued that the public-utility investor is and should be interested in obtaining a fixed and steady dollar return upon his investment. This contention is valid for bondholders, because they enter a contract stipulating a fixed monetary return. Stockholders, on the other hand, do not make such a contract; they usually accept the risk of ownership in return for the possibility of returns higher than those current for bonds. Indeed, in recent years more and more "conservative" investors have purchased common stock or participating preferred stock because they believe that dollar returns on it will increase as general prices rise. Buying such stocks as a hedge against inflation is an increasingly important motive behind stock purchases.

ECONOMIC ASPECTS OF VALUATION

The economic necessities of a sound rate level make any original-cost method of calculating the rate base subject to some infirmity. The rate base, fixed upon original cost, is more or less frozen to the amount of money invested, and the return calculated upon it tends also to be fixed in terms of dollars. In the face of an increasing price level, this would seem to place a public utility at a disadvantage so far as obtaining stock capital is concerned. If prices should change substantially, or show promise of doing so, the matter for bonds might also be affected adversely.

Use of a value measure taking into account present costs would make for a rate base changing with the price level; allowable return would likewise vary. The economic difficulty with a present-cost measure lies in the fact that public utilities are customarily financed with about half their

[51] *West Ohio G. Co. v. Public U. Com. of Ohio*, 294 U.S. 73 (1935).
[52] *Driscoll v. Edison L. & P. Co.*, 307 U.S. 120–121 (1939).

capitalization in bonds. If prices rise and the rate base and return in dollars are increased, the dollar return to bondholders remains the same, and the stockholders receive a more than proportionate enlargement of their dollar income at the expense of rate payers. If prices fall, the contracted dollar return to bondholders stays at the same level, and dollar earnings for stock fall precipitously, or disappear, or become deficits endangering the payment of fixed interest bondholders.

If one looks to the economic nature of public-utility investment, the argument runs, the present-cost measure of value has greater validity. While an investor's contribution is measured in dollars, what he really invests is capital or that which dollars will buy. He does not hold title to dollars but claims against physical and intangible property. It is an elementary concept of economics that original cost, stated in dollars, has no particular significance as value, except at the time the expenditure is made. As price levels change, original costs may come to have little more importance than an interesting historical fact.

However, there are certain fallacies in this real-income argument which should be pointed out.[53] No distinction is made between different kinds of price-level changes. Some changes might be temporary, others permanent. Cyclical changes may not appreciably affect investments. Furthermore, investors know that utility earnings are more stable than nonutility returns and they may not expect equivalent incomes from utility and nonutility stocks. Moreover, from the standpoint of flow of needed capital into the industry, the utility companies have had little difficulty selling their bonds and notes. Finally, this argument implies that the only important variable of earnings regulation is property valuation, which is not the case. The rate of return itself is also flexible.

ADMINISTRATION ASPECTS OF VALUATION

One of the goals of regulation is effective control. In addition to meeting certain economic requirements, public-utility rate regulation should meet the test of sound and efficient administration.

If accounts have been prescribed by commissions for a long enough time and have been subject to inspection and audit by the government, they may show original costs fairly accurately. In ascertaining these costs for rate-base purposes, a public-utility commission is faced with a fairly simple task. Although adequate accounting control takes much time of the commission and requires sizable appropriations for an accounting staff both in the office and in the field, it is useful in nearly every aspect of public-utility control. Hence, regulation of accounts for valuation purposes need not place an unreasonable burden upon a commission.

[53] Following Emery Troxel, *Economics of Public Utilities* (New York: Rinehart & Company, Inc., 1947), pp. 297–298.

Where accounts have not been prescribed or policed to any appreciable extent, or where the accounting regulation has not been in effect long enough, books of public-utility companies may not give an accurate picture of original cost. In cases of this kind, the commission is faced with expensive investigations and a resort to unsatisfactory estimates for the ascertainment of original cost. Where this is true, the administrative problem of determining original cost makes this method little less difficult than computing present costs. Nevertheless, once a record of original cost is computed or estimated, accounting control thereafter can keep the original cost up to date without much trouble.

Calculation of reproduction cost new is a complicated administrative task, as has been indicated by the discussion of how reproduction cost is obtained. The process of inventorying thousands of articles from poles to desks and applying unit prices is complex enough. Add to this the laborious task of estimating intangible items of property and the honest differences of opinion that can exist between experts, and one can understand how expensive this method is. The company ordinarily makes an estimate of reproduction cost, as well as the commission. Often, interested municipalities make estimates. Mosher and Crawford refer to a case where a company spent $5 million to appraise a property finally valued at $500 million.[54] Expenditures of 1 per cent of the valuation by one party in a valuation dispute are not at all unusual. Furthermore, the hypothetical character of cost of reproduction lends itself to conflicts in judgment and resort to legal processes. These ordinarily involve delays in settling a rate case, a decade or more having elapsed in some instances before final decision.

Critics also point out that cost-of-reproduction estimates cannot accurately reflect present costs. By the time an investigation is completed, the prices used are obsolete; to keep cost of reproduction up to date, such estimates would have to be made continually. As a matter of fact, this is an extreme criticism. No one familiar with rate regulation expects detailed accuracy. Cost-of-reproduction estimates need be made, moreover, only when a rate change is contemplated, whether by the company or the commission. Even then, the dispute may not be of such a nature as to force resort to measuring value anew, and often data of previous valuations reduce the complexity of the task in making a new estimate of fair value.

ECONOMIC ASPECTS OF A FAIR RATE

An economically sound rate of return is one which is high enough to safeguard the credit of public utilities so that needed capital may be

[54] W. E. Mosher and F. G. Crawford, *Public Utility Regulation* (New York: Harper & Brothers, 1933), p. 205.

readily obtained. The rate, consequently, should be such that capital structure may be safeguarded for future financing, as well as for the present. A rate of return based upon bond-interest rates only, and fixed in contemplation of debt financing, shortsightedly overlooks the possibly deleterious results of too great a burden of fixed charges.

As one might expect, the economically proper rate of return is not necessarily the same as between companies or as between different times. Thus, any particular fair rate must be judged in the light of the individual company and the time at which it is made. There is a danger, however, that too much attention may be given to a certain capital market and that rates may be influenced by a temporary status of capital demand and supply.

ADMINISTRATIVE ASPECTS OF A FAIR RATE

Among the many factors to be considered by regulatory commissions in fixing rates of return, three may be noted: (1) the rate necessary to attract capital to the utility company; (2) the rates earned by comparable, but unregulated, industries; (3) the historical cost of the capital to the utility company.

The first factor focuses on the current cost of borrowing. The relevant information about what rate of return would attract new lenders is obtained from current sales of new utilities securities, the yield rates on outstanding utilities securities, and the general character of the capital market. As for the second factor, the earnings of industries with comparable risks and the prices of securities of these industries would appear to be pertinent, but most attempts at comparable studies have been clumsy and superficial. Therefore, the commissions have shown no great inclination to consider this factor.

The third factor emphasizes the financial commitments of the utility company. This may be measured by the interest rates on outstanding bonds and notes, the fixed dividend for preferred stock, and a "substantial" return on common stocks.

The record of the public utility itself and the probable effects of taxation, competitive enterprises, and future government regulatory policies might well influence the judgment of a commission. Because some companies are small, or are located in a relatively unknown geographic area, they may be unable to finance on as favorable terms as other companies.

Some states provide that a commission consider efficiency of management in fixing the rate of return. Plans have been devised whereby the rate is increased or decreased according to efficiency and satisfactoriness of service. This method involves a fixed rate of return which is agreed upon by the company and the commission. If service is maintained at a high level and rates are reduced, the percentage of return allowable is automatically increased. The principal difficulty with this plan lies in obtaining objective measurement of service standards agreeable to the public and the private companies. Moreover, if a rate of return becomes high under this plan, the public may feel that it has cause for complaint. If incentives to efficient management can best be given by such a plan, there is much for which it can be commended. In formulating a plan of this sort, care should be taken that the company does not obtain too great a reward for technological progress, with which a management may have little to do.

State Regulation of Rates

All states have some measure of power to regulate utility rates. This authority does not extend to certain utilities in a number of states. For example, 6 states have no power to regulate electric rates; 8 states, no authority over the rates of manufactured gas; and 8 states, no power over rates of natural gas. The rate authority of 15 states does *not* extend to street railways; of 13 states, to interurban railways; of 6 states, to motor busses; of 8 states, to trucks; of 7 states, to water; and of 2 states, to telephone and telegraph companies.[55] In a majority of states the power is not applicable to municipally owned utilities. Since the general scope of rate regulation is practically identical to that of service regulation, the exceptions need not be pointed out here.

Where any sort of rate regulation exists, the laws are more uniform as among states than in any other aspect of public-utility control. They generally provide that rates must be just and reasonable, that unreasonable discrimination is unlawful, that schedules must be filed and adhered to, and that changes may be made only after due notice to the commission. Nearly all commissions are given power to suspend changes in rates pending investigation. Most states also empower commissions to undertake investigations, upon their own motion or upon complaint, as to the reasonableness of rates, and to fix a reasonable rate in the place of any found unreasonable; in a few states this power is limited to maximum rates.

An interesting rate-regulation device has become law in several states. This is the temporary-rate order.[56] It enables a state commission to set rates which a utility must charge during the pendency of a case before the courts. Commissions have used it to meet emergency conditions, to test a rate when there are uncertainties concerning the revenue that may

[55] Council of State Governments, *Book of the States, 1954–1955* (Chicago, 1954), p. 218.

[56] For a detailed treatment see Irston R. Barnes, "Temporary Rates in Utility Regulation," 34 *Illinois Law Review* 929–955 (April, 1940).

be expected, and to correct unreasonable rates pending the final determination of the just and reasonable rate. State laws usually permit the temporary rate to be made on the basis of commission data as to reasonableness. When the case is decided, the temporary rate is changed to the price arising from the litigation. If the rate finally allowed is above the temporary one, the utility is allowed to make up the deficiency by a temporary higher charge. In 1942, the Supreme Court expressly approved this device as a reasonable commission procedure.[57] However, the Court emphasized that the temporary rates must be based on factual data and that the procedures of due process must be observed.

Federal Regulation of Rates

The power of the states to regulate utility rates is not dependent upon any specific constitutional grant of power but is derived from that residue of power that inheres in the states. This residual power is the "police power" to protect the health, safety, and morals of the people. It cannot be exercised if it conflicts with the powers delegated to the federal government, and it cannot contravene the due-process and equal-protection safeguards of the Fourteenth Amendment. Nor can it violate the obligation of contracts and privileges-and-immunities clauses of the Constitution. However, the federal government has no such police power which might serve as basis for rate regulation. Since the federal government is a government of "limited and enumerated powers," authority for rate regulation (as well as all economic regulation) must be found among the delegated powers of Congress. No legislation may be enacted if it cannot be reasonably derived from these powers. The due-process protection of the Fifth Amendment serves as the principal limitation.

COMMUNICATIONS

Acting under the interstate-commerce clause, Congress enacted the Mann-Elkins Act in 1910 which placed interstate (but not foreign) transmission of messages by wire or wireless under the Interstate Commerce Commission and within many of the provisions of the law applicable to railroads. Charges were required to be just and reasonable, and making or giving any undue preference or advantage to persons, places, or kinds of traffic was forbidden. The Commission was empowered to prescribe maximum and minimum rates and to require periodic reports and uniform accounts. Effective rate regulation, however, was practically impossible because of numerous omissions in the law. The Commission could not require companies to file and post rates, nor could it investigate or suspend proposed changes in rates, classifications, or other practices pending final

[57] *FPC v. Natural Gas Pipeline Co. of America*, 315 U.S. 583–584.

action. It had no authority to require through rates. Without such essential powers, the Interstate Commerce Commission could not have done much even if it had had the staff and the inclination to do so.

By the Communications Act of 1934, the newly formed Federal Communications Commission was given authority over the rates charged by wire- and wireless-communications companies, except that it was granted no power to fix the charges of radio and television broadcasting. The law of 1934 provides that all charges of communications common carriers must be just and reasonable, and it specifically declares that the services of each carrier may be classified and different charges made for each class of service. Rate discrimination against persons and places is forbidden if found to be undue or unreasonable. Common carriers are required to file their rates with the Commission, to post them for public inspection, and to abide by them. Changes in charges, classifications, or practices concerning rates must be filed with the Commission and thirty days' notice given unless modified by its action. Any such change may be suspended by the Commission, pending investigation of its reasonableness, for a period of three months. The burden of proving reasonableness rests on the carrier.

To aid the Commission in fixing a reasonable rate level, the law provides for valuation of the property of companies subject to the act. The companies are required to furnish information as to cost of reproduction new, less depreciation, and original cost. It is interesting that the law demands a rather detailed breakdown of this information, depicting clearly how any resultant valuation is obtained. In showing the detail of original cost, companies must report as a separate item any costs incurred in obtaining a franchise or license from any public authority, and the Commission is directed to include in its figures at original cost nothing except lawfully incurred and reasonably necessary expenditures. The Commission is instructed "to adopt any method of valuation which shall be lawful."

The Commission also has the authority to investigate the prices that communications companies pay for equipment, supplies, managerial or construction services, and research work. This provision was apparently aimed at transactions between telephone companies affiliated in the Bell system. Like other holding companies, the American Telephone and Telegraph Company provides contract services, such as engineering, accounting, and legal services, for subsidiary systems.[58] In addition, there is an arrangement by which the Western Electric Company, a subsidiary of American Telephone and Telegraph Company, manufactures 90 per cent of the telephonic equipment. Since the Bell system owns Western Electric,

[58] These practices led to an extensive congressional investigation in 1936 and 1937. See *Investigation of the Telephone Industry in the United States*, H. Doc. 340, 76th Cong., 1st Sess. (1939).

it can control the equipment prices on which Bell companies expect returns.

Since the creation of the Federal Communications Commission in 1934 there has been a steady movement toward uniform message toll telephone rates throughout the United States. By 1941, this uniformity was substantially achieved. Certain deviations in the five-state area served by the New England Telephone and Telegraph Company were eliminated in 1952.[59]

ELECTRICITY

The authority of the Federal Power Commission to regulate electric rates hangs on two constitutional pegs. Jurisdiction over the rates charged by hydroelectric licensees is based on federal power over navigable waters and waters on public lands. Authority over the rates of interstate electric utilities is derived from the interstate commerce power.

Regulation of hydroelectric licensees. By legislation passed in 1920, federal power licensees have been required to adhere to the system of accounts prescribed by the Federal Power Commission, to allow government inspection of accounts, and to make such reports as the Commission demands. One of the chief purposes of accounting control is to allow the government to police investment accounts so that the net investment may be fairly and accurately determined from the records of the company. An equally important purpose is to provide a basis for regulation of rates (and security issues), both by the state public-utility commissions and by the Federal Power Commission. Examination of the records of the Commission indicates that, particularly since 1930, this control has been carefully administered and that the Commission has insisted upon the books of a licensee showing no more than a fair net-investment cost.[60]

Licensees which are public utilities must abide by regulations of states on matters of rates (as well as service and securities), where intrastate commerce is concerned. If the state is not empowered to regulate these matters, the license terms confer jurisdiction upon the Federal Power Commission. When the licensee is engaged in interstate commerce, the Federal Water Power Act requires rates and services to be reasonable and nondiscriminatory. The guide used is a fair return on "net investment." When reasonable rates and services cannot be obtained by state action, or when a state with jurisdiction over the company has no law regulating security issuance, the Commission has been given jurisdiction.

[59] FCC, *18th Annual Report, 1952*, pp. 43–44.

[60] See, for example, *Re Alabama Power Co.*, P.U.R. 1932 D 345 (1932), and *Clarion River Power Company v. Smith* (District of Columbia Court of Appeals), 59 F.2d 861 (1932).

Regulation of interstate electric rates. The Federal Power Commission's rate-fixing powers over interstate electricity were not extensive until the enactment of the Federal Power Act of 1935. This law requires all rates by any electric public utility operating as a federal licensee or engaged in interstate transmission or interstate wholesale sales to be just and reasonable.[61] Rates which discriminate unduly between persons, classes of service, or localities are forbidden. All utilities subject to this portion of the law must file their rates with the Commission for public inspection, and new or changed rates may not be made effective unless with thirty days' notice, except by permission of the Commission. While the Commission is charged to decide the question as speedily as possible, the law allows the suspension to be effective for five months.

Rate reductions may be ordered immediately where a preliminary investigation reveals that existing rates are unjustifiably high. The company is advised of the tentative findings which the Federal Power Commission proposes to adopt in a final order. To prevent the order from going into effect, the company must be able to "show cause" why the findings should not be made final. To aid the Commission in determining a reasonable rate, it may investigate and ascertain the "actual legitimate cost" of the properties under its jurisdiction, the "depreciation therein," and other facts which bear upon the determination of cost, depreciation, or fair value. So that the Commission may perform this task, every utility under its jurisdiction is required, when requested by it, to file an inventory of property and original-cost data and to keep it informed as to the cost of additions, betterments, extension, and new construction. The Commission has shown a preference for the original-cost method of determining fair value, rather than cost of reproduction. Specifically, it has favored the prudent-investment variation.

The authority of the Federal Power Commission extends only to wholesale rates charged in interstate commerce. In the case of electric companies for which the Commission has no rate-regulation power, it may, however, upon request of a state commission, investigate and determine the cost of producing or transmitting electric energy by means of the facilities under its own jurisdiction. Thus, an electricity-producing or -distributing company operating in interstate commerce but not selling at wholesale may be subject to investigation as to cost of electricity. This provision is for the benefit of state commissions which are unable to reach interstate company operations, although they do have power to fix a local retail public-utility rate.

[61] By declaration of policy in Title II of the Public Utility Act of 1935, Congress stated that such regulation was "to extend only to those matters which are not subject to regulation by the states."

NATURAL GAS

The regulation of the rapidly expanding natural-gas industry, which now supplies one-fourth of the nation's energy, is complicated by the distinct phases which separate production from ultimate consumption. Natural gas is produced from gas and oil wells and is then assembled through a network of gathering pipelines. The next major phase is the transportation of gas to local distribution companies. Some pipeline companies own their own natural-gas reserves and are commonly known as "integrated" companies. Other transportation companies purchase from producing companies all or part of the gas they transmit and sell. Producers who have no affiliation with pipeline companies and sell their gas to the pipelines in arm's-length transactions are called "independent" producers. The local distribution of natural gas to the ultimate consumer is the final phase of the industry. Because of the multiphase character of the industry, there are three different marketing transactions in which the rates might be regulated: (1) the field sale of producers and gatherers; (2) the city-gate sale at wholesale by pipeline companies to local distribution companies; and (3) the retail sale by the distribution company.

Before 1938 retail sales were subject to state public-utility regulation, but city-gate rates were found to be beyond the jurisdiction of the states because of the constitutional limitations which prevent state regulation from burdening interstate commerce. Furthermore, the states were at a disadvantage both in ascertaining the facts with respect to the costs applicable to city-gate rates and in coping with exorbitant charges by pipeline companies. The utility companies often preferred to take their profits from the pipeline companies rather than from the local distributing companies which were subject to state regulation.

Congress enacted the Natural Gas Act in 1938 to fill this gap. The Federal Power Commission is authorized to fix just and reasonable rates, eliminate undue preferences, and maintain reasonable differences in rates between localities and classes of wholesale customers for the companies subject to its jurisdiction. It can also ascertain "actual legitimate cost of property" and prescribe the measurement of depreciation charges.

The jurisdiction of the Commission extends to "the transportation of natural gas in interstate commerce" and the "sale in interstate commerce of natural gas for resale." The local distribution and the production or gathering of natural gas are specifically exempted. Unfortunately, Congress did not make clear whether the field prices paid by interstate pipe lines were to be regarded as sales in interstate commerce or as a part of production and gathering and hence exempt. A bitter controversy developed over this question that has ranged from the hearing rooms of the

Federal Power Commission, up to the Supreme Court, and back into the halls of Congress.

In fixing the wholesale rates charged by pipeline companies that produce their own gas, the Commission has chosen to take into account the cost of gas to the transportation companies.[62] This choice puts the Commission very nearly in the position of regulating production, because it has treated production and gathering facilities as an integral part of utility property. Until 1954, the Commission computed the value of production facilities at depreciated original cost. The companies have complained strenuously. Many natural-gas leaseholds were acquired at a negligible value before the existence of natural gas was proven. This cost was used rather than the enhanced value after the gas was discovered. The position of the Commission was justified on the grounds that the enhanced value was produced by fortuitous circumstances unrelated to efforts of the company. However, in 1954 the Commission abandoned the original cost of reserves in favor of "fair yield value," thereby permitting the elements of real value, as indicated by proven reserves, to have an important influence in rate making.[63]

The Commission did not attempt to fix the rates charged by independent producers or gatherers.[64] In 1947, however, the Supreme Court ruled that *all* sales in interstate commerce were subject to federal regulation and that the exemption of production or gathering should be narrowly interpreted.[65] Immediately certain Congressmen from the Southwestern gas- and oil-producing states, prodded by gas and oil interests, launched a campaign to amend the Natural Gas Act to prohibit federal regulation of the price of natural gas before it entered the pipeline. In 1950, Congress passed a bill to exempt independent producers from Commission jurisdiction.[66] President Truman, however, vetoed the legislation.

The next year a case involving the Phillips Petroleum Company was before the Commission. The total sales by Phillips in 1950 were 500 billion cubic feet (8 per cent of total marketed production). Of this, 324 billion cubic feet was sold to interstate pipelines. Moreover, Phillips

[62] *In the Matter of Billings Gas Co.*, 2 F.P.C. 288 (1940).

[63] In a decision involving the Panhandle Eastern Pipeline Company. See *New York Times*, Apr. 16, 1954, p. 30.

[64] See, especially, *In the Matter of Columbian Fuel Corp.*, 2 F.P.C. 200 (1940).

[65] *Interstate Natural Gas Co. v. FPC*, 331 U.S. 682 (1947).

[66] In an endeavor to break the majority opposition of the Federal Power Commission to this legislation and deliver a personal rebuff to Leland Olds, chairman of the Commission, gas and oil interests joined forces with the proponents of the legislation in the Senate to defeat the confirmation of Olds, who had been reappointed for another term. For an excellent discussion of this action, see Joseph P. Harris, "The Senatorial Rejection of Leland Olds: A Case Study," 45 *American Political Science Review*, 674–692 (September, 1951).

owned approximately 4,380 miles of gas lines in five states. Yet the Commission refused to regulate the company's rates.[67] The case was appealed to the Supreme Court, which held that the Commission does have authority over the prices charged by an independent producer to interstate pipelines.[68]

Congressional efforts to reverse a Supreme Court interpretation of Commission jurisdiction in another area were more successful. The Natural Gas Act exempted the local distribution of natural gas from regulation by the Federal Power Commission. In 1950, the Supreme Court ruled that the sales of the East Ohio Gas Company were subject to Commission jurisdiction.[69] The East Ohio Gas Company owns and operates a natural-gas business wholly within Ohio and sells only to Ohio consumers. Most of the gas is transported into Ohio from other states through interstate pipelines owned by other companies. The Court held that the company was engaged in the transportation of interstate gas even though it sold the gas directly to consumers rather than for resale. In 1954, Congress passed a law exempting from Commission regulation interstate carriers engaged chiefly in local operations where they are subject to state regulation.[70]

Regulation of Utility Rates: Conclusions

The regulation of public-utility rates has now run the full course of domination by each of the three branches of government. The legislative phase was set in motion by *Munn v. Illinois*.[71] This phase ended when it became apparent that legislatures did not have the special competence to make fine economic adjustments to do justice to the customer, investor, and company. The phase of judicial supervision of rate fixing was ushered in by *Smyth v. Ames*.[72] However, implementation of the Court's decision in the Smyth case required expert, specialized bodies with jurisdiction to make continuous adjustments in light of changing economic conditions. So state, and eventually federal, regulatory commissions came into existence. Yet, for over forty-five years, these bodies functioned under the shadow of judicial supervision. The Supreme Court instructed the regulatory commissions how to handle such complex matters as fair

[67] *In the Matter of Phillips Petroleum Co.*, 90 P.U.R. (n.s.) 325 (1951). As a result of the Commission's past practice of regulating the prices of integrated companies but not of independent producers, many integrated companies have been divesting themselves of their producing and gathering holdings to escape regulation. By 1954, over 90 per cent of all natural-gas reserves were in the hands of independents.

[68] *Phillips Petroleum Co. v. State of Wisconsin*, 74 Sup. Ct. 794 (1954).

[69] *FPC v. East Ohio Gas Co.*, 338 U.S. 464 (1950).

[70] *New York Times*, Mar. 28, 1954, p. 72.

[71] 94 U.S. 113 (1877).

[72] 169 U.S. 466 (1898).

property valuation, reasonable rate of return, and reasonable operating expenses.

During this long period the overriding problem in rate regulation was the determination of fair value to satisfy the Smyth rule. Yet, as one author put it: "The whole doctrine of *Smyth v. Ames* rests upon a gigantic illusion. The fact which . . . the court has been vainly trying to find does not exist. "Fair value" must be shelved among the great juristic myths of history, with the Law of Nature and the Social Contract. As a practical concept, from which practical conclusions can be drawn, it is valueless." [73]

Many of the commissions used the original-cost formula—or a variation of it, the prudent-investment formula—for arriving at the rate base, but the Supreme Court often insisted that fair value meant only reproduction cost, in spite of the fact that original cost was also identified as a method in the Smyth case. The absurdity of this requirement was revealed when the Court said that reproduction cost "may be less than, equal to, or more than, present cost of plant plus depreciation plus necessary supplies and working capital." [74]

An era of administrative regulation was launched in 1944 when the Court handed down the decision in the Hope Natural Gas case.[75] The Court ruled that the commissions should be allowed to choose whatever property-valuation method they wanted. No single formula for measuring value is "right." Attention should be directed to "end results." A problem still remains of determining when an "end result" is fair and reasonable. The advantage of the Hope decision is that it realistically focuses attention on the most immediate and significant aspect of the whole valuation problem—the final determination. The standards for judgment may not be any more precise than the various methods for measuring fair value, but the discussion is shifted to real issues that can be clearly identified rather than being concerned with sometimes abstract questions of method.

Many of the state and federal commissions have long resisted the mandatory reproduction-cost rule. Hereafter, unless restricted by statutory or constitutional limitations, the commissions may determine their own formula for rate making, and its validity depends upon its effect "viewed in its entirety." Where state law requires it, of course, reproduction cost will continue to be used. But regulatory commissions in the remaining states may now base their rate orders on other evidence, which can be assembled and presented more quickly, at less cost, and which is generally

[73] G. C. Henderson, "Railway Valuation and the Courts," 33 *Harvard Law Review* 1051 (1920).

[74] *Denver Union Stock Yards Co. v. United States*, 304 U.S. 479 (1938).

[75] *FPC v. Hope Natural Gas Co.*, 320 U.S. 591 (1944).

deemed more satisfactory than evidence based on reproduction figures. Even though original-cost or prudent-investment methods may be subject to shortcomings from an economic point of view, they do have the administrative advantages of being convenient and workable and are being favored today. The economic drawbacks might be eliminated if commissions would keep in mind the fact that a fundamental purpose of regulation is to see that rate levels are kept high enough to maintain, under efficient management, the standards of service demanded by the public.

The results of public-utility rate regulation have been somewhat better than the results of regulating carrier rates, if the financial stability of the operating companies is used as the measure. Despite reduced earnings in the depression following 1929, the record of these companies, with the exception of street railways, has been remarkably good. Few of them have been forced into bankruptcy, and most have been able to pay interest on bonds and moderate to good dividends on stock.

Whether this test is a proper measure of successful regulation is another question. The indispensable nature of public-utility service, the fairly monopolistic position of the companies, and their high standard of business management have probably been the principal factors in this relatively successful record.

In dealing with regulation of rates, commissions are faced with many problems. Considering the character and diversity of tasks before them, they have been notoriously understaffed. As for the state commissions, W. E. Mosher found evidence that total appropriations were so low that not only could not enough staff members be hired, but also salaries high enough to attract highly qualified experts were not often paid.[76] Robert Cushman reported similarly on the federal commissions.[77] As a result, commissions frequently were reduced to awaiting protests of organized consumer groups and sitting as judges in deciding the disputes, instead of exercising a continuous supervision over rate and other matters. Since the Hope decision, which placed greater emphasis on commission supervision of rates, the regulatory bodies have attained a higher professional character and have been able to spend resources, once allocated to legal work, to the economic and business evaluation of the rate problem.

Selected References

Barnes, Irston R., *The Economics of Public Utility Regulation*, chaps. 9–17. New York: Appleton-Century-Crofts, Inc., 1942.

[76] "Defects of State Regulation of Public Utilities," 201 *Annals of the Academy of Political and Social Science* 105–110 (1939).

[77] *The Independent Regulatory Commissions* (New York: Oxford University Press, 1941), pp. 750–758.

Bauer, J., and Peter Costello, *Public Organization of Electric Power: Conditions, Policies, and Program.* New York: Harper & Brothers, 1949.

Bauer, John, and Nathaniel Gold, *Public Utility Valuation for Purpose of Rate Control.* New York: The Macmillan Company, 1934.

Bonbright, James C., "Contributions of the FPC to the Establishment of the Prudent Investment Doctrine of Rate Making," 14 *George Washington Law Review* 136 (December, 1945).

———, "Utility Rate Control Reconsidered in the Light of the Hope Natural Gas Case," 38 *Proceedings, American Economic Review* 465–482 (May, 1948).

———, *The Valuation of Property.* New York: McGraw-Hill Book Company, Inc., 1937.

Clemens, Eli Winston, *Economics and Public Utilities*, chaps. 6–16. New York: Appleton-Century-Crofts, Inc., 1950.

———, "Some Aspects of the Rate-of-return Problem," 30 *Land Economics* 32–43 (February, 1954).

Esser, Charles A., "State Laws in Relation to the Hope Natural Gas Decision," 34 *Public Utilities Fortnightly* 69–83 (July 20, 1944).

Smith, Nelson Lee, *The Fair Rate of Return in Public Utility Regulation.* Boston: Houghton Mifflin Company, 1932.

Troxel, Emery, *Economics of Public Utilities*, chaps. 10–19. New York: Rinehart & Company, Inc., 1947.

Welch, Francis X., "Impact of the Hope Natural Gas Decision on Commission Regulation," 33 *Public Utilities Fortnightly* 139–151 (Feb. 3, 1944).

12

REGULATION OF PUBLIC-UTILITY FINANCE AND COMBINATIONS

There are many aspects of regulation of public-utility accounting and financial practices that need be given little attention here. So far as operating companies, as distinguished from holding companies, are concerned, much of the discussion undertaken in connection with the control of transportation is applicable here. The reasons for government control and the problems encountered in regulation of security issuance are practically identical with those already discussed in connection with transport finance. Likewise, accounting control is similar to that imposed upon carriers by the Interstate Commerce Commission and the Civil Aeronautics Board. The regulation of railroad accounting undertaken by the federal government has clearly influenced the character of state accounting provisions in respect to public utilities.

In the field of combinations and financial transactions, the holding company has dominated the public-utility industry. Although non-holding-company aspects may be found, the major portion of regulation of combinations and financial transactions is closely related to that of the holding company. Because of this prevailing influence, and the far-flung nature of holding-company transactions, one finds the field of finance regulation occupied by both state and federal governments.

Accounting and Reports

Accounting regulation and the requirement of periodic reports provide the means, but not the purposes, of effective control of public utilities. If the purposes are to ascertain reasonable rates, approve security issues, prevent falsification or distortion of financial records, or limit combinations to those in the public interest, the regulatory commission must have accurate, systematic, and uniform information about operating expenses and capital expenditures.

SCOPE OF CONTROL

Most state commissions have statutory authority to prescribe uniform accounting. All commissions having power to regulate rates of electric and gas utilities, a total of forty, have the power. Of the forty, all but four have adopted or permit the use of classifications prepared by the National Association of Railroad and Utilities Commissioners or the Federal Power Commission for electric utilities; for gas utilities, all but nine have done so.[1]

All communication common-carrier companies operating in interstate or foreign commerce are subject to rather complete regulation of accounts and reports by the Federal Communications Commission. Prescription of the forms of these accounts is provided for in the Communications Act of 1934, and adequate legal grounds for policing the accounts are included. These provisions are similar to the corresponding requirements of the Interstate Commerce Act and the better state public-utility laws.

Hydroelectric licensees are required to adhere to the system of accounts prescribed by the Federal Power Commission, to allow government inspection of accounts, and to make such reports as the Commission demands. The Federal Power Act also gives the Commission strict control over the accounts and reports of those interstate electric utilities subject to its jurisdiction. It has the authority to prescribe accounting forms and regulations necessary or appropriate to the administration of the law. Preservation of certain memoranda and filing of reports are required. The Commission is given access at all times to the books of companies for purposes of inspection or examination. Even books of persons controlling one of these public utilities may be inspected by the Commission in so far as they relate to transactions with a public utility under its jurisdiction.

The Federal Power Commission has also prescribed a uniform system of accounts for natural-gas companies under its jurisdiction. This system follows the pattern adopted for electric-utility companies and provides, among other things, for a detailed restatement of accounts in terms of original cost.

LEGAL ASPECTS OF ACCOUNTING CONTROL

The power to require uniform accounting has been adequately upheld by the courts.[2] They have shown a tendency to defer to commission discretion in this field probably more than in any other. So long as the classifications and instructions are not so at odds with accepted business and accounting principles "as to be the expression of a whim rather than an exercise of judgment," [3] the courts have upheld commissions.

[1] FPC, *State Commission Jurisdiction and Regulation of Electric and Gas Utilities* (1948), pp. 4–5.

[2] *ICC v. Goodrich Transit Co.*, 224 U.S. 194 (1912); *Kansas City Southern Rwy. Co. v. United States*, 231 U.S. 423 (1913); *American Tel. and Tel. Co. v. United States*, 299 U.S. 232 (1936).

[3] *American Tel. and Tel. Co. v. United States*, 299 U.S. 237.

SOME PROBLEMS OF ACCOUNTING CONTROL

The most difficult aspect of accounting control arises from the need for proper policing and interpretation of classifications. Transactions are so diverse and entries so subject to varied interpretation, even by qualified accountants, that accurate and comparable accounts do not automatically result from prescribing classifications. Then, too, to prescribe classifications does not mean that the amounts charged to certain accounts will be reasonable. Furthermore, effective accounting regulation would necessitate periodic audits, and most commissions do not have the staff to make such inspections often and thoroughly enough, if at all.

Perhaps the major portion of policing work is done in rate cases. Where a commission inquires into the reasonableness of data presented in support of such a case, it is given an opportunity to pass upon accounting practices of the utility in question. The sporadic character of this control, even if it should influence a company to change its book entries, is not adequate for effective regulation.

One of the principal abuses of accounting, which has caused much difficulty in rate cases, is the practice of writing up asset accounts above fair and reasonable costs. Since original cost, as shown by books, is one of the measures used in arriving at a rate base, there is clearly a strong motive to make it as high as possible. Write-ups may result in several ways. Construction work may be undertaken by a company affiliated in a holding-company system with an operating company, and excessive costs may be charged. In transferring property from one company to another, especially during consolidation, the assets may be written up in value. Properties have been reappraised and book values written up. Intangible values have been written into books at high figures. Results similar to write-ups occur, too, when a public utility does not retire worn-out or obsolete equipment from its books.

These write-ups have occurred over the entire public-utility field in varying degrees, but apparently most of them have been made in companies controlled by public-utility holding companies. The amounts concerned have been considerable, as is evident from an investigation of the Federal Trade Commission completed in 1935. In ninety-one operating companies in sixteen holding-company systems, it found write-ups amounting to $3,300 million.[4] Granting that the figures of the Commission may not be entirely free from criticism as to their accuracy, these write-ups are important evidence of the shortcomings of accounting control. They show how it is possible for *amounts* charged to accounts to be inaccurate, even though the *forms* of accounts are prescribed, especially if accounts are not policed.

[4] FTC, *Utility Corporations,* S. Doc. 92, part 72A (1935), p. 298.

Regulation of Financing

The same motives which led to control of railroad finance and securities can account for the regulation of public-utility financing. The objectives are prevention of overcapitalization and maintenance of a proper balance in capital structures between debt and equity. Utility financing is so intimately related to the level of rates, the quality of service, and the interests of the investor that regulation of utility financing is an important adjunct to effective utility regulation.

SCOPE OF STATE CONTROL

State regulation of utility financing dates from the early laws of Massachusetts, enacted during the 1850s, by which railroad and other corporations were not allowed to issue stock for less than par value. Other laws were passed within the next few decades, and in 1894 Massachusetts enacted a fairly comprehensive plan of regulation. Until 1910 most laws passed by other states were rather pioneering in nature, and effective state control dated after that time. Even many of these laws were ineffective until the depression of 1929 to 1933 revealed weaknesses in the financial structure of many utilities, after which more states gave commissions fairly complete authority over financial transactions. By 1948, the public-utility commissions in thirty-three states had power over security issuance of gas and electric companies. The amount of security regulation over other utilities varies greatly.[5]

State laws vary from the mere requirement of publicity for new issue to detailed supervision, including power to approve the nature of securities, use of proceeds, and terms of sale. Where strict security regulation is provided for, approval before issue is normally required, except for a limited amount of short-term notes. The company must show that the proceeds are necessary and appropriate in the public interest, that the method of raising the funds is consistent with sound finance, and that the terms of sale are fair and reasonable. Where securities are issued for considerations other than cash, the commission is generally empowered to inquire into the reasonableness of the amount paid for such acquisitions. Other regulations require competitive bidding among investment bankers, attempt to restrict the issuance of more debt securities, give careful attention to corporate reorganizations, limit the payments of common-stock dividends, and oversee financial relations with affiliates.

SCOPE OF FEDERAL CONTROL

In common with business generally, limited control over the issuance of public-utility securities is exercised by the Securities and Exchange Com-

[5] FPC, *op. cit.*, p. 6.

mission under the Securities Act of 1933. The purpose of this law is to protect investors by requiring full and accurate disclosure of information regarding the sale of a proposed issue.[6] In contrast to state public-utility laws, the object is to see that the investor is well informed as to the nature of an issue and not to ensure that the issue will safeguard rates and service.

The Public Utility Holding Company Act, which will be discussed below, gave the Securities and Exchange Commission extensive control over the securities and finances of holding companies. Through regulation of holding companies, the control of the federal government is being extended to local operating-company finances in cases in which these companies are in a holding-company system. Since so many companies are a part of some interstate holding-company system, the authority of the Securities and Exchange Commission in financial matters tends to overshadow that of the Federal Power Commission.

Electric companies subject to the Federal Power Commission's jurisdiction may not issue any security, or assume any obligation or liability with respect to any security, unless authorized by the Commission. In granting this permission, the Commission is instructed, as are most state commissions, to find the issue or assumption of obligation to be (1) for a "lawful object" compatible with the public interest and necessary and appropriate for or consistent with the proper performance of the applicant as a public utility, and (2) "reasonably necessary" and appropriate for such purposes.

The Federal Power Commission's authority over the financing of natural-gas firms operating in interstate commerce is less complete than its power over electric companies. The Commission is not authorized to regulate the issuance of securities, purchases of property, payment of dividends, and other financial matters. The financial transactions of natural-gas companies that are subject to federal control, those arising when a company is a subsidiary falling under the Holding Company Act of 1935, fall under the jurisdiction of the Securities and Exchange Commission.

The jurisdiction of the Federal Communications Commission over communication common-carrier companies operating in interstate and foreign commerce extends to rates, service, accounts, and reports. But the Commission has no power to regulate the terms of transactions between operating companies and affiliated companies with respect to service, purchase, financing, or construction contracts. The Commission can only investigate these matters with a view to recommending legislation. Furthermore, the Federal Communications Commission has no jurisdiction over issuance of securities.

[6] See Chapter 18.

Corporate Integration

Unification of operating companies has been an inevitable development in the growth of the utility businesses because of the economies often present in large-scale production. Consolidation was initially accomplished through merger or through lease or stock control by operating public utilities. Combinations effected through holding companies constitute a more recent development and will receive separate treatment below.

ECONOMICS OF COMBINATION

Consolidation and combination in the public-utility industries have many economic advantages, especially where physical integration of properties is effected. The advantages are not so great if the combination is one of unified management of scattered operating properties. But where operations can be merged or coordinated, it is possible not only to reduce costs but to improve service. Large production and distribution plants can be operated more efficiently than small ones, and the larger companies, through a diversity of customer demand, have a better opportunity fully to utilize them. Other economies come from the ability to hire superior management, to float securities on more favorable terms, and to purchase supplies and equipment at lower prices. Finally, as has already been pointed out in Chapter 10, there are certain advantages of monopoly in the public-utility field, such as the elimination of duplicating systems, ruinous competition, and so forth.

It should not be inferred that there are no limits to the economic growth of public utilities. A company may become so large that it cannot be operated effectively and efficiently as a unit. The diseconomies of large-scale enterprise are well known. As the size of a business increases, management becomes more difficult and expensive, the organization becomes less flexible, and less enterprise may be shown in adopting new techniques of production and distribution. A business may also become so large that the needed regulation becomes difficult, if not ineffective. The tendency also for competition in purchasing new companies may mean that the company desiring control is forced to pay so much that overcapitalization results. Except possibly for telephone companies, there are limits, too, beyond which improvement of service is negligible.

SCOPE OF STATE CONTROL

State commissions did not carefully regulate the integration of operating companies before 1930. Because unifications of operating utilities require the issuance of new securities, commission control of corporate integration has been practically identical with that of security issuance. In addition, the more progressive states, like Illinois and New York, have special laws placing all kinds of consolidations, leases, acquisitions of control, and operating contracts under definite control of utility commissions. The commissions are directed to make a finding as to whether the proposed combination is in the public interest; if it is, they may grant approval. In certain cases they may impose conditions with which the company must comply before the combination is consummated. The laws usually provide that consolidation may not increase the capitalization of a new company beyond the total value of bonds and stocks in the combining companies. Where a purchase price is involved, some statutes require that the value of assumed obligations, or new stocks and bonds, must not exceed the reasonable cost of the facilities to be purchased. By 1948, thirty-five state commissions had the authority to regulate mergers and consolidations of gas and electric companies.[7]

On the whole, commission regulation has not stood in the way of economic development of combination. If anything, commissions have permitted combinations which have had little economic justification. Some commissions have probably conceived their function to be the supervision of terms and procedures of combination rather than approval of the economic wisdom of the move. In a number of cases, however, commissions have required that the combination have real economic advantages in the public interest.

SCOPE OF FEDERAL CONTROL

A rather weak control over telephone consolidations and combinations has been vested in the Federal Communications Commission. If, after hearing, the Commission holds a combination to be in the public interest, laws of the federal government against combinations in restraint of trade will not apply. However, nothing limits the power of the states in this regard. Thus, a company could consolidate, if a state authority approved, in the face of a refusal by the Federal Communications Commission. The only restraint apparently is possible prosecution under the federal antitrust laws. Somewhat stronger is the provision which prohibits any person from holding the position of officer or director in more than one communication company subject to the Commission, unless authorized by the Commission upon a showing that neither public nor private interests will be adversely affected thereby. Thus, except for the limitation on interlocking directorates, the law as it now stands is little more than a restatement of federal acts making unreasonable restraint of trade unlawful for any business.

[7] FPC, *op. cit.*, p. 6.

Companies engaged in radio broadcasting are forbidden to acquire, own, or control any wire-communication company (telephone, cable, or telegraph) where the result is substantially to lessen competition, to restrain commerce, or to tend to create a monopoly in any line of commerce. The penalty for disobedience is revocation of, or refusal to reissue, a license for operation. But before the Commission may take this action, the restraint of trade must be proved in a federal court.

Public utilities subject to the Federal Power Act may not sell, lease, or otherwise dispose of facilities without approval of the Federal Power Commission; nor can they purchase or acquire the securities of any other public utility without its permission. The Commission is empowered to allow such transactions upon such terms and conditions as it finds necessary or appropriate to secure the maintenance of adequate service and the coordination of facilities under its control.

Combination activities effected through interlocking officers or directors are also closely regulated. The law forbids any person to hold the position of officer or director in more than one public utility subject to the Commission; or to hold such position and the position of officer or director of any bank, trust company, or firm authorized by law to underwrite or market public-utility securities; or to hold such position and the position of officer or director of any company supplying electrical equipment to the public utility in question. But such interlocking holding of positions may be authorized by the Commission upon a showing that neither public nor private interests will be adversely affected thereby.

The Federal Power Commission is not authorized to regulate mergers and consolidations of natural-gas companies that are otherwise subject to its jurisdiction. If the gas companies are part of a holding-company system, however, such combinations fall under the Securities and Exchange Commission's jurisdiction.

The Public-utility Holding Company

An important development in the public-utility field has been the emergence of the public-utility holding company. Through this device, numerous scattered operating utilities have been brought under the control of a relatively small number of holding-company systems. By 1932, the 3 largest holding companies controlled nearly half the electricity sales; and the 15 largest systems controlled about 80 per cent of the total sales.[8] Virtually all the telephone utilities have been in one holding-company system for some years, with the American Telephone and Telegraph Company controlling 83 per cent of the telephone stations in service in

[8] FTC, *op. cit.*, p. 38.

the United States by 1935.[9] By 1934, 54 holding companies controlled production of 31 per cent of natural gas and 56 per cent of artificial gas in the United States.[10]

THE NATURE OF THE PUBLIC-UTILITY HOLDING COMPANY

The holding company, as a form of organization, is found in all fields of business enterprise. It is a corporation empowered by charter to hold, as assets, stocks of other corporations. As distinguished from a pure investment company, the holding company owns the stocks for the purpose of controlling other companies.

The holding company is possible by virtue of the arrangement in any business organization, and particularly in the corporation, that permits a majority of the investors to control the capital lent by the minority. If the stockholders are widely scattered and unorganized, a few individuals might well gain working control even if they hold much less than a majority of the stock. This control is made even easier by the tendency of small stockholders to assign their voting power, if they use it at all, to others, usually the inside management. In enterprises issuing securities, this control is further extended by selling ownership interests in which there is little or no right to control. An example is the nonvoting preferred stock. These features of business enterprise make it possible for certain individuals to control far more than the capital they invest.

The holding-company device is merely a means for magnifying the concentration of control already inherent in large business corporations. Suppose that company A is a holding company that has as its base four operating companies (B, C, D, and E) engaged, say, in the business of generating and selling electricity. Assume, also, that these four companies were financed in each case with $4 million in 4 per cent mortgage bonds, $2 million in 5 per cent nonvoting preferred stock, and $2 of common stock. Hence, each of the four operating companies might have $8 million in generating and distributing assets.

If company A owns one-half of the common stock in companies B, C, D, and E, its control of these operating companies would be easily assured; as a matter of fact, much less than a majority ownership in each might do so. But if the total capital of company A is $4 million, this might be raised by the issuance of $2 million in 5 per cent collateral trust bonds, $1 million in 6 per cent preferred stock, and $1 million of common stock. Since company A can be controlled by one-half (or perhaps much less) of its common stock, an investment of $500,000 in its stock would ensure control. Thus company A could control companies B, C, D, and E, with assets

[9] FCC, *Investigation of the Telephone Industry in the U.S.*, H. Doc. 340, 76th Cong., 1st Sess. (1939), p. xxiii.

[10] FTC, *op. cit.*, pp. 29–33.

aggregating $32 million, by means of an equity investment of $500,000. On top of A might be pyramided a second-degree holding company in which an investment of much less than $500,000 would be sufficient for control; and so on to third-, fourth-, and fifth-degree holding companies.

There have been instances where a few individuals controlled operating assets thousands of times greater than their small investment. The Federal Trade Commission noted that the equity of owners in the top of one very large holding company amounted to from 0.02 to 0.05 per cent of the book value of the securities in controlled operating companies.[11] Through a network of holding companies organized under the Associated Gas and Electric System as it existed in 1929, about 200 operating companies of various sorts were brought under the control of two men. With an exceedingly small personal investment, these individuals gained control of a system with nearly a billion-dollar capitalization.

STATE CONTROL OF HOLDING COMPANIES

Although a few states had laws which dealt with holding-company activities in the public-utility field before 1930, most state legislation followed this date. More than half the states now have some kind of legislation for regulating holding companies. However, most holding-company transactions are in interstate commerce, and state jurisdiction cannot generally be extended over them. Regulations designed to keep foreign (out-of-state) corporations from doing a public-utility business or from owning securities in local public utilities seem to be within the power of a state; and power to investigate holders of a substantial interest in operating companies has not been seriously contested. Yet these regulations have been easily circumvented.

Even if it had authority to do so, a single state can hardly be expected to deal efficiently with the broad character of holding-company operations. Limitations in staff and appropriations for regulation make efficient regulation almost impossible. Also, states differ too much in scope and character of regulations affecting utility holding companies to make the regulation effective.

FEDERAL CONTROL: THE PUBLIC UTILITY HOLDING COMPANY ACT

Not until the federal government entered the field by enacting the Public Utility Holding Company Act (Title I of the Public Utility Act) was holding-company regulation effective. After a vigorous fight in Congress, and with a bare majority of one in the Senate, the Act was passed in 1935. The Securities and Exchange Commission was vested with its administration. This law is one of the most aggressive regulatory statutes found in the entire field of government control of the economy. It is also

[11] *Ibid.*, p. 161.

one of the most complex and thoroughgoing pieces of financial legislation ever enacted.

Coverage. The Act applies to all gas and electric holding companies, their subsidiaries, affiliates, and mutual-service companies. A holding company is defined as any company owning, holding, or controlling 10 per cent or more of the voting stock of a public-utility operating company or of any holding company doing so. In addition, other companies not having this percentage of control may be declared by the Securities and Exchange Commission to be within the purview of the law, if they exercise such control over management as to make their regulation in the public interest. The Commission is empowered to exempt certain holding companies from the provisions of the Act, if it is the public interest to do so.[12]

Registration. As a first step in regulation, the holding companies subject to the Act are required to register with the Securities and Exchange Commission. A holding company that does not register is forbidden to engage in any business in interstate commerce or to use the mails to conduct any business. In registering, holding companies are required to file information concerning all corporate and other contracts, corporate organization, financial data, information as to control and persons controlling, and other similar data.

The "death sentence." The core of the Act, and the primary concern of the Commission since its enactment, is the section that requires the physical integration [section 11b(1)] and financial simplification [section 11b(2)] of holding-company systems. Each system subject to the law is directed to limit its operations to a single integrated operating system—one whose operating assets are capable of being physically interconnected and economically run as a single coordinated system in a single area, but which would not be so large as to impair the advantages of localized management, efficient operation, and effectiveness of regulation.

To accomplish simplification of intercorporate relationships and the financial structures of holding-company systems, reorganizations can be ordered by the Commission. The purpose of reorganization is to ensure that the corporate structure or continued existence of a holding company does not unnecessarily complicate the structure or inequitably distribute

[12] Criteria for granting exemptions are: (1) the company is predominantly intrastate in character and carries on its business substantially within a single state; (2) the company is predominantly an operating company carrying on business in the state of organization and in states contiguous thereto; (3) the company is only incidentally a public-utility holding company, deriving a material part of its revenue outside the public-utility field; (4) the company is temporarily a holding company because of acquisition of securities in liquidation of debt previously contracted or in connection with distribution of securities; (5) the company derives the material part of its income outside of the United States.

voting power among security holders. To eliminate complications, the Commission is empowered to prohibit a holding company from operating through more than two tiers. In other words, a holding company may have no more than one holding company between it and the operating utility company. Once a company has met these requirements, it is released from the jurisdiction of this section.

Financial operations. Several sections authorize the Securities and Exchange Commission to govern the financial operations of holding companies and their subsidiaries. The issuance of securities, the acquisition and disposition of interests and securities by such companies, their accounting practices, intrasystem servicing arrangements, and other intercompany transactions in holding companies are subject to Commission scrutiny and control.

Political activities. Financial contributions for political purposes are prohibited. The law provides regulation by the Commission of activities which "present, advocate, or oppose any matter affecting" registered holding companies or their subsidiaries before Congress or its members, the Securities and Exchange Commission, the Federal Power Commission and their staffs. Persons employed or retained by a holding company or subsidiary for these purposes must register with the Commission and submit to its rules and regulations in respect to the subject matter of their employment, its nature and character, and the amount of compensation received.

Enforcement. Finally, there are a number of sections designed to accomplish the above provisions and to ensure that the newly created holding companies or affiliated relationships that result from the enforcement of the "death sentence" clause shall meet certain standards prescribed by the act. Other provisions require a limited degree of surveillance over exempt systems. The Commission may make studies and investigations, call witnesses, hold hearings, and prosecute offenders in court. An order of the Commission is enforceable only by application to the federal courts. But the role of the courts, the procedure to be used, and punishments for nonconformance to be meted out are provided for in detail by the law.

CONSTITUTIONALITY OF THE ACT

In passing the Holding Company Act, Congress relied on its interstate commerce and postal powers. The first test of the constitutionality of the act involved the registration requirement. In the Electric Bond and Share Company case, decided in 1938, the Supreme Court held that the registration requirements of the act were within the constitutional powers of Congress.[13]

The validity of section 11b(1) under which the Securities and Exchange Commission can order a holding company to conduct its opera-

[13] *Electric Bond and Share Co. v. SEC*, 303 U.S. 419.

tions in a single integrated public-utility system was questioned by the North American Company a few years later. The Supreme Court responded that the section was a legitimate exercise of Congressional authority and that, although its enforcement did result in a destruction of property values, Congress had weighed the actual and potential damage to the public and found that it outweighed the economic advantages of a scattered holding company.[14]

Section 11b(2), which requires the dissolution of holding companies which unduly complicate the holding-company system, was upheld in the American Power and Light Company case.[15] The Court found that the carrying out of the "death sentence" was a valid exercise of the commerce power and did not constitute a deprivation of property without due process of law.

FEDERAL CONTROL: CORPORATE SIMPLIFICATION

The Securities and Exchange Commission has always regarded the enforcement of the "death sentence" provision as the most important segment of its responsibilities under the Holding Company Act.[16] There are a great number of ways that financial reorganization has been accomplished to achieve simplification of intercorporate relationships and the financial structure of holding companies.

Some holding companies have been dissolved by action of the Commission under Section 11b(2). If a system did not voluntarily undertake simplification of its corporate structure, the Commission has ordered dissolution of extra holding companies. These powers have been upheld by the courts.[17] In addition, the Commission has liquidated companies because of unsound financial practices, such as overcapitalization, pyramiding, or write-ups of asset values. Holding companies that did not provide necessary and economical managerial services for their subsidiaries were subject to liquidation, as were companies with excessive debt securities and large amounts of preferred stocks.

As a matter of policy, however, the Securities and Exchange Commission has encouraged holding companies to exercise their own initiative in formulating, developing, and presenting their proposals to achieve compliance with the standards of the act.[18] Some companies have been voluntarily liquidated by the sale of plants and securities in the open market or to other companies. The proceeds have been used to pay off stockholders and retire any debt.

[14] *North American Co. v. SEC*, 327 U.S. 686 (1946).

[15] *American Power and Light Co. v. SEC*, 329 U.S. 90 (1946).

[16] SEC, *18th Annual Report, 1952* (1953), p. 82.

[17] See *American Power & Light Co. v. SEC* (U.S. Dist. Ct. of Appeals), 53 P.U.R. (n.s.) 16 (1944).

[18] SEC, *op. cit.*, p. 86.

A simple method of company dissolution has been to distribute the securities of operating companies to the stockholders of the holding company. In some cases the holding company has been turned into an operating company and merged with the subsidiaries. On occasions holding companies have been turned into investment companies. Such a procedure must stay within the requirements that ownership by the investment company must be of less than 10 per cent of the voting securities issued by any operating company or holding company and that it cannot exercise controlling influence over the subsidiaries.

FEDERAL CONTROL: PHYSICAL INTEGRATION

The companion to the requirement of corporate simplification is the requirement of physical integration of holding-company operations. Section 11b(1) authorizes the Commission to assure that each holding company limits its operations to a single integrated public-utility system and to such other businesses as are reasonably incidental, or economically necessary to the operations of such integrated system.

Under certain conditions, the Commission might permit a registered holding company to control additional integrated systems. These conditions, as determined by the Commission, are as follows: (A) each additional system cannot be operated as an independent system without loss of substantial economies which could be obtained by retention of control; (B) all additional systems are located in one state or in adjoining states, or in a contiguous foreign country; and (C) the combination of systems is not so large as to impair the advantages of localized management, efficient operation, or the effectiveness of regulation.

These provisions of section 11—known as the "ABC clauses"—could obviously be subject to a wide range of interpretations. The holding companies, naturally, supported the interpretations that would be the least damaging to their established structures. In a number of cases the Commission, with Court support, ruled differently.

The single-utility rule. To the utility companies, a single integrated system could include both gas and electric properties. The Securities and Exchange Commission established the rule that gas and electric interests could not be integrated in the same system, unless substantial economies were assured from such combined operation.[19] Only the American Water Works Company was allowed to retain both its gas and electric businesses, because the gas business was such a small part of the total operation.[20]

The one-area rule. The utility companies maintained that section 11

[19] *Columbia Gas & Elec. Corp., United Gas Improvement Co.*, Releases Nos. 2477 and 2692.

[20] *Re American Waterworks & Elec. Co.*, 2 S.E.C. 972 (1937).

allowed a two-area organization; i.e., a principal integrated system and at least one additional integrated system, even though they were in widely separated parts of the country. The Commission has insisted on a one-area location of the principal system and, if permitted, the additional system. At issue in this dispute are "ABC clauses" set down to guide the Commission in permitting registered holding companies to control additional systems. The companies recognized that clause B might prohibit two-area organization. But they argued that if the standards of either clause A or C were satisfied, two-area organization should be allowed. The Commission ruled that not just one standard, but all three, must be met if an integrated system is to be permitted to control an additional system.[21] Moreover, the Commission has given clause B, which requires all additional systems to be located in one state or in adjoining states, a very narrow interpretation. For example, the North American Company was prohibited from retaining interests in Michigan and Illinois because the states are separated by Lake Michigan.[22]

In one case the Commission prohibited the Lone Star Gas Corporation from controlling another system, even though both principal and additional systems were located in the state of Texas.[23] The Commission was here being guided by more than the one-area rule. An integrated system must also have an economic and technical relationship between the principal and additional system.

Size. In addition, size may be considered. On the grounds that a proposed integrated system, extending from Wyoming to New Mexico and Arizona, did not meet the standard of localized management, the Commission turned down a plan of the Cities Service Power and Light Company.[24] On the other hand, the American Gas and Electric Company was allowed to control interconnected properties that were scattered over seven states—Michigan, Indiana, Ohio, Tennessee, Kentucky, Virginia, and West Virginia. Although this system approached maximum size, it was not inconsistent with efficient operation and localized management.[25]

"Other businesses." Section 11b(1) also included the provision that "other businesses" could be retained by a holding-company system if the Commission found them ". . . appropriate in the public interest or for the protection of investors or consumers and not detrimental to the proper functioning . . ." of integrated systems. It had been common practice for a public-utility holding company to include within its system interests in

[21] *Re Engineers Public Service Co.*, 9 S.E.C. 768 (1941); see also *Engineers P.S. Co. v. SEC*, 51 P.U.R. (n.s.) 65 (1943). *Re Standard Power & Light Corp.*, 9 S.E.C. 774–883 (1941).

[22] *Re North American Co.*, 43 P.U.R. (n.s.) 257 (1942).

[23] *Re Lone Star Gas Corp.*, 12 S.E.C. 292–296 (1942).

[24] *Re Cities Service Power & Light Co.*, Holding Co. Act Release No. 4489.

[25] *Re American Gas & Electric Co.*, Holding Co. Act Release No. 6333.

steam and street railways, busses, oil, coal, ice, real-estate, and nonutility businesses. In general, the Commission has interpreted this provision very narrowly and strictly. Only rarely has it permitted a holding company to retain other businesses, and then only because they were small relative to the principal business or directly and functionally related to the principal business. On occasions, railroads, steam-heating, and oil-production properties have been permissible "other businesses," but street railway and bus systems, real-estate businesses, bridge companies, water and irrigation, and ice and rice-farming properties had to be eliminated from the system.[26]

Divestments. In bringing about the physical integration required by the Holding Company Act, holding companies were faced with problems similar to those in dissolution actions. The interests and securities of holding companies had to be sold, exchanged, or distributed to accomplish integration. Similarly, divestment could be ordered by the Commission or the holding companies could voluntarily submit physical-integration plans. Initially, there was considerable unwillingness on the part of holding companies to prepare plans voluntarily. By 1940, only a few systems submitted plans. Therefore, the Commission took the initiative and indicated to the major systems the changes that would be necessary to fulfill the requirements of the law.

The Commission did not indicate the specific divestment methods to be followed, but it did regulate the divestments that were undertaken. Security allocations, selling prices and selling costs, fees, and expenses of divestment plans were all subject to Commission investigation.

FEDERAL REGULATION OF HOLDING COMPANIES: CONCLUSIONS

There were valid economic reasons for resort to the holding-company mechanism. But with its growth came abuses that cried for correction. On the basis of its commerce and postal powers Congress enacted one of the most stringent and far-reaching pieces of economic regulation in the history of this country. The keystone of the Holding Company Act is section 11—the "death sentence" to holding companies.

Vigorous administration has resulted in the liquidation of a large number of unnecessary holding companies, with the return of their subsidiaries to individual ownership, and the streamlining of a number of others into compact regional systems. By such actions consumers and investors have been afforded the benefits of large-scale centralized generation and transmission of electric power and of integrated long-distance transmission and distribution facilities for natural gas. The task of bringing about compliance with section 11 did not begin until 1940 and is now, in

[26] See E. W. Clemens, *Economics and Public Utilities* (New York: Appleton-Century-Crofts, Inc., 1950), p. 518.

the words of the Commission, "nearing completion." [27] An entire industry which represents an investment of billions of dollars and which serves millions of people has been completely reorganized in a space of twelve years. This herculean labor was accomplished with a staff that has been steadily declining from 175 in 1940 to 35 in 1952.[28] When this work is finally completed no further expense will be imposed on the taxpayer to administer this portion of the Act. The objective of the law will have been accomplished.

This record of accomplishment can be briefly reviewed by reference to a few statistics. In the early 1930s, 15 holding companies controlled 80 per cent of all electric-energy generation in the United States; 20 systems controlled 98.5 per cent of all transmission of electric energy in interstate commerce; and 11 holding companies controlled 80 per cent of all natural-gas pipeline mileage. By June 30, 1952, the electric utility plant owned by holding-company systems registered under the Act was 30 per cent of the aggregate dollar amount of plant owned by all private utility companies. The manufactured- and natural-gas plant (including transmission properties) owned by registered systems was 28 per cent of the total. When reorganization under section 11 is completed, these figures will be 23 per cent and 18 per cent respectively. At one time, 2,197 companies were subject to the Holding Company Act (214 holding companies, 929 electric or gas utilities, and 1,054 nonutility companies or utilities other than gas and electric). By June 30, 1954, that total stood at 324 (35 holding companies, 133 gas and electric utilities, and 156 other companies).[29] Table 12–1 shows how this reorganization was accomplished.

As activity under section 11 nears completion, attention of the Securities and Exchange Commission is shifting to the implementation of another portion of the law—section 30, which has lain dormant until recently. This section authorizes the Commission to make investigations of public-utility companies to determine the size, types, and locations of companies which do or can operate most economically and efficiently in the public interest. On the basis of these studies the Commission is instructed to recommend the size and type of geographically and economically integrated public-utility systems which can best promote and harmonize the interests of the public, the investor, and the consumer. In a sense, this section is the obverse of section 11. Section 11 directs the Commission to reduce uneconomical holding companies to an integrated system; section 30 directs the Commission to report on how utility facilities may be more economically combined. Hence, the Commission

[27] SEC, *op. cit.*, p. 82.
[28] *Ibid.*
[29] SEC, *20th Annual Report, 1954* (1955), p. 50.

Table 12–1. *Companies Released from Active Regulatory Jurisdiction of the Securities and Exchange Commission. Period from June 15, 1938 to June 30, 1952*

Type of company	*Total companies subject to Act during this period*	*Divestments of nonretainable companies*	*Dissolution not part of divestment transactions*	*Absorbed by merger or consolidation*	*Miscellaneous disposals*	*Exempt by rule or order*	*Total released from jurisdiction*	*Companies subject to Act as of June 30, 1952*
Holding	214	15	67	25	9	41	157	57
Electric and/or gas	929	381	70	172	48	66	737	192
Nonutility, plus utility other than electric and/or gas	1,054	365	183	150	103	65	866	188
Total	2,197	761	320	347	160	172	1,760	437

SOURCE: SEC, *18th Annual Report, 1952,* p. 84.

has the power not only to destroy uneconomical systems but also to construct more economical ones.

Section 30 has broader investigatory powers than those under section 11. In many respects, it is the most penetrating intrusion of government into business. Not only is a business regulated, but its economic planning tends to become the function of government.

During 1952 the Commission initiated the first study under section 30. The investigation is a pilot model of a limited size which is being used to determine the scope of future examinations, the source of data, analytical procedures, and other aspects. This function will also be partially self-liquidating over a period of years.[30]

Selected References

Accounting and Reports

Barnes, Irston, *The Economics of Public Utility Regulation,* chap. 8. New York: Appleton-Century-Crofts, Inc., 1942.

Clemens, E. W., *Economics and Public Utilities,* chap. 19. New York: Appleton-Century-Crofts, Inc., 1950.

[30] SEC, *18th Annual Report, 1952,* p. 110.

Kohler, E. L., "The Development of Accounting for Regulatory Purposes by the Federal Power Commission," 21 *Accounting Review* 19 (January, 1946).

——, "Development of Accounting for Regulatory Purposes by the FPC," 14 *George Washington Law Review* 152 (December, 1945).

Morehouse, E. W., "Innovations in Public Utility Accounting Regulation," 46 *Yale Law Journal* 955 (April, 1937).

Paton, W. A., "Accounting Policies of the Federal Power Commission—A Critique," 77 *Journal of Accountancy* 432 (June, 1944).

Sanders, T. H., "Government by 'Accounting Principles,'" 22 *Harvard Business Review* 270 (Spring, 1944).

Troxel, Emery, *Economics of Public Utilities*, chap. 6. New York: Rinehart & Company, Inc., 1947.

Regulation of Financing

Barnes, Irston, *The Economics of Public Utility Regulation*, chap. 20. New York: Appleton-Century-Crofts, Inc., 1942.

Clemens, E. W., *Economics of Public Utilities*, chap. 20. New York: Appleton-Century-Crofts, Inc., 1950.

Pegrum, D. F., *The Regulation of Public Utility Security Issues in California*. Berkeley, Calif.: University of California Press, 1936.

Taylor, W. H., "Regulation of the Issue Price of Public Utility Securities," 8 *Journal of Land and Public Utility Economics*, 418 (1932).

Troxel, Emery, *Economics of Public Utilities*, chap. 7. New York: Rinehart & Company, Inc., 1947.

Regulation of Corporate Integration and the Holding Company

Anderson, W. H., "Public Utility Holding Companies: The Death Sentence and the Future," 23 *Journal of Land and Public Utility Economics* 244–254 (August, 1947).

Barnes, Irston, *The Economics of Public Utility Regulation*, chap. 19. New York: Appleton-Century-Crofts, Inc., 1942.

Blum, Robert, "SEC Integration of Holding Company Systems," 17 *Journal of Land and Public Utility Economics* 423–439 (November, 1941).

Clemens, E. W., *Economics and Public Utilities*, chap. 19. New York: Appleton-Century-Crofts, Inc., 1950.

Cook, Donald C., "SEC Plans under Section 30 of the Holding Company Act," 50 *Public Utilities Fortnightly* 333–395 (Sept. 11, 1952).

Fournier, L. T., "Simplification of Holding Companies under the Public Utility Act of 1935," 13 *Journal of Land and Public Utility Economics* 138–152 (May, 1937).

Lobell, N. D., "Fifteen Years of the Holding Company Act," 47 *Public Utilities Fortnightly* 292–299 (Mar. 1, 1951).

Ritchie, Robert F., *Integration of Public Utility Holding Companies*. Ann Arbor, Mich.: Michigan Legal Publications, 1954.

Securities and Exchange Commission, *The Problem of Maintaining Arm's-length Bargaining and Competitive Conditions in the Sale and Distribu-*

tion of Securities of Registered Public Utility Holding Companies and Their Subsidiaries. 1940.

Troxel, Emery, "Capital Structure Control of Utility Companies by the SEC," 15 *Journal of Business* 225 (1942).

———, *Economics of Public Utilities*, chap. 8. New York: Rinehart & Company, Inc., 1947.

Welch, F. X., "Functions of the FPC in Relation to the SEC," 14 *George Washington Law Review* 81 (December, 1945).

PART FOUR

MAINTAINING COMPETITION

13

PUBLIC POLICY AND THE DECLINE OF COMPETITION

From the earliest days of government control of business until recently, public policy has been based on the assumption that two categories of business exist—businesses affected with a public interest, and businesses of a private nature. A more accurate interpretation in view of recent court decisions is that lawmaking bodies have preferred, as a matter of public policy and with court approval, to regulate certain businesses in great detail. The previous chapters have been concerned with the regulation of these businesses which, for historic reasons, are still known as "public utilities" (including transportation agencies). For the most part, but not entirely, these enterprises have been considered to be natural monopolies, and regulatory policy has been designed to control them in such a way that the public interest would be served. Prices and services in these businesses have been regulated by government, in principle at least, to bring about results as they presumably would be under competition, and entry into and departure from service have not been left to individual initiative. To be sure, regulated prices and services have also been influenced by competitive factors, and in certain instances, as with the railroads and industrial electric power, this influence has been a major one.

For the so-called private businesses, the traditional approach of government has been based upon the belief that competition is the best means of obtaining efficient production, equality of business opportunity, and fair prices to consumers. Consequently, public policy has been concerned with business activities that result in a decline of competition. By breaking up already existing monopolies and preventing practices that restrain trade or tend toward monopolies, government has sought to enforce competitive conditions.

The Competitive System: Myth and Model

Much of the confusion and misunderstanding over the characteristics of the competitive system arise from the fact that it is both a myth and a model.

By myth is meant "the value-impregnated beliefs and notions that men hold, that they live by or live for." [1] Every society is held together by myths; social relations are born and sustained by them. The term is used in an entirely neutral sense and does not question the validity of the belief. In this sense, the competitive system is the motivating value of American life in the economic sphere. It assumes that man knows his own best interests and is motivated by them. It believes that the pursuit of self-interest will serve community interest and places faith in the efficacy of private property, freedom of contract, and profit as the major incentive. Competition is the prime regulatory force that assures that consumers and society will in fact be protected against excessive profits, inefficiency, and poor quality.

In the other sense, the competitive system is only a concept, a model by which to measure the varying degrees of imperfection that characterize the actual market condition. Perfect competition presupposes a homogeneous commodity, many sellers and buyers, all acting independently and with full information of market conditions, mobility of productive factors, and no artificial barriers to entering or leaving an industry. Under such conditions keen rivalry between buyers and between sellers would result, for no individual buyer or seller would be able to gain market dominance. Price would be determined by the free interaction of both demand and supply. In the long run, a price above lowest average total unit costs of production would not be possible, for entry of new firms or willingness of existing sellers to accept a price equal to average total unit cost (including a return on capital and wages of management) would bring the price down. Nor could prices long remain below this cost since losses would force a reduction in the number of firms and curtail the amounts the remaining firms would be willing to offer for sale.

Under this kind of competitive system, the quality of goods would be protected by rivalry between sellers and by the shunning of goods of inferior quality at similar prices by buyers. Those businesses which produced things people want would tend to be the most profitable, and existence of returns over cost would tend to draw new enterprises into such fields. Resources would be directed to the most productive uses, as measured by consumer marginal utilities.

Where a free system of competition operated, unused productive capacity, whether of capital or labor, could hardly exist except for short transitional periods. If capital or labor were unused, its price would fall, until at some level employment would be profitable.

This, then, in oversimplified terms, is the competitive model. There is

[1] Robert MacIver, *The Web of Government* (New York: The Macmillan Company, 1947), p. 4.

an important difference between the myth and the model. The model has never existed. As will be noted, there is a considerable variance between reality and the competitive system as a model. However, the model is a useful device, because it provides a standard against which existing conditions can be measured. The competitive system as a myth, on the other hand, is neither a theoretical model nor a description of reality. It is the expression of value goals, a prescription rather than description, a statement of what "ought to be" rather than of what "is."

Public policy that does not recognize this distinction is doomed to failure, because any attempt to achieve, as the goal of public policy, a system that did not, does not, and cannot exist is futile. Perhaps somewhere between the model of perfect competition and pure monopoly there is an area of "effective" competition that is both a feasible and desirable goal of public policy. But before considering that problem the extent of the departure from the competitive model must be examined.

The Apparent Decline of Competition

Evidence of the decline in the apparent vigor of competition is not hard to find. An impression of the decline can be gained from data concerning the emergence of big business, the concentration of economic power in the hands of a few sellers, rigidity of prices, and the introduction of nonprice competition.

RISE OF CORPORATE ENTERPRISE

The American economy is characterized by the predominance of the corporate form of organization, with its typical divorce of ownership from control, tight centralization of power in corporate management, and enormous financial resources. In 1800, there were some 335 corporations in the United States, and most of these were operating banks, insurance companies, canals, turnpike roads, waterworks, and toll bridges. Only a few corporate charters were granted to firms in general business. The corporate device did not become a widely used means for conducting business activity until after 1860. Its use in the industrial field before the War between the States was largely confined to textiles. By 1897, there were 44 corporations, or allied groups of corporations, with capital of $50 million or more. Of these, only 8 were industrial corporations, 11 or 12 were public utilities, and the majority were railroads.[2] By 1948, $122 billion of national income (54.3 per cent) originated in corporations.[3]

[2] *Big Business: Its Growth and Its Place* (New York: The Twentieth Century Fund, Inc., 1937), pp. 1, 27.

[3] *Business Size and the Public Interest* (New York: National Association of Manufacturers, 1949), p. 8.

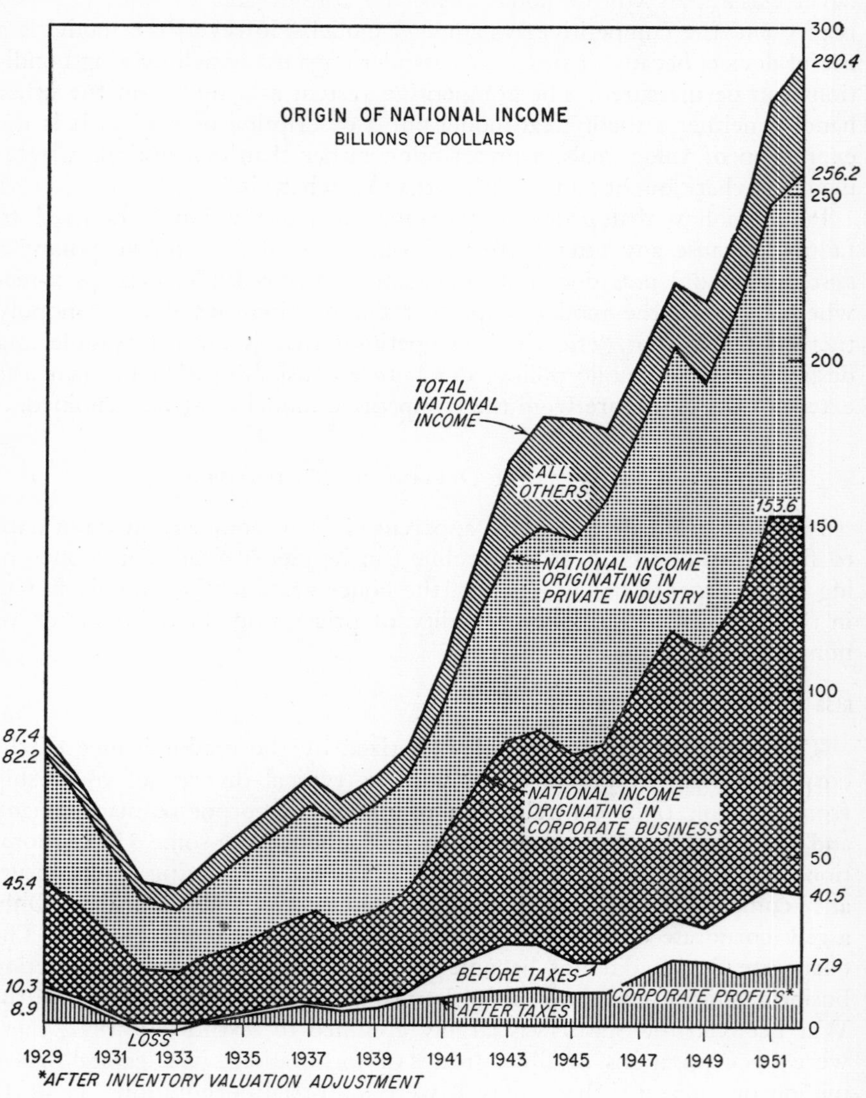

Figure 13-1

Source: Reprinted from Robert K. Carr and others, *American Democracy in Theory and Practice* (New York: Rinehart & Company, Inc., 1955), p. 718. National Industrial Conference Board, Inc., *Profits in Perspective*, prepared for 37th annual meeting (New York: The Board, 1953).

Single proprietorships, partnerships, and other private businesses originated 33.7 per cent of the national income, and the remainder was accounted for by government, households, nonprofit institutions, and other sources. Out of an estimated total of 500,000 corporate businesses there were 601 corporations (0.12 per cent of the total) with assets of $100 million or over in 1948, having a net income before taxes of $13.2 billion (5.8 per cent of national income).[4]

Although only slightly more than half the production of the nation takes place under the administrative control of corporations, in the fields of manufacturing, mining, and public utilities almost all activity is carried on by corporations. In 1937, the percentage of business done by corporations in communications, electric light, power, and manufactured gas was 100; in mining, 96; in manufacturing, 92; in transportation, 89; and in finance, 84.[5]

Corporate profits have shown a sharper increase than those of noncorporate enterprises. In 1951, corporate profits were almost four times their 1929 levels, while noncorporate income had increased only threefold.[6] Undoubtedly, the corporate sector of the economy carries more tangible weight than the noncorporate. The authors of a study of the modern corporation concluded: [7]

> The rise of the modern corporation has brought a concentration of economic power which can compete on equal terms with the modern state—economic power versus political power, each strong in its own field. The state seeks in some aspects to regulate the corporation, while the corporation, steadily becoming more powerful, makes every effort to avoid such regulation. Where its own interests are concerned, it even attempts to dominate the state.

The rise of corporations in itself is not significant in considering the decline of competition. What is important is the fact that the corporate device has facilitated the growth of business giants possessing a tremendous economic power.

EMERGENCE OF BIG BUSINESS

Large-scale enterprises also characterize the American economy. Evidence of the growth of big business can be found in the statistics of consolidations. Watkins found that, in the period from 1890 to 1904, 237 industrial consolidations were consummated, involving a total capitaliza-

[4] A. D. H. Kaplan and Alfred E. Kahn, "Big Business in a Competitive Society," 47 *Fortune Magazine* (sec. 2) 10 (February, 1953).

[5] David Lynch, *The Concentration of Economic Power* (New York: Columbia University Press, 1946), p. 94.

[6] Kaplan and Kahn, *op. cit.*, p. 9.

[7] Adolph A. Berle and Gardiner C. Means, *The Modern Corporation and Private Property* (New York: The Macmillan Company, 1933), p. 357.

tion of nearly $6 billion.[8] Thorp reported a total of 1,268 mergers in the decade following 1918 in manufacturing and mining industries.[9]

Between 1940 and 1947, more than 2,450 formerly independent manufacturing and mining companies disappeared as a result of mergers and acquisitions. The asset value of these companies was $5.2 billion, roughly 5.5 per cent of the total assets of all manufacturing corporations in the country during 1943. In this recent merger movement nearly one-third of the companies merged were absorbed by corporations with assets exceeding $50 million. The distinctly small firms, those with less than $1 million of assets, made only 11 per cent of the acquisitions. Of the nation's 200 largest corporations, 123 alone acquired 27 per cent of all firms bought up since 1940.[10] Furthermore, high profits have led to a sharp increase in the funds available for the purchase of other companies. As of June, 1947, according to the Federal Trade Commission, 78 giant corporations had sufficient net working capital to buy up the assets of 90 per cent of all manufacturing corporations in the nation.[11]

The position of big business has been strengthened also because the greatest number of recent mergers occurred in fields that in the past have been predominately small-business fields—textiles and apparel, and food and kindred products.

Increase of business size is also indicated by employment data. In 1909, only 15 per cent of the manufacturing plants hired more than 1,000 workers, but by 1929 over 24 per cent of the plants were in this class.[12] By 1939, the firms with 1,000 or more employees accounted for 39 per cent of all manufacturing employment; by 1948, for 50 per cent. As for all businesses, 1/6 of 1 per cent (6,400 firms) employed 44 per cent of all workers in 1948. In 1940, they employed only 40 per cent of all workers.[13]

However, the size of a corporation is not itself necessarily an index of its market power. Assets of over $100 million will put a business within the list of the 200 to 250 largest industrials (excluding financial and public-utility corporations). But $100 million in assets would be a competitive handicap for an automobile manufacturer. In carpets, on the other hand, the biggest company falls $30 million short of that figure—yet it embraces one-fourth of the industry. A grocery chain with $100 million of assets has annual sales of $1 billion or more; but those sales are less than 4 per

[8] Myron W. Watkins, *Industrial Combinations and Public Policy*, as cited in *Big Business: Its Growth and Its Place*, p. 29.

[9] W. L. Thorp, "The Changing Structure of Industry," in *Recent Economic Changes in the U.S.*, cited in Watkins, *op. cit.*, p. 31.

[10] FTC, *Report of the F.T.C. on the Merger Movement: A Summary Report* (1948), p. 28.

[11] *Ibid.*, p. 21.

[12] *Big Business: Its Growth and Its Place*, p. 38.

[13] Kaplan and Kahn, *op. cit.*, p. 6.

cent of the total sales of all retail grocers. It is necessary to examine additional evidence to understand the decline of competition, because bigness may be, but is not necessarily, a sign of concentrated economic power.

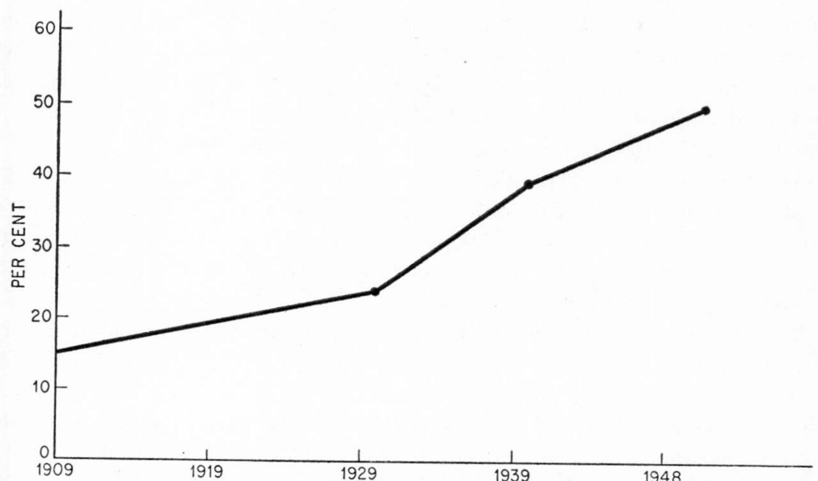

Figure 13-2. Increase in Manufacturing Firms Employing More than 1,000 Workers

Source: Twentieth Century Fund, *Big Business: Its Growth and Its Place* (New York: The Twentieth Century Fund, Inc., 1937), p. 38; A.D.H. Kaplan and Alfred E. Kahn, "Big Business in a Competitive Society," 17 *Fortune*, §2, 10 (February, 1953).

CONCENTRATION OF BUSINESS ACTIVITY

Many studies of economic concentration have been made in the past twenty years.[14] It would be impossible to review the findings of all

[14] Berle and Means, *op. cit.; Big Business: Its Growth and Its Place*; National Resources Committee, *The Structure of the American Economy*, part I, *Basic Characteristics* (1939); Clair Wilcox, *Competition and Monopoly in American Industry*, TNEC Monograph 21 (1940); Smaller War Plants Corporation, *Economic Concentration and World War II*, Report to the Special Committee to Study Problems of American Business, S. Doc. 206, 79th Cong., 2d Sess. (1946); FTC, *Report of the F.T.C. on the Merger Movement*; Harrison F. Houghton, "The Growth of Big Business," 38 *American Economic Review* 72–93 (May, 1948); House of Representatives, Committee on Small Business, *United States versus Economic Concentration and Monopoly*, Staff report to the Monopoly Subcommittee, 79th Cong. (1949); FTC, *The Concentration of Productive Facilities, 1947* (1949); FTC, *The Divergence between Plant and Company Concentration, 1947* (1950); House of Representatives, Subcommittee on Study of Monopoly Power of the Committee on the Judiciary, *The Mobilization Program*, H. Rept. 1217, 82d Cong., 1st Sess. (1951); FTC, *Monopolistic Practices and Small Business*, Staff Report to the F.T.C. for the Subcommittee on Monopoly of the Select Committee on Small Business (1952); G. W. Stocking and M. W. Watkins, *Monopoly and Free Enterprise* (New York: The Twentieth Century Fund, Inc., 1951).

these investigations here. In general, they have reported that concentration, in terms of operating units, corporate wealth, corporate income, and total value of shipments has steadily increased for the last fifty years.[15] Some of the evidence may be highlighted briefly.

As early as 1909, the 200 largest nonfinancial organizations owned one-third of the assets (exclusive of intercorporate securities) of all nonfinancial corporations. By 1929, they controlled 48 per cent, and their control had risen to 55 per cent in the 1930s. On the other hand, self-employed enterprisers constituted 36.9 per cent of the gainful workers in 1880, but only 18.8 per cent in 1939.

Giant corporations expanded their control in basic industries. For example, the big three automobile producers accounted for 42 per cent of the output in 1909 and over 90 per cent in 1939. The four largest iron and steel producers owned 25 per cent of the rolling-mill capacity in 1880 and 64 per cent in 1938.[16]

As a result of economic expansion and defense programs in World War II, industrial concentration increased above the prewar level. The nation's manufacturing facilities in existence in 1939 cost $40 billion to build. By June, 1945, $26 billion worth were added. Two-thirds of this plant expansion was provided for directly from federal funds. The 250 top manufacturing corporations gained 79 per cent of the new facilities. The 63 largest manufacturing corporations, with assets of over $100 million, increased their net working capital to nearly $10 billion—more than that of all listed manufacturing corporations in 1939. Such highly liquid working capital would then have been sufficient to buy the assets of 84 per cent of the total number of manufacturing corporations in the United States.

While the defense programs during World War II and the decade since that war clearly contributed to concentration of business in many large firms, one should recognize that the larger companies were naturally in the best position to assume responsibility for heavy expansion in aircraft, munitions, atomic power, mobile ground equipment, electronics, and other requirements of modern war. It is likewise understandable that a high portion of the research and development contracts should be given to these firms with their readily available research facilities, organizations, and manpower.[17] Moreover, in concentrating attention on the value of

[15] For a critical view of some of these studies, see *Studies on Concentration: The F.T.C. versus the Facts* (New York: National Association of Manufacturers, 1951); for somewhat conflicting results, see *Business Size and the Public Interest* (National Association of Manufacturers), and Kaplan and Kahn, *op. cit.*

[16] House of Representatives, Committee on Small Business, *op. cit.*, p. 96.

[17] For facts as to the extent of this, see *ibid.*, pp. 71, 72, 211. Also see Corwin Edwards, "Antimonopoly Policy during Rearmament," 42 *American Economic Review* 404–417 (May, 1952).

government prime contracts given to the very large firms, it should not be forgotten that these contracts led to subsidiary contracts to many other firms. It is probable that the post-World War II period has led to a resurgence of small business in large numbers, especially since these smaller

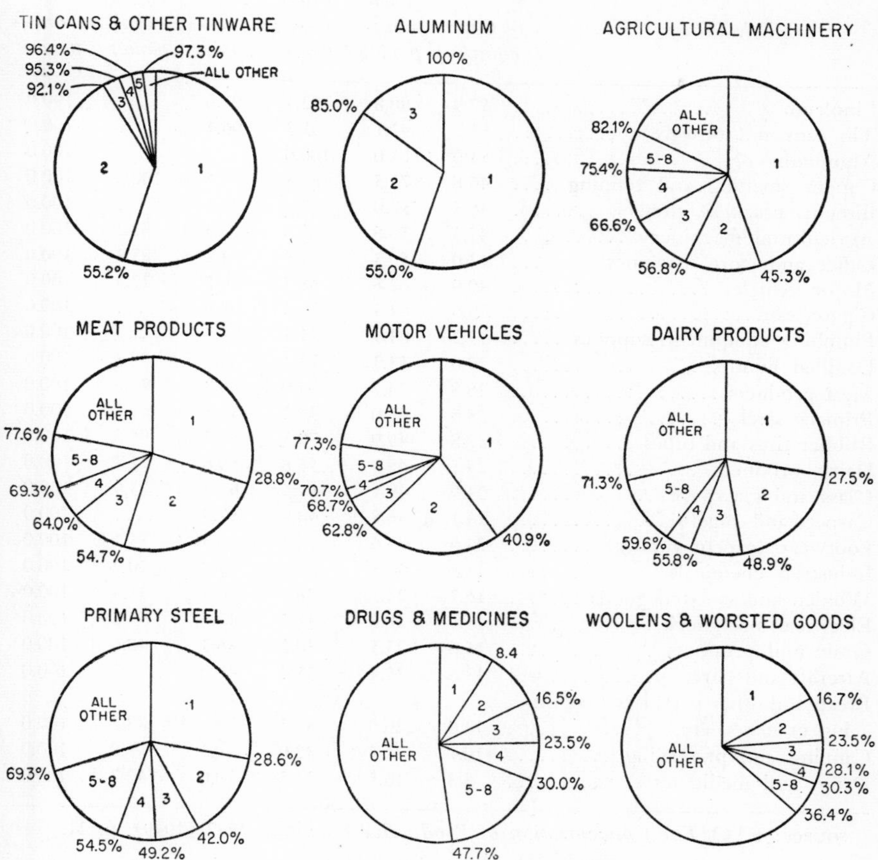

Figure 13-3. Concentration of Productive Facilities

Cumulative percentages of net capital assets owned by largest corporations, 1947.

Source: Reprinted from John H. Ferguson and Dean E. McHenry, *The American System of Government* (New York: McGraw-Hill Book Company, Inc., 3d ed., 1953), p. 633, as adopted from FTC, *Report . . . on the Concentration of Productive Facilities, 1947* (1950).

businesses are not fettered with the managerial and labor problems and many of the organizational and economic inflexibilities of the larger firms.

By 1948, the most recent year for which figures are available, $50 billion worth of economic resources were centered in the hands of 100

Table 13–1. *Twenty-six Selected Manufacturing Industries, Proportion of Net Capital Assets Owned by Leading Concerns,* 1947

Industry	*Per cent of net capital owned by*					
	One company	*Two companies*	*Three companies*	*Four companies*	*Eight companies*	*All companies*
Linoleum	57.9	80.8	92.1	93.6	....	100.0
Tin cans and tinware	55.2	92.1	95.3	96.4	....	100.0
Aluminum	55.0	85.0	100.0	....	....	100.0
Copper smelting and refining	46.8	73.5	88.5	94.6	100.0	100.0
Biscuits, crackers, pretzels	46.3	57.0	67.7	71.4	....	100.0
Agricultural machinery	45.3	56.8	66.6	75.4	82.1	100.0
Office and store machines	42.0	56.3	69.5	74.3	85.3	100.0
Motor vehicles	40.9	62.8	68.7	70.7	77.3	100.0
Cigarettes	36.6	64.4	77.6	87.8	....	100.0
Plumbing equipment, supplies	33.2	64.9	71.3	74.3	....	100.0
Distilled liquors	29.0	53.3	72.4	84.6	94.3	100.0
Meat products	28.8	54.7	64.0	69.3	77.6	100.0
Primary steel	28.6	42.0	49.2	54.5	69.3	100.0
Rubber tires and tubes	27.8	49.9	70.3	88.3	94.8	100.0
Dairy products	27.5	48.9	55.8	59.6	71.3	100.0
Glass and glassware	24.9	49.1	57.4	62.2	73.9	100.0
Carpets and rugs	24.1	36.8	48.9	57.9	....	100.0
Footwear (except rubber)	23.6	39.6	43.4	46.8	53.1	100.0
Industrial chemicals	21.5	36.5	45.5	51.8	70.2	100.0
Woolen and worsted goods	16.7	23.5	28.1	30.3	36.4	100.0
Electrical machinery	15.8	28.8	41.7	47.5	55.2	100.0
Grain-mill products	15.6	23.5	30.2	36.3	48.6	100.0
Aircraft and parts	13.6	25.4	35.2	44.0	73.7	100.0
Bread and other products (excluding crackers, etc.)	13.0	20.0	35.4	30.6	38.2	100.0
Canning and preserving	10.7	21.4	32.0	39.4	51.0	100.0
Drugs and medicines	8.4	16.5	23.5	30.0	47.7	100.0

SOURCE: FTC, *The Concentration of Productive Facilities, 1947* (1949), p. 21.

managements. The 100 largest corporations, of all kinds, accounted for 12 per cent of all income originating in private business and 10.6 per cent of the total national payroll, public and private.[18]

As for manufacturing, there were 113 corporations with assets of over $100 million in 1947. These companies owned $16,093 million of net capital assets, or 46 per cent of the total for all manufacturing, corporate and noncorporate. Table 13–1 indicates the percentage of net capital assets owned by the leading concerns in 26 selected industries. The range in these industries is from 57.9 per cent ownership of net capital assets

[18] Kaplan and Kahn, *op. cit.*, p. 10.

Table 13–2. *Percentage of Total Value of Product of All Manufacturing Industries Accounted for by the Largest Manufacturing Concerns, 1935 and 1950*

	1935	*1950*	*Change*
First 5 companies	10.6	11.4	0.8
First 50 companies	26.2	26.6	0.4
First 100 companies	32.4	33.3	0.9
First 200 companies	37.7	40.5	2.8

SOURCE: FTC, *Changes in Concentration in Manufacturing, 1935 to 1947 and 1950* (1954), p. 17.

by one company to 8.4 per cent ownership. In one instance, 3 companies own the entire assets of an industry. Certainly, what individual enterprises do in some of the above industries may affect the whole complexion of the industry concerned.

The Federal Trade Commission measured the change in concentration between 1935 and 1950, using as a measure the total value of shipments for manufacturing enterprises. Table 13–2 compares the percentage position of companies which occupied the top places in 1935 with that of companies which occupied the top places in 1950. The difference in the level of concentration as between the years 1935 and 1950 is revealed in greater detail in Figure 13–4, which presents the cumulative concentration curves in intervals of five companies.

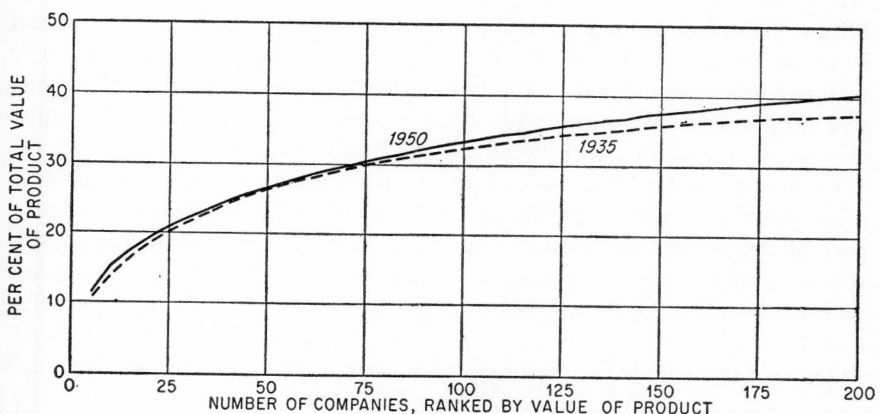

Figure 13-4. Concentration in Manufacturing

Cumulative percentages of total value of product accounted for by the 200 largest manufacturing companies.

Source: FTC, *Changes in Concentration in Manufacturing, 1935 to 1947 and 1950* (1954), p. 18.

While the Federal Trade Commission's study reveals a tendency toward increasing concentration of industry, one cannot but be impressed with the slow rate of increase displayed, particularly for the largest 100 manufacturing companies. When it is recalled that the period 1935–1950 encompassed a depression recovery, a war, and a postwar recovery, the slow rate of relative growth is probably more startling than the absolute increase in concentration. It discloses that considerable vigor still exists in the medium-large, medium, and smaller manufacturing companies.

Data of the Federal Trade Commission and of students of industrial concentration must not be taken as prima-facie evidence of a decline in competition.[19] Existence of a few large firms in an industry does not necessarily imply that workable competition does not exist among them. One would hardly say, for example, that the automobile industry or the refrigerator industry has not been vigorously competitive. The very definition of an industry has become less clear as competition has taken various forms. Jacoby points to the refrigerator "industry" as an example.[20] The largest producers of this commodity include two firms from the automobile industry, two from the electrical-equipment industry, two from the radio-television industry, and one from the farm-machinery industry. This is evidence of the way firms cross industry lines to take advantage of favorable prospects which may utilize their facilities and know-how. Other examples could be cited to illustrate the constant actual and potential threat which faces the typical firm in a "concentrated industry."

Thus, the assumption by many economists that oligopoly results in an unaggressive and stabilized market does not always square with the facts. Often, if not indeed as a normal matter, the existence of a stable situation is an invitation for one of the firms of the industry or for a newcomer to upset this stability and gain a better share of the market by an aggressive program of sales promotion, by innovation or invention, or by some other device designed to take advantage of the situation.

Furthermore, the role of mergers in the concentration of business is often greatly overrated. While they were doubtless important in the latter part of the nineteenth century and the turn of the present one, their significance in the past four decades may not be as great. Had all business mergers between 1900 and 1948 been prohibited, the degree of concentration found in these industries would have been only slightly changed, since most increase in power has been achieved through internal growth.[21]

[19] For an excellent and persuasive analysis of this and similar points, see N. H. Jacoby, "Perspectives on Monopoly," 59 *Journal of Political Economy* 514–527 (December, 1951).

[20] *Ibid.*, p. 524.

[21] *Ibid.*, p. 526. See also J. F. Weston, *Mergers and the Rise of Business Firms* (Berkeley, Calif.: University of California Press, 1953).

It should not be overlooked also that mergers or the growth of large firms may actually sharpen competition in an industry by equalizing size, efficiency, and the availability of markets to the firms.[22]

Finally, it should be noted that only 36 of the 100 largest corporate enterprises in 1909 were on the same list in 1948, and many of these dropped to a comparatively low place on the list.[23] The large majority of gainfully employed persons are still in smaller businesses (under 500 employees) or in the nonbusiness field, and there are probably more businesses in relation to population than there were a half century ago.[24] There is evidence not only that a fair degree of competition and freedom of opportunity among smaller firms has gone hand in hand with the growth of large firms but that the large firms themselves carry on a virile kind of competition to a greater extent than is given credit in the somewhat oblique reports of the Federal Trade Commission and the Anti-trust Division.

PRICE RIGIDITY

Although stable prices over a considerable period of time are not conclusive evidence that the vigor of competition has been impaired, the existence of such stability raises questions. When producers are in a position to fix their prices, regardless of changes in general price levels, costs, and consumer demand, the prices are referred to as "administered prices," [25] rather than market prices.

Burns found in 1936 rigidity to be characteristic of the prices of some fifty goods, including aluminum, bananas, bread, canned milk, cement, chemicals, crackers, drugs, fertilizer, gasoline, glass, iron ore, nickel,

[22] A study of the domestic trunk airlines indicated that certain mergers which would equalize size and the ability of firms to serve markets more efficiently and adequately would tend to increase competition. See Harold Koontz, "Economic and Managerial Factors Underlying Subsidy Needs of Domestic Trunk Line Air Carriers," 18 *Journal of Air Law and Commerce*, 127–156 (Spring, 1951).

[23] Kaplan and Kahn, *op. cit.*, p. 5.

[24] *Ibid.*, p. 6. Note that Dun & Bradstreet listed 1,170,000 businesses in 1900, or 15.4 per thousand persons; and 2,020,000 in 1950, or 18 per thousand. It must be admitted that these data may present a somewhat more favorable picture in 1950 because of the more complete reporting coverage which probably existed then as compared with 1900.

[25] The term used by Gardiner C. Means in *Industrial Prices and Their Relative Flexibility*, S. Doc. 13, 74th Cong., 1st Sess. (1935). For other studies, see A.C. Neal, *Industrial Concentration and Price Inflexibility* (Washington, D.C.: Public Affairs Press, 1942); Saul Nelson and Walter G. Keim, *Price Behavior and Business Policy*, TNEC Monograph 1; J. K. Galbraith, "Monopoly Power and Price Rigidities," 50 *Quarterly Journal of Economics* 456–475 (May, 1936); Don D. Humphrey, "The Nature and Meaning of Rigid Prices, 1890–1933," 45 *Journal of Political Economy* 651–661 (October, 1937); Rufus S. Tucker, "The Reasons for Price Rigidity," 28 *American Economic Review* 41–54 (March, 1938).

paper, steel, sugar, and tin cans.[26] During the depression from 1929 to 1932 only slight price declines occurred in concentrated industries. For example single producers controlled all the output of nickel and aluminum; nickel prices remained unchanged, while aluminum declined only 4 per cent. Two producers in each field controlled the markets for sulphur, plate glass, and bananas. Sulphur prices showed no change, plate-glass prices dropped 5 per cent, and banana prices decreased only 2 per cent. On the other hand, in lumber, where the largest four producers accounted for only 5 per cent of the output, prices fell 36 per cent. In cotton textiles, where the top four concerns produced 8 per cent of the total, prices declined 42 per cent.[27]

Of even greater significance to economic welfare is the extent to which, over an extended period of time, the benefits of technological improvements are passed along to consumers in the form of lower prices. Price reductions are not extensively used in concentrated industries as a means of increasing output to compensate for decrease in unit labor requirements, whereas in the nonconcentrated industries price decreases tended to parallel reductions in unit labor requirements.

In each of six concentrated industries (iron and steel, nonferrous metals, cement, motor vehicles, cigarettes, and electric light and power), prices failed to decrease from 1920 to 1936 by as great an extent as unit labor requirements were reduced. On the other hand, in nonconcentrated industries (cotton goods, woolen and worsted goods, and furniture), prices fell more than unit labor requirements.[28]

The existence of price rigidities is not always due to an absence of competition. As one writer has pointed out, other factors may be responsible.[29] Some prices are affected by custom, so that competition tends to be reflected in quality rather than price. In some cases, goods are produced under conditions in which variable costs are high in relation to fixed costs. Hence, total cost per unit does not vary considerably over different ranges of output. Or, conceivably an industry could be faced with a stable demand and be made up of firms all operating at minimum average total unit costs.

IDENTICAL PRICES

There are numerous instances, well known to any observer of prices, in which prices of the same products are identical. A lack of competition

[26] A. R. Burns, *The Decline of Competition* (New York: McGraw-Hill Book Company, Inc., 1936), pp. 198–240.

[27] House of Representatives, Committee on Small Business, *op. cit.*, pp. 92–93.

[28] *Ibid.*

[29] R. S. Tucker, "The Essential Historical Facts about 'Sensitive' and 'Administered' Prices," 51 *The Annals* 195 (Feb. 4, 1938).

is not always implied in identical prices, since the necessary result of perfect competition would be a single price for a certain good in a given market. But where the price of an article sold in different markets or produced under different cost conditions is the same, the existence of identical prices gives credence to the belief that price leadership, adoption of price schedules, open price reporting, allotment of sales territory, trade-association services, or collusion (explicit or tacit), are operating to short-circuit the competitive system.

When the Denver office of the Bureau of Reclamation opened 17 bids for reinforcement bars, 14 of them were for $1,144.16. When the United States Engineers at Los Angeles opened 12 bids for the same product, 11 of them were for $194,051.89. When the purchasing agent for the Fort Peck Dam opened 10 bids, each was for $253,633.80.

A survey was made of 331,851 bid openings made by 45 agencies of the federal government in connection with purchases aggregating more than $860 million. In 23.1 per cent of these openings, involving the expenditure of more than $87 million, 2 or more bids were identical. In 4.1 per cent of the openings, all the bids were identical. In another 5.7 per cent, 2 or more of the lowest bids were identical. Thus, 9.8 per cent of the contracts awarded went to bidders who had submitted identical bids.[30]

The use of basing points in such industries as steel and cement, by which prices are given as of a certain producing point plus freight costs to the consuming point regardless of actual shipping costs, has often resulted in identical prices.

Policies of "follow the leader" and "live and let live" in such fields as steel, gasoline, copper, cigarettes, tin cans, and agricultural implements have resulted often in price uniformity.[31] Collusion may not exist, and the leader is not always the same seller at all times. But such practices do result in a decline of price competition.

While it should be recognized that identical prices often result from restrictions placed on competition, many business managers responsible for company pricing policy feel bewildered at the charge of monopolistic practice arising from such instances. They properly ask how, in a competitive system, they may be expected to sell a standardized product in a market above the going price and even to sell a differentiated product much above the market. They also point to the futility of undercutting a market unless this will clearly increase their share of the market and augment their profits, an advantage which no competitor would permit if the price-cutter were an important factor in the market.

[30] Wilcox, *op. cit.*, p. 301.

[31] For an excellent discussion of price leadership in cigarettes and tin cans, see Stocking and Watkins, *op. cit.*, chap. 6.

NONPRICE COMPETITION

A basic tenet of the competitive system is that prices will be set by the free play of forces in the market. An evidence of the decline of traditional competition is the development of nonprice competition.[32] Companies, instead of competing with one another to produce or sell a better item at a lower price, attempt to outdo each other in advertising programs, packaging, style, brand names, special services, and real or psychic improvement in quality. But the prices offered the customer are approximately the same. In a very real sense, this development might be called a transformation of competition instead of a decline of competition. In its essential vigor and extent, this competition may actually be as strong and as conducive to economic improvement as any system of competition based on price alone.

Nonprice competition is most likely to occur when personal efforts play a part in marketing or when products can be differentiated, i.e., made to appear unique from the products of competitors. A principal reason for product differentiation is the rise of advertising and salesmanship. The bigger the corporation is, the greater its financial resources to promote its product and expand its market. This advantage has the effect of increasing the enterprise's size and concentration of control. Moreover, to the extent that the seller is successful in differentiating his product he moves toward a semimonopolistic position, for in the minds of buyers his product tends to become the "only" one available.

The paradox of product differentiation is that it is a response to mass production which standardizes products. But mass production also emphasizes cheapness, in order to reach a wider market. However, cheapness is seldom a good theme for an effective advertising campaign. Instead, advertising tends to emphasize style, fashion, and novelty. Where a product is capable of differentiation, the seller tries to stabilize his price over fairly long periods of time. One has only to look at the steadiness of prices of branded goods to note how true this is. The producer may even seek government guarantee of his price through resale-price-maintenance laws. In support of these laws, many manufacturers contend that a stable resale price is a component of the good will which the article has and that price cutting tends to reduce the respect of buyers for it.

The Means for Limiting Competition

To the extent that competition has declined—and this extent is often exaggerated—the reasons can be classified as economic and political. The economic causes are found in the activities of business enterprises that create monopolies, restrain trade, and coerce competitors. The political

[32] For a detailed discussion, see Burns, *op. cit.*, chap. 8.

reasons are found in the actions of government that contribute to the decline of competition.

Monopoly or industry dominance may develop as a result of the growth of large-scale enterprises, a contraction of the number of competitors through horizontal combinations, or the emergence of differentiated products. Through these means, single businesses may achieve sufficient power to adopt monopolistic policies toward those with whom they deal and to coerce, overawe, or exclude competitors or potential competitors.

LARGE-SCALE ENTERPRISE

The economic advantages of large-scale enterprises in certain industries have frequently been described. Where the product is one which can be fairly standardized and where the market is broad and and stable enough, large plants can take advantage of economies through specialization and division of labor. Where the product is adaptable to the use of machinery, such plants gain by the specialized employment of expensive machines. Large output requires extensive organization for marketing, and only the large enterprise can achieve the advantages to be thus derived. It may also be able to pay high salaries for men of special ability, to conduct experimentation and research, and to utilize by-products more efficiently than a smaller company. Advantages may further accrue in the quantity purchases of raw materials and supplies.

The financial advantages of large size should not be overlooked. Generally, large, well-known companies find it easier to sell their securities. There are also economies for a large company when it borrows. A computation in 1937 revealed that bond issues of less than $1 million cost the borrower 8.8 per cent on the proceeds of the loan, while for bond issues of over $1 million the average flotation cost was 3.7 per cent.[33]

By combining successive stages in the process of production and distribution (vertical integration) additional economies are often available. A continuous supply of raw materials may be assured, and coordination of manufacturing and distribution processes may result in savings.

The economies of large-scale production and combination do not apply only to manufacturing enterprises. They may be found also in marketing, as well as in many service industries. The chain-store movement, for example, has resulted from economies brought about because the combining of numerous retail and wholesale plants has lowered costs.

To be sure, not all economic activity lends itself to the attainment of economies through large size. Where labor is of exceptionally great importance, or a commodity cannot be standardized, or a market is limited, the most efficient size of an enterprise may be relatively small.

Furthermore, there are limits to the advantages of size, even where

[33] Stocking and Watkins, *op. cit.*, p. 76.

initial advantages accrued. Conceivably, specialization may be carried too far. For workers, monotony and ennui may set in when specialization reduces tasks too near to a mechanical routine, with resulting decline in efficiency. For management, the problem of keeping all the specialized units working effectively together and in balance may become too great.

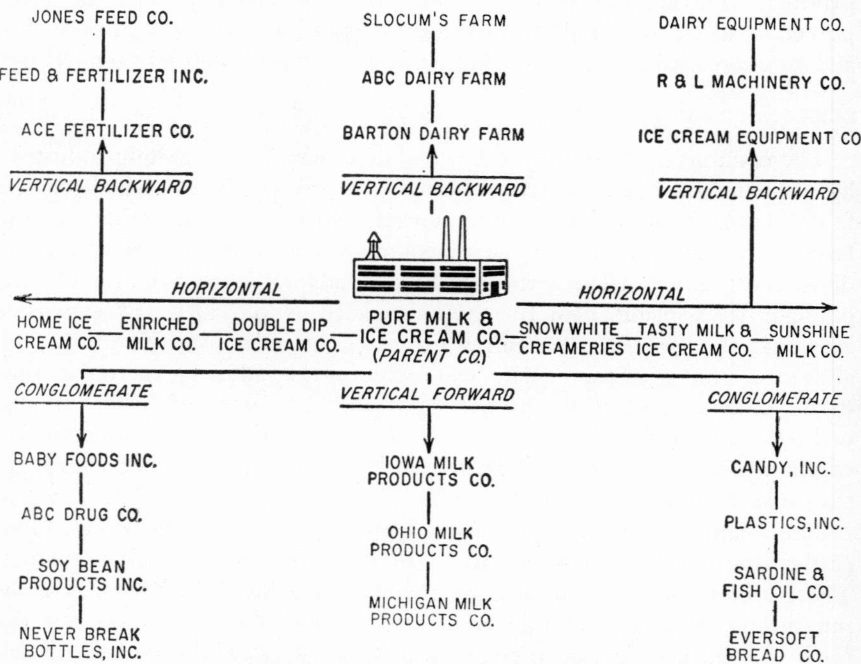

Figure 13-5. Types of Business Acquisitions

This hypothetical milk and ice-cream company has grown big by acquiring a variety of enterprises. American businesses have adopted many variations of this pattern. For illustrations of what has been happening in particular companies and industries, see FTC, *Report of . . . on the Merger Movement* (1948).

Source: Reprinted from John H. Ferguson and Dean E. McHenry, *The American System of Government* (New York: McGraw-Hill Book Company, Inc., 3d ed., 1953), p. 696.

Indeed, the problem of managing large enterprises has come increasingly to be recognized as one of the most significant causes of diseconomy in size.

The Federal Trade Commission, in a study that has been severely criticized,[34] compared the unit costs of production by large and small

[34] *Relative Efficiency of Large, Medium-sized and Small Business*, TNEC Monograph 13 (1941). For criticisms, see Robert N. Anthony, "Effect of Size on Efficiency," 22 *Harvard Business Review* 290–306 (Spring, 1942); John Scoville and Noel Sargent, *Fact and Fancy in TNEC Monographs* (New York: National Association of Manufacturers, 1942), pp. 190–200.

companies. The Commission concluded: "The largest companies made, on the whole, a very poor showing . . . medium size in itself did not insure a low cost. . . . But certain efficient medium-sized units . . . generally made the best showing." [35]

Stocking and Watkins make a more cautious statement: "The conclusion to which recent studies appear to point is that unit costs decline with increasing size of plant up to a certain point, then level off until, in some industries at least, a scale of operations is reached beyond which increasing size is attended with rising unit costs. . . ." [36] Available evidence suggests that the consolidation movement has carried the expansion of many big business units beyond the size essential for economical operation.

Although there is ready agreement that many economic causes lie behind the growth of large-scale enterprises, there is much dispute over the contention that size, in itself, gives monopolistic advantages. Big companies, of course, contest this assertion. J. Howard McGrath, when he was Attorney General in 1949, stated that the Department of Justice has "never instituted a case solely on the question of 'bigness.' Size in and of itself presents no antitrust problem." [37]

The significance of bigness alone in contributing to the decline of competition lies in the fact that size gives power. A large-scale enterprise has vast resources which it can command and a great variety of tactics which it can employ. It can endure relatively big losses that might ruin smaller organizations, and it may do so to destroy competitors. Difficulties for new rivals who may wish to enter the market may be created.[38] Even if intentional obstacles are not placed in the way of new competitors, the capital requirements of modern large-scale production are enough to limit free entry into the market.

A big business may also have a more stable operation in that it depends on a wider market and its profits are derived from more diverse commodities. It has more power as a buyer of raw materials, transportation, credit, labor, and advertising. Moreover, vertical integration may be accomplished to obtain these benefits. The large enterprise is then in a position to supply itself to the disadvantage of its competitors, which it also may serve.[39] Finally, it can afford expensive litigation under the

[35] *Ibid.*, pp. 10–11.

[36] *Op. cit.*, pp. 68, 498.

[37] "Bigness Itself Is No Crime: An Interview with J. Howard McGrath," *U.S. News and World Report*, Nov. 25, 1949, p. 26.

[38] See *Problems of Small Business*, TNEC Monograph 17 (1941).

[39] At the same time this integration may constitute a disadvantage if the units of the firm are not forced to meet the standards of outside competition. There is hardly any "monopoly" more complete than that of a division or subsidiary which has an assured customer in the form of another division or subsidiary of the same company.

various regulatory laws which small operations may not be able to endure.[40]

HORIZONTAL COMBINATION

Whereas vertical integration is the joining of different stages in the process of production and distribution, horizontal combination is the bringing together of competitors at the same stage of the business process. Horizontal combination may be accomplished by uniting former rivals under a single ownership or control, or by independent businesses coming to an agreement or understanding to restrain competition.

Horizontal combination achieves commercial savings by eliminating duplication in buying and selling, and by reducing the amount of fact finding, account keeping, inventory storing, and advertising in which independent competitors engage. A big single enterprise can buy materials and supplies in larger quantities, solicit business over a wider area, eliminate crosshauling, reduce delivery costs, and effect similar economies. Great cost savings can result from one nationwide advertising program, rather than separate campaigns. Furthermore, to take advantage of the nationwide coverage of the radio and magazine advertising media, the firm needs to operate on a nationwide basis.

When the integration is accomplished by merging with a competitor, competition between the two is undoubtedly eliminated. Moreover, such consolidation may threaten the viability of nonintegrated businesses. Their financial resources may be more limited, their markets smaller, and the diversity of their products less. A diversified firm can take high margins on products for which customer preference is secure and carry on cutthroat competition for other products. An integrated enterprise can take higher profits in markets where competition is weak and cut margins where it meets nonintegrated independents. The financial resources of the wealthy corporation can be used to conduct research, expand markets, and outbid competitors for supplies. More money can be poured into advertising to build consumer good will, channelize consumer tastes, and make buying habits relatively inflexible.

Consolidation reduces the number of sellers in the market. If the remainder are few enough, the seller may keep prices high and maintain them by curtailing sales. Or, he may choose to reduce the quality of the goods sold. Such power may be enjoyed by several consolidated firms that find it to their advantage not to compete. The nonintegrated enter-

[40] For the classic statement on the problem of size, see Louis Brandeis, *The Curse of Bigness* (New York: The Viking Press, Inc., 1934); cf. T. K. Quinn, *Big Business: Threat to Democracy* (New York: Exposition Press, 1953). For an interesting and conflicting statement, see David E. Lilienthal, *Big Business: A New Era* (New York: Harper & Brothers, 1953).

prises may learn that it is in their interests to follow the leader. If they do not, discriminatory discounts, local price cutting, exclusive dealing, and geographic price discrimination may be employed to bring them into line.

EMERGENCE OF DIFFERENTIATED PRODUCTS

Monopoly power is also created by the practice of making products which are physically similar seem different to buyers. This differentiation is accomplished by selling efforts designed to individualize products. For example, while several brands of cigarettes are practically identical, sellers are able to create the feeling among buyers that one brand is different from another. Coffee of practically identical quality is differentiated by brand names, so that buyers do not purchase coffee of a certain grade, but coffee of a certain brand. The legal protection given to trade-marks and trade names supports monopolistic positions such as these. The result of product differentiation, as has already been described, is that price competition may become secondary to competition in the use of sales devices, advertising, packaging, and special services.

RESTRICTIVE TRADE AGREEMENTS

Another economic cause for the decline of competition is the practice of reaching agreements among independent businesses to avoid competition or to prevent others from competing. To be sure, restrictive agreements to restrain trade are often stimulated by the growth of monopolistic power. Where the number of sellers are few, it is easier to conclude such agreements; and when power rests in the hands of giants, they can be required of small competitors. Even in the absence of monopolistic or concentrated power, companies may find it to their advantage to limit competition and freely enter into restrictive agreements. They are by far the easiest way of eliminating competition.

Corwin D. Edwards classifies restrictive agreements as exploitative and regulatory.[41] Exploitative agreements have the objective of substituting the large profits that come from joint action for the more moderate returns which individual competitors might receive. Sometimes the agreement may be to fix prices at higher than competitive levels; sometimes prices are raised or prevented from falling by agreements to increase the scarcity of goods or to limit future increases of supply; sometimes the agreements allocate markets among the participating concerns, each being permitted to adopt its own price and production policies without fear of competition; and sometimes agreements are reached to share profits or combine sales agencies.

The purpose of regulatory agreements is not to obtain unusual profits

[41] *Maintaining Competition: Requisites of a Governmental Policy* (New York: McGraw-Hill Book Company, Inc., 1949), pp. 19–25.

or eliminate all competition which threatens profits but to prevent or regulate only those types of competitive action that are regarded as undesirable or harmful. Agreements may seek to avoid variations between one market and another in their policies toward prices and profits; or to regard particular markets as suitable for low prices and others for high prices. Regulatory agreements may be concluded to limit the impact of a recession or depression, promote stability, prevent cutthroat competition, or cushion the impact of surplus capacity. The codes entered into under the National Industrial Recovery Act were types of regulatory agreements.

Trade associations have been widely used instruments to promote both exploitative and regulatory agreements. Dating from the War between the States, trade associations reached a high point in their growth in the environment of business self-regulation of the 1920s. Then, under the National Recovery Act in 1933, they were incorporated into the processes of government. The codes that the President signed under the National Industrial Recovery Act were usually initiated by the trade groups that were affected by them.

It is true that the trade associations provide many services that are unrelated to the decline of competition, such as conducting industrial and marketing research, engaging in public relations and advertising programs, bettering employer-employee relations, lobbying before governmental bodies, and establishing commercial tribunals. However, through data collected and distributed on such matters as cost-accounting methods, production, inventories, productive capacity, unfilled orders, and sales, the trade associations may make available to sellers information by which they can set their own price and production policies in line with others. These data also help members to share markets. Even the standardization of products, which has the effect of reducing costs and eliminating waste, may help ensure uniform prices among trade rivals.

It is not necessary to dwell on the effects of restrictive agreements on competition, because the purpose, explicit or implicit, of all such agreements is to limit competition. There can be no doubt about this fact in the case of exploitative agreements. Some doubt may be raised that regulatory agreements similarly contribute to the decline of competition. Desirable competition is actually promoted, according to certain observers. However, once a regulatory agreement is concluded, regardless of how worthy its initial purpose, the participants have a device which might easily be extended to less worthy objectives. A restrictive agreement against price discrimination can also be used to raise prices. It is impossible to leave private groups, such as trade associations, free to regulate without leaving them also free to exploit.

COERCIVE PRACTICES

The destructive effects that coercive practices have on competition are so obvious that it is sufficient merely to describe the various types. Coercive behavior may be identified as attempts to coerce or destroy competitors, or discipline them through fear.[42]

The policy of buying more than one needs in order to take supplies off the market or to become the source of supply for one's competitor is a coercive method of destroying competition. Discriminatory sharpshooting, predatory price wars, squeezing the nonintegrated concern, tying arrangements, and reciprocal buying are other methods.[43]

Discriminatory sharpshooting is the action of a large concern serving many territorial markets when it selects local competitors for destruction and reduces its prices in their local markets. The company maintains its financial solvency from its sales at higher prices elsewhere. The destruction of a rival by deliberate price cutting is predatory price warring. Squeezing the nonintegrated concern is possible when a vertically integrated concern has so large a control of one of the successive steps in production or distribution that its products or services are sold to its nonintegrated competitors. The transactions may be conducted to the benefit of the integrated enterprise and to the harm of the nonintegrated concern.

A tying arrangement is a device by which the buyer is forced to take products that he does not want in order to obtain products that he wants to buy. Related to this is the exclusive-dealing contract which binds a buyer to make all his purchases from a particular seller. Finally, reciprocal buying is an arrangement in which the buyer agrees to purchase one commodity from a seller provided the seller will purchase another from the buyer.

EFFECT OF PUBLIC POLICY

Although the fact is frequently overlooked, government itself has contributed to the decline of competition. The development of corporation laws which make possible the gathering together of large amounts of capital under one corporate roof has aided the growth of large business units. Without favorable forms of business organization, making convenient the conduct of business enterprises on a large scale and making investment in the enterprises appealing to a large class of owners and

[42] For the following discussion the authors rely on Edwards, *Maintaining Competition*, chap. 5.

[43] For current examples of these practices, see FTC, *Monopolistic Practices and Small Business.*

creditors, it is inconceivable that many, or any, of the $50 million and larger firms could exist.

Without the protection of patent laws, there is doubt that the striking technological development of the past would have occurred. But these same laws influence the decline of competition. The idea of granting monopoly powers to holders of a patent is in itself in conflict with competition. The power to hold patents over a period of years has often been instrumental in giving one firm a dominance in an industry and enabling it to become so strong that it could not be overcome by would-be competitors even after the original patents had expired. Such has been the case in the wire-communication, sewing-machine, shoe-machinery, and aluminum fields, to mention only a few.

The power over certain basic patents has sometimes given concerns control over the whole development of an industry, the prices charged, the output produced, and the entry of firms. The Temporary National Economic Committee disclosed in 1938 that control of patents by two companies allowed them to dominate completely the glass-container-manufacturing industry.[44]

The tremendous cost of developing many patented improvements to the point where they are ready for commercial production, and the cost of maintaining suits against infringement of valuable patents, are generally beyond the resources of individuals. As a result, there is a strong tendency for patents to be assigned to businesses already large, even if the inventor happens to be working outside the research laboratories of these concerns. This tends to place many patents in the hands of single business enterprises, thereby accentuating their monopolistic nature.[45]

As has already been discussed, the decisions government has made in awarding production, research, and other contracts in time of war have been a contributing factor. The allowance of generous tax write-offs to promote wartime plant expansion further assists the limited number of firms that receive the big contracts.

Various forms of government-erected trade barriers have been instituted which restrain competition and discriminate between competitors. One type discriminates between producers on a territorial basis and awards the benefits of monopoly to those in the home market. Milk-inspection laws are one illustration of this type. A second kind is designed to favor producers of one product against those of a substitute. Regulatory taxes, such as the oleomargarine tax, are an example. In international trade, tariffs are outstanding examples of trade barriers which promote monopoly. According to one study, of 317 products whose concentration

[44] *Investigation of Concentration of Economic Power*, part 2 (1939).

[45] See Stocking and Watkins, *op. cit.*, chap. 14; Walton Hamilton, *Patents and Free Enterprise*, TNEC Monograph 31 (1941).

ratios exceed 75 per cent, 27.7 per cent by value would have lower prices if tariffs were reduced, because monopolistic elements in domestic prices would be offset.[46]

Many observers believe that the antitrust laws themselves—those laws designed to break monopoly—have had something to do with the decline of competition. Because any kind of cooperation between producers might be interpreted as combination in restraint of trade, and because of a belief, possibly erroneous, that consolidated businesses would not so easily run afoul of the law, cooperation of independent sellers has often given way to outright consolidation. Although cooperative methods between separate sellers may become highly destructive of competition, the completeness and permanence of such reduction in competition is likely to be far greater under outright consolidation. In addition, many exemptions to the antitrust and fair-trade-practice laws have allowed monopolistic elements to continue to exist in certain sectors of the economy.

The Goals of Public Policy

The social and economic justification for competition lies in the belief that under a freely competitive system goods wanted most by consumers will be produced by those who can produce them at least cost, and that consumers will pay no more than the cost necessary to bring goods into being in such form and at such place as desired by consumers. There is also often the feeling that a freely competitive system encourages democratic equality by equalizing the freedom to enter the market place as an entrepreneur.

Certainly, even the most enthusiastic advocates of competition would not contend that the economist's model of perfect competition should be the objective of public policy. If this model were to become a value goal, fundamental changes in the present economic system would have to be made. Business would have to be atomized so that no seller acting alone could influence the market. Goods would have to be so standardized that no seller could gain a semimonopolistic position through trade names or trade-marks. Or, measures might have to be taken to limit size or influence by trade names whenever perfect competition is threatened. Unless such steps are taken, it would seem fruitless to try to enforce perfect competition by law.

Such a drastic policy would clearly not be beneficial to consumers. Production at lowest cost calls for large firms in many lines of economic activity. In certain areas, monopoly, or near monopoly, may be justified upon a cost basis, owing to the lower cost incident to size and the elimination of wastes involved in competitive duplication of facilities. Production

[46] *Export Prices and Export Cartels*, TNEC Monograph 6, p. 82.

of branded articles and the giving of special services under monopolistic competition may increase consumer satisfaction out of all proportion to any additional cost involved.

An economically sound public policy should recognize that underlying economic factors are such that perfect competition is not feasible or desirable in most markets. There may be some industries in which a monopoly would be the most efficient producing unit. There may be others in which one firm of the most efficient size could not produce enough for the market. In such a case an oligopoly of large firms might be socially desirable. Moreover, in some industries where consumers' tastes vary, and individualized products with different service or psychic qualities satisfy these tastes best, conditions of monopolistic competition may be desirable. After these industries are determined, a large field for effective competition between small business units would still be left.

In view of such considerations, public policy should be molded to suit diverse underlying conditions. Criteria should be developed for measuring the comparative advantages and disadvantages of operation at sizes involving various degrees of concentration of control. These criteria might set forth such tests of social performance as relative waste and economy in the use of resources, efficiency of production and unit costs of output, expansion of an industry's total output and sales, improvement of quality and service, progress through invention and innovation, and stability of operations over time.[47]

Where a monopoly is allowed, price and service regulation should be undertaken to ensure protection of buyers. In industries earmarked for an oligopoly of large producers, public policy should depend upon the degree of competition existent. If independent rivalry between sellers is not adequate to ensure consumer prices consistent with costs and economical utilization of resources, regulation to gain these ends should be enforced. However, it should never be assumed that mere size or fewness of firms in an industry is conclusive evidence of a lack of competition; there are too many industries where competition under such circumstances is vigorous and real.

Competition among sellers, even though imperfect, may be effective or workable if it offers buyers even more numerous, varied, and significant market alternatives sufficient to enable them, by shifting their purchases from one seller to another, substantially to influence quality, service, and price.[48] To be effective, competition need not involve the standardization

[47] See Stocking and Watkins, *op. cit.*, p. 543.

[48] See Blackwell Smith, "Effective Competition: Hypothesis for Modernizing the Anti-trust Laws," 26 *New York University Law Review* 405–450 (July, 1951); John M. Clark, "Toward a Concept of Workable Competition," 30 *American Economic Review* 241–256 (June, 1940).

of commodities. It does, however, require the reasonably ready substitution of one product for another. Effective competition depends, also, upon the general availability of essential information. Buyers cannot influence the behavior of sellers unless alternatives are known. Therefore, public policy should be formulated to encourage enlightenment of buyers as to what they are receiving. The government could insist upon accurate description of the article in all advertising and labeling. In certain cases, methods of grading might be devised, dishonest claims outlawed, packaging regulated to indicate size accurately, and special services required to be billed separately from the cost of the article.

One may justly insist that such a program represents a vast incursion of government into the field of business. This may be true. But many of the advantages of large business enterprises and of product differentation come from the special protection which government has placed around business. The laws regarding patents, trade-marks, protection of good will through resale-price maintenance, and limited liability of corporate stockholders which has made incorporation so valuable, have accounted for much of the imperfection in the competitive system.

The significant fact from an economic and political point of view is that the consumer will be protected either by selfish rivalry among competitive firms or by some instrument of public policy. As a general thing, breaking up business into small competitive units does not appear to be wise or feasible. While there may be some cases in which competition can and should be restored, namely, those of monopolistic collusion between independent sellers in which the buyer has nothing to gain, it would seem to be better in other instances, if economically justified, to protect the consumer through regulation. If the objectives of protecting the consumer and of promoting the public welfare dominate antimonopoly law and administration, rather than an unrealistic attempt to restore nineteenth-century competition and penalize size and progress, public policy can be made consistent with efficient individual enterprise.

Although it may be true that the public complains about the curse of bigness and that American business has often been the whipping boy of publicist and politician, effective and vigorous action to enforce workable competition has been taken only sporadically and hesitantly. Only when the consequences of loss of competitive vigor, a loss which does not necessarily result from bigness, are truly impressed on the public, consumer, and businessman alike will there be a real demand for action. It should be recalled that the experience of countries such as England and France has been that, when action was not taken to preserve workable and responsible competition, ownership and control by government followed. This experience should serve as a warning.

Selected References

Berle, Adolph A., Jr., and Gardiner C. Means, *The Modern Corporation and Private Property*. New York: The Macmillan Company, 1935.

Brandeis, Louis, *The Curse of Bigness*. New York: The Viking Press, Inc., 1934.

Burns, A. R., *The Decline of Competition*. New York: McGraw-Hill Book Company, Inc., 1936.

Chamberlin, Edward H., *The Theory of Monopolistic Competition*. Cambridge, Mass.: Harvard University Press, 1933.

Edwards, Corwin D., *Maintaining Competition: Requisites of a Governmental Policy*. New York: McGraw-Hill Book Company, Inc., 1949.

Fellner, William J., *Competition among the Few: Oligopoly and Similar Market Structure*. New York: Alfred A. Knopf, Inc., 1949.

Federal Trade Commission, *Report on the Merger Movement; A Summary Report*, 1948.

Hamilton, Walton, *The Pattern of Competition*. New York: Columbia University Press, 1940.

Kaplan, A. D. H., *Big Enterprise in a Competitive System*. Washington, D.C.: Brookings Institution, 1954.

Lilienthal, David E., *Big Business: A New Era*. New York: Harper & Brothers, 1953.

Lynch, David, *Concentration of Economic Power*. New York: Columbia University Press, 1946.

National Resources Committee, *The Structure of the American Economy*, part I, *Basic Characteristics*. Government Printing Office, 1937.

Quinn, T. K., *Giant Business: Threat to Democracy*. New York: Exposition Press, 1953.

Robinson, Joan, *The Economics of Imperfect Competition*. New York: St. Martin's Press, 1933.

Smaller War Plants Corporation, *Economic Concentration and World War II*, Report to the Special Committee to Study Problems of American Business, U.S. Senate, S. Doc. 206, 79th Cong., 2d Sess. (1946).

Stocking, George W., and Myron W. Watkins, *Monopoly and Free Enterprise*, chaps. 2–6. New York: The Twentieth Century Fund, Inc., 1951.

14

REGULATION OF MONOPOLY AND RESTRAINT OF TRADE

There are two aspects of public policy designed to maintain competition. Laws have been enacted to forbid combinations in restraint of trade or attempts to monopolize business. Regulations have also aimed at maintaining a plan of business behavior conducive to effective competition; in some ways, they attempt to curtail practices, regarded by a given standard of business ethics as unfair, which lead to monopoly in some form or other. A clear distinction between the two sets of regulations is not always possible. For purposes of discussion, the program directed toward monopoly and restraint of trade will be considered in the present chapter. Regulation of competitive practices will be surveyed in the next chapter. The final chapter in this section will discuss special areas of trade regulation.

Common-law Regulation

Much of the early business regulation of England, either by courts or by statutes, did not find its way into modern common law. This fact was due in large part to enactments by Parliament, and to the fact that many business cases did not reach the King's Bench Courts and so did not come down in the court records. But two rules of regulatory effect did get into modern common law and became a basis for some regulation of the trusts. These had to do with conspiracy to monopolize trade and with agreements to restrain trade.

CONSPIRACY TO MONOPOLIZE

The common-law doctrine making conspiracy to monopolize unlawful finds its roots in the old judicial principle of conspiracy. Conspiracy involved the joining together of two or more parties with the purpose of inflicting harm upon a third party. The common law did not hit monopolies developed by the natural growth of an individual business; yet it did touch upon practically all attempts to monopolize, since such attempts almost invariably were carried on by means of a conspiracy.

Contracts made to effect a conspiracy to monopolize were not enforceable in the courts. Any party injured by such a conspiracy had a case for the collection of damages. Moreover, conspiracy was a criminal offense in the common law, punishable by fine or imprisonment, but the criminal penalties were not generally applied.[1] As a matter of fact, where the common law was used against industrial combinations in this country, the conspiracy doctrine was seldom the basis for legal action. By far the greater number of cases by which common-law regulation was applied had to do with agreements to restrain trade.

AGREEMENTS TO RESTRAIN TRADE

At the outset the courts regarded all contracts with a purpose of suppressing competition, or contributing to such purpose, as unenforceable. In time, however, they came to the position that only contracts in unreasonable restraint of trade should be outlawed. When contracts were ancillary to the main purpose of the agreement—for example, when a man sold a business and agreed not to enter the same type of business within the same market area—the restraints were regarded as reasonable. A restraint was regarded as reasonable if it was limited as to time, space, or scope. The time and space limitations must be for the protection of the person for whose benefit the restraint was imposed and not an undue burden upon the person restricted. The scope limitation meant that it must not infringe upon the interests of the public by creating a monopoly controlling prices or by limiting production artificially.

Contracts which constituted unreasonable restraints of trade were not illegal in the sense that they could not be made. They merely could not be enforced at law. Hence the law of agreements to restrain trade did not stop the forming of combinations. It did, however, make many combination transactions risky and ineffective. If any participant in a combination plan should break away from an agreement, the group had no legal means of forcing him to live up to his agreement.

WEAKNESSES OF THE COMMON LAW

As a method of protecting the public against the existence and abuses of monopoly, the common law had serious shortcomings. The fact that agreements to restrain trade were not made illegal has been mentioned. So long as participants in a combination scheme live up to their obligations, or methods of enforcement outside the courts are found, there is little in the common law which would regulate the combination. And all

[1] Common-law criminal conspiracy has been used by a few states to attack combinations. See, for example, *State v. Erickson,* 54 Wash. 472, 103 Pac. 796 (1909); *State v. Craft,* 168 N.C. 208, 83 S.E. 772 (1914).

too often it had been profitable for participants to abide by agreements made to suppress competition.

Even if the conspiracy doctrine had been rigorously applied, the common law would have been somewhat weak. In the first place, not all agreements to suppress competition might fall under the doctrine, for the essence of conspiracy is the acting in concert for purpose of damaging third parties. In the second place, the common law provided no definite program upon which the administrative branch of government might be required to operate, nor did it provide any facilities for continuous supervision of business practices.

Since the common law was practically limited to voiding agreements in restraint of trade, it provided for no punishment of those combining. So long as members to an agreement were willing to live up to it, there was no way by which the public might be protected from its harmful or uneconomic results. However, the common-law precedents are important, for they determined the interpretation of the Sherman Act. For example, Chief Justices White and Taft assumed that the statute merely codified the common law and imposed penalties on monopoly and restraint of trade.[2]

State Antitrust Laws

As public opposition to the trusts crystallized and the shortcomings of the common law came to be realized, the state governments as well as the federal government attempted to break up these combinations by statutory enactments. The constitutions of many of the states had long included declarations against monopolies, but these provisions seemed to have been designed to forbid the state governments themselves to grant monopoly privileges. Acting under their powers to legislate in the general welfare and to prescribe the conduct of corporations operating within the state, states passed antitrust laws, the first such law being placed on the statute books of Kansas early in 1887.

In that year twelve more states enacted some kind of antitrust law, either by statute or by constitutional amendment, and by 1891 nineteen states had done so.[3] At present all but seven states have prohibitions against attempts to monopolize, restrain trade, or fix prices. A group of

[2] See Milton Handler, *A Study of the Constitution and Enforcement of the Federal Antitrust Laws*, TNEC Monograph 38 (1941), p. 7.

[3] R. E. Curtis, *The Trusts and Economic Control* (New York: McGraw-Hill Book Company, Inc., 1931), p. 116. Authorities are in disagreement as to how many states had passed laws at this time. See discussion of the point in H. R. Seager and C. A. Gulick, *Trust and Corporation Problems* (New York: Harper & Brothers, 1929), p. 342, note.

twenty-seven states have included these prohibitions in their constitutions, while the rest rely on statutes.[4]

PROVISIONS OF STATE LAWS

While the terms of state laws differ, the purposes of their provisions are surprisingly uniform. All arrangements, contracts, agreements, or combinations designed to restrain trade are made unlawful. Most states indicate that the actions condemned are those which would suppress trade with a view to increasing prices or reducing production. These laws likewise forbid any person to enter such an arrangement upon penalty of fine or imprisonment, or both. Typical penalties are fines from $500 to $5,000 and imprisonment up to one year.

Almost all states provide for forfeiture of the charter of a convicted domestic corporation, and ousting of a convicted foreign corporation. Some make officers of the corporation liable along with the corporation. A few provide that anyone injured by an unlawful combination may receive damages equal to three times the sustained loss.

EVALUATION OF STATE ANTITRUST LAWS

Most authorities seem to be agreed that the state laws have not had very great effect in stopping growth of combinations in restraint of trade or breaking up those existing. Few states have attempted to enforce them. Even where attempts have been made to do so, little has been accomplished except the ousting of a few corporations and levying fines against others. So far as meeting the threat to trade which some combinations have presented, the record of the states has not been impressive.

There are many reasons for the impotence of state antitrust regulation. Perhaps the greatest single cause has been the inherent inability of state authorities where interstate activities are concerned. Big combinations have often been nationwide and are seldom found to be operating entirely within a state. A charter can be forfeited only by the state granting it. Nor does fining the corporation solve the fundamental problem much better. Fines have seldom been large enough to deter combination activities, and they have come to be regarded as fees for doing business. Where fines are large, the penalty really falls upon investors, most of whom are innocent of wrongdoing.

The machinery of law enforcement in most states is not adequate to the task of meeting the combination problem. Enforcement is usually left to the attorney general, or at best to some commission with general supervision over corporate activity. Such agencies often have neither the time nor the inclination to enforce the law, especially in the face of the tremendous difficulties encountered. The interstate nature of combination

[4] Marketing Laws Survey, WPA, *State Antitrust Laws* (1940).

activities makes it impracticable, if not impossible, to get complete and accurate information for law-enforcement officers to use.

The Federal Antitrust Laws

When the nature of the combination or trust problem is considered, there can be no doubt that the federal government is the only level of government capable of dealing with it. This fact was recognized almost as soon as the states enacted their antitrust laws and has been well confirmed by the experience of succeeding years.

The federal government entered the field with the enactment of the Sherman Anti-trust Act in 1890. This statute was a product of growing concern over the concentration of business and industry and a public hostility against the giants of the 1880s, such as the Standard Oil and the sugar trusts. Competitors were frozen out of the market, and consumers suffered. Public antagonism was increased by the public-be-damned attitudes of certain aggressive business leaders. The inadequacies of common-law protection and the weakness of state regulation were recognized. Hand in hand with the movement for government control of the railroads emerged pressures that could not be denied. By 1888, all four major political parties were in agreement about the need to curb combinations designed to suppress competition. As a result, the antitrust legislation passed both houses of Congress in 1890 with only one dissenting vote.

THE SHERMAN ACT, 1890

The Sherman Anti-trust Act is not a complicated piece of legislation, for it contains only eight brief sections. Section 1 of the law made illegal "every contract, combination in the form of trust or otherwise, or conspiracy in restraint of trade or commerce among the several States, or with foreign nations." This section was directed against the practices of two or more parties. Section 2 was more inclusive, because it was not limited just to two or more concerns. Section 2 declared that "every person who shall monopolize or attempt to monopolize or combine or conspire with any other person or persons to monopolize any part of the trade or commerce among the several States, or with foreign nations, shall be deemed guilty of a misdemeanor." This section was also broader than section 1, because it was designed to curb monopolies secured by means other than contract, combination, or conspiracy in restraint of trade. A monopoly, regardless of whether it restrained trade, was thereby declared illegal.

No definition was provided of what constituted "restraint of trade" or "monopoly." The vagueness and uncertainty of the law made it necessary for the courts to look to the common law for guidance in interpreting these terms. However, not every restraint of trade or every monopoly was illegal at common law. If reasonable, they were valid. Yet by its terms the Sherman Act outlawed *every* "restraint of trade" and "attempt to monopolize."

THE CLAYTON ACT, 1914

In 1903, Congress established a Department of Commerce and created a Bureau of Corporations within it. The elaborate reports and extensive investigations of this research organization disclosed a number of questionable business practices. Businessmen, as well as enforcing officials of the Sherman Act, could attribute the existence of these practices to the ambiguity in the antitrust law. No one could be certain just what practices were illegal. The Clayton Act was consequently passed in 1914 primarily to strengthen the Sherman Act by prohibiting certain specific monopolistic practices.

Sections 2, 3, 7, and 8 of the Clayton Act, respectively, outlawed price discrimination, exclusive-dealing and tying contracts, intercorporate stock acquisition, and interlocking directorates, where the effect was to lessen competition or tend to create a monopoly.[5] The purpose of this law was to prevent a business from becoming a monopoly by curtailing certain monopolistic practices.

OTHER ANTITRUST LEGISLATION

The Federal Trade Commission Act of 1914 established an independent regulatory commission with powers of investigation and authority, shared with the Anti-trust Division of the Department of Justice, to enforce the prohibitions in the Clayton Act. The act added little to the basic law against monopoly and restraint of trade, since its substantive provisions were directed toward maintaining a certain plan of competitive behavior. Nevertheless, the Federal Trade Commission has done much to thwart monopoly and has furnished the Department of Justice with information for proceeding under the antitrust laws.

A great number of highly specialized antitrust laws have been passed from time to time. Most read the antitrust doctrine into other areas of control or public aid. The Wilson Tariff Act of 1894, as amended in 1913, declared unlawful combinations or conspiracies in restraint of trade by persons engaged in the import of goods into the United States. In 1912, Congress specified that any vessel owned or operated by a concern doing business in violation of the antitrust laws should not be permitted to pass through the Panama Canal. A series of acts required the forfeiture of mineral lands or deposits leased from the United States if subleased to

[5] There are certain refinements and exceptions to these sections which will be discussed in detail in the next chapter.

form part of an unlawful trust, of oil and gas pipeline right of way in Arkansas if any corporation taking advantage of the law was violating the Sherman Act, and of coal deposit lands acquired from the United States in Alaska if controlled by unlawful trusts.

The Communications Act of 1934 declared the antitrust laws applicable to the manufacture and sale of radio apparatus and to interstate or foreign radio communications. In authorizing the formation of corporations to engage in foreign banking and financial operations, the Federal Reserve Act prohibited price fixing in connection with the commodities handled. The Federal Power Act of 1920 banned agreements to limit output of electric energy, restrain trade, or fix, maintain, or increase prices for electric energy or service.

The Public Utility Holding Company Act of 1935 granted the Securities and Exchange Commission supervision over the purchase and sale of utility properties and required the Commission's approval of reorganizations, mergers, and consolidations. The Federal Alcohol Administration Act of 1935 prohibited exclusive outlets and purchasing arrangements with retailers of distilled spirits, wine, and malt beverages. Monopolies and trade restraints in packers and stockyard industries were declared illegal in 1921. By the Fisheries Cooperative Marketing Act, the Secretary of Interior was authorized to issue cease-and-desist orders if commerce is restrained or monopolized in this industry.

The Atomic Energy Act of 1946 directed the Atomic Energy Commission to refuse licenses or to establish conditions where monopolies or restraints of trade might be fostered. Legislation in 1947 declared that a fair proportion of total purchases and contracts for armed forces supplies and services shall be placed with small-business concerns. Another law prohibited the Post Office from granting contracts to persons who have prevented others from bidding on contracts or who engaged in price fixing. In 1949, Congress required consultation with the Attorney General to see whether antitrust laws would be violated by each surplus plant disposal of over $1 million.

EXEMPTIONS FROM THE GENERAL ANTITRUST LAWS

The sweeping character of the prohibition against "every" restraint of trade and attempt to monopolize has led Congress to retrench in a number of specific areas and grant exemptions from the provisions of the antitrust laws. The Clayton Act provided that labor unions should not be held conspiracies in restraint of trade, although many years passed before this exemption was effective.

Other laws extended exemptions to agriculture. The Capper-Volstead Act of 1922 permitted agricultural producers to form cooperative associations to process, handle, and market their products. The Cooperative

Marketing Act of 1926 permitted the dissemination of past, present, and prospective crop, market, statistical, and other information. Marketing agreements entered into by the Secretary of Agriculture with processors, producers, associations of producers, and others engaged in the handling of any agricultural commodity were exempted from the antitrust laws by the Agricultural Marketing Agreement Act of 1937.

In the transportation field, the Shipping Act of 1916 exempted agreements if they were approved by the Maritime Commission (now Maritime Board). Associations entered into by marine-insurance companies were exempted by the Merchant Marine Act of 1920. Exemption has been granted to railroads when consolidation is authorized under the Transportation Act of 1920. The Reed-Bulwinkle Act of 1948 suspended the antitrust laws respecting certain agreements between common carriers, if approved by the Interstate Commerce Commission. The Civil Aeronautics Act of 1938 exempted parties to agreements approved by the Civil Aeronautics Board.

The Webb-Pomerene Act of 1918 exempted export-trade associations, provided that no restraint of domestic trade resulted. In 1943, Congress provided that telegraph-company mergers approved by the Federal Communications Commissions are not subject to the antitrust laws. Insurance companies were exempted by the McCarran Act of 1945, if they are subject to state control.

Judicial Interpretation of the Federal Antitrust Laws

Although the Sherman Act clearly and specifically forbade *every* combination, contract, and conspiracy that restrains trade and *every* attempt to monopolize, its meaning has long been the subject of debate and uncertainty. The role of the courts has been of extraordinary importance in the development of antitrust regulation. Judicial interpretation of the laws has served not only to give them meaning for future use but also to thwart effective enforcement at some times and to place teeth in the laws at other times.

It would be desirable to review the facts and decisions in the leading cases in which the Supreme Court has dealt with the antitrust laws. However, space prohibits such treatment, and this review has been well done elsewhere.[6] For present purposes, it is sufficient to summarize the factors the courts have considered in interpreting the antitrust laws.

[6] See, among others, Handler, *op. cit.*; Walton Hamilton and Irene Till, *Anti-trust in Action*, TNEC Monograph 16 (1940); E. P. Hodges, *The Anti-trust Act and the Supreme Court* (St. Paul, Minn.: West Publishing Company, 1941); Thurman Arnold and others, "The Sherman Antitrust Act and Its Enforcement," 7 *Law and Contemporary Problems* 1–160 (January, 1940).

PURPOSE OF THE LAW TO PROTECT COMMERCE

The first case to reach the Supreme Court under the Sherman Act involved a combination of sugar manufacturers that controlled 98 per cent of the sugar-refining industry in the United States. In 1895, the Court held, with only one dissent, that the combination was in *manufacturing* rather than *commerce* and so did not fall under the Act.[7] The interpretation that manufacturing affected commerce "only incidentally and indirectly" disillusioned those who believed that the Sherman Act might curb large industrial combinations, and the belief became prevalent that it had no real meaning.

Some vitality was given the Sherman Act by decisions involving railroad rate agreements. In the Trans-Missouri Freight Association case, handed down in 1897, a closely divided Supreme Court held that an agreement between railroads whereby rates were fixed was a clear case of direct restraint of trade and was forbidden by the Sherman Act.[8] A like decision was announced in the Joint Traffic Association case the next year.[9] A holding company which had brought about a combination of two large competing railroads was dissolved in 1904.[10] The railroads in these cases were clearly in interstate commerce. However, these cases are a distinct and separate group because they involved franchised companies and the Court took a strict view that the franchise should not be extended beyond the scope of the grant. Thus, these decisions added little to the scope of the Sherman Act to protect interstate commerce.

The first industrial combination to be found illegal under the Sherman Act involved a minor pooling arrangement among six cast-iron-pipe producers.[11] The Court held that, while control of manufacturing was involved, the combination had not limited itself to such control, as had the sugar refiners, but had exerted an immediate and direct effect upon the selling of pipe.

The Supreme Court gradually broadened its interpretation of the commerce power over the years, so that the fact that the antitrust laws are limited to the protection of interstate commerce ceased to be a definitive restraint. With the decisions involving the National Labor Relations Act in 1937,[12] most of the limitations under the commerce power were swept away. For example, at one time the insurance business was not subject to regulation under the Sherman Act.[13] However, in the Polish National Al-

[7] *United States v. E. C. Knight Co.*, 156 U.S. 1 (1895).
[8] *United States v. Trans-Missouri Freight Assn.*, 166 U.S. 290 (1897).
[9] *United States v. Joint Traffic Assn.*, 171 U.S. 505 (1898).
[10] *Northern Securities Co. v. United States*, 193 U.S. 197 (1904).
[11] *Addyston Pipe and Steel Co. v. United States*, 175 U.S. 211 (1899).
[12] See pp. 29–30 and 557–558.
[13] *Paul v. Virginia*, 8 Wall. 168 (1868).

liance case [14] interstate insurance companies were held to be subject to the National Labor Relations Act. Thereafter the interstate insurance business was declared to be subject to the antitrust laws.[15]

It should be noted that, while the trade affected must be interstate or foreign, the persons threatening the freedom of commerce need not be in interstate commerce themselves. If they are in the flow of commerce, or if they do things which have a direct effect upon commerce, their actions may be brought within the federal law. As an illustration, in 1948, the operators of a chain of motion-picture theaters were found guilty of engaging in practices which interfered with commerce even though they themselves were not engaged in commerce.[16]

ONLY UNREASONABLE RESTRAINTS OF TRADE FORBIDDEN

In interpreting the act before 1911, the majority of the Supreme Court held to the position that the antitrust laws forbade *every* agreement, combination, or conspiracy in restraint of trade. In the Trans-Missouri Freight Association case, handed down in 1897, the majority of the Court held that the Sherman Act outlawed all restraints and monopolies directly affecting interstate commerce. Four justices dissented from this position, arguing that the law should have been construed to forbid unreasonable restraints of trade only. They pointed to the fact that only unreasonable restraints of trade were illegal at common law. Again, in 1904, in the Northern Securities case the Court reiterated that the Sherman Act embraced *all* restraints of trade.

The rule of reasonableness was read into the antitrust laws in the Standard Oil decision of 1911.[17] Although the statement of the rule in this case had little if anything to do with the decision—for under any interpretation of the law the Standard Oil Company was clearly a combination in restraint of trade—the dictum did serve to lay the legal framework for an interpretation of the law which has prevailed to the present day. In this case the Supreme Court pointed out that the language of the law must be interpreted in the light of the "existing practical conception of the law of restraint of trade," and that it did not intend to forbid every contract which might have a restraining effect upon trade but only those contracts which, as judged by a "standard of reason," unduly restrained trade.[18] The same interpretation was given the Sherman Act in the American Tobacco case of 1911.[19]

[14] *Polish National Alliance v. NLRB*, 322 U.S. 643 (1944).

[15] *United States v. Southeastern Underwriters' Association*, 322 U.S. 533 (1944).

[16] *Schine Chain Theaters v. United States*, 334 U.S. 110 (1948).

[17] *Standard Oil Co. v. United States*, 221 U.S. 1 (1911).

[18] 221 U.S. 59–60.

[19] *United States v. American Tobacco Co.*, 221 U.S. 106, 179 (1911).

Even though the introduction of a rule of reason may be justifiable as bringing to the law a practical interpretation, it does place words in the antitrust laws which were not there. It makes the determination of reasonable or unreasonable restraints an element of uncertainty in virtually every case. Whether a combination falls under the ban of the antitrust laws has become a matter for determination of the courts in view of facts existing in certain individual cases. This construction has made it necessary for the courts to find standards of reasonableness. The remaining factors discussed in this section are standards the courts have devised.

THE FORM OF THE COMBINATION

Both restraints of trade and attempts to monopolize are prohibited by the Sherman Act. Although Chief Justice White treated restraint of trade as synonymous with monopoly in the Standard Oil case,[20] there are vital distinctions between the two concepts. As has been pointed out in the Socony-Vacuum case,[21] every monopoly may constitute a restraint of trade, but not every restraint of trade is monopolistic. In practice, the doctrine of restraint of trade has been applied principally to loose-knit combinations and agreements, such as trade associations and pooling arrangements, whereas the monopoly concept has been of major importance in the field of mergers and consolidations.

The courts have strictly applied the antitrust laws to loose-knit combinations. Where competition was restrained by agreement, formal or informal, between ostensibly independent competitors, the courts have ruled adversely, even though the cooperators lacked monopoly power. The agreement did not have to cover all firms in the field. Power to affect the market, even in the absence of predatory practices, was applied as a standard and emphasis placed on economic effects rather than on motives.

In marked contrast with their attitude toward loose-knit combinations, where competing businesses have been fused by merger or consolidation, the courts have usually not regarded the consequent disappearance of competition as serious. It is ironic that the cases which resulted in the formulation of the rule of reason were also the cases that ordered the dissolution of two great combinations that dominated their industries—the Standard Oil Company and the American Tobacco Company. Not until the Alcoa case of 1954 [22] was the Sherman Act again successfully applied to a dominant firm falling short of complete monopoly.

The explanation of this striking contrast can be found in the law to be

[20] *United States v. Standard Oil Co.*, 221 U.S. 53 (1911).

[21] *United States v. Socony-Vacuum Oil Co.*, 310 U.S. 150, 226 (1940).

[22] *United States v. Aluminum Co. of America*, 148 F.2d 416 (1945). See discussion below, pp. 339–340.

applied and in the economic effects of dissolution of large combines. The long-standing doctrines of conspiracy were more applicable to loose-knit combinations than to mergers. The traditional legal meaning of monopoly was narrow and difficult to apply. Furthermore, dissolution of a large, well-established consolidation might seriously disrupt the entire industry as well as affect the entire economy. It was far easier to order the end of an agreement or dissolve a trade association.

A great diversity of forms of combinations have been used in the history of American business. Although loose-knit combinations may have been found illegal more frequently, the form of the combination has not been a constant guide in determining whether certain combinations violate the law. Moreover, since 1947 the Supreme Court appeared to abandon the distinction between loose and tight combinations and return to the doctrine of the American Tobacco Company case when it ruled that the Sherman Act "is aimed at substance rather than form." [23]

INTENT OF THE PARTIES

One of the earliest standards the Supreme Court developed in deciding cases under the Sherman Act was the intent of the parties concerned. In the Addyston Pipe Pool case, the Court pointed out as evidence of unlawfulness the fact that the combination had a "direct, immediate and *intended* relation to and effect upon the subsequent contract to sell and deliver the pipe." [24] In the Standard Oil case, it found a "*prima facie* presumption of intent and purpose to maintain the dominancy over the oil industry" as the result of the whole history of the company and the general policy of excluding competitors.[25] The element of intent was likewise pointed out in the American Tobacco Company case.[26] Intent of parties to suppress competition has been an important aspect of numerous other decisions.[27]

Intent has been used to acquit as well as to convict. Although the case did not turn on this finding alone, the Supreme Court found in 1920 that the United States Steel Corporation had not intended to monopolize but had desired to effect economies associated with large size.[28] A cooperative selling agency whose members were independent producers of bituminous coal was upheld by the Court in 1933, partly on the finding that the association intended to remove certain well-recognized evils in the coal

[23] *United States v. Yellow Cab Co.*, 332 U.S. 218, 227 (1947).

[24] *Addyston Pipe & Steel Co. v. United States*, 175 U.S. 243 (1899). (Italics added.)

[25] *United States v. Standard Oil Co.*, 221 U.S. 75 (1911).

[26] 221 U.S. 182 (1911).

[27] See *United States v. Paramount Pictures, Inc.*, 334 U.S. 131 (1948); *United States v. Columbia Steel Co.*, 334 U.S. 495 (1948) for recent examples.

[28] *United States v. U.S. Steel Corporation*, 251 U.S. 417 (1920).

industry and not unduly to restrict competition.[29] A labor union, attempting to unionize a hosiery factory, forcibly took possession of a mill and thereby interrupted an $800,000 shipment of goods. The union was not subject to suit for damages under the Sherman Act, because the delay of shipments was not *intended* to have an effect on prices of hosiery in the market but to compel the company to accede to the union's demands.[30]

The concept of intent is highly unrealistic in many cases, because it emphasizes an ethical criterion rather than the actual economic situation. Certainly, from the point of view of maintaining competition the fact that trade has been restrained or monopolized is basic regardless of the intent of the parties.

OVERT ACTS OF THE PARTIES

Closely related to the factor of intent, but more important, is the consideration of overt acts of parties in achieving or maintaining a market position in violation of the Sherman Act. These two factors usually go hand in hand, and overt acts attest to illegal intent. As the Supreme Court said in the American Tobacco Company case: [31]

> Indeed, the history of the combination is so replete with the doing of acts which it was the obvious purpose of the statute to forbid, so demonstrative of the existence from the beginning of a purpose to acquire dominion and control of the tobacco trade, not by the mere exertion of the ordinary right to contract and to trade, but by methods devised in order to monopolize the trade by driving competitors out of business, which were ruthlessly carried out upon the assumption that to work upon the fears or play upon the cupidity of competitors would make success possible.

The Court went on to enumerate the practices of the tobacco combination by which it had unfairly come to a position of dominance.

Unfair and suppressive acts were used as the basis for finding many combinations unlawful under the antitrust laws. This was especially true of cases in the lower federal courts.[32] Only a few examples can be mentioned here. In many instances, a combination has gained dominant position by buying out competitors and forcing them to agree not to compete for long times in the future. At times, rather liberal payments have been made by a combination for a competitor's business. But even where this has been true, monopolistic groups have often been able to force sale

[29] *Appalachian Coals, Inc. v. United States*, 288 U.S. 344 (1933).

[30] *Apex Hosiery Co. v. Leader*, 310 U.S. 469, 500–502 (1940).

[31] *United States v. American Tobacco Co.*, 221 U.S. 181–182 (1911).

[32] See, for example, *United States v. Eastman Kodak Co.*, 226 Fed. 62 (1915); *United States v. E. I. DuPont de Nemours & Co.*, 188 Fed. 127 (1911); *Patterson v. United States* (National Cash Register case), 222 Fed. 599 (1915).

by a competitor under threat of destructive competition. Trade wars have been promoted by certain groups in order to force competitors to withdraw from the field. Buying up plants and then closing them down as a means of controlling supply have also indicated attempts to monopolize. When combination actions are undertaken and then attempts are made to cover up these operations through dummy corporations and competitors, the natural inference is that restraint of trade is intended. Finally, there is the whole group of unfair competitive practices with which the Federal Trade Commission has come to deal, which may denote the development of a combination in restraint of trade.

There are cases, however, where a large company has been developed by the aid of acts designed to gain dominance for it and yet where the courts have not held these acts grounds for finding the combination guilty of antitrust-law violations. The United States Steel Corporation had admittedly engaged from 1901 to 1911 in certain practices aimed at curtailing competition. Before 1907 it had led in obtaining cooperation among steel producers by pools, associations, and various trade meetings. For several years after 1907, the famous Gary dinners were used to effect a gentlemen's agreement in the trade. But six months before the government brought a suit under the antitrust laws, these activities were abandoned. Finding that the abandonment was not in prophecy or dread of the suit and that the corporation was not engaging in such acts at the time of the suit, the United States Supreme Court did not allow these acts to be taken as presumptive evidence of restraint of trade.[33]

The existence of overt acts does not make a conclusive case of restraint of trade. If such practices are being engaged in at the time of the suit, doubtless they would have great weight in determining the result. If, however, a combination is to be freed from the antitrust laws merely because it has discontinued practices regarded as tending toward monopoly, the laws might be circumvented unless prosecution can be started while the combining or monopolizing is taking place. But this does not seem to be the necessary import of the United States Steel case. In this case, and in others where past overt acts have been overlooked, there were other reasons why the Court was unwilling to order dissolution. Where competition has not been stamped out and where the combination has appeared to be economically justified, some trusts have been looked upon as "good" trusts.

THE PROBLEM OF SIZE

In the Northern Securities Company case, before the introduction of the rule of reason, the Supreme Court held that the mere existence of a large combination with power over a great part of trade constituted a

[33] *United States v. U.S. Steel Corp.*, 251 U.S. 444–445 (1920).

"menace to, and a restraint upon, that freedom of commerce which Congress intended to recognize and protect."[34] Yet, after the rule of reason was adopted, its application brought into being the principle that mere size is not an offense under the antitrust laws.

The first case in which the Supreme Court enunciated this principle was that in which it refused to find the United States Steel Corporation a combination in restraint of trade.[35] Two important principles stand out in this case. The first is the very significant one that under a reasonable construction of the antitrust laws mere size is not an offense. The second has to do with the introduction of the idea of a "good" trust. A "good" trust is apparently one which has abandoned its objectionable practices and which, at the same time, is efficiently conceived, so that breaking it up would actually cause a loss to the public. The notion that the public may have an interest in the maintenance of a large and efficient organization is so important that it might well be treated as a separate factor which the courts have come to recognize in antitrust-law enforcement.

In the years following the decision concerning the United States Steel Corporation, the Supreme Court has had a number of occasions to repeat its stand. There is evidence that this concept of size and "goodness" has been a basis for the courts' allowing the existence of enterprises which are economically and ethically defensible. In the International Harvester Company case, in spite of the fact that the company controlled 64 per cent of the harvesting-machinery business, the Court held that trade was not unduly suppressed and implied that it was not in the public interest to dissolve the company.[36] Similar conclusions were reached in 1936 in a case involving the manufacture of women's dresses.[37]

In 1945, an important break was made from this principle. In the

[34] *Northern Securities Co. v. United States*, 193 U.S. 327 (1904). Typical of early court opinion is the statement of a lower federal court in *United States v. Patten*, 187 Fed. 664 (1911). At p. 672 the court declared that "trade and commerce are 'monopolized' within the meaning of the federal statute, when, as the result of efforts to that end, such power is obtained that a few persons acting together can control the prices of a commodity moving in interstate commerce. It is not necessary that the power thus obtained should be exercised. Its existence is sufficient."

[35] *United States v. U.S. Steel Corporation*, 251 U.S. 417 (1920). In 1916, a lower federal court decided in favor of the American Can Company on pretty much the same grounds as those used by the Supreme Court to uphold the United States Steel Corporation. In *United States v. American Can Co.*, 230 Fed. 859 (1916), the court showed a reluctance to disturb the organization of the American Can Company, merely because it was big or had been developed by questionable practices, since abandoned. The Court frankly stated that it felt the company was an efficient organization doing an excellent public service.

[36] *United States v. International Harvester Co.*, 274 U.S. 693 (1927).

[37] *Filene's Sons Co. v. Fashion Originator's Guild of America*, 14 F. Supp. 353 (1936).

Alcoa [38] case the Circuit Court held that "to have combined ninety per cent of the producers of ingot would have been to 'monopolize' the ingot market." [39] There, mere existence of this power was sufficient basis to find the company in violation of the Sherman Act, regardless of how the power was exercised. Evidence of specific intent was also regarded as unnecessary. To read the Sherman Act as "demanding any 'specific' intent, makes nonsense of it, for no monopolist monopolizes unconscious of what he is doing." Guilt of monopolizing was found in the fact that Alcoa was able "to embrace each new opportunity as it opened, and to face every newcomer with new capacity already geared into a great organization, having the advantage of experience, trade connections and the elite of personnel." The court refused to limit their interpretation of "exclusion" of competitors to "manoeuvres not honestly industrial, but actuated solely by a desire to prevent competition," because such interpretation "would emasculate the Act; would permit just such consolidations as it was designed to prevent." [40]

The next year the Supreme Court used this new criterion in the new American Tobacco Company case.[41] This case differed from the Alcoa case, which involved only one company, because it was concerned with a group of three independent companies. The Court ruled that "no formal agreement is necessary to constitute an unlawful conspiracy. The material consideration in determining whether a monopoly exists is not that prices are raised and that competition is actually excluded, but that power exists to raise prices or to exclude competition when it is desired to do so." The tactics of American Tobacco, Reynolds, and Liggett and Myers made competition difficult for smaller companies. Moreover, the Court said: "Neither proof of exertion of the power to exclude nor proof of actual exclusion of existing or potential competitors is essential to sustain a charge of monopolization under the Sherman Act."

If the precedents of the Alcoa and American Tobacco cases are followed, the rule of reason will be markedly modified. The Sherman Act will be directed against the *power to abuse* rather than the *abuse of power.*

[38] *United States v. Aluminum Co. of America*, 148 F.2d 416 (1945). The case was originally tried in the District Court for the Southern District of New York. The Supreme Court granted a writ of certiorari, but because of lack of a quorum of six justices qualified to hear the case, it certified the appeal to the Circuit Court for the Second Circuit under a 1944 amendment to the Judiciary Act.

[39] 148 F.2d 416, at 429. Actually, Alcoa had control of only 66 per cent of *all* ingot, virgin and secondary, although it did control 90 per cent of virgin ingot. The court emphasized the 90 per cent monopoly, but a sounder case economically could be built in regard to the 66 per cent position, since virgin and secondary ingot are perfect substitutes.

[40] 148 F.2d 429–432.

[41] *United States v. American Tobacco Co.*. 328 U.S. 781 (1946).

Intent and overt acts of parties will assume less significance as attention is directed to situations in which one or a few sellers, whether or not they agree to act in concert, have size and market power enough to dominate.[42] What size and how much market power remain unknown quantities. Since the word "monopoly" was left undefined in the Sherman Act, its only meaning, pending clarification by Congress, is the degree of control the Supreme Court deems unlawful.

EFFECTS UPON PRICE

One of the factors which has bearing upon the finding of antitrust violation has been the effect of a combination agreement upon price. In the early cases on railroad rate agreements and the Addyston Pipe Pool, the Supreme Court emphasized that agreements to foreclose competition and fix prices were clearly forbidden by the Sherman Act. The importance of price fixing by combination methods as an indication of violation was also pointed out in cases involving trade-association activities [43] and resale-price maintenance.[44]

Price fixing may present conclusive evidence of an unlawful restraint of trade, even though the resulting prices are reasonable. In a case in 1927, the Supreme Court held that a restraint of trade does not become reasonable merely because the prices so fixed are reasonable.[45] Pointing out that the Sherman Act was based upon the assumption that maintenance of competition is desirable public policy, the Court declared that the important thing is the restraint of competition and the power to fix prices

[42] However, the Supreme Court refused to declare unlawful the acquisition of assets of "the largest independent steel fabricator on the West Coast" by a subsidiary of U.S. Steel. *United States v. Columbia Steel Co.*, 334 U.S. 495 (1948). Justice Douglas, in dissent, called this the most important antitrust case in years. He said (at pp. 536–537): "We have here the problem of bigness. Its lesson should by now have been burned into our memory by Brandeis. The *Curse of Bigness* shows how size can become a menace—both industrial and social. . . . Size in steel is the measure of the power of a handful of men over our economy. That power can be utilized with lightning speed. It can be benign or it can be dangerous. The philosophy of the Sherman Act is that it should not exist."

[43] See, for example, *American Column and Lumber Co. v. United States*, 257 U.S. 377 (1921). At p. 409 the Court said, "These quotations are sufficient to show beyond discussion that the purpose of the organization, and especially of the frequent meetings, was to bring about a concerted effort to raise prices regardless of cost or merit, and so was unlawful. . . ."

[44] In *Dr. Miles Medical Co. v. John D. Park and Sons Co.*, 220 U.S. 373 (1911), the Supreme Court condemned resale-price contracts as involving a restraint of trade, primarily because of an attempt to fix dealer prices of an article which was in the channels of commerce. This doctrine has been somewhat modified. See discussion below, p. 393.

[45] *United States v. Trenton Potteries Co.*, 273 U.S. 392 (1927). See also *United States v. Bausch & Lomb Optical Co.*, 322 U.S. 707 (1944).

and that what is a reasonable price at one time may become an unreasonable price later.

The importance of price fixing as denoting unlawful restraint of trade was again emphasized by the Supreme Court in 1940. In a case involving price-fixing activities by a combination of oil refiners, the Court held that the artificial fixing of prices by a combination of private parties cannot be justified under the antitrust laws, even if such action seems desirable to remove competitive abuses or evils.[46] The Court pointed out that it had "consistently and without deviation adhered to the principle that price-fixing agreements are unlawful per se under the Sherman Act" and that the reasonableness of the prices so fixed is of no legal importance, since "those who fixed reasonable prices today would perpetrate unreasonable prices tomorrow. . . ."[47]

One of the most important and recent rulings against price fixing was handed down in the Cement Institute case of 1948.[48] In this case the Court declared that the basing-point system constituted conspiracy to restrain competition in violation of section 5 of the Federal Trade Commission Act outlawing unfair methods of competition. By the basing-point system, a company quotes delivered prices so that the prices all consumers pay in a given area are identical, regardless of the origin of the goods bought. The price consists of the factory price plus a transportation charge, but the latter, instead of being the actual cost to deliver the goods from the factory to the consumer, corresponds to the cost from a designated production center, known as the "basing point," to the buyer. Sometimes several basing points may be used. Thus, the consumer is actually paying a phantom freight, while all sellers in the area are assured that no one will have a competitive advantage because his factory is located closer to the market.

JUDICIAL INTERPRETATION: CONCLUSIONS

In spite of the apparent ban in the Sherman Act against *every* restraint of trade and attempt to monopolize, the rule of reason set the pattern for the judicial interpretation of the antitrust laws throughout most of their history. Under this doctrine, restraints of trade and attempts to monopolize as such were not illegal, unless intent to monopolize or abuse of power were proved. For example, the Supreme Court required proof of intent and overt acts in the United States Steel case. However, the rule of reason

[46] *United States v. Socony-Vacuum Oil Co.*, 310 U.S. 150 (1940). See also, *Kiefer-Stewart Co. v. Seagram & Sons*, 340 U.S. 211 (1951).

[47] *United States v. Socony-Vacuum Oil Co.*, 310 U.S. 150, 218 (1940).

[48] *FTC v. Cement Institute*, 333 U.S. 683. Actually, this case found the multiple-basing-point system illegal. The single-basing-point system had been invalidated three years earlier in *Corn Products Refining Company v. FTC*, 324 U.S. 726 (1945), as price discrimination in violation of the Robinson-Patman amendments to section 2 of the Clayton Act.

did not apply in cases where there was conspiracy to fix prices, as in the Addyston, Trenton Potteries, Socony-Vacuum, and Kiefer-Stewart decisions. In such instances, price fixing was illegal per se.

Recent judicial interpretations are revising these principles. A new restraint-of-trade concept is the principle of implied conspiracies. Originally conspiracies were not illegal unless there was actual agreement to conspire. Voluntarily following the price leader was no offense. However, recently the power of three tobacco companies was ruled illegal in the new American Tobacco case, even though the companies did not conclude a formal agreement.[49] The courts are coming to view similar marketing policies of firms in a few-firm market resulting in undue restraints of trade as illegal, even though the classical requisite of conspiracy or agreement is not present.[50] Thus, conscious parallelism of action may be illegal in oligopolistic markets. The courts need only determine (1) whether there existed similar or parallel action, (2) whether the firms were aware of each other's adherence to such marketing policies, and (3) whether the marketing or price policies and their resulting market conditions were noncompetitive.

Judicial thinking is also shifting to the position that monopolization per se is illegal, just as is conspiracy to fix prices. This attitude was implicit in the Pullman Company case, a district court decision.[51] In the Alcoa and new American Tobacco cases the courts came near to holding that size and market power in and of themselves were offenses. The distinction between monopolistic power and its exercise was regarded as "purely formal." The possession of power rather than abuse of power was determining. Indeed, a newspaper publisher was found guilty of the attempt to monopolize in 1951 when the Court held that it was unnecessary to show that the attempt was successful.[52]

Enforcement of the Antitrust Laws

Enforcement of the antitrust laws devolves primarily upon the Department of Justice. The Department has sole responsibility for the enforcement of the Sherman Act, shares concurrent jurisdiction with the Federal

[49] The first case to abandon the requirement of some plan or organization activity as proof of illegal restraint of trade was *Bigelow v. RKO Radio Pictures, Inc.*, 150 F.2d 877 (1945), reviewed as to proof of damages, 327 U.S. 251 (1946). Consciously parallel action in restraint of trade reached complete acceptance as a legal rule in *Milgram v. Loew's, Inc.*, 192 F.2d 579 (1951), certiorari denied, 343 U.S. 929 (1952).

[50] For a detailed discussion, see Michael Conant, "Consciously Parallel Action in Restraint of Trade," 38 *Minnesota Law Review* 797 (1954).

[51] *United States v. Pullman Co.*, 50 F. Supp. 123 (1943).

[52] *Lorain Journal Co. v. United States*, 342 U.S. 143 (1951).

Trade Commission to enforce the substantive provisions of the Clayton Act, and has supplementary responsibilities under thirty-seven other acts.

THE ANTI-TRUST DIVISION

The purposes of the Sherman Act were deemed sufficiently comparable to the traditional obligation of government to prosecute crimes against the public and to vindicate private rights which might be invaded that the use of the traditional techniques for law enforcement seemed warranted. No special investigative body was set up, and no special investigative powers were conferred. The prosecuting task was assigned to the Department of Justice with authority to proceed either by criminal prosecution or by suits in equity.

The courts are authorized to entertain private suits by those who might be injured by illegal acts and, upon proper showing, to assess triple damages on the offending party. Property of an unlawful combination being transported across state lines is subject to seizure.[53]

An antitrust case has its beginnings in a complaint. Although the Antitrust Division may initiate a case, it is largely dependent upon private information for its knowledge of violations of the law. The great bulk of these complaints come from businessmen who feel they have been injured by acts prohibited under the law. The Division, in cooperation with the Federal Bureau of Investigation, conducts an investigation which, where appropriate, leads to criminal or civil action. The criminal action may be instituted in lieu of or in addition to the civil action.

Criminal action. A person found guilty as a result of a criminal prosecution may be fined $5,000, or imprisoned for a term of one year, or both. Rather than undergo a trial, a person may enter a plea of *nolo contendere*. If this plea is accepted by the court, the person makes no admission of guilt but concedes that the court may impose a penalty and satisfies the law simply by paying a fine.

Down to July, 1950, the Anti-trust Division had brought 507 criminal cases as compared to 551 civil cases. Seldom has a case resulted in imprisonment of the guilty party. Penal sentences were imposed in only 31 cases by July, 1946. Of these, 13 involved labor unions, 2 had to do with war spies, 15 with business racketeering, and only 1 case with businessmen who had run afoul of the law. The latter was the Trenton Potteries case. Short sentences were pronounced on eight individuals, but they were suspended and the terms were never served.[54]

[53] Up to 1939, this section has been used only three times, and in all cases the issue was settled out of court before the case went to trial. Hamilton and Till, *op. cit.*, p. 8.

[54] House of Representatives, Committee on Small Business, *United States versus Economic Concentration and Monopoly*, Staff Report to the Monopoly Subcommittee, 79th Cong. (1949), p. 257.

Although less sparingly used, the fines imposed have not been severe. By July, 1946, fines had been imposed in 245 cases. The earliest of these amounted to only $200. The largest was the $638,000 fine levied against the Protective Fur Dressers Corporation in 1936.[55]

The purpose of the Sherman Act is to prevent monopolistic practices and restore competition. Criminal penalties have not proved to be adequate sanctions. Imprisonment is a nonexistent threat. Because of their infrequency and small size, the fines offer no effective deterrent to the businessman who may profit from his illegal action far more than the fine he pays. But most important of all, as the Justice Department is frank to admit, criminal action is not an effective means of restoring competition where preponderant economic power already exists.[56] The real punishment tends to be the stigma of the indictment, for no respectable citizen wishes to have his name tainted by the formal charge of crime. But since punitive action does not bring about economic changes, remedial action through suits in equity is necessary.

Civil procedures. Three civil procedures are available to the Anti-trust Division: the injunction; the consent decree; and dissolution, divestiture, and divorcement proceedings.

Attempts to restrain trade or monopolize may be enjoined. However, since the aim of the injunction is to prevent a future recurrence of illegal activities, it may not operate as a positive deterrent. Unless disobeyed after issuance, an injunction never punishes and may leave the wrongdoer free to repeat his action when the injunction is lifted. Moreover, it applies only to the parties named in the suit.

Nevertheless, the House Small Business Committee has reported that the antitrust decree [57]

> . . . has become in effect an instrument of administrative control. As the official authors of the decree the courts have tended to be more liberal with its terms than they have with the cease-and-desist orders of the Federal Trade Commission. A large measure of affirmative relief can usually be written into a decree if this is necessary—as it usually is—to provide an adequate remedy for the situation under attack. Positive requirements of a far-reaching character can be placed on the offending parties. It is not too much to say that it is in these civil decrees issued under the Sherman Act that the real protection of the American public against monopoly lies today.

A novel device that was not provided for in the Sherman Act has attained widespread use. This is the consent decree, which is a quasi-

[55] *Ibid.*, pp. 258–261.

[56] *Ibid.*, p. 35.

[57] House of Representatives, Select Committee on Small Business, *Antitrust Law Enforcement by the Federal Trade Commission and the Antitrust Division, Department of Justice--A Preliminary Report*, H. Rept. 3236, 81st Cong., 2d Sess. (1951), p. 62.

administrative device whereby the Anti-trust Division can achieve civil relief from violations of the antitrust laws upon agreement with the defendants to the terms of the decree. The use of this device dates from 1906, when the Otis Elevator Company consented to have a judgment entered against it. Since that time, approximately one-half of the civil cases have ended in victory for the government by consent. This percentage is even larger if only cases filed within the last ten years are considered.[58] Walton Hamilton describes it as an instrument that [59]

> . . . has a sweep which no process of law could ever impart. It can go beyond sheer prohibition; it can attempt to shape remedies to the requirements of industrial order. . . . It can reach beyond the persons in legal combat to comprehend all the parties to the industry. . . . It can, unlike a decree emerging from litigation, take into account the potential consequences of its terms.

The most extreme civil action the Anti-trust Division may bring is dissolution, divestiture, and divorcement proceedings. The Anti-trust Division reports that between 1890 and 1948 some eighty-seven judgments have been entered containing provisions for dissolution, divestiture, and divorcement.[60] In an increasing number of cases in recent years, the Division has come to the conclusion that the only permanent relief to be secured is through the decentralization of economic power.

However, the courts have used this technique cautiously, and the cases in which it was employed have not on the whole produced the desired results. Firms found guilty of possessing and exercising monopoly power have often escaped dissolution. However, others such as the motion-picture companies [61] have felt the sharp ax of dissolution. As one authority put it, in spite of "many legal triumphs, economic relief has generally been unimpressive." [62] Remedial actions have in most instances failed to lessen concentration and to restore effective competition. The Standard Oil and American Tobacco cases did not lessen concentration or restore competition as much as had been hoped, although they certainly forced the existence of several firms where one had been dominant. Among the recent illustrations might be listed the Alcoa, National Lead,[63] and Pullman cases [64] where the results have not been extensive.

[58] *Ibid.*, p. 66.

[59] Hamilton and Till, *op. cit.*, p. 88.

[60] Antitrust Division, Department of Justice, *Judgments Containing Provisions for Dissolution, Divestiture, and Divorcement in Cases Filed from July 2, 1890 to March 25, 1948* (1948).

[61] *United States v. Paramount Pictures, Inc.*, 334 U.S. 131 (1948). This case has been termed the greatest economic victory in sixty years of antitrust enforcement.

[62] Walter Adams, "Dissolution, Divorcement, Divestiture: The Pyrrhic Victories of Anti-trust," 27 *Indiana Law Journal* 5 (Fall, 1951).

[63] *United States v. National Lead Co.*, 332 U.S. 319 (1947).

[64] *United States v. Pullman Co.*, 53 F. Supp. 908 (1944).

The reluctance of the courts to order drastic reorganizations is usually attributed to their unwillingness to disturb property relations. Another explanation may be that judges lack sufficient training in economic affairs. Certainly, the Securities and Exchange Commission, more skilled in economics, was able to bring about a drastic reorganization of the public-utility industry under the Holding Company Act of 1935. The courts may also properly fear the results of dissolution in terms of removing from the economic scene some large firms which have contributed heavily to the high productivity and mass distribution of the American economy.

Evaluation. In addition to the inadequacies of sanctions and the ineffectiveness of the relief available under the Sherman Act, there have been other weaknesses in its enforcement.

Historically, one of the major reasons for enforcement failures was the lack of sympathy with the purposes of the Act on the part of the officials who were responsible for its administration. During the administrations of Presidents Harrison, Cleveland, and McKinley, only eighteen antitrust actions were brought. The Attorney General from 1893 to 1895 was openly hostile to the law. When Theodore Roosevelt became President he declared himself to be a trust buster, but only forty-four suits were instituted under his administration. Seventy-eight suits were begun during Taft's administration, as compared with only sixty-two during the entire prior period, but Taft was deeply opposed to a criminal suit until the possibilities of equity had been fully explored.

Wilson's intention to enforce the law was interrupted by World War I. During the 1920s the Act fell into disuse, and it was virtually abandoned during the Depression and the period of the National Recovery Administration. The Act was revived by Thurman Arnold in 1939, and since then, except for war years, it has been enforced more vigorously than at any time in history. Between 1890 and 1939, 443 cases were instituted. During Arnold's incumbency as Attorney General between 1939 and 1943, 342 cases were instituted. In 1951, 48 cases were started; in 1952, 36; and in 1954, 181. As the Small Business Committee has commented: "Until recently the enforcement of the Sherman Act was largely a matter of a policeman looking the other way." [65]

Given the desire to enforce the Sherman Act, another weakness the Anti-trust Division has always suffered has been a lack of sufficient appropriations and personnel. Prior to 1935, the appropriation of the Division never exceeded $300,000 and frequently was only $100,000. The number of attorneys on the staff never exceeded twenty-five. Beginning in the late 1930s appropriations passed $1 million, and by 1950 and 1951 they reached a high of $3.75 million.

Even these funds are not adequate for thorough enforcement. For ex-

[65] House of Representatives, Committee on Small Business, *op. cit.*, p. 4.

ample, in the Hartford-Empire case the Division estimates that the defendants spent considerably over $2 million, whereas the entire appropriation for the Division was less than $2 million. The Division had five attorneys working on the case against approximately thirty for the defense. In the case against Paramount Pictures the Division had ten lawyers pitted against fifty. And in the Socony-Vacuum case the odds were 5 to 103. A few big cases could easily tie up the entire Division for years. The Division estimates it is able to take action on only about 20 per cent of the justifiable complaints which come to it.[66]

Another consequence is delay in processing major cases. The United States Steel case took nine years, the International Harvester case nine years, and the Alcoa case was in the jurisdiction of the courts eighteen years.

More generous appropriations alone are not enough. The money must be spent wisely, i.e., in the prosecution of cases which will make significant contributions in realizing the basic objectives of the antitrust laws. The Division must have a coordinated plan for spending its appropriations on cases that will yield maximum returns in eliminating monopoly and reducing undesirably concentrated economic power. One of the problems of the Anti-Trust Division is that its efforts have sometimes been expended in tackling large companies whose size makes a publicly interesting target rather than in prosecuting more clear-cut cases of monopoly and restraint of trade.

In conjunction with this factor is the lack of a suitable machinery for the detection of violations. The present restriction of investigation to complaints as they are received is not adequate. Moreover, the availability of the grand jury and the power to subpoena books and records leads too often to criminal prosecution, since equally effective investigatory procedures are not available in civil actions.

THE FEDERAL TRADE COMMISSION

The Federal Trade Commission derives its antitrust responsibilities from the Federal Trade Commission Act and the Clayton Act. Only about 15 per cent of all formal cases in which the Commission issues complaints are antitrust cases.

The procedures of the Commission will be described in the next chapter. Here brief comment is made in evaluation of its antimonopoly work. The Commission has failed to accomplish one of the primary reasons for its establishment—avoidance of the lengthy procedures of the courts. Of the 143 formal complaints settled in 1950, one-fourth had been pending for five years or more.[67] While it is true that the Commission lacks the men

[66] *Ibid.*, pp. 47–48.

[67] House of Representatives, Select Committee on Small Business, *op. cit.*, p. 19.

and money to handle its heavy case load, the House Small Business Committee reports that the principal reason for delay has been bad commission management.[68]

The Commission has also been criticized for giving little attention to the most serious areas of concentration. The reason for this deficiency, the Committee feels, is that the Federal Trade Commission operates as a kind of court, handling complaints as they come to it, rather than initiating action in areas where its investigations reveal the need for action.[69]

Another complaint concerning the Commission's enforcement of the antitrust laws has been that it provides little opportunity for the businessman to receive a fair and impartial trial.[70] Commissioner Lowell B. Mason has commented: "We lost the confidence of industry. We were reviled and berated by House and Senate. We allowed our staff to roam the halls of Congress, spreading discord, discontent and disrespect for our vain pretensions." [71]

Public Policy and the Trust Problem

In the previous chapter, the decline of competition in American industry was noted. If the antitrust laws were designed to restore competition in the traditional sense of many firms competing aggressively in the market place without restraint on entry or withdrawal, they must be regarded as having been ineffective. The Federal Trade Commission reported in 1946 that the ". . . present, and still growing, concentration of economic power in the United States constitutes today's greatest domestic challenge to the American theory of competitive enterprise. . . ." [72] And the Justice Department characterizes the monopoly problem as "more serious and widespread than at any time since the passage of the Sherman Act in 1890." [73]

While the law has been effective in smashing a few of the larger monopolistic combinations and has certainly acted as a severe brake on many other combinations, it has not been able to enforce competition of the kind traditionally thought to be characteristic of the American competitive system. In other words, the law has not been able to halt the growth of large-size firms. Moreover, there are doubtless many restraints not related to concentration or size which the antitrust laws have been

[68] *Ibid.*, p. 21. [69] *Ibid.*, p. 22.

[70] W. Simon, "The Case against the Federal Trade Commission," 19 *University of Chicago Law Review* 335 (Winter, 1952).

[71] Quoted in *ibid.*, p. 336. Such criticisms by Mason led to a demand by the National Federation of Independent Business for his removal. *New York Times*, May 18, 1952.

[72] House of Representatives, Committee on Small Business, *op. cit.*, p. 144.

[73] *Ibid.*, p. 209.

unable to reach, some of which have been placed beyond the purview of the laws by numerous exemptions, so that in the sense of combinations in restraint of trade or attempts to monopolize, a trust problem still exists.

CONFUSION OF SIZE AND MONOPOLY

In reviewing the experience of the United States in antitrust enforcement, one is struck with the confusion which exists between size and monopoly. There has been a persistent undercurrent of thought that the growth of large business enterprises necessarily results in the destruction of competition, and such matters as economic power and identical prices are taken as obvious evidences of the passing of competition.

There is no doubt but that there have been material changes in the manifestations of competition, particularly in industries dominated by large firms or in industries where firms have been able to gain advantages through product differentiation. There is also no doubt that size, combination, cooperation, and even collusion have on occasion been used to destroy competition and gain monopolistic advantages. However, the mere fact of size, fewness of firms in an industry, or product differentiation does not necessarily mean the passing of the competitive system. Large firms can and do compete as aggressively with each other as small firms. Industries with few firms can be as strongly competitive as those with many firms; one of the authors, who has studied several oligopolistic industries from the inside, has examined them too closely to agree that fewness of firms necessarily makes for competitive sterility. On the contrary, such firms often recognize that their continuance in business on a profitable basis depends upon aggressive product development and promotion, reduction of cost, and expansion of markets. The fact that the competition does not manifest itself in day-by-day price battles is in itself no evidence that the competition is nonexistent or unreal.

Size is, therefore, in and of itself no proof of the lack of competition. Where effective competition exists and where size becomes a prerequisite for efficient development, production, and marketing, it is difficult to see how the purposes of social welfare would be served by limiting size. The large firms in the chemical, oil-processing and -marketing, and automobile industries are cases at point. Not only does the march of progress in new products, the efficiency of production, and the ready supply of goods to the market attest to the advantages of size in these and other industries, but the experience of these large firms in defense production during and since World War II also dramatizes their social desirability.

The real question is whether size leads to such trade restraints that society is paying a higher price, both in costs and freedom of the individual, for the output of the large firm than would be necessary under a system of more and smaller firms. Even if some of the larger firms should be able to exert monopolistic power and should take advantage of this ability, there might be question as to the social desirability of dissolving them and enforcing competition. In the public-utility field the inherent advantages of monopoly have been often recognized. Indubitably in other fields the large firm or even a combination of firms approaching monopoly might be justified upon grounds of economies of size and elimination of wastes of competition.

On the other hand, if left unregulated, large combinations may tend to keep the economic system from operating effectively. If prices are kept at inflexible levels or are fixed to bring monopoly profits, capital and labor resources may not be utilized efficiently, because constant pressure on the part of competing producers and competing buyers is likely to be required in order to force operations at lowest cost and production most wanted by purchasers.

If large firms or combinations of firms do have economic advantages in certain fields, it may be well to allow them to continue, *if* the lower costs of large size can be passed on to consumers. This is a problem for public policy. If the stimuli of competition do not exist, it would seem that the only alternative would be to erect safeguards in the form of government controls. This would not mean any wholesale regulation of industry in the pattern of public-utility control, for there would be few businesses of which it would be true both that size was socially desirable and that competition was ineffectual.

ALTERNATIVES IN GOVERNMENT TRUST POLICY

If the complete enforcement of competition outside the field of business affected with a public interest were desired, the government would seem to have the power to obtain it. This would mean a much more restrictive law and a much more vigorous enforcement than have been the case. In effect, the law and its enforcement would have to be drawn so as to obtain the virtual atomization of industry. Each industry would have to be broken up into such small units that competition would be the natural result, and attempts of these units to cooperate in any way would have to be forbidden or regulated.

As a matter of fact, there are those who believe that the proper government policy is rigorous enforcement of an antitrust law which would restore competition by making business units small and independent.[74] The attitude of this group is that competition is necessary for the maintenance of a free capitalistic system, and that unless competition is en-

[74] See, for example, the discussion of the ideas of former Justice Brandeis in A. T. Mason, *The Brandeis Way* (Princeton, N.J.: Princeton University Press, 1938), and the attitude of the Federal Trade Commission in *Investigation of Concentration of Economic Power,* part 5, pp. 1647–1656 (1939).

forced totalitarian controls will result. Some in this group would admit that where economies of combination or monopoly are so great as to be in the social interest, legal monopolies might be allowed, but they believe that these should be kept within as narrow limits as possible. Some of those who subscribe to this view declare that an arbitrary limitation must be placed upon size, the percentage possibly varying with the industry but being small enough to ensure competition.

An alternative policy is to give up antitrust law enforcement as such and to substitute self-regulation of industry along the pattern of the codes under the National Industrial Recovery Act. This self-regulation would involve provisions dealing with price and production policies of all kinds and would be a recognition that competition is no longer practical or desirable. To protect the public interest, however, such schemes of so-called self-regulation would seem to necessitate government supervision of the content of codes and perhaps extensive government regulation as a part of the codes themselves.

Another possible policy is to keep the antitrust laws much as they are but to set up means for determining whether a combination is in reasonable or unreasonable restraint of trade. If believed to be wise, some definition of reasonableness might be determined by a commission in view of the facts in each case of combination; apparently the concept of reasonableness would be dependent upon the social good. If a combination could effect economies, took no advantage of its position to exploit consumers, and engaged in no practices regarded by business as unfair, it might be a reasonable combination. This kind of policy would be similar to that now followed, except that the determination of reasonableness would be left to a commission rather than to the courts, and social welfare would become a definite hallmark of reasonableness.

It has occasionally been suggested that the concept of businesses affected with a public interest be extended to all fields of business in which effective competition has become impracticable. In other words, by this policy monopoly or quasi monopoly would be tolerated or encouraged. To protect the public, however, these industries would be subject to regulation of prices and service by some government agency, much in the way railroads are regulated by the Interstate Commerce Commission. This would mean widespread extension of government control. While it may be an ultimate solution, it would present tremendous problems of administration. The difficulty of solving price- and service-regulation problems has already been noted in the chapters on railroads and public utilities. If this sort of control were extended to many more businesses, the job of continuous supervision of many thousand firms would be exceedingly complex.

Another approach which has gained some favor is based upon the belief that there is no single standard of competitive behavior suitable to all industries alike and that the antitrust laws should undertake an industry-by-industry approach. This policy would admit that free and complete competition can hardly be obtained in all industries and that, even if industries could be atomized, the diseconomies resulting might not be in the public interest.

The foundation of this suggested policy is to make a realistic study of each industry and, on the basis of the economic situation in the industry, decide what degree of competition is feasible or economically and socially desirable. Where it does not seem wise to require free competition, the industry would be placed under some kind of government supervision, to an extent necessary to protect the public. In industries in which competition can be restored by removing artificial restraints without loss of economies of size or combination, competition would be enforced through strict application of antimonopoly or anticombination laws.

In view of the economic nature of the forces behind the present decline of competition, as discussed in the previous chapter, the last approach seems to have much in its favor. Competition has not declined simply because grasping combinations, by fair means or foul, have driven the independents out of an industry. Underlying economic developments and the economic forces which have determined size have been influential. A return to traditional free competition would surely necessitate atomization of business. That the breaking of business into small enough units to ensure competition would hinder productive efficiency is hardly open to doubt. If this be the case, as it seems to be, then abandonment of the single standard of free competition has much in its favor.

On the other hand, the industry-by-industry approach necessarily involves increased government supervision of business. Nevertheless, this approach does not require regulation of all business along the pattern of public-utility control. Many industries would be left as they are, for if competition is found to be desirable in a particular industry, about all government need do is to remove monopolistic restraints. In industries in which the firms are few and relatively large, and in which this is found to be economically desirable, a program of regulation might need to do no more than to investigate and to supervise in a general way. Protection of the public might well be of enough concern to the industry and enough seeds of competition might remain to make detailed regulation unnecessary. Other industries in which a single firm or a very few firms dominate might have to be placed under regulation similar to that now imposed on businesses affected with a public interest.

Of course, another alternative, and one which has something to be said for it, is to leave the antitrust laws as they are. Admittedly, the present laws have not been very effective either in restoring competition or in regulating it. But they do furnish a basis for prosecution of unreasonable restraints of trade. Flagrant cases in which the public interest is disregarded may be brought under the antitrust laws without much trouble. Moreover, the meaning of these laws has been greatly clarified over the years, and a willing enforcement agency can find much in them to thwart unreasonable combination. Furthermore, even though competition may be diminished by business growth and other economic developments, this is not in itself proof that society is being harmed so much that more drastic measures are necessary.

THE NECESSITY OF A PUBLIC POLICY

Examination of the antitrust laws and the experience under them points abundantly to the desirability of a clear public policy in this area. As it is now, business managers are often confused as to whether the mere fact of being large and efficient involves legal risks; yet few businesses can stand still, since stagnation is an invitation to inefficiency and loss of position. Government officials, including both the staff members of the Anti-trust Division and the Federal Trade Commission, are likewise often puzzled as to just what the public wishes them to do by way of enforcing the laws. And the public, clearly in favor of suppressing "trusts" and monopolies, finds itself confused when the government uses the law to attack large companies generally believed by the public to be efficient, competitive, and producing both civilian and military goods necessary for the welfare of the nation.

Some of the confusion stems from a lack of understanding as to the real extent and nature of competition and from the search for an eighteenth-century kind of small-firm competition which economic events have changed. Some of the confusion arises from the law itself with its vagueness and exemptions. And one gets the impression that some of the confusion is engendered by the officials and staff members of the enforcing agencies, who see in publicity and attacks on well-known giant companies a means for receiving budget support in Congress.

A review of present policy as it has been administered and a re-examination of the criteria of competition would go far toward removing this confusion. The welfare of the public appears to require that private business be regulated to the minimum extent possible and that advantages of large size in business be retained, while maintaining freedom from the restraints and powers of big business. Among the world powers, the American antitrust laws are virtually a unique institution. It is perhaps not too extravagant to say that much of the continuing vigor of American industry, the freedom in business affairs, the rise of new firms from small beginnings, and the extensiveness of small businesses in the economy of this country—features which stand in sharp contrast to the economic situation in most large foreign countries—have been due to the policy of outlawing industrial cartelization and enforcing a level of competition.

Selected References

American Economic Association, *Readings in the Social Control of Industry*. New York: Blakiston Division, McGraw-Hill Book Company, Inc., 1942.

Arnold, Thurman, and others, "The Sherman Antitrust Act and Its Enforcement," 7 *Law and Contemporary Problems* 1–160 (January, 1940).

Commerce Clearing House, Inc., *The Federal Antitrust Laws with Summary of Cases Instituted by the United States, 1890–1951*. New York: The Clearing House, Inc., 1952.

Cook, Franklin H., *Principles of Business and the Federal Law*, chaps. 12, 14. New York: The Macmillan Company, 1951.

Edwards, Corwin D., *Maintaining Competition: Requisites of a Governmental Policy*. New York: McGraw-Hill Book Company, Inc., 1949.

Hamilton, Walton, and Irene Till, *Antitrust in Action*, TNEC Monograph 16. Government Printing Office, 1940.

Handler, Milton, *A Study of the Construction and Enforcement of the Federal Antitrust Laws*, TNEC Monograph 38. Government Printing Office, 1941.

Machlup, Fritz, *The Political Economy of Monopoly: Business, Labor and Government Policies*. Baltimore: Johns Hopkins Press, 1952.

Mund, Vernon, *Government and Business*, chaps. 10–14. New York: Harper & Brothers, 1950.

Oppenheim, S. Chesterfield, *Cases on Federal Antitrust Law*. St. Paul, Minn.: West Publishing Co., 1948.

———, *Federal Antitrust Laws*. Ann Arbor, Mich.: Michigan Legal Publications, 1954.

Stocking, George W., and Myron W. Watkins, *Monopoly and Free Enterprise*, chaps. 8, 9, 14, 15, 16. New York: The Twentieth Century Fund, Inc., 1951.

U.S. Congress, House of Representatives, Select Committee on Small Business, *Antitrust Law Enforcement by the Federal Trade Commission and the Antitrust Division, Department of Justice—A Preliminary Report*, H. Rept. 3236, 81st Cong., 2d Sess. (1951).

———, *Congress and the Monopoly Problem: Fifty Years of Anti-trust Development, 1900–1950*, H. Doc. 599, 81st Cong., 2d Sess. (1950).

U.S. Department of Justice, Anti-trust Division, *Judgments Containing Provisions for Dissolution, Divestiture, and Divorcement in Cases Filed from July 2, 1890 to March 25, 1948*. Government Printing Office, 1948.

15

REGULATION OF COMPETITIVE PRACTICES

In a sense, regulation of restraint of trade and attempts to monopolize is a regulation of competitive practices. The trade-practice regulation discussed in this chapter has additional purposes. Originally, the purpose of all trade-practice regulation was to prevent those practices which stifled competition and led to monopoly. While this purpose is still very important and special monopolistic practices have been singled out for control, the regulation of competitive practices has been broadened to include two other objectives: (1) regulation to protect the businessman by prohibiting practices which are regarded as unfair, and (2) regulation to protect the consumer by eliminating deceptive practices and preventing false and misleading advertising. Thus, trade regulation takes for granted the existence of competition and attempts to make it more effective.

Common-law Regulation

The common law affords some protection against competitive practices which invade property rights or the freedom of competitive activity. Damages are allowed in cases of "palming off"—the practice of a seller representing his product to a buyer as that of his competitor. Not only is this practice regarded as an invasion of property rights—good will or trade name—but also it is regarded as deception upon the buying public.[1] The common law makes misappropriation and misrepresentation the essence of the offense, whether it is accomplished by word of mouth, by advertising, or by simulation of labels, packaging, color, form, or appearance of goods.

Another actionable offense at common law is the misappropriation of trade secrets or other intangible trade values. Imitation is accepted by the courts as inherent in the competitive system, but if a seller obtains knowledge of certain confidential information or secret processes by fraud, by breach of contract, or by inducing an employee of a competitor to disclose such secrets, he might be enjoined from using them to the disadvantage of the original owner.

[1] Milton Handler, "Unfair Competition," 21 *Iowa Law Review* 183 (January, 1936).

Under the common law, malicious interference with competitors might also be restrained and suits for damages entertained. As a general rule, to obtain redress an aggrieved competitor must prove that attacks on his reputation or the integrity of his products have been made willfully to injure the reputation of his business or product and that the utterance has caused him a definite loss. Such proof was often difficult to obtain. Where malicious interference resulted from threats or physical violence against a competitor or his customers, the common law allows redress as a means of avoiding a wrong to the injured party, and such proof of interference has not been so difficult to establish. Occasionally, misbranding or false advertising is also held to constitute unlawful competition under the common law.

As an instrument for enforcing a level of fair competition, the common law leaves much to be desired. Often malicious intent must be proved. Usually specific damage must be shown by a competitor or a purchaser. Moreover, resorting to judicial process to remove instances of unfair competition is not satisfactory. Suits for individual cases are so expensive that many unlawful activities will not be prosecuted. Actions deceptive or harmful to buyers, even where unlawful under the common law, may not be contested at all unless a seller is damaged.

Furthermore, the scope of unlawful competitive activity is very limited under the common law. Deceptive practices which harm the public rather than a competitor are clearly not actionable at law. Even where the common law has applied, it has served only to bring adjudication of particular controversies and the levying of damages in individual cases; it has not been an effective instrument for prevention. Thus, the common law lacks breadth to cover the whole area of that which society may believe to be fair competition; it has proved to be an expensive and annoying means of forcing compliance with the law; and it has been deficient in furnishing supervision by which unfair competition might be prevented.

State Regulation

Dissatisfaction with the common law as an instrument of regulation of competitive standards led to the reliance on statutory control. Between 1900 and 1915, twenty-three states outlawed local price discrimination. In the same period a smaller number of states prohibited exclusive-dealer contracts and a variety of other unfair practices, such as commercial bribery and malicious interference with a rival's business.[2]

Some states set minimum requirements of wholesomeness and of labeling

[2] Joseph E. Davies, *Trust Laws and Unfair Competition* (Government Printing Office, 1914), p. 187.

for specific kinds of products, such as milk, meats, and medicines.[3] In a few states monopolistic trade practices were spelled out in great detail and outlawed.

However, as in the case of the antitrust laws, effective regulation of a national economy could be accomplished only by federal action.

Federal Regulation

Pressure for federal regulation of competitive practices came from two divergent forces which were both dissatisfied with judicial enforcement of the Sherman Act. The liberal forces of the country were disillusioned with the Supreme Court's announcement in 1911 that the antitrust law prohibited only unreasonable restraints of trade. They wanted more vigorous enforcement of the law and felt that an administrative commission would be more able to cope with each new unfair trade practice on a continuing basis. The business community wanted greater certainty and more specific standards as to the lines of legitimate conduct. To businessmen a commission was desirable as a body to review in advance potentially illegal acts. Congress did not hesitate in satisfying these forces. In 1914, it created the Federal Trade Commission, the first independent regulatory commission to be established since the creation of the Interstate Commerce Commission in 1887.

The Federal Trade Commission draws its authority from the Federal Trade Commission Act and the Clayton Act, passed at the same time to supplement the Sherman Act. These acts have been partially amended in subsequent years. In addition, the Commission has jurisdiction over certain other laws.

The regulatory authority of the Commission under the Federal Trade Commission Act is derived from section 5, which prohibits "unfair methods of competition" in interstate commerce. This section was extended by the Wheeler-Lea Act of 1938 to provide for protection of the consumer against "unfair or deceptive acts or practices in commerce," regardless of their effect on competition. This amendment also prohibited false and misleading advertising of foods, drugs, curative devices, and cosmetics. The Oleomargarine Act of 1950 modified the Wheeler-Lea Act to include misleading advertisements for oleomargarine.

Regulatory jurisdiction of the Commission extends to the substantive portions of the Clayton Act, which it enforces concurrently with the Department of Justice. Section 2 of this law, as amended by the Robinson-Patman Act of 1936, forbids certain price discriminations between purchasers and provides that the granting as well as the receipt of such dis-

[3] *Ibid.*, pp. 521–526; S. P. Kaidanovsky, *Consumer Standards*, TNEC Monograph 24 (1941), chap. 4.

criminations shall be unlawful. Section 3 outlaws exclusive-dealing arrangements and tying contracts, if they substantially lessen competition or tend to create a monopoly.

Sections 7 and 8 forbid certain intercorporate relationships. Section 7, as amended in 1950, bans mergers or consolidations where the effect may be to substantially lessen competition or tend to create a monopoly, regardless whether they are accomplished by the acquisition of capital stock or by the purchase of assets. Prior to 1950, the purchase of assets was permitted. Section 8, as amended in 1935, provides that interlocking directorates may not exist between industrial corporations any one of which has capital, surplus, and undivided profits of more than $1 million, if elimination of competition would result.

The Commission has authority under a miscellany of other acts. The Commission administers the Export Trade Act of 1918, commonly known as the Webb-Pomerene Act, which exempts export-trade associations from the Sherman Act, provided that their activities have no restraining influence upon domestic trade. The 1940 Wool Products Labeling Act and the 1951 Fur Products Labeling Act also fall under the Commission's jurisdiction.

Certain provisions of the Lanham Trade-Mark Act of 1946 are enforced by the Federal Trade Commission. The Commission may apply to the Commissioner of Patents for a cancellation of registered trade-marks which are deceptive, immoral, or scandalous; which have been obtained fraudulently; or which are in violation of other provisions of the Lanham Act. Finally, the Commission has jurisdiction over the Flammable Fabrics Act of 1953, which makes the manufacture and commerce in certain inflammable fabrics illegal, an unfair method of competition, and an unfair and deceptive practice.

In general, the Federal Trade Commission is vested with responsibilities in four areas: (1) regulation of special monopolistic practices which the antitrust statutes forbid; (2) regulation of unfair methods of competition and unfair or deceptive trade practices; (3) conduct of investigations of business; and (4) since 1919, promotion of business self-regulation by holding trade-practice conferences. These functions will be discussed in the remaining sections of this chapter.

Regulation of Special Monopolistic Practices

The prosecution of special monopolistic practices is conducted by the Federal Trade Commission, in cooperation with the Department of Justice. These practices are specifically prohibited by the substantive portions of the Clayton Act, and they differ from the unfair methods of competition and deceptive practices outlawed by the Federal Trade Commission

Act, as amended by the Wheeler-Lea Act. The latter practices are not defined in the statute, and the Commission, which has sole jurisdiction over them, is granted the discretion of placing given practices within or outside of the general prohibition. The illegal practices in the Clayton Act are more clearly defined.

Furthermore, the matters outlawed by the Clayton Act are in extension of the Sherman Act, whereas the Federal Trade Commission Act is not technically an antitrust law. Those things forbidden by the Federal Trade Commission Act are generally connected with the ethical plane of competitive activity rather than practices tending toward monopoly. While this distinction can often be made, there are cases where a practice may tend toward monopoly and at the same time be an unfair method of competition. For example, basing points were found to be a device tending to create a monopoly in opposition to certain features of the Clayton Act, and also a means of unfair competition.

PRICE DISCRIMINATION

One of the specific practices forbidden by the Clayton Act of 1914, as amended by the Robinson-Patman Act of 1936, was discrimination in price by a seller between different purchasers of commodities of like grade and quality, where any of the purchases involved were in interstate commerce, and where the effect was substantially to lessen competition. Because the original provision of the Clayton Act has been materially changed by the amendments of the Robinson-Patman Act, it may be well to note the meaning of the original law before undertaking an analysis of the amendments.

Regulation under the original section. Under the original section 2 of the Clayton Act, price discriminations made by sellers in interstate commerce were forbidden (1) where such differences were not based upon variations in grade, quality, quantity, selling or transportation costs, or the necessity of meeting bona fide competition; and (2) where the effect of such discrimination was substantially to lessen competition or to tend to create a monopoly in any line of commerce.[4] The original section also reserved to sellers the right to select their customers as they wished unless the purpose of doing so was to restrain trade.

Section 2 was aimed at destructive price cutting among competing sellers, as well as at the favoring of one buyer over another, where the purpose was monopolistic. Note that it did not compel sellers to charge

[4] A "line" of commerce is a portion of a trade or industry on the same level of competition. Thus, drug retailers and drug wholesalers are in the same industry, but since they do not compete directly with each other, they are not in the same line of commerce. A line of commerce would be presented by retailers of the same kind of drug, or manufacturers of a certain product, or wholesalers in the same field.

all buyers the same price. Besides the justifiable causes for variations allowable under the law, the sales had to be in interstate commerce, and until 1929, the courts held that the discrimination must injure sellers rather than buyers.[5] Since most of the evils of price discrimination arose from that between buyers, the corresponding provisions of the Clayton Act became a dead letter for a time. In 1929, however, application of price discriminations to lessening of competition between purchasers was made effective in a case decided by the United States Supreme Court.[6] The Court held that the action of a can company in selling tin cans at a lower price to one food packer than to others enabled the buyer to secure a monopolistic advantage in the packing industry and was within the prohibition of the Clayton Act.

While this case gave the Federal Trade Commission increased power to proceed against price discrimination, the provisions of section 2 of the Clayton Act were still open to objection by certain parties. Independent retailers had been alarmed at the amazing growth of chain stores after World War I. Believing that their rapid increase in the grocery, drug, tobacco, and other fields was due in part to unreasonably advantageous price concessions from manufacturers and wholesalers, the independent retailers pushed for an amendment of section 2 which would prevent these discriminations. As a result, Congress directed the Federal Trade Commission in 1928 to make a study of the development of chain stores. The Commission made its report in 1934.[7]

As was expected, the report disclosed many instances where advantageous prices helped the chain stores to undersell their independent competitors. Price concessions for volume purchases were common, these discounts often bearing no relation to costs and sometimes being refused to groups of independent retailers who pooled their purchases. Special promotional allowances were often made; these included allowances for advertising, counter display, and dressing of windows. Allowances for services performed by the purchaser were also made. The most widely practiced of these were concessions made for brokerage and sales commissions where the chain-store organization dealt directly with manufacturers, rather than through customary middlemen with whom independent retailers dealt. These price discriminations were generally believed to be beyond the powers of the Federal Trade Commission under the original section 2 of the Clayton Act.

[5] *Mennen Co. v. FTC*, 288 Fed. 774, certiorari denied, 262 U.S. 759 (1923), and *National Biscuit Co. v. FTC*, 299 Fed. 733, certiorari denied, 266 U.S. 613 (1924).

[6] *Van Camp and Sons Co. v. American Can Co.*, 278 U.S. 245 (1929).

[7] FTC, *Final Report on the Chain Store Investigation*, S. Doc. 4, 74th Cong., 1st Sess. (1934). This report was preceded by thirty-three volumes of factual data.

The Robinson-Patman Act, 1936. The Robinson-Patman Act was drafted to fill the gaps existing in the original price-discrimination law. It was also designed to curtail the growth of the chain store and preserve the independent retailer and wholesaler. The dominant motive behind its enactment was the fight against chains and other large sellers.

The Robinson-Patman amendments made material changes in the scope and effectiveness of price-discrimination regulation. Of its six sections, the first is a revision of section 2 of the Clayton Act and the other five are new. The changes may be summarized as follows:

Section 2a. Price discrimination is forbidden which harms competition between sellers, between sellers and buyers, or between buyers; i.e., which injures a particular competitor. Proof of injury to a line of commerce is no longer necessary.

Differences in price based on quantity of purchases is allowed only if due allowance is made for differences in the cost of manufacture (the same limitation that had previously applied only to price differences based on differences in selling methods and transportation costs).

The Commission is authorized to fix maximum discounts where large buyers are few and quantity discounts would be unjustly discriminatory or promotive of monopoly.

Differences in price are allowed in response to changing conditions affecting the market for or the marketability of goods concerned, such as imminent deterioration of perishable goods, obsolescence of seasonal goods, distress sales under court process, or sales in good faith in discontinuance of business in the goods concerned.

Section 2b. A bill of particulars charging a person with a violation is taken to be prima-facie evidence of guilt and places the burden for proving innocence upon the accused.

Section 2c. Allowances made by the seller for brokerage are prohibited, where payments are not made to the person actually performing such service and where the broker is not independent of the purchaser. Hence, making price concessions under the guise of brokerage, even through a firm under the control of the purchaser, is prohibited.

Section 2d. Allowances made by the seller for services performed by a purchaser are forbidden, unless available on proportionately equal terms to other buyers.

Section 2e. Granting services and facilities to some purchasers and not to others is forbidden.

Section 2f. The buyer, as well as the seller, may be found guilty if he "knowingly" receives a discrimination or induces a seller to grant a discrimination.

The law applies to sales which affect interstate commerce, and probable or possible injury to competition must be proved. The right to select customers, in absence of a purpose of restraining trade, is still granted sellers.[8]

Proof of application of the law has been made easier, since the Commission now must show only that the parties are engaged in interstate commerce and that the practice complained of has tended to harm competition between directly interested persons. Prior to 1936, the Commission had to prove that competition in a line of commerce was substantially lessened. Under such a requirement, the courts had taken the position that the industry generally must be affected, or at least a large part of it, and that a price discrimination affecting only a few competitions was not within the prohibitions of the law.[9] Since such proof was difficult, the Robinson-Patman Act makes injury to any party concerned an adequate basis for prosecution. To a competitor engaged in the same line of business the injury may be because the price is too low. In practice, such predatory local price cutting has become uncommon. Or, the injury may be to the customer, because the price is too high as compared to other customers who bought the product for a lower price.[10] In effect, where unrestrained competition has become too severe or too "hard" the Robinson-Patman attempts to "soften" it so that competition would not be harmed.

A new enforcement section provides that certain types of price discrimination shall be criminal offenses, punishable by a $5,000 fine, one year's imprisonment, or both.

It is apparent that the breadth and complexity of these amendments create a tremendous enforcement problem for both the Federal Trade Commission and the courts. One judge said of the law: "I doubt if any judge would assert that he knows exactly what does or does not amount to violation of the Robinson-Patman Act in any and all instances." [11]

Enforcement of the Act. All sections of the Robinson-Patman Act have not been invoked with equal vigor. Generally, two kinds of price discrimination fall under the act—geographic and personal. The Commission's concern with geographic price discrimination, i.e., the basing-point system of quoting delivered prices, has consumed much of its energy and resources. It should be noted that the basing-point system, which will be discussed in the next chapter, was also prosecuted as an unfair method of competition. By far the greatest number of cases of personal price dis-

[8] Refusal to sell per se does not amount to price discrimination. *Jarrett v. Pittsburgh Plate Glass Co.*, 42 F. Supp. 723 (1942). However, if such refusal is part of a concerted plan to drive competitors out of business, it does. *Hershey Chocolate Corp. v. FTC*, 121 F.2d 968 (1941).

[9] See, for example, *American Can Co. v. Ladoga Canning Co.*, 44 Fed. 763 (1930), certiorari denied, 282 U.S. 899 (1931).

[10] See *FTC v. Ruberoid Co.*, 343 U.S. 470 (1952).

[11] *United States v. Atlantic & Pacific*, 67 F. Supp. 677 (1946).

crimination has involved brokerage allowances and quantity discounts. Approximately 80 per cent of orders entered by the Commission pertained to brokerage payments.[12] The Commission has had considerable success in clarifying the law and applying it to this form of discrimination. Although a significant number of quantity discount cases have been prosecuted, the interpretation of this section is not clear. These two categories of cases will be considered below.

Under section 2d, which prohibits the granting of discriminatory allowances for services or facilities rendered by the buyer, only a few orders have been issued. Most of the allowances were for advertising. The Commission's policy is obscure on this section and little is being done to eradicate the offensive practices.

A negligible number of orders have been entered under section 2e, which prohibits granting services or facilities to some customers and not to others. Although the law is reasonably clear on this point, the difficulty of proving violation is great.

Only a few orders have been issued under section 2f, which makes it unlawful for buyers knowingly to induce or receive a price discrimination. The interpretation of this section is unsettled, and enforcement has been weak.

Brokerage allowances. Chain stores and other mass distributors have customarily dealt directly with manufacturers. Under section 2c, they may not be granted an allowance in lieu of the brokerage which would have to be added to the cost of dealers buying through a commission house. The abuses to which brokerage allowances led were responsible for this prohibition. The courts have uniformly upheld the Commission's strict and vigorous application of this section. But the courts, at the same time, acknowledged that it may impose hardships when, for example, an intermediary acting in good faith renders services of value to both the seller and the buyer.[13]

Quantity discounts. The application of that portion of section 2a having to do with quantity discounts is uncertain as a result of conflicting court rulings. In the Bruce's Juices case the Supreme Court refrained from outlawing quantity discounts unless the Federal Trade Commission could find

[12] For these data on extent of enforcement the authors rely on House of Representatives, Select Committee on Small Business, *Anti-trust Law Enforcement by the Federal Trade Commission and the Anti-trust Division, Department of Justice—A Preliminary Report*, H. Rept. 3236, 81st Cong., 2d Sess. (1951), pp. 37–38, and Annual Reports of the FTC.

[13] See, *Biddle Purchasing Co. v. Federal Trade Commission*, 96 F.2d 687 (1938), certiorari denied, 305 U.S. 634 (1938); *Oliver Bros. v. Federal Trade Commission*, 102 F.2d 763 (1939); *Southgate Brokerage Co. v. Federal Trade Commission*, 150 F.2d 607 (1945).

substantial injury to competition. The Court said: "The economic effects on competition of such discounts are for the Federal Trade Commission to judge. . . . It would be a far-reaching decision to outlaw all quantity discounts. Courts should not rush in where Congress feared to tread." [14]

In the Morton Salt case the Supreme Court appeared to rule differently. The Morton Salt Company, selling table salt in carload lots to wholesalers, jobbers, and large retailers, granted quantity discounts. The manufacturer argued that this practice had no effect on competition between purchasers, because less than 1 per cent of their total sales were under carload lots, and that salt was but a small part of the total grocery trade. The Court was satisfied that the Commission had evidence that a price differential existed and held that the manufacturer did not prove that the discount was based on actual cost differences. The Robinson-Patman act "does not require that the discriminations must in fact have harmed competition, but only that there is a reasonable possibility that they 'may' have such an effect." [15] The broadening of the section to include "possible" injuries to competition and the elimination of the distinction between price differences and price discrimination may have significant effects.

The Commission has been hesitant about establishing quantity limits under section 2a. A beginning was made in 1947 when it ordered an investigation of the quantity limits existing in the rubber-tire industry. In 1949, the Commission announced that it was setting up procedures to determine at what point quantity discounts become discriminatory or monopolistic. However, the Commission did not intend to launch an immediate campaign to regulate such discounts.[16]

Proof under the Act. An important interpretation was given to section 2b in 1951. This section provides that a seller may rebut the charge that his exercise of discrimination is prima facie illegal by showing that his lower price was made in good faith to meet the equally low price of his competitor. The sponsors of the law had intended this section to give an accused seller the right to show good motives in explanation of an offense. The Federal Trade Commission, on the basis of this congressional intent, took the position that "good faith" was only a procedural aid, and not absolute defense for discrimination. The Standard Oil Company of Indiana, which was under prosecution for price discrimination, argued that discrimination in good faith was an absolute defense. The Supreme Court upheld the company: "Congress did not seek by the Robinson-

[14] *Bruce's Juices, Inc. v. American Can Co.*, 330 U.S. 743, 746 (1947).
[15] *FTC v. Morton Salt Co.*, 334 U.S. 37, 47 (1948).
[16] *New York Times*, Jan. 15, 1949, p. 20.

Patman Act either to abolish competition or so radically to curtail it that a seller would have no substantial right of self-defense against a price raid by a competitor."[17] In some quarters of Congress this decision has been objected to on the grounds that "bad faith" is difficult to prove. Attempts have been made to eliminate the use of "good faith" as a defense when the practice complained of is intended to eliminate competition.[18]

TYING CONTRACTS AND EXCLUSIVE-DEALING ARRANGEMENTS

Section 3 of the Clayton Act makes it unlawful for a person engaging in interstate commerce to sell or lease a good on the condition that the purchaser shall not use or deal in the goods of a competitor of the seller, where the effect is substantially to lessen competition or to tend to create a monopoly. The Federal Trade Commission and the Department of Justice have interpreted this provision as applying to tying contracts and exclusive-dealing arrangements. In the case of the tying contract, a seller or lessor agrees to sell or lease a good only on the condition that another good be purchased and used with the first. This type of contract has generally arisen when a seller has a patented article which calls for the use of nonpatented supplies. The exclusive-dealing arrangement is one in which the seller or lessor forces the purchaser not to deal in the goods of a competitor.

In administering this portion of the Clayton Act, the Commission has often combined it with section 5 of the Federal Trade Commission Act, under which it has power to prohibit unfair methods of competition. One reason it has done this is that the Federal Trade Commission Act requires a showing of hindrance to competition and not necessarily a substantial lessening of competition in a *line* of commerce.

The government has had mixed success in applying these prohibitions. The Department of Justice was successful in its suit against the United Shoe Machinery Company and forced it to give up certain clauses in contracts whereby the lessee of shoe machinery was required to use United machines for other operations and to purchase supplies from the company for the machines leased.[19] The government also caused the International Business Machines Company to give up requiring persons using its patented tabulating machines to buy supplies from it exclusively.[20] Like-

[17] *Standard Oil Co. (Indiana) v. FTC*, 340 U.S. 231, 249 (1951).

[18] For example, Senator Estes Kefauver introduced a bill to this effect in 1953. See *New York Times*, Mar. 19, 1953, p. 45.

[19] *United States v. United Shoe Machinery Co.*, 258 U.S. 451 (1922).

[20] *International Bus. Machines Corp. v. United States*, 298 U.S. 131 (1936). For other cases of similar import see *Radio Corp. of America v. Lord*, 28 F.2d 257, certiorari denied, 278 U.S. 648 (1928), and *Standard Fashion Co. v. Magrane-Houston Co.*, 258 U.S. 346 (1922).

wise, the requirement that users of International Salt Company vending machines must use International salt was voided.[21]

The most important exclusive-dealing case involved an arrangement by which Standard Oil Company of California entered into exclusive-supply contracts with independent dealers in petroleum products and automobile accessories, in which dealers agreed to purchase from the company all their requirements of one or more products. The Court held that the requirement that a violation of section 3 of the Clayton Act must show an actual or potential lessening of competition or tendency to establish a monopoly was adequately met by proof that the contracts covered a substantial number of outlets and a substantial amount of products.[22] Justice Douglas, in dissent, feared that by outlawing this "relatively innocuous" device companies would be induced to build service-station empires of their own which would be far worse from the point of view of small business units.

All these cases were instituted by the Department of Justice under the Clayton Act. The Federal Trade Commission has also had some success in prosecuting exclusive-dealing and tying contracts, especially when the seller's possession of partial monopoly makes these practices destructive of competition.[23]

In several important cases under section 3, the Commission has not been so successful. In 1919 it issued complaints against the Sinclair Refining Company and some forty other refiners and wholesalers with respect to the practice of leasing pumps and tanks to dealers at normal prices on the condition that the equipment be used only with gasoline supplied by the lessors. Twenty-seven cease-and-desist orders were issued against the oil companies, and the case was carried to the Supreme Court.[24] That Court held that the Commission had failed to prove that the lease contracts caused a substantial lessening of competition. It pointed out that the dealers could buy wherever they chose, could lease as many pumps as they wished, and could buy outfits of their own and use them without hindrance.

Further difficulty encountered by the Commission in applying the clause is shown by the case involving exclusive-dealing contracts of the

[21] *International Salt Co. v. United States*, 332 U.S. 392 (1947). This case, and others of the same type, involve a patentee's trying to tie unpatented articles to patented ones, thus extending a granted monopoly beyond the scope of the grant.

[22] *Standard Oil of California v. United States*, 337 U.S. 293 (1949); see also *United States v. J. I. Case Co.*, 101 F. Supp. 856 (1951).

[23] See *Carter Carburetor Co. v. FTC*, 112 F.2d 722 (1940); *Signode Co. v. FTC*, 132 F.2d 48 (1942); *Judson Thompson v. FTC*. 150 F.2d 952 (1945), certiorari denied, 326 U.S. 776 (1945).

[24] *FTC v. Sinclair Refining Co. et al.*, 261 U.S. 463 (1923). See also *Pick Mfg. Co. v. General Motors Corp.*, 299 U.S. 3 (1936).

Curtis Publishing Company. This company had a practice of requiring its agents not to sell copies of magazines except those published by it. The Commission found this practice to be unlawful under the Clayton Act and issued a cease-and-desist order. The company appealed the case, maintaining that the contract restrictions were lawful agreements between principal and agent and, not being sales or lease contracts, were not contrary to the Clayton Act. The United States Supreme Court agreed with the company's position.[25]

While section 3 may be used to thwart some of the more dangerous types of monopolistic tying devices, the power is not without its shortcomings. To be unlawful under this portion of the Clayton Act, an arrangement must be between seller and buyer or between lessor and lessee. Agency arrangements do not fall within the prohibitions of the law. Companies wishing to obtain the benefits of tying arrangements can easily circumvent the law by resorting to agency contracts. Moreover, to prove a substantial lessening of competition is not easy. The dealer may have alternatives, in which case the contract does not substantially reduce competition; or the dealers concerned may not represent such a large proportion of a trade as to endanger the working of competition generally.

INTERCORPORATE RELATIONSHIPS

Other practices specifically prohibited by the Clayton Act are certain intercorporate relationships which tend to reduce competition. Section 7 originally prohibited in certain instances the purchase of stock by one corporation in another, where the effect of the purchase was substantially to lessen competition, or to restrain commerce in any section or community, or to tend to create a monopoly in any line of commerce. The 1950 Anti-merger Act amended this section to outlaw mergers or consolidations where the effect may be substantially to lessen competition or to tend to create a monopoly, whether they are accomplished by the acquisition of capital stock or by the outright purchase of assets. The purchase of assets was not prohibited prior to 1950. Purchase of stock solely for investment or to establish subsidiaries for carrying on immediate lawful business, where the effect is not substantially to lessen competition, is permitted. Likewise, purchase by common carriers, subject to the Interstate Commerce Commission, is not outlawed where necessary to acquire feeder or branch lines, or to extend lines.

Section 8 makes unlawful the interlocking of directors or employees between two or more banks, banking associations, and trust companies, where they are organized under federal law and the total deposits, capital, surplus, and undivided profits aggregate more than $5 million. This practice is also forbidden between two or more industrial corporations in

[25] *FTC v. Curtis Publishing Co.*, 260 U.S. 568 (1923).

interstate commerce, any one of which has capital, surplus, and undivided profits totaling more than $1 million. Likewise, interlocking relationships between railway companies are restricted, the section forbidding the making of securities, supply, or construction contracts in an amount of more than $50,000 between two companies with such relationships, unless in accordance with competitive bidding as prescribed by the Interstate Commerce Commission.

Neither section 7 nor section 8 has been particularly effective to date. In 1949 the Federal Trade Commission frankly admitted that it had been a total failure in preventing mergers under section 7.[26] For one thing, the Supreme Court distinguished between acquisition of stock and acquisition of assets. In 1926, it held that the Commission has no power to force the divestment of assets acquired by two competing concerns, even though this acquisition followed upon an unlawful purchase of stock.[27] Since 60 per cent of the major mergers consist of acquisition of assets rather than stock, the jurisdiction of the Commission was considerably weakened. As for the remaining 40 per cent, as soon as the Commission moved against a merger involving the acquisition of stock, the company could quickly move to acquire the assets.[28]

Since 1926 the Commission had recommended that the loophole in section 7 be closed. No real action was taken on this recommendation until 1945, and the Anti-merger Act did not pass Congress until 1950. The first case under this new amendment was initiated in 1952 against Pillsbury Mills, the second largest flour milling company in the United States, when it acquired the assets of Ballard and Ballard and the Duff Baking Mix Division of American Home Foods.[29] The Commission subsequently found the action of Pillsbury Mills to be a violation of section 7. In so deciding, however, the Commission rejected the "substantiality" test as a measure of illegality and said, "There must be a case-by-case examination of all relevant factors in order to ascertain the probable economic consequences" of corporate mergers. Thus, the section 7 prohibition was not "to be added to the list of per se violations." [30] In 1954 the Department of Justice ruled against a proposed merger of Bethlehem Steel Corporation and Youngstown Sheet and Tube Company.[31]

[26] House of Representatives, Committee on Small Business, *United States versus Economic Concentration and Monopoly*, Staff report to the Monopoly Subcommittee, 79th Cong. (1949), p. 30.

[27] *FTC v. Western Meat Co.*, 272 U.S. 554 (1926).

[28] See, for example, *Arrow-Hart and Hegeman Electric Co. v. FTC*, 291 U.S. 587 (1934). The FTC proceeded against a holding company that was formed to acquire the stocks of the two competing corporations. Upon Commission action, the holding company was dissolved and the assets of the competitors merged into a new company, which put it beyond FTC jurisdiction.

[29] FTC, *Annual Report, 1952*, p. 31.

[30] FTC Press Release, Dec. 28, 1953.

[31] *Los Angeles Times*, Oct. 1, 1954.

The prohibition of interlocking directorates in section 8 has been of no practical significance. Few actions have ever been undertaken by the Commission. In 1951, the Commission concluded an extensive study of interlocking directorates,[32] in which certain defects in the present law were noted, but no action has resulted from the investigation.

Regulation of Unfair Competition

When the Federal Trade Commission Act was enacted in 1914, the need was felt for a ban on unfair competition so that practices which might eliminate competition could be prevented. However, the futility of a specific definition of "unfair competition" was recognized, because it would be impossible to specify in law all the unfair practices that could be devised. Therefore, Congress enacted a broad prohibition against "unfair methods of competition in commerce" and authorized the Federal Trade Commission to issue a complaint "if it shall appear to the Commission that a proceeding by it in respect thereof would be to the interest of the public." The Wheeler-Lea Act of 1938 amended the law to prohibit "unfair or deceptive acts or practices" in interstate commerce. It also specified that false or misleading advertising of foods, drugs, cosmetics, and devices was an unfair or deceptive act.

A competitor injured by an unfair competitive practice has the common-law right of action to stop the practice and recover damages, but he cannot sue for treble damages as he can under the Clayton Act.[33] Or he can file a complaint with the Commission to institute formal proceedings such as will be described below. Under the Wheeler-Lea Act the Commission may enjoin the use of false and misleading advertisements in the food, drug, cosmetic, and device field when it believes that such action would be in the public interest. Persons who falsely advertise with an intent to mislead or who produce a product that is injurious to health may be fined up to $5,000, or given a prison sentence of not more than six months, or both, for the first offense. Succeeding convictions carry a penalty of not more than $10,000, or not more than one year's imprisonment, or both.

UNFAIR METHODS OF COMPETITION

The Commission has followed two distinct courses in enforcing section 5 of the Federal Trade Commission Act. One course has been to prosecute

[32] FTC, *Report of the Federal Trade Commission on Interlocking Directorates* (1951).

[33] See, for example, *Standard Oil Co. of New Mexico v. Standard Oil Co. of California*, 56 F.2d 973 (1932).

unfair methods of competition that stifled competition and restrained trade. In this sense, the Commission was implementing the antitrust laws. The other course has been to attack practices that fell below a desired plane of competition. In time the second course of action has become the Commission's main interest, and major emphasis has been placed on preventing injury to the consumer rather than to other competitors.

Since the phrase "unfair methods of competition" was left undefined, the Commission's first task was to specify the practices which it prohibited. In the Sears, Roebuck case the court said that the commissioners are "to exercise their common sense, as informed by their knowledge of the general idea of unfair trade at common law, and stop all those trade practices that have a capacity or a tendency to injure competitors directly or through deception of purchasers, quite irrespective of whether the specific practices in question have yet been denounced in common-law cases." [34] Taking heart from this decision, the Commission announced in 1919 that it felt itself "empowered to leave the shores defined by the common law and . . . embark on an uncharted sea, using common sense and the common law for its compass." [35] However, the Federal Trade Commission suffered a serious blow when the Supreme Court ruled the next year: "The words 'unfair methods of competition' are not defined by the statute and their exact meaning is in dispute. It is for the courts, not the commission, ultimately to determine as matter of law what they include." [36] The effect of this decision was to make of the Commission little more than a body to enforce the traditional concept of fair trade, with no authority to identify new practices which should be regarded as unfair.

Another setback was suffered in the Raladam case.[37] The Raladam Company had been manufacturing an obesity "cure" and advertising the product as one which could be safely taken as a reducing agent. The Commission found that the product could not be taken safely by all individuals without medical direction and advice, and it ordered the company to cease and desist from its misleading advertising. The Supreme Court refused to uphold the Commission on the ground that, although the advertising might damage the public, there was no evidence that competition was injured to a substantial extent. The Court declared that an unfair method of competition must meet three requirements before the Commission might proceed against it:

[34] *Sears, Roebuck & Co. v. FTC*, 258 Fed. 307 (1919).

[35] Quoted in Merle Fainsod and Lincoln Gordon, *Government and the American Economy* (New York: W. W. Norton & Company, Inc.. 1941), p. 509.

[36] *FTC v. Gratz*, 253 U.S. 421, 427 (1920).

[37] *FTC v. Raladam Co.*, 283 U.S. 643 (1931).

1. The method complained of must be unfair. A practice is not unfair merely because it gives a concern an advantage over its rivals; it must be oppressive, fraudulent, deceptive, or in bad faith or restrain competition or tend to a monopoly.

2. A practice must affect competition in interstate commerce. Practices which were unfair or injurious to purchasers did not thereby fall under the law unless they affected competition, as well as being in interstate commerce.

3. The Commission could prevent practices only where such proceeding appeared to be in the public interest. This interest must be specific and substantial, and the power of the Commission could not be used to interfere in a private controversy.[38]

The Raladam case turned on the second requirement, the Court finding that it had not been shown that the Raladam Company's advertising affected competition.

The 1938 amendments changed this formula in one respect. The Federal Trade Commission is no longer required to show a relationship between an unfair or deceptive act or device and competition. A deceptive or unfair practice which does not necessarily affect competition but which merely harms the public and is interstate commerce may be forbidden. Hence, both competitors and the public may be protected under the new law. When the second Raladam case[39] reached the Supreme Court in 1942, the Commission was sustained in the order it had issued against Raladam for making misleading and deceptive statements.

The Commission has found the unfair-methods section of the law useful in attacking many business practices. Among the noteworthy victories of the Commission has been the successful attack on the multiple-basing-point system,[40] to be discussed in the following chapter. The Commission was also upheld by the Supreme Court on finding that the exclusive contracts which the producers and distributors of advertising motion pictures had with 40 per cent of the theaters in thirty-seven states exhibiting such films violated section 5 of the Federal Trade Commission Act.[41] The Commission also has had considerable success in attacking resale-price-maintenance practices as unfair methods of competition—so much success, in fact, that legislation was passed in 1937 exempting such practices from prosecution by the Commission. This special area of trade regulation will be discussed in the next chapter.

[38] See, for example, *FTC v. Klesner*, 280 U.S. 19 (1929). The Court dismissed a case involving a controversy between two sellers of lamp shades over the use of the firm name "The Shade Shop" on the ground that the interest concerned was primarily a private one.

[39] *FTC v. Raladam Co.*, 316 U.S. 149 (1942).

[40] *FTC v. Cement Institute*, 333 U.S. 683 (1948). See below, pp. 403–405.

[41] *FTC v. Motion Picture Advertising Service Co., Inc.*, 344 U.S. 392 (1953).

DECEPTIVE ACTS AND PRACTICES

By far the most numerous of the cases the Federal Trade Commission has instituted have involved misrepresentation, misbranding, deceit, bad faith, oppression, and the like. Prior to the addition of the phrase "unfair or deceptive acts or practices" in 1938, the deceptive practices had to be injurious to competition to fall under the common-law doctrine of unfair competition, a point emphasized by the first Raladam case. This common-law doctrine did provide a basis for attacks on false and misleading advertising. After 1938, injury to the consumer was sufficient basis for prosecution of deceptive practices.

Only a few of the many cases that the Commission has prosecuted can be mentioned here. Misbranding has been prohibited. In the Winsted Hosiery case [42] the respondent was ordered to stop calling its partly cotton textile products "woolen" or "worsted." In the Algoma Lumber case [43] the order was directed against the use of the term "white pine" to describe another kind of wood. The General Motors Corporation and Ford Motor Company were ordered to discontinue advertising a "6 per cent" plan for financing the sale of automobiles when the actual interest rate—calculated on the unpaid balance—amounted to 11½ per cent.[44]

Misrepresenting the geographic origin of goods was limited in a number of cases. For example, advertising American-made perfumes as of French origin has been attacked,[45] as has the misuse of the name Havana on cigars.[46] Misrepresentation of the business of mixing and blending flour under the name "milling company," where no grinding was done, was stopped.[47] Fraudulent endorsements, approval of products, and certification have often suffered attack.[48]

Over thirty different business practices have been identified as unfair or deceptive.[49] It is impracticable to discuss the entire list here, but some of the more important and usual ones can be noted briefly.

1. The use of false and misleading advertising, calculated to mislead and deceive the purchasing public to their damage.
2. Misbranding of fabrics and other commodities with respect to their

[42] *FTC v. Winsted Hosiery Co.*, 258 U.S. 483 (1922).

[43] *FTC v. Algoma Lumber Co.*, 291 U.S. 67 (1934).

[44] *General Motors Corp. v. FTC*, 114 F.2d 33 (1940); *Ford Motor Co. v. FTC*, 120 F.2d 175 (1941).

[45] *Parfums Corday v. FTC*, 120 F.2d 808 (1941).

[46] *H. N. Heusner v. FTC*, 106 F.2d 596 (1939).

[47] *FTC v. Royal Milling Co.*, 288 U.S. 212 (1933); see also *Herzfeld v. FTC*, 140 F.2d 207 (1944).

[48] See, for example, *In re Hearst Magazines, Inc.*, 32 F.T.C. 1440 (1941); *FTC v. Army & Navy Trading Co.*, 88 F.2d 776 (1937); *FTC v. Standard Education Society*, 302 U.S. 112 (1937).

[49] See FTC, *Annual Report, 1952*, pp. 113–118.

materials or ingredients, their quality, origin, attributes or properties, history, or nature of manufacture.

3. Passing off goods for well and favorably known products of competitors through misappropriation or simulation of trade names, labels, or packaging.

4. Selling rebuilt or secondhand products as new.

5. Bribing buyers and employees of customers to secure patronage.

6. Procuring business or trade secrets of competitors by espionage or bribery, or by similar means.

7. Making false and disparaging statements respecting competitors' products and business.

8. Using merchandising schemes based upon lot or chance.

9. Combinations or agreements of competitors to enhance or maintain prices, or divide territory, or cut off competitors' source of supply, or otherwise restrain free and fair competition.

10. Various schemes to create the impression in the mind of a prospective customer that he is being offered an opportunity to make a purchase under unusually favorable conditions when such is not the case.

11. Using containers ostensibly of the capacity customarily associated in the mind of the buying public with standard weights and quantities, so as to make the purchaser believe that he is receiving standard weight and quantity when such is not the case.

12. Misrepresenting the position of the seller so that the buyer is led to believe that he is especially fortunate to deal with the seller. (Making claims to be an "authorized distributor," or a "manufacturer," or an "importer" when such is not the case.)

13. Use by associations of businesses of standard cost-accounting systems, price lists, or guides, calculated to result in observance of uniform prices.

14. Giving products misleading names so as to give them a value to the purchasing public they would not otherwise possess. (For example, representing products as being inspected by the government when such is not the case.)

Investigatory Activities of Federal Trade Commission

The Federal Trade Commission Act gave the Commission sweeping powers to conduct investigations of business, either on its own initiative or at the request of the Attorney General, the President, or either house of Congress. In making these investigations the Commission may require both regular and special reports from businesses using the channels of interstate commerce. In effect, the Commission took over the investigatory functions of the old Bureau of Corporations that was established in the Department of Commerce and Labor in 1903.

The investigatory activities of the Commission have been numerous.[50]

[50] For a complete account, see the Annual Reports of the FTC and the reports themselves. A compilation may be found in *Investigation of Concentration of Economic Power,* part 5A, pp. 2373–2417 (1939), and one for the five years preceding 1946 in House of Representatives, Committee on Small Business, *op. cit.,* pp. 149–165.

The initiative for these investigations has usually come from Congress. The bulkiest study made by the Commission was that of the public-utility holding companies; its findings totaled nearly 60,000 pages in ninety-five volumes. The report on chain stores was thirty-four volumes long. Other important general investigations include reports on the agricultural-implement and -machinery industry, the causes of decline in agricultural income, the packing and stockyard industry, cooperative marketing, open-price trade associations, the motor-vehicle industry, the petroleum industry, and the use of basing-point methods. During World War II many studies were conducted at the request of the Office of Price Administration. Among the recent postwar investigations are *The Merger Movement*, *The Concentration of Productive Facilities*, *The Divergence Between Plant and Company Concentration*, and *Interlocking Directorates*. By 1954 the Commission had conducted 113 published and 40 unpublished investigations.[51]

In addition to these general investigations, the Commission has studied certain features of a large number of industries, with a view to finding the extent of questionable competitive practices.

The results of some of these investigations have been significant. Disclosure of questionable business practices has led to their modification without resort to legal process. Antitrust suits against the meat packers in 1920, the International Harvester Company in 1923, and several lumber trade associations in the early 1920s resulted from other investigations. Most noteworthy perhaps were the major pieces of legislation that received their stimulus from Commission investigations. Out of the study of the meat-packing industry grew the Packers and Stockyard Act of 1921. The public-utility investigation for the Senate brought about the enactment of the Securities Act (1933), the Public Utility Holding Company Act (1935), the Federal Power Act (1935), and the Natural Gas Act (1938). The chain-store study pointed the way to the enactment of the Robinson-Patman Act of 1936.

On the other hand, the investigatory activities of the Federal Trade Commission have not fully lived up to expectations. The program has not been sufficiently integrated into the regulatory work of the Commission and other governmental agencies. Some of the legal victories on the antitrust front, for example, might have had the desired economic effects if the Commission's studies had indicated solutions of some of these economic problems.[52] Congress has been reluctant to provide the Commission with sufficient funds to undertake investigations, and in 1934 it provided that no new investigations were to be launched in compliance with a legislative resolution, unless moved by *both* houses of Congress.

[51] FTC, *Annual Report, 1954*, pp. 78–102.

[52] See House of Representatives, Committee on Small Business, *op. cit.*, pp. 22–23.

A rider attached to the act granting the Commission funds for 1954 provided that "no part of the foregoing appropriation shall be available for a statistical analysis of the consumer's dollar." [53] The Commission was thus forestalled from investigating the gap that sometimes exists between the price received by the producer of goods and the price the consumer must pay.

Trade-practice Conferences

Another way by which the Federal Trade Commission regulates competitive practices is by means of the trade-practice conference. In 1919 the Commission announced that it would cooperate with business groups in the formulation of codes of fair practice through trade-practice conferences. To obtain such a code, trade associations or representatives of a substantial portion of an industry are invited to apply to the Commission for a conference. With the Commission acting as sort of adviser and referee, such conferences are held and codes of fair competition drafted. If the Commission finds the conference to be representative of an industry and the code provisions not tending to restraint of trade or monopoly but conducive of fair competition, it approves the code. From that point, the rules so formulated become a basis for lawful business behavior, with the implication that the Commission will not proceed against members of the group who live up to the code. The Commission also cooperates with the trade to obtain compliance.[54]

Business at first adopted the trade-practice conference and codes resulting from it with enthusiasm. Many industries held such conferences and adopted codes. However, the program never recovered the vigor which it had possessed during the 1920s, except for the brief period from 1933 to 1935 when the National Industrial Recovery Act was in effect. This law, enacted by Congress as a means of combating the competitive excesses of the Depression, provided for business control through codes of fair competition established by trade groups of businessmen and approved by the government.[55] By 1952, only 179 industries or segments of industries were

[53] Public Law 176, July 31, 1953.

[54] This does not mean that the Commission has affirmatively enforced all the rules of a trade conference. The rules included in a code are of two sorts. Those which constitute settled interpretation of the law have been enforced by the Commission; those which have been recognized by it as constituting good business ethics but are believed to lie outside its jurisdiction are left to enforcement by the trade itself through the influence of business opinion and enlightened leadership.

[55] The code regulation established under the NRA was much broader than that carried out under the FTC. Many practices which have been held by the Commission to constitute unfair competition became fair competition under the codes. For example, the Commission has always held basing-point price systems to be unfair

operating under trade-practice agreements. In spite of the interest business has shown in the conferences, the actual promulgation of rules proceeds slowly.

There are a number of distinct advantages in this practice of regulation. For one thing, the trade-practice conference is a flexible instrument of control, allowing businessmen to have a part in determining fair practices in industry. Those in a business are often best qualified to define practices which are harmful to fair trade and deceptive to the customer. Generally the practice in question is one which only a minority may favor, although a majority may be forced to employ it to meet competition. Furthermore, the trade conference, by leaving some of the rules to be enforced by the trade itself, represents business self-regulation at its best in a way which is not subject to secretiveness.

From the point of view of the individual businessman, the trade-practice conference has the advantage of making him certain of the government's attitude toward questionable trade practices. Many businessmen may not even be aware that a given practice is unlawful or unethical. The conference and the resulting code may be of great educational value to those who wish to conduct their businesses in line with the principles of fair play but who would not otherwise know the rules until actually proceeded against by some governmental agency.

The code system of regulation is also helpful to the Federal Trade Commission and any other governmental agency concerned. In enforcing its authority to forbid unfair practices in interstate commerce, the Commission must proceed against individuals rather than against the practice itself. This often means that orders must be directed against a large number of individuals all of whom may be guilty of the same kind of offense. The trade-practice agreement tends to reduce the amount of such duplication. By outlawing certain practices in codes of fair competition for an industry, the members are more likely to know what practices are unlawful and are less likely to take their chances of being prosecuted.

On the other hand, practices which involve conspiracy or concerted action can rarely be corrected by industry cooperation on a voluntary basis. The well-disciplined industries such as cement, salt, steel, and most nonferrous metals are generally opposed to rules issued by a government agency. The usefulness of rules is limited by the distrust, if not open hostility, of many industries to the conference procedure. It is significant that in the three decades of its use so few industries have resorted to the conference.

---

competition, but many codes included them as methods of fair competition. In many instances the codes under the NRA seemed to be drawn for the purpose of eliminating competition rather than enhancing it and were not inaccurately termed "codes of *no* competition."

Furthermore, the codes must be supplemented by government supervision. In its absence, businessmen, in their zeal to curb competitive practices which harm them, whether fairly or unfairly, may tend to control competitive activity by the elimination of competition itself. The experience under the National Industrial Recovery Act supports this conclusion. The ever-present danger of self-regulation is that the broader interests of the consumer and the general public will be overlooked.

Procedures of the Federal Trade Commission

Action before the Commission originates through a complaint filed by consumers, by competitors, by government agencies, or by the Commission itself. If the complaint merits investigation it goes to the Bureau of Investigation. Upon completion of investigation, the Bureau makes a recommendation (1) to close the case, (2) to negotiate a stipulation, (3) to issue a formal complaint, or (4) to send the case to the Division of Trade Practice Conferences.

STIPULATION PROCEDURES

If the Commission feels that there has been no fraudulent intent, it may offer businessmen the opportunity of entering into a voluntary agreement to discontinue the practice considered in violation of the law. This is the stipulation procedure. The stipulation is similar to the consent decree used by the Anti-trust Division. The offender admits the facts and promises to cease and desist from the objectionable practice. The requirement of admission, however, is unlike the consent decree. Since there is the possibility that these admissions may be used in damage suits by private parties, resistance is often raised to this procedure, and it tends to be a time-consuming process.[56]

The stipulation is used primarily to enable the Commission to close relatively unimportant matters without the necessity for the still more lengthy and expensive formal proceedings. This saves the offender money and possible unpleasant publicity. Since 1954, a person may settle with the Commission at any stage in the case. Before that time settlement could be agreed upon only before taking of evidence was begun. Also, since 1954 the stipulation can cover just some of the issues instead of having to cover all issues.

If the stipulation is refused, the case moves to the formal complaint stage. If accepted it has no standing in law and carries no penalties for noncompliance. However, the Commission may then proceed to issue a formal complaint.

[56] To meet this problem, the Commission adopted in 1954 a new rule permitting use of consent orders which do not require admission of facts.

CLOSING BY TRADE-PRACTICE CONFERENCE

In some cases complaints may be presented to the Trade Practice Conference Division. While the Commission may call a conference, it ordinarily requires that the interested members request the conference and that a majority of the industry be represented. Trade practices are discussed at the conference, and with the advice of the Commission, the industry may draw up a code of fair practice. Where applications for complaints are satisfied by the adoption of such a code, and offending members of an industry agree to comply with it, the proceedings are usually dropped.

The value of this technique to settle a case is a matter of some controversy. The advantage is that, through the spur of self-regulation, an industry may be able to eradicate many questionable practices as the result of the conference. Hence, instead of having to wait for a number of individual cases to be brought before the Commission, members of the industry may more easily and quickly find out what the proper interpretation of the law of unfair competition is. To the extent that the code resulting from a trade conference leads to its wide acceptance, the Commission itself is saved the time and trouble of prosecuting a host of isolated infractions.

On the other hand, the rules resulting from such a conference are only interpretative and advisory, for the Commission has no coercive rule-making power. Therefore, the question arises whether the violator of the law should be freed from prosecution because he accepts rules that interpret the law he has broken. Nearly every set of rules includes prohibitions of practices already forbidden by law. Furthermore, there is the danger that comes from the pressure from industry to include objectionable practices. At most, a rule expresses the law in greater specificity; but the more specific the rule, the greater the difficulty of expressing it accurately.

FORMAL HEARING PROCEDURE

Most complaints do not proceed beyond the informal stage, formal complaints being issued by the Commission only after careful consideration of the facts developed by the investigation. Where evidence is to be taken in a contested case, the matter is set for hearing before a hearing examiner with the Bureau of Litigation prosecuting the case. It should be noted that the trial examiners are lodged administratively in a separate bureau, so that the same office does not both prosecute and try the case.

The trial examiner issues an "initial decision" on the basis of these hearings. He draws up a statement of facts and recommends either dismissal of the complaint or the issuance of a cease-and-desist order. The accused parties are allowed to file exceptions to his findings. After study of the proposed report and the exceptions, the Commission issues its own report. If it finds the charges to be supported and the alleged action to be unlawful, it issues an order requiring the accused party to cease and desist from such action.

In cases arising under the Federal Trade Commission Act and the Wool, Fur, and Flammable Fabrics Acts (i.e., unfair and deceptive practices cases) the cease-and-desist orders become final sixty days after the decision without judicial review of the Commission's proceedings, unless within that period one of the parties appeals to an appropriate United States Court of Appeals. If, on appeal, a federal court finds an order inconsistent with the law or grounded upon findings not supported by evidence, the court may modify it or set it aside.

The legal sanction for cases arising under the Clayton Act is somewhat weaker. The cease-and-desist orders do not become final simply by the lapse of time. If an order is not obeyed, the Commission must petition a Court of Appeals to affirm its order. Only after the order is affirmed does noncompliance constitute contempt of court and can appropriate sanctions be imposed.

Federal Trade Commission Regulation of Competitive Practices: Conclusions

Of all the independent regulatory commissions, the Federal Trade Commission has been subject to greater criticism perhaps than any other. Its defects have been the inadequacies of its organic legislation and jurisdictional authority, the weaknesses of its organization and procedure, the quality of its personnel, and the lack of sufficient appropriations. These defects can be remedied. A more fundamental problem is one that confronts all regulatory commissions. As agencies charged with control of sectors of the economy, they inevitably operate in an atmosphere of antagonism.[57] In the case of the Federal Trade Commission the problem is more acute, because its area of operation is not limited to one portion of the economy as is that of the Interstate Commerce Commission, Federal Communications Commission, Federal Power Commission, and so forth. The jurisdiction of the Federal Trade Commission extends over almost the entire American business world.

Unfortunately, the Commission is ill equipped by its organic legislation to perform its task. The substantive provisions of the Clayton Act which it enforces are specific enough, but jurisdiction must be shared with the

[57] See Robert M. Cooper, "Techniques of Public Control–An Appraisal of Methods," 201 *The Annals of the American Academy of Political and Social Science* 1–16 (January, 1939).

Department of Justice and adverse court rulings on some sections have made of them virtually dead letters. The attempt to identify and codify those practices which fall under the vague phrase "unfair methods of competition" has been restricted by the courts' assumption of that responsibility. Therefore, the Commission has been content to limit its operations largely to its one area of successful prosecutions—false advertising and misbranding. The Hoover Commission Task Force criticized the Commission for "prosecuting trivial and technical offenses and . . . failing to confine these dockets to cases of public importance." [58] As a former commissioner remarked, the Federal Trade Commission today prevents "false and misleading advertising in reference to hair restorers, anti-fat remedies, etc.—a somewhat inglorious end to a noble experiment." [59]

Consequently, the attempts of the Commission to restore competition and prevent the growth of monopolies have been of slight effect. Myron Watkins explained: ". . . The diversion of the thrust of administrative regulatory policy from unfairness to trade competitors to unfairness to trade customers reflects the general shift in public opinion from the trust-busting sentiment of a previous generation to resignation to the inevitableness of economic concentration and to the endeavor to find such protection as may be had in the exercise of public control rather than in the restoration of free competition." [60]

Until its complete reorganization in 1950, serious problems of coordination arose because different bureaus were responsible for different stages of its cases and were relatively autonomous. The new organization should greatly strengthen the ability of the Commission to expedite its business. The Commission's procedures are complex, cumbersome, and tedious. Its complaints, findings, and orders are worded in highly legalistic language. Moreover, until recently the Commission did not make public any of the opinions written by its members. Davis criticizes the Commission for being "glaringly deficient in its failure to prepare reasoned opinions and to develop a reliable body of case law." [61]

The Commission has also suffered from a lack of adequate appropriations. Although the general trend of appropriations has been upward since 1914, the increase has not kept pace with the rising cost of operations. With the exception of a brief period in 1941, the Commission had a larger

[58] Commission on Organization of the Executive Branch of the Government, *op. cit.*, p. 128. See also similar earlier criticisms: E. Pendleton Herring, *Public Administration and the Public Interest* (New York: McGraw-Hill Book Company, Inc., 1936), p. 115; J. C. Blaisdell, *The Federal Trade Commission* (New York: Columbia University Press, 1932), p. 225.

[59] Quoted by Herring, *op. cit.*, p. 115.

[60] "Unfair Competition," *Encyclopedia of the Social Sciences*, vol. 15, p. 177.

[61] Kenneth Culp Davis, *Administrative Law* (St. Paul, Minn.: West Publishing Co., 1951), pp. 547–548.

staff in 1918 than at any time since.[62] In spite of the fact that the Federal Trade Commission is charged with the duty of maintaining the general plane of competition throughout the entire American economy, it ranks near the bottom of the list of independent regulatory commissions in respect to the size of its appropriations.

Thus, while the Commission may have fallen short of expectations as an agency to restore and maintain competition, it has emerged as a vigorous agency for the protection of the consumer against unfair and deceptive practices. The defects that have been identified can be remedied. The major need is for policy guidance as to whether the two objectives—maintaining competition and protecting the consumer—should be pursued by the same agency, and if not, what the distribution of functions should be. The Hoover Commission Task Force on Regulatory Commissions concludes on a positive note: [63]

> . . . The conception of the Commission seems to us a sound one for this field. The developments in industry in recent decades have only reenforced the need seen in 1914 for an administrative agency devoted to a vigorous program to maintain effective competitive conditions and to eliminate and correct restrictive practices. But if the Commission is to perform the significant functions intended by Congress a number of basic changes will have to be made in its organization and program. Fortunately, the Commission itself has become aware of the need for reform and has taken some measures in this direction.

Selected References

Blaisdell, T. C., *The Federal Trade Commission.* New York: Columbia University Press, 1932.

Commission on Organization of the Executive Branch of the Government, *Task Force Report on Regulatory Commissions* (Appendix N). Government Printing Office, 1949.

Cook, Franklin M., *Principles of Business and the Federal Law*, chaps. 13, 15. New York: The Macmillan Company, 1951.

Edwards, Corwin, *Maintaining Competition: Requisites of a Governmental Policy*. New York: McGraw-Hill Book Company, Inc., 1949.

Federal Trade Commission, *Control of Unfair Competitive Practices through Trade Practice Procedure of the Federal Trade Commission,* TNEC Monograph 34. Government Printing Office, 1941.

Henderson, G. C., *The Federal Trade Commission.* New Haven, Conn.: Yale University Press, 1925.

McFarland, C., *Judicial Control of the Federal Trade Commission and the Interstate Commerce Commission.* Cambridge, Mass.: Harvard University Press, 1933.

[62] House of Representatives, Select Committee on Small Business, *op. cit.*, p. 18.

[63] Commission on Organization of the Executive Branch of the Government, *op. cit.*, p. 120.

Miller, J. P., *Unfair Competition.* Cambridge, Mass.: Harvard University Press, 1941.

Mund, Vernon, *Government and Business,* chaps. 16–19, 22, 23. New York: Harper & Brothers, 1950.

Stocking, George W., and Myron W. Watkins, *Monopoly and Free Enterprise,* chaps. 7, 10, 11. New York: The Twentieth Century Fund, Inc., 1951.

U.S. Congress, House of Representatives, Committee on Small Business, *United States versus Economic Concentration and Monopoly,* Staff Report to the Monopoly Subcommittee, 79th Cong., (1949).

Watkins, Myron W., *Public Regulation of Competitive Practices in Business Enterprise.* New York: National Industrial Conference Board, Inc., 1940.

16

SPECIAL AREAS OF TRADE REGULATION

Certain major areas of regulation under the laws directed against monopoly, restraint of trade, and unfair competitive practices have been singled out for separate treatment in this chapter. These areas are trade associations, resale-price maintenance, patents and copyrights, and basing-point systems. In addition, because the regulation of competitive practices under the food and drug laws is related to some of the activities of the Federal Trade Commission, that problem will also be discussed here.

Trade Associations

Although organization of businessmen on a trade basis has existed at least since 1850, new impetus to this form of combination came in 1912 with the publication of a book entitled *The New Competition*, by Arthur J. Eddy, a Chicago corporation lawyer. Eddy's thesis was that competition could be made more free and open if businessmen could have information about the price and production policies of competitors. This idea was adopted by many trade associations, and compilation and dissemination of trade data became one of their principal functions. In addition, trade associations have generally engaged in cooperative research, advertising, and lobbying and have done much to encourage uniform accounting methods, codes of business ethics, and standards of size and quality.

Under government aid and encouragement, trade associations grew rapidly during and after World War I. The Department of Commerce cooperated with them in compiling business statistics, and the Federal Trade Commission worked with them in formulating business-practice codes. The heyday of the trade association came with the enactment of the temporary National Industrial Recovery Act of 1933. In forming the codes of fair competition under this law, the trade associations in the various industries performed the principal task of drawing up the codes and furnishing the government with data and personnel for making them workable.

There are some 12,000 trade associations in the United States, of which almost a quarter are national or international in scope, and there are some 4,000 local chambers of commerce which represent a kind of territorial form of trade association.[1] The trade association is frankly a device to obtain cooperation among businessmen who are generally in competition with each other. Since it can hardly be expected that the antitrust laws were devised to forbid all such cooperation, the problem of trade-association activities is primarily to divide the unlawful activities from the lawful. Obviously, the trade association can be used as a means for working a destruction of competition. Just as obviously, it can be used to sharpen competition and to reduce wastes to society by spreading business information.

LAWFUL ACTIVITIES OF TRADE ASSOCIATIONS

Scrutiny of trade-association activities for antitrust law violations has been rather generally limited to those matters by which the degree of price competition in an industry might be affected. Cooperation for advertising, research, business ethics, and standardization of size and grade has not been the basis for violation of the antitrust laws. It is in the realm of price and production statistics and policy that such violations have come.

The scope of permissible activities is given in several cases where trade-association programs were upheld. One of the first of such cases was concerned with the Maple Flooring Manufacturers' Association.[2] This trade association, among other things, distributed information on flooring inventories of manufacturers, current production, shipments, costs, freight rates, and prices in actual sales. It was attacked as being in effect a combination the purpose of which was to restrain trade. The Supreme Court found in favor of the trade association, holding the dissemination of information by it did not constitute violation of the law. The Court found no restraint of trade from the mere fact that dissemination of information enabled individual producers to "stabilize prices or limit production through a better understanding of economic laws and a more general ability to conform to them, for the simple reason that the Sherman Law neither repeals economic law nor prohibits the gathering and dissemination of information." [3] The Court insisted that [4]

> We decide only that trade associations or combinations of persons or corporations which openly and fairly gather and disseminate information as to the cost of their product, the volume of production, the actual price which the product has brought in past transactions, stocks of merchandise on hand,

[1] U.S. Department of Commerce, *National Associations of the United States* (1949), p. viii.

[2] *Maple Flooring Manufacturers Assoc. v. United States*, 268 U.S. 563 (1925).

[3] 268 U.S. 563, 584.

[4] 268 U.S. 563, 586.

approximate cost of transportation from the principal point of shipment to the points of consumption as did these defendants and who, as they did, meet and discuss such information and statistics without however reaching or attempting to reach any agreement or any concerted action with respect to prices or production or restraining competition, do not thereby engage in unlawful restraint of commerce.

A like decision was reached in a case involving the Cement Manufacturers' Protective Association in 1924.[5]

UNLAWFUL ACTIVITIES OF TRADE ASSOCIATIONS

The activities of many trade associations have been held to constitute an unlawful combination in restraint of trade. The program of the American Hardwood Manufacturers' Association resulted in such a decision.[6] In this case, however, more than mere dissemination of information was attempted. Weekly reports were required of each member, and the association audited these reports to ensure complete accuracy. Information published by the association identified every member's price and production policies, so that each member knew exactly what every other member was doing. Market letters were sent out by the association suggesting restriction of output and maintenance or increase of prices. By exposing members who were engaging in price-cutting tactics and by holding meetings at which future price and production policies were discussed, the association was actively engaged in fixing uniform price and production practices for the trade. Hence, the Supreme Court found that the association was not only spreading information for its members but also restraining interstate commerce by concerted action to curtail production and increase prices.

Similar conclusions were reached by the Supreme Court in 1923 with a like plan of the Linseed Crushers' Council, a trade association of linseed-oil producers.[7] This association had gone even farther than the Hardwood Association and had levied fines on members for nonattendance at meetings, had forced members to explain departures from published prices, and had put recalcitrants "on the carpet." Likewise, practices of the Sugar Institute, a trade association of sugar-refining companies, whereby attempts were made to fix prices and enforce adherence to these prices, were enjoined by a decision of the Supreme Court in 1936.[8]

As might be expected, actions of trade associations to enforce trade policy through the use of boycotts or other concerted action have been held to be unlawful. As early as 1914, the Supreme Court declared unlaw-

[5] *Cement Manufacturers' Protective Assoc. v. United States*, 268 U.S. 588 (1925).

[6] *American Column and Lumber Co. v. United States*, 257 U.S. 377 (1921).

[7] *United States v. American Linseed Oil Co.*, 262 U.S. 371 (1923).

[8] *Sugar Institute, Inc. v. United States*, 297 U.S. 553 (1936).

ful the action of an association of retail lumber dealers in circulating black lists of wholesalers selling directly to consumers as a boycott to force the entire trade through the hands of retailers.[9] More recently, a trade association of manufacturers of women's garments sought to protect the original designs of its members from "style piracy." It did not attempt to fix prices or to allocate or restrict production. Despite its objective to stop a practice clearly regarded as unethical, at least in the trade, the association was held to be in violation of the Sherman Act, because it exercised sufficient control in the industry to exclude manufacturers and distributors who did not conform to the rules and regulations of the association.[10]

TRADE-ASSOCIATION ACTIVITIES: CONCLUSIONS

The courts have applied both the rule of reason and the per se principle in trade-association cases.[11] The rule of reason has permitted broad latitude in the presentation and analysis of information by business groups. The trade-association cases give businessmen confidence in the legitimacy of cooperative collection, compilation, and dissemination of trade statistics which contribute to enlightened competition by acquainting both buyers and sellers with the basic facts that govern market forces. Trade associations will not be molested so long as they do not deliberately and collectively tamper with market forces to restrict competition. Thus, the per se principle has been applied only to conspiracies to fix prices. The principles enumerated in the Maple Flooring case still govern.

Resale-price Maintenance

Resale-price maintenance is a selling arrangement under which the manufacturer fixes by contract the minimum price at which the wholesaler or retailer who handles his product may sell it. As a practical matter, fixing resale prices by contract can be accomplished only where the good is trade-marked or otherwise differentiated and not subject to free competition. The same end may be accomplished by legislation making it unlawful for a dealer to sell below the cost of the good to him, or below that cost plus a markup to cover a reasonable cost of selling. In contrast with the *horizontal* price-fixing practices of some combinations, resale-price maintenance represents a *vertical* price-fixing arrangement between persons at different stages of the business process.

[9] *Eastern States Retail Lumber Association v. United States*, 234 U.S. 600 (1914).

[10] *Fashion Originators' Guild of America, Inc. v. FTC*, 312 U.S. 457 (1941).

[11] For an exhaustive analysis, see George W. Stocking, "The Rule of Reason, Workable Competition, and the Legality of Trade Association Activities," 21 *University of Chicago Law Review* 527–619 (Summer, 1954).

SOCIAL AND ECONOMIC ASPECTS OF RESALE-PRICE MAINTENANCE

The pressure for resale-price-maintenance laws comes from the small dealers, especially in those fields threatened by competition of the chain store, the supermarket, the large department store, and the mail-order house. Faced with competition from large retailing outlets, the small dealer has desired a system which protects him from the inroads of competition.

Many manufacturers have also supported resale-price maintenance, principally because of the pressure of retailers, but partly to protect the value of the good will attached to their trade-marked products. It is sometimes argued that, if retail price cutting should drive the small seller from the field, the manufacturer might well sell as much as before; but dealing with a few large buyers does not give him the independence he has when his retail outlets are legion. Moreover, if good will is built about an article at a sales price of $1, reducing the retail price to 59 cents by a price-cutting retailer tends to make the public believe either that profits are too large or that the product is not worth the dollar. It is further argued that cutting retail prices may bring pressure on the manufacturer to lower his price to wholesalers and retailers. This could mean that he would be forced to skimp on quality or selling effort, or to take a cut below a reasonable profit margin. If quality or selling effort is curtailed, the market may fall off; if profit margins are cut too close, losses may result. On the other hand, an increasing number of manufacturers are finding that lower retail prices due to aggressive price rivalry do not affect their profits but rather, through increasing the volume of sales, lower their costs and increase profits.

The idea of resale-price maintenance and of forcing selling at cost or cost plus a merchandising profit has also appealed to many individuals who are not manufacturers, wholesalers, or retailers. Many people fear the consequence to social stability of growing size in the merchandising field and the squeezing out of the independent merchant.

From an economic point of view, resale-price maintenance is usually viewed in a different light. It is true that a good case can be made for saying that the manufacturer has a property right of value in the good will surrounding his differentiated product, that the price cutter uses this property as an unfair means of getting customers into his store, and that he destroys it through the mere lowering of price itself. From the point of view of society, however, resale-price maintenance, by forcing prices to be higher than necessary economic costs, makes the consumer pay too high a price for the good he receives. If the resale price is high enough to give all retailers a reasonable profit margin, it is probably high enough to shield the inefficient middleman. Indeed, it is this protection of the inefficient through protecting them against effective competition that gives rise to the primary social criticism of resale-price maintenance.

On the other hand, if resale-price maintenance contributes to the maintenance of competition, there may be some social and economic justification for it. If the small retailer would be driven out of the field without it, and if marketing outlets would become few and large so that competition would decline, consumers might be subject to the dangers of oligopoly pricing. This eventuality seems remote, however, especially in view of the competition between large distributing units, as well as the ability of many smaller units to keep in the competitive stream even where resale-price maintenance is ineffective.

FEDERAL REGULATION BEFORE 1937

Prior to 1937, resale price fixing fell under the prohibitions of both the antitrust and the fair-trade-practices laws.

Impact of the antitrust laws. The Dr. Miles Medical Company attempted to fix resale price of its medicines by entering into contracts with jobbers and wholesalers who agreed not to sell to any retailer unless the retailer in turn agreed to sell at prices fixed by the company. In 1911, the Supreme Court found these contracts to be a restraint of trade in violation of the Sherman Act.[12] Similar arrangements to control resale prices of patented goods were held to be an unlawful restraint of trade in 1913.[13] Likewise, resale-price maintenance under copyrights has been turned down by the Supreme Court.[14]

However, when the Colgate Company undertook to fix resale prices by persuasion, the Supreme Court found no unlawful restraint of trade.[15] The company used no contracts or other agreements to establish resale prices. Instead, it circulated price suggestions to dealers and asked for their cooperation in maintaining these prices. If a dealer was found not to be charging these prices, the company merely refused to sell him additional stocks. The Court held that manufacturers or wholesalers have a right to deal or refuse to deal with whomever they please. Since the company was not binding its dealers to sell on specified terms, its later refusal to deal was held not to constitute any unlawful restraint of trade.

Impact of the Federal Trade Commission. Before 1937, the Federal Trade Commission took the position that fixing of resale prices was a method of unfair competition as prohibited by section 5 of the Federal Trade Commission Act.

At first, it insisted that all attempts of manufacturers to fix resale prices

[12] *Dr. Miles Medical Co. v. John D. Park & Sons Co.*, 220 U.S. 373 (1911); see also an earlier case, *Bobbs-Merrill Co. v. Straus*, 210 U.S. 339 (1908).

[13] *Bauer v. O'Donnell*, 229 U.S. 1 (1913).

[14] *Straus v. Victor Talking Machine Co.*, 243 U.S. 490 (1917).

[15] *United States v. Colgate & Co.*, 250 U.S. 300 (1919).

by whatever method were unlawful. The Beech-Nut Packing Company followed the general pattern of the Colgate Company's resale-price-maintenance policy, but it announced in advance its refusal to deal with price cutters and kept a black list of dealers who did not charge the suggested prices. The Commission's cease-and-desist order against this practice was upheld by the Supreme Court.[16] The Court made clear that not all attempts to fix resale prices were unlawful.

After the decision in the Beech-Nut case, the Federal Trade Commission proceeded more slowly against attempts to fix resale prices. However, where it had reason to believe that any coercive measure beyond mere refusal to deal had been employed, until 1937 it proceeded vigorously against the parties concerned.[17] Even since then the Commission, while being debarred from proceeding against resale-price-maintenance contracts, has taken the position that the damage to the public from such contracts is probably far more than any damage that may come to producers through price cutting.[18]

LEGALIZATION OF RESALE-PRICE MAINTENANCE

Legalization of resale-price maintenance came first through state legislation.

State fair-trade laws. Largely because of fear of unbridled competition engendered by the Depression and the belief that the chain store would drive the independent retailers out of business, public pressure led to the enactment of state fair-trade laws. The first was passed by California in 1931. This statute merely permitted resale-price fixing on a voluntary basis. In 1933, it was amended to make a resale-price contract binding even on nonsigners who had not voluntarily agreed to abide by the price.

Some of the codes of fair competition under the National Industrial Recovery Act of 1933 included provisions allowing resale-price maintenance by manufacturers. When the codes were invalidated in 1935, a new impetus to the passage of fair-trade laws was experienced in many states.

By 1937, forty-one states had laws allowing manufacturers to fix resale prices by contract, and by 1955 forty-five states had them.[19] Some of

[16] *FTC v. Beech-Nut Packing Co.*, 257 U.S. 441 (1922).

[17] See, for example, *Toledo Pipe-Threading Mach. Co. v. FTC*, 11 F.2d 337 (1926); *Moir v. FTC*, 12 F.2d 22 (1926); *Cream of Wheat Co. v. FTC*, 14 F.2d 40 (1926). But the Commission has been overruled many times. See, for example, *Harriet Hubbard Ayer, Inc. v. FTC*, 15 F.2d 274 (1926).

[18] See *Investigation on Concentration of Economic Power*, part 5, pp. 2170–2172 (1939).

[19] All states except Missouri, Texas, and Vermont have resale-price-maintenance laws; however in Florida, Georgia, Michigan, Nebraska, and Arkansas the state Supreme Courts have held that nonsigner clauses violate the state constitutions.

these laws allow the manufacturer to fix the minimum resale price, while others permit the fixing of the price itself. Most of them provide that a manufacturer of a branded or trade-marked product may make a contract with wholesalers and retailers (directly or through the wholesalers) binding the retailers to sell the good at a certain price. These laws generally provide that contracts need not be made with all sellers but that a contract made with any becomes binding on all upon notice to the sellers. In order to avoid evasion of established prices by special concessions, the newer type of law forbids offering to sell a price-fixed article with a "gift" of any item of value or any other concession. They provide for selling below the fixed price only under the following circumstances: (1) sales of goods which have been damaged and are sold as such; (2) sales to close out a stock for purpose of discontinuing a product, although often state laws provide that the manufacturer must be given an opportunity to repurchase this stock;[20] and (3) sales made by an official acting under orders of a court.

In addition to laws allowing resale-price maintenance by contract, many state laws have set up limitation upon sales of any good below cost. These laws are ordinarily called "unfair-practices" or "unfair-sales" acts. By late 1950, such laws had been passed in thirty-one states. While these laws vary somewhat, they are all designed to require wholesalers and retailers to sell at no less than invoice cost,[21] or at invoice cost plus some percentage markup, or at invoice cost plus the cost of doing business. Sales below these limits are usually allowed where necessary to meet competition, to close out a line of merchandise, or to sell upon orders of a court. The purpose of the laws is largely to supplement resale-price-maintenance laws by placing a floor under prices of goods which are not branded or trade-marked.

These loss-limitation laws are generally difficult to enforce where the minimum is placed at invoice or replacement cost plus the cost of doing business. While the items of cost incurred by the retailer are usually listed in the law,[22] computations are not necessarily uniformly made, and costs differ so much and enforcement is so difficult that this type of law has been found fairly unsatisfactory. Most laws consequently required a definite percentage markup, generally 6 per cent. For example, an Oregon

[20] This chance is being eliminated by some manufacturers because of a question that has been raised whether it applies to nonsigners as well as signers. Some nonsigners have been using it as a dodge to cut the prices of fair-traded goods. *New York Times*, May 16, 1953, p. 23.

[21] Generally invoice cost or replacement cost, whichever is lower.

[22] The cost of doing business is usually defined as including the following: all wages and salaries, rent, interest on borrowed capital, depreciation, maintenance, selling costs, delivery costs, accounting and auditing costs, losses, cost of licenses and fees, taxes, insurance, and advertising.

amendment placed the minimum markup for retailers at 6 per cent above invoice price. Where invoice prices differ as between stores or over a period of time, a dealer, of course, has the right to place his price at a level to meet competition.

A loss-limitation law which merely requires that a dealer sell at a price equal to or above his invoice price would seem not to be open to criticism, since it merely stops the use of loss leaders and the more vicious types of cutthroat competition. But laws which provide for a minimum percentage markup do not take into account either the possibility that an efficient merchandiser may not need such a markup, or the fact that fast-moving goods may require, on a basis of cost, a lesser markup than slow-moving ones. As for laws which require that the markup be equal to the average cost of doing business, little favor can be found from an economic point of view. Such laws require in effect that an equal percentage of total average costs, including both fixed and variable costs, must be applied to every dollar's worth of merchandise sold. They overlook the very nature of fixed costs, and of cost allocation where fixed costs exist.

Rather than lose business (and after all, consumers' demands are often very elastic), it might well be in the interests of most profitable operation to sell some goods at a markup below the average cost of doing business. Moreover, if the purpose of this kind of legislation is to curtail price competition which tends toward monopoly, to require markups equal to the cost of doing business is to overshoot the mark. Such a requirement seems to go beyond mere prevention of price cutting and becomes a device for ensuring profits to independent sellers.

Exemption under the federal antitrust laws. The state laws give a manufacturer no power to make resale-price-maintenance contracts in interstate commerce. The Miller-Tydings Act authorizes the use of resale-price-maintenance contracts in interstate commerce, provided they are for trade-marked or branded products and are lawful in the state in which the resale takes place. At the time the Act was passed, forty-one states authorized sellers of branded merchandise to fix resale prices by contract. The federal law merely allowed these contracts to be effective in interstate commerce without danger of running afoul of the antitrust laws.

A number of state laws contained "nonsigner" provisions which required *all* retailers to abide by the resale price agreed upon by the manufacturer and just one retailer, even though the rest of the retailers had not signed such a contract. The Supreme Court ruled in 1951 that enforcement of a resale price against a nonsigner violates the Sherman Act, since only voluntary minimum-price agreements were exempted by the Miller-Tydings Act. "Contracts or agreements convey the idea of a cooperative arrangement, not a program whereby recalcitrants are dragged in by the heels and compelled to submit to price fixing." [23]

Congress reacted to this decision by enacting the McGuire Act the next year. This statute amends the antitrust laws to exempt price-fixing contracts that apply to all sellers, whether a party to the contract or not, when such contracts are lawful under state law. Thus, nonsigners in states with fair-trade laws containing a nonsigner clause can be required to observe resale prices set by a manufacturer in interstate commerce in a signed contract with only one retailer in any state.

Legality of state fair-trade laws. The United States Supreme Court in 1936 held unanimously that state laws allowing for resale-price-maintenance contracts were valid.[24] Mr. Justice Sutherland, speaking for the Court, pointed out that while a retailer buying a product from a manufacturer owned the commodity, he did not own the good will which a trademark or brand symbolized. If fixing of resale prices is necessary to protect the value of this good will, then, he declared, legislation allowing such contracts to be made is a reasonable measure for protection of the manufacturer's property.

It is interesting to note that Justice Sutherland found no fault with the nonsigner provision in the state law. The retailers were not obliged to buy, he said. However, the nonsigner clause was attacked as a violation of the due-process and equal-protection clauses of the Fourteenth Amendment in the Old Dearborn case. A question of its legality under the Sherman Act was not raised until 1951 in the Schwegmann case, in which it was found illegal. In the same year the Michigan Court of Appeals found the nonsigner provision of the Michigan Fair Trade Act a violation of the due-process and equal-protection clauses of the Michigan constitution, even in an intrastate transaction.[25]

After the enactment of the McGuire Act, Schwegmann Brothers Giant Markets, still nonsigners, continued to sell fair-traded products below the minimum fixed prices. Schwegmann contended that the previous Schwegmann case had overruled the Old Dearborn case. However, a Louisiana District Court said that the retailer of a trade-marked product does not fully own it to fix prices as he pleases. The good will that inheres in the product belongs to the manufacturer, entitling him to fix its price. Furthermore, the court said, nothing in the first Schwegmann case indicated that Old Dearborn had been overruled.[26]

[23] *Schwegmann Bros. v. Calvert Distillers Corp.*, 341 U.S. 384, 390 (1951).

[24] *Old Dearborn Distributing Co. v. Seagram Distillers Corp.*, 299 U.S. 183 (1936); *Pep Boys v. Pyroil Sales Corp.*, 299 U.S. 198 (1936).

[25] *Shakespeare Co. v. Lippman's Tool Shop Sporting Goods Co.*, 54 N.W.2d 268 (1952).

[26] *Eli Lilly & Co. v. Schwegmann Bros. Giant Markets,* 109 F. Supp. 269 (1953); cert. denied, 74 Sup. Ct. 71 (1953).

In recent years state courts have tended to take an unfavorable view of state fair-trade laws. The Florida Supreme Court held the Florida Fair Trade Act invalid in 1949 on the ground that the law was enacted at a time when there were surpluses and a general need for such a law in certain basic commodities.[27] After the McGuire Act was passed another case arose in Georgia where a fair-trade law had been held illegal under the Sherman Act in 1936.[28] The Georgia Supreme Court ruled that neither the Miller-Tydings nor the McGuire Act validated the earlier statute without the legislature's taking action to reenact it.[29]

The legality of state resale-price-maintenance laws is clouded by conflicting court decisions. It may be several years before the issue is finally settled, if it is settled at all. In any event, it should be noted that state legislatures are less inclined to enact fair-trade laws than they were. In 1953, the Vermont Senate rejected a resale-price law and the Michigan legislature refused to strengthen its fair-trade laws by voting down an amendment that would have required nonsigners to charge the minimum prices.[30]

Under federal antitrust and competitive-practices legislation, resale-price-maintenance is illegal in the absence of state exemption. The Miller-Tydings and McGuire Acts permit vertical price fixing only if state law has authorized it. It should be emphasized that these acts and the various state fair-trade laws legalize only vertical price fixing. Should agreements be made to fix prices of similar products in competition with each other, the antitrust restrictions would clearly be valid.[31]

STATE FAIR-TRADE LAWS AND THE FEDERAL TRADE COMMISSION

There never has been any doubt of the adverse position of the Federal Trade Commission with respect to the state fair-trade laws. However, the Commission never made a policy statement regarding these laws until 1955, even though it continually watched to see that these laws were not utilized as a device to accomplish unlawful restraints on competition. In 1955, in a policy-making decision rejecting a request that it enforce state fair-trade laws on price-cutting discount stores, the Commission made it clear that the federal government had only given the states enabling legislation through exempting fair-trade laws from the antitrust statutes.[32]

[27] *Liquor Store, Inc. v. Continental Distilling Corp.*, 40 So.2d 371 (1949). The next month the state legislature passed a new fair-trade law. *New York Times*, Apr. 8, 1949, p. 37.

[28] *Harris v. Duncan*, 67 S.E.2d 692 (1936).

[29] *Grayson-Robinson Stores, Inc. v. Oneida, Ltd.*, 75 S.E.2d 161 (1953).

[30] *New York Times*, Apr. 19, 1953, sec. 3, p. 1.

[31] See *Kiefer-Stewart Co. v. Joseph E. Seagram & Sons, Inc.*, 340 U.S. 211 (1951).

[32] *Los Angeles Times*, part I, p. 8 (Feb. 21, 1955).

But in the statement issued in 1955, the Commission went farther than merely informing some complaining jewelers that enforcement of these laws was a matter for the states. The commission made clear that the exemption of these laws would be narrowly construed and that arrangements under state laws which are not clearly lawful and are "an integral part of a greater restraint" can be attacked under the antitrust laws. In addition, the Commission counseled jewelers who complained of lax enforcement of resale-price laws by manufacturers to resort to various means of self-help, including suits for injunctive relief against the price cutting by discount houses or disregarding the resale-price contracts by cutting prices to compete with the discount houses. The Commission noted in this connection that "it cannot be suggested that price competition is morally reprehensible." [33]

RESALE-PRICE MAINTENANCE: CONCLUSIONS

Whether resale-price maintenance can be successful without some degree of horizontal price agreement is open to question. When one manufacturer of a branded product in general competition with other goods refuses to fix his resale prices, the success of competitors' fixing prices by contract is endangered. Under the pressure from distributors who handle the goods of rival manufacturers, as well as pressure from the other manufacturers themselves, a horizontal price line tends to be held. Moreover, when goods are generally competing, the fixed prices would have to be in line so that consumers might not be influenced too much by price, and so that dealers might not find it so advantageous to cut prices.

While collusive tactics may not be employed in connection with the fixing of resale prices, there is tremendous pressure to engage in activities clearly forbidden by the antitrust laws. The fact that only vertical price agreements are made valid should not obscure the possibility that horizontal agreements may easily accompany resale-price maintenance.

The wisdom and desirability of fair-trade laws may be judged from three points of view. The first, and by far the most important, has to do with the questions of efficiency in marketing and production and of low prices to the consumer. If fixing of resale prices, whether by contract or by markup laws, places a protective "umbrella" over both the efficient and inefficient, society must pay for this encouragement to inefficiency. If these laws encourage the raising of prices above necessary costs, the consumer is forced to pay more or turn to products not favored by the law. As compared to prices existing before the state laws, even after

[33] *Ibid.*

allowing for a rise in the price level, there does seem to be evidence that the consumer has paid more.[34]

A second consideration of great importance to society is whether this type of program is in the direction of protecting the small businessman from monopolistic tendencies in marketing and, even if it is, whether such protection is wise. A question might be raised as to whether without resale-price maintenance monopolistic conditions would arise. If mere unreasonable price discrimination between a manufacturer and his customers is erased and if predatory price cutting below invoice or replacement cost is restricted, perhaps the small retailer does not need more protection. Even if he should, is it wise, even as a political measure, to subsidize one group of entrepreneurs over another? Moreover, the small businessman and the manufacturer who have asked for some degree of price control may have opened the way for a greater program of government regulation of their businesses in the future. Government regulatory schemes have a way of making themselves more effective by introducing more far-reaching controls.

Finally, there is the practical consideration of the effect of these laws on the retailers who presumably desire them. The size of their margin is determined by contract and made universal. The result is to divert retailers to competition in sales effort, in providing various types of distributive services, and in pricing goods not covered by contracts. Where contracts apply to most goods which retailers carry, only sales effort and service competition remain, and as a result the cost of distribution is likely to rise. Moreover, there is some tendency for new retailers to be attracted into the trade where the margins are fixed and generous and for the average volume per distributive outlet to be correspondingly reduced.[35]

Patents and Copyrights

In order to encourage invention and the advancement of the arts and sciences, inventors are allowed by law to have the exclusive use or control of patented devices. The patent holder may assign his patent rights as he chooses and may attach such conditions to the use of the patents as he wishes. In other words, to the extent of the matter covered and for the life of a patent, the patent laws confer an individual monopoly on the holder.

[34] E. H. Gault, "Fair Trade," *Michigan Business Studies,* vol. 9, no. 2 (Ann Arbor, Mich.: University of Michigan, 1939), pp. 41 ff; *Investigation of Concentration of Economic Power,* part 8, p. 3371 (1939).

[35] Corwin D. Edwards, *Maintaining Competition* (New York: McGraw-Hill Book Company, Inc., 1949), p. 71.

If control is exerted by the individual acting alone over matters directly pertaining to the patent, administration of patent rights involves no question of violation of the antitrust laws. Questions arise when the patent right is used as a means of restraining trade beyond the lawful power of the patentee, or when patent holders join together in doing something in concert which restrains trade.

EXTENSION OF CONTROL UNDER PATENTS

The monopolistic rights which patent holders enjoy do not justify the extension of the monopoly control to matters not immediately concerned with the patents. The fixing of resale prices and the making of tying contracts in connection with patents are really cases in which patent holders have used their monopoly powers to extend their control beyond the exclusive rights granted under the patents.[36] But the unlawful extension of power under patents may go much further. For example, in 1940 the United States Supreme Court found that a company which owned patents for a good had used the patent monopoly as a means of building up a combination and controlling prices.[37] This company, the Ethyl Gasoline Corporation, producing under patent a fluid to increase the octane rating of gasoline, not only had controlled gasoline-selling policies of refiners but had forced gasoline jobbers into contracts by which jobbers' prices were fixed and competition between jobbers was suppressed. The Supreme Court pointed out that such contracts or combinations, which were used to obstruct the free flow of interstate commerce, were in violation of the Sherman Act, even in the case of a patented article, after the article is sold by the patentee or his licensee.

Two schemes closely resembling that outlawed in the Ethyl case were ruled invalid in 1942.[38] In the same year, the Court invalidated two attempts by patentees to extend their respective monopolies on patented devices by monopolozing unpatented materials used in conjunction with them.[39] Two years later, a patent-licensing scheme for uniting under the domination of one holding company all manufacturers of thermostatic control devices was voided.[40] In 1947, the patent-license system of Inter-

[36] See *Motion Picture Patents Co. v. Universal Film Manufacturing Co.*, 243 U.S. 502 (1917); *United Shoe Machinery Co. v. United States*, 258 U.S. 451 (1922); and *Standard Fashion Co. v. Magrane-Houston Co.*, 258 U.S. 346 (1922).

[37] *Ethyl Gasoline Corporation v. United States*, 309 U.S. 436 (1940).

[38] *United States v. Univis Lens Co.*, 316 U.S. 241 (1942); *United States v. Masonite Corp.*, 316 U.S. 265 (1942).

[39] *Morton Salt Co. v. Suppiger*, 314 U.S. 488 (1942); *B. B. Chemical Co. v. Ellis*, 314 U.S. 495 (1942).

[40] *Mercoid v. Mid-Continent Investment Co.*, 320 U.S. 661 (1944); and *Mercoid v. Minneapolis-Honeywell Co.*, 320 U.S. 680 (1944).

national Salt Company received the same Court treatment that was accorded Morton Salt.[41] The next year the Court disapproved two patent-licensing schemes that involved combinations among otherwise competitive manufacturers mutually to fix prices.[42] In 1952, the Court held illegal a conspiracy to fix uniform minimum prices and eliminate competition throughout substantially all the wrinkle-finish industry of the United States by means of patent agreements.[43]

CROSS-LICENSING AND PATENT POOLS

As the number of patents has increased in many lines of industry, producers have found it generally advisable to pool patents. By doing so all producers of a certain commodity may obtain the latest mechanical devices without danger of patent infringement and the costly suits which arise. Since so many goods involve a number of patents, and an individual producer seldom has all the needed patents, the system of pooling patents often works to the advantage of all patent holders.

Patents may be pooled in several ways. Patent holders may work out cross-licensing agreements on a reciprocal basis, or they may assign the patents to a trustee or a corporation which is authorized to issue licenses for the use of patents. Patents are also pooled sometimes by giving powers of attorney to a central administrative association, which in turn licenses users.

Patent pools have grown up in many industries. Patents have been pooled in the automobile industry since 1914 through a cross licensing agreement of members of the Automobile Manufacturers Association. In 1938, there were nearly 1,100 patents covered by these agreements.[44] Of course there were many additional patents not placed in the pool. The Radio Corporation of America has been an agency whereby many radio and other communication patents have been pooled. Patents have also been pooled in such industries as hosiery, aviation, oil refining, and motion pictures, to mention only a few.

The legal status of patent pools depends upon whether the patents are pooled primarily to limit competition or for the purpose of increased efficiency and decreased patent litigation. For example, a pool of patents held by manufacturers of enameled ironware was formed in 1910. The manufacturers agreed not to sell except at certain fixed prices and not to deal with jobbers except those who resold at prices fixed by the pool. The United States Supreme Court found this arrangement to be a combina-

[41] *International Salt Co. v. United States*, 332 U S. 392 (1947).

[42] *United States v. U.S. Gypsum Co.*, 333 U.S. 364 (1948); and *United States v. Line Material Co.*, 333 U.S. 287 (1948).

[43] *United States v. New Wrinkle, Inc.*, 342 U.S. 371 (1952).

[44] *Investigation of Concentration of Economic Power*, part 2, p. 292 (1939).

tion in restraint of trade in violation of the Sherman Act, since these agreements were hardly necessary to protect the use of a patent but were designed to restrain competition in the industry.[45]

Perhaps the leading cases in which patent combinations were held to be lawful were the United Shoe Machinery and the Standard Oil cases. In the United Shoe Machinery case,[46] the company had gained control, partly through consolidation with other shoe-machinery producers, of patents covering practically every basic operation of shoe manufacture. As a result, although other shoe machines were built, the United had under its control the manufacture of every important kind of machine used in certain fundamental shoemaking processes. It was attacked as being a monopoly in restraint of trade, but the Supreme Court, in a close decision, refused to order its dissolution. The ground for upholding the combination was that it represented a combination of supplementary, rather than competing, patents. The Court claimed that competition would not be increased if the combination was broken up, for the machines for which patents were held were not in competition with each other. If seven or eight companies held these patents, the monopoly aspect of the patent privilege would mean that competition would not be enhanced.

However, a recent District Court decision, subsequently affirmed by the Supreme Court,[47] ruled that United Shoe Machinery now has substantial market power to give it effective control of the shoe-machinery market, a power which has adverse effects on competition. By 1953, United maintained through leases a network of contacts with approximately 90 per cent of all shoe factories and supplied more than 75 per cent of the demand for shoe machinery. The court held that United fell within the doctrine applied in Alcoa and subsequent cases, because it exercised effective market control. Its business practices were not predatory, immoral, or discriminatory as between different customers, but they did operate as barriers to competition. The court refused to dissolve United into three manufacturing concerns but did rule that United must (1) offer for sale every type of machine it leases; (2) discontinue acting as distributor of other companies' supplies and dispose of its branches and subsidiaries which manufacture nails, tacks, and eyelets; and (3) make its patents available upon reasonable royalty basis to those wishing to manufacture shoe machinery and supplies.

[45] *Standard Sanitary Mfg. Co. v. United States*, 226 U.S. 20 (1912). Other cases in which a like result was reached include *United States v. New Departure Mfg. Co.*, 204 Fed. 107 (1913), and *United States v. Motion Picture Patents Co.*, 225 Fed. 800 (1915), certiorari denied, 247 U S. 524 (1918).

[46] *United States v. United Shoe Machinery Co.*, 247 U.S. 32 (1918). See also *United States v. Winslow* 227 U.S. 202 (1913).

[47] *United States v. United Shoe Machinery Corp.*, 110 F. Supp. 295 (D. Mass., 1953), affirmed per curiam, 347 U.S. 521 (1954).

Another interesting example of a legal patent pool is supplied by the Standard Oil of Indiana decision.[48] In 1920 and following, several prominent oil companies worked out an agreement by which certain patents used in refining might be shared. This cross-licensing combination was organized for the purpose of avoiding patent litigation. The government moved for the dissolution of the combination on the ground that it was in restraint of trade. The Supreme Court found that the companies made no attempt to restrain trade, in that the advantages of the combination were open to all upon reasonable terms; that the companies concerned were in real competition with each other; and that there had been no attempt to fix prices or do anything else beyond the agreement to pool patents. The Court consequently upheld the pool as a proper case of patent cooperation without evidence of restraint of trade.

From the examples noted here, it appears that a patent pool may or may not be unlawful under the antitrust laws, depending upon what it does. If it suppresses competition by price or production agreements, or by conspiracy against those outside the pool, then it is illegal. If it is made up of complementary, as distinguished from competing, patents, no question of violation exists. If it does not stamp out competition, by fact or deed or intent, but is formed for cooperative purposes in avoiding patent litigation and sharing of patent benefits, it is a perfectly legal arrangement.

COPYRIGHTS AND THE ANTITRUST LAWS

The Supreme Court has found that the federal copyright laws do not protect combinations in restraint of trade from prosecution under the antitrust laws. In 1913, the Court ruled against a trade association of book publishers and sellers which attempted to restrict the sale of copyrighted books to persons who agreed to maintain the fixed net retail price.[49]

An unusual arrangement by which buyers, in this instance two chains of motion-picture theaters, were able to combine to force the lessor of copyrighted films to prescribe certain practices for the independent operators who also leased the films, reached the Court in 1939.[50] The Court ruled that the holding of a copyright does not give the owner the right to dictate admission prices or that other films may not be shown with the licensed films.

In 1948, the Court ruled that the practice of "block booking" of motion pictures was invalid because it added to "the monopoly of the copyright." The refusal to license one or more copyrights unless another copyright was accepted was held illegal.[51]

[48] *Standard Oil Co. (Indiana) v. United States*, 283 U.S. 163 (1931).

[49] *Straus v. American Publishers' Association*, 231 U.S. 222 (1913).

[50] *Interstate Circuit v. United States*, 306 U.S. 208 (1939).

[51] *United States v. Paramount Pictures*, 334 U.S. 131 (1948).

Geographic Price Discriminations: Basing Points

A subtle form of price discrimination that was found illegal under section 2a of the Robinson-Patman Act as well as under section 5 of the Federal Trade Commission Act is the basing-point system of quoting delivered prices. Prices are calculated at factory cost plus transportation (usually rail) from one or more basing points to the point of delivery. Where every producing point is a basing point, the system becomes merely one by which the sale price is the delivered price to the purchaser. As a matter of fact, beginning in the 1880s the use of only one or a few basing points became widespread in the American economy, especially in heavy industry. By 1940, sixty industries were using the system or one of its variations.[52]

To illustrate, under the Pittsburgh-plus system of pricing, the user of steel in Chicago paid the base price plus freight from Pittsburgh to Chicago, even though the steel was produced in the Chicago area. If the

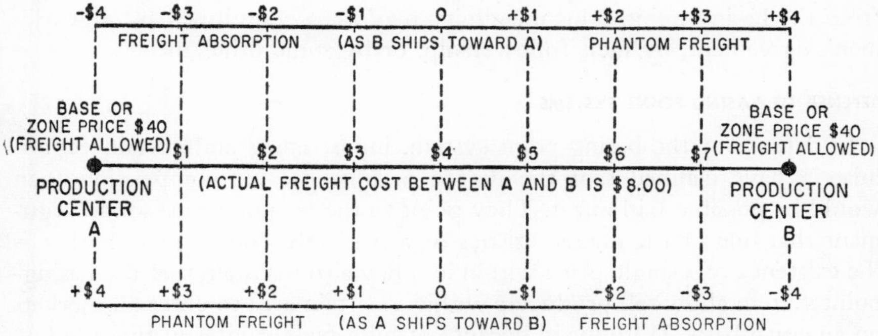

Figure 16—1. The Freight-allowed or Zone-delivered Pricing System

The base or zone prices include a sum to cover the "average freight" from the mill to the points in the zone, and a uniform price is made to all customers within that zone. In this example the average freight is assumed to be $4 per unit. The upper line shows the fictitious freight differentials of sellers at *B* as they ship toward *A*. Up to a point midway between the two production centers, sellers at *B* charge *more* for freight than the freight actually costs (phantom freight). In shipping beyond the mid-point, they charge *less* for freight than it actuallly costs (freight absorption). The lower line represents the fictitious freight differentials of sellers at *A* as they ship toward *B*. It may be noted that the "advantage of location," which under normal competitive conditions is enjoyed by consumers located at production points, is appropriated by producers through a system of discriminatory prices. Source: Reprinted from Vernon A. Mund, *Government and Business* (New York: Harper & Brothers., 1950), p. 362.

[52] *Competition and Monopoly in American Industry*, TNEC Monograph 21 (1940), pp. 147–148. The variations include zone pricing, by which uniform delivery prices are set within given regions, such as east and west of the Mississippi River; and freight equalization, by which a manufacturer charges base price plus a freight charge adjusted to equal the lowest delivered price of his competitor.

steel mill were located in the Chicago area, the transportation charge in excess of the actual cost was "phantom freight." Under such a situation, an independent steel fabricator was at a disadvantage in relation to a fabricator in Pittsburgh. But if a Pittsburgh corporation had a subsidiary in Chicago which used steel ingots or sheets produced by another subsidiary, this subsidiary fabricating company was in a better position than an independent concern. Even if the subsidiary were charged Pittsburgh-plus, it was only a paper charge, in that both steel producer and fabricator were in the same business organization. When the basing point is nearer the customer than the point of origin of the shipment, then the producer absorbs the excess of the actual freight paid by the seller over the amount in calculating base price plus Pittsburgh. Thus, a Chicago fabricator selling in Cleveland would receive a lower base price, as he absorbs the higher freight charge.

The basing-point system makes possible a uniform price policy in an industry. All producers, whether at the basing point or not, charge the same price to customers, by using the same base price plus freight charges from the basing point. This unanimity may be accomplished by a gentlemen's agreement, by tacit followership, or by some other means.

DEFENSE OF BASING-POINT SYSTEMS

In defense of the basing-point system, industrialists and certain economists [53] have claimed that the device permits greater competition than would be possible without it. They point to the economically sound argument that one of the characteristics of a perfectly competitive market is the existence of a single price within it. They also maintain that the basing-point system allows all producers within a certain area to enter all markets on an equal basis. Without it, because of high freight rates in those industries using basing points, local mills would tend to have a monopoly within the vicinity of their operations.

Steel men insist that in actual practice there is little cross-hauling or selling in a local market at prices based upon freight from a distant point. They maintain also that the number of basing points has so increased that most principal places of steel production have a base price, and they hold that this price does not generally represent a differential from Pittsburgh. Assertions of similar import are made by representatives of other industries using the basing-point system.

Those who support the use of basing points also maintain that the system makes for fair competition. If all pricing were f.o.b. the mills, and

[53] See statement of representatives of the steel industry, in *Investigation of Concentration of Economic Power*, part 27, pp. 14. 619–670 (1940). Also see C. R. Daugherty, M. G. de Chazeau, and S. S. Stratton, *The Economics of the Steel Industry* (New York: McGraw-Hill Book Company, Inc., 1937), vol. II, pp. 579–732.

if the custom of observing uniform prices and differentials were abolished, the result might be competitive chaos. Owing to large fixed costs in the industry, competition would tend to become cutthroat, and the larger and stronger firms would drive the weaker from the field. This vigorous type of competition would not necessarily mean the survival of the more efficient producers but that of the producers having the strongest financial position.

CRITICISM OF BASING-POINT SYSTEMS

The Federal Trade Commission has found many specific objections to basing-point systems. The Commission has pointed out that basing points cause wasteful cross-hauling. Since all sellers in a certain basing-point area are placed on an equal price basis, any advantage of location is not passed on to customers in the form of lower transportation costs. Mills may deliver their product in the neighborhood of other mills, and these in turn may ship to the vicinity of their rivals. The system artificially distorts the area of distribution of each mill, with resultant higher costs. Moreover, customers are usually charged base plus *rail* freight, even though a lower-cost transportation facility may be available. This, of course, increases the cost to customers and aids sellers in maintaining a system of uniform delivered prices.

The Commission has also claimed that the basing-point system, by permitting the fixing of higher prices, places an "umbrella" over high-cost producers and tends to cause existence of unused productive capacity when goods will not be purchased at the fixed price. The position of the Commission is that this encourages inefficiency in use of natural resources, capital, and labor. Hence, its objection to basing-point systems is that by aiding in the restraint of competition they contribute to inefficiency and higher prices.

GOVERNMENT ATTACK ON BASING POINTS

The Commission proceeded against the basing-point system as being in violation of the price-discrimination section of the Clayton Act and the unfair-methods-of-competition section of the Federal Trade Commission Act. Its action began hesitantly and without full knowledge of the effects of the system, but it gained momentum, and in the past decade its prosecution has been vigorous.

In 1924, the Commission ordered the United States Steel Corporation and its subsidiaries to cease and desist from pricing their goods on a Pittsburgh-plus-freight system.[54] The corporation did not contest the Commission's order—although it claimed that it had adequate grounds to do so—and it increased the number of basing points in compliance therewith. In

[54] *FTC v. United States Steel Corp.*, 8. F.T.C. 1 (1924).

practice the order was openly violated, but not until 1938 was court action resumed. In that year the Wheeler-Lea Act made Commission orders automatically final, so the corporation immediately petitioned for an appeal against the 1924 order. United States Steel did not consent to sign a "decree of affirmance and enforcement" until ten years later.[55] It has been suggested that the reason for the delay was that the Commission was expecting a favorable court decision in several cases it had pending against the glucose, cement, and conduit industries.[56]

As early as 1925, in antitrust cases, the Supreme Court took the position that dissemination of basing-point information, without outright collusion, was not action in restraint of trade.[57] Not until 1945 did the

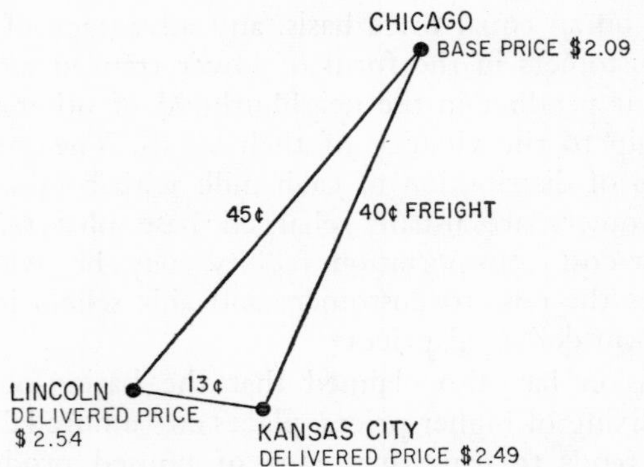

Figure 16–2. The Basing-point System Condemned by the Supreme Court in the Corn Products Case

The Corn Products Refining Company has plants in Chicago and Kansas City. Its pricing policy was to sell glucose at a Chicago base price plus rail freight from Chicago to the customer's location, even through the product was made in Kansas City and sold in adjoining territory. Source: Reprinted from Vernon A. Mund, *Govrnment and Business* (New York: Harper & Brothers, 1950), p. 379.

Court, in the Corn Products case, rule against a pricing system that used a basing point.[58] In the same year the Supreme Court held that the single-basing-point system used by the Staley Manufacturing Company violated section 2a of the Clayton Act,[59] and a Court of Appeals ruled that eighteen manufacturers of malt who quoted prices on the basis of a single

[55] *United States Steel Corp. v. FTC, Decree of Affirmance and Enforcement,* U.S. Court of Appeals for the Third Circuit, Oct. 5, 1948.

[56] See Vernon A. Mund, *Government and Business* (New York: Harper & Brothers, 1950), p. 378.

[57] See *Maple Flooring Mfrs. Assn. v. United States,* 268 U.S. 563 (1925); and *Cement Mfrs. Protective Assn. v. United States,* 268 U.S. 588 (1925).

[58] *Corn Products Refining Co. v. FTC,* 324 U.S. 726 (1945).

[59] *FTC v. A. E. Staley Mfg. Co.,* 324 U.S. 746 (1945).

basing point were violating section 5 of the Federal Trade Commission Act.[60]

The Corn Products and Staley cases found illegal only the single-basing-point systems and phantom freight. In 1948, the Supreme Court upheld the Commission's case against the Cement Institute and, in so doing, ruled that the multiple-basing-point system was an illegal method of pricing under the Federal Trade Commission Act and that freight absorption, as well as phantom freight, was illegal under section 2a of the Clayton Act.[61]

In the Conduit case of 1949 the Court sustained the charge of the Commission that the use of the basing-point system here both was tainted with conspiracy and was illegal without the element of conspiracy.[62] The importance of this decision is noteworthy. The task of proving conspiracy has become increasingly difficult as trade members have become more sophisticated and secretive in their agreements. Now the conspiracy need not be proved to find the use of basing points a restraint of trade. Furthermore, in the past, users of the basing-point system could continue to use it after an order to cease and desist, claiming that it had been modified and that they were now acting individually. More effective relief is possible under this decision because, even without conspiracy, its continued use is illegal.

However, the House Small Business Committee reported in 1951: ". . . the Commission is making very little real progress in actually ridding industry of discriminatory delivered-pricing systems. Even when one form of discriminatory pricing is outlawed, industry shifts to a slightly modified form. Industry is always a few jumps ahead and years of time elapse while investigations are being made." [63]

BASING POINTS: CONCLUSIONS

It may be expected that the controversy over basing-point pricing will continue for some time to come. After the Cement case, the battle was transferred to the halls of Congress, where legislation was introduced in 1948 and 1949 to legalize the system. In 1950, a bill was passed that would amend the antitrust laws to enable manufacturers to absorb shipping costs in order to quote uniform delivered prices throughout the country, so long as conspiracy was not involved. President Truman vetoed this

[60] *United States Maltsters Assn. v. FTC*, 152 F.2d 161 (1945).

[61] *FTC v. Cement Institute*, 333 U.S. 683 (1948).

[62] *Clayton Mark & Co. v. FTC*, 336 U.S. 956 (1949), sustaining by a 4 to 4 vote, *Triangle Conduit and Cable Co. v. FTC*, 168 F.2d 175 (1948).

[63] House of Representatives, Select Committee on Small Business, *Anti-trust Law Enforcement by the Federal Trade Commission and the Anti-trust Division, Department of Justice—A Preliminary Report*, H. Rept. 3236, 81st Cong., 2d Sess. (1951), p. 36.

bill, saying that, although it was intended to clarify the producers' rights, it would actually obscure existing law. He felt it was susceptible to conflicting interpretations and would require years of complex litigation. "Meanwhile," the President continued, "some individuals might be encouraged to resume practices which are now prohibited. During this period, doubt cast on the previous decisions of the courts would impair effective enforcement of the anti-trust laws." [64]

Special Regulation of Competitive Practices: Food, Drugs, and Cosmetics

The activities of the federal and state pure food and drug administrations constitute another aspect of the regulation of competitive practices and are closely related to the activities of the Federal Trade Commission. They differ slightly from the activities of the Commission in two ways. First, the Federal Trade Commission prohibits unfair and deceptive practices to protect competitors as well as consumers, whereas the food and drug administrations are primarily interested in the welfare of consumers. Second, the Commission polices false advertising, whereas the food and drug administrations prevent adulteration and misbranding but not false advertising.

FEDERAL PURE FOOD AND DRUG ACTS

Public opinion, aroused by the revelations of muckracking literature such as Upton Sinclair's *The Jungle* and by the experiments of Dr. Harvey Wiley's "poison squad," induced Congress to enact the Pure Food and Drug Act of 1906. This act was substantially amended by the Copeland Act of 1938 to include cosmetics and therapeutic devices.

As amended, the law prohibits the shipping or receipt in interstate commerce of any food, drug, device, or cosmetic which is adulterated or misbranded. It also prohibits the alteration, mutilation, destruction, or removal of any label while the article is held for sale after shipment in interstate commerce which results in such article being misbranded. The Act declares that a food product is adulterated if it contains any poisonous, filthy, or decomposed substance, if it is mixed with an inferior substance so as to reduce quality, if it is mixed with a substance to increase weight or bulk, or if it is manufactured so as to conceal damage or inferiority. A food product is misbranded if it is labeled so as to deceive or mislead the purchaser through imitation of another article, through replacement of original content of a package by another substance, or through packaging which leads the buyer to believe the contents to be different in quantity or quality from what they are. In addition, labels must bear an accurate

[64] *New York Times*, June 17, 1950, p. 18.

statement of weight or other measure of contents. Any other information required under the administration of the Act must be shown on the label, and all information must be plainly expressed. The use of coloratives and preservatives must also be noted on the label.

If one food sold under the name of another, it must be clearly marked "imitation." The use of artificial flavoring or coloring and of chemical preservatives must be shown on the label. Food must not be prepared under unsanitary conditions. If it is to be used for special dietary purposes, it must contain information concerning its vitamin, mineral, and other properties.

The Food and Drug Administration is authorized to fix standard grades for specific kinds of food products. A manufacturer of such foods must either mark the correct grade on his product or plainly label it as ungraded.

The present law holds a drug or device to be adulterated if it contains filthy or decomposed substance, is manufactured under unsanitary conditions, or falls below the standard of strength and quality recognized by the United States Pharmacopeia or the National Formulary. The latter requirement applies only if the drug or device is described in terms of standard meaning. The same qualifications found in the definition of misbranding of food apply to drugs. In addition, drugs containing any habit-forming ingredients must be labeled as such. Drugs must be labeled with adequate directions for use and with adequate warnings where mistaken use might be dangerous to health.

In connection with the regulation of drugs, it is interesting that the Food and Drug Administration is given power to forbid the channels of interstate commerce to new drugs if it finds that the methods of manufacture, processing, or packaging have not developed to the point where the identity, purity, strength, or quality of the drug cannot be preserved. The Administration is also given the power to deny entry to interstate commerce of new drugs which are not yet safe for use.

Regulation of cosmetics is entirely new with the 1938 amendment. The law interestingly excepts soap from its definition of cosmetics, making the term apply to other preparations intended to be rubbed, poured, sprinkled, or otherwise applied to the human body for purpose of cleansing it, beautifying it, or altering its appearance. The description of what may make a cosmetic adulterated or misbranded is similar to that given in the law on food and drugs. One minor exception may be noted. Hair dyes may include harmful coal-tar colors if the label conspicuously notes this and warns users as to the deleterious effects which may follow.

Confusion results from the fact that the Federal Trade Commission has statutory authority over false and misleading advertising and the Administration has responsibility in the field of false labeling of food, drugs, and cosmetics. Stipulations on advertising accepted by the Commission have precluded proceedings by the Food and Drug Administration against similar labels, and testimony given before the Commission has led to constitutional immunity in court proceedings brought by the Administration.

Most of the responsibility in the food, drugs, and cosmetics industries is held by the Administration, which has a substantial staff, research laboratories, and field agents. The Commission has only a small fraction of the work and has no research facilities, no field staff, and only three technical specialists. As a result, since the technical problems are dominant in the investigation of false advertising, the Task Force on Regulatory Administration (of the Hoover Commission) recommended that authority over false and misleading advertising of foods, drugs, and cosmetics should be transferred to the Food and Drug Administration.[65]

OTHER FEDERAL FOOD LAWS

In addition to its authority over foods, drugs, cosmetics, and devices, the Food and Drug Administration has power to control adulteration of insecticides, proper branding of caustic poisons designed for household use, standards for milk and imported tea, and inspection and grading of naval stores, such as turpentine and rosin. Not all the regulation to prevent deception or harm in the preparation of foods is under the Administration. The part played by the Federal Trade Commission has already been noted. Inspection of the preparation of meats for entry into interstate or foreign commerce is placed under the Bureau of Animal Industry of the Department of Agriculture. Other regulations under various agencies of the Department include the inspection and grading of many agricultural commodities, and the regulation of importation of seeds. Special regulation of branding and grading of alcoholic beverages is also found under the Federal Alcohol Administration.

FOOD, DRUG, AND COSMETICS REGULATION: CONCLUSIONS

The special regulations of deception involved in pure food and drug acts and the other legislation noted above are primarily designed to protect the purchaser. As such, they represent prime evidence that the forces of competition are not sufficient to furnish such protection, because of the ignorance or indifference of buyers. In other words, society has attempted to supplement consumer discrimination by regulatory control where it appears that the consumer cannot or will not protect himself.

But these activities, helpful as they are, should not lull the consumer into feeling that the government has guaranteed him against being deceived or harmed by careless or unscrupulous business enterprises. Government

[65] Commission on Organization of the Executive Branch of the Government, *Task Force Report on Regulatory Commissions* (Appendix N) (1949), p. 133.

laws are not broad enough to cover all such cases. Administration of these laws is not effective enough to eliminate all violations, even if the statutes are adequate. One authority has pointed out that the annual advertising budget of a single toothpaste manufacturer has been larger than the enforcement budget of the Federal Food and Drug Administration.[66] Federal and state governments have not attempted to set up machinery which could even approximate complete enforcement of these laws. Perhaps to do so would be too expensive and would involve too detailed regulation. However, if these agencies can give publicity to types of abuses, the greatest hope for eradication lies in an intelligent and discriminating buying public and an enlightened business leadership.

Control of Competitive Practices: Conclusions

The government's part in controlling the level of competitive behavior has been becoming broader and based upon somewhat different factors. Common-law regulation of competition was founded primarily upon fraud practiced by the seller against the buyer or another seller. Regulation under the Clayton Act was based largely upon the premise that certain specified practices accounted in large part for the growth of monopolistic combinations. This was also the primary purpose behind the creation of the Federal Trade Commission and the endowment of it with powers to prohibit unfair methods of competition.

To a great extent, the fear that certain practices may enable a seller to get such an upper hand that he may drive competitors out of business or force them to combine with him still lies behind the laws concerned with competitive practices. But these laws have developed along other lines, and other motives have been introduced. The Federal Trade Commission itself has come to feel that its job is not alone to keep business on a nonmonopolistic level of competition but also to raise the standards of business morality and protect the buying public from the dishonesty and guile of the irresponsible seller. This attitude of the Commission, often difficult to apply before 1938, was given a sounder legal basis for action when unfair or deceptive methods in commerce were outlawed along with unfair methods in competition in interstate commerce. The result is that now the work of the Federal Trade Commission and that of such agencies as the Pure Food and Drug Administration are rapidly approaching the same end. A seller guilty of infraction of the federal pure food and drug laws could in most cases be found guilty of an unfair or deceptive practice in interstate commerce by the Federal Trade Commission.

Another interesting development of the laws has to do with the concept of fair trade. From the notion that discrimination in prices by a seller to

[66] C. F. Phillips, *Marketing* (Boston: Houghton Mifflin Company, 1938), p. 690.

injure his competitor often leads to monopoly and suppresses competition, the law has undergone changes so that now a seller may not discriminate between purchasers except on the basis of differences in cost or service rendered. Hence, the supposition is made that differences in selling price not justified by differences in cost must be made with the intent or effect of reducing competition and creating monopoly. State laws making it unlawful for retailers to sell at less than invoice cost, or replacement cost plus a markup to cover the cost of doing business, have also been justified as a means of curtailing price competition which tends toward monopoly by driving honest competitors out of a field. Legalization of privately made resale-price-maintenance contracts, surprisingly found lawful as a means of protecting a manufacturer's good will—a property right which he does not sell with the physical good—has also been defended as a means of protecting sellers and manufacturers from the inroads of conscienceless competitors.

While practically all recent developments can be justified as means of preserving competition through curtailing unfair competition, there is a danger that the results similar to monopoly may follow. If the law against unfair competition develops to the stage where competition is made sterile and where price is not determined by the laws of demand and supply, the results may be a system in which the inefficient, rather than the efficient, are protected. If laws tend to make all sellers sell at prices determined not by themselves but a legislature or a manufacturer, what is to happen to the vigor of competition? Does it matter too much for the consumer whether prices are fixed by a law requiring horizontal uniformity or by a combination of sellers? To be sure, the legislature may be more careful in looking out for a consumer's interest, but a large combination might be more effective in obtaining efficient production and gauging the elasticity of buyers' demand. Care must be exercised lest, in the name of regulation of competition, competition itself be destroyed.

From an economic and social point of view, there is one rather hopeful sign in the regulation of competitive practices. By eliminating fraud and deception in the selling process and by educating the consumer as to the nature of things he buys, the laws may be making for a wiser expenditure of the consumer's dollar. To the extent that the consumer need not rely upon deceptive names or misleading advertising, he may be better able to compare different brands upon their merits and select the one that yields him satisfaction at the lowest cost. If he becomes so educated, or if the laws protect him against his own ignorance, the demand facing the seller of a particular good may become far more elastic than is now the case, and conditions more like perfect competition may be approximated. The drawback to such a development lies in the "fair"-trade restraints by which the individual seller is kept from engaging in price competition and by which prices may not be forced down to the level of the most efficient. To the extent that these developments go beyond the rules of fair play necessary to maintain honest competition, they tend to operate in opposition to movements aimed at protecting the consumer from his own ignorance.

Selected References

Barnett, O. R., *Patent Property and the Anti-monopoly Laws*. Indianapolis: The Bobbs-Merrill Company, Inc., 1943.

Clark, J. M., "Law and Economics of Basing Points," 39 *American Economic Review* 430–447 (March, 1949).

Federal Trade Commission, *Report on Resale Price Maintenance*. 1945.

———, *Open-price Trade Associations*. 1929.

Fox, H. G., *Monopolies and Patents*. Toronto, Canada: University of Toronto Press, 1947.

Grether, E. T., *Price Control under Fair Trade Legislation*. New York: Oxford University Press, 1939.

Hamilton, Walton, *Patents and Free Enterprise*, TNEC Monograph 31. Government Printing Office, 1941.

Latham, Earl, *The Group Basis of Politics: A Study in Basing Point Legislation*. Ithaca, N.Y.: Cornell University Press, 1952.

———, "The Politics of Basing Point Legislation," 15 *Law and Contemporary Problems* 272–310 (Spring, 1950).

Lyon, L. S., and Victor Abramson, *The Economics of Open Price Systems*. Washington, D.C.: Brookings Institution, 1936.

Machlup, Fritz, *The Basing Point System*. New York: Blakiston Division, McGraw-Hill Book Company, Inc., 1949.

"The New Food, Drug, and Cosmetic Legislation," 6 *Law and Contemporary Problems* 1–182 (January, 1939).

Sage, George R., *Basing Point Pricing Systems under the Federal Antitrust Laws*. St. Louis: Thomas Law Book Company, 1951.

Wilson, Stephen, *Food and Drug Regulation*. Washington, D.C.: Public Affairs Press, 1942.

PART FIVE

PROTECTING THE INVESTOR

17

REGULATION OF FINANCIAL ORGANIZATIONS

In the regulation of many privately owned businesses, the government has sought to protect investors as well as consumers. This objective has been a major consideration in the regulation of public utilities and transportation agencies. A primary purpose has been to safeguard their credit and thereby make the production of services economical. To a very great degree, the same motives dominate the regulation of financial organizations and exchange institutions. But the major interest of public policy in this area arises from the fact that they are custodians of public funds and distributors of the financial resources of society. Moreover, the policies they follow have widespread effects upon business prosperity and the fluctuation of prices.

Attention is now directed to the regulation of those financial and exchange institutions that are under private ownership. The present chapter deals with the regulation of financial organizations, and the following two chapters will discuss the regulation of security issuance and of stock and commodity exchanges.

Financial Organization and the Regulatory Problem

Among financial organizations are included enterprises commonly known as banks, businesses engaged in group-investment activities, those underwriting the sales of new securities, and those which are forced into group investment as a corollary of insuring risks.

TYPES OF FINANCIAL ORGANIZATIONS

The leading types of financial institutions in private ownership are (1) deposit and loan banks, (2) investment banks, (3) trust companies, (4) investment trusts, and (5) insurance companies. While separate companies engage in these functions, it is not unusual for two or more of them to be carried out by the same company.

In terms of numbers and extensiveness of regulation, the deposit and loan banks are the most important of these financial organizations. There are many kinds in existence, but the most significant types are the commercial bank, the savings bank, the mortgage bank, and the consumptive credit bank (including Morris Plan banks), finance or installment credit unions, and the personal-loan departments of commercial banks.

Investment banks are not really banks in the popular sense of the term but are organizations engaged in the distribution or merchandising of securities. They are primarily engaged in financing the needs of governments and private businesses for long-term capital. New bonds and stocks are ordinarily distributed by investment banks. They may purchase the securities outright and resell them at a profit through their own sales organization or through independent dealers. They may merely underwrite an issue, attempting to sell it and agreeing to purchase on their own account any portion unsold at a certain time; or they may occasionally do little more than guarantee to take an unsold portion of the securities in return for a certain fee.

Trust companies are generally corporations, the chief function of which is to act as trustees to accept and execute trusts. A trust is a common-law arrangement whereby one party (the creator) grants legal title to property to a second party (the trustee) to manage that property in the interests of a third party (the beneficiary). Trusts are established for a variety of reasons, and any kind of property can be placed in trust. Trusts are created often to provide an income for support of dependents after the death of the creator, or even during his life. They are often established to ensure the carrying out of an educational or other project. Trusts may also be formed by order of a court to hold property of any person adjudged to be incompetent. They may further be set up to hold a mortgage title under a bond indenture.[1]

Trust companies, by virtue of their trustee and agency work, are naturally concerned with the management and safeguarding of investment. It is not surprising, therefore, to find trust functions and commercial or savings-bank functions carried on by the same companies. Many commercial and savings banks have trust departments. Likewise, many trust companies do a regular banking business.

The investment trust is a company, either incorporated or in the form of a trust, which sells shares of ownership and occasionally bonds to investors and uses the proceeds of these sales to invest in securities of other companies. It differs from the holding company in that the holding of stock is primarily for purposes of investment rather than control. While investment trusts always attempt to gain safety through diversification of holdings, some of them diversify over a field of many industries, while

[1] Clearly, trusts need not be handled by a trust company, since trusts may be administered by any legally competent individual. However, because of the need for expert treatment of many trusts, this field has been found to be a useful and lucrative one for specialized trust companies.

others diversify within the field of one industry, such as insurance, railroads, aviation, or chain merchandising.

Although insurance companies are engaged in pooling risks of a large number of individuals and in levying the average cost of these risks plus a management charge to individuals, they are primarily financial organizations. They gather funds from policy holders and pay them out to those persons upon whom the loss has fallen. They consequently collect funds from many sources for the payment of current losses to the few. More than that, because premiums for protection are paid to cover a period in advance and losses occur over the whole period, the insurance companies become custodians of funds contributed by the insureds for the period that the insurance is in force. This fact makes it wise for insurance companies to make investments so that such reserve funds may be earning a return and the cost of insurance may be reduced.

One cannot stress too much that the above discussion of financial organizations is functional and attempts to describe briefly the principal types of functions of financial organizations. Individual companies generally carry on several of the above functions. Commercial banks usually have savings departments and trust departments, and they often make mortgage and personal loans. Savings banks occasionally have a commercial banking department, sometimes offer life insurance, and often have trust departments. Other intermixtures of functions may be found. While investment trusts and insurance companies seldom carry on functions of other financial institutions, it is not at all unusual for close relationships to exist between them and commercial banks and investment banks.

PUBLIC INTEREST IN FINANCIAL ORGANIZATIONS

This brief description of the leading kinds of financial organizations is adequate to indicate the great public interest in the conduct of these organizations. They solicit funds from nearly every business and individual in the nation. They act as custodians of these funds, whether the funds are deposited for repayment upon demand, invested in securities or mortgages, or pooled to remove a contingent loss. The borrowing public is also interested in these organizations. Business has to a large degree become dependent upon insurance and short-term credits; home and farm owners, as well as the construction business, have relied on these organizations to supply credit needs; and individuals requiring funds to meet an emergency or buy a good for consumption have looked to them for their help.

The interest of investors and users of credit is primarily in obtaining a safe, continuous, adequate, and efficient financial system. They want deposited funds to be safe from dishonest or incompetent hands. They want the system to furnish a flow of funds to meet legitimate production and distribution needs. They desire that the system be operated efficiently, so that interest rates paid by borrowers may be no higher than necessary and returns to investors may be as high as economically feasible, without sacrificing safety.

But the public interest in financial organizations is even greater than the reasonable desires of individual investors and borrowers. These organizations all have a part in directing the flow of society's capital. The wisdom of their choice in making investments or encouraging investment by others is a matter of the greatest concern. Contrary to the belief of many uninformed people who confuse capital with money or credit, capital is a scarce good, and it is a good necessary for efficient production and higher material living standards. Those who undertake to direct its flow are charged with a duty of the highest public importance.

The public interest in financial organizations also springs from the fundamental nature of money and credit. Since the latter are not themselves capable of producing anything or satisfying the wants of many consumers but are merely means for gaining title to such useful goods, the demand for them depends upon the volume of exchange transactions for which they are needed. If money and credit should be increased beyond the normal need for them, the result would tend to be a drop in the value of dollars and a resultant rise in price levels. The upward spiraling of prices, fed by unwise credit expansion, can have disturbing effects upon business and the efficient operation of the economic machine. Likewise, an abnormal contraction of credit can contribute disastrously to interrupting the smooth functioning of the economic system through causing a downward spiral of prices. Furthermore, the structure of credits built upon credits, caused by such practices as lending funds backed by credit, may build a false superstructure of values which, when liquidation is attempted, dislocates sensitive economic equilibria. Financial organizations have much to do with the expansion and contraction of this credit structure, and they must accept responsibility.

THE LEGAL BASIS FOR CONTROL

Regulation of financial organizations by the states has never been seriously questioned. This is particularly true with banking companies, but little difficulty has been encountered in extending regulation to other types of financial organizations. From the earliest days of the Union the Constitution has placed no bar in the way either of state ownership or of state regulation of banks. Likewise, the power of states to regulate virtually every aspect of the insurance business under the state police power is recognized, and the basis for federal regulation was laid by a Supreme

Court decision in 1944.[2] State regulation of such matters as insurance rates and commissions paid to brokers has specifically been upheld by the Supreme Court.[3] The fiduciary nature of the businesses of financial organizations and the public interest in their honest and sound operation make ample grounds for their regulation by the states.

The legal basis for federal ownership and regulation of banks was established by the famous case of *McCulloch v. Maryland*.[4] In this case, Chief Justice Marshall carefully reasoned that the power of the federal government to establish a bank could be implied from the powers to tax, to borrow money, and to regulate interstate commerce, even though no specific authority over banking was granted by the Constitution.[5] As a result of expanded interpretations of the commerce power and by reliance on other powers, such as the postal power, federal regulation has been extended to holding companies, investment bankers, security issuance, insurance companies, and other financial organizations and operations.

Regulation of Loan and Deposit Banks

Regulation of loan and deposit banks is complicated by the wide variety of financial organizations which make loans, accept deposits, or do both. Government regulation includes the control over entry into business, the functions of the federal reserve banks, the supervision of operation, the control of centralization and combination, and the relationship of these banks to a system of central banking.

REGULATION OF ENTRY INTO BUSINESS

The public character of the banking business makes it desirable for the government to control the number and kind of banking companies and to pass upon the moral and business qualifications of persons interested in starting banks. Unnecessary duplication of banking facilities, undue competition between banks, and dishonesty or incompetence in bank management are contrary to the public interest.

The federal government in recent years has set up fairly effective

[2] *United States v. Southeastern Underwriters Association*, 322 U.S. 533 (1944); see p. 439.

[3] See *German Alliance Ins. Co. v. Lewis*, 233 U.S. 389 (1914); and *O'Gorman & Young v. Hartford Fire Ins. Co.*, 282 U.S. 251 (1931).

[4] 4 Wheat. 415 (1819).

[5] On the monetary powers of the federal government, see *Federal Reserve Bulletin*, March, 1933, pp. 166–186; T. J. Anderson, *Federal and State Control of Banking* (Cambridge, Mass.: Bankers Publishing Co., 1934); and Charles S. Tippetts, *State Banks and the Federal Reserve System* (New York: D. Van Nostrand Company, Inc., 1929).

standards for regulating the entry of persons into the commercial banking business. A national bank may be chartered by any group of five or more natural persons who meet the minimum capital requirements. The group applies to the Comptroller of the Currency for a national charter. The Comptroller turns the application over to a bank examiner, who investigates the necessity for the proposed bank and the character of the applicants. If the examiner's investigation presages probable success and public need for a new bank, he recommends that the charter be granted. Every national bank must become a member of the Federal Reserve System by subscribing to capital stock in the Reserve bank of the district and must also become a member of the Federal Deposit Insurance Corporation.

In general, state banking laws are not as strict or complete as those of the federal government. In many of our states the banking business is still within the reach of groups of persons with as little as $10,000 capital and perhaps little talent for banking. However, in the more progressive states, particularly those in the northeastern section of the country, requirements at present pretty much parallel those of the federal government.

THE FEDERAL RESERVE SYSTEM AND CONTROL

To effect centralized banking while leaving numerous independent and privately owned banks in existence, the Federal Reserve System was established by Congress in 1913. Although the legislative basis of the System has undergone many changes since 1913, its framework remains practically the same.[6]

The Federal Reserve banks. The Federal Reserve Act divides the United States into twelve districts with a Federal Reserve bank in each district. The twelve banks have twenty-four branches. The banks were set up by capital subscriptions from member banks within the district. Up to the present, however, only 3 per cent of the capital and surplus has been paid in, the remainder being subjected to call. All national banks are required to join the System as member banks or give up their national charter. State banks are permitted to join upon meeting requirements similar to those demanded for the chartering of national banks.

The twelve Federal Reserve banks are really bankers' banks. They are managed much like other banks. Their deposits are made up almost entirely of deposits of member banks. They also act as depositaries for the United States government and have a few individual business depositors.[7]

[6] For a detailed account, see E. W. Kemmerer and D. L. Kemmerer, *The ABC of the Federal Reserve System* (New York: Harper & Brothers, 1950).

[7] Under the Bretton Woods Agreements Act of 1945, Federal Reserve banks can act as depository or fiscal agent for the International Monetary Fund and the International Bank for Reconstruction and Development.

They make loans to member banks on the security of bonds, commercial paper, and occasionally upon real estate, and discount commercial paper which member banks have received from business in support of loans. They issue Federal Reserve notes, which are the principal kind of paper currency in circulation.

Member banks. By the middle of 1953, there were 4,874 national bank members and 1,891 state bank members. They comprised less than one-half of all commercial banks and controlled three-fourths of commercial banking assets.

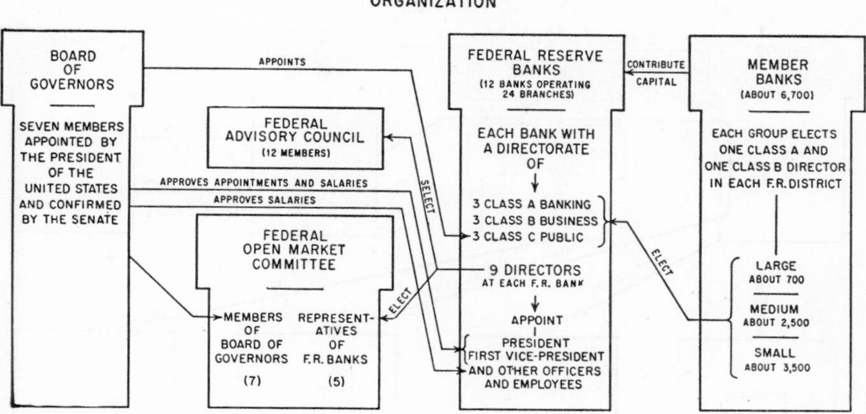

Figure 17—1

Source: Board of Governors of the Federal Reserve System, *The Federal Reserve System: Purposes and Functions,* p. 82.

Each member bank of the Federal Reserve System, in addition to abiding by the various rules and regulations of the System, must deposit its legal reserves in the district Federal Reserve bank. Each member bank has its checks cleared through the Reserve bank and carries a deposit in that bank for such purposes. This privilege is also open to nonmember banks upon the meeting of certain requirements.

The Board of Governors. The agency charged with coordinating and controlling the entire Federal Reserve System is the Board of Governors. It is made up of seven members appointed for fourteen-year terms by the President of the United States, by and with the consent of the Senate.

The Board has been given broad powers over credit policy and banking regulations. To control the flow of credit in the country, it has power to approve rates at which the twelve Federal Reserve banks will discount commercial paper of member banks, to change the percentage of cash assets to deposit liabilities that member banks must have, and to fix the policy to be followed by Federal Reserve banks in buying or selling securities, commercial paper, or real-estate mortgages. In the sphere of banking regulation, the Board may make examinations of all banks in the Federal Reserve System, pass upon admission to membership, suspend banks from membership, regulate interest rates of member banks, regulate the use of a bank's discount privilege, control interlocking directorates, pass on requests to establish branch banks, suspend or remove officers of any Reserve or member bank, and take other steps to improve the caliber of

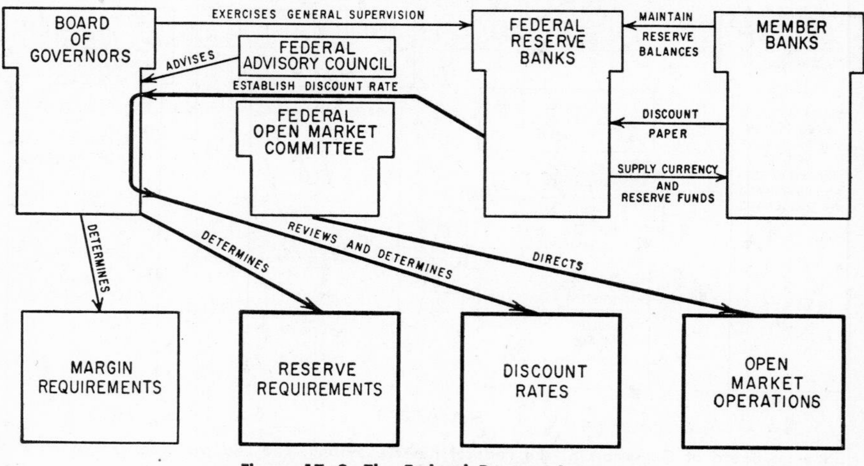

Figure 17–2. The Federal Reserve System

Source: Board of Governors of the Federal Reserve System, *The Federal Reserve System: Purposes and Functions*, p. 83.

banking operations. In addition, the Board has power to control the issuance of most of the country's currency through its authority over the leading type of paper money, the Federal Reserve notes. While these notes are issued by the Reserve banks, the control of conditions of issuance rest with the Board, subject to certain definite legal requirements for the notes.

The Open Market Committee. The Federal Reserve banks in each district have authority to engage in open-market operations with a view to expanding or contracting the volume of credit. These operations involve the buying or selling of government bonds, commercial paper, and occasionally other types of securities. The theory of open-market operations is that, if the Federal Reserve banks buy, cash reserves of banks will be increased through such purchases and greater credit expansion will be

Figure 17–3

	Federal Reserve did this	Intended effect on credit and money	Why action was taken—official explanation
July-December, 1952	Reduced buying of government securities in open market	Restrictive	To tighten up a bit on banks' capacity to lend when demand for credit was heavy
January-April, 1953	Sold $800 million worth of government securities	Restrictive	To prevent a rise in amount of money available for loans by banks
January, 1953	Raised discount rate from 1¾ to 2 per cent	Restrictive	To discourage banks from borrowing money from Federal Reserve and making more loans
February, 1953	Cut margin requirement on stock purchases	None	To allow maximum freedom without encouraging excessive use of credit
May-June, 1953	Bought about $900 million worth of government securities	To ease market tension	To provide money when market was strained, and seasonal needs were coming
July, 1953	Reduced reserve requirements for banks	Expansive	To ease up on bank money available for loans, in view of coming seasonal demand
July-December, 1953	Bought $1.7 billion worth of government securities	Expansive	To set off a policy of "active ease" because of the business downturn
January-June, 1954	Limited sales of United States securities to about $900 million	Expansive	To absorb only part of seasonal rise in reserves, thus easing banks' position
February-May, 1954	Cut discount rate twice, to 1¾, then to 1½ per cent	Expansive	To encourage banks to borrow from Federal Reserve and make more new loans
June-July, 1954	Cut banks' reserve requirements again	Expansive	To supply banks with money needed for seasonal demands
July-October, 1954	Sold $1 billion of United States securities, then bought $400 million	"Cushioning"	Sales were to avoid increasing bank funds "unduly." Purchases resumed as new needs developed

SOURCE: Reprinted from the Dec. 10, 1954, issue of *U.S. News & World Report*, an independent weekly news magazine published at Washington. Copyright, 1954, United States News Publishing Corporation.

possible; and that if the banks sell, cash reserves will be reduced and credit expansion facilities will be curbed.

Under present law, a Federal Open Market Committee has been established with powers to control the policy to be followed by reserve banks in their open-market operations. It is made up of the Board of Governors plus five representatives of the twelve Reserve banks. Since the Board of Governors dominates the Open Market Committee, through having seven members on it, any policy unanimously desired by the Board can be forced on the Reserve banks.

SUPERVISION OF OPERATION

Practically all kinds of loan and deposit banks are subject to regulation of certain aspects of their operation. The supervision of commercial banks is generally more complete than that of other loan and deposit organizations, although states customarily exercise close control over certain aspects of other banking organizations, such as the investments of savings banks. The supervision of bank operation is carried on by several government agencies. States customarily have a banking department headed by a superintendent who administers the state banking laws. Since this supervision is largely administrative in character and calls for little judicial determination of questions, the single commissioner and an administrative staff, rather than the commission of several members, are usually found. The Comptroller of the Currency supervises the operation of nationally chartered banks. Members of the Federal Reserve System are subject to supervision of the Board of Governors and the officers of the district Federal Reserve bank. Any bank, whether national or state, which has taken out insurance on deposits in the Federal Deposit Insurance Corporation is also subject to supervision by the corporation's staff: a bank may consequently be supervised by more than one government agency, and as a general rule is so regulated. While it is impracticable to separate the supervisory work of each agency toward each type of bank, the general subjects of regulation can be noted.

Reports and examinations. One of the most important features of supervision of bank operation, both as an end in regulation and as a means of exercising other controls, is the periodic examination of bank affairs. Nationally chartered banks are required to make at least three reports of their financial condition to the federal government each year and must publish abbreviated reports in the newspapers. In addition, the Comptroller of the Currency may require reports whenever he believes them to be necessary for a more complete exposition of conditions. Reports are also required of banks which are members of the Federal Reserve System or of the Federal Deposit Insurance Corporation. Moreover, loan and deposit banks which are chartered by the states are required to make reports to the state banking department, although the requirements differ somewhat among states and among different kinds of banking organizations.

Banks of all kinds are subject to periodic examination by examiners from the state banking department or the federal government control agencies. Examinations are usually made at least twice during a calendar year, and examiners arrive unannounced. Besides making a study as to the existence of assets, the legality of the bank's holdings, and the value of the assets, they attempt to discover practices which are illegal or unsound, or operations which involve inefficiency or carelessness, and to make suggestions to bank officials for the improvement of their holdings and operating practices. Where circumstances warrant, the examiner may report serious infractions of the law or evidences of bad practices to the state or federal regulating agency concerned. If further investigation makes such a course desirable, operation of the bank may be suspended or a change in policy may be ordered. In other cases, the examiner may merely suggest changes informally to bank officials without any formal actions being taken by the chief regulatory agency.

Loans and investments. The most thoroughly developed phase of bank regulation [8] has been in the control exerted over loans and investments. Under their discretionary powers bank examiners do much to improve the character of loans and investments. The federal law can serve to illustrate the kind of statutory regulations covering them. State laws have differed somewhat from the federal laws, and many state legislative standards fall below federal requirements, but the more progressive states have followed the lead of the federal government.

According to the federal law, the total liabilities of any one person or corporation to a bank must not exceed 10 per cent of the bank's capital stock actually paid in and unimpaired, plus 10 per cent of its surplus. This limitation is subject to the exception that more liberal loans or investments may be made where the borrower pledges as security bonds of the United States government or where the loans are backed by actually existing values arising out of business transactions. Loans by a bank to its own officers are restricted to a maximum of $2,500, and any such loan must be approved by a majority of all the directors. No loans may be made to examiners who examine or are authorized to examine the bank.

Of all loan and deposit banking companies, the mutual savings banks have had their investment policies most rigorously regulated, particularly by the more progressive states, such as Massachusetts and New York. These banks may place their funds only in certain high-grade bonds and

[8] Because nearly all kinds of deposit banks have been accepted in the coverage of the Federal Deposit Insurance Corporation, most federal laws apply to some extent to state and nationally chartered commercial banks, savings banks, trust companies, and other companies receiving deposits.

mortgages and occasionally in commercial paper. Commercial banks have not had quite the degree of regulation of quality of their portfolios that savings banks have had. Until 1935, the power of commercial banks to invest in bonds was practically unrestricted. More control over portfolios was provided at that time when the federal Banking Act of 1935 authorized the Comptroller of the Currency to regulate the security purchases of national banks.

Interest payment and charges. The government regulates both the payment of interest by banks to their depositors and the interest charged by lending institutions to their borrowers. The principal purpose of regulating interest paid to depositors is to conserve the resources of banks by eliminating the competitive stress of paying too high returns and the danger of speculative loan or investment practices. The regulation of interest charges has a twofold purpose. The public desires to keep lending agencies from charging an extortionate rate of interest to those who need funds, for much the same reason that public-utility consumers are protected from too high or discriminatory rates. The government has also intervened in the setting of interest rates on loans to encourage or discourage the flow of credit and thereby influence the course of business.

Insuring deposits. The wholesale failure of banks during the Depression [9] aroused political pressure which induced Congress to establish the Temporary Deposit Insurance Fund in 1933. It was made permanent in 1935 as the Federal Deposit Insurance Corporation. Its purpose is to protect depositors from losses encountered by bank failure and to aid the banking system to meet the threat of mass withdrawal of deposits.

All national banks and banks which have taken out membership in the Federal Reserve System are required to become members of the Federal Deposit Insurance Corporation. Commercial banks, mutual and stock savings banks, Morris Plan banks, and trust companies, not members of the Federal Reserve System, have been permitted to join the insurance plan if they measure up to the requirements of the Corporation.

The Federal Deposit Insurance Corporation provides for insurance of deposits for each depositor in an insured bank to the extent of $10,000; deposits in excess of this amount are not insured. The cost of the deposit insurance is provided for by a levy of 1/12 of 1 per cent annually [10] on the deposits of each insured bank. These assessments plus the $150 million capital subscription by the United States Treasury and the subscription

[9] Between 1920 and 1932 the losses amounted to $1,600 million. See L. A. Rufener, *Money and Banking in the United States* (Boston: Houghton Mifflin Company, 1934), p. 715.

[10] Although assessments were still technically made at this rate in 1955, the actual rate was much less. Beginning in 1951 the Corporation transferred each year 40 per cent of its net assessment income to capital account, and the balance has been credited pro rata to insured banks with this credit applying to future assessments.

of $139 million in stock by the Federal Reserve Banks, along with interest on investments, constitute the assets of the Corporation. By 1948, the Corporation was able to repay the capital advances made by the Treasury and the Federal Reserve Banks and in effect became a mutual organization. A sizable fund has been built up from net assessments and is invested primarily in government securities. Should the needs require, the Corporation can borrow up to $3 billion from the Treasury.

When an insured bank is unable to meet the demands of depositors, the Federal Deposit Insurance Corporation *must* be appointed as receiver in the case of national banks, and it *may* be appointed as receiver if the bank is chartered by a state; actually, it is usually appointed in either event. The Corporation is required by law to pay the insured-deposit liabilities as soon as possible, either by making available a transferred deposit in another bank, or by the payment of cash outright. The Corporation acquires the rights of the depositors and attempts to collect the amount of the deposit insurance in the liquidation of the closed bank.

If the Deposit Insurance Corporation believes it to be in the public interest, loans may be made to insured banks to help them to reopen or to banks which take over their assets. Or, the Corporation may purchase assets from or make deposits in an insured bank that is in danger of closing. These are important optional powers in that they make it possible for the Corporation to encourage the continuance of a banking business without the expense and trouble of liquidation of assets. Through the use of these optional powers, the Corporation has forestalled the necessity of any insured bank being placed in receivership since 1944.

Savings and loan associations are given almost identical protection by the Federal Savings and Loan Insurance Corporation. All federal savings and loan associations must (and state-sponsored building and loan associations may) become members of this organization by paying an initial fee of $400 and annual premiums of $\frac{1}{12}$ of 1 per cent of all accounts. In emergencies the Corporation is authorized to borrow up to $750 million from the Treasury. It is managed by the Home Loan Bank Board, which also supervises the savings and loan and building and loan associations. If an insured member association is forced to close or unable to meet depositor withdrawals, depositors are given either equal-sized accounts in another insured association, or full cash payment by the Corporation, in liquidating the assets of an insured member. The maximum protection given a person who is a depositor in a savings and loan association is $10,000.

The program of deposit insurance is not without criticism. Some insured banks complain because the assessment is based on both insured and uninsured deposits and because it falls on all banks without regard to financial strength. Their feeling is that strong and stable concerns are underwriting the losses that accrue from the inept management of smaller and weaker ones. A more fundamental criticism is that deposit insurance is a poor alternative to reforms that would prevent bank failure. While many reforms for sounder banking have been effected since 1933, there is always the question, particularly in the light of two decades of inflation and prosperity, as to how depression-proof modern banking practices are.

Reserve ratios. To meet cash demands in connection with the withdrawal of deposits, banks must keep on hand or as a deposit in other banks enough cash to make such payments promptly. While savings banks and savings departments of commercial banks have a legal right to demand notice in advance of a withdrawal, this right is not generally enforced. Practically all banks of deposit have to be able to pay out any deposit in cash when desired by the depositor. The bank cannot, of course, operate profitably and keep enough idle cash on hand to pay off all depositors' claims simultaneously on demand. Since the portion of deposits which tend to be withdrawn on any business day or in any business week is likely to be a very small part of the total deposits, and since new deposits are continually being made, it is obvious that the cash reserve necessary to meet withdrawals would normally not be large. The ratio of such cash reserves to the total amount of deposits for which they exist is known as the "reserve ratio."

Ordinary business prudence would dictate that an adequate reserve ratio be maintained by a banking organization. But this has seemed so important to bank stability that legislation has been provided fixing minimum reserve ratios. It might be mentioned that the purpose of some of this regulation has been the control of credit as well as regulation for safety. If minimum reserve ratios are increased, the same cash reserve held by a bank will support a smaller volume of deposits than before. Because deposits of commercial banks, at least, result largely from loans made by them, to curtail deposits by increasing reserve ratios is to limit expansion of loans. Likewise, a reduction in the reserve ratio may tend to encourage loan expansion.

For more than 100 years state governments have required banking companies to hold minimum cash reserves. Nearly every state fixes minimum reserve ratios for commercial banks, savings banks, and trust companies. In many of the states the reserves follow the federal regulations. In some, however, the competitive urge remains, and state banking is made to seem more favorable to private enterprise by making state reserve ratios lower than those required by the federal government.

Since the introduction of nationally chartered privately owned banks by the National Banking Act of 1863, the federal government has regulated the minimum reserve ratios of national banks. At present, such regulation is under the Board of Governors of the Federal Reserve System.

The minimum reserve ratios are fixed by law, but the Board is given power to raise them to not more than twice the amount fixed by law if necessary to prevent injurious credit expansion. To prevent contraction of credit which might be harmful, the Board may lower the ratios, but it may not put them below the minima fixed by law.[11]

Payment of dividends. Banking organizations are not free to pay dividends to stockholders as desired even if such dividends be earned. The national banking law and the laws of many states require the accumulation of a surplus from earnings. Thus, the federal law declares that banks must carry one-tenth of their annual net profits to surplus until the latter amounts to 20 per cent of capital stock. This provision, like so many of the regulations affecting operation of loan and deposit banks, is designed to increase the financial strength and stability of these organizations.

CONTROL OF CENTRALIZATION AND COMBINATION

As compared to most foreign countries, the lack of centralization in American banking is striking. Where Canada has 10 commercial banks, and Great Britain has 11 commercial banks, each with many branches, the United States has some 14,100 separate commercial banks with a relatively small number of branch offices. This large number of banks, many of which necessarily have small financial resources, not only has complicated banking business and regulation but has probably been the largest single contributing cause of the sad record of bank failures.

While banks should not be allowed to combine with each other, or with other kinds of financial organizations, without government supervision, government policy has tended to discourage bank combinations and has thereby tended to retard the building up of more large and sound banking companies.

Such centralization of banking in this country as has been effected has been carried on through the use of branch banks and consolidations. In addition, a problem has arisen as to the combination of commercial or savings banks and investment banks. Combination of other kinds has not presented a serious problem.

Branch banking. Branch banks are banking offices subject to the control of a single owning company and may be operated on a state-wide or city-wide basis. Although branch banking prevailed in the United States before the depression of 1837, the system fell into disrepute because of the failures of that panic. The national banking law of 1863 did not authorize the establishment of branch banks, and few states permitted it

[11] For table showing member-bank reserve requirements between 1917 and 1951, see *Federal Reserve Bulletin*, March, 1951, p. 282. On June 24, 1953, Federal Reserve reduced reserve requirements to 22 per cent for Central Reserve city banks, 19 per cent for Reserve city banks, and 13 per cent for country banks.

until recent years. In 1927, Congress enacted legislation permitting very limited branch banking by national banks. Since that time, and especially after 1933, both state and national governments have liberalized the laws regarding branch banking.

Federal law permits national banks to establish branches in any part of any state where and to the extent that this is permitted by state law. Although national banks must have the permission of the Comptroller of the Currency in addition, this law leaves the real control of branch banking to the states. Only 18 states, principally in the West, and the District of Columbia permit state-wide branch banking, 17 allow it in restricted areas, 9 do not permit it, and 4 have passed no legislation on the subject.

With the loosening of restrictions on branch banking, especially in states such as California, branches have been rapidly developed. It may be that the future will see a rapid development of branch banking and the growth of a far more centralized banking system. However, insurance of bank deposits by the Federal Deposit Insurance Corporation so protects the reputation for safety of small banks that they may be able to exist in almost as large numbers as at present. Proponents of centralized banking have pointed out that a strong system of a few large banks with numerous branches would remove the need for and the cost of deposit insurance.

Control over consolidation. Consolidation of two or more banking organizations is usually subject to control by both the states and the federal government. Such consolidation ordinarily requires permission by the Comptroller of the Currency or the state banking superintendent. As a general rule, consolidations are fairly readily permitted if the banks are located in the same city, village, or county. By legislation passed in 1927, Congress permitted national banks to consolidate with state banks under the supervision of the Comptroller of the Currency. While many consolidations have been effected in the last few decades, many of them have been consummated to provide for the taking over of financially embarrassed banks by stronger institutions.

Divorcement of commercial and investment banking. Many commercial banks have found it advantageous to organize investment-banking affiliates. Investment banking by affiliates of commercial banks grew so important by 1930 as almost to dominate the field.

The depression following 1929 brought to light many evils of the combination of investment and commercial banking functions. Furthermore, commercial banking, with its concern for short-term credit, and investment banking, with its interest in long-term capital, are inconsistent in purpose. These factors, taken together, led to adoption of legislation to divorce the two functions.

Under the Banking Act of 1933 and the Banking Act of 1935, member banks of the Federal Reserve System are forbidden to have investment affiliates and to participate in the underwriting of new securities, except for domestic government securities. To make the requirement of divorcement more effective, the federal law provides that investment-banking companies engaging in interstate commerce or using the mails may not engage in a deposit-banking business. Member banks are still permitted to act as agents for any customer in the purchase or sale of securities, but this is a brokerage function, not to be confused with the business of dealing in securities.

REGULATION OF LOAN AND DEPOSIT BANKING: CONCLUSIONS

For a business so greatly affected with the public interest, the regulation of loan and deposit banking presents a picture of some confusion. The regulations of the federal government and of some state governments seem well designed to gain safety and soundness in banking practices. Yet altogether too many banking organizations are under the control of state governments which have tended to compete with each other in laxity of regulation. Perhaps the greatest move toward uniformity and adequacy of regulation has come from the development of deposit insurance under the Federal Deposit Insurance Corporation. Because of the obvious value to a bank of pointing out to depositors that their accounts are insured, many banking companies which found the regulations of the Federal Reserve System too restrictive and its benefits of questionable value have gone into the insurance scheme. Nevertheless, the very adoption of deposit insurance is evidence of the danger of unsound practices.

It must be recognized that no system of regulation can ensure sound banking. Regulation may eliminate certain abuses and set standards conducive to good banking. But the question of extending credit to a borrower must be answered in the light of the facts in each case. The determination of eligibility of persons for loans is a part of the broader problem of sound investment. Legal formulas cannot determine sound investment, but what is sound must be primarily a function of management. Thus, good banking must stem from competent bank management. The law may establish minimum standards and create aids to good banking, but it can hardly be expected to solve the problem of managerial mistakes or incompetency.

The tradition of free private enterprise in banking and the fear of "Wall Street" dominance have militated against the growth of a strong system of central banking in the United States. While sound banking might require exclusive regulation by the federal government, it has been politically unfeasible to put such a policy into practice. The constitutionality of dominance by the federal government in the banking field is hardly open to doubt, but the full use of such powers has been blocked by local interests. The picture of federal government employees as controllers of credit is admittedly not appealing to local users.

At the same time, certain developments point to the ultimate growth of more centralized banking under stronger and more uniform federal government control. The role of the Federal Deposit Insurance Corporation has been mentioned. Liberalization of branch banking laws has already led, and will probably continue to lead, to larger banking systems; and large banking systems can hardly escape eventual federal regulation.

Regulation of Trust Companies

Trust companies, which have been called "the omnibus of financial institutions" because of their widespread activities, exist in large numbers as departments of commercial and savings banks and also as separate organizations. Even where trust companies are found as separate organizations, they often do a deposit-banking business and fall under the regulation of federal and state laws. Owing to the close relationship ordinarily existing between trust companies and deposit banking, these companies are under regulations which apply primarily to loan and deposit banks. There are a few regulations, however, which are aimed primarily at the trust business.[12]

In their capacity as trustees of various kinds, trust companies are subject to close supervision by the courts. According to the common law, a trustee is bound to discharge his duties honestly and to exercise such care over the property entrusted to him as an ordinarily prudent man would exercise over his own property. He is liable for losses caused by dishonesty, misconduct, or gross negligence.

Besides the regulation of trust-company deposit business, the principal control of these organizations has had to do with the holding and management of assets in trust accounts. Trust funds must ordinarily be invested in securities taken from a list which state authorities compile as being safe for that purpose, although some states allow discretion to the trustee where the deed of trust so specifies. Trust companies are generally required to submit to periodic examination of accounts and investments. Trust funds must be separated from other funds of a trust company, and in many states deposits of trust funds in commercial-banking accounts of the same company must be secured by placing readily marketable collateral with the trust department.

[12] It should be made clear that not all uses of the trust are subject to regulation, although companies specializing in trust activities are. The courts closely supervise some trusts, such as testamentary trusts, but many private trusts have nothing to do with a court unless there is a dispute.

In addition, many states control the fees charged by trust companies. They are also under strict supervision in connection with their work as transferors or registrars of corporate securities. In fact, it can be said that nearly all the multifarious duties of the trust company are under some degree of state or federal supervision.

The work of trust companies in acting as trustees of mortgages in corporation bond issues has been subjected to special legislation. To make the position of trustee one of greater responsibility, the Trust Indenture Act of 1939, among other things, defined the obligations of trustees of corporate mortgages. Since one of the trustees for a corporate mortgage is required to be a trust company, this law is partly a regulation of trust institutions. By the law the trustee must furnish periodic and special reports to bondholders regarding the mortgage and other matters, must obtain evidence from the corporation as to financial matters pertaining to the mortgage, must notify security holders of any defaults from the mortgage, and must take active steps to protect them in case of such default. In short, this law imposes on trust institutions acting as bond trustees the legal obligation to carry out these duties actively.

Regulation of Investment Banks

The investment-banking business was practically free of government regulation until 1933. Since that time several legislative acts have tended to bring it under government control. Because these banks are not banks of deposit, it is not surprising that government regulation has been so slow in overtaking them. As merchandisers of securities, they have been caught in the wave or regulation of security issuance, with most of the reasons attaching to this regulation also accounting for control of investing banking.[13]

Investment bankers are naturally subject to some regulation under all the laws regarding the issuance of securities. Since these laws are discussed in the following chapter, only the special regulations affecting investment banking will be noted here. The prohibition against investment bankers' operating a deposit-banking business has already been mentioned.

The Federal Securities Act of 1933 makes investment bankers liable, along with corporation executives, accountants, engineers, and others signing a registration statement, for losses incurred by security purchases as the result of omission of a material fact or inclusion of a misleading statement in the registration statement filed with the Securities and Exchange Commission before the issuance of a new security. Investment

[13] An excellent analysis of the business of investment banking can be found in H. G. Guthmann and H. E. Dougall, *Corporate Financial Policy* (New York: Prentice-Hall, Inc., 1948), chap. 14.

bankers are also made liable for including misleading information in a prospectus by which a new issue is advertised to a possible purchaser. The law requires merely full and accurate disclosure of information and makes the investment-banking house one of the parties responsible for fulfillment of this requirement. This provision, applicable to almost all new securities sold in the channels of interstate commerce or through the mails, has served to make investment bankers far more responsible in their investigation of new security issues.

Although the fees of investment bankers are not generally subject to regulation, the federal law requires that publicity be given to the amount of compensation to be received so that investors may take this fact into consideration. In the case of public-utility and railroad securities, many state commissions and the federal commissions having jurisdiction over them have powers to fix the compensation or to refuse to authorize an issue if the compensation proposed is too high. As a condition for authorization, too, they may apparently require that the issue be opened to competitive bidding among bankers, and commissions have occasionally done this. As for the evils connected with market manipulation, even the federal securities law allows restricted manipulation to support the price during the period of distribution of a security.

Regulation of Investment Trusts

The investment trust is a comparatively recent development in the United States. While a few such trusts were organized before 1924, the period from 1924 to 1929 witnessed a mushroom growth. The investment trust, with its emphasis upon investment in common stocks and capital gain, as well as security through cooperative investment and diversification, harmonized with the speculative tenor of the latter 1920s. In the anxiety for speculative profit, the fundamentally sound principles of this form of organization were sometimes forgotten, and promoters organized investment trusts rapidly and without careful consideration of the character of the investments made. As a result, the investment trusts were caught in the sweeping fall of security prices after 1929 and came into disrepute in the Depression. After the failure of some of the more unstable investment trusts and the rise of security prices in recent years, the attitude of investors toward the better-managed companies has improved, and the investment trust has returned to a position of prominence and prestige. As a matter of fact, following World War II public awareness of inflation and desire for diversification in stockholding have led to a rapid growth of investment trusts in recent years. In 1949, for example, there were 1 million shareholders in 124 investment companies, as compared with only 750,000 shareholders just eight years before.

ABUSES OF INVESTMENT TRUSTS

Past experience with investment trusts has disclosed certain abuses for the treatment of which legislation has been enacted. Some trusts have been too careless in their selection of securities and have been managed by individuals who have used the funds at their disposal to engage in market operations in utter disregard for even the more elementary principles of sound investment. Investment-banking houses and other firms interested in the sale of securities have sponsored investment trusts and have used them as a device for unloading poor securities which they themselves could not sell, at prices far in advance of reasonable market prices. Brokerage houses have sponsored investment trusts and have drawn large commissions from them for the needless shiftings of investment holdings. Officers and promoters of investment trusts have raided their funds by charging excessive fees and have abused the responsibility placed in them by borrowing securities of the trusts for personal loans. Some investment trusts have employed unsound accounting practices whereby they have made earnings seem better than was actually the case and have paid dividends to investors out of capital. Trusts have sold securities on a rising market and have paid dividends from the profit, rather than building a reserve to meet losses in a falling market. They have sometimes followed the policy of considering the proceeds from the sale of stock dividends, stock rights, and additional stock resulting from the splitting of shares, as earnings, and distributing these funds as dividends to their investors.

REGULATION OF INVESTMENT TRUSTS

The investment trust was first subjected to comprehensive regulation in 1940. However, the trusts were not entirely free of government regulation before that date. The companies had to live up to their charter provisions like any other corporation, if incorporated, and if they were set up in the trust form, the trustees had the fiduciary obligations attached thereto. Moreover, under the Securities Act of 1933 the investment trust marketing its securities in interstate commerce or through the mails had to make full disclosure of pertinent information, and if its securities were registered on a nationally regulated stock exchange, it was required to keep this information up to date.

The Investment Company Act of 1940 was passed partly at the instigation of the investment trusts themselves. The sounder and better-managed trusts saw in regulation a means of ridding the business of firms which had been unethically managed and of gaining a degree of public confidence. The lack of opposition to the passage of the law grew largely out of this attitude and out of the general feeling that the Act represented a fair program of regulation.

The law provides for control over investment counselors and advisory services, as well as investment trusts. The administration of the Act is placed in the hands of the Securities and Exchange Commission. Investment companies must register with the Commission and give current information relative to their size, financial structure, and investment policies. In order to prevent indiscriminate formation of companies, minimum net worth is fixed for future companies at $100,000.

Investment trusts are required to eliminate the evils of complex financial structures, to apportion voting power equitably among security holders, and to prevent unfair dilution of stockholders' interests by flotation of securities or loans with prior claims. The law provides strict regulation of the financial structure of investment trusts for the future and attempts to safeguard actual stockholder control of their management. For issuance of any securities other than common stock, strict and conservative asset-coverage requirements must be met. As a general rule, the law allows only one class of funded debt or preferred stock to be issued.

Investment activities of the trusts are closely regulated. Their funds may not be used to finance affiliated investment bankers and offerings of affiliated security merchandisers unless a majority of the directors are not personally affiliated with the bankers and this majority approves the arrangement, or unless it is approved by holders of a majority of the voting stock.

Loans to outside corporations are subject to government supervision, and purchases of securities from companies in the same investment-company system are likewise supervised. Investment trusts are limited in buying securities in other investment trusts, thereby reducing pyramiding of companies.

Strict control over management is also provided. Except in unusual cases as defined by the law, not more than 60 per cent of the board of directors of an investment trust may be investment advisors of, or officers or employees in, the company. Transactions with companies in which directors or officers have a pecuniary interest are forbidden, unless approved by directors not so interested, who must form a majority of the whole board, or unless approved by stockholders. Managerial fees and commissions are subject to regulation to ensure reasonableness. Uniform accounting and auditing methods may be prescribed, as well as periodic examination of records by the Securities and Exchange Commission, and the requirement of reports to stockholders. The payment of dividends from sources other than net income from interest and dividends is prohibited, unless such payment is accompanied by a written statement which adequately discloses the source or sources of such payment.

The Investment Advisers Act of 1940 provided for regulation of investment counselors and sellers of investment services. The law requires registration of advisers with the Securities and Exchange Commission. Such registration must disclose pertinent information as to the nature of the organization, the character of its personnel, and the methods of operations employed. Counselors are specifically forbidden to defraud or deceive customers, or to represent themselves unlawfully as counselors or advisers unless registered with the Commission. If they have any interests in the securities bought or sold, they must tell these facts to their clients.

The law has been judiciously administered by the Securities and Exchange Commission, and public faith in investment companies has gradually returned. Most investment companies belong to the National Association of Investment Companies, which has worked closely with the Commission to improve standards in the field.

Regulation of Insurance Companies

Most of the insurance business in the United States is under private ownership. Social-insurance plans operated by the states and the federal government, especially insurance against industrial accident, unemployment, and old age, account for a growing portion of total insurance and may in the future eclipse in reserves and volume that of private companies. But the fact is that the insurance business in the United States is still predominantly privately owned. The character of the services rendered by insurance companies, the obvious public interest in insurance, the technical nature of the business, and the immensity of its operations require some form of government regulation. Because of the technical aspects of insurance, the policyholder is at a great disadvantage. Moreover, the insurance companies have become custodians of large sums of society's savings. In 1954, life-insurance companies alone held over $84 billion in assets. The amount of life insurance in force was almost $350 billion.

The first regulation of the insurance business in the United States was through corporate charters granted to insurance companies as early as 1794. In the following half century several states attempted to tax insurance companies. The first state to set up a special commission to regulate insurance was New Hampshire in 1851. By 1890, seventeen states had established supervisory authorities. However, most of the important regulation of insurance has come in the twentieth century. In all cases, the control was performed by the states as an exercise of their police power.[14]

[14] See Edwin W. Patterson, *The Insurance Commissioner in the United States* (Cambridge, Mass.: Harvard University Press, 1927).

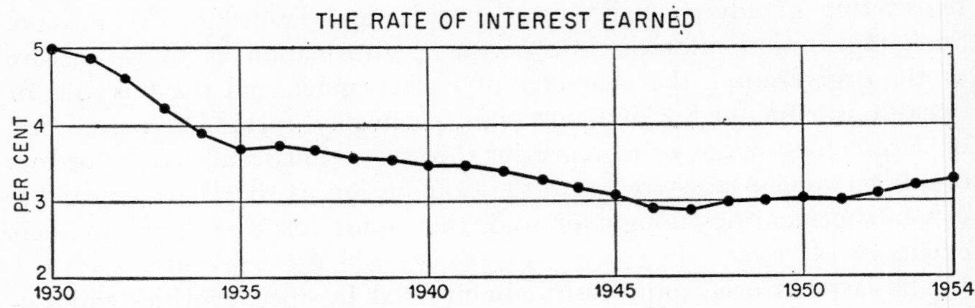

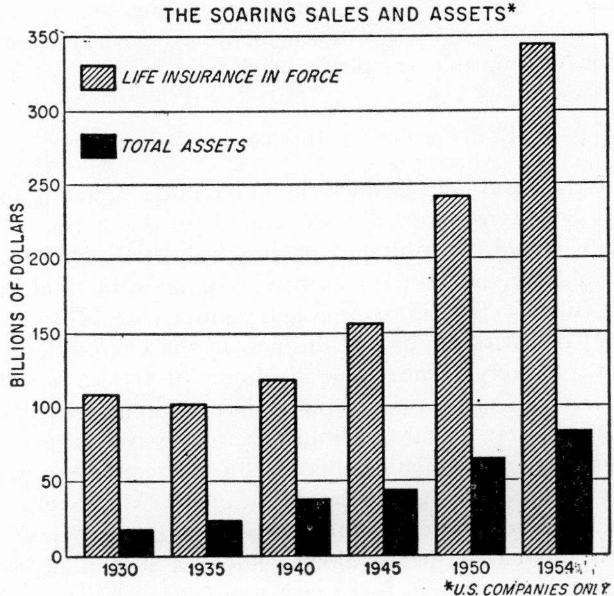

Figure 17—4. The Life-insurance Billions—How They Grow, and Where They Go

In recent years life-insurance sales have been expanding even more rapidly than the rapidly expanding United States economy. As the lower chart shows, life-insurance assets are rising spectacularly, too. But prosperity intensifies a problem that each year grows more pressing: how to find for these funds investments that are safe enough to guarantee policy payments and profitable enough to keep the cost of life insurance reasonable. Note the low net rate of interest earned (after taxes and investment expenses) even in the best of times. Source: Reprinted from the February, 1955, issue of *Fortune Magazine* by special permission of the editors. Copyright, 1955, Time, Inc.

THE CONSTITUTIONAL BASIS FOR REGULATION

The Supreme Court's decision in *Paul v. Virginia*[15] acted as an inhibiting influence on regulation by the federal government. In that case the Court decided that "issuing a policy of insurance is not a transaction of commerce" and that insurance policies "do not constitute a part of the commerce between the states." Consequently, the regulation of insurance appeared to be an activity reserved to the states.

In 1944, the Supreme Court surprised the insurance world with its holding in the Southeastern Underwriters case that the business of insurance is interstate commerce.[16] The effect of this case was to make insurance companies immediately subject to such federal regulatory statutes as the Sherman Act, the Clayton Act, the Federal Trade Commission Act, the Robinson-Patman Act, and the like. To the extent that these acts were applicable to the business of insurance, all state laws in conflict with them would have immediately become invalid.

Congress did not hesitate long in the face of the confusion that this decision created in the state insurance commissions as well as in the insurance business itself. In 1945, Congress passed the McCarran Act placing a moratorium on the operation of federal laws until July 1, 1948, as they might apply to insurance companies. The above-listed laws were among those mentioned as subject to this moratorium. After that date, federal laws were to be applicable in so far as insurance was not regulated adequately by the states.[17]

The Council of State Governments set up a Committee on Insurance which, in cooperation with the National Association of Insurance Commissioners, prepared model state insurance laws. During 1947 and 1948 legislative activity was great as most of the states adopted those parts of these model laws that were not already covered by existing legislation. By 1952 every state had passed rate-regulation laws in the fire and casualty fields; 24 had adopted model fair-trade-practice legislation, while most had laws prohibiting unfair trade practices; 15 had passed accident- and health-insurance laws; and 23 had passed unauthorized-insurers process acts, 4 states having previously enacted legislation providing for service of process on unlicensed insurers. The purpose of the latter laws is to get at unlicensed insurers who are writing insurance through the mails or have no authorization to do business in the state. Most of this legislation was patterned after the model laws recommended by the National Association of Insurance Commissioners.[18]

[15] 8 Wall. 168 (1868). [16] 322 U.S 533, 552.

[17] For a general discussion of these developments, see Elmer W. Sawyer, *Insurance as Interstate Commerce* (New York: McGraw-Hill Book Company, Inc., 1945).

[18] Bernard R. Stone, "State Regulation of Insurance," in Council of State Governments, *The Book of the States, 1952–1953* (Chicago, 1952), pp. 444–446.

The legality of continued state regulation of insurance in light of the Southeastern Underwriters case was tested in 1946. In *Robertson v. California*,[19] the Supreme Court upheld state regulatory power over insurance, *without* regard to the McCarran Act. In *Prudential v. Benjamin*,[20] the Court relying on the McCarran Act, upheld the power of a state to impose a premium tax on the aggregate premiums received from business done in that state even though the tax applied only to foreign (out-of-state) and not to domestic companies. The constitutionality of the McCarran Act itself was upheld in 1950.[21]

An important decision for the future of state regulation of insurance was handed down in 1950. The Supreme Court upheld in *Travelers Health Association v. Virginia* the legality of unauthorized-insurers service-of-process legislation, by which a state might stop unauthorized companies from selling insurance in a state by mail.[22] If such laws were enacted generally, a major complaint about the inadequacy of state regulation might be partially eliminated and the demand for federal control mitigated.

State regulation of insurance has resulted in a variety of laws which large insurance companies find troublesome to follow. This diversity makes it impracticable to study insurance regulation in detail here, but state regulations follow similar patterns, and a fair picture can be gained by noting the general provisions and principles of such controls.

The administration of state control of insurance companies is conducted through state insurance departments, with a commissioner or superintendent at the head. The predominantly administrative character of insurance regulation, in contrast to the judicial and legislative aspects of railroad or public-utility control, probably accounts for this kind of administrative device in the field of insurance as it does in the regulation of banks.

CONTROL OVER ENTRY INTO BUSINESS

Insurance companies are ordinarily chartered under special incorporation laws. But the most important means of controlling entry into service is the requirement of a license or certificate of authority. This is required of every company doing business within the state, whether it was incorporated there or in another state. Licenses are ordinarily restricted to short periods of time, such as a year, although they are renewable by application. This short period makes it possible for the burden of proof to be placed on the company if the state insurance department refuses

[19] 328 U.S. 440 (1946).

[20] 328 U.S. 408 (1946).

[21] *North Little Rock Transportation Co. v. Casualty Reciprocal Exchange*, 85 F. Supp. 961, affirmed in 181 F.2d 174 (1950) and 71 Sup. Ct. 56 (1950).

[22] 339 U.S. 643 (1950).

for some cause to renew a license, rather than upon the department, as would be the case with revocations of licenses.

The license serves several purposes. It is a test of qualifications, an instrument for enforcing continuous regulation, and a basis for collecting taxes from operating companies. In applying for a license, companies are required to agree to regulation, to make reports to the insurance commissioner, to show evidence of financial responsibility, and often to deposit securities in a certain amount with the state to ensure proper performance of their contracts.

In some states insurance departments have wide discretion in revoking licenses of insurance companies, particularly of out-of-state corporations. The insurance commissioner need only show that continuance of the business is not in the public interest. In other states definite grounds for revocation must be specified, including violation of the law, unsound financial practices or condition, failure to meet contractual obligations, and nonpayment of taxes.

REGULATION OF INSURANCE-COMPANY OPERATION

In most respects, insurance-company operation is subject to regulations similar to those applied to loan- and deposit-banking organizations. The investment of insurance funds is frequently regulated. State laws require that reserves be adequate, some states defining this requirement as certain percentages of insurance liability, and others leaving the definition to the administrative discretion of the insurance commissioner.

States have also undertaken to regulate operating expenses and dividend policies. A few states, like New York, give their commissioners this authority. In most states, however, the commissioners exert influence on these matters through their general power to revoke or refuse to renew licenses.

States customarily have given their authorities power to regulate insurance premiums. This matter is generally handled in the first instance by the insurance companies themselves through rating bureaus—cooperative organizations financed by the companies for the purpose of establishing just and equitable rates. After the bureaus have agreed upon the premiums to be charged by insurance companies for each kind of insurance, the rates are recommended to the insurance commissioners for their approval.

In addition, states have undertaken to regulate the commissions paid to agents and insurance brokers. Since these commissions are often a material portion of the premium paid for insurance, and since insurance companies might engage in dangerous competition to obtain business, the regulation is clearly in the public interest.

Most states provide for regulation of the form in which policies are drawn. The exact wording of different kinds of policies may be prescribed by the legislature or by the insurance department; or the insurance commissioner may be given the authority to approve or disapprove policy forms drawn up by the companies.

The settlement of claims is ordinarily left to the courts, but in several states disputes between policyholders and companies must be submitted to arbitration.

As in the case of loan and deposit banks, insurance companies are subject to periodic examination by state insurance officials. In addition, they must make reports to the state insurance department, to stockholders, and often to policyholders. These devices, important as means of obtaining data for control of operation, are also significant in their regulatory effect.

REGULATION OF INSURANCE: CONCLUSIONS

In the states with more advanced insurance laws, insurance businesses are fairly adequately regulated. States in which are located the home offices of the larger companies almost invariably have good systems of regulation.

The state insurance departments and officials who carry the burden of regulation, since Congress has chosen to leave the authority over insurance in the states, have a wide range of duties. The most pressing problem in the administration of state regulation is that of maintaining the technical staffs necessary to regulate so large an industry. A number of states have enlarged their insurance departments in recent years, but the turnover is so great that it is difficult to maintain continuity of policy. During 1952 alone, there were sixteen new insurance commissioners–one-third of the total number in the United States. In Nebraska, for example, during a four-year period, there were three different chief clerks, four different actuaries, five different attorneys, and five different rate men.[23]

The diverse nature of the state regulatory laws has created a problem which plagues the insurance companies and results in uneven protection of the public. The National Association of Insurance Commissioners, established in 1870, has as one of its main objects the promotion of uniformity in legislation and administrative rulings affecting insurance. The Association, especially under the impetus of the McCarran Act, has had considerable success in increasing the uniformity of state regulatory provisions in recent years.

The question of the role of the federal government in the regulatory picture in the future is still indeterminate. Congress does have the constitutional authority to impose uniform regulation should the need arise. In the meantime, the Federal Trade Commission stands ready to enforce the Federal Trade Commission Act and the Clayton Act against the

[23] Stone, *op. cit.*, p. 446.

practices of insurance companies that violate these laws and are not regulated by state statutes. After the moratorium of the McCarran Act ran out, the Commission promulgated rules relating to advertising and promotion of mail-order insurance. The Commission then began hearings looking toward the promulgation of fair-trade-practices rules for the auto-finance business. In so doing the Commission sought to govern insurance companies and insurance rates and coverage in connection with the sale of automobiles. The National Association of Insurance Commissioners protested this latter action as an invasion of the field already regulated by the states, and the proposed rule was withdrawn.[24] Thus, while serious gaps exist in positive regulation of insurance companies because of the varying nature of state laws, and abuses continue to exist, particularly with mail-order insurance and lax laws in certain states, the strong tradition of states' rights in this industry appears to thwart effective federal control.

Selected References

Anderson, Thomas J., *Federal and State Control of Banking*. Cambridge, Mass.: Bankers Publishing Company, 1934.

——, *Powers of Congress over Currency, Banking and Security Distribution*. Cambridge, Mass.: Bankers Publishing Company, 1935.

Bach, G. L., *Federal Reserve Policy-making*. New York: Alfred A. Knopf, Inc., 1950.

Chapman, John M., and Ray B. Westerfield, *Branch Banking*. New York: Harper & Brothers, 1942.

Comptroller of the Currency, *Federal Laws Affecting National Banks*. 1950.

Cook, Franklin H., *Principles of Business and the Federal Law*, chap. 23. New York: The Macmillan Company, 1951.

Foster, Major B., Raymond Rodgers, J. L. Bogen, and Marcus Nadler, *Money and Banking*. New York: Prentice-Hall, Inc., 1953.

Goldenweiser, E. A., *American Monetary Policy*. New York: McGraw-Hill Book Company, Inc., 1951.

Guthmann, H. G., and H. E. Dougall, *Corporate Financial Policy*, chap. 14. New York: Prentice-Hall, Inc., 1948.

Hall, Ford P., *Government and Business*, 3d ed., chaps. 13, 14. New York: McGraw-Hill Book Company, Inc., 1949.

Harris, S. E., *Twenty Years of Federal Reserve Policy*. Cambridge, Mass.: Harvard University Press, 1933.

Haven, T. K., *Investment Banking under the Securities and Exchange Commission*. Ann Arbor, Mich.: University of Michigan Press, 1940.

Kemmerer, E. W., and D. L. Kemmerer, *The ABC of the Federal Reserve System*. New York: Harper & Brothers, 1950.

Patterson, Edwin Wilhite, *The Insurance Commissioner in the United States*. Cambridge, Mass.: Harvard University Press, 1927.

[24] *Ibid.*, p. 445.

Prochnow, Herbert V. (ed.), *American Financial Institutions*, chaps. 2, 3, 6, 14, 15, 16, 17, 20, 21. New York: Prentice-Hall, Inc., 1951.

Sawyer, Elmer W., *Insurance as Interstate Commerce*. New York: McGraw-Hill Book Company, Inc., 1945.

Szymczak, M. S., *The Federal Reserve in World War II*. Detroit: Burroughs Clearing House, 1945.

18

REGULATION OF SECURITY ISSUANCE

No competitive business is as highly regulated as the securities business. Government control of security issuance by transportation agencies and other public utilities has already been studied as an aspect of regulation of these quasi-public businesses. There, however, the primary reason for regulation has been the necessity of preserving efficient entry into capital markets, so that a ready flow of capital to expand and improve service would be forthcoming and so that the cost of capital would be kept down in order to protect consumers against high rates. The protection of the investment public has been of secondary importance.

In the regulation of security issuance by business generally, the government has been concerned above all with the protection of the investor against fraud or loss caused by misguided choices. In a sense, general regulation of security issuance is also motivated by the desire to lower costs of production to society by preserving capital from loss and by aiding its flow into the most efficient channels.

General governmental regulation of security issuance is a relatively new development, largely because widespread public interest in business securities is a new phenomenon. Statutory regulation of security issuance dates from the passage of a law by the state of Kansas in 1911; by 1933 most other states had followed suit. The federal government did not enter the field with a systematic scheme of regulation until 1933, although the law prohibiting use of the mails to defraud had occasionally brought it into contact with fraudulent security sales. Likewise, the common law had long made fraudulent transactions of all kinds subject to legal retaliation by the victims.

In emphasizing the control of security issuance by state and federal governments, one is likely to lose sight of the regulatory work of private business itself. The New York Stock Exchange and other privately operated exchanges have taken a leading part in encouraging honesty in security sales, as have local better-business bureaus and associations of security dealers. The salutary effect of the growth of a business morality which will not tolerate dishonest and deceitful practices should never be overlooked in an enthusiasm for solving social problems by legislation.

Public Interest in Security Issuance

The public interest in security issuance has both its individual and its social aspects, although practices harmful to the individual investor have probably had more to do with the passage of regulatory legislation than questions concerned with the efficient use of society's stock of capital.

HARMFUL PRACTICES IN SECURITY ISSUANCE

Until after the turn of the twentieth century and even until World War I, the number of purchasers of business securities in the whole population was relatively small, and those who did buy them were deemed to be a small class of the well-to-do who could take care of themselves. This picture changed with the advent of business opportunities after 1900 and the wide public sale of government bonds during World War I. The unregulated sale of stocks and bonds led to certain practices which investors found objectionable and costly. By 1920, the American public had become "security-minded," and promoters took advantage of this appetite for stocks and bonds during the speculative 1920s; people bought securities blindly and often became victims of sellers of fraudulent and highly speculative stocks and bonds. The loss to the investing public by purchase of worthless securities between 1923 and 1933 was placed as high as $500 million annually in New York State alone, and as high as $25 billion in the entire country.[1]

Hand in hand with the promotion of fraudulent securities went the misrepresentation of the prospects of securities. Although fraud is basically a kind of misrepresentation, there are other kinds as well. Many highly speculative business enterprises have been launched and securities sold to an unsuspecting public through misrepresenting the nature of the business, its assets, the dividends that have been paid, and its prospects and possible future dividends.

Until the passage of thorough federal regulation in 1933, requiring disclosure of information, conservative and sound business corporations, as well as the speculative and unsound ventures, rather generally followed the practice of withholding information concerning their business affairs. These corporations held that if they gave out too much information, their competitors would get valuable information, or stockholders and bondholders might misunderstand the significance of the data. The investor in a private business in the 1920s did well if he could obtain a highly abbreviated income statement and a sketchy balance sheet to use as the basis for making his decision. Although there is no assurance that investors would make use of more information, its disclosure makes it possible for

[1] *Regulation of Securities,* S. Rept. 47, 73d Cong., 1st Sess. (1933), p. 2.

investment-advisory services to make a more accurate analysis of corporation issues. Moreover, many investors do take advantage of more complete information when it is available to help them make wise selection among various opportunities for security purchase.

SOCIAL JUSTIFICATION OF CONTROL

As in the case of regulation of financial organizations, the basic social justification of control over security issuance is that the supply of capital is limited. Society has an interest in seeing that this resource, so important to a high material standard of living, is rationed into efficient uses. Standards of living and efficient use of capital would not be advanced, however, if capital were not allowed to flow into speculative enterprises. The willingness of owners of capital to assume risks is a prerequisite of progress. Without this characteristic those new industries which have now materially raised the standard of living would never have been started. But if society is to rely on individual interests to choose where capital shall be placed, the investing public should be protected from fraud and misrepresentation, and efforts should be made to give the investor as full information as possible. If the investing group can be informed and sheltered from dishonesty and deceit, there is hope that individual self-interest will make good use of capital.

The alternative to regulations which will help the individual in his investment problems seems to be legislation which will specifically allocate capital resources to particular uses.

The Background of Security Regulation

Where individuals invest directly in a business or make a direct loan on a mortgage, they are likely to scrutinize the object of their investment closely. The need for regulation of security issuance arose with the development of the joint stock company, the corporation, and similar forms of business. These forms have made possible the accumulation of large sums of capital under one management; this accumulation has followed because certain characteristics, such as free transferability of shares, long life, and limited liability, have been appealing to countless small and large investors.

Moreover, if the power to incorporate or to set up a joint stock company or similar organization had been used sparingly, the problem of regulating security issuance as such might never have arisen. If legislatures had set up rigid requirements of disclosure of information, of the character of promoters, and of the prospects of the business before granting charters to corporations and like companies, the problem of separate security issue control might have been avoided. But actual experience has been different; the powers and privileges of incorporation have been granted indiscriminately by state governments in the United States, many states publicly carrying on competition in making incorporation easy and free from legal restraints.

The system of security-issuance regulation in the United States has been patterned on the English model to a large extent. The common law provided certain remedies to purchasers of securities. For example, at common law the purchase price of a security was returnable if the seller had misrepresented the security and the buyer had relied upon this misrepresentation in making his purchase. However, the burden of action rested on the buyer. If he had tried to resell the security or had accepted dividends, he was unable to act because he was held to have ratified the sale. A purchaser might also sue for damages for malicious deceit by the seller, and if the suit met with success, criminal penalties, as well as civil damages, might be levied against the seller. However, the buyer had to prove that in purchasing the security he had relied upon deliberate misrepresentations which the seller knew to be false. While these common-law principles were often effective, the obtaining of proof was far too uncertain and prosecution too expensive to give the general securities purchaser much protection.

Common-law regulation in England gave way to statutory control. The Company Act of 1929 is a consolidation and revision of statutes having to do with incorporation and security issuance that date back to the early part of the nineteenth century.[2] The Act makes it a criminal offense for corporate officers or directors to publish false statements of a "material" fact about the status of a company. Promoters, directors, officers, security sellers, and experts whose information is relied on are made liable for the accurate and full disclosure of information in the prospectus by which securities are sold.

In the United States the principle of "Let the buyer beware" in security dealings received its first modification at the hands of state governments. The first blue-sky law—so called because of the belief that unscrupulous promoters would even sell shares in the blue sky—was passed by Kansas in 1911, and similar laws by other states followed shortly after. When in 1917 the United States Supreme Court upheld the constitutionality of the early laws,[3] impetus was given to the passage of such laws in other states, and by 1922 more than half the states had blue-sky laws on their statute books. The decline of security prices following 1929 led to further agitation for regulation, so that in 1933 every state except Nevada had enacted legislation controlling security issuance.

[2] See Seigvald Nielson, "The Issuance of Securities under the English Companies Act," 20 *Virginia Law Review* 88–102 (1933).

[3] *Hall v. Geiger-Jones Co.*, 242 U.S. 539 (1917), and *Merrick v. N. W. Halsey & Co.*, 242 U.S. 568 (1917); *Caldwell v. Sioux Falls Stock Yards Co.*, 242 U.S. 559 (1917).

State Regulation of Security Issuance

State laws vary considerably in regard to the extent, objectives, and the means of control over new securities. They range from statutes which merely strengthen the common law in respect to fraud to those which make the state a sort of paternalistic guardian of its investors by granting power to a commission to qualify securities suitable for sale. The laws of the forty-seven states which currently regulate security issuance may be roughly classified as three types: (1) the "fraud" type, (2) the type requiring licensing of sellers, and (3) the type requiring registration of securities. The laws of certain states combine two or more of these types. New York, New Jersey, and Delaware, have the "fraud" type of law. Connecticut, Maine, Pennsylvania, and Rhode Island place sole reliance on the licensing of dealers. The rest require some kind of registration of new securities, while some of them supplement this control by regulation of dealers.[4]

THE "FRAUD" TYPE OF LAW

The so-called "fraud" type of law merely provides criminal penalties for frauduluent action. The attorney general is empowered to stop the sale of any security which appears to be fraudulent and to start criminal prosecution against the dealers or other persons who have anything to do with it. Dealers convicted of fraud not only are subject to fine or imprisonment but also are permanently enjoined from future security sales in the state.

Because fraud is not capable of close definition, this kind of law has led to little punishment and not much prevention. Infractions are seldom discovered until investors have been cheated out of their savings. Moreover, since this kind of law is directed against fraudulent practices only, the investor is left unprotected from losses incurred from incompetent judgment, inadequate investigation of prospective investment, or sheer ignorance.

LAWS LICENSING SELLERS

Under the second type of law, dealers, brokers, and others participating in the sale of securities must obtain a license before selling securities in the state. These licenses are usually granted for short periods, such as a year, and are invariably subject to revocation by the state agency in charge. To obtain a license, sellers must file information establishing that they are persons of "good repute." Revocation or refusal to renew licenses is left largely to the discretion of the licensing commission.

[4] F. P. Hall, *Government and Business* (New York: McGraw-Hill Book Company, Inc., 3d ed., 1949), p. 378.

Licensing laws are subject to the same deficiencies as the "fraud" laws. Some prevention results from careful qualification of sellers, but the real effect of the law is more likely to be felt *after* a seller has defrauded the public. However, if a state licensing commission would take great care in licensing sellers and not make the granting of licenses a perfunctory task of approving applications, the law could be fairly effective.

LAWS REQUIRING REGISTRATION

The great majority of state blue-sky laws require that securities be registered, and most of them in addition require that they meet certain definite qualifications. Laws in some states permit certain securities, generally those of well-established corporations or bonds adequately secured by a first mortgage on physical property, to be sold immediately upon registration and the filing of designated information. Usually, however, the securities must be filed, and approval for sale must be granted before sale can be made. Fairly complete information has been required by most state laws. The state agency—which may be a corporation commission, securities commission, banking commission, or even the office of the secretary of state, depending on the state—examines these data and approves or disapproves the registration.

Altogether too few state laws provide for an accurate checkup on prospectuses or other advertising matter. While the information required may be adequate, it is too often placed in the files of the commission and not made readily available to the investor. Moreover, those laws which impose a duty on the commission of passing judgment as to the soundness of a security are seldom accompanied by appropriations which will permit thorough examination and analysis. The result is that securities commissions are forced on too many occasions to pass upon a security on the basis of the general appearance of information filed and are not able to make an analysis which would enable them to fulfill the requirements of the law. The same difficulties arise from laws which authorize approval on grounds of adequacy of information, questions of fraud, or the soundness of business principles of the issuer. Appropriations for administration have been too low to allow considered and accurate judgments based on a full analysis of information. Unless the administration of the laws is adequately financed and carried on by experts, the protection to investors may turn out to be delusive.

STATE SECURITY REGULATION: CONCLUSIONS

It is difficult to assess the value of state blue-sky legislation. Although these laws have not been successful in removing fraud or deception in security sales, there can hardly be doubt that they have had beneficial effects. The large number of issues disapproved by states with well-drawn and well-administered registration laws is evidence of this fact. Perhaps one of the greatest accomplishments has been the discouragement of fraudulent promotion before any attempt has been made to register or sell securities. Although this benefit cannot be measured, its value should not be overlooked.

Nevertheless, state regulation of security issuance has fallen far short of the high purposes of the legislation. The principal underlying causes of the inadequacy of state regulation are not difficult to find. In the first place, state laws have not been uniform in purpose or requirements, and the character of their administration has varied considerably. Those states with lax laws or enforcement agencies have furnished a refuge for unscrupulous promoters and have consequently impaired the fairly thorough programs of other states. States with proper legislation but inadequate enforcement have unwittingly aided in the deception of investors.

A second weakness of state regulation has been the inability of authorities to detect and apprehend sales across state lines, especially where done by direct mail and through advertising in magazines or newspapers sent into a state. Third, state security laws and their administration have failed to get information to investors regarding new security issues.

In the fourth place, state regulation at best only attempts to see that an offering is not dishonest or deceptively handled at the *time* the security is to be sold. Avoidance of fraud and deception and aid to investors demand that regulation continue after the first offering. The task of regulation is only half completed when a security is offered for sale.

Finally, it should be noted that the problem of state control of security issuance is closely related to state incorporation requirements. Many American states have vied with each other in making the chartering of corporations easy.[5] This laxness has resulted in an important privilege being given to groups of individuals, with relatively little control placed over them in return. Regulations respecting security issuance, financial practices, and adequate reports to investors, as well as other business matters now subject to separate regulation, could be made requisites of incorporation. However, as long as the business of chartermongering is looked upon by legislators as a rich source of state income, reforms in incorporation procedure are not likely to come. It may be that control over incorporation will have to be placed in the hands of the federal government, as has been done with regulation of security issuance.

[5] Justice Brandeis refers to this competition among states in enacting favorable corporation laws in a dissenting opinion: "The race was not one of diligence but of laxity." *Liggett v. Lee,* 288 U.S. 517, 541 (1933).

Federal Regulation of Security Issuance

The federal government first entered the field of security-issuance control in 1909 by making it a criminal offense for persons to use the mails to defraud. This law applied to general cases of mail fraud, but it has been especially helpful to the states in combating fraudulent sales of securities. However, the law was at best only punitive and furnished no continuing supervision of security issuance. The real entry of the federal government into this field came in 1933 and 1934. The inadequacies of state control of security issuance in the face of widespread abuses which the Depression highlighted prompted Congress to enact the Securities Act in 1933 and the Securities Exchange Act in 1934.[6] To protect the investor, the first of these laws is designed to oversee the public offerings of new securities.[7] The second law is concerned with the regulation of the national stock exchanges and the listing of securities and will be treated in the next chapter.

The Securities Act has been aptly called the "truth in securities act," because its stated purpose is "to provide full and fair disclosure of the character of securities sold in interstate and foreign commerce and through the mails. . . ." To this end, (1) the issuer is required to file a registration statement with the Securities and Exchange Commission containing certain prescribed information about the security issue, and (2) the distribution of the security to the investor must be accompanied or preceded by a prospectus containing in condensed form most of the information given upon registration. If these requirements are not met or if the Commission disapproves the registration statement or prospectus, the mails and the channels of interstate commerce are denied to the security. Thus, the law does not propose to pass on securities as being good or bad for investment, and makes no attempt to protect the investor against his own folly, incompetence, or lack of considered analysis. It merely attempts to ensure that investors will be fully informed of facts relating to a security offered for sale. Violation of either of the two prohibitions is subject both to civil liabilities and to criminal penalties, if the violation is willful.

Enforcement of the act was originally placed in the Federal Trade Com-

[6] The 1934 law included numerous amendments to the Securities Act of 1933, principally in the exemption and civil-liability provisions. No attempt will be made to distinguish the original act from its amendments, so the discussion of the Securities Act will be of the law as it exists today.

[7] For one of the most detailed treatments of the Securities Act, see Edward T. McCormick, *Understanding the Securities Act and the S.E.C.* (New York: American Book Company, 1948).

mission. When the Securities and Exchange Commission was created in 1934, administration was transferred to the more specialized agency.

EXEMPTED SECURITIES AND TRANSACTIONS

Like the state blue-sky laws, certain securities and transactions are exempt from the operation of the federal law. Securities issued by the following are exempt: (1) federal, state, and municipal governments and their instrumentalities; (2) national banks and properly supervised state banks; (3) persons organized exclusively for religious, charitable, educational, fraternal, benevolent, or reformatory purposes; (4) building and loan associations; (5) farmers' cooperative associations for marketing of farm produce and purchasing of farm supplies and equipment; (6) common and contract carriers whose securities are regulated by the Interstate Commerce Commission; (7) trustees or receivers issuing certificates of indebtedness under court approval; (8) state-regulated insurance companies issuing insurance, endowment, and annuity policies; and (9) by a 1949 amendment, securities issued or guaranteed by the International Bank for Reconstruction and Development.

In addition, the law exempts ordinary commercial paper (bank notes, drafts, bills of exchange, and acceptances) which arise from current business transactions. The Securities and Exchange Commission may also exempt securities because of the size of issue or the limited distribution.

Some securities fall outside the law if they involve certain transactions. Exempt are (1) transactions by an issuer not involving a public offering; (2) transactions which are issued in reorganization following bankruptcy and which are subject to supervision by the courts or other administrative body; (3) transactions more than a year after the security was first offered to the public; (4) transactions by persons other than an issuer, underwriter, or dealer; and (5) intrastate sales of securities.[8]

REGISTRATION REQUIREMENTS

All new offerings, except for exempt securities, must be registered. Registration is accomplished by filing a statement with the Securities and Exchange Commission, accompanied by a fee. [9] The registration statement must contain the following: [10]

[8] For a discussion of some of the questions that have been raised about these exemptions, see A. E. Throop and C. T. Lane, "Some Problems of Exemption under the Securities Act of 1933," 4 *Law and Contemporary Problems* 89–127 (January, 1937).

[9] The fee is equal to 1/100 of 1 per cent of the aggregate amount at which the securities are proposed to be offered for sale, subject to a minimum fee of $25.

[10] Drawn largely from Brunson MacChesney and R. H. O'Brien, "Full Disclosure under the Securities Act," 4 *Law and Contemporary Problems* 133–153 (April, 1937).

A. Information relating to promoters.
   1. Names and addresses of promoters.
   2. Stock interest of promoters.
   3. Amount and nature of payments to promoters.

B. Information relating to underwriters.
   1. Names and addresses of underwriters and other distributors.
   2. Price at which underwriters are to buy securities from the issuer.
   3. Price or prices at which underwriter proposes to sell to the public.
   4. Profits of underwriters and other distributors of securities.
   5. List of preferred buyers who are given a special price and the price they will pay.
   6. Subscriptions of securities by persons affiliated with the management of the company and the price at which they will subscribe.
   7. If security is a part of an existing substantial block, agreements made to keep existing securities off the market pending sales of new securities must be disclosed.
   8. Activity by sellers to support the market price must be disclosed.

C. Information relating to experts who have aided in drawing up the registration statement (accountants, engineers, lawyers, etc.).
   1. Professional qualifications of experts.
   2. Relationship of experts to issuing company.

D. Information relating to the management of issuing company.
   1. Names of directors, principal officers, and other "insiders" with some power in managing the company.
   2. Stockholdings of the management in the company.
   3. Interest of the management in property purchased by the company or in business contracts made by the company.
   4. Remuneration of directors and persons receiving more than $25,000 annually.
   5. Business experience of management in five years previous to registration.

E. Information relating to disposition of proceeds of issue.
   1. Purposes to which proceeds will be devoted and amount to be allocated to each purpose.
   2. Priority of application of proceeds to the purposes.

F. Information relating to capitalization of issuing company.
   1. Rights investors will acquire in proposed new security (dividends, voting powers, priorities and preferences, underlying security, sinking funds, etc.).
   2. Balance sheets (where company is established) for several years in proper detail and with explanations to show the nature of the assets, liabilities, and proprietorship clearly.
   3. Income statements (where company is established) for several years in adequate detail.

The registration statement must not contain an untrue statement of material fact, or omit a material fact, or omit such facts as will make a statement misleading. These requirements are backed up with ample penalties and place responsibility upon those connected with issuance of securities to furnish the necessary full disclosure. The Commission has further interpreted the law to require that the registration statement or the prospectus as a whole must not be misleading. It has found that a registration statement furnishing too much or too detailed information can present a misleading picture of the enterprise. In describing assets or intended use of proceeds from an issue, issuers have sometimes given such detail as to the possibilities of the company that they may overstate the future to the investor. Or if information is made purposely detailed and complex to confuse the investor, the registration statement or prospectus may be declared misleading as a whole.

If no action is taken by the Commission, the statement becomes effective twenty days after the filing date.[11] The Commission may, after notice and opportunity for hearing, refuse to permit registration before the effective date or revoke registration after the effective date if it finds the statement to be inaccurate or incomplete. Actually, there are few formal hearings of this type, because the Commission may notify the registrant in a letter of deficiency and allow the registration to be completed when the deficiency is satisfied. This informal procedure is especially useful where there is evidence of an honest and sincere effort to comply with the law.

THE PROSPECTUS

A new security must be accompanied by an approved prospectus as well as be registered before it can be offered publicly. The law stipulates that a prospectus must be given to every person solicited and to every purchaser either before or at the time of sale.

The prospectus is the real selling document and the basis for circulating the information to investors. It is a digest of the registration statement, and while it should be readable and not too long, it should contain all the information of material importance in the statement. Supporting data, except for balance sheets and income statements, necessary for full disclosure in the statement may often be left out of the prospectus. However, the prospectus is subject to the requirement that it must not make misleading assertions or omit material facts important to the making of judgments by the investor.

The issuing company and the distributors of securities are responsible for digesting the material in the registration statement to prepare the prospectus, subject to some suggestions and possible amendments by the Commission. An interesting dilemma has been presented by the prospectus. The Commission has desired that it be concise and plainly worded, so that

[11] By amendment in 1940, the Commission is given discretion to shorten the waiting period where it finds that the requirements of full disclosure have been met.

the investor will read and understand it. On the other hand, issuers are made liable for inclusion of untrue statements or omission of material facts necessary to make the statements in the prospectus not misleading. In order to play safe, the issuers have tended to make the prospectus lengthy, so that they may not be subject to liability under the law. The result has been that prospectuses have often been documents of 200 or more pages, crammed full of detailed information which would leave anyone except the expert rather bewildered, even if they were read.

The answer to this dilemma is not easy to find. Information upon which an intelligent investment can be made is not often capable of concise and clear statement. The fact that the prospectus is complicated and must probably continue to be so is not entirely a matter for discouragement. If investors can be encouraged to obtain prospectuses, they may at least realize the difficulties of competently selecting investment, and if they cannot comprehend the prospectus themselves, they may make wider use of expert advice and assistance than many have in the past.

Furthermore, since all the registered information is not included in the prospectus, the complete data on every security are on file at the office of the Securities and Exchange Commission. Investors and investment advisory agencies can consult these files and obtain photostatic copies of the registration statements at cost.

LIABILITY OF REGISTRANTS

In addition to the power of the Securities and Exchange Commission to issue a stop or refusal order in connection with registration, the federal law provides other means of bringing about compliance with the law. These are divided between criminal and civil penalties.

Criminal penalties. When a person connected with the issuance of a security wilfully mistakes or omits facts, or disregards the law or regulations adopted by the Commission, the latter may bring action in a federal court to enjoin such activities; or it may transmit available evidence to the Attorney General, who may begin criminal proceedings. A fine not to exceed $5,000, imprisonment up to five years, or both, may be imposed for wilful violation of the law.

Civil penalties. The civil penalties are more complicated and technical. Liability may arise because a seller fails to file a registration statement or send a prospectus to a buyer. The immediate purchaser may be refunded the purchase price or be paid damages in this event.

Liability may also arise when there is omission of a material [12] fact or

[12] The Commission has defined "material" as the information of "which an average prudent investor ought reasonably to be informed before purchasing the security registered." See A. H. Dean, "The Lawyer's Problems in the Registration of Securities," 4 *Law and Contemporary Problems* 154–190 (April, 1937).

the inclusion of an untrue or misleading assertion in the registration statement. The right to sue under such circumstances extends not only to the first purchaser but also to subsequent purchasers of securities. Damages which a purchaser can collect are limited to the difference between the price paid for the security and the market price at the time of the suit or the price realized upon sale of the security. However, a defendant is given the right to prove that the loss in value occurred because of circumstances not related to the faulty portion of the registration statement, and to the extent that he can so prove, the damages are to be reduced. Ordinarily the purchaser need not prove that he bought the security relying upon the registration statement, and he need never prove that he read it or the prospectus. But if suit is brought after the issuing company has made available to security holders an earning statement covering a period of at least twelve months beginning after the effective date of the registration statement, the purchaser must prove that he acquired the security relying upon the misrepresentation in the registration statement, even though he need not prove that he read it. In no event, however, may the damages collectible exceed the price at which the security was offered to the public.

Finally, a right of action exists in favor of the immediate purchaser against a person who sells a security on the basis of an oral communication or a prospectus which includes an untrue statement of material fact or a misleading statement of fact. The remedy is the same as for failure to file a registration statement or to send a prospectus at all.

Actions for damages under the law may not be maintained unless brought within one year after the discovery of an untrue statement or misrepresentation. In no event may suits be brought more than three years after the public sale of the security.

Liability for failure to register or for omissions or misstatements in the registration statement or prospectus runs against not only the signatories of the registration statement[13] but also the following: (1) every person who was a director of, or partner in, the issuing company at the time it was filed; (2) every person who has consented to be named as being as about to become a director or partner; (3) every expert who has consented to be named in the registration statement as having prepared or certified data which were used in it and which have turned out to be faulty; (4) every underwriter of the issue; and (5) every person who controlled any of the above, unless the controlling person had no knowledge of, or reasonable grounds to believe in, the existence of the facts giving rise to the liability.

[13] The statement must be signed by the issuer of securities, its principal executive officer or officers, its principal financial officer, its comptroller or chief accounting officer, and a majority of the board of directors or persons performing similar functions.

Except for the issuing company, which has no defense against a suit beyond those previously mentioned, the law does not make the liability of other persons absolute. Persons who resign from any relationship described in the registration statement before its effective date and have advised the Commission that they would therefore take no responsibility under it may be allowed to escape liability. Public notice that a registration statement became effective without an official's knowledge may also furnish grounds for competent defense. Persons other than the issuer who can prove that, after reasonable investigation, they had reasonable grounds for believing that the data in the registration statement were accurate and complete may also escape liability. The law sets up as a standard of reasonableness that care which would be required of a prudent man in the management of his own property. In every case of a person using the above defenses, the entire burden of proof is placed upon him.

In spite of the declaration by many businessmen that the liability provisions of the securities law place intolerable burdens even on the honest and careful seller of securities, the record of successful suits for civil damages has been so negligible that the original fear of the act does not seem justified.[14] Its main purpose was to force full disclosure by terrorizing sellers with the liabilities which *might* be incurred if the registration statement, prospectus, or other means of sales solicitation were untrue or misleading; the act was not designed primarily to give security purchasers machinery for recouping their losses. In accomplishing its main purpose, the law has been successful.

PREVENTION OF FRAUD

Under the Securities Act, the Securities and Exchange Commission is not concerned with the speculative character of a security. If the information is adequate and accurate, the Commission has no power to refuse registration of a security no matter how risky it may seem. However, the law does go beyond full disclosure by outlawing fraudulent sales of securities in interstate commerce or by use of the mails. It provides that none of the exemptions of the act apply in cases of fraudulent practices, transactions, or courses of business which operate as fraud or deceit upon the purchaser. Included, therefore, in its scope are attempts to defraud in sale of securities, whether such securities are new or not.

CORRELATION WITH STATE LAWS

The Securities Act does not supersede state blue-sky laws. As a matter of fact, it specifically declares that nothing shall affect the jurisdiction of

[14] Between 1933 and 1940, the civil remedies were invoked only sixteen times; recovery was obtained in only three cases. "Civil Liability under the Federal Securities Act," 50 *Yale Law Journal* 90–106 (November, 1940).

the various state commissions. A federal court said that this provision did not indicate an intention on the part of Congress to limit the Securities Act to activities solely in interstate commerce but merely gave concurrent jurisdiction to the Securities and Exchange Commission and state commissions.[15] The offering of new securities by a corporation in one state through underwriters and dealers in another state places the issue under the federal government, and because the actual sales are likely to be made between a seller and purchaser within the state, the transaction often falls under the state law. Consequently, the larger portion of the new securities subject to federal control are also under the jurisdiction of the states. On the other hand, the federal government has not taken control over purely intrastate security sales, and the state governments have not often attempted to regulate interstate aspects of security issuance. Thus, there is a certain part of the new security business in which the regulations of the two levels of government do not overlap.

Even where overlapping does exist, regulation is not necessarily duplicated. Many state regulations are based upon control over sellers, elimination of fraud, and qualification of securities for investment. These are matters only incidentally subject to federal control. Only in those state laws which require registration of the securities before issuance is there serious duplication.

In this last class of legislation, some confusion and needless expense to sellers of securities exist. Many sellers have to go to the expense of registering under several state laws and the federal laws; they also have to be sure that they are complying with both regulations. In cases of this kind, it might well be wise for Congress to exert its superior power and remove such interstate transactions from the registration requirements of state law.

CONSTITUTIONALITY OF FEDERAL CONTROL OF ISSUANCE

The legal basis for federal security-issuance control is the interstate-commerce power and the postal power. In view of early decisions of the Supreme Court holding that contracts for insurance were not commerce,[16] there was some misgiving in Congress as to the legal justification for the Securities Act. For this reason, Congress provided that the instrumentalities of interstate commerce and the facilities of the Post Office should be forbidden to those who refused to abide by the provisions of the law. Hence, the legal approach was not to regulate security issuance as commerce itself but to prohibit the channels of commerce and the Post Office to per-

[15] *SEC v. Timetrust, Inc.*, 28 F. Supp. 34 (1939). See R. A. Smith, "State 'Blue-sky' Laws and the Federal Securities Acts," 34 *Michigan Law Review* 1135–1166 (June, 1936).

[16] See p. 439.

sons who disobey the law. The commerce power has often been used in the past to achieve a moral end: e.g., the prohibition on the interstate transportation of lottery tickets, of impure foods and drugs, of kidnapped children, of stolen automobiles, and of women for immoral purposes.

Many lower federal courts have upheld the constitutionality of the Securities Act [17] and the Supreme Court has denied certiorari in a number of cases.[18] The courts have also almost invariably upheld the Securities and Exchange Commission where review of its orders has been sought.[19]

FEDERAL REGULATION OF SECURITY ISSUANCE: CONCLUSIONS

When the Securities Act was passed, the framers of the legislation could hardly have foreseen the magnitude of the task they were imposing on the Securities and Exchange Commission.[20] The Commission has made an enviable record for efficient and fair administration. The Hoover Commission Task Force on Regulatory Commissions concluded: "It has combined knowledge of the field, judgment and reasonable consistency of policy with freedom from partisan political pressures. The Commission on the whole has been notably well administered. Even its critics concede that its staff is able and conscientious, and that the Commission generally conducts its work with dispatch and expedition where speed is most essential." [21]

However, the provisions and operation of the Securities Act have not been beyond criticism.[22] In the first place, it has been claimed that the registration requirements necessitate going to great trouble and expense and that this places an unneeded burden upon well-established corporations. Question may be raised, however, whether the expense of selling

[17] See, for example, *SEC v. Wickham*, 12 F. Supp. 245 (1935), and *Jones v. SEC*, 79 F.2d 617 (1935).

[18] See SEC, *Annual Report, 1939*, pp. 114–115.

[19] *Ibid.*, pp. 3 and 96–115; and SEC, *Annual Report, 1940*, pp. 292–313, where are listed numerous proceedings where the SEC has been upheld.

[20] Actually, the Commission did not assume responsibilities under the Securities Act until the Securities Exchange Act of 1934. In addition, it administers the Public Utility Holding Company Act (1935), the Trust Indenture Act (1939), the Investment Company Act (1940), the Investment Advisors Act (1940), and chap. X of the Bankruptcy Act (1938).

[21] Appendix N prepared for the Commission on Organization of the Executive Branch of the Government (1949), p. 144. Among its most eminent commissioners have been numbered Joseph P. Kennedy, James M. Landis, William O. Douglas, Ferdinand Pecora, and Sumner T. Pike.

[22] For an excellent discussion of some of the defects in federal security regulation and recommendations for improvement, see Willard E. Atkins, George W. Edwards, and Harold G. Moulton, *The Regulation of the Security Markets* (Washington, D.C.: Brookings Institution, 1946), pp. 92–123; and McCormick, *op. cit.*, pp. 285–295.

securities has really been increased, although it must be conceded that probably the care and detail needed for the registration statements impose troublesome burdens. Some writers have even pointed out that the costs have been lower under the securities law and have shown that the spread between the public offering price and that received by the corporation has been less since 1933 than it was in the previous decade.[23] The question of whether the law has materially increased the cost of selling securities is rather inconclusive. In cases of well-established corporations where underwriting firms in the past felt little investigation to be necessary, the requirements of the law have probably increased the cost of selling securities. In other cases the investigation required by law is no greater than than that made by the better underwriters before it was enacted. But the fact that the cost of selling may have increased in some cases is of no consequence, since this cost may be amply justified by the purposes of the law.

The law has been criticized for its strictness and for its leniency in respect to its civil-liability provisions. On the one hand, it is claimed that directors and others cannot know whether they have included all matters of material fact, especially in the light of subsequent developments, and that the law is too hard on them. On the other hand, critics have declared that most persons subject to liability under the law can too easily escape it through the defenses provided. Whether the law is too strict or too lenient has not in reality been a serious matter. The fewness of liability cases and the success of full disclosure have as yet made these arguments of little more than academic importance.

The exemptions of the law have been criticized as being too broad. Between 1948 and 1952, only 14 to 16 per cent of all new offerings were registered under the Securities Act. The rest were exempt. Many securities exempt under this law were issued by railroads and therefore were subject to the jurisdiction of the Interstate Commerce Commission. Particularly criticized has been the exemption of state and municipal issues. As an authority connected with one large institutional investor has pointed out, "Sins of omission and commission have occurred in this field as flagrantly as in any other." [24]

Many critics of the Act attribute the large amount of privately placed securities to the desire on the part of issuing corporations to escape the necessity of meeting the registration requirements.[25] During the ten-year

[23] P. P. Gourrich, "Investment Banking Methods Prior to and Since the Securities Act of 1933," 4 *Law and Contemporary Problems* 69 (January, 1937).

[24] C. J. Kuhn, "The Securities Act and Its Effect on the Institutional Investor," 4 *Law and Contemporary Problems* 86 (January, 1937).

[25] A privately placed issue is also free from the restrictions of the Trust Indenture Act of 1939.

period ending in mid-1944, about one-sixth of the new corporate securities were exempt from registration because they were privately placed, many of them with insurance companies. The Securities and Exchange Commission, however, maintains that "the real causes for the growth of private placements will be found in the unfolding of certain broad economic forces totally unrelated to the registration requirements of the Securities Act." [26]

The securities law has further been criticized because it does not really attain its principal objective of building up a group of adequately and accurately informed investors. The complicated mass of information included in the registration statements and prospectuses do not inform the investor unless he reads it and understands the inferences from it. There are those who claim in this connection that a positive danger exists by having the investor believe that he is trading in securities which are approved by the government or which must necessarily be good because of the detailed information made public.

As a matter of fact, the effect of the law on the investor group is of the utmost importance. If it fails to inform the investor, it has failed in its primary purpose. Granting that few investors read registration statements or prospectuses and that fewer still are capable of drawing accurate inferences from them, it does not follow that the federal securities law has been fruitless. The disclosure requirements of the law have made available much pertinent information to financial advisory agencies and to the small distributor of securities, information which was generally closely held before 1933. Pertinent data and interpretations are often passed on to investors by these parties. Some of this information finds its way into the financial columns of newspapers and magazines, and the average investor often becomes better educated thereby. Furthermore, the investing group cannot avoid being helped by the improvement in accounting standards and financial practices which the administration of the law has brought about. This benefit is made greater by the introduction of a degree of uniformity in a field previously characterized by diverse state laws. While state laws have not lost their diverse nature, superimposing a uniform federal law upon them has reduced the opportunity for defrauding or deceiving investors.

The greatest harm may result if the securities law creates a confidence among investors that risks of investment are virtually eliminated. No full-disclosure law can protect the investor against investment losses caused by other things than the lack of adequate information. With the course of progress relatively uncontrolled and the fallibility of human judgment in business matters unchanged, investment losses are sure to continue. Moreover, the get-rich-quick promoter has not been stamped out. Exemptions

[26] SEC *Annual Report, 1944,* p. 6.

of intrastate and small issues place many of them beyond the federal law, and state laws are not always adequately enforced. Even if the laws were comprehensive and well enforced, the possibility of making an easy, albeit dishonest, dollar will ever encourage unscrupulous promoters to risk the penalties of the law. The investor cannot forget that the buyer, as well as the seller, must beware.

Selected References

Ashby, F. B., *Economic Effects of Blue Sky Laws.* Philadelphia: University of Pennsylvania Press, 1926.

Cherrington, H. V., *The Investor and the Securities Act.* Washington, D.C.: Public Affairs Press, 1942.

Cook, Franklin H., *Principles of Business and the Federal Law,* chap. 21. New York: The Macmillan Company, 1951.

Edelman, J. M., *Securities Regulation in the 48 States.* Chicago: Council of State Governments, 1942.

Flynn, John T., *Security Speculation.* New York: Harcourt, Brace and Company, Inc., 1934.

Husband, William H., and James C. Dockeray, *Modern Corporation Finance,* chap. 20. Homewood, Ill.: Richard D. Irwin, Inc., 1952.

Jome, Hiram L., *Corporation Finance,* chap. 22. New York: Henry Holt and Company, Inc., 1948.

Loss, Louis, *Securities Regulation.* Boston: Little, Brown & Company, 1951.

McCormick, Edward T., *Understanding the Securities Act and the S.E.C.* New York: American Book Company, 1948.

Prentice-Hall Securities Regulation Service. New York: Prentice-Hall, Inc.

Securities and Exchange Commission, *A Proposal to Safeguard Investors in Unregistered Securities.* 1946.

Smith, R. S., "State 'Blue-sky' Laws and the Federal Securities Acts," 34 *Michigan Law Review* 1135 (1936).

Stein, E., *Government and the Investor.* New York: Rinehart & Company, Inc., 1941.

19

REGULATION OF SECURITY AND COMMODITY MARKETS

A market may be described as an area in which buyers and sellers make exchanges with each other. Wherever goods are bought or sold a market exists. Some markets are far more organized than others. The most thoroughly organized consist of associations of individuals established for the principal purpose of furnishing a place for the transaction of purchases and sales in a certain few kinds of goods. To make the process orderly, such associations restrict to their own members the privilege of trading in the market place they furnish. The members may buy and sell on their own account or, as is more usual, as agents of parties outside the exchange membership; in other words, members of organized exchanges may be dealers or brokers.

The most widely used organized exchanges are the stock and commodity markets. The stock exchanges furnish facilities for buying and selling not only common and preferred stocks of business corporations but other types of securities as well. The commodity exchanges provide a place for organized trading in such goods as wheat, oats, rye, and other grains, cotton, hides, sugar, coffee, copper, rubber, and other raw materials.

The operations of organized exchanges have greater public significance to the economic organization than the mere fact that many people use them. The prices paid for securities and raw materials have their effects upon the efficient operation of the economic system. Just as fair stock or bond prices facilitate the flow and transfer of capital resources in business enterprises, fair commodity prices, by influencing cost and price, affect the flow of raw materials into production and consumption. The function of the organized exchange is to furnish facilities for making exchange at prices fairly determined by demand and supply. The public interest in these exchanges is based on the desire to see that practices by individuals will not impede the orderly setting of fair prices by the market. In any system relying in large part upon free private enterprise, price is of the utmost importance, and the conditions under which it is set, including facilities for transfer, bargaining, and buyer and seller information, are impressed with a public interest.

The relationship between regulation of security exchanges and that of new security issuance is particularly close. Under the federal program of regulation, full disclosure of information is required of new issues only. This requirement is supplemented by the regulations connected with trading which apply to all securities handled by registered exchanges. In the case of both security and commodity exchanges, virtually all the governmental regulation has been under the federal government.

Regulation of Organized Stock Exchanges

Most of the dollar volume of security purchases and sales is handled through nineteen stock exchanges in the United States; [1] a larger number of issues, but a smaller dollar volume of business, is traded by some 4,500 security brokers and dealers. The transaction of security sales and purchases by these brokers, without use of organized exchanges, is called the "over-the-counter market." Since special regulation has been provided for this vast unorganized market, it will be touched upon in the succeeding section.

THE NEED FOR GOVERNMENT REGULATION

The end of the speculative orgy of the 1920s with the stock-market crash of 1929 brought in its wake a demand for regulation of the stock exchanges. In spite of the fact that most stock exchanges had provided high-grade self-regulation and that many of the evils of speculation could not be laid at the door of the exchanges, which merely furnished the facilities for trading, there were several considerations which pointed to the need for regulation, especially by the federal government.

Margin trading [2] was a practice which appeared in need of regulation

[1] By far the largest and most important exchange is the New York Stock Exchange, which, since 1935, has done between 85 and 90 per cent of the business done by all exchanges.

[2] The criticisms of stock-exchange operation given here are drawn from *The Security Markets* (New York: The Twentieth Century Fund, Inc., 1935), chap. 17. Margin trading is the purchase of securities by the aid of borrowed funds. The usual procedure is for the purchaser to put up a portion of the cost of securities bought through his broker and for the latter to use the purchased securities as collateral in borrowing funds to finance the rest of the cost. So long as the market value of the securities is above the amount of borrowings, the loan is well secured and easy for the broker to get. When the market price falls below the purchase price, the broker may ask the purchaser to contribute more funds or may sell the securities to satisfy the loan. The amount the purchaser contributes is called his "margin." Thus, if he buys a share of stock at $100 and makes a payment of $60, his margin is said to be 60 per cent. Obviously, the amount of margin varies with the subsequent market price of the security.

in 1934. Purchasing stocks on the margin increases the volume of purchases any individual can make with the same amount of capital and thereby contributes to the activity of a market. Because the credit base in the American banking system is capable of great elasticity, and because loans on stock as collateral have been regarded as very safe, brokers have generally had no trouble in obtaining adequate funds for margin trading. The result has been that, especially in a rapidly rising market, loans have been expanded to furnish funds for security purchases. But increased security purchases contribute to rising prices, and higher security prices make more collateral value for larger loans. This spiral of increasing prices and increasing credit has a tendency to be self-generative and to lead to an inflated level of security prices and credit. When adverse circumstances cause prices to fall, collateral values decline, and loans must be liquidated, causing further price declines, further falls in collateral value, and further loan liquidation. The distress indicated by selling of securities causes a rapid credit deflation and a more than normal depression of security prices. The criticism of margin trading, then, is that it contributes to market instability and is instrumental in causing detrimental credit expansion and deflation. The criticism of exchanges in the operation of margin trading is that they have not insisted upon high enough margin requirements to minimize its dangers.

Upsetting to the normal equilibrium of markets has been the practice of short selling,[3] which has been subject to more criticism and complaint than has margin trading. The reason, of course, is that most speculators among the general public purchase for a rise in the market and hence are likely to feel that short sellers, by offering a supply of securities on the market which they do not own, tend abnormally to depress market price. Ordinary short sales do not have material effects upon the normal functioning of markets, and they are even necessary to eliminate abnormal fluctuations caused by occasional large purchases; but there has been a feeling that excessive short selling may interfere with the proper functioning of a market, particularly if it is aimed at a certain stock or is performed on a certain day.

Security exchanges have also been criticized for not exercising better control over manipulative operations. Manipulation involving deliberate interference with the free action of demand and supply is generally car-

[3] One sells short when he orders a broker to sell a security which the seller does not own. In order to consummate the sale, the broker borrows the security and holds the selling customer responsible for replacing it at some time in the future. This device has possibilities of profit (and loss) to the seller. If he sells, say, at $50 per share and purchases the same security later at $30 per share, he has made a profit. However, should the security go up in price, he would stand to lose.

ried on by pools.[4] The purposes of pools vary from a desire to make a profit for a certain group of speculators, by forcing the price of a security up, to a desire to sell a large block of securities without causing their price to fall unduly. Some of the operations of pools may be perfectly legitimate, such as the support of a market while a new issue of securities is being distributed or while a large block of securities owned by an individual or an investing institution is being methodically liquidated. The objection to the manipulation of security markets has been that a false activity may be created and that investors and speculators may be deceived by it, the market thus being subjected to artificial controls and not being allowed to reflect genuine demand and supply forces.

Those in charge of security exchanges before 1934 were severely criticized for not publishing more adequate data of interest to traders and for not requiring companies whose securities were listed on the exchanges to publish financial information helpful to investors. The need for regulation of security exchanges became more apparent after the program of control over new security issuance was adopted in 1933. By requiring full disclosure of information at the time a new security was issued, the government could do much to help investors make sound security selections and to eliminate financial practices which might delude them. But for securities already issued and those outside the classification of a new issue, the program provided no means of continuing and extending the principle of full disclosure. The Securities Exchange Act of 1934 did much to fill this gap.

SECURITIES EXCHANGE ACT OF 1934: GENERAL OBJECTIVES

The Securities Exchange Act of 1934 brought under federal control the large security exchanges of the nation and placed most of the regulatory authority in the care of the Securities and Exchange Commission, with jurisdiction over a few matters in the Board of Governors of the Federal Reserve System. There are three principal objectives of the law: (1) to prevent the excessive use of the nation's credit facilities to finance speculation, with its disturbing effects upon security prices and the entire economic system; (2) to provide for regulation of those unfair practices in security trading which interfere with the orderly establishment of

[4] Pools are usually formed by a group of speculators banding together for the purpose of buying or selling large blocks of securities. The resources of the group are usually placed at the disposal of a manager. If the purpose of the pool is to drive the price of securities up, its members mass their buying, create an active market which encourages others to buy, and when the price is high enough liquidate their securities. In order not to cause the market price to fall, pool managers are generally forced to sell cautiously and to make purchases during the process of liquidation in order to support the market.

security prices; (3) to make available to the average investor accurate and adequate information about the financial affairs of the companies whose securities he may buy or sell.

The legal basis upon which this law rests, as in the case of the Securities Act of 1933, is the power of the federal government over interstate commerce and the mails. Both laws stress adequate disclosure of relevant information; both require registration statements; both ban fraudulent and deceptive practices and provide penalties for violation. However, the 1934 law goes much further and provides for a greater measure of federal control than the 1933 act. Moreover, the exchanges are not deprived of their incentive for self-government; in fact, the 1934 law virtually insists on its continuance, subject to government supervision.

REGISTRATION OF NATIONAL EXCHANGES

The Securities Exchange Act makes it unlawful for any broker, dealer, or exchange, directly or indirectly, to make use of the instrumentalities of interstate commerce or the mails for the purpose of effecting security transactions through an exchange, or reporting such transactions, unless the exchange is registered with the Securities and Exchange Commission or exempted from registration by it. The Commission is empowered to grant exemptions to any exchange if it finds that the volume of transactions is so limited as to make registration impracticable, unnecessary, or inappropriate for the protection of the public interest.

If the Commission finds that the applicant exchange is so organized as to be able to comply with the law and its own rules and regulations and that the rules of the exchange will ensure fair dealing and protection to investors, it is empowered to register the applicant as a national security exchange. Under this power, by 1954, the Commission had registered fifteen national security exchanges and had granted exemption from registration to four.[5]

REGISTRATION OF SECURITIES

The law forbids exchange members, brokers, and dealers to make any transaction in any security, other than an exempted one, on a national security exchange unless the security has been properly registered with the Securities and Exchange Commission. The law applies to all securities bought and sold by exchange members. Although the requirements for

[5] The registered exchanges are the Stock Exchanges of Boston, Cincinnati, Detroit, Los Angeles, New Orleans, New York, Philadelphia-Baltimore, Pittsburgh, Salt Lake City, San Francisco, Spokane; the Chicago Board of Trade, Midwest Stock Exchange, American Stock Exchange, and San Francisco Mining Exchange. The following are exempt: the Stock Exchanges of Colorado Springs, Honolulu, Richmond, and Wheeling. SEC, *20th Annual Report, 1954* (1955), p. 22.

unlisted[6] securities traded by exchange members are for all intents and purposes the same as those for listed securities, there is some leeway in the requirements for the former through a measure of discretion granted to the Commission.

Exempt securities. Certain securities are exempt from the registration requirements of the law. These exemptions are similar to those of the Securities Act of 1933 applying to new issues but are somewhat more limited. Insurance policies, receivers' certificates, and securities of building and loan associations are not exempt, probably because they are seldom traded on the exchanges. Securities authorized by a court in reorganization or by the Interstate Commerce Commission are also not exempt. This difference is probably due to the belief that, although registration may not be needed for these securities at the time of their issuance, that the continued publicity of corporate affairs after issuance may make registration on the exchanges desirable.

Registration requirements. The requirements for registering securities for trading on stock exchanges are somewhat similar to those for registering new issues. They undertake to force disclosure of information of interest to investors.[7] The registration provisions of the Securities Exchange Act have resulted in widespread publicity for most of the important business securities.

Periodic reports. Issuers of securities registered for trading on national stock exchanges are required to file periodic and other reports with the Commission. These reports are intended to keep the information in the registration statements reasonably current. The Commission is given full authority to prescribe forms for these reports and the methods to be followed in preparing them.

Under its authority to pass upon the adequacy of information for registration or periodic reports, it may go beneath the reports themselves and require that information be stated in such manner as seems to it to be in the public interest. The exercise of this power tends to bring about uniformity in accounting practices, and exerts a strong deterrent influence upon those business practices which are deceptive and unsound.

Liability of registrants. The Securities Exchange Act provides for civil liability of persons responsible for false or misleading statements, but it is not quite so strict or so specific in the matter of liability as is the Secu-

[6] A "listed" security is simply one which may be traded on the floor of an exchange. Listing involves furnishing the exchange with certain information regarding the issue and promising to keep this information up to date, making reports to stockholders, and other matters designed to keep the investing public informed as to the issue. An "unlisted" security is one which is traded by members of the exchange but which has not met its listing requirements. For some years the New York Stock Exchange has not permitted trading in unlisted securities.

[7] See pp. 453–458.

rities Act of 1933. Any person may sue for these damages if he, not knowing the statement to be false or misleading, relies on the statement and purchases or sells a security whose price is affected by it. However, he must prove that he relied upon the misleading or fraudulent statement and that it affected the price of the security so as to cause him loss. Under the Securities Act, it will be recalled, the injured party need not prove that he acquired the security relying upon the false or misleading statement until after an earnings statement, covering a period of twelve months following issuance, has been made public.

REGULATION OF EXCHANGE PRACTICES

An important part of the Securities Exchange Act of 1934, and of the regulations made under it by the Securities and Exchange Commission, refers to the practices involved in exchange transactions. Regulation of exchange practices may be summarized under controls over margin trading, short-selling manipulation, trading by "insiders," and special offerings and secondary distribution.

Margin trading. Brokers are forbidden by the law to extend credit to a customer without collateral. In making loans to customers for trading on a margin, the brokers are subject to regulation under rules established by the Board of Governors of the Federal Reserve System. The law gives the Board power to fix margin requirements from time to time, and it has raised or lowered the percentage of margin required as it feels that speculative activity should be increased or decreased.

Short selling. Many persons have strongly advocated the abolition of short sales. In the 1934 act, however, Congress wisely refrained from prohibiting them and instead placed supervision of them in the hands of the Securities and Exchange Commission with instructions to eliminate abuses. Pursuant to these powers, brokers have been required to obtain the permission of an owning customer before borrowing a customer's stock for use in making a short sale. To restrain short selling on a falling market, the Commission for several years permitted it only at a price *above* the last sale price. In 1939, at the suggestion of the New York Stock Exchange, this rule was amended to permit short sales at the price of the preceding sale, provided that the last sale price was itself higher than the last different price which preceded it. Under this rule, short sales may only be made on a fairly stable or rising market and short sellers are not permitted to "raid" a rapidly falling market. This meets most of the criticism of short sales and still preserves them as a safety valve for too rapid price rises in buyers' markets.

Manipulation and deception. Placing orders to buy and to sell at the same time for the purpose of creating a false appearance of market activity is made unlawful. Also unlawful are (1) effecting a series of such transactions alone or in concert with others to raise or lower prices artificially, (2) circulating rumors that security prices are likely to rise or to fall because of the market activity of certain persons, and (3) making false or misleading statements of material fact by purchasers or sellers to induce a sale or purchase.

Any attempt to stabilize the price of a security by a series of purchase or sale transactions must be in accordance with the rules and regulations of the Commission. This provision recognizes that in certain circumstances, especially when a block of new securities is being sold by underwriters and dealers, price-stabilization activities may be necessary. The Commission allows them to be undertaken by an underwriting group for a limited time and with provision for publicity of the pegging operations. The acquisition and making of options are also subject to Commission supervision to safeguard against their abuse.[8] Performance of the business of arbitrage is likewise subject to its rules.[9] Just to make sure that no device which ingenious traders may find advantageous to use in the future is overlooked, the Commission is given power to regulate any manipulative or deceptive device or contrivance when necessary or appropriate in the public interest or for the protection of investors.

The penalties for willfully violating any portions of the law respecting manipulation are fairly severe. Besides the danger of criminal prosecution for disobeying any rules and regulations of the Commission, guilty persons may be sued for damages by persons injured by the manipulation. Such actions must be brought by persons who purchased or sold a security whose price was affected by the manipulation, and they must be brought within one year after the discovery of the violation and within three years after the violation. Any person found guilty of manipulation may be sued by a multitude of speculators who were affected by the manipulated price. Strangely enough, however, the prohibitions against manipulation do not apply to any exempted security, and such activities in government issues, while unlikely by private parties, would be outside the scope of the law. This exemption may have been granted, partly at least, to protect the Federal Reserve banks in their purchases and sales of government bonds to control the prices of these securities.

Trading by "insiders." For the purpose of preventing the unfair use of corporate information by insiders of a corporation, special regulations are provided for trading in its stock by officers, directors, and persons owning directly or indirectly more than 10 per cent of any class of the company's stock. These insiders must file information monthly with the

[8] Options are devices whereby a person, for a consideration, agrees to deliver or buy securities in the future at a price fixed in the agreement.

[9] Arbitrage is the practice of buying a security on one exchange and selling it on another.

securities exchange and with the Commission showing their ownership interest in the company and any changes which have occurred during the month.

Any profit realized by such insider in buying and selling a security, or selling and later buying it, within a period of six months becomes recoverable by the company. If the transaction is made within the six-month period, it is assumed that it was made because of the advantage obtained from the knowledge of advance or confidential information, irrespective of the real reason for it. The only exception is the circumstance where the security is acquired through a previously contracted debt. Suit to recover may be brought by any stockholder or by the company, but it must be brought within two years after the date that the profit was realized.

Special offerings and secondary distributions. As long as securities are traded in relatively small amounts, the effect of each individual transaction on the current market price is small. But there are times when a holder of a relatively large block of securities may desire to dispose of the holding in a relatively short time at a price consistent with the current market price. For example, an estate may be required to dispose of a large block of securities for the purpose of meeting tax payments.

Recognizing this problem, in 1942 the Securities and Exchange Commission issued Rule X-10B-2, providing for what are known as "special offerings." A security may be the subject of a special offering when it has been determined that the auction market on the floor of the exchange cannot absorb a particular block of that security within a reasonable period of time without undue disturbance to the current price of the security. Provided a special offering is made according to a plan which has been filed with and approved by the Commission, it may be made at a fixed price consistent with the existing auction market price of the security, and brokers are paid a special commission by the seller which ordinarily exceeds the regular brokerage commission. Buyers of the security are not charged any commission on their purchases.

The same rule permits distribution of comparatively large blocks of previously issued and outstanding securities in over-the-counter trading. The term "secondary distribution" is used to apply to such over-the-counter trading of securities, which may be listed or unlisted. Secondary distribution is resorted to when it has been determined that it would not be in the interest of the parties involved to sell their shares on an exchange in the regular way or by special offering. Secondary distributions are generally made after the close of exchange trading.

REGULATION OF EXCHANGE MEMBERS

The Securities Exchange Act requires dealers and brokers who transact business in securities not registered on a regulated exchange to register with the Securities and Exchange Commission. Brokers or dealers doing business only through a registered exchange are not required to register, but they are effectively controlled through their membership in the exchange, the control of the exchange over membership, and the supervision of the Commission over the rules of the exchange.

Obviously, all the regulations of the law applicable to manipulation or deception include members of exchanges within their scope. Most of the special regulation of members is left to the exchange, but a few definite restraints are placed in the law. Since a broker acts as an agent of the customer in executing a sale or a purchase, and a dealer is naturally interested in selling securities which he carries, members of exchanges (and others who transact business through them) who are both brokers and dealers may not extend credit to a customer to purchase a security in the distribution of which the dealer participated until a period of six months beyond the offering date has passed. Brokers who are dealers as well must also disclose to customers in writing the capacity in which they are acting when they sell them securities which they offer as dealers. This restriction seems to be wise in safeguarding the customer against being influenced, or being charged unduly, for a security which the combined broker-dealer is selling.

The Commission also has power to regulate and prescribe functions of members of security exchanges, to regulate floor trading, and to prevent excessive speculation by members. It may prescribe such rules as are found necessary for increasing the solvency of dealers and brokers, rules regarding the commingling and pledging for loans of customers' securities held by the member, and regulations governing the keeping of books and records by brokers and dealers.

The Commission has relied to a great extent upon the self-regulation of exchanges in controlling member activities. It has often informally suggested changes to be made in the regulations of exchanges and has accepted suggested changes made by them. The practice of regulating member conduct by cooperation of the exchanges and the Commission is especially commendable in this field of business. Security exchanges customarily have complete control over membership, and rules may be enforced without resort to legal process or other complicated procedures. Moreover, the regulation of security trading is a highly intricate task. Wise and competent government control does well to rely upon the knowledge and experience of those in the exchange business.

SECURITY-EXCHANGE REGULATION: CONCLUSIONS

The Securities Exchange Act fulfills its objectives reasonably well. Thousands of companies are making available to the investing public important information that was published by only a few prior to 1933. The

Securities Exchange Act has ensured that these data will be kept current and that pertinent financial information can become the basis for sound comparisons and conclusions which were not possible a few years ago. Recognizing the great strides made by such private organizations as the New York Stock Exchange to make security trading honest and not detrimental to the best public interests, the Securities Exchange Act consolidates and advances these gains by extending the controls and making them more uniform over the country.

The security-exchange regulations, as well as control over security issues, have not escaped criticism. Some criticisms are justified. Thousands of security issues are not covered under either set of laws, but the laws may lead the investing group to assume a completeness of regulation that does not exist. Moreover, the law cannot guarantee that the purchase of a listed security on a registered national security exchange will always be a wise investment. The authors doubt that it would be either desirable or possible for a law to attempt such guarantees, but the advent of such strict regulation as is now imposed may mislead investors into believing that they exist.

The law has been criticized on the ground that it does not make speculative excesses impossible. While controls over credit and margin requirements place restrictions on such excesses, this does not mean that dangerous speculation cannot occur. For one thing, the law still allows use of credit in the purchase of securities, and one cannot be sure that the Board of Governors of the Federal Reserve System will be willing or able to stop the impetus of a rising market. Furthermore, if people want to speculate wildly or to gamble, neither the law nor the sincere attempts of exchanges to abide by it can prevent them from doing so.

Regulation of the Over-the-counter Security Market

As was pointed out in the previous section, a large number of security issues are traded outside the organized exchanges. The importance of this trading can be seen in the fact that there were only 3,500 issues listed in the organized exchanges in 1952, whereas the National Quotation Bureau [10] daily lists approximately 7,000 different securities and semiannually approximately 30,000. This trading, referred to as the "over-the-counter market," is carried on by some 4,481 registered brokers and dealers who buy or sell unlisted securities either for their own account or for customers.[11] As dealers, these individuals may purchase securities and hold them for possible resale at higher prices. As brokers, they keep in constant

[10] A private organization which reports bids and offers in over-the-counter trading filed with the Bureau. These quotations are available to brokers and dealers for a fee.

[11] SEC, *Annual Report, 1952*, p. 61.

communication with each other, and when an order to sell or buy comes from a customer, the possible market price to be expected is obtained by telephoning other brokers or dealers who are believed to have a market in the security. Some large over-the-counter houses maintain a file of thousands of issues with data as to the persons owning or desiring to buy them, and their probable sales or purchase price.

The very individualistic nature of the over-the-counter market makes abuses possible and causes regulation to be difficult. Customers should know whether a trader is acting as a dealer or as a broker in certain transactions, so that they can weigh the fairness of the price offered and the expense involved in making the deal. Because of his position of trust in security trading, the over-the-counter dealer should be a person of integrity and financial soundness. The fact that over-the-counter traders deal in many relatively unknown securities has in some instances led them, with or without intention, to foist highly speculative or fraudulent securities on an unsuspecting investing public. Moreover, since the companies whose securities they handle are often obscure and do not publicize their affairs for the investor, the public interest in a well-informed class of investors necessitates that some scheme for requiring full disclosure be worked out. With the market for such securities so unorganized, this is extremely difficult.

If the over-the-counter market were left unregulated, a means of evading regulation of securities and trading on the organized exchange would be furnished. Since regulation of this market appeared to be so complicated and expensive, the Securities Exchange Act of 1934 made no effort to prescribe rules for its regulation. Instead, the law gave the Securities and Exchange Commission broad authority to regulate in the public interest and to investigate and report upon further possible legislation. This the Commission has done, with the result that the Act was amended in 1936 and 1938 to provide for more definite regulation. The problem has been approached through requiring registration of over-the-counter traders and by providing for supervised self-regulation under an organization of these traders.

REGISTRATION OF BROKERS AND DEALERS

All security brokers and dealers not members of a national security exchange must register with the Securities and Exchange Commission if they use the mails or instrumentalities of interstate commerce, unless their business is exclusively intrastate or entirely in securities exempt from exchange regulation. In applying for registration, traders must file information about themselves, their business, and the securities in which they deal. The Commission is empowered to require these brokers and dealers to keep such information current and is thus placed in a position where it can obtain needed information about securities not traded on organized exchanges. This broad power is supplemented by the legal provision that issuers of new securities aggregating more than $2 million and registered under the Securities Act of 1933 must file supplementary information and make periodic reports such as those made by issuers with securities registered on national security exchanges.

Most of the regulation of registered brokers and dealers is left to the code provisions of a national organization. A few specific regulations are provided in the law. Brokers and dealers are forbidden to use the mails or instrumentalities of interstate commerce to effect or induce any purchase or sale of securities by means of any manipulative, deceptive, or fraudulent device or contrivance. Other rules have been set up by the Commission. These include the definition of manipulative and deceptive devices similar to those forbidden to members of exchanges and the requirement that dealer-brokers must disclose to customers whether they are acting as dealers or as brokers in any given transaction.

The registration of any broker or dealer may be denied or revoked by the Commission whenever it finds that such action would be in the public interest and that the applicant or registrant is guilty of certain objectionable practices. Such practices include infractions of the rules for fair and equitable trading which the Commission or the association has provided.

The history of the regulation of over-the-counter trading illustrates that the most important law to an administrative agency may consist of common-law precedents established long before the statutes being administered were enacted. The attempts by Congress and the Securities and Exchange Commission to solve the over-the-counter problem were not effectual until the principles of common law were employed to supplement statutes and administrative rules. The construction and enforcement of these laws and regulations required application of the common law of torts regarding what constitutes fraud to warrant recission, the law of equity on what constitutes fraud or misrepresentation in equity, and the law of agency on what constitutes the agency relationship and abuse of its fiduciary obligations of such character as to amount to fraud.

The standards now invoked by the Commission make it clear that a security firm can no longer claim to have acted in a capacity free from fiduciary obligation except in very narrow circumstances. Firms engaging in over-the-counter transactions must therefore undertake compliance with the fiduciary obligations to which they have always been subject by fundamental, even elementary, principles of the law of agency.[12]

[12] W. T. Lesh, "Federal Regulation of Over-the-counter Brokers and Dealers in Securities," 59 *Harvard Law Review* 1237–1275 (October, 1946).

SELF-REGULATION THROUGH ASSOCIATIONS

Most of the detailed regulation of over-the-counter brokers and dealers is left to self-regulation under Commission supervision. The Maloney amendment to the Securities Exchange Act passed in 1938 provides for a system of regulation through formation of one or more voluntary associations of investment bankers, brokers, and dealers doing business in the over-the-counter markets. As a result, the National Association of Securities Dealers, Incorporated, filed application to become a national security association in 1939, and it is the only such association organized to date. The Commission granted the application, finding that the Association was national in scope and that it had formulated rules of fair practice for the protection of the public interest and the investors. In 1952, its membership was 2,950. In addition, there were 33,053 registered representatives employed by or associated with the member firms in capacities which involved their doing business directly with the public.[13]

The National Association of Securities Dealers has adopted rules for its members and has provided for the financing of the expense of self-regulation through a schedule of dues. It is thus somewhat similar to the organized exchanges in its controls over members. The rules which have been adopted aim to prevent fraudulent and manipulative acts and practices, to promote just and equitable principles of trade, and to provide safeguards against unreasonable profits and charges. They have been approved by the Securities and Exchange Commission, and the Commission has undertaken a series of informal conferences with the Association to study the need for further rules and regulation. Penalties for violation of the rules of fair practice include suspension, expulsion, fines, and censure. Although membership in the Association is voluntary, nonmembers may be barred from obtaining brokers' discounts.

Regulation of Commodity Exchanges

In many respects the characteristics of trading on the organized commodity exchanges are similar to the transaction of business on the security exchanges. As a result, much of the regulation of the two types of exchange corresponds. However, trading on commodity exchanges is accompanied by widespread use of the futures contract. Commodities may be bought or sold for immediate or future delivery. If the deal calls for future delivery, a futures contract is made and there is said to be trading in "futures." For example, a person may purchase wheat through a broker in February at a price fixed in that month but for delivery on a

[13] SEC, *Annual Report, 1952*, p. 66.

specified date in May. Trading in futures is primarily speculative in nature in that purchases or sales are made not for immediate use or disposal but for the purpose of gaining through future changes in commodity prices. Even contracts for future delivery are in fact seldom delivered, but speculative accounts are closed out by offsetting purchases and sales. Because not every agricultural product is capable of accurate grading, durable, and produced in large enough quantities to engage wide public interest, only relatively few of these commodities are systematically traded for future delivery on the organized security exchanges. However, those so traded include the leading agricultural produce of the country, such as wheat, barley, corn, oats, rye, rice, cotton, flaxseed, wool, butter, eggs, and potatoes.

The public interest in organized commodity exchanges arises from the number of important commodities traded on them and the fact that the prices established there are used as the basis of pricing these products throughout the nation. The interest of farmers in the fair determination of commodity prices is obvious but others have a vital business interest in such prices. The merchant buying or selling these commodities and the businessman furnishing storage service have a direct interest. Not only is the manufacturer or processor affected by the price he pays for raw materials, but his business stability is affected because he often finds it economical to deal in futures.

Dealing in futures is of economic significance to these producers and to society in general because of the device referred to as a "hedge." Prices of finished goods tend to reflect those of raw materials. If a processor buys raw materials in November and cannot effect sale of finished goods until the following May, his ordinary business profit may be wiped out if raw-material prices are substantially less in May. To eliminate this risk and to safeguard his manufacturing profit, the processor would sell for delivery in May a quantity of his raw material equal to his purchase for immediate delivery in November. If the price fell by delivery time in May, he would make a profit by purchasing the commodity at that time. This profit would tend to counterbalance the loss he would probably incur on the sale of his finished goods. If the price rose, he would lose on his short sale, but make a profit from the selling of the finished goods. In either case, he would protect his manufacturing profit. Obviously, unless short sales or dealing in futures existed the processor would have to assume the risk of price changes in the basic raw material.

Trading in commodities has been highly speculative and has attracted many individuals who like to pit their judgment or luck against gains or losses to be made from future prices. The result has been that speculative transactions on the commodity exchanges have been voluminous. It has not been unusual for them to be far greater in a year, before a crop has ever reached the market, than the entire year's output; for example, market transactions in wheat in a year may be fifteen or twenty times the year's crop. The chances of gains from commodity speculation have arisen out of the violent fluctuations which occur in commodity prices, and these very fluctuations have often been magnified by speculative activity. Occasionally speculators have been able to band together and systematically drive prices of commodities up or down to suit their plan for profit.

As a result of the extensive speculation and the violent changes in commodity prices, the public has long believed in the regulation of commodity exchanges. When agriculture suffered depression after World War I and prices never thereafter even approximately satisfied the mass of farmers, the commodity exchanges were one of the institutions for which regulation was insisted upon. Irrespective of the motives which crystallized the insistence of the public for regulation, however, the control of commodity exchanges is definitely in the public interest, since the free and fair fixing of prices of such importance can hardly be entrusted to unregulated private business.

EVOLUTION OF COMMODITY-EXCHANGE REGULATION

Government control of trading on commodity exchanges was inaugurated with the passage of the Future Trading Act in 1921. This act placed a tax of 20 cents a bushel on all contracts for sale of grain for future delivery but exempted all transactions upon a "contract market." Any grain exchange could receive the designation of contract market if it registered with the Secretary of Agriculture and submitted to certain regulations of its business. This law was declared unconstitutional by the United States Supreme Court in 1922, on the grounds that it was not a valid use of the taxing power and that it did not limit itself to trading in interstate commerce.[14]

Congress immediately set to meeting the objections of the Supreme Court and passed the Grain Futures Act in 1922. Under this law, regulation of trading in grain futures was established as a means of removing obstructions and burdens upon interstate commerce. As in the Future Trading Act of 1921, the Secretary of Agriculture was empowered to limit to contract markets trading in grain futures which affected or were in interstate commerce. The designation of contract market was given only to those exchanges trading in grain futures in interstate commerce which would agree to provide information as to market transactions and to prevent unfair and deceptive market practices. The Secretary was authorized to define the grains to which the regulation of future trading might apply. The constitutionality of the Grain Futures Act was upheld

[14] *Hill v. Wallace,* 259 U.S. 44 (1922).

by the United States Supreme Court in 1923 as a proper regulation of interstate commerce.[15]

Although passed as an amendment to the Grain Futures Act, the Commodity Exchange Act of 1936 is practically a new law governing trading on commodity exchanges. The scope of the regulation was extended to cover trading in a large list of commodities, including cotton, rice, corn, oats, barley, rye, flaxseed, grain sorghums, mill feeds, butter, eggs, and Irish potatoes. Wool tops were added to this list in 1938, and fats and oils, cottonseed, cottonseed meal, peanuts, soybeans, and soybean meal were added in 1940. The 1936 act placed regulation of the commodity exchanges in the care of the Commodity Exchange Administration (now the Commodity Exchange Authority), a semi-independent agency under the supervision of the Department of Agriculture. The requirements of the Grain Futures Act as to contract markets were kept in the law, along with its other provisions, but the character and application of commodity-exchange regulation were extended.

CONTRACT MARKETS

In order to obtain the contract-market designation, a commodity exchange must register with the Commodity Exchange Authority, furnishing copies of its bylaws and regulations, agreeing to keep its records in a form prescribed by the Authority, and agreeing to cooperate with it in the enforcement of the laws regarding manipulation and misrepresentation. The exchange must also agree to admit farmers' cooperative marketing associations as members, if any such association meets the qualifications imposed upon other members of the exchange.

Up to 1955, seventeen commodity markets had registered and been designated as contract makers.[16] These include all the leading commodity exchanges of the country in which future trading in agricultural produce is carried on. Some exchanges are permitted to do such trading in four or five commodities covered by the act, while others are limited to one commodity. Thus, the Chicago Board of Trade may deal in futures on wheat, corn, oats, rye, and cotton, while the Seattle Grain Exchange may handle such transactions only in wheat.

REGISTRATION OF COMMISSION MERCHANTS AND FLOOR BROKERS

The law requires that all commission merchants dealing in futures and all floor brokers on the contract markets register annually with the Commodities Exchange Authority. These exchange members must make periodic reports to the Authority on such matters as the volume of business they do, the volume and character of future trading, and the quan-

[15] *Board of Trade v. Olsen,* 262 U.S. 1 (1923).

[16] Commodity Exchange Authority, *Annual Report, 1955.*

tities and grades of commodities delivered on future contracts. In 1955 the Authority reported the registration of over 1,500 merchants and floor brokers.[17]

REGULATION OF COMMODITIES TRADING

Besides the extensive information of the nature and volume of commodities trading required of exchanges and their members, the dealings on commodity exchanges are subject to close governmental regulation. These regulations may be classed as those designed to prevent manipulation of prices, to prevent excessive speculation, and to protect customers from unethical practices of commission merchants and floor traders.

The regulation of manipulative practices is similar to that provided for the security exchanges. Fraudulent devices are prohibited, as is the dissemination of false or misleading information. Manipulation of the market by causing false activity from such fictitious transactions as wash sales is prohibited.[18] Manipulating prices by getting a corner on a commodities market is also outlawed.[19]

Control over excessive speculation is provided for in the power of the Commodities Exchange Authority to fix limits to the amount of trading in futures that can be done by one person. These restrictions apply only to purely speculative transactions, although separate and different trading limits may be fixed for spread and straddle transactions. Hedges are specifically exempted. The restrictions have been defended as eliminating unusually large operations which might tend to force the price of grains above or below proper levels, with injury to farmers and customers.

Closely allied to the government's regulation of excessive speculation is that undertaken by the exchange organizations themselves. Several exchanges have undertaken to rule against excessive speculation. Regulations have been made, for example, to protect traders caught in a "squeeze" in making good on delivery under futures contracts, by extending the allowable time during which such contracts may be met. Perhaps the most striking instance of exchange regulation for reducing excessive speculation has been the fixing of limits allowable for daily price fluctuations. The prescription of limits means that, in a falling or rising market for wheat futures, traders may not drive the price up or down by taking advantage of the momentum gained.

The price-limitations regulations of the Chicago Board of Trade and

[17] *Ibid.*

[18] Wash sales are transactions involving the purchase and sales of a commodity at the same time by the same party.

[19] A corner occurs when one party or a cooperating group obtains a quantity of a good large enough so that those desiring to buy must purchase from that party or group.

other exchanges, and other rules adopted by exchanges looking to reducing speculation, represent cases of business self-regulation. However, it is well known that many such rules are instituted at the request of the government regulating agency, as well as by the mere pressure of public opinion. Such a drastic rule as the price-limitation regulation may almost surely be traced to governmental influence. As such, it might be regarded as a kind of regulation by government itself.

Members of the commodity exchanges are forbidden to enter into a transaction at any other price than the true one existing on the exchange at the time of the transaction, thereby protecting customers against traders charging or giving a price not in accordance with the market. Commission merchants often handle money that has been deposited by customers for the fulfillment of a contingent obligation arising under a futures trade. The law requires that the commission merchant must separate such deposited funds from his own assets and that he may not use the funds of one customer for temporary loans to another customer. Defrauding customers in any way is forbidden, as is the willful making of false reports of transactions to the customer, to the exchange, or to the Commodities Exchange Authority.

In the enforcement of the regulations applying to the members of the exchanges, particularly that respecting the segregation of and caring for customer deposits, the Authority must make a comprehensive audit of the members' books. In order for these audits to be as effective as one might wish, they should be made frequently. In 1953, 605 audits were conducted, showing generally a good record of compliance.[20]

ENFORCEMENT OF THE LAW

The Commodities Exchange Authority is given adequate authority to enforce the law governing commodity exchanges. Their registration, or that of their individual members, may be revoked or suspended. For most violations of the law or any rules made under it, the Authority may issue a cease-and-desist order against the offending person. If compliance is not forthcoming, it may go before a federal court and have the offender fined as much as $10,000 or imprisoned for one year, or both. Furthermore, it should be remembered that commodity exchanges, like security exchanges, are generally voluntary associations with rules and regulations and with adequate powers to punish members for misconduct. There is also fairly reasonable assurance that their rules will be complete enough for most purposes and that they will enforce these rules as best they can, because the right to grant or withhold designations as contract markets gives the government a strong basis for supervising the elements of self-regulation in exchange administration.

[20] Commodity Exchange Authority, *Annual Report, 1953,* p. 17.

REGULATION OF COMMODITIES EXCHANGES: CONCLUSIONS

The objectives and many of the means of regulating commodity exchanges parallel those found in the case of security exchanges. The principal gain of such regulation to the public is a free and accurate determination of commodity prices. No one can deny the benefit to producers and consumers alike of having the exchange mechanism free from manipulation or excessive speculation which makes prices inaccurate and unstable. If the market becomes a playground for speculators to match their wits against each other and against the future for their own chance of gain, the public interest in free price determination is subordinated to the selfish interests of a small group.

On the other hand, there is danger that restrictions on the markets may become so great as to make the price determined in them an inaccurate reflection of supply and demand forces. Nevertheless, most of the regulations are clearly justified as being necessary for the public interest, even if it can be shown that they may introduce some inflexibilities into the price-fixing process. Furthermore, the question of accurate competitive price determination in a free market is broader than the mere matter of control of commodity exchanges. Some aspects of the general regulation of production and marketing of farm products have a far greater and more disturbing effect upon the determination of price.

Selected References

Atkins, Willard E., George W. Edwards, and Harold G. Moulton, *The Regulation of the Security Markets*. Washington, D.C.: Brookings Institution, 1946.

Baer, J. H., and O. G. Saxon, *Commodity Exchange and Futures Trading*. New York: Harper & Brothers, 1949.

Commodity Exchange, Inc., *Trading on the Commodity Exchange in New York*. New York: The Exchange, 1947.

Cook, Franklin H., *Principles of Business and the Federal Law*, chap. 22. New York: The Macmillan Company, 1951.

Dice, C. A., and W. J. Eiteman, *The Stock Market*, 3d ed. New York: McGraw-Hill Book Company, Inc., 1952.

Husband, William H., and James C. Dockeray, *Modern Corporation Finance*, chap. 21. Homewood, Ill.: Richard D. Irwin, Inc., 1952.

Lesh, W. T., "Federal Regulation of Over-the-counter Brokers and Dealers in Securities," 59 *Harvard Law Review* 1237–1275 (October, 1946).

Loeser, John C., *The Over-the-counter Securities Market*. New York: National Quotation Bureau, Inc., 1940.

Prochnow, Herbert V. (ed.), *American Financial Institutions*, chaps. 10–12. New York: Prentice-Hall, Inc., 1951.

Securities and Exchange Commission, *Report on the Feasibility and Advisability of the Complete Segregation of the Functions of Dealer and Broker.* 1936.

———, *The Work of the Securities and Exchange Commission.* 1944.

Twentieth Century Fund, *The Security Markets.* New York: The Twentieth Century Fund, Inc., 1935.

PART SIX

LABOR

20

REGULATION OF TERMS OF EMPLOYMENT

Legislation for the protection of workers has been one of the earliest forms of government interference in business. Massachusetts and Connecticut enacted laws in 1842 limiting labor of children under twelve years to ten hours per day in manufacturing establishments. Pennsylvania led with prohibition of child labor in manufacturing plants by a law in 1848 forbidding such labor to children under twelve. A ten-hour day for women was prescribed by legislation in New Hampshire in 1847. But the real development of labor legislation belongs to the twentieth century.

The acceleration in labor laws in recent years has made the role of government in the relations of workers and management exceedingly important. Every businessman must reckon with government today in making a labor contract. He must take note of the hours for which he employs workers, the conditions under which they work, and the wages which they are paid. He must provide for their insurance against accidental injury, occupational disease, old age, and unemployment. And when he hires or discharges workers, or enters into a contract of any kind for the use of labor, he may have to take into account the rights which government guarantees to workers to organize and bargain collectively. These areas of labor regulation will be discussed in the next three chapters.

Public Interest in the Protection of Labor

As in the case of most government controls over economic enterprise, a strong public interest must exist in such regulation and the public must be aroused to the need for such interference. Without this broad public interest, limitations in so far-reaching an area as conditions of work would hardly have come, particularly in the face of the long-standing American traditions of freedom of property and contract.

PUBLIC INTEREST IN REGULATION OF HOURS

The earliest regulation of hours had to do with women and children. The most compelling basis of public interest is found in the health and moral aspects of the problem. It has been easy to convince the public that long hours worked by women and children are deleterious to their health. The effect of long hours and of night work upon moral tone has also been easily understood. As for men, the ill effects of long hours upon health and morals have not been so well established. However, in certain trades, such as mining, transportation, and a few other hazardous occupations, the limitation of hours has often been based upon safety, as well as health.

Public interest in shorter hours for men and women alike has been due to an increasing extent to considerations of good citizenship and economy. Long hours mean little time for leisure activities, for attention to home life, or for mental and physical betterment and are consequently looked upon as a threat to a stable and intelligent citizenry. They have also been of doubtful economic justification. Since human beings are subject to fatigue, there is a limit to efficient working periods. The lesson that long hours do not pay has been brought home to many industrialists, notably since World War I. Numerous investigations have indicated that reduction of hours to eight per day not only tends to increase hourly output but often increases daily output.[1]

PUBLIC INTEREST IN REGULATION OF WAGES

Although the effect of long hours on health and safety is clear, the close relationship is not so evident in regard to wages. As a result, laws requiring employers to pay a minimum wage have been slow to develop, the first such law being one applicable to women and passed by Massachusetts in 1912. But the motives which have prompted the public to demand minimum-wage laws have been similar to those which have resulted in other labor regulation more closely related to considerations of safety and health.

The evils of low wage payment are to be found in the need for a certain minimum of material means for subsistence on a level of health and decency. Low income may mean inability to have proper food, shelter, clothing, and medical attention. It may lead to immorality. It often means social instability, unhappiness, irritability, and the willingness to listen to and support any kind of social nostrum purporting to solve economic ills. The payment of wages below some accepted standard of social subsistence may well be fraught with such social evils that the community is justified in setting a minimum below which wages may not fall.

The fixing of minimum wages has sometimes rested upon other grounds.

[1] J. R. Commons and J. B. Andrews, *Principles of Labor Legislation* (New York: Harper & Brothers, 4th ed., 1936), pp. 87 ff. It might be noted that some studies of the increased efficiency due to shorter hours fail to take into account other factors, such as improved equipment, which may increase productivity.

The lower-paid groups are likely to be the more unskilled and ignorant workers whose lack of bargaining power allows them to be easily exploited by an unscrupulous employer.[2] This situation, it is said, leads to inefficiency in production and slackness in adopting improved methods of production. Moreover, the lack of bargaining power of certain workers and their low wages tend to depress wages in general and thereby to extend the evils of economic insufficiency.

PUBLIC INTEREST IN MINORITY GROUPS

The members of various minority groups have often suffered the effects of job discrimination. While prejudice and discrimination against minority groups did not begin in business, and businesses are naturally subject to the standards of their social environment, a major portion of the public has believed that the social and economic consequences of job discrimination are of such a magnitude as to justify public action.

Although some of the concern over discrimination has been politically inspired by a desire on the part of certain office seekers to obtain votes of these large groups, a substantial public interest lies in the economic and social costs induced by such discrimination. Where a well-qualified member of a minority group is deprived of the opportunity to use his abilities in the most productive channels, national productivity is reduced and the efficiency of the economic system impaired. Moreover, society must shoulder the costs of relief payments, crime, delinquency, and social maladjustment which often grows out of the inability of minority groups to obtain employment on terms equivalent to their abilities.[3] Incalculable are the losses that result from increased social tension, poor morale, and the psychological effects of prejudice. However, perhaps the most serious consequence is the corrupting influence of job discrimination on the democratic ideals of freedom and equality of opportunity.

Regulation of Child Labor

There has been little dispute that the limitation or outright prohibition of child labor is properly within the jurisdiction of states' police powers. For many years the matter was regarded as one exclusively for state control.

[2] From an economic point of view, it would seem that such an employer is not only unscrupulous, but foolish. If he can get labor at a price below its productivity, his most profitable course would seem to lie in hiring more of it until the marginal product of labor just equals its wage.

[3] It has been estimated that these costs amount to $30 billion annually. See Elmo Roper, "Discrimination in Industry: Extravagant Injustice," 5 *Industrial and Labor Relations Review* 590 (July, 1952).

STATE REGULATION OF CHILD LABOR

Following the lead of Massachusetts and Connecticut in 1842, other states passed child-labor laws, until by the time of the War between the States, seven states had legislation fixing hours of labor for children.[4] These laws represented little more than a gesture, however, since they were loosely drawn and were not well enforced. They often provided punishment only for "knowingly" violating the law, or allowed longer hours with the consent of parent or guardian, or merely required that children could not be "compelled" to work longer than the stated maximum.

More effective regulation of hours for children did not come until after 1900. Beginning with an Illinois law in 1903, all states by now have child-labor laws. Twenty-three states set sixteen years as the basic age minimum below which employment in manufacturing, mining, and mercantile establishments is prohibited. All but five states set eight hours as the maximum for children under sixteen. Most states forbid employment in dangerous occupations, and many have extended the protection to the age of eighteen. Nightwork is ordinarily forbidden. Other limitations applicable to children are found in laws providing for physical examination or completion of a minimum of education for the granting of an employment certificate.[5] Generally exempt from child-labor laws of states is employment outside school hours in agriculture, in the home, in street trades, and in canneries.

State regulation of child labor has not been subject to serious question on the score of constitutionality. The law regards minors somewhat as wards of the state, which has power to act in any way for their protection. Moreover, since a minor has no legal right to enter into a free contract, the due-process clause can hardly act as a deterrent to state regulation. Regulation of hours of child labor cannot be said to take away any rights to sell labor, because children have no such right in law.[6]

FEDERAL REGULATION OF CHILD LABOR

State laws regulating child labor varied widely in effectiveness and the standards fixed. States with relatively high standards have complained that they were at a competitive disadvantage as compared to those states with relatively low standards, and the states with low standards were, of course, not moved to raise theirs. Only a uniform federal law could raise

[4] Commons and Andrews, *op. cit.*, p. 95.

[5] Council of State Governments, *The Book of the States, 1954–1955* (Chicago, 1954), pp. 392–396.

[6] The leading case on these points is *People v. Ewer*, 36 N.E. 4 (1894).

the level of child-labor regulations in all states. Furthermore, there was a need for national action to place the United States on a par with other nations in the world and to meet international commitments.

Having no specific constitutional authorization to regulate employment, Congress relied on the commerce power to pass the Owen-Keating Act in 1916. This Act forbade the transportation in interstate commerce of the products of any mine in which children under sixteen had been employed, or the products of any factory employing children less than fourteen years old. The Supreme Court had previously upheld the use of the commerce power to prohibit the interstate transportation of lottery tickets, impure and adulterated foods, and white slaves,[7] but in the case of *Hammer v. Dagenhart* [8] the Court ruled that the child-labor law was unconstitutional. The Court reasoned that although the legislation purported to be a regulation of commerce, its actual intent was to regulate production, which was regarded as a matter reserved to the states and beyond the scope of federal authority.

Balked at its first effort, Congress enacted a second child-labor law based upon the tax power. In 1919, Congress levied a tax of 10 per cent on the profits of any mine or factory employing children contrary to the standards enunciated in the 1916 law. Again the Supreme Court declared the legislation invalid, arguing in the case of *Bailey v. Drexel Furniture Company* [9] that the law was not enacted to raise revenue but was designed to regulate a matter that was completely the business of the states. It is interesting that, in other cases in which the tax power has been used for regulatory purposes, the Court was content to accept the tax without looking below the surface to see its effects. Thus, the regulatory taxes on state bank notes, on shipping companies bringing in aliens, on colored oleomargarine, and on narcotics were all upheld.[10]

The Walsh-Healey Act of 1936 met part of the problem by prohibiting the employment of girls under eighteen and boys under sixteen on work being done on all government contracts subject to the Act. Not until 1938 was a general ban on child labor enacted by Congress in the Fair Labor Standards Act. In 1941, the entire Act was upheld without a dissenting vote, and *Hammer v. Dagenhart* was specifically overruled.[11]

The child-labor section of the Fair Labor Standards Act set the general

[7] *Champion v. Ames*, 188 U.S. 321 (1903); *Hipolite Egg Co. v. United States*, 220 U.S. 45 (1911); *Hoke v. United States*, 227 U.S. 308 (1913).

[8] 247 U.S. 251 (1918).

[9] 259 U.S. 20 (1922).

[10] *Veazie Bank v. Fenno*, 8 Wall. 533 (1869); *Head Money Cases*, 112 U.S. 580 (1884); *McCray v. United States*, 195 U.S. 27 (1904); *United States v. Doremus*, 249 U.S. 86 (1919).

[11] *United States v. Darby Lumber Co.*, 312 U.S. 100 (1941).

minimum age for employment in industry at sixteen years. Outside manufacturing and mining, and where such employment does not interfere with schooling, health, or welfare, the Children's Bureau in the Department of Health, Education, and Welfare may lower the age limit to fourteen. In any occupation found to be particularly hazardous or detrimental to the health or well-being of minors, it may raise the age limit as high as eighteen.

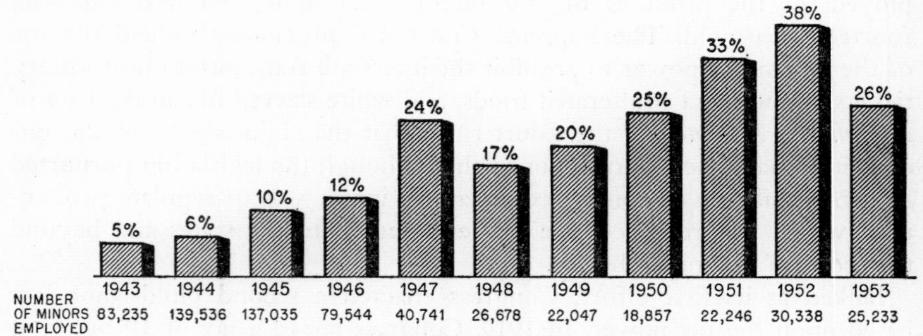

Figure 20—1. Child-labor Violations, 1943 to 1953

Source: Wage and Hour and Public Contracts Divisions, *Annual Reports.*

Child labor in retailing, personal service, street trades, motion pictures, and theaters is not covered by the law. Children employed in agriculture were also exempt until a 1949 amendment specified that agricultural labor for children is permissible only outside school hours. Moreover, except in manufacturing and mining, children working for their parents are excluded.

Fair-employment-practices Legislation

One of the most recent developments in labor legislation is the passage of laws designed to eliminate discriminatory employment practices by employers, employment agencies, and unions because of race, color, creed, or advancing age. During World War II the federal government made the first attempt to prevent discrimination in employment by establishing as a temporary agency in 1943 the Committee on Fair Employment Practices. Vigorously opposed in many quarters, the Committee, nevertheless, was fairly successful. A bitter fight developed after the war over giving the Committee permanent status, and it went out of existence.[12]

A few of the more progressive jurisdictions followed the pattern set by

[12] See Louis Kesselman, *The Social Politics of FEPC. A Study in Reform Pressure Movements* (Chapel Hill, N.C.: The University of North Carolina Press, 1948).

the Fair Employment Practices Committee. Between 1945 and 1953, eleven states and twenty-five municipalities adopted some form of fair-employment-practices legislation. New York and New Jersey led off in 1945, followed by Massachusetts in 1946 and Connecticut in 1947. In 1949, New Mexico, Oregon, Rhode Island, and Washington adopted similar laws as did Alaska and Kansas in 1953. Massachusetts amended its statute in 1953 to prohibit discrimination against persons because they are between forty-five and sixty-five years of age. These laws are similar in coverage, types of discrimination prohibited, and methods of administration. It is estimated that enforceable fair-employment-practices laws are in effect in areas that include one-third of the nation's total population and one-eighth of the nation's non-whites.[13]

In six states, boards or commissions administer the laws. The Oregon statute is administered by the commissioner of labor, and a special division in the Department of Education is the responsible agency in New Jersey. These agencies are authorized to attempt by education and conciliation to eliminate discriminatory practices. Where efforts fail they may, after public hearing, issue cease-and-desist orders which are enforceable in the courts. Indiana and Wisconsin have laws against discrimination providing for voluntary compliance. Colorado uses the educational and conciliatory approach to discrimination problems encountered in private industry; cease-and-desist orders may be issued only against public employers.

In addition to the fair-employment-practices laws of general application, several states have antidiscrimination laws designed to eliminate discrimination in specific fields. Nine states prohibit discriminatory practices where employment is undertaken in connection with public-works contracts. Four states have legislated against discrimination in work under defense and war contracts, and two have done so in the public-utility field. Four states prohibit discriminatory practices of unions which result in denial or restriction of employment opportunities. The right of a state to prohibit discrimination by labor unions against Negroes was upheld by the Supreme Court in 1946.[14]

A fairly small number of complaints alleging discrimination has been filed in recent years. However, a period of a tight labor market does not provide a true test. The temptation to discriminate is greater under adverse economic conditions. By far the greatest majority of complaints are settled without the need to resort to court action. A recent congressional report stated: "Many [employers] have . . . expressed their belief that

[13] Mary Bedell, "Employment and Income of Negro Workers–1940–52," 76 *Monthly Labor Review* 596–601 (June, 1953).

[14] *Railway Mail Association v. Corsi*, 326 U.S. 88 (1945).

such legislation has not prevented them from hiring the most competent employees available and has had positive beneficial effect."[15]

Regulation of Wages and Hours

STATE REGULATION OF HOURS

Regulation of hours of work by the states vary so much that all that will be attempted here is to indicate the general extent and nature of these laws and to discuss their administrative and constitutional aspects.

Hours limitation for women. Following the lead of New Hampshire in prescribing a ten-hour day for women in 1847, five states had similar legislation before the War between the States. But these laws were largely made ineffective by the clause that ten hours was the limit in the absence of a contract requiring greater time. Massachusetts passed an hours law for women in 1874 which, after amendment in 1879, became the first effective regulation in this direction.

By 1954, forty-three states and the District of Columbia had laws limiting the daily and weekly hours that women work in one or more industries.[16] One-half of these jurisdictions have set eight hours a day and/or forty-eight hours a week or less as the maximum time a woman may be employed in one or more industries. Nine states have set a maximum nine-hour day for women and a weekly maximum of fifty or fifty-four hours. Moreover, nine states have set a maximum of ten hours a day and fifty to sixty hours a week.

The above restrictions on hours do not mean that all trades are so covered or that the maxima mentioned are the same for all those trades which are covered. All the states having laws limit the hours in manufacturing establishments, and nearly all states with such laws make them apply to mercantile businesses.

Agricultural and domestic employments are usually exempt from application of hour maxima. Nurses are also customarily exempt, as are telephone operators and restaurant employees. Other exemptions are made in many states where the employment is not looked upon as dangerous or conducive to ill health.

Hours limitation for men. The majority of states have fixed an eight-

[15] U.S. Senate, Committee on Labor and Public Welfare, *State and Municipal Fair Employment Legislation*, Staff Report to the Subcommittee on Labor and Labor-Management Relations, 82d Cong., 2d Sess. (1953). See also Morroe Berger, *Equality by Statute: Legal Controls over Group Discrimination* (New York: Columbia University Press, 1952).

[16] Alabama, Florida, Indiana, Iowa, and West Virginia do not have such laws. Council of State Governments, *op. cit.*, pp. 398–399.

hour day for men employed in state work. A good many of these states have also provided for a forty-hour week for their employees. Nearly as many states have insisted that those persons furnishing the state with materials, supplies, or services under contract also abide by similar requirements for their employees. Purchases in the open market do not require that the goods so bought be produced under the stipulated hour condition. Two-thirds of the states also have maximum-hours laws for employees in city and intrastate transport. In those industries regarded as particularly hazardous or unhealthful, the limitation on hours tends to run far below those allowed in public transportation. States usually place a maximum of eight hours per day in mining and smelting businesses. Many states also limit hours in industries in which work under air pressure is required. Other scattered examples of special hours limitation may be found in stamp mills, concentrating mills, chlorinating processes, cyanide processes, cement works, rolling mills, rod mills, coke ovens, and blast furnaces, mines, and smelters.

There is a tendency to increase the scope of hours laws. For years, states have undertaken to regulate hours only where a definite danger to the public or to labor tended to result. Inclusion of all manufacturing businesses and retail establishments within hours-limitation legislation seems to denote a tendency toward restricting hours in business where the length of the working day does not present a particular hazard. These broader laws are consequently justified on the ground that too long hours for any worker may be deleterious to physical or mental health or may result in a citizenry with too little time for recreation and community upbuilding.

Constitutionality of state hours regulation. The power of the government to fix the hours of work of its own employees and employees of government contractors doing work for it has not been questioned since 1903. In that year, the United States Supreme Court held that the state has the power to control its affairs and make contracts for public work on whatever terms it pleases.[17] A private contractor doing work for the government, the Court declared, was subject to the conditions the state wished to impose.

The constitutionality of other hours regulation was not so easily settled. Some courts held hours regulation for women to be a valid exercise of the police power,[18] and others found that the regulation caused deprivation of property without due process of law.[19] In 1908, however, the Supreme Court found no difficulty in holding constitutional the ten-hour law for

[17] *Atkin v. Kansas*, 191 U.S. 207 (1903).

[18] Note especially *Commonwealth v. Hamilton Mfg. Co.*, 120 Mass. 383 (1876).

[19] See *Ritchie v. People*, 155 Ill. 98 (1895).

women in Oregon.[20] The Court, faced with able briefs showing the effect of long hours upon the health of women, agreed that the limitations placed on contractual powers of women were far outweighed by the public's interest in healthy motherhood. A few years later, the Supreme Court upheld a California law which limited the hours of work for women to eight each day.[21] The constitutionality of hours laws for women has consequently been long accepted.

Where hours of men are limited in the transportation industry the constitutionality is not open to doubt. If the laws are reasonable—and none in this field has been found to be so restrictive as to be unreasonable—the courts have taken the position that protection of the safety of employees, travelers, and property through such means is eminently within the police power of the states.[22] In the field of transportation, conflict between state and federal laws is most likely to occur; but the United States Supreme Court has made it clear that state laws must give way where federal laws exist.[23]

Regulation of hours of work in distinctly hazardous undertakings has also long been regarded as within the reasonable exercise of state police power. As early as 1898, the United States Supreme Court upheld an Oregon law which limited work to eight hours daily in underground mines, smelters, and ore-reduction works.[24] Admitting that the law interfered with freedom to contract, the Supreme Court nonetheless held that a state might limit the hours of workmen in employments reasonably adjudged by the legislature to be detrimental to health when pursued for too long a working day. The Court commented: "The law is, to a certain extent, a progressive science."

In spite of a decision against a New York eight-hour day for bakers in 1905,[25] the United States Supreme Court in 1917 upheld an Oregon law which established a ten-hour day for both men and women in any mill, factory, or manufacturing establishment.[26] The Court emphasized

[20] *Muller v. Oregon*, 208 U.S. 412 (1908). The briefs in this case were prepared by L. D. Brandeis (later of the Supreme Court) and Josephine Goldmark and were noteworthy for emphasizing the consequences of excessive hours rather than mere legal precedents.

[21] *Miller v. Wilson*, 236 U.S. 373 (1915). In allowing the eight-hour law to stand, the Court recognized that hours limitation could be pressed to "indefensible" extremes but agreed that eight hours was a reasonable limitation.

[22] See *Baltimore and Ohio R.R. Co. v. ICC*, 221 U.S. 612 (1911). Although this decision by the Supreme Court upheld the right of Congress to legislate hours limits of employees on interstate trains, it has furnished an adequate precedent for state regulation, since it involved an interpretation of due process.

[23] *Erie Rwy. Co. v. New York*, 233 U.S. 671 (1914).

[24] *Holden v. Hardy*, 169 U.S. 366 (1898).

[25] *Lochner v. New York*, 198 U.S. 45 (1905).

[26] *Bunting v. Oregon*, 243 U.S. 426 (1917).

that the record of the case did not include any facts to support the view that the law was not necessary to preserve health.

The question of reasonable regulation of hours has not been open to question since 1941. In that year the United States Supreme Court upheld the Federal Fair Labor Standards Act which provides for a forty-hour week.[27] While this case involved a federal statute, the interpretation made there would clearly apply to state controls under the police power.

Administration of state hours laws. Because of the size of the labor force and the large number of businesses employing workers, the possibilities for infractions of hours laws are great. Consequently, the problems of administration are tremendous.

One of the most generally used administrative methods is publicity. State laws usually require posting of notices as to hours and rely to a large extent upon complaints to aid in enforcement. Where workers are ignorant of the law, notices are not conspicuous, or workers are afraid to make complaints, this type of enforcement procedure often breaks down. Even when states make periodic inspections, infractions of hours laws are difficult to discover. To aid in this inspection, a few states require the use of record books of hours and place strong penalties against falsifying these records. This is perhaps one of the best means of enforcing hours limitation.

State hours regulation: conclusions. With all its advantages and contribution to progress, state hours regulation is not without faults. State laws still do not cover all employments in which hours limitation might be justified. To meet the deficiencies of legislative selection of occupations to which hours laws should apply, a few states have established commissions with power to determine for women the length of the working day and week and to select the occupations to which such limitation should be applicable. These states usually provide by law that women are not to be employed for periods dangerous to their safety, health, or welfare. A commission is authorized to investigate conditions in different industries and to establish such limitations as the facts indicate to be necessary for protection from the dangers of long hours.

The use of commissions to establish such standards seems to be a logical development in control of hours. In public-utility and railroad regulation, the legislature generally states only that rates shall be "reasonable," and the determination of reasonableness itself is left to a commission. The reason for making such provision is that the question of reasonableness is eminently one for commission determination after an analysis of all pertinent facts. This same reason should justify the use of a commission to establish labor standards. At least if the limitation of hours is to be based upon the protection of health, safety, and welfare, the differing con-

[27] *United States v. Darby Lumber Co.*, 312 U.S. 100 (1941).

ditions in various occupations would seem to make such a system advisable.

STATE REGULATION OF WAGES

The first state minimum-wage law was passed by Massachusetts in 1912, the only sanction being publication of the names of employers paying less than the recommended minima. Not until twenty-five years later could it be said that any state had an enforceable wage-regulation law. Until 1937 the Supreme Court failed to find that the state police power could justify legislation fixing minimum wages.

Nature of state wage laws. The states have enacted wage regulations in three general areas: government contracts, private industry, and methods of wage payment. While the regulation of methods of wage payment is not a restriction of the wage itself, it does amount to a limitation upon certain features of the wage contract. Nearly all the states control methods of wage payment, usually requiring the wages to be paid at least twice a month. A few require weekly payments, while some allow monthly intervals between payments.

Regulations regarding government contractors require that they pay a certain minimum, usually the "prevailing wage" in a locality. This provision has generally meant that they must pay the union scale where a union exists; if a community is not unionized, the contractors are sometimes given complete freedom from government influence in fixing wages.

As for wage regulation in private industry, by 1954 twenty-six states plus the District of Columbia, Puerto Rico, Hawaii, and Alaska had minimum-wage laws.[28] In all states these statutes apply to women and minors, but in only seven states do they apply to men as well. As will be seen presently, expansion of state legislation has become largely unnecessary in view of the wide application of the federal minimum-wage law.

Six states and Alaska and Puerto Rico establish specific minimum wages by statute, although in three of these, variations can be made by the wage boards. In the other states, the fixing is left to a commission, committee, or labor commissioner. The legislatures in the latter states have prescribed either a "cost-of-living" standard or one calling for a "fair wage." The cost-of-living standard, which is by far the most popular, requires that the minimum wage selected must be sufficient to meet the minimum cost of living necessary for health. The fair-wage standard is one which takes into account the work performed with the wage representing a fair and reasonable return for such work.

Administration of state wage laws. Administration of state minimum-wage laws is generally placed either under an industrial commission of three to six members or under the state commissioner of labor. Except in

[28] Council of State Governments, *op. cit.*, p. 401.

those few states where a flat rate is specified in the statute, these agencies have authority to issue wage orders directing compliance with wage findings, to follow up with suits for their enforcement, and to supervise the wage regulation generally. In selecting occupations for imposition of the minimum wage and in establishing the minimum wage itself, the customary procedure is to use wage boards. These boards, ordinarily made up of representatives of labor, management, and the public, act in an advisory capacity. The state authority may accept or reject the findings of the wage board or may appoint a new one to study the problem. If the findings are acceptable, the state commission or commissioner, after public hearing, issues a wage order for the occupation under consideration.

Compliance with the wage orders is obtained by means of inspection by the state labor department or through complaints from workers. The penalty for infraction may include fine or imprisonment of the employer, and it almost always includes the right to collect back wages for employees who have been paid less than the minimum rate. Some states provide for punishment by publicity for a specified period before nonconformance is punishable by fine or imprisonment.

Constitutionality of state wage laws. In 1923, the Supreme Court held that a District of Columbia minimum-wage law applying to women deprived them of their liberty to contract for the sale of their labor without due process of law.[29] Following the Adkins case, the United States Supreme Court consistently held unconstitutional state laws requiring minimum wages based upon a cost-of-living standard to be paid to women.[30] With the new wave of minimum-wage legislation following 1933, several states attempted to ensure constitutionality by outlawing only wages which were both below a minimum standard of living and below the fair value of the labor. A New York law drawn along such lines was brought to the Supreme Court in 1936, and by a closely divided vote of 5 to 4 was found to be unconstitutional.[31]

The next year the Court reversed its line of decisions resting upon the Adkins case when it upheld the Washington minimum-wage law.[32] Although the Washington law was practically identical with the New York one, the change of opinion of Mr. Justice Roberts, who voted with the majority in the New York case, turned the tide in favor of constitutionality. As an excuse for the change in attitude, Mr. Chief Justice Hughes, presenting the majority opinion, claimed that the Court had not been

[29] *Adkins v. Children's Hospital*, 261 U.S. 525 (1923).

[30] See *Murphy v. Sardell*, 269 U.S. 530 (1923) (Arizona law), and *Donham v. West Nelson Mfg. Co.*, 273 U.S. 657 (1927) (Arkansas law). It should be noted that these decisions merely invalidated minimum-wage legislation for adult women. No question was raised as to the validity of wage regulation for children.

[31] *Morehead v. People ex. rel. Tipaldo*, 298 U.S. 587 (1936).

[32] *West Coast Hotel Co. v. Parrish*, 300 U.S. 379 (1937).

asked to reverse the Adkins ruling in the New York case. But the reasoning by which the majority sustained the Washington law was essentially that which the minority had used in all the cases from the Adkins case of 1923. The majority pointed out that the evils of sweating were so generally recognized that it could no longer be denied that minimum-wage regulation was within the competency of the state police power. Upon this reasoning the majority frankly stated that the decision in the Adkins case "should be, and it is, overruled."

Thus after years of unconstitutionality, the fixing of minimum wages of adult women has been held to be a valid use of the state police power. In 1941 the United States Supreme Court upheld minimum-wage regulations by the federal government under the Fair Labor Standards Act as being within due process of law.[33] Since this law applied to men and women alike, and since the Court maintained that no constitutional question exists as to the validity of such regulation, the due-process clause of the Fourteenth Amendment would appear not to limit the states in this respect any more than the Fifth Amendment restricts the federal government.

State regulation of minimum wages: conclusions. Because of the difficulty of generalizing about the effects of minimum-wage legislation, it is hard to draw any meaningful conclusion. The dangers that opponents of minimum wages emphasize are that unemployment may result or that some businesses may be driven into bankruptcy if the minima are placed too high. The fact is that the minima in most states are so low that these dangers are slight. Some of these laws are restricted in coverage or nearly inoperative. In addition, twenty-two states are without any wage regulation. When such legislation has the effect of pushing wages up, the profits of low-paying firms may be decreased. But better wages and higher living standards increase the efficiency of workers and attract more capable employees. Furthermore, employers are inclined to improve their methods of production, eliminate waste, and use workers to greater advantage. Therefore, higher wage costs may be dissipated and price increases need not result. A few inefficient workers may be forced out of jobs, but the operation of seniority rules may mitigate some of this result. The experience with the Fair Labor Standards Act indicates that relatively few persons were forced out of work by the minimum wages that were set.[34]

The persistence of statutory minima once they have been established is perhaps the major objection to such legislation. Prices and the cost of living usually vary much more rapidly than wage minima. Legislatures are often too slow to take action when the floor under wages needs to be

[33] *United States v. Darby Lumber Co.*, 312 U.S. 100 (1941).

[34] 52 *Monthly Labor Review* 969 (April, 1941); 54 *Monthly Labor Review* 318 (February, 1942).

raised. Since the objective is the elimination of poverty, greater flexibility is essential. Therefore, more reliance upon administrative action is desirable.

FEDERAL WAGE AND HOUR REGULATION

By the 1930s the problems of minimum wages and maximum hours had taken on a national aspect because of the country-wide economic considerations involved and the variations in state regulation. Consequently, in 1938 Congress enacted the Fair Labor Standards Act.

Even before 1938, however, the federal government exerted some control over hours and wages of certain types of employees. An eight-hour day was established for government employees as early as 1869. In 1912, Congress provided that an eight-hour provision be inserted in certain public contracts made by the federal government for work done by laborers or mechanics. The Davis-Brown Act was enacted in 1931 establishing minimum-wage standards for mechanics and laborers employed on public works contracts which exceed $2,000. The Walsh-Healey Act of 1936 provides that all contracts made by the government for the furnishing of any materials in excess of $10,000 must include the stipulation that the contractor not hire any person for more than forty hours a week and eight hours a day. The contractor must also agree to pay wage rates prevailing in the industry and not to hire males under sixteen years of age and females under eighteen years of age.

Since 1907, the federal government has regulated the hours of service of persons engaged in or connected with the actual movement of interstate trains. The Adamson Act of 1916 fixed a basic eight-hour day for railroad trainmen. Hours of work of employees in water, motor, and air transportation have also been subject to regulation.[35]

Although it was short-lived, the National Industrial Recovery Act of 1933 undertook the most extensive federal regulation of wages and hours before 1938. Even the Fair Labor Standards Act did not attempt to cover as many employees as did the Recovery Act. In the codes of fair competition through which the law was enforced, certain minimum-wage and maximum-hours standards were included. If an industry did not make up a code, a limitation of thirty-five to forty hours a week and thirty to forty cents per hour applied. Even though the Recovery Act lasted only two years, there is evidence that it contributed to a general rise in wages and a reduction of the work period—gains which were not lost when the Supreme Court invalidated the law.

When the Recovery Act was overturned by the Court, Congress and the administration began a new drive to eliminate substandard labor con-

[35] By the Merchant Marine Eight-hour Day Act of 1915, the Motor Carrier Act of 1935, and the Civil Aeronautics Act of 1938.

ditions. This movement suffered a setback when the New York minimum-wage law was declared unconstitutional in 1936. The desire for an accepted constitutional basis for labor legislation and other reform measures led President Roosevelt to suggest enlargement of the Supreme Court. Although this proposal did not win popular support, the President won his point. In 1937 the Court found the Wagner Labor Relations Act to be constitutional and reversed itself on the constitutional basis of state minimum-wage regulation by finding the Washington law to be within the reasonable limits of the police power. With this background Congress proceeded to draft the Fair Labor Standards Act which became law in 1938.

General provisions of the Fair Labor Standards Act. The hours provisions are relatively simple, the maximum now being forty hours per week.[36] If a covered employee works more than forty hours in a week, he must be paid at overtime rates of time and a half. Some elasticity is provided as a result of special exemptions, which will be discussed below, and of longer hours permissible in seasonal industries and businesses operating under guaranteed-employment contracts.

The minimum-wage rates for all employees subject to the act were 40 cents an hour,[37] except where a lower rate is prescribed by the Administrator of the Wage and Hours Division (located in the Department of Labor). In 1949, the law was amended to raise the minimum wage rate to 75 cents an hour, and in 1955, Congress approved a proposal to raise it to $1.

Constitutionality of the Act. In a unanimous decision handed down in 1941 the United States Supreme Court upheld the constitutionality of the Fair Labor Standards Act.[38] The Court held that the power of Congress over interstate commerce is complete in itself and extends to the exclusion of articles whose use is conceived to be injurious to the public health, morals, or welfare. The Court asserted that, even though manufacture is not itself interstate commerce, the power to exclude goods extends to shipments made by employers whose wages-and-hours practices do not measure up to the federal law.

Coverage of the Act. The commerce power of Congress was the constitutional peg on which the legislation was hung. However, Congress did not intend that federal regulation should extend to the furthest reaches of its authority. The coverage of the wage-and-hour provisions of the Act

[36] For the first year, the law established a forty-four-hour week; for the second year, forty-two hours; and in the third year the forty-hour maximum was reached.

[37] For the first year, minimum rates were 25 cents an hour; from 1939 to 1945, 30 cents an hour; and 40 cents an hour thereafter.

[38] *United States v. Darby Lumber Co.*, 312 U.S. 100 (1941).

is determined by the application of a general coverage formula and a series of exemptions.

Type of work done by the employee—not the nature of the employer's business—determines coverage. It is therefore possible for an employer to have some workers who are covered and others who are not. The minimum-wage and overtime-pay benefits of the Fair Labor Standards Act, as amended in 1949, extend to employees in two types of work: (1) "engaged in commerce"; and (2) "engaged in the production of goods for commerce," including fringe workers in occupations "closely related" and "directly essential" to such production. However, even though a worker may be within the coverage formula, he may still be outside the scope of the Act if he comes under one of the exemptions enumerated in the Act.

To be engaged in commerce, the employee must participate in the actual movement of commerce.[39] In defining the scope of employment in commrce, the Administrator has pointed out that it includes typically, but not exclusively, employees in interstate transportation and communication industries, as well as those working in establishments that are instrumentalities in the stream of commerce, such as warehouses, stockyards, storage facilities, and some grain elevators.[40]

The application of the Act to employees engaged in the production of goods for commerce and fringe workers has necessitated certain fine distinctions. Certainly the provisions apply to employees in manufacturing, processing, and distributing plants a part of whose products go into interstate commerce. But they also cover workers engaged in a process or occupation "directly essential" and "closely related" to production for commerce or for movement in commerce. Thus included are maintenance workers, watchmen, clerks, stenographers, messengers, as well as workers making cartons, boxes, containers, and the like. For example, in *Kirschbaum v. Walling*[41] the Supreme Court applied the Act to elevator operators and maintenance workers of various types for a loft building in which the tenants are "principally engaged in the production of goods for interstate commerce." In *Borden Co. v. Borella*[42] the Court extended coverage to similar employees for an office building owned and used as a central office building to the extent of 58 per cent of the total rentable space by a corporation engaged in the production of goods for interstate commerce. However, the Supreme Court repudiated the application of

[39] For illustrative cases see *Walling v. Jacksonville Paper Co.*, 317 U.S. 564 (1943); *McLeod v. Threlkeld,* 319 U.S. 491 (1943); *Overstreet v. North Shore Corp.*, 318 U.S. 125 (1943).

[40] Wage and Hours Division, Interpretative Bulletin 1 (Oct. 12, 1938).

[41] 316 U.S. 517 (1942).

[42] 325 U.S. 679 (1945).

the Act to the operating and maintenance employees of a building which was exclusively used as an office building and which was rented to a great variety of enterprises, although a number of them happened to be engaged in the production of goods for interstate commerce, in the case of *10 East 40th Street Building v. Callus.*[43] In *Martino v. Michigan Window Cleaning Company* [44] the Court held that the employees of a corporation engaged in washing windows and similar maintenance work were covered by the Act, as the greater part of their work was done on premises used by the employer's customers in the production of goods for interstate commerce.[45]

An employee is not beyond the reach of the Act merely because his employer is engaged in interstate operations only to a limited degree. Regardless of how minor such operations are, if they take place regularly, the Act applies. For example, a daily newspaper with a circulation of 10,000, of which only ½ of 1 per cent was out of state, was held to be engaged in the production of goods for interstate commerce, so its employees fell under the Fair Labor Standards Act. However, sporadic, unsubstantial interstate activity on the part of an employer does not bring employees within the terms of the law. Moreover, applicability does not depend upon the location of work. Employment done at home is covered.

The question of when goods are intended for interstate commerce has caused some difficulty. It is often hard to tell whether a given good will enter interstate commerce. The Administrator has ruled that an employer falls under the Act when he has reason to believe that the goods he produces will move in interstate commerce. Even if a producer within a state sells the goods to a vendor within the state and the vendor distributes them in the channels of interstate commerce, the producer may be liable under the law. The question, as interpreted by the Administrator, is not whether the goods stop after being produced before they enter interstate commerce, but whether they enter interstate commerce at some later time.

The exemptions from the Fair Labor Standards Act may be classified as partial and complete for both the minimum-wage provisions and the overtime-pay provisions. It should be noted that the amendments of 1949 broadened some exemptions and added other new ones, so fewer employees benefited by the increase in minimum wages.

Specifically exempt from both the wage and hour portions of the law

[43] 325 U.S. 578 (1945).

[44] 327 U.S. 173 (1946). This case illustrates a situation in which the courts will no longer be able to hold the Act applicable since its coverage was narrowed by the 1949 amendment.

[45] See also *Mabee v. White Plains Pub. Co.*, 327 U.S. 178 (1946); *Schulte Inc. v. Gangi*, 328 U.S. 108 (1946); *Roland Electric Co. v. Walling*, 327 U.S. 657 (1946); *Boutell v. Walling*, 327 U.S. 463 (1946).

are executive, administrative, and/or professional employees, or those engaged in local retailing or in the capacity of outside salesman; employees of retail or service establishment the greater part of whose sales are intrastate, laundries, and dry cleaners; employees engaged in catching and processing fish; agricultural employees and employees of nonprofit irrigation companies; employees of semiweekly or weekly newspapers with a circulation of less than 4,000 (previously 3,000); employees of street, suburban, or interurban railways or bus systems; any switchboard operator in a telephone exchange having less than 750 stations (previously 500); taxicab operators; employees of telegraph agencies where message revenue does not exceed $500 per month; seamen; employees in forestry and lumbering operations where the total number of employees does not exceed twelve; and persons employed in handling, packing, storing, ginning, compressing, pasteurizing, drying, or processing materials in their raw or natural state, or canning agricultural or horticultural commodities, or preparing cheese, butter, or other dairy products.

Completely exempt from the overtime-pay provisions are employees of motor carriers, railroads, or pipelines subject to the Interstate Commerce Commission; employees of air carriers subject to Title II of the Railway Labor Act; employees engaged in the canning of fish; buyers of poultry, eggs, or dairy products; and employees engaged in the first processing of dairy products, ginning and compressing cotton, processing cottonseed and sugar beets, sugar-beet molasses, sugar-cane, or maple sap into sugar or syrup.

Partial overtime-pay exemption extends to employees in seasonal industries and businesses operating under guaranteed-employment contracts. In the case of seasonal industries, the Act permits employment for as much as fifty-six hours a week for not more than fourteen weeks in a year. Special arrangements for particular industries can also be made by collective bargaining agreements. If the total hours worked do not exceed 1,040 in a twenty-six-week period, no overtime has to be paid for up to twelve hours a day and fifty-six hours a week. This exception can be as high as 2,080 hours in a calendar year where the agreement contains a provision for guaranteed employment or an annual wage.

Partial minimum-wage exemption applies to learners, apprentices, messengers, handicapped workers, Puerto Ricans, and Virgin Islanders.

By 1953, the Act applied to approximately 715,000 establishments employing about 20 million covered workers. With the establishment of regional and field offices, the Wage and Hour Division seeks to keep administration and enforcement close to the people. Under general policy guidance from Washington, the local office carries on inspections, gives legal advice, handles litigation, and selects cases to close on payment of restitution. In the first ten years of the Act's operation, 3 million employees received more than $111 million as restitution for minimum wages or overtime pay illegally withheld.[46]

Federal wage and hour regulation: conclusions. Any student of government control of business cannot but be surprised at the wide application of federal government regulation of wages and hours since the Act was held to be constitutional in 1941, particularly after so many decades of limited control. In the application of this law, perhaps more than in that of any other, one can see and appreciate the expansion of the interstate commerce power. Except where an occupation is specifically exempted, the law has come to mean that even the most local activity has fallen subject to the power of the national government.

There can be no doubt that the broad coverage of the federal law has tended to overshadow state control except in those cases, such as the regulation of hours of work for women, where state laws are more stringent than the federal law. The application of federal law to such a large portion of business has tended to simplify the task of compliance, particularly in the case of companies with operations in several states. In other cases, the federal law has tended to place the cloak of central government control over small local businesses and has limited their freedom and flexibility in operating. With a full-employment economy enjoyed since the law became effective and with more than a decade of rising prices, the limitation of hours and the establishment of minimum wages have not themselves caused much difficulty. But the problems of the small local business involved in meeting detailed regulations of a central government agency, in attempting to distinguish between exempt and nonexempt employees, in meeting the requirements of operating without overtime premium, and in many other ways, have caused more hardship than living up to the purely economic and social objectives of the law.

At the same time, it must be admitted that, if the problems of wages and hours are to be dealt with in as closely knit an industrial economy as that in the United States, some kind of uniformity is probably wise. While there are certain fallacies in arguing that one segment of an economy is harmed by "cheap" labor of another, much as there are fallacies in the same argument advanced in international trade, it is certainly true that uniform floors and ceilings have social benefits which a nation such as the United States should support.

Regulation of Terms of Employment: Conclusions

The past century has brought about tremendous changes in public attitude toward the sanctity of the labor contract. From a belief that inter-

[46] W. S. Tyson, "Fair Labor Standards Act of 1938: A Survey and Evaluation of the First Eleven Years," 1 *Labor Law Journal* 282 (January, 1950).

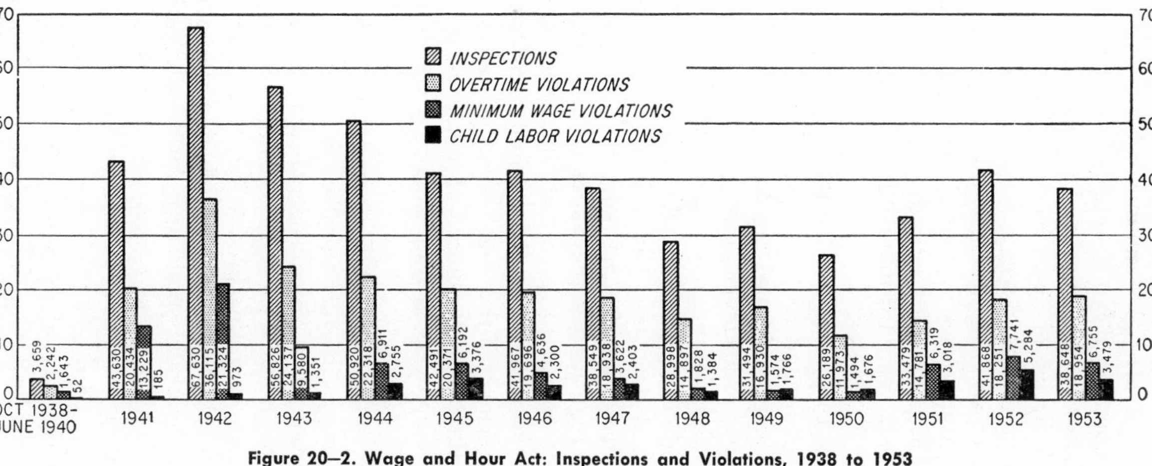

Figure 20–2. Wage and Hour Act: Inspections and Violations, 1938 to 1953

Source: Wage and Hour and Public Contracts Divisions, *Annual Reports.*

ference with hours of work for children under twelve years was dangerous meddling with private rights and inexorable economic laws, public opinion has come to condone, if not to support, prohibition of most child labor, limitation of hours for both men and women, and minimum wages for most workers. Limitation of hours in more progressive states led the way to legislation fixing minimum wages. Regulation of hours for women and minors and for men working in unhealthful or hazardous occupations has been extended in some states to control over hours of practically all industrial workers. The progressive attitude of many states has even been outdone in the last few years by more rigorous control by the federal government.

Although the desire to protect the working members of society from the hazards of long hours and too low wages is still probably the most dominant motive for wage and hours regulation, in recent years the wish to solve basic economic problems of unemployment and underconsumption has furnished a strong incentive for such controls. Even if in the long run the material standard of living should be impaired, improvement of individual physical and economic health and welfare may more than justify such governmental interference with the labor contract. Even if the motive for some regulation is the assurance of adequate income and leisure for workers to enjoy a fuller life and become better citizens, the possible loss in material welfare may be a minor consideration. Furthermore, it should be remembered that much wage and hours regulation may not adversely affect the material standard of living but may merely force a few unenlightened employers to adopt measures which improve labor's productivity.

From an economic point of view, the practice of lowering hours and increasing minimum wages in order to solve unemployment and overproduction or underconsumption, or similar economic ills, does not seem to be sound. An increasing material standard of living for a people as a whole can come only through increasing production. Curtailing output may be advantageous for a small monopolistic producing group faced with an inelastic demand, but generally speaking it can hardly enrich society. In the ardor to lift oneself by one's bootstraps, this simple truth is often overlooked. It is true that mechanical and social inventions and efficient management of the factors of production have brought forth a higher material production in the face of measures which tend to increase labor cost per unit of output. In fact, pressures, both governmental and union, to increase wages and reduce hours have stimulated efficiency in the use of labor. These pressures plus the rise of prices generally have consequently so softened the impact of wage and hour legislation that the actual economic effects have been minor.

Wise social policy would appear to demand a balancing of the desirability of fewer hours and higher minimum wages against that of material production. Many social reforms, to which wage and hours laws are no exceptions, cost society something in terms of the total production of goods and services. Yet this loss may be far outweighed by humanitarian considerations. These facts should be realized and well understood so that the legal fixing of hours and wages may proceed along lines indicated by an intelligent balancing of material and humanitarian factors.

Selected References

Berger, Morroe, *Equality by Statute: Legal Controls over Group Discrimination.* New York: Columbia University Press, 1952.

Burstein, H., "Federal Regulation of Hours and Wages," 28 *Chicago-Kent Law Review* 107–129 (March, 1950).

Daugherty, Carroll R., *Labor Problems in American Industry.* Boston: Houghton Mifflin Company, 1948.

Davisson, M. M., "Coverage of the Fair Labor Standards Act," 41 *Michigan Law Review* 1060–1088 (1943).

Dodd, E. Merrick, "The Supreme Court and Fair Labor Standards, 1941–1945," 59 *Harvard Law Review* 321 (1946).

Helsell, Frank P. "The Law against Discrimination in Employment," 25 *Washington Law Review* 225 (1950).

Kaplan, A. D. H., *The Guarantee of Annual Wages.* Washington, D.C.: Brookings Institution, 1947.

Kelly, Matthew A., "Early Federal Regulation of Hours of Labor in the United States," 3 *Industrial and Labor Relations Review* 362–374 (April, 1950).

Kesselman, Louis C., *The Social Politics of F.E.P.C.* Chapel Hill, N.C.: The University of North Carolina Press, 1948.

Marshall, Leon, *Hours and Wage Provisions in N.R.A. Codes.* Washington, D.C.: Brookings Institution, 1945.

Ruchames, Louis, *Race, Jobs and Politics. The Story of F.E.P.C.* New York: Columbia University Press, 1953.

Stigler, George, "The Economics of Minimum Wage Legislation," 36 *American Economic Review* 358–365 (June, 1946).

Tyson, W. S., "Fair Labor Standards Act of 1938; A Survey and Evaluation of the First Eleven Years," 1 *Labor Law Journal* 278–286 (January, 1950).

———, "Fair Labor Standards Amendments of 1949—Wage and Hour Coverage," 28 *North Carolina Law Review* 161–172 (February, 1950).

21

HEALTH AND SAFETY REGULATION AND SOCIAL INSURANCE

The individual worker and his family are seldom able to absorb the losses that result from sickness, disability, unemployment, or old age. Whether these are caused by industrial conditions, by natural causes, or by dislocation of the economic system is of no great moment. They all lead to suffering to an extent great enough to cause public concern. Some risks are more directly attributable to business and the conditions under which people work than others. Most, however, can be traced to the social or economic environment.

Labor legislation is no longer based upon mere protection of workers' physical health and safety but has become a means for protecting labor against economic risks. Lying back of this broader program of protection is the not unreasonable assumption that society should assume some of the burdens of economic risks that lie beyond the individual's control.

Public Interest in Reduction of Labor's Economic Risks

The seriousness of these risks is not difficult to show. In 1950, for every 1,000 workers there was an average of 117 men and 258 women who were disabled for eight days or more because of sickness or nonindustrial injuries.[1] The average number of person-years lost because of sickness and nonindustrial injuries of more than eight days' duration was 173,881 for men and 14,113 for women.[2] Moreover, about 3 million persons between fourteen and sixty-four years of age had long-term disabling illnesses.[3]

Industrial accidents also present a serious risk. In 1951, there were 2 million disabling injuries. Of these, 16,000 were fatalities; 1,600, permanent-total; and 89,400, permanent-partial. These injuries were responsible for a loss of 42 million man-days in the year of injury and 177 million

[1] This average had increased from 99 men and 151 women in 1937. The President's Commission on the Health Needs of the Nation, *Building America's Health, America's Health Status—Needs and Resources*, vol. III, *A Statistical Appendix* (1951), p. 108.

[2] *Ibid.*, p. 109.

[3] *Ibid.*, vol. II, p. 35.

man-days in subsequent years.[4] This loss has been estimated to be worth $4 billion.[5]

Although accident or disease generally strike at an individual with greater severity than does loss of a job by a person able and willing to work, unemployment is probably the greatest of all labor's risks and one of the most important problems which society has to face. The official estimates indicate that over 14 million persons were unemployed in March, 1933; that 7 million were unemployed in July, 1937; and that in October, 1938, the number was around 10 million.[6] Even in a year as prosperous as 1953 the average number of unemployed amounted to 1,602,000.[7]

Even more striking are the losses involved. It has been conservatively estimated that wage losses due to unemployment in nonagricultural employment alone amounted to $119 billion in the nine years from 1930 through 1938.[8] This tremendous total is the equivalent of the total wages and salaries actually paid out in the three years of 1936 through 1938.[9]

The problem of indigent old age is one of the important risks of labor, and it has been steadily increasing in severity. With increasing longevity and a declining birth rate, a larger portion of the population is falling within the age bracket above sixty-five. In 1900, only 3 million persons were sixty-five years and older, compared to 13 million in 1952, and an anticipated 18 million aged persons in 1975.[10] Meanwhile, modern economic conditions have sharply increased the economic dependency of aged persons. Industry has tended more and more to prefer younger men, and individuals over forty-five or fifty are usually too old to find new employment if once they lose their jobs. The shift of employment from agriculture into other industries has also had its effect in increasing old-age insecurity, since the man on a farm can usually find something to do, even though he may be over sixty-five. With the dissolution of the family as the central economic unit, older members can no longer so easily take refuge in the support of younger ones.

The losses to labor in health and in economic status are indicative not only of the great risks which labor faces but of the compelling public

[4] U.S. Department of Labor, *Handbook of Labor Statistics*, Bulletin 1016, 1951 Supplement (1952), p. 57.

[5] U.S. Department of Labor, *Annual Report, 1952* (1953), p. 73.

[6] See TNEC, *Investigation of Concentration of Economic Power*, 75th Cong., 3d Sess. (1939), part 1, p. 160. These estimates include, as unemployed, individuals working on work relief projects but not on public works.

[7] *Economic Report of the President* (1955), p. 153.

[8] *Investigation of the Concentration of Economic Power*, part 1, p. 13.

[9] *Ibid.*, p. 196.

[10] Robert Carr and others, *American Democracy in Theory and Practice* (New York: Rinehart & Company, Inc., 1955), p. 803.

interest in these risks. Individuals are seldom able to absorb them. Even the thrifty worker who makes a fair rate of pay may be unable to stand the financial cost of layoff due to accident, sickness, or unemployment. If a worker has been earning even an average wage, he is seldom able to save enough to pay doctor's bills and maintain the expense of a household, if he happens to be one upon whom the misfortune of sickness or unemployment falls. The risks of laborers not only are great but tend to fall

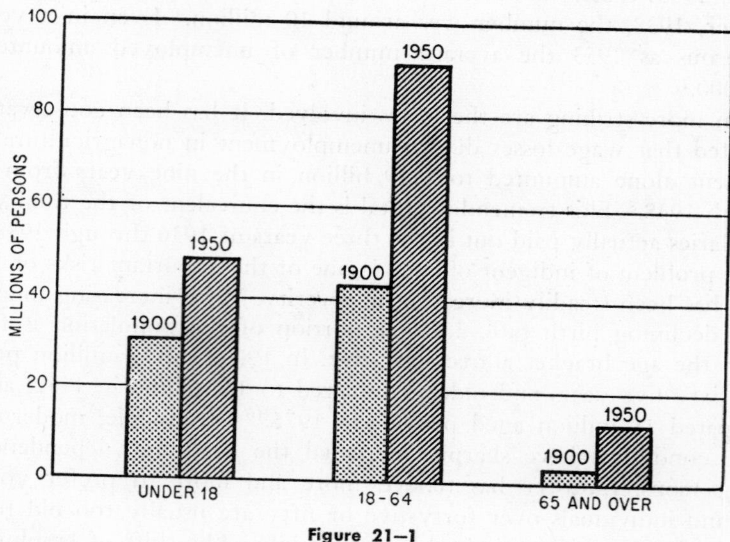

Figure 21–1

In fifty years the number of aged persons in the population has increased fourfold. Source: Social Security Administration, *Social Security in the United States* (1953). Reprinted from Robert K. Carr and others, *American Democracy in Theory and Practice* (New York: Rinehart & Company, Inc., 1955), p. 804, by special permission.

rather unevenly and to bear particularly heavily upon some individuals. The result, without some sort of cooperative risk-bearing scheme, is that the worker and his family are reduced to pauperism and to a standard of existence which may make them disgruntled and useless members of society.

The development of social legislation in the United States to protect the worker from the hazards of disease, accident, unemployment, and old age has trailed behind most European nations. By the latter part of the nineteenth century, many leading European governments passed legislation providing for safety prevention, accident compensation, compulsory health insurance, old-age pensions, and old-age and invalidity insurance. Shortly after the turn of the century European nations passed laws providing for occupational-disease compensation and compulsory unemployment compensation.[11]

Despite the recentness of most American social legislation, the development has been greatly accelerated in the past two or three decades. Both federal and state governments have passed extensive social measures in behalf of health and safety and to protect against the risks of unemployment and old age.

Health and Safety Regulations

STATE HEALTH AND SAFETY REGULATION

Legislation to deal with risks arising from accident and disease has applied largely to those misfortunes resulting directly from workers' occupations. The preventive aspects of regulation have been devoted to reporting and publicity, to limitations placed on persons, and to requirement of safety standards in the working environment. In addition, compulsory insurance, usually financed by the employing group, has supplemented these regulations in certain areas.

Limitations on persons. In the interests of health and safety some states exclude certain persons from dangerous occupations. Most common of such limitations is the exclusion of women and children from many jobs. Most mining states prohibit work of women in mines. Other states prohibit women from quarries, steel mills, smelters, poolrooms, freight or baggage services, and delivery services. In addition, occasional states prohibit women from working in businesses requiring constant standing and from employment on moving or otherwise dangerous machinery. Some states also forbid employing women for stated periods before and after childbirth. The most general method of protecting the health and safety of minors is through limitations placed upon the age at which children may enter certain jobs.

Exclusion of men from employment in the interest of safety and health has been conditioned upon physical and technical qualifications. A few states require physical examination to determine fitness of workers in work done under air pressure and on lead and lead products. Many more states, but far from all, require examination of workers in food-preparation industries for the existence of any diseases which might be communicated to consumers. Some states require other physical qualifications for entry

[11] For an excellent discussion of foreign experience, see J. R. Commons and J. B Andrews, *Principles of Labor Legislation* (New York: Harper & Brothers, 1936), chaps. 4 and 5; and H. A. Millis and R. E. Montgomery, *Labor's Risks and Social Insurance*, vol. II of *The Economics of Labor* (New York: McGraw-Hill Book Company, Inc., 1938), chaps. 3, 4, 6, and 8.

into an occupation. These requirements are usually designed to protect the general public; for example, eyesight tests are often required for employees in transportation industries.

Harmful working conditions. Regulation of the conditions under which labor works has been the principal means whereby government has attempted to prevent the occurrence of industrial disease and accident. State laws at first specified safety and health measures to be taken in manufacturing, among which were generally included machine guards, proper ventilation and lighting, fire safeguards, boiler inspection, and requirements of sanitation in washrooms and toilets. Numerous safety measures for mining are also provided by state laws. While state laws still establish definite minimum safety and health standards, the recent tendency is for the specific rules and regulations to be formulated and enforced by administrative agencies provided by the laws. In this way, as new conditions arise requiring regulation, the labor authority can draw up appropriate rules and not have to wait for the tedious process of state legislatures.

State regulation of harmful working conditions calls for administration of a high order to be effective. Many states place fairly adequate laws on the statute books but fail to provide enough funds for effective enforcement. Most state laws require a minimum of one annual inspection in each establishment per year, but even this altogether inadequate minimum cannot be realized in some states. Several states hire only one inspector for the entire state. In other states the number may be much greater but still be insufficient. Moreover, safety and health inspection requires a high degree of competency, and even the most expert inspector may not be able to pass accurately upon the many technical matters which safety and health laws provide.

Fortunately for the cause of safety and health, many employers have come to find out that measures to reduce disease and accident result in savings that far surpass the basic outlay. Since compensation laws often levy costs in accordance with the accident and disease records of businesses, and since insurance payments often vary with the existence of hazards, accident and disease prevention has been found to be economical.

STATE WORKMEN'S COMPENSATION LAWS

Accidents and occupational disease can be reduced by safety regulation, but it is too much to expect that they can be eliminated. These risks are now compensated for in most states through some sort of insurance which employers are required to carry. Prior to the enactment of compensation legislation the worker was protected only by the common-law principles of employer's liability. If the employer did not use reasonable care in protecting the safety of workers he laid himself open to the possibility of legal suits for damages. In practice, certain common-law doctrines often freed the employer from liability.[12]

The common law of employer's liability was modified from time to time by statute, but the technique of compensating injuries by resort to legal suit proved to be unjust, inadequate, and uncertain. Moreover, the system of employer's liability did not encourage accident prevention. So long as industry did not have to meet the costs of the physical risks of employment, employers had little interest, or found little profit, in prevention.

Development of compensation laws. Europe led the world in the enactment of compulsory insurance for work injuries. Germany passed such a bill in 1884 and Great Britain in 1897. The first compensation laws passed in the United States were those of Maryland in 1902, Montana in 1910, and New York in 1910. While these laws were held unconstitutional by state courts and the issue in favor of constitutionality was not settled by the United States Supreme Court until 1917,[13] twenty states had enacted compensation laws by 1913, and ten more states had such laws by 1915. By 1948 every state as well as the territories of Hawaii, Alaska, Puerto Rico, and the Philippine Islands, and District of Columbia, and the United States government (for civil employees and harbor workers) had some kind of workmen's-compensation legislation in effect.[14]

General nature of the laws. Workmen's compensation is compulsory in one-half of the states and territories. In the other twenty-six jurisdictions it is elective. In some cases where it is elective, the employer and workers are covered unless the employer—in some states, the worker—individually rejects it. In others, the employer must positively elect to be covered by workmen's compensation so as not to come under employers' liability laws. However, if an employer elects to stay under employers' liability, the customary legal defenses are generally not permitted, so that elective laws tend in reality to be compulsory.

[12] These doctrines absolved the employer of liability if the accident was due to any negligence on the employee's part, if injury to a worker was caused by negligence of a fellow servant, and because the employee was held to assume the ordinary risks incident to his work when he took the job.

[13] *New York Central Railroad Co. v. White*, 243 U.S. 188 (1917).

[14] These and other details of compensation legislation are drawn from the following: C. F. Sharkey, "Principal Features of Workmen's Compensation Laws, as of January 1, 1940," 50 *Monthly Labor Review* 574–600 (March, 1940); Max Kossoris, "Workmen's Compensation in the United States, I—An Appraisal," 76 *Monthly Labor Review* 359–366 (April, 1953); Kossoris, "IV—Occupational Disease," 76 *Monthly Labor Review* 709–713 (July, 1953); Bruce Greene, "V—Medical Services," 76 *Monthly Labor Review* 826–829 (August, 1953); S. Bruce Black, "The Anomalies of Workmen's Compensation," 7 *Industrial and Labor Relations Review* 43–50 (October, 1953).

Workmen's-compensation insurance may be carried in state funds where they exist, in private companies, or by the employer, if he can convince state authorities that he has ability to pay possible benefits. Studies have indicated that the cost of administering insurance has been lowest in exclusive state funds, and lower in competitive state funds than in any private insurance company, whether stock or mutual.[15]

Regardless of the way the insurance has been handled, the effect has been to encourage accident and disease prevention. In practically all insurance schemes, rates have been based upon merit rating. The employer's insurance cost has been based upon his accident and disease record. Consequently, employers have found it to their pecuniary advantage to reduce the cases of compensation loss. Not only has this led to safety and health devices and campaigns, but the employer has taken a far greater interest in minor accidents and sickness, where at all attributable to employment, so that carelessness in immediate treatment may not lead to larger claims later.

Coverage. State laws vary considerably in the character of employment which they cover. In principle, if workmen's compensation is sound, all employments and all employees should be covered. Actually, exceptions are made for small establishments, exceptions result from laws applicable only to hazardous employments, and employees are removed from the protection of these laws by specific exclusion of certain employments, such as agricultural work, domestic employment, casual work, and often work in charitable institutions. These exemptions leave one-third of the employees in the United States without coverage.

The primary object of state compensation legislation has been to insure workers against the risks of industrial accident. Obviously, there is equal justification for insuring workers against the hazard of disease contracted because of the nature of employment. Today it is generally accepted that the worker suffering disability through occupational disease should be entitled to the same protection as the worker disabled through accidental injury. There is some provision for such protection in fifty-two of the fifty-four laws in the United States and territories. More than one-half of the jurisdictions cover all diseases. Others limit coverage to specifically listed diseases. The recent trend is toward full or general coverage. Much of the objection to full coverage (that it might include even the common cold) can be overcome through proper administration. The settlement of an occupational disease claim need be no more difficult than the adjudication of an accidental injury case.

Benefits. Compensation benefits are usually of three kinds: death benefits, disability benefits, and payments for medical care. The amounts paid for death and disability benefits are usually determined by three factors:

[15] Commons and Andrews, *op. cit.*, p. 254.

the benefit rate, ordinarily a percentage of wages; the term of payment; and the maximum total set by law.

Most states have not been very liberal in allowance for death benefits when the economic value of the loss of a wage earner to his family is considered. In two-thirds of the states the worker's life is worth $10,000 (i.e., approximately two and one-half years' earnings) or less. Only seven states provide for payments to the widow for life, or until remarriage, and for minor children until a specified age is reached. Additional amounts for burial expenses vary from no provision at all in Oklahoma to $500 in Connecticut and Rhode Island.

Most state laws generally provide for a three- to seven-day waiting period before disability payments are made, to discourage malingering or false claims. This safeguard is probably not very important, for few workers would care to feign illness and lose regular wages in return for the small compensation benefits.

Payments for disability may be classified under the four kinds of disability: permanent-total, permanent-partial, temporary-total, and temporary-partial. Benefits for permanent disability are often higher than death benefits. In view of the necessity of caring for the injured, this provision is perfectly reasonable. A few states allow benefits to continue for the life of the injured worker, but most states limit them to periods ranging from 240 to 600 weeks.

For permanent-partial disability, payment is usually a percentage of the wage loss for fixed periods varying with the type of disability. This method is open to criticism as being unfair. The loss of a finger or a hand to one worker whose job requires digital skill may involve more economic loss than it would to another worker.

Temporary-partial and temporary-total disability benefits follow pretty closely the provisions of permanent disability. The main difference is that the waiting period becomes of primary significance because temporary disability does not often last more than a week or two. Furthermore, nearly all cases of temporary disability are likely to be total, or to be treated as such. If the worker is forced to leave his job because of industrial accident or disease, the disability usually involves complete discontinuance of work for a time. Another difference between temporary and permanent disability benefits is that in the former time limits have little effect, although the weekly maximum pay allowed may be very important to the worker.

The greatest advances in the field of workmen's compensation have been in the provision for medical benefits. By July, 1953, full medical aid was provided in thirty-six jurisdictions. The remaining jurisdictions impose limits on the cost of medical aid or a period of time during which it may be rendered—or both. All but a few include the furnishing of artificial appliances whenever necessary. In 1951, medical payments accounted for about one-third of the total benefits.[16]

Only about one-third of the state workmen's-compensation acts contain specific provisions for tiding a permanently impaired worker over a period of vocational rehabilitation. In the rest of the states the task of rehabilitating a permanently disabled worker is left to public or private agencies.

Workmen's compensation: conclusions. While it is probably true that workmen's compensation has been responsible for the reduction of injuries and has certainly been an improvement over employer's-liability laws, it still has many shortcomings. In many states, the basic statute is antiquated, holding fast to the more limited objectives of experimental legislation of earlier days. The laws and their administration have not grown with a more enlightened social point of view. Many administrators serve only as adjudicators of contested claims and are handicapped by limited tenure of appointment. Few states are concerned with rehabilitation of permanently impaired workers, and fewer still take an active part in accident prevention. Two-thirds of all workers still are not subject to planned, organized safety efforts.

Benefit payments are grossly inadequate. Average benefits probably do not exceed one-third of wage loss. When the weekly earnings average $72, the weekly maximum for benefit payments is $30 or less in more than one-half of the states. Only two states permit more than $40 for single workers, and only five allow that much or slightly more for workers with a large number of dependents. Only one state attempts to relate for all injured workers the degree of permanent impairment to disability payments, taking into account a worker's age, his occupation, and the extent to which impairment will limit his future earning power.

As the authors of a recent appraisal put it: "The evidence is clear that workmen's compensation has left unfulfilled most of its major original objectives." [17] Some workers, such as railway employees and seamen, who originally complained about their omission now resist inclusion, and labor is pressing for outside supplementation through welfare provisions in the labor contract.

DISABILITY INSURANCE

Few workers have long-term protection against loss of income from permanent and total disability, especially if the injury or sickness is not connected with work. Yet, among the civilian population of working age, approximately 2 million persons have total disabilities that keep them from

[16] Herman Somers and Anne Somers, "Workmen's Compensation. Unfulfilled Promise," 7 *Industrial and Labor Relations Review* 32–42 (October, 1953).

[17] *Ibid.*, p. 33.

work more than six months. In addition, another 2 million between the ages of fourteen and sixty-five are away from work because of injuries and illnesses that have lasted less than six months.

Those persons who have protection against loss of income from disability owe it to the fact that industrial pension plans commonly provide for a pension at a reduced rate in case of permanent-total disability—usually at an advanced age. Only if the condition is due to work-connected injury or illness may workers count on receiving payments under workmen's compensation. But a third of the workers are not under workmen's compensation, inadequate as it is.

To meet the risk of income loss due to short-term non-work-connected illness and injury, four states have established temporary-disability-insurance programs—Rhode Island, California, New Jersey, and New York. In three states, the program is coordinated with the unemployment-compensation program and the benefits are the same. In Rhode Island, the payments come from a special fund, which is collected by a 1 per cent tax on employees. Employees in New Jersey and California may enter into arrangements with private companies, provided the benefits are at least as good as under the state plan.

HEALTH INSURANCE

Whether or not disabling illness arises indirectly from employment, the costs of medical care constitute a social problem which society can hardly overlook long. While the federal and state governments do much to aid in the prevention of illness, and private organizations, such as insurance companies and the National Safety Council, have made great progress in education for prevention, compulsory health insurance is still not provided by law in any jurisdiction of the United States.

When the federal Social Security Act was passed in 1935, there was some agitation for a program of compulsory health insurance. Such insurance had been provided in many European countries,[18] and it was recommended by the Committee on the Costs of Medical Care [19] and the President's Committee on Economic Security.[20] After World War II the issue

[18] For a good discussion of these developments, see Millis and Montgomery, *op. cit.*, chap. 6.

[19] Organized in 1927 and financed by several large foundations, this committee reported in 1932 in favor of placing health insurance on a compulsory basis. See *Medical Care for the American People* (Chicago: University of Chicago Press, 1932).

[20] *Report to the President of the Committee on Economic Security* (1935), pp. 41–43. Other investigations and reports supporting compulsory health insurance have been made. See Technical Committee on Medical Care of the Interdepartmental Committee to Coordinate Health and Welfare Activities, *The Need for a National Health Program* (1938). For a good summary of investigations, see J. S. Falk, *Security against Sickness* (New York: Doubleday & Company, Inc., 1936).

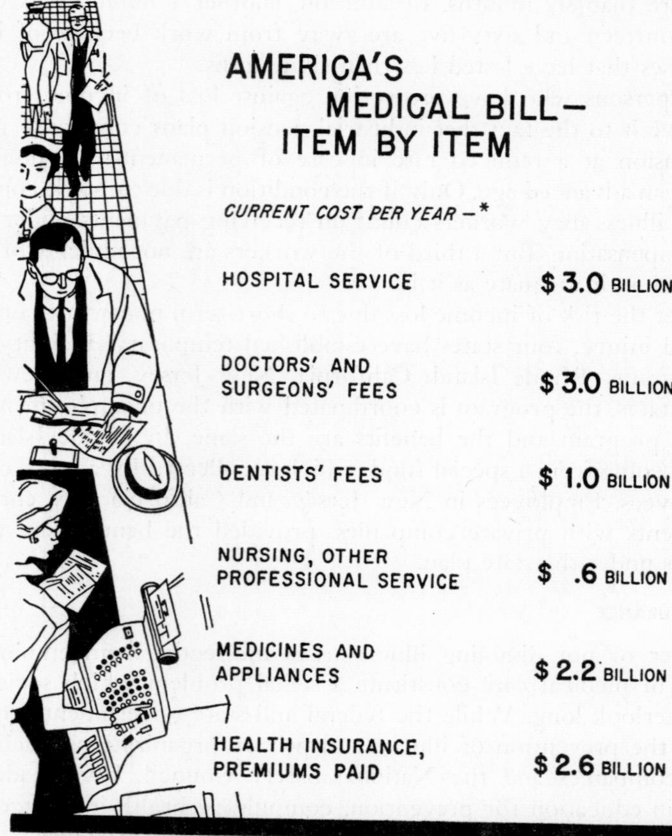

AMERICA'S
MEDICAL BILL–
ITEM BY ITEM
CURRENT COST PER YEAR –*
HOSPITAL SERVICE $ 3.0 BILLION
DOCTORS' AND SURGEONS' FEES $ 3.0 BILLION
DENTISTS' FEES $ 1.0 BILLION
NURSING, OTHER PROFESSIONAL SERVICE $ .6 BILLION
MEDICINES AND APPLIANCES $ 2.2 BILLION
HEALTH INSURANCE, PREMIUMS PAID $ 2.6 BILLION
TOTAL OUTLAY $12.4 BILLION
BENEFITS RECEIVED FROM HEALTH INSURANCE $ 2.1 BILLION
OUT-OF-POCKET COST $10.3 BILLION
*PAYMENTS BY INDIVIDUALS AND COMPANIES, EXCLUDING WORKMEN'S COMPENSATION AND OTHER PAYMENTS REQUIRED BY LAW

Figure 21–2

Source: Reprinted from the Dec. 24, 1954, issue of *U.S. News & World Report,* an independent weekly news magazine published at Washington. Copyright, 1954, United States News Publishing Corporation.

became the subject of much discussion and controversy. In 1948, the Federal Security Administrator proposed a program of national compulsory prepaid health insurance.[21] Still more recently, in 1952, the President's Commission on the Health Needs of the Nation recommended a system of prepaid medical care on a federal-state-regional basis.

Perhaps the most important reason why some kind of health insurance has not been adopted under governmental auspices is the opposition of certain strong groups. Private insurance companies, drug and patent-medicine manufacturers, employers' organizations, and the medical profession have registered strong opposition to compulsory health insurance. Insurance companies and the drug industry fear loss of business and curtailment of profit margins. Private industry, although not entirely opposed, has generally fought the insurance because of the increased tax costs. The medical profession, with the exception of certain groups, has been against it on account of fear that doctors' fees and freedom might be restricted by government control. These real reasons were not always given in publicly opposing a health-insurance law. Instead, health insurance was branded as socialistic and un-American, as designed to encourage malingering and hypochrondria, to interfere in the personal relationship of doctor and patient, and to discourage medical research and diminish the attractiveness of the medical career through government control over fees.

As the benefits of social-security programs are more widely experienced and as fears regarding schemes once regarded as radical—such as compensation insurance, unemployment insurance, and old-age insurance—fail to materialize, it seems that the time will soon arrive when compulsory health insurance will be a part of the national and state social-insurance program. It may be difficult to pass such legislation unless strong safeguards are placed in the law and individuals are given the right to choose between public and private insurance. If measures are included to safeguard the personal relationship of doctor and patient, however, and to prevent waste of time and money in treating imaginary ills, the real bases for fear of the law should disappear. The main difference between the present system and a compulsory health-insurance plan lies in the allocation and distribution of costs. Even if the portion of the national income going to prevention and treatment of illness should increase, the benefits might well be worth the costs.

FEDERAL HEALTH AND SAFETY REGULATION

Because of the local nature of the problem, and because the constitutional power of state governments in matters of safety and health is broader than that of the federal government, most of such regulation has

[21] *The Nation's Health, A Report to the President* (1948).

been under the states. The federal government has had some part in the program, however, mainly in terms of aid rather than regulation, although in certain fields, such as transportation, its activities have been predominant.

Efforts by the federal government in the field of compensation legislation have been limited to civil-service employees and to harbor employees, although an employer's liability act applies to employees in interstate transportation. Compensation legislation for civil employees is of little regulatory concern, for it is simply the plan of a large employer for establishing definite accident and disease benefits for his employees. Congress has placed all employees in interstate transportation under an employer's liability law which makes the employer liable for all accident hazards involved in the employment. Because longshoremen were held not to be under this law, or under state compensation laws when injured aboard vessels, Congress passed a special compensation law for these workers. It does not differ in any material respect from typical state legislation. In 1941, the employees of certain private employers in contractual work for the government outside the United States were covered. By May, 1953, 3.2 million workers were covered by these laws, which are administered by the Bureau of Employees' Compensation in the Department of Labor.[22]

Publicity and education. One of the most significant contributions of the national government to the cause of occupational safety and health is its publicity and education work. The Bureau of Labor Statistics of the Department of Labor has compiled information needed to guide legislatures and interested parties in passing laws on behalf of safety and health. The Bureau of Labor Standards has initiated various conferences with organizations of state labor commissioners, with a view to developing legislation and administrative techniques. The Bureau also aids states in the effective training of factory inspectors by developing training courses and making studies of industrial hazards. The Bureau further cooperates with private state and national safety organizations. The research and advisory work of the Children's Bureau in the Department of Health, Education, and Welfare and the Women's Bureau of the Department of Labor is also an important source of aid in bettering working conditions dangerous to health and safety.

Nearly every regulatory agency of the national government carries on some kind of investigatory and advisory work related to safety and health. The activities of the Interstate Commerce Commission, the Civil Aeronautics Board, and the Maritime Commission are especially well known, and work of this kind is also performed occasionally in bureaus of gov-

[22] John Petsko, "III—Workmen's Compensation in U.S. Federal Legislation," 76 *Monthly Labor Review* 602 (June, 1953).

ernment administrative departments other than the Department of Labor.

Public-health services. The activities of local, state, and federal government agencies to promote public health have been so varied and extensive that they cannot be more than mentioned. Some idea of these may be gained from the fact that expenditures by federal, state, and local governments in 1951 for health and medical services amounted to $2,512 mil-

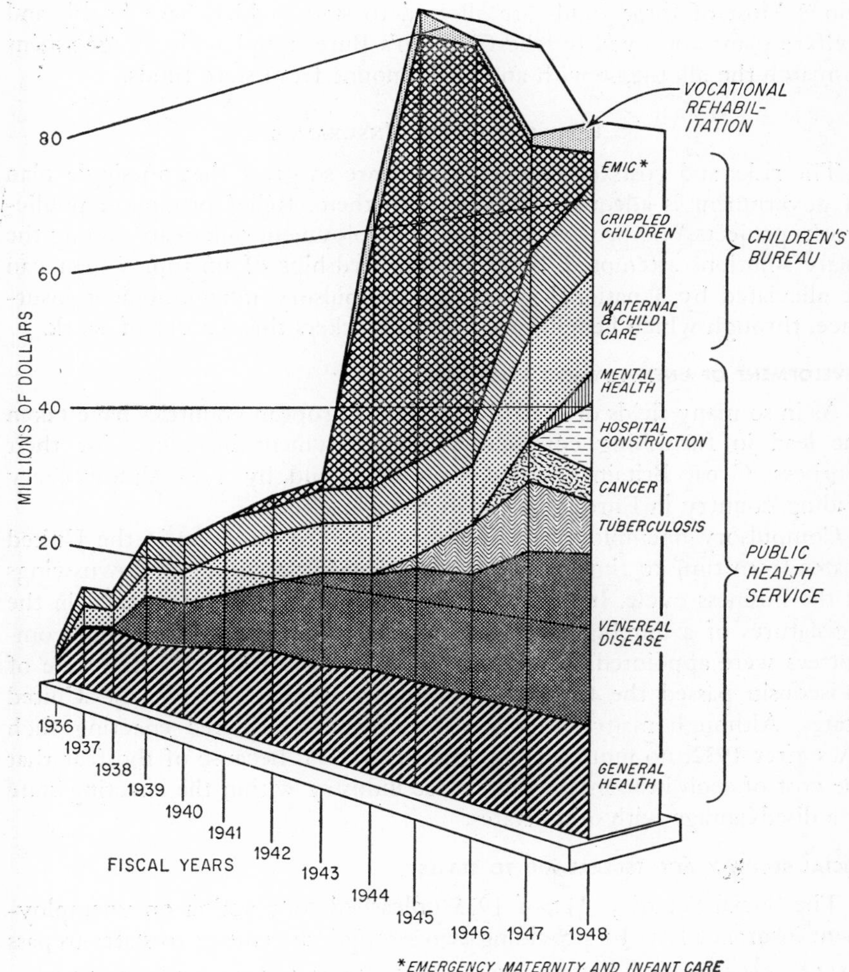

Figure 21–3. Allotments of Federal Grants-in-aid to States for Health Programs

Fiscal Years 1936 to 1948. Source: Commission on the Organization of the Executive Branch of Government, *Task Force Report on Public Welfare* (1949), p. 149.

lion.[23] The United States Public Health Service has made a great number of surveys and has engaged in numerous researches of methods of disease control. In 1954, $266 million was granted to the Public Health Service for such research and for allotment to states for public-health work.[24] The Children's Bureau (now in the Department of Health, Education and Welfare) has also been granted funds, since 1935, for maternal and child health services, services to crippled children, and child-welfare services. In 1954 appropriations for these services amounted to over $30 million.[25] Most of these funds are allotted to states which have health and welfare plans approved by the Children's Bureau and with an agreement to match the allotment with an equal amount from state funds.

Unemployment Insurance

The risks and costs of unemployment are so great that no single plan of government is adequate to cope with them. Relief programs, public-works projects, and provision of public employment offices are among the many solutions attempted. Some of the hardships of unemployment can be alleviated by a national system of compulsory unemployment insurance, through which benefits are paid to workers thrown out of work.

DEVELOPMENT OF UNEMPLOYMENT INSURANCE

As in so many fields of social legislation, European countries have taken the lead in furnishing compulsory unemployment insurance for their workers. Great Britain adopted it in 1912, and by 1927 almost every leading country in Europe had such plans in effect.

Compulsory unemployment insurance received attention in the United States from time to time after 1912, particularly at times of downswings in the business cycle. In 1931, compensation bills were introduced in the legislatures of a number of states, and several special investigating committees were appointed to study the problem. Early in 1932, the state of Wisconsin passed the first unemployment-insurance law in the United States. Although many other states seriously considered enacting such laws after 1932, no more were passed until 1935, because of the fear that the cost of such insurance would place industry within the enacting state at a disadvantage with other states.

SOCIAL SECURITY ACT: FEDERAL AID TO STATES

The Social Security Act of 1935 unleashed state action on unemployment insurance laws by providing two strong inducements to states to pass

[23] Ida Merriam, "Social Welfare Programs in the United States," 16 *Social Security Bulletin* 8 (February, 1953).

[24] *Annual Report of the Department of Health, Education, and Welfare, 1954* (1955), p. 104.

[25] *Ibid.*, p. 65.

them: (1) the tax-offset provisions of the law, and (2) the federal subsidy of state administrative costs under an unemployment-insurance plan. Thus, while the federal law did not directly establish a national system of unemployment insurance, it made it highly unwise for a state to refuse to enact a law. The incentive was so strong that by 1937 every state and territory had enacted unemployment-insurance statutes.

Tax and offset provisions of the federal law. Under the Social Security Act, a 3 per cent excise tax is levied on the payrolls (up to $3,000 per employee) of employers within covered industries who employ eight or more employees for twenty weeks within the taxable year. No tax is levied on employees. Certain kinds of employment are exempted, such as agricultural labor, domestic service, public employment, work for parents or spouse, and work for nonprofit institutions.[26]

Up to 90 per cent of the federal unemployment tax reverts to the state for use in its unemployment-compensation program, if the state has an unemployment-compensation law which meets certain requirements. The unemployment fund of each state, which is kept as a deposit in the Unemployment Trust Fund in the United States Treasury, is invested by the Treasury and bears interest at the average rate paid the United States on interest-bearing obligations. A separate account is maintained for each state, and states make requisitions for funds for benefit payments against these accounts.

Federal grants for administration. From the 10 per cent of the unemployment tax held by the federal government, grants are made to the states to aid in meeting the costs of the unemployment-compensation program. The amount granted to each state is determined in light of the population of the state, the number of persons covered by the state law, the proper cost of administering the plan, and other factors deemed to be relevant by the Social Security Administration.

To be eligible for federal grants, the states must meet certain administrative standards, including, since 1940, a merit system for administrative and technical personnel, the provision of opportunity for a fair hearing before an impartial tribunal for individuals whose claim for compensation is denied, and the submission of adequate reports as required by the Social Security Administration. The Administration is authorized, after reasonable notice and hearing, to revoke administrative grants to states if it finds that the provisions of the law are not being complied with or that

[26] Note the differences from the old age and survivors insurance portions of the Social Security Act. The unemployment-compensation law retains the $3,000 tax base, which has been raised to $4,200 for OASI. Also, the exclusion of domestic and agricultural workers and the narrower definitions of employee and agricultural labor are continued in the unemployment-compensation law. But the most important difference is the restriction to employers of eight or more. See pp. 533–537.

a substantial number of persons entitled to compensation are being denied it.

THE NATURE OF STATE LAWS [27]

The state and territorial unemployment-compensation laws present so many variations in detail that generalizations are difficult. At the same time, the federal act and the influence of the Social Security Administration in formulating model bills make it possible to summarize some of the more important aspects of these laws.

Coverage. State laws follow fairly closely the coverage provisions found in the federal law. All states cover employers of eight or more individuals, and twenty-nine states have extended the system to employers of fewer than eight workers. Practically all states exclude those employments exempt from the federal tax.[28] The total coverage is in excess of half the normally gainfully occupied persons.[29]

Tax provisions. All states levy a payroll tax on employers, generally at a rate of 2.7 per cent. [30] A few states levy taxes on employees in addition, but the tendency is away from such taxes.[31]

Financing arrangements and merit rating. All state funds must be deposited with the United States Treasury. This provision in and of itself precludes any system of financing by private insurance companies or by the employer, as is so often the case in accident- and health-compensation laws. But the setup of the state fund varies as between "pooled funds" and "employer reserves." In the former case, all contributions of employers in the state are maintained in a general state account, and benefits are charged to this account or fund irrespective of the employer who laid the workers off. In the case of employer reserves, each employer has a separate account with the state fund; his contributions are credited to this account and the costs of compensation for employees laid off by him are charged to it. According to the latest figures available, all states except Kentucky

[27] See "State Unemployment Insurance Laws, September 1, 1952," 75 *Monthly Labor Review* 623–625 (December, 1952).

[28] However, a number of states now include some types of "industrialized" farm labor. Idaho covers domestic service, and New York does so when four or more are employed. Wisconsin covers certain state and local employees.

[29] In 1952, 34.3 million of the 61.2 million employed civilians were covered by federal-state unemployment insurance. In addition, 4 million railway workers were protected by an unemployment-compensation program. U.S. Department of Labor, *Annual Report, 1952* (1953), p. 61.

[30] This rate is based upon 90 per cent of the federal tax of 3 per cent, the maximum allowable credit. Thus the employer customarily pays 0.3 per cent to the federal government and 2.7 per cent to the state government.

[31] In 1937 ten states required contributions from employees, often at a rate of one-half the employer's contributions. By 1945 only four states still required employees' contributions.

and North Carolina have pooled funds. In the two states named, a combination of a partial pool and reserve accounts is used.[32]

Under the employer-reserve type of fund, each employer pays for the unemployment caused by his own action, so that employers with good employment records have lower insurance costs. To guard against the depletion of an individual employer's fund, state laws allowing for such reserves usually provide that an employer's tax rate be raised as soon as his reserve falls to a certain point and appears to be in danger of depletion.

Because there is the real possibility that an individual employer's reserve may be depleted in spite of safeguards, nearly all laws have provided for state pooled funds. These plans represent insurance principles at their simplest, all contributions being pooled and all costs being charged against the pool. As long as funds remain in the state fund, payments may be made to unemployed workers. Yet a simple pooled plan means that all employers, both those with good employment records and those with poor ones, pay the same rate. This has not seemed too fair. Furthermore, it seems desirable because it produces no economic incentive for an individual employer to undertake methods to prevent unemployment.

To meet the objection to simple pooled funds, most states now apply a merit-rating principle to govern individual-employer contributions.[33] These plans operate through statistics of the employment record of each employer. Employers with good records may have their tax reduced below the standard, and those with poor records may have their tax increased above it, though not usually higher than 4 per cent of payrolls. Strictly speaking, pooled plans cease to be such if they involve merit rating. They are really closer to employer-reserve plans, even though all contributions are credited to, and all costs are charged to, a single fund.

Computation of benefits. The greatest variation in state and territorial laws is found in the methods of computing benefits, yet the results are surprisingly similar. Benefits in virtually all states and territories average between $20 and $30 a week. Mississippi has a minimum of $3, and nine other states have a $5 minimum. A minimum of $10 or more is found in sixteen states. Only seven states have maximums above $30, while the highest maximum is $48 in Alaska. Most laws make provision for benefits for partial unemployment, to encourage workers to take any part-time employment they can get. These benefits are usually equal to the difference between the amount earned and the benefit for full unemployment, plus a

[32] U.S. Department of Labor, *Comparison of State Unemployment Insurance Laws as of October, 1949* (1950), p. 14.

[33] Where a state's merit-rating program meets federal government standards, the tax levied against an employer may be lower than 3 per cent. It, of course, could not be lower than 0.3 per cent, as this latter amount is a federally collected tax against which there is no offset.

small addition, often $2 per week or one-sixth of partial-employment earnings.

Qualification for unemployment-insurance benefits depends upon several factors, including a waiting period, the amount of earnings previous to being unemployed, and the reasons for the unemployment. All states but Maryland, North Carolina, and Nevada require at least a one-week waiting period. Commonly the waiting period is just one week. Most states require for qualification a certain minimum-earnings record in the previous calendar year, or the first four of the last five quarters preceding the claim for compensation. The requirements differ between states, but usually provide for a minimum of eight to ten weeks' full-time wages in the year preceding application for benefits. This provision is to safeguard the fund from the expense of carrying workers who do not have much of an employment record. Some states refuse unemployment benefits to workers who leave a job voluntarily without a good reason, are discharged for misconduct, refuse suitable employment (as limited by the national law), or participate in a labor dispute. In many states, however, the benefits are not entirely denied in these cases, but the waiting period is merely extended.

To economize reserve funds and to make possible adoption of actuarial principles in calculating costs, all laws limit the total payment of benefits to a qualified unemployed worker. In only six states is the maximum duration less than twenty weeks. For the rest it ranges between twenty and twenty-six weeks, with more than one-half being twenty-two weeks or more.

CONSTITUTIONALITY OF UNEMPLOYMENT COMPENSATION

Both the state and the federal laws have been upheld by the courts as being within the constitutional powers of government. The highest courts of many states have upheld state unemployment-insurance laws,[34] and the United States Supreme Court has upheld both the state and the federal laws.

The law of the state of Alabama was upheld by the Supreme Court in 1937.[35] On the same day the Court upheld the constitutionality of the unemployment-insurance provisions of the federal law.[36] The majority held that employment was a perfectly proper object for excise taxes and

[34] See, for example, *Chamberlin v. Andrews,* 271 N.Y. 1 (1936), and *Gillum v. Johnson* (California), 62 P.2d 1037 (1936).

[35] *Carmichael v. Southern Coal and Coke Co.,* 301 U.S. 495 (1937).

[36] *Steward Machine Co. v. Davis,* 301 U.S. 548 (1937). Both this decision and the one in the Alabama case were decided by a 5-to-4 vote. Mr. Justice Roberts, who had voted against social-security measures for railroad employees in 1935, sided with the majority in the social-security cases of 1937.

that the exemptions were not so arbitrary as to vitiate the tax. The Court found that the tax-credit provisions did not unlawfully coerce the states to set up unemployment-insurance plans. Admitting that "every rebate from a tax, when conditioned upon conduct, is in some measure a temptation," the Supreme Court declared that under the law states did not have to adopt unemployment-insurance plans.

UNEMPLOYMENT INSURANCE: CONCLUSIONS

Most state unemployment-insurance laws provide only for employer contributions. This practice is supported on the ground that unemployment is an industrial hazard, the cost of which should be included in the cost of producing goods. Unemployment is a social problem which is the concern of all industry, not to mention society in general. However, if the concept of insurance is to be kept as the central thesis of unemployment compensation, the advent of merit rating raises certain problems. If each employer pays only the costs of unemployment occasioned by his own experience, the unemployment risks of society are not really pooled. Moreover, merit rating assumes too much that individual employers are responsible for and can control unemployment.

Benefit provisions are needlessly complicated in most present laws. Calculation of percentages of wage payments often involves more detail than is necessary. In the interests of simple administration, the flat-rate system of payment might well be adopted universally. Most European laws provide for flat rates, or a series of flat rates based upon certain defined wage groups. Whether a worker should get $18.67 a week or $19.01 a week does not seem to be a very vital matter.

A question might be raised about the adequacy of the whole system of benefits. A large part of the working population is outside the laws. Weekly benefits are so small, waiting periods so long, and benefit periods so short that a relatively small cost of unemployment is borne by the system. It may not seem to matter much whether the unemployed are supported by government relief, by unemployment insurance, or by other means of assistance. But in the interests of uniformity, adequacy, and self-respect of recipients, the scope of unemployment insurance should be materially broadened.

Finally, the difficulty of the federal-state approach to this problem might be noted. A definitely national problem is being attacked through a great many different jurisdictions operating under laws which vary widely in details. The system of federal-state laws means that some states will have ample funds to pay unemployment-insurance benefits and that others —those unfortunate enough to have industries in which employment is variable—may have to restrict benefits because of inadequate funds.

Old-age Assistance and Insurance

Germany instituted a system of compulsory old-age insurance for workers as early as 1889, and England enacted an Old Age Pension Act in 1908. The latter was made contributory in 1925 and expanded into a new, comprehensive national insurance system, pursuant to the Beveridge report, in 1946.

Not until the enactment of the Social Security Act in 1935 did the United States become committed to the policy of contributory old-age benefits. But because it takes time to bring an insurance plan into effect, and since not all old persons in need will always be able to qualify for contributory benefits, this policy has been supplemented by a plan of noncontributory pensions.

STATE OLD-AGE PENSIONS BEFORE 1935

The first old-age pension plans in the United States, except for pensions to war veterans and government employees, were enacted by state and territorial governments. The first permanent old-age pension law was enacted by Alaska in 1915, and the first state to pass an effective law was Montana in 1923. By 1929, ten states and Alaska had such laws. Under the impetus furnished by the Social Security Act, however, every state had an old-age pension law in operation by 1938.

Until 1929, many state old-age pension laws were of the optional type, giving county commissioners the authority to choose whether indigent old people should be supported by almshouses or by a system of pensions. The result was that few people were granted pensions, in spite of the fact that they were generally less costly than support in almshouses. After 1929 nearly all effective laws required payment of pensions, but as late as 1934 many state pensions were grossly inadequate. During 1934, the average monthly pension paid in North Dakota was only 69 cents; in Nebraska, $1.22; and in Indiana, $4.50. More than half the twenty-seven states and territories paying pensions in 1934 expended an average of less than $10 per month per pensioner.[37]

FEDERAL GRANTS FOR STATE OLD-AGE ASSISTANCE PLANS

The Social Security Act allows federal grants-in-aid to the states[38] for payment of pensions to needy persons sixty-five years of age or older. In addition, the federal government grants to states an amount equal to 5 per

[37] Millis and Montgomery, *op. cit.*, p. 381.

[38] The states now receive four-fifths of the first payments up to $25, plus half the amount in excess of $25 up to $55. Originally, the law provided for grants equal only to one-half the total pension up to $30 per month; in 1939, the maximum was raised to $20.

cent of the pension grant for administering the state system. In order to get the grant, the state plan has to be mandatory on all subdivisions of the state, to provide for financial participation by the state, and to be administered by an agency approved by the federal Social Security Admin-

CRADLE-TO-GRAVE BENEFITS — THEY GROW AND GROW

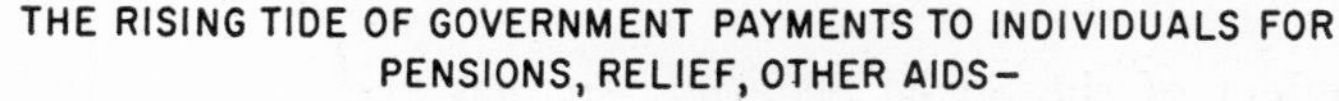

THE RISING TIDE OF GOVERNMENT PAYMENTS TO INDIVIDUALS FOR
PENSIONS, RELIEF, OTHER AIDS—

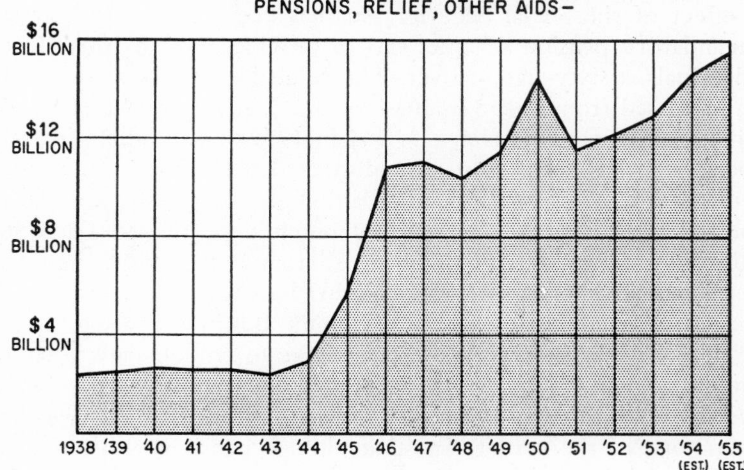

PAYMENTS BEING MADE IN 1954

BY THE FEDERAL GOVERNMENT:

PENSIONS FOR NONVETERANS . . .	$4,600,000,000
PAYMENTS TO VETERANS	$4,300,000,000
UNEMPLOYMENT BENEFITS	$2,200,000,000
OTHER	$ 400,000,000

BY STATE AND LOCAL GOVERNMENTS:

RELIEF	$2,400,000,000
PENSIONS	$ 600,000,000
OTHER	$ 200,000,000

Figure 21–4

Source: Reprinted from the Dec. 10, 1954, issue of *U.S. News & World Report*, an independent weekly news magazine published at Washington. Copyright, 1954, United States News Publishing Corporation.

istration. The state administration, to be approved, is required to allow a fair hearing for any applicant whose pension is denied, to provide for such methods of administration (including, since 1939 those relating to selection, tenure, and rating of personnel) as are found necessary for efficient administration of the plan, and to make such reports to the Social Security Administration as are found desirable by that agency. State plans are further forbidden to place an age limit above sixty-five, to exclude any citizen of the United States, or to fix residence requirements higher than five years in the nine years immediately preceding application for a pension.

The effect of the Social Security Act has been to cause all states to adopt mandatory pension schemes and to provide pensions for all qualified individuals at sixty-five or over. The result has been that the average pension increased from $14.53 in 1934 to $51.45 in 1954 and that the total number of pensioners rose from 235,265 in 1934 to 2.6 million in 1954.[39] The Social Security Act has also caused marked reduction in the residence requirements for pension qualification, although many states are still perhaps too strict in fixing the degree of economic dependency. These states generally use a means test for fixing pension amounts and attempt to set each pension at an amount which, with other income of the pensioner, will make a monthly income close to the maximum. But in estimating the other income of the pensioners, state administrators often calculate what relatives ought to contribute. While this may seem fair, state laws have often been administered so that a real burden is placed on relatives or on pensioners, one of the very things that old-age pensions are designed to prevent. The wisdom of considering any other means than those of the applicant or spouse is questionable.

Except for residence and age requirements, the federal government has little to say about the qualifications of these pensioners. The question of adequacy of the pension is left to the individual states, although amendment in 1939 required that applicants' income be considered. As a result, standards vary considerably from state to state. In 1954 monthly pensions averaged as low as $28.19 in Mississippi (and $7.71 in Puerto Rico) and as high as $81.90 in Connecticut. Of the pension laws now in effect, four average below $30 a month, ten between $30 and $39, eleven between $40 and $49, fourteen between $50 and $59, nine between $60 and $69, and four above $70.[40] Moreover, in some states in which local government units share in the financing of the program, there is a difference in average payments from county to county which is not explainable solely on the basis of living costs.

[39] *Annual Report of the Department of Health, Education, and Welfare, 1954* (1955), pp. 39–41. Note that, in addition, there were some 2.4 million pensioners under the old-age insurance program.

[40] *Ibid.*, p. 39.

RETIREMENT PROVISIONS OF THE SOCIAL SECURITY ACT

To supplement and eventually largely to replace straight state pensions, the federal government provided in the Social Security Act of 1935 for a national system of contributory retirement benefits. Strictly speaking, the plan does not provide for direct connection between contributions and benefits and does not represent a contractual system of retirement insurance. The law is set up in two parts, one levying taxes which go into general funds, and the other providing benefits under yearly appropriation laws. However, since this separation was made primarily to ensure constitutionality, and since amendment in 1939 provided for automatic annual appropriations equal to tax revenues, the law may be regarded as a compulsory and contributory retirement-insurance scheme.

Coverage. With certain exceptions which have been narrowed by successive amendments, the Social Security Act covers most employed and self-employed persons in the United States. Amendments between 1950 and 1954 extended available coverage from 35 million to approximately 58 million individuals, including a large number of self-employed persons and others who may accept coverage on a voluntary basis.

To be covered a self-employed person must make at least $400 a year. Some self-employed, such as physicians, dentists, veterinarians, and lawyers, are still excepted. Agricultural workers must earn at least $100 a year or more from the same employer to be eligible. Therefore, many casual agricultural workers, like seasonal and migratory workers, who are probably in greater need of social insurance than the regularly employed, are not yet covered. Domestic workers must be employed by any household employer in a given quarter with wages of at least $50 to be included. Obviously, the administrative problem in collecting taxes from such casual workers and their employers is extraordinarily great.

Not all the new coverage is compulsory. Ministers and employees of nonprofit organizations and state and local governments are subject to voluntary coverage. Approval of a majority of the employees of these organizations is needed before coverage is extended.

Method of financing. The original act provided for income taxes on employees and excise taxes on employers of 1 per cent for each (total 2 per cent) on wages paid in any calendar year up to $3,000. This rate was to increase in succeeding years, but Congress refused to allow the scheduled increases to go into effect, so Congress provided for an entirely new schedule. The income tax on employees in 1955 was 2 per cent on all wages and salaries up to $4,200. In 1960, this rate will rise to 2½ per cent, and to 4 per cent in 1975. An equivalent excise tax is levied on employers. For self-employed persons, since there is no matching amount, the income tax runs somewhat higher. In 1955 self-employed persons paid

Figure 21–5

Source: Adapted from the Sept. 3, 1954, issue of *U.S. News & World Report*, an independent weekly news magazine published at Washington. Copyright, 1954, United States News Publishing Corporation.

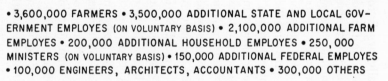

3 per cent on their earnings up to $4,200; by 1975 this rate will rise to 6 per cent.

These taxes are paid into the general funds of the United States and then appropriated for benefit purposes. In 1939 an old age and survivors trust fund was established to which the tax receipts are automatically appropriated. This trust fund must be invested in bonds of the United States or bonds fully guaranteed by it.

Retirement benefits. Retirement benefits are not paid to every fully insured person as soon as he reaches his sixty-fifth birthday. Because benefits are a partial replacement for loss of earnings, they are payable only when a fully insured person retires from covered employment, or after he reaches seventy-two. To become "fully insured" a person must meet certain requirements as to previous employment.[41] A worker must have credit for (1) forty quarters of coverage; or (2) one-half the number of quarters since 1950 until his retirement or death, subject to a minimum of six quarters of coverage; or (3) *all* the quarters elapsing after 1954 and before mid-1956 or (if later) before the quarter in which he retires or dies, subject to a minimum of six quarters of coverage.

The amount of retirement benefits that a fully insured person receives is computed by reference to a basic sum, called "primary insurance amount." Under the 1954 formula the primary insurance amount consists of two elements: 55 per cent of the first $110 of the average monthly wage or self-employment earnings, plus 20 per cent of the next $240 of the average wage or self-employed earnings. Thus, a worker who received an average monthly wage in covered employment of $350 would receive monthly retirement benefits of $60.50 plus $48, or $108.50.

The 1954 amendment also established a "dropout rule" which permits, in figuring "average monthly earnings," the dropping out of up to four years of the work record. This will allow leaving out of computation as many as four years in which the person may not have been working or may have been earning low pay or may have been working in employment not covered by social security. Those who show a work record of five or more years will be permitted to drop out as many as five years. If, however, the remaining months after the "dropout" are less than eighteen, the total earnings must be divided by 18 to arrive at the monthly average.

A person under seventy-two years of age can earn as much as $1,200 in a year in a covered employment without losing old age and survivors benefits. A person under seventy-two whose annual earnings exceed $1,200 in a covered employment but do not exceed $2,080 will lose monthly benefits depending on the amount earned within those two

[41] The Social Security Act also provides for a "currently insured status" which depends upon a generally shorter but more recent coverage than the "fully insured status."

figures. A person who earns more than $2,080 annually will not be entitled to any social-security payment for that year. After the age of seventy-two an insured person receives full benefits regardless of his income.

Family benefits. Benefits are also provided for wives (or husbands) reaching the age of sixty-five during the life of the retired worker, for the wife of a retired worker if she cares for a dependent child (under eighteen), and for dependent children of a retired worker. Upon the death of an insured worker, the widow (or widower) and dependent children receive benefits or, if no widow or child is entitled to benefits, dependent parents over sixty-five receive them.

If a worker retires he receives the primary insurance amount. When his wife reaches the age of sixty-five, she receives a supplementary benefit equal to one-half of the worker's benefit,[42] and dependent children under eighteen get a like amount.

If a worker dies either before or after retirement, benefits are provided for survivors. If an insured worker leaves no children, his widow receives benefits at the age of sixty-five equal to three-fourths of the primary insurance amount. If an insured worker leaves a widow with one or more dependent children in her care, she immediately receives a benefit equal to three-fourths of her husband's benefit,[43] plus a like amount for the first dependent child. If there is more than one dependent child, each child receives one-half the primary insurance amount plus one-fourth of such amount divided by the number of children.[44] These benefits remain the same until the children reach eighteen or leave school to go to work, or the widow remarries. Each parent who was dependent upon an insured worker when he died is eligible to receive an amount equal to three-fourths of the primary insurance amount, if the worker did not leave a widow or dependent children. Lump-sum payments are made to relatives paying burial expenses, or under certain conditions, to friends who do so. In 1955, these lump-sum payments amounted to three times the primary insurance amount.

The benefit provisions of the amended Social Security Act indicate an attempt to protect the whole family, rather than the individual, from the insecurity of old age or the loss of the family provider. Each amendment also strengthens the principle that the lower-paid workers should draw relatively higher allowances than the higher-paid, so that a certain minimum necessary for subsistence can be paid to every insured worker. A fully insured worker earning an average of $100 per month would receive $55 a month as retirement benefit, while a worker earning twice that much would retire on only $78.50 a month. Furthermore, insured persons

[42] The maximum benefits for a man and wife are $162.80.

[43] The maximum widow's benefit is $81.40 a month.

[44] The maximum for a widow with dependents is $200.

do not receive benefits commensurate with the period over which taxes are paid. The 1950 amendment eliminates length of covered employment as a factor in calculating benefits. This system, therefore, tends to make the cost of insurance to the worker who retires soon much lower than to the one who pays taxes for many years.

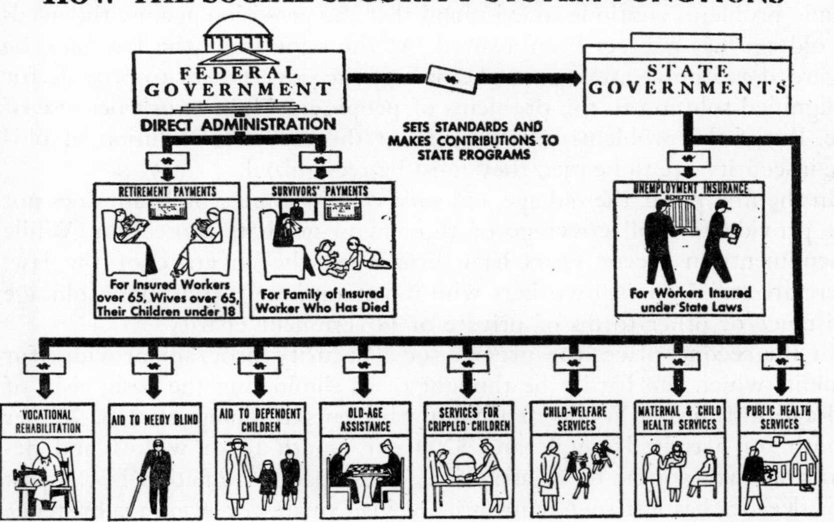

Figure 21–6

CONSTITUTIONALITY OF OLD-AGE ASSISTANCE AND INSURANCE

The power of the state to care for the poor, and hence to pay old-age pensions, has long been held to be proper.[45] Moreover, the power of the national government to aid states in paying old-age pensions has not been seriously questioned.

When the old-age insurance plan of the national government reached the Supreme Court in 1937, the minority view in the railroad retirement case prevailed, and the law was held to be within the constitutional power of Congress.[46] The Court ruled that the tax on payrolls was a proper one and that the power of Congress to tax for the general welfare included the power to spend funds for the general welfare. The majority insisted that the problem of old age was "national in area and dimensions" and that expenditures for old-age insurance were clearly for the general welfare.

[45] See, for example, *Kelly v. Pittsburgh*, 104 U.S. 78 (1881).
[46] *Helvering v. Davis*, 301 U.S. 619 (1937).

OLD-AGE ASSISTANCE AND INSURANCE: CONCLUSIONS

The old-age insurance provisions of the Social Security Act represent a revolutionary change in the concept of the role of government in the United States. Contemplating the virtual solution of most of the problem of old-age insecurity by one piece of legislation, it is no wonder that the original law has been amended many times, that administrative and economic problems continue to exist, and that the provision against the needs of old age has not yet been assured. At the same time, the law may be regarded as a noble attempt on the part of the government to provide for a dignified solution to the problems of people unable to work because of age. But if the problems which confront the successful solution of old-age insecurity are to be met, they must be recognized.

In the first place, the old age and survivors insurance program does not yet provide for full coverage of those who need its protection. While amendments in recent years have broadened the coverage of the law, there are still 5,900,000 workers who must continue to rely upon old-age assistance or other forms of private or government charity.

In the second place, the present social-security program provides for benefits which can hardly be thought of as eliminating the basic risks of old-age insecurity. While maximum payments reaching to $162.75 per month for a retired couple and $200 per month for a widow and dependents may appear to be attractive, the impact of inflation in the past two decades has left such sums grossly inadequate for even a subsistence level of existence. But what is most distressing is that few persons can qualify for the maximums, as is indicated by the fact that the average payment after the 1954 amendment was $59 per month. Thus, there is less real security in the program than is often believed.

At the same time, the retired worker who has a home in which to live or some small outside income from savings may find that his social-security check spells the difference between the indignities of public charity or dependence upon relatives and the dignity of independent, though moderate, subsistence. Moreover, especially since World War II, there has been a tendency in all forms of enterprise to supplement social security with various forms of private pension plans. This development, almost surely given impetus by the concentration on old-age insecurity in the Social Security Act, may well make the difference between intolerably low government-pension benefits and payments necessary for subsistence.

A third and perhaps the most important single problem lies in the economics of financing and supporting even the present inadequate program. Although referred to as insurance and often naïvely believed to be insurance in the usual sense of the term, with actuarially calculated reserves to ensure future payments, the present plan is not such an arrangement.

The original act provided for the establishment of reserves similar to those used by private insurance companies. However, by amendments in 1939 and succeeding years, Congress has held taxes below that level necessary for a reserve to cover risks, although higher than that required for current payments. Thus the present program is a compromise between a reserve program and one based on "pay-as-you-go" principles. For example, by 1954, the Old Age and Survivors Trust Fund held $19 billion in government bonds, and benefits had been paid out to more than 6 million persons. As large as this trust "fund" appears to be, it is only a fraction of the actuarially computed reserve which a private insurance company would have to provide for such a plan.[47]

Tax rates provided in the present law, which reach 8 per cent (for both employees and employers) in 1975, will probably be inadequate to finance the program. For example, one analyst of the problem estimates that there will be some 36 million persons over sixty-five in the United States in the year 2000 and that, if 60 per cent of these persons were pensioners with pension allowances averaging a modest $94 per month, the cost would be more than $24 billion per year.[48] On the other hand, should there be 80 million in the work force with an average monthly taxable wage of $250, the tax collected at the 8 per cent rate would be less than $21 billion. At an average taxable wage of $300, the collections would exceed $23 billion.

However, it is probable that some of the dire financial predictions of the financial impact of the old-age insurance program may be softened by the tendency of individuals not to retire, a tendency which seems reasonable in view of the smallness of the benefits, and also by the almost certain march of continued inflation which will always tend to keep payrolls and tax income higher than benefits. Nevertheless, should benefits be increased to a size which would give minimum subsistence to retired persons, the problem would appear to become almost unmanageable. If the average pension were assumed to be raised to $250 per month, application of this benefit level to the estimates given for the year 2000 would disclose a cost of more than $64 billion if 60 per cent of those over sixty-five retired and received this benefit and $32 billion if only 30 per cent retired.

Whether social-security benefits can be maintained at a level to pay

[47] This has been variously estimated, the difficulty of an exact estimate being due to such unknowns as the number of persons over age sixty-five who will continue to work rather than to take social security, the level of wages, and the changes which continue to be made in coverage and benefit provisions.

[48] Matteson, *op. cit.*, p. 90. The author comes to the conclusion that, should 60 per cent of the eligible individuals retire on social security, the cost would be 17 per cent of payrolls.

OLD-AGE PENSIONS —UNDER TWO KINDS OF PLANS

HERE'S ONE EXAMPLE:

UNDER SOCIAL SECURITY—

EMPLOYE, SINGLE, HAS BEEN "COVERED" SINCE SYSTEM STARTED IN 1937. HE WILL BE 65 AND ELIGIBLE TO RETIRE ON HIS PENSION IN JANUARY, 1957.

HIS MONTHLY OLD-AGE PENSION CHECK: . . . . . $ 108.50

WHAT PENSION COST HIM, IN PAY-ROLL TAXES: . . . . . $ 837

(NOTE: EMPLOYER ALSO PAYS $837, MAKING TOTAL TAXES $1,674.)

UNDER A PRIVATE PLAN—

EMPLOYE BOUGHT IN 1937 AN ANNUITY TO START PAYING OFF IN JANUARY, 1957, WHEN HE REACHES AGE 65.

HIS MONTHLY OLD-AGE ANNUITY CHECK: $108.50

WHAT ANNUITY COST HIM, IN PREMIUMS: $8,200

HERE'S ANOTHER EXAMPLE:

UNDER SOCIAL SECURITY—

FARMER, SINGLE, EARNING MORE THAN $4,200 A YEAR, ENTERS SYSTEM JAN. 1, 1955, AT AGE 63½. HE WILL RETIRE AT AGE 65 IN MID-1956.

HIS MONTHLY OLD-AGE PENSION CHECK: . . . . . $ 108.50

WHAT PENSION COST HIM, IN SELF-EMPLOYMENT TAXES: . . $189

UNDER A PRIVATE PLAN—

FARMER, AT AGE 63½, BUYS LIFETIME ANNUITY, STARTS DRAWING BENEFITS AT AGE 65.

HIS MONTHLY ANNUITY CHECK: $108.50

WHAT ANNUITY COST HIM, IN PREMIUMS: $16,200

Figure 21–7

Source: Reprinted from the Sept. 3, 1954, issue of *U.S. News & World Report*, an independent weekly news magazine published at Washington. Copyright, 1954, United States Publishing Corporation.

bare subsistence and to realize the hopes of the millions of workers who place their future risks against the hazards of old age in the program is difficult to say. It is probable that this program will give rise to important tax and political problems in the future, and one cannot be too sure that the larger number of younger workers will be willing to assume the heavy tax load necessary to support a reasonable retirement pay for those over sixty-five. Of course, private pension plans of various sorts may serve so to supplement social security as to keep the government-financed benefits down in the future, but the slight impact of these plans and their inability to preserve investment from the eroding effects of inflation diminish the hope in this direction.

One of the difficult problems of the present is that old-age benefits seem to be so generous to those who have recently retired. This is indeed the case. The present social-security program clearly favors the older and the lower-paid worker. Many individuals have retired at minimum allowances with negligible tax costs. Others have received relatively generous allowances at low costs. A couple retiring in 1954 at the age of sixty-five can receive a pension of $162.75 per month, which has a value of nearly $28,000 at current annuity rates, and yet not have paid in more than approximately $600 in taxes since 1937. This kind of experience can lead the unthinking to believe that the old-age insurance plan is a tremendous bargain for all. Yet a young worker entering the plan might well find that, had he invested his money in a good private plan, the benefits would exceed those promised under the present social-security program.

Selected References

Black, S. Bruce, "The Anomalies of Workmen's Compensation," 7 *Industrial and Labor Relations Review* 43–50 (October, 1953).

Burns, Eveline M., *The American Social Security System.* Boston: Houghton Mifflin Company, 1949.

Dodd, Walter F., *Administration of Workmen's Compensation.* New York: The Commonwealth Fund, 1936.

Falk, J. S., *Insurance against Sickness: A Study of Health Insurance.* New York: Doubleday & Company, Inc., 1936.

Gagliardo, Domenico, *American Social Insurance.* New York: Harper & Brothers, 1949.

Haber, William, and Wilbur J. Cohen (eds.), *Readings in Social Insurance.* New York: Prentice-Hall, Inc., 1948.

Harris, Seymour E., *Economics of Social Security.* New York: McGraw-Hill Book Company, Inc., 1941.

Heinrich, H. W., *Industrial Accident Prevention,* 3d ed. New York: McGraw-Hill Book Company, Inc., 1950.

Malisott, Harry, "The Emergence of Unemployment Compensation," 54

Political Science Quarterly 237–258, 391–420, 577–599 (June, September, December, 1939).

Manning, Lucy, and N. Diamond, *State Child-labor Standards*. Bureau of Labor Standards, 1949.

Meriam, Lewis, *Relief and Social Security*. Washington, D.C.: Brookings Institution, 1946.

Millis, H. A., and R. E. Montgomery, *Labor's Risks and Social Insurance*, Vol. II of *The Economics of Labor*. New York: McGraw-Hill Book Company, Inc., 1938.

Perlman, Jacob, "Changing Trends under Old-age and Survivors Insurance, 1935–1950," 4 *Industrial and Labor Relations Review* 173–186 (January, 1951).

———, "The Federal Social Security Programs," 70 *Monthly Labor Review* 1–8 (January, 1950).

Pollack, Jerome, "A Policy Decision for Workmen's Compensation," 7 *Industrial and Labor Relations Review* 51–62 (October, 1953).

Reede, Arthur H., *Adequacy of Workmen's Compensation*. Cambridge, Mass.: Harvard University Press, 1947.

Reticker, Ruth, "The Financing of Unemployment Insurance," 70 *Monthly Labor Review* 257–262 (March, 1950).

Riesenfeld, Stefan A., and Richard C. Maxwell, *Modern Social Legislation*. Brooklyn: The Foundation Press, Inc., 1950.

Ross, James S., *The National Health Service in Great Britain*. New York: Oxford University Press, 1952.

Sinai, Nathan, Odin Anderson, and Melvin Dollar, *Health Insurance in the United States*. New York: The Commonwealth Fund, 1946.

Wandel, William H., "Insurance against Unemployment in the United States," 70 *Monthly Labor Review* 9–13 (January, 1950).

22

REGULATION OF LABOR-MANAGEMENT RELATIONS

Labor has sought to improve its bargaining position so that it may obtain better working conditions and avoid some of the risks which imperil its standard of living. The individual worker cannot afford to bargain on equal terms with an individual employer, since he generally lacks the resources with which to support himself and his family if he fails to make a contract. The employee, acting alone, can seldom place any pressure upon the employer to modify the wage or other conditions of work, because often his only alternative to employment at the terms offered is unemployment. Moreover, individual workers have often been afraid to make complaints to employers for fear of being regarded as trouble-makers and being discharged. The individual out of work is also in a poor bargaining position. He may not always know where a market exists for his labor, and he may not know what are fair and reasonable terms upon which to sell it.

Workers long have resorted to collective means to increase their bargaining power.[1] Trade unions have been organized in crafts and in industries. These organizations have generally sought a large membership so that the employer may be obliged to deal with a unified front. They have also become mediums through which laborers have been able to impress their views upon legislators and leaders in government.

Government is now dedicated to the policy of encouraging collective bargaining as a solution to the traditional conflict between labor and management. This encouragement has taken the form of legislation drawn to protect labor in the right of organizing and bargaining, without hindrance by management, through representatives chosen by the workers. This policy has been extended in recent years to provide for protection of management, as well as labor, from the abuses of collective bargaining. It has meant that virtually all employers must consider the rights of or-

[1] For an extensive treatment of union growth, see John R. Commons, David J. Saposs, and others, *History of Labour in the United States* (New York: The Macmillan Company, 1926–1935), 4 vols.

ganized labor in dealing with employees and that unions must recognize certain rights of individual employees and employers.

The Theory and Justification of Collective Bargaining

Collective bargaining is simply a method by which a group decision is reached. Under such an all-inclusive definition, the members of a family reaching an agreement about the kind of car to buy, legislators drafting a bill, or diplomats negotiating a treaty are all bargaining collectively. But as the words have come to be used, the term "collective bargaining" applies almost exclusively to relations between working people, or their representatives, and those who employ them.

Collective bargaining, therefore, is a process of give-and-take. The union has something to offer which the employer needs—labor. The employer has something which workingmen need—jobs. Each party in the industrial bargain uses its power to press for acceptable terms. Labor may withhold its work by striking or engaging in other forms of concerted action; management may withhold the jobs at the terms demanded by labor. The outcome is a contract acceptable to both parties. In actual practice the economic weapons of both labor and management are rarely used relative to the number of contracts that are successfully concluded without resort to the strike, lockout, boycott, slowdown, and the like. Unfortunately, the average citizen knows more about the breakdown of collective bargaining machinery than he does about the many cases where it works well to preserve industrial stability.

An obvious justification for collective bargaining is that peaceful discussion has been substituted for industrial conflict. But force is not the only underlying element in collective bargaining. If collective bargaining is regarded merely as a substitute for force, whatever agreement is reached is simply a truce. However, each side needs the other. As S. T. Williamson points out, the around-the-table process reconciles the conflicting interests of two sides which cannot get along without each other. The resulting agreement is actually a treaty and even an alliance.[2]

Another justification for collective bargaining is found in the weak economic position of the individual laborer. This lack of "withholding" power often means that, while there may be real and effective competition between individual laborers, bargaining between the buyer and seller of labor service may be virtually nonexistent. If it can be assumed that

[2] *Trends in Collective Bargaining: A Summary of Recent Experience* (New York: The Twentieth Century Fund, Inc., 1945), p. 2. See pp. 218–222, for a discussion of the functions and advantages of collective bargaining. See also George W. Taylor, *Government Regulation of Industrial Relations* (New York: Prentice-Hall, Inc., 1948), pp. 13–18.

effective bargaining is an important element in the American system of capitalism and is significant as a goad to efficiency in production, low prices, and a high standard of living, the public interest in effective collective bargaining is clear. Without it, sellers of labor become an easy prey to unfair and inefficient employers of labor. The result may very well be that the economic system will not function as efficiently as might be desired. A system of individual bargaining between buyers and sellers of labor is practically a system of no bargaining.

Collective bargaining has other advantages for society. Strong unions and fair collective contracts make for greater stability in labor supply, tend to reduce sporadic stoppage of work, and make it possible for employers to calculate their future labor costs more accurately, with resultant curtailing of risks in future production. Through the relative standardization of labor costs, employers tend to be placed on a fairer competitive level. From a political and social point of view, collective bargaining may be in the public interest. Discontent of workers over the results of the labor bargain may be lessened. Jobs may be made more secure, and exploitation of labor may be reduced. Associations of workmen large enough to have some voice in the decisions of industry may raise the morale of labor and introduce a higher sense of self-respect.

On the other hand, collective bargaining may lead to results not altogether in the public interest. Organizations of employees may become so strong as to be able to dictate business policies. Laborers may insist upon terms so high as to increase the cost of production and limit output. If costs are increased too much, or output unduly restricted, the public pays a higher price for goods and services than may be economically justifiable. Labor organizations may restrict membership and adopt monopolistic policies, with harmful effects upon the consuming public similar to those which have made monopolies of capital feared. Combination of labor presents many of the same problems and hazards that combination of capital has shown.

Restraints on Labor

The history of industrial relations reveals that many governmental restraints have been placed from time to time on the right of workers to organize and bargain collectively. These have varied from the application of the common-law doctrine of conspiracy and the use of the injunction to prevent irreparable damage following from union action to specific legislation designed to limit or define the activities of unions. While most of these restraints have been superseded by modern labor-management-relations legislation, some of them are still in effect, and an analysis of the major restraints is advisable to appreciate the present program of government controls in the industrial-relations field.[3]

THE CONSPIRACY DOCTRINE

Beginning with the famous Philadelphia Cordwainers' case of 1806, America's first labor case, the doctrine evolved that if as few as two persons working for the same person combined their efforts to improve their working conditions they were engaging in a conspiracy and guilty of a misdemeanor. The very act of combining was a crime, even if no other action had been committed by the group. In a number of cases prior to 1842 workers were fined or imprisoned for nothing more than joining a union.[4]

In 1842 the burden of conspiracy was largely lifted from the shoulders of organized labor. In that year the highest court of Massachusetts ruled that a combination seeking to raise wages was not unlawful per se.[5] This case did not abolish the common-law doctrine of criminal conspiracy, but it never again played a prominent part in judicial control of labor unions. Some cases of criminal conspiracy arose even after the War between the States, but they became increasingly rare as a more effective means of control was discovered.

THE LABOR INJUNCTION

The new device to limit unions came into use in the 1880s. Employers who felt that a strike or other form of concerted action endangered their property requested the courts to issue an injunction, a writ in equity designed to prevent irreparable harm or injury before it has occurred.

The usual procedure in granting a labor injunction was for the employer to present a formal complaint to the appropriate judge, detailing the activities which threatened his property with irreparable damage. Since the judges of that day were likely to be sympathetic to employers, they usually issued a temporary restraining order requiring all parties to maintain the *status quo*, which meant that the union had to stop activities tending to endanger the property of the employer. Frequently these orders were issued without any notice or hearing to the union or its officials. Often the actions forbidden were exceedingly vague, and the orders were

[3] For an extensive discussion of the legal aspects of labor activity, see Harry A. Millis and Royal E. Montgomery, *Organized Labor*, vol. III of *The Economics of Labor* (New York: McGraw-Hill Book Company, Inc., 1945), chaps. 11, 12; and Charles O. Gregory, *Labor and the Law* (New York: W. W. Norton & Company, Inc., 1946).

[4] John R. Commons and E. A. Gilmore, *Documentary History of American Industrial Society* (Glendale, Calif.: Arthur H. Clark Company, 1910), vol. III, p. 19.

[5] *Commonwealth v. Hunt*, 4 Metc. 111 (1842).

directed to general groups so that it was difficult to tell who was affected.

Eventually the case might go to trial to determine whether a temporary or permanent injunction should be allowed. During all this procedure, which often lasted many months, the temporary restraining order remained in effect. Both sides were represented at the trial, which was held before a judge without a jury. Many judges got into the habit of making findings of threatened violence whether or not it existed. Often the judges signing these injunctions did not draft them personally but permitted counsel for the complaining employers to prepare them instead.

If the strike continued in the face of either the temporary restraining order or the injunction, the workers were fined or jailed for contempt of court. These contempt cases were almost always tried in the court of the judge who had issued the injunction. Therefore, either the restraining order, the injunction, or the contempt action broke the back of the strike.[6]

THE ANTITRUST LAWS

The federal government did almost nothing to help or hinder organized labor in the first 100 years of this country's existence.[7] It is ironical that the basis for the most extensive regulation of labor by the federal government was found in a law that was directed primarily against the monopolistic practices of business.

Whether Congress intended the Sherman Act to cover the activities of organized labor is still a much-debated question. Senator Sherman maintained that labor was not included and argued against an amendment specifically exempting labor on the ground that it was unnecessary.[8] However, the courts interpreted the law differently. In its early history, the

[6] While the number of injunctions which have been issued against labor cannot be ascertained accurately, Witte found records in 1931 of 508 cases in federal courts and 1,364 cases in state courts where injunctions had been issued at the instigation of employers. See E. E. Witte, *The Government in Labor Disputes* (New York: McGraw-Hill Book Company, Inc., 1932), pp. 84–85. For a detailed discussion and criticism of the labor injunction, see Felix Frankfurter and N. Greene, *The Labor Injunction* (New York: The Macmillan Company, 1930).

[7] Almost the only assistance that can be noted was the creation in 1884 of the Bureau of Labor in the Department of Interior. Its function was solely to gather information concerning wages and hours of employment and means of promoting labor's prosperity. It had no regulatory function. In 1888, the Bureau was made an independent establishment with the name of "department," but it was not of Cabinet rank. The Department of Commerce and Labor with Cabinet rank was formed in 1903, and the separate Department of Labor in 1913.

[8] See Edward Berman, *Labor and the Sherman Act* (New York: Harper & Brothers, 1930).

Act was invoked against labor as frequently as it was used against business trusts and restraints of trade. In 1908, the Supreme Court specifically upheld its application to labor activities in the famous Danbury Hatters' Case.[9]

Seeking to eliminate this obstacle from its path, labor succeeded in having certain provisions incorporated in the Clayton Act of 1914, an amendment to the Sherman Act designed to improve its effectiveness against business combinations. Sections 6 and 20 of this act were hailed as labor's "Magna Charta." The labor of human beings was declared not to be a commodity or article of commerce. Section 6 further stated that the antitrust laws should not be construed to forbid the existence of labor organizations, or to forbid their members from "lawfully carrying out the legitimate objects thereof." Section 20 prohibited the federal courts from issuing labor injunctions except to prevent irreparable injury to property or a property right.

In practice, these provisions changed nothing. Moreover, the Clayton Act made injunctions available not only to government but also to private parties as well.[10] Labor soon found this out. In attempting to organize the Duplex Printing Press Company, a machinists' union called a strike against a manufacturer and attempted a secondary boycott by inducing printers not to use presses manufactured by the Duplex Company and by urging truckers not to haul them. The Supreme Court held that it was not the intention of Congress to legalize the secondary boycott. All the Clayton Act did was to enact into law existing practice. Since the secondary boycott was illegal before 1914, it was still illegal after 1914. Therefore, the Clayton Act did not prevent the issuance of an injunction against the machinists' union because only the "lawful" and "legitimate" actions of unions were exempt from the antitrust laws.[11] The Court reaffirmed the issuance of an injunction against a secondary boycott in the Bedford Cut Stone case.[12] In another leading case, the Supreme Court found that an attempt by coal miners to hinder the production and distribution of nonunion coal was an unlawful interference with interstate commerce.[13]

Thus, the effect of the Clayton Act, in spite of the apparent intention to remove organized labor from the coverage of the antitrust laws, was to grant antiunion employers another reason for wielding the injunction as well as to permit large damage suits against unions for engaging in union practices generally believed to be normal.

[9] *Loewe v. Lawlor*, 208 U.S. 274 (1908).

[10] Such actions soon became more numerous than criminal prosecutions, damage suits, and government applications for labor injunctions combined.

[11] *Duplex Printing Press Co. v. Deering*, 254 U.S. 443 (1921).

[12] *Bedford Cut Stone Co. v. Journeymen Stone Cutters' Assn.*, 274 U.S. 37 (1927).

[13] *Coronado Coal Co. v. United Mine Workers of America*, 268 U.S. 295 (1925).

To prevent the abuse of labor injunctions by federal courts, Congress passed the Norris–La Guardia Anti-injunction Act in 1932.[14] The law did not outlaw the labor injunction. But it did enumerate acts which no federal court has jurisdiction to restrain, and it made certain specific findings and court procedures necessary before any temporary or permanent injunction might be issued. Other changes were made in contempt proceedings, the issuance of temporary restraining orders, and the liability of union officers.

The major cases arising under the Norris–La Guardia Act have been concerned with its interpretation rather than its constitutionality. Not until 1938 did the Supreme Court rule on the constitutionality of the Act.[15] The court simply held: "There can be no question of the powers of Congress . . . to define and limit the jurisdiction of the inferior courts of the United States."

After many years of being subject to the federal antitrust laws, labor received virtual liberation from these laws by a changed Supreme Court in 1940. During the course of a sit-down strike a union changed the locks on the plant doors of a company, management was not permitted to enter the plant or to remove stock to fill orders on its books, and considerable damage was done to machines. The District Court applied the antitrust laws and assessed triple damages, but the Circuit Court of Appeals reversed this judgment and was affirmed in so doing by the Supreme Court.[16] In spite of the fact that the Court recognized that the strike was conducted by illegal means, damages were not awarded because the Court felt that substantial restrictions on interstate commerce had not been proved and that the antitrust laws were not intended to apply to such a labor dispute.

Moreover, in 1941, the Supreme Court ruled that the original antitrust law had been modified in its application to labor by both the Clayton and Norris Acts.[17] The Court said: "Whether trade union conduct constitutes a violation of the Sherman Law is to be determined only by reading the Sherman Law and Section 20 of the Clayton Act and the Norris–La Guardia Act as a harmonizing text of outlawry of labor conduct." The Court took judicial notice of the desire of Congress to remove labor

[14] Since the Norris–La Guardia Act does not affect the issuance of injunctions in state courts, organized labor pushed for state anti-injunction legislation also. By 1940, approximately half the states had such laws, most of which followed the federal law. However, a reaction against labor soon set in, and several of these laws were modified to impair their value as anti-injunction measures. By 1948, only sixteen states had effective anti-injunction legislation on the books. In those states without anti-injunction laws, injunctions may be issued as freely as ever by state courts.

[15] *Lauf v. E. G. Shinner & Co.*, 303 U.S. 323 (1938).

[16] *Apex Hosiery Co. v. Leader*, 310 U.S. 469 (1940).

[17] *United States v. Hutcheson*, 312 U.S. 219 (1941)

disputes from the realm of federal government restrictions by the Norris–La Guardia Act and concluded that such legislation indicated that Congress desired a policy less restrictive of union actions.

These decisions do not mean that organized labor is entirely exempted from the Sherman Act. In 1945, the Supreme Court upheld a prosecution of certain union practices under the Act. In this case [18] a union had agreements with electrical manufacturers and contractors in the New York metropolitan area. The contractors bought only from local manufacturers who had closed-shop contract agreements with the union, and the manufacturers also agreed to supply only those contractors who had such agreements with the union. The system expanded until it became industry-wide, involving price and market control as well as control over wages and hours. These practices were held to be a restraint of trade, and the fact that a union was a party to the combination did not make the arrangement any the less a violation of the Act.

However, an illustration of the exclusion of purely labor activity from the antitrust laws occurred on the same day, when the Supreme Court refused to permit prosecution of a union under the Sherman Act for virtually forcing a trucker out of business. The union refused to sign a contract with an independent trucker with whom it had a long-standing grudge and prohibited its members from working for him. Since the union had agreements with customers of the truckers in the area to the effect that they should patronize only truckers who had contracts with the union, this trucker could get no business. Yet the Supreme Court saw no violation of the Sherman Act in this case.[19]

Thus, by mid-1940 the courts had gone a long way toward freeing unions from prosecution under the Sherman Act. The Taft-Hartley Act, however, altered labor law by outlawing specific practices which the courts were no longer regarding as antitrust violations and once again made the injunction available for restraining many union activities.

Protection of Collective Bargaining Prior to 1935

Government guarantee of the right to organize and bargaining collectively is the culmination of a long development in public policy that began with suppression, passed through toleration, then acceptance, and finally became one of encouragement. Public labor policy was slow in evolving. Each stage of development produced appropriate legislation on both the state and federal level.

[18] *Allen-Bradley Co. v. International Brotherhood of Electrical Workers,* 325 U.S. 797 (1945).

[19] *Hunt v. Crumboch,* 325 U.S. 821 (1945).

STATE ACTION

In the states the trend was to deprive employers of some of their antiunion weapons and to limit the judicial power to regulate union activities. Between 1892 and 1921 legislatures in various states passed laws limiting the issuance of injunctions in labor disputes, exempting unions from conspiracy laws and antitrust laws, legalizing peaceful picketing, and outlawing such antiunion devices as discrimination, black-listing, and yellow-dog contracts.[20] Most of these early state laws were either declared unconstitutional or rendered meaningless by the courts. Beginning in 1929, renewed state efforts to protect the right to organize were more favorably received by the courts.[21]

World War I marked a turning point for the role of the federal government in industrial relations. With the outcome of the war depending heavily upon uninterrupted production, the War Labor Board was established to intervene in disputes which might lead to strikes and other work stoppages and to ease the strain upon mediation machinery. The Board laid down a policy which recognized the right of unions to organize and bargain collectively. Employers were warned against preventing employees from joining unions, or discriminating against union members; and employees were warned against coercing fellow workers into joining unions, or coercing employers into dealing with unions. Since this policy was justified on the basis of the war powers, it was abandoned at the end of hostilities.

RAILWAY LABOR ACT OF 1926

The first permanent peacetime law to establish collective bargaining as the accepted device for conducting labor-management relations, and one which has served as a pattern for modern labor legislation, was restricted to one industry only, the railroad industry. Congress took this important step in 1926 when it enacted the Railway Labor Act. The government guaranteed the right of railway workers to organize into unions of their own choosing and to bargain collectively with management free from any interference or coercion. If necessary, elections were to be held, under government supervision, to determine the bargaining agent, and by amendment in 1934, the employer was clearly obligated to negotiate with the designated agent.

In 1930, the Supreme Court held that a railroad could be enjoined from

[20] A yellow-dog contract is one made by an employer with an employee under which the employee agrees, as a condition for employment, to refrain from joining an independent labor union while he is employed.

[21] Charles C. Killingsworth, *State Labor Relations Acts: A Study of Public Policy* (Chicago: University of Chicago Press, 1948), pp. 10–11.

establishing a company union and coercing its employees by threats of discharge to give up their membership in unions of their own choosing and join the new organization.[22] Without specifically overruling the Adair case of 1908, which had permitted the railroads to discharge employees for union membership, this decision established a new precedent that was more favorable to unions.

SECTION 7A OF NATIONAL INDUSTRIAL RECOVERY ACT

The National Industrial Recovery Act was a spectacular effort to cope with the unemployment, declining standard of living, and insecurity of the Great Depression. Section 7a of this statute provided that every code drawn up under the provisions of the law should contain a guarantee of the right to bargain collectively. This protection of organized labor was a necessary corollary to the provisions of the act which relaxed the antitrust laws to permit agreements concerning fair competition.

No agency was provided for in the original law to enforce Section 7a. However, President Roosevelt created a National Labor Board in 1933, which was later formalized by Executive order. The following year Congress authorized the President to establish a National Labor Relations Board. Both boards combined the function of mediating disputes with that of enforcing the guarantee of collective bargaining. But since the boards had no means of requiring employers to bargain collectively other than withdrawing the Blue Eagle—the symbol of compliance—the policy was largely a failure. When the National Industrial Recovery Act was declared unconstitutional in 1935,[23] this first effort to establish collective bargaining as a national labor policy by law came to an end. The value of section 7a was that the experiences of the boards which had to administer this policy were useful to Congress when it came to consider a longer-range policy, and many of these experiences were reflected in the National Labor Relations Act.[24] The section was also in a very real sense a precursor to the National Labor Relations Act, for this, like other portions of the Recovery Act program, furnished the basis for a new law reconstructing this part of the defunct National Industrial Recovery Act.

The National Labor Relations Act, 1935

In 1935, Congress enacted the National Labor Relations Act, one of the most controversial laws in recent times. Based on the assumption that

[22] *Texas & New Orleans Railway Co. v. Brotherhood of Railway and Steamship Clerks*, 281 U.S. 548 (1930).

[23] *Schechter Poultry Corp. v. United States*, 295 U.S. 495 (1935).

[24] See Harry A. Millis and E. C. Brown, *From the Wagner Act to Taft-Hartley* (Chicago: University of Chicago Press, 1950), p. 26.

collective bargaining is the best method of conducting industrial relations, the Act guaranteed workers the right to organize and bargain collectively through representatives of their choosing. Since the Act is limited in its objective to protecting this right, the law did not cover all aspects of industrial relations. Even conciliation and mediation activities were outside the scope of the law, on the theory that industrial disputes should be settled through collective bargaining.

GENERAL PROVISIONS

To make its guarantee effective, Congress listed five "unfair practices" which employers were prohibited from committing:

1. Interfering with employees in the exercise of their right to organize, bargain collectively, or engage in concerted action.
2. Dominating or interfering with labor organizations, or contributing financial or other support to them (a ban on company unions).
3. Discriminating against workers in hiring or firing because of union membership.
4. Discriminating against an employee because he filed charges or gave testimony under the Act.
5. Refusing to bargain collectively with properly qualified representatives of employees.

To enforce the Act, also known as the Wagner Act, the law created the National Labor Relations Board, an agency of three members appointed by the President with the consent of the Senate. The scope of the Board's jurisdiction was broad, applying to matters "affecting commerce," that is, to matters by which the free flow of interstate or foreign commerce might be obstructed, burdened, or impeded.[25] It is worth noting, however, that the Wagner Act, like its successor the Taft-Hartley Act, did not apply to railroads or airlines, since these carriers are covered by the Railway Labor Act.

The Board was entrusted with two main tasks: (1) aiding in the determination of proper bargaining agents for organized employees, and (2) protecting employees against the specified unfair labor practices of employers.

DETERMINATION OF BARGAINING AGENTS

The Wagner Act provided that a majority of the employees in a unit appropriate for collective bargaining may select representatives who should be exclusive bargaining agents for employees in such units, except that any other group or individual might present grievances to an employer. The Board was authorized to determine whether the employer

[25] Exempted from the law were agricultural workers, domestic workers in a home, and individuals employed by a parent or spouse.

unit, a plant unit, a craft unit, or some other unit was the appropriate grouping of employees to ensure full bargaining rights. Furthermore, the Board was authorized to investigate any controversy respecting the proper representatives of employees and to certify, after election or other suitable method, the names of representatives designated by employees.

The greatest portion of the case work of the National Labor Relations Board under the Wagner Act has been concerned with the problem of representation.[26] One of the most difficult problems facing the Board was the determination of the proper bargaining unit. At times the Board has set up large plant units; at other times, it has found craft units to be appropriate; and sometimes it has broken off strong craft units from the rest of an industrial plant and set up several divisions of employees as appropriate units. Since the unions affiliated with the American Federation of Labor have generally been organized along craft lines and those affiliated with the Congress of Industrial Organizations have tended to follow industrial or plant organization, the Board has been necessarily thrust into the dispute between these two rival factions. Although the craft-versus-industrial-union controversy is not identical with the struggle between the American Federation of Labor and the Congress of Industrial Organizations, since these labor groups were not developed completely along either craft or industrial union lines, in given cases the determination of the appropriate unit has had much to do with the selection of the actual union—or so it has been charged. Where the Board has felt that "evenly balanced factors" made either unit appropriate, it has, since 1937, referred the question of an appropriate bargaining unit to the employees.[27]

Once the appropriate unit is determined, the Board may be called upon to investigate and certify the proper representatives for it. The Board certifies the representatives either after an election or after a cross-check of union membership cards against payrolls. If the union does not submit membership cards that have been voluntarily signed, or if there is doubt of the accuracy of the membership list and cards submitted, the Board will hold an election by secret ballot. The ballot allows employees to vote in favor of the union they desire, or to vote against all the unions.[28] If a

[26] During the twelve years of the Wagner Act, American workers and their representatives filed nearly 60,000 representation petitions with the Board, as compared to more than 45,000 charges of unfair labor practices. The Board conducted almost 37,000 elections or checks of union cards against payrolls to determine whether a union had been chosen as bargaining agent and counted the votes of more than 7½ million workers in representation elections. Millis and Brown, *op. cit.*, p. 76.

[27] This doctrine of "self-determination of homogeneous groups," was adopted by the Board in *Re Globe Machine and Stamping Co.*, 3 N.L.R.B. 294 (1937).

[28] Of the total of 36,969 elections and cross-checks conducted by the Board in its twelve years, 30,110, or more than four out of every five, were won by unions. Millis and Brown, *op. cit.*, p. 89. After 1939, the elections were normally used, although cross-checks continued to be used in some informal cases. *Ibid.*, pp. 133–134.

majority of the employees voting vote against the unions, then no organization on the ballot can be certified as representative of the employees. If there are two or more unions on a ballot, the one polling a majority of all votes cast is certified as the representative. If neither union obtains a majority of the votes cast, but a majority of the employees vote for some union, the practice is to have a runoff election between the two unions receiving the highest votes.

To most unions, by 1947, the representation procedures were the most important of the Board's functions. H. A. Millis and E. Brown conclude: [29]

. . . A study of the Board's handling of representation cases leads to the conclusion that on the whole the Board built soundly in developing a common law which would protect the right of employees freely to choose their bargaining representatives. Handicapped by inadequate staff and by the enormous difficulties presented by the divided and competing labor movements, and faced by a tremendous volume of cases which made it difficult to apply the rules as flexibly as was most desirable, the Board nevertheless achieved a very large degree of respect and acceptance of its work in this field. It made an outstanding contribution toward the establishment of collective bargaining on a freely chosen and democratic basis.

UNFAIR LABOR PRACTICES

The second class of cases the National Labor Relations Board handled under the Wagner Act has dealt with allegations of unfair labor practices on the part of employers.[30] The procedure established for the Board to handle these charges is similar to the procedure of the Federal Trade Commission in respect to unfair trade practices. Whenever a complaint is received, the Board investigates and takes testimony through an examiner. Cases may be decided informally without trial before an examiner, they may be decided by resort to a stipulation, they may be dismissed or withdrawn, or as a last resort, the Board may issue an order to cease and desist.[31] If this order is not obeyed by the employer, the Board may proceed for its enforcement in the United States Court of Appeals. On the other hand, if the employer feels that the Board has exceeded its jurisdiction or has misconstrued the Act, he can appeal the order to the nearest Court of Appeals.

Violations of the section forbidding discrimination against employees

[29] *Ibid.*, p. 173.

[30] See the list of unfair labor practices, p. 553.

[31] During the twelve years of the Wagner Act from 1935 to 1947, more than nine-tenths of the unfair labor practice cases closed and nearly three-fourths of the representation petitions were handled informally. Only 3,154 decisions in complaint cases and 11,419 decisions in representation cases, including decisions based upon stipulations, were issued in the more than 100,000 cases closed. Millis and Brown, *op. cit.*, p. 80.

for union activity were responsible for the greatest number of unfair-practice proceedings under the Wagner Act. About 30,000 charges, or two-thirds of all those filed during the twelve years of the Act's existence, included charges of discrimination, and this proportion continued steady throughout the years.[32] While this section did not contemplate interference with the right of an employer to hire, fire, transfer, lay off, or change wage rates or hours, it did forbid him to take such action because of his attitude toward unions. When such cases have come before the Board, it has attempted to find the real reason for the discharge or other change of status of the employee.

Of great importance for the development of free collective bargaining has been the elimination of company-dominated unionism. Charges under the section prohibiting domination or other interference with or support to a labor organization were involved in about one in five of the complaint cases filed in the first three years, but after that they decreased and were less than one in ten cases filed in the recent years. As this part of the law has been applied, an employer might not in any way contribute to or help a labor organization, allow officials or other supervisory employees actively to solicit aid for or disparage a labor union, advance money to workmen to pay membership fees, or grant any facilities, such as bulletin boards, office space and equipment, or mailing lists to preferred labor organizations.

Numerically more important were the charges of refusal to bargain, almost 15,000 of them over twelve years. Half the cases in the first year involved this charge. As interpreted by the Board, this provision required that the employer negotiate in good faith with the union and make reasonable efforts to reach an agreement for a fixed period of time. The employer has been expected to meet with union representatives, receive their proposals, and put forth counterproposals of his own. Negotiations with an intent to delay and postpone a settlement do not constitute bona fide collective bargaining.

However, the employer has not been required to continue bargaining collectively when negotiations have already made it plain that further meetings would be futile. But the duty to bargain collectively does not end if new proposals are offered by either side, and the existence of a strike does not extinguish the duty of the employer to negotiate. The duty to bargain collectively does not require that any agreement be reached but simply that the employer shall have acted in good faith in negotiating with the certified union representatives. Where an agreement has been reached between an employer and a union, the employer might be required to put the agreement in writing, and a refusal to do so has been interpreted as an attempt to forestall the union in collective bargaining.

[32] These, and the statistics that follow, have been drawn from *ibid.*, pp. 78–79.

Some cases arose under the catchall provision which outlawed general interference with the right to organize, bargain collectively, and engage in concerted action. These cases were few in number in the early years, but as employers learned to avoid specific violations of the other sections of the Act, this type of charge increased in number and amounted to more than 10 per cent of all filed in the later years. Statements by employers to the effect that a union will not be tolerated, threats to close a plant if unionized, bribes, black-listing, employer-instigated threats or acts of violence, and general schemes of employers to discredit the union fall in this class.

The final unfair labor practice, discrimination against an employee because he made charges to the Board or because he testified before it, has been the source of a negligible number of cases.

As a result of these cases, management over the years has tended to adopt the new standards set by the Act, recognizing the right of employees to organize and bargain collectively. The fight against collective bargaining ended in many instances, and labor and management began to work and live together.

CONSTITUTIONAL ASPECTS OF WAGNER ACT

When one considers the status of constitutional law in 1935 and the revolutionary character of the Wagner Act, the successful legal record of the National Labor Relations Board has been extraordinary. No other administrative commission has had better support from the courts in its formative years, although the lower courts hamstrung the Board until the Supreme Court upheld the Act in 1937. The change in philosophy of those on the bench and the infusion of "new blood" into the judiciary after 1937 do not entirely explain this success. Much of the credit can be laid at the door of the able group of lawyers and economists who handled these early cases. The National Labor Relations Board had never lost sight of the fact that it was limited to labor matters affecting interstate commerce, and in pleading its cases it had taken great pains to show that this relationship existed.

The Wagner Act was first upheld in a rather surprising group of decisions in 1937.[33] In the leading case of this group, the United States Supreme Court held that the Jones and Laughlin Steel Company, in view of its "far-flung activities," was in the flow of interstate commerce and that a law designed to reduce stoppages of work in such a business was constitutional as legislation for the protection of interstate commerce from

[33] *NLRB v. Jones and Laughlin Steel Corp*, 301 U.S. 1 (1937); *NLRB v. Fruehauf Trailer Co.*, 301 U.S. 49 (1937); *NLRB v. Friedman–Harry Marks Clothing Co.*, 301 U.S. 58 (1937); *Associated Press v. NLRB*, 301 U.S. 103 (1937); *Washington, Virginia, and Maryland Coach Co. v. NLRB*, 301 U.S. 142 (1937).

obstruction. The Court found no reason to question the methods of the labor law, finding them to be related to the ends in view and adequate for protection against arbitrary and capricious action by an administrative board. In the other cases decided simultaneously, the Supreme Court upheld the Labor Board in applying the Wagner Act to a commercial-trailer company with about 80 per cent of its business interstate, to a clothing manufacturer with more than 80 per cent of its business interstate, to a national news-gathering agency, and to an interstate bus company.

All the above cases involved enterprises doing a major part of their business through the channels of interstate commerce. The cases still left open the question as to how much business a company must do in interstate commerce to fall within the provisions of the Wagner Act. By a series of subsequent cases, the scope of the law was extended until enterprises with a minor share of their purchases and sales in interstate commerce have been brought under the scope of the law. In 1938 the Supreme Court upheld the Labor Board in applying the law to an agricultural packing company which sold 37 per cent of its products to customers outside of the state.[34] And in a decision handed down the same year, the Court supported the Labor Board in finding an electric-power company, selling a small part of its power purely in intrastate commerce to an interstate electric railroad company and other interstate instrumentalities, to be within the law.[35] In this case it is significant that the sales were to an interstate railroad, since this fact had much to do with making the Court see a direct and substantial relationship of the continuity of the power company's local business to interstate commerce. Another business was found subject to the Act by the Supreme Court because it received materials to be processed across state lines and shipped the product to points outside of the state, even though it never owned the goods and only processed them under special contract.[36] This business was a small shop hiring only sixty persons. The Court pointed out that the volume of interstate trade was not important but that the significant thing was whether the employer was in interstate commerce to an extent that an unfair labor practice might lead to a labor dispute which would obstruct that commerce. No percentage of business done in interstate commerce can be taken as the criterion of whether the business falls within the law. The fundamental question is whether the business is one in which a stoppage of work occasioned by a labor dispute would have a tendency to burden or obstruct the stream of interstate commerce.

Not only was the Wagner Act generally held to be constitutional and most of the Labor Board's interpretations supported, but in several cases

[34] *Santa Cruz Fruit Packing Co. v. NLRB*, 303 U.S. 453 (1938).

[35] *Consolidated Edison Co. v. NLRB*, 305 U.S. 197 (1938).

[36] *NLRB v. Fainblatt*, 306 U.S. 601 (1939).

certain portions of the law were upheld. In one case the Supreme Court claimed that the inclusion within the category of employees of persons who have struck for wage increases was perfectly proper.[37] The Board has been upheld in its definition of the requirements for collective bargaining in good faith, even to the extent of the necessity for putting an agreement in writing if the agreement is reached.[38] A Board order directing a company to hire a man who had never been employed by the company was supported by the Court. Since the employer was guilty of discrimination in refusing to hire the worker, he was also ordered to compensate the worker for loss of pay.[39]

In a few cases, the Labor Board has been rebuffed by the Supreme Court. In one case, the Board had ordered a company to reinstate certain strikers who had been discriminated against because of union activity, despite the fact that these strikers were guilty of unlawful conduct in seizing the employer's property by a sit-down strike. The Supreme Court held that when the employees unlawfully seized the employer's property they placed themselves outside the protection of the Wagner Act.[40] Moreover, the Board was reversed by the United States Supreme Court on the ground that it had made a finding contrary to the evidence presented in a case.[41]

ACHIEVEMENTS OF THE WAGNER ACT

Until the Wagner Act became law, the federal government regarded union organizational campaigns and labor-management relations as economic struggles between workers and employers, with practically no holds barred, except for violations of the antitrust laws. This hands-off policy perpetuated the employer's position of dominance, so that individual bargaining characterized most employer-employee relations. The Wagner Act used federal power to prevent long-established practices of interference with the efforts of workers to organize, and it encouraged the practice of collective bargaining. The law did not automatically put all workers in unions or require that they join unions. It did not require that the labor contract prescribe the closed shop or union shop. An open shop was equally permissible. It did not attempt a detailed regulation of employer-employee relations. Instead, it left the details of this relationship to be worked out by the parties in the labor negotiations. Thus, the Wagner Act was an enabling law which made collective bargaining possible and

[37] *NLRB v. Mackay Radio and Telegraph Co.*, 304 U.S. 333 (1938).

[38] *H. J. Heinz Co. v. NLRB*, 311 U.S. 514 (1941).

[39] *Phelps Dodge Corp. v. NLRB*, 313 U.S. 177 (1941).

[40] *NLRB v. Fansteel Metallurgical Corporation*, 306 U.S. 240 (1939).

[41] *NLRB v. Columbian Enameling and Stamping Co.*, 306 U.S. 292 (1939), and *NLRB v. Sands Mfg. Co.*, 306 U.S. 332 (1939).

prohibited interferences with it, although it must be admitted that by so doing the law greatly strengthened and aided the organizing efforts of the unions.

Judged purely in terms of its objective, as an enabling law, the Act has clearly been successful in encouraging bargaining through union organizations. Union membership increased from less than 4 million in 1935 to

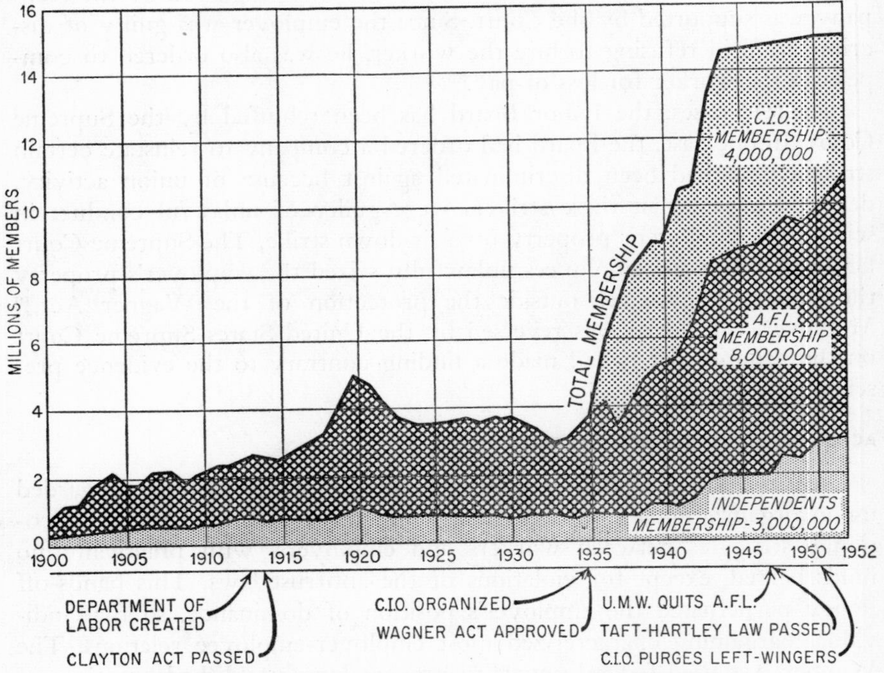

Figure 22–1. Growth of United States Labor Movement since 1900

Two events of 1935 greatly stimulated organizing efforts of labor: the enactment of the Wagner Act and the launching of the Congress of Industrial Organizations.

Source: Reprinted from John H. Ferguson and Dean E. McHenry, *The American System of Government* (New York: McGraw-Hill Book Company, Inc., 3d ed., 1953), p. 767, as adapted from the *New York Times*, Nov. 16, 1952.

almost 15½ million by 1947.[42] The extent to which workers were covered by collective-bargaining agreements between unions and employers increased from an estimated 19.5 per cent in manufacturing industries and

[42] While the National Labor Relations Act undoubtedly encouraged the growth of unions, it should be noted that the competition from the newly created CIO as well as the vigorous character of the union movement in this period promoted union growth also.

26.1 per cent in all industries in 1935 to 69 per cent of the workers in manufacturing and 48 per cent of all workers in occupations (where unions were organizing and seeking collective-bargaining agreements) in 1946. In that year, although more strikes occurred than ever before, there were nine labor-management contracts renewed or revised peacefully for every one that broke into a work stoppage.

The Act has been criticized for failing to eliminate strikes and, in fact, for promoting industrial strife. The Act made no attempt to guarantee that agreements would be reached by negotiation but merely tried to eliminate strikes to obtain union recognition and the right to negotiate. Strikes over this issue were 30 per cent or more of all strikes in 1934 and the first years of the Act, but they decreased during World War II to less than 10 per cent and to 16 per cent in 1946. Disputes about wages, hours, and other conditions of work continued to be beyond the scope of the Wagner Act. Therefore, it is misleading to judge the Act by the quantity of industrial strife, for strikes are due to other factors than those which the Act was designed to prevent. Nevertheless, during the life of the Act, the percentage of all employees who were engaged in strikes during any one year never reached the 1919 level of 20.8. From 1935 to 1941, it fluctuated between 2.3 and 8.4 per cent in different years. However, in 1945 and 1946, years of postwar adjustment, it reached 12.2 and 14.5 per cent, respectively.

CRITICISMS OF THE WAGNER ACT

Of the criticisms of the law that merit attention, two general types may be noted: (1) those which attacked the law itself, and (2) those which, while accepting the purpose of the Act, contended that its administration was faulty. Sometimes it is difficult to determine whether the philosophy of the statute or the way it was administered was under fire.

The one-sidedness of the law. A common criticism of the Wagner Act was that it was one-sided, because it restricted antiunion activities of employers while protecting union activities. In this sense, the law was deliberately one-sided. Its avowed policy was encouragement of collective bargaining through union organizations, because individual bargaining was believed to be a source of industrial strife. Collective bargaining is impossible without some kind of organization; therefore, employees who wanted to organize were protected in their activities. Such a charge of one-sidedness strikes at the very purpose of the Act.

Other criticisms were more favorable to the Act's objective but pointed to inequalities within the Act. Critics charged that it did not outlaw coercion, intimidation, and violence on the part of the unions, while it prohibited coercion by employers. In response, it was argued that these actions by employees were already illegal and were better handled by local law-enforcement authorities than by a federal administrative commission.

Another complaint was that unions were not prevented from coercing employers into violating the law. Although this was not a common occurrence, the need for a restriction on unions in this regard was clear. Similarly, an equalizing extension to employers of the right to petition for representation elections was justifiable, although its need was not pressing.

Two allegations of inequality which received widespread attention were that unions were not obligated to bargain in good faith, as employers were, and that employers were denied free speech while unions had freedom to say what they pleased. The reason for the absence of a requirement that unions bargain in good faith was undoubtedly that experience had proved that employers, not unions, were more commonly unwilling to negotiate. However, since healthy industrial relations require both parties to bargain in good faith, a parallel obligation for unions seemed necessary.

The charge that employers were being denied the right to present their case to workers was appealing as being in the interests of fair play and free speech. The employer, it was argued, should not have to sit by and see his employees duped by an unscrupulous organizer or see his labor policies misrepresented without being able to respond. On the other hand, it is difficult to separate honest and fair employer advice, which does not intimidate or coerce workers, from attempts to interfere unfairly with employees' rights of self-organization. The danger is that the employer, in exercising his free speech, may achieve ends that are contrary to the Wagner Act. However, in the absence of acts indicating a motive to interfere with the rights of employees, an employer should be able to present his case to his employees.[43] Such a change was desirable even if it did nothing more than eliminate a grievance of employers.

Violation of individual and minority rights. The Wagner Act was criticized for requiring individuals and minority groups to accept the will of a majority of the workers. Especially where the appropriate bargaining unit is large, there are likely to be employees who do not wish a union elected by the majority to bargain for them. Moreover, the majority of workers may even consummate a closed-shop or union-shop contract with the

[43] As a matter of fact, in the latter years under the Wagner Act, employers were generally permitted to express their views on labor problems and policies, unless the statements constituted restraint or coercion of the rights of employees. See, e.g., *NLRB v. John Engelhorn & Sons*, 134 F.2d 553 (1943); *NLRB v. Virginia Electric & Power Co.*, 314 U.S. 469 (1941).

employer under which dissenters would have to join the union or give up their jobs.[44]

There appears to be an elementary fairness in giving minorities the right to bargain individually or through representatives of their own choosing. But this fairness is rather specious. Rule by majority is not a strange principle in democratic government. Furthermore, bargaining can hardly be collective if small groups are permitted to bargain with the employer on matters of general interest to all workers. Employers themselves would find this system burdensome, for they would be forced to bargain on wages, hours, and working conditions with a number of independent groups, rather than with one representative union. Actually, in attempting to protect the dissenting minority, danger exists that the whole process and effectiveness of collective bargaining may be weakened.

Bias in the Board. Probably the most common criticism was that the Wagner Act was acceptable but that the Board was biased in its administration. The charge of bias came from employers and labor unions alike. Some of the complaints were directed at the Board for administering the law as it was written and were, therefore, criticisms of the Act itself.

Employers particularly attacked the Board. They alleged that it was judge, jury, and prosecutor all rolled up into one, because it investigated complaints, passed on their validity, and prosecuted them by orders in the Court of Appeals. Many commissions have been attacked at some time on this score. These critics misunderstand the nature of the administrative process, the advantages in the use of independent commissions, and the safeguards that are provided. The flexibility and informality of handling complaints, the development of a specialized staff, and the continuous supervision offered by an administrative commission are all positive values. Moreover, administrative commissions, including the National Labor Relations Board, have divided their staffs into groups, with some members responsible for investigation, others responsible for prosecution, and still others sitting in judicial capacities. Every precaution is taken to keep these groups as independent as seems wise.

Labor unions contended that the Labor Board was biased against them whenever it made a decision which placed one union at a disadvantage in relation to another, and employers generally claimed that the Board was

[44] Under a closed-shop contract, the employer agrees to hire only members of the union with which the contract is signed. Under a union-shop contract, the employer has free choice in hiring, but all workers must join the union with which the contract is signed within a specified time after being hired, usually thirty or sixty days. Closed-shop contracts with minority unions were prohibited by the Board under the Wagner Act.

"labor-minded." The basis for the criticism from labor unions arose primarily from the function of the Board in determining the appropriate bargaining unit; the American Federation of Labor claimed that the Board favored the Congress of Industrial Organizations, and the latter declared that the Board broke down genuine national collective bargaining by favoring the craft organizations of the former. The basis for employer criticism lay in the whole gamut of Board decisions; the employers felt that the Board extended the meaning of unfair practices so as to take away employer rights and to be lenient with labor to a much greater extent than was ever contemplated by the law.

It must be remembered, in appraising the charges of bias, that appeals were possible from the decisions of the Board. The major policies developed by the Board stood remarkably well the test of court review, although it must be admitted that bias is largely a matter of interpretation of facts rather than of law, and appellate courts tend to limit their review to the law.

The Labor Management Relations Act, 1947

Ten years of constant criticism of the Wagner Act culminated in the enactment of the Labor Management Relations Act of 1947, commonly known as the Taft-Hartley Act. During that period some 230 bills were introduced in Congress to amend or seriously modify national labor policy. Intensive criticism began when the constitutionality of the Wagner Act was upheld and reached a climax before World War II in the investigation of the National Labor Relations Board by a special committee of the House of Representatives.[45]

After the war the campaign gained momentum. The limited success of the President's Labor-Management Conference of 1945, the epidemic of postwar strikes, the conservative shift in public opinion, and the Republican victory in 1946 all contributed to the enactment of the Taft-Hartley Act, which was passed over the veto of President Truman. The campaign to amend the Wagner Act was under the leadership of such groups as the National Association of Manufacturers and the Chamber of Commerce, which saw the enactment into law of most of the principles they had been advocating for the previous ten years.[46]

The Taft-Hartley Act is a complex omnibus measure which retains por-

[45] See U.S. House of Representatives, Special Committee to Investigate the National Labor Relations Board, *Intermediate Report,* H. Rept. 1902, part 1, 76th Cong., 3d Sess. (1940).

[46] For a description of the role played by the NAM, see Richard W. Gable, "NAM: Influential Lobby or Kiss of Death?" 15 *Journal of Politics* 254–273 (May, 1953).

tions of the Wagner Act, amends some of its provisions, and adds new provisions.[47] The new measures provide for detailed regulation of the internal affairs of unions, bargaining procedures, dispute settlement, and the content of labor-management agreements.

CHANGES IN THE BOARD

The size of the National Labor Relations Board was increased from three to five members. Moreover, the Board was split into two authorities. The administrative work of the Board is now vested in the General Counsel, who has final authority over investigation of charges, issuance of complaints, and prosecution of unfair labor practices. The Board itself is now primarily a judicial agency.

The jurisdiction of the Board is extended to cover new types of cases, such as unfair-labor-practices cases filed against unions, and new types of elections, such as union-shop elections. Moreover, supervisors in businesses that are subject to the Act are excluded from the jurisdiction of the Board.[48] However, like the Wagner Act, the Taft-Hartley Act permitted the railroads and the airlines to remain under the Railway Labor Act. Consequently not all the restrictions of the Taft-Hartley Act apply to these carriers.

EQUALIZING AMENDMENTS

In an effort to redress the balance of powers in industrial relations, the Act removes certain restraints upon employers and imposes certain restrictions upon unions and their agents.

Freeing employers from restraints. The five unfair employer practices listed in the Wagner Act are left unchanged in wording but are modified in other ways. The types of activities which can be held to justify effective discharge of an employee without having to reinstate him later are extended to include engaging in one of the newly listed unfair union practices, striking within the sixty-day notice period at the end of a contract, or engaging in certain specified unlawful practices. The Supreme Court recently upheld the discharge of a worker for disparaging statements concerning his employer that were viewed as "disloyal."[49]

The Act grants the employer the right to petition for a representation election when one or more unions claim a majority. Under the Wagner

[47] Since portions of the Wagner Act were incorporated in the Taft-Hartley revision, it will be unnecessary to repeat the discussion of those provisions. Attention hereafter will focus on the significant changes in national labor law.

[48] This provision reversed a Supreme Court decision handed down earlier in 1947 that foremen had the right to bargain collectively. See *Packard Motor Car Co. v. NLRB*, 330 U.S. 485 (1947).

[49] *NLRB v. Local Union No. 1229, Int. Brotherhood of Elec. Workers*, 74 Sup. Ct. 172 (1953).

Act, the employer could petition for an election only where two or more unions asked recognition.

A "free-speech" amendment is included which permits employers to express their opinions to employees without danger of prosecution for unfair labor practices, if such expression contains no threat of reprisal or force or promise of benefits. Actually, by 1947, the Board had reversed an earlier tendency to view antiunion remarks or speeches of employers with suspicion. In view of the more reasonable attitude of the Board and the courts toward employers' statements, it is doubtful whether the "free-speech" amendment was necessary. One authority concludes that the provision casts "clouds of uncertainty over theretofore basically satisfactory doctrine produced by the National Labor Relations Board and the courts through a long and careful process of testing under the original act." [50]

Although two Courts of Appeals have stated that the "free-speech" amendment is no more than a restatement of principles embodied in the First Amendment,[51] the Board interprets it as going beyond the protection contemplated in the Bill of Rights. The Board has reversed its position on captive audiences [52] and now holds that the technique of presenting the employer's side of a dispute to employees is legal,[53] even where similar opportunity to address the employees is not accorded the union.[54] Moreover, the use of noncoercive statements as evidence of some other unfair labor practice is no longer permissible.[55] In fact, it appears that a statement may not be used against the employer unless, standing alone, it is itself an unfair labor practice within the express terms of the Act.

Unfair and illegal practices by unions. The original list of unfair employer practices included in the Wagner Act is balanced by the specification of union practices which are declared unfair.[56] These practices do not, in every case, correspond to the unfair employer practices. The Taft-Hartley Act prohibits unions from engaging in the following unfair labor practices: (1) restraining or coercing employees in the exercise of

[50] Frank Elkouri, "Employer Free Speech," 4 *Labor Law Journal* 78–84, 84 (February, 1953).

[51] *NLRB v. LaSalle Steel Co.*, 178 F.2d 829 (1949); *NLRB v. Bailey and Co.*, 180 F.2d 278 (1950).

[52] *Re Clark Bros. Co.*, 70 N.L.R.B. 802 (1946). According to the captive-audience doctrine, employers who required employees to attend an antiunion speech during working hours were, by this action, guilty of restraining and coercing their employees.

[53] *Re Babcock and Wilcox Co.*, 77 N.L.R.B. 577 (1948).

[54] *Re Bonwit Teller, Inc.*, 96 N.L.R.B., 608 (1951).

[55] *Pittsburgh Steamship Co. v. NLRB*, 180 F.2d 731 (1950).

[56] Unfair labor practices are not a crime; they are a statutory "wrong" and are somewhat akin to a common-law tort. They may be prosecuted only in the designated agency by an injured party.

their right to organize or refrain from organizing (except in the case of an approved union-shop arrangement); (2) causing or attempting to cause an employer to discriminate against a worker for any other reason than failure to pay his fees or dues; (3) refusing to bargain collectively; (4) engaging in a secondary boycott, jurisdictional strike in violation of rulings of the Board, or strikes to force an employer to deal with a union other than the one which has been duly recognized as the bargaining agent; (5) requiring the payment of initiation fees which the Board has found to be excessive or discriminatory; and (6) causing or attempting to cause an employer to pay for services which are not actually performed (featherbedding).

Another section of the law declares illegal any strike or concerted action in support of a secondary boycott or featherbedding. Strikes to force an employer to recognize or bargain with a union other than the one that has been certified are also unlawful. An employer injured by these illegal practices may sue and recover the damages sustained.

REGULATION OF INTERNAL AFFAIRS OF UNIONS

The equalizing amendments were intended to adjust the alleged one-sidedness of the Wagner Act and its administration and can, therefore, be properly regarded as amendments to that Act. Certain provisions in the Taft-Hartley Act do not modify its predecessor but go beyond anything contained in that statute. Among these are provisions extending government supervision over certain internal union practices.

The National Labor Relations Board will not perform the services of investigating a complaint of unfair labor practices or certifying a union unless the union involved has filed with the Secretary of Labor the name and address of the union, the names of its three principal officers, their pay and method of selection, the union's dues schedule, a detailed statement of the union's rules and operating procedures, and a financial report. Copies of the financial report must also be furnished to all members of the union. In addition, each officer of a union must file with the National Labor Relations Board a statement that he is not a member of the Communist party and that he does not believe in or teach the forceful overthrow of the United States government. The non-Communist affidavits must be renewed annually.

An outright ban is imposed on political contributions or expenditures by unions in connection with any federal election. Any union which violates this prohibition is subject to a $5,000 fine, and any officer of a union who permits such contributions or expenditures may be fined $1,000, or imprisoned for one year, or both.

The constitutionality of the section requiring financial reports, description of procedures, and the like was immediately upheld by the Supreme

Court as a reasonable incident to public policy.[57] The requirement of a Communist affidavit created much more controversy. Its constitutionality was vigorously attacked by many unions, including those most forthright in their opposition to communism, and some prominent labor leaders, notably John L. Lewis, refused to sign. When the question reached the Supreme Court in 1950, the charge that the non-Communist affidavit violated the guarantees of free speech in the First Amendment was denied.[58] By a 5-to-1 majority, with two members of the majority not going along with the whole opinion, the Court held that the provision regulates harmful conduct which Congress has reasonably determined is carried on by persons identifiable by their political affiliation and beliefs and that it is therefore fully within congressional power.

The question arose whether officers of the national labor federations, American Federation of Labor and Congress of Industrial Organizations, were required to file affidavits, or only those of the international unions to which local unions were affiliated. The General Counsel of the Board took the position that all top officials of the American Federation of Labor and Congress of Industrial Organizations must sign, while the Board itself overruled this interpretation. The Supreme Court upheld the General Counsel's view,[59] but doubt was cast on all contracts which had been negotiated without the officials of the national federations having signed. Congress clarified the situation by passing a law in 1951 validating such contracts.

The Supreme Court has not ruled on the constitutionality of the ban on political contributions and expenditures, because the case that reached the Court in which the question was raised did not involve an offense under the Act. Union expenditures for the publication of a newspaper containing statements in support of candidates for federal offices were held to be valid.[60]

The apparent intention of the ban on political contributions and expenditures is to limit union activity to the field of collective bargaining. However, the effect of the Taft-Hartley Act has been to transfer major segments of industrial relations into the political sphere. The paradoxical fact, therefore, is that the Act stimulates greater political activity while limiting the right of one of the parties to engage in it.

[57] *National Maritime Union v. Herzog*, 334 U.S. 854 (1948).

[58] *American Communications Association v. Douds*, 339 U.S. 382 (1950).

[59] *NLRB v. Highland Park Mfg. Co.*, 341 U.S. 322 (1951). This case also held that the national federations also have to meet the requirement in regard to financial and other reports.

[60] *United States v. CIO*, 335 U.S. 106 (1948). On the basis of this decision a lower court upheld union expenditures for radio and newspaper advertisements opposing political candidates where the union published no newspaper. *United States v. Painters Local Union No. 481,* 172 F.2d 854 (1949).

REGULATION OF BARGAINING PROCEDURES

Making the agreement. Apart from protecting collective negotiation from employer interference, the Wagner Act did not specify the procedure or content of collective bargaining. The parties were on their own to work out acceptable procedures for negotiation and the scope of the joint discussion. The Taft-Hartley Act, on the other hand, specifies that management and union representatives have a mutual obligation "to meet at reasonable times and confer in good faith with respect to wages, hours, and other terms and conditions of employment, . . . and the execution of a written contract incorporating any agreement reached if requested by either party." [61]

The necessity of deciding what constitutes bargaining "in good faith" and what lies within "other terms and conditions of employment" brings government into the bargaining procedure. Case-by-case litigation has been required to determine the character of "good faith" bargaining. The problem is one of preventing refusal of either side to bargain in good faith and at the same time avoiding undesirable regulation of collective bargaining procedures. George W. Taylor suggests that a more even-handed law might have been secured by eliminating the unilateral requirement to bargain collectively, instead of extending the requirement to cover unions. That requirement for employers was incongruous with the rest of the Wagner Act anyway, Taylor contends.[62] However, if it is to be required of employers, justice demands that it be required of unions.

Borderline cases of what falls within the "other terms and conditions of employment" that are within the scope of collective bargaining must be submitted to the Board for determination. The Board has held, for example, that pension plans and group health- and accident-insurance are within the scope of collective bargaining. But what will happen if certain issues are held to be outside the scope of collective bargaining? The alternative to dropping the issue is a political campaign to amend the law to broaden the scope of labor negotiations. Congress, rather than the interested parties, thus becomes the judge of the appropriate subjects for bargaining.

The National Labor Relations Board under the Taft-Hartley Law is more narrowly circumscribed in defining the appropriate unit: (1) craft and professional groups must be separately established unless a majority vote decides otherwise; (2) guards must be set up as a separate unit and can be represented only by a union which does not admit other classes of employees; (3) supervisors must be excluded from all units; (4) the degree or extent of union organization must not be the deciding factor in setting up bargaining units.

[61] Section 8d.

[62] Taylor, *op. cit.*, p. 283.

Representation procedure is also more closely prescribed by the Act. A petition may be filed by any individual, employee, or labor organization claiming the right to be recognized, or asserting that the existing bargaining agent is no longer representative. The employer also may petition on the grounds that *one or more* individuals or unions have presented a claim to be recognized. Under the Wagner Act the employer could petition only if *two or more* unions presented such claims. The petitions from employers or employees to decertify a union must be given the same consideration by the Board as a union's petition for certification. If, after investigation, the Board believes that a question of representation exists, it holds a secret election and certifies the results. No election may be held if one was held within the preceding year.

Furthermore, the Taft-Hartley Act provides that employees on strike who are not entitled to reinstatement are not eligible to vote. Under the Wagner Act the Board had developed the policy that during a strike caused by unfair labor practices only the strikers were eligible to vote, since they were entitled to reinstatement, but in a strike over economic matters (wages and the like) any replacements *and* those still on strike were eligible. Under the Taft-Hartley provision the Board has ruled that economic strikers, when replaced, are permanently replaced (that is, are not eligible for reinstatement) and therefore are ineligible to vote.[63] The Board has also decided that strike replacements are eligible to vote.[64] The possibility that this provision might be used to break strikes or even to break unions is apparent.

Upon petition of at least 30 per cent of the union, the Board holds a secret election to determine whether the existing bargaining representative should be decertified. Such an election cannot be held within a year after the previous representation election. If a majority of the employees vote to decertify, a nonunion condition is restored. During the first four years of the law's existence, the incumbent union was decertified in less than 20 per cent of the cases.[65]

Keeping the agreement. Further government regulation covers the action of parties after an agreement has been reached. Both parties to a labor contract are legally obligated to meet at reasonable times and to confer in good faith with respect to any question arising under the agreement.

If one party alleges that the other has broken the agreement, that party

[63] *Re Pipe Machinery Co.*, 76 N.L.R.B. 247; 79 N.L.R.B. 1322 (1948).

[64] *Re Triangle Publications, Inc.*, 80 N.L.R.B. 835 (1948); *Re Dadourian Export Corp.*, 80 N.L.R.B. 1400 (1948).

[65] John R. Foley, "Decapitate the Decertification Petition," 4 *Labor Law Journal* 87 (February, 1953). Similar results under the union-shop-election requirement convinced Congress to eliminate the union-shop election in 1951, but the decertification provision remains.

may bring suit for contract violation. The purpose for this provision was undoubtedly to deter wildcat strikes. However, if it should result in court supervision of day-to-day issues, in place of adjustment by the interested parties, industrial stability would not be promoted.

REGULATION OF DISPUTE SETTLEMENT

General procedures. An existing collective-bargaining contract cannot legally be modified or terminated unless the party desiring the change (1) serves a written notice upon the other party of the desired change at least sixty days prior to the termination of the contract or date of desired change; (2) offers to negotiate the change with the other party; (3) notifies the Federal Mediation and Conciliation Service within thirty days after notice of the existence of a dispute; and (4) continues the existing contract in full force and effect for sixty days after such notice is given. Any employee who engages in a strike within the sixty-day "cooling-off" period loses his status as an employee, unless the employer chooses to retain him.

Federal employees are absolutely prohibited from striking. Anyone who does strike loses his job, loses his civil-service status, and is not eligible for reemployment with the United States government for three years.

Procedure for national-emergency strikes. The Taft-Hartley Act provides for a special procedure to force a settlement, if possible, in labor disputes that constitute a threat to national health and safety. When the President finds that an actual or impending strike imperils national health and safety, he may appoint a board of inquiry to make a written report to him containing the facts and circumstances of the dispute. After receiving this report, which must not contain any recommendations, the President may seek an injunction of eighty days' duration. During this time, with the help of the Federal Mediation and Conciliation Service, the parties endeavor to settle the dispute. If the controversy persists, the President reconvenes the board of inquiry, which continues its investigation and submits its final report by the sixtieth day of the eighty-day period. This report, again without recommendations, describes the current positions of the parties and the employer's last offer. Within the next fifteen days the National Labor Relations Board takes a secret ballot of the employees to determine whether they wish to accept the final offer of settlement made by their employer. In the remaining five days, the Board certifies the results of the election, but regardless of its outcome the injunction is discharged. The parties are then free to take any action they see fit. The President makes a comprehensive report on the dispute to Congress. Senator Taft suggested that Congress should then enact "on the spot" legislation if a serious threat continues.

This machinery has been invoked on ten occasions between the passage of the law and June, 1953. In only two instances did the use of the injunction bring about an end to the strike. In two instances strikes occurred after injunctions were discharged, two strikes continued in spite of injunctions, and three of the threatened strikes did not result in work stoppages. In none of these disputes did the vote of the employees on the last offer of the employer result in a settlement.

After a careful study of these cases, Charles M. Rehmus concludes that the emergency provisions have been almost a complete failure in stopping critical strikes. He attributes the failure to the effect of the provisions on the collective-bargaining process, for "they neither aid collective bargaining nor create the conditions necessary for amicable agreement between labor and management." [66] This conclusion is explained by the facts that the parties have sometimes relied upon the injunction as a part of their strategy, that the injunction may come at a poor time in the negotiation procedure, and that excessive restrictions have been imposed on the boards of inquiry. The cooling-off period, imposed by the injunction, is found to be "at best meaningless and at worst harmful in relation to the collective bargaining process." In practice, it is used as a "warming-up period." [67]

Jurisdictional disputes. Conducting or encouraging a jurisdictional strike is declared an unfair labor practice. Moreover, the Taft-Hartley Act directs the National Labor Relations Board to "hear and determine" jurisdictional disputes, unless the parties work out a voluntary adjustment of the dispute within ten days after the filing of a charge. The Board has construed this provision as requiring the Board to "hear and determine" *all* complaints involving jurisdictional strikes.[68]

However, the Board members have been divided over the powers they have been granted in the case of jurisdictional disputes. The majority has held that this section was designed to facilitate the settlement of jurisdictional disputes and not to enjoin a union from committing an unfair labor practice. They expressed the view that the Board is prohibited from going further to grant a union exclusive rights to a job. One member expressed the view that Congress assigned the Board the power to determine which of the conflicting unions is entitled to the disputed work. The majority rejected this view as tantamount to awarding a union a closed shop and as a violation of other provisions of the act.[69]

[66] Charles M. Rehmus, "The Operation of the National Emergency Provisions of the Labor Management Relations Act of 1947," 62 *Yale Law Journal* 1052 (June, 1953).

[67] *Ibid.*, p. 1059.

[68] *Re Moore Drydock Co.*, 81 N.L.R.B. 1108.

[69] S. A. Levitan, "Jurisdictional Disputes," 4 *Labor Law Journal* 136 (February, 1953).

In general, therefore, after a hearing, the Board either quashes charges, or determines that the union accused of an unfair labor practice has no lawful right to force or require a work assignment, or determines the unit to which the disputed work belongs. The union gets ten days to comply with the Board's determination. If it does not, a complaint is issued and the case proceeds before a trial examiner like any other unfair-labor-practice case.

The conclusion reached by one commentator is that this procedure "probably encourages labor unions to settle their intra-family squabbles and establish voluntary machinery for reconciling disputes over work assignments." [70] In the construction industry, for example, the Building and Construction Trades Department, American Federation of Labor, and two employers' associations formed the tripartite National Joint Board for the Settlement of Jurisdictional Disputes. During the first four years of its operation the joint board helped settle close to 2,000 jurisdictional disputes. Similarly the Congress of Industrial Organizations provided in 1951 for a method of settling all jurisdictional disputes that may arise among its affiliates within the organization.

Provision for mediation. Mediation and conciliation under government auspices are made an integral part of the bargaining procedure under the Taft-Hartley Act. The old Conciliation Service in the Department of Labor was abolished, and its functions transferred to a new independent agency called the Federal Mediation and Conciliation Service. The motivation behind this change was to make the agency more impartial.

REGULATION OF THE CONTENT OF THE AGREEMENT

Under the Wagner Act not only were the procedures for collective bargaining and dispute settlement to be worked out by the interested parties, but also the substantive issues of the contract were matters to be determined by these parties. By the Taft-Hartley Act the actual terms and conditions of employment, in a number of instances, are either specified directly by law or made subject to determinations by the National Labor Relations Board. Revision of these terms and conditions now requires further congressional action rather than a joint decision of union and management. Thus, although the Taft-Hartley Act goes further than the Wagner Act in requiring both parties to bargain collectively, the parties are deprived of some latitude of decision in their attempts to solve certain problems, and political power assumes importance alongside of economic power.

Union security. The Taft-Hartley Act fixes a number of limitations on the right of employers and unions to negotiate and implement union-

[70] *Ibid.*, p. 140.

security agreements.[71] Under the Wagner Act the negotiation of union-security agreements was handled through the process of collective bargaining. The Taft-Hartley Act outlaws the closed shop entirely and allows the union-shop and maintenance-of-membership agreements only under certain conditions.

Union security can be of importance not only to the union but also to the employer who wants to deal with a responsible representative of his employees. A union-security contract, in a given situation, is defensible if a majority of employees support it and the employer approves of it. Prior to the Taft-Hartley Act union-security agreements were widely accepted by both employees and employers.

It is estimated that 33 per cent of all workers covered by collective-bargaining contracts in 1946 worked under agreements providing for the closed shop.[72] In some industries it was a long-standing practice, yet all closed-shop agreements were prohibited by the Taft-Hartley Act. The efforts of the National Labor Relations Board to eliminate the closed shop from American industry have been only partly successful. So firmly entrenched was the closed shop that it continues to flourish in the face of legal prohibition.[73] It is apparent that some employers as well as unions feel that it fits their needs, and they continue to use it. A better policy for national labor law might be to attack the abuses of the closed shop rather than impose a universal ban on an arrangement that is acceptable under certain circumstances.[74]

Union-shop or maintenance-of-membership clauses are lawful under the Taft-Hartley Act only if membership in a labor organization is available to the worker on the same terms generally applicable to other members. Furthermore, these provisions cannot compel a worker to join a union as a condition of employment unless at least 30 days have elapsed from the effective data of the contract or the beginning of employment.

[71] Union-security agreements require union membership as a condition of employment, and include closed-shop, union-shop, or maintenance-of-membership agreements. A closed-shop agreement requires that a worker be a member of the union before he is hired. An open-shop agreement requires that a worker join the union within a specified time after he has been hired. Under a maintenance-of-membership agreement a worker is free to elect whether or not he desires to join a union. However, once he does join, he must maintain his membership in the union for the duration of the contract or lose his job.

[72] U.S. Bureau of Labor Statistics, *Extent of Collective Bargaining and Union Recognition*, Bulletin 909 (1946), p. 3.

[73] The Senate Committee on Labor and Public Welfare reported in 1949: ". . . notwithstanding the provisions of the Labor Management Relations Act, closed shop contracts continue to be observed over a wide area of industry." U.S. Senate, Committee on Labor and Public Welfare, S. Rept. 99, to accompany S. 249, 81st Cong., 1st Sess., p. 20.

[74] See Fred Witney, "Union Security," 4 *Labor Law Journal* 111 (February, 1953).

As originally enacted, the Taft-Hartley Act prohibited including a union-security agreement in a contract unless, upon petition of 30 per cent of the employees in the unit, the Board held a secret election and a majority of workers eligible to vote (not merely a majority of those voting) approved of the agreement. In 1951, Congress amended the Act to eliminate the requirement of an election before union-shop or maintenance-of-membership clauses could be included in a contract. In a little over four years' time, the Board has conducted 46,119 polls at a cost of over $3 million. In 97 per cent of the elections, union-shop agreements were authorized.[75]

The Taft-Hartley Act further provides that if any state has an anti-union-shop law, the state law takes precedence over the federal law. By 1953, thirteen states had outlawed all forms of union security.[76] Actually, twelve of these laws were on the books when the Taft-Hartley Act was passed. In the interest of a uniform union-security formula, Congress could have invalidated these state statutes for conflicting with national law. However, Congress did not choose to do so and therefore permits the states to nullify a policy which it feels to be desirable for federal law. Some states, in fact, require the union-shop election (with, in some cases, a two-thirds or three-fourths majority) which Congress has seen fit to eliminate.

The Supreme Court has ruled, in a case involving a Wisconsin law that requires a two-thirds vote for a union shop, that a state union-shop-election requirement must be complied with despite the fact that the federal law no longer provides for the union-shop election.[77] Lower courts have upheld state bans on the union shop.[78] The Supreme Court has also denied the claims of unions that the constitutional guarantees of free speech and assembly protect them in their formation of a closed shop and has upheld the validity of state laws prohibiting it.[79]

[75] NLRB, *16th Annual Report* (1951), p. 10. This amendment, however, continues in effect the provision that permits employees, upon petition of 30 per cent of the workers in the unit, to vote on continuing the union-shop or maintenance-of-membership agreement in their contract. At least one year must elapse before such an election can be held, but if a majority of the employees disapprove of the union-security agreement, it must be deleted immediately, even if the contract has more time to run. See *Great Atlantic and Pacific Tea Co.*, 100 N.L.R.B., 1494 (1952).

[76] Witney, *op. cit.*, p. 118.

[77] *Algoma Plywood and Veneer Co., v. Wisconsin Employment Relations Board*, 336 U.S. 301 (1949).

[78] *State v. Whitaker*, 45 S.E.2d 860 (1947); *Finney v. Hawkins*, 54 S.E.2d 872 (1949).

[79] *American Federation of Labor v. American Sash and Door Co.*, 335 U.S. 538 (1949); *Lincoln Federal Labor Union v. Northwestern Iron and Metal Co.*, 335 U.S. 525 (1949).

The checkoff[80] is another form of union security. Like other union security provisions it can benefit the employer as well as the union, because it avoids the nuisance and impaired productive efficiency resulting from dues-collecting activities as a more or less continuous process in and about the plant. The Taft-Hartley Act prohibits the employer from using the checkoff arrangement unless he has written authorization from each employee.[81] Workers must renew their authorization each year. Compliance with this requirement has been rather general.

Finally, union security is weakened by the provision which relieves the employer of the obligation to enforce union discipline by discharging an employee for any reason except failure to pay union fees and dues. Thus, even where a union-shop arrangement requires union membership as a condition of employment, expulsion from a union for any reason other than nonpayment of dues or fees cannot result in loss of employment. The ability of unions to enforce the discipline necessary to maintain responsible unionism is thereby weakened.

Welfare funds. Welfare funds as a subject for collective negotiation are placed under certain limitations. Employers are prohibited from contributing to union health and welfare funds unless the following requirements are met: (1) contributions must be held in trust for payment of medical or hospital care, insurance, pensions, or injury benefits to employees or their dependents; (2) the plan of the fund must be worked out in detail and stated in writing; (3) the fund must be audited annually; (4) contributions for pensions or annuities must be segregated and used only for those specific purposes; and (5) employers and employees must be equally represented in the administration of the fund.

Featherbedding. The practice known as "featherbedding" is removed from the sphere of collective negotiation. Causing or attempting to cause "an employer to pay or deliver or agree to pay or deliver any money or other thing of value, in the nature of an exaction, for services which are not performed or not to be performed" is declared an unfair labor practice.[82]

In the face of this provision, the Supreme Court declared that the insistence of a musicians' union that a theater hire a local orchestra to play in the pit when a traveling orchestra played on stage was legal, even though the theater operator did not want to hire the local orchestra.[83] In another case, the Court held that this provision does not outlaw union

[80] The checkoff is a procedure by which an employer agrees with a union to deduct from his employees' wages union dues and other financial obligations and turn these sums over to the appropriate union officials at regular intervals.

[81] Violation of this provision by the employer carries a fine of $10,000, or one year's imprisonment, or both.

[82] Section 8(6).

[83] *NLRB v. Gamble Enterprises, Inc.*, 345 U.S. 117 (1953).

demands that newspaper printers be paid for setting "bogus" type.[84] "Bogus" type is type which duplicates advertising matter received by the newspaper already set in type. The "bogus" type is not used. The Court ruled that the Act is not violated when pay is demanded for work done. The question whether the work done was useful to the employer was considered immaterial.

THE JOINT COMMITTEE ON LABOR-MANAGEMENT RELATIONS

The possibility that the Taft-Hartley Act would not completely satisfy the nation's need for an effective labor policy is recognized in the provision for a Joint Committee on Labor-Management Relations. This Committee, composed of seven members from each house of Congress, is responsible for conducting "a thorough study and investigation of the entire field of labor-management relations." [85] The duty of this Committee is to make recommendations as to necessary legislation.

EVALUATION OF THE TAFT-HARTLEY ACT

The insistent demands for reform of the Wagner Act resulted in a new labor policy which, while limiting certain abuses, went beyond the elimination of inequities in the Wagner Act and its administration. While avowing their faith in collective bargaining, the framers of the Taft-Hartley Act (1) weakened collective bargaining, (2) encouraged individual bargaining, and (3) thrust government into the labor bargain further than ever before.

Collective bargaining weakened. Collective bargaining is certainly not abandoned as a goal of public policy, for many of its principles are enunciated in the Taft-Hartley Act.[86] However, union power in collective bargaining is weakened by certain restraints placed on the procedure and content of the labor bargain as well as by restrictions imposed on unions. The limitations placed on union security and the curtailment of the union's power to control its members lessen the ability of unions to maintain responsible relations with employers. The ban on the closed shop, including the hiring hall, interferes with a well-established relationship satisfactory to the parties or worked out on the basis of experience. The procedures for settlement of disputes introduce rigidities, especially in the case of national emergency strikes, which have not promoted peaceful relations and have, in some cases, interfered with them.

[84] *American Newspaper Publishers Assn. v. NLRB,* 345 U.S. 100 (1953).

[85] Section 402.

[86] One labor authority disagrees vigorously that collective bargaining is preserved. Archibald Cox writes: ". . . the Taft-Hartley Amendments represent an abandonment of the policy of affirmatively encouraging the spread of union organization and collective bargaining." "Some Aspects of the Labor Management Relations Act, 1947," 61 *Harvard Law Review* 44 (November, 1947).

The Act provides the employer with certain legal weapons which could be used to weaken unions or break strikes. Among these are provisions that allow the employer to petition for a collective-bargaining election or to instigate a decertification petition by employees, permit injunctions to restrain picketing, grant the strike replacement the right to vote in a representation election while the strikers are held ineligible, require the government to certify and enforce a "no union" vote if this is the outcome, and protect the employer for one year against further efforts to obtain recognition should an election go against the union.

The fact that the Taft-Hartley Act has not had some of the adverse effects on unions that these provisions might imply can be explained by the high level of employment since 1947, the restraint exercised by employers in using the Act, and the hostility toward the Act shown by the Truman administration that was entrusted with its execution during the first five years of the law's existence. *Business Week* magazine, a journal that is sympathetic to the philosophy of the Taft-Hartley Act, editorialized shortly after its passage: "Given a few million unemployed in America, given an administration in Washington which was not pro-union—and the Taft-Hartley Act conceivably could wreck the labor movement." [87]

Individual bargaining encouraged. The meaning of the Act is that it is immaterial whether employees join unions or not. Moreover, on the assumption that the interests of employees and their unions may not coincide, workers are extended legal help against unions. The guarantee of the right to refrain from organizing, the provision for union decertification elections, the check-off requirements, and the provision that employees vote on accepting the employer's last offer in a national emergency strike are expressive of this assumption. The full protection of the desires of dissenting individuals and groups, even to the extent of encouraging dual unionism, further indicates this belief. The total effect is to extend government protection to individual bargaining.

Government-regulated labor relations. The entire framework within which labor-management relations are conducted is changed. Government now supervises certain internal affairs of unions, regulates portions of the content and procedure of collective bargaining, and enters into deadlocked dispute situations even to the extent of strongly influencing the nature of settlements in disputes of national concern. Free collective bargaining is hedged in by a substantial body of governmental rules and regulations.

What was once regarded as a matter for private negotiations between interested parties is now subject to government direction. By the Taft-

[87] *Business Week*, Dec. 18, 1948, p. 124.

Hartley Act the federal government assumes authority "to prescribe the legitimate rights of both employees and employers in their relations affecting commerce, to provide orderly and peaceful procedures for preventing the interference by either with the legitimate rights of the other, . . . to define and prescribe practices on the part of labor and management which affect commerce and are inimical to the general welfare. . . ." [88] Private problems are made public problems; political power is substituted for economic power; the area for negotiation is shifted from the bargaining table to Washington. Modification of basic elements in employer-employee relations now appears to require another act of Congress instead of a new contract between union and management. This fact is apparent when one recalls that revision of the Taft-Hartley Act has been a major issue in each of the presidential elections and some of the off-year congressional elections since 1947.

The Act will continue to be a subject of controversy as long as certain newly created inequities continue to be a part of the law of the land. The internal affairs of unions, but not of companies, are subject to detailed supervision. Provision is made for the use of the injunction during a labor dispute, but no provision is made for plant seizure. Company officials are not required to sign the non-Communist affidavit as union officials are. It is obvious that once government becomes involved in the details of collective bargaining to the extent that it prescribes the procedures, terms, and conditions of negotiation, a political tug-of-war will follow in an endeavor to keep the scales balanced.

While the Taft-Hartley Act clearly places some impediments in the process of free collective bargaining and while it regulates certain union operations more severely than those of employers, a decade of experience has furnished no evidence that this has weakened the labor movement. If anything, the Act has appeared to bring a greater sense of responsibility to the labor-union movement. Moreover, with the broad public interest in the proper functioning of a full-employment economy, as free as possible from crippling strikes in essential industry, one can expect increased government participation in the collective-bargaining process.

State Industrial-relations Regulation

The states have often been looked upon as laboratories for experimentation in legislation and government. In the field of industrial-relations legislation the states have played a significant role as a preliminary testing ground.

Twelve years after embarking on a strong policy obviously designed

[88] Section 1b.

to encourage independent unions, the federal government placed certain limits on the application of this policy. This departure, however, was anticipated in a number of state industrial-relations and other regulatory acts that were passed in the decade between 1937 and 1947. The experiments in several states, especially in Wisconsin and Minnesota, provided the framers of the Taft-Hartley Act with a number of specific suggestions for modifying the Wagner Act.

DEVELOPMENT OF STATE INDUSTRIAL-RELATIONS ACTS

Disenchantment with the Wagner Act did not affect state legislatures immediately. The initial industrial-relations acts were patterned after the Wagner Act. In 1937, five states enacted such acts. These laws prohibited certain unfair labor practices of employers, set up an election and certification machinery to settle representation disputes, and created an administrative board to enforce these provisions.

In the next ten years, beginning in 1939, five more states enacted industrial-relations laws, but most of these statutes contained provisions designed to control unions. Three of the earlier laws were also amended to make them more restrictive of unions. Thus, as a reaction against labor set in, alternative policies were worked out in several states which inclined toward individual bargaining, with some reliance on government regulation of industrial negotiations. The lack of a specific alternative to collective bargaining that characterized some of the state laws was reflected in many of the provisions of the Taft-Hartley Act.

The variation in these state labor-relations laws is so great that it is impossible to describe them all in general terms. The significant point is that in these laws enacted before 1947 can be found most of the provisions that were later incorporated into the Taft-Hartley Act. Added to the list of unfair employer practices were unfair labor practices by unions, including coercing an employee into joining a union, engaging in a secondary boycott, picketing without the approval of a majority of the union, striking without giving notice or observing a cooling-off period, and striking with less than majority approval of the union. In some instances union-security agreements were subjected to restrictions, jurisdictional disputes were outlawed, stranger picketing and picketing in the absence of a labor dispute were declared unlawful, and strikes in violation of an agreement were banned. Certain states required unions to register and file certain reports, distribute financial reports to members, and charge only reasonable dues. In a few instances political contributions by unions were outlawed and detailed dispute-settlement procedures, including a cooling-off period, were specified in some states.[89]

[89] For an excellent digest of all union-regulatory laws passed by states, 1937 to 1947, see Killingsworth, *op. cit.*, pp. 267–298.

A wave of reaction against unions swept through the states in 1947, at the very time that Congress was writing the Taft-Hartley Act. In one year's time fourteen states passed laws prohibiting the closed shop and, in all cases except Maine, the union shop as well.[90] Twelve states restricted or regulated picketing and other strike activity, eleven states banned the secondary boycott, and six imposed restrictions on jurisdictional disputes. Disputes in public utilities were regulated in ten states, and strikes by public employees were prohibited in six states. In the same year three states also required registration and financial reports of unions.

By September of 1947, a tabulation of state industrial-relations laws revealed the following: 15 states banned the closed shop and other union-security agreements; 22 restricted picketing and other strike activity; 16 prohibited the secondary boycott; 9 restricted jurisdictional disputes; 12 regulated disputes in public utilities; 11 required registration and a financial report of unions; and 7 outlawed strikes by public employees.[91]

After the passage of the Taft-Hartley Act, in spite of the failure of its critics to amend or repeal it, a surprising reversal occurred in the states. In 1948 and 1949, several state legislatures enacted bills to repeal the anti-closed-shop laws and other union-restrictive statutes they had passed during the past few years. Four states repealed such laws, two of which had been based on the Taft-Hartley Act. In three states the voters, in referendum elections, defeated proposals to ban the closed shop and other union-security agreements. Several states amended their industrial-relations laws, making them less restrictive of unions.[92]

The trend continued into 1951 and 1952 when three states passed measures to facilitate union activity and two states amended anti-injunction laws to restrict further their use in labor disputes. Nevada, however, in 1952, became the first state since 1947 to take advantage of the provision in the Taft-Hartley Act and prohibit all types of union-security agreements. Two other states passed mild restraints on picketing, prohibiting picketing in or near courthouses for the purpose of interfering with the administration of justice.[93]

CONSTITUTIONALITY OF STATE LAWS

The cases involving state labor laws fall into two groups: (1) those in which state statutes or decisions affecting labor unions are attacked as

[90] In New Hampshire union-security contracts were prohibited only with respect to employers having five or less employees.

[91] Council of State Governments, *The Book of the States, 1948–1949* (Chicago, 1948), p. 454.

[92] Council of State Governments, *The Book of the States, 1950–1951* (Chicago, 1950), p. 443.

[93] Council of States Governments, *The Book of the States, 1952–1953* (Chicago, 1952), p. 419.

violations of due process, and (2) those in which such statutes are alleged to be inconsistent with congressional policy.

Many of the cases in the first group deal with the constitutional right to picket. That right was established in 1940 when the Supreme Court characterized picketing as a form of speech and held that an Alabama statute which had been so construed as to make it a substantially complete prohibition of all picketing violated the Fourteenth Amendment by unconstitutionally interfering with the fundamental right of free speech.[94] However, in terms of its effects on the lower courts, the Thornhill bombshell was a dud. Many lower courts ignored it, and a variety of limits on picketing was upheld, such as picketing to enforce discharge of nonunion employees, to achieve a union shop or closed shop, and the like.

The Supreme Court itself retreated from the Thornhill doctrine. In 1941, picketing was prohibited because of a fear of future coercion flowing from past violence.[95] In 1942 picketing was prohibited because it did not follow the subject matter of the dispute.[96] Picketing was prohibited in 1949 on the grounds that it was for illegal purposes; that is, it conflicted with a state law prohibiting restraint of trade.[97] In 1950 three more important decisions were handed down in which picketing was limited.[98] During this period there were also cases in which the Supreme Court permitted picketing.[99]

There is much to indicate that the Court has been charting a course that will take it back to the position where it began before rendering Thornhill. The problem is that picketing is obviously more than speech. The primary function is often not to inform but to turn away persons who might deal with the employer. Since picketing is more than speech, it is argued that it should be subject to regulation under state police power and that the Supreme Court should not interfere with state action.

In the other group of cases, state statutes regulating union activities or some action taken under them were attacked on the ground that they conflicted with federal law. In the earliest case to reach the Court a union attacked an order to cease mass picketing issued under the Wisconsin Employment Peace Act. The Court held that such an order in no way con-

[94] *Thornhill v. Alabama*, 310 U.S. 88 (1940).

[95] *Milk Wagon Drivers' Union v. Meadowmoor Dairies*, 312 U.S. 287 (1941).

[96] *Carpenters & Joiners Union v. Ritter's Cafe*, 315 U.S. 722 (1942). Ritter was picketed in his capacity as a café owner, although the dispute was with Ritter in his capacity as home builder; hence the Court regarded him as a neutral.

[97] *Giboney v. Empire Storage & Ice Co.*, 336 U.S. 490 (1949).

[98] *International Brotherhood of Teamsters, etc., Local 309 v. Hanke*, 339 U.S. 470 (1950); *Hughes v. Superior Court of Calif.*, 339 U.S. 460 (1950); *Building Service Employees v. Gazzom*, 339 U.S. 532 (1950).

[99] *AFL v. Swing*, 312 U.S. 321 (1941); *Bakery & Pastry Drivers Union v. Wohl*, 315 U.S. 769 (1942); *Cafeteria Employees' Union v. Angelos*, 320 U.S. 293 (1943).

flicted with the Wagner Act.[100] However, a Florida statute making it a misdemeanor for a person, without obtaining a license, to act as a business agent of a labor organization was ruled invalid as conflicting with the Wagner Act.[101] Similarly, a Wisconsin law denying employees of public utilities the right to strike for higher wages was held unconstitutional as infringing upon rights guaranteed in national labor law.[102]

On the other hand, the Court handed down decisions in 1949 involving the anti-closed-shop provisions of Arizona, Nebraska, and North Carolina laws. Unanimously in regard to two of the laws, and with only one dissent in the third, the Court declared that it was within the province of the states to determine their own policy with regard to labor unions.[103] These cases involved the Wagner Act, and therefore it would seem that the provision in the Taft-Hartley Act banning the closed shop would be upheld.

In 1953 the Supreme Court decided that state courts were barred from issuing injunctions to enforce state labor laws which parallel the Taft-Hartley Act.[104] The Court unanimously upheld the view of the Pennsylvania Supreme Court that Congress intended that, if a union activity might be held to be an unfair labor practice under the Taft-Hartley Act, the power to determine that question and to act should rest solely with the National Labor Relations Board.

Collective Bargaining: Conclusions

Public policy has undoubtedly been subject to more controversy in the area of collective bargaining than in any other on the domestic scene in recent decades. The policy of government, originally enunciated in the Railroad Labor Acts of the 1920s and broadened to include all industry by the Wagner Act of 1935, clearly encouraged collective bargaining as the most desirable solution to the management-labor conflict. A result of this legislation placing strict safeguards on the right of employees to organize has been the growth of national unions. The original policy which was purposely one-sided in order to encourage labor organization, led to some abuses and unnecessary throttling of employers which were largely removed by the Taft-Hartley law of 1947. While this Act was passed over

[100] *Allen-Bradley Local No. 111 v. WERB*, 315 U.S. 740 (1942).

[101] *Hill v. Florida*, 325 U.S. 538 (1945).

[102] *Amalgamated Assn. of Street, Electric Railway and Motor Coach Employees v. WERB*, 340 U.S. 383 (1951).

[103] *Lincoln Federal Labor Union v. Northwestern Iron and Metal Co.*, *Whitaker v. North Carolina*, 335 U.S. 525 (1949); *AFL v. American Sash and Door Co.*, 335 U.S. 538 (1949).

[104] *Garner v. Teamsters, Chauffeurs and Helpers Local Union No. 776, A.F.L.*, 346 U.S. 485 (1953).

the heated objections of labor unions and with the prophecy that it would seriously impair these organizations, nearly a decade of experience under it has proved that the fears of union leaders were unfounded, since national unions have apparently lost none of their strength in the meanwhile. It appears that the recent laws have resulted in an effective and reasonably fair kind of collective bargaining, and even though problems still exist, the original objective of government policy can be said to have been attained.

In making collective bargaining truly effective, however, a number of problems have resulted. If employers are to have a strength equal to that of national unions, with the possible exception of such very large national employers as General Motors, private business management tends to find it necessary to join together and present a united front in union negotiations. In other words, individual companies, particularly smaller companies, acting alone cannot normally withstand the tremendous economic power of strong national unions. This power, therefore, can practically be equalized only by industrial bargaining.

The existence of industry-wide bargaining, however, presents some difficult public-policy questions. In the first place, combinations of employers dealing with combinations of labor tend to establish a pattern inconsistent with this country's traditional competitive private-enterprise system. In the second place, and perhaps an even more serious problem, industry-wide bargaining sometimes leads to strikes which, because of their widespread effect, may cripple the entire economy. This is obviously most true in the case of industries such as steel, coal, and transportation. But because the American industrial economy has become increasingly interdependent, industry-wide strikes in almost any important field of activity tend seriously to hamper the operation of the entire economy.

The problem of crippling strikes is especially serious in the case of those essential service industries, such as transportation, where the complete lack of any inventory of product brings immediate hardship. In other words, inventories of steel or coal may keep work stoppages in these industries from causing serious public harm for weeks, but a total work stoppage in the railroad, motor trucking, telephone, or electrical-power industries brings almost immediate halt in the operation of the entire economic system.

As a matter of fact, even though public policy has been successful in encouraging collective bargaining and even though collective bargaining, through providing a framework for negotiation by parties of approximate equal power, has generally resulted in sound adjudication of labor disputes, the technique itself does not necessarily solve wage disputes, settle strikes, or maintain production of essential services. There have been many strikes of serious public import since 1935, and there have been many disputes where the government has been forced, by one device or another, to halt the strike.

If, in solving the problem of collective bargaining, public policy has not solved the problem of labor strife or work stoppage harmful to the public interest, one may ask what the alternatives are. Certainly a return to individual bargaining is hardly the answer, because an individual workman typically does not have the economic power to make his negotiating position effective. It is recognized that the shortage of labor since 1941 and the increased enlightenment of management in the importance of human relations since World War II have made collective bargaining somewhat less necessary than was the case in the 1930s and before. Nevertheless, these developments are neither extensive nor thorough enough in their application to safeguard the rights of labor.

Another policy which has sometimes been advanced is one of outlawing industry-wide bargaining in order to localize strikes and maintain a more truly competitive system. While this course of action has much to commend it, there is a question whether it would be acceptable public policy. In the first place, national unions might well claim with justification that this would so weaken their position as to amount to their destruction. In the second place, in some industries the pattern of industry-wide bargaining has been fairly well established, and outlawing this practice might be very disruptive. Nevertheless, this alternative is one which deserves careful study.

In recent years, particularly during the administration of President Eisenhower, the government has tended to follow a laissez-faire policy in handling labor disputes. The philosophy back of this policy is that neither labor or management should look to government for the solution of its problems but that they should come to their own terms through the process of negotiation and even, if necessary, through pitting their economic strength against each other by permitting a strike to run its course. The difficulty with this policy is that a strike in an essential industry may so cripple the economy as to make a work stoppage intolerable to the public.

As the result of the problem of work stoppage in essential industry, and as a result of the increased interrelations in the economic system, a further alternative has often been recommended. In the case of essential industries, it is sometimes believed that the best policy is to require compulsory arbitration of labor disputes by an established government agency and the outlawing of strikes. Although this policy is approached in the fact-finding proceedings under present laws, especially where these fact-finding proceedings have been followed by extraordinary government pressure or positive government action, this approach to solving labor problems has tended to be distasteful to the American public. There is a belief that the right to strike should not be hampered and that the government should not take such a controlling position in labor relations. Yet, government has consistently refused to permit a strike against its own activities, and there appears to be only a small difference in degree in extending this attitude to privately owned essential industry.

Perhaps the best alternative of all, although one which may be too optimistic, is that enlightened and responsible management and union leadership will realize, at least in essential industries, the public dangers involved in strikes and will work, as reasonable parties honestly seeking a fair settlement, until an agreement is reached. While there may be some grounds for not being too hopeful that this kind of approach to union-management negotiations will be adopted widely, there are evidences pointing in this direction. One of these is the greater sense of responsibility found in the leadership of many labor unions and the greater responsiveness of this leadership to the real interests of their members. Another is an enlightened leadership and a recognition of the productivity of labor found in the managements of many industrial firms. If both parties to a dispute can realize that wages must and should be based upon productivity, if ways can continually be found to improve labor productivity, and if a high enough degree of intelligence can be brought to bear on this problem, it is not completely improbable that the public interest in the maintenance of stable labor relations will be satisfied within the present framework of collective bargaining.

Selected References

Bernstein, Irving, *The New Deal Collective Bargaining Policy*. Berkeley, Calif.: University of California Press, 1950.

Berman, Edward, *Labor and the Sherman Act*. New York: Harper & Brothers, 1930.

Bowman, D. O., *Public Control of Labor Relations, A Study of the National Labor Relations Board*. New York: The Macmillan Company, 1942.

Cohen, Sanford, *State Labor Legislation, 1937–1947*. Columbus, Ohio: Bureau of Business Research, Ohio State University, 1949.

Commons, J. R., and J. B. Andrews, *Principles of Labor Legislation*, 4th ed. New York: Harper & Brothers, 1936.

Frankfurter, F., and N. Greene, *The Labor Injunction*. New York: The Macmillan Company, 1930.

Fisher, Thomas R., *Industrial Disputes and Federal Legislation*. New York: Columbia University Press, 1943.

Gregory, C. O., *Labor and the Law*. New York: W. W. Norton & Co., Inc., 1946.

Hartley, Fred A., *Our New National Labor Policy*. New York: Funk & Wagnalls Company, 1948.

Kaltenborn, H. S., *Governmental Adjustment of Labor Disputes*. Brooklyn: The Foundation Press, Inc., 1943.

Killingsworth, Charles G., *State Labor Relations Acts*. Chicago: University of Chicago Press, 1948.

Leiserson, William M., "For a New Labor Law—A Basic Analysis," *New York Times Magazine*, Feb. 6, 1949.

Lindblom, Charles, *Unions and Capitalism*. New Haven, Conn,: Yale University Press, 1949.

Lorwin, Lewis L., and Arthur Wubrig, *Labor Relations Boards*. Washington, D.C.: Brookings Institution, 1935.

Mathews, Robert E., *Labor Relations and the Law*, 2 vols. Boston: Little, Brown & Company, 1953.

Metz, Harold W., *Labor Policy of the Federal Government*. Washington, D.C.: Brookings Institution, 1945.

———, and Meyer Jacobstein, *A National Labor Policy*. Washington, D.C.: Brookings Institution, 1947.

Miller, Glenn W., *American Labor and the Government*. New York: Prentice-Hall, Inc., 1948.

Millis, Harry A., and Emily Brown, *From the Wagner Act to Taft-Hartley. A Study of National Labor Policy and Labor Relations*. Chicago: Univerversity of Chicago Press, 1950.

———, and Royal E. Montgomery, *Organized Labor*, vol. III of *The Economics of Labor*. New York: McGraw-Hill Book Company, Inc., 1945.

Mueller, Stephen J., *Labor Law and Legislation*. Cincinnati: South-Western Publishing Company, 1949.

Perlman, Selig, *A Theory of the Labor Movement*. New York: The Macmillan Company, 1928.

Seidman, Joel, *The Yellow-dog Contract*. Baltimore: Johns Hopkins Press, 1932.

Taylor, Albion G., *Labor Problems and Labor Law*. New York: Prentice-Hall, Inc., 1950.

Taylor, George W., *Government Regulation of Industrial Relations*. New York: Prentice-Hall, Inc., 1948.

Werne, Benjamin, *The Law of Labor Relations*. New York: The Macmillan Company, 1951.

Witte, E. E., *The Government in Labor Disputes*. New York: McGraw-Hill Book Company, Inc., 1932.

Witney, Fred, *Government and Collective Bargaining*. Philadelphia: J. B. Lippincott Company, 1951.

Wollett, D. H., *Labor Relations and Federal Law*. Seattle: University of Washington Press, 1949.

PART SEVEN

PUBLIC PROMOTION AND OWNERSHIP OF ECONOMIC ENTERPRISE

23

GENERAL AIDS TO BUSINESS

Government assistance to business enterprise, like government regulation of the economy, is based on the assumption that such a policy will contribute to the general welfare. It is not always easy to distinguish between government controls and government aids, since government assistance may have an important regulatory effect on the groups being aided. The establishment of standards of weight and measure clearly controls the conduct of business enterprises. The granting of credit or outright subsidies and the provision of such facilities as patent privileges are accompanied by duties and obligations which control business behavior. Moreover, some measures are often effected to assist a certain group, but in doing so they regulate other groups. The fair labor standards that government established to help workers amount to regulation of the employment policies of business. Resale-price-maintenance legislation may help small, independent retailers but acts as a restraint on the pricing policies of other enterprises. Sometimes a program of control is accomplished through assistance measures. The program of agricultural control discussed in the next chapter is actually dominated by a desire to aid the farmer, and extensive subsidies are used to effectuate the plan.

Certain types of government aid have existed since the earliest days of the United States, among which are tariff protection, government-established standards of weight and measure, and patent privileges. Land grants for education and transportation, funds for encouraging and improving farming, and services to foreign trade were among the aids furnished long before 1900.[1]

The present system of government aids is so complex that it is impossible to note all the significant promotional activities. While the state and local governments have done much to aid business, the program of assistance of the federal government has been more important and will be emphasized in this chapter. Also, only those aids which bear rather directly upon economic activities will be discussed; promotion of public health

[1] For a historical account of government promotion of economic activities, see Merle Fainsod and Lincoln Gordon, *Government and the American Economy* (New York: W. W. Norton Company, Inc., 1941), chaps. 4, 5, and 6.

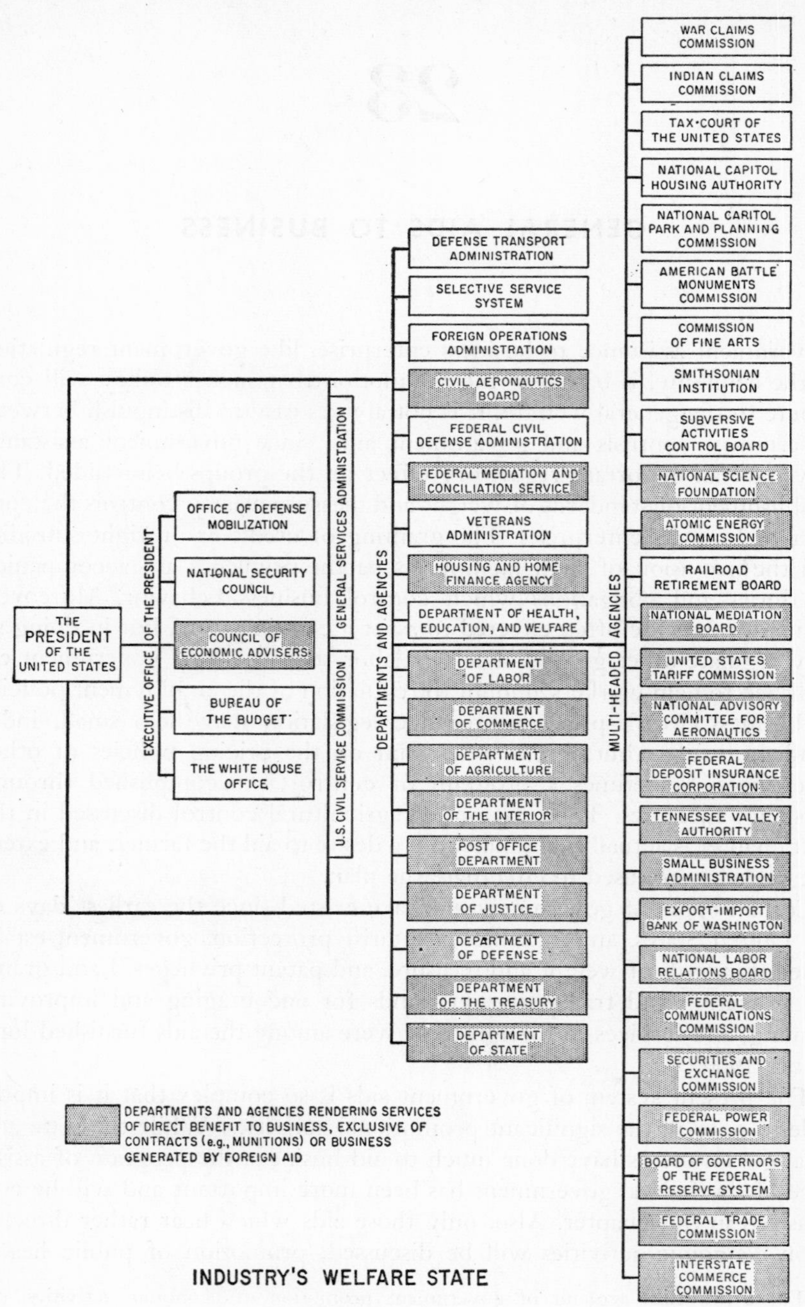

Figure 23—1

Source: Reprinted from Robert K. Carr and others, *American Democracy in Theory and Practice* (New York: Rinehart & Company, Inc., 1955), p. 726, as adapted from the February, 1952, issue of *Fortune Magazine* by special permission of the editors; copyright, 1952, Time, Inc.

and education, it is true, is of great significance and has an important influence on human activity, but since it is not so closely related to economic affairs, such promotion will not be treated here.

Many of the aids extended by the federal government rest upon specific constitutional provisions. Among the powers specifically granted to Congress is the authority to establish a national currency, fix the standard of weights and measures, establish bankruptcy procedures, and provide for patent and copyright protection. Most of the other types of assistance given to business rest on the commerce power or the power to tax and spend, although some have been justified on the basis of the war powers and the postal power.

Government assistance to business, for purposes of discussion, may be classified along the following lines: (1) establishment of a framework for business operation; (2) establishment of standards; (3) special services to business; and (4) financial aids, including the indirect assistance of the tariff, provision of credit facilities, and direct subsidies. In some cases, aids to business have already been treated in discussion of regulation; these aids need only be noted in this chapter.

Establishment of a Framework for Business Operation

Many of the ways in which government assists business are so basic to our constitutional democracy that they may escape attention as being aids to business. Yet without them it would be virtually impossible for the American economic system to function. The Constitution of the United States and many congressional enactments have provided a framework within which business can organize and operate. This framework includes the protection of private property and the obligations of contract, the establishment and maintenance of a monetary system, provision for incorporation and bankruptcy procedures, and the protection of ideas by patents, copyrights, and trade-marks.

PROTECTION OF PROPERTY AND CONTRACT

The right to own, use, and dispose of private property forms the basis for the free-enterprise system. Contracts are the principal way that property, or the services of individuals, are acquired, used, or disposed of. A private-enterprise system could not exist unless property rights and the obligations of contracts were enforced.

The Fifth Amendment to the Constitution protects a person against the deprivation of property by the federal government without due process of law. The states, according to the Fourteenth Amendment, cannot deprive a person of his property without due process of law. Corporations have been viewed as legal persons and therefore have been assured of the same protection.

The right to enter into contracts, whether with regard to persons or to property, has been held to be an incident of the right, not only of property, but also of liberty. Thus, although there is no express constitutional prohibition against the impairment of the obligation of contracts by Congress, since contracts are a form of property (and liberty) protected by the due-process clause, federal encroachments on contracts would probably be held unconstitutional if due process were denied. Assuming, however, that there is no denial of due process, the federal government may impair contract obligations and has done so.

The states, on the other hand, are specifically prohibited in the body of the Constitution from passing any law impairing the obligation of contract. The contract clause of the Constitution has been the subject of interpretation in the Supreme Court more frequently than any other limitation upon the states except that relating to due process.

Thus, through the establishment of the rights of property and their enforcement through the law of contracts, government assists business enterprise and business transactions are made more certain, definite, and secure. At the same time, the power to protect property and enforce contracts carries with it a degree of control, for government also has the power to establish limits to private contracts.

MAINTENANCE OF A MONETARY SYSTEM

The exchange of goods and services is at the heart of any economic system. Business can be conducted by barter, but an economy of the size and volume of the American economy could not be so handled. A definite, reasonably stable, and widely accepted medium of exchange is absolutely indispensable. Therefore, the establishment and maintenance of a monetary system is of utmost importance.

In most countries, including the United States, the provision of money is a function of the government. The Constitution delegates to Congress the exclusive authority to coin money, to regulate its value, and to punish counterfeiting.[2] In providing money, the government has had to define the meaning of the monetary unit, to furnish the monetary instruments to be used in exchange, to limit the agencies which may issue money, and to set up requirements of legal tender.

[2] The monetary powers of the federal government have been used as the constitutional basis for Congress to charter a bank [*McCulloch v. Maryland*, 4 Wheat. 316 (1819)]; make paper bills legal tender in the payment of debts [*Hepburn v. Griswold*, 8 Wall. 603 (1870)]; *Knox v. Lee*, 12 Wall. 457 (1871), and *Juilliard v. Greenman*, 110 U.S. 421 (1884); and cheapen the value of the dollar so that it buys more [*Norman v. Baltimore & Ohio R.R. Co.*, 294 U.S. 240 (1935), and *Perry v. United States*, 294 U.S. 330 (1935)].

The American dollar is defined as the equivalent of a certain amount of gold—a commodity which is generally acceptable by the peoples of the world. Before 1933 any paper or silver money called a "dollar" by the government was the equivalent of a fixed quantity of gold and could be exchanged for it. However, when many people began to withdraw their bank deposits in gold during the depression, bank reserves declined and the stability of banks was seriously endangered. Congress met this problem by abrogating the gold standard. The gold content of the dollar was reduced to 59 per cent of what it had been, the government bought all gold produced in the United States, and the coinage of gold ceased. Now, one may not obtain gold for his paper or silver money, and all gold bullion is stored by the federal government.

Money is legal tender when, according to law, it must be accepted in payment of debt expressed in terms of the monetary unit, and when it is acceptable in settlement of taxes and court decrees. This characteristic means only that if a debtor offers legal-tender money in payment of debt expressed in terms of the monetary unit, the creditor must accept that money or forgo any power to force payment. Strictly speaking, the debt still exists after refusal of legal tender, but the creditor cannot force payment in any other medium, and the statute of limitations would eventually outlaw the debt. Since 1933, all money in the United States has been legal tender.

Obviously, the power of the government to control the issuance of money and to fix the value thereof, along with its power to regulate credit through its supervision of banking, is of tremendous significance to the public. These powers may be used to influence the quantity and character of money and thereby to determine to a large degree its value. Money is not exempt from the law of supply and demand. If the supply of money increases, its value tends to fall—unless, of course, the demand for it likewise increases. If business should decline, or if people should lose confidence in the soundness of money and make their exchanges with some other medium, its value would tend to decrease. Or factors influencing the demand for, or supply of, money could cause a rise in its value. Since a fall in the value of money is expressed through an increase in the number of dollars which all other commodities will command in exchange for dollars, a decline in the value of money results in a rise in prices. An increase in the value of money likewise causes a fall in prices.

Because most contracts for exchange and many claims against economic goods are expressed in terms of the monetary unit, changes in the value of money materially affect these economic relationships. If a debt is contracted for $1,000 at one time, and if at a later due date the price level has fallen by half, in terms of the purchasing power of money at this later time, the debtor is obligated to pay back twice as much as he received. Opposite results follow when prices rise.

In every period of falling prices there has been a demand for governmental monetary control to increase prices and ease the burden of debt. Following every war and financial panic, the government has been pressed to increase the quantity of money. In almost every instance, this has been done. These measures have ranged from expansion of state bank notes after 1837 to the silver purchases since 1890 and the devaluation of the dollar in 1934. This last expedient is an interesting example of the character and importance of the government's monetary power.[3]

PROVISION FOR INCORPORATION

Business has received almost indispensable aid from the government through the passage of legislation which has allowed property rights to be pooled in advantageous organizational forms. In a sense, all forms of business organization exist because the government tolerates them. The procedures, rights, and restrictions upon forms of business organization are often provided by legislation. But the corporation is a form of business which, in itself, has been created by legislation and which does not exist as a common-law right. Thus, incorporation represents a privilege granted by the government through special enabling laws. As yet, in the United States, general incorporation laws are found only in state legislation, although the federal government has incorporated businesses for special purposes.

A corporation is an artificial or fictitious person created by the state for the purpose of owning and using property. The corporate form implies, and legislation has granted to the corporation, certain characteristics which businessmen find to be advantageous. In the first place, ownership of property and the making of contracts in the name of the corporation make possible a continuity and permanence not possible with natural persons, since corporations do not die and need come to an end only when they are dissolved by stockholders or the government. A second advantage is that stockholders are not liable for the debts of the corporation and cannot lose more than the value of their investment (in some cases other possible liabilities exist, but they are relatively unimportant). A third feature advantageous to the stockholders is that shares of stock can ordinarily be transferred freely without affecting the stability of the cor-

[3] Many other governmental policies designed to control the value of the monetary standard might profitably be discussed. For purposes of this book, however, an understanding of the nature and importance of the power of the government to fix the monetary standard and furnish the monetary medium is adequate. For the student interested in a study of government monetary policy, any good money and banking textbook will give an introduction to the subject and will also furnish references for further study.

porate form. Furthermore, as the corporation has developed, the stockholding owners delegate managerial functions to a board of directors which in turn selects the management, thereby making it possible for the stockholder to become an owner without assuming the responsibilities of management. These features of the corporation make it advantageous for long-term business operations and also conduce to obtaining large funds of capital through the appeal of the organizational features to investors.

Every state has enacted a general incorporation law. While these laws differ in details, all follow the same general procedure in allowing natural persons to create a corporation. Three or more natural persons make application to a state official, often the Secretary of State, setting forth in detail certain information about the corporation which they intend to form: the corporate name, location of principal office, purpose of the corporation, capitalization, original stockholders, life of the corporation, and rights and obligations of stockholders. The information is drawn up with regard for the state law and what it allows corporations to do. When the application has been filed, fees paid, and other legal requirements met, the state official customarily approves the application automatically. It then becomes a charter by which the state contracts for the creation of a corporation. Most states grant such broad powers to corporations and place so few restrictions upon incorporators, directors, and stockholders that the choice between states is often made on the basis of taxation or mere convenience. Some few states are far more restrictive than others, limiting the privilege of owning stock in other corporations, forbidding the issuance of nonvoting stock, limiting the power of directors in acting on matters without specific stockholder approval, or forbidding certain questionable financial practices. The real difference in the laws of the great majority of states lies in taxation.

The very fact that the element of taxation, in the absence of the convenience or necessity of being incorporated in the state where most of the business is done, plays the dominant part in the selection of a state for incorporation is a striking commentary upon state incorporation laws themselves. The states have engaged in an almost unwholesome competition in giving to private individuals an important public privilege.

As a corrective for overly lax state incorporation laws, suggestions have been made and bills introduced into Congress providing for federal incorporation or federal licensing of corporations. Although the federal laws could probably reach only those corporations engaged in or affecting interstate commerce, the breadth of interstate commerce arising from recent interpretations of the courts would appear to make it possible for the federal government to reach most business corporations. Possibly a more practical plan would be the licensing of corporations, closing the channels of interstate commerce to those businesses which refuse to take a federal license. This measure would avoid the problem of usurpation of state incorporation privileges and the political importance of incorporation taxes to the states. The conditions for licensing could be made broad and strict enough to allow the federal government to make corporation regulation uniform and effective. The power to incorporate is a valuable social privilege, and society should make sure that it is used to achieve desirable social objectives.

DEBT RELIEF

The government has contributed to orderly and efficient business operation by the enactment of legislation and the establishment of judicial process allowing businesses to be released from debt burdens which they no longer can support, or to adjust debt claims so that they may be continued as producing social mechanisms. This orderly liquidation or readjustment of property rights has been provided for by bankruptcy and reorganization laws and procedures. Although these have sometimes been used to allow incompetent or even unscrupulous individuals to escape their obligations, it is nevertheless in the social interest that the burden of insupportable debt be economically and systematically adjusted. A business unable to meet its obligations tends to impair the proper functioning of other businesses. If creditors were simply allowed to sue according to their common-law rights, the result would be delay and confusion in the number of suits, with advantages in obtaining satisfaction of claims lying with creditors who make the first suits. Moreover, if businesses had always to be liquidated upon their inability to meet claims when due, many economic units would be forced to withdraw resources from production, and capital would be lost in the process. As a general rule, if an economic organization can be kept as a going concern, the capital sunk in the enterprise can be made to produce far more effectively than if it must be liquidated.

The purpose of bankruptcy and reorganization procedures is to provide for the orderly adjustment of debt in a situation where the debtor is incapable of meeting his obligations. The procedures should allow creditors fair and reasonable protection of their claims and should enable them to obtain the greatest possible satisfaction of these claims in the salvaging process. These procedures should be designed for expediting the process of readjustment and for conserving the economic resources of society.

Bankruptcy procedures. Bankruptcy procedures derive from long-accepted judicial practice, as well as from specific enabling legislation. Both the liquidation and the reorganization of financially embarrassed businesses may be handled by resort to courts of equity. Under this procedure, a judge of a court of equity, upon request of a creditor or the company, may appoint a receiver to manage the business for the court. The judge does not ordinarily appoint the receiver, unless he is convinced that the company is insolvent or in danger of being unable to pay its debts, and unless he believes that an appointment is necessary to preserve the property rights in the interests of all creditors. An equity receivership does not generally arise unless there are many creditors, for otherwise one or two creditors could simply sue for their claim and attach such property as necessary for their satisfaction. But where there are many creditors, as is likely to be the case in the modern business corporation, allowing damage suits to be filed would make it possible for the creditors who sued first to receive full compensation of their claim and other creditors to receive nothing.

The receiver in equity simply acts to conserve the assets of the business until the court is ready to make a judicial sale of the property to satisfy the claims of the creditors. In most business receiverships involving large businesses, the receivership period is used to obtain an agreement between creditors as to the proper share of their claims and to allow for the setting up of a new corporation to take over the assets of the defaulted business. When the judicial sale is made, the assets are sold to a creditor or stockholder group, which turns them over to a new corporation. The business is continued as a going concern, and claims are adjusted to satisfy creditors and owners and to enable the new corporation to fulfill its obligations. This process is referred to as "reorganization." In some cases the receiver may realize that the business cannot be reorganized. He then liquidates the assets, and the court distributes the proceeds to creditors according to the priority and size of their claims. Since liquidation usually involves sacrifices of the assets far below their book values, creditors are generally quite willing to assume a reduction in their claims if the business can be reorganized and continued.

The equity procedure has been modified and supplemented by state and federal legislation. Until 1898, except for laws with temporary effect passed on several occasions during the preceding century, the several states dominated the field of bankruptcy legislation. The federal government was given a specific constitutional grant of power to enact bankruptcy legislation, but such laws as were passed between 1800 and 1898 either were repealed or became ineffective. In 1898 a permanent federal bankruptcy law was passed, and since 1933 the scope of such laws has increased until they supersede the state laws in importance for the treatment of business failure.

There have been several reasons for superseding equity procedures with bankruptcy legislation. The procedure under equity was advantageously flexible, but in many cases this very flexibility led to abuses. Receivers and bankers and lawyers on reorganization committees sometimes took excessive expenses and fees from the bankrupt companies. Occasionally, one group of creditors was able to take unfair advantage of another. Reorganizations were often held up for long periods of time by the power of dissenting creditors to hold out from the plan in the hope of getting a larger share of the proceeds than they would get by accepting reorganization plans. In other cases, the price set for judicial sale was so low as to squeeze out junior creditors and stockholders who had real property rights in the failed company. Difficulties also arose from equity receiverships because of the conflict of jurisdiction between state and federal courts and between federal courts in different districts. Businesses with properties in many localities often faced the complex task of obtaining reorganization through parallel bankruptcy proceedings going on in several judicial districts. Not only did this conflict retard the completion of reorganization, but it increased the expense.

The reasons for having federal laws for bankruptcy rather than state laws are also clear. With business operating in several states, the problem of jurisdiction impedes reorganization. Moreover, the courts have held that state bankruptcy laws could not discharge a debtor in one state from his full obligation to a creditor in another state, so complete bankruptcy proceedings were necessary in every state in which a company did business or had creditors.

For purposes of analysis here, it will be sufficient to note the more important provisions of federal bankruptcy legislation. This legislation has provided for a general bankruptcy law and for laws which enact special procedures for certain types of businesses.

General-business bankruptcy legislation. The general-business bankruptcy law enacted in 1898, and revised in some minor details since that time, defines the procedure and the rights of claimants in case of bankruptcy but does not work very material changes in previous equity procedure.

Special bankruptcy procedures for railroads, moneyed corporations, and farmers. Federal laws have provided for special bankruptcy and reorganization procedures for interstate railroads, which have been designed to expedite railroad reorganization and place the Interstate Commerce Commission in a role whereby it can influence the reorganization plan and control the costs involved. Although the operation of this legislation has not speeded up railroad reorganization, primarily because of the necessity for plans to shuttle between the Commission and the courts, the Commission has been instrumental in paring down railroad debt and reducing capitalizations.

A bank or insurance company may not be liquidated or reorganized under general bankruptcy or reorganization laws. To protect the investing public, states and the federal government require that liquidation or reorganization of moneyed corporations be under the supervision of the government agency empowered to regulate them. Moreover, where a bank has its deposits guaranteed by the Federal Deposit Insurance Corporation, that agency naturally participates and exerts much control over the bankruptcy process.[4]

Special bankruptcy procedures also apply to farmers who are unable to pay agricultural mortgages. After an earlier mortgage-relief law was declared unconstitutional as a deprivation of the creditor's property,[5] Congress passed a farm-mortgage-relief law in 1934 which has been upheld by the United States Supreme Court.[6] In this law, Congress provided that a farmer unable to pay his mortgage could be adjudged a bankrupt in the federal courts and that the court could stay legal proceedings for three years. At any time during this period, the court could order that the property be appraised, allowing the farmer to obtain clear title to it by paying the appraised value. During the period when the foreclosure proceedings might be stayed, the farmer is obligated to pay fair rental to the mortgage holder. Protection to the creditor is further furnished by the provision that he can insist upon the sale of the mortgaged farm at auction, although the law gives the dispossessed farmer the privilege for ninety days to regain ownership by paying the auction price and 5 per cent interest.

Special general-business-corporation procedures. Section 77b, passed as an amendment to the bankruptcy law in 1934 and amended by the Chandler Act of 1938, has established a special bankruptcy procedure for general business corporations. While business corporations can still have their insolvency difficulties resolved by resort to equity receiverships, the advantages of the new procedure have been such as to encourage businesses to use it. The new special bankruptcy legislation attempts to remove the stigma from bankruptcy, to provide simpler and less expensive procedures, and to provide methods designed to aid in the sound reconstruction of a corporation.

Either voluntary or involuntary proceedings may be initiated under the new law. Upon the approval of a bankruptcy petition, the judge must appoint one or more disinterested trustees in cases where the debtor's indebtedness amounts to $250,000 or more. In the case of smaller indebtedness, he may appoint disinterested trustees or he may appoint the existing management or others interested in the property. The requirement of disinterested trustees for the larger corporations has been introduced to remove from the control of a bankrupt corporation those who managed it before the insolvency. Of course, if the distinterested trustee desires,

[4] See above, p. 427.

[5] *Louisville Joint Stock Land Bank v. Radford*, 295 U.S. 555 (1935).

[6] *Wright v. Mountain Trust Bank*, 300 U.S. 440 (1937).

he may continue the old management in office for purposes of operating the property.

The trustee is charged with the formulation of a reorganization plan within a time fixed by the court and with the assistance of suggestions by interested parties. Hearings are held on the plan, at which all parties interested may offer suggestions or modifications. If the judge believes a plan to be worthy of consideration, he must submit it to the Securities and Exchange Commission for an advisory report if the corporation has indebtedness in excess of $3 million; in other cases, he may or may not submit the plan to the Commission, as he wishes. After an advisory report from the Commission, which is not binding upon the judge, any plan deemed by him to be equitable, fair, and feasible may be submitted to the creditors and stockholders included within the plan. If two-thirds in amount of the classes of security holders included within the plan approve of it, the court may make it effective.

The law lays down numerous provisions which must be included in a reorganization plan. These are partly of a definite regulatory character and partly to protect nonassenting security holders. The regulatory features insist upon provisions in the new corporate organization for equitable selection of officers and directors compatible with the interests of security holders and the public, equitable distribution of voting power and prohibition of issuance of nonvoting stock, fair distribution of rights and privileges of classes of security holders, and (for companies with an indebtedness of $250,000 or more) periodic issuance of financial statements. The protective features required are the fair and reasonable treatment of dissenting creditors and the just protection of claims of stockholders who are left out of a reorganization plan.

The new law also provides for safeguards against abuses by protective committees and others soliciting proxies or deposits of securities. These provisions are designed to prevent exploitation of the bankrupt corporation's estate by persons who make it a business of interfering in reorganizations and attempting to obtain high fees for services of questionable worth. The law also attempts to stop misrepresentation by interested parties in getting creditors and stockholders to assent to reorganization plans.

PATENT PRIVILEGES

One of the most valuable of government aids to business is the grant of temporary monopolies to persons who invent devices. The federal government has allowed inventors to have the exclusive right to their inventions since the first general patent law was passed in 1790. This law was based upon the definite power granted to Congress by the Constitution to secure "for limited times to authors and inventors the exclusive right to their respective writings and discoveries." From time to time since 1790, the federal patent law has been revised, but the general principles of granting a patent to any person who could prove an invention and the general outline of patent procedure remain essentially the same. The rights of patent holders have, of course, undergone modification with legislative amendment and judicial interpretation, and the many problems of patents have undergone some changes.

Patent requirements. With the single exception of persons employed by the U.S. Patent Office of the Department of Commerce, any person who has made an original and patentable discovery may apply for a patent. The patent law defines as patentable the invention or discovery of any useful art, manufacture, engine, machine, composition of matter, ornamental design, or botanical plant. The scope of patentable things is so broad that almost any idea which can be put into tangible form [7] can be patented. In addition to the general character of articles which may be patented, the law insists that they be novel and useful.

The granting of a patent secures, under present law, to the inventor exclusive rights for a period of seventeen years, except in the case of design patents, in which the period ranges from three and one-half to fourteen years. By means of various devices, however, the actual period of patent monopoly may be extended, although it takes an act of Congress to extend the basic patent monopoly beyond the stated seventeen-year period. The monopoly period does not begin until the patent is issued, and since patents may be pending for a number of years in which the monopoly is practically effective, the total monopoly period may be much longer than seventeen years. By resort to amendment of patent claims by the inventor and protracted litigation, the period of pendency may be very long. A patent may also be used publicly for two years before the inventor even need make an application. Moreover, where a device depends upon the combination of several patents, by spacing the application or issue of these patents, or by superimposing new and essential patents upon old patents, the period of actual patent monopoly may be extended for a long period of time.

Rights of patent holders. A patent holder has the exclusive right to the use of his invention during the period of effectiveness. This includes the right of the holder to use it himself, or to license others to use it, or not to use it at all, or to assign full rights for use to other persons. The patent is a property right, and as such it can be used in the same way as can any

[7] Even a design must be expressed in a tangible object. Thus, a dress design or a silverware design is patented, but it must be expressed in the dress or the silverware. However, what is actually patented is the design and not the object.

other property right. While corporations cannot apply for patents or have them issued to them, they may have patents assigned to them by inventors immediately upon issuance.

Use of the patent by others without permission of the patent holder subjects the user to liability for infringement of the property right. To establish the liability, however, the patent holder must have marked the patented articles properly and the patent must be valid in every respect. Even though a patent is issued by the Patent Office, it may not be valid, and a person accused of infringement has the right to contest the validity of the patent in the courts. An interesting example of escape from liability for infringement is represented by the famous defense of the Ford Motor Company in a suit for infringement of the so-called Selden patents.[8] These were issued to cover the idea of an automobile as a unit, and for a time they were used to require all automobile manufacturers to be licensed by Selden interests and pay royalties for production of automobiles. On appeal to the courts, the Ford Motor Company effectively broke the Selden monopoly by having it restricted to an automobile of a particular design.

The damages which may be claimed for infringement are greater than those which can be obtained under most property-appropriation suits. The patent holder may claim damages for losses he has suffered as well as profits made by the infringer in the use of the patent. Or a court may enter judgment for damages, in excess of those suffered by the patent holder and allowed by a jury, up to three times the verdict.

Criticisms and proposed reforms of patent laws. The operation of the patent laws has indubitably aided the development of efficiency and progress in American industry. But the laws have not operated without serious criticism.[9] The chief criticisms which have been advanced involve the questions of volume and social merit of patents, of long monopoly periods, of cost and delay in obtaining patents, of suppression of patents, and of patent concentration. Problems which have arisen from patent pooling have already been discussed in connection with the operation of the antitrust laws.[10]

Most authorities seem to be agreed that a large percentage of patents are issued which have little or no social value and which represent improvements in trifling details that should not be regarded as inventions. There are several causes for the low standard of invention. The Patent Office has neither the staff nor the funds to examine all patent applications

[8] See *Investigation of Concentration of Economic Power* (1939), part 2, pp. 267–271.

[9] For an interesting discussion of the United States patent system, see the testimony of numerous experts in the hearings before the Temporary National Economic Committee (the Monopoly Inquiry), printed in *ibid.*, parts 2 and 3, pp. 253–1159.

[10] See above, pp. 396–400.

and to make a technical judgment of the worth of an invention. Even where the Office has refused patents on account of lack of novelty or social value, the courts have occasionally overruled the Office. Patent attorneys sometimes encourage the patenting of useless inventions in order to obtain revenue. But even a frank and well-meaning attorney can exercise only a limited restraint upon poor patents, because of the natural enthusiasm of the inventor and his suspicion that the attorney is attempting to "steal" his invention. Moreover, the proper standard of quality for a patentable invention can hardly be defined. This problem presents such difficulty that probably all a law can do is to set up in unequivocal terms the necessity for patents to possess a positive degree of social utility. Such a change in legislation would not necessarily solve the problem, because it would still leave the definition of certain terms to the discretion of administrative and court officials. However, if the new legislative standards were accompanied by appropriations to increase the investigatory work by the Patent Office, they might serve to warn these officials of the proper standards which should apply. As the law has developed, the standard has become one of absence of social disutility, and if an invention promises not to work harm, it will be allowed irrespective of any positive advantages.

Another prominent criticism of the patent laws is the long monopoly periods which are sometimes enjoyed. Because of the possibility of pending applications and other devices, patent holders have been known to extent their patent privileges beyond the statutory seventeen years. One patent monopoly extended for forty-four years, the seventeen-year term following upon twenty-seven years of litigation.[11] Pendency of application for five to ten years preceding issuance of patent is not unusual, with such delays more likely to be encountered in the case of patents of high social value, because of the conflict of interests and the desire of the applicant to extend the monopoly.

The suppression of patents by groups interested in keeping them off the market has been subject to criticism. Many patents are purchased to exclude other persons from developing a product which might compete with an existing one. Patents are also suppressed to keep existing machinery or processes in which a company has a large investment from becoming obsolete. This suppression is made possible by the legal right of a patent holder to use or not to use a patent, as he sees fit. Some suppression of patents may be socially desirable in order to reduce capital losses and labor displacement from too rapid technological changes, but this retardation of progress can be dangerous in private hands. Some withholding of patents may be desirable to allow a group of producers to build up accep-

[11] *Investigations of Concentration of Economic Power* (1939) part 3, pp. 853–855, 1132–1137. Data concerning other instances are found in this investigation.

table standards in a new industry. Suppression of patents which have military significance may also be justifiable in the interests of national defense.

To meet the danger to social progress through undue suppression of patents, various proposals for compulsory licensing have been made. The most usual proposal is to require issuance of a license under a patent if it has not been used by the holder for a certain period of time. Proposals for compulsory licensing raise many questions. In view of the constitutional grant of power to Congress to give "exclusive rights" to inventors, compulsory licensing might not be constitutional. Moreover, it might interfere with the development of an invention. Many inventions must be used in connection with others, and the development of a good employing several patents may require extended research along several lines. Compulsory licensing has also been opposed by many licensing companies on the ground that, if they were forced to license competitors at a reasonable fee, they might actually be forced out of business by a stronger and larger licensee. Compulsory licensing has hence been criticized as tending to remove some of the incentive for invention.

A further important criticism of the American patent system is found in the contention that patents tend to be concentrated in few hands and to promote monopoly. Since so many patents are assigned to corporations and this practice has been growing,[12] many people are led to believe that patents are becoming concentrated in too few hands. The sheer number of patents held by individual corporations does not necessarily show the importance of the patents held, and the fact remains that the increase in patents assigned to corporations is not yet very alarming. Most of the corporations holding patents are small ones, a perfectly understandable phenomenon in view of the risk of patent development. The majority of unexpired patents are also held by small corporations. Moreover, the existence of many cross-licensing agreements have made patents widely available.

To meet the possible threat of concentration, it has been proposed to limit the number of patents which any person may hold. This proposal seems to be arbitrary and rather unnecessary. For one thing, the problem of patent concentration does not seem to be very great, and the use of patents in combination for purposes of monopolizing trade might better be dealt with through the antitrust laws. Consideration should also be given to the economic necessity of the development of patents by corporations and large businesses. Patent development not only is risky but often requires much research and the expenditure of large sums of money. Individual inventors and small companies cannot always furnish these facilities. Efficient development of patents is almost sure to result in some

[12] In 1921, approximately 27 per cent of issued patents went to both small and large corporations, while in 1938 over 57 per cent went to them. See *ibid.*, p. 1127.

concentration of them. But until this concentration appears to be abused more than it is at the present, or until the government is unable to deal with abuses through the antitrust laws, modification of the patent laws to prevent concentration does not seem to be desirable.

COPYRIGHT PRIVILEGES

The federal Constitution also gives Congress the power to grant authors exclusive rights to their work for a limited period of years. To secure these rights for authors, Congress has enacted copyright laws since 1890. Copyright legislation does not have as much business significance as do patent laws—except, of course, in the case of the publishing business. Hence, it will be necessary here only to note the main provisions of copyright laws.

The law provides that any of the following may be copyrighted: books, periodicals, newspapers, lectures, sermons, public speeches, dramatic compositions, musical compositions, works of art, maps, drawings, photographs, including moving pictures, and other kinds of pictorial works. While any of these articles may be copyrighted, not every expression of an idea included in them may be protected. The expression must represent some artistic or intellectual work. Moreover, the copyright covers only the particular expression of the idea and not the idea itself. The copyright holder obtains no proprietary interest in the idea, as in the case of patent holders, and can claim infringement only if the expression itself is copied. In the case of such writings as newspapers, the newspaper cannot copyright the news itself, although it can copyright a way of expressing the news which has artistic merit. A photographer cannot copyright the subject of his photograph, but can merely be protected against others' copying the photograph itself.

Copyrights give exclusive privileges to the author, his kin upon his death, or an assignee of the copyright, for a period of twenty-eight years. Except for assignees of copyrights, other copyright owners may renew the privilege for an additional twenty-eight years. The copyright may be assigned to others, although the assignment is void if not registered with the Copyright Office. The copyright gives to the holder the right to print or reprint a work in any language, or to convert it into some other form of artistic expression (a book copyright owner retains the right to convert the book into a drama), or to perform or present the work to the public for profit. Any interference in this right by other persons constitutes an infringement and may be the cause for damages.

TRADE-MARK PRIVILEGES

The Constitution gave Congress no special power for the registration of trade-marks, probably because important product differentiation did not develop until more recent years. Moreover, even under the common law, misrepresentation and appropriation of trade-names were causes for damage suits by aggrieved parties. Not until 1870 did Congress enact legislation for the registration of trade-marks. This early law was found constitutional as a valid use of the interstate-commerce power in 1879,[13] and later trademark laws of 1881, 1905, 1920, and 1946 have been presumed to be constitutional. State legislation also provides for registration of trade-marks and generally covers those which would be used only in intrastate commerce. State laws, however, follow pretty closely the pattern of federal law.

Federal registration of trade-marks. The Lanham Trade-mark Act of 1946 codifies and simplifies, and to a certain extent revises and liberalizes, common and federal statutory law on trade-marks. Provision is made for the registration of service marks, collective marks, and certification marks, in addition to trade-marks.[14]

These marks can be registered with the U.S. Patent Office upon application and the payment of a $25 fee. Those which cannot be registered are marks which show the flag or symbol of any government agency, or which are immoral or obscene, or which are merely descriptive, deceptively misdescriptive, or merely geographical, or which are closely similar to marks previously registered.

Registration of trade-marks and other marks lasts for twenty years, but it may be renewed for like periods of time. The holding of a registered federal trade-mark entitles the holder to sue for damages in the federal courts, under a law which allows the judge to grant damages up to three times the amount incurred and supported by a verdict. Furthermore, the holding of a registered trade-mark establishes a valuable claim for priority in its use, in case a damage suit or a suit to enjoin appropriation by a competitor is sought.

The significance of trade-marks. The government's assistance to trade-mark maintenance and protection, provided by the trade-mark–registration laws, has been of invaluable aid to business. Product differentiation would be virtually impossible without trade-marks. The general development of monopolistic competition depends to a large extent upon them. The fixing of resale prices by a manufacturer or wholesaler would hardly be feasible without some kind of product distinction. While the common law would

[13] *The Trade-Mark Cases*, 100 U.S. 82 (1879).

[14] A trade-mark is a word, name, symbol or device which identifies and distinguishes goods; e.g., Chevrolet for cars, or Zenith for radios. A service mark identifies or distinguishes a service; e.g., Greyhound for bus transportation. A collective mark is one used by a group to identify or distinguish goods or services of members; e.g., Sunkist for oranges. A certification mark is one used for goods and services of any person other than owners to certify regional origin, quality, accuracy, mode of manufacture, and the like; e.g., the "Good Housekeeping Seal of Approval."

protect property rights in trade-names, and the law against unfair competition would also limit unfair use of a trade designation by a competitor, the registration procedure systematizes trade-marks and offers government recognition of the ownership in them. Perhaps it might be said that the government in protecting property in a trade-name has contributed to the breakdown of the freer and more perfect competition.

Establishment of Standards

The system of buying and selling goods is materially aided by the assurance that the goods exchanged meet certain government prescribed standards of weight, measure, and quality.

STANDARDS OF WEIGHT AND MEASURE

The federal Constitution authorizes the national government to fix standards of weight and measure. But in spite of the completeness of the power of the national government to fix such standards, the setting of practically all lawful standards is left to the state governments. This anomalous situation may seem difficult to understand, but there are several reasons which may explain it. The standards of measurement in existence in the states at the time of the establishment of the federal government varied somewhat, and difficulty was encountered in arriving at an agreement. Moreover, disagreement was encountered as to whether to adopt standards according to the English system, which was in preponderant use in the United States about 1800, or according to the metric system. The lack of federal control may also be explained by the difficulties the young government had in meeting other problems and by the fact that state governments voluntarily followed federal government recommendations, thereby developing a surprising uniformity throughout the nation.

The federal government has, however, played a substantial role in the fixing of standards of weight and measure. By legislation passed in 1894 and 1915, standards for electrical measurement and for the barrel were definitely prescribed by the law. As early as 1836, Congress ordered the Secretary of the Treasury to provide the states with detailed lists of weights and measures used in the calculation of import duties. Since 1901, when the National Bureau of Standards was created (placed a few years later in the Department of Commerce), the national government has assumed increasing leadership over the establishment and maintenance of uniform standards. Moreover, the standards used by various federal agencies, especially the many regulatory agencies, the Public Health Service, the Army, the Navy, and many service bureaus, have been made uniform and have influenced the establishment of like standards by the states.

The leading part in the establishment of standards has been taken by the Bureau of Standards. The Bureau not only maintains testing and experimental laboratories but encourages assistance from scientists and businessmen in the setting and modifying of standards. It operates scale- and measure-testing services to check upon and aid in the administration of state weight and measure laws.

STANDARDS OF QUALITY

Consumers and business have been aided by state and federal specification of standards of quality. A bushel of wheat of one quality is a different good from a bushel of another quality, and one pound of butter or a drug may differ materially from another pound. Hence, if standards are to mean anything for purposes of exchange, it is practically necessary to have uniformity in quality classifications. Requirements of grading and description may be onerous to businessmen, but business in general stands to gain from standards which make it difficult for a product to be passed off as being of a quality superior to that which it is. Establishment of standards of quality is closely related to the maintenance of fair competition, discussed in Chapter 15, in that the proper description and classification of goods remove one of the principal bases for practices which are unfair to competitors and deceptive to consumers.

The federal government has done most of its work in establishing quality standards in the field of agricultural products; foods, drugs, and cosmetics; and certain commercial goods. It has taken more definite action in establishing quality standards than in fixing standards of weight and measure. The state governments, however, still exercise an important degree of control, even in regard to quality.

Special Services to Business

The government gives so many special services to business that one can hardly present a complete picture of them. Many of the regulatory agencies give such services as accounting advice to business in the normal course of supervising it. Their published statistical reports and opinions often contain information of great usefulness. Furthermore, regulatory functions are sometimes intermixed with promotional ones, and in many instances the government aids have been discussed along with the regulation. This has been especially true in the previous discussion of government regulation in behalf of labor, and further treatment at this point is believed to be unnecessary. Some of the governmental aids to transportation have also been noted previously, and only the special services to maritime shipping need be noted in this chapter.

STATISTICAL INFORMATION

Government is the chief source of statistical information. Nearly every agency of the federal government, as well as other levels of government, contributes in some way to the collection and dissemination of statistical information that is valuable to business. The primary function of many agencies is to make this information available. Other agencies furnish it as a by-product of their normal reporting of activities.

The principal statistical aids to business may be classified according to the subject matter of the data, such as national income, money, population, foreign commerce, manufacturing and distribution, mining, transportation, agriculture, banking, labor, investment information, and consumer information. In fact, so extensive are the statistical data available from government sources that business of all kinds would doubtless be crippled in many areas of their management, particularly major policy formulation, without them. On the other hand, there often appear to be many relatively useless studies and statistical data produced by government agencies. Yet experience has shown that whenever any government agency suggests deletion of various reports or statistics, there is almost always a strong objection from some segment of the economy which has found the data useful.

SPECIAL SERVICES TO SHIPPING

The federal government has long given certain special services to shipping. These include various kinds of inspection activities, survey and map work, and lighthouse services. Inspection of marine equipment is entrusted to the United States Coast Guard of the Treasury Department. The Coast Guard carries on regulatory functions in inspecting merchant vessels for safety and seaworthiness and in its administration and enforcement of rules and regulations governing construction, equipment, operation, and manning of vessels. While these inspection duties are helpful to shipping companies, the Coast Guard has in addition a technical division which makes studies of and recommendation concerning naval architecture, marine engineering, and electrical engineering.

Another service which only government is able to furnish is the aid to water and aerial navigation by lighthouse, buoys, and radio beacons. These aids are administered by the Lighthouse Service, since 1939 consolidated with the Coast Guard. This service includes not only the furnishing of many navigation aids but research into new methods to make navigation safe and efficient.

An aid to the government which is practically indispensable for shipping is the surveying and mapping work of the Coast and Geodetic Survey of the Department of Commerce. Geographical data could hardly be developed upon such a broad scale by a private enterprise, and the wide sweep of shipping operations makes full and complete geodetic surveys a necessary and justifiable function of the government. The Coast and Geodetic Survey carries on extensive surveying operations and produces charts needed for safe navigation on the coastal and intercoastal waters of the United States. Aeronautical charts are prepared for airmen. Seismological studies are made for aid in designing structures to withstand earthquakes. Studies are made of tides and currents, of the earth's magnetism, and of gravitational and astronomical observations. Many of these studies are utilized for shipping and some for other businesses.

SPECIAL SERVICES TO FOREIGN TRADE

The Department of State carries on a well-organized system of assistance to the operation of foreign trade throughout the world. Through the establishment of consular offices in numerous cities of the world, the government furnishes facilities for the expedition of foreign trade with this country. These officers help businesses by furnishing them information of trade conditions, by aiding domestic firms to meet foreign buyers and sellers, by watching out for property rights of American businessmen in foreign nations, and by assisting in protection of American trade-marks and patents.

The Office of International Trade aids foreign trade by seeking to reduce obstacles and restriction abroad to international trade, bringing specific trade opportunities to the attention of exporters and importers, and helping resolve trade disagreements. The Office helps administer foreign trade zones—those port areas designated by Congress where foreign goods may stop temporarily, without tariffs, for repacking and reshipment. The Office also worked with the United Nations in setting up the International Trade Organization and helps formulate reciprocal tariff agreements.

SPECIAL SERVICES TO FISHERIES

Because of the common-ownership character of fishing grounds and the inability of private enterprise to control them, the special assistance of the government to the fishing industry is not difficult to understand. The Fish and Wildlife Service of the Department of Interior is charged with a variety of government aids, and also administers some regulatory functions respecting interstate shipments of fish and fishing in certain territorial waters. The aids include investigations of catches, propagation conditions, and marketing practices; technical assistance to fishery and hatchery administrators of the states; the operation of experimental hatcheries; and conservation of fur seals.

SPECIAL SERVICES TO MINING

Besides the statistical help given the mining industry by the Bureau of Mines, other assistance is granted through technical investigations carried on by the Bureau. These have centered about activities to promote safety and health of mining, and researches to show operators methods for efficiency mining and treating minerals. The constant research activities have contributed much to mine safety, one discovery alone, the use of rock dusting, having resulted in highly improved mine operation. Causes of accidents and disease have been studied, and the Bureau has recommended many safety devices and has also established safety stations and mine rescue cars to be used in cases of disaster. The conduct of experimental mines has also brought about improved methods of mining and the elimination of much waste of natural resources.

FINANCIAL AIDS

INDIRECT FINANCIAL AID—THE TARIFF

While all governmental aids involve the expenditure of a portion of the national income for the purpose of helping a particular group, there are certain kinds which place funds in the hands of the recipients. The more obvious type is the subsidizing of an industry, for example, of the merchant marine and the aviation industry. A little less obvious, but nevertheless real, is the extension of credit to private groups through governmentally furnished facilities and upon the strength of government credit. Definitely in the same class of government aids is the imposition of protective or prohibitory tariffs [15] upon articles imported into the country. Tariffs do not involve government expenditures to aid a particular industry, but by eliminating or lessening competition from foreign industry, they permit a protected industry to charge higher prices and thereby obtain a larger share of the national income. As such, tariffs, when protective, are the equivalent of government subsidies. The incidence of a tariff is, however, ordinarily different from that of taxation to raise government

[15] A tariff is simply a tax levied upon goods imported into the country. While it may be levied to obtain revenue, and often is, it may also be "protective" or "prohibitory." Technically, a protective tariff is one which is high enough to make the foreign price of the good, plus transportation charges, plus the tariff, equal to the domestic price of the good. This supposedly places foreign and domestic sellers on an equal competitive basis. A prohibitory tariff is one high enough to make it practically impossible for foreign sellers to compete in the domestic market. To the extent that a tariff is really prohibitory, no imports of the good come into the country and no customs revenue accrues to the government. Since a domestic producer or seller is not really protected from foreign competition by a protective tariff, the tendency in this country has been to make "protective" tariffs prohibitory.

funds for outright subsidies. Its burden really falls upon the consumers of goods produced by the protected industry, while the burden of government subsidies will fall generally upon the taxpayers of the country.

Development of the American tariff. Customs duties have been levied upon a varying list of imports since the first tariff act of 1789. The demand for tariff protection continued, especially after the War of 1812, when foreign trade increased rapidly, until by 1828, in the so-called "Tariff of Abominations," protectionism dominated the formulation of import duties.

The Southern and Western planters, whose products were exported and who gained nothing and lost much by tariff duties which allowed

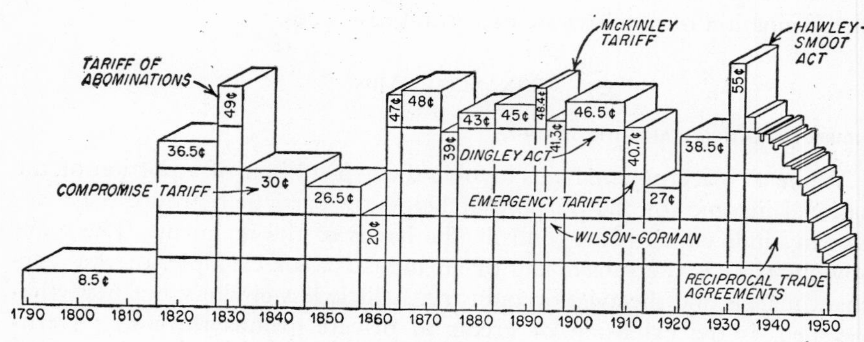

Figure 23–2

Source: Reprinted from Carl Brent Swisher, *The Theory and Practice of American National Government* (Boston: Houghton Mifflin Company, 1951), p. 505.

high prices for manufacturers, opposed the high-tariff policy and forced downward revision between 1833 and 1861. These lowered duties, however, did not remove the fundamentally protectionist character of the American tariff. In the period between the beginning of the War between the States and the Wilson administration in 1913, tariff rates were raised to high levels and almost consistently maintained on a strongly protectionist basis. Throughout this period, the tariff was one of the leading political issues, with the Democratic party insisting upon tariff for revenue only, and the Republican party declaring for protection.

With the advent of a Democratic administration in 1913 and the apparent popular desire for downward tariff revision, a policy of real protective, or "competitive," tariffs was adopted. During the eight years of the Wilson administration, tariff duties fell until average rates were about 16 per cent of the value of dutiable goods in 1920. Through the increased admission of goods free of duties and the lowered rates, tariff rates became lower than they had been for more than a century.

With the return of peace and increased production abroad after World War I, popular opinion in America again favored upward tariff revision. The result was a series of tariff acts culminating in the infamous Hawley-Smoot tariff of 1930.[16] While this tariff enacted high rates upon agricultural products to appease farmers, most of these rates were ineffective because of the export situation. However, it also placed very high rates upon a long list of manufactured articles. The result was to raise average rates on dutiable goods to about 59 per cent, to cause retaliation against American exports by foreign governments, to reduce American imports and hence the purchasing power of foreign countries, and to all but ruin the export market for American agriculture.

Flexible tariffs and reciprocal agreements. Throughout most of the history of the protective tariff, the rates were rigid, being fixed by Congress and subject to change only by further act of Congress. The act of 1922, however, authorized the President to raise or lower the tariff to the advantage of American producers to the extent of a 50 per cent increase or decrease, if the Tariff Commission[17] found a difference between foreign and American costs of production.

In 1934, the Democratic administration enacted the Reciprocal Trade Agreements Act. By this law the President is authorized to enter into foreign trade agreements with countries willing to make satisfactory concessions. In return, the President is empowered to modify tariff duties within 50 per cent of the duties fixed in 1930. Furthermore, when duties are lowered to one country, they shall be also lowered on the same item to any other country which does not discriminate against American exports (the most-favored-nation provision). These agreements resemble treaties but do not require Senate approval.

The original act had a three-year life. It was renewed in 1937 and 1940 without change and in 1943 with one minor amendment. In the Extension Act of 1945 an important change was made. The President was authorized to base tax concessions, subject to the 50 per cent limit, on the rates

[16] This act occupies nearly 200 pages in the statutes-at-large and contains over 3,200 dutiable items. When the "catchall" clauses are taken into account, it has been estimated that more than 25,000 commercial articles ordinarily imported into the United States are covered by the law. See the Attorney General's Committee on Administrative Procedure, *Administration of the Customs Law* (1940), vol. 1, pp. 2–3.

[17] The Tariff Commission, a bipartisan body created in 1916, has the duty of conducting research and furnishing information to Congress and the President on tariff matters. Its membership, which was originally twelve, was reduced to six in 1930. The members serve six-year terms, and no more than three can come from the same political party.

in effect on January 1, 1945. Thus, if duties had already been reduced 50 per cent before 1945, they could be lowered another 50 per cent, bringing about as much as a 75 per cent reduction. The 1948 extension contained an important escape clause, which, however, was repealed in 1949. It provided that the President must first supply the Tariff Commission with a list of articles upon which the United States will consider granting concessions. The Commission must investigate and report to the President the limits to which concessions may be granted without causing or threatening serious injury to domestic industry or where increases are needed to avoid injury.

The Extension Act of 1951 reenacted the escape clause and at the same time shortened the life of the act to two years. When the Reciprocal Trade Agreement Act came up for renewal again in 1953 it was extended for only one year, but a motion to increase the size of the Commission was defeated. Congress gave the program another year's life in 1954.

Although the program of reciprocal trade agreements has brought about reduced tariffs, it has not drastically modified the structure of American tariffs. The tendency in recent years, moreover, is to restrict the flexibility of the program and, in fact, threaten the very life of reciprocal trade agreements by requiring more frequent renewals.

Defense of tariffs. A number of arguments in defense of protective tariffs have been advanced over the years. One of the strongest has been the "infant-industry" argument, which contends that protection is necessary to help young industries become established until they can compete with older foreign industries. However, in practice these protected industries seldom "grow up," and irrespective of their strength in the market, they demand continued protection against foreign competition. Moreover, "infant-industry" protection should only be given to those industries which show promise of becoming self-sustaining. In the United States, such protection has been granted almost indiscriminately.

Another argument for protectionism has been the claim that high protective tariffs preserve the American standard of living, and especially American wage levels, from impairment by the importation of competitive foreign goods produced by cheap labor. This argument claims that high wages necessitate high cost and that high cost makes necessary high prices, which must be protected from foreign competition. The real flaw in the standard-of-living argument is that high wages do not necessarily cause high prices; high wages result from efficient production and the high value productivity of labor. One might ask in this connection how otherwise American exporters could sell billions of dollars' worth of domestic goods to foreign countries, the wage levels of which are so much lower than American wages. Moreover, the standard of living depends upon the volume of material goods and services which can be purchased with money wages. If a protective tariff raises money costs of those things which labor buys, the net result may be to lower the real wages of labor and the material standard of living.

Finally, the home-industry argument contends that if a country does all its buying at home, it keeps the money there with consequent maintenance of property. The absurdity of the buy-at-home argument is readily seen if one follows it to its logical conclusion. If it is sound to buy only from domestic producers, it also should be sound for the people of New York State to buy only from New York producers, for the people of Buffalo to buy only from Buffalo producers, and for the people of Seneca Street to buy only from Seneca Street producers. As a matter of fact, as one economist has pointed out, this argument comes down to the absurd conclusion that the sound thing for a buyer to do is to buy only from himself.[18]

The confusions over protectionism arise largely from the misunderstanding of the economic advantages of trade. Although money acts as a medium of exchange and goods are generally paid for by it, a moment's reflection will prove that, in any system of exchange, goods are really exchanged for goods. A nation cannot export indefinitely unless it imports goods to pay for the exports. For a period of time, the exports can exceed the imports, the balance being paid for by the shipment of gold or the shipment of notes (foreign bonds, for example) payable to the exporting country. But if a country receives gold or IOUs, these are really imports which balance the exports and which obviously have no great worth in increasing the standard of living of the importing country. If goods are exchanged for goods, then a country's stock of goods would seem to be increased to the extent that it will produce those things which it can produce most efficiently, and trade those goods for goods of other countries. This simple principle of comparative advantage is easily illustrated. It would hardly increase the standard of living for people in Detroit to produce only the automobiles they need and also produce all their foodstuffs, clothing, and building materials, and for the people of Iowa to limit their production to the corn and pork they would use and attempt to build their own automobiles. Even if people in Detroit should prove to be better farmers than those in Iowa, it would still not pay them to curtail automobile production in order to raise their own pork, since they can produce more value output by manufacturing automobiles than by producing corn. These simple advantages of specialization and trade are relatively obvious when dealing with the United States alone, but the

[18] A. L. Meyers, *Modern Economic Problems* (New York: Prentice-Hall, Inc., 1939), p. 202.

principles are just as sound from an economic point of view when speaking of international specialization.[19]

Some evils of the American tariff system. Apart from any of the professed bases for tariff protection and their questionable economic validity, there are other evils in the tariff system as it has developed in this country. Legislation has not been drafted according to any well-considered plan but has degenerated into a system of pressures exerted by interested producers, of economic favors to producers for political contributions and influences, and of legislative logrolling through trades of votes by legislators interested in obtaining tariff doles for producers in their constituencies. About the only consistency in tariff policy has been the granting of protection for anybody and everybody, in the naïve belief that if a tariff helps one person, then tariffs for all will help everyone. The methods of drafting tariffs and the lack of consistent plan have meant that the tariff policy has been an ever-vacillating one. This instability has made it difficult for business to adjust itself to trade conditions and has introduced an unnecessary element of risk into the economic system.

The tariff also often has repercussions in foreign economic and political policy. A restrictive tariff policy not only leads to retaliation by foreign countries but may actually cause the countries affected to feel less friendly toward the nation which has impaired their export markets. Moreover, restriction of trade by high tariffs has intensified the demand of countries without colonies for the natural resources and markets of colonies. The scramble for colonies, which had so much to do with causing World War II, might have been avoided had freer trade been allowed.

Government control through tariffs. Tariff legislation involves government controls as well as government aids. The size of an import duty not only controls domestic supply but acts to regulate domestic prices of a good subject to import. Through its power to change tariff duties, the government is able to exert indirectly a wide influence upon prices. In addition, the power to levy and change tariffs places a sort of economic planning authority in the hands of the government. By changing, withdrawing, or imposing tariffs, it is able to encourage or discourage domestic production in certain fields. Where industries are subject to effective

[19] For more complete discussions of the economics of tariffs, the student is referred to the large volume of competent writing on this subject. See, for example, F. W. Taussig, *Principles of Economics* (New York: The Macmillan Company, 4th ed., 1939), vol. 1, chaps. 34–37; by the same author, *Some Aspects of the Tariff Question* (New York: The Macmillan Company, 3d ed., 1931); P. T. Ellsworth, *International Economics* (New York: The Macmillan Company, 1938); and Bertil Ohlin, *Interregional and International Trade* (Cambridge, Mass.: Harvard University Press, 1935). Practically any good elementary economics text has a concise and accurate treatment of the economics of protectionism.

foreign competition in the absence of a tariff, the government has wide power to decide to what extent an industry may grow.

CREDIT FACILITIES FOR BUSINESS—THE RECONSTRUCTION FINANCE CORPORATION AND THE SMALL BUSINESS ADMINISTRATION

Government aids to business have also taken the form of credit facilities established for the benefit of certain groups; they normally supplement private lending agencies, which are generally under government regulation, and replace some of the customary investment of private funds in business. The usual scheme is to set up an agency to administer loans, the funds for which are obtained by direct appropriation or the floating of bonds, guaranteed either by definite legal provision or by an implied moral obligation.[20]

In some instances, all the government aims to do is to act as a channel for investment of private funds, by borrowing at advantageous rates from the public and lending these funds to businesses at a lower rate than the latter could obtain directly. Many of the loans are made directly or indirectly through some kind of lending organization, and many are made to individual consumers to enable them to purchase goods from business. In either case, the credit facilities are advanced at least in part to aid business. In some cases, loans are made at rates to cover their full cost; while in others, such as many of the loans made to farmers, the rate is not high enough to cover the costs. In such a case, of course, the loan involves in part an outright subsidy.

The extension of credit for aiding those engaged in production is a development of this century. After World War I the federal government lent more than $350 million to the railroads for making additions and betterments and for refunding maturing obligations. Beginning with special legislation in 1916, the government embarked upon a program of encouraging and furnishing special credit facilities for agriculture. It has also indirectly furnished credit facilities for business by the establishment of the Federal Reserve System and by its power to force Federal Reserve banks to expand the credit base through open-market operations.

The principal government agency providing for the extension of credit to business was, until recently, the Reconstruction Finance Corporation, established by legislation in 1932. Intended to operate during an emergency in which private lending agencies appeared to be inadequate for business credit demands, the Corporation had its life periodically extended until 1953, when its lending functions were terminated; it was abolished in 1954.

[20] For an excellent account, especially of the theoretical basis for government financial assistance, see D. R. Fuller, *Government Financing of Private Enterprise* (Stanford, Calif.: Stanford University Press, 1948).

As originally set up, the Reconstruction Finance Corporation was endowed with a subscription of $100 million of capital stock by the federal government and with power to borrow, by means of bonds or notes guaranteed by the government. Under the direction of a five-man board of directors, the Corporation could, much like a private bank, extend financial aid to commercial, industrial, or agricultural concerns to which private banks might not want to lend money. Loans had to be adequately secured, at rates fixed by the board of directors, for periods up to five years. Amounts to any borrower were limited to 2 per cent of the capital and authorized bonds of the Corporation.

The lending powers of the Corporation were steadily extended after 1932, so that it had authority to lend funds to many types of businesses, including banks, trust companies, building and loan associations, and other loan organizations. Loans to insurance companies could be made only upon the recommendation of the Secretary of the Treasury. The Corporation was empowered to make loans to railroads upon certification by the Interstate Commerce Commission that certain carriers could not obtain the loans upon favorable terms through private channels and were not in need of financial reorganization, and with approval of the Civil Aeronautics Board, it could lend to air carriers. It also had the authority to lend to state, county, and municipal governments as well as to federal agencies like the Export-Import Bank, federal home-loan banks, and the farm-credit agencies. However, attention is here focused only on the extension of credit to private businesses.

During World War II the Corporation was given more extensive lending authority. It was given power to aid in the national defense program by lending funds to government or private plants manufacturing arms and other strategic materials deemed by the President to be necessary for the war effort. A great many industrial plants were built with money furnished by the Corporation. In 1945, the functions, assets, and liabilities of the Defense Plant Corporation, Metals Reserve Company, Rubber Reserve Company, and Defense Supplies Corporation were transferred to the Reconstruction Finance Corporation for liquidation purposes. Through the Office of Synthetic Rubber the Corporation operated synthetic-rubber plants, and through the Office of Tin and Fiber it operated a tin smelter in Texas and certain abacá (Manila-hemp) plantations in Panama, Honduras, Guatemala, and Costa Rica.

When the Korean War began, the Defense Production Act of 1950 empowered the Corporation to make loans to private business for the expansion of capacity, the development of technical processes, the production of essential materials, and the mining of strategic and critical metals and minerals. The Act also authorized loans for financing projects for civil defense. The Small Defense Plants Administration could recommend to the Corporation that loans be made to enable certain small businesses to finance plant construction, conversion, and expansion.

The same act which terminated the lending functions of the Reconstruction Finance Corporation created, on July 30, 1953, the Small Business Administration with authority to make loans to small businesses and victims of disasters. Legislative authority for these programs expired in June, 1955, but extensions have since been granted.

The Administration, which also takes over the functions of the Small Defense Plants Administration, is financed by a revolving fund of $300 million. Of this sum, $150 million is earmarked for small-business loans, $25 million for disaster loans, $25 million for loans to municipal and other public agencies, and the balance for the purpose of entering contracts with the armed forces and subletting contracts to small-business firms.

The maximum loan to any small-business borrower is $150,000, and maximum maturity is generally ten years. Loans may be made only if financial assistance is not otherwise available on reasonable terms and if there is reasonable assurance of repayment. There is no limit on the amount that may be loaned to disaster victims. Loans for housing under this disaster provision may have maturities up to twenty years, but other loans are limited to ten years. By 1955, appropriations of $80 million had been made to finance the small-business- and disaster-loan programs since the Small Business Administration was established.

On the whole, the Reconstruction Finance Corporation was ably managed as it loaned $50 billion between 1932 and 1954. Except for loans which were made to government agencies at the direction of Congress and for which the Corporation can hardly be held accountable, the loans made by it were fairly well secured and were liquidated without serious loss to the government. On some business loans, of course, the Corporation suffered loss, but in the case of some advances of funds made upon securities, it resold the securities at a profit.

The operations of the Reconstruction Finance Corporation furnish an interesting example of government control effected through aids. Railroad borrowers have been called upon to make changes in financial practices as a condition for receiving a loan. Banks and insurance companies have similarly been called upon to effect changes in policy, and the Corporation insisted upon the right to examine the books of borrowing companies. The effect of competition of the government corporation with private lending agencies is also important. On several occasions, the Chairman of the Reconstruction Finance Corporation intimated to private banks that they must adopt a more liberal business-loan policy, or undergo the danger of severe government competition in the loan field.

In 1955 the Hoover Commission Task Force on Lending Agencies recommended that the lending activities of the Small Business Administration be completely discontinued. Only the loans to defense contractors and to persons suffering financial hardships resulting from floods, tornadoes, and drought should be continued, according to the Task Force, and these loans should be made by the Treasury Department.[21]

CREDIT FACILITIES FOR FOREIGN TRADE—THE EXPORT-IMPORT BANK

The Export-Import Bank was established in 1934 by Executive order and has been continued by acts of Congress from 1935. For a time it was lodged in the Federal Loan Agency, but since 1945 it has been a permanent, independent establishment incorporated by Congress. Governed by a board of directors consisting of the Secretary of State ex officio and four full-time members, the Bank has a capital stock of $1 billion owned entirely by the federal government. In addition, the Bank may borrow from the Treasury on its own obligations up to, but not more than, three and one-half times its authorized capital stock.

Originally created to help finance trade with the Soviet Union, the Export-Import Bank now aids in financing and facilitating export and import and the exchange of commodities between the United States or any of its territories or insular possessions and a foreign country. Beginning in 1939 and during the war years, its principal operations were in Latin America. The Bank lends money to exporters and importers who cannot obtain the funds they need from private banks, and it makes loans to foreign governments to help develop resources, stabilize their economies, market products, and recover from war. The Bank may not have outstanding at any one time loans and guaranties in aggregate amount in excess of four and one-half times its authorized capital stock. Between 1934 and 1953 the Bank made loans totaling $4.5 billion. Loans outstanding at the end of 1953 reached a new high of $2.8 billion.[22]

The Hoover Commission Task Force on Lending Agencies recommended that the Export-Import Bank be shorn of its lending authority and that it be placed in liquidation as promptly as possible.[23]

CREDIT FACILITIES FOR HOUSING

The government has sought to encourage home ownership by aiding persons to buy or build new homes and remodel existing houses and by assisting those who have difficulty in meeting mortgage payments. An equally important motive has been to assist mortgage-banking institutions and the construction industry. Many government planners have believed that stimulation of the construction industry is one of the most effective means to combat declines in business activity.

[21] Commission on Organization of the Executive Branch of the Government, *Task Force Report on Lending Agencies* (Appendix R) (1955), pp. 71–73.

[22] *Ibid.*, p. 247.

[23] *Ibid.*, pp. 83–85.

An array of agencies have been created, beginning in 1932, to accomplish four objectives in the housing field: (1) the Federal Home Loan Bank system, including the federal savings and loan associations, the Federal Savings and Loan Insurance Corporation, and the Federal National Mortgage Association, were created to provide more adequate credit facilities; (2) the Home Owners' Loan Corporation was established as an emergency device to relieve homeowners in mortgage difficulties; (3) the Federal Housing Administration was created to encourage home construction and modernization; (4) a program of subsidization of slum clearance and low-cost housing, which is now under the authority of the Division of Slum Clearance and Urban Redevelopment and the Public Housing Administration, was instituted. In 1942, seventeen agencies carrying on housing activities in the federal government were consolidated into the National Housing Agency. In 1947, this agency was combined with the housing credit agencies to form the Housing and Home Finance Agency,[24] the operating divisions of which are the Home Loan Bank Board, the Federal Housing Administration, the Federal National Mortgage Association, the Public Housing Administration, and the Division of Slum Clearance and Urban Redevelopment.

The federal home-loan banks. The Federal Home Loan Bank Act of 1932 was enacted to assist both home-financing institutions and borrowers. Patterned along the lines of the Federal Reserve System, the law created a Federal Home Loan Bank Board and twelve (now eleven) federal home-loan banks. The Board, consisting of three members, appointed by the President for four-year terms, administers this law and has since been charged with administration of other credit facilities which have been provided for homeowners. The banks were originally financed partly by stock subscriptions of member institutions and partly by federal funds, but by 1951 the members had bought out all federal interest, so all stock is now held by the member institutions. All federal savings and loan associations are required to be members of the home-loan-bank system and any other savings and loan association, building and loan association, insurance company, cooperative mortgage bank, or savings bank may become a member bank of the system by subscribing to stock of a regional home-loan bank and by meeting the requirements and regulations of the system. By 1955, there were 4,234 members having assets estimated to total over $30 billion.[25]

These banks are authorized to borrow funds upon debentures or bonds

[24] In 1955 the Hoover Commission Task Force on Lending Agencies recommended that the Housing and Home Finance Agency be discontinued and that its components be divided into three separate establishments. For a detailed discussion see *ibid.*, pp. 31–49.

[25] *U.S. Government Organization Manual, 1955–1956*, p. 424.

guaranteed by the United States and may lend to any member institution on the security of selected real-estate mortgages. Thus, credit facilities for home modernization and building are made available through loans to member lending institutions. These banks can also lend to loan institutions which cooperate with other aspects of the housing credit program. The actual loans to persons building or improving their homes come from these member or cooperating institutions.

Federal savings and loan associations. The federal savings and loan associations, which must be members of the federal home-loan-bank system, are mortgage-lending institutions incorporated by the federal government. They may be entirely new organizations, or they may be state building and loan associations converted into federal organizations with the consent of the state concerned. These associations received capital stock subscriptions from the government and obtained other funds by sale of shares to savers and by borrowing from the home-loan banks. Some 1,613 federal savings and loan associations were chartered by 1954, with assets amounting to $14.5 billion. These associations are permitted to lend on first mortgages up to 80 per cent of the appraised value of homes and combinations of homes and business properties, in amounts not exceeding $25,000 for each borrower.

Savings accounts in the federal associations, as well as the state-chartered building and loan, savings and loan, and homestead associations and cooperative banks which apply and are approved, are insured up to $10,000 under legislation of 1935 and 1950, providing for the Federal Savings and Loan Insurance Corporation. Like the Federal Deposit Insurance Corporation in the commercial-banking field, it is financed by assessments on insured institutions and in other regards functions similarly. In 1947 the functions of the Corporation were taken over by the Home Loan Bank Board. By 1955 there were 3,433 insured institutions, with total assets of $28.4 billion.[26]

The Home Owners' Loan Corporation. The Home Owners' Loan Act of 1933 directed the Home Loan Bank Board to create a new corporation as an emergency device to refinance mortgages upon urban real estate at a time when foreclosures were taking place at the rate of 1,000 a day. The Home Owners' Loan Corporation was set up with a capital of $200 million from the United States Treasury and with power to borrow $4.8 billion more.

The Corporation was empowered to refinance home mortgages at low interest rates to homeowners in urgent need of funds to save their homes from foreclosure and to make mortgage loans to homeowners for reconditioning of homes. The Corporation was directed not to make the loans

[26] *Ibid.*

unless the borrower was unable to borrow upon fair and reasonable terms from private lending institutions.

The lending operations of the Corporation were terminated in 1936 with nearly $3.5 billion advanced to over a million homeowners. As might be expected, the majority of loans made by the Corporation were for refinancing mortgages. About one out of five of all mortgages on urban owner-occupied homes were refinanced. The Corporation often exchanged its bonds for the mortgages held against the homeowners. In

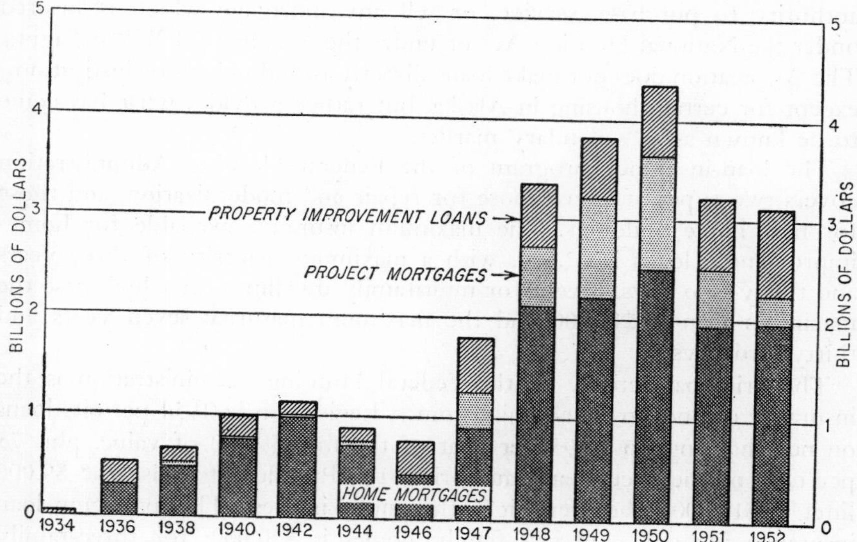

Figure 23–3. Annual volume of loans insured by Federal Housing Administration

Source: FHA, *19th Annual Report, 1952* (1953), p. 9.

other cases it paid off a portion of the mortgages in cash or made advances for payment of taxes, maintenance, or repairs.

The Home Owners' Loan Corporation did succeed in bringing down interest rates to homeowners and in extending maturity dates on mortgages. Since the Corporation was permitted to make loans for periods up to fifteen years, it did not go out of business until 1951. At that time it showed a surplus of nearly $14 million, this amount representing a financial gain from the $3.5 billion loaned during the Great Depression.[27]

The Federal Housing Administration. Further aid to homeowners is offered through the Federal Housing Administration, created by legisla-

[27] Legislative Reference Service, Library of Congress. *Your Congress and American Housing*, H. Doc. 532, 82d Cong., 2d Sess. (1952), p. 5.

tion in 1934, with authority to insure lending companies against losses which they might incur on loans to modernize buildings and to construct new farm and urban homes, apartments, and certain other buildings. The National Housing Act provided for two activities to assist in this program. A Mutual Mortgage Insurance Fund has been established, with the aid of government funds, to make commitments for mortgage insurance, to collect fees for this insurance, to compensate lenders for mortgage losses, and to distribute excess premiums to borrowers on a mutual basis. The Act also provides for a Federal National Mortgage Association which has authority to purchase, service, or sell any mortgage which is insured under the National Housing Act or under the so-called GI Bill of Rights. The Association does not make loans directly to individuals or institutions, except for certain housing in Alaska, but rather provides what has come to be known as a "secondary market."

The loan-insurance program of the Federal Housing Administration covers two types of loans: those for repair and modernization, and those for new home buildings. The maximum insurance available for home-improvement loans is $2,500, with a maximum maturity of three years and thirty-two days, except for multifamily dwellings, in which case the maximum loan is $10,000 and the maximum maturity seven years and thirty-two days.

The principal activity of the Federal Housing Administration is the insurance of one- to four-family homes. Legislation in 1954 permits loans on new housing up to 95 per cent of the first $9,000 of value, plus 75 per cent of the excess, and authorizes the President to raise the $9,000 limit to $10,000 if he deems it in the public interest. The maximum loan insurance for one- and two-family homes is $20,000; for three-family residences, $27,500; and for four-family dwellings, $35,000. The maximum mortgage maturity for new home mortgages is thirty years. Loan insurance on existing housing is available up to 90 per cent of the value of the first $9,000 plus 75 per cent of the excess. The maximum mortgage maturity is thirty years, or three-fourths of the remaining useful life of the house. Other loan insurance is available for cooperative housing, rental housing, defense housing, and loans to manufacturers of prefabricated houses.

As a condition for obtaining mortgage insurance, the Federal Housing Administration sets certain requirements. Loans must be made at low interest rates, the maximums varying from 4½ to 5 per cent. Insurance premiums are fixed at ½ of 1 per cent upon unpaid principal. The mortgage transaction must be economically sound, and the mortgage amount is limited by the Administration's estimate of appraised value. The Administration is given full discretion in determining whether a loan will be insured, and it has the power to turn down applications if the structure does not meet specifications of the Administration or if the loan does not appear to be economically sound.

Between 1934 and 1952, the Federal Housing Administration insured loans totaling $29 billion, of which $18.6 billion were mortgages on homes, $6.1 billion on property improvement, and $4.4 billion on rental and cooperative projects.[28] Losses amounted to only 2/100 of 1 per cent

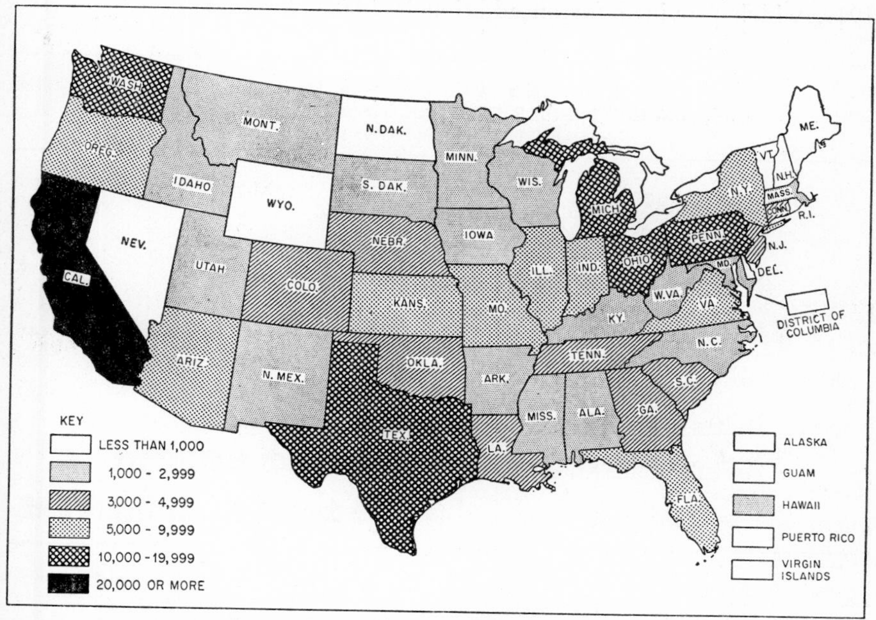

Figure 23–4. Number of Home Mortgages Insured by Federal Housing Administration, 1952
Source: *FHA, 19th Annual Report, 1952* (1953), p. 36.

during that time. Approximately 18 per cent of all outstanding home mortgages in 1955 were insured by the Federal Housing Administration. In 1956, it is estimated that the outstanding guaranties and insurance will amount to $22.6 billion.[29]

Public Housing Administration. The Public Housing Administration is a successor agency to the United States Housing Authority, which was created in 1937 to administer the low-rent public housing program. The Public Housing Administration has responsibility for five separate housing programs. The first is the low-rent public housing program instituted in 1937. This is a long-run program of federal loan and subsidy assistance

[28] FHA, *19th Annual Report, 1952* (1953), p. 8.

[29] *The Budget of the United States Government for the Fiscal Year Ending June 30, 1956.*

to local public housing agencies to enable them to build and operate housing for rent to families that cannot afford adequate private housing. The basic legislation was amended by the Housing Act of 1949 to perfect its details and to increase the amount of federal assistance available. However, in succeeding years Congress imposed limitations on the number of units to be authorized for construction in specified periods. Consequently, construction fell far behind the six-year program of the Housing Act of 1949, which provided for an additional 810,000 low-rent dwellings (see

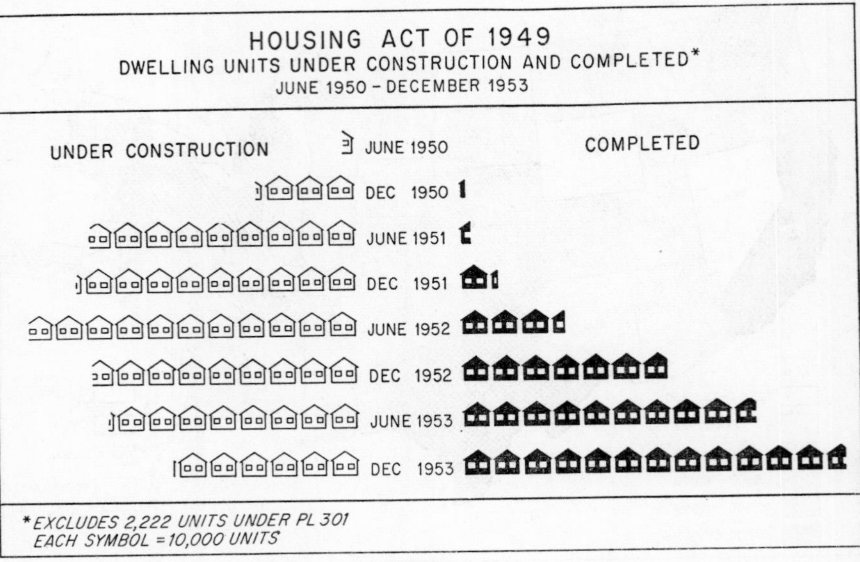

Figure 23—5
Source: Public Housing Administration, *7th Annual Report, 1953,* p. 20.

Figure 23–5). By the end of 1953 the accumulated total of federally aided low-rent housing, including that authorized as long ago as 1937, was 344,000 homes, housing 1¼ million persons.[30]

The other four programs conducted by the Public Housing Administration are emergency programs destined for liquidation. Two are war housing programs, one being the program to provide housing for war workers and military personnel during World War II under the Lanham Act, and the other being the program developed under the Defense Housing and Community Facilities and Services Act of 1951. The latter provided temporary or mobile housing for immigrant defense workers and military personnel required in connection with the national defense activities in critical defense areas. The Administration is responsible for

[30] Public Housing Administration, *7th Annual Report, 1953,* p. 1.

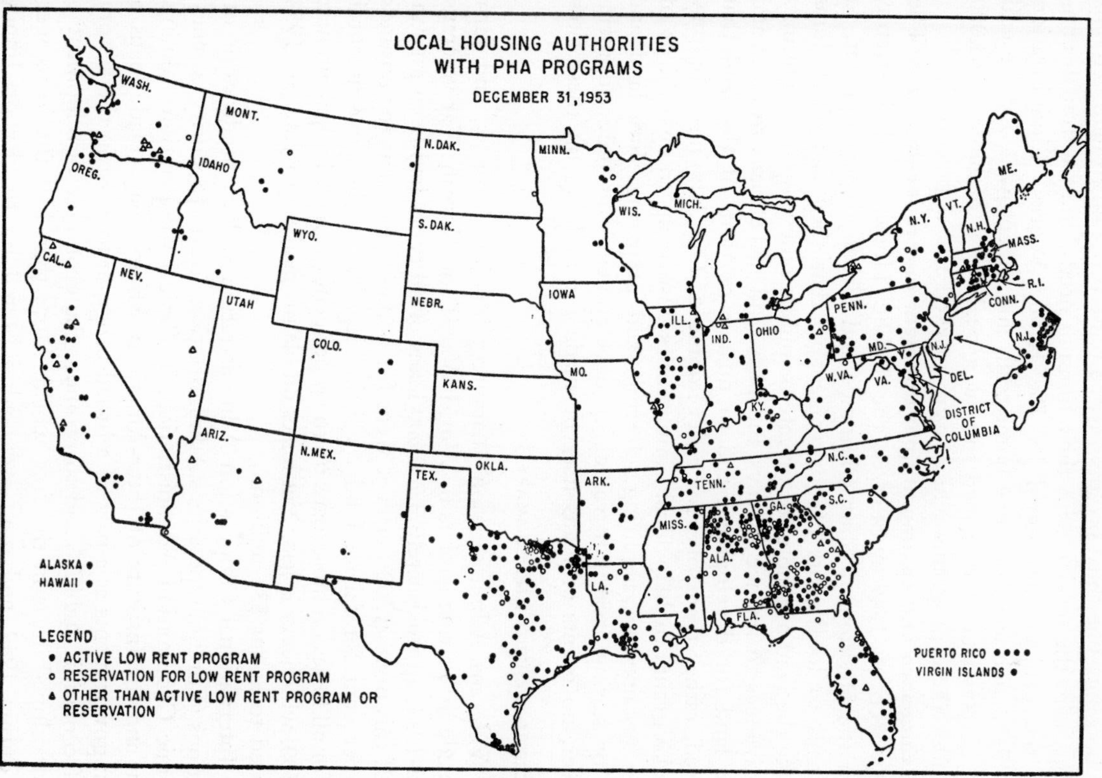

Figure 23—6

Source: Public Housing Administration, *7th Annual Report, 1953*, p. 7.

the management of the housing included in these programs, either by direct operation or through local agencies, and for the orderly disposition of such housing. The third program is the reuse program to help veterans returning from the service with their housing needs, and the fourth consists of the projects developed by the Public Works Administration before 1937, such as subsistence homesteads and greentowns. By the end of 1953, 226,500 units remained out of a peak total of almost 963,000 units under these programs which were marked for disposition.[31]

Slum clearance and community development and redevelopment. The Housing Act of 1949 authorizes the Public Housing Administrator, through the Division of Slum Clearance and Urban Redevelopment, to make loans to local units of government so that they can clear slums and make the land available for private or public redevelopment. He may make advances to finance surveys and plans and make loans to clear and prepare land for development and to finance portions of the land that are leased, rather than sold, for redevelopment. The Administrator may also make grants to help local communities absorb up to two-thirds of the loss sustained in acquiring, clearing, and preparing slum land and selling or leasing it at fair value for development and redevelopment. However, no grants or loans may be made for building on these sites.

OTHER CREDIT FACILITIES AND SUMMARY

The Veterans Administration guarantees housing, business, and farm loans made by private lenders to World War II and Korean War veterans. By mid-1954, approximately 3,720,000 loans of all types had been guaranteed. Of this number, 92 per cent were for homes, 6 per cent for business, and 2 per cent for farms. Under existing legislation, the government is liable for all losses on most loans up to 60 per cent of the principal amount, or $7,500, whichever is less. Net losses on claims paid up to June 30, 1954, amounted to about $32 million.

The International Cooperation Administration and its predecessor organizations (Foreign Operations Administration, Mutual Security Agency, Economic Cooperation Administration, Technical Cooperation Administration, and the Institute of Inter-American Affairs) have made loans to foreign governments as a part of a broad program to assist in the restoration of economic stability and to promote the economic development of underdeveloped areas in the free world. More than half the loans were made during 1949, and most were administered by the Export-Import Bank.

The Commodity Credit Corporation, Rural Electrification Administration, Farmers' Home Administration, and the Federal Intermediate Credit Banks all provide farmers with special credit facilities for various purposes.

[31] *Ibid.*

Since these programs will be discussed at greater length in the next chapter, they need only be mentioned here.

Table 23–1 shows the commitments and expenditures of the various federal credit programs. A majority of them began during the Depression. Since then their size and scope have mounted until the total of outstanding loans and guaranties is expected to reach $57 billion by the end of fiscal 1956.[32] Of this amount, $41 billion will consist of outstanding guaranties and insurance, and $16 billion will consist of direct loans and investments. About 95 per cent of the guaranties and insurance will be for guaranties of mortgage loans by the Veterans Administration and the Federal Housing Administration and guaranties of local housing authority loans by the Public Housing Administration. Foreign loans, including $3.5 billion to the United Kingdom, $2.7 billion through the Export-Import Bank, and $1.8 billion through the Foreign Operations Administration, will account for about one-half of the outstanding direct loans and investments.

The Hoover Commission Task Force on Lending Agencies was extremely critical of many of the lending and loan-guaranty programs of the federal government. The Task Force found no fault with the use of government credit to stimulate the organization and development of new facilities needed in the nation's credit system. Nor did the Task Force find fault with the use of government credit to serve the legitimate needs of procurement for defense and war. The principal criticism was directed toward those programs which the Task Force viewed as helping individual people and businesses to improve their competitive positions and, in this way, as discriminating against those who did not qualify for similar assistance.[33] The feeling was that such programs burden the government with risks of business and that it encourages people to seek riskless investments for their savings. Instead, the Task Force felt "that the Federal Government should curtail its lending and that it should encourage the direct investment of savings in property ownership and in the equity shares of business enterprises." [34]

It can be anticipated that the Hoover Commission Task Force Report on Lending Agencies will generate considerable debate and opposition. The premises on which the Task Force builds its recommendations are by no means universally accepted. In fact, there has been, and still is,

[32] The Tax Foundation, Inc., *Tax Review,* February, 1955.

[33] The Task Force included in this category the lending programs of the Rural Electrification Administration, Reconstruction Finance Corporation, Small Business Administration, Farmers' Home Administration, Export-Import Bank, Commodity Credit Corporation, the loan guaranties of the Veterans Administration, and the lending and subsidy programs of the Public Housing Administration.

[34] Commission on Organization of the Executive Branch of the Government, *op. cit.,* p. 5.

Table 23–1. Federal Credit Programs

Commitments and Expenditures by Agency or Program
Fiscal Years 1954–1956
(In millions of dollars)

	Commitments							
	New commitments [a]			Outstanding June 30, 1956 [b]		Net budget expenditures		
	1954	1955 [b]	1956 [b]	Direct loans and investments [c]	Guaranties and insurance [d]	1954	1955 [b]	1956 [b]
Housing and Home Finance Agency:								
Federal Housing Administration	$ 4,648	$ 6,967	$ 8,305	$ 208	$22,587	$ 33	$ 31	$ 27
Federal National Mortgage Association	710	136	568	2,424	270	—181	189	—151
Public Housing Administration	770	754	896	160	3,195	—410	—85	4
Slum clearance, urban renewal, and college housing	96	179	349	190	86	45	50	60
Veterans' Administration	3,507	5,170	4,942	642	12,742	102	139	156
Department of Agriculture:								
Commodity Credit Corporation	3,356	2,400	2,069	143	865	—512	—215	—1
Rural Electrification Administration	242	240	265	2,451	....	151	141	146
Farmers' Home Administration	192	186	217	675	146	71	31	19
Disaster loans	93	87	40	90	....	50	24	—38
Farm Credit Administration:								
Federal Intermediate Credit Banks	1,790	1,864	1,966	857	....	39	26	41
Expansion of Defense Production	145	129	121	243	320	50	66	—71
Small Business Administration	28	78	72	72	54	2	37	19

Treasury Department:								
Reconstruction Finance Corporation liquidation	4	....	....	80	5	−250	−92	−97
Loan to United Kingdom	....	....	....	3,519	....	−46	−47	−48
Export-Import Bank	250	460	665	2,670	232	158	17	−31
Foreign Operations Administration	111	200	[e]	1,803	....	14	167	75
Subtotal, major agencies or programs	15,942	18,850	20,475	16,227	40,502	−762	479	110
Other agencies or programs	[e]	[e]	[e]	[e]	[e]	−40	135	40
Adjustments for repayments going directly into miscellaneous receipts	....	....	....	....	....	220	244	269
Total	$15,942	$18,850	$20,475	$56,729		−$582	$858	$419

[a] Includes direct loans and investments and guaranties and insurance of private loans. Because of the overlap in new commitments (especially for housing credit), the totals may overstate by $1 or $2 billion the net amount of credit assistance by the Federal government.

[b] As estimated in *The Budget of the United States Government for the Fiscal Year Ending June 30, 1956.*

[c] Excludes undisbursed commitments.

[d] Excludes commitments outstanding but not in force. Also excludes the unguaranteed portion of outstanding loans, almost all of which is under the veterans' loan-guarantee program.

[e] Not available.

SOURCE: The Tax Foundation, Inc., *Tax Review*, February, 1955.

widespread agreement that aid and assistance to selected groups in the community can, under the proper circumstances, actually contribute to the welfare of all. Most of the lending activities that draw Task Force fire have been inaugurated and continue to operate on that premise. From a political point of view it has always been extremely difficult to withdraw programs of aid and assistance once they have received public support and have become entrenched in our system of values. In any case, the Task Force Report has clearly drawn the battle lines for a struggle that every citizen should follow with keen interest.

DIRECT SUBSIDIES

Direct subsidies have been given for business purposes on a number of occasions. The more important ones have been granted in the field of transportation. Every kind of transportation agency has at some time received direct subsidies from federal or state governments. Railroads have received generous land grants. It has been estimated that land grants to railroads by 1940 totaled 183 million acres.[35] Pipelines have also received land grants, though the amounts have been negligible as compared to those received by railroads.

Both federal and state governments have contributed liberally to the development of waterways which have greatly aided the shipping industry. Rivers and harbors have been improved, and shipping terminals and lighthouses have been constructed. Many billions of dollars have been spent for navigation facilities. In addition, the maritime industry has been aided by subsidies for the construction and operation of ships.

Public construction of roads and highways greatly helps the motor-carrier industry. Promotion of the air-transport industry has received some impetus by the states, though most of the promotional activities are financed by the federal government. By far the greatest part of state aid has come from municipal expenditures for airports. State aid has also been given by way of constructing auxiliary landing fields for emergency use. Federal funds have provided for meteorological information, lighted airways, beacon lights, radio range beacons, radio informational services, airports, and other airway facilities.

Generous payments for carrying the mail have aided the water, rail, and especially the air-transport industries. So important were the air-mail contracts to air carriers that commercial flying could hardly have advanced to its present status without them, and in the early days an airline carrying no mail had little chance for financial success. The extent of the subsidy included in air-mail contracts was always difficult to determine. It was not simply an excess of the payments for air-mail service

[35] Federal Coordinator of Transportation, *Public Aids to Transportation,* vol. I, p. 13.

over air-mail revenues, because this excess may prove only that air *mail* is subsidized, not that the business of air *transportation* is subsidized. In 1953 the subsidy and the service elements in air-mail contracts were separated. The Civil Aeronautics Board was made responsible for paying the subsidy element, and the Postmaster General was made responsible for paying the service element. A summary of the mail-pay data is set forth in Table 23–2.

Table 23–2

Fiscal year	*Domestic trunks*	*Local service*	*Helicopters*	*International overseas and territorial*	*Total*
		Service mail pay (in thousands)			
1951	$25,432	$1,151	$ 907	$17,177	$44,667
1952	31,806	1,139	891	17,979	51,815
1953	32,315	1,136	1,814	18,629	53,894
1954	33,410	1,245	322	22,006	56,983
1955	34,708	1,283	331	23,471	59,793
1956	36,674	1,313	338	23,768	62,093
		Subsidy (in thousands)			
1951	$18,881	$17,244	....	$39,173	$75,298
1952	6,325	19,057	....	45,823	71,205
1953	3,527	21,778	....	49,471	74,776
1954	3,808	25,095	$2,647	48,898	80,448
1955	4,830	25,870	2.685	46,041	79,426
1956	4,439	25,970	2,928	45,763	79,100

SOURCE: CAB, *Annual Report, 1954* (1955), p. 14.

The below-cost postal rates for mailing newspapers and periodicals may be regarded as a subsidy to publishers. Preferential tax treatments, especially in periods of defense or war, amount to subsidies to encourage industries to expand their plant and productive facilities and take war contracts. These subsidies are justified as necessary to promote the welfare of the nation. The transport subsidies are regarded as necessary to develop a transportation system adequate for the needs of the nation. The subsidy to publishers promotes a better-informed citizenry, and, of course, the wartime subsidies were imperative to win the war.

In some cases, the subsidies, especially those for inland waterways, have been of questionable economic justification and have followed from pork-barrel tactics of legislators representing local interests. Other transport facilities have been constructed, in some cases, without determining the social need for them. Regulation has sometimes been hampered by government subsidies which are economically unjustified and which do not consider transportation needs generally. Some wartime subsidies and tax write-offs actually contributed to the concentration of control in business and industry which the antitrust laws were enacted to prevent.

Selected References

Beckett, Grace, *The Reciprocal Trade Agreements Program.* New York: Columbia University Press, 1941.

Bennett, W. B., *The American Patent System.* Baton Rouge, La.: Louisiana State University Press, 1943.

Commission on Organization of the Executive Branch of the Government, *Task Force Report on Activities and Organization of Lending Agencies of the Government* (Appendix R). 1949.

———, *Task Force Report on Lending Agencies.* 1955.

Cooper, John C., *Government Financial Aid to Foreign Air Carriers.* Library of Congress, 1950.

Fuller, D. R., *Government Financing of Private Enterprise.* Stanford, Calif.: Stanford University Press, 1949.

Galloway, George B., *Major Government Lending Agencies.* Library of Congress, 1947.

Harriss, C. Lowell, *History and Policies of the Home Owners' Loan Corporation.* New York: National Bureau of Economic Research, Inc., 1952.

Letiche, John M., *Reciprocal Trade Agreements in the World Economy.* New York: King's Crown Press, 1948.

Straus, Nathan, *Two-thirds of a Nation. A Housing Program.* New York: Alfred A. Knopf., Inc., 1952.

Toulmin, Harry A., *Patents and the Public Interest.* New York: Harper & Brothers, 1939.

U.S. Board of Investigation and Research, *Public Aids to Domestic Transportation.* H. Doc. 159, 79th Cong., 1st Sess. (1945).

Warren, Charles, *Bankruptcy in United States History.* Cambridge, Mass.: Harvard University Press, 1935.

24

GOVERNMENT AIDS FOR AGRICULTURE

The paradox of American agriculture is that it is characterized by conditions approaching pure competition and free enterprise and yet is subject to more government programs than almost any other sector of the economy. The large number of producers and relatively easy entry of newcomers, the fact that the products have been capable of a high degree of standardization, and the fact that no single producer can affect appreciably the price of the products he buys or sells have created problems necessitating programs of aid and regulation of agriculture.

Historically, the first efforts to aid agriculture took the form of high tariffs. Then, in 1839, Congress appropriated a small sum for the purpose of prosecuting agricultural investigations and procuring agricultural statistics. The Department of Agriculture was created as a service agency for farmers in 1862. The Land Grant College Act of the same year laid the basis for a system of agricultural colleges, and the Hatch Act of 1887 provided further aid for agricultural research. A system of extension education was established by the Smith-Lever Act of 1914. During this period since 1862 the general assumption was that if the farmer were aided by means of educational and demonstration programs he could solve his problems himself. As the farmer's position worsened, special credit facilities for farmers were created in 1916 in the belief that the individual farmer could adjust to price fluctuations if he had proper credit. Only after these self-help programs proved inadequate did the government resort to the more heroic measures of the 1930s—surplus removal, storage, and production and marketing controls.

THE PROBLEMS OF AGRICULTURE

The major agricultural problems are related to farm prices and income, namely, instability of prices and income, uneven distribution of income, and low level of prices and income. After a brief description of the role of agriculture in the American economy, each of these problems will be analyzed.

AGRICULTURE IN THE AMERICAN ECONOMY

Agriculture is the largest single industry in the United States, as it is in the world. No other single industry has an investment that can compare with agriculture's $160 billion investment (in 1954) in land, buildings, livestock, and machinery.

The economy of the United States was originally agricultural. In 1820, 71.8 per cent of the labor force of the nation worked in agriculture. With the growth of business and industry, the proportion of the gainfully em-

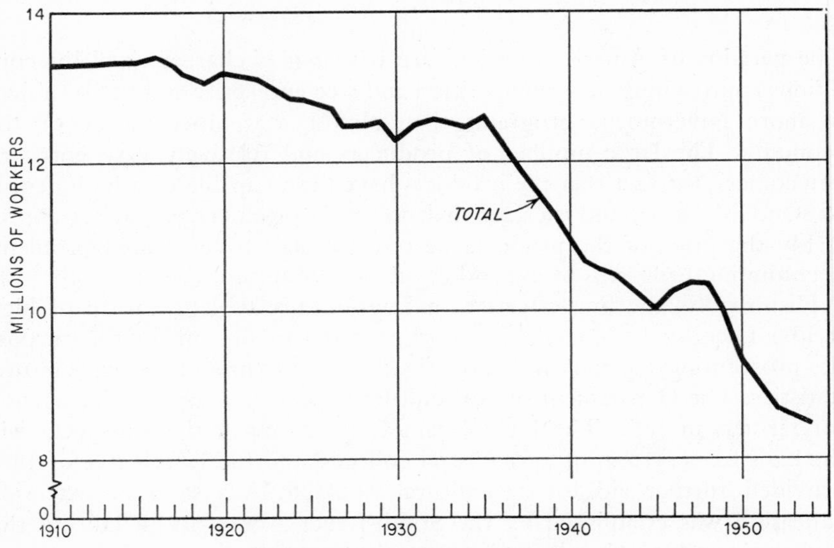

Figure 24–1. Workers on Farms

Source: U.S. Department of Agriculture, *Agricultural Outlook Charts, 1955* (1954), p. 29.

ployed persons found in farming declined until it was only 13 per cent (8,499,000) in 1954. The number of people working on farms has declined almost steadily since 1910, but the rate of decline has accelerated measurably since 1935, largely because of the greater use of machinery on farms and because of increased opportunities for nonfarm jobs (see Figure 24–1). In 1954 the farm population was 13.5 per cent of the total population. Since the peak of farm population in 1916 (32,530,000), the trend in the number of people living on farms has been generally downward also. Changes in farm population have been particularly marked since the beginning of World War II. The number of persons living on farms fell over 5 million during the war; there was some increase after the war, but the downward trend was resumed after 1948 (see Figure 24–2).

The decline of both farm population and farm employment is not, however, evidence of the declining importance of agriculture. Agriculture is still the foundation of our economic structure. It furnishes the materials by which human beings are able to survive and, in addition, many of the raw materials used for production of shelter, transportation, and other goods of general use. The whole nation is dependent upon the output of agriculture. Moreover, the farmer has always been a social and political force in American life.

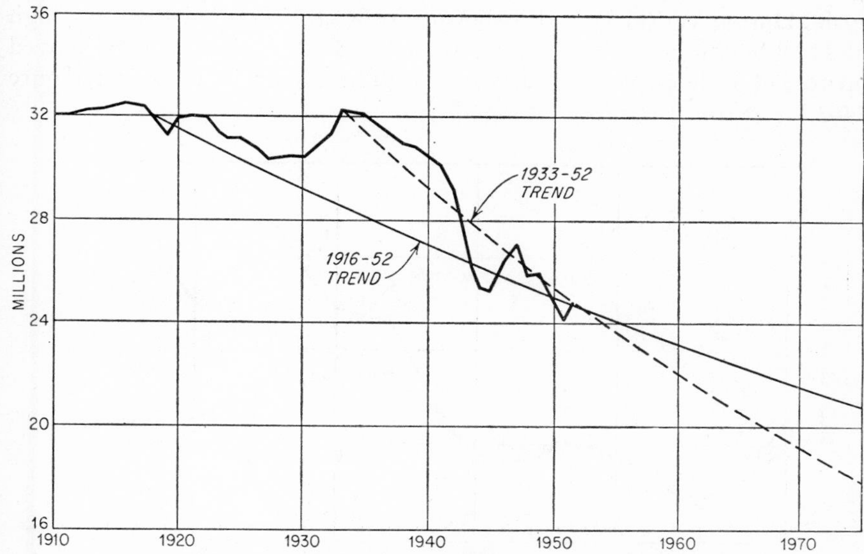

Figure 24—2. Decline in Farm Population, with Projections to 1975

Based on cooperative estimates of the Bureau of Agricultural Economics and the Bureau of the Census (1952 revision). Source: U.S. Department of Agriculture, *Agricultural Outlook Charts, 1954* (1953), p. 28.

In spite of the decline in farm population and employment, agricultural production increased at a steady rate of about 1 per cent a year between 1910 and 1954.[1] This upward trend in production corresponds roughly with the trend of population growth in the United States over the past fifty-four years. With the improvement of agricultural techniques, fewer people engaged in agriculture can provide for the needs of an expanding population, thus releasing farmers for other essential tasks. The importance of agriculture to the national economy as well as the political influence of such a large segment of the population easily account for the development of government programs to remove elements of general dissatisfaction in the industry.

[1] Except for the period during World War II when the annual rate of increase jumped to 3 per cent.

INSTABILITY OF FARM INCOME

One of the most serious problems of farm income and the reason for most price-support legislation is the wide fluctuation of net farm income. Net farm income rose from $3.6 billion at the beginning of World War I to $9.3 billion by 1919. In two years' time it collapsed to $3.7 billion. During the 1920s it increased slightly, but it fell off from $6.1 billion to $1.9 billion between 1929 and 1932, after which it gradually recovered again. During World War II it shot up from $4.3 billion in 1940 to a high of $16.8 billion in 1947. Again it dropped to $12.4 billion by 1950, moved up to $14.6 billion in 1951, and fell to $12.5 billion in 1954 (see Figure 24–3.)

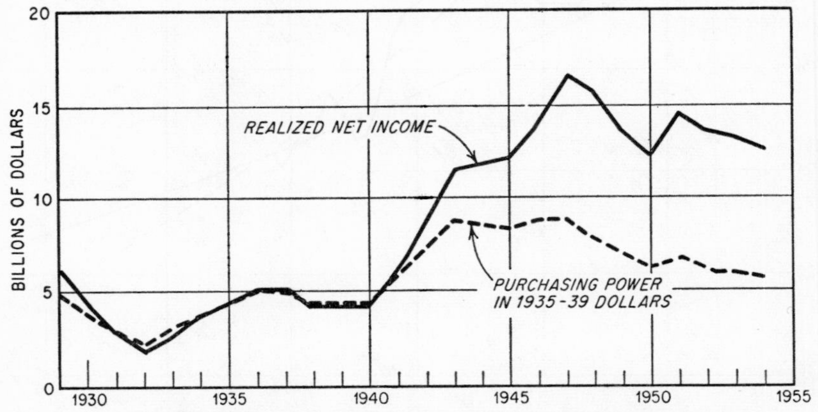

Figure 24—3. Farm Operators' Realized Net Income and Its Purchasing Power

Source: U.S. Department of Agriculture, *Agricultural Outlook Charts, 1955* (1954), p. 15.

This instability of income reflects the instability of agricultural prices. Business and industry have been able to meet the problem of severe price fluctuations more successfully than agriculture.[2] It is true that business prices fall in depressed times and rise in prosperous times, but agricultural prices fall and rise far more precipitously. The comparatively greater amplitude of price variations in agriculture is the result of the movement of demand around a relatively fixed supply.[3]

[2] In the three years from 1929 to 1932, farm prices dropped 54 per cent while industrial prices declined only 25 per cent. The 1938 recession forced farm prices down 22 per cent as compared to 7 per cent in industrial prices. Again, farm prices fell 11 per cent from 1948 to 1949; industrial prices, 4 per cent. U.S. Department of Agriculture, *Agricultural Outlook,* October, 1949, p. 1.

[3] For a more detailed analysis, see Theodore W. Schultz, *Agriculture in an Unstable Economy* (New York: McGraw-Hill Book Company, Inc., 1945), chaps. 3–7; by the same author, *Economic Organization of Agriculture* (New York: McGraw-

The unbalancing force in the economics of agriculture is consumer demand. Changes in demand are related primarily to variations in personal income. Income is, of course, related to the general state of the economy. In good times personal income increases so that the ability and willingness to consume farm products expands markedly.[4] When the economy is depressed the reverse is true.

Other possible determinants of demand, such as ability to substitute and changes in consumers' tastes and preferences, do not affect greatly the total demand for agricultural commodities. Moreover, since there is a continuing need for farm products and there is a lack of close substitutes, demand tends to be relatively inelastic at a given time; that is, aggregate demand is not greatly affected by price changes. The elasticity of demand for particular farm products understandably differs considerably. The amount of wheat, cotton, tobacco, milk, sugar, and potatoes that is consumed is only slightly affected by changes in price. The elasticity of demand for barley, corn, oats, rye, and hay is somewhat higher. The demand for meats, fruits, and vegetables is still more elastic. But even in the case of those products for which demand is most elastic, a point is soon reached at which price change has little effect on quantity purchased.

Whereas demand fluctuates widely over time and as between certain products, agricultural supply does not. The vagaries of weather, disease, pests, and the like may seriously affect the output of individual farms or specific regions, but total farm production seldom varies because of these factors or the movement of price and demand. During the droughts of 1934 and 1936, total farm output fell off only 10 per cent. In the boom years between 1924 and 1929, agricultural output moved from an index

---

Hill Book Company, Inc., 1953), chaps. 11–14; Harold G. Halcrow, *Agricultural Policy of the United States* (New York: Prentice-Hall, Inc., 1953), chaps. 2–11; Walter W. Wilcox and Willard W. Cochrane, *Economics of American Agriculture* (New York: Prentice-Hall, Inc., 1951), chaps. 21–24; John D. Black, *Introduction to Economics for Agriculture* (New York: The Macmillan Company, 1953), chaps. 22–23; Geoffrey S. Shepherd, *Agricultural Price and Income Policy* (Ames, Iowa: Iowa State College Press, 1952), chaps. 1–3; Rainer Schickele, *Agricultural Policy: Farm Programs and National Welfare* (New York: McGraw-Hill Book Company, Inc., 1954), chaps. 9–10.

[4] However, the demand for every agricultural commodity does not rise at the same rate. The various income groups of the population buy differing amounts of certain farm products. Low-income groups spend a relatively large proportion of their food dollar on cereals and cheaper vegetables. The higher-income groups spend a larger proportion on meats, certain dairy products, and the higher-priced fruits and vegetables. Therefore, when personal incomes increase, the demand for meats, fruits, vegetables, and similar products rises at a faster rate, because the low-income groups can afford more of these products. The reverse is true as income falls off. The consumption of certain products like fats and oils (except for butter) is not materially affected by income variation.

of 98 to 99, while industrial output jumped from an index of 82 to 110. In the succeeding years of depression (1930 to 1932), industrial output fell from an index of 110 to 58, whereas farm production dropped from 99 to 96. Again, from 1933 to 1937, agricultural output increased only to an index of 106 at the same time that industrial production soared from 58 to 113.[5]

The principal determinants of a steadily expanding agricultural production have been factors related to technological advances. For example, the introduction of mechanical power released 62 million acres from raising horse feed, thereby increasing crop area for human foodstuff by 17 to 20 per cent. Hybrid corn, new fertilizers, soil-conserving practices, and new methods of crop-pest and disease control have further stimulated production. The pressure of two world wars within recent times forced agriculture to employ these developments to expand production beyond peacetime demand. But once there is an expansion, contraction is virtually impossible. New land has been put into production, improvements have been added to the farm, and new machinery has been bought. The cost of maintaining these improvements as well as paying off the loans used to make them requires continued high-level production.

Thus, even though farm output does not expand proportionately as much as business production, when prices fall off production is not reduced as in industry. Agricultural supply is highly inelastic over time. There are many reasons for this inability of farm output to reflect price changes. First, production begins long before the time of marketing. The farmer cannot predict what prices will be. It is not possible to shift easily from one product to another when the price of the one in production falls off. It is difficult to shift, let us say, from wheat to apples, or from dairying to hogs. Furthermore, a farmer finds it difficult to lay off workers, usually members of his own family, to cut down production. In fact, in depressed times, the farmer is stimulated to work harder and harvest a larger crop to bolster his income. Even when production expenses do fall off, they fall off more slowly than does gross income. Hence, the net income is proportionately less than the net income for other industries which can cut back expenses immediately. For instance, at the depths of the Depression in 1932, 72 per cent of the gross agricultural income went for production expenses. By contrast, in the peak year of 1947, only 48 per cent of gross income went for expenses.

Labor constitutes roughly seven-tenths of the cost of farm production. Unfortunately, labor does not leave agriculture in response to falling farm prices which would help reduce costs. In fact, only two limited periods of net movement from the city to the farm coincide with periods of falling prices—1932 to 1933, and 1945 to 1946. The competitive struc-

[5] Schultz, *Agriculture in an Unstable Economy*, p. 135.

ture of agriculture forces family labor to stay employed, which is not the case in much of industry. During a depression farmers are better off on the farm than in the city, where jobs are short. Migration away from the farm generally occurs only when there are job opportunities in the city, which is during prosperous times.

The excess supply of labor on the farm is further aggravated by the fact that the major technological improvements have been laborsaving. Between 1910 and 1954 total farm output increased from an index of 61 to 106, while during the same period the man-hours of work required on the farm fell from an index of 132 to 86. In other words, farm mechanization and the widespread adoption of improved farming practices has increased the output per man-hour from an index of 46 to 123.[6]

The oversupply of farm labor does not, however, result in unemployment, except for migrant workers. Farm workers are usually continuously employed regardless of the level of farm prices. In fact, during poor times the farmer is stimulated to put more members of his family to work to increase his yield in the hope of raising his income. The consequence of excess labor on the farm is that the already disproportionately small share of the national income that farmers receive must be spread among too many people, thereby reducing the per capita income of farm workers.

The basic agricultural problem, therefore, rises from the fact that farming is still highly competitive and farm prices are determined by the interaction of supply and demand. However, it is impossible for the farmer to produce just enough to meet the quantity demanded at a price profitable to him. Demand fluctuates freely as a result of the movement of personal income. Supply is not basically affected by a change in price, and because of the steady increase of farm output due to technological advances, supply at profitable prices has tended to exceed the amount demanded at these prices. It should be emphasized that this does not mean that there is too much production. As long as famines occur and people anywhere in the world go hungry, the problem is not one of agricultural surpluses. Even in the United States, where famine has been rare, consumption could greatly expand if all persons received a more balanced and nutritious diet. The real farm problem is that the ability and willingness of the consumer to buy farm products at prices which cover the cost of production have not kept pace with the expansion of agricultural output.[7] Then, when demand falls off in depressed times, prices drop much

[6] U.S. Department of Agriculture, *Agricultural Outlook Charts, 1955* (1954), pp. 1, 30.

[7] For example, by 1953 farm production was 44 per cent above prewar production, while the nation's population had increased already 24 per cent in that time. Furthermore, the export market has been contracting since 1900. In short periods, especially after the two world wars, these reductions have been very great. For example, in 1953, exports fell off 31 per cent from the previous year. See U.S. Department of Agriculture, *Report of the Secretary of Agriculture, 1953* (1954), p. 7.

more than proportionately because of the existence of a relatively inelastic supply. Since expenses go on, farm net incomes decline precipitously. Few workers can be laid off, and limited urban opportunities mean that movement off the farm does not keep pace with the decreasing need for farm labor.

UNEVEN DISTRIBUTION OF FARM INCOME

The second problem of farm income is the disparity in the distribution of income. According to the 1950 Census of Agriculture, there were 5,380,127 farms of all types in the United States.[8] Some 3.9 million farms (73.2 per cent of the total) were operated by owners or by farmers who owned part of the land and rented the rest. Tenant farmers operated 1.5 million farms (26.8 per cent of the total). The general upward trend in farm tenancy since 1880 was reversed in 1935. By 1950, farm tenancy was almost as low as it was in 1880.[9]

Of the total farm units, 29 per cent (1.6 million farms) were classified as part-time or residential farms and produced only 2 per cent of the total value of farm products sold. Farms with a value of sales of farm products amounting to $1,200 or more are classified as commercial. In 1950, commercial farms amounted to 71 per cent of the nation's farms and produced 98 per cent of the total value of farm products sold.

A breakdown of these statistics reveals that a great percentage of the farms in the country contribute little or nothing to the total agricultural output. At one extreme, 43 per cent of the nation's farms produced only 4 per cent of the total value of products sold; 60 per cent produced only 11 per cent of the products sold. At the other extreme, 9 per cent of the farms produced 50 per cent of the total value of products marketed. Expressed in terms of dollars, only 9 per cent of the farms produced over $10,000 worth of commodities, whereas 60 per cent of the farms counted in 1950 had gross farm sales that amounted to less than $2,500.

The relatively small gross sales of farm products by 60 per cent of the nation's farms raise doubt as to the adequacy of incomes available to many farm families. Furthermore, total cash income is lower than gross income, because cash operating expenses must be deducted. Total cash income for 28.1 per cent of the farm-operator families in 1950 amounted to less than $1,000. Less than $2,000 total cash income was earned by 52.9 per cent of the farms. Only 17.5 per cent of the farms earned a total cash income of over $4,000.[10]

[8] The statistics used in this section have been drawn from U.S. Bureau of the Census, *Farms and Farm People* (1953). See also K. L. Bachman and R. W. Jones, *Size of Farms in the United States*, U.S. Department of Agriculture Technical Bulletin 1019 (1950).

[9] U.S. Department of Agriculture, *Agricultural Statistics*, 1952, p. 623.

[10] The disparity of distribution of income is even wider for whites and Negroes

THE LEVEL OF FARM INCOME

The problem of farm income is further complicated by the lag of farm income behind nonfarm income. The dissatisfaction with this lag has been responsible for much of the effort to achieve "equality" for agriculture.

There are several ways of showing the relatively low level of farm income. Agricultural income as a percentage of national income has varied

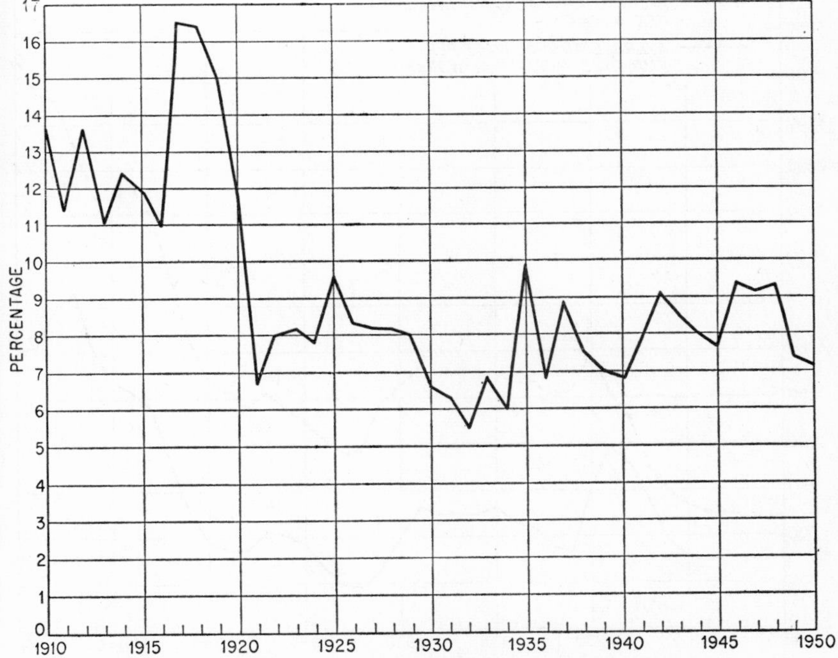

Figure 24—4. Agricultural Net Income as a Percentage of National Income

Source: U.S. Department of Agriculture, *The Farm Income Situation* (July-September, 1951), p. 19.

from a high of 16.5 per cent in 1917 to a low of 5.5 per cent in 1932 (see Figure 24–4). The percentage is somewhat higher in time of war, but the long-run trend seems to be downward. The percentage during and immediately after World War II was never as high as during and after World War I. It should be remembered that this income goes to a farm population which, although constantly declining, is still 15 per cent of the

in the South. Whereas 39 per cent of the whites made under $1,000, 72 per cent of the Negroes earned under $1,000. Only 1 per cent of the Negroes made over $3,000, whereas 15 per cent of the whites in the South made over $3,000.

nation's population. In 1950, for example, 17 per cent of the population received an income from farming which was only 7.1 per cent of national income.

Another comparison shows that in recent years the average income per worker in agriculture has been only about half as high as the average income per worker in industry (see Figure 24–5). It should be recognized

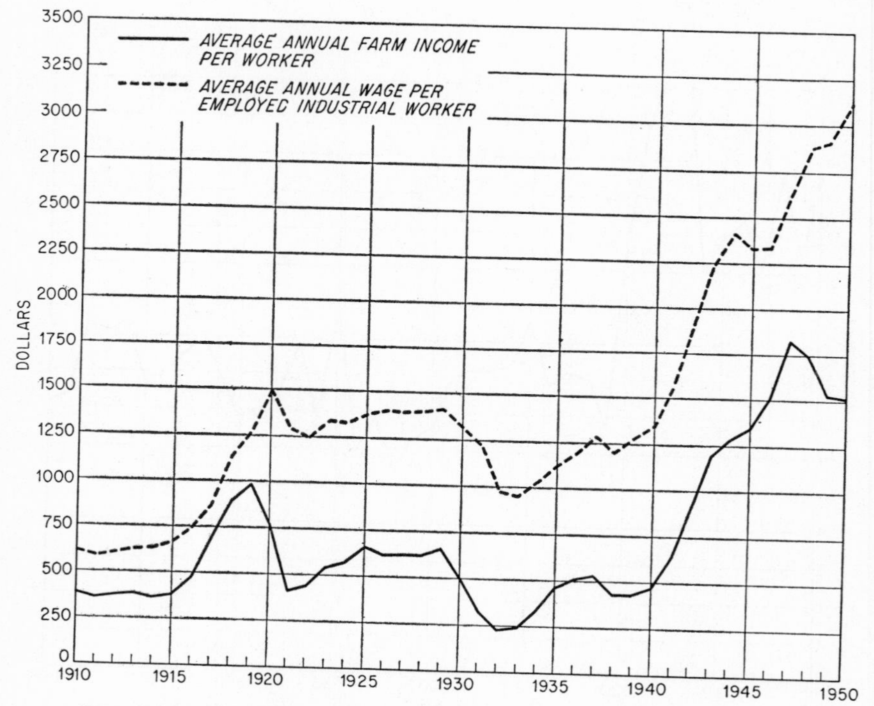

Figure 24—5. Per Capita Income of Farm and Nonfarm Workers, 1910 to 1950

Source: U.S. Department of Agriculture, *The Farm Income Situation* (July-September, 1951), p. 19.

that farming has a number of advantages which offset to a certain extent this disparity of income. The real income of the farmer is actually higher because he grows much of his food and does not have some of the transportation, entertainment, utility, and tax expenses that accompany city living. In addition, there are intangible values in rural living which cannot be evaluated in monetary terms. Nevertheless, the fact remains that the income of farmers has tended to be much lower than nonfarm income.

As a consequence of the lag of farm income behind nonfarm income and its uneven distribution, the income of fully half the people engaged in farming has been held to be too low to permit them to have housing, health facilities, education, and even diets that are regarded as adequate.[11]

AGRICULTURAL PROBLEMS AND PUBLIC POLICY

Problems relating to farm prices and income set the goals of agricultural policy. Farmers need a rather large source of credit because the annual return relative to the investment is low, there is a recurring need for new equipment, seed, and other capital requirements, and the income from farming is not predictable. Regular commercial sources of credit have not been adequate. The terms are too short, the interest is too high, the sources are undependable, and the payments cannot be timed with fluctuations in income. Therefore, in response to insistence by farmers that the government should furnish more adequate and less costly credit facilities than those available from private sources, the federal government embarked upon a program of credit aid to agriculture in 1916.

As a result of a serious disparity in the distribution of farm income and the lag of farm income behind nonfarm income, many farm families suffered from a low level of income and inadequate essentials of life. Government has endeavored to aid low-income farmers and improve the general conditions of rural life by means of special programs.

Because of the distinctive characteristics of farm supply and demand, free competition in agriculture has resulted in great instability of prices. Prices have often been lower than the cost of production. Moreover, the long-run level of farm income has been considerably lower than nonfarm income. Therefore, government has designed a number of programs to stabilize and raise the level of farm income, including storage programs, control of agricultural production, food-consumption programs, crop insurance, and price- and income-support programs.

Farm Credit Programs

FEDERAL FARM CREDIT BEFORE 1933

After three years of debate Congress passed in 1916 the National Farm Loan Act creating a system of farm land banks, one in each of twelve districts, and supervised by the Federal Farm Loan Board. The Act also provided for the formation of local cooperative farm loan associations. Land-bank loans, amounting to up to 65 per cent of the normal value of the farm, are made through the associations, which are organizations of ten or more owners or prospective owners of farm land. When a farmer borrows from an association, he is required to buy stock in the association

[11] See Theodore W. Schultz, "Reflections on Poverty within Agriculture," 58 *Journal of Political Economy* 1–15 (February, 1950).

equal to 5 per cent of the loan. The association in turn subscribes for a similar amount of stock in the federal land bank, which endorses the loan and furnishes the funds for it. Initially, in 1916, the government made a subscription of $9 million capital stock in the banks. In time all this capital has been repaid, and the federal land banks are now entirely owned by the member-borrowers. The land banks can also raise money by selling bonds to the public.

Since the land banks were limited to the long-term loan field, farmers still had to go to private lenders for short-term and intermediate-term loans necessary to finance purchases of equipment and livestock and to finance harvest needs. In 1923, Congress established a system of twelve intermediate-credit banks under the management of the land banks. They are authorized to make loans to farmers for periods from six months to three years through two types of agencies: they can discount or purchase notes representing loans made by banks, livestock companies, cooperative marketing companies, or agricultural credit associations; or they can make direct loans to cooperative marketing associations. Unlike the land banks, they are wholly owned by the federal government which supplies the capital,[12] and they do not deal directly with individual farmers. They are banks of rediscount.

The Depression seriously shook the entire farm-credit structure. Farmers were unable to meet their payments, banks failed, foreclosures multiplied, and the land banks themselves were threatened. The agriculture loan system was reorganized early in the Roosevelt administration.

REORGANIZATION AND EXPANSION OF FARM CREDIT AFTER 1933

In 1933, the Federal Farm Loan Board was abolished and the Farm Credit Administration was created to supervise practically all the farm-credit facilities of the government. The Emergency Farm Mortgage Act of 1933, the Farm Credit Acts of 1933, 1935, and 1937, and other acts have enlarged the government program of credit assistance.

The new legislation continued the system of federal land banks and intermediate-credit banks and added to the lending facilities of the land banks by authorizing the Land Bank Commissioner to make direct loans to borrowers in localities in which cooperative associations did not exist or were not functioning properly. The Federal Farm Mortgage Corporation was created with government capital of $200 million and power to borrow up to $2 billion on bonds guaranteed by the government. The resources of the Corporation have been used to allow farmers to purchase their mortgages, to make new mortgages, to repurchase farms lost through foreclosure, and to provide farm working capital.

[12] They also have raised funds by selling short-term debentures to the public and by reselling notes obtained from borrowers.

Intermediate- and short-term credit facilities were expanded by establishment of special banks for cooperatives in each land-bank district and by creation of production-credit corporations. Under the legislation existing prior to 1933 the intermediate-credit banks were authorized to make loans to cooperative marketing associations, but the arrangement proved inadequate. The special banks for cooperatives were authorized to make loans to cooperatives. These banks are owned by the government, and their paper is discounted with the intermediate-credit banks.

The production-credit system consists of twelve production-credit corporations and twelve production-credit associations, one in each of the land-bank districts. The production-credit associations operate analogously to the farm loan associations, and their loans are discounted by the intermediate-credit banks. Their purpose is to provide short-term loans, but none may be less than $50. The production-credit corporations are government-owned bodies which give aid in organizing production-credit associations, assist in capitalizing them by buying preferred capital stock in them, and supervise their operations.

The operations of the production-credit system and the banks for cooperatives are assuming greater importance as time goes by. During the 1930s the long-term loans of the land banks were the principal loans being made, as private lenders were withdrawing from the field. In the period between 1932 and 1936 these loans averaged $254 million a year, totaling almost $2.2 billion. In 1954, farmers and cooperative associations used $2.2 billion in credit supplied by units operating under supervision of the Farm Credit Administration. However, only $306 million were loaned by the land banks. The production-credit associations loaned $1.3 billion and the banks for cooperatives loaned $483 million in 1954.[13]

Aiding Low-income Farmers and Improving Farm Welfare

The low level of farm income relative to nonfarm income, coupled with the uneven distribution of income within agriculture, results in an extraordinary amount of poverty and near poverty among many farm families. In 1948, which was one of the best years agriculture in the United States ever experienced, 6 million farm people had incomes little above subsistence level.

The low level of earnings in agriculture is caused to a considerable extent by the excess supply of labor. Too many people with insufficient capital to make improvements are working farms that are too small to be productive. The long-run need is to encourage the movement of some underemployed farmers into other jobs where they can be assured of a higher income and to increase the efficiency of the low-income producers

[13] *United States Government Organization Manual, 1955–56* (1955), p. 356.

who stay on the farms so that they can make an adequate income. The immediate need is to treat the consequences of rural poverty until the causes of it can be eliminated.

INCREASING THE EFFICIENCY OF LOW-INCOME FARMERS

Since proposals and programs to encourage migration out of agriculture have never solved the problem of underemployment and low income, something must be done to increase the efficiency of low-income farmers to improve their level of income. The major cause of underemployment and low income appears to be the inadequate size of many family farms. For historical and legal reasons the basis for settling in many areas in the United States provided farm families with plots of land that are too small for profitable farming. The objectives of farm programs to increase the efficiency of low-income farmers are to promote the farm family and strengthen farm ownership.

Promoting the family farm. Promotion of farming on land owned and operated by independent families has long been the goal of land-settlement and tenure programs in the United States. Rooted in the agrarian philosophy of Thomas Jefferson, this ideal still dominates agricultural policy, in spite of the growth of corporate and factory farming. It has been estimated that over one-third of all bona fide farms do not meet the size criterion of an adequate family farm.[14]

Financial aid. Prior to the New Deal, financial aid to low-income farmers consisted almost entirely of emergency loans and grants to tide farmers over unusually adverse circumstances. Generally loans or grants were made to farmers only if they were destitute. As a result, defaults and deficiencies were common.

Beginning in 1933 the government launched a series of programs to strengthen the position of farm families, particularly those at the low end of the income scale. Resettlement projects; farm ownership, enlargement, and development loans; and farm-debt-adjustment programs were designed to strengthen farm ownership. To assure farmers access to capital resources, the government provided farm-operating (rehabilitation) and group service loans.

In 1946, Congress created the Farmers' Home Administration. All the grant and lending programs for low-income farmers were consolidated in this one agency. By 1953, the Farmers' Home Administration and its predecessor agencies had made loans totaling $2.9 billion.[15]

[14] For a definition of the family farm, see Joseph Ackerman and Marshall Harris (eds.), *Family Farm Policy* (Chicago: University of Chicago Press, 1947), p. 389.

[15] Commission on Organization of the Executive Branch of the Government, *Task Force Report on Lending Agencies* (1955), p. 183.

IMPROVING FARM WELFARE

Until the problem of underemployment on farms can be solved and the efficiency of low-income producers raised so that all farmers are making an adequate living, there is need to improve the status of farmers and better the conditions of rural life. The need to improve and develop rural facilities applies not only to low-income farmers but also to all rural dwellers.

The rural health problem is serious. One of the most significant governmental efforts to ease the burden of medical expense and make medical care available in rural areas was the program operated by the Farm Security Administration between 1936 and 1947. The program was conceived principally on a voluntary-insurance basis. The government made loans to farmers to be used for paying membership fees in locally organized and controlled prepayment plans for doctor care, hospitalization, drugs, and dental care. The pressures of the war and postwar legislative changes brought the program to an end.

The social and political environment became hostile to group health plans after the war, and the Farmers' Home Administration no longer assists in making medical care available. But this does not mean the problem is solved. At present the Farmers' Home Administration is limited to encouraging families to improve their diets, construct better sanitary facilities, and safeguard their water supply against contamination.

Lack of adequate housing has been another problem. Congress enacted a rural housing act in 1949 by which the Farmers' Home Administration can make financial and technical assistance available to farmers to provide themselves and their tenants with more adequate housing.

A great boon to farmers has been the service provided by the Rural Electrification Administration. Only 11 per cent of farm families had electricity in 1934. Congress passed the Rural Electrification Act in 1936 authorizing the Administration to make loans for rural electrification and the furnishing of electric energy to persons in rural areas. By 1954, almost $3 billion in electrification loans had been approved, and 90 per cent of farmers had electricity in their homes.[16] Congress extended the authority of the Administration in 1949 to provide credit to finance rural telephone service. In addition to loaning funds, the Administration also makes technical and managerial assistance available and establishes standards for construction, operation, and financial management.

The problem of helping the aged on farms has been materially improved by the 1954 amendment to the Social Security Act. An estimated 3 million farm operators and 2 million farm employees may now receive the benefits of old age and survivors insurance.

[16] *Ibid.*, pp. 3, 63.

Storage Programs

When demand for farm products falls off, as has already been shown, prices drop because production remains relatively constant. Government storage programs have been devised as a means of removing a certain portion of farm output from the general market, thereby reducing the amounts offered for sale and increasing the market price. Storage programs serve several related purposes. They may be used to stabilize income, stabilize supply, or carry out a price-support program.

It should be pointed out that, although the commodities that are removed from the market are usually referred to as surpluses, they are "surplus" only in a certain sense. If prices were allowed to fall freely, there would almost always be some price at which total production could be taken off the market. Therefore, the term "surplus" refers to the amount which it is believed should be removed from the market to force prices to a certain level.

THE FEDERAL FARM BOARD, 1929 TO 1933

Early efforts in Congress to establish a storage program in 1926 and 1927 failed. Not until 1929, the worst possible time to inaugurate such a program, did Congress provide for surplus removal and storage. A Federal Farm Board with a revolving fund of $500 million was created by the Agricultural Marketing Act of 1929. The Board was authorized to make loans through cooperatives and so-called stabilization corporations to enable farmers to hold surpluses off the market. While the Board had power to advise restriction of production and methods of increasing sales, it had no power to require adoption of this advice.

The Board failed to maintain prices, and the acquisition of huge stocks of goods caused practical abandonment of the plan in 1931 and 1932. There are several reasons for this failure. In the first place, the operations were conducted at a time when conditions were exceedingly unfavorable to stabilization. The world-wide depression beginning in 1929 caused prices of agricultural products to fall far below normal levels. In the second place, stabilization of prices can hardly be attained if the approach is entirely from the demand side of the market, unless the government is prepared to buy commodities unsparingly and to keep these commodities off the market indefinitely. Real price stabilization must also reduce the supply offered on the market, and this can be accomplished only through control over production. Furthermore, a large holding of a commodity by a government agency tends to have a depressing effect upon market price, since operators in the market never know when the supply will be increased by sales of government holdings.

COMMODITY CREDIT CORPORATION

Just five months after the Federal Farm Board was abolished, President Roosevelt created the Commodity Credit Corporation by Executive order. Like its predecessor it has the objective of keeping products off the market under certain circumstances while assuring farmers a cash income. The Corporation was operated as an independent agency financed by funds from the Reconstruction Finance Corporation until 1939, when it was transferred to the Department of Agriculture.

Commodity loans are made to farmers on the assurance that the commodities offered for collateral have been placed in storage and the farmer has joined the production-control program set up by law. These loans are made "without recourse" at stated price-support levels. The term "without recourse" means that the borrower has the option of selling the commodity and paying off the loan if the market price of the commodity rises above the loan value. On the other hand, if the market price should stay below the loan value, the borrower turns the commodity in storage over to the Commodity Credit Corporation, which cancels the loan without holding the borrower to the difference between the loan value and the market price.

The loan program of the corporation is similar to the stabilization operations which were conducted by the Federal Farm Board, with the exception that goods may be stored on the farm or in warehouses and that farmers obtaining loans must be cooperating in the program for restriction of production. As time went on, loans were not confined to commodities under production control and direct purchases were made of nonstorable commodities.

At first loans were offered only to producers of corn and cotton, but they were extended after 1937 to include a great variety of other products. Prior to 1937, loan rates were set by administrative decree, usually by the President himself. In 1938, Congress adapted the commodity loan program to the concept of an "ever-normal granary" which the Agricultural Adjustment Act of that year established. At the same time Congress took the setting of loan rates out of administrative hands and wrote into law that loan rates should be set between 50 and 75 per cent of parity. In 1941, Congress established the loan rates for basic crops at 85 per cent of parity. The next year the figure was raised to 90 per cent of parity for the duration of the war and two years afterward. A schedule of flexible loan rates was established in the acts of 1948 and 1949, but their application was postponed so that the rates continue to be 90 per cent of parity until 1955.[17] Between 1933 and 1950, the Commodity Credit Corporation

[17] The parity concept as well as the various price- and income-support programs will be discussed in more detail in a later section.

made loans totaling over $10 billion, two-thirds of which were on cotton and wheat alone.[18] By October, 1953, Commodity Credit Corporation investments stood at $4.5 billion.[19]

What the plan of commodity loans has really done is to allow the farmer to sell his products to the government at a fixed price, set by the loan value, and to receive in addition any profits which might accrue if market price rose above the loan value. The experience of the Commodity Credit Corporation has been more fortunate than that of the Federal Farm Board, because the Corporation has operated in a period of generally rising demand and price levels, so storage commodities have been sold at generally higher prices than the Corporation paid for them. The potato-storage program and, more recently, the butter-storage program have been notable exceptions which resulted in heavy losses.

An evaluation of the storage program administered by the Commodity Credit Corporation must take into consideration the various objectives pursued by such a program. It has not proved to be an effective way of raising farm prices over a period of years. At any one time the loan value of a commodity may be higher than the market price so that farm income rises if the commodity is stored rather than sold on the market. But what is put in storage must eventually come out of storage, and when it does it may depress prices about as much as it has raised them. Moreover, where the loans are made on commodities sold in the export market as well as in the domestic market, the higher loan values tend to put domestic prices above world prices and make the export of the commodities difficult or impossible. If the domestic price is higher than the world price, foreign importers tend to purchase from other countries and foreign production tends to be stimulated. Thus, unless the government is prepared to accumulate supplies indefinitely or to subsidize domestic consumption and foreign export, the increased quantities held by it become a threat to the market and the price-supporting effect of the loans tends to disappear.

Where prices happen to rise above loan values so that loans can be liquidated, farmers often believe that the government can support prices at almost any level and pressure is brought to bear for even higher loans. Even where the loans have to be taken over by the government, this pressure for higher rates is likely to be maintained as long as farmers believe the price they are receiving to be unsatisfactory. The result is that a vicious circle is set up. Higher loan rates tend to discourage export and to increase domestic supplies, which in turn has a depressing effect on domestic prices. But unless domestic prices respond upward to levels

[18] U.S. Department of Agriculture, *Agricultural Statistics*, 1951, p. 660.

[19] U.S. Department of Agriculture, *Report of the Secretary of Agriculture, 1953*, p. 23.

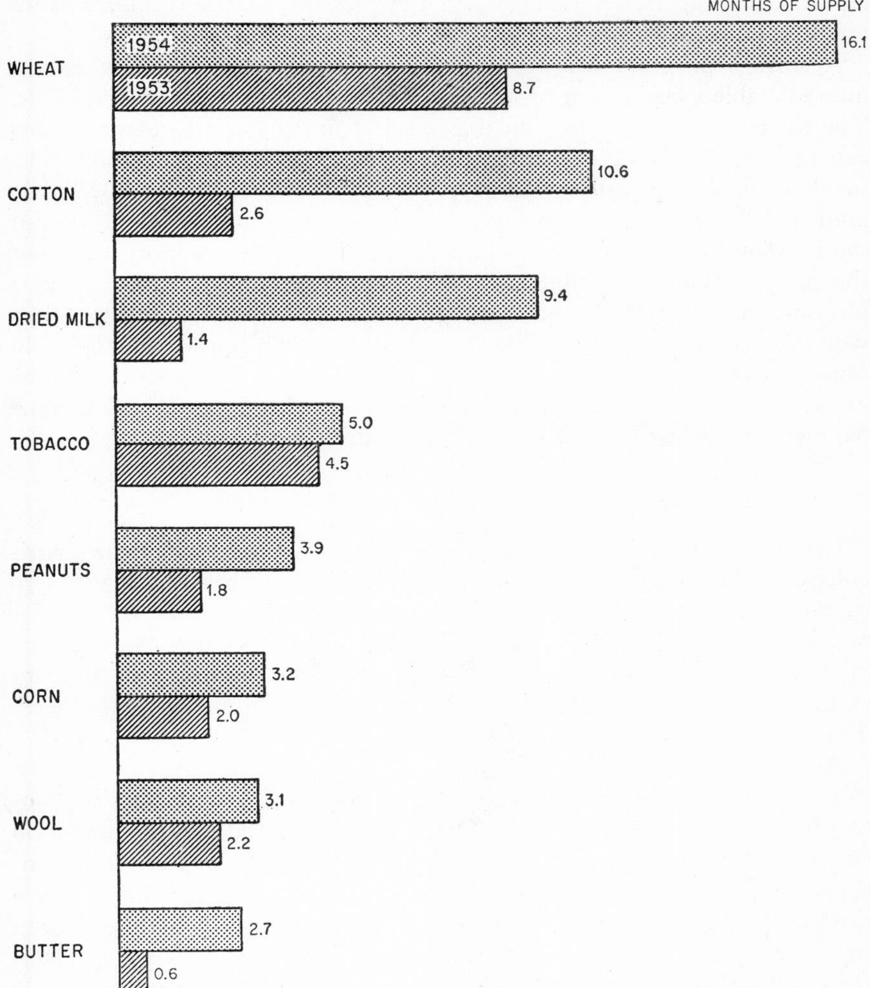

Figure 24—6. Farm Products in Government Inventory and Pledged for Loans, February 28, 1954, and February 28, 1953

Wheat held by the government or under government loan at the end of February, 1954, was sufficient to supply the United States for more than sixteen months at recent consumption rates. A year earlier, this supply was about half as large. Increased stocks of farm products are due largely to slackening in foreign demand, which has strongly contributed to the falling off in farm prices. The government's investment in the products shown here at the end of 1954 was $5.5 billion, and the total of all items under price support programs was $6.2 billion. Wheat alone accounted for $2.2 billion. Source: The Conference Board, *Road Maps of Industry,* No. 956, Apr. 23, 1954.

regarded by farmers as satisfactory, the pressure for more liberal loans tends to increase.

A storage program is a very effective way to stabilize prices against unpredictable variations in production due to weather, pests, and the like. The fluctuations in production that result from these unforeseen factors can be evened out by controlling the flow of products to market. The surpluses of an unusually good crop year can be stored to be released in poor production years. However, a storage program aimed at output stabilization need not have any loan at all, so the price-support aspect of the program could be eliminated. The program could be handled as a physical matter, and the quantity put in or taken out of storage then would determine the price. The Department of Agriculture could simply remove and later return the proper quantities of commodities to the market by buying and selling rather than by granting loans. Direct income payments might be used, if necessary, to raise farm income.[20]

Control of Agricultural Production

Ever since the unfortunate experience of the Federal Farm Board, agricultural policy makers have agreed that surplus-purchasing programs to raise farm prices would not be effective as long as the supply offered for sale is not limited. Control of agricultural production has been undertaken by two kinds of government programs. One approach has been to contract with farmers for limitation in acreage planted or units produced. This technique is obviously production control.

Another line of attack has been to limit the amount that a farmer can offer on the market. While this is, strictly speaking, not production control but marketing control, the effect is practically the same as limitation of production. If a farmer can market only a certain amount and contracts to do so, he does not find it advantageous to produce more. As a matter of fact, acreage reduction or other restrictions in volume have been suggested to those who enter into marketing agreements. As we shall see, the principal reason for employing the marketing-agreement device has probably been that it is superior to direct control from the point of view of constitutionality.

AGRICULTURAL ADJUSTMENT, 1933–1936

Production-control contracts. The Agricultural Adjustment Act of 1933 established a system of production control for certain "basic" commodities.[21] The Secretary of Agriculture was empowered to enter into

[20] Shepherd, *op. cit.*, pp. 116–117.

[21] Originally wheat, cotton, rice, tobacco, field corn, hogs, and milk. By legislation in the next two years, the list was increased to fifteen by the addition of rye, flax, barley, grain sorghums, cattle, peanuts, sugar, and potatoes.

contracts with producers of basic commodities by which they agreed to cut down acreage or livestock production by a certain amount. In return, farmers received rental or benefit payments which were financed by taxes levied on the processors of agricultural products.

The amount of output reduction as well as the amount of the benefit payments were left to the determination of the Secretary. Obviously, the payments had to be high enough to induce farmers to enter into a production-control contract. The payments were intended to make up the difference between the current market price and the parity price.

Marketing agreements. The act of 1933 also gave the Secretary of Agriculture the power to enter into marketing agreements, as a method of control alternative to production control.[22] The law authorized the Secretary to issue licenses to processors, associations of producers, and others, permitting them to engage in marketing of goods moving in interstate or foreign commerce. It allowed him to set up requirements, as a condition for licensing, for the removal of those unfair practices which might prevent the operation of a marketing agreement. The power of the Secretary to issue licenses gave him authority to enforce marketing agreements upon recalcitrant minorities of producers, simply by not licensing them to market goods.

Numerous marketing agreements were put into effect after 1933 for several basic commodities as well as for general crops. Following the Supreme Court decision in 1935 invalidating the National Recovery Administration, the marketing-agreement program broke down. As a result, Congress amended the law in 1935 giving the Secretary of Agriculture authority to use "marketing orders" instead of the licensing powers granted in the original act. A marketing order is an order by the Secretary that an agreement is approved by him, by the requisite two-thirds of growers, and by handlers of one-half of market volume, and that henceforth all handlers of products covered by the order are to comply with it. Orders could also be issued in the absence of marketing agreements. Most of the marketing agreements were local or regional in scope, and only two—those for dried and evaporated milk—were placed on a national basis. Many marketing agreements were temporary in nature and were succeeded in 1934 and 1935 by adjustment contracts for production control. The lack of producer solidarity in many fields, the fear that definite controls under agreements were illegal, the fact that marketing agreements did not impose controls on production, and the too ambitious coverage of many plans made the experience in marketing agreements between 1933 and 1936 not too significant in solving the basic agricultural problem.

[22] See E. G. Nourse, *Marketing Agreements under the AAA* (Washington, D.C.: Brookings Institution, 1935).

Constitutionality of the first AAA. The early agricultural adjustment program met with legal difficulties when the Supreme Court, in the famous Hoosac Mills case [23] of 1936, held the processing-tax provisions to be unconstitutional. The Court found that the processing-tax and benefit provisions involved a system of regulation of agriculture and, as such, represented an invasion of states' rights. The majority of six justices argued that the tax and benefit provisions did not involve a lawful use of taxing and spending powers in that they coerced local producers to yield to government regulation. The minority, on the other hand, insisted that the tax was for the general welfare and that the hope of gain by compliance with the program did not result in economic coercion.

While this decision did not affect the constitutionality of marketing agreements or the operations of the Commodity Credit Corporation, it struck at the heart of the New Deal's first agricultural program, making necessary a new approach to production adjustment.[24]

THE SOIL-CONSERVATION PROGRAM

The soil-conservation program was developed to replace the production-control measures found unconstitutional in 1936. The soil-conservation program owes its beginnings to a relatively obscure act passed in 1935. The Soil Erosion Act of 1935 attempted to bring together the several features of previous government plans to curb erosion, prevent floods, and otherwise preserve the soil. Shortly after the invalidation of processing taxes and adjustment contracts, Congress passed the Soil Conservation and Domestic Allotment Act, technically as an amendment to the 1935 act, authorizing the Secretary of Agriculture to make payments to farmers who would agree to participate in soil conservation.

Soil-conservation payments. Instead of contracts and payments for acreage adjustment, as provided in the 1933 act, the new legislation called for acreage adjustment oriented to conservation objectives and payments for making these adjustments. Two kinds of conservation payments were established. By far the most important of these were the payments made to farmers for decreasing acreage in "soil-depleting" crops and increasing acreage in "soil-conservation" crops. In addition, payments were made to farmers to aid them in adopting approved methods of restoring soil fertility such as strip cropping, terracing, new seeding of leguminous plants and grasses, and the use of limestone.

It is hardly surprising that the crops classed as "soil-depleting" were the basic crops for which production control was provided under the

[23] *United States v. Butler*, 296 U.S. 561 (1936).

[24] For a comprehensive analysis of the first AAA, see E. G. Nourse, J. S. Davis, and J. D. Black, *Three Years of the Agricultural Adjustment Administration* (Washington, D.C.: Brookings Institution, 1937).

first Agricultural Adjustment Act. The shift in orientation to conservation was an expedient to gain support for a more popular objective and to assure that public funds would be spent for a purpose that would be regarded as constitutional. If soil conservation had been the primary objective, the logical action would have been to expand and modify the work of the Soil Conservation Service, a principal agency already established for that purpose.[25] Instead, the payments have been made by the Agricultural Conservation Program within the Production and Marketing Administration, which also administered the production and marketing controls established in 1938.[26]

The general pattern of conservation payments has continued down to the present day with only a few significant adjustments. Since 1945 the payments have amounted to about $250 million, or about $80 per cooperating farmer.[27]

Evaluation of the program. Although the objective of soil conservation is laudable, the program must be judged from the point of view of production control as well, since that is its primary objective. Evaluated in these terms the program is open to many of the criticisms which were aimed at the earlier Agricultural Adjustment Act, and it is subject to criticisms which were not leveled at the earlier program.

In the first place, soil conservation and production control are in some respects inconsistent. Soil renewal and control of erosion tend to increase the productivity of land. By financing the building up of soil productivity, the government may be creating a production problem when farmers come to realize that it may be more profitable to use the soil for production of soil-depleting, or cash-market, crops than to accept benefits to conserve the soil further. To meet this problem, additional production controls will have to be instituted (as has actually happened under the marketing laws) or benefits for soil conservation will have to be increased.

In the second place, there is some question as to whether the program, by subsidizing one type of agricultural crop, may not cause surpluses of certain commodities. For example, planting crops in grasses and leguminous products led to increased dairying, with depressive influence in that in-

[25] The Soil Conservation Service does not disburse payments but mainly renders technical assistance to individual farmers and soil-conservation districts. The Service has encouraged the states to enact legislation setting up conservation districts as government subdivisions with powers to protect farm lands from misuse and erosion. It should be emphasized, however, that the conservation payments have made it possible for farmers to adopt the conservation measures recommended by the Soil Conservation Service and the conservation districts.

[26] The Eisenhower administration separated the Agricultural Conservation Program from the Production and Marketing Administration in 1953. See Charles M. Hardin, "The Republican Department of Agriculture—A Political Interpretation," 36 *Journal of Farm Economics* 210–227 (May, 1954).

[27] Schickele, *op. cit.*, p. 108.

dustry. Consequently, in 1938, Congress provided that benefit payments should be granted only on the condition that diverted acres were not used to produce dairy products for the market.

A third criticism which has been advanced is that soil fertility is not necessarily lost through utilization. Proper fertilization and planting methods may stop depletion, even if the production consists of those basic crops regarded as soil-depleting.

THE MARKETING-CONTROL PROGRAM

The conservation approach to production control was only a stopgap until more comprehensive legislation could be formulated. Since 1937, marketing controls have been the principal means by which agricultural supply has been regulated. The soil-conservation program was enlarged and integrated with marketing controls.

The Agricultural Marketing Act of 1937 gave congressional reaffirmation, plus a broader grant of authority, to the marketing-agreement plan set up in 1933. The Agricultural Adjustment Act of 1938 provided for a new device—marketing quotas—by which marketing of farm products could be controlled.

Marketing quotas and acreage allotments. Marketing quotas are a means of limiting the amount of a product a farmer may market in a given year without a penalty. This device, which was originally provided for in 1938, has been perpetuated in subsequent agricultural acts.

Whenever an "overproduction" of a particular product exists or threatens, the Secretary of Agriculture may poll the producing farmers to determine whether compulsory marketing quotas should be put into effect. Overproduction is declared by law to exist whenever the supply of a commodity is or promises to be a certain percentage above "normal." [28] If the referendum is approved by two-thirds of the producers, the quotas go into effect.[29] The Secretary calculates the marketing requirements to make the supply normal and apportions this to individual states, counties,

[28] Under the law, this allowable departure from normal supply is 7 per cent in the case of corn, 7 per cent for cotton, 10 per cent for rice, 30 per cent for wheat, and 0 to 5 per cent for tobacco. Note, however, that the law defines "normal supply" to be a normal year's domestic consumption and exports of the commodity plus 7 per cent in the case of corn, 40 per cent in the case of cotton, 10 per cent in the case of rice, and 15 per cent in the case of wheat, as an allowance for a normal carry-over. The "normal supply" of tobacco is a normal year's domestic consumption and exports plus 175 per cent of a normal year's domestic consumption and 65 per cent of a normal year's exports as an allowance for a normal carry-over. The normal year's domestic consumption and exports are calculated for yearly averages ranging from five to ten years.

[29] See L. V. Howard, "The Agricultural Referendum," 2 *Public Administration Review* 9–26 (Winter, 1942).

and farms. All producers are bound to comply or face the loss of conservation payments and commodity loans, as well as the imposition of a penalty.[30]

If a farmer markets more than the quota allocated to him, he must pay a penalty ranging from 2 cents a pound for cotton to 25 cents a pound for rice. Commodities produced in excess of the marketing quota may not be given away, used for feed on the farm, or bartered for other goods, unless the penalty tax is paid to market them. These excess commodities must be placed in storage for future sale within quota allotments.

In general, farmers have accepted the imposition of quotas when the matter has been submitted to them for a vote. Only in rare instances has it been turned down.

To aid farmers in producing only the quantities allowed by their quotas, provision is also made for a system of acreage allotments. First, a total national acreage goal is set, taking into account carry-overs, prospective demand, and parity price. The national total is then broken down into state totals, which in turn are allotted to individual farms on the basis of their crop history, thus tying the acreage allotment of each farm to what the farm has been producing. Farmers are not bound to produce in accordance with these allotments, but they find it practically necessary to do so in order to be sure that production will keep within marketing quotas as well as to derive the benefits from direct payments, crop loans, reduced prices for fertilizers, and crop insurance.

Marketing orders and agreements. Whereas marketing quotas and acreage allotments may be used for storable commodities, they would not be effective for perishable crops like fruits, vegetables, and milk. Marketing agreements and orders proved more effective for perishables, so the Agricultural Marketing Act of 1937 restated and broadened the earlier program.

The Secretary of Agriculture may issue a marketing order setting forth the terms and conditions under which a commodity should be marketed. An order may cover a wide range of matters from the total quantities to be marketed to various kinds of grade and size regulations and, in the case of milk, a schedule of minimum prices. An order does not become effective until a public hearing has been held and the order has been accepted by two-thirds of the producers and the handlers of at least half the total volume marketed.

Marketing orders may or may not be issued in conjunction with marketing agreements. Usually they are accompanied by agreements between

[30] Prior to the AAA of 1938, the Bankhead Cotton Control Act of 1934, the Kerr-Smith Tobacco Control Act of 1934, and the Warren Potato Act of 1935 contained provisions for penalty taxes on marketing in excess of individual quotas.

producers and handlers in which the marketing terms and conditions are specified in some detail. Such agreements are exempt from the antitrust laws.

Marketing agreements have been concluded for a number of commodities, including potatoes, citrus fruits, pecans, certain vegetables, and tobacco. Most important have been the milk-marketing agreements, which, unlike other agreements, must be approved by three-fourths of the producers supplying the market. In 1953, forty-nine milk-marketing areas operated under marketing orders and agreements, and twenty-five agreement and order programs covered twenty different fruits, vegetables, and tree nuts.[31]

Constitutionality of marketing controls. In 1939, the Supreme Court upheld the New York and Boston milk-marketing-agreement programs and confirmed the constitutionality of the Agricultural Marketing Act of 1937 under which the agreements were made.[32] The Court declared that the authority of the federal government over interstate commerce is complete and that, since most of the milk under agreements moved in interstate commerce and the intrastate milk was inextricably mixed with interstate milk, the regulation of prices of all milk in the New York and Boston markets through marketing agreements was a valid exercise of the commerce power.

The marketing-quota provisions of the Agricultural Adjustment Act of 1938 were also upheld by the Supreme Court early in 1939. In a case testing the quota restriction as applied to the marketing of tobacco, the Court held the regulation to be a proper use of the power to control interstate and foreign commerce.[33] It pointed out that the statute does not purport to control production but merely aims to control the sales of tobacco in interstate commerce so as to prevent the flow of commerce from working harm to the people of the nation.

War and postwar developments. Prior to World War II, as a product of the Depression, the main concern of farmers was with surpluses and how to avoid them. Such a policy was totally unsuited to the needs of a nation at war. The shift-over to programs to expand production was actually impeded by the surplus phobia. In time the transition was made, and production controls were sparingly used during the war, except for tobacco and cotton. The major emphasis was placed on price supports and production subsidies to expand output.

Postwar agricultural legislation continued the program of acreage allot-

[31] U.S. Department of Agriculture, *Report of the Secretary of Agriculture, 1953*, p. 25.

[32] *United States v. Rock Royal Co-operative*, 307 U.S. 533 (1939), and *H. P. Hood and Sons v. United States*, 307 U.S. 588 (1939).

[33] *Mulford v. Smith*, 307 U.S. 38 (1939).

ments for basic crops, with provision for marketing quotas and agreements. But the major emphasis was on price supports. The provisions for acreage allotments, except for tobacco and more recently for cotton, peanuts, and wheat, have not been brought into general use. Marketing quotas for wheat, peanuts, cotton, and some types of tobacco have been put into effect in recent postwar years. The 1954 crop of cotton and wheat was under allotments and quotas. Marketing quotas were approved for the 1953 peanut crop and some tobaccos.[34]

EFFECTS OF PRODUCTION CONTROL

The various programs of production control have been designed for three purposes: (1) to curtail production and, assuming a relatively inelastic demand, thus raise income; (2) to reduce the misuse of soil; and (3) to form a basis for supplementing farm incomes with government payments. At this point, attention will be focused only on the first two objectives, drawing examples from the period 1933–1942 when production control was in widest operation.

Effects on production. There is no doubt that the program of acreage allotments reduced the acreage planted and harvested for the basic crops. Of the four major crops under allotment (wheat, cotton, corn, and tobacco), the reduction in acreage between 1933 and 1942 totaled about 46 million acres, a reduction in total acreage of about 21 per cent.[35] In spite of the reduction in acres, production actually increased, except for cotton. While cotton output declined 17 per cent, tobacco production rose 4 per cent, corn production 5 per cent, and wheat production 21 per cent.

The explanation of this increase is that a farmer has several alternatives if he wants to maintain production in the face of acreage reduction. He may remove his poorest acres from production and intensify the use of his better land by using improved seed, more fertilizer, improved tillage, and more labor. On the restricted acres he may produce substitute crops for feeding cattle. He may forgo present outputs for future outputs by adopting crop rotation and other practices that will build up his soil.

Consequently, the program of acreage allotments did not achieve its objective of reducing production. The most that can be said for the program is that it prevented acreage expansion in certain commodities, thus preventing even larger surpluses.

Effects on income. During the period when production control was extensively tried for certain crops, the general level of farm prices and

[34] U.S. Department of Agriculture, *Report of the Secretary of Agriculture, 1953*, p. 21.

[35] Halcrow, *op. cit.*, p. 294–299; see also Schultz, *Agriculture in an Unstable Economy*, pp. 167–175, for a discussion of the effects of production adjustment.

income rose. However, the improved condition of agriculture in 1941 over 1933 should not be taken as an indication of the success of production adjustment alone. For one thing, other government programs were also in operation. Perhaps the most important cause for production decreases and price rises was the severe drought and dust storms of 1934 and 1936. In the case of most crops, except cotton and tobacco, the weather accounted for the major portion of production control. Furthermore, the return of general business from the low levels of the Depression greatly contributed to an increased demand for farm products, with resulting effects upon prices. Since production control did not decrease outputs of most of the controlled commodities, let alone alter materially the total output of farm products, it is unlikely that production adjustment played a significant part in raising farm income. Another important consequence should be noted. The personal-income effect of production control was regressive, because benefit payments were tied to acreage allotments. As a result the larger farms and farm families in better income brackets received proportionately larger payments than did smaller farms and poorer farm families.

Effects on resource use. As a result of production-control programs, partly because of better farming practices which were introduced as a result of crop-control programs and partly because of the supplementary income which farmers derived through benefit payments, more capital was invested in soil productivity. Land was improved.

On the other hand, a misuse of resources also resulted. Farmers acquired a vested interest in their acreage allotments. Consequently, shifts among crops that normally take place during a span of years were arrested.

Food-consumption Programs

The agricultural programs that have been discussed thus far have been directed mainly toward a reduction of supply. Storage programs remove certain commodities from the market, and production and marketing controls attempt to cut down the flow of products at the source. Other programs have met the agricultural problem by stimulating the demand for farm products. Among these have been export-encouragement programs, diversion and new-use programs, direct food distribution for relief, food-stamp programs, and school-lunch and penny-milk programs.

Like other agricultural programs, the food-consumption programs are not single-purpose programs. In addition to stimulating demand and providing nutritional diets for needy families, they provide means for removing price-depressing surpluses from the market. The simplest method of removing surpluses, once they have appeared and threaten the market, is to destroy them. But whether such action is taken voluntarily by individual farmers or through the coercion of government, it is morally indefensible when millions of people are in want of adequate and nutritious diets. Therefore, some of the food-consumption programs are on sounder moral and economic grounds.

EXPORT ENCOURAGEMENT

As has been noted previously, one of the needs facing American agriculture is to increase exports, and one of the drawbacks to commodity loans is that exports are discouraged. To meet this deficiency, the government has abandoned traditional opposition to export subsidies and has subsidized shipments to foreign nations.

Until 1938 actual export facilitation was engaged in rather cautiously. Large-scale assistance to wheat exports was begun by the Department of Agriculture in 1938.[36] Export assistance for cotton became effective in 1939.

Between 1941 and 1949 a total of $20.7 billion of agricultural exports were financed by the government through lend-lease, British loans, the Marshall Plan, and similar activities. The activities of the International Monetary Fund, the International Bank for Reconstruction and Development, and the Export-Import Bank are also relevant because agriculture is one aspect of the total economic program that concerns these bodies.

The original intention was that export-subsidy plans would be temporary and that other means might be found to solve the problem of agricultural surpluses. However, as long as government policy is designed to place domestic prices above world prices in the face of a surplus, about the only feasible way is to subsidize the export market.

DIVERSION AND NEW-USE PROGRAMS

Agricultural policies since 1933 have included many programs which have sought to develop and encourage new uses for farm products and to divert excess supplies into channels for use outside the main use of the products. A number of new-use programs have been financed by agricultural appropriations as well as through the use of tariff revenues allocated to the Secretary of Agriculture. Peanut producers and potato growers have been encouraged by the use of these funds to feed their production to livestock. Experimental use of cotton in bituminous-road construction has been supported, and potatoes have been diverted to the production of starch and alcohol.

[36] The basis for continuing export subsidies was provided for in section 32 of Public Law 320 (1935). Congress allocated 30 per cent of the revenues collected from tariffs to the Secretary of Agriculture for use to encourage export of agricultural commodities, as well as other activities. This provision has been continued in effect, and in 1953, $11.5 million were spent to encourage exports. U.S. Department of Agriculture, *Report of the Secretary of Agriculture, 1953*, p. 24.

In general, diversion of food and feed crops into industrial uses at below-market prices results in economic waste. People would be better off if such agricultural products were distributed among families in nutritional need of such foods.

The diversion of food surpluses into feed uses is more economically justified, because it transforms one kind of food into another. When, however, such diversion occurs as a part of a price-support program, the diversion may be more costly than producing an equivalent amount of other feed grains. Such was the case in 1946 to 1949, when potatoes were diverted into feed use.[37]

DIRECT DISTRIBUTION FOR RELIEF

The direct distribution of foods to needy families is one of the more cheerful aspects of the government's agricultural program. If surpluses are to be disposed of or demand increased, it is obviously in the public interest to do so by raising the material well-being of substandard families in the United States. The program of relief distribution has been financed largely from customs receipts assigned to the Department of Agriculture under section 32 of a 1935 law. These funds, as well as monies appropriated for relief, are used to buy up food surpluses, which are then turned over to state relief agencies for distribution to needy families.[38]

The program of relief distribution has been criticized because it cannot absorb large enough amounts of surplus food to be really effective in any major price-support program. Moreover, neither government nor local relief agencies are equipped to handle a large volume of food for distribution to the needy. On the other hand, the program is certainly more defensible morally than production control or diversion to less economic uses, and it raises none of the international problems associated with the dumping of farm products on overseas markets.

SCHOOL-LUNCH AND PENNY-MILK PROGRAMS

In addition to relief distribution, the government used section 32 funds for a national school-lunch program. Originally the program was devised in 1935 as a means by which food surpluses that were purchased for price-support purposes could be made available to school children. By 1943, farm surpluses ceased to be a serious problem but the need was felt for maintaining the school-lunch program. The program was continued, and since that time the purpose has shifted to improving the nutrition of school children. In 1946, the program was put on a permanent basis by

[37] Schickele, *op. cit.*, pp. 222–225.

[38] Peak expenditures under this program were $66 million in 1939. In 1953, almost $57 million of section 32 funds were spent for direct distribution. U.S. Department of Agriculture, *Report of the Secretary of Agriculture, 1953*, p. 24.

the enactment of the National School Lunch Act. Although provision is made for the direct distribution of surpluses, the program is assured of continuity by the provision for regular congressional appropriations. The program is now operated on a grant-in-aid basis, and the states are required to match federal funds dollar for dollar.

A penny-milk program for school children was conducted between 1940 and 1943. The schools purchased the milk and sold it for a penny a half pint to pupils. The government then repaid the schools for the loss they sustained. About $7 million was spent on this program before it was absorbed into the school-lunch program.

Crop Insurance

None of the agricultural programs discussed thus far deals with the problem of income instability arising out of fluctuations in production on individual farms. The other programs might succeed in stabilizing income for farmers as a group, but the income of individual farmers might vary greatly because of weather, pest and disease damage, or drought. The stability of income for individual farmers is promoted by crop insurance that protects them against income loss resulting from low yields caused by natural phenomena.

As early as 1899 a Minneapolis fire-insurance company undertook to write all-risk crop insurance, but the venture was a failure. Again, in 1917, two companies entered the field, only to abandon efforts after heavy losses. Between 1911 and 1930 five states undertook to provide hail insurance, but again the results were not encouraging.[39]

After disastrous crop failures in the 1930s and as a result of the study by the President's Committee on Crop Insurance in 1936, Congress passed a Federal Crop Insurance Act in 1938. The Act created the Federal Crop Insurance Corporation with a capital stock of $100 million and authority to write all-risk crop insurance. The amount of insurance which may be taken is from 50 to 70 per cent of the actual or appraised yield of any farm in bushels or pounds, and the amount of the premium is calculated in bushels or pounds in accordance with an actuarial study of the loss experience for the farm for a base period. In case of an unavoidable loss which reduces the insured crop below the amount of insurance, an indemnity is paid out of the reserve, equivalent to the difference between the actual production and the insured yield. All calculations, premium payments, and indemnities are figured in bushels or pounds, although indemnities may be paid for the sake of convenience in the cash equivalent.

Initially insurance was written only on wheat, but in 1941 the program

[39] Murray Benedict, *Farm Policies of the United States, 1790–1950* (New York: The Twentieth Century Fund, Inc., 1953), pp. 382–383.

was extended to cotton. The results of the first five years of the programs were disappointing. Participation was not high, especially in high-risk areas. The loss claims paid out surpassed premiums collected, although the losses might have been lower if the coverage had been more comprehensive. In Congress criticisms of the insurance were so great that it was abandoned in 1943. The following year reestablishment was authorized for cotton, wheat, and flax, and for corn and tobacco on a limited experimental basis. However, the program was restricted by a limitation which specified the maximum number of counties within which insurance on each commodity could be offered and by a requirement that insurance could not be written in a given county unless there were at least fifty applications. In 1948, the program was transformed from one of national coverage to a limited operation, the entire program was put on an experimental basis, and multiple-crop contracts were written.

By 1950, six crops were covered by all-risk insurance. Yet, a maximum of only 6 per cent of the total number of farmers in the United States were carrying insurance, with a range from 10 per cent of the wheat acreage to 1 per cent of the corn acreage covered. Each year between 1939 and 1946, the total indemnities paid out exceeded the total premiums collected. The year 1947 was the first year without a deficit, but a deficit was again incurred in 1949.[40]

Crop insurance appears to be emerging as one of the more settled features of farm policy. However, Harold G. Halcrow, after careful study, concludes that it is doubtful whether all-risk insurance, with indemnities based on individual farm yield experience, can be designed to attract the large majority of farmers and to be self-supporting over several years' operations. Believing that actuarial structures are at the root of the difficulty, he nonetheless feels that area insurance would avoid most of the actuarial difficulties of all-risk insurance. Premium rates would be established by area, rather than by farm, and indemnities would be paid on all insured acreages in an area when the average yield for a given area falls below the insured level for the area.[41] Nevertheless, experience indicates that much more experimentation is necessary before it can be finally settled whether it is preferable to maintain an insurance program or to meet major farm disaster out of direct appropriations for disaster relief.

PRICE AND INCOME SUPPORT

Each of the programs that have been discussed is directed toward some immediate goal and these goals sometimes overlap and occasionally conflict with each other. The immediate goals have been identified as removal

[40] Halcrow, *op. cit.*, pp. 409–410; see also, by the same author, "Actuarial Structures for Crop Insurance," 31 *Journal of Farm Economics* 418–443 (August, 1949).

[41] *Ibid.*, pp. 414–417.

of current market supplies by means of purchases, loans, and surplus disposals; curtailment of production and marketing; improvement of nutrition; soil conservation; and crop insurance. All these programs are tied together by being means to achieve the ultimate goal of income support.[42] Under certain programs income support has been accomplished by direct payments, such as benefit, rental, production adjustment, and parity payments. Other programs have indirectly supported farm income by restricting imports and encouraging foreign and domestic consumption.

THE PURPOSE OF SUPPORTS

The purpose of income support is to raise the level of farm income, bringing it in line with the level of nonfarm incomes, and to induce farmers to adjust production to current and prospective demand. Since the relationship between farm and nonfarm income which prevailed between 1909 and 1914 was regarded as desirable, that historical relationship set the goal of income equality, or parity. Income can be raised by increasing output, lowering production costs, or increasing prices. Since farm production and costs tend to remain stable, the decision was made to support farm prices to achieve income parity. However, because income is related to the volume of production and cost of production as well as to prices received, price parity may or may not achieve income parity, depending on general economic conditions and the productive abilities of individual farmers. Moreover, income parity depends on the income from every farm commodity, but price parity has been sought only for certain crops. Finally, the actual level at which the prices of individual crops have been supported has usually been somewhat less than 100 per cent of parity. Therefore, price parity cannot be expected to achieve the desired goal of income parity.

The other purpose of income-support programs, i.e., production adjustment, has been a secondary consideration to price supports, except for the war period, when price supports were used to stimulate output to meet greatly expanded demand. Indeed, production adjustment was used as a *means* of price support instead of being the objective. As will be shown below, parity prices actually hamper production adjustment.

THE LEVEL OF SUPPORTS

Parity price is the price a farmer would have to receive to be able to purchase at today's prices as much of the things he needs as he was able to buy in some historic period. If the prices of things farmers buy increase by a certain percentage over the same period, the price he received for a farm product would have to increase by the same percentage. Since the period

[42] See Reed L. Frischknecht, *Farm Price and Income Support Programs, 1933–1950* (Salt Lake City: University of Utah, Institute of Government, 1953).

from August, 1909, to July, 1914, was one of stable prices and a favorable price relationship, it was selected as the historic period.[43] Support price is a certain percentage of parity below which prices are supported by government action. Support levels may be fixed by law as a specific percentage of parity or determined by a sliding scale, or, for certain commodities, they may be set by the Secretary of Agriculture operating under the authority granted him by law.

Early efforts to support farm prices were made by the War Food Administration during World War I to stimulate farmers to produce more wheat and meat, and later by the Federal Farm Board. However, the parity concept did not find its way into law until the enactment of the first Agricultural Adjustment Act in 1933. The 1936 Soil Conservation and Domestic Allotment Act also contained a legislative definition of parity, but a more precise formulation was contained in the 1938 Agricultural Adjustment Act. This law authorized the Secretary of Agriculture to make parity payments to producers of corn, wheat, cotton, rice, or tobacco. Peanuts were added to this list in 1942. The support of these basic commodities was required at a designated percentage of parity, usually 90 per cent.[44]

The Steagall amendment of 1942 assured support prices at 90 per cent of parity for basic commodities (later 92.5 per cent of parity for cotton) during the war and for two years afterward. The same support level was extended to certain "Steagall" commodities: hogs, eggs, chickens, turkeys, milk, butterfat, dry peas, dry beans, soybeans for oil, peanuts for oil, flaxseed, American-Egyptian cotton, potatoes, and cured sweet potatoes. In addition, the Secretary had the authority to announce price supports on a large number of other commodities, but these commodities were not eligible for postwar price protection.[45] The purpose of this amendment was to stimulate wartime production while reducing the fear of a postwar slump.[46]

The Steagall supports expired at the end of 1948. Without congressional action, supports would have reverted to the lower levels provided in the 1938 legislation. New legislation was enacted in 1948 extending price support at 90 per cent of parity for the basic commodities and certain other

[43] Except for tobacco, for which the base period was from August, 1919, to July, 1929.

[44] The 1938 act specified that commodity loans were to be made at rates ranging between 52 per cent and 75 per cent of parity. The 1941 act made all loans mandatory at 85 per cent of parity.

[45] In 1945, for example, price supports were announced for 166 different commodities.

[46] The nation's farmers responded effectively to the appeals of the "food-for-freedom" campaign. In a six-year period output expanded one-third, aided also by good weather and accumulated feed-grain reserves.

products. A sliding scale was to go into effect in 1950, but before it could do so, Congress passed the act of 1949 which continued for another year price supports at 90 per cent of parity, *if* marketing quotas were not disapproved and *if* acreage allotments or marketing quotas were in effect.

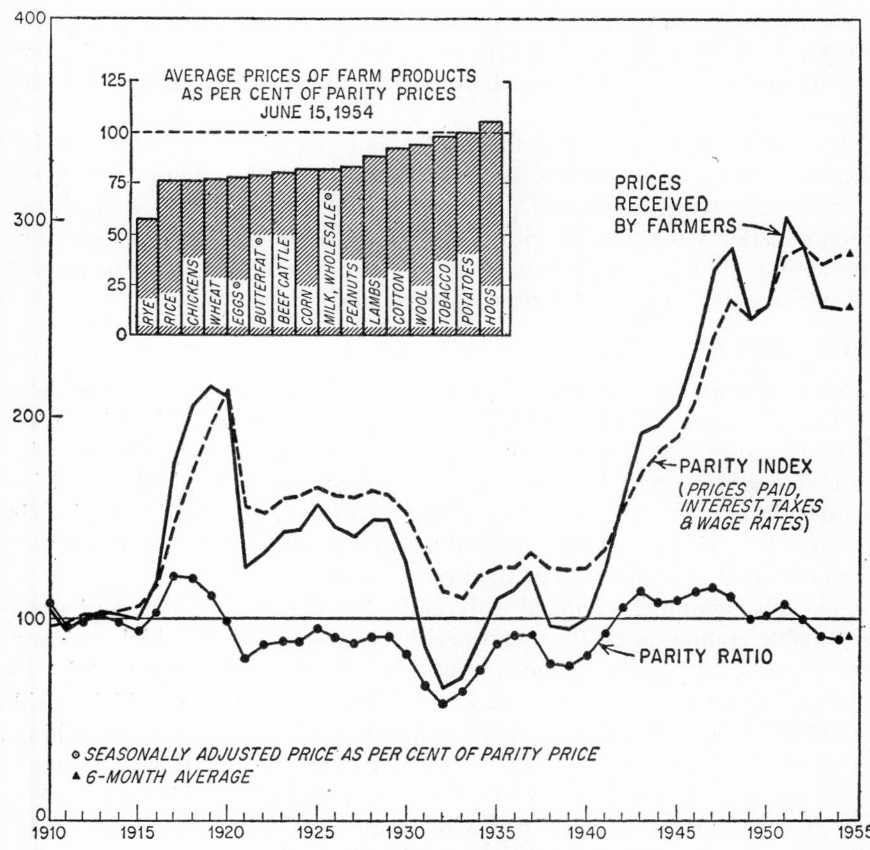

Figure 24—7. Prices Paid and Received by Farmers, 1910 to 1954

Index numbers, 1910 to 1914 = 100. In 1954, prices received by farmers were well below the wartime and postwar peaks. Prices paid by farmers for goods and services, however, were hovering near their all-time high. The parity ratio was at the lowest point since the early 1940s. Source: The Conference Board, *Road Maps of Industry,* No. 970, July 30, 1954.

The act provided for another sliding scale to take effect in 1952, but again its application was postponed, and Congress agreed to support prices at 90 per cent of parity until 1955.

In 1954, Congress enacted a flexible price-support law fixing supports at 82½ per cent to 90 per cent of parity for the basic farm products (except tobacco, which remained at 90 per cent). The new law also modernized the parity formula, recognizing that the present formula is based upon the relation of farm prices to industrial prices which existed forty years before. The immediate operation of the new parity formula would mean a decrease in the price of most grains relative to the prices for meat, milk, and eggs. In order to soften the blow of this decrease in price, the law stated that the parity level will be decreased only 5 per cent each year beginning in 1956 until the gap between the old and new parity has been bridged.

It must be emphasized that farm price and income do not move to the levels set by these various agricultural acts without some additional specific action being taken. If market prices are above support levels, there is no problem. But when market prices fall below supports, acreage controls, marketing quotas, commodity loans, or surplus-removal programs must be put into action to push prices up to support levels.

THE BRANNAN PLAN

Secretary of Agriculture Brannan proposed a plan which was widely debated during 1949 and 1950, although it was not approved by Congress. Unlike any of the previous support programs, the Brannan plan sought to maintain not prices but income. The price-support standard would be the level of prices of farm commodities which would produce total cash receipts in a subsequent year with the same purchasing power as average cash receipts of the first ten of the preceding twelve years.

The plan would be applied differently for perishable foods and nonperishable commodities. Prices on perishable commodities, which account for 75 per cent of farm income, would be allowed to fluctuate freely. If they fell below the income-support standard, the farmer would be paid in cash the difference between the support level and the average selling price for each commodity. Thus, consumers would be allowed to purchase goods at lower prices while the farmer would still be assured of a fair purchasing power. The prices of nonperishable commodities would be supported generally by purchases and loans as they are now, but at the new income-support level.

The Brannan plan also provided for a new list of ten basic commodities having first claims on funds available for price supports.[47] These ten products make up about three-fourths of all cash receipts from farm marketings. The present six basics make up less than one-fourth.

The most common criticism of the Brannan proposal was that it would cost too much. It is true that the plan would be more costly to administer, because it would make supports mandatory for more commodities than

[47] Corn, wheat, cotton, tobacco from the old list, plus whole milk, chicken eggs, farm chickens, hogs, beef cattle, and lambs.

currently receive support. Whether the benefits farmers would receive for any given crop in any given year would cost more is difficult to calculate. If they should cost the government more, the savings to consumers in lower retail prices for perishable commodities would have to be balanced against that increased cost. The shift to a standard that is influenced by aggregate farm output changes in the preceding ten-year period was a significant improvement over the standard then being used, but calling it an income standard does not make it one. It is still a price standard and, moreover, one that seriously overvalues farm products.

Farm leaders criticized the use of direct payments to farmers, rather than the use of other supports in the market place. Although the other supports are certainly indirect, and sometimes direct, subsidies, farm leaders argued that they are earned, instead of being given as charity. They also feared that the Brannan plan would introduce many new and more stringent controls over agriculture. Actually, production payments are an improvement over concealed subsidies.

The plan has also been criticized for continuing the regressive features of previous programs in that it would benefit farmers exactly in proportion to the volume of products sold. It would not come to grips with the fundamental problem of poverty in agriculture. However, one provision in the Brannan plan would slightly modify its regressive nature. Very large producers would be entitled to support payments only up to cash farm incomes of about $26,000 per farmer.[48]

The agricultural act of 1954 in effect enacted the Brannan plan for the wool industry. Price supports have not helped the wool industry as much as was intended. High prices encouraged the import of foreign wools and the use of synthetic fibers. Therefore, the new law provided that the government will no longer support wool prices at some arbitrarily determined level. The price of wool will fall to its free market level. Wool producers will receive government payments equal to the difference between the market price of wool and 90 per cent of parity. Money available from tariff duties on wool and wool products is used to make the payments.

EVALUATION OF PRICE SUPPORTS

The program of supporting prices for nonperishables, like wheat, cotton, corn, rice, tobacco, and peanuts, has been more successful than

[48] For further analysis, see Harold G. Halcrow and Roy E. Huffman, "Great Plains Agriculture and Brannan's Farm Program," and D. Gale Johnson, "High Level Support Prices and Corn Belt Agriculture," 31 *Journal of Farm Economics* 487–519 (August, 1949); Stewart Johnson and George Brinegar, "What about the Brannan Plan?" 2 *Farm Policy Forum* 9–12 (October, 1949); Theodore W. Schultz, *Production and Welfare of Agriculture* (New York: The Macmillan Company, 1949), chap. 15.

the program for perishables. While stocks of storable commodities have built up in government hands, they have not been unmanageable. The total cost of government price-support activities for storables between 1935 and 1950 amounted to $588 million, of which wheat market-price supports absorbed almost one-half.[49] By contrast, the price-support programs for perishables cost the government almost twice as much, involved a great amount of waste, and has had adverse political repercussions. The total price-support activities for perishables between 1935 and 1950 cost the government $1,489 million. Almost half this sum went for potatoes alone.

If government expenditures under production control and conservation programs are added to the cost of price-support activities, the total for the 1935–1950 period is $8,048 million, or an average of $518 million a year.

Price supports should not be judged solely in terms of their costs. The objective of farm price supports has been to achieve equality for farmers and adjust agricultural production. The fundamental criticism of price supports, therefore, is not that they cost too much, great as the expenditures have been, but that they cannot achieve their purpose and, furthermore, that they have adverse effects on agriculture. The government's entire price program is directed toward the achievement of parity prices. But prices are not a suitable means for stabilizing farm income from one year to the next or for lessening the inequality in income among farmers. Furthermore, to rely upon the pricing system to perform those functions reduces its capacity to facilitate and guide economic activity. Prices are appropriately used in the economy to guide production and channel products into consumption.[50] For example, the price of corn, compared with the price of pork, plays a big role in helping farmers decide how many pigs to raise. Also, prices help the consumer to decide which products to buy and in what amounts. Parity prices misdirect production and consumption, because they hinder the maintenance of a good produc-

[49] This summary of the cost of price supports is based on Schickele, *op. cit.*, pp. 279–282; see also *Price Supports for Perishable Products: A Review of Experience*, a staff report, printed for the Senate Committee on Agriculture and Forestry, 82d Cong., 1st Sess. (1951).

[50] For a discussion of the difference between the use of prices as goals and as directives, see T. Schultz, *Redirecting Farm Policy* (New York: The Macmillan Company, 1943), chap. 3. For other criticisms of the parity approach, see T. Schultz, "Needed! A Production and Marketing Price Policy," 1 *Farm Policy Forum* 35–37 (April, 1948); Report of the Committee on Parity Concepts, "Outline of a Price Policy for American Agriculture for the Postwar Period," 28 *Journal of Farm Economics* 380–397 (February, 1946); Geoffrey Shepherd, "A Rational System of Agricultural Price and Income Controls," 28 *Journal of Farm Economics* 756–772 (August, 1946), and the references therein cited.

tion balance within agriculture and prevent adjustment of current consumption of various products to existing supplies.

The price relationships that prevailed in a historic period are perpetuated in current parity prices. No account is taken of the changes in the relative costs of producing the different agricultural commodities or of the changes in the relative demands for them which have occurred since the base period.

The parity approach tends to impede needed adjustments in production and to reduce efficiency in agriculture by keeping prices above market levels. Unwanted production is encouraged. Production control, export subsidies, storage, and like programs must then be relied upon. But production controls have been shown to be inadequate means of achieving price-support goals. High support goals act as a stimulant to produce more products on fewer acres. Benefit payments for acreage reduction, as well as for conservation, go to farmers with larger incomes and acreage. Likewise, farmers with the most crops and land gain more from commodity loans and purchases. Furthermore, price supports do not attempt to keep the level of living of individual farmers above any specified level, even a starvation one. Parity price supports raise the average cash income of some farmers but do not necessarily relieve poverty in agriculture.

Finally, the parity prices weaken demand because the consumer, faced with supported market prices, balks at paying high prices. Hence, more surpluses develop. Also, the parity approach tends to price United States products out of the export market.[51] Thus, parity prices attack only one of the symptoms of a general disease that afflicts agriculture without curing the disease. In some ways they aggravate the disease.

ALTERNATIVES TO PRICE SUPPORTS

Fundamentally, the problem of low income for farmers and wide fluctuations of farm income is a reflection of the instability of the nation's economy. The ultimate solution of the broader economic problem requires a general fiscal-monetary policy that is designed to stabilize the whole economy at a high level of production and employment. The discussion of such a policy is beyond the scope of this chapter. Agricultural policy should supplement, but not conflict with, that general policy.

In the past, the fear of crop surpluses and poor markets, growing out of the experience of depressions and wars, has motivated federal farm policies. Therefore, income parity and income stability for farmers have

[51] See Committee on Agricultural Policy of the Association of Land-Grant Colleges and Universities, "Long-run Effects of Price-maintenance Policy for Agricultural Products," in O. B. Jesness (ed.), *Readings on Agricultural Policy* (New York: Blakiston Division, McGraw-Hill Book Company, Inc., 1949), pp. 222–228.

been sought almost exclusively by programs designed to curtail supply. Yet a steady, high level of agricultural output is a major asset to the nation. A more desirable approach would be to place more emphasis upon maintaining consumer purchasing power and expanding consumption, rather than enforcing scarcity through restrictions on production. A positive farm policy would begin with consumption goals rather than production goals. If the amount that consumers will buy with anticipated incomes plus what foreign countries will buy is less than anticipated production, it would be desirable to attempt to expand consumption. Then, if surpluses are still anticipated, output control might be considered—or programs to dispose of surpluses after they have appeared. On the other hand, if shortages are anticipated, as in the time of war, efforts can be directed toward expanding output.

Existing farm price policy, being based upon a historic relationship, does not provide the farmer with satisfactory production guides to meet current and expected demand. There is widespread agreement among agricultural economists that the parity price approach should be abandoned. To guide farmers in their production, prices should be forward-looking, not backward-looking. Serious attention should be given to the proposals leading farm economists have made for using a system of forward prices.[52]

Forward prices were used for a limited time during World War I and the price programs adopted by Congress during 1941 and 1942 for certain commodities were, in effect, a system of minimum forward prices. Forward prices are a system of relative prices which would call forth no more than the quantities of farm products for which there is an effective demand at full employment. The determination of production goals is the first step. Then the price which is necessary to induce farmers to produce enough to meet production goals is determined and announced far enough in advance to enable farmers to make their production plans. The forward price should be established for only one production period ahead and should be sufficiently precise in terms of grade and quality of the commodity and the time and place at which the price would be in effect so that every farmer could interpret the price in terms of his operations.

Forward prices alone would not be enough. Storage and purchase programs would still be needed to help commodities clear the market as well as to adjust for the effects of weather on farm output. However, the Com-

[52] See T. Schultz, "Economic Effects of Agricultural Programs," 30 *American Economic Review* 127–154 (February, 1941); *Redirecting Farm Policy*, chap. 5; *Agriculture in an Unstable Economy*, chap. 12. See also the award and honorable mention papers in the Price Policy for Agriculture Contest, *Journal of Farm Economics*, vol. 27 (November, 1945). For the most complete discussion, see D. Gale Johnson, *Forward Prices for Agriculture* (Chicago: University of Chicago Press, 1947).

modity Credit Corporation should not be required to operate under mandatory levels for loans and purchases. In time of full employment, therefore, income payments would not be made to farmers.

However, if employment fell off,[53] income payments would have to be made to farmers to make up for the decline in prices or the loss of markets. The rate of payment for each commodity would be equal to the difference between the current market price of the commodity and some specified percentage of its predepression price. The greater the decline in employment, the higher the payments would be until unemployment is relieved. Thus, these payments are calculated to be countercyclical in nature and would be an important supplement to a broader fiscal-monetary program to stabilize the nation's economy.

Selected References

American Farm Economic Association, *Readings on Agricultural Policy*. New York: Blakiston Division, McGraw-Hill Book Company, Inc., 1949.

Benedict, Murray R., *Farm Policies of the United States, 1790–1950*. New York: The Twentieth Century Fund, Inc., 1953.

Black, John D., *Introduction to Economics for Agriculture*. New York: The Macmillan Company, 1953.

———, *Parity, Parity, Parity*. Cambridge, Mass.: Harvard University Press, 1942.

———, and Maxine E. Kiefer, *Future Food and Agriculture Policy*. New York: McGraw-Hill Book Company, Inc., 1948.

Blaisdell, Donald G., *Government and Agriculture*. New York: Rinehart & Company, Inc., 1940.

Gee, Wilson, *The Social Economics of Agriculture*. New York: The Macmillan Company, 1954.

Gold, Bela, *Wartime Economic Planning in Agriculture*. New York: Columbia University Press, 1949.

Halcrow, Harold G., *Agricultural Policy in the United States*. New York: Prentice-Hall, Inc., 1953.

Hardin, Charles M., "Reflections on Agricultural Policy Formulation in the United States," 42 *American Political Science Review* 881–905 (October, 1948).

Johnson, D. Gale, *Forward Prices for Agriculture*. Chicago: University of Chicago Press, 1947.

———, *Trade and Agriculture*. New York: John Wiley & Sons, Inc., 1950.

Nourse, Edwin G., Joseph S. Davis, and John D. Black, *Three Years of the Agricultural Adjustment Administration*. Washington, D.C.: Brookings Institution, 1937.

Parks, W. Robert, "Political and Administrative Guidelines in Developing Public Agricultural Policies," 33 *Journal of Farm Economics* 157–168 (May, 1951).

[53] Schultz suggests, as a criterion, a 5 per cent decline in employment.

Schickele, Rainer, *Agricultural Policy*. New York: McGraw-Hill Book Company, Inc., 1954.

Schultz, Theodore W., *Agriculture in an Unstable Economy*. New York: McGraw-Hill Book Company, Inc., 1945.

———, *The Economic Organization of Agriculture*. New York: McGraw-Hill Book Company, Inc., 1953.

———, *Production and Welfare of Agriculture*. New York: The Macmillan Company, 1949.

———, *Redirecting Farm Policy*. New York: The Macmillan Company, 1943.

Shepherd, Geoffrey S., *Agricultural Price Analysis*. Ames, Iowa: Iowa State College Press, 1950.

———, *Agricultural Price and Income Policy*. Ames, Iowa: Iowa State College Press, 1952.

U.S. Department of Agriculture, *Agricultural Outlook*.

———, *Agricultural Statistics*.

———, *The Farm Income Situation*.

———, *Price Programs in the Department of Agriculture, 1949*, Miscellaneous Publication 683, March, 1949.

Wilcox, Walter W., *The Farmer in the Second World War*. Ames, Iowa: Iowa State College Press, 1947.

———, and Willard W. Cochrane, *Economics of American Agriculture*. New York: Prentice-Hall, Inc., 1951.

25

GOVERNMENT OWNERSHIP OF BUSINESS

The basic values of American economic life are individualism and free enterprise, and private enterprise is the predominant characteristic of the American economy. Yet, numerous examples can be found of public enterprises,[1] i.e., businesses owned and operated by federal, state, or local units of government. By definition, government ownership and operation of economic enterprise is socialism.

The motivation for government ownership depends to a great extent upon the kind of political and economic values to which a society adheres. If a society is committed to the tenets of socialism, then government ownership may be justified as an objective of that system. But in the United States, although some people may be motivated by an ideological attachment to socialism, public enterprise has always been resorted to on a case-by-case basis to solve special problems involved in each instance. As a result, public ownership has been justified as being within the framework of a pragmatic conception of *laissez faire* and free private enterprise.

Reasons for Public Enterprise

Social and political considerations rather than strictly economic considerations have more frequently motivated government to engage in a business enterprise. Perhaps the most important reason for government entrance into an essential business operation is that private persons cannot or will not provide the good or service. Military considerations may lead the government into the production of atomic bombs, arms, munitions, and ships, the operation of communication and transportation facilities, or such widespread enterprise as is found in the Canal Zone. These businesses may be so important to national defense that private enterprise cannot be relied on, or the returns may be so uncertain that private enterprise is unwilling to produce adequate facilities except at costs regarded

[1] Public enterprises, sometimes called "government proprietary enterprises," differ from ordinary government services according to the means by which they are financed. Public enterprises are financed wholly or in part by the fee or price charged for the good or service. Other government activities, such as police and fire protection, health and safety inspection, and national defense, are financed by taxes.

as excessive. There are also essential services in which the capital outlay is too great or the return too uncertain for private enterprise to undertake them. Such are atomic energy, canals, harbor improvements, wharves, city markets, power and irrigation dams, bridges and tunnels, forests, airports, housing, insurance, and certain kinds of credit.

Closely allied to this reason is the entrance of government into business where private enterprise has proved incapable or inefficient. The emergence of government ownership of railroads in most countries of the world has come after financial failure of private companies. For example, the federal government took over the operation of the barge lines on the Mississippi River, the Alaska Railroad, and the Panama Railroad after they fell into financial difficulties.

In other instances private enterprise may have been capable of providing such essential services as power, communications, transportation, or credit, but then operation under private ownership, even with public regulation, has led to serious public dissatisfaction. Private profit making in certain of these areas has sometimes been viewed as harmful or undesirable. As a result, going private businesses have sometimes been taken over, especially by municipal governments.

Certain economic activities have come to be acknowledged as public functions. For example, the conservation of natural resources is generally accepted as being a responsibility of government. In the interests of more efficient utilization of natural resources, projects like the Tennessee Valley Authority have been undertaken, forests and grazing lands acquired, and irrigation projects constructed. Interest in public health, welfare, and safety may lead government to own and operate water-supply and distribution systems, liquor enterprises, housing projects, and garbage-collection services. For reasons of convenience, economy, and efficiency the federal government operates the largest printing establishment in the world, the Government Printing Office.

Sometimes public enterprise arises when social policy dictates that particular groups in the community should receive special aid and assistance from government. This decision has led government into making available the services offered to farmers by the fertilizer program of the Tennessee Valley Authority and the Rural Electrification Administration and to other groups through the many lending services government has provided.

Another purpose of government ownership has been to provide a stimulus to higher efficiency and lower prices in private enterprise. The government has on occasion entered the production and distribution of electric energy to furnish a "yardstick" for private enterprise, thereby stimulating privately owned plants to improve service and lower costs. With the same motive the government has gone into other businesses, such as street-railway and bus services, grain elevators, gasoline retailing, banking, and insurance.

To be realistic, one should recognize that an important basis for government ownership of business lies in political motives. Irrespective of any other justification, the political value of having government funds spent in a given locality and of having government jobs available for reward may well account for some of the extension of government ownership in the United States.

The record of American experience in the field of public ownership supports the conclusion that the impelling motives have been not ideological but pragmatic. In virtually every case where government ownership exists, it is because this course seemed more desirable in the particular instance, in spite of a general philosophical objection to socialism. Any discussion of public enterprise in the United States which is based on a dogmatic and ideological attack on, or support for, government ownership is, therefore, unrealistic and not in accord with the facts.

Government Ownership: Federal Enterprises

In describing the extent of government ownership of business in the United States, it is proposed to select outstanding examples of public enterprise at the federal, state, and local levels. The reader will realize that these lists are not exhaustive. Practically every government activity results in some economic production, and many examples of aids to business, discussed in the two previous chapters, may be looked upon to some degree as cases of public ownership.

THE UNITED STATES POST OFFICE

The Constitution authorized the establishment of a postal service, which has since become the largest government-operated enterprise in the world. When the first Congress of the United States carried over the organization, already existing in the colonies, there were only seventy-five post offices. By 1955, there were about 40,000 post offices in the United States, employing more than 500,000 workers. During 1954 the Postal Service had gross receipts of approximately $2¼ billion.[2]

While the original purpose of the Postal System was to provide the best means for conveying letters and intelligence throughout the nation, the Post Office Department was ultimately enlarged to include other services. Among the more important developments of the Postal Service were postage stamps (1847), registered mail (1855), railway mail service (1862), city delivery service (1863), postal money orders (1864), special delivery (1885), rural delivery (1896), postal savings (1911), village delivery

[2] *United States Government Organization Manual, 1955–56,* p. 197.

(1912), parcel post, including insurance and collect-on-delivery service (1913), and air mail (1918). In addition, certain free services are given. Officials, departments, bureaus, commissions, and other agencies of the federal government are given the privilege of sending mail free; and reading matter for the blind and bulletins and reports from certain agricultural experiment stations and colleges may be mailed without charge. The privilege of free delivery is also granted to newspapers within the limits of the county in which they are published when mailed at or to post offices which have only rural delivery service.

Although the Post Office did not become a separate executive department until 1872, being responsible to the President and submitting reports to the Treasury Department before that time, the Postmaster General was admitted to the cabinet by President Jackson in 1829. The Postmaster General manages the business of the Department and executes all laws relative to the Postal Service.

In most matters, except those relating to personnel under civil service, prices, and the introduction of new services, discretion is left to the Postmaster General. He may make regulations regarding operation and, in the case of fourth-class mail (parcel post), regarding weight limits, rates, and other matters, subject to approval by the Interstate Commerce Commission. The Postmaster General also makes all contracts for the transportation of mail, although the Interstate Commerce Commission is given authority to fix reasonable rates for carriage of mail by carriers under its jurisdiction, and the Civil Aeronautics Board may fix them for the handling of air mail. Other matters, such as the extension of urban delivery and the routing of rural delivery, are left to the Postmaster General—subject, of course, to restrictions laid down by Congress. Congress has reserved to itself the right to fix rates on all mail except parcel post, and has undertaken to define the general character of services offered by the Post Office Department.

As a result, one has an interesting case of a business enterprise which has little power to price its service or to expand or restrict it. It cannot enter into contracts for transportation of mail without gaining the approval of charges by an outside agency, and it cannot hire and discharge employees without following the rules and regulations of another government agency. This division of policy-making authority could hardly be tolerated in private business, and it may well be a cause for some inefficiency and inflexibility in the postal service. On the other hand, the size of the postal business and its social and economic importance may be so great that too much power should not be allocated to a single agency.

For the first quarter of a century after 1789, the Post Office was operated along private-business principles and a profit was shown practically every year. However, since that time the fiscal record of the Post Office has been one of constantly recurring operating deficits. If any privately owned business had such a record, it would be regarded as a dismal failure. However, in all fairness, it should be pointed out that the Post Office Department is not in business primarily to cover its costs or to make a profit. If that were desired, the government monopoly of letter mail and the relatively inelastic demand for that service, as well as the business feasibility

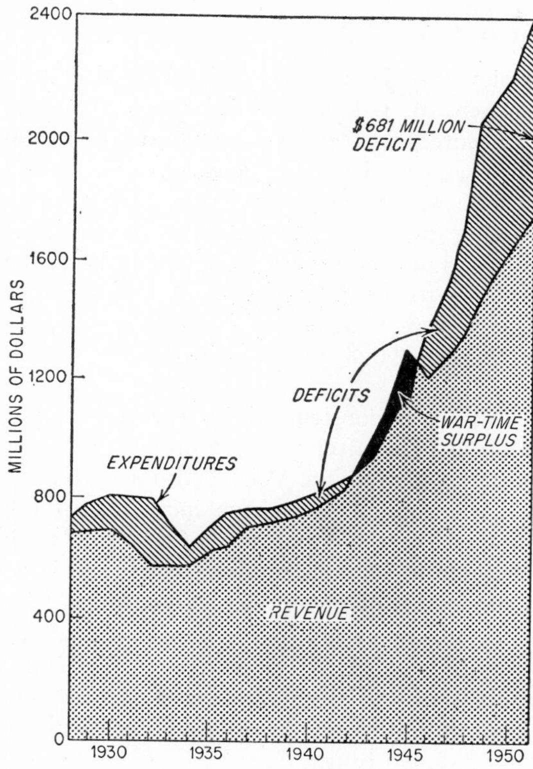

Figure 25—1. Post Office Deficits, 1928 to 1951

Source: Reprinted from John H. Ferguson and Dean E. McHenry, *The American System of Government* (New York: McGraw-Hill Book Company, Inc., 3d ed., 1953), p. 738.

of dropping second-class mail, would make a profit possible. But the Postal Service is a socializing and unifying force in the nation. Cheap transportation of periodicals, newspapers, and other matter may well be justifiable from the point of view of promoting and unifying the culture of the American people.

The very fact that the Post Office has become a means of broadening and unifying culture indicates that when the government takes over a business, social motives, rather than economic ones, are likely to prevail. The business tends to become an instrument of social policy, rather than a mere producer of goods and services which the consumer desires and can pay for. While the authors have no quarrel with the interjection of such a motive into production, noneconomic production gives rise to costs which must be borne by taxation, and the problem arises whether people wish to have their resources spent in that way or in some other.

THE PANAMA CANAL COMPANY

The most completely socialized area under United States governance is the Canal Zone, where the federal government owns and operates one of its largest business enterprises, the Panama Canal Company. Like other government businesses, the Panama Canal was not built primarily for commercial purposes; it was constructed as a means for aiding national defense by facilitating the interocean mobility of the nation's fleet. Nonetheless, the Canal is an important business enterprise providing a thoroughfare from the Atlantic to the Pacific Ocean for world shipping. In addition, the federal government owns and operates a number of other business enterprises in the Canal which are run by the Panama Canal Company.[3]

The Panama Canal was constructed by the federal government and placed in operation in 1914, after years of difficult work and an original expenditure of nearly $400 million. With additional construction expenditures after 1914, the capital assets have increased to more than $706 million.[4] When one realizes the importance of the Canal to defense and the difficulties and expense in its construction, its history is one to give encouragement to supporters of government ownership of business.

The maintenance and operation of the Panama Canal and the conduct of business operations incident to such maintenance and operation and the civil government of the Canal Zone are the responsibility of the Panama Canal Company. The company is wholly owned by the United States, which is represented by the Secretary of the Army, referred to as the "stockholder." The management of the corporation is vested in a board of directors appointed by and holding office at the pleasure of the stockholder. The president of the corporation, who is also the Governor of the Canal Zone, is the chief executive officer of the corporation.

Partly because of limitations of space and the need for facilities to care for operating personnel, and largely because of the defense importance of

[3] In 1951 the Panama Railroad Company was renamed the Panama Canal Company, and all activities other than those of a strictly governmental nature were transferred to the new company. Governmental functions previously performed by the Panama Canal were transferred to a new agency—the Canal Zone government.

[4] *Annual Report of the Governor of the Panama Canal, 1951*, p. 5.

the Canal, private parties are not allowed to own any land in the Zone and private businesses do not operate there. Therefore, the many other businesses in the Zone other than the Panama Canal are maintained and operated by the Panama Canal Company. These businesses include a steamship line between New York and the Isthmus of Panama; a railroad across the Isthmus; the cargo docks and piers and harbor terminal facilities on the Isthmus; a coaling plant for ships; an oil-handling plant; commissary stores, including cold-storage plants, supplying employees and ships; a hotel; electric-power, water, and telephone systems; procurement and storehouse facilities; motor-transportation services; a printing plant; restaurants, theaters, bowling alleys, and miscellaneous merchandising activities; marine and general repair shops; and an employees' housing system.

These enterprises have been carried on in a highly creditable manner.[5] The quality of goods and service has been superior in general to that of private business, the prices even after allowing for tax and other differentials have been reasonable, the operation of the enterprises has been efficient, and the employees have appeared to be exceptionally well treated. On the other hand, the operating units have not been given enough independence, the executives were not always picked with a view to their ability but according to somewhat unsuitable civil-service requirements, and the enterprises have failed to give sufficient attention to public relations.

THE ALASKA RAILROAD

The Alaska Railroad is one of those business projects in which the government was forced to engage because private enterprise was unwilling to go into it, and because government regarded the service as desirable for the economic and social development of one of its territories. Although privately owned railroads existed in Alaska before the government constructed the Alaska Railroad, they were not profitable. Some of them went into bankruptcy, and they did not extend their lines to open up the interior of Alaska. As a result, Congress provided in 1914 for the construction and operation of a government railroad under the direction of the President. The act appropriated $35 million for a line not to exceed 1,000 miles which was to connect one or more ice-free Pacific Coast harbors with navigable waters and coal mines in the interior. With an additional $17 million, a new line was constructed and certain existing lines purchased, until the government had by 1922 a line 500 miles long reaching from Seward to Fairbanks. In addition, the company now owns and

[5] M. E. Dimock, *Government-operated Enterprises in the Panama Canal Zone* (Chicago: University of Chicago Press, 1934). See also U.S. Federal Coordinator of Transportation, *Public Aids to Transportation* (1940), vol. I, p. 24.

operates telephone and terminal facilities along the line, river boats on the Yukon, and petroleum barges; promotes Alaskan agricultural and industrial development; and investigates minerals and other resources.

The Alaska Railroad is headed by a general manager and is located for administrative purposes in the Office of Territories, Department of Interior. In spite of low rates, the railroad never earned its operating expenses until 1940. However, by 1952 it had a net operating revenue of $18 million, even though it was allowed no rate increase since 1937.[6]

INLAND WATERWAYS CORPORATION

During World War I, the federal government through the United States Railroad Administration undertook the operation of a barge line on the Mississippi and Warrior Rivers. Because much money had been spent on the line and in improving the rivers for navigation, and because inadequate private barge service existed, the government after the war turned the barge line over to the War Department for operation. It desired to prove that private operation of the line would be feasible, and it was assumed that the government would sell the line to a private operator as soon as a suitable one was available. Because of the burdensome regulations of the War Department, Congress created the Inland Waterways Corporation in 1924 to take over and operate the barge line.

In 1939, the Corporation was transferred from the War Department to the Department of Commerce, to be administered under the supervision and direction of the Secretary of Commerce.

The Inland Waterways Corporation has been the object of frequent attacks by opponents of government ownership and operation. Unfair competition was charged, and the profits which have been alleged in recent years were attributed to government subsidies rather than efficiency of operation. Transportation economists pretty generally agree that the Corporation has not been a financial success, and in 1949 the Hoover Commission recommended its liquidation.[7] At that time, an accumulated deficit of $8,192,104 was reported by the Commission, and it estimated that $18 million would be required to rehabilitate an obsolete fleet. On the credit side, it should be noted that the Inland Waterways Corporation helped improve and develop navigation facilities along its routes; its facilities made an important contribution during the war; and by the prod of competition it helped lower rail and other transportation rates in the area.

[6] Secretary of the Interior, *1952 Annual Report*, p. 436.

[7] The Commission on Organization of the Executive Branch of the Government, *Reorganization of Federal Business Enterprises* (1949), p. 64. Liquidation was also recommended by the Committee on Small Business of the House of Representatives in 1947 and by the General Accounting Office.

In 1953, the Eisenhower administration, committed to a policy of reducing government ownership of business enterprises wherever possible, sold the Corporation to the privately owned Federal Waterways Corporation of Delaware.

THE MERCHANT MARINE

During World War I, Congress authorized the establishment of the United States Shipping Board Emergency Fleet Corporation in 1917 to engage in the construction, maintenance, and operation of merchant vessels. The activities of this corporation were continued after the war by the Merchant Fleet Corporation. Later its activities were transferred to the U.S. Shipping Board Bureau and in 1936 to the Maritime Commission. In 1950, the Commission was abolished and its activities transferred to two agencies within the Department of Commerce, the Federal Maritime Board and the Maritime Administration. The former, composed of three members appointed by the President, exercises regulatory control over rates, services, practices, agreements, charges, classifications, and tariffs of common carriers by water engaged in foreign commerce and persons engaged in forwarding or furnishing wharves, docks, warehouses, or terminal facilities to such common carriers. The Maritime Administration administers all programs of government aid to shipping, purchases ships when needed for government operations and, if necessary, charters them to private operators, maintains national-defense reserve fleets of government-owned ships, maintains four shipyards in inactive condition to be used for ship construction in emergencies, and trains young men to become merchant-marine officers.

The basis for the financing of merchant vessels by the federal government, both during the war and since, has been primarily national defense, although there has naturally been some desire to increase the amount of commerce carried in American ships. Merchant vessels are often easily convertible to wartime use, either as armed raiders or as supply ships, and the part a large merchant fleet would play in defense has aided in getting Congress to vote large sums for the merchant marine.

The policy of the merchant marine since 1917 has shown a wavering between federal ownership and operation, and federal subsidies for the building of ships to be owned and operated by private companies. During World War I, the government embarked on an ownership plan and leased ships to operators or operated them through the Fleet Corporation. After the war it operated a large part of the merchant fleet but began immediately to dispose of the ships on the best possible terms. In spite of liberal prices the Shipping Board still had 149 vessels in 1936.[8] By 1940, all had

[8] Commission on Organization of the Executive Branch of the Government, *Task Force Report on Revolving Funds and Business Enterprises of the Government* (Appendix J) (1949), p. 110.

been disposed of, and as the nation approached another world war, for the first time since World War I the federal government was not engaged in direct operation of merchant shipping.

The demand for merchant ships during World War II forced the Maritime Commission to embark in the largest shipbuilding program in history. Between 1937 and mid-1944, the Commission supervised the construction of 4,910 vessels costing over $8 billion and had an additional 1,855 under construction or contract in mid-1944.[9] At the outset of the war a few of these ships were built for operation by the Commission, but later most were sold to private shipping interests.

In 1942, the War Shipping Administration was established to acquire by purchase or charter all private ships in the United States merchant marine. Thereafter, the Maritime Commission built exclusively for the War Shipping Administration. However, the Administration did not operate any ships. Rather, the ships were chartered to private companies to operate.

Federal construction and operation of a merchant fleet has been extremely costly. However, as in the case of a number of government enterprises, the objectives sought are national defense, international prestige, and so forth, and the attainment of these goals cannot be judged in dollars-and-cents terms.

THE TENNESSEE VALLEY AUTHORITY

The entry of the federal government into the business of producing and selling electric energy may be traced to the search for power to produce the nitrates needed to make munitions during World War I. Under the National Defense Act of 1916, the government undertook the construction of Wilson Dam at Muscle Shoals, Alabama, for the purpose of supplying electricity to two of its nitrate plants. The war ended before the project was completed, leaving the government with an investment, by 1925, when the dam was finished, of $80 million, totaling the cost of the nitrate plants, an auxiliary steam-generating plant, a limestone quarry, and a connecting railroad.[10]

Creation of the Tennessee Valley Authority. For years, dispute raged over the disposition of the Muscle Shoals properties. Henry Ford, among others, offered to buy the nitrate plants and the accompanying steam power plants. Lease or sale of the facilities to private operators was blocked by a small group of senators, primarily through the efforts of George W. Norris. However, bills to provide government operation

[9] John H. Ferguson and Dean E. McHenry, *The American Federal Government* (New York: McGraw-Hill Book Company, Inc., 2d ed., 1950), p. 707.

[10] G. L. Wilson, J. M. Herring, and R. B. Rutsler, *Public Utility Regulation* (New York: McGraw-Hill Book Company, Inc., 1938), p. 417.

were vetoed by Presidents Coolidge and Hoover. Not until the election of F. D. Roosevelt could enough political support be mobilized for public operation. One of the first New Deal measures to be enacted provided for the creation of the Tennessee Valley Authority, to take over and operate the disputed properties and foster the "orderly and proper physical, economic, and social development" of the Tennessee Valley, a region of 40,000 square miles covering parts of seven states.

By the terms of the Act, a corporation was created, with three directors appointed by the President to direct the activities of the Authority and appoint the general manager, who was to be in immediate charge of operations. President Roosevelt characterized the Tennessee Valley Authority as "a corporation clothed with the power of government but possessed of the flexibility and initiative of a private enterprise."[11] The Authority was directed to take over the Muscle Shoals properties and operate them in the interest of the national defense and for the development of new types of fertilizers for use in agricultural programs. The statute further provided for the development of the Tennessee River and its tributaries in the interest of navigation, the control of floods, and the generation and disposition of hydroelectric power. The generation and distribution of electric energy appeared to be given little emphasis, probably for reasons of constitutional "window dressing," and was therefore conceived of as a means of avoiding the wastage of water power and meeting the cost of the project. The Authority was authorized to construct dams, reservoirs, powerhouses, and transmission lines. The law further provided for unified agricultural and industrial development of the Tennessee Valley through fertilizer production, reforestation, national-defense preparations, experimentation, and other means for the social and economic promotion of the area.

Administration of the Tennessee Valley Authority. The corporation has the power to sue and be sued, enter into contracts, purchase or lease real and personal property, and exercise the right of eminent domain. However, it is not financially autonomous like, for example, the Panama Canal Company. It does not have capital stock and must rely on Congress for appropriations. It may spend the income from the sale of fertilizer and electric power, but the amount above that necessary for its business operations must be returned to the Treasury. The reason for this reliance on Congress is that the Tennessee Valley Authority is more than just a government-owned and -operated enterprise. Its navigational, flood-control, and other defense activities are not in themselves revenue-producing and must be supported by appropriations. The Comptroller General of the United States has always been empowered to make a postaudit of all accounts of the corporation, and under the Government Corporation Con-

[11] 77 *Congressional Record,* 2282 (1933).

trol Act of 1945 he is now directed to make an annual commercial-type audit. However, appropriations control is the most important continuing control that Congress exercises over the Authority.

In the field of personnel administration the Tennessee Valley Authority was permitted considerable corporate freedom from traditional civil-

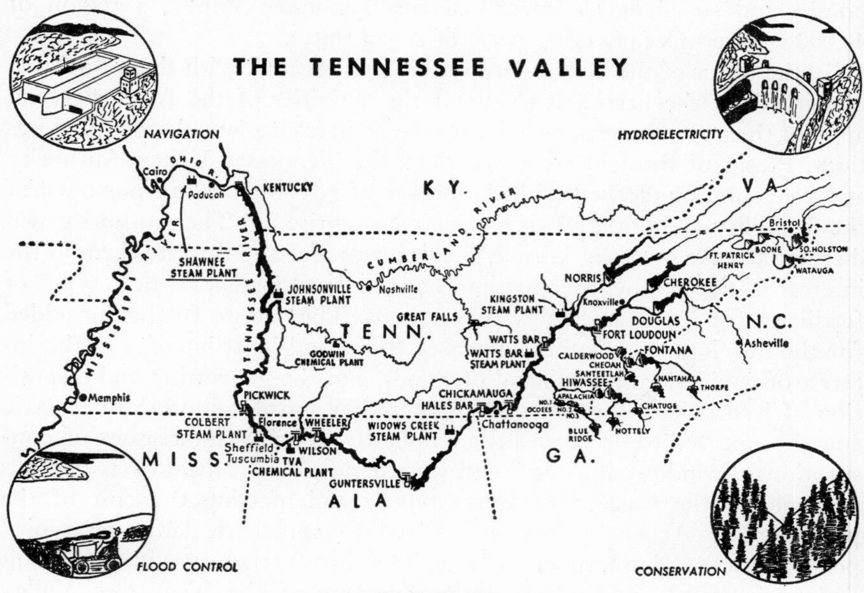

Figure 25—2

Source: Reprinted from John H. Ferguson and Dean E. McHenry, *The American System of Government* (New York: McGraw-Hill Book Company, Inc., 3d ed., 1953), p. 742.

service methods, and it achieved greater success in this field perhaps than in any other administrative area. In summarizing the extent of corporate freedom, one author has written: [12]

> The T.V.A. certainly has not achieved "the essential freedom and elasticity of a private business corporation," which the congressional committee so hopefully forecast in 1933. That is, in fact, a goal to which a government agency cannot and should not aspire, for it is not consonant with the claims of public responsibility. But the T.V.A. has been granted a reasonable measure of autonomy which it has on the whole used so wisely as to defeat all efforts to force its administration back into the regular departmental mold.

The physical plant of the Tennessee Valley Authority has been continually growing since it took over the dam and nitrate plants and other

[12] C. Herman Pritchett, *The Tennessee Valley Authority: A Study in Public Administration* (Chapel Hill, N.C.: The University of North Carolina Press, 1943), p. 266.

assets at Muscle Shoals. By 1954, there were nine major dams in operation on the Tennessee River, a system of twenty-one dams on the tributary rivers, and a series of steam plants at which electric power may be generated by fuel instead of water. The main dams on the Tennessee River not only develop a waterhead for the generation of electricity but also contain locks so that the 630-mile distance from Paducah, Kentucky, to the Ohio River can be navigated. The tributary dams are essentially storage dams and have no navigation locks, but all except two have hydroelectric generating plants. The Authority also maintains a network of transmission lines, a switchyard at each hydro or steam plant to put the

Figure 25—3. Facts about the Tennessee Valley Authority

What the TVA system includes:

30 major dams—9 on Tennessee River, 21 on tributaries—harnessing the fourth-largest river system in the United States.

12 steam plants, built or building, to produce electric power.

9,000 miles of transmission line, distributing power throughout a marketing area of 80,000 square miles.

630 miles of navigation channel from Knoxville, Tenn., to the Ohio River.

Artificial lakes with more than 10,000 miles of shore line.

Two chemical plants.

How TVA has grown:

In 1933, original plan called for a power capacity of 1 million kilowatts.

In 1954, the TVA system had a capacity of 5.1 million kilowatts.

By 1956, TVA will be capable of producing 10 million kilowatts.

What TVA has cost:

$1.6 billion in 21 years—$925 million for power, $157 million for navigation, $182 million for flood control, $35 million for chemical plants, $22 million for other buildings, $275 million for operation and other costs.

What TVA has paid back:

$81 million has been repaid to U.S. Treasury. $145 million has been reinvested in new power projects.

What customers pay for power:

	TVA area—average homeowner	Entire country—average homeowner
Electricity used per year	4,314 kwh	2,257 kwh
Electric bill per year	$56	$62
Cost to consumer per kwh	1.3¢	2.7¢

SOURCE: Adapted from the July 30, 1954, issue of *U.S. News & World Report*, an independent weekly news magazine published at Washington. Copyright, 1954, United States News Publishing Corporation.

power on the lines, substations throughout the power-service area for taking power from the lines, chemical plants for the production of fertilizer, and nurseries for growing seedling trees for reforestation and soil-conservation purposes.

Yardstick rates. The greatest controversy over the Tennessee Valley Authority focuses on the generation and sale of electric energy. Under the law the Authority must give preference in the sales of power to publicly owned distributing systems, that is, either cooperatives or municipal utilities, but other sales may be made to government plants, private industries, and privately owned utilities.

The Tennessee Valley Authority fixes not only the wholesale rates of the electricity it sells distributors but also the rates to be charged the ultimate consumer (retail rates). The retail rates charged by municipalities and cooperatives distributing electricity purchased from the Authority and fixed by the Authority are the much-debated "yardstick" rates.[13] In 1933, the Tennessee Valley Authority announced its schedule of yardstick rates. These rates were extremely low in comparison to the prevailing rates of private companies. Their objective was to provide a standard for measuring the service and rates of private power companies. The intent was to force private companies, through the prod of competition, to lower their rates. It was anticipated that a general decline in all rates would lead to an increased demand for electricity with a resulting expansion in use and production. However, "the conditions imposed by the T.V.A. in its power contracts ensure that the financial experience of the contractors is accumulated under conditions which do not make possible a measure of comparison with the experience of private distribution agencies." [14]

Writing in 1944, David E. Lilienthal, who served as a director of the Authority from 1933 to 1946 and as chairman from 1941 to 1946, revised the meaning attached to the yardstick rates. Yardstick rates are not, according to him, "an absolute standard of precisely what should be charged for electricity anywhere and everywhere in the country, with the implication that any company charging more than the T.V.A. rate was therefore proved an extortionist." The rates are, instead, "a yardstick in a much more important sense. It has been demonstrated here, to the benefit both of consumers and utilities, that drastic reductions in electric rates result in hitherto undreamed-of demands for more and more electricity in homes and on farms. . . . The yardstick in its correct sense has served and continues to serve a public purpose. It has led all over the country to a

[13] For a discussion of the arguments over the yardstick formula, see Pritchett, *op. cit.*, pp. 99–104; Merle Fainsod and Lincoln Gordon, *Government and the American Economy* (New York: W. W. Norton & Company, Inc., 1941), pp. 357–361; U.S. Congress, Joint Committee to Investigate the T.V.A., *Investigation of the Tennessee Valley Authority*, S. Doc. 56, 76th Cong., 1st Sess. (1939).

[14] Pritchett, *op. cit.*, p. 101.

realistic re-examination of the financial feasibility of low rates." [15] In other words, the Authority used public risk capital to prove to private enterprise the elasticity of demand for electric power in rural areas, a speculation that private industry would not hazard.

Table 25–1. Tennessee Valley Authority Rates Compared with National Average

Year (June 30)	*Average annual use of electric power, kilowatthours*		*Average cost per kilowatthour, cents*		*Average annual bill*	
	TVA area	United States	TVA area	United States	TVA area	United States
1948	2,520	1,505	1.57	3.03	$39.68	$45.60
1949	2,765	1,625	1.54	2.98	42.50	48.43
1950	3,079	1,765	1.48	2.91	45.59	51.36
1951	3,612	1,917	1.38	2.84	49.96	54.44

SOURCE: Tennessee Valley Authority. Reprinted from John H. Ferguson and Dean E. McHenry, *The American System of Government* (New York: McGraw-Hill Book Company, Inc., 3d ed., 1953), p. 745.

In this sense, the yardstick rate is more acceptable to private companies and has accomplished its purpose. Shortly after the Tennessee Valley Authority announced its schedule of resale electric rates, which were in some cases as much as 50 per cent below existing rates, neighboring private power companies followed suit. The immediate result was a phenomenal increase in consumer demand for electricity. Before the power program of the Authority was put into effect, the Tennessee Valley had the lowest per capita use of electricity of any part of the nation. Ten years later it was second highest in the nation, and the rate of increase was twice that of the country as a whole. In 1933, only 15,000 farms were served in the entire area. There was electricity on only one Mississippi farm out of every 100; one out of 26 farms in Georgia; and one out of 25 in Tennessee and Alabama.[16] By 1953, electric power was being furnished to 423,000 farms in seven states. In 1953, 90 per cent of the farms in the Tennessee Valley region had electric service, compared to 3 per cent in 1933 and 16 per cent in 1940. The average Valley region home in 1953 used nearly double the national average. Comparative bills were $56 in the Valley and $62 in the nation.[17]

[15] David E. Lilienthal, *TVA: Democracy on the March* (New York: Harper & Brothers, 1944), pp. 3–4.

[16] *Ibid.*, p. 19.

[17] *Annual Report of the Tennessee Valley Authority, 1953*, pp. 4, 25.

Another far-reaching result of the yardstick rates has been the stimulating effect of reduced rates on the production and sale of electric appliances used in the home and electric equipment for the farm and factory. With the adoption of the mass-consumption electric rates, the volume of manufacture and sale of electric appliances increased enormously.[18]

Perhaps even more startling is the fact that instead of the widespread bankruptcy which private power operators predicted would occur, the revenues of private companies have increased since the inauguration of the yardstick rates. In fact, net profits higher than those in 1933 have been reported for the Georgia, Alabama, and Tennessee power companies in every year since the introduction of Tennessee Valley Authority competition into the private power market.[19] Although comparable increases in profits have not occurred in every instance, the introduction of reduced rates has greatly expanded the income and improved the financial condition of the private power companies, including those affected by the Authority's program. To the extent that the Authority's policies brought rate reductions and expanded sales, it can certainly be given credit for success in obtaining the objectives. Of course, one cannot be sure that private companies might not have done the same in the course of normal aggressive business operations. It seems almost certain, however, that the Authority's program accelerated this development.

Tennessee Valley Authority: conclusions. The Tennessee Valley Authority has weathered the storm of court suits, internal dissension of directors, a congressional investigation, and continuous public scrutiny by private power interests and others, many of whom are naturally prejudiced against its program. In the face of such difficulty, one might wonder that the program has survived. Yet it survived, and with exceedingly high credit. Tales of political corruption and inefficiency were blasted by the facts turned up in the congressional investigation.[20] The record of the directors and the responsible employees is a credit to the public service.

The primary difficulty in assessing the Authority lies in its multiple-purpose program. It combines governmental services in the interests of conservation and navigation with business enterprise. The directors are forced to administer a part of the program as a business enterprise and the

[18] For example, the state of Tennessee, with only 1.95 per cent of the United States consumers of electricity, purchased 2.66 per cent of the electric refrigerators, 3.44 per cent of the electric water heaters, and 5.53 per cent of all the electric ranges sold in the United States in 1952. *Ibid.*, p. 26.

[19] Lilienthal, *op. cit.*, p. 3.

[20] See U.S. Congress, Joint Committee on the Investigation of the T.V.A., *Hearings before the Joint Committee on the Investigation of the T.V.A.*, Pursuant to Public Res. 83, 75th Cong., 3d Sess. (1939).

rest as an economic-planning and social-rehabilitation program. In any such project, one is likely to find difficulty in weighing the merits of each. Thus, it is extremely difficult, if possible at all, to tell whether the electric production proves either the efficiency or the inefficiency of government in business.

Nonetheless, the social and economic rehabilitation of the areas in and about the Tennessee Valley has proceeded with remarkable success. New capital has been attracted to the area, industry diversified, and population stabilized. The experiments in fertilizer production have produced new forms, and their use on farms has been promoted. Soil has been conserved, navigation improved, and successful reforestation accomplished.

The power policy of the Authority has very clearly stimulated the use of electricity, and has aided in showing to private public-utility companies that the demand for electric energy may be so elastic as to make low rates more profitable than high rates. Thus, the project furnishes an interesting and valuable addition to regulation. As may be recalled, regulatory authorities cannot usually force private utilities to charge lower rates to stimulate consumption unless they can prove that these will yield operating expenses plus a fair return on utility investment. Often, regulatory authorities have their hands tied in forcing mass-production and mass-consumption policies on private utilities. But an experimental program like that of the Tennessee Valley Authority not only has shown that these policies can succeed but has acted to put the pressure of potential competition on private companies to get them to adopt such policies.[21]

HOUSING

In addition to assistance to private builders of houses and other buildings, the federal government has gone into the business of constructing and operating housing projects. In order to stimulate low-cost housing developments, it supplemented its favorable loan policy by actual construction of many housing projects.

The government first entered the housing business in 1917 during World War I. At that time, two agencies were concerned with the work. The United States Housing Corporation in the Department of Labor carried on forty housing projects in twenty-six localities, and owned and operated accommodations for 6,000 families and 8,000 single men and

[21] Other federal agencies engaged either in construction and distribution of electric power or in lending money for that purpose are the Army Corps of Engineers; the Bureau of Reclamation, the Bonneville Power Administration, the Southwestern Power Administration, the Southeastern Power Administration, all located in the Department of Interior; and the Rural Electrification Administration. The Corps of Engineers and Bureau of Reclamation have combined efforts in the Colorado River Project, the Missouri Valley Project, and the Columbia River Power System.

women.[22] The United States Shipping Board also constructed houses for 28,000 individuals. At the end of the war, the government withdrew from its low-cost housing operations.

In 1932, the Reconstruction Finance Corporation was empowered to make loans to self-liquidating building projects undertaken by limited-dividend corporations under state and municipal control. In 1933, the Public Works Administration was authorized to promote low-cost housing. At first, the Administration undertook to stimulate construction by loans to limited-dividend housing corporations set up under state law, but the failure of the loan policy led to direct construction of low-cost housing by the Administration. When the United States Housing Authority was created in 1937, the fifty projects in thirty-five cities undertaken by the Public Works Administration were taken over by the Authority, which was directed by law to sell or lease the Public Works Administration projects as soon as possible.[23] By 1940, all the projects, except seventeen operated temporarily by the Housing Authority, had been leased to publicly owned housing agencies. In addition to its function to sell or lease the Public Works Administration projects, the Authority was given power to make loans to public housing agencies in the states to enable the latter to erect and operate low-cost housing. The law authorized loans to be made up to 90 per cent of the developmental cost and also provided for an annual subsidy to permit rentals consistent with incomes.

With the advent of World War II, federal housing activity was directed toward meeting the needs of war workers and their families. A number of agencies helped with home construction for war projects. Federal housing activities grew so rapidly that the National Housing Agency was created in 1941 to absorb all existing programs in the field. After the war an acute housing shortage had to be relieved and the housing needs of veterans met. In 1947, the various federal housing agencies were again regrouped into the Housing and Home Finance Agency. Legislation in 1949 and 1950 set the framework for the present housing program.

Major emphasis is now placed on private enterprise, with government aid in the way of credit to home builders, home buyers, and mortgage lenders. The slum-clearance and urban-development program is promoted by federal loans and grants to local communities. The low-rent public housing program started in 1937 is continued by means of loans and grants to state and local housing authorities, under the management of the

[22] M. H. Schoenfeld, "Progress of Public Housing in the United States," 51 *Monthly Labor Review* 269 (August, 1940).

[23] The PWA projects were located in twenty states, the District of Columbia, Puerto Rico, and the Virgin Islands, and involved a cost of approximately $127 million. *Ibid.*, pp. 271–272.

Public Housing Administration. During 1953, only 3 per cent of the total housing starts were accounted for by public housing. Of the 35,600 units put under construction, 31,269 were in federally aided programs and the remaining 4,311 were divided among state- and city-aided programs. Less than fifty public authorities are permitted to proceed with the award of construction contracts in fiscal 1954 because of the 20,000-unit ceiling imposed by Congress.[24]

The federal government has hardly entered the field of housing construction and operation as a business. Where it has, the dominant motive has been to provide needed low-cost housing for social betterment and at the same time to give employment to workers in the construction and allied industries. The housing program thus represents another type of governmental economic activity which is dominated by noneconomic motives.

OTHER CASES OF FEDERAL ENTERPRISES

Other examples of federal ownership and operation of business might be mentioned. Some of the executive departments compete with private manufacturers by producing firearms, ammunition, uniforms, ship stores, stationery, and innumerable other goods.[25] The Virgin Island Company, created in 1934 and incorporated in 1949, has the purpose of promoting the general welfare of the inhabitants of the Virgin Islands through the economic development of the Islands. Its operations have been largely the production of sugar and the manufacture of rum from molasses.

The Federal Prison Industries, Incorporated, was created in 1934. It operates forty-three shops in federal prisons and makes twenty-eight different types of products, including mail sacks for the Post Office. Government agencies buy most of its products, and there is little competition with private enterprise.

The Puerto Rico Reconstruction Administration was established in 1935 to administer projects for providing relief and for increasing employment in Puerto Rico. The Administration manages and maintains housing projects, constructs additional rural housing units, services loans to cooperatives, and operates a demonstration farm for assistance to needy resettlers. It was liquidated in 1955.

[24] *The Municipal Year Book, 1954* (Chicago: International City Managers Association, 1954), pp. 323, 325.

[25] A congressional investigating committee found in 1933 that the federal government was competing with private enterprise in some 225 lines of industrial activities. See *Government Competition with Private Enterprise*, H.Rept. 1985, 72d Cong., 2d Sess. (1933). See also Commission on Organization of the Executive Branch of the Government, *Task Force Report on Revolving Funds and Business Enterprises of the Government* (1949), pp. 135–163, and *Reorganization of Federal Business Enterprises* (1949), pp. 67–70.

Government Ownership: State Enterprises

Although at present the state governments are not widely engaged in business, there have been many notable incursions into state businesses in the past. State banks were common, and many states constructed turnpikes and canals in the early nineteenth century. State governments also contributed to or constructed railroads. But the depression of 1837 to 1842 brought most of these enterprises to a halt, and involved the states in tremendous losses from operations by which it had been hoped to make profits capable of supplementing, or making unnecessary, tax revenues. The lack of business administrative techniques and of an appreciation of business methods and judgment doomed these state enterprises from their beginning.

Of the present instances of state ownership of business, perhaps the most important are special transport facilities, state liquor stores, housing activities, and state-owned insurance funds. The diverse business operations of the state of North Dakota are a striking example of state enterprises. Although a number of states operate canals and provide harbor facilities, toll bridges, and ferries, perhaps the most representative and largest such enterprise is the Port of New York Authority.

PORT OF NEW YORK AUTHORITY

One of the most successful government-owned businesses is the Port of New York Authority. This agency, the first public authority in the United States, was jointly created by means of an interstate compact between New York and New Jersey in 1921.[26] Its purpose was to prepare plans for port development and to construct and operate toll bridges and tunnels leading into New York City. The two states concerned provided capital funds of $17.5 million with the provision that the Authority should repay this investment with interest. All other funds have been obtained through development of its own revenues and by selling its own bonds on the open market. The Authority must depend solely on its own credit, because the states do not guarantee the bonds of the Authority and it does not have the power to tax or assess. Bonds are secured by a first lien on the net revenues of all existing facilities, and payments to the states are subordinated to the claims of the bondholders. Consequently, the Authority has been able to borrow needed funds easily and at low rates of interest.

The Port of New York Authority operates seventeen terminal and transportation facilities representing an investment of $450 million. Of

[26] See Frederick L. Bird, *A Study of the Port of New York Authority* (New York: Dun and Bradstreet, Inc., 1949).

the seventeen, six are interstate vehicular crossings, designed to facilitate the interstate movement of passengers and commerce across boundary rivers within the district. The four terminals are the Union Railroad Freight Terminal, the New York and Newark Union Motor Truck terminals, and the Port Authority Bus Terminal in Manhattan, the last being the world's largest bus terminal. The Port Authority also operates the Grain Terminal and Columbia Street Pier in Brooklyn, La Guardia and International Airports in New York City, Newark Airport and Port Newark, Teterboro Airport, and the Hoboken–Port Authority Piers.

In the ten-year period from 1943 to 1952 the Port of New York Authority has experienced annual net operating revenues ranging between $11.2 million and $29.3 million.[27] These revenues have been used largely to amortize investments and to accrue reserves. As resources have increased, they have been applied consistently in accordance with the two states' statutory program that (1) surplus revenues from each facility be pooled in the General Reserve Fund and pledged to the support of the financial obligations of any and all Port Authority facilities, and (2) that the General Reserve Fund be maintained at all times in an amount equivalent to 10 per cent of outstanding Port Authority bond indebtedness.

STATE LIQUOR STORES

Following the repeal of the Eighteenth Amendment and the legalization of sale of intoxicating beverages, a number of states entered the business of dispensing liquor to customers. Of the forty-six states in which the sale of alcoholic beverages is legal (all except Mississippi and Oklahoma), sixteen states have a monopoly on the retail sale of packaged liquor [28] and a seventeenth [29] has a wholesale monopoly. A great majority of these states allow sales by the glass by any licensed vendor.[30]

The establishment of state-owned liquor stores has been justified as a measure to supplement regulation of manufacture and use, to avoid the perplexing problems arising in connection with sale of liquor, and to provide revenues to the states. In addition, state operation has sometimes been justified as a means of getting the good to customers at low cost, and prices are generally lower in the states having a monopoly on the retailing of packaged intoxicants.

[27] *32d Annual Report of the Port of New York Authority* (1952), pp. 70–71.

[28] Alabama, Idaho, Iowa, Maine, Michigan, Montana, New Hampshire, North Carolina, Ohio, Oregon, Pennsylvania, Utah, Vermont, Virginia, Washington, West Virginia.

[29] Wyoming.

[30] For a discussion of the state stores and their operation, see G. A. Shipman, "State Administrative Machinery for Liquor Control," 7 *Law and Contemporary Problems* 600–620 (October, 1940).

State operation of liquor stores has been uniformly profitable and has probably meant lower distribution costs than in states in which private stores operate. Although states with private enterprise in retailing liquor get large income from license fees, and in a few this return may be as high as or higher than profits which would be obtained from state stores, the operation of the latter usually means that retail outlets are fewer and that savings can be obtained from volume purchases. Moreover, state stores have not been bound by resale-price-maintenance contracts and hence have not been forced to charge the high markups prevalent on many nationally advertised brands. However, the quality of service of state stores is often inferior to that of privately operated stores.

Although state operation of retail liquor stores opens the way for political influence which may lead to inefficiency, the retailing of intoxicants is a kind of business in which a state may profitably engage. The state need not bother with advertising or state promotion. Moreover, the demand for intoxicating beverages is relatively inelastic and fairly stable, so that price policies and inventory problems are relatively unimportant. From a business-management point of view, the retailing of liquors, especially with a state monopoly, is not particularly complex.

INSURANCE

In analyzing workmen's-compensation insurance and unemployment insurance, the existence of state-owned insurance systems was discussed.[31] With the advent of unemployment insurance on a national scale, such systems have in reality become so much a part of the national government program that they can hardly be regarded as examples of the state government in business. The state does its own accounting for the unemployment-insurance scheme, but the plan is under close supervision of the Social Security Administration and the funds are kept in the federal treasury. But for the handling of compensation insurance, many of the states requiring it operate funds which virtually put them in business. Experience indicates that they have generally administered these plans effectively and efficiently, although in some states costs and service have been inferior to those of private companies.

Occasionally other kinds of insurance are handled by the state governments. Wisconsin has a state life-insurance system, and North Dakota, South Dakota, and Oklahoma have had state hail insurance for crops. Moreover, in certain states, such as Massachusetts, systems have developed under state guidance for the insurance of deposits in savings banks. Beyond compensation insurance, however, the entry of states into the insurance business has not been great enough to warrant much attention.

[31] See above, pp. 516, 524–525.

HOUSING

To an increasing extent, especially with encouragement by the federal government, the state governments have been going into low-cost housing. They have done so through authorizing the formation of housing authorities, state corporations with power to investigate housing conditions, to construct projects, and to operate them. In a few states, a housing authority is given a wide jurisdiction and most of the low-cost developments are handled by it. In most cases, however, the state authorizes localities desiring low-cost developments to set up housing authorities.

These local and state housing authorities are the agencies referred to in the discussion above on the federal government and housing. They receive the construction funds, up to 90 per cent of the cost, from the Federal Housing Administration and also obtain subsidies to allow rentals to be low enough for the low-income classes. Since the program has been treated above,[32] further attention need not be paid to these subsidies here.

Government Ownership: Municipal Enterprises

Municipal governments have entered into a wide array of business enterprises, most of which fit into the category of public utilities. In fact, the municipality is the chief governmental unit which owns and operates utilities. Municipalities have the power to engage in business operations only in so far as it is conferred upon them by the state constitution or the state legislature.

THE TREND OF MUNICIPAL OWNERSHIP

Of those enterprises which are more likely to be regarded as businesses, the most important in which the municipalities have entered are those furnishing water supply and electric service. The supplying of water service by municipal enterprise has shown a consistent increase since the opening of the nineteenth century, when most of the existing waterworks were privately owned. Water utilities are simple to operate, and the industry is not subject to dynamic technological changes. Moreover, the service is essential to fire protection, and the public has an interest in the quality and purity of the water. Hence, water service is well suited to public ownership. Almost 70 per cent of the cities with a population of 5,000 or more own their own water systems. Birmingham and Indianapolis are examples of larger cities in which water service is supplied by private companies.[33]

[32] See above, pp. 695–697.

[33] Eli W. Clemens, *Economics and Public Utilities* (New York: Appleton-Century-Crofts, Inc., 1950), p. 549.

The trend in municipal ownership of electric-power facilities has been rather mixed. From a beginning of four municipal plants in 1882, the number increased to 3,066 by 1923.[34] After 1923 the number declined until there were only 1,849 plants in 1932. Since 1932 the number has been constantly increasing. In 1935, 16.3 per cent of the cities over 2,500 were served by publicly owned electric plants; by 1945, the percentage was 21.9.[35]

The reversal of the downward trend since 1932 has been interesting. Not only has the number of municipal enterprises and generating plants increased, but the production of electric energy has increased faster than has that of privately owned utilities. The explanation is found largely in

Table 25–2. Percentage of Cities with Publicly Owned Utilities
(Cities over 5,000 population)

Services	*Percentage publicly owned*
Utility:	
Water supply and distribution	68.4
Water distribution only	6.2
Electric generation and distribution	13.1
Electric distribution only	8.3
Gas manufacturing and distribution	2.2
Gas distribution only	2.0
Bus or trolley system	1.8
Street railway	0.6
Other services	
Sewage treatment plants	47.2
Incinerators	26.5
Auditoriums	19.8
Airports	16.3
Port facilities	4.0
Slaughterhouses	2.4

SOURCE: *Municipal Year Book, 1947*, p. 49. Data for incinerators and airports are for cities of over 10,000 population.

the policy of the federal government to encourage municipal ownership by Public Works Administration grants and loans,[36] and by the generation

[34] H. B. Dorau, *The Changing Character and Extent of Municipal Ownership in the Electric Light and Power Industry* (Chicago: Institute for Research in Land Economics and Public Utilities, 1929), p. 12.

[35] Clemens, *op. cit.*, p. 556.

[36] The influence of the Public Works Administration can be seen from the fact that by 1939 it had allocated $205 million to help finance local public ownership, of which $98 million represented outright grants. PWA, *America Builds: The Record of P.W.A.* (1939), p. 278.

of hydroelectric power by such agencies as the Tennessee Valley Authority, which give preference to publicly owned distribution enterprises. In addition to the encouragement of the federal government, state governments have removed some of the legal barriers to effective municipal ownership by allowing municipalities to finance public-utility enterprises through revenue bonds, outside the municipal debt limit and supported by revenues from electric operations, and by allowing them to serve customers living beyond their boundaries.

Municipal ownership of gas-generation and -distribution facilities has shown a downward trend. By 1947, only 2.2 per cent of the cities over 5,000 owned and operated gas-manufacturing and -distribution systems. Among the large cities only Omaha and Memphis own gas plants. The technical nature of gas production and its relative unprofitability have not made it an attractive field for municipal enterprise. However, in 1953, 45 Alabama municipalities established publicly owned gas-distribution systems, adding to the 35 already in existence.[37]

Municipal ownership of street-railway and bus lines has shown some tendency to increase, although such cases have never been very important. The number of street-railway enterprises operated by municipalities increased from 1 in 1907 to 20 in 1927, and declined to 10 in 1940, but the number of bus operations had increased to 22 in 1940, thereby making the total of street-transportation enterprises owned by municipalities 32 in 1940.[38] Detroit, Seattle, and San Francisco are the leading examples of cities which own their street-railway and bus lines.

Municipal ownership of telephone utilities is of little consequence in the United States. Of the 23,500,000 telephones in service in 1943, only 3,800 were publicly owned by five companies—four cities, and one county in Nevada. This compares with 144 systems publicly owned by municipalities in Canada. The experience of Brookline, South Dakota, for example, provides ample evidence that telephones can be administered by a municipality to provide good service at a low rate and bring in a substantial revenue for the municipality.[39]

One other example of municipal enterprise might be noted. In 1952, 360 of the 805 Minnesota cities and villages operated liquor stores. These operations were very profitable, bringing in a net income of $5.9 million.[40]

[37] *The Municipal Year Book, 1954*, p. 372.

[38] E. Jones and T. C. Bigham, *Principles of Public Utilities* (New York: The Macmillan Company, 1932), p. 736; and *Municipal Year Book, 1941* (Chicago: International City Managers Association, 1941), p. 41.

[39] Floyd R. Simpson, "Public Ownership of Telephones in the United States," 19 *Journal of Land and Public Utility Economics* 99–102 (February, 1943).

[40] C. C. Ludwig, "Liquor Sales Aid to Cities," 42 *National Municipal Review* 497–501 (November, 1953).

SOME PROBLEMS OF MUNICIPAL OWNERSHIP

In addition to the drawbacks facing any government industry, which will be summarized presently,[41] municipal public-utility enterprises have faced certain special problems which have hampered them in serving adequately and efficiently. One of these is the practice of furnishing services free to the municipality. Water service may be given without cost to the fire department and the city departments, and electric power may be made available for street lighting and other services without charge. The result of such practices is often to make the municipal enterprise appear to be less profitable than it is. Or if the rates to customers are made high enough to cover these services, some of the cost of government is levied on the users of utilities rather than upon the general taxpayers. In this connection, it is pertinent to note that financing of government costs by high rates to users of utilities is not necessarily consistent with the best application of the tax principle of ability to pay.

Closely related to the problem of free services is that of a successful municipal enterprise charging its customers too much and using the profits to replace tax costs of government. Profitable operation is often not difficult, especially with such services as gas, water, and electricity, the domestic demand for which may be relatively inelastic in the upper price ranges. The making of an excess profit is subject to the same objections on the score of sound tax principles as is the granting of free utility services to municipal government departments. However, it would seem reasonable to allow the municipality to charge rates which would cover operating expenses, a payment equivalent to taxes which a private company would pay, and a fair return on the investment. If these items were allowed in calculating rates, the user of municipal utility service could hardly feel injured, the rates charged would present a fairer yardstick for measuring results under private ownership, and the taxpayers could obtain a reasonable benefit from business revenues of the municipality.

Another difficulty which has thwarted many municipalities in the entry or expansion of utility service is the practice of most states of placing debt limitations on their local subdivisions. While one cannot deny that limitation of municipal debts contracted for non-revenue-producing services is highly desirable, this has sometimes meant that a municipality cannot enter the business of furnishing utility service or, if already engaged in it, has been unable to finance extensions and betterments. Since expenditures may be necessary to make a municipal enterprise efficient and to enable it to serve adequately, debt limitation may not be wise in all cases. If a municipal utility is well operated, the addition to a locality's debt for purchase of utility assets may be a sound move. To ease the burden of debt

[41] See below, pp. 714–716.

limitations, some states in recent years have been allowing bonds for utility enterprises to be floated outside these limitations, if the indentures bind the municipality to payment of interest and principal from income of the utility services only.

Until the development of publicly owned power districts or power areas receiving energy from some large public power-production plant, and the growth of interconnection between municipal utilities and private utilities, one of the greatest obstacles facing municipal utilities was to have a plant large enough to be efficient. With technological changes in the industry making large plants most efficient, many small systems found that they could not generate and distribute power as cheaply as could a private company with its far-flung connections. The inefficiencies of small size, particularly in generation of electricity, had much to do with the decline of municipal ownership in the 1920s, and they still constitute a serious drawback to its institution in many smaller localities. The development of diesel-powered electric generation plants has served to modify this disadvantage to some extent, however.

STATE REGULATION OF MUNICIPALLY OWNED UTILITIES

As a general rule, operations of municipally owned utilities are not subject to regulation by state public-utility commissions. By 1954, only fourteen states placed municipal utilities under the jurisdiction of their commissions, and in a few instances this regulation applied only to electric or telephone utilities or excluded water utilities. A few additional states assume jurisdiction only over municipal utility operations outside of corporate limits.[42]

The lack of public regulation of municipally owned utilities is explained by the general belief that a city owning its utility services is subject to direct control of the customers through the polls and that these customers do not need state intervention to protect them. Although this may be true in very many cases, the authors question whether such control is adequate to allow municipalities to be free of regulation. With political control existent in many municipalities and with very little real power in the hands of unorganized individuals, there are often as great possibilities for abuse as exist in privately owned enterprises. Perhaps the possibilities are even larger, since the operators of a publicly owned enterprise need not fear the competition of private ownership, as the privately owned company often fears public ownership. If for no other reason than to prod officials to adopt accurate and modern accounting methods and to take an aggressive interest in promotion of service through experimentation with rates, state regulation would seem to be advisable. When

[42] Council of State Governments, *The Book of the States, 1954–1955* (Chicago: 1954), p. 423.

it is realized that it may remove abuses which can creep into municipal business enterprises, there appears to be reason to believe that it might do good and certainly should cause no harm.

MUNICIPAL OWNERSHIP: CONCLUSIONS

Most of the questions regarding the advantages and disadvantages of municipal ownership of public utilities are also applicable to government ownership generally, and they will be discussed as aspects of the wider problem. Perhaps the most significant question is that having to do with charges under public ownership as compared to private ownership. Except for such cases as public markets and auditoriums, municipalities have generally entered the public-service business to make total costs and perhaps a profit, at the same time furnishing adequate service at reasonable rates to customers.

On the question of reasonable rates under municipal ownership, unfortunately the only studies available were made a number of years ago in reference to electric utilities. The Federal Power Commission collected information pertaining to rates charged by publicly owned electric-power companies in comparison to rates of privately owned companies. Data on average electric bills in several size groups have indicated that the rates of publicly owned utilities were generally lower than those of privately owned companies.[43] This was true for all size groups of communities above 2,500 population. In communities of less than 2,500 population, the privately owned companies indicated lower rates.

In order to meet the criticism of private companies that public enterprises pay no taxes and hence do not have as high costs, the Federal Power Commission also made a study of taxes and tax equivalents. It found that in 1936 the privately owned plants paid on the average 13.2 per cent of their gross revenues in taxes. Publicly owned enterprises, on the other hand, paid through taxes and net cash contributions an average of 17.3 per cent of their revenues. In addition, publicly owned utilities were paying the equivalent of 8.5 per cent of their revenues in free services, while the corresponding payments by privately owned utilities were negligible.

Consequently, the studies of the Federal Power Commission indicate that, on the average, municipally owned electric utilities furnish service at as low cost as privately owned companies—if, indeed, they are not doing so at a lower cost, especially when the extra burden of free services is considered. However, the averages of the Commission leave much to be desired. Study of individual companies and public enterprises show results

[43] See FPC, *Rates, Taxes, and Consumer Savings—Publicly and Privately Owned Electric Utilities—1935–1937* (1939); FPC, *Average Electric Bills, 1939* (1939); and FPC, *19th Annual Report* (1939), pp. 12–14. The average bill groups are for sales of 25 kilowatthours per month, 100 kilowatthours, and 250 kilowatthours.

widely diverse from the average. The average rates and results of municipally owned enterprises tend to be brought down by some of the outstanding cases where the municipality is furnished with low-cost hydroelectric service from federal projects. Furthermore, the Federal Power Commission study does not take into account the assistance which has been rendered to municipal enterprises by advantageous federal government loans and grants, nor does it give a basis for accurately weighting the quality of service involved. Nevertheless, the light cast by the detailed data which the Commission has published makes it far more difficult for proponents of private enterprise in the electric-utility business to flout public ownership on grounds of excessive rates, high costs, inefficiency, or the advantages of lower taxation.

Organizational Forms of Public Enterprise

Publicly owned and operated enterprises may be administered as a part of the traditional departmental structure of government or by government corporations. The latter organizational form is the most controversial and will be examined at greater length.

DEPARTMENTAL ADMINISTRATION

The traditional administrative arrangement is to group related activities together into a department and vest over-all administrative responsibility for those activities in a single executive. Responsibility and authority reach downward to every echelon of the departmental hierarchy and upward to the chief executive on top. The operation of public enterprises is sometimes fitted into the departmental structure and is subjected to the direction of the department executive.[44] Under such an arrangement the personnel procedures that apply to other government agencies apply to the public enterprise. The government-owned business is dependent on appropriations by the legislature, follows the regular budgetary procedure, and is subject to the legislative postaudit.

The Post Office is the outstanding example of a government-owned enterprise that is organized along departmental lines.[45] A number of public power projects also follow this pattern. The far-flung operations of the Bureau of Reclamation are fitted into the Department of Interior, as are the Bonneville Administration and the Southwestern Power Administration.[46] The Army Corps of Engineers, which operates a few power plants,

[44] For a more complete discussion, see Fainsod and Gordon, *op. cit.*, pp. 673–681.

[45] See C. Herman Pritchett, "The Postmaster General and Department Management," 6 *Public Administration Review* 130–136 (1946).

[46] See C. Herman Pritchett, "Administration of Federal Power Projects," 18 *Journal of Land and Public Utility Economics* 379–390 (1942).

is a part of the Department of Defense.[47] At the municipal level many publicly owned utilities are administered as a department of the municipal government.[48]

The advantage of departmental organization of public enterprise is the control that is possible over the policy-making process of the enterprise. Since political rather than economic motives usually dictate the resort to government ownership, policy control is necessary to ensure that these motives are satisfied. But this political control is, at the same time, the chief disadvantage of departmental organization. This disadvantage magnifies as government ownership extends into more and more areas. Under departmental administration the public enterprise is subject to political change and political attack; it cannot spend money as it sees fit; there is little possibility that it can be run in a businesslike fashion; and the formulation of long-range business policy is difficult. In addition, such businesses have to conform to general governmental practices respecting the appointment of personnel, the making of contracts, and the keeping of accounts.

The Post Office has suffered the effects of departmental administration of a business-type operation. The Hoover Commission reported that the Post Office lacks the freedom and flexibility essential to good business operation, its administrative structure is obsolete and overcentralized, and a maze of outmoded laws, regulations, and traditions freezes progress and stifles proper administration.[49] The methods of budgeting and appropriation, the Commission pointed out, are entirely unsuited to a business of the size and character of the Post Office. Therefore, the Commission recommended that the Post Office be taken out of politics. The Postmaster General should not be an official of a political party, and a permanent Director of Posts should be appointed to be operating head of the Post Office, responsible to the Postmaster General. The Postal Service should be decentralized into fifteen regions under Regional Directors of Posts and District Superintendents, and the provisions of the Government Corporation Control Act of 1945 in respect to business management, budgeting, accounting, and audit should be applied to the Post Office.[50] By 1955 a number of these recommendations had been carried out.

GOVERNMENT CORPORATIONS

Since the departmental organization of public enterprise does not provide for autonomy and flexibility felt to be necessary in carrying out a

[47] Prior to the reorganization of the Panama Canal Company in 1950, the Panama Canal was a bureau of the War Department and the Panama Canal Railway was a government corporation.

[48] See John Bauer, "Metropolitan Utility Supply and Organization," 5 *Public Administration Review* 127–134 (1945).

[49] Commission on Organization of the Executive Branch of the Government, *The Post Office* (1949), p. 3.

[50] *Ibid.*, pp. 7–15.

business enterprise, the government corporation [51] has been developed as a method for effective public ownership. The device came into common use during World War I, when several corporations were established to perform business functions.[52] Most of these were liquidated in the postwar years, but others appeared during the Depression and in great numbers during World War II. A peak of over 110 corporations, with an investment in excess of $20 billion, was reached in 1946, but a contraction has set in since that time. The Hoover Commission found 75 active government corporations and 12 in the process of liquidation as of June 30, 1948.[53] Of the 75, the Farm Credit Administration group alone accounted for 51 corporations and the Housing and Home Finance group was next with 13. The remaining corporations included the Commodity Credit Corporation, the Federal Crop Insurance Corporation, the Export-Import Bank of Washington, the Federal Deposit Insurance Corporation, the Panama Railroad Company, the Tennessee Valley Authority, the Virgin Islands Company, and the Federal Prison Industries, Incorporated.[54]

Characteristics of the government corporation. The characteristics which originally distinguished a government corporation from the traditional organization forms were the nature of activity, the method of financing, and operating practices.[55] A government corporation engages

[51] For a detailed discussion see, among others, John Thurston, *Government Proprietary Corporations* (Cambridge, Mass.: Harvard University Press, 1937); John McDiarmid, *Government Corporations and Federal Funds* (Chicago: University of Chicago Press, 1938); Ruth Weintraub, *Government Corporations and State Law* (New York: Columbia University Press, 1939); C. Herman Pritchett, "Government Corporations in the United States," 19 *Southwestern Social Science Quarterly* 189–200 (September, 1938); David E. Lilienthal and R. H. Marquis, "The Conduct of Business Enterprises by the Federal Government," 54 *Harvard Law Review* 545–601 (1941); Marshall E. Dimock, "These Government Corporations," 190 *Harper's Magazine* 569 (1945), and "Government Corporations: A Focus of Policy and Administration," 43 *American Political Science Review* 899–921, 1145–1164 (October, December, 1949).

[52] These included the War Finance Corporation, the Emergency Fleet Corporation, the United States Grain Corporation, the United States Housing Corporation, the United States Sugar Equalization Board, and the United States Spruce Production Corporation. The first United States Bank, chartered in 1791, and the Panama Railroad Company, acquired in 1904, are examples of government corporations dating before World War I.

[53] Commission on Organization of the Executive Branch of the Government, *Task Force Report on Revolving Funds and Business Enterprises of the Government* (Appendix J) (1949), pp. 172–173.

[54] Since 1948, the Reconstruction Finance Corporation has been abolished, the Inland Waterways Corporation sold, and the Federal National Mortgage Association transferred to the Housing and Home Finance Agency raising the number in that group to fourteen.

[55] The modifications of these characteristics which have occurred since 1935 will be discussed in the next section.

in business operations (for which there are usually well-established trade practices) and deals with the public as an entrepreneur rather than as a sovereign. Being engaged in a business enterprise which produces revenue, a government corporation, before 1935, was permitted to be financially self-sufficient. It was usually set up by Congress with a capital fund and was allowed to retain and use its earnings. Thus, unlike other government operations, it depended on an income from consumer payments for goods and services rather than from taxes, although taxes were sometimes used to supplement the former. Since expenditures necessarily fluctuated with consumer demand and could not be predicted accurately or realistically kept within annual limitations, the corporation was freed from the obligation of submitting an annual budget to the Bureau of the Budget and Congress. In addition, corporations were exempt from accounting controls and in varying degrees relieved from the audit by the Comptroller General.

A government corporation is a distinct legal body, usually having a board of directors [56] which sets policy and a manager who is responsible for day-to-day administration. By appointing directors with staggered terms it is possible for the corporation to weather political changes and still maintain some continuity of policy. Since a government corporation carries on commercial transactions with the public that allow it to be financially self-sustaining, it was originally given the right to manage its own affairs. Like other business enterprises it was given the freedom to sue and be sued, hold property, borrow money, purchase goods and enter into contracts, and hire and fire people free from the restraints that apply to other government organizations. This autonomy was felt to be necessary so that the corporation could experiment in new areas of government operation, exercise initiative and judgment in business affairs, and have the flexibility of operation that characterizes similar private enterprises.

The decline of corporate autonomy. The characteristics that distinguished the government corporation, one author has observed, "have been disappearing before our eyes, like the Cheshire cat. Soon there may be nothing left but the smile to mark the spot where the government corporation once stood." [57] In 1935, a number of corporations were required to submit their budget for "administrative expenses" to the Bureau of the Budget for review.[58] The requirement was extended to the rest of the cor-

[56] The Inland Waterways Corporation did not have a board of directors, and the boards of directors of the Reconstruction Finance Corporation and the Export-Import Bank were later replaced by single administrators.

[57] C. Herman Pritchett, "The Paradox of the Government Corporation," 1 *Public Administration Review* 389 (Summer, 1941).

[58] For this section the writers rely on V. O. Key, "Government Corporations," in

porations in 1942. Beginning in 1936 Congress prohibited government corporations from incurring administrative expenses except in accord with annual appropriations. By presidential and congressional acts between 1938 and 1941, all positions in government corporations except the Tennessee Valley Authority were brought under the civil-service system. Under the Reorganization Act of 1939 the existing corporations, except for the Tennessee Valley Authority and the Federal Deposit Insurance Corporation, were brought into a department. The final step was taken in 1945 when Congress enacted the Government Corporation Control Act. Further incorporation under state law was prohibited, and all corporations were ordered to reincorporate under federal law. Each corporation was obliged to present a "business-type budget" through the Bureau of the Budget to the President and the Congress, setting forth its plan of operations with due allowance given to the need for flexibility. Estimates were required of the amount of government capital which might be returned to the Treasury or which might be required for restoration of capital impairment. The General Accounting Office was authorized to audit the accounts annually in accordance with the customary commercial-corporation auditing practices.

C. Herman Pritchett concludes that the Control Act of 1945 "goes far toward completing the task of eliminating the features which have made government corporations useful instruments for enterprise purposes . . . The pattern of control imposed means that, for good or ill, American experience with autonomous public corporations is substantially at an end."[59]

It would seem that the central issue in the controversy over corporate autonomy is whether social purpose or administrative technique should be the controlling criterion. On one hand, since the activities performed by government corporations require flexibility, businesslike efficiency, and opportunity for experimentation, corporations should be vested with a certain amount of autonomy and financial self-sufficiency. On the other hand, fulfillment of the corporation's objectives requires that it be subject to policy guidance and be held responsible for its actions. The assumption underlying the present legal status of the government corporation is that administrative integration to assure responsible performance is more important.

F. Morstein Marx (ed.), *Elements of Public Administration* (New York: Prentice-Hall, Inc., 1946), pp. 236–263; and C. Herman Pritchett, "The Government Corporation Control Act of 1945," 40 *American Political Science Review* 495–509 (1946).

[59] Pritchett, "The Government Corporation Control Act of 1945," p. 509.

Government Ownership of Business: Conclusions

In drawing conclusions respecting government ownership of business, the observer should distinguish the motives which have prompted it. Most government production is undertaken as a means of performing a public service with certain broad social or economic gains to be made, not as a means to sell goods or services at a profit, or even at cost. In such enterprises, one cannot be too concerned with the relative efficiency of government ownership in relation to private ownership, since the chances are that private enterprise could hardly be induced to take over the business and operate it on the same basis upon which the government operates. Thus, a private enterprise could hardly be expected to enter low-cost housing without government subsidies and charge the same rents that the government charges. But in the case of those services which the government furnishes free or below cost, and hence finances partially or wholly out of taxation, one should ask whether the service is worth the tax cost. Conclusions on such matters are not subject to objective determination but must be left to individual evaluation in special cases.

But where the government enters into business in competition with private enterprise, or takes over a business which could be operated as efficiently under private enterprise, or goes into business with the avowed purpose of making it pay, then the taxpayer, worker, or consumer has a right to know whether public or private enterprise is the proper course of action. Moreover, even if the government believes that a service should be given to the people at a price below the full economic cost, one may question whether in every case it is wise to have it enter the business, or whether it would do better to subsidize private industry to undertake the task.

Answers to such questions of public policy can be determined sometimes in the light of the usual advantages and disadvantages of government ownership of business. But to obtain informed judgment, the advantageous and disadvantageous aspects of government ownership of business must be modified by the particular project in mind. The motives which lead to government ownership, the results to be obtained, and the costs to be incurred are matters the validity of which must be judged by reference to special cases of public enterprise.

ADVANTAGES OF GOVERNMENT OWNERSHIP

Governmentally owned enterprises often have certain advantages in cost over private businesses. As a general rule, not only has the government ready access to the capital market to obtain funds adequate to any enterprise, but interest rates on government borrowings are lower than the cost of capital for private enterprise. The lower capital cost results from lower interest rates on government bonds, as well as from the fact that private enterprise must obtain some of its funds by share capital in which the investors have the hope, if not the promise, of materially higher returns than those available on bonds. The difference between the low interest rates on government bonds or even bonds of governmental corporations, whether such securities are fully guaranteed by the government or not, and the lowest rate of return allowed by the courts to regulated private companies is ample evidence of the lower cost of government capital. On the other hand, it can be stated that sometimes government enterprises are not constructed and financed with as low investment costs as are private enterprises, and that the savings in interest costs may be dissipated in the larger amount of capital required.

The governmentally owned enterprise may also obtain some economies through being able to unify operations and to make larger producing organizations than may be possible or feasible under private ownership. In certain cases, the government might be able to avoid the duplication of facilities and effort which competitive private enterprises entail. For example, many of the problems of wasteful duplication could be eliminated by government ownership of the railroads or all transportation facilities. Moreover, the unification of operations may result in larger-scale producing plants, with resultant economies, and in larger organizations, with economies of large-scale management. The unified ownership and operation of electric plants under some kind of government ownership broader than the ordinary municipality could, for example, result in the adoption of the most efficient size of plant and could also give rise to economies from pooling purchases, research, and expert assistance.

A third possible economy from governmentally owned business might come from the use by the enterprise of existing government services. Virtually every government needs corps of engineers, architects, construction experts, lawyers, financial experts, and numerous other individuals of special training and ability. A government enterprise having only occasional need for such services could obtain them from other government departments at little or no additional cost. A private business, on the other hand, would have to maintain staffs for such purposes, or hire, usually at high fees, the assistance when needed.

Another advantage of government ownership of business arises from the reduced cost of regulation. If the government takes over a business on which it has previously had to expend much effort and money in regulating, the lessening or discontinuance of regulation would result in material savings. However, it should be recognized that government ownership may not denote the complete lack of need for regulation. Regulation may be made easier through the control over the business being more direct, but the necessity for checking upon possible abuses of power, dishonesty or incompetence in personnel, and policies not conducive with the purposes of the government business means that some part of the funds now spent on regulation would have to be used for control even of a government business. The fact that funds are spent for financial audits, civil-service techniques, or legislative investigations should not conceal the real nature of the regulatory function. In many cases of government ownership, full protection of the public interest would appear to justify setting up an independent regulatory commission with many of the duties such an agency now has toward privately owned companies.

The government would also perhaps enjoy some advantages in labor costs and a less difficult labor problem. Although many individuals in the government receive wages or salaries higher than would be paid to them in private industries, other government employees, especially those in the middle and upper pay brackets, often work for less pay than they would obtain in private business. The security of government employment, the advantageous pension systems, and the favorable working conditions, especially when the employment is covered by an effective civil-service system, are inducements which private employment has not always offered. But it is in the lesser labor problem that government enterprise would probably enjoy its more important advantage. The tradition and legal principle that workers may not strike against the government have led to fewer labor disturbances in government employment than in private employment, where such disturbances are causes for great expense in many industries.

DISADVANTAGES OF GOVERNMENT OWNERSHIP

Most of the disadvantages associated with government ownership of business arise from the lack of profit motive and the natural tendency for political influences to play too large a part in functions which are predominantly economic. In too few cases is government enterprise judged by its ability to make a profit. As a result, the lack of motivation from profit seeking may cause inefficiency and sluggishness to impede the progress of an activity which should be dominated by imagination, vision, and aggressiveness. In this connection, however, two rather pertinent observations can be raised. Perhaps the public pressure to make an enterprise pay and to accomplish results efficiently is greater in certain cases of government ownership than has been realized; and it is a well-known fact that there are many capable individuals in government enterprise who are motivated to such an extent by the desire to serve that the profit motive could add little or no stimulus to their efforts. In the second place, the modern large corporation with its thousands of unorganized stockholders and its management responsible only to itself can hardly be regarded as dominated by a very strong profit motive, at least by the persons who would be expected to gain most by the making of handsome profits.

A second drawback to government ownership may be mentioned. In the zeal to develop controls in government, legislators and administrators have sometimes built up systems of red tape which hamper the efficient operation of business enterprise. A business which under federal ownership must seek appropriations from Congress each year before it can spend anything, which must deposit its funds in the national Treasury, which must have every pay voucher approved by the office of the Comptroller General, which must select personnel through channels of the civil service, and which must have specific legislative authorization for changes or extensions in policy is an enterprise which must necessarily lose much of its efficiency. The persistent efforts to restrict the autonomy of government corporations do not help overcome this problem.

Perhaps the greatest disadvantage in government ownership of business is the tendency for political considerations to impair the securing of economic results. The application of the spoils system to the selection of government personnel, with its resultant uncertain tenure and filling of positions with incompetent individuals, is one of the principal causes for inefficiency in government enterprise. The extension of civil-service qualification for positions may help rid the government of this fault, but these requirements do not ensure competent personnel. Civil-service examinations are often too much concerned with technical skills and not enough with personal qualities of leadership and capability to guarantee high-grade personnel. Furthermore, civil-service employees are not easily removed from their positions, in the absence of proof of dishonesty or great incompetency, so a government enterprise under civil service might not be able to keep the most capable persons in responsible positions.

Political influences make themselves felt in government enterprises in other ways than through the spoils system. In the making of contracts for the purchase of materials and supplies and for the sale of goods, political pressure and considerations do on occasion cause uneconomic transactions to be made. In some cases, the law may be adequate to guard against these influences, and in others the fear of unfavorable publicity may act as a deterrent. But to expect that political considerations can be eliminated from the transaction of business in a government enterprise is to expect the impossible.

Political influences of pressure groups of one kind or another may undermine the efficiency of public ownership in business. Organized labor may inflate costs by pressing for high wages and exceptional working conditions, not by means of a strike threat but through the offices of legislators. Local pressure groups may demand that the government business expand its services or lower its prices, or increase its construction in their locality. Users of the government service may band together to bring about a reduction of prices, on the curious theory that, somehow, if the government pays for it individuals will not have to. In the long run, perhaps this sort of tampering with the economic operation of a government business, on the ground that departure from serving at cost is in the "public interest," is the chief danger of public ownership.

Selected References

Commission on Organization of the Executive Branch of the Government, *Reorganization of Federal Business Enterprises.* 1949.

———, *The Post Office.* 1949.

———, *Task Force Report on Activities and Organization of Lending Agencies of the Government* (Appendix R). 1949.

———, *Task Force Report on Revolving Funds and Business Enterprises of the Government* (Appendix J). 1949.

Dahl, Robert A., and Ralph S. Brown, Jr., *Domestic Control of Atomic Energy.* New York: Social Science Research Council, 1951.

Dimock, Marshall E., *Developing America's Waterways; Administration of the Inland Waterway Corporation.* Chicago: University of Chicago Press, 1935.

———, "Government Corporations: A Focus of Policy and Administration," 43 *American Political Science Review* 899–921, 1145–1164 (October, December, 1949).

———, *Government-operated Enterprises in the Panama Canal Zone.* Chicago: University of Chicago Press, 1934.

Eldridge, Seba, and Associates, *Development of Collective Enterprise.* Lawrence, Kans.: University of Kansas Press, 1943.

Fainsod, Merle, and Gordon Lincoln, *Government and the American Economy,* chaps. 18, 19. New York: W. W. Norton & Company, Inc., 1941.

Field, Oliver P., "Government Corporations: A Proposal," 48 *Harvard Law Review* 775 (March, 1935).

Goldberg, Sidney, and Harold Seidman, *The Government Corporation: Elements of a Model Charter.* Chicago: Public Administration Service, 1953.

Key, V. O., "Government Corporations," in Fritz Morstein Marx (ed.), *Elements of Public Administration,* chap. 11. New York: Prentice-Hall, Inc., 1946.

Lilienthal, David, *TVA: Democracy on the March.* New York: Harper & Brothers, 1944.

———, and R. H. Marquis, "The Conduct of Business Enterprises by the Federal Government," 54 *Harvard Law Review* 545–601 (1941).

McDiarmid, John, *Government Corporations and Federal Funds.* Chicago: University of Chicago Press, 1938.

Persons, Warren M., *Government Experimentation in Business.* New York: John Wiley & Sons, Inc., 1934.

Pritchett, C. Herman, "The Government Corporation Control Act of 1945," 40 *American Political Science Review* 495–509 (1946).

———, "Government Corporations in the United States," 19 *Southwestern Social Science Quarterly* 189 (September, 1938).

———, "The Paradox of the Government Corporation," 1 *Public Administration Review* 381–389 (Summer, 1941).

———, *The Tennessee Valley Authority*. Chapel Hill, N.C.: The University of North Carolina Press, 1943.

Seidman, Harold, "The Government Corporation: Organization and Controls," 14 *Public Administration Review* 183–192 (Summer, 1954).

———, "The Theory of the Autonomous Government Corporation: A Critical Appraisal," 12 *Public Administration Review* 89 (1952).

Thurston, John, *Government Proprietary Corporations in the English-speaking Countries*. Cambridge, Mass.: Harvard University Press, 1937.

PART EIGHT

PUBLIC CONTROL OF THE TOTAL ECONOMY

26

WARTIME ECONOMIC CONTROLS

Under normal peacetime conditions the primary objective of the economic system is to produce the goods and services which provide maximum satisfaction of human wants. The operating assumption in a basically free-enterprise economy such as ours is that the satisfaction of material desires will result from the relatively free play of market forces and from allowing considerable freedom in the making of economic decisions. Government normally intervenes only in limited areas and for specific reasons, as has been discussed in the above chapters.

But the mechanisms of a free market are inadequate to meet the needs of a nation engaged in total war. To a great extent, victory in modern war goes to the side which can quickly mobilize its economy to produce the greatest volume of goods and services and channel this output into the most essential military and civilian uses. Freely moving prices may ration and allocate resources in peacetime, but they are not enough to direct production in time of war. Even with the incentive of high prices for military goods, some manufacturers would prefer to produce civilian goods. The competition for strategic materials would inevitably lead to rising prices at a time when government expenditures to wage a war are mounting. Under free-market conditions the quantity of goods available at a reasonable price tends to equal the demand for them, but in wartime producers may hesitate to expand output and workers may resist war-production job offers, so the quantity available may be inadequate to meet requirements at reasonable prices. The adjustments that occur in a free economy in normal times are often slow in coming and may appear only in the long run. But a nation at war cannot wait for the long run to supply troops at the front with the weapons necessary to win a war. The incentives of the free market must be supplemented or supplanted by extensive and widespread economic controls.

Wartime economic controls represent the maximum government involvement in a free economy. A study of these controls, which is the subject matter of this chapter, is important not only for the impression it conveys of such controls under conditions of total mobilization in the past but also because it sketches the controls that might be expected in the event of another war or during a prolonged period of limited mobilization. Moreover, many of these controls are patterned after established peacetime control, and others have a way of becoming an established part of the public program to regulate enterprise.

THE OBJECTIVES OF WARTIME CONTROLS

MAXIMUM BALANCED SUPPLY

The single overriding objective of a nation at war is to win the war. Therefore, the primary aim of economic mobilization is to organize and utilize most effectively all the nation's resources to produce enough goods and services to wage the war successfully. Existing plants must be reconverted, new factories built, and the work force expanded so that planes, ships, tanks, weapons, ammunition, uniforms, and all the other necessary supplies may be turned out.

Various military needs compete with one another for the limited supply of manpower and other productive resources. The division of military output among its many alternative uses involves difficult decisions and often leads to serious controversy. Should steel be used to produce tanks immediately, or should it be used to expand plant facilities for a larger output in the future? Should planes or ships be built with the limited resources? Should facilities be reconverted to produce a new rifle, or should existing tools be used to turn out the old rifle? A balance must be struck between the limited resources and the various military demands made upon them. Moreover, these goods and services must arrive on a time schedule at the proper time and in the right amount to be most effectively used.

Another goal, which may interfere with or divert production from the attainment of a maximum war output, is the satisfaction of civilian requirements, because even in time of war, the civilian economy cannot be allowed to deteriorate unduly. Obviously, the resources of any nation are limited so that it cannot have both guns and butter under total mobilization. Decisions must be made about how much of the total productive system can be spared to turn out civilian goods, recognizing that the larger the civilian output, the smaller the military output will be, except to the extent that the total production can be expanded. At the same time, since military output must be obtained primarily through the use of civilian labor and since it is militarily dangerous to allow civilian morale to fall too low, it is important to maintain the civilian economy at a level to meet military objectives.

ECONOMIC STABILIZATION

The demands upon the economy to ensure the maximum, balanced supply of military and civilian goods and services generate serious inflationary pressures. The reason for these pressures is not hard to find. Fundamentally, the cause is the tremendous expansion of money and credit which attends the financing of production for total war while at the same time the supply of goods for which people ordinarily spend their money is contracting.

The great rise of government expenditures increases the effective money demand for output. This rise adds to private money incomes and spending power. Moreover, since part of the monies spent by government must be obtained by borrowing from commercial banks, total purchasing power is further increased. As long as the economy has idle resources to draw upon, this increased demand is not felt. But as soon as productive resources are fully utilized, the pressure is apparent. Once full employment is reached, the necessities of the military program require a reduction of civilian production and the supply of goods and services available for private purchase is curtailed. A decline of imports in wartime further cuts down supplies. As government purchases increase, the expectation of shortages and price increases makes people increasingly willing and anxious to buy.

The result of all these conditions is a seller's market in which there is a tendency to bid up both prices and wages. A price increase generates a wage increase, which again leads to a price increase. And so the spiral mounts.[1]

Therefore, another general objective of wartime economic controls is economic stabilization. Such a goal is important not only in the interest of equity in distribution of wealth and income and the costs of the military effort but for the achievement of maximum war production and for the channeling of output into the most essential military and civilian uses.

Types of Wartime Controls

INDIRECT CONTROLS

In general, two kinds of controls may be resorted to in time of war—direct controls and indirect controls. Direct controls are legal devices for directing, guiding, or restraining some aspect of economic behavior. Indirect controls rely upon action through intermediate devices.[2] The pur-

[1] The evils of inflation, especially in time of war, are ably described by Lester V. Chandler and Donald H. Wallace, *Economic Mobilization and Stabilization* (New York: Henry Holt and Company, Inc., 1951), pp. 180–181. See also Donald H. Wallace, *Economic Controls and Defense* (New York: The Twentieth Century Fund, Inc., 1953), chap. 2.

[2] In a sense, any control is indirect in that it usually has other final objectives. For example, price control has broader objectives than stable prices. See Robert C. Turner, "Recent Development and Evaluation of Direct Controls," 5 *Journal of Finance* 3 (March, 1950).

pose of indirect controls is to limit the total spendable income and credit funds to approximately the amount that can buy the expected consumer output at noninflationary prices. This objective is accomplished through tax and credit measures. When taxes go up or credit is restricted, people have less money to spend. Likewise, if people can be induced to increase their savings, either voluntarily through bond-selling drives or through coercive measures, they can spend less.

The advantage of indirect controls is that potential spenders are deprived of the cash which they might use in competition with government while at the same time the government, through taxes and bond sales, gets the money it needs to finance the war effort. Indirect controls are more generally acceptable to the public, they do not require the extensive administrative machinery necessary to apply direct controls, and they are not likely to affect basic institutions and patterns of behavior as much.

However, under conditions of total mobilization, indirect controls are not enough. No tax and credit program could completely close the inflationary gap and ensure the proper allocation of productive resources. Credit funds cannot be cut off entirely, because some must be kept available to allow for necessary expansion of the economy. The political objections to a tax high enough to drain off excessive purchasing power are almost insurmountable. Voluntary savings can never be relied upon to take enough money out of circulation, and compulsory savings meet the same objections as a high tax program.

If a brake is not put on excess demand there is the danger that nonessential production will compete for these monies and that hoarding and inequitable distribution of scarce consumer goods will follow so that the goal of maximum, balanced production will not be attained. Therefore, direct controls must be added.

DIRECT CONTROLS

Direct controls are of two general types: (1) those that directly affect the use of specific materials, facilities or kinds of manpower, or place restrictions on production or consumption of particular things; and (2) those that directly restrict movement of specific prices or income.[3] The former includes priority regulations and allocations to channel materials into specified uses, measures to channel labor into particular uses, orders directing production and delivery of specified types of products, orders prohibiting or limiting output of some end products to divert production to other things, orders prohibiting or limiting the use of scarce materials (such as copper or rubber) in some end products to divert them to more

[3] Wallace, *op. cit.*, pp. 10–11.

essential uses, and rationing of consumer goods. The latter include ceilings on prices, rents, and wage and salary rates. However, if prices are fixed below levels that would prevail in a free market, some higher-cost supplies may not be produced. To prevent the loss of necessary higher-cost supplies and to stimulate rapid conversion to war production, it becomes necessary to supplement price controls with the payment of subsidies, short-term amortization of plant expansion, and private operation of government-built and -owned plants.

The obvious advantage of direct controls is their directness. They can be applied rapidly and effectively at the particular places where they are needed. They can be imposed piecemeal as specific crises develop and need not be the result of an over-all plan. Their results are more immediate than those of indirect controls, and they are relatively easier to manipulate. By holding down prices and wages, the cost of waging the war is reduced. The wealth of experience gained from their use in the past provides valuable guidelines for their use again. In spite of a general hostility to direct economic controls in American culture, they have been accepted and successfully used when the overwhelming objective of winning a war submerges motives of private interest.

Direct controls also have many disadvantages. Government decisions replace market decisions about prices, wages, profits, what to produce, and how much of each product to produce. It is virtually impossible for government to reflect the myriad of pressures that affect market decisions, and in fact, new pressures intrude in the decision-making process. These new pressures come from private-interest groups which seek rulings, exceptions, or changes in regulatory policies that benefit their particular groups. A continued program of direct controls would probably heighten intergroup competition, with the possible result that the major decisions would embody the desires of the contending interest groups rather than reflect the needs of a nation at war.

Yet, these interest-group pressures cannot be denied the right of free expression and the right of petition. Any system of far-reaching economic controls will freeze certain inequities into the system. Sale prices or low prices in an industry experiencing a slump may become the ceiling prices under a general price freeze. Therefore, machinery must be provided by which these and other inequities can be adjusted.

Direct controls can seldom be confined to a limited number of controls. When one is imposed, others become essential. The setting of maximum prices may require rationing control, because under the free-market system of pricing a higher price performs the function of cutting off some demand. Wage controls may become necessary to hold down the pressure for price increases. But if wages are controlled they are useless in allocating manpower, so other controls are needed to divert manpower into war production and to restrict workers from taking nonessential jobs.

Moreover, direct controls must be linked with indirect controls. If one of the reasons for imposing direct controls is the existence of a gap between demand and supply, then higher taxes, credit restrictions, and similar controls must be used. Otherwise, direct controls alone will give a false sense of security that the basic economic problem confronting the country is being dealt with when only the superficial manifestations of the problem are being controlled.

Another shortcoming of direct controls is that they are more generally resisted than indirect controls, especially by the groups that suffer the greatest regulation. The task of administering direct controls is difficult enough, but when it must be done in the face of outright or covert resistance it becomes all the more difficult. If the appeals for special concessions which further increase the administrative burden are not handled to the satisfaction of the groups, they may attempt to evade the law. Successful evasion of the law in one area may lead to widespread evasion in other areas. Black markets were not uncommon during World War II. Other evasions of the law were more subtle, taking the form of lower standards of quality and service or a shift from low markup to high markup goods, e.g., from dress shirts to sport shirts. If direct controls are to be successful, the people must be sold on the necessity of them.

The most serious danger of direct controls is the possibility that free institutions may suffer during a period of prolonged total mobilization. If extensive government management of the economy should harden into a permanent arrangement as a result of a long war or protracted build-up for war, free competitive activity and free collective bargaining might be lost. It is by no means certain that in the long run direct government controls could do a better job than the free-market system in meeting shifts in consumer demand and in advancing productivity.[4]

In spite of these dangers and shortcomings, direct controls have been successfully used without destroying the viability of free institutions in the United States. The problems of administering direct controls were satisfactorily worked out in most cases. Goods and services were produced in the amount and at the time needed to win the war. Perhaps the most serious objection that can be raised against their use in World War II is that they were removed too rapidly and not according to plan before the inflationary gap had been sufficiently closed. As a result, the inflation which was largely forestalled during the war burst forth on the economy after the removal of controls.

[4] For an excellent discussion of the dangers of direct controls and of which direct controls to use in a period of limited mobilization, see Wallace, *op. cit.*, chaps. 3, 4.

Controls to Ensure Maximum Balanced Supply

The discussion in this and the succeeding section will be directed to an examination of the particular controls that have been employed to achieve the twofold objective of maximum, balanced supply and economic stabilization. Principal emphasis will be on the controls developed during World War II, with somewhat less emphasis placed on the unique problems that arose in the limited mobilization during the Korean War.

PRODUCTION PROGRAMMING

The heart of a system of materials controls is production programming.[5] Programming is the calculation of time-phased production goals, determined by reference to the requirements of the armed forces to wage the war successfully and of essential civilian needs and modified by the feasibility of meeting those requirements with the limited facilities, materials, and manpower available.

The determination of what must be produced to meet both essential military and civilian requirements is a tremendous problem. Estimates are made of the need for guns, shells, planes, tanks, and the rest, and of the time schedule on which they are needed. These needs must be balanced, because too much of one item will mean a shortage of another, which could result in waste or delay, or even military disaster. Vital civilian requirements must also be fitted into estimates of over-all production goals. Production goals must be continually revised in light of changing military requirements.

Production goals must then be converted into requirements in terms of productive facilities, materials, and manpower necessary to meet the goals. Estimates must be made of existing and potential sources of materials and manpower, and an inventory must be made of the nation's productive facilities. A determination is necessary of the extent to which facilities can be expanded or converted to meet war needs and the amount of new facilities needed. The problem of balance arises from the decision as to whether it is better to use scarce materials and manpower in current production or in converting and expanding facilities.

The estimates of facilities, materials, and manpower are compared with the estimates of requirements. Feasibility now becomes the central issue, because in a total war the combination of unrestricted military and civilian demands will certainly exceed the maximum feasible output of the econ-

[5] For an excellent discussion of the problems involved in production programming, see John E. Brigante, *The Feasibility Dispute* (Washington, D.C.: Committee on Public Administration Cases, 1950), reprinted in Chandler and Wallace, *op. cit.*, pp. 63–91.

omy. Cutbacks must be made in production goals where gaps between demand and feasible output are shown. These cutbacks will of course be heaviest in civilian requirements. Actual production goals result from the modification of over-all requirements by the feasibility of their accomplishment.

Production programming is necessary even during a period of limited mobilization, because although the percentage of total national output that

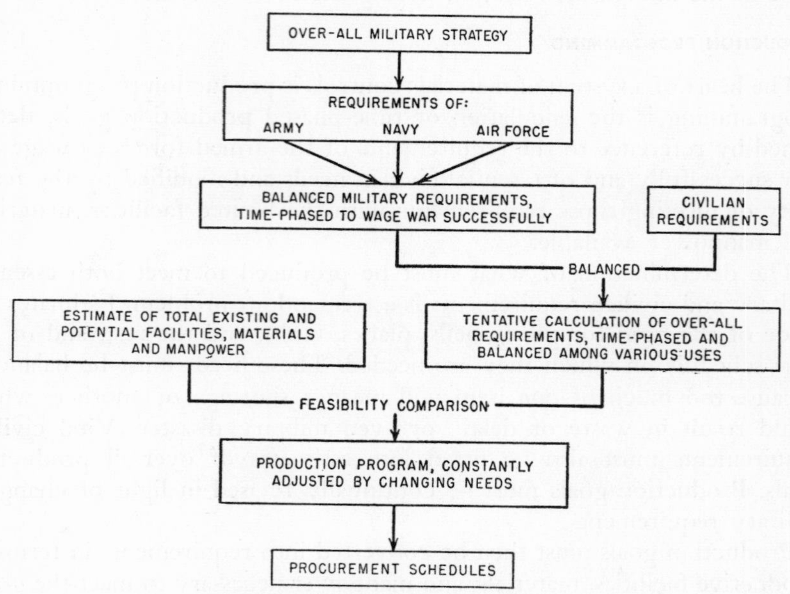

Figure 26–1. Production Programming

is required may be small, the percentage needed of specific minerals, metals, or chemicals may be large. However, civilian production need not be programmed to a high degree if the needs of the armed forces can be filled without seriously affecting civilian output.

Programming of production, then, is the concrete expression of the maximum feasible production goals, scheduled over specific time periods. Once formulated, production programs become procurement schedules. The procurement process translates the total production program for each item into individual company production schedules, as well as establishing the terms of the production contract.

EXPANSION OF PRODUCTIVE FACILITIES

Production programming sets the objectives of military and civilian production on a time schedule. With these schedules determined, direct wartime controls ensure that actual production meets the time-phased goals. Since the peacetime productive ability of the nation is inadequate to meet these goals, the purpose of government controls is to expand and convert productive facilities, control and allocate the use of materials, and direct the utilization of manpower.

Total industrial mobilization requires that the existing productive facilities be used at maximum capacity and that, where necessary, industrial plants be converted or expanded, or new ones be constructed. In 1939 to 1941, the nation's industrial plant had a considerable amount of unused capacity coupled with a rather high degree of unemployment. This cushion allowed a significant increase in output until converted, expanded, and new facilities could be made ready.[6] Today the nation is operating at a level of near full employment and has little cushion of unused capacity to absorb the initial shock of another war. Should war come, the nation faces the prospect of having to rely almost entirely on new and expanded industrial capacity, increased productivity, and sharp cutbacks in civilian production.

Government may promote industrial expansion and conversion by granting priorities or allocating scarce construction materials, aiding in securing an adequate number of construction workers, assisting private financing of plant expansion, or actually building and operating or allowing private operation of government-constructed plants. Since facilitating the acquisition of necessary materials and manpower for plant expansion is an aspect of the general materials procurement and manpower controls, it will be treated in the following subsections, and the latter two aids will be discussed here.

Assisting private financing. Private industry is actually unable to finance the necessary expansion of facilities that a modern war requires. In addition, a certain reluctance on the part of private industry to provide the necessary investment capital is understandable in that the expansion is for wartime requirements and may surpass civilian peacetime needs. Therefore, government financial assistance becomes imperative.

Three methods of helping private industry obtain the needed additional capital to expand plant facilities were used during World War II.[7] The

[6] It has been estimated that merely by using the unused facilities and supply of labor that existed in 1939, manufacturing production could have been increased by about 26 per cent, railroad traffic by 31 per cent, electric light and power output by at least 44 per cent, and bituminous coal mining by 47 per cent. J. Frederic Dewhurst and Associates, *America's Needs and Resources* (New York: The Twentieth Century Fund., Inc., 1947), pp. 629–630.

[7] Here the authors rely on George A. Lincoln, William S. Stone, and Thomas H. Harvey, *Economics of National Security* (New York: Prentice-Hall, Inc., 1950), pp. 221–225. For a more detailed discussion, see Douglas R. Fuller, *Government Financing of Private Enterprise* (Stanford, Calif.: Stanford University Press, 1948), pp. 115–166.

first method was to provide industry with the money directly through advance payments, progress payments, or direct loans. Advance payments were interest-bearing loans by government to contracting producers before work was begun. These payments, limited to 30 per cent of the contract price, were deposited in special accounts and the money could be withdrawn only with the approval of the government contracting agency. Almost $10 billion was advanced in this manner between 1940 and 1945.

Progress payments were made on many major contracts. These are immediate payments made upon the completion of designated parts of a contract and, not being loans, require no payment of interest. Since they were particularly applicable to ship construction, they were widely used by the Navy and Maritime Commission. Direct loans were occasionally made by the procurement agency to contractors, but because of the competition with commercial banks they were soon abandoned. Their total was only $76 million during the entire war.

Since the first method did not increase the flow of idle private capital out of banks into the productive system, government sought to stimulate private investment. The Board of Governors of the Federal Reserve System issued Regulation V by which a government contractor could get a bank loan (known as a "V-loan") with the government guaranteeing repayment up to 90 per cent of the principal.

Another incentive to corporations to invest surplus funds in plant expansion was the acceleration of amortization for tax purposes. By a 1941 act, corporations were permitted to amortize additional facilities necessary to the war effort over a five-year period. This inducement attracted a total of $7 billion in private capital, almost 20 per cent of the total investment in manufacturing facilities in 1939.

Assisting new plant construction. In addition to relying on private construction, with public financial assistance, the government itself spent $16 billion during World War II expanding the nation's industrial plant.[8] The Defense Plant Corporation, a subsidiary of the Reconstruction Finance Corporation, proved to be the most important single agency for assisting new plant construction. Through this corporation the government constructed approximately $8 billion worth of new facilities and leased them to private contractors for war production. The rental was low, and the contractor was given the option of purchasing the plant when it was no longer required.

Supply bottlenecks in the procurement of certain critical items were broken by the procurement agency financing directly the construction of necessary facilities. Over $7 billion were spent from special "expediting production" funds for this purpose.

[8] Lincoln, Stone, and Harvey, *op. cit.*, p. 223.

Accomplishments and evaluation of construction program. Since the nation had virtually no facilities to produce war materials in 1940, the production goals staggered a nation that had to start from scratch in building up a munitions capacity. Facilities expansion and military construction reached their peak in 1942, when construction constituted almost one-third of the total war output. The total value of construction and installations of equipment put in place by the end of 1942 was over $40 billion, and it exceeded $60 billion by mid-1945. Approximately $25 billion of the final total went into manufacturing facilities, while the rest went into military and nonmanufacturing facilities.[9]

A succession of bureaus and committees attempted to oversee the construction of facilities during the war, with varying degrees of success.[10] The official history of the War Production Board concludes that the Board [11]

> . . . was relatively unsuccessful in programming facilities construction, in appraising objectively the relative essentiality of industrial facilities projects, and in guiding the geographical distribution of plant expansons. Deficiencies in forward planning of productive capacity forced WPB to look at each facilities project individually, instead of as a part of a total facilities program. WPB had no authority over military command construction, had difficulty in obtaining authority over the equipping of plants with new machine tools, and found it difficult to apply rigorous tests of essentiality to projects sponsored by the Army and the Navy. WPB and its predecessor agencies had relatively slight influence on the location of new plants, largely because review by the central production agency came at too late a stage in the negotiations for plant construction.

CONTROL OF USE AND DISTRIBUTION OF MATERIALS

Wartime controls over productive facilities are designed to assure their conversion and expansion, but they do not attempt to control directly their use, except in the case of limitation orders which restrict or prohibit the production of certain consumer durable goods like automobiles. Material controls indirectly limit and direct the use of industrial capacity, but their fundamental purpose is somewhat different. When the supply of essential materials is insufficient to meet wartime production goals, materials controls must conserve materials and direct their flow into essential production.[12]

Conservation of materials. The purpose of conserving essential mate-

[9] Civilian Production Administration, *Industrial Mobilization for War: History of the War Production Board and Predecessor Agencies, 1940–1945*, vol. I, *Program and Administration* (1947), p. 385; Lincoln, Stone, and Harvey, *op. cit.*, p. 219.

[10] See *Industrial Mobilization for War*, pp. 386–409, 652–659.

[11] *Ibid.*, p. 985.

[12] See David Novick, Melvin Anshen, and W. C. Truppner, *Wartime Production Controls* (New York: Columbia University Press, 1949).

rials is to assure their availability for war production. The most drastic device used during World War II was the limitation order (L-order) prohibiting or limiting the output of certain civilian products.[13] The first of the limitation orders, issued in August, 1941, applied to certain truck and bus manufacturers. Soon after this order the production of passenger automobiles and light trucks was limited. Later in the year the manufacture of refrigerators and domestic laundry equipment was restricted to a quota expressed as a percentage of previous annual output.

M-orders restricted the uses to which specific materials might be put, either by absolute prohibition or by a percentage limitation. Among items affected by these orders was the use of copper in building construction and for other purposes, the use of chromium steel in certain products, and silk and rubber in certain articles. Under the pressure of M-orders ingenuity of manufacturers was tested as substitute materials were sought, such as cardboard containers for tooth powder and plastic for lipstick cases.

Simplification and standardization in certain articles also conserved scarce materials. Cuffs were eliminated from men's trousers, fancy trim and gadgets were removed from refrigerators and washing machines, and women's garments were designed to save materials. Inventory controls forbade the accumulation of manufacturers' inventories beyond minimum levels to prevent hoarding.

While each of these conservation devices can greatly reduce the demand for scarce materials, they may not conserve the right amounts of materials, nor will they channel the materials into essential production and at the proper time to meet production schedules. Other material controls are necessary.

Priorities and preference-rating orders. Preference ratings are a simple method of directing the flow of materials into more essential uses. There are generally two types: individual preference-rating certificates, and blanket preference-rating orders. The former were used at the beginning of the defense build-up in 1940 and issued by procurement officers of the Army and Navy and the War Production Board to show the relative urgency of end products. Urgency was indicated by ratings such as A-1, A-2, A-3, . . . , B-1, B-2, B-3, . . . , and so on, as a means of putting the most essential war orders at the head of shipping schedules. Otherwise orders would be filled on the peacetime basis of first come, first served. Manufacturers were soon permitted to extend their preference

[13] For a discussion of these and other devices, see John Lord O'Brian and Manly Fleischmann, "The War Production Board Administrative Policies and Procedures," 13 *George Washington Law Review* 1–60 (December, 1944); David D. Levine, "Administrative Control Techniques of the War Production Board," 4 *Public Administration Review* 89–96 (May, 1944).

certificates to cover orders they placed with suppliers of raw materials and components of end products.

The individual character of preference certificates made administration an impossible burden, so a more general procedure was developed. The new procedure took the form of the General Preference Order (P-order) which was inaugurated in March, 1941. The P-order assigned a blanket preference rating to whole categories of end products rather than to individual manufacturers and permitted manufacturers to translate such blanket authorizations into ratings on specific orders for parts and materials.

Both kinds of preference ratings were merely means of asserting a prior claim, but they did not assure allocations of scarce materials. They were issued without regard to the need to balance essential needs against limited supplies. Therefore, although they served a worthwhile purpose in the early stages of the defense build-up when supplies were still plentiful, they were useless when supplies were inadequate to meet the needs of manufacturers, even those who had top priority ratings. Under such circumstances pressure mounted to constantly upgrade ratings until the distinction between varying degrees of urgencies was destroyed. Furthermore, preference ratings were worthless as a means of coordinating the flow of different materials into urgent uses, so that a manufacturer could obtain the varying amounts of several materials and components at the time he needed them to turn out a completed product on schedule. The preference-rating system broke down in 1942, and it became apparent that some method of allocating scarce materials was required if scarce materials were to be channeled into the most essential uses.

Allocation orders. As early as 1941 certain shortages were so apparent that no serious question was raised as to the need for some mandatory form of distribution. In February, 1941, mandatory priority orders for aluminum were issued which actually allocated the metal. As the priority system began to collapse in mid-1941, the Office of Production Management moved toward general allocations but the system for each material operated independently, so coordination of the flow of materials was completely lacking.

The Production Requirements Plan. When the War Production Board came into existence at the beginning of the war, it inherited a variety of materials-distribution controls, including conservation and limitation orders, the preference-rating system, and a group of allocation schemes for particular materials. The Board was also the beneficiary of the Production Requirements Plan, which was announced in December, 1941. The Production Requirements Plan joined the preference-rating system to the allocation idea, and added the principle of coordinating the allocation of all essential materials to assure a balanced flow to the manufacturer. The plan was originally voluntary, but the War Production Board soon made it mandatory.

As the plan operated, all producers using more than $5,000 worth of certain critical materials in any one quarter-year were required to submit to the War Production Board properly supported estimates for each quarter of their need for scarce materials. The estimates of needs from all users for each material were totaled and compared with the estimated

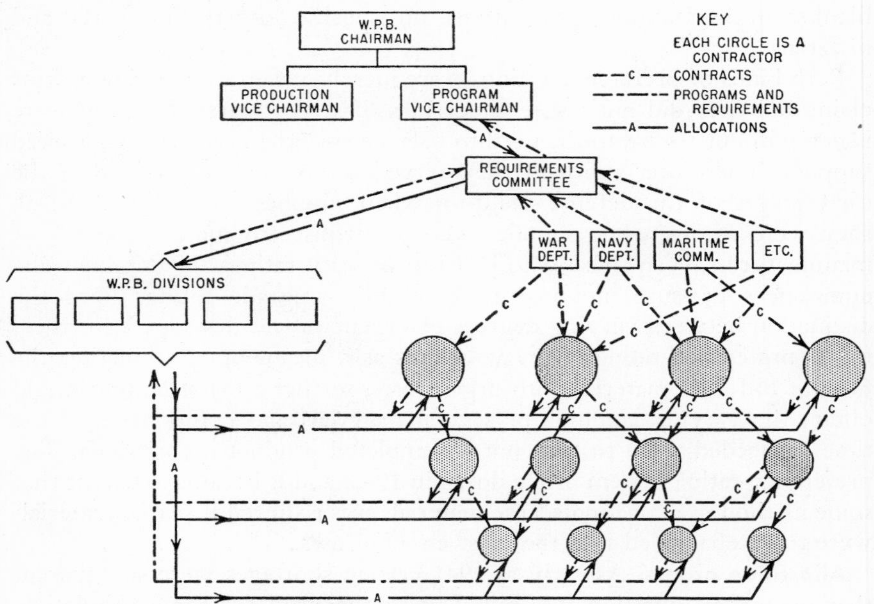

Figure 26–2. Production Control under Production Requirements Plan

General scheme. Source: U.S. Bureau of the Budget, *The United States at War* (1946), p. 309.

available supplies of each material. If the total demand for the quarter exceeded available supply, individual requests were scaled down on the basis of the importance of the product, the inventory position of the manufacturer, and his record of past consumption of allocated materials. The manufacturer was then allocated the amount of material that had been calculated by this procedure.

Despite the revolution in materials control envisaged by the Production Requirements Plan, the system did not do away with either preference ratings or individual allocations by materials branches. Limitation and conservation orders were not eliminated either. Furthermore, the plan did not cover all manufacturers, all materials, or even all requirements of manufacturers falling under the plan. The most serious defect of the plan was that, since it was a horizontal system of allocation which divided limited supplies among users on the basis of their needs, it did not take into account the effect of any particular reduction on successive stages of production. The plan imposed a tremendous administrative burden on the War Production Board which the Board was not prepared to undertake. A simpler allocation procedure was needed which would balance all material requirements at every production stage from metal mills to final assembly plants.

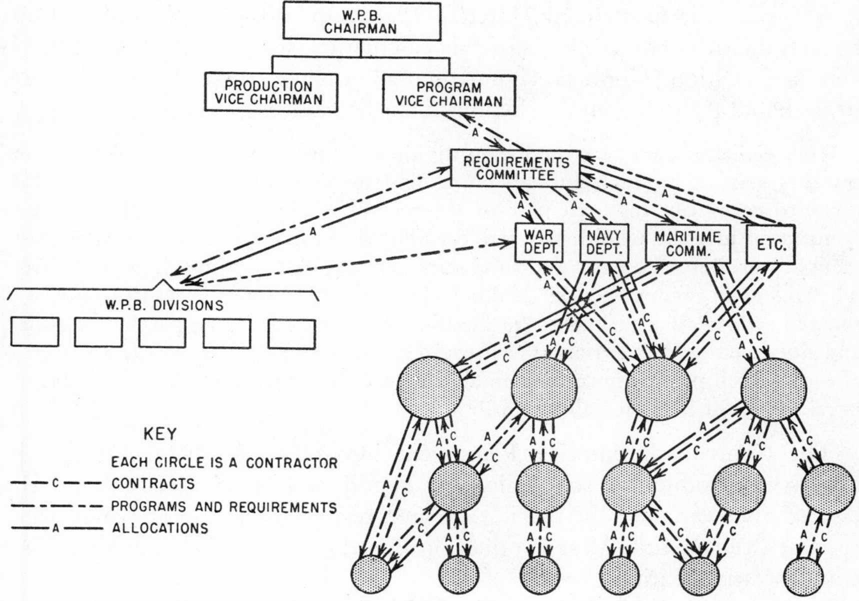

Figure 26–3. Production Control under Controlled Materials Plan

General scheme. Source: U.S. Bureau of the Budget, *The United States at War* (1946), p. 311.

The Controlled Materials Plan. In November, 1942, a vertical system of allocation was announced. The Controlled Materials Plan, as the new procedure was called, was a method of turning the whole country "into an integrated national arsenal" by dealing with the entire productive plant of the country "as one vast company." [14]

The plan was organized around total production programs that involved the use of steel, copper, and aluminum. By tying control over these materials together with control over schedules, the War Production Board could keep demand in line with supply and balance production. Prime contractors were made responsible for obtaining the material requirements

[14] Statement by Ernest Kanzler, Director General for Operations, as quoted in *Industrial Mobilization for War*, p. 487.

of their subcontractors, so that the Board was in a position to scale down schedules and materials not only for complete end products but also for all the essential parts, subassemblies, and components of the end products.

The procedure was simple. The claimant agencies estimated the kinds and quantities of end products they needed. These requirements were translated into needs for the specific forms and shapes of steel, copper, and aluminum. These material requirements were totaled, compared with available supply, and necessary adjustments made.

Although the Controlled Materials Plan emphasized vertical allocations to manufacturers on the basis of this calculation, it also incorporated horizontal allocation. Upon receiving their allotments, each claimant agency brought its programs and schedules into line with its allotment.

> Each claimant agency would then divide its allotment among its prime contractors, passing to each enough controlled material under his adjusted allotment to carry out his own part of the agency's whole program. Each prime contractor in turn would proceed to give his subcontractors sufficient allotments to produce the parts and subassemblies required by the prime contractor. The claimant agency, besides making allotments to its prime contractors, was to assign preference ratings to be used in procuring necessary parts, assemblies, and noncontrolled materials. With each allotment, the claimant agency would also give each prime contractor an allotment number, which was the claimant's break-down of its major allotment.[15]

The Controlled Materials Plan went into effect in 1943 and greatly improved production scheduling. It functioned satisfactorily until the end of the war and, by placing greater responsibility on the procuring agencies, relieved the War Production Board of some of its overwhelming administrative duties.

In the event of a future war, the Controlled Materials Plan could easily be revived and, if necessary, extended to other essential materials.

Materials control in the Korean War.[16] During the Korean War a program of materials-distribution control was reinstituted. Under the direction of the National Production Authority, conservation orders were issued restricting the nondefense use of copper, aluminum, zinc, and a number of other materials, chiefly metals. Priorities were also used, but their issuance was limited. Moreover, in contrast to the great number of finely distinguished ratings in World War II, only a single rating (DO—defense order) was used, indicating no degree of preference among rated defense orders. Contractors were permitted to extend their DO rating to their suppliers. In mid-1951, the Controlled Material Plan was reestablished to allocate steel, copper, and aluminum. A number of other materials were also brought under allocation.

[15] *Industrial Mobilization for War*, pp. 489–490.

[16] Following Wallace, *op. cit.*, pp. 124–128.

MANPOWER CONTROLS

Expansion and conversion of productive facilities and control of the use and distribution of materials must be accompanied by the assurance of an adequate supply of manpower. However, workers cannot be moved from one job to another, prohibited from certain employment, and allocated to essential work on a time schedule with the same ease that materials can be controlled. The danger of infringing upon human freedom and the resistance of workers to such controls present serious difficulties.[17] The United States has never had to resort to a manpower draft or compulsory work assignment, although it is conceivable that the urgency of some future emergency might require such drastic measures. Other less severe controls can go a long way toward relieving the manpower problem.

The purposes of a manpower program in total mobilization are to increase the total labor force, make more effective use of labor so that output will increase, and ensure that an adequate supply of labor is available at the particular place and time it is needed.

Increasing the labor force. The unemployed are, of course, the first great reservoir of manpower to be tapped when total mobilization requires that the labor force be increased. In addition, the labor force itself must be expanded by making greater use of women, youths, older people, the handicapped, and similar groups. Immigrant labor and prisoners of war are other possible sources of manpower, although the United States has not been inclined to make extensive use of these workers. It is conceivable, in the event of a future war and a critical manpower shortage, that the vast untapped reservoirs of manpower in underdeveloped friendly nations might be tapped by locating productive facilities there. The labor force can in effect be further expanded by lengthening the work week. An average work week in 1939 of 37.7 hours was lengthening to 46.6 hours by 1943, a 23 per cent increase.

Increasing the effectiveness of labor. Greater production will result from utilizing workers more intensively and effectively. Various methods of increasing the effectiveness of the use of labor have been employed. Appeals to patriotism have succeeded in raising individual output. The productivity of groups of workers has been increased by better organization and management practices, increased specialization of workers, and greater use of machinery. Members of minority groups who, for reasons

[17] Other problems are the following: How can a program of compulsory assignment be administered so that each worker is assigned where his skills are best used? How can personal and family problems be solved? Can a worker be expected to be assigned to a job where the pay is lower than he has been earning? What happens to a worker's seniority and other rights if he must leave his present job?

of prejudice, were underemployed have been allowed to work in jobs where their skills are more fully utilized.

Training programs [18] were widely used during World War II to increase the output of workers. Training was a necessity for the many persons who were drawn into the labor market during the war but who had never worked before or had never worked at the particular kinds of jobs that were essential. Training programs also served to upgrade many workers so that they could be more effectively employed to produce war goods.

A great wastage of manpower occurs because of labor turnover. By September, 1943, the monthly quit rate reached a peak of 6.3 per cent, while total separations were 8.2 per cent—a rate of almost 100 per cent per year. The Boeing plant in Seattle, for example, employed only 39,000 workers yet had hired 250,000 workers between 1940 and 1943. Since the reasons for high turnover vary so widely, no single solution to the problem is possible. Higher wages, improved working conditions, adequate housing, clarification of the selective-service regulations, and training programs are among the many measures that have been taken to attempt to lower the turnover ratio.

Controlling the use of labor. By far the most difficult problem in mobilizing manpower for defense is ensuring that an adequate supply of labor is available at the time and at the place or in the industry where it is most needed. The solution to this problem requires that some control be exerted over the use to which particular workers are put. These controls range from measures which encourage voluntary movement into essential war jobs to the possible extreme of national service and compulsory allocation of labor.

Major effort was placed initially on voluntary movement from nonessential to essential war jobs during World War II. The United States Employment Service provided the necessary job information for voluntary transfers. The incentive of high wages which existed in many war industries was then often sufficient inducement for workers to shift to essential jobs.[19] The lack of adequate housing deterred some workers from migrating to war jobs, so the Division of Defense Housing Coordination, later the National Housing Agency, was created with the responsibility of ensuring provision of housing for war workers. Other services such as transportation, child care, medical care, and recreational facilities were also provided to attract workers. Draft deferments for essential jobs further encouraged workers to take up war jobs. In fact, as the war pro-

[18] See War Manpower Commission, *The Training within Industry Report, 1940–1945* (1945).

[19] The limitation and conservation orders discussed above, although concerned with the allocation of materials, have the effect of encouraging the movement of labor to more essential jobs, since employment falls off in nonessential industries when materials are not available.

gressed, voluntary enlistments were prohibited so that skilled workers in necessary work could be kept on the job through the mechanism of the draft deferment.

A lack of urgency kept government from establishing a procedure for coping with the manpower crisis that was sure to come. Fortunately, the war ended before a serious shortage developed. When the problem did become somewhat critical in late 1943 and 1944, it was difficult to get action because of a general feeling that the war was soon going to be over.

A rudimentary system for allocating labor developed in a number of areas where the scarcity of labor was particularly pressing—notably on the Pacific Coast.[20] The West Coast program did not succeed in balancing the labor budget on an area basis or in reducing turnover, but it did have other significant results. Controlled referral channeled a larger proportion of the manpower flow through the Employment Service, and the priority system directed this flow to the points of greatest need. Adoption of the program caused procurement officials in Washington to give increased attention to labor supply in placing contracts. A good deal of future work was canceled, and many contracts which would have been crammed into the area were placed elsewhere. For the first time a program and administrative framework were provided within which the efforts of procurement, production, and manpower agencies could be organized to meet manpower shortages at the local level. Once the West Coast program had demonstrated its ability to survive, other areas outside the West Coast set up systems of manpower priorities, employment ceilings, and controlled referral.

Economic Stabilization

The second general objective of wartime controls is economic stabilization. Without stabilization controls the nation would suffer from spiraling prices, wages, and cost of living. The average individual would suffer greatly under mounting inflation, and the nation's war effort would be disrupted by increasing costs.

As has been already described, inflation results because the total effective demand of government, business, and individuals greatly exceeds the available supply. A simple measure of the inflationary gap is the excess of income available to be spent on consumer goods, minus taxes and savings, over the consumption goods available at prevailing prices.[21] The inflation-

[20] For a detailed discussion of this plan as well as of the general problem of allocating labor supply, see U.S. Bureau of the Budget, *The United States at War* (1946), chap. 14.

[21] Seymour E. Harris, *The Economics of Mobilization and Inflation* (New York: W. W. Norton & Company, Inc., 1951), p. 100.

ary gap is especially large in time of war because military needs greatly expand the demands of government for output and the rise of government spending increases employment and contributes increasing amounts to private money incomes. At the same time, the amount of consumer goods and services on which this greater income may be spent cannot be proportionately increased, and in some cases it must be curtailed.

In 1939, total federal expenditures amounted to $8.9 billion, of which only $1.3 billion were devoted to war goods and services (1.4 per cent of annual gross national product). By 1944, federal war expenditures reached $88.6 billion, or 41.5 per cent of the gross national product, thus leaving $125.1 billion for nonwar expenditures. During the war disposable personal income (personal income minus taxes) rose from $70.2 billion in 1939 to $146.0 billion in 1944 and $150.7 billion in 1945. The difference between disposable personal income and the value of goods available is the inflationary gap.

It is apparent that inflation can be suppressed if the amount of purchasing power in the hands of consumers is brought into some reasonably close relationship with the supply of commodities available. There are a number of means by which the inflationary gap may be reduced. The supply of consumer goods and services might be increased to approximate existing demand. This solution is possible only if an unused manufacturing capacity exists and an adequate supply of raw materials and labor is available at the outset of a war. This was the situation in early 1941, one year after the beginning of the defense program, when the nation was using only one-eighth of its productive effort to turn out war materials. The expansion

Table 26–1. *Total Federal Government Expenditures, Federal War Expenditures, Annual Gross National Product, and Apportionment to Federal War Expenditures—1939 to 1945*
(In billions of dollars)

Year	*Total federal government expenditures*	*Total federal war expenditures*	*Gross National Product*	*Percentage of GNP devoted to federal war expenditures*
1939	8.9	1.3	91.3	1.4
1940	10.0	2.2	101.4	2.2
1941	20.5	13.8	126.4	10.9
1942	56.1	49.6	161.2	30.8
1943	86.0	80.7	194.3	41.4
1944	95.6	88.6	213.7	41.5
1945	84.9	75.9	215.2	35.3

SOURCE: U.S. Department of Commerce, Office of Business Economics.

of total output was so great that consumer purchases of goods and services were somewhat larger in each of the war years than in 1939. In 1944, for example, consumer purchases were 12 per cent greater than in 1939.[22]

Table 26–2. National Income, Personal Income and Disposable Personal Income, 1939 to 1945
(In billions of dollars)

Year	*National income*	*Personal income*	*Disposable personal income* *
1939	72.5	72.6	70.1
1940	81.3	78.3	75.7
1941	103.8	95.3	92.0
1942	136.5	122.2	116.2
1943	168.3	149.4	131.6
1944	182.3	164.9	146.0
1945	182.8	171.6	150.7

* Personal income minus taxes.
SOURCE: U.S. Department of Commerce, Office of Business Economics.

However, a sufficient amount of consumer goods and services to close the inflationary gap can never be produced if the basic wartime objective of maximum supply of military goods and services is to be accomplished. Moreover, under conditions of full employment the total output of goods and services available for civilian needs must decline if the maximum supply of military goods is to be assured. Therefore, purchasing power must be curtailed by means of increased taxes, voluntary or compulsory savings, and credit controls. At the same time, government must hold down its demand for manpower, goods, and services by curtailing or ceasing programs that are not essential to the war effort.[23]

FISCAL-MONETARY CONTROLS IN WARTIME

Tax increases and government borrowing accomplish two objectives: (1) personal income is reduced, closing the inflationary gap in the interests of economic stabilization; and (2) necessary revenue is raised to finance a war.

Total federal expenditures during the six years ending in June, 1946, amounted to $383.4 billion, or more than twice as much as the federal government had spent during the preceding 150 years. Taxes financed 51.3

[22] *Industrial Mobilization for War*, p. 964.

[23] Nonwar federal expenditures were reduced from $3.9 billion in 1939 to $1.0 billion in 1945.

per cent of total federal expenditures and were an anti-inflationary instrument. Prior to the defense effort, federal tax receipts were about $6 billion a year. Tax collections rose to a wartime peak of $51 billion in fiscal 1945, and brought in a total of $196.7 billion in the six years following June, 1940. The excess of federal expenditures over tax receipts for the six-year period amounted to $186.7 billion. These deficits were a major inflationary pressure, because they represented the government's net contributions to private money incomes after taxes.

Taxes are an effective stabilization control because they are compulsory.[24] In addition to curtailing purchasing power, taxes, such as luxury taxes, also can direct consumer spending away from nonessential goods so that the production of those goods will be restricted. Taxes, of course, should not be so high as to discourage workers from coming into the work force or from working overtime. However, they may have to be somewhat more regressive in time of war than in peacetime. Since the greatest bulk of consumption spending is done by the lower and middle income groups, their purchasing power must be markedly reduced.

Credit controls seek to limit the expansion of credit for the purchase of consumer goods. Expansion of credit is inflationary, since it increases purchasing power. Credit controls include restrictions on charge accounts, regulation of installment buying, and elimination of buying on margin on the stock market. For example, during World War II the Board of Governors of the Federal Reserve System issued Regulation W, which restricted the purchase of consumer durable goods through installment payments, charge accounts, and other forms of credit. However, since this regulation did not reach people who could afford to pay cash for the goods they wanted, it was of minor importance in the fight against inflation.

Indirect fiscal-monetary controls cannot operate effectively without direct controls which establish ceilings on prices, wages, and rents. Tax increases that are sufficient to siphon off excess demand have been politically unacceptable even in times of war. Moreover, because of the time lag between their adoption and effectiveness, there tends to be a period of great excess demand. Furthermore, taxes are a blunt instrument which might interfere with the allocation of resources and the expansion of essential output. The public is not likely to save enough on a voluntary basis to close the inflationary gap, and compulsory savings are subject to the same shortcomings as taxes. Borrowing must therefore tap the resources of commercial banks, thereby adding to the inflationary pressure. The conclusion seems inescapable that direct controls must supplement indirect controls in times of heavy and rapidly expanding defense

[24] See the discussions in Chandler and Wallace, *op. cit.*, p. 43, and in Lincoln, Stone, and Harvey, *op. cit.*, pp. 387–389.

expenditures. But direct controls cannot do the job alone, nor can they make up for the shortcomings of indirect controls. This was clearly recognized in the statement which accompanied the General Maximum Price Regulation of 1942 which pointed out that without adequate taxation, savings, and wage stabilization "the ceilings would in the long run become administratively unenforceable and socially harmful." As Seymour Harris put it, the pricing system is more important than the mimeographing machine.[25]

DIRECT CONTROL OF PRICES

No wartime economic control is better known or the subject of more controversy than price control. Scarcely a person in the nation escapes the impact of government price fixing. The immediate purpose of price control is to place a ceiling on inflationary price increases. However, unlike the fiscal-monetary controls that are used to combat inflation, price control does not attack the sources of wartime inflation. Instead, it is directed at the effects of inflationary pressures and attempts to control them.

During World War I price control of consumer goods at retail was not attempted or was mainly hortatory. Price control at the producer level, except for a brief experiment with shoes and the pricing of government purchases, was limited to a few strategic commodities.[26]

World War II experience. Price control during World War II developed through several organizational and policy phases. The Advisory Commission to the Council of National Defense, resurrected in 1940, included a Price Stabilization Division under Leon Henderson. There was also a Division of Consumer Protection, which was concerned with the threats of rising retail prices and the dangers of quality deterioration as a concealed form of price increase. This division merged with the Price Stabilization Division when the Office of Price Administration and Civilian Supply was formed in 1941. Later in the year the civilian supply function was moved to the Office of Production Management, leaving the price control agency with the short and widely known title "OPA."

During the period prior to Pearl Harbor none of the agencies had adequate authority to control prices. The Advisory Commission relied on persuasion and publicity. The two succeeding control agencies were based only on Executive orders and relied on voluntary adherence to the price schedules they issued. Consequently, between September, 1939, and Pearl Harbor, commodity prices rose 25 per cent. In January, 1942, Congress put the price-control program on a legislative basis by enacting the Emergency Price Control Act. This law conferred authority to fix prices

[25] *Op. cit.*, p. 18.

[26] For a description of price control during World War I, see George P. Adams, *Wartime Price Control* (Washington, D.C.: Public Affairs Press, 1942).

ceilings that were "generally fair and equitable." But rather than permit general price control, Congress provided for selective controls. Wages were exempt, not all sales of real estate were covered, and authority over agricultural prices were sharply restricted. Therefore, the act "was better suited to the situation prevailing when it was introduced in August, 1941, than to the conditions of the following winter." [27]

It soon became apparent that a broader approach was needed to bring about real stabilization. In April, 1942, the Office issued the General Maximum Price Regulation. The regulation, covering all commodities and services not specifically excluded or not covered by another regulation of the office, was simple. It established the highest price charged in March, 1942, as the ceiling for all commodities sold to consumers. Although a general price freeze is easy to prepare, the handling of claims can be burdensome. In the months following the issuance of the general regulation, the Office of Price Administration was flooded with requests for adjustment and lacked the staff to handle them.

Prices continued to rise, and still more drastic action was imperative. In October, 1942, Congress passed the Economic Stabilization Act directing the President to stabilize prices at the levels which existed on September 15, 1942. The act permitted the fixing of agricultural prices at a somewhat lower level, and wages were subjected to control. The President immediately established the Office of Economic Stabilization and appointed Supreme Court Justice Byrnes as its Director. The new law permitted 90 per cent of the typical consumer's food budget to be controlled at the retail level, as compared with only 60 per cent under the General Maximum Price Regulation.

When prices still continued to move upward, the President issued the "Hold-the-line" order of April 8, 1943. This order prohibited the Price Administrator from allowing any further upward price adjustments unless such increases were required by law and did not exceed the minimum amount the law required. Any increase above that minimum level had to be approved by the Economic Stabilization Director. This order, Harvey Mansfield writes, "marked a turning point in OPA operations, legally, psychologically, and administratively. . . . It signalized a new and this time successful assault . . . on rising food prices." [28] Between the spring of 1943 and April, 1945, the Bureau of Labor Statistics Index of Consumers' Prices rose less than 2 per cent, or at one-sixth the rate of the preceding two years. Food prices actually declined at retail by more than 4 per cent. The only significant increases in the cost of living during this period were in clothing (slightly more than 11 per cent) and housefurnishings (not

[27] Harvey C. Mansfield, *A Short History of OPA* (Government Printing Office, 1949), p. 39. This section relies heavily on this excellent work.

[28] *Ibid.*, p. 55.

quite 16 per cent). Some quality deterioration occurred in certain goods, and black markets occasionally were troublesome, but the over-all accomplishment was impressive.[29]

During the entire war the rise in prices was 25.9 per cent, whereas prices went up 64.6 per cent in World War I. Yet the second war cost 10 times as much as the first.[30]

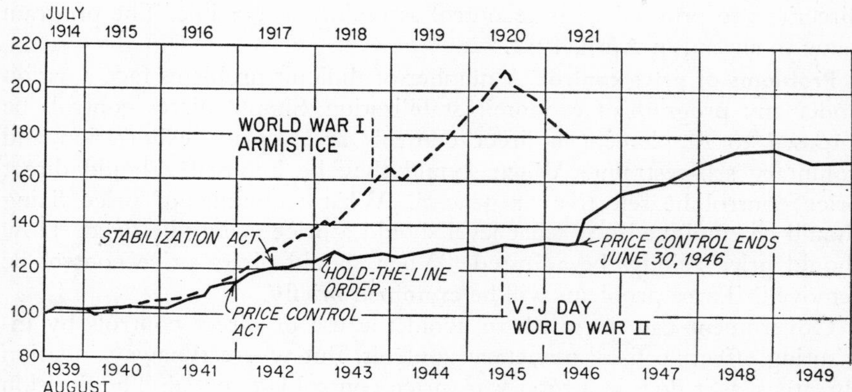

Figure 26—4. Living Costs in Two Wars

Source: Office of Price Administration.

Korean War experience. In two months after the Korean War began, the wholesale commodity index rose from 264 to 307.6 The President was desirous of imposing controls gradually and sought wide discretion and flexibility rather than a rigid congressional schedule for instituting them. Congress, prodded by the recommendations of Bernard Baruch, granted the President more powers than he asked for, but nowhere near the authority that Baruch suggested he should have. The Defense Production Act of 1950 authorized the production and credit controls the President requested and also provided him with the power to impose price and wage control and to order rationing of consumer goods. This legislation became effective in September, 1950, but the Office of Price Stabilization was not created or a general price freeze regulation issued until the following January. Rationing was never imposed.

The original price-stabilization authority expired in mid-1951, and new legislation weakened price control. Congress disapproved a further rollback of beef prices (permitting a rollback to 90 per cent of the freeze level to continue), forbade slaughtering quotas, required historic margins to be preserved for retailers, and required the adjustment of ceiling prices

[29] *Ibid.*, p. 56.
[30] Harris, *op. cit.*, p. 214.

of individual manufacturers to reflect all costs, up to the date of the new legislation. The latter provision, called the Capehart amendment, struck down the Office of Price Stabilization policy of cost absorption of post-freeze cost increases and its requirement that approved cost increases be "passed through" the various levels of distribution without an increase of previous per-unit dollar margins.

Price legislation was continued in 1952 with more restrictions and with directions to proceed with decontrol as rapidly as possible. The program came to an end in April, 1953.

Problems of price control. A number of difficult problems face a nation under any program of economic stabilization. Should direct controls be imposed to supplement indirect controls and replace exhortation and voluntary self-restraint? When should they be imposed? Should direct price control be selective or general? What technique of price fixing should be employed? At what level should a price ceiling be fixed? How should price ceilings be adjusted? When should direct price control be removed? These problems will be examined briefly.

Government can do much to avoid the use of direct controls by instituting effective fiscal-monetary controls. But where runaway inflation threatens, as it does in a total war, price control is essential. The decision to supplement fiscal-monetary controls with direct control in a partial mobilization like the Korean War is far more difficult. Since indirect controls do not become effective immediately, there is a time lag before they shrink spending power. Furthermore, when the economy is operating close to full employment and inflationary pressures are introduced, fiscal-monetary controls may not be adequate. Therefore, in a partial mobilization, direct controls may be necessary at least until indirect controls have time to take effect and are adequate to restrain inflation.[31]

In an all-out war there is little doubt that the controls must be general and cover practically everything. If they did not, large profits in uncontrolled areas might attract manpower and material so as to interfere with the achievement of production goals. Selective price controls might be sufficient in a defense period or limited mobilization, if the inflationary pressures impinged only on sectors of the economy. Luxury taxes could be used to prevent an excessive shift of materials and facilities to certain exempt articles. More stringent production controls would have to be employed where uncontrolled items used scarce materials.

Types of price ceilings. Three basic types of maximum-price ceilings have been utilized: freeze, dollars-and-cents, and formula. Each has certain

[31] Arthur M. Ross, *The Lessons of Price and Wage Controls* (Berkeley, Calif.: Institute of Industrial Relations, 1953), p. 4. For a presentation of the arguments for and against the imposition of price control, see Jules Backman, *Government Price-fixing* (New York: Pitman Publishing Corporation, 1938), pp. 567–572.

advantages and disadvantages. The freeze ceiling is by far the quickest and easiest to impose and is the most effective way of checking an upward movement of prices by a single act. The freeze ceiling simply fixes the maximum legal price at the level at which a particular commodity (or group of commodities) was selling in a specified base period. Both the General Maximum Price Regulation of World War II and the General Ceiling Price Regulation of January, 1951, were of the freeze type. A freeze ceiling has the advantage of preserving price differentials that arise out of competitive conditions, product differentiation, and other economic conditions.

On the other hand, the freeze ceiling is difficult to enforce because only the seller knows what his ceiling is, and it is unlikely that the buyer knows what the ceiling was during the base period. Temporary inequities, such as sale prices, seasonal prices, and depressed prices, are frozen into the ceiling. Moreover, a commodity may be altered in style, quality, or composition to escape the ceiling. At most, it is only a stopgap.

The dollars-and-cents ceiling, being more precise, is more easily enforced. The maximum price for a commodity is specifically established. The dollars-and-cents technique has the disadvantage of being very complicated.[32] It requires the collection and analysis of much data to arrive at the ceiling. It cannot be used very effectively where quality can be changed easily, where costs vary widely among sellers, where products cannot be defined precisely, or where transportation cost is a factor in pricing. The administrative burden is so great that neither under the Office of Price Administration nor under the Office of Price Stabilization was the technique widely applied. Nevertheless, the dollars-and-cents ceiling was employed in the retail food field during both emergencies, and the development of precise ceilings was recognized as a significant achievement in combating inflation.

A formula ceiling is arrived at by applying a prescribed formula. This determination may be made either by the seller or by the price agency using information supplied by the seller. The formula technique is useful in determining the price of nonstandardized products, new products, or old products if the materials used or methods of production have been changed. For example, the regulation issued in 1951 to place ceilings on different manufactured products required use of the cost elements and formulas which firms had employed in 1950.[33]

[32] For example, fixing retail prices for ham during World War II involved ten zones, four grades of meat, and seventy-two different cuts, for a total of 2,880 price quotations. Backman, *op. cit.*, p. 567.

[33] This regulation was later superseded by the Capehart amendment to the Defense Production Act of 1951, which allowed the addition of all cost increases up to a more recent date.

The flexibility of the formula ceiling is its principal advantage. It can be adapted to any particular commodity or company. The disadvantage is the difficulty of enforcement because of the problem of checking individual calculations. Moreover, the formula ceiling may not prevent price increases, if increases of the elements of cost are permitted to be reflected in the maximum price.

Administering price ceilings. Imposing a general freeze ceiling is a relatively simple task. The biggest problems follow the price freeze. Detailed dollars-and-cents or formula regulations must be issued, and then prices must be adjusted to correct inequities and alleviate hardships.

Under the general freeze of March, 1942, the highest price charged during that month was used to determine the ceiling price, not only for each commodity sold at that price during March, but also for any "similar" commodity. If a seller of a new commodity could not find that it was "similar" to one for which he had a ceiling, then he would use as the ceiling the price for that commodity when sold by "the most closely competitive seller of the same class." Obviously, these standards allowed a wide range of interpretation. In the months that followed many new products appeared as businessmen searched for higher price ceilings.[34]

Toward the end of 1942 the administration of price control improved, and enforcement became more vigorous. The "Hold-the-line" order of 1943 provided more objective standards on which to base decisions concerning price adjustments, since the order prohibited increases beyond the "minimum requirement of law." Any increase that was authorized had to meet the standard "necessary to aid in the effective prosecution of the war." The minimum standards of law were met

> (1) if they would permit the industry to earn, before taxes, the same aggregate dollar profits (proportionately adjusted for changes in investment) that were earned in a normal peacetime period, and (2) if on all significant product lines they were adequate to permit the recovery of at least out-of-pocket costs for the output of all but the high-cost marginal fringe of producers.[35]

The years 1936 to 1939 were ordinarily taken as a normal peacetime period for any industry.

Subsidies were sometimes used to give necessary price relief to marginal producers without raising the price level for the entire commodity. Among the most successful subsidy programs during World War II were the industrial-alcohol-subsidy program and the premium-price plan for nonferrous metals. The best-known and most expensive stabilization sub-

[34] The president of W. T. Grant Company testified in 1944: "The present $1.98 cotton dress is the equivalent of the former 59¢ dress with approximately 10¢ of styling added." Cited by Harris, *op. cit.*, p. 222–223.

[35] Mansfield, *op. cit.*, p. 67.

sidies were those that supported the meat-price rollbacks and kept flour prices stable. The latter did not aim at production increase by stimulating marginal production, as did the former. The purpose of rollback subsidies was simply to reduce the cost of living.

DIRECT CONTROL OF WAGES

There is an obvious relationship between prices and wages. When wage rates rise, unit labor costs increase, and these increases must normally be reflected in prices. Mounting prices increase the cost of living, which generates demands for wage boosts. Therefore, if prices are stabilized it is logical also to stabilize wages to prevent the wage-price spiral and hold down government costs. The need for wage control is especially apparent when there is a scarcity of labor and workers can demand and receive wage increases.[36] Wage control also prevents the competitive bidding for manpower that would interfere with the attainment of programmed production goals. Finally, by limiting the increase in aggregate wage income, wage stabilization restricts the total demand for goods which are in short supply in wartime.

In the early phases of mobilization, wage increases may be desirable in essential war industries to attract workers to war jobs. But as labor shortages develop, wage raises in war industries lose their value as means of channeling labor. Between 1939 and 1941, the average hourly earnings of factory workers increased 16 per cent,[37] and by fall of 1941 a strong case could be built for imposing checks on wage raises. However, the country was not yet at war, and the political climate was not favorable for the introduction of wage-stabilization measures.

The tripartite National War Labor Board was created by Executive order in January, 1942, with authority to settle labor disputes based on the no-strike pledge given the previous month. But it had no wage-control policy or power. The labor members and, to a lesser extent, the public members of the Board were opposed to the imposition of wage controls. By the spring of 1942, the increase in average hourly earnings was greater than the increase in productivity, and when the General Maximum Price Regulation was issued in April, the problems created by the lack of control over voluntary wage agreements were apparent.

In July, the Board evolved the Little Steel formula, which became the

[36] This is a partial explanation for the delay of ten months after World War II began before imposing wage control, whereas it was incorporated in the Defense Production Act passed immediately after the start of the Korean War. In 1940, there was a surplus labor force of 9 million, but in July, 1950, it was no more than 1½ million.

[37] H. M. Douty, *Problems and Policies of Dispute Settlement and Wage Stabilization during World War II*, U.S. Bureau of Labor Statistics, Bulletin 1009 (1950), cited in Chandler and Wallace, *op. cit.*, p. 326.

cornerstone of the wartime wage program. Under this formula straight-time hourly earnings were permitted to be increased 15 per cent above the January, 1941, levels. But the Board still had no authority over voluntary wage agreements. Not until Congress enacted the Stabilization Act the following October did the Board receive a mandate to regulate wages. Wages were stabilized by the law at the level existing in September, 1941, and departures were permitted only if the President found adjustment necessary "to aid in the effective prosecution of the war and to correct gross injustices."

The "Hold-the-line" order of April, 1943, forbade wage increases except to correct abuses. The World War II effort to restrain wage raises was reasonably successful, especially after the issuance of the "Hold-the-line" order. Between October, 1942 and August, 1945, manufacturing wage rates rose 13.9 per cent, while consumers' prices went up 8.7 per cent. Between April, 1943, and August, 1945, the increases were only 10.6 per cent and 4.2 per cent, respectively. In the much briefer period from January, 1941, to October, 1942, wage rates mounted 17 per cent and consumers' prices 18.1 per cent.[38]

In the Korean War, as in World War II, wage control was handled by the same agency which was concerned with industrial disputes. It is understandable that one agency should handle both matters, because wage stabilization and the settlement of labor disputes are inseparable problems. Many disputes involve wage matters or are in one way or another related to wages. However, during the Korean War the handling of disputes by the same agency assigned the task of administering wage control became the most controversial issue during the Wage Stabilization Board's brief history. In 1952, the Board's jurisdiction over industrial disputes was limited by law. Thereafter, it could only give advice on request to the affected party or government agencies as to the interpretation or application of policies relating to wage stabilization.

Unlike price control, wage stabilization must be general when it is imposed. Even in a partial mobilization it would not be feasible or equitable to control wages on a selective basis. The freeze ceiling, applying to wage rates, fringe benefits, and the conditions of employment in a specific base period, is the most suitable technique of wage control. In contrast to the situation under a price freeze, employers and employees are likely to know the level of wages in the base period, because of the importance of wage rates to both parties. In many instances, wage contracts are in existence. Consequently, enforcement is easier and more effective. The contracts themselves, where they are in effect, are instruments of enforcement.

Since it is not possible to change the type of ceiling or the coverage of wage control—as is possible in the case of price control—adjustments in

[38] *Ibid.*, p. 385.

wage stabilization must be introduced by changing wage standards.[39] A number of standards have been devised to permit wage adjustments. During World War II much more rigid standards were needed than during the partial mobilization during the Korean War.

In the interests of justice and fairness, wage adjustments were necessary, even during total mobilization, to assure that the relative position of labor was not depressed during the war. Therefore, adjustments were permitted to keep up with living costs. The catch-up formula was a useful device to allow wage increases, both in the interests of equity and as part of the general guarantee that the relative position of labor would not fall behind others in the economy. The Little Steel formula was such a catch-up device used during World War II. During the Korean War the Wage Stabilization Board permitted all wage rates to rise 10 per cent above the January, 1950, levels.

Adjustment of particular occupation rates that had an inequitable relationship to each other in some plants was permitted, as well as adjustment of particular occupational rates in certain plants that were below the minimum rate for these occupations in specific labor markets. It was also felt desirable to allow wage adjustments to reflect increases in productivity when this standard could be applied without increasing inflationary pressures. Such adjustments should not exceed the average increase in productivity for the economy as a whole. The Wage Stabilization Board used this standard in addition to the catch-up adjustments during 1951.

Finally, adjustments were permitted to ease manpower shortages. These adjustments were necessarily worked out on a case-by-case basis in the smallest amount necessary to attract workers to essential industries where shortages existed.

RATIONING OF CONSUMER GOODS

In total mobilization, rationing of certain consumer goods[40] is a necessary supplement to price control. With prices held down by price control and with the rise of personal income that occurs during production expansion, people will wish to buy more goods at the lower prices. By limiting demand for certain commodities to correspond to available supply, rationing reduces inflationary pressures and helps make price control effective.

Other purposes of rationing are to assure a fair share of scarce goods to everyone and to assure the distribution of commodities in short supply to persons who need them for reasons of health, contribution to the war effort, and the like. Whereas fairness in the former case is simply a matter

[39] Here the authors rely on Wallace, *op. cit.*, pp. 230–240.

[40] Rationing of materials essential to war production is usually referred to as "allocation" and was treated as an aspect of production control. See above, pp. 727–736.

of equity of distribution, in the latter case fairness calls for differential rationing dependent upon the difference in the needs of persons. Differential rationing permits doctors and war workers to obtain needed gasoline and tires, nursing mothers and children to receive milk, or very young children to get oranges. Finally, rationing of specific commodities helps conserve goods that are in short supply.

Since shortages of consumer goods has never been severe in past wars,[41] selective rationing has been sufficient to achieve the various objectives of rationing. Total mobilization in time of full employment would undoubtedly require more extensive rationing. Selective rationing has been instituted where severe shortages developed in essential commodities. During World War II sugar and tires were in short supply because of import deficiencies; petroleum products were scarce because of the high military consumption and transportation difficulties; and automobiles and typewriters were scarce because the productive facilities of these goods were turned to war production. Therefore, these commodities were rationed. Since rationing has also been introduced with an eye to its administrative feasibility (rationing that cannot be enforced is useless), it has been imposed generally where the number of producers is small and is subject to public scrutiny. Meat rationing was introduced because demand mounted as personal incomes increased, but the many small producers and the ease by which new producers could enter the field made effective rationing difficult.

Since rationing is closely related to price control and since the Office of Price Administration had the administrative machinery to do the job,[42] it was logical to combine consumer-rationing and price-control functions in the same agency. The Defense Production Act of 1950 authorized rationing during the Korean War, but the power was never invoked.

Two kinds of rationing were employed during World War II. "Certificate" rationing involved the specific allotment of a single commodity on the showing of a specific need in accordance with certain prescribed standards of eligibility. If a person met the requirements, he was issued a certificate allowing him to buy the commodity. The rationing was on a one-at-a-time basis and applied to automobiles, tires, stoves, typewriters, and the like.

The second type of rationing was "coupon" or "stamp" rationing, which applied to foods, fuel oil, gasoline, and shoes. This type assured the allotment of a certain quantity of an individual commodity in a given period

[41] During World War II civilian consumption increased about 25 per cent above 1939.

[42] The Office of Price Administration had 5,600 local boards, employing 35,000 clerks, most of whom worked on rationing. In addition 150,000 to 200,000 people worked as volunteer board members and clerks.

of time. The consumer was issued a book of coupons—e.g., a sugar-ration book—which he could spend at designated rate within a given time period. A more flexible variation on "coupon" rationing was group rationing, or point-system rationing. Several similar products—e.g., meat, butter, cheese, and fats—were grouped together, each having a certain point value. The consumer had the choice of what combination of products he wanted to buy up to a specified quantity. The point values of commodities were changed to increase demand for goods that were piling up on shelves or to decrease demand for goods found to be in short supply. The advantages of the point system are the freedom of consumer choice it allows, the greater ease of administering a program for a group of items over separate schemes for individual commodities, and its flexibility.

The certificates or coupons were collected by the merchant at the time of the sale. Through a system of ration banking that was developed in 1942, the merchant deposited these certificates and stamps in the commercial bank where he did his banking. A separate account was maintained for each rationed commodity in the name of the merchant. Depositors would then draw ration checks on these accounts and use them to buy rationed goods from their suppliers. The suppliers would in turn deposit these checks in their accounts and draw on them to buy from producers and manufacturers. This process came to be known as a "flowback system."

Wartime Economic Controls: Conclusions

Judged by the most important single criterion, the war effort of the United States during World War II was a success—the enemy was defeated. There can be no doubt that the wartime economic controls which were imposed contributed to this success. The production controls contributed to a production achievement that stands without parallel. The industrial-plant capacity of the United States was expanded 50 per cent between 1939 and 1945. By 1944, 18.7 million more people were employed than in 1939, 11 million in the armed forces and 7.7 million in the civilian working force. Of the total, 10 million were net additions to the labor force, and 8.7 million were persons who had been a part of the labor force but unemployed in 1939. Productivity of labor increased about 25 per cent between 1939 and 1944, as a result of such measures as lengthening the work week, increasing worker efficiency, installing up-to-date plant equipment, and appealing to individual incentives in helping to win the war.[43]

With these facilities and manpower, the nation's industrial machine was able to produce the staggering total of 300,000 warplanes, 124,000 ships

[43] *Industrial Mobilization for War*, p. 965.

of all types, 41 billion rounds of ammunition, 100,000 tanks and armored cars, 2.4 million trucks, 434 million tons of steel, and 36 billion yards of cotton textiles[44] (see Figure 26–5). War production, which amounted to less than 2 per cent of total national output in 1939, rose to over 41 per

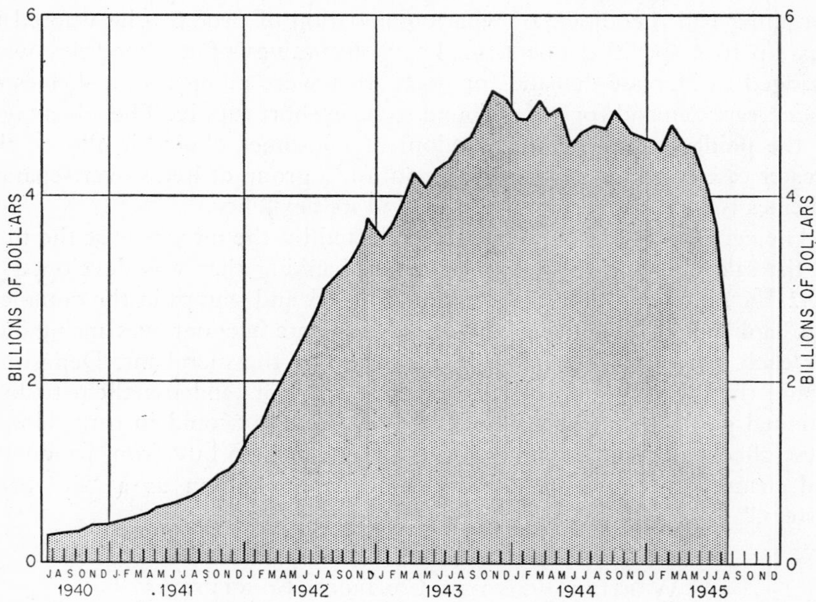

Figure 26—5. United States Munitions Production, July, 1940, to August, 1945

In standard 1945 munitions dollars. Source: Civilian Production Administration, *Industrial Mobilization for War* (1947), p. 961.

cent by 1943 and 1944 (see Figure 26–6). Yet the expansion of total output was so great that consumer purchases were larger in the war years than in 1939. Consumers suffered very little from the impact of World War II, although particular items were in short supply, and inflationary pressures were contained better than ever before. Equally important is the fact that the wartime economic controls did not damage basic democratic institutions and processes.

Although it [the War Production Board] had necessarily exercised sweeping controls, the Board had maintained both flexibility of structure and a clear perception of the need for democratic procedures; industry, labor, civilian economy, and the Armed Services had each participated in the formulation of

[44] Donald Nelson, *Arsenal of Democracy* (New York: Harcourt, Brace and Company, Inc., 1946), foreword.

policy. Whatever the problems the Nation faced on its return to peace, it could face them with the means for democratic action unimpaired.[45]

During the Korean War the demands on the economy were not so great. At the peak of that effort, only 15 per cent of total national output was devoted to war. Many of the World War II production controls had

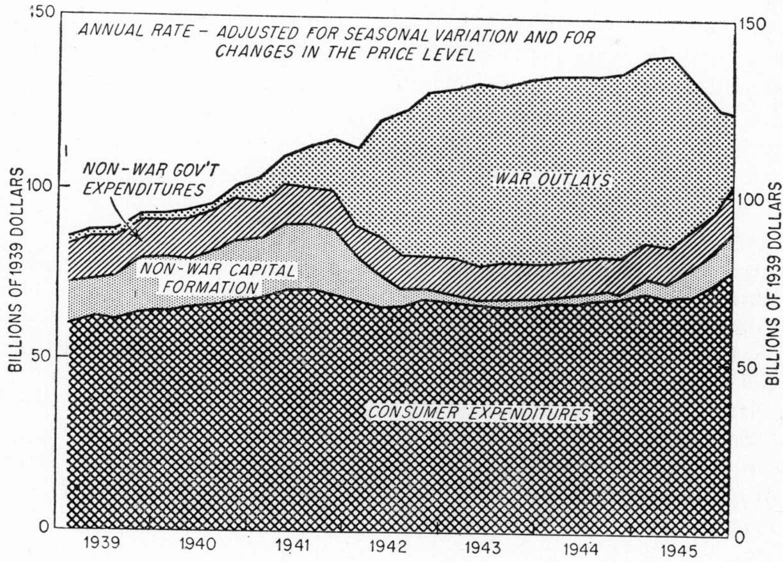

Figure 26–6. United States Gross National Production

Total output of goods and services. Source: Civil Production Administration, *Industrial Mobilization for War* (1947), p. 963.

to be invoked to mobilize the economy, and stabilization measures were imposed as inflation mounted. In spite of the relatively limited scope of the Korean mobilization, the problems faced were in some ways more difficult. About nine-tenths of the additional resources for World War II came from additional output. It was not possible in 1950, under conditions approaching full employment, to expand and divert production for war without soon generating inflationary pressures. But the nation was not prepared to accept stabilization measures which, more than any other wartime control, depend upon wide popular support for their success. Fortunately, maximum effort was not necessary, and hostilities were concluded before serious dislocation occurred.

The Korean War ominously pointed to the serious problems that would confront the nation in the event of a war that required total

[45] *Industrial Mobilization for War*, p. 986.

mobilization. The effort might well require a higher portion of national output than occurred during the peak of World War II, and it might last much longer. Under conditions of full employment, it would not be possible to expand greatly the work force or increase military production without tremendous diversions from nonwar consumption and investment. The inflationary pressures would be so strong that the most stringent and far-reaching controls in history might have to be imposed. The lessons learned in three wars provide the building blocks for a program of indirect and direct controls. But whether they would be effective depends on the will of the public to make them work as much as (and perhaps more than) on the nature and administration of the controls.

Selected References

Backman, Jules, Antonin Basch, Solomon Fabricant, Martin Gainsbrugh, and Emanuel Stein, *War and Defense Economics.* New York: Rinehart & Company, Inc., 1952.

Catton, Bruce, *The War Lords of Washington.* New York: Harcourt, Brace and Company, Inc., 1948.

Chandler, Lester V., and Donald H. Wallace, *Economic Mobilization and Stabilization.* New York: Henry Holt and Company, Inc., 1951.

Civilian Production Administration, *Industrial Mobilization for War: History of the War Production Board and Predecessor Agencies, 1940–1945,* Vol. I, *Program and Administration.* 1947.

Connery, Robert H., *The Navy and the Industrial Mobilization in World War II.* Princeton, N.J.: Princeton University Press, 1951.

Corwin, Edward S., *Total War and the Constitution.* New York: Alfred A. Knopf, Inc., 1947.

Harris, Seymour E., *The Economics of Mobilization and Inflation.* New York: W. W. Norton & Company, Inc., 1951.

———, *Price and Related Controls in the United States.* New York: McGraw-Hill Book Company, Inc., 1945.

Janeway, Eliot, *The Struggle for Survival.* New Haven, Conn.: Yale University Press, 1951.

Lincoln, G. A., W. S. Stone, and S. H. Harvey (eds.), *Economics of National Security.* New York: Prentice-Hall, Inc., 1950.

McMillan, S. Sterling, *Individual Firm Adjustments under O.P.A.* Bloomington, Ind.: The Principia Press, Inc., 1949.

Mansfield, Harvey C., *A Short History of O.P.A.* Office of Price Administration, 1947.

Nelson, Donald A., *Arsenal of Democracy.* New York: Harcourt, Brace and Company, Inc., 1946.

Novick, David, Melvin Anshen, and W. C. Truppner, *Wartime Production Controls.* New York: Columbia University Press, 1949.

O'Brian, John L., and Manly Fleischmann, "War Production Board Administrative Policies and Procedures," 13 *George Washington Law Review* 1–60 (December, 1944).

Rossiter, Clinton L., *Constitutional Dictatorship: Crisis Government in the Modern Democracies*. Princeton, N.J.: Princeton University Press, 1948.

Scitovsky, Tibor, Edward Shaw, and Lorie Tarshis, *Mobilizing Resources for War—The Economic Alternatives*. New York: McGraw-Hill Book Company, Inc., 1951.

Somers, H. M., *Presidential Agency: OWMR, the Office of War Mobilization and Reconversion*. Cambridge, Mass.: Harvard University Press, 1950.

Thompson, Victor A., *The Regulatory Process in O.P.A. Rationing*. New York: Columbia University Press, 1950.

U.S. Bureau of the Budget, War Records Section, *The United States at War*. 1947.

U.S. Congress, Joint Committee on the Economic Report, *The Economic and Political Hazards of an Inflationary Defense Economy*, 82d Cong., 1st Sess. (1951).

Wallace, Donald H., *Economic Controls and Defense*. New York: The Twentieth Century Fund, Inc., 1953.

War Production Board, *Wartime Production Achievements and the Reconversion Outlook*. 1945.

Witney, F., *Wartime Experiences of the National Labor Relations Board, 1941–1945*. Urbana, Ill.: University of Illinois Press, 1949.

27

PUBLIC CONTROL FOR ECONOMIC STABILITY AND GROWTH

Although they may have widespread effects on the economy, the areas of public control of enterprise discussed in the previous parts of this book have been aimed at particular problems. They have been primarily controls designed to regulate such specific matters as prices, quality of service, competitive behavior, bank operation, or collective bargaining. They are thus normally limited in their application, although in such areas as agriculture and labor they are so broad as to amount almost to control of the entire economy. But despite the far-reaching effects of these controls, they are still not aimed at the economy as a whole.

When the Great Depression following 1929 ravished the nation and caused widespread unemployment, economic loss, and human distress, the public, through its national, state, and local governments, undertook to combat the depressed conditions of the 1930s with varying activities designed to bring return to prosperity. Yet these actions, gigantic as they were as compared to pre-Depression government programs, were largely inadequate to solve the problem. There were still more than 10 million unemployed persons in 1938 and 8 million in 1940. Gross national product, which reached $181 billion in 1929 (1954 prices) and dropped to $126 billion in 1933, had risen only to a level of $206 billion by 1940. Per capita product remained virtually constant between 1929 and 1940, despite a rise in productivity in the eleven-year period.

During World War II the government's purchase of goods and services (1954 prices) rose from $31 billion, or 15 per cent of gross national product, in 1940 to $150 billion, or 47 per cent of gross national product, in 1944. At the same time, unemployment dropped from approximately 8 million to 0.67 million, despite a rise in the total labor force of 10 million persons and only a slight decline of 1 million persons in the civilian labor force. This experience went far in convincing the public, as well as economists and politicians, that government activity could clearly increase gross national product and that, if this could be done for war purposes, it could likewise be done for purposes of peace.

Moreover, the war experience so increased taxes and government debt as to make government, particularly the national government, a major factor in the economy. Even with the decline in defense expenditures after World War II, the government has retained a dominant role in the economy. Government expenditures have maintained an important position, as may be noted from the fact that since 1949, when they totaled $51 billion or approximately 16 per cent of gross national product, they have remained high, being 22 per cent of gross national product in 1954.

Public opinion has been influenced by the realization that gross national product, in constant prices, has almost doubled since 1939 and that personal consumption expenditures have risen nearly 70 per cent in the same time. This unparalleled prosperity has seemed to indicate that a full-employment economy, through its encouragement of technical innovation and full utilization of human resources, can afford an extraordinary level of consumption expenditures as well as a huge expenditure for defense and nondefense government services. At the same time, the very size of government expenditures and taxes, as well as the size of national debt, has furnished a tool whereby the national government, at least, can assert exceptional control on the economy.

The Objective of Control for Economic Stability and Growth

Against the background of economic experience obtained primarily from the period of World War II, it became apparent that means were available for combating depressions. Moreover, the very growth of the economy during World War II and the rapid rise of prices brought on by deficit financing of the war led the public also to fear the recurrence after World War II of a depression reminiscent of the Great Depression following 1929, or at least a major economic readjustment of the dimensions of the 1920–1921 depression. These factors combined toward the establishment of a public policy in which there was an understandable degree of unanimity, a policy of promoting stable prosperity.

THE EMPLOYMENT ACT OF 1946

This policy was given statutory definition by the Employment Act of 1946, which states clearly the objectives of control for stable prosperity. Section 2 of this Act incorporates the following declaration of policy:

> The Congress declares that it is the continuing policy and responsibility of the Federal Government to use all practicable means consistent with its needs and obligations and other essential considerations of national policy, with the assistance and cooperation of industry, agriculture, labor, and State and local governments, to coordinate and utilize all its plans, functions, and resources for the purpose of creating and maintaining, in a manner calculated to foster and promote free competitive enterprise and the general welfare, conditions under

which they will be afforded useful employment opportunities, including self-employment, for those able, willing, and seeking to work, and to promote maximum employment, production, and purchasing power.

The Act also provides, as a means of implementing this policy, that the President must transmit to the Congress at the beginning of each regular session a report outlining current and foreseeable trends in the level of employment, production, and purchasing power, as well as reviewing the economic programs of government and establishing new programs for putting this policy into effect. To assist the President and Congress in this aim, the law provides for two agencies. One is the Council of Economic Advisers, established as a staff agency for the President to assist in this task; the other is the Joint Committee on the Economic Report of the Senate and House, whose primary function is to study the President's economic report and program proposals and guide the various committees of Congress in effecting legislation needed to meet the economic objective.

THE ELEMENTS OF ECONOMIC STABILITY AND GROWTH

It will be noted that the Employment Act of 1946 lists three basic elements in defining the objective of public control for economic stability and growth. These are full employment, stable prices,[1] and maximum production. Public policy has thus recognized that full employment is not, as is so often believed, the sole objective of over-all economic control. A highly inflationary or a very inefficient economy might provide full employment, but at great cost in terms of inequitable distribution of wealth or at a low standard of living. For this reason the objective is properly stated to include, in addition to full employment, price stabilization and maximum production. The harmful effects of rapid inflation or deflation, with the hardships wrought on persons who rely on prices under fixed price contracts, are well known. Moreover, it has wisely been understood that a public policy which does not promote increased productivity would be one which would result in stagnation of the nation's standard of living.

While not, strictly speaking, one of the objectives of the Employment Act of 1946, the provision that the federal government should accomplish these economic goals in a framework of competitive private enterprise is significant. It has clearly been the intent of the public, an intent so well expressed by Congress, to accomplish these goals without expanding gov-

[1] Although the Act refers to "maximum" purchasing power rather than stabilized prices, it is believed that what Congress intended is a stable price level. It is possible, however, to argue that Congress meant to encourage increasing income to the worker or low-income groups and thereby increase the purchasing power of the masses. However, through increased production and a stabilized level of prices, this goal would appear to be possible unless artificial restraints are placed on the distribution of income.

ernment ownership of business, which would involve utilizing some of the methods of the totalitarian states.

Economic Requisites of a Control Program

Because such broad national controls must naturally be operated with regard to basic economic factors, it might be well to review some of the economic requisites of such a program. Moreover, these controls must operate within an environment of political institutions, and there are consequently political requisites for successful operation. The economic requisites will be discussed in this section and the political ones in the following section.[2]

The objective of economic stability may be achieved through certain basic economic requisites.

DYNAMIC STABILITY OF TOTAL MONEY INCOME

If national output is to grow at an optimum rate, depending upon the size of the work force, the number of hours worked, and the increases in productivity, it is important that total money income grow at approximately the same rate of growth as national output, if a stable price level is desired, or at a rate which differs upward or downward depending upon whether it is wished to increase or decrease the level of prices. This is apparent from a simple analysis of the national economic income statement. The dollar value of gross national product must naturally equal in any year personal consumption expenditures plus private investment (for new construction, producers' durable equipment, and addition to inventories) plus government expenditures, plus net foreign investment. If, because of the availability of more or fewer dollars, this balance is not obtained, the result is necessarily either an inflation in prices, if more expenditure dollars are available than product, or a deflation in prices, if fewer expenditure dollars are available. This indicates that either government or private action (but probably government action) which changes the relationship involved could induce inflation or deflation of prices in the economy and through such action tend to encourage or discourage spending. There is strong doubt that changes in the supply of money at optimum rates can automatically be produced in the economy, thus indicating that this is an area where government action is essential.

The national-product-and-expenditure approach (see Table 27–1) also indicates that if public action can be taken to balance consumer expendi-

[2] The writers follow here the excellent analysis by G. L. Bach, "Economic Requisites for Economic Stability," 40 *American Economic Review* 155–164 (May, 1950); and Roy Blough, "Political and Administrative Requisites for Achieving Economic Stability," 40 *American Economic Review* 165–178 (May, 1950).

Table 27–1. *National Product and Expenditures, Selected Years*

(In billions of dollars, 1954 prices)

	1929	*1939*	*1944*	*1949*	*1954*
Production:					
Gross private product: farm	$ 16.7	$ 18.1	$ 20.2	$ 20.1	$ 21.3
Gross private product: nonfarm	155.0	154.9	236.1	248.3	304.1
Gross government product *	9.3	16.3	60.8	23.0	31.6
Total Gross National Product †	$181.0	$189.4	$317.1	$291.4	$357.0
Expenditures:					
Personal consumption expenditures:					
Durable goods	$ 14.6	$ 13.2	$ 8.8	$ 25.1	$ 29.0
Nondurable goods	66.4	78.3	96.3	108.2	120.5
Services	46.5	46.2	56.1	70.9	84.5
Gross private domestic investment:					
New construction	20.9	12.1	4.7	20.4	27.6
Producers' durable equipment	11.2	8.6	9.1	20.7	22.1
Changes in business inventories	2.8	0.9	—1.4	—3.4	—3.6
Net foreign investment	0.5	0.6	—6.1	—0.6	—0.6
Government purchases of goods and services:					
Federal	2.7	10.4	136.2	28.2	50.0
State and local	15.4	19.0	13.3	22.0	27.5
Total Gross National Product †	$181.0	$189.4	$317.1	$291.4	$357.0

* Includes compensation of general government employees and excludes compensation of employees in government enterprises whose operating costs are at least to a substantial extent covered by sale of goods and services. Compensation of employees of the latter type are included in gross private product, since these enterprises are essentially commercial in nature.

† Detail will not necessarily add to totals because of rounding.

SOURCE: Council of Economic Advisers, *Economic Report of the President* (January, 1955), pp. 138–141.

tures and investments with gross national product at a level of full employment, then full employment must occur. As simple as this product-and-expenditure relationship is, however, it can readily be seen that it introduces a number of complex factors. In the first place, one cannot be sure how consumers will divide their disposable income between expenditures for consumption and saving. In the second place, both private and government investment programs are subject to degrees of uncertainty in their accomplishment and to administrative problems which may thwart the attainment of a given level.[3] A third factor of extraordinary importance is the difficulty of measuring and forecasting the components of gross national product. The components themselves are simple, but it is difficult to forecast exact changes in productivity, in size of the labor force, or in the average work week beyond one or two years into the future. With these uncertainties a fairly simple economic principle becomes difficult to apply, although the statistical and analytical work which has been done in recent years by both government and private agencies shows promise of refining the data upon which action must be taken.

CONSISTENCY BETWEEN INCOME CLAIMS AND MONEY INCOME

In addition to the uncertainties pointed out above in measuring the elements of the national income statement and in effecting action to carry out a given policy, there are problems as to whether the owners of production resources, including labor, will actually offer their resources at prices consistent with the optimum gross national product under conditions of free employment. One of the requisites is that they do so. Obviously, if inflexible prices of any production resource exist, whether inflexibly high or inflexibly low, there is danger that resources will not be utilized to their fullest extent. While perfect price flexibility is probably unnecessary, administered pricing, if carried far enough to affect the entire economy, is certainly inconsistent with maximum resource utilization.

In other words, if an industry sets its prices at a given level and productivity increases materially, there is a danger that the increased productivity cannot be passed on to consumers because of their unwillingness or inability to buy. Or if wages are increased faster than rises in productivity,

[3] For example, Secretary of Defense C. E. Wilson is believed to have found that simple administrative frictions made it impossible for him to change policy direction readily in 1953 and 1954. In 1953, his laudable attempt to make sure that the American taxpayer received a full dollar's worth for each dollar of expense slowed up the granting of defense contracts considerably. In late 1953 and early 1954, when a recession became apparent, he is believed further to have found that a policy favoring rapid acceleration of letting contracts required many months to effectuate through the huge administrative structure of his Department, merely because of the time required to change policy, procedure, and administrative action through so large an organization.

the same danger exists, because sellers of products may be forced to increase their prices disproportionately so as to cause unbalances in the structure of prices and production, with probable reduction in amount of product demanded. Also, such increases may adversely affect incentives for risk capital, with consequent reduction in production.

These types of inflexibility have been fairly well camouflaged in recent years because of the rise in price levels which tends to act as a corrective. With stabilized prices there is ever the danger that price inflexibility may interfere seriously with the operation of the economic system. This economic principle does, as the reader will immediately see, argue in favor of a vigorous kind of competition.

The inflexibilities which may cause the most difficulty are those which are accomplished under government sponsorship. The support of agricultural prices may be cited as a case at point. While agricultural productivity is increasing and the need for agricultural products remains high, government-supported prices for food and other items have tended to restrict consumer purchases of these commodities. This kind of thing can, of course, be upsetting to the balance of the nation's economy, especially where the resources committed to a supported industry cannot be easily shifted to another use.

PROGNOSIS

One of the truly important requisites, which is both economic and administrative in nature, is a proper prognosis of the immediate and long-range future. As in any case of control, one cannot control the past. But if a program of public policy must be aimed at controlling the future, it then becomes important to be able to forecast the future so that action can be taken which will modify any undesirable trends detected. The necessity for such action was well recognized in the Employment Act of 1946 when it required the President to report "foreseeable trends in the levels of employment, production, and purchasing power." But foreseeing the future is inadequate unless such a forecast is accompanied by a skillful diagnosis of the economic factors causing deviations from a desired course and of the actions required in returning the economy to it.

The approach to such an analysis is facilitated by calculation of economic models. These are simply tabulations of the various elements of gross national product, national income or expenditures under assumptions of full employment, stable prices, or a predetermined level of productivity. On the basis of these models and a considerable skill in analysis, judgments can be reached as to the course the economy is expected to follow and the steps which should be taken to force a modification of this course, if the forecast indicates an otherwise undesirable future.

Political Requisites of a Control Program

If, as seems almost certainly to be the case, stabilization for prosperity cannot be obtained without considerable government action, questions as to the political and administrative requisites of such a control program arise. As many technical experts have found in both business and government, it is one thing to be able to analyze a problem and come up with a feasible measure for its solution and often quite another to be able to put these measures into effect. In all kinds of group activity there are problems involved in getting a policy accepted and understood by the group, in getting the solution coordinated with other programs, and in translating policy or program into effective action. Government, being the largest and most complex organized group of all, understandably gives rise to political and administrative questions and difficulties of extraordinary proportions. Even so large an industrial empire as the General Motors Corporation shrinks into relative insignificance when compared to the size and complexity of the federal government of the United States.

ECONOMIC UNDERSTANDING

One of the primary, and often least understood, political prerequisites for a control program is a fairly high degree of economic sophistication on the part of government policy makers and administrators. Economic programs have tremendous impact on various interest groups and on other government programs. Under the American democratic system both the legislative and executive branches owe their position of leadership and influence to the ballot box. As a result, they are naturally influenced by constituent group reactions to economic policy and by the effects of this policy on government programs in which they have an interest. Moreover, what those in Congress, in the presidency, or in charge of the various branches of government do not understand, they are not likely to support, as they might thereby risk their political standing. This reluctance is clearly greater in the case of economic phenomena than in that of the natural or physical sciences. The very social nature of economics and its immediate concern to so many people, plus the fact that most people feel that they know something about the subject, accentuate the natural disinclination to follow economic advice unless it is fully comprehended.

There exists, then, a need for the politician and the government administrator to develop a fairly high degree of comprehension in economic analysis and policy. While this can never be expected to reach the level of the professional economist, the degree must be adequate for understanding of the nature and solution of economic problems. Effective business managers have found that subordinates more enthusiastically and efficiently follow out a course of action which they understand. This would seem to be a good objective for government economic policy. In fact, it appears to the authors to be a requisite.

Moreover, since the voting public must be satisfied with economic policy and since the ramifications of government action in this area reach into the everyday lives of so many people, it appears to be a requisite also that a reasonably adequate degree of economic understanding be possessed by the public. As one writer has said: [4]

> I suggest that in the absence of spectacular achievements comparable to the discovery of the atom bomb, the economist will not achieve the confidence of the public until its members are more highly sophisticated in economics than they are today. It is only too easy for a clever man running for office or sponsoring a bill to make fools of the economists in the eyes of an uninformed public.

The need for economic understanding has been made even more important by the lack of agreement among economists themselves in matters of public economic policy. Some of this difference stems from the rather crude state of economic science and the fact that social action does not lend itself to the techniques of the laboratory or the exactness of higher mathematics. Some of the difference has been due also to a failure among economists to distinguish between matters of data, where the lack of exact information may cause real differences of opinion, and matters of analysis. However, on this score, not only have strides been made in perfecting basic economic data but the national-income approach to analysis has brought forth a very considerable uniformity in analytical techniques and principles.

Furthermore, some of the lack of agreement among economists is more apparent than real. There are many persons who pose as economists and who seem to the uninformed to be such but who neither have been properly trained nor have studied carefully the data upon which economic judgments have been made. It is true that the record of economists leaves much to be desired, and both the public and government legislators and administrators have, at times, rightfully been disillusioned by economic analyses and predictions. In all, however, there does seem to be arising an improved public understanding of national economics and a much higher level of professional economic analysis, with far greater unanimity of conclusions among economists.

FLEXIBLE GOVERNMENT ACTION

A second major requisite of government control of the economy for stable prosperity is the need for speed, definiteness, and thoroughness of

[4] Blough, *op. cit.*, p. 170.

government action. It obviously does little good to foresee difficulties and to know what to do to avoid them and thereby gain desired goals if the government, as an organizational entity, cannot move. The problem of flexibility arises primarily from two factors. In the first place, the American government, being a representative democracy with a plural policy-making body in the form of the Congress, suffers from the delays inherent in all group decision making, delays which are augmented by the traditional reluctance of elected representatives to give too much power to the executive branch. In the second place, the very size of the national government establishment makes it administratively difficult to translate a policy into effective action quickly.

The problems of legislative and administrative flexibility and celerity are exceedingly disquieting. Particularly for the short run, quick action is imperative if recessions or dangerous booms are to be controlled. Large business firms attempt to maintain a degree of flexibility whereby moderate changes of plans can be made in periods of one to six months, since they know that market, sales, or cost conditions can undergo important changes in that short a period. This kind of flexibility appears to be required of the government. The recession of early 1954 became apparent to many business and government economists some six months before it occurred. Yet, as will be discussed later in this chapter, the government found it difficult to shape necessary policy to combat it and was unable to do so until the recession was well under way.

COORDINATION OF GOVERNMENT ACTION

The complexity of the structure of government and the variety of programs in effect make difficult the task of effectuating control of economic policy. But this complexity and variety require that effective control be obtained through coordination of government actions. There are few areas of government activity which do not affect employment, prices, or productivity. In these areas, the goal is normally not to increase employment, stabilize prices, or encourage productivity but rather to protect investors, aid farmers, regulate public utilities, eliminate unfair competitive practices, or purchase defense matériel. There are thus many completely legitimate goals other than stable economic prosperity. One cannot blame an agency in placing uppermost in its planning the attainment of objectives which Congress has established for it and by which Congress and the people judge its performance. Yet the objective of stable prosperity can normally not be achieved unless every major resource of the government is utilized in that direction. This clearly requires coordination and integration of government policy.

Government Tools of Control for Economic Stability and Growth

The tools by which government can control the entire economy are many and varied. The very size and importance of the government in the economy naturally gives it leverage whereby its actions will influence materially the direction of employment, prices, and productivity. The principal tools may be summarized largely by reference to their effect upon gross national product and upon the expenditure of this product. In other words, the economy may be influenced upward or downward by measures which tend to increase or decrease gross product or measures which tend to augment or diminish expenditures for personal consumption, for private domestic or foreign investment, or for government uses. Some of these tools, such as mortgage insurance to encourage residential construction, are specific in their application; other tools, notably monetary and fiscal policies, tend to be so general in their application as to affect most phases of production and expenditure.

MONETARY POLICY

One of the most far-reaching tools of government control of the economy is the regulation of the volume of money and credit and the terms upon which they are available to consumers and investors. While economists differ as to the major effectiveness of monetary policy in controlling the economy,[5] none would deny its pervasiveness. The instruments of government monetary policy may be grouped into those which encourage or discourage lending institutions to grant credit and those selective credit controls which tend to act directly on the consumer or business spender of funds.

In its program to encourage or discourage bank lending, the government may lower or raise the rediscount rate of the Federal Reserve banks, it may engage in open-market operations, or it may change member-bank reserve requirements. The Federal Reserve Act under which the central banking system of the United States was established provided for the rediscounting of commercial paper (commercial bank loans made by member banks) by member banks with the various Federal Reserve banks. By so doing, the member banks are given funds which bolster their reserves

[5] R. A. Gordon, in his *Business Fluctuations* (New York: Harper & Brothers, 1952), p. 513, states that "there has been some renewed emphasis on monetary policy during the inflationary years since World War II, but most economists today (though not all) assign to it a secondary place in their proposals for stabilizing the economy." On the other hand, the President's Council of Economic Advisers in 1955 rated monetary policy as a "powerful instrument of economic recovery." (See *Economic Report of the President, January, 1955*, p. 22.)

and enable them to make additional loans. In a sense, then, the Federal Reserve banks act as wholesalers of credit—on an expansible basis, however, since member banks' loans can be much greater than their reserves. The Federal Reserve banks exercise control not only through their ability to review the quality of paper subject to rediscount but primarily through the rate at which the paper is discounted. Thus, if credit expansion is deemed desirable, the Reserve banks may lower the rediscount rate; if contraction of credit is desired, they may raise the rate. Moreover, since the funds obtained or withheld by rediscount become a part of the member bank's reserves and can be used for multiple deposits, the freeing or limiting of funds through rediscount is designed to have a far more than proportionate effect on bank lending. As a matter of fact, however, banks have preferred to hold their commercial paper and to obtain funds to expand reserves in other ways, primarily through sale of government bonds, so that the direct effect of the rediscount rate has been negligible because of the extremely small volume of paper submitted for rediscount. Yet the raising or lowering of the rediscount rate has had an important psychological influence on credit, since it has been regarded as an indicator of government monetary policy.

Perhaps the principal reason why the rediscount rate has not been a strong tool of control is the dominance in monetary expansion of a second tool, open-market operations. The Federal Reserve banks have the power to sell or buy government securities. If the Federal Reserve banks buy government securities in the open market, they create additional funds in cash or deposits which usually become bank deposits, increase the reserves of the member banks, and thereby expand their power to lend. If, for example, member banks need have only 20 per cent reserves back of deposits, the sale of 1 million of government securities can result in support for $5 million in bank loans. If the Federal Reserve sells securities, the reverse takes place. It is interesting to note in this connection that the Federal Reserve banks tend to have a virtually inexhaustible supply of reserves for buying government securities, since the law allows them to use these securities as a part of their reserves.[6]

Thus the government, through the Board of Governors of the Federal Reserve System, has a strong instrument for expanding or contracting credit. But, as a practical matter, this power has some limitations. After all, member banks have a considerable voice in the affairs of the Federal Reserve banks, and they, in turn, have much influence on the Board of

[6] In 1955 the law required the Federal Reserve banks to hold reserves of 25 per cent of their deposits in gold certificates, but the remainder could be made up of government bonds and eligible commercial paper. However, Congress has shown a ready willingness to increase or decrease this reserve if greater or less expansion is desired.

Governors. Moreover, the Treasury Department, with its concern for keeping the cost of financing government bonds low, has tended to press for an easy money policy and to ask the Federal Reserve to buy bonds in the open market when prices show a tendency to fall.[7] In addition, the acquisition of a tremendous volume of government securities by the banks and insurance companies during and after World War II tended to make it inexpedient from the standpoint of investment to allow the price of governments to fall to any great extent.

A third tool of monetary policy is the power of the Federal Reserve Board to change reserve requirements of member banks. While currently limited by statute to a range of legal reserves of 10 to 20 per cent of deposits, the Federal Reserve Board can order changes within this range. Clearly, if the reserve requirements are increased, member banks are forced to restrict their loans, and if the requirements are decreased, they have the lending base to increase loans. Changes in reserve requirements have been frequently made in recent years and have served as a powerful tool of credit control.

A fourth type of monetary control which has often been effective is the selective control of credit. Since 1934, the Federal Reserve has had the power to regulate the percentage of margin necessary in the purchase of securities. It has likewise had at various times the power to regulate the terms on which banking institutions can make consumer loans (for example, automobile, appliance, and similar loans), and in recent years the Federal Reserve has established controls over noninsured mortgages. Since the 1930s, the federal housing agencies have had control over the insurance of loans for new residential and commercial construction and improvements; in exercising this control under the various statutes, these agencies have greatly influenced credit through establishing such conditions as the amount required for down payment and the length of the loan repayment period. Credit controls have existed also through the many credit facilities available to agriculture, railroads, and other businesses. Clearly, the government, in establishing the terms under which credit is granted, may encourage or discourage its use.

It can be readily seen that monetary controls are much more effective in controlling a boom than in pulling the economy out of a depression. If banks have made loans in amounts approaching their limits, reduction of reserves is likely to be very effective in curbing an expansion. How-

[7] During World War II and until 1951 the Treasury Department was fairly successful in prevailing on the Federal Reserve to support the government-security market by purchases. In 1951, after several years of conflict between the Treasury and the Federal Reserve, an "accord" was reached by which the Federal Reserve Board was relieved of its obligation to act as a market-pegging agency for the Treasury Department.

ever, even in a period of credit expansion, banks may have sizable reserves so that monetary controls are often far less sensitive than the above recital of the machinery might imply.

In a depressed economy, such as existed in the 1930s, banks may not be willing to lend even though they have the reserves to do so, and businesses may be unwilling to borrow even if the credit is available. Likewise, lowering credit restrictions may not make the market investor willing to buy stock or the consumer willing to buy automobiles. On the other hand, an environment favorable to credit expansion is important in encouraging utilization of credit if other measures can be taken to stimulate spending or if the psychological resistance to expansion is not too great.

FISCAL POLICY

Government fiscal policy has to do with the volume and management of government expenditures and tax receipts. With the national government taking such a major role in the economy, particularly during and since World War II, the amount which government spends and taxes has become a major determinant of the level of employment and prices and, through its effect on demand and profits, a major force influencing productivity. Note that the level of government expenditures and taxes must be high to ensure this control. When the federal government operated on a budget of $4 billion, as it did in the early 1930s, and spent less than 3 per cent of the gross national product, it could not be a determining factor in the national economy. But with the level of expenditures of recent years, the power of government fiscal policy, so well illustrated during World War II, has become exceedingly great.

There are several ways that government fiscal policy can control the economy. Even with a balanced budget, a rise or drop in government expenditures can increase or decrease employment. While the locality and industry affected will naturally reflect the kind of product for which the government increases or reduces expenditures,[8] the effect on the economy is definite and positive. However, the effect is relatively greater if the government spends more than it receives in taxes, thereby tending to stimulate private spending and increase prices through an increase of the money supply relative to production. Unless the "inflationary gap" created by a deficit in the cash budget [9] is so great and continues so long as to undermine seriously the confidence of the public in its monetary system, this stimulation can be expected to continue. By the same token, a policy of taxing heavily relative to spending and creating a cash budget

[8] For example, when defense spending was slowed in late 1953 the effect was keenly felt in such areas as Detroit and Los Angeles.

[9] Note that it is the unbalance of the cash budget which has the fiscal effects discussed here. "Paper" expenditures or receipts obviously do not affect money supply.

surplus reduces the supply of funds available for private spending and tends to discourage such spending. The more positive and definite effects on the economy thus come primarily from budget deficits or surpluses, rather than any change in a level of government spending—assuming, of course, that the amounts involved are large enough to influence the total economy.

To some extent, the elements of the government fiscal program provide automatic stabilization of the economy. As incomes fall, taxes fall, thereby reducing some of the effect of the fall in incomes. At the same time, because government spending programs do not usually fall so fast as taxes, there tends to be a budgetary deficit which, in turn, acts as a stimulant to spending. The reverse tends also to be true. Furthermore, government expenditures for unemployment-insurance benefits, for old-age insurance, and for agricultural aids under parity programs tend to rise automatically with a drop in income and a rise in unemployment.

But there are few who believe that the automatic stabilizers in government fiscal policy are adequate to control the economy and fewer still who believe that the public should take a chance that they are adequate. Clearly, a positive program of either increasing government expenditures or reducing taxes, or both, would furnish a strong weapon against recession; and an opposite program would be a potent force against excessive boom. Within the area of government expenditures are such projects as public-works expenditures (although these are difficult to get under way speedily), increased defense expenditures, accelerated stockpiling of materials for defense uses, liberalization of unemployment compensation (although the key role of the states in these makes quick action difficult), or furnishing freer credit aids to businesses and consumers.

Perhaps the most readily available weapon for attacking threatened recession or boom is the income tax. If it were politically feasible, a quick lowering or increasing of income taxes, patricularly at the low and middle ranges of the income scale, could have an immediate and strong influence on the economy. With the use of withholding taxes, a rise in the level of personal exemptions could place dollars in the hands of every wage earner in the country within a very short period of time. Likewise, a reduction in exemptions could do the reverse. While this kind of tool, being fairly regressive in nature, is probably politically unfeasible, at least as regards increasing taxes, it does demonstrate how quickly expenditures could be influenced through the use of the tax system. Obviously, this is not the only means by which taxes could be reduced or increased, although it appears to be one of the most practicable if immediate results are desired.

The income tax can also be useful as a means of stimulating private investment. Major examples of government policy in this direction include lowering the tax rate on high incomes, liberalizing provisions whereby businesses can charge off depreciation on new investment, and lowering corporate taxes so that more funds are available for expansion and new investment becomes more attractive.

It must be recognized that fiscal policies should be integrated with monetary policies. The financing of deficits or surpluses necessarily affects the money market. With a federal government debt of approximately $279 billion in 1954, there were approximately $229 billion held by others than the federal government. Of the total held outside the various investment accounts of the federal government, the Federal Reserve and com-

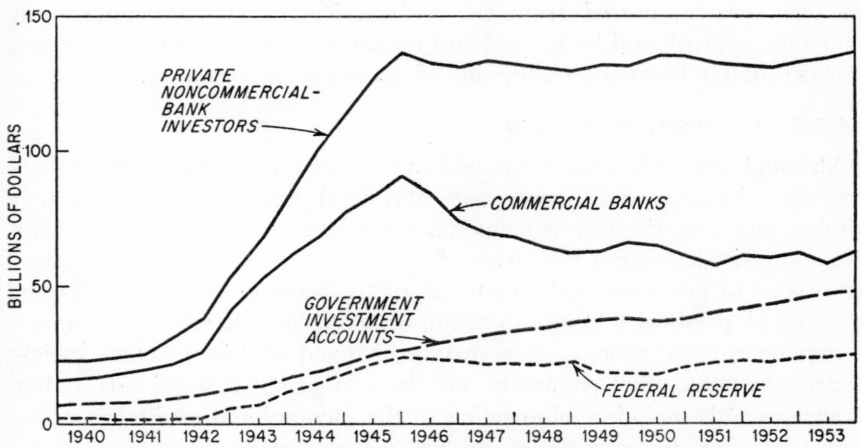

Figure 27–1. Ownership of United States Government Securities

Source: The Conference Board, *Road Maps of Industry*, No. 962 (June 4, 1954).

mercial banks held $95 billion and savings banks and insurance companies an additional $24 billion. Thus, deficit financing has been heavily supported by the banks of the nation. This has both good and bad effects from the point of view of economic stabilization. If the debt were held by the public and if deficit financing were handled by sale of government securities to the public, a deficit spending policy would have limited effect in stimulating spending. It would also be much more difficult for a budget surplus to be used as a means of curtailing private spending. On the other hand, the very fact that so much of the debt has been financed through the banks, particularly the commercial banks, creates other problems. The ability of the banks to sell their securities, particularly to the Federal Reserve banks, gives them a means of rapidly increasing their loan base through increasing their reserves. If the Federal Reserve does not support the price of government bonds, the result is some financial disorganization through drop in asset values of the banks and other institutional investors and considerable difficulty for the Treasury to finance the debt.[10] With rises in interest rates, the expense of financing the debt rises, and the Treasury understandably tends to do more short-term financing, thus increasing the amount of borrowing that must be done each year.

Yet, as was found in the postwar years to 1951, if the Federal Reserve pegs government-bond prices at a high level in order to reduce interest costs, its purchase of bonds increases bank reserves. In so pegging the prices, the Federal Reserve loses much of its power to expand or contract credit. Fortunately, from the standpoint of economic control, the Treasury desire for stabilizing government-security interest rates at low levels has been partly severed from the Federal Reserve Board's interest in monetary control, and both fiscal and monetary controls can be expected to work better from the standpoint of economic stabilization.

CONTROL OF ECONOMY EXPENDITURES

Although the subject has already been discussed in large part in connection with the basic tools of monetary and fiscal policies, it may be worth emphasizing that the government has many methods at its disposal for increasing or decreasing the levels of spending for personal consumption for private or governmental investment or for foreign investment. Within the area of personal consumption, important tools whereby the amount of income available to consumers may be changed are income taxes, social-security benefits, relief payments, and the various agricultural aids. Other means available include the changing of the income- and excise-tax structures to make them more or less progressive, so that funds are granted to, or withheld from, low-income families, since they are more sensitive to consumer expenditures than the families with higher incomes. While changes of this kind can effectively be made in the long run, they may not be very feasible in the short period. It may be possible to grant tax relief to low-income families to combat a recession, but to apply this regressive principle in times of boom may prove to be difficult. Even though most tax experts and social scientists tend to believe that this tool has serious limitations in practice, it is not at all uncertain that, once an informed public recognized the immediacy and effectiveness of such a tool, it would prove to be impracticable.

The propensity to consume can also be influenced by a government policy favoring high wages even at the expense of profits. However, unless an economy is expanding and opportunities for profits still exist despite such pressures, there is a danger that a wage-increase policy, if not con-

[10] The magnitude of this job even in times of fairly stable budgets can be ascertained from the fact that in 1954 nearly two-fifths of the privately held marketable federal debt was due within one year. See *Managing the Federal Debt* (New York: Committee for Economic Development, 1954), p. 10.

sonant with increases in productivity, will discourage expenditures for private investment and thereby defeat the stabilizing effects of higher consumer expenditures. Also, because of the fact that wages, particularly with the existing degree of unionization, are especially inflexible on the down side, this tool is useful only as a stimulant to the economy.

An important tool for the control of consumption expenditures is the direct control of consumer credit. Rules for the amount of down payment and payment period for consumer durable goods have been especially influential in stimulating or discouraging consumer expenditures.

Control of the private-domestic-investment segment of national expenditures must recognize the existence of the three basic components: business plant and equipment, residential construction, and inventories. As for business plant and equipment, perhaps the major tool which has been used is tax policy. Through such devices as permitting accelerated depreciation in calculating business earnings and reducing the rate of taxes on business, as well as through the pervasive effects of monetary policy, the government has influenced private investment in plant and equipment. However, perhaps the greatest influence has been in the imposition or removal of roadblocks to the operation of private investment, a point to be discussed presently.

The principal tools for controlling residential construction have, of course, been connected with credit aids. Mortgage insurance and the conditions under which it is granted, including the size of down payments, interest rates, and the period for repayment of principal, have been relied on primarily in this area. In addition, various aids to builders, the sale or lease of government land, encouragement to rural electrification, and other aid programs have furnished means for stimulating residential construction.

Controls to expand or contract inventories have been largely in the field of monetary policy. But aids through credit facilities, such as the guaranteed defense loans of World War II and after, have played an important part. Perhaps the principal controls over business inventories have occurred as the result of the economic program as a whole. Periods of inflation tend to encourage expenditure for inventory and periods of deflation the opposite. But, as can be seen, the influences of inflation are not in the direction of economic stability; instead, they run counter to it. On the other hand, if the government should desire inventory accumulations, the creation of a rising price level, along with adequate credit facilities, would certainly stimulate such a rise.

Foreign investment has tended to receive government attention disproportionate to its economic importance to the domestic economy because of the international political implications involved. Various credit aids for foreign investment exist, and the government has undertaken at times to give direct subsidies to foreign investment. From an economic point of view, the effect of such expenditures is primarily that they tend to create shortages and so support or increase prices. This stimulation may consequently be a significant factor in increasing production and employment, but the same effect could be obtained if the production were dumped into the ocean. Thus, foreign investment has generally been only of moderate importance as a tool of economic stability, although the Marshall Plan did stimulate domestic production and remove many agricultural surpluses after World War II, thereby doubtless doing much temporarily to stabilize prices.

As has already been noted in the discussion of fiscal controls, a major factor in controlling the economy is the level and nature of government spending. Experience with wartime expenditures and the high level of defense expenditures in recent years cannot but impress one with the power of government expenditures. In fact, the programming of public-works expenditures is generally looked upon as one of the powerful economic stabilization tools of the federal, state, and local governments of the nation. There have been many attempts to program public works so that they may act as counterweights to economic booms and depressions. It has properly been reasoned that, if expenditures are to be made for public facilities over any given period of years, they might as well be programmed to coincide with periods of recession.

There are several difficulties with the use of public works as instruments of national economic control. In the first place, public works require considerable planning, and even when projects are planned for in advance, months may elapse between a decision to go ahead and the actual commencement of work. They are, then, not suitable for quick action to combat a threatened business downturn. In the second place, because of the immobility of labor, it may not be possible quickly to move the unemployed skills in the localities of unemployment to the area and for the employment for which the public-works program is desired. A third problem is that, unless public-works programs are combined with deficit spending, the stimulating effect may be lost in the rise in government taxes. Finally, it is often not possible to delay public works until a recession appears to be at hand. The experience of the past fifteen years indicates that many public programs for highways, water supply, and public schools have been so badly delayed that public need requires their building whether or not the economy requires the stimulus of such construction. But from the standpoint of combating any possible recession or depression in the foreseeable future, it can be said that the need for additional public assets is so great as to furnish a stimulating backlog for production and employment providing the political and administrative machinery are available to make expenditure possible.

ENLARGING THE OPPORTUNITIES OF COMPETITIVE ENTERPRISE

In analyzing the major tools available for government control of the entire economy, the importance of enlarging the opportunities for competitive enterprise should not be overlooked. This is especially important for meeting the objective of full employment and increased production. It does rather little good to manipulate monetary and fiscal policy for the benefit of economic stability and growth under the guidance of private enterprise if government policies in other areas either place, or fail to remove, obstacles in the path of private enterprise. To be sure, public enterprise *can* replace private enterprise, and some of the goals of economic stability and growth can be attained. But in the interests of freedom and the kind of efficiency and happiness which the American system has proved can come from freedom, a major objective of control of the economy should be to encourage the operation of private competitive enterprise.

A number of government policies operate in this direction. The policy of the government to encourage competition and restrict monopolistic practices tends to give to the American economy a vigor and efficiency which can hardly be possible under government regulation of the management decisions of industry. Experience has amply proved that rivalry, freedom, and individual reward in the operations of business enterprise lead to results superior to those under centralized control and planning. In obtaining new products and their development, low costs, and low prices, history has proved the efficacy of a private-enterprise system.

The policy of government in enforcing competition wherever possible leads to a flexibility in the adjustment of production to demand, while maintaining incentives for increasing production, that no authoritarian system—in peacetime, at least—has been able to achieve. One of the reasons, of course, why the dispersal of decision making involved in competitive enterprise is so important in peacetime is that the precise objectives of planning are so diverse that a central government authority is a poor substitute for the action of millions of consumers expressing their demands through price and the market place. On the other hand, during war, the goals of an important portion of the economy are rather clear and centralized planning is more effective.

Even in the regulated industries, such as the public utilities, where competition is limited or eliminated through government policy, American traditions have favored utilization of private rather than public enterprise. Consequently, in these industries as well as in competitive industries, an important government tool leading to stability and growth is the removal of roadblocks to the operation of private enterprise and encouragement to private investment and industrial expansion.

The national and state governments can contribute to growth of private enterprise in a number of ways. In addition to curbing monopolistic tendencies, not only of business but of labor, agriculture, and other segments of the economy, the government may encourage private enterprise by limiting its own expansion into fields where private enterprise can operate. The encouragement of private enterprise, rather than government operations, in the field of atomic energy may be cited as a laudable case in point. Through providing for accelerated depreciation, the expense write-off of research and development, the protection of advantages from capital gains, and the fair treatment of corporate taxes and taxes on dividends, tax laws may be revised so as to furnish a climate for industrial growth.

Another major area in which government may contribute to growth and stability of competitive enterprise is in the removal of regulations, unnecessary for the protection of important public interests, which strangle private enterprise in its operations. Many regulations have grown from past needs which no longer exist. Others have been imposed at the insistence of interest groups and have little or no justification from the broad public interest. Perhaps an example of the strangling effect of regulations, many of which are obsolete and which interfere unnecessarily with the operation of private enterprise, are the detailed controls of the railroad industry, dealt with earlier in this book. Similar question may be raised with respect to the state fair-trade laws which limit price competition at the retail level.

Furthermore, in its proper scope of activities the government itself can contribute to private-enterprise growth. One such area is the field of education in all its applications, from mere literacy to scientific investigation and research. As was pointed out in the 1955 *Economic Report of the President*: [11]

> Among the activities essential to economic progress and in which there is a large public interest is the field of education, extending from education for literacy to the highest reaches of theoretical inquiry. Scientific and technical knowledge, research and development programs, and industrial innovation and its diffusion are the wellsprings of an increasing output per man-hour, upon which our hopes for a better life and more leisure in the future largely depend. An enlightened public policy must therefore focus attention upon augmenting the number of young people who have scientific, engineering, and technical skills; upon encouraging creative thinking and invention; upon inducing business enterprises and nonprofit organizations to support expanding programs of research; upon enlarging the range and depth of Federal research and development programs in fields that cannot be covered adequately by private efforts; and upon hastening the industrial application of new methods and ideas through new investments.

[11] P. 4.

But to encourage innovation and advance will be of questionable value if public policy is not also designed to encourage a spirit of enterprise by protecting the fruits of such enterprise. Reasonable protection afforded through patents and copyrights and a tax system which will make it possible for innovation and enterprise to be rewarded by retention on the part of individuals of a significant part of these fruits are among some of the most powerful tools for economic growth.

Managing Controls for Growth and Stability

The preceding sections have briefly analyzed the major tools available to government for control of the economy in the interest of maintaining stability while encouraging growth and have outlined some of the more important requisites for such control. In so doing they have highlighted the problem of managing these controls. There is every reason to believe that the economy can be controlled in the interest of growth and stability, while maintaining a system predominantly one of private competitive enterprise, if we have the political, economic, and administrative adeptness to do so. There is always the danger of doing too much too late or too soon, or of doing the wrong things because of honest differences of opinion or on account of political considerations which reflect individual or local interests rather than the broad public interest.

MACHINERY ESTABLISHED BY THE EMPLOYMENT ACT OF 1946

As was noted at the beginning of this chapter, the Employment Act of 1946 (1) required that the President submit to Congress an economic report setting forth economic trends and prospects and a program for meeting the objectives of economic stability and growth; (2) created a Council of Economic Advisers (comprised of a chairman and two other members) to assist the President in the development of his economic program; and (3) established a Joint Committee on the Economic Report with members from both the Senate and House of Representatives to evaluate the President's economic program and to develop means of coordinating the various programs of Congress so that the goals of the Employment Act may be attained.

While the Employment Act of 1946 creates very little new authority for the management of the national economic program, it does provide means whereby the programs established by Congress and administered by the President may be designed so as to focus attention on the objectives of economic stability and growth. It thus establishes staff service agencies in the executive branch and in the Congress whereby the powers already residing in these major segments of government can be harnessed toward the goals desired. It really adds no new authority for centralized management of the economy, and there is little of an automatic nature in the law or the agencies created. But by establishing agencies which must study and recommend and which must appraise the various programs of government in their impact upon stability and growth, the law does establish important advisory machinery for better management of the economy through already established means.

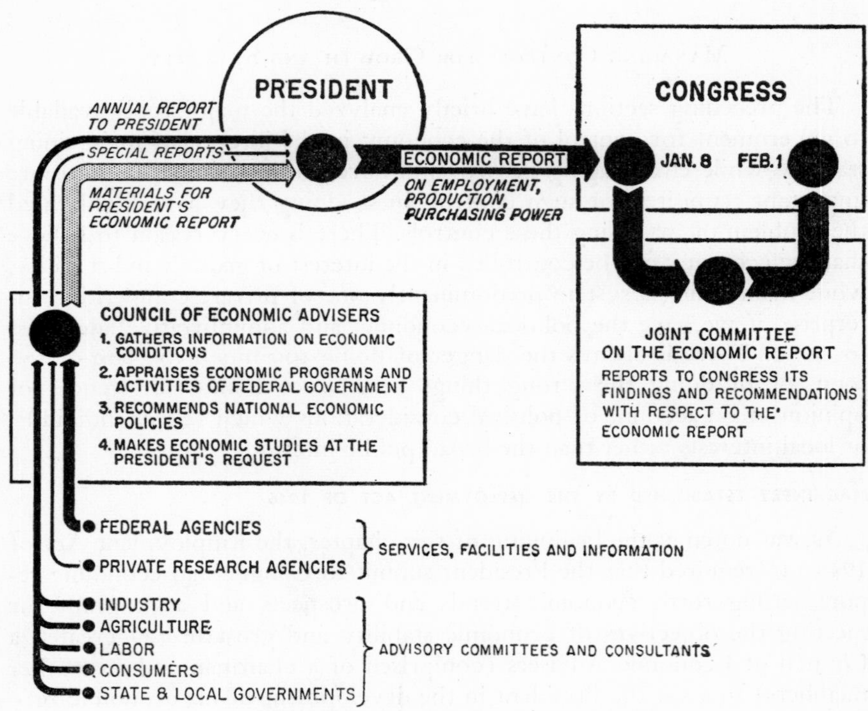

Figure 27–2. Mechanics of the Employment Act of 1946

Source: *Report of Council of Economic Advisers* (December, 1947).

From the standpoint of the executive branch of the federal government, the Council of Economic Advisers is the key instrument.[12] In addition to assisting the President in the preparation of the Economic Report, the Council is empowered by law (1) to gather timely and authoritative information concerning economic developments and trends, both current and prospective; (2) to analyze and interpret this in the light of the objectives of the law; (3) to submit studies relating to such data to the

[12] For assistance in analyzing the work of the Council, the writers are indebted to former member Neil H. Jacoby, whose addresses and unpublished papers in the first half of 1955 have been extremely helpful.

President; (4) to appraise the various programs and activities of the federal government and make appropriate recommendations to the President as to how these programs may contribute to the goals of the law; (5) to develop programs for growth and stability and recommend them to the President; and (6) make such other economic studies and recommendations as the President may request. In addition to these statutory duties, the President, by Reorganization Plan No. 9 of 1953, established an Advisory Board on Economic Growth, headed by the Chairman of the Council of Economic Advisers and including (as later amended) top representation (usually at the Undersecretary or Assistant Administrator or Director level) from the Departments of the Treasury, State, Agriculture, Commerce, and Labor, the Bureau of the Budget, the Board of Governors of the Federal Reserve System, and the White House Office. This body, which meets regularly, has been an important instrument for regular coordination of government activities and policies with the program and goals of the Employment Act.[13]

From the standpoint of the legislative branch of the government, the Joint Committee on the Economic Report is the key agency of the program. This Committee, comprised of seven members from the Senate and an equal number from the House, has the statutory functions of (1) making a continuing study of matters relating to the Economic Report; (2) studying means of coordinating legislative programs in the interest of economic stability and growth; and (3) guiding the various committees of Congress considering legislation bearing upon the problems and recommendations of the Economic Report. It is thus a staff service agency for the legislative branch as the Council is for the executive branch. Like the Council, it has no specific authority to effectuate any of its findings except through its ability to sell its recommendations to Congress.

OPERATION OF THE COUNCIL OF ECONOMIC ADVISERS

Like any staff service agency, the Council of Economic Advisers will be successful only to the extent that the members and their staffs are competent to deal with the problems involved and that the agency's superior, the President, will utilize their services. Technical competence in analyzing and appraising economic forces and programs is naturally an indispensable quality of the Council members. But it should also be recognized that the Council, like any staff organization, must be able to communicate technical advice and to sell ideas effectively if it is to succeed.

[13] The Advisory Board has been backed by an Auxiliary Staff Committee, composed of top economists of the agencies represented on the Board. The Board has also been assisted by interagency task forces established by the Council to investigate special economic problem areas and report to the Board or the Council.

In the first few years of the Council's life, the members often regarded themselves as individuals and took different points of view on the proper direction of economic policy. This tended to lead to some public confusion and to some lack of confidence in the Council. Also, there were evidences that the President attempted to use the Council as an instrument of selling legislative programs, rather than as a staff advisory agency.[14]

These factors highlighted a fundamental dilemma of the Council. If its members were to be three of the most distinguished economists of the nation, one might expect them to act honestly and independently in recommending economic action for the people of the United States.[15] On the other hand, if the Council's responsibility is to act primarily as an adviser to the President, there would appear to be some obligation for the members to express their independent views internally, rather than publicly, with the President having the full right to reject or accept any or all of their views. Moreover, there seems to be much merit in former member Roy Blough's suggestion that, since the Council is in an advisory role to the President, it cannot be so independent as to undermine the position of the President with Congress or the public and that the advisory relationship with the President is such as to require "in the usual case only people with the same general pattern of values and beliefs as the President." [16]

When President Eisenhower came to the White House in 1953, there were grave doubts whether the Council would be continued, and for a time the President operated with an Economic Adviser. After a few months, however, the President stated his determination to utilize the Council with one major change—that the Council would act through its Chairman who was made responsible for transmitting the recommendations and advice of the agency to the President and, through him, to the Congress and the public. The President also carefully selected other members, not with a view to obtaining persons who would rubber-stamp his ideas, but rather to appointing members whose basic set of economic values coincided with his. These moves have proved to be wise, and the Council has become a respected and useful staff agency for the executive branch.

There is evidence that the Council has been listened to by President

[14] For an able paper criticizing the Council on this and other scores, see P. J. Strayer, "The Council of Economic Advisers: Political Economy on Trial," 40 *American Economic Review* 144–154 (May, 1950).

[15] As former member E. G. Nourse pointed out, in opposing the suggestion that a member should be otherwise, "I myself am one of those old-fashioned girls who has no liking for the idea of being a 'kept' economist, even of the White House." See his discussion of papers in 40 *American Economic Review* 189 (May, 1950).

[16] *Op. cit.*, p. 174.

Eisenhower [17] and, through the Advisory Board on Economic Growth and Stability as well as the active support of the President, has been a powerful coordinating force in government control of the entire economy. The reports of the Council have shown, on the whole, accurate analysis of the economic situation and of the programs of the government for economic progress. In recent years, the Council has been more careful than before in limiting its analysis to government programs definitely related to economic stability and growth rather than to many reform issues which have little or no bearing on these goals. For example, in the 1955 *Economic Report* the Council dealt primarily with government programs relating to fiscal policies for economic expansion, assisting new and small business, freeing the channels of trade and fostering foreign investment, improving social security and otherwise "building the floor of personal and family security," expanding and coordinating public works, and developing measures for meeting business fluctuations.

However, in one major area the Council's work leaves much to be desired. Even though it has furnished government and private agencies with some of the most authoritative employment, production, and income statistics and has done an able job in examining the trends disclosed, the economic reports have not furnished any projections of these essential indicators of economic stabilization and growth. There can hardly be any doubt that the Council does make forecasts of the future under various assumptions of future public policies. But if it does so, these are not included in the *Economic Report*. Since the *Report* is used as the basis for executive and legislative action to control the economy, it would seem that such forecasts should be available to policy makers and administrators. It is probable that the Council will do so in the future. Having just been revitalized in 1953 and having been faced immediately with the pressing problem of a recession, the Council had not had much time by 1955 to pay much attention to longer-run projections.

OPERATION OF THE JOINT COMMITTEE ON THE ECONOMIC REPORT

The Joint Committee on the Economic Report is an important part of the machinery of economic control because it is designed to furnish the leadership and coordination for molding legislation which will further the aims of the Employment Act of 1946. The operations of this commiteee follow those of most congressional committees. Witnesses are heard, staff studies are submitted, and reports are made. These have furnished a forum for the divergent views of economists, government officials, industry and labor groups, and others interested in the direction of eco-

[17] In an address to Town Hall of Los Angeles on March 8, 1955, former Council member Neil H. Jacoby stated, "I can testify that President Eisenhower does rely heavily upon the Council."

nomic events. As experience is gained with economic stabilization, the work of this committee shows increasing promise, and as one economist said of the 1954 hearings: ". . . one cannot help but be impressed by the relatively high level of economic understanding of the members of the Committee. There is still much room for improvement in this regard but in contrast to the behavior of other Congressional committees the level of discussion is high." [18]

It is difficult to weigh the influence of the committee in the molding of legislation. But if the committee continues to gain in stature and understanding as it has, particularly in recent years, there is reason for optimism that it will be a potent force toward making the objectives of economic stability and growth important considerations in pertinent congressional legislation. Other than the guiding leadership of the President, there seems to be little hope for a better organizational device in the nation's legislative processes. The committee system is in integral part of the legislative process. The implications of over-all economic control for stability and growth are so far-reaching that one can hardly expect all legislation with such implications to be referred to a single committee for action. It may be possible in the future for this committee to be given an opportunity to review all such legislation, but at present the hope seems to lie in using the Joint Committee as a service and advisory agency for Congress. It is to be hoped that its prestige and understanding of economic issues will continue to grow, and that it may be manned by the most influential members of Congress.

Control for Economic Stability and Growth: the Case of the 1954 Recession

To illustrate the effects of public controls for economic stability and growth, the case of the 1954 recession furnishes an interesting example. This recession was not severe, and there are those who could argue that recovery by late 1954 and early 1955 would have resulted without government action. Nevertheless the recession was severe enough to influence the congressional elections in the fall of 1954 and to cause some concern that this might be the beginning of the long-feared postwar depression. There is no doubt, in the opinion of the authors, that the recession was in large part brought on by government policy and that recovery was likewise influenced by government action.

ECONOMIC HISTORY OF THE RECESSION

The economic recession which began to be felt in the final quarter of 1953 and gained momentum in the first half of 1954 did not represent a

[18] P. J. Strayer, in "Full Employment—1954 Model," 44 *American Economic Review* 891 (December, 1954).

severe reversal of the economic indicators of stability and growth. This can be seen by reference to Table 27–2, which summarizes by years for 1950 to 1952 and by quarters in 1953 and 1954 the trends in gross national product, national expenditures, personal income, unemployment, and prices.

The rapid growth of gross national product reached a peak of $369.9 billion per year in the second quarter of 1953 and declined to a level of somewhat less than $356 billion in the first three quarters of 1954, after which it began a slow increase toward the high levels of 1953. As can be noted, this is a drop in gross national product of only 4 per cent, but when the normal rise in the productivity of approximately 3 per cent is considered,[19] the actual loss in gross national product was somewhat greater compared to what would have been the case had normal improvement in productivity taken place.

However, as can be readily noted, personal consumption expenditures and total personal income remained fairly constant throughout the latter part of 1953 and in 1954, despite a drop in employment, thus indicating that labor rate increases approximately offset the drop in employment. Even so, the annual rate of labor income fell some $5 billion between the third quarter of 1953 and the first quarter of 1954. Analysis of consumer expenditures showed that consumers' purchases of durable goods, as distinguished from services, dropped somewhat during the period, thus tending to increase the inventories held by retailers. However, in one important part of the economy, agriculture, lowered food prices and inadequate exports caused a substantial decline in farm incomes. It will be noted that farm incomes dropped from a level of $16 billion in 1951 to $11.1 billion in the third quarter of 1953 and, after a rise to $13 billion in the first quarter of 1954, settled to $11 billion by the final quarter of that year.

The most important expenditure features of the contraction in 1953–1954 were two, however. One was the rapid decline in government defense spending, which dropped from an annual rate of $54.3 billion in the second quarter of 1953 to $50.6 billion in the fourth quarter and continued its decline to $40.6 billion in the fourth quarter of 1954. The second factor was the change in inventories. Business inventories, which had built up rapidly in 1950 and 1951 and had maintained a fair growth through the first three quarters of 1953, turned downward thereafter and showed fairly rapid liquidation throughout the final quarter of 1953 and 1954, although by the final quarter of 1954 the liquidation was almost complete. From a practice in the second quarter of 1953 of adding to inventories at an annual rate of $5.4 billion, businessmen reduced their inven-

[19] Normally, one would expect a rise in the work force, but this was negligible during the period.

Table 27–2. *National Production, Income, Expenditures and Unemployment*, 1950 to 1954 *

(Product, expenditures, and income in billions of current dollars; unemployment in millions; quarterly data at annual rates)

				1953				1954			
	1950	1951	1952	1st	2d	3d	4th	1st	2d	3d	4th
Gross National Product	$285.1	$328.2	$346.1	$361.8	$369.9	$367.2	$360.5	$355.8	$356.0	$355.5	$361.0
Personal consumption expenditures	194.0	208.3	218.4	228.6	230.8	231.2	229.7	230.5	233.1	234.8	237.5
Gross private investment	51.2	56.9	50.7	51.9	55.9	52.4	45.5	44.5	45.6	45.3	49.2
Residential construction	12.6	11.0	11.1	11.7	12.2	12.1	11.7	11.7	12.8	14.0	14.8
Other construction	10.1	12.4	12.6	13.3	13.7	13.5	13.9	14.3	14.2	14.2	14.3
Producers' durable equipment	21.1	23.2	23.3	24.1	24.6	24.8	24.0	22.7	22.4	21.8	21.6
Net change in inventories	7.4	10.4	3.6	2.8	5.4	2.0	−4.2	−4.2	−3.8	−4.8	−1.5
Net foreign investment	−2.2	.2	−.2	−1.8	−3.3	−1.8	−.6	−1.1	−1.0	−.2	.0
Government purchases	42.0	62.8	77.2	83.0	86.6	85.4	86.0	81.9	78.3	75.6	74.3
Federal national security	18.5	37.3	48.5	51.0	54.3	52.3	50.6	46.9	44.7	42.1	40.6
Federal other †	3.6	3.8	5.4	7.2	7.9	8.0	9.3	8.1	6.6	5.9	5.5
State and local	19.9	21.8	23.2	24.9	24.4	25.1	26.2	26.9	27.0	27.7	28.2
Total personal income	227.1	255.3	271.2	283.3	286.4	287.5	287.3	285.1	285.7	286.2	289.0
Labor income	150.3	175.6	190.6	201.3	205.2	206.9	204.3	201.3	201.6	202.2	204.0
Proprietors' income: farm	13.3	16.0	14.2	13.4	12.1	11.1	12.3	13.0	12.2	11.6	11.0
Proprietors' income: non-farm	22.9	24.8	25.7	26.5	26.3	26.1	25.9	25.6	25.9	25.9	26.2
Rental income of persons	8.5	9.1	10.0	10.5	10.5	10.6	10.8	10.8	10.9	10.9	11.0
Dividends	9.2	9.1	9.1	9.1	9.3	9.5	9.6	9.6	9.6	9.8	10.4
Personal interest income	10.6	11.6	12.3	12.8	13.3	13.7	14.1	14.2	14.4	14.6	14.7
Transfer payments ‡	15.1	12.6	13.1	13.6	13.6	13.6	14.3	15.2	15.8	15.7	16.4
Less: Personal contributions for social insurance	2.9	3.4	3.8	3.9	4.0	4.1	4.0	4.7	4.6	4.6	4.6
Unemployment: No. of unemployed	3.1	1.9	1.7	1.8	1.5	1.3	1.8	3.5	3.4	3.3	2.8
Per cent of labor force	5.0	3.0	2.7	2.8	2.3	2.1	2.8	5.5	5.2	5.0	4.4
Prices: Wholesale price index	103.1	114.8	111.6	109.8	109.6	110.8	110.0	110.6	110.6	110.3	109.7
Consumer price index	102.8	111.0	113.5	113.6	114.1	115.0	115.1	115.0	114.9	115.0	114.6

* Details will not necessarily add to totals because of rounding. † Less government services ranging from 0.2 to 0.4.

‡ "Transfer payments" include government interest payments, government transfer payments (social-security payments, pensions, benefits to veterans, etc.), inheritances and gifts, sale of personal assets, and similar transfers where the payment does not result from production.

SOURCE: *Economic Report of the President* (January, 1955), pp. 137, 147, 153–154, 176.

tories at an annual rate of $4.2 billion by the first quarter of 1954. At the same time, net federal government spending for goods and services dropped from an annual rate of $62.2 billion in the second quarter of 1953 to $55 billion in the second quarter of 1954 and continued to drop so that it fell to an annual rate of $46.1 billion by the fourth quarter of 1954.

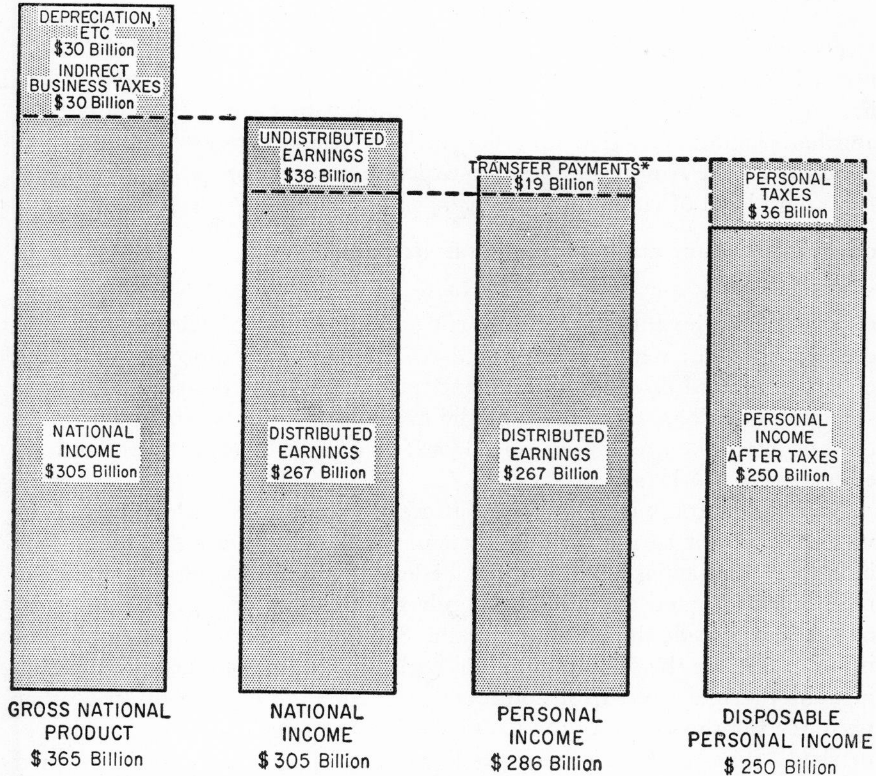

Figure 27–3. Relationship of National Output, Income, and Consumer Purchasing Power in 1953

Source: U.S. Department of Commerce, Office of Business Economics, *National Income, 1954 Edition* (1954), p. 3.

Between inventory liquidation, then, and the decline in federal spending, the result was a drop of some $17 billion in the annual rate of expenditure in nine months. This rather sharp drop, concentrated as it was in the durable-goods industries, accounted for most of the unemployment during the recession. It also accounted for the fact that this unemployment was made to seem larger because of its concentration in certain manufacturing areas.

The result, as can be seen from Table 27–2, is that unemployment increased from a phenomenal low of 1.3 million in the third quarter of 1953, or some 2.1 per cent of the civilian work force, to 3.5 million in the first quarter of 1954, or 5.5 per cent of the labor force. The reaction from this unemployment, concentrated as it was in industrial areas, along with the effect of dropping farm income, unquestionably influenced the election results in the fall of 1954. This is a good indication that the American electorate is not willing to accept what was once regarded as a fairly normal level of unemployment or a fairly prosperous level of agricultural income. One can only come to the conclusion that the full-employment and high-income experience of World War II and the postwar years has conditioned the American public to expect a government policy providing for a high level of economic stability.

GOVERNMENT POLICY CONTRIBUTING TO THE RECESSION

While the recession of 1953–1954 was not severe and has often been regarded as an inventory-readjustment period, one can detect several government policies which contributed to the recession. One of these was clearly the rapid drop in government spending. While desirable from the standpoint of channeling more of the nation's product to nongovernment uses, it was too precipitous to allow for normal readjustment, and its effects were too localized.

Another factor which certainly affected the business situation in 1953 was the attempt to use both credit and fiscal policies for the control of inflation.[20] In January of 1953, the Federal Reserve System increased the rediscount rate and the Treasury undertook special efforts to finance its obligations outside the banking system. The result was a general tightening up of credit. At the same time, despite plans to reduce government spending, the President asked for continuance of the high income-tax and other tax rates for the year. As the Council of Economic Advisers so aptly remarked, "The restrictive monetary and debt management policies pursued in the early months of the year had, however, a more potent effect than was generally expected." [21] As events did prove, these policies did have such an effect and showed the sensitivity of the economy to monetary and fiscal controls. Of course, it is probable that the economy was more sensitive in 1953 than would normally be the case because of the fear of inflation at that time and the uncertainty as to whether government controls could avoid recurrence of the depressions of 1920–1921 and 1929 to 1933.

[20] For a description of this development, see *Economic Report of the President, January, 1954*, pp. 49–53.
[21] *Ibid.*, p. 50.

GOVERNMENT POLICY CONTRIBUTING TO RECOVERY

As a result of the rise in unemployment and the drop in gross national product and expenditures, the national government did undertake in late 1953 and 1954 a number of actions designed to stem the recession and return the economy to an upward rise. A few of these were, of course, automatic. The drop in personal incomes was at an annual rate of $4.4 billion between mid-1953 and mid-1954. At the same time, social-security payments increased at the rate of $2.2 billion and personal income taxes dropped at the rate of approximately $1 billion.[22] Also, the drop in corporate income at the rate of $7.4 billion was cut by $4.5 billion by the application of the tax laws (including excess-profits taxes) then in effect.

Several positive steps were taken by the national government, however. In May of 1953, the Federal Reserve undertook to ease credit, both by expanding the reserves of commercial banks through open-market operations and by reducing the reserve requirements. The Treasury undertook to handle government financing in a manner designed not to compete with mortgages and other long-term private issues. While the Secretary of the Treasury announced in the fall of 1953 that he would recommend elimination of the excess-profits tax for 1954 and reduction of personal income taxes, these programs were not written into the tax laws until 1954. In addition to these tax reductions and the reduction of excise taxes by approximately $1 billion effective in mid-1954, the new tax law provided several structural changes designed to encourage business expansion. These included more liberal depreciation allowances, permission to treat research and development expenses as expenses, token relief of double taxation of dividends, and lengthening of the period over which business losses could be carried back for tax purposes. At the same time, the coverage of social security was extended.[23]

Later in 1954, additional steps were taken. The Federal Reserve lowered the rediscount rates and again reduced member-bank reserve requirements. The government stockpiling program was revised to assist lead and zinc mining. Shipbuilding was assisted through a new construction program. The Defense Department—particularly the Air Force, which had lagged badly in the placing of orders against approved funds—accelerated its commitment of contracts by the fall of 1954. Another important action was taken by Congress when, by the Housing Act of 1954, it liberalized the terms for insured residential construction mortgages, increasing the maximum amount of cost which could be insured and providing for "open-end" mortgages to permit additional loans for home improvement.

[22] *Economic Report of the President, January, 1955*, p. 18.

[23] And tax rates increased, thus taking away somewhat the benefits of the reduction in personal income taxes.

RESULTS OF GOVERNMENT POLICY

The halting of the recession by the latter part of 1954 and the continuation of stable prosperity in 1955 have appeared to prove the efficacy of government policy to control the economy, at least in a relatively minor economic contraction. As the Council of Economic Advisers rather exultantly declared in 1955: [24]

> What gave them [the government actions] a special character was their promptness and heavy reliance on monetary policies and tax reductions. The shift from credit restraint to credit ease before an economic decline had begun, the announcement of sizable tax reductions before it was generally appreciated that an economic decline was actually under way, the submission to the Congress of a comprehensive program for encouraging the growth of the economy through private enterprise—these early measures to build confidence were by far the most important. For they strengthened confidence when it was needed, and they thereby rendered unnecessary any later resort to drastic governmental programs in an atmosphere of emergency.

While this statement gives comfort to those concerned about the ability of government to control the economy, and the resultant recovery justifies the optimistic feeling that such control can be achieved, the statement raises an important question. If it was not, in fact, generally appreciated that a recession was under way at the time the tax cuts were announced in the fall of 1953, one wonders whether an adequate job of forecasting was done. There were indications in the spring of 1953 that credit restrictions were too severe, and certainly by the middle of 1953 many business forecasters prophesied a decline in the latter half of the year and in the first half of 1954. Since government action requires time both for putting it into effect and for making its effect felt throughout the economy, planning based on careful forecasting would appear to be an urgent requirement of controls for stability and growth.

It is true, however, that the government measures did have important results, even though these results did not come until a recession had been experienced and the electorate had registered its disapproval at the polls in the 1954 elections. Personal income was supported by tax reductions, both from automatic decreases and from the lowering of rates, and by an increased level of unemployment-insurance benefits and other social-security benefits. This was so successful that the *Economic Report of the President* for January, 1955, reports that disposable personal income increased $1 billion at a time when industrial production declined 10 per cent, a result which, according to the *Report*, "has no parallel in our

[24] *Economic Report of the President, January, 1955*, p. 20. Material in brackets added.

recorded economic history."[25] The reduction of corporation taxes by the elimination of the excess-profits tax had a marked effect on many corporate income reports for 1954, ballooning net income after taxes of many corporations to record levels and bringing on higher dividend rates and a feeling of confidence with respect to future corporation earnings.

Relaxation of credit, particularly in the residential construction field, also had marked effects. Mortgage debt outstanding rose from $101 billion in the fourth quarter of 1953 to $113 billion one year later, and housing starts went from approximately 1.0 million in 1953 to 1.2 million one year later. At the same time, total loans and investments of commercial banks rose some $10 billion.

Control for Economic Stability and Growth: Conclusions

Perhaps there is no area so directly affecting business where there is less dispute that the government has a proper role than in the control of the economy for stability and growth. Certainly the power of the government in this area is unavoidable if government is to play a large role in the utilization of gross national product, in financing of debt, and in controlling money and credit. These appear to be unavoidable attributes of modern big government. Moreover, this is a power which only the government can exercise. It is amply evident that the public has given its governmental representatives a clear mandate to do what they can within the framework of traditional American liberties and institutions to ensure economic growth and stability. While the question may be raised whether it is possible for the national government to ensure such stable prosperity without taking an increasing part in the actual management of the economy and its business elements, there is certainly reason for optimism that government action can be limited. In other words, there is reason to believe that big government need not become an encompassing authoritarian regime, planning the major details of economic life, and that government control of the economy in the interest of stability and growth can remain compatible with a high degree of freedom and private enterprise.

Perhaps the greatest safeguarding against the rise of predominantly authoritarian government is the avoidance of economic crises. It is doubtful that the American people would stand for a serious depression of the order of that following 1929 without insisting that government take over the active management of large areas of business decision-making and operations which are now in private hands. If this be true—and the demonstrated unwillingness of the public to stand for much unemployment would seem so to indicate—one is forced to the conclusion that those responsible for national government policy must take advantage of every

[25] *Ibid.*, p. 21.

proper tool within the present institutional framework of the nation for management of the economy toward the goals of economic stability and growth.

The national-income approach to national economic problems and more intelligent use of monetary policy appear to offer the tools. With greater knowledge of the components of gross national product, expenditures, and income, and with a clearer perception of how to control the economy, the techniques of control seem to be available. If the techniques can be wisely applied, there does seem to be no reason for a major depression which might sap the interest of the public in continuing to support a relatively free private-enterprise economy.

But there are several causes for concern as to whether the public, through its national government, will actually be able so to manage the economy. Good control requires careful planning. Careful planning, in turn, requires reasonably accurate forecasting and the ability to make and administer plans to avoid undesired consequences. There is little evidence that the national government, either through its Council of Economic Advisers or through some other agency, has developed short-range forecasting, not to mention equally significant longer-range projections, which is widely understood by the policy makers or in which there is enough confidence to furnish the basis for action.

Of perhaps greater concern is the ability of the government to act quickly. Even in those areas where the President has considerable influence, as in the rate of defense spending, Treasury financing, or the credit policies of the Federal Reserve System, there is an inherent tendency for the government to move slowly. This was indicated in the actions taken to combat the 1953–1954 recession. And it is understandable. The national government is a very large enterprise and suffers the problems of communications and inflexibility which characterizes all large organizations. There are many agencies and interested parties to be consulted before a course of action is agreed upon. Then, once a top policy decision is made, much time is required to make detailed plans and to have effective actions filtered down through the organization to persons who must put them into effect. One does not quickly change the policies and course of action of a department of several hundred thousand people.

But in addition to the problems of planning and effectuating plans in so large an organization, the American political system reserves to the legislative branch the power to make many decisions. Particularly in financial areas, such as taxes and expenditures, Congress has been understandably loath to delegate powers to the President or the executive establishment. But to pass laws through Congress takes time, time which may be of strategic importance in quickly changing a course to meet a threatened recession or boom.

These problems are not easy to solve. The inflexibilities involved may well be insuperable. But there does appear to be ground for some hope. If the President and the Council will place greater emphasis on forecasting and planning and, if at all possible, encompass a future period adequate to allow for the time necessary for translating forecasts into action, undesirable economic events might be avoided. However, public policy should not overlook the possibility that it might be wise to lodge certain discretionary powers in the executive branch. It would not seem unrealistic or dangerous to place in the President limited power to change the size of personal-income-tax exemptions, to modify government procurement and spending, or to undertake other measures which influence the economic climate under which business firms operate.

In addition, the increasing strength of the Committee on the Economic Report offers some hope that, through this committee, more intelligent, more public-minded rather than individual-interest-minded, and more expedient legislative action will be forthcoming. Perhaps the greatest degree of hope must lie in an increasing sophistication in economic affairs on the part of the public generally and of legislative and executive members of the government. This, in turn, will depend much on a high order of economic understanding and teaching, as well as careful analysis of trends and effects by those economists who are influential in public affairs.

At the same time it must be recognized that complete elimination of economic fluctuations is not feasible. Because the economy is dynamic, innovation is certain to be a disturbing factor. The goal of public policy should be to keep these fluctuations within limits of moderate severity and modest duration so that long-range plans are little disturbed. One of the encouraging factors in control of the economy during the recession of 1953–1954 was the confidence displayed by business firms in the long-range soundness of the economy and the ability of government to make the recession a minor interruption in the trend toward stability and growth. The clear demonstration that public economic policies can provide for a high degree of stability has, in itself, encouraged business and consumer investment and spending plans which reinforce the tendencies toward stability.

Selected References

Bach, G. L., "Economic Requisites for Economic Stability," 40 *American Economic Review* 155–164 (May, 1950).

Blough, Roy, "Political and Administrative Requisites for Achieving Economic Stability," 40 *American Economic Review* 165–178 (May, 1950).

Bowman, M. J., and G. L. Bach, *Economic Analysis and Public Policy*, 2d ed., chaps. 11, 36–41, 48. New York: Prentice-Hall, Inc., 1949.

Committee for Economic Development, Research and Policy Committee, *Defense against Recession: Policy for Greater Economic Stability*. New York: The Committee, 1954.

———, *Managing the Federal Debt*. New York: The Committee, 1954.

Dewhurst, J. Frederic, and Associates, *America's Needs and Resources: A New Summary*, chaps. 4, 18, 25, 26. New York: The Twentieth Century Fund, Inc., 1955.

Economic Report of the President, January, 1954.

Economic Report of the President, January, 1955.

Gordon, Robert A., *Business Fluctuations*, chaps. 16–19. New York: Harper & Brothers, 1952.

Gross, B. M., and J. P. Lewis, "The President's Economic Staff during the Truman Administration," 48 *American Political Science Review* 114–130 (March, 1954).

Hansen, Alvin H., *Business Cycles and National Income*, chaps. 25–31. New York: W. W. Norton & Company, 1951.

Jacoby, Neil H., *Can Prosperity Be Sustained?* New York: Henry Holt and Company, Inc., 1956.

Samuelson, Paul A., *Economics: An Introductory Analysis*, 3d ed., chaps. 6, 7, 10, 16–18, 36. New York: McGraw-Hill Book Company, Inc., 1955.

Shultz, W. J., and C. L. Harriss, *American Public Finance*, 6th ed., chaps. 27–29. New York: Prentice-Hall, Inc., 1954.

Strayer, Paul J., "An Appraisal of Current Fiscal Theory," 42 *American Economic Review* 138–146 (May, 1952).

———, "The Council of Economic Advisers: Political Economy on Trial," 40 *American Economic Review* 144–154 (May, 1950).

———, "Full Employment—1954 Model," 44 *American Economic Review* 884–893 (December, 1954).

28

PUBLIC CONTROL OF ECONOMIC ENTERPRISE: CONCLUSIONS

Since the ability of the economic system to function efficiently and to improve the material position of individuals is closely related to the happiness and welfare of every member of the community, the significance of government controls of economic enterprise should be understood by every citizen. Individual economic well-being is virtually a prerequisite for effective freedom, and economic liberty is closely related to political liberty. If democracy is to succeed, it must solve problems of economic welfare and, at the same time, preserve a governmental framework which leaves the maximum of individual freedom consistent with that welfare.

However, democracy does not imply what the economic policies of government should be. Strictly speaking, democracy as a form of political association should be distinguished from any special form of economic association or organization. Democracy is a political arrangement by which the people may establish the goals of the state and, out of conflicting and divergent views, select the programs to achieve them. A democratic government is thus committed to no economic system or doctrine of state function. Decisions regarding the relation of government to the economy are worked out through the democratic political process. That is not to say that one economic system may not be more wise or reasonable than another in terms of such community values as freedom, efficient enterprise, material welfare, or happiness.

Perhaps a chart [1] will make this point clearer. Governments classified as to the *location* of political authority range from democracy through oligarchy, in which political power is concentrated in the hands of a few, to autocracy, in which power is arbitrarily assumed by one man. The various political doctrines which range from anarchism, through individualism and socialism, to totalitarianism, refer to the *extent* of power exercised by government over the economy. The actual practical application of these doctrines range from rugged individualism of the nineteenth

[1] Adapted from John M. Swarthough and Ernest R. Bartley, *Principles and Problems of American National Government* (New York: Oxford University Press, 1951), p. 12.

century through the mixed economy of the New Deal and contemporary experiences, the welfare or service state, the limited socialism of Great Britain, to the extensive socialism practiced in the Communist Soviet Union.

Figure 28–1

Extent of power
Totalitarianism
↑ Socialism
Welfare state
↓ Rugged individualism
Anarchism

By distinguishing between democracy, as a political arrangement which locates political power in the people's hands, and the extent of economic control that may be exerted by a democratic government, the relation of government to the economy can be properly regarded as a problem of public policy to be worked out through the democratic process.

The scope and nature of economic control are proper subjects for public debate and political decision under a democratic government. The decision, on one hand, to have no economic regulation, and the decision, on the other hand, to have extensive and detailed aid, regulation, or ownership of particular economic enterprises or transactions are conceivable policy decisions that could be made through the democratic process. The substance of democratic economic controls is limited by the restraints inherent in the process by which democratic decisions are made and by the predominant values of the people. If other restraints existed, the ability of the people to work out the problems of their economy through public means would be impaired.

The examination of government control of economic enterprise undertaken in this book makes it possible to give summary answers to certain fundamental questions that are frequently asked about government intrusion in the economy. What, in general, have been the patterns of economic control? What have been the motives leading to control, and are these motives sound reasons for control? In instituting controls, what problems have been created? What have been the effects of government controls upon economic activity and the institutions of capitalism? Finally, what can be said of the future of public control of economic enterprise?

The Patterns of Control

Out of the complex of government controls of business, a few principal patterns of control seem to emerge. These patterns do not account for all kinds of government controls. But it does appear that the major programs fall into one or more of the following categories: control to determine the degree of competition, control of price, control of output, control of business conduct, control to reduce personal economic risks, and control to stabilize the economy as a whole. As can readily be appreciated, these controls are not independent of each other but are often intermingled in any given program of government intervention.

CONTROL TO DETERMINE THE DEGREE OF COMPETITION

A great many government control measures are designed to establish a certain kind or degree of competition between sellers. In some fields monopoly has been encouraged, in others competition has been restrained but not eliminated, and in still others the government has attempted to maintain effective competition. In the transportation industry, the federal government has restricted competition by requiring certificates or permits before entry into service and has encouraged the lessening of competition through rate and service limitations; at the same time, it has not allowed carriers to gain a position which would "unduly" suppress competition. In the public-utility industries, state governments have encouraged the growth of local monopolies to a much greater extent than they have been promoted elsewhere, although incursions of government ownership in the electric-power field have tended to restore some of the respectability of potential or actual competition.

The attitude of the government toward private businesses—those not "affected with a public interest"—has been one of insisting upon competition. The antitrust laws and the fair-competition laws have been passed by the federal and state governments with such an end in view. But as the antitrust laws have been interpreted, they do not restore completely competitive conditions. Large producers or sellers, even formed as the result of combination, may still lead a lawful existence, and price competition may give way somewhat to service competition, although the apparent lack of rivalry in oligopolistic industries has been greatly overestimated. Sellers may retain the monopolistic advantages of trade-marked and advertised merchandise, or of goods produced under a patent. In such cases, with resultant price leadership, product differentiation, and reluctance to engage in price competition, the vigor of competition may be reduced. Fair competition laws both encourage and discourage competition. Removal of deception, misrepresentation, or other restraints upon trade may sharpen competition, while insistence upon equal treatment of buyers irrespective of economic advantages—as found in the Robinson-Patman Act—and application of state "fair-trade" laws may dull it.

In agriculture, competition is also reduced by market agreements, control of output, fixed-price commodity loans, outright price fixing, and other means to ensure farm producers a certain share of the national income. Competition between workers for jobs and between employers for labor is diminished by legislation fixing working conditions and wages and protecting labor unions which speak for the majority in bargaining for the entire group of workers in a craft or industry. Government aids to business tend both to increase and to decrease competition. Promotion of standards and dissemination of information, for example, encourage more effective competition, but protective tariffs, subsidy policies, and provision of patents and trade-marks retard its operation.

Often overlooked is the fact that protection of society demands either the restraining hand of competition or the restrictions of government control against abuses of monopolistic power. If the government allows or encourages monopoly or the moderation of effective competition, government control of price and service is a natural result. Sellers who seek refuge from competition should realize that the public has never long permitted monopolistic power to continue unregulated. On the other hand, governmental policy should take into account the extent to which competition exists and should not impose restrictions on private businesses where competition can do the regulating.

CONTROL OF PRICE

For many years government control of price was restricted by the interpretation of the national Constitution and by generally accepted policy to those businesses clothed with a special public interest, such as transportation agencies and local public utilities. In addition there had been some price control involved in regulation of interest rates which financial organizations might charge borrowers and scattered, though largely ineffective, regulation of minimum wages of certain classes of workers. More recently, however, the scope of price control has been extended to include minimum wages of workers generally and the price of agricultural products. In the case of most agricultural products these controls have been indirect, with regulation coming through marketing agreements, production controls, and other plans for maintaining price through influencing supply. Moreover, the resale-price-maintenance laws, the laws providing for minimum retail markups, and the Robinson-Patman price-discrimination law tend to result in fixing of price under government auspices. Furthermore, government ownership and promotion of such facilities as waterways and electric-power plants have been used as means for reducing prices charged by private enterprise. Also, in time of war under conditions of full mobilization, and often under limited mobilization, price control has been regarded as essential to ensure maximum, balanced supply of needed goods and services and to promote economic stabilization.

Where peacetime price controls are well developed, as they are in the transportation and public-utility industries, they involve the administrative problems of fixing reasonable rate levels and reasonable and nondiscriminatory individual rates or prices. Commissions have followed the principles, largely as dictated by legal and economic necessity, that the level of prices should cover total costs, including reasonable operating expenses and a fair return on the capital used in the business, and that individual prices should cover out-of-pocket costs plus a contribution toward overhead or joint costs. The determination of such reasonable prices by administrative action has been shown to be an extremely difficult and complicated task. Similar difficulties are likely to be encountered in any field to which price regulation may be extended.

The difficulties of price control have led to additional regulations. Thus, accounting regulation has been found necessary, largely as an incident of fixing reasonable prices. Strict regulation of security issuance by carriers and public utilities has been held to be essential for protection of rates and service, because of the destructive results of overcapitalization and of deterioration of credit standing. The regulation of other financial practices, reorganization procedures, and combination also has a definite relationship to the need for reasonable rates and adequate service. Indeed, once the government undertakes to regulate price, the way is open, through the sheer necessity of making price regulation effective, to bring under control many practices of management and labor.

CONTROL OF OUTPUT

Output controls of various kinds have generally been found along with price controls, especially in time of war. The quantity of output may be regulated as a means of obtaining price control, as is the case in agriculture, or as a means of securing adequate service under monopolistic conditions, as is the practice with the public utilities. Interesting, too, is the control of quantity of output involved in maximum hours for labor; often such hours laws have been justified as a method of increasing the demand for labor and hence increasing the value of workers employed. The quality of output may also be subject to government regulation. Thus, the usual public-utility and transportation laws require that service be of a certain minimum standard and be rendered without unreasonable discrimination between customers.

To be effective, output controls necessarily require strict and detailed supervision of business operation. They not only cause a heavy burden on government administration but are likely to be irritating to enterprisers. As the scope of output-control increases, the questions of what to produce, how much to produce, and by whom it should be produced naturally mean the replacement of profit-seeking initiative of individual enterprisers by government economic planning.

CONTROL OF BUSINESS CONDUCT

Although all government controls entail intervention into the character of business conduct, certain controls are instituted by society, or at least by organized groups within society, to place business operations on a plane which is regarded as ethically correct. The requirement that competition be fair, the regulations to prevent fraud and deception, and the controls to protect labor against maltreatment fall into this class. These regulations are based generally upon the feeling that certain courses of conduct are inimical to the well-being of society and that other courses are "fair" or "good." Because these controls rest upon ethical considerations, and such grounds depend upon group attitudes of right and wrong, or good and bad, the substance of control of business conduct is likely to undergo change. For example, the fixing of resale prices and placing of other restrictions on price competition between ordinary businesses, which are now regarded as necessary for price competition to be "fair," and which a few decades ago were thought of as unfair, are again being questioned as unfair. And the establishment of the company-dominated unions in the 1920s was viewed as sound and just business practice, but such domination of union organization a decade later became an unfair labor practice.

CONTROL TO REDUCE PERSONAL ECONOMIC RISKS

Many programs of control have as their primary motive the reduction of economic risks with which persons may be faced. Controls to ensure economic security have assumed greater importance in recent years. The wave of labor legislation to provide minimum wages, maximum hours, and social insurance against risks of accident, disease, unemployment, and indigent old age began many years ago, but it gained real momentum in the last two decades. The renewed vigor with which financial institutions have been regulated, security issuance supervised, and holding companies controlled represents a program to protect investors. Most of the agricultural program of aids and controls has constituted a broad plan for ensuring an economic status for the farmer which is thought to be desirable. Fair-trade laws have been used as devices to protect the small independent seller against the danger of crushing competition from mass distributors. Government assistance programs, such as a protective tariff, a transportation subsidy, or a program of credit aids, may be means whereby groups are protected from the rigorous effects of competition and the danger of economic failure.

If, in reducing economic risks, the government succeeds in eliminating fraud, misrepresentation, or the exploitation which comes from superior bargaining power, the control may improve the efficiency of the economic system. However, as has been pointed out in the discussion of labor regulation, agricultural controls, and certain cases of government promotion and ownership, the sympathy felt for certain groups of society may well be justified, but a policy giving effect to that concern must not overlook the consequences upon the ability of the economic system to function efficiently. Regulation to reduce economic risks should take care lest the vigor of individual initiative be undermined or people come to believe that security can be guaranteed for society by restraints upon production.

CONTROL TO STABILIZE THE ECONOMY AS A WHOLE

Out of the New Deal attempts to combat the effects of economic depression and the experience of World War II there has emerged a pattern of control aimed at regulating the economy as a whole in the interests of economic stability and growth. The disheartening experience of high unemployment in the 1930s and the realization during and after World War II that full employment and economic growth could be effected through government programs have led to a public demand for government control to accomplish the objectives of economic stability and growth. At the same time, the development of economic knowledge and the rise of "big" government have placed in the national government the tools for exerting important influence on the economy as a whole. One of the advantages of a national government spending some 20 per cent of the national product, as it has done recently, compared to one spending some 3 per cent, as it did in 1929, is that its expenditure, fiscal, and monetary policies can be used with telling effect for economic control of the economy. Although there can be no positive assurance that these tools will be expeditiously and accurately used, their existence plus experience in recent years furnish grounds for optimism.

To some extent, this pattern of control is an extension of the control to reduce economic risks. However, an important distinction can be drawn. In using its powers over expenditure, fiscal, and monetary policy, the government can reduce the risks of persons and business firms generally, and thereby establish an economic environment which improves the efficiency of the entire economic system. These controls need not place umbrellas over selected groups at the expense of other groups. If used in the broad public interest they need not interfere seriously with economic and political liberty, although one must recognize that government expenditure policy, tax programs, debt financing, and controls over interest rates and the use of credit involve controls and therefore tend to limit freedom. At the same time, if these controls are not abused to gain undeserved privileges for certain persons or segments of the economy, and if they are wisely employed for promoting the health of the economy as a whole, the loss in economic freedom appears to be a small price to pay for the efficiency engendered in the economic system.

Economists have long believed that the material standard of living of the American nation could be vastly increased if means could be found to harness human and technical abilities to the great natural resources available. While a major portion of this job must be done through effective management, at all levels, of the business enterprises of the nation, it has become apparent that only the government has the power to control the economy as a whole in the interests of stability and growth.

As far as competition is concerned, there is every reason to believe that control of the economy as a whole in the interests of economic stability and growth will sharpen business rivalry. It should be noted that this expansion is expected to take place primarily under private ownership and enterprise. An expanding economy will doubtless bring improved technology, lower costs, higher labor productivity, and better products. With the probability that improvements in technology will be widely shared and that business firms, both large and small, will be operating in an economic environment freed from the fears of serious depression, there appear to be strong forces tending toward increase in the vigor of competition.

The Motives of Control

As a general rule, government policies do not materialize unless they are supported by the public. This does not mean that the public generally must actively support every policy adopted by the government. It does mean that, for a policy to succeed, either a large segment of the public must believe the policy to be wise, or a small segment must press actively for a program which is not strongly opposed by the larger group. Such a latter possibility is of real importance. With the tendency of pressure groups to influence legislators, programs may be adopted largely because the general public is indifferent or uninformed.

BROAD SOCIAL OBJECTIVES

If one were to read the preamble of most important control measures passed by federal or state legislatures, he would be impressed with the broad social objectives there expressed. He would find there that a transportation law was passed to encourage a transportation system adequate to meet the needs of the country. He would find that a resale-price-maintenance law, which can hardly be regarded as a means of encouraging price competition, is justified as a law to prevent destruction of competition. Or he would note that the purpose of an agricultural production-and price-fixing law is to remove an economic emergency arising from the disparity between prices of agricultural and other commodities, with consequent destruction of farmers' purchasing power and a breakdown in orderly exchange. In fact, it is difficult to find a regulatory law, a government aid measure, or an instance of government ownership which is not put forth in large part as a means of protecting the public health, morals, safety, or welfare, or of contributing to national defense, or of collecting necessary revenue.

In most cases of government control laws, broad social objectives do actually exist and the desire to fulfill them is the predominating motive behind the institution of control. There can be no doubt that the public desire to remove abuses which interfered with equal, adequate, and reasonably priced services motivated and justified regulation of railroads. The honest insistence upon competition and the belief in the social value of competition did surely account very largely for the Sherman Anti-trust Act, the Clayton Act, and the Federal Trade Commission Act. The desire to protect labor from the harm of too long hours and too low wages was the principal reason for the state and federal wage-and-hours laws. Likewise, one must admit that the belief that free collective bargaining would aid orderly manufacture and commerce had much to do with the passage of the Wagner and Taft-Hartley Acts. And public interest in reasonably priced and adequately furnished public-utility services explains why legislation has been adopted to regulate public-utility operating companies and to place holding companies under strict control. Nor can it be denied that the needs of national defense and the promotion of flood control and navigation had something to do with the creation of the Tennessee Valley Authority. One could go over the entire field of regulation and find a broad social objective apparently acting as the principal motive for control, if not constituting the entire motive.

The primary reason for having to bring government controls into play for protecting the welfare of society is the abuse of individual freedom by persons responsible for business policy. While the abuses which often give rise to government regulation have sometimes had a degree of justification from the point of view of individual property rights, the destructive influence of certain practices upon the welfare of many persons has made regulation necessary or desirable. The railroad managements of the nineteenth century who took a "public be damned" attitude might have sincerely believed that their principal duty was to their stockholders, rather than to the public which depended so much upon fair and adequate transportation service. The promoters of large combinations in the latter part of the same century may have honestly thought that they had a right to combine businesses for profit and for preservation of property rights against destructive competition, but they did not reckon with the broader public interest in the maintenance of free competition and fair opportunity for other individuals to do business. Many of the promoters of the public-utility holding companies of the 1920s may well have felt that they were within their rights to increase profits, to protect their interest in construction companies or investment banks, and to enlarge their sphere of influence and power by combining control over many public-utility operating companies. But these promoters either did not consider how their actions affected investors and users or did not realize that the device they had built up could be used by the unscrupulous to defraud customers and investors through questionable, if not unlawful, practices.

The abuses which have called forth control have been the thoughtless or dishonest practices of persons in positions of business responsibility. Had these individuals been more careful to see and promote the public interest, as opposed to narrow private interests, or had they been able to rid themselves of the dishonest or otherwise unethical element in their midst, many of the government controls would not have come. Although the honest and public-spirited businessman must chafe under regulation along with the dishonest and selfish, businessmen must realize that certain members of their own group have necessitated many of the controls.

Nevertheless, it must be recognized that such concepts as public welfare, health, morals, safety, conservation, and national defense are so broad that virtually any policy might be justified as promoting their betterment. While one must grant that these social interests have been real and important in bringing about control, there have seemed to be some far more definite motives which have strongly influenced the legislative course of government control of business.

PROTECTION OF BUSINESS GROUPS AGAINST COMPETITION

One of these more definite motives is the desire by certain producing groups to be protected against competition. Manufacturers of products competing with foreign imports struggle to obtain passage of tariff laws and other legislation designed to place a foreign competitor at a disadvantage in the local market. Railroad managements have encouraged more regulation of water carriers and motor carriers so that their competitors may be held in check. More recently, common-carrier truckers have vigorously opposed relaxing railroad rate regulation for fear that the resulting competition would be destructive. Farmers support legislation giving the government power to enforce marketing agreements so that competitors in a market will not drive prices down. Independent retailers promote legislation to require their competitors to abide by resale prices fixed under manufacturers' contracts or to charge prices equal to some formula of cost. Other businessmen in many fields support legislation to limit size and curtail monopoly, with a hope of reducing the competitive advantages of a large producer. Or businessmen may encourage the government to legalize codes of competitive behavior which may reduce the vigor of competition which they face, even though such codes mean greater business controls. Likewise, labor may wish to eliminate competition of unorganized workers or workers in certain unions by insisting that the government pass legislation outlawing company-influenced unions and allowing organized labor to speak for majorities in collective bargaining.

When producers themselves desire to have legislation passed to protect them against competition, government control is invited by the very parties which have traditionally resisted it. A business group asking for legislation to protect itself against competition does not, of course, wish the government to enlarge its field of control very much. But these groups forget that, if a precedent is made for protecting one group against competition, another group may find a way of soliciting government aid in its behalf. The manufacturers who have so strongly supported a protective tariff have given the farmers a good case for having their prices protected by legislation. The retailers who wish prices controlled by or through the government may not see that they are creating a basis for other sellers to push for legislation to fix their prices at profitable levels. What has happened in many cases is that organized groups of producers and sellers have gone independently to the government for legislative assistance, not realizing that the combination of efforts of many such groups can result in a large extension of government control over business.

Moreover, the businessman or farmer who asks for legislation which may protect his competitive position often brings down upon himself a program of government control which may be more complete and irritating than he had ever realized. The farmers who saw in the Agricultural Adjustment Acts a means for improving their lot apparently did not realize that they were assuming the burden of having government inspectors check their planting; and the support of marketing agreements meant that many farmers lost the traditional freedom of planting what they desired and marketing the quantity of goods they wished. Moreover, retailers and manufacturers who supported the resale-price-maintenance laws and the Robinson-Patman Act may not have realized that the operation of these laws would mean increased governmental supervision of their businesses, with an enlarged list of government rules to observe and a multiplied volume of reports to make. Whenever government assumes a field of control, not only does it have to put in many irksome rules and enforcement procedures but the government control tends to become broader and more intensive. As the problems of control become better understood, gaps in laws and procedures are discovered, and additional legislation involving added control ordinarily results.

PRESERVATION OF SMALL BUSINESS

Back of many of the government controls of business may be found the desire to protect and preserve the small businessman. Although the desire to maintain competition was perhaps the principal motive for the antitrust laws and the many trade-regulation laws which have followed, a motive of almost equal importance has been the wish to protect the small businessman from extermination. This motive has become stronger during the development of the laws against combination and unfair competition. The curious twists taken by the Clayton Act through the Robinson-Patman Amendment and by the resale-price-maintenance and sales-below-cost laws indicate that the program to maintain a certain plane of competitive activity has become more and more a program to keep the small seller from being destroyed by the efficiency and power of the mass distributors.

Other policies of control can be pointed to as illustrating this motive. The refusal of the federal government to take over the banking field and the reluctance with which such a practice as branch banking has been permitted indicate an unwillingness on the part of government to allow the smaller business unit to be edged out of banking. The agricultural program, both as respects control and assistance, also apparently aims to maintain farm ownership with small units by protecting the profit margin of the average producer and by aiding farmers to improve production methods and rehabilitate themselves. The various "grandfather" clauses in the new federal regulations of carriers are another indication of the desire to protect the small businessman.

The preservation of small business units has something to be said for it. The experience of ownership and control of business not only encourages individuals to put forth their best productive efforts but, by maintaining economic independence, aids in conserving political democracy. Effective competition, with its merits of price and quality control, is also more easily realized the smaller the business unit. On the other hand, government control policies should be careful not to give up too much by the way of efficiency and costs in order to protect the smaller businesses. Intelligent policy should carefully weigh the relative advantages to be obtained against the possible losses to be incurred.

PROTECTION OF CONSUMERS

Many governmental control programs put into effect to promote the social welfare may well be for the protection of the consumer. The regulation of railroad and other public-utility rates and services, the regulation of banks and banking, and the controls over insurance have decidedly protective results for the consumer. But consumers have seldom been thought of as a class and have even more rarely been given much consideration in the framing of governmental control policies. Yet in spite of the fact that the protection of consumers has not been a very important motive leading to government control of business, it appears to be gaining somewhat in importance.

The work of the Federal Trade Commission is especially noteworthy as illustrating a desire to protect consumers. Through opposing price-fixing schemes as methods of unfair competition and outlawing various deceptive devices in selling, the Federal Trade Commission has contributed handsomely to consumer protection in the United States. Also worthy of note are the administration of pure food and drug laws by the Food and Drug Administration and the influence of the Department of Agriculture to have uniform standards of measurement and grading adopted. The increasing role of consumer protection is illustrated by the passage of legislation in 1938 to extend the jurisdiction of the Federal Trade Commission over deceptive and harmful practices as well as unfair methods of competition. The Food, Drug, and Cosmetic Act of 1938 also enlarged the scope of consumer protection by giving the Food and Drug Administration much more power to protect the public against dangerous drugs, devices, and cosmetics.

However, it may well be emphasized that the desire to protect the consumer has not been as strong a motive behind government control of business as the importance of the consumer class should justify. The fact that consumers have not been organized and that other groups have been well organized to press their cases before legislatures accounts for this apparent inconsistency in government policies. The desire to protect shippers, laborers, independent retailers, agricultural producers, and other producing groups has had a greater part in determining government policies, simply because they have been better organized than consumers in presenting their cases.

THE DESIRE FOR ECONOMIC SECURITY

One of the strongest motives behind government control of business, particularly in recent years, is the desire of certain groups in society for economic security. In a sense, this motive is not altogether separate from those already mentioned. The businessmen who have pressed for tariff laws, protection from monopoly, protection from too vigorous competition, or financial and other assistance from the government desire to preserve their income, investment, or position. Farmers have demanded an agricultural program which would protect their "fair share" of the national income. Investors have desired security from incompetent, dishonest, or unfortunate managers of financial organizations and from sales of fraudulent or misrepresented securities. The desire of workers for security has led them to insist upon laws guaranteeing collective bargaining, fair minimum wages and maximum hours, unemployment compensation, and retirement benefits.

The desire for security is a human motive which is easily understood. Most of the struggle of mankind throughout history has been dominated by a desire for economic and political security. With the complications introduced by a wage system and by industrialization, the maintenance of individual security has been increasingly more difficult. When the world-wide depression occurred after 1929, with its decline in employment, business profits, wages, and production, the impairment of security led inevitably to a demand for government action. In response to this demand the government has instituted programs of social security, regulation, and business aids which have accounted for much of the expansion of government control over economic activity.

The demand for government action to alleviate the effects of depression has been supplemented in the period following World War II with a demand that the government take action to avoid depression. The public which tolerated unemployment running to 19 per cent of the labor force in 1938 showed strong displeasure at the polls in 1954 when unemployment stood at a little more than 5 per cent. Thus the desire for economic security is a desire not merely to protect those harmed by economic fluctuation but to ensure that the fluctuation, at least in any major sense, not occur at all and that the nation's economy be guided along the path of stability and growth.

Some Basic Problems of Control

In dealing with the fields of public control of economic enterprise, much attention has been given to the problems encountered therein. Some of the more important problems were briefly noted earlier in this chapter in the summary of programs of control. There seem, however, to be a few problems which are characteristic of government control generally. Among the more important of these basic problems are those having to do with encouragement to competition or monopoly, encouragement to economic inefficiency, conflicting interests in control, and the effectiveness of administration.

SHALL GOVERNMENT ENCOURAGE COMPETITION OR MONOPOLY?

One might ordinarily expect that, in certain fields of regulation, the government would either support the maintenance of competitive conditions or encourage monopoly. The theory behind regulation of railroads and public utilities has been that they have monopoly power, that monopoly is most efficient, and that regulation is to furnish the safeguards which competition would otherwise provide. The theory back of regulation of other business has been that competition is desirable and that, if the law will maintain competitive conditions, fair prices and adequate service will follow.

Much can be said for regulation dividing businesses between those which are monopolistic, and in which monopoly is the most efficient, and those which are competitive, and in which the best output at the lowest costs can be obtained under competition. But what has actually happened in government regulatory policy? In the transportation field businesses have been regulated as monopolies, but competition has been allowed to flourish and is even encouraged. In the public-utility industries, a much higher degree of monopoly is found, with the preeminent position of one telephone system throughout the nation and the usual local monopolies in electricity, transit lines, water, and gas.

In other businesses, one finds a curious mixture of competitive and monopolistic governmental control policy. The antitrust laws have the purpose of enforcing competition, but they do not cause businesses to be broken down into small enough units so that completely effective competition may in fact be secured, nor do they outlaw loose combinations, such as those furnished by trade associations, cooperatives, and joint selling agencies. The laws regulating competitive practices encourage competition to a great extent, but many obstructions to its free operation have resulted from the strange interpretation given to fairness under resale-price-maintenance legislation, restrictions on mass distributors, and other legislation. Moreover, along with laws to enforce competition may be found other laws giving strong protection to patent rights and trademarks.

In the agricultural industry, the traditional freedom of competition has given way in part to various kinds of price and production controls. Competition in the labor market is made to diminish or disappear through encouragement to monopolistic labor organizations and partial removal of wages, hours, and conditions of work from the field of competitive bargaining. Furthermore, by aiding and entering business either directly or as a major purchaser on an ever-increasing scale, the government has tended to reduce the effectiveness of competition between private parties.

Not only has the government policy of control appeared to be inconsistent in regard to the support of competition and monopoly, but the mixture of policies has tended to introduce an unnecessary element of confusion in the operation of the economic system. What is needed is a canvass of the entire field of economic activity, with a view to determining where monopoly should be permitted to prevail, where competition should be enforced, and where oligopoly or monopolistic competition might yield desirable results. After such a determination, regulatory policy should be designed to promote the ends sought. If it is believed that social and economic advantages lie in making an industry monopolistic, then government policy should encourage monopoly and regulate the prices, services, and conduct of the business in great enough detail to protect the public interest. If competition appears to be the best policy in another industry, then government policy should be designed to promote effective competition on a plane of socially desirable behavior. If other industries may better be operated with monopolistic elements but with a degree of competition, then the control policy should be created to safeguard the public against the abuses of monopoly which the existing competition cannot eliminate. If the report on transportation policy made by the President's Cabinet Committee in 1955 is any indication, the pendulum of public policy seems to be swinging toward more, rather than less, competition.

THE PROBLEM OF ENCOURAGEMENT TO INEFFICIENCY

In previous chapters, a number of cases have been pointed to in which the government has encouraged inefficiency. The tendency to place an "umbrella" over the costs of inefficient producers, whether in transportation, retailing, agriculture, or elsewhere, means that society is deprived of the advantages of getting goods at their lowest cost and that the efficient producer may be handicapped by regulations to protect his inefficient competitor. Such policies are obviously not in the interests of the efficient operation of the economic system and the improvement of the material welfare of society. They have been introduced at the behest of politically vocal groups who wish to be guaranteed their costs and their "share" of the national income, irrespective of whether they may justify such returns by their value to the economic system. The requests of these groups have been aided by the rather naïve belief, apparently so widely entertained, that somehow all can become richer by giving everyone a stable or increasing proportion of a national income which he does not help to augment.

There may be cases where it is in the social interest to protect inefficiency. If society may ultimately be harmed by the rise of monopolistic businesses and the destruction of the small businessman, government controls to protect small businesses may well be justified. Or if farmers might become impoverished with unhampered operation of a competitive system, the importance of this group to social and economic stability might justify legislation which may reduce material output. And if tariffs or subsidies are necessary for national defense, the costs may be warranted. Nevertheless, any governmental policy which tends to impair economic efficiency should be closely scrutinized to ascertain whether the advantages are worth the costs.

THE PROBLEM OF CONFLICTING INTERESTS

The very nature of representative government in America means that regulations are usually passed piecemeal, in response to the demands of organized groups, and that the problem is seldom seen as a whole. It is therefore not surprising that government controls produce many conflicting policies. The inconsistency of measures dealing with competition and monopoly has been discussed. The conflict between the desire to protect certain groups and the desire to make for efficiency in production has been noted. Throughout the programs of government control, one finds conflicting interests. In order to give the farmers better prices, consumers are called upon to pay higher prices for their goods. Users of transportation and public-utility services find their interests in lower rates in conflict with the need of management for higher revenue.

Conflicts of interest also exist between producers. Industries producing goods for export are harmed by protective tariffs on imports, which impair the ability of foreign buyers to make purchases in the United States, but other industries demand them. Railroad companies feel themselves harmed by government subsidies to waterways and airlines, but manufacturers and other producers using transport services find benefits in the lower rates resulting. Power companies find their interests damaged by strict regulation and by government hydroelectric production, but industrial users of electricity are helped by the low rates made possible. Labor regulations and security programs bring improvement in the status of labor groups which are employed, but they may raise costs to consumers and other producers and may tend to limit the volume of employment available to other workers. Fair-trade laws may yield benefits to a large class of retailers but may take away advantages of mass distributors.

Many more conflicts of interest could be found in the present program of government control, but perhaps the most prevalent conflict is between the interests of producers and those of consumers. Since producing groups are much better organized than consumers, and since individual groups of producers feel that they have more to gain by getting regulations favorable to them as producers rather than as consumers, the tendency for government controls is to reflect their needs. While conflicts may be inevitable in government and there may be no means of eliminating conflicting interests in control policies, the problem should be recognized and attempts should be made to see government controls from the point of view of their effects on the broader social interest in heightened production, lower costs, and wider participation in economic security.

THE PROBLEM OF ADMINISTRATION

The extension of government controls over economic activity gives rise to difficult problems of administering these controls intelligently, fairly, and with the public interest in mind. As government controls have been broadened and regulation has become more specialized, commissions and other administrative agencies have multiplied and have received more discretion in applying the laws. At first, the legislatures defined the scope of administrative discretion narrowly, but as the number of such cases increased, definite legislative rate fixing gave way to discretionary requirements of reasonableness. Vast discretion came to be given in matters of entry and abandonment of service, accounting, finance, adequate service, investigation, wages, hours, fair competition, and other objects of regulation. Government administrative agencies were bound only by the requirements that their actions be "reasonable," "just," or "in the public interest."

The broad field of discretion left to administrative agencies and the complications of applying an ever-enlarging field of regulation have raised critical problems of administration. If commissions or other administrative agencies are inexpert, biased, or arbitrary in the application of their authority, the public purpose behind many regulations can be thwarted, economic liberty can be curtailed unwisely, and government controls can become greater burdens on the effective operation of the economic system than was ever conceived by legislators.

In many fields of administration, a "right" or "correct" application of the law cannot be expected. The concepts of "reasonableness," "fairness," "justness," or "public interest" are so indefinite that it is virtually impossible to give them a meaning in practice which is beyond criticism. But because these concepts are indefinite and their application may be colored by the prejudices or incompetency of administrators, safeguards must be placed about the administration of regulation. These may come from several directions. The legislature may define the jurisdiction and duties of administrative agencies more closely or may broaden the basis for appeal to the courts. The courts themselves, in interpreting the requirements of due process of law, may widen the grounds upon which appeals may be accepted. And the legislative and administrative branches of government may undertake measures to ensure greater competence and impartiality of administrative personnel and may enlarge administrative staffs so that adequate findings may be made before laws are applied.

However, during the past two decades there have been developments in the direction of giving administrative agencies of government more, rather than less, power. Led by the interpretations of due process by the United States Supreme Court, the courts—the federal courts, at least, and many of the state courts—have refused to review the substantive findings of commissions and the other agencies of the administrative branches of government. When the courts limit, as they have been doing, their review of administrative action to the requirements of procedural due process and to questions of the statutory bases of administrative power, the result is to place in the administrative agencies tremendous power from which there is no appeal other than through the polls or the legislature itself. Findings of fact give the real meaning to such vague terms as "reasonableness," "fair," or "undue." If, as a matter of practice, there is no effective appeal from these findings of fact for the individual business firm, it is at the mercy of the administrative agency.

This development in the administration of control can lead, and on occasions has led, to arbitrariness and abuse of the regulatory process. Appeal to the legislature or to the polls has little practical meaning to the individual business enterprise. Abuses of administrative interpretation of the law cannot often be corrected until they so affect a material segment of an industry or the public as to force change on the agency directly or through the lawmakers who define its authority. This tendency to place so much power in the hands of administrative bodies seems to point to several modifications in the control machinery. In the first place, legislatures should give more attention to defining the requirements of regulatory policy, so that findings of fact may more nearly reflect wise public policy. In the second place, both legislatures and the public should exercise greater control over the quality of membership and staffs in these commissions. A third safeguard would appear to be some means, through periodic investigation, for the public, probably through the legislature, to audit the findings and administration of these agencies to ascertain whether, in fact, the power residing there is abused.

Some Effects of Control

The effects of government controls of business are numerous and widespread. They have influenced the very form and importance of government. They have reached out into every branch of economic activity and have modified the production and distribution of economic goods. They have forced changes in the concept and philosophy of capitalism and have had significant effects upon economic freedom. Moreover, this very development has tended to cause the further expansion of control. While other effects of government intervention into economic activity may be pointed out, these effects seem to be the most noteworthy from the point of view of social interest.

THE ASCENDANCE OF THE FEDERAL GOVERNMENT

The expansion of government control of business has been accompanied by the ascendance of the federal government over state and local governments. In broadening the sphere of regulation and in attempting to make it more effective, it has been found that the federal government is the agency which can best accomplish the task, so it has become the chief regulatory authority. Railroad regulation started with state and local government controls but was soon brought under the fold of the federal government. Regulation of highway carriers likewise has been placed in part under the federal government, although state and local controls are still predominant. State regulation to prevent monopoly and to enforce a level of fair competitive practice has been to a great extent superseded by federal regulation. Failure of state governments to solve the interstate aspects of communication, electric-power, and gas-industry regulation resulted in the shift of many phases of control of these industries to the federal government. State and local governments hardly dared attempt the regulation of agricultural production, because of the difficulties encountered in the fact that economic boundaries transcend political boundaries. Moreover, in the fields of government assistance to business and government ownership of business, the federal government has emerged as the dominant agency.

This ascendance is not at all difficult to understand. As economic activities cease to be local in nature and become interstate and national, the limited political boundaries of the state and local governments and the practical impossibility of cooperation between so many governments have made the federal government the logical authority to create and administer controls. This tendency has certainly not reached its limit in practice. The rise of increasingly bothersome interstate trade barriers in recent years will probably call forth federal action. The relationship of many transportation agencies, now regarded as local, to the national system of transportation is likely to result in further enlargement of federal control in this field. The importance of interconnected and coordinated electric-power production and distribution to national welfare and national defense seems to presage the continued growth of federal-government influence in this field. As a matter of fact, the awakened interest of government in national welfare indicate that its role will continue to increase.

ECONOMIC EFFECTS OF CONTROL

The economic effects of government control over business are difficult to trace and to evaluate. Those of many individual government policies have been noted in the discussion of separate regulations, aids, and cases of government ownership. But to attempt to assess the entire program of government control as it affects the level of economic activity is fraught with difficulties. For one thing, economic results in any industry or in the whole economic system are subject to many other forces than the actions of government. Industrial managements determine the course of economic activity by the decisions they make, as do trade unions, trade associations, cooperatives, and other nongovernmental elements in society. Furthermore, government controls may tend both to increase economic efficiency and to reduce it, so that the balance of effects on material welfare may be hard to strike.

The question of economic results of control revolves around the influence of the government policies on maximum production at lowest cost. Has the government enacted legislation which increases costs without proportionately increasing output? Has it put programs of control into effect which have reduced society's supply of natural and capital resources? Have the government controls restricted the full utilization of resources and manpower? In surveying the field of control, many cases of increased cost, decreased output, impairment of capital, and operation at less than capacity can be found in which these controls have caused or contributed to such economic effects. The duplication of transportation facilities encouraged in some areas by the government, the reduction of price competition in retailing that it has made possible, the obstructions to international and national trade through tariffs and regulations, the arbitrary limitation of agricultural production and price fixing to guarantee income, the limitation of hours of work, the tolerance or encouragement of business and labor monopolies, and the sometimes spendthrift allocation of resources to questionable government aids and public works are some of the examples of government policies which appear to bring about negative economic results.

On the other hand, many of the government control policies have indubitably added to the ability of the economic system to produce at low costs. The curbs placed upon private selfishness and incompetency not only may lower costs to buyers but may aid in the preservation of economic resources. The enforcement of order in such fields as transportation and public utilities, and elsewhere, may bring economic saving through not permitting the competitive squandering of resources and through not allowing private persons to gain positions of unregulated economic power. The insistence on publicity, fair dealing, or competition may have the effect of allowing consumers and investors to make choices which will yield them greater satisfaction at lower costs. Furthermore, the program of government to bring economic stability and growth in an enterprise system, predominantly privately operated and characterized by fluctuations induced by innovation and change, has unquestionably contributed to the rapid advances in national productivity, particularly since 1940.

Moreover, it must be recognized that human values may be more important than the improvement of material standards of living. The limitation of working hours, the betterment of wages and working conditions, or the reduction of labor's risks may involve costs to society, but the results in human happiness and health may more than justify these costs. The preservation of independent businessmen or farmers from the destructive effects of too strong competition may cost society some loss of efficiency, but the existence of an independent middle class of owners may be of greater value than the cost. Military or defense considerations, improved housing for submerged classes, or other policies for social or political betterment may mean economic costs and losses, but may still be good public policy. However, when government controls are considered, their economic effects should be studied along with their other advantages, and a decision should be made as to whether the benefits accruing to society are worth the costs.

EFFECTS ON CAPITALISM

It can hardly be open to doubt that the vigor engendered by the desire for profits found in the capitalistic system has been in large part responsible for the economic prosperity of the United States, although the abundance of natural resources and the large area of free trade should not be overlooked. Moreover, in spite of the tendency of many persons to look with disdain on capitalism or free private enterprise as representing codes of the jungle, the fact remains that the American people still predominantly believe in a system which is fundamentally capitalistic, a system which allows freedom to individual enterprise, profits to business owners, and competitively determined prices.

To say that government control of business has modified the essence of capitalism is to put the effect lightly. Virtually every government control restricts the private-property rights upon which capitalism has been based. But many of these controls contribute to the more effective operation of capitalism. If competition is encouraged by government action, the effectiveness of the system of private enterprise to produce at lowest cost and in the greatest quantities tends to be improved. If the government controls result in the reduction of dishonesty, deception, or incompetence in business, they encourage the efficient use of private property. If government requirements increase the fund of information available to consumers and producers, the government may aid in the operation of intelligent competition and economic business policies.

While many of the government controls may help free private enterprise in business, the very restrictions involved tend to diminish the freedom which has characterized capitalism. Private property becomes far less private. Business policies must consider government regulations, and business practices may be modified by the aids and ownership of government. But in spite of these restrictions on business, the owner of property in the United States still has a large area of freedom. In fact, it may be that the government program of controls, by eliminating the more glaring abuses and shortcomings of capitalism and by providing for an environment of fairly stable business conditions, will serve to ensure a high degree of business freedom and to protect capitalism from the complete destruction which it has met in many parts of the world.

THE SELF-GENERATIVE TENDENCY TO EXPANSION OF GOVERNMENT CONTROL

One of the interesting results of government control of business is that programs of control have a tendency to expand. Even if no new fields are opened, government control in existing ones tends to enlarge. One program of regulation discloses gaps in control and leads to further regulation. This extension may also generate more control by bringing to the light the need for additional regulation to make the control more effective. For example, the regulation of railroads proposed by the Interstate Commerce Act of 1887 was planned primarily to maintain fair and reasonable rates and rate practices. But experience showed that maximum- and minimum-rate powers, accounting control, supervision of security issuance, regulation of combinations, control over service, and other restrictions were necessary to effect the purposes which the framers of the Act had in mind. Then, to make railroad regulation fair and equitable and to bring substitute transportation services under government supervision, it was not difficult to prove the wisdom of extending railroad controls to other transportation agencies.

The ever-increasing control of electric-power companies has extended to regulation of holding companies and interstate operations of the power industry, primarily to make possible government supervision of rates and services to consumers. The regulations against monopoly were supplemented by measures restricting practices conducive to monopoly. The rather innocuous assistance to farmers by credit aids and tariffs led to stricter control of production and marketing, because the earlier measures could not solve the problem. The failure of state blue-sky laws to protect investors has given rise to controls by the federal government.

Many other examples of this self-generative tendency in government control of business could be mentioned. The significant point about this tendency is that a minor and rather harmless policy of control may develop into a major and highly restrictive program, through the natural desire of the public and legislators to fill the gaps in government control policy and to accomplish the ends sought by it. This tendency has meant that the government has seldom reversed the direction of its policies. The disposition to maintain extensions of control is well illustrated by the experience with the National Industrial Recovery Act. This legislation provided for government supervision of wages, hours, and collective bargaining for labor and for measures of fair competition which reduced competition for businesses. When this law was invalidated by the United States Supreme Court, the government replaced almost all its controls, bit by bit, with other legislation. The Wagner Act guaranteed collective bargaining rights. The Wage and Hour Act provided for regulation of wages and hours. The various state fair-trade laws received the blessing and support of the federal government, which also passed the Robinson-Patman Act limiting competition between mass distributors and small retailers.

Public Control and the Future

The history of public control does seem to support, and the events of the past quarter century to prove, the generalization that, once government assumes a function, it is seldom, if ever, relinquished. However, there have recently been some signs that the government may withdraw somewhat from the economic scene. A number of government-owned enterprises have been sold since World War II, and prominent groups, including the Hoover Commission Task Force on government enterprises, have recommended further withdrawal. The same is true of government lending and loan-guarantee services, and the well-known Reconstruction Finance Corporation has been abolished, although its lending functions with respect to smaller businesses have been continued in the Small Business Administration. Even in well-established fields of government regulation, serious proposals have recently been made to lessen regulatory controls. For example, the Presidential Advisory Committee on Transport Policy and Organization has urged that certain powers of the Interstate Commerce Commission be curtailed and more reliance be placed on the play of competitive forces. Proposals are being studied to limit the jurisdiction of the Federal Power Commission over the field prices of natural gas. Still other movements are on foot to replace government decision making with private-management decision making, particularly where competition can act as an effective brake on price and quality of essential services.

It is doubtful, however, that one will see any real reversal in the general pattern of public control, and it is probable that these recent trends are but eddies in the on-moving tide of government regulation. On the other hand, if public policy succeeds in bringing stability and growth to the economy under a system of private enterprise, the very success of privately operated business may lead to public demand for less reliance on the government. If public confidence in private enterprise and competitive action grows enough, it is not unreasonable to expect that there may be a material deregulation of business and a withdrawal of the government from business operations and aids.

At the same time, it must be recognized that many of the problems which have impelled government action still exist, and in many cases the growing complexity of the nation's expanding economy produces problems demanding government attention. There is little evidence of any change, also, in the social values which have motivated government controls. In spite of a traditional public aversion to government regulation, there is an undiminishing tendency to look toward government for guidance, aid, and regulation. And when government policies aid or control one group more than another, there is a natural disposition to obtain from the government further assistance and regulation to remove this discrimination.

In view of the growth of authoritarian governments in many parts of the world, there is good reason for the citizen, alert to the advantages of liberty, to consider carefully the growth of a powerful welfare state in this country. While it is entirely possible to retain freedom at the polls while permitting extensive government regulations, aids, and ownership, there is ever the danger that the inevitable limitations on economic freedom involved in government control may affect political freedom. But whether or not political freedoms are impaired, the segment of personal freedom which is economic is great enough that the intelligent citizen must be prepared to weigh gains from government activity against losses.

Admittedly, the choice is not easy. On the one hand, to reject government controls because of certain inherent shortcomings or dangers may lead to even more serious results, such as monopoly control, destruction to small enterprises, injury to consumers and stockholders, or dislocations in the economic system. On the other hand, to embrace government action without careful study of results might be to drift unwittingly into the totalitarian state, with eventual destruction of political as well as economic liberties.

Fortunately, the history of public controls over economic enterprise has indicated that the American public has not embraced any particular dogma or ideology in seeking solutions for its problems. The most distinctive American philosophy has been pluralism and pragmatism, which is the philosophy that truth lies in practice and experimentation. One sees in this philosophy and its application to the relationships of government and business a reliance upon analysis of problems and the evolving of solutions suitable to the objectives. The result is often that formulas and answers are unavailable for the solution of many problems when urgently needed. It also leads often to less than perfect solutions of many problems. But such a philosophy does keep the way open for change, for consideration of solutions in the light of facts, and for more unprejudiced exercise of the public will.

In view of the pragmatic approach which has characterized American public control of enterprise and the importance of these controls, the citizen must be prepared to analyze their nature and effects so that economic efficiency may not be hampered and liberty may not knowingly be traded for security and protection. Even with a system of controls which encompass so much of economic life, and even if these controls should grow in intensity and scope, it is still possible for the citizen to retain for himself, through intelligent voting and exercising enlightened influence on others, the ability to guide these policies into desirable channels and to safeguard himself and others against arbitrary usurpation of liberty.

Selected References

Clark, J. M., *Social Control of Business*, 2d ed., chaps. 28–32. New York: McGraw-Hill Book Company, Inc., 1939.

Galbraith, J. K., *American Capitalism.* Boston: Houghton Mifflin Company, 1952.

Hayek, Friedrich A., *The Road to Serfdom.* Chicago: University of Chicago Press, 1944.

Hyneman, Charles S., *Bureaucracy in a Democracy.* New York: Harper & Brothers, 1950.

Koontz, Harold, "Government Control: The Road to Serfdom?" *Education,* January, 1951, pp. 1–8.

Lilienthal, David, *Big Business: A New Era.* New York: Harper & Brothers, 1953.

Merriam, Charles E., *The New Democracy and The New Despotism.* New York: McGraw-Hill Book Company, Inc., 1939.

Schumpeter, Joseph, *Capitalism, Socialism, and Democracy*, 2d ed. New York: Harper & Brothers, 1948.

Stone, H. F., *Public Control of Business.* New York: Howell, Soskin and Company, 1940.

Wilcox, Clair, *Public Policies toward Business*, Homewood, Ill.: Richard D. Irwin, Inc., 1955, chaps. 30–31.

LIST OF CASES

INDEX